How Dark Was Our Valley

James Durose Rayner

Published by New Generation Publishing in 2020

First Edition

ISBN: 978-1-80031-420-7

www.newgeneration-publishing.com

 New Generation Publishing

Contents

Continued…

James Durose-Rayner - Scarborough 1969

1.   The Target, The Mechanism, The Fix

Here is a narrative in three parts, which I am hoping will help you navigate the story that you are about to read.

I rarely come back home. For that to happen, it must be some family event or something bad that needs addressing, as rarely would I make an impromptu visit. It is just how I am.

Part 1. The Target. 16 February 2008

I remember being in a car and sat outside a semi-detached property in the Mexborough area. It was a dark and cold Wednesday evening. The street had several points of entry and a main thoroughfare at one of its ends that linked Doncaster with Rotherham. It was all part of the mechanism of a plan that was being worked out. If I could describe how I felt, I suppose emotionless would be the word.

The owner of the property was a huge unit. He was in excess of 240 lbs, over six feet tall and was someone that had form for extreme violence.

Did I know him? No, not really – just of him.

So, how did I know? If you know how and where to look, you can find out almost anything. I am extremely fortunate that I know how to do both. This is a large part of what I do.

He had been incarcerated for malicious wounding with intent to cause grievous bodily harm some years earlier. In short, he was an aggressive piece of manpower – a bully, and my purpose being there, was quite one-dimensional.

Taking down such a huge unit can be fraught with problems. If you are aware of your capabilities or indeed your limitations, it poses none. No matter how big they are, they will always go down. Always remember that. The idea, however – is to do it both as quickly and efficiently as possible. My remit was to knock on his door and let him have two blasts rip through him at close range but have him survive the hit.

Why? If he survives, the upshot is, is that you get half a dozen police looking into it for a couple of weeks before they draw a blank and focus their attention elsewhere. If it goes the wrong way and you end up taking out a major artery and he dies, it then becomes a manhunt with the hundred or so police that are deployed putting their two and two's together and forming what I always term as a series of building blocks – the first one being motive.

The complicated part was in the mechanics – mainly, getting home safe. That was not my plan, but the man in the passenger seat sitting next to me and a man who had done this sort of thing dozens of times before.

After emptying the guts of the both pipes into him I would be whisked away to a property on Bolton-Dearne's Ingsfield Lane to destroy the evidence and have a scrub down. Whilst all this was going on my mobile phone would have been conveniently pinging a transmitter over fifty miles away.

Life is full of common denominators and connections and this was one.

The safe house was the home of the second born son of my uncle Paul and auntie Anne (Durose). "No problem," our Steve had told me.

To this day, I am certain that he had absolutely no idea what I had meant when I had mentioned "banging someone".

The last time our Steve had been at my home he had brought his mate with him – who rather interestingly was the youngest son of Goldthorpe's *Body in the Boot Murderer* – Raymond (Ray) Vernon Billam. I knew the family, but not well. The lad's father had been a bit pissed off and killed his wife. Every relationship has its problems, altercations or whatever, but once a husband does-in his beloved and then begins trying to hide the body – well, that spells intent. That takes a three-year wrap for manslaughter with diminished responsibility up to a life sentence for murder, which in Ray's case, that is what exactly what happened.

The job at Mexborough had been live for three or four weeks, when frustration set in. The problem was solely in its mechanics and not the job itself. If I rightly recall, it boiled down to money. A person picks you up and drops you off from something this serious and gets implicated – well, they are doing time. As that was the case, you need a bit more than some muppet and that is exactly what I got told. Money buys a lot of things – I am not so sure about loyalty, though. Personally, I felt that I was being shaken down.

As it was, I hit the bastard on three separate occasions over a period of eight days – one of which produced pure carnage. The last one, however, told him exactly *what* was knocking and *why*.

Unfortunately, I had showed my hand, which is something that I rarely do.

The job that I had planned, could not go ahead in its original form. The question of why was a simple one. He knew he had been targeted, therefore there was no fucking way this clown would be answering any unsolicited knocks on his door late at night – especially from someone wearing a ski mask and wielding a chopped-down twelve gauge.

My hobby of his misery had stalled, or so I thought.

Next up: 2 Lancaster Street, Thurnscoe.

This is a property that I had walked past maybe a thousand times, but one that I had never been inside.

Here had lived an unlikely source that would give me a solution to my problem. I had to admit, this lad had absolutely no fucking idea what he had in his possession and he just gave them me. No requests for money, no quid pro quo, no nothing. What a top kid. It is such a shame how it all ended. However, I will touch on that later.

I was hardly in the league of the IRA but through my past life in mining I knew enough about both the priming and use of explosives. That being the case, I was more than capable of blowing up a vehicle. The problem that I had, however, was that I wanted it to detonate when the target was in it – and this, especially given the amount of shrapnel I intended attaching to it, could have culminated in one of those said manhunts.

So, why attach shrapnel? If you don't, it is just a big bang followed by a fireball that will give the target nothing more than the feeling of having the backside fall out of his trousers.

The shrapnel – the nails (or screws) were intended to rip through the undercarriage of the vehicle and fuck up everything from below his knees. It sounds horrific, but it was nothing that he did not deserve.

Again, the problems were in the mechanics. No-one fancied getting caught planting it. Well, they didn't for less than three-grand! Have you ever tried crawling under a truck in the middle of the night whilst some Halogen intruder light that the vehicle is parked under, keeps coming on?

Unfortunately, this must have rattled him and straight after, he fled to Thailand.

Part 2. The Mechanics. 28 April 2007

From memory, it had been a beautiful Saturday morning, as I sat eating breakfast in the conservatory of Wath-on-Dearne's Sandygate Hotel – a lovely structure that at one time sat above several stone farm buildings and overlooked the Dearne and Dove Canal. The sun had been shining through its glass as I sipped at my coffee, whilst at the same time I listened to the good-humoured banter coming from the table opposite. It was just one of those days when you feel good about yourself.

The night before had been great. It had been a Durose family birthday. Plenty of camaraderie, plenty of drink and literally half of Bolton-on-Dearne calling in throughout the night, with my young lad and his mate running riot around the hotel along with his two second cousins – Amy and Sheridan. To top it off, my wife had drunk too much and had slung her guts up in the bedroom. As I said – a cracking night.

Our Steve (Durose) can tell you more to the story in how he came to stay that night, as he certainly wasn't intending to. More to the point, however – was that it had been straight after, when I had put to him the question that forms the first part of this mini-trilogy. "I could do with a favour," I said. "I'm on about banging someone local and I need a place to be dropped."

He never asked who or what and just said: "Yeh – no, problem."

2

The people that I surround myself with are second to none.

My wife and I had arrived at the hotel in separate cars as the following morning I had to do something that required me driving into the Hillsborough area of Sheffield and which eventually saw me emptying the contents of someone's wheelie bin into two black sacks.

In the first part, I had supposedly been the one delivering the misery. In this instance I was part of its mechanics.

Here was a person that South Yorkshire Police had had tucked away. My remit had always been to find the safe house that they had stashed him in. I knew I had found it as I had been chasing this kid for weeks. The fact that I was being called on it had pissed me off.

"I've had people around there and there's been no sight of him," I was told.

I therefore needed it confirming. A letter from the DHSS, a hospital appointment – anything with his name on it would do.

"I don't think anyone lives there," I was further advised.

That statement was wrong. I had waded through all the empty packets of shit food such as microwave meals, Chinese take away cartons, empty pizza boxes, lager and pop cans along with old magazines etc. All the evidence pointed to someone living on-the-fly.

In the first part I was serving justice. The second had been a plain case of perverting it.

My target had been a sexual predator – a nonce. This one was a witness for the prosecution. The first part was to inflict considerable harm. The second – much more serious. This target, I was informed, had to go.

How did I feel about it? Much the same as I had in the first part – emotionless.

Vague is how this story is currently playing out, therefore I will add some sauce into the mix.

If I told you that I could link the person in the first part with the murders of two children – one of who had been raped beforehand, you would probably think that as far-fetched as this story itself. Unfortunately, it is not.

You may be living what you consider as some ordinary life, but if you were made aware of what is actually going on all around you, the reality of it would perhaps frighten you to death. No-one really knows who the person is, that they are sitting or standing next to – say on an aeroplane, train or even in a supermarket or restaurant. The reality is, is that you just don't know.

So, am I career criminal? God, no.

It is something that the police have never understood about me and nor are they likely to.

"Here you have the picture of respectability with a vicious underlayer of menace."

That wasn't me who said that. That was Rebecca Dolby – the Crown Prosecutor at Scunthorpe Magistrates Court on the Saturday morning of 2 October 2010, whilst urging the judge to refuse me bail. "I am asking you to remand this man in prison, because if not, there is no doubt in my mind that he will intimidate witnesses."

Part 3. The Fix.

For five days I had been holed up in a flat in the north of Sheffield signing off on a load of work-related stuff before I went to the police station with my solicitor and duly handed myself in.

There had been an altercation whereby a man ended up in intensive care with an embolism on his brain, following what was described as a sustained and violent attack. The police made it sound much worse than it was, that is for sure. Their helicopter unit trawling the skies looking to pinpoint the assailant certainly didn't help my case either. Nor did my name being splattered all over the front pages of the local newspapers.

"You don't look like someone who should be in here," said one of the inmates in HMP Hull.

This is what I get all the time.

My legal team of Wilford Smith and Co., along with my wife and rather strangely, my nana (Minnie Durose) had worked like hell during the five days that followed, and on the Friday morning of 8 October 2010, I was granted bail.

The one thing I don't have, is a face for radio.

After I had sifted through the rubbish that had been lifted at the safehouse, I called at the Fish and Chip Shop, had the girl make me up a fish-patty in a bap and ended up at an address back at Fearn House Crescent in Hoyland. This had been the home of my nana – my eldest surviving relative.

When I had been a small child, she and my granddad Sam had lived at 9 The Crescent, Bolton-on-Dearne. She was my gateway into the past and possessed something of a family loyalty that I have rarely seen matched.

I could be out in her back garden burying a corpse and there she would be rattling on the kitchen window: "Are tha coming in – thee tea's getting cold."

Is that an exaggeration? Certainly not. Ask any of my younger cousins.

There had been some debate within the family about a briefcase that I had dropped off at her house along with a cardboard box during the heady summer of 2005. "Nan, can you save this lot for me?" I had asked.

I'd had the pleasure of having my home searched on four separate occasions. Thinking about it, I had also had my offices searched twice along with a gym and fight club that I owned in Scunthorpe's Ten Foots – a series of backings which are located behind Frodingham Road – although the latter had been nothing to do with me. Anyway, this had been straight after the second search, whereby the police found stuff that even I didn't know I had.

As for the briefcase, my auntie Anne – who was never one to mince her words, thought it was drugs and told me as much. This was not only wrong but something that I have had aimed at me all the fucking time. This, I assume, is down to the lifestyle that I lead – half of which is spent outside the UK. Oh yeah – and it has often been said that I also keep unbelievably bad company.

I had told my nana that it was legal documentation – some of which related to property and banks over in Cyprus, which in part, it was.

"I've had to shift that box," she told me. "It was stinking the bedroom out. I've put them in the shed."

"I bet you've had a look in it," I said.

"Yes, I bloody did."

As for the briefcase, you need to ask my auntie Anne or her children what was really in it, because if I told you, you would certainly never believe me.

In later life I tried to visit my nana on a regular basis. There is a reason for this which you will pick up on as the story progresses.

As for the second part of the story, although the witness survived several attempts on his life – to my knowledge at least two shootings, the intimidation failed. The case eventually went to trial and the Crown Prosecution Service got the result that it wanted.

I approached my problem much differently, but before I go on to explain, you must always keep looking at how I use the words.

My case was always going to trial of that there was never any doubt.

The intimidation of witnesses and jury tampering are serious offences and although I certainly had the means to carry both through, I did not. It was alleged that I had tested the water with the former, as on the first day of the trial there had been whispers between the Crown Prosecutor and my barrister in relation to a threatening phone call. Intimidating the witnesses pre-trial, I always knew was futile, as the police always give them a false sense of security. Just like politicians they will lie through their back teeth to get what they want. They guarantee them everything. Yours truly taking the full force of the tariff for grievous bodily harm – that being a seven-to-ten-year stretch and they, personal safety – having their homes fitted with panic alarms and meticulously placing panda cars outside their properties.

Never trust the police because they do not care. After it is done, they will walk away and leave you to deal with the consequences.

Just prior to the end of Day 2 of the trial, I turned around in the dock and looked directly into the gaze of the lead detective in the case. The day before he had looked arrogant and self-assured. In this instance, he shot out of the court. I, through my barrister, had turned the trial on its head. The Fix had been set in motion. I had ramped up the pressure and from thereon in, the case was always going to collapse.

I remember whilst being out on bail – I had been down to a job on the M25 and on my return – around the Stamford turn off on the A1, I had a police car drive up behind me, chuck on its blue lights and flash me to stop. I wasn't speeding. I wasn't on my phone. The car was taxed. And I was insured. Therefore, the question was always going to be: Why would he stop me?

He requested my presence in the rear of his vehicle. "You are driving while disqualified," he told me.

"Disqualified? What are you on about?" I shrugged. "I've not even got any points on my licence."

He then started reading me my rights, which was the point when I went fucking ballistic. "Do your job and contact the DVLA – because this is bullshit," I told him.

He did as I asked before contacting his control unit, after ten minutes of which, he began scratching his head. He certainly knew I hadn't been having him over.

"Have you got three cars?" he asked.

I nodded.

"Are you in some sort of trouble – drugs?"

Again, with the fucking drugs! It is always the drugs.

"I'm due in Crown Court next month," I told him. "GBH."

"Well, I'll just let you know," he said. "Humberside Police have got markers on all three of your vehicles."

That certainly had me thinking, but all the same, I thanked him for the heads-up.

"How do you think you'll get on at court?" he inquired.

"I will be very unlucky if it goes the wrong way," had been the last thing that I ever said to him.

Next up: 47 Hanover Street, Thurnscoe.

This is a property that I knew well and to describe its owner, three things immediately spring to mind. Although his lifestyle resembles a fucking car crash, he is possibly the most honest and thoughtful person you could meet, although I wouldn't be lying if I said that I know two or three dozen females that would firmly state the opposite. He is also a highly capable unit who became part of the dynamics in the obliteration of all the work that had been undertaken by the police.

All through my questioning by the two detectives prior to being charged I had never once showed my hand. As with the trial, I was always going to be remanded. My idea was to go with the flow, hopefully be granted bail and get my barrister – Chris Tonge from Sheffield's Bank House Chambers, to play all my cards in court.

"This is a highly intelligent and scheming individual who has been responsible for at least a half a dozen recent car bombings," Rebecca Dolby had told the judge, prior to my remand. "Some of whose vehicles belonged to serving police officers. And only the other year he was the prime suspect in an attempted murder."

"Have you been charged with any of this?" asked a rather aghast David Kempshall – the Duty Solicitor who had been in court that Saturday morning.

"Scheming?" I shrugged. "What does she mean by *scheming?*"

"Never mind that, just answer my question," he said.

"I have never even been questioned about any of these offences – never mind charged," I told him.

He knew I was being set up – however, there was a problem. He also knew who I was and told me as much.

Remember, when I mentioned the second thorough search of my property? This had been part of a very high-profile case when on 27 September 2005 it made all the local newspapers including ITN's regional weekday news programme, *Calendar*. It was a case that had the police scratching their heads as how to prosecute me and as such, my depositions (DEPS) got sent down the Attorney General at the time – the Baroness Scotland of Astha. As part of these case files, there had been a thirteen-page Victim Impact Statement handwritten by a corrupt and lying piece of shit that paraded as a serving policeman – basically stating how mean I had been to him.

After six months, the Baroness finally made a decision and had me lumbered with a Section 4 charge of harassment, which I then had to defend – and which my brief – the Managing Partner of Wilford Smith & Co., Steve Smith, absolutely ripped to shreds in court.

Can you guess who had been the Crown Prosecutor that day? Yeah, none other than Ms Dolby.

Make no mistake about it, both she and the police wanted me banged away.

In Crown Court during early 2011, there had been no better feeling than watching the smug lead detective in my case scurrying about trying to get a connection on all six defence witnesses at the last minute. Remember what I said: Never ever show your hand. I have to say that it was quite humorous. I sat back and like the rest of the court, just watched on.

After what was a six-day trial, it took less than twenty minutes for the jury to reach a verdict. The very next day, three-quarters of a million pounds worth of property was put on the market.

Now, that could easily be construed as witness intimidation.

So, what did I do? Nothing. I didn't have to. The police had done it for me.

"If I were you, I would think about moving." It is their stock advice to any witness post-police blunder.

Unfortunately, after five or six months the 'For Sale' sign on one of these properties was taken down. Its proprietor was a woman that had been proved a liar on the triple-nine call that had been played in court. Unfortunately, she had then had to make another similar call, but this time she managed to tell the truth. Having three fire engines outside her property in the early hours of the morning ultimately eased her into rented accommodation a few villages away.

I look back, and these handful of events don't even begin to scratch the surface.

On 8 January 1998, I had handed over a banker's draft for £17,500 (£32,139, circa 2020) in an upstairs office, opposite Sheffield Cathedral. It was a day when all my industry and hard work would pay off. The deposit had been paid to my corporate solicitor's – Norrie Waite & Slater, and I would be leaving my comfort zone forever.

Unfortunately, what I never bargained for was the amount of god-awful luck that I would have bestowed up on me during the following few years. It is often said that bad luck is brought on by the individual, but I don't believe that for one second. Just ask the families of Valerie Barrett, Diane or Neil Hudson or indeed Jade and Alex Goddard – the list is endless. They, as you will see as the story unfolds, never deserved any of the hurt and misery that would burden their lives. As for me, my move away started with the loss of my fifteen-year-old daughter, but I have to say – as much hurt as that caused – and it did, it was in no way the same as those five poor souls.

I would be badly let down by the authorities, the judicial system and eventually have to deal with a corrupt police force. It certainly did not happen overnight, but over time, a dark side of my personality, that in the past, had only made brief appearances throughout my life, would fully reveal itself. I wouldn't exactly say that I became judge, jury, and executioner – but an awful lot of people ended up getting hurt.

It was a situation borne of frustration.

The hardest thing about starting something such as this, however – is that it tends to spiral out of control, which is exactly what it did do. It is then a case of – how do you make it all stop?

2. All God's Children

When something huge happens at a particular moment in time – for example, some life-changing event, you tend to know where you were and what you were doing. Ask most people where they were when they heard the news of the death of Princess Diana or the World Trade Centre getting hit and they could probably tell you.

Most memories are built on emotion.

If you look back in time, we can easily remember some of the Christmases that have long since passed, the holidays that we spent in our youth and the parents and grandparents that are no longer with us. No matter what emotions these generate, memories such as these rarely leave us.

The weekend of **3 March 1985** was no different.

The new model village (pit estate) in Thurnscoe's East end had been built in between 1921 and 1926 and in part, had aged badly since its final construction. By the mid-1970s the National Coal Board (NCB) had begun recouping money by selling off some of its assets in bricks and mortar and whereas at one time you had red bricked buildings with their white multi-paned steel framed windows, now you did not. Miners who had bought their homes had commenced putting their own personal stamp on them – taking away their quaint uniformity and creating something of an untidy rag bag of disorderly structures. In some instances, the red brick had been replaced by a grey or sandy mock stone facing, or even worse, a white, cream or magnolia paint. The multi-paned windows had been ripped out and replaced with larger singular paned UPVC, aluminium or wooden ones or at worst, there was a mix of both, where front windows had been replaced and the back ones had not. And what at one time had been a series of low peripheral red brick walls bordering blossoming front gardens now they were not. Many of these charming, arced borders had been knocked down and their gardens replaced by makeshift drives.

Thurnscoe, like many other mining villages, suffered at the hands of progress.

I lived in one of these houses, set back on the left-hand side of a cul-de-sac – the sixteenth house of twenty. Briton Square was situated on the north-west side of Thurnscoe's East end and a couple of hundred yards away from the bridge that crossed the Sheffield-York (Swinton-Knottingley) railway line, which provided pedestrian access into what was at that time, the prefabricated REEMA (Reed & Mallick) estate that had been constructed in the 1960s.

I had made that walk hundreds of times, possibly thousands. I knew Thurnscoe inside-out and back to front, as I did Goldthorpe and Bolton-on-Dearne. These were the villages within the eastern Dearne Valley that I had grown up in.

The hundreds of smoking chimney stacks always made sure that from autumn going into winter, there was always a thick blanket of smog, which you could taste at the back of your throat. Whether you were coming in from school, walking home from work, the smoke and the darkness made those dimly lit houses, with the smell of fat often being fried as you walked past, rather strangely – look quite appealing.

As I was growing up, I knew exactly what I wanted. I was hardly ambitious, and my wants at that time never really exceeded a wife, a house, and a car.

I remember a time during the early summer of 1976 – a Friday evening, and of my mum and (step)dad bundling us into the back of their six-year-old blue Ford Escort estate (SET 125J) and of us being taken shopping to a supermarket in Denaby.

The Fairway (Gateways) was part of a small regional chain of supermarkets owned by Harry Round. This one had been located on Doncaster Road and was on the site of the former Drill Hall and which had opened in 1965.

Whilst Paul McCartney's *Silly Love Songs* had been playing over the speakers my mum had been navigating the trolley around the supermarket's narrow aisles, with all three kids in tow – me being the eldest, with the ultimate treat of us being able to pick something that we wanted and put it in the trolley. It was basically nothing, yet all I ever wanted to do when I left school was to replicate that moment in time, as in my mind, it had been something that I must have seen as being quite perfect. I suppose there is a reason for that, which will maybe become apparent as you read on.

I could say that the **said** Sunday on the **said** weekend in March 1985 was like many others, as even though the days were becoming longer, it was still as cold, damp and gloomy inside the house as it was outside, which always made the option of being somewhere else, the much better option. Therefore, that night, I hadn't been in my house on Briton Square, but in a property a few hundred yards away.

The streets that made up what was once the pit estate, were in the main, of a historical theme and whereas my place of residence was on Briton Square, the house I was in on that night was on Dane Street. This was a street which was often termed as The Bullring: a series of houses that had been built to form a circle, which both looked out onto a green and which was accessed from four other streets – those being that of Norman Street to its north and Saxon Street to its south, Tudor Street to its east and Stuart Street to its west.

The street may have had one of the worst histories in the village – however, this house was neither cold, damp nor gloomy. On the contrary.

As the TV seemingly played to itself, the property's owner had been an unwilling recipient of telephone call and was partaking in some strained dialogue and offering a series of nod's and yes's in response to whatever questions were being asked at the other end. Whilst this was happening, the embers in the fireplace were being momentary shielded by the owner's wife, whose attention had solely been fixated on me. As had been her twelve-year-old son's, who had been seated opposite, dressed in just his shorts and T-shirt, whilst his pretty seventeen-year-old sister had been sat next to me, smiling as she watched me juggle with eating a sandwich and reciprocating in a conversation with her mum, that bordered on a mild interrogation. I remember it like it was yesterday – however, there is a big part that I am missing.

The phone call ended, and it was then that the man of the house turned his attention to his daughter. The conversation he had been having, had with her boyfriend, ex-boyfriend or soon-to-be ex-boyfriend (not sure which), and he gave her what he considered to be both barrels of verbal.

Her stepfather was a vociferous little guy with a handlebar moustache who possessed an uncanny resemblance to the comedian Bobby Ball of the comedic duo *Cannon and Ball*. It was hardly a case of him being that mad that he could have bitten a banana in half (sic), nevertheless he did raise his voice to offer an opinion. His wife, however, gave me a wry wink and smile, which indicated that this was the norm and that there was no real malice in his assessment of the situation.

As for the TV, it had been an extended edition of the *Six O'clock News* of which its subtitles were stating that the year-long Miners' Strike was over.

On that evening, I felt what was possibly one of the greatest feelings that I had ever had. Nowadays, I suppose that emotion is hard to gauge as I have had so many great things happen in my life, and a thirty-odd year passage of time does tend to dilute things somewhat. Nevertheless, I have no doubt – that even now, that that evening was well *up there*.

The girl – Debbie Davidson (now Howell).

I had known of her quite some time and on the Friday night that kicked off that weekend, we all had an idea what was going down. I remember being in the Halfway Hotel – a public house that has long since gone, but which once proudly stood on the junction of the A635 at Highgate crossroads, opposite what was once *Ian's Car Sales*, and talking with an old school mate and fellow miner at Hickleton Main, Tony (Wuffy) Waugh. "We'll be back next week," he told me.

All I wanted at that time, was for him to be right.

As was the norm in the latter part of the strike, I had been out with Colin Hunter and Brian Latham, both of who I had known since starting school, and who as the story progresses, you will get to know much more about. How we ended up in the old Empress Ballroom's down on Mexborough's West Street, no matter how I try, I really cannot remember.

As a child, I often remember standing at the bus stop outside the old Empress building, which at that time had housed a café within its frontage, and I fondly recall waiting for the buses to come into Hope Street and drop off at the end of John Street before the driver changed the destination on the black and white roll above his windscreen. I had seen that sequence of events occur literally hundreds of times throughout my childhood – and one that I remember was of me wanting to ride on the No 18 Yorkshire Traction bus.

"Mam, where's Newhill?" I remember asking. "Can we go?"

Nowadays, Newhill is just an extension of Wath-on-Dearne, but in the past had been a village in its own right – even possessing its own colliery up until leasehold problems arose.

If you look at the area between Newhill Road and Wombwell Avenue – just up the hill from The Crown public house – there used to be a place called Pottery Yard, part of which contained a lodging house capable of rooming over forty navvies, which during 1886 – the year the colliery ceased production, had been run by a sixty-five-year-old by the name of James Devine.

Devine, born in India to Irish parents, was a small, rotund, and extremely violet man. Standing at 5'1", with his face heavily scarred, he would be sentenced to seven years penal servitude the very same year.

On 6 August 1886, a twelve-year-old girl by the name of Martha Longbottom had been raped in one of the rooms of the lodging house – a place where she had been sent to work by her Irish-born stepmother, Bidelia (nee Carroll).

Whereas Devine ended up in Dartmoor Prison, Martha got sent to St John Baptist's Home, Newport, Monmouthshire – a children's home for neglected and abused children and one that closed its doors in 1940.

In 1985, the Empress', was in name only and was run as some shady night club. There were a few similar establishments scattered around the eastern Dearne Valley – The Kiss of Life, which became The Staithes on Manvers Way and the short-lived McCartney's, which was basically part of The Dearne Hotel in St. Andrews Square, Bolton-on-Dearne – none of which I ever went into.

Debbie had been in the Empress' with two other friends that night. One was a girl who at the time appeared an upmarket version of the lead singer out of the punk band Siouxsie and the Banshees. She had been in a serious relationship with a kid a year above me at school, who lived next door to my uncle Steve (Carman), down on Bolton-on-Dearne's Concrete Canyon.

Brian was the most laid-back of my friends and was just a nice genuine lad. He hadn't been a miner, therefore nor had he been on strike. My thoughts were, that unlike his elder brother Keith who was one year older than me, he had missed signing on as one of the last intakes into the pits as he had been moved down a year at school, due to his birthday falling on the very last day of August. He should have been part of the Class of 1981 but was not.

Brian was the unwilling poster boy for what at the time was Margaret Thatcher's Britain. One of the three million unemployed, something which at times he became quite aggrieved about – especially when his emotions got the better of him. All he ever got was scheme after scheme after scheme and the lad deserved much better.

This night however, he had got talking to the leather clad pseudo-punk that was Jeannie Allinson and Colin being the gentleman that he was (sic) ended up with all six of us in his car, with me offering to see Debbie the day after.

Like Jeannie, Debbie had also been in a relationship and with a lad from Goldthorpe who I had gone to school with by the name of Glenn Battersby.

Glenn was a decent looking lad – small and stocky, with a bit of a square-jaw and blond hair. Just another nice lad, but without sounding conceited, he was totally different to me. He may have been the same age and a miner –

however, that is where the similarities ended. I was never overly involved in the politics of pit life. I went to work, and I got paid, end of. I had no interest whatsoever in the rudimentary workings of what made everything tick. And I would have rather be seen dead than wear a flat cap. Glenn had been typical of a lot of the lads who went down the mines at a similar time to me, in that they immediately became middle-aged tap room politicians, whose main line of conversation was – yeh, you've guessed it – the pit.

Debbie informed me that they as a couple were going through a sort of cooling off period.

It's strange looking back at the situation as she was a girl with such a lovely demeanour and that being the case, I could never imagine her hurting anyone's feelings. She did, however, certainly hurt Glenn's.

The following day, all that had been on my mind was the strike ending and I remember standing outside Martin Morrell's grocers shop on Roman Street with Debbie at my side and talking at length with Carl Eades, who is another person you will get to know as the story progresses.

"It looks like we are going back," was my line of conversation.

"Is that a new jumper?" was his.

I had just had a similar question aimed at me from Debbie.

"No – I've had it a while," I told him.

I had. A white jumper with yellow sleeves. £9 (£29, circa 2020) off the sales rail at Topman.

I hadn't realised how shite it looked until I got it home, with my first thoughts being – *that's really bright.*

As for Debbie, her mum had apparently told her that she wanted to meet me, and her daughter had therefore asked me if I would go to their house.

"I've met your mam," I told her.

"No, you haven't," she said.

Yes, I had.

I had met her in the spring of 1982, when she had been a part-time cleaner in the offices at Hickleton Main colliery. At the time, the blow-back machine for the brass checks had gone down and I had spent a week on Afternoon shift post-my sixty days underground training fetching and carrying them from the No 3 shaft side to the Time Office. Since then, however, she had moved on and possessed the same supervisory job as my mum at the English Rose, which was a sewing factory that was once located within the industrial estate that sat in the shadow of the embankment that once carried the long-since dismantled Wath Branch Line extension of the Hull and South Yorkshire Railway at the bottom of Highgate Lane.

"Well, she wants to meet you, again then," she said.

By the time I had walked her home on Saturday night, they had all been in bed. However, on the said Sunday she certainly made sure that I would indeed meet her mum. Firstly, by calling at my house around two o'clock in the afternoon with her ten-year-old sister, Helen and then literally dragging me through mine and their back doors around four hours later.

I liked her mother a damn sight more than she ended up liking me – that is for sure. Yvonne could come over sharp and abrupt, but she was both a fantastic mother and a woman quite typical of a miner's wife. I also liked her stepfather, Eric – or *Dabba* rather, as he liked to be known, and who like mine, worked as an Official (Deputy) at Hickleton Main.

You notice the similarities?

Debbie's home was a vibrant household and full of lovely people, one of which included her younger brother, Dean – who was someone that I would get to know much better in later life. It's strange looking back at it, as I thought the family to be extremely nice and why I didn't stick around, I really don't have an answer to.

"I'm a Conley," her mum had told me.

"Like Brian Conley, the Union man?" I shrugged.

"That's right," she said. "And my mother was an Exley."

The Exley's were a family that I had certainly heard of and one that had had their share of heartache.

Yvonne's grandparents – Sam and Elizabeth Exley (nee Baines), had married in 1924 and between them had moved into a house on King Street and were looking forward to their first child, which was due around the New Year. Elizabeth did give birth to the child on 29 December – however, it was born dead.

Never think that you only get one major upset or heartache throughout your life, because you don't. As sad as it is, back then, a child being born dead or indeed the death of a child, was nothing out of the ordinary and it happened all too often – and that includes my family.

The cemeteries at Thurnscoe and Bolton-on-Dearne are full of dead children.

The couple went on to have a further seven children – the first who was Yvonne's mother – Joyce, who was born two years later and the second of whom, was Derek.

The layout of Thurnscoe's King Street hasn't changed much in over one hundred years, except for one side of the street being demolished to make way for a series of new-builds and a substantial facial uplift of the remaining properties opposite.

Derek had lived at No 19 whilst his best friend, Herbert Gilthorpe, had lived five doors up at No 9.

Not only did the street end where Hickleton Main's colliery sidings were – it also backed onto what is now referred to as The Drum playing field, which back in May 1937 was the Wath Branch Line along with a railway station, which served the Sheffield-York line. In fact, the station master's house is still there, which in 2019 operated as a community nursery.

As you will see, Thurnscoe can be a hard and vicious place and in my humble opinion much more so than either Goldthorpe or Bolton-on-Dearne. I have no real idea as to why – it is just how it is.

Derek and his mate were mischievous eight-year-olds that were being subjected to a bit of bullying from an elder lad. To get away from him, they split up and Derek slipped under the platform and on to the main line where he was hit by an oncoming train, which ended up dragging him several hundred yards down the track. It wasn't the first and certainly wouldn't be the last. It was tragic, but avoidable. Back then the colliery sidings and the railways were a great source of interest – and to children, they were something of a playground.

Not only did I know of the Exley's, I also got to know about Derek's mother's family – the Baines's, who were from Bolton-on-Dearne – however, that would be a case of me jumping too far ahead of myself as that is a story in its own right.

"So, Derek would have been your uncle?" I asked.

Yvonne nodded and smiled.

The whole East end of Thurnscoe was like this. Everyone tended to know one another or was related to someone, somewhere along the line. All the good, the bad and the ugly. However, one thing I could always do, was interact with a miner's wife.

For me, the Miners' Strike had been in two parts, which I will hope to explain as the story progresses. During its latter months, I developed something of a routine, where I would come in from a picket, and Colin, Carl and myself would share breakfast – either at mine or at Carl's just around the corner at 27 Briton Street, where we would be joined an hour or so later by John Gratton – who due to his arrest at Haworth Colliery and the conditions of his bail, picketed well-away from where the violence was. It may have only been tea, toast, and breakfast TV, but the craic and humour were quite something else. And the stories we picked up from Carl used to have us all in stitches.

Imagine Rik Mayall's *Flashheart* character from the *Blackadder* TV series and that is probably the closest comparison you could ever get to him. He would often play out his alter-ego as the devilishly handsome, loud, brash and treacherous playboy, who was not just a sex symbol to pretty much every woman that he came across but was also amazingly experienced and utterly perfect at everything he did – from lovemaking to driving, through to him being the world's most complete miner. It was a great act that he played out time and time again and his treachery knew no bounds. In truth, he was very witty, articulately spoken and extremely clever – and more importantly he was someone that I could listen to all day.

During those breakfast times, Carl told us a rather eerie story of something that had happened circa 1968/69, when he and his family had lived close to one part of the Exley family on Thornley Crescent. It was also something I relayed to Debbie's family: The story of Mad Lettie.

Thornley Crescent and Taylor Street were the main part of a sweeping estate on which the Thurnscoe UDC commenced its construction in 1919 and which was rightly named after the benefactor of the land, who was Rev Thomas Thornely Taylor, MA.

The huge Crescent arced all the way from opposite The Thurnscoe Hotel (New 'Un) on Houghton Road, sweeping around the rear of its infant and junior school and what was the site of Houghton Road's Garden City, which was not only intersected from west to east and sort of half way up by Taylor Street, but from north to south by School Street, the latter of which was one of the two vehicular accesses into what would become the REEMA Estate.

As with The Crescent in Bolton-on-Dearne, it has long since been redeveloped to bring the structures in line with metropolitan borough council modernisation. What was different in Thurnscoe, however, is that the names were completely erased and what is left, now forms Stotfold Drive, Ashberry Close, Orchard Way and what is now an extension of John Street.

The clergyman's generous donation of the Thornley Crescent site doesn't even scratch the surface of what he did during the development of Thurnscoe – both its village and East end, so it is a bit of a headscratcher as to why the great man's kindness was in effect thrown back in his face?

It is true to say that Thornley Crescent and Taylor Street did possess an indifferent history, the latter possibly more so – but so did other streets.

In the main, its houses were made up of blocks of terraces, with ginnels to access the rear yards or gardens. Carl's parents – Laurence and Lilian (nee Liversidge) – or Lol and Lil rather, had moved from Bolton-on-Dearne's Maori Avenue and lived in one of these blocks of terraces with his two elder sisters, one of whom was their Debbie – a girl that had been a couple of years older than us.

Also living on one of the houses within the terraced block, was a woman by the name of Letitia – or Lettie, rather.

Lettie Corbett, had originally been from Butcher Street and in 1950 had married a man from 44 Deightonby Street, by the name of George Norman and sometime after their marriage became locally regarded as someone who had, what would now be termed as, mental health issues.

If you want a blunt appraisal: "It was the husband who fucked up her head," I was candidly told by one of her then-near-neighbours.

During the early 1960s, she was often seen wielding a stick and chasing kids through gardens. Nowadays, that would be construed as an offence of violence towards a minor and a psychiatric evaluation would precede any sentence a judge would have to offer. Back then it was different. Parents just told you to avoid anyone who was viewed as not being a *full shilling*.

On this night in question, however – and whilst everyone was asleep, Carl's sister awoke in panic, and literally screamed her lungs out. Her father Lol, raced into the bedroom thinking that his daughter had just had a nightmare. What she had witnessed, however – had certainly been no figment of her imagination. It had been something very real. Her sleep had been disturbed by a noise in the bedroom and she had awoken to see the head and shoulders of a woman hanging through the ceiling of her bedroom. After Lol had managed to compose his daughter, she pointed up to the loft hatch, which he noticed had been displaced. On him climbing up into the roof of the house he saw that a couple of the brick partitions that separated the lofts of each house had had bricks removed at one of their ends. It hadn't been much but had certainly been enough for a person to travel between each property. The police were called and according to Carl, 'Mad Lettie' ended up being 'put away'.

Debbie's mum apparently knew of the woman who had lived at 27 Thornley Crescent and was the one returning the conversation – however, it was the expression on her son's face that I recall the most.

Dean was possibly one of the greatest young lads that I had ever known, and I could kick myself up the backside in the fact that I should have got to know him better. He was a brave, fearless and an incredibly talented goalkeeper – who had played with the all-conquering Thurnscoe Hill junior side and who could have, and who should have, played at a completely different level.

I remember circa 1990 playing the last half of the pub-football season with The Fairway – not the supermarket, but the big East end pub at the bottom of Lancaster Street and our coach Albert Hey coming up to me at the season's end and asking, "Who's your pick for our Player of the Year, Jamie?"

"Dean," I told him.

I had brief spurts in and out of football all though my life, which altogether probably added up to about three, maybe three-and-a-half seasons – and although I stood out at this level, my heart was never really in it and my job and my family always dictated where my priorities lay. In the main, I worked weekends and as was the norm, I was generally out on a Saturday night.

As for Dean, he walked the Player of the Year award, and there was no-one happier for him than me.

Thinking back to that evening and the Strike's end, his mum had brought up the sensitive subject of all the rioting that had gone on in the village in late-November 1984, and I remember watching Dean's expression as I explained my involvement, therefore dispelling most of the rumours that had been circulating within the village: Those of which who had actually done *this and that*.

I may not have been interested in pit politics, but out on the street, I had been one of these so-called miners that the tabloid media referred to as headcases. More importantly, from my perspective, I was one of those headcases who never got caught!

I certainly never looked like one, however. I appeared clean, courteous, said "Please" and "Thank-you" when needed, and as I relayed the tale of how a few dozen striking miners created huge blockades and caused carnage everywhere, headlining on the ITN News after an attempt on the life of two police officers, that twelve-year-old lad was in complete awe.

"At Hickleton Colliery police were drawn into a potentially lethal ambush. They arrived to move a private car which had been overturned alongside a railway bridge. As they set about the job, several sections of railway track were thrown on top of them from a height of thirty feet. A police vehicle took the full impact from one of them, but no-one was injured.

"The police said it was an amazing escape as the railway line was so heavy it took seven men to lift each piece and haul it clear of the road which led to the nearby pit. Other officers were used to scour the area in a vain bid to find their attackers."

Terry Lloyd, *News at Ten.* 21 November 1984.

"I heard it was *so and so* who threw that railway line on top of the police car," Yvonne had inquired.

"That's definitely not what happened," I told her, and my explanation literally had them all aghast.

As I have often said, time passes and things that were important back then tend to either have their importance diluted or at worst get forgotten. And they shouldn't do.

Mine was a surreal sight as I stood in the waste land and the ash-tips that was once the lovely Lidget Wood (The Bluey). At around 3.00 a.m., I recall looking up the hill and past the entrance to Hickleton Golf Course and seeing police van after police van after police van after police van arriving and tactfully parking up on the hill. I counted fifty-two of them – all of which would have contained anything between twelve and eighteen officers, all of whom would have been decked out in riot gear. They knew what they were coming to.

I had been one of those lads who had helped create the eastern blockade of the village, but what happened at the western end could have had severe ramifications if it had gone the wrong way. It could have easily resulted in the death of a police officer or officers and several thirty-year sentences handed out.

Thurnscoe rarely gets mentioned in any history books of the strike, which is strange as the village (and its pit) was more solid than anywhere in the UK. To my knowledge, there is only one pit – a pit in South Wales, that could claim to have been more so, and that had no miners go back to work whatsoever.

That morning would be a catalyst of invention which a few days later made all the national headlines for all the wrong reasons as it saw two miners from South Wales – Dean Hancock and Russell Shankland, receive life sentences for the murder of a taxi driver who had been taking a scab into work at Merthyr Vale mine.

In Thurnscoe, a similar method was used – however, it hadn't been a taxi driver that had been targeted, it had been the police. After failing to ignite a car, which had been pushed from the car park of The Station Hotel (The Drum) to the site of the underbridge – a structure that had been tunnelled beneath the Sheffield-York railway at the turn of the century, a concrete railway sleeper had been hurled from height and onto the roof of a police Range Rover. This created panic beneath and saw the vehicle scream forward to safety in first gear – its roof being severely crushed.

Nowadays, the move from open analogue to the encrypted digital Airwave system in the UK has made it practically impossible to listen in on police radio – however, back then you could easily pick their conversations up on any decent Medium Wave system.

"We have an abandoned car partially blocking the access to the bridge," stated one of the officers in the Range Rover, as it tentatively navigated around the white car, with a rag crudely hanging out of its petrol tank before partially mounting the kerb before moving to drive beneath the underbridge.

"I think there are some people on the bridge."

Then it came. Bang!

"…We've been hit – we've been hit… requesting assistance… a railway line has been thrown off the bridge and hit us… requesting immediate assistance."

It hadn't. It had been a concrete railway sleeper. One second earlier and it would have gone through the windscreen and possibly killed those occupying its two front seats.

As the crumpled Range Rover pulled up around fifty yards from the scene of the crime, every available railway line and concrete sleeper was thrown off the underbridge. Thurnscoe East had been completely cut off.

Due to the severity of what had just taken place, all the striking miners – maybe around twenty-five of us, quickly dispersed.

Some of the stories that emanated from that night and the day after bordered on exaggeration to complete falsehood, and in later life some claimed to have had been there who had not.

The frightening thing about that night is that it had been seen by the police as attempt on two of their colleague's lives and became the catalyst for them becoming out of control and as such, someone could have easily been killed.

Colin Hunter and I were the only miners that never totally left the scene of the western blockade. From a personal angle and being inquisitive, I wanted to see what was happening – therefore, we stood back, both hidden by the shadow of darkness on the old infilled railway bankings that once carried the Wath Branch Line past the rear of Deightonby Street.

It was a mess, but nowhere near as bad as the eastern blockade, which saw over a dozen mine cars lifted from the colliery sidings and slung across Lidget Lane, along with every other movable object. I remember Frankie Feast – a big lad who had been a year older than me at school, saying that he had never worked as hard as he had in helping set up that blockade.

The blockade at the western end had been far easier as the thirteen-foot high (not thirty as claimed by ITN) underbridge had always been regarded as something as a bottleneck. The bridge not only suffered regular bridge strikes, but often had HGVs or high-sided vans getting stuck beneath it. As kids the tailbacks generated by these, was always a great source of interest.

Our inquisitive nature however, soon changed, when dozens of policemen who were all decked out in riot gear arrived on site to clear the debris. This was swiftly followed by four Ford Escort police vans that pulled up in The Drum car park.

"We need to fuck off," Col exclaimed. "They're the dog handling units."

He wasn't wrong.

On the back doors of the vans being opened we heard the dogs barking and snarling, and on them getting out saw them jumping around with their handlers trying to restrain them. It was as though they had known what had happened.

We didn't hang around and shot off up the rear of Deightonby Street and back to the safety of my house on Briton Square – or so we thought.

Never ever think that a police dog doesn't know the subject that it is tracking, because it does. Ten minutes later there were about a dozen officers with dogs standing at the end of the cul-de-sac and staring into the Square. Why they didn't go into it I still don't know. Maybe they thought it could lead into an ambush? As for us, both Col and I had been knelt under my front room window in both total darkness and silence, whilst trying to watch developments from behind the net curtains.

In both our minds we thought they were just waiting for reinforcements before getting ready to come on to the street. However, the mess that had been made at either end of Thurnscoe East was thankfully taking hundreds of police to clear. Therefore, as soon as the police decided against coming on to the cul-de-sac and focused their interest on moving further up Briton Street, we left the house and cut through the back garden of the empty tenth house on the Square. This was a property that had been the former home of an elderly lady by the name Annie Whittaker, who must have had over a dozen cats living with her.

Never ever forget what I said in that each house on every street in Thurnscoe East has a tale to tell and 10 Briton Square is one such property and one that could usurp most.

Off the top of my head, I knew of at least eight children that had died on the Square – but none in the circumstances which five-year-old Brenda Cole did on 27 January 1942.

She had lived at No 9 – the house in the far-right hand corner, but had been playing in the next-door neighbour's house along with her elder sister Sarah and Josephine Billam – whose parents John and Minnie (nee Nortcliffe) were the occupants of No 10.

According to the neighbours, the children had been playing around lighting paper in the fireplace and Brenda had unwittingly set her clothing alight, with the quick-thinking of an insurance man visiting a nearby property coming to the aid of the burning child. The damage, however – had been done. Brenda suffered extensive burns to her body, face, arms, hands, and thighs and was pronounced dead on arrival at Mexborough Montagu Hospital. It was stated that the daughter of Francis and Mary (nee Gaskell) had died from shock.

What is more upsetting is that little Brenda had had two elder sisters that had died: Joyce aged nineteen months in November 1936 and Margaret some sixty-three days later, aged four.

Never think that the suffering in that property was just confined to the Cole family. The dark cloud of misery has hovered over that house at 9 Briton Square a long time and has seen families come and go – one of whom who were a lovely couple by the name of Paul and Susan Hollinshead (nee Davies) who sadly lost their seven-month-old daughter on 24 October 2001.

If you ever want to witness a pure and unadulterated sadness, you need look no further than the funeral of a child. To the parents, it is an emotionally crippling feeling of hopelessness and despair. The mother propped up by her husband and her father completely heartbroken at the sight of his granddaughter's casket being carried towards the altar and unable to deal with the hurt, ending up on his knees outside St Hilda's Church, sobbing his heart out.

With regards to upset, I don't think anything can ever come close.

As for the Billam's – they would have six children all in all, one of whom would have the notoriety of eventually being found guilty of Goldthorpe's *Body in the Boot murder* on 6 October 2011 and which is a story that I will certainly go on to explain.

As for Colin and myself, we sought sanctuary down at the NUM Office, which was a huge mistake as there were police everywhere, some of whom had lost control with one officer, in particular – being well and truly off the scale. "There's a fucking load of them in there," he said on climbing up at the window.

I knew the senior NUM Official at Hickleton Main, quite well. A lovely man with a slicked-back Elvis-style haircut, by the name of Billy Hayes. However, this would be the only time I ever saw panic in his face. The situation was as scary as hell and the said officer had been riling up his colleagues. My thoughts were that they were going to start smashing skulls and it was only his commanding officer who stopped that from happening.

"Have you seen what they've done down at the bridge?" he screamed.

"I've told you once," said his commanding officer. "Get back in line."

It took the said officer being told quite a few times, before he eventually backed off – and even then, he was still snarling and spitting.

We got off unscathed – however some did not.

Billy Coulson, who is another person that you will also get to know as the story progresses, had been totally unaware of what had happened during the small hours and as he had most mornings from late-summer into winter, had been walking up to the pit for what was generally a 6.00 a.m. picket (unless otherwise stated). Unfortunately, Billy got accosted on The Drum playing field, just yards from where little Derek Exley had lost his life forty-seven years earlier. It was something that resulted in thirteen stitches in his forehead, along with his wrongful arrest.

It is hard to imagine over one thousand police officers camped in Thurnscoe East and patrolling its streets, but that is exactly what happened as more and more police got drafted in throughout the day.

Later that morning, things never let up and I remember standing outside a store on Lidget Lane opposite its Hickleton Terrace, which had always been referred to as the *Pit Shop*, along with around thirty or forty lads who were a similar age to myself. This had been no picket – it never was. The irony was, that although we were easily outnumbered, our sole intention had been to draw out the riot police.

You could throw all the bricks that *you* wanted, but those long shield police units were virtually impenetrable, and it wasn't until the short shield police made their presence known that you could actually hurt them. There was a downside to this, however – as it was they, that were after hurting *you*.

The police had been camped behind the huge wall that surrounded the colliery grounds and every now and again a handful of them came to the top of Pit Lane to monitor the situation of the slowly swelling crowd. As I recall, the crowd weren't all miners. I think most people there, were simply curious and stood back watching as events unfolded. They weren't to be disappointed.

Around 11.00 a.m. the long-shield riot police began to be deployed across Lidget Lane, possibly gearing up for the scab coming out of the pit – or possibly not. Unfortunately, for us we were limited to what we could achieve. As we were on the busy thoroughfare that traverses the village, and barring ripping some innocent persons wall down there wasn't much aggregate around to throw. It had therefore been a case of slowly transporting it around from the site of the old Coronation WMC – that had once stood opposite the park behind the Whitworth Buildings and which had closed its doors on 31 July 1958. However, even then, there hadn't been that much.

As the riot police set up to block the road everything that could be hurled at them, was. They were bombarded for a good ten minutes – however, as was always the story – they were organised, and we were not. Their sole aim had been to soak up everything we had – which as I have said, hadn't been a lot. Suddenly, their lines parted and around fifty short shield police came charging at us, screaming at the top of their voices, and beating their shields.

I would be the first to admit, that if you have never seen it before it is quite an intimidating sight.

Apart from the odd missile being thrown, we had nothing. Even if we would have stayed and gone hand to hand, we would have only had our heads pummelled and ultimately been arrested. Have you ever tried hitting someone with a crash helmet on and who is bulked up with body armour? I have. You cannot hurt them. Add the fact that they have a rubber shield in one hand and are wielding a great stick in the other, it only left one option.

I remember the crowd scattering – the majority down Lidget Lane and towards The Drum with various pods of miners breaking off through the village's eight northern terraces and some racing across the car park of the Coronation WMC.

My *pod* had been a retreating dash up Coronation Street with Colin Tutin, guiding the escape party. I may claim to know Thurnscoe inside-out, but at the juncture in my life the back gardens of Saxon Street and Dane Street South were a completely new territory to me.

Saxon Street was one of the first to be built as part of the new pit estate – being constructed in 1921. It was, however, one of those streets that you never really had to go down unless you lived there, and in the twenty-eight years that I had lived in the village I could count on one hand the times that I had walked down it.

I may not have traversed its undulating tarmacked thoroughfare between the *Houses of Stuart and Tudor*, but I certainly knew of it, as very few streets had witnessed the amount of misery that this one had. To my knowledge there are at least twenty-five children off Saxon Street buried in the cemetery. These range from a two-year-old by the name of Alen Atkinson who had lived at No 9 and who had literally been boiled alive in February 1922 to the unfortunate Cook twins – John and Brian, the sons of Lawrence and Frances (nee Holland) at No 3, who both died as babies a few days before Christmas 1940.

Never let anyone tell you that Thurnscoe wasn't founded on blood, sweat and tears.

We had been directly opposite No 33 – which had been another house on the street with a lousy history, and vaulting over a few rear fences, before concealing ourselves. Waiting for them to go or knelt there in anticipation of any one or two policemen breaking rank and becoming isolated? I have no idea. It could have been either. During the late autumn of 1984 this had become the norm. Just eleven days earlier we had been in Brampton Bierlow and I recall us being chased through some old-aged pensioners bungalows by a couple of dozen or so police and three or four of them becoming separated from the rest of the pack. These hadn't been dressed in riot gear, however – on the contrary, they were just normal Bobbies from the South Yorkshire Police force. It was hardly a case of us dragging them to the floor and beating them senseless. They were just attacked with anything that could be thrown at them – dustbins, milk bottles, bricks, stones etc.

Although the police were on Saxon Street in numbers, I cannot recall any of them presenting themselves in the rear gardens for anything more than a brief glance. They just wanted us away from the colliery.

We had been up all night and although our industry created nothing short of a mess at either end of Thurnscoe East and a massive police presence in the village for a few days, our actions were futile. In life, history as a tendency to repeat itself and everything – and I mean everything, comes to an end.

Almost sixty years earlier the miners at Hickleton Main had returned to work after the lockout of 1926 and still out of work after suffering from influenza, and with Christmas a only few days away and a pile of debts that couldn't be paid, the fifty-eight-year old head of the household at No 33 – George Henry Goddard, had decided that he'd had enough. He took a carving knife from a drawer in the kitchen and didn't just slit his own throat but almost completely severed his head from the trunk of his body before collapsing on the kitchen floor in a pool of his own blood.

I could certainly think of a much better way of committing suicide – however, it hadn't been the first time that someone had done it by cutting their throats. Far from it.

i) On 5 May 1910, Alice Stockton – the fifty-three-year-old wife of the Caretaker at Houghton Road school, in some frenzy of depression, slit her throat in the attic of 3 Orchard Street, Thurnscoe almost severing the head from her body.

ii) On 2 November 1916, a thirty-eight-year-old by the name of Charles Lane of 5 Beever Street, Goldthorpe was found collapsed on the hearth rug in the kitchen with a table knife in his hand. According to his landlady, Clara Coates – he too had nearly sawn his head off.

iii) A sixty-two-year-old miner off Thurnscoe's Spike Island by the name of James Spencer was found in a semi-conscious state, collapsed and half naked in some undergrowth off Lidget Wood a short way away from his home at 86 George Street. He was found to have had two lacerations in either side of his throat and died from loss of blood on 3 July 1920.

iv) On the Friday morning of 10 September 1922, one of the bedrooms at 9 Main Street, Goldthorpe set the scene for the suicide of a forty-eight-year-old miner by the name of Alfred John Bulgin. He was found by his fellow lodger, George Rowley, slumped at the side of his bed with his throat cut.

v) A sixty-year-old by the name of George Goodman of 49 High Street, Thurnscoe had survived a roof fall at Goldthorpe Colliery on 4 September 1923, which had crushed his rib cage. According to his wife, Annie, he never truly recovered from the injury and continually suffered violent pains. On the Sunday morning of 13 January 1924, it appeared that he had had enough and slit his throat – his wife finding him laid in a pool of blood on the kitchen floor.

vi) Although he had been born in Tullamore in County Mayo, George Patrick Conway had, like many miners living in Thurnscoe, gone to fight in the First World War. George had served with the Fifth Lancashire Regiment but at thirty-four years of age and following severe head injuries, had been discharged on 17 January 1916. He had married Elizabeth Bootland in 1910 and after initially living in Shafton, had set up home at 69 Church Street, before moving into one of the newly constructed houses at 6 Westfield Crescent in 1928. After the war, he had been employed by Thurnscoe UDC as a lamp lighter – however, since the war, he had been known to suffer from severe bouts of depression. At 3.20 p.m. on 12 December 1929, he was found dead on the kitchen floor of his home. He had cut his throat.

vii) Joe Barstow was the elder brother of George – a miner who had resided at 33 Butcher Street with his wife Alice, and who between them ended up seeing five of their children buried in Thurnscoe Cemetery: two-year-old Samuel (d. 1904) and Rhoda (d. 1906); eleven-month-old Nellie (d. 1911); three-year-old George (d. 1915) and nine-year-old Harry (d. 1925). Joe – a sixty-four-year-old miner, had lived at 4 Whyn View, with his wife Emma and on 29 July 1932, he had been one of the 750 men that were laid off from Hickleton Main due to a dramatic downturn in the coal industry. After six months without work, Joe had had enough and at 7.20 p.m. on 11 January 1933, he was found in the lavatory – his throat being slit with so much force, that the carving knife had to be dislodged from his spine.

viii) On 28 April 1934, and unable to take any more pain from a serious internal problem that had left him almost bedridden, sixty-eight-year-old Harry Taylor – who lodged at 18 Hickleton Terrace, with Herbert and Mary Ann Carr, was found bleeding in the kitchen. He had slit his throat. Dr Francis Boyle was called and stitched up the wound – but Harry died shortly after.

ix) The strangest one was perhaps the slow and painful death of the great grandfather of one of the lads that had been part of the mayhem in Thurnscoe on 21 November 1984 and someone who would become a good friend – Steve Bradley. Eighty-two-year-old Benjamin (Ben) Sims was one of those poor souls whose life mirrored that blood, sweat and tears philosophy, and who had seen six of his kids die – five as children, one as a thirty-two-year-old. Ben finally succumbed to life at 12.10 p.m. on 15 September 1941. Three weeks prior he had tried gassing himself but failed. This time he not only slit his own throat but made sure of his death by self-mutilation, in that he literally disembowelled himself. Even then, it was hardly instantaneous. An ambulance had been called to his home at 72 Houghton Road, Thurnscoe and on him being admitted to Mexborough Montagu Hospital at 11.15 a.m. his body defied all odds. "He was in a semi-conscious condition and there was a severe incision in the abdomen," explained House Surgeon Dr Abraham Greenberg. "Numerous coils of intestine were lying outside the body cavity and there had been another serious incision that had exposed both the liver and stomach."

x) The last one takes us back into the story in that this was one was one of George Henry Goddard's near-neighbours at 19 Saxon Street. Sixty-two-year-old Percy Fred Ensor worked on the colliery surface at Hickleton Main and had been employed as a wagon lowerer until the summer of 1958, when he suffered a mental breakdown. At 12.40 p.m. on 13 September 1958, Percy – who had been a capable local footballer in his younger days, had been found lying in the bushes of his back garden, with cuts to his wrists, groin, and throat – the latter causing his death through haemorrhage and shock.

"My husband was a very moody man and very often went for hours without speaking," spouted the wife of George Henry Goddard, to anyone who would listen to her. "There is insanity in his family and both his sister, and a cousin are in asylums."

There was a passage that was cited by the literary master of the irrational, the demonic and the macabre. Edgar Allan Poe was quoted as saying: Believe nothing what you hear, and only half of what you see. Poe may well have had his issues, but he hadn't been that far from the truth. There is always another angle to every story.

Although George Henry Goddard had supposedly been married a total of nineteen years and to a woman that was twenty years his junior – it certainly hadn't been the happiest of unions. I say supposedly, as rather strangely, there are no records of George and Martha's marriage, which can mean one of two things: Either they were never married, or I just can't find the records.

Their marriage had made worse by the presence of a man by the name of John Arthur Dickenson – who, reading between the lines, was nothing more than a ponce.

George had been a forty-two-year-old single miner living alone with his father in a two-up-two-down in the Eckington area of Sheffield. A year later he had a twenty-two-year-old woman in tow by the name of Martha (nee Hayes) and had lived in numerous addresses in Bolton-on-Dearne – not at least a property at 164 Furlong Road and just next-door-but-one to what would bear witness one of the oddest incidents that ever occurred in the area. However, that rather strange episode would be around sixty-five years into the future. It was here, however, where Martha gave birth to a boy on 7 November 1912 – who was named after the father.

As with her husband, Martha had been from the Eckington area – however, my thoughts are – and that is all they are – is that she had been married before, and that she needed out quickly. Therefore, it is assumed that she hooked up with George and fled the area for the eastern Dearne Valley.

As for Dickenson – he was originally from Bradford and in December 1907 had signed up for twelve years with the Royal Navy. His military career was nothing short of a disaster, and with just fourteen months on the clock and whilst serving on board HMS Charybdis, he got slung out on his ear. "He is a shore undesirable," his discharge sheet read. "He is also dirty, troublesome and very untrustworthy."

His career away from the Navy didn't bode too well either, being sentenced to twelve months hard labour for committing a burglary in 1913 by the grandfather of Baron Peter Hardy of Wath-on-Dearne – that being Sir Reginald Hardy.

How he got to Thurnscoe is anyone's guess – as is how he found the Goddard family in 1922. Firstly, living at 10 Dane Street South then both 41 and 22 Saxon Street, before firmly getting his feet under the table at No 33.

He was four years younger than Martha and possessed dark brown hair, deep blue eyes and a fair complexion – but at 5'3", it could hardly be said that he cut a dashing figure.

It was well-noted that Martha went everywhere with him. "When he first came to us," she had said of Dickenson. "He had an enemy who was threatening him, and my husband agreed that wherever he should go, I should go with him."

There was a lot of truth in that – not so much the "being stalked by an enemy", but the fact that they went everywhere together. It was even stated that Martha's husband gave them money to go to the cinema.

On 24 October 1925, Martha gave birth to a child in the large bedroom of 33 Saxon Street – however, that child was born dead. At fifty-seven years old it is not inconceivable for George Henry Goddard to have been the father – just unlikely.

The pieces of the jigsaw were coming together.

With the General Strike and the subsequent lockout of the miners, 1926 had been a year like no other, but George had left for a while. This was something that had been confirmed by his wife.

Her father-in-law had been a coal miner at Eckington – the exact same place where her husband had worked, which during the said lockout had witnessed terrible scenes of violence. Scab labour had been imported into Eckington's Moor Lane and Plumbley Wood Collieries as early as June – with the latter having around 100 striking miners wrecking the place, to such an extent that it had had to be abandoned.

"Even when my husband went away, he sent us money," she had said.

Was the reason George Henry Goddard had left the village because he had scabbed at his old pit?

"He never worked during the lockout, though," his wife candidly stated.

I am not so sure about that.

By 23 December 1926, however and with Hickleton Main beginning to turn coal, George had finally had enough.

With both the child and lodger out, George had come downstairs to find his wife sat at the kitchen table eating breakfast and something inside him obviously snapped. Without saying a word he attacked her with a knife, stabbing her five times around the head, once in the neck and whilst trying to stop the flurry of blows, she had received several defensive wounds in her arms and hands, before managing to escape the assault and run out on to the street screaming – eventually getting sanctuary at their next-door neighbour's house, the home of Harry Smith.

At the coroner's inquiry at The Drum, all the fingers were pointing at Martha Goddard and her inappropriate relationship with Dickenson.

"People are saying that our lodger Mr Dickenson caused the trouble," she said. "The reason why we always went out together was so that I could be a witness in case anything happened from the man who had been threatening him."

PC Stones, who had been first on the scene and had opened the house to find her dead husband, explained that he had been called to the property several times due to family quarrels, but rather strangely, never a quarrel between George Henry and Dickenson. "It was either with the deceased and his wife or Dickenson and the wife – never between the two men."

"You know it is suggested that you are the cause of this, trouble," the coroner Frank Allen told Dickenson – which was something that he totally refuted.

After the inquiry, Martha Goddard told reporters: "When the matter is cleared up, I shall try to forget my husband and teach my boy that he never had a father."

She moved out of the house and along with her son took up temporary residence at 52 Church Street – the home of Herbert and Rose Crowley, where low and behold on 18 February 1928, she gave birth to another son, which she again duly named after its father – this time John Arthur Dickenson Goddard. Unfortunately, the child died after just two days.

This was a tragic tale, but never think that the story ends there.

Rather strangely, Dickenson didn't move to Church Street with Martha and stayed in the house at 33 Saxon Street, quickly befriending a twenty-one-year-old by the name of Violet May Goodlad – a girl that he ended up marrying and setting up home in Thurnscoe's Avenue's with.

As with Martha Goddard, Violet became pregnant but unfortunately their child was born dead, only to get caught on immediately after – this time with twins.

The Dickenson's moved from Marlborough Avenue and onto Kingsway – close to Violet's mother, Annie – however, it was not to be. His wife gave birth to a son and daughter – Jack and Violet (Jnr). Their joy, however, was short-lived as the twins survived only two days, dying on 9 December 1930.

As for what happened to the remainder of the Goddard family, the son – George Henry Goddard would marry a girl from Chapeltown by the name of Ivy Pell. However, don't ever think that the Thurnscoe connection goes away.

Ivy Mary Pell was also from a big mining family and had a cousin a year older than herself by the name of Arthur, whose great grandson knew Thurnscoe and much of its elderly population extremely well, and had walked its streets during the time that I and several others had been evading the riot police in those rear gardens of Saxon Street.

Tall and studious in appearance, Graham Pell had been selling policies on behalf of the United Friendly Insurance Company. He did, however, work at a completely different level and befriended some of the older generation, and after carefully hand picking his victims, took out loans on their policies, which led to both his arrest and imprisonment for embezzlement in the early 1990s.

Rather strangely his imprisonment led to something of a company shake-up and one of the people to eventually step into Pell's shiny shoes was one of Thurnscoe's Class of 1981 and a striking miner, who lived but a short walk over Dane Street's infamous Bullring – Kevin (Chammy) Chambers.

Kevin was a very smart and witty lad who I would get to know quite well. I suppose it is starting to sound as though everyone I knew was a great kid. That, however, is most definitely not the case. If you believe what these the socialist history books state, you will find yourself being sucked into thinking that mining and its communities was one of solidarity in the face of adversity. There is of course a lot of truth in that, but if you look deeper, the exact opposite could be also said.

By the Strike's end, I had turned twenty years old and I knew a hell of a lot of people. There were also a lot of these who I regarded as friends – not at least Chammy. That was certainly never the case when my mum in her wisdom, decided to cross the divide that is the A635 Doncaster-Barnsley road and uproot the family from Bolton-on-Dearne in early-February 1977.

In September 1976, I had started school at Dearneside Comprehensive – the huge red-bricked building off Goldthorpe Green that was rectangular in shape and which stood close to Barnsley MBC's Goldthorpe *Town* Hall – the latter of which is a contradiction in term as Goldthorpe is a village.

The royal blue jersey, white shirt and striped tie may well have brought something of a false equality amongst its students, but on moving to Thurnscoe, it certainly made sure that I stood out like a sore thumb – especially as it was at the height of the Goldthorpe-Thurnscoe rivalry, where village gangs fought to establish, who were the Kings of their crumbling castles.

Our move to Thurnscoe was around the time that one of our Fourth or Fifth Year-lads had been involved in some altercation on Pit Lane and had had his skull fractured. A student by the name of Doddy – Andrew Dodd, I think. This had created tensions between the two rival factions and being a kid in Thurnscoe's East end and wearing the uniform of Goldthorpe – I had been immediately singled-out. The first-time had been one late Friday afternoon whilst walking up Stuart Street, where on its junction with Norman Street I came across two lads – one of who was none other than Kevin and his minder, Martin Finbow.

I may have described him as articulately spoken – however, back then he was nothing more than a fast-talking, trouble-causing motor-mouth. Dressed in a V-neck jersey, grey trousers and propped up by a pair of black slip-on shoes, he had fast-tracked my induction into what would be three or four years of hatred, which a day or so later, became very much full-on.

We had moved into a four-bedroomed pit house at the far end of Lancaster Street. Why we had moved from what a newly constructed four-bedroomed house on Bolton-on-Dearne's Flower Estate is anyone's guess. I always saw it as a sheer act of folly. My mum had said that the council had increased the rent on the house and that the rent for the pit house was much cheaper. There was certainly a reason for that! Just a couple of months had passed since my twelfth birthday and all I saw, was that the move made absolutely no sense at all. In my mind, the house on Lancaster Street was nothing short of a fucking dump. The only good thing about it was the shed. And even that was falling to bits.

I had the option of moving schools – however, I had been halfway through my first senior year (Year 7), and as I had done in the last year of Carfield Juniors, I was thoroughly enjoying it. Looking back, 1976 was without doubt, the best year of my childhood. When you have a good home life, everything follows suit.

Hanover Street is quite a long street and joins both Tudor Street at its east and Briton Street at its west, whilst the dirty old *House of* Lancaster cuts right through its centre. In early 1977 its western end contained St Hilda's Church, with its tape-recorded chimes along with its park, playing field and two heavily graffitied, brick-built bus stops. The western stop for the Barnsley-Doncaster buses – the eastern stop for the Thurnscoe-Mexborough ones, or in the 107 or 276's case as it was later to become – the Mexborough-Doncaster bus, which only ran on a Saturday.

The following Monday morning, whilst waiting to board the 8.25 a.m. 273 bus for school, and whilst all the non-uniformed kids from Thurnscoe's Comprehensive were hanging around the western stop to board their schools-chartered transport, over twenty lads – some much older than myself, made their presence known. It was something that as a kid you should never have to encounter. I was jostled, kicked, and spat at, so much so, that the driver of the bus, had to issue threats to some of the kids. This had been my first real taste of Thurnscoe's East end and it would only get worse.

The rivalry between the two fractions had also reared its head at Dearneside.

As I have said, 1977 was the height of Thurnscoe *Mob*-legend, and one of the lads that always seemed to be mentioned was the heavy-set and chisel-jawed lad that was Colin Tutin. I recall one dinnertime, whilst stood around in Dearneside's school playground of him and Keith Waite turning up at the entrance to the school and of why I still have no idea.

It was quite an eerie moment, as all the noise in the playground suddenly stopped. Within what was literally minutes, most of the lads from the Fifth Year (Year 11) ROSLA block came out and commenced walking towards the entrance to the school. It was the stuff of legend – and as for me – I was the kid who had to walk (and at times run) between the two.

We all expected some fight breaking out – some form of payback for the brain damage caused to Doddy. I can't quite remember which teachers they were – possibly our headmaster Mr (Leonard) Dickinson or maybe Mr (Howard) Baxter, the deputy headmaster, but whoever it was, they did a first-class job of calming the situation, both sending Colin and Keith on their way and getting their Fifth-Year students to go back inside.

As for Debbie Davidson, at that point in time I was someone who was beginning to move too quickly and had become extremely selfish. And if there is one golden rule in life, it is that you should never shit on your doorstep. This would be the first time, but certainly not the last that this would happen. She was an extremely nice girl and deserved far better than what I gave her. What is also true is that her mum mirrored those exact sentiments.

I really liked Yvonne and my thoughts of her now is one of admiration. Back then, however, and as a kid who didn't give a shit, I just saw her as some loose-talking firebrand of a woman. She did, however, have a side to her that you had to respect.

The Strike had been over a few weeks when I answered a phone call up at my mum's. Rather strangely it had been Yvonne. "Ah, now then young man, you are just the person I want to speak to," she said in a rather well-thought out, if not eerie tone. "Now, what have you been saying about my daughter?"

I hadn't been saying anything about her daughter. There was nothing to say. Debbie was just a pretty girl with an extraordinarily nice demeanour. There was nothing bad that anyone could ever say about her.

I ended up on the receiving end of a few barrels of verbal, until I cut her dead and told her to put their Debbie on. "I've said nothing, Deb," I shrugged. "Honest."

I hadn't. The upshot was that her mum just wanted to give me a bollocking and boy did she give me one. And it didn't end there. The next thing that happened is that I then had my mum on my case.

"Someone's got to marry these poor lasses after you've done with them," she shouted.

I had treated Debbie badly and I would be the first to admit it – however, her mum still wasn't done. Around nine or ten months down the line I had a pregnant girlfriend grizzling at me after Yvonne had kindly sent us down their Debbie's wedding album. We were using the same photographer for our wedding as Deb had had for hers, and Yvonne obviously thought my future wife should see what a good photographer (sic) he was.

As for Yvonne, she died not so long ago, and what I heard – whether this is right or not, is that she and Debbie hadn't been on speaking terms for quite a while before her death. Now, if that was the case, it is tragic. I thought them a genuinely great family – and Yvonne, one hell of a woman.

The Hunter children of 123 Thornley Crescent, Thurnscoe.
Left to right. Andy, Jane, Colin and Steve

23

Top. The rear yards of Thurnscoe's Terraces (Grange, York and Clarence) with Hickleton Main's No 1 and 2 headgear in the background - 1973 (c. Kevin Holt). Bottom. Thurnscoe's Market Place (and former Cinema building) - 1985.

24

3.   1981

At just sixteen-years-old, I signed on at Hickleton Main colliery in November 1981, along with a Catholic kid from Thurnscoe's Whinwood Estate by the name of Steve Handley and a lad off the East end's Windsor Street, by the name of Darren Eades. There had been a fourth lad, who the training officer, Ron Lester sent back for not having the appropriate eye wear and who ended up getting set on later. He had been another lad off Windsor Street by the name of Dave Helm.

The intakes into Britain's coal mining industry were becoming fewer and fewer and that *Friday the Thirteenth's* version of the Fab Four, would not be far off being the last. I had got in by the skin of my teeth, but the reality of it was – it was something which should never been allowed to happen.

In my mum's mind, me going into mining was never an option as I was seen by her as being a very clever lad and that being the case, she thought that there were other jobs I could do. I was, I just never used it. I had gone up into Dearneside Comprehensive in September 1976 as one of the most promising students from Carfield Primary School and had left with a load of mediocre O-Levels that in truth, were not worth a dot. I had excelled in English, but even then, it had been a case of rushing to complete a heavily backloaded set of assignments, as throughout the first part of my final two years, I had been both lazy and disruptive.

My mum had initially refused to offer her parental signature for me to apply for the NCB's Junior Management scheme, even though I'd had it filled-in some ten months earlier and I had to endure an unsuccessful interview down in Mexborough for the same position in some local travel agency, where I had been one of over 200 applicants for the job.

Me being knocked back for a job in Allied Travel, was obviously the catalyst for my mum finally giving-in and offering her signature to complete my application form. This would eventually be processed over at the NCB's Area Headquarters at St. George's on Doncaster's Thorne Road – though rather strangely, mine never got sent in by post. It got handed in to the training officer at Goldthorpe Colliery, by the father of my best mate through school – Pete Bright.

Little did I realise during the long hot summer of 1981, that in just over seven years' time, I would be in conversation at those exact same headquarters trying to force the end of my employment, as I saw the Board's newly re-branded British Coal as doing its absolute damnedest to hold me back.

I was backwards and forwards to the Area Training Centre at Armthorpe's Markham Main colliery for exams and medicals throughout the spring and summer of 1981, passing every test that they gave me – however, my mum's reluctance to sign that form when I had first handed it her, made sure that my easy path to being a mining engineer and/or undermanager had been blocked. For their part, the NCB offered me an alternative placement as a general miner – however, that route was also nearly blocked when their letter arrived during my family's two-week vacation in Torremolinos.

In my life, I gauge 1981 nearly on par with 1976, as things at home, and school, had been quite good.

My mum made sure that I would be driving come my seventeenth birthday and just to move that line of thought along, a near-neighbour on Lancaster Street who had also been a supervisor at the English Rose sewing factory, Christine Walton (nee Cruise, now Hobson) had had begun a relationship with a man who originated from Sheffield by the name of Frank St. Clair.

The story was, that her husband Tony, who had been a miner – had walked out on both their marriage and young daughter Nicola (now Cornes).

Frank was not only a fantastic bloke in general – he was also a qualified driving instructor.

What made him special is that he was a thoughtful character who treated me as a grown-up and took time to speak with me about a variety of subjects – with cars and aeroplanes being something of a passion. He was quite tall, therefore at times he could appear to stoop, and possessed slicked back – if not a greasy-looking dark brown hair. He did, however, possess quite a rather cool Mexican moustache.

All through the summer, Frank would drive us over to Sandtoft aerodrome on the Isle of Axholme and at the request of my mum, teach me to drive. I fondly remember him buying me half-a-pint of bitter and sitting outside The Reindeer public house in Sandtoft.

Little did I know at the time, that just over twenty-six years later, amid national media interest, a mobile incident room would be set up in its car park, whilst around fifty policemen combed the fields opposite. It would be a time when I had been implicated in a botched murder attempt on some shitbag career criminal. According to the police, two armed men and gone into a property several hundred yards away with intention of killing its owner.

It was allegedly all part of some strange puzzle that had seen around half a million pounds worth of property destroyed over several isolated incidents, two of which saw both the ITN and BBC *News* outside my home and sort-of culminated with the two-would be killers – one who originated from the High Green area of Sheffield, trying to put a bullet in the man's forehead.

Fortunately, I had been in Paris for the weekend, therefore my role as alleged gunman was downgraded to that of orchestrator, with the police insisting that I come in for questioning and my phones seized.

Did I go? You must be fucking joking. That is why I use the best solicitor in the north of England.

What the media never reported on, however, could be construed as two-fold. The fact that the owner of the property had been hanging out of the upstairs window returning fire with an automatic weapon and the fact that during the Crown Court trial of the two would-be killers, one of the North East circuit judges who had been presiding over the case – Justice John Reddihough QC, referred to the witness as being a "paid police informant". This was something that had the trial put back several times as the prosecution had been purposely withholding evidence.

After a bit of plea bargaining the two lads got hit with a six and a five-year sentence – not for attempted murder, but for reckless arson. Whilst the owner had hit the triple-nine these would-be assassins had gone on to torch his property – and whilst he was still inside it. It is where the phrase *smoking him out* could be used.

As for Frank – I saw him as something of a big brother, rather than just my mum's mate's new bloke and that line of thought was further stamped, on our immediate return from Spain.

While we had been away my mum had obviously asked Christine to keep an eye on the house and Frank had been nipping over on a regular basis – to feed the cats I think, and on us opening the door on our return there had been a hand-written note waiting for me on the kitchen table.

"I hope James didn't mind," it read. "He had a letter from the NCB and me thinking that it was important I thought I should open it."

There had been some problem with a chest X-ray that I'd had. Not a medical problem, just the fact that it hadn't been developed properly. As that was the case, they wanted me to go in for another, prior to me signing on. Frank had phoned up the Area Headquarters at St George's, told them who he was and of course where I was, and had requested that they reschedule the X-ray for when I got back. It may sound like nothing, but most people would have ignored that letter. Frank being Frank did not and his overly humble explanation for opening my mail and the thoughtfulness shown in taking time out to call St George's, said absolutely everything about man.

However, just I was about to go in for my driving test during the spring of 1982, I was tipped the wink from my mum to look out of our room window, only to see him packing up his car. He and Christine's relationship had come to an end, and he was leaving. Not only would I only see him a further two or three times, it was also the catalyst for me not taking my driving test. Some of life's impressions may only be small, but no matter how big or small those impressions are, some can last a lifetime.

Life is a series of sliding doors and timing – well, timing is everything.

The reality, is that I never ever saw mining as a career. And being honest, I was initially as lazy and disinterested in mining as I had been at school. The money was the only thing good about undertaking the morning ritual of catching two buses: the first into Doncaster's North Bus Station and the second from the Christ Church bus stop opposite Cooplands bakers on East Laithe Gate into Armthorpe, where sixty days of training took a damn sight longer to undertake than the said twelve weeks it advertised. This was mainly to do with bad weather prior to and throughout the Christmas period of 1981, along with the regional strikes.

Our instructor had been a guy by the name of Derek Rawson. He was a rather sharp-witted fellow who possessed a highly sarcastic nature and was someone that I had bumped into just before the Strike. If I am being brutally honest, he wasn't someone who left a lasting impression on me, as if he had, I would have certainly remembered it.

Training was boring and monotonous and only the thought of going underground made it bearable. Half the time we were shipped out to the colliery screening plant over in Askern where we shovelled shit and mud all day. There was a day at Bentley Colliery doing the exact same thing springs to mind as well.

There were some other good local lads in our group – Ian Dickinson from Goldthorpe and Mark Swales from Thurnscoe – both who ended up at Goldthorpe Colliery. The blond-haired Ian had a penchant for beef dripping sandwiches whilst Mark had a battered complexion and spoke with a broad Yorkshire accent.

The horrific weather throughout December 1981 might have drawn out the training but being sent back to your own pit was quite the eyeopener. All the trainees were charged with gritting the pit yard, sweeping the lamp cabin or pit baths, and in some cases, washing the managers car. There was certainly no mining involved. After being sacked from baths duty by a bespectacled man by the name of George Cartwright, for not respecting the chain of command and having over-elaborate snap times, which ran into hours rather than the allotted twenty minutes, Tim Bright and myself were excommunicated and sent out into the freezing cold to work over in the stockyard where there was a smell of diesel all around. It was a job you could do standing on your head. Building up fires in the massive steel drums was great fun, which along with the snowball fights quickly forced our transfer out of the stockyard and over to the pit top drainage, where we were put under the supervision of a man by the name of Billy Burton.

Billy was from *The Spike*. This is basically a part of Lidget Lane opposite the blacksmith and wagon shop, its central point being a street which at one time ran up the side of the colliery brickworks. What is rarely, if indeed, ever said is that this was in fact the second brickworks. The first was built on the same site as the mine around the same time it was being sunk and was located in more or less the exact same spot as the Parkgate No 3 shaft which was sunk to a depth of 820 yards in 1921/22.

Billy was also an amateur Radio Ham, but more notably, he had a high-pitched speech impediment, which made him sound as though he was talking through his nose. Both Tim and I thought he was a wonderful guy, made more to do with the fact that he treated us like his long-lost grandson's than anything else. He basically let us do whatever we wanted, such as rolling into work at 8.00 a.m., having hour-long snap times and knocking off at 1.15 p.m. And this was nothing compared to the easy life underground.

If you wanted a perfect example of a nationalised industry and the main reason why the government wanted to get shut, then this was it.

Tim had been my best mate throughout school. While I had been living on the Flower Estate, he had moved into one of the even-numbered prefabricated houses at the end of Carr Field Lane which, along with part of Hall Broome Gardens and Crofton Drive had been built straight after the Second World War. He was part of a family that had come together via two divorces.

His father Pete was a Thurnscoe lad. He was the son of Charles and Sally (nee Jarvis) and the middle of two brothers that worked at Hickleton Main – Derek (b. 1929) and Keith (b. 1939).

Pete had been born on The Avenues and had several sisters including an elder one by the name of Brenda who sadly died from Dilated Cardiomyopathy – heart failure, at the age of thirteen. It had been something that had been brought on by both Mitral Stenosis and Asthma. He also had two more siblings which had been sadly born dead – in 1935 and 1946.

Rather strangely, Pete's family had moved from 24 York Street to 8 Salisbury Avenue and then onto 85 Brunswick Street, with the time spent down on The Avenue's being when his father hadn't been employed at the pit.

Tim's mother had walked out on not just her husband, but he and his younger sister Catherine, whilst his stepmother, Jill, had split from her husband Ronald who she had married in 1958. She came to the union with her two daughters – Beryl and Linda.

Tim's mum was a woman by the name of Jean Parry, who I had only ever seen the once. This was around 1979 at her mother's and Tim's nan's – the end bungalow off Calder Road and opposite Bolton-on-Dearne Railway Station.

My first recollection of his dad was winning the parents 90-yard dash on Sports Day at Carfield School in the summer of 1973, whilst wearing, what appeared to me at the time, a pair of platform-heeled shoes. It must have been a chip off the old block as their Tim – a bit of a rank outsider, had won the First-Year lads 60-yard dash beating Darren Mitchell into first place. As for me, I slipped after the starting pistol had been fired, courtesy of a cheap pair of pumps that I'd been bought purely for the occasion and I just managed to beat Darren Hughes into fifth place.

The contrasting emotions was of Tim – who at that time had a quite a stutter – getting a medal of sorts and me bawling my eyes out as my mum had come down to watch, and had brought my sister and baby brother.

Other contrasting emotions from the First-Year's that day was of the diminutive Carol Parr winning the girl's sixty-yard dash by at least twenty yards and Julie Atkinson (now Link) losing her footing and falling over in the girl's walking backwards race and being as miserable as I was.

It was in the Second Year (Year 8) of Dearneside that Tim and I became good friends, something which has lasted a lifetime, although as you will see as the story progresses, it is a relationship that has not been without its ups and downs.

Due to both my mum's reluctance to sign on the dotted line and the glitch with the chest X-ray, Tim had been part of an earlier intake of lads, which wasn't just a case of him starting six weeks earlier than me – he had made it onto the NCB's Junior Management scheme – which was something that I would come to resent during the year-long Miners' Strike, as his going to Barnsley Technical College one day a week allowed him a standard fortnightly payment of £27 from the DHSS. As for me, I would receive absolutely nothing. Zilch.

The course was dubbed *Mining Craft* and as I would see throughout my short life with the NCB, those who had both made and stayed the course, jumped to the top of Face Training lists, paving the way for much better wages. This was always a constant bug bear with me, both before the Strike and after it. Some lads appeared to get on without trying. As for me, I had always been made to fight.

The reasoning behind the failure of the Strike is put down to miners in Nottinghamshire being reluctant to come out as they were earning better wages than those in Yorkshire. There is of course, a lot of truth in that, but in my mind, the disparity of pay at colliery level, always fucking stunk. The money was never brilliant and the most that I ever took home in my pay packet, whilst at Hickleton Main was £93 (£331, circa 2020).

During the sixty days training, my wages hadn't been touched by HM Revenue and the majority of the regular £51 (£221, circa 2020) I picked up on a Friday, was being spent on my way through Doncaster's town centre. Lester's – a young man's clothing shop, which was located off Waterdale on the top right-hand side of Duke Street and opposite what is now The Colonnades shopping centre, was generally my first port of call. This was always followed by half-an-hours browsing in my favourite shop. Fox's Record's was located on the upstairs landing of the Arndale Centre and opposite *The Lovers* bronze statue. It was a huge place of interest for any audiophile as it held a vast catalogue of records and if, for some reason they didn't have it in the shop – they would always order it for you. Fox's also had a sister shop further down the landing which specialised in musical instruments – their forte being pianos and keyboards.

On leaving the shopping centre via the escalators, amid the rush of people shopping and going home from work you had to negotiate the subway tunnel beneath the A630 that led into the town's North Bus Station with its distinct stench of urine along with its heavily graffitied walls, with *Skellow Suedeheads*, being the one to greet you as you came into the underpass. There were also illegally fly-posted advertisements everywhere with *Afghan Rebels* live at *Japs Wine Bar* and *Orpheus in the Underworld* being the ones that immediately spring to mind. And at the end of the subway there was a café to the right along with steps up to the Trades and Labour WMC as well as a well-stocked newsagent with a front and rear access to the left. How I miss how things were!

Buses were our only way of completing the journey home as very few of us had a car.

At 14p (61p, circa 2020), the 212 was easily the best option or 18p (78p, circa 2020) if I caught the 213. Both buses provided a Doncaster-Hanover Street route on their way to Barnsley, with the more expensive ride taking in the longer journey through Sprotborough, High Melton, Barnburgh and Goldthorpe.

Everything was dependent on timing, and more often than not, it was a case of jumping on either the 279 or X19 and a stop outside (Barry) Taylor's shoe shop at Goldthorpe. This meant a walk over Pit Lane – or in Darren Eades' case, a run.

Darren was the son of Frank Eades and the nephew of Fred, the latter who I knew, not just from him living in Briton Square in later life, but from him being the husband of Shealagh. Whilst we lived on the Flower Estate, they had lived on Stumpcross Gardens, which was a cul-de-sac off the western leg of Crossway – two streets which dissect the Ringway council estate. Shealagh had worked regular nightshift with my mum at either one of two places – that being Lyons Bakery in Carlton or United Biscuits (KP Nuts) in Rotherham.

Apart from being a very smart, good-looking kid that possessed a lovely demeanour, Darren had been a very capable schoolboy footballer. His childhood sweetheart had been Cheryl Adams (now Marsh). She was a year younger than us and lived near-opposite him on Windsor Street and that being so, was the sole reason of his haste.

Although we were never at the same school, I knew him quite well – sometimes through playing football, but mainly through my popularity (not) at being the uniformed kid that was kicked, spat and flagged at by the kids from Thurnscoe Comprehensive.

Just prior to me signing on at the pit, I had got involved in a relationship with a girl who lived at the east end of Chapel Lane. This is the long street which runs along the very top of Thurnscoe's East end, and that in reality ran south to north from Lidget Lane as solely a untarmacked bridle path of sorts, then as a street with the odd-numbered houses looking out onto the countryside and linking the top of Brunswick, Lancaster and Briton Streets and ending at which was at one time the old wooden bridge over the Wath Branch Line.

Prior to the pit being sunk, it was a lane which ran through greenbelt land known as Chapelfields, hence why its name didn't follow the regal pattern of naming as the other streets.

Colleen Evans was, in part, the template for the girl that I would marry. She was exactly two years younger than I and had an elder sister by three years who was employed as a sewing machinist. Her father worked at the pit, whilst her mother was on the local authority's Home Help. To complete that template – even though the younger daughter was far less aggressively spoken, she was by far the more headstrong and more to the point, certainly the more volatile.

Her father, Johnny had been born in the Betts Building's part of Lidget Lane and next-door-but-one to a property that possesses an indifferent history – not at least, its inhabitants down the years witnessing aggressive and violent paranormal activity, which had (wrongly) been put down to an old miner hanging himself on 21 July 1961. In fact, during the 1970's, the local vicar – a Rev Ken Emmerson refused point-blank to go upstairs and fully exorcise the house.

"The Cunningham family had lived in it and they fled one night never to come back," explained Kevin Feast, the grandson of the people that moved in shortly after.

As for Johnny, he sadly lost his parents when he was a child. His mother when he was five years old and his father when he was eleven – leaving him to be brought up as an orphan.

On 1 December 1938 and at just thirty-two years old, his mother Sarah had died of Mitral Stenosis following pneumonia. As for his thirty-seven-year-old father, George – he died in Crookhill Hall, Conisbrough on 8 November 1944. This was a facility that had been purchased by West Riding County Council in 1926 to use as a sanatorium for people suffering with Tuberculosis.

Johnny had therefore, for a time, been brought up with the family of Bill (Smokey) Watson at 79 Brunswick Street. He was also another who suffered from a speech impediment that saw him stutter badly – which was something that his wife Joyce (nee Roper) attributed to the fact that he had been an orphan.

As for Joyce – she had an uncanny resemblance to her part-namesake – that of Yootha Joyce's lovable on-screen character that was Mildred Roper. She was also, and rather conveniently, the younger sister of Elsie – the wife of Bill Watson, who between them also had two daughters – Denise and Diane.

In the main, the pit houses in Thurnscoe East had been built in blocks of two's and three's with the Evans family living in the middle house of a block of three at No 9, which was a grey mock-stone faced property, with a ginnel running down its side.

Johnny had been a Faceworker at Hickleton Main who had been injured during the 1970s – something which had forced him onto what would be regarded as a lower-paid job. As this was the case, he received some lump-sum compensation for his injury along with a weekly hardship payment that kicked up his wages to what they would have been if he had still been on the coal face. Therefore, I wouldn't be wrong in saying that both he and his wife appeared to be more affluent than most miners living up in the East end. It could also be said that this, had been a contributing factor to both daughters coming over as being spoiled, which at times led them to get away with murder. Personally, I didn't think that was solely the case. Far from it. There had been a younger child by the name of Martine who had been born around Christmas 1968, and who had died in Rotherham's Moorgate Hospital aged just three months old. Losing a child can give you a different perspective on life, especially where your other children are concerned.

Joyce was another who was very typical of a miner's wife in that she was a lady who always had an opinion and more to the point, a lady who was never afraid to voice it. She also suffered badly from a deformed spine, which I recall one time in particular – of her being bedridden for a couple of weeks and having to wear some immobilisation support corset to help keep her body straight.

Like most of the NCB properties that had been bought by its miners, they had put their personal stamp on it. Whereas our house was a series of bad attempts at DIY by my (step)dad, with mismatching windows and an interior that was held together by Artex, their house was not. Apart from the mock stone facing there was a small white conservatory that had been constructed around the front door which matched perfectly with the windows. Their kitchen had also recently been modernised to such an extent that it had been totally knocked through and the bathroom moved upstairs. Their home was a classic example of miners embracing progress.

In early 1982, my mum had put our house on Lancaster Street up for sale and rather strangely someone actually put in an offer to buy it. Our destination was supposedly an empty bungalow on Thurnscoe's High Street, a few properties down from the Thurnscoe WMC (The Ship). I wasn't fussed about moving as it would have meant my board going up from £10 (£38.71, circa 2020) to £15 (£58, circa 2020) and sharing a bedroom with my younger brother, Joel, as it would have with a similar property my parents had focused their attention on in Swinton.

As much as I hated living on Lancaster Street, neither move appealed to me and I was glad when it broke down. However, what would follow would be the catalyst for me leaving home.

I personally think that my (step)dad had got cold feet, as any house move would have meant them over-extending themselves – and what was always known, is that there was some huge industrial dispute lurking on the horizon. If this had been in my (step)dad's mind at the time it would, from a financial point of view, prove to be a very shrewd move. From a personal point of view, however – it was nothing short of matrimonial suicide.

As a teenager you rarely understand what is going on between parents, but I immediately noticed a change. Although I loved her, and I really did, I would be the first to admit that my mum was not only extremely volatile but very high-maintenance, and more to the point, living a life that, although she was its architect, she absolutely despised.

I mention the last years of Carfield Primary and Dearneside Comprehensive in 1976 and 1981 respectively with an affection, as they were times when family life was good. That wasn't always the case.

As I have said, you may never fully understand what is going on, but you certainly notice things, and I often looked at how other families interacted.

I thought Tim's parents, Jill and Pete, were quite perfect, given the circumstances of what was a union of two separate families under one roof. You need the two people at the heart of the family to make things work and even though there must have been a multitude of problems to overcome, Tim's parents worked hard at it. Mine on the other hand, did not.

My mum wanted things which my (step)dad could never ever give her.

My (step)dad had been born during the early years of the war to a wonderful woman who I thought was beautiful, both inside and out. His father was a war hero, wounded in North Africa and one of the under-commanders of the Second Battalion of the Bedfordshire And Hertfordshire Regiment who engaged in the Fourth Battle of Monte Cassino. Unfortunately, after his battalion crossed the Gari river during the advance into the Liri Valley he had been mortally wounded, dying some days later, on 21 May 1944, aged twenty-nine.

Major Sidney Francis Rayner had been born into a military family in 1915. His father was Henry, who had been a highly decorated soldier who had served in both the Boer and First World Wars and of which the evidence (medals) is mounted in a walnut frame in one of the alcoves of my lounge. He married a lady from 57 Windsor Street on 8 April 1939 by the name of Elsie Cowen. Exactly seven years after the death of her husband this lady would remarry a near-neighbour from 2 Windsor Square by the name of Eric Ellis and who sometime during early-1968, I would come to know as my granddad.

Her son and my (step)dad, Richard (Dick), had followed a similar route in the Army, joining up with the King's Own Yorkshire Light Infantry at an early age and serving in overseas campaigns in Malaya, Borneo and Aden, and which during one of these, he had someone's gun discharge in his face, causing partial blindness in one of his eyes.

I often wondered how he and his best mate, fellow soldier and Thurnscoe-lad Mick Lowe, were never knighted for their services to Queen and Country. His exaggerated stories of fighting off sharks in the Persian Gulf and wading through leech-infested swamps and shooting crocodiles in Malaya were the stuff of legend. As a kid I thought he was a brilliant man who in later life I would regard as a great friend. Unfortunately, it was not always like that.

In 1982 and on me going underground at Hickleton Main, I was part of a crew engaged as slave labour, to clean up the conveyor belt spills down near a new development into the Parkgate seam labelled PO2s, when I came across a three-man team, part-comprising Nigel Evans – a huge well-set man who would play an active role in the Miners' Strike, and Ronnie Rich, who were undertaking a back-rip and replacing bent and tired tunnel supports with wooden props. I knew Ronnie, as he lived across the road from us on Lancaster Street and had worked with my (step)dad as a miner. He explained that my (step)dad had become concerned about the discs in his back and mentioned that this had been the main reasoning behind him going on some management course in early 1980 – in the hope of becoming an Official (Deputy) at the colliery.

Although I was lazy, disinterested, acted rather foolishly at school and therefore at times felt the wrath of his tongue – mainly in that he referred to me as either *stupid* or *thick*, this was certainly was never the case. Although he was never a nasty man, he had a highly sarcastic nature about him, which on one hand could be extremely humorous and the other, not so. He was also a man who became easily frustrated at failure. I recall one Friday evening of him coming home from his management training course at Doncaster's Bessacarr College with a load of homework and slinging it across the room floor and candidly stating that he was going to pack it all in. The problem he had concerned standard mathematics. He didn't know how to undertake the division of fractions.

You leave the first fraction in the equation alone. Turn the division sign into a multiplication sign. Flip the second fraction over and multiply the top numbers (numerator) of the two fractions together and then do the same with the bottom numbers (denominators).

"Basically, you just turn the end one upside-down and times them," I told him.

"And that's it?" he shrugged.

If no-one shows you how things are done, how on earth do you learn?

Mining, just like maths, was a huge learning curve and although I never fully appreciated it at first, there were good reasons behind the boring and monotonous training course, the on-site induction, the close personal supervision and the long wait, which felt like an eternity, before we were allowed underground. Most of the spring of 1982 was spent with Darren Eades over in the colliery screening plant and washery, cleaning-up conveyor spills and removing debris. Again, basically shovelling shit. Although it was boring, monotonous and filthy work, it gave you a huge insight into how everything worked on the surface, and my (step)dad's stepfather – my granddad Ellis, who had both recently retired and who had formerly been a fitter on the washery and coal prep plant, used to be in his element at my tales of who was doing this and who was doing that.

My grandma and granddad lived on Thurnscoe's Lindley Crescent, an estate of prefabricated concrete pit houses that were constructed in 1954 and which theirs – No 63, backed onto the Sheffield-York railway line as well as the railway sidings into the pit.

Their house was the exact replica of the several hundred that the NCB had built along Thurnscoe Bridge Lane and down Derry Grove and at either side of Ingsfield Lane in Bolton-on-Dearne around the exact same time.

Even now, I can close my eyes and recollect the smell of the house as I walked in through its front door to see the stairs and its landing right in front of me. There was the lounge door to my left that was rarely ever used apart from Christmas and New Year and a further walk down the passage took *you* into a busy kitchen-cum-dining room via a door with a fizzy lime popsicle handle. There was sink under the window, an open fire, a settee and a chair and a sky-blue Formica dining table that always had a teapot and sugar bowl on it. How I loved that house and the people who lived in it.

As my grandma rarely threw anything away there was absolutely no uniformity about the house whatsoever. From the magazines and comics that got delivered on a daily basis and got stuffed down the side of the chairs to the varied shaped glasses and cups in a cupboard beneath the sink along with a miniature wooden barrel with its multi-coloured plastic-sword cocktail sticks on the windowsill.

As a young child, I was allowed to toast bread over the fire's hot coals and often asked by my grandma to look over at the colliery's red-bricked chimney stack, which stood 200-feet tall, as that is where my granddad would be. The treat of treats would be around 2.30 p.m. when the Deltic-hauled Flying Scotsman would trundle past their house on its way to Edinburgh, and which at one time, would have been a Gresley steam engine. And around five o'clock my granddad would come through the door off his ten-hour shift to a lovingly set table of a ham salad and celery sticks.

My grandma's house was extremely vibrant and heavily-trafficked, with neighbours such as George and Margaret Marples (nee Bruce) regularly calling around with their dog – a snappy terrier by the name of Whiskey, both of whom, just like my grandma and granddad, were just lovely genuine people.

George was a huge jolly balding fellow with a lump on the side of his head. He had been a Rope man at the colliery – a profession that involved the complex splicing of steel wires and which could appear like rocket science to anyone not au fait with it. His main love was crown green bowling on the snooker table-like surfaces of the greens off Houghton Road's junction with Shepherd Lane, that were snugly positioned to the rear of both the library and Liptons (Broughs) supermarket.

I remember exactly where I was, when I was relayed the news of his death at just sixty-three years of age. On an underground Tannoy system talking with my (step)dad after spending most of the morning cleaning up some coal spills from the huge conveyor which transported mineral from T02's main gate and the P02s development down to the bottom of Number 3 conveyor, which had recently been the scene of possibly the largest coal spill in Hickleton Main's history.

"What's up with the belt?" asked Joe Roper, the compact albeit moustachioed District Overman with the all-guns blazing attitude.

"I've got a bit of a spillage," said the TPA (Transfer Point Attendant), rather understating it somewhat.

"Do you want me to send a couple of lads down to help you shift it?" asked Joe.

"Yeah – and can you send down an Eimco bucket down as well?"

"Why, is it a big one?"

"A bit – you could put a flag on top of the fucker."

It wasn't word for word, but it summed up the enigma that was the affable and extremely funny lad that was Eddie Lockwood – a lad from the bottom end of Thurnscoe, who was a couple of years older than me. Rumour had it, that he had fallen asleep down the mine. The NUM explanation to the Colliery Manager was much different however, in that "he had gone for a shit".

The west side of Parkgate had been stopped from working for a couple of shifts, costing the colliery hundreds of thousands of pounds in lost production and all Eddie received was a fine of £30 (£116, circa 2020).

A Transfer Point Attendant was an over-elaborate name for a Button-Man, which to me was the most boring and monotonous job in the colliery. Eddie's job was certainly one of the worst in the pit and which was one that he shared with similar aged lads on the two other shifts in Tony Morley and Phil Lloyd, the latter of who was an extremely good local amateur footballer. It was also the lowest paid job, but one which was an integral part of some unqualified apprenticeship towards the greater good. It may have sounded par for the course, but the reality was post-strike, that once you were on this type of job – you would never get off it.

The thoughts of me being on one were straightforward. It was easy work and therefore money for old rope.

My girlfriend had asked, on me on starting at Hickleton Main, a similar question that most people had aimed at me after I had signed on: "Are you going to make mining your career?"

I remember it, like it was yesterday – walking their dog on the huge playing field opposite their house – a Rough Collie by the name of Duke, one freezing evening during late-November 1981.

"I don't think so," I replied. "I'm going to give it five years and I'll see what happens."

Now, that was exactly word for word.

4.   The Drowning Pool

As I have said, Martin Finbow had been one of the first kids that I bumped into on my return to Thurnscoe on that afternoon in February 1977. The Finbow's roots can be traced back to the turn of the century, when Walter and William came down from Thornhill Lees in Dewsbury, to work at Hickleton Main and their being here and through marriage – to Emily Willets and Rose Simpson in 1908 and 1911 respectively, provided the foundations for its future generations.

The family was not without its misfortunes, however – as the cemetery in Thurnscoe gives a stark reminder to how things were. Ten children bearing the name of Finbow are buried there – one of which was Martin's ten-year-old cousin, John, who along with his eight-year-old friend and neighbour, Stephen Dolan of 90 Deightonby Street, both drowned in the colliery reservoir (Reser) in July 1963.

These weren't the only tragedies in the deep dark pond that innocently backs on to the rear of both Tudor and George Street, as well over one hundred bodies have been dragged out of its watery abyss. Some who had accidentally drowned and some not so.

If you want a similar occurrence, an eleven-year-old William Redvers Kelly and nine-year-old Stephen Brown of 26 and 24 King Street respectively, suffered the exact same fate on 17 August 1911. They had waded out into the pond to waist height before stepping off one of its ledges and being sucked into its depths – with the words, *sucked into*, giving stark meaning to what lies beneath.

Lessons would not be learned. On the Sunday morning of 6 September 1914, several boys from South Elmsall and Moorthorpe had walked over to Thurnscoe, with the sole purpose of going for a swim in the Reser – which back then was plainly referred to as the *clay pit*. Ten-year-old Elias Brown went into the deep end and immediately got into difficulties, with his friend – a thirteen-year old by the name of George Whitehead, going to his aid, and being pulled under with him.

A seventeen-year-old Army recruit from 116 Main Street, Goldthorpe by the name of Richard Moore (Andy Moore's great uncle) – went to the rescue of both boys but could only save one of them – the younger lad being the one that drowned.

The Reser was at one time a deep circular tank which was situated immediately to the rear of No's 10-14 Tudor Street. This preceded the pond that you see now and was still present up until after the Second World War, when it was both capped and backfilled. Even though the irregular pentagonal-shaped pond was built over 110 years ago, it is not the original structure and is indeed the second part of the Reser.

As you will come to understand, the clay bed of the pond and its extremely steep sides – the latter of which have been severely reprofiled over the years, were far more treacherous than depth.

i)   In late January 1899 – Alice Ann, the two-year-old daughter of Harry and Emma Hardman, went missing. After an all-night search it was ascertained that she had wandered from her home at 26 Butcher Street and up to the East end, which was still under construction and whose body ended up being recovered from the deep circular reservoir. It was the start of a series of misfortune that would follow the family around for years to come – culminating in one of her nephew's being charged with murder in 1968. Prior to that, her parents would have to bury a further three children following the death of two bothers and a sister. Tom and Frank died aged just one and eight months in 1906 and 1915 respectively, whilst Hilda died one year later aged two. Alice also had over a dozen nieces and nephews that died as children – all who are buried in Thurnscoe's cemetery, one of whom was two-year-old Mary Hardman. She lost her life at 100 George Street – a property that was not only part of the local authority's slum clearance in 1956, but one, which shortly after her death, would become the home of Ben Sims – the ex-miner who ended up disembowelling himself some ten years later.

ii) On the hot Thursday afternoon of 2 July 1908, seventeen-year-old Walter Firth of 58 Church Street was one of around 50 bathers in the Reser, but the only one not to return. Around 10.00 p.m. the pond was dragged by several miners – one of the men being forty-six-year-old George Sheppard of 6 Whitworth Buildings, and a body recovered. At a coroner's inquest in the Butcher's Arms, it was ascertained that Walter had got into difficulty after getting cramp.

iii) On 12 August 1909, a similar occurrence happened to a twelve-year-old by the name of John Connor, whose parents had been visiting friends in Thurnscoe East. He had got into difficulty after he became stuck in the clay bottom. Just a week later, on 17 August, two-year-old Lily Evelyn Hall of 27 Butcher Street fell into the pond and drowned.

iv) On Friday 19 August 1910 – a few days before a two-year-old child by the name of Alice Trueman died in a bath tub at 35 Chapel Street, Thurnscoe, an eighteen-year-old who was up from North Staffordshire visiting family, went bathing in the Reser, got into difficulty and drowned. William Brundle's body was retrieved by the relentless diving of a young miner from 10 Hickleton Terrace, by the name of William Jackson – whose son and namesake lived at 21 Merrill Road up until his death in 1983.

v) On 30 August 1913, Edward Rookledge of 21 King Street, Thurnscoe was commended by the Royal Humane Society and handed a certificate along with ten shillings and six pennies (£60.50, circa 2020) at the Doncaster West Riding Police Court. On 19 July 1913, he had dived into the Reser and saved the life of a seventeen-year-old girl from Goldthorpe by the name of Emmeline Cullingworth. She had attempted to take her own life.

vi) A nineteen-year-old, by the name of John Owen of 11 Gosling Gate Road, Goldthorpe had gone missing from his home on Christmas Day 1920 only to be found floating in the Reser three days later. Although, an open verdict was given by the District Coroner, it was stated that he had had been off work after suffering some form of Apoplexy – a stroke.

vii) Never think that it ends there, however. John's father – a man by the same name, had moved into 14 Tudor Street – a property that backed on to where his son had met his end. John Owen (Snr) had not worked in five years and suffered from violent bouts of tinnitus – noises in the head and ears, which had become more volatile than normal. Around 8.45 p.m. on 20 April 1934, he left the house and was found around 3.00 p.m. the very next day part-floating in around three foot of water by Fred Johnson of 3 Dane Street. Although John's hands had been bound with string, there were no signs of violence. He had committed suicide. He is buried along with his namesake and his other son, Thomas, who had died aged twenty-eight, two years prior.

viii) John Corley – a greengrocer who lived at 84 George Street found a body floating in the eastern corner of the Reser around 1.15 p.m. on Tuesday 5 April 1927. Rather strangely, twelve-year-old Robert Allington of 34 George Street had found a cap, coat and letter the day before – and had handed it his mum, Priscilla (nee Willetts), who duly handed it into the police station. Reading between the lines, both the contents of the letter and the state of the bloated body of twenty-one-year-old Joseph (Joe) Henry Briggs Jeffels of 25 Dane Street caused some alarm. The Coroner, Frank Allen, candidly advised against Joe's parents reading it and stated: "It is time there was a mortuary in Thurnscoe as in a case such as this, it is better that the body should not be taken home until it was in a coffin."

ix) At 9.30 a.m. on 16 August 1929, the body of twenty-six-year-old James Wood of 79 Deightonby Street was found floating face-down in the Reser. According to his parents – their son – who was a joiner by trade, had become paranoid and said that everyone was talking about him and saying that he was no good. Yet, another suicide.

x) On 22 May 1930 a nine-year-old boy, by the name of Harvey Slack was stood in shock watching Dr Francis Boyle trying in vain to resuscitate his seven-year-old brother, Leonard, after he had fallen into the Reser, whilst playing around the periphery of its then-steep banks. The scenes of panic with kids screaming and people racing from houses on Tudor Street, George Street and Lidget Lane were described during the inquest at The Drum, as was the fact that men employed at the brickyard, had been continually chasing children away from the pond. "We were racing each other round," Harvey explained to the Coroner, W.H Carlile. "Leonard was throwing stones into the water and he slipped in. I jumped in after him and brought him to the side, but I could not get anyone strong enough to help me. In the end I had to let him go as the mud was pulling us both under." The Reser at that time, possessed banks so, steep, that once you fell in, it was near-impossible to get out. A twenty-two-year-old, from 93 Lidget Lane, John Ratchus, was cycling towards the colliery when he noticed lots of people running towards the pond and after being told there was a boy in the water, stripped off and dove in. "I dove twice and on the second attempt I managed to find him," he told the coroner. "I handed him up to others on the bank who applied artificial respiration for an hour and a half. These were ambulance men from the pit and then the doctor."

The first time I had been to the Reser had been on a hot summer's day during 1977, with one of our near-neighbours and part of Thurnscoe Comprehensive's Class of 1981 – Neil Hopkinson.

Although its shape was very much the same, it looked absolutely nothing like it does now. Back then, the pond was nothing short of filthy. There also seemed to be rubbish everywhere – something which was further matched by the rear of part of the street that ran alongside of it.

A tall girl stood at the water's edge wearing only a brown bikini, while a couple of anglers had been positioned at the other end of the pond. The girl was Gail French – the youngest child of Leonard and Gladys (nee Cunningham). These were a couple who had married in 1944 and who had had her some twenty years later. Gail was also the younger sister of Terry, who a year later would marry his pregnant eighteen-year-old girlfriend – a girl from 23 Pitt Street, Darfield by the name of Carol Lofts.

It would be fair to say that at that moment in time I did not know her. That would certainly change, however.

Their marriage would inevitably break down, the reasons of which, I have no idea. It was mentioned that he had *gone off* with Sandra Griffiths – a short, disabled lady with wiry hair, who I had often seen trundling around Windsor Street in a wheelchair.

Without sounding facetious, this could give you a slight indication of the level *we* are working at.

Carol would hook up with my (step)dad's half-brother and therefore, my uncle – Pete Rayner, circa 1983, and eventually move into his house, which was a stone-built property on Wath-on-Dearne's Fitzwilliam Street. How they met I could only put down to only one thing. One of my uncle Pete's best friends had been an Official (Deputy) at Hickleton Main, who after the Miners' Strike went on to work at Bentley Colliery before being paid off and ultimately becoming the landlord of The Fairway. Geoff Morris was a lovely fellow – burly in stature and gregarious in nature. He also possessed an uncanny resemblance to the actor Gene Wilder – hence why he often got referred to as *Willy Wonka*. Geoff had been in a steady relationship with a lady who he would eventually marry in 1991. Diane Lofts was the elder sister of Carol by three years – however, that is where any similarities ended.

The last time I had seen Carol had been one afternoon in The Boy and Barrel – a rough-arsed pub on Mexborough's High Street, which had been the scene of several knifing's and where a twenty-five-year-old by the name of Robert Pears was brutally killed in the early hours of 2 August 2009.

Carol had come to the relationship with two young children – Gavin and Gareth, both of whom I regarded as extremely outgoing little lads who were nothing short of balls of fire. I would never get to know them as adults, however, as after a few years, their mum's relationship with my uncle Pete well and truly hit the rocks. It would be something that would see him waiting outside The Fairway and brandishing half-a-yard of lead pipe. Carol had been having an affair. She had been using her sister's pub to pursue a married man from 20 Lancaster Street.

I knew Jimmy Bridgen, more from my time private contracting in the mines – him with the Amalgamated Construction Company (AMCO) and I with Cementation Mining, as opposed to us living on the same street. He was originally from Bolton-on-Dearne – his parents firstly living at 56 The Crescent – a house where they lost their one-month-old son, Peter and which stood opposite a property which held an extremely dark secret, and one which I will get on to later.

The family moved shortly after, with Jimmy and his younger brother, Barry growing up at the bottom end of Lowfield Road.

Jimmy married and set up his marital home at the foot of Thurnscoe's Chapel Street around four years after Albert Jones at No 61 had abruptly ended his life on 29 May 1967, by putting a gun to his head and pulling the trigger.

Jimmy's wife, Irene, was the elder sister of one of Thurnscoe Comprehensive's Class of 1981. Tony Taylor was a freckled-faced lad with long hair who had been an integral part of the welcoming party on my first morning at the Hanover Street bus stops, which, in truth, never let up for weeks. It is strange looking back at it, as with Kevin Chambers, first impressions are quite often wrong. In the summer of 1979, Tony's quick thinking would save the life of a man on Brunswick Street when a car he had been working beneath, came off its jacks. However, during in my early days back in the East end Tony had been one of the first to feel my anger and frustration.

Although marriages break down, Irene certainly never deserved the humiliation that she would suffer, something which was compounded further by the fact that her marriage didn't just end in divorce. In December 1992, Jimmy, for some strange reason, married Carol.

I saw it as nothing more than a sheer act of recklessness. Without wishing to sound facetious (again), there are women that you can stake your life on and there are those you cannot. However, the twist in the tale was that Irene would somehow become the common-law wife of my uncle Pete and therefore my aunt, with Pete's son candidly stating: "Noel Edmonds couldn't have done a better job!"

I totally agreed.

Irene was the oldest daughter of Willie and Violet (nee Gillan) and who, along with her brothers and sisters, grew up at 27 Brunswick Street. The family, however, were another to suffer a tragedy in the dark pond.

Irene's great grandfather was Willie Taylor who had been born in Hoyland and had married a girl by the name of Harriet (Fanny) Hinchliffe (not to be confused with the surname Hinchcliffe) from the same village at the turn of the century and moved to Thurnscoe – the family being the very first people to occupy the newly constructed property at 12 Windsor Street in 1926.

This was the final piece of the jigsaw that saw Windsor Street complete the inner-arc of the East end and via Grange Crescent at its top, link with Stuart Street which had been built in 1921 as part of phase one, and therefore create a thoroughfare for traffic.

The couple had several children – one of who was twenty-nine-year-old Willie (Jnr) who had lived next door with his wife Emma at No 10 – another being nineteen-year-old Harold who lived at 52 Deightonby Street.

At 4.00 p.m. on Saturday, 15 March 1930, Willie – who was a tunnelling contractor at Hickleton Main, left his home on Windsor Street and was never seen alive again. The very next day his jacket and cap were found hanging on a fence at the side of the colliery reservoir by a PC Turner, who ordered the pond to be dragged. Willie's body was retrieved at 2.50 p.m. He had committed suicide.

His wife had died eighteen months prior and it was something which had hit him badly. According to both his sons and his thirty-seven-year-old housekeeper – Florence Grist, he had become even more depressed following the recent death of his seventy-three-year-old mother, Hannah, who had passed away over in Hoyland on 9 February.

To make matters worse the Taylor family would have more misery heaped on them as in August that year, his son Willie (Jnr), would lose his wife Emma Elizabeth at just twenty-nine years old.

Rather strangely though, he would go on to marry twenty-three-year-old Evelyn Eyre – the daughter of Herbert – the latter who had been President of the Kingsway Branch of the Cooperative Society. I say strangely, as his marriage came just a few months after the death of his wife.

Even though it was the newest part of Thurnscoe's East end, Windsor Street would not be left behind where people's misery was concerned. Just ask any of the surviving Lowther, Turner or Calland families – the latter which had two children, Joseph and Elizabeth, die on the same day – on 17 July 1939, and just before their respective seventh and third birthdays.

In November 1926, a twenty-nine-year-old lady by the name of Elsie May Hipwell (nee Woodson) of 3 Windsor Street became the first recorded person to die on the street. She was the grandmother of both Les (b. 1935) and Eddie Hipwell (b. 1939) – both who had contrasting roles at Hickleton Main when I had started there – the former as NUM Treasurer and the latter as a District Overman – the latter of which would have been the job I would have been looking to aim for.

Mick Tucker had been one of the supposed bright young things that had signed on as part of the earlier Class of 1981 intakes at Hickleton Main and embodied everything that the Doncaster Area's Junior Management course had been all about. Although we had been in the same year in Houghton Road school – he was not really someone that I could ever really recall.

His parents had lived on Thurnscoe's Whinwood Estate at 144 Merrill Road.

He appeared quite a tall, decent-looking kid and the first thing I recall on seeing him, was that he had The Human League chalked on his pit helmet. He also appeared quite outgoing, going-on-brash, and never wasted anytime in delivering a few verses of his favourite band.

"You were working as a waitress in a cocktail bar – When I met you. I picked you out, I shook you up and turned you around – Turned you into someone new – Oh, don't you want me…"

He could also do Buck's Fizz.

"Run for the sun, little one – you're an outlaw once again…"

First recollections, eh?

This had been during our winter solstice in the Pit Baths during December 1981. A heavy snow had come down during the night and never really let up through early morning, and had in places, been up to two- and three feet-deep. Being that our industry took place underground, nothing ever stopped. All the trainees – me included, had been charged with both clearing paths and spreading rock salt and as such, we had taken a ten-minute break (skive) down at the canteen, which was situated at the entrance/exit into the baths.

Mick had been on one of the first draws out of the pit on day shift and had been getting showered whilst talking to a few of the lads who had recently left Thurnscoe Comprehensive.

He was one of those kids that once working at the pit – every conversation they had, reverberated around it. *Pit-pissed* is what this was always referred to as. He was, however, the golden boy of the Class of 1981 in that he went farer than any of us – to an Undermanager, I believe.

The only thing I knew of him, was that his current girlfriend had attempted to slash her wrists. Certainly not because of his singing, more to do with an ex-boyfriend from off The Spike who had recently dumped her. This is a story that I will relay later, as she would go on to lose her life in very suspicious circumstances.

Mick's grandfather had been Horace Victor Tucker – a man who was one of the many poor souls who had endured the hardship of the eastern Dearne Valley and someone who had had to deal with much upset.

Horace had married a girl by the name of Jane Johnson on 16 February 1920 at St Helen's Church.

Looking at the place now, it is hard to imagine that Horace's marriage took place when Thurnscoe was being looked upon as a place of envy. That very month, Thurnscoe UDC – along with their contractors Messrs Jackson & Potts, had started the construction of a major housing scheme that would become Taylor Street and Thornley Crescent, and by September that year, 178 properties would ready for occupation, whilst on the street where Horace lived – that of George Street, they were in the process of adding a further eighteen properties.

It would be on the Wednesday evening of 12 May 1920 that more history would be made, when the council approved plans submitted by the owners of Hickleton Main for the construction of 238 colliery houses as part of the first phase of its development on the north side of Lidget Lane.

One of the first things on the agenda, however, was to provide a supporting infrastructure and as such, Notice's to Quit were given to several residents of Lidget Lane in August that year, with a view to transforming those properties into shops.

Things never run smoothly, and problems with tenders and contracts put pressure on Joseph Ledger Hawksworth – the Clerk for both Bolton-on-Dearne and Thurnscoe UDC who in October, appeared to have had enough and handed in his resignation. It was, however, immediately knocked-back. He had recently signed off on the sinking of a new water supply borehole at Miles Wood on the villages border with Great Houghton, which was to provide extra supply into Thurnscoe.

The very first houses to be constructed in 1921 as part of the vast pit estate, would be Tudor Street moving west towards Stuart Street, whilst its long-term plans would complement the development as part of the second phase with the construction of a new infant school (Thurnscoe Hill). This was a building that eventually opened on Monday 21 June 1926.

Horace set up home in the newly constructed property at 29 Tudor Street, with his wife and new-born son Tommy – having a further child by the name of Billy, who was born in spring 1923.

As both Horace and Jane's families lived over on The Spike – not at least at 51, 80 and 82 George Street, a quick walk over the back and around the brickworks appeared the easiest route of getting from A to B. Unfortunately, however, at 11.30 a.m. on 27 March 1924, his wife's body was recovered from the Reser. It was assumed that on the night before, and whilst moving between Tudor and George Street's, part of her clothing had got caught on a tree and she had lost her footing, slipped, and drowned.

Although Horace would remarry a lady from Goldthorpe's Orchard Street by the name of Olive Doore on 23 January 1926 – misery would still follow him.

The family moved on to 25 Thornley Crescent – the house sandwiched to where Carl Eades and Mad Lettie would come to live many years later – however, their experience would be much worse. Tommy, aged just eight-and-a-half years old and extremely inquisitive, had uncoupled a gas pipe in one of the bedrooms and ended up dying of asphyxiation.

Always a smile and never a frown. Always a hand when one was down.

He never complained, he wasn't that kind. He was one of those sons who are hard to find.

It could have been written for Tommy – but it wasn't. He wrote it for another of his sons – Wilfred, who died on 28 December 1954, aged twenty-two.

Horace died in Late-February 1970. He had moved around a considerable amount of times – three times on the old Council estate and ended up on the Whinwood Estate at 32 Burnside – less than one hundred yards from the home of his grandson, who at that time would have been in the First Year of Houghton Road's infant school.

Houghton Road Infant School 1969/1972. Top. Mrs Gilbert's class - Mick Whitehurst, Colin Hunter and Andy Moore (brick in hand) amongst the pupils. Bottom Left. Chris Lyons painting whilst Carl Eades is leaning on a desk and looking at the camera. Bottom Right. Headmistress, Mrs Andrews at the piano and the kids ready for singing.

5. The Evil That Walks Among Us

"Keep away from that house," we were often told.

However, we were rarely given explanations. It is only when you get older that you realise as to the reason or reasons why.

My house at Briton Square backed on to one at Hanover Street, which during the late 1980s had its occupier labelled a paedophile. According to neighbours, he had been charged with having sex with his daughter. This wasn't just idle tittle-tattle, everyone knew. There had been a similar situation on Lancaster Street during the late-1970s where a rather macabre suicide formed the catalyst for a lot of vicious gossip.

During 2008, I was approached to find a person quite local to the area. I don't know the specifics, but some smack heads had come across a (stolen) laptop, and as they do, turned it around for a quick thirty or forty pounds. Its contents, I was told, were **bad** and therefore its new owner wanted to find the address of its original one – hence the telephone call to me, which a week or so later, culminated in a couple of paragraphs in the *Sheffield Star*.

I used to get requests such as these all the time.

If you think that is bad, during the spring of 2019, I was asked by a seventy-three-year-old lady if I could arrange for some man off Truro's Pensilva Road, and one who just happened to be her nephew, to be severely harmed.

Without going into specifics, I declined and advised her to see a solicitor and take it through the proper channels.

She had told me, that when he had been nineteen years old, he had raped her eleven-year-old daughter.

It does happen. On 23 April 1940, twenty-four-year-old William Farrar of 23 Wellington Street, Goldthorpe – the son of James and Edith (nee Croft), was sentenced to fifteen months at Leeds Assizes for something not too dissimilar.

The daughter of the lady, who is now in her thirties, possessed some form of Histrionic Personality Disorder (HPD) – an excessive attention-seeking behaviour, and I wasn't totally convinced that she was telling the truth.

That hadn't been the real reason I knocked her back, however.

This had been one of three requests that I'd had at that time and was one of two which I never took forward. The other had been some guy who had been arrested and charged with embezzlement from a company that even now, is located off Scunthorpe's Hebden Road and is one which a friend owns. What made this worse, is that whilst this guy had been in his youth, he had severely disfigured a child after setting it on fire.

There are people out there that are just no good.

So, why did these people ask me? One reason only. They would never get justice from the system.

What had happened – and quite recently, is that I'd had something of a divine intervention, whereby during a carol service at Belton All Saints Church I had been called out to the front – and introduced to the congregation by the vicar. We had met over the internet whilst being on different islands in the Mediterranean – he in Malta and I in Cyprus, and we both shared similar interests, the irony being that in the UK we lived less than 800 yards apart.

At the time I had been contemplating getting involved in something that could have had severe ramifications – not at least for the target.

A mid-range Sheffield-based drug dealer had called my phone and expressed his desire to meet with me as according to him, I had put his life in danger. Most of these gangster-types I come across have a tendency for the melodramatic, but nevertheless, I understood his upset. I did, however, take exception to the threatening undertones of the conversation and whilst still on the phone listening to his diatribe I had tracked him down through his common-law-wife (as he didn't exist on paper) and had been on Google Maps looking at the layout of the cul-de-sac in which he lived and taking note of all the points of entry and exit.

"I don't believe in coincidences," said the vicar, who had his hand on my shoulder. "Everything happens for a reason."

After I sat down, he continued: "Good will to all men, isn't just for Christmas – it is for all year round."

This had been my watershed moment.

Not only was I getting too old, I had also had enough. One of the last sorties I had been on, had been the first of a three-stage process that had partly involved a 1,000-yard hike over fields and scrubland with a ski mask over my head along with the humping of 14 lb sledgehammer and around two gallons of accelerant.

The final one certainly wasn't as illuminating and showed just how low I had sunk. A discourteous driver giving me the bird and I ended up putting through the window of his brand-new land cruiser and threatening to bounce his head off the bonnet. It all needed to stop.

The Sunday evening of 18 December 2016 was when it did.

Am I religious? Not really, but it would be nice if there is something up there. Nevertheless, if that is indeed the case, I will certainly be elsewhere, that is for sure – most probably deployed deep underground on the eternal night shift shovelling coal.

The vicar in the story? The Rev Cliff Kay. He is on Facebook.

I am sure Cliff had heard a lot of the local gossip (most probably wrong) as he put a great deal of time into me. One of the nicest moments, however – came after I had returned from a site in Kilmarnock. The previous day he had sort of touched base and texted me asking if we were all okay. I told him that I was going to Scotland and would be calling at John Dawson's butcher's in Muirkirk and just to make conversation I asked if he wanted a haggis bringing back.

"I've never had haggis," he said.

At 4.00 p.m. next day I drove onto the long sweeping drive into the vicarage and there he was, with his wife Jane, chatting to some of his flock.

"Fresh from Scotland," I said, as I handed him the haggis.

"How much do I owe you," he smiled.

"Nothing – just ask the big man upstairs to keep on looking out for us," I winked.

"That's my job," he told me. "That's why I am here. I have been put here to look after you."

Now, that was some statement. How could I not be impressed?

There had been a third job that I mentioned. This had been based in Thurnscoe East and was something that certainly aroused my interest and is something that I will touch on later.

Anyway, I'm digressing.

A few years ago, I was told a tale by a man whose name was in the frame for several local high-profile robberies during the 1950s. These were at the Doncaster Woodlands branch of the Co-op on 5 October 1952, the Co-op on Mexborough's Main Street on 21 December 1957 and the Empire Cinema in Wombwell on 22 June 1958. There was also a raid on A Kay & Sons on Church Street in Ecclesfield on 22 January 1959.

In each of these robberies the safes were blown – the detonators of which, were possibly part of another robbery at the Maltby Metallic Brick Co. in Ravenfield around Christmas 1951.

Albert Hattersley had lived on St Margaret's Road in the Ecclesfield area of Sheffield and came to national media attention on 19 December 1953.

The thirty-year-old miner had been sent down by Justice Sir James Dale Cassels at Leicestershire Assizes the previous May after the police had charged him with blasting a safe at a post office in the Birstall area of the city. With Christmas on the horizon, he made an audacious escape from Leicester Gaol where he scaled a 50-foot wall, breaking his ankle in the process and duly went on the run (sic) for a couple of days.

During his twilight years, Albert had lived off Green Gate Lane in the High Green area of Sheffield with his wife Kath (nee Phillips), and told me that during one such raid, that he had unwittingly opened a safe and come across a selection of lurid photographs, which didn't just incriminate its owner – they had made him physically sick.

I never got to know the rest of the story, but knowing Albert, I'm sure there would have been violence at the end of it.

One raid he hadn't been made culpable for had been the failed robbery at Goldthorpe Town Hall in the early hours of Monday, 7 December 1959.

The robbers had parked up on Washington Road and accessed the building from the rear using some form of skeleton key. There had been £400 (£9,448, circa 2020) in two safes – £100 in the largest and £300 in a smaller one. The big safe was primed with gelignite but failed to blow, with the Treasurer for the Dearne UDC, George Fordham glibly telling reporters: "I doubt if the intruders were very expert, as considering they used gelignite, they didn't do a deal of damage."

A robbery which took place around a similar time had been that of the St John's sub-post office in Wakefield during October 1957, of which the proceeds of the haul – namely a safe containing £1,006 (£25,397, circa 2020) of Premium Bonds and National Savings certificates, ended up being dumped in the Dearne & Dove Canal at Wath-on-Dearne.

Interestingly, the Area Mechanical Engineer at Manvers Main, Albert Fairhurst – who lived just a few hundred yards away at 37 Sandygate, arranged for it to be craned out of the watercourse and transported over to Swinton Police Station.

Anyway, I am digressing… again.

My auntie Anne's parents – Milton and Margaret Watson, had moved into a property at 12 Pickhills Avenue, after her father had taken on the role as Chief Electrical Engineer at Goldthorpe Colliery on 1 November 1959.

It was the last street in Goldthorpe with an easterly outlying view of Barnburgh Park and Bella Wood and certainly appeared plusher than the rows upon rows of terraces that stood between it and the village's vibrant shopping centre – which during the following year would see the construction of Arndale House with FW Woolworths as its anchor store. This would be something that would supplement Dewhurst's Butchers, Carlines Cash and Carry, the Cavendish Woodhouse furniture shop, Clay's electrical store, Timothy White's chemist and the huge Laws supermarket on the corner of Lockwood Road.

Milton was the son of Fred Watson – a former Blacksmith at Hickleton Main and the younger brother of Harold – a man who had been a hero of the Second World War and who had had stints working down the pits at Hickleton and Kilnhurst Colliery, before going on to work with John Laing & Co. (now Laing O'Rourke).

Harold had married Doreen Pressley in 1940, and after the war, set up home at 24 The Crescent, Bolton-on-Dearne. On the Tuesday afternoon of 4 September 1951, however – his family would receive the news that he had lost his life after suffering horrendous injuries after becoming trapped beneath the tracks of an excavator on the huge opencast mining site down on Lowfield Road.

An inquest was opened, then strangely adjourned by the Deputy District Coroner C.R Marshall, with a verdict of accidental death being clouded by the fact that the thirty-one-year-old father of three had severe money troubles – something which was put down to his heavy gambling.

He not only left a twenty-nine-year-old wife but two sons – Derek aged eleven and Alan aged five and a two-year-old daughter, Shirley.

Rather strangely, Doreen 's sixty-one-year-old grandfather Joseph Arthur Pape had committed suicide the year she had married Harold Watson.

In the early hours of 8 May 1940, there had been a strong smell of gas in his home at 123 The Crescent. Joseph, who was a road sweeper for Bolton UDC, was found under the bedsheets in the large bedroom along with a length of flexible tubing in his mouth.

It was said that he had been depressed since to the loss of his wife Sarah and was (wrongly) under the assumption that he had some serious internal complaint.

Doreen's mother – Edith Ann Pressley, explained at the coroner's inquest that he often wished that he could join her mum.

What should be noted is that Joseph had already suffered tremendous heartbreak in the house back in January 1932.

He and his wife had been looking after their daughter-in-law, Evelyn Clara (nee Smith) who had just given birth to their twin baby granddaughters – Mary and Margaret. Unfortunately, they died – the first after just six hours and the second after a week.

Joseph and his wife had been here before as just prior to the Christmas of 1917 – when they had lived at 9 Ladycroft, they had had a daughter that had sadly been born dead.

As for his son, Frank – he and his wife, Evelyn had lived up near the library at 2 Carr Head Lane when I had first moved back to Bolton-on-Dearne in 1972.

As for my auntie's move to the more salubrious surroundings of Pickhills Avenue, it occurred at the time when improvements were being undertaken to widen the A635 Doncaster-Barnsley Road between the end of their street and Hickleton village. However, it certainly wasn't the first thing that my ten-year-old aunt recalled.

During 1942, a man by the name of Robert Dobie had moved from Oxcroft No 3 Colliery near Bolsover to Goldthorpe, after taking up the post as a Mechanical Engineer at the colliery.

His neighbours were Clifford Bishop – who was a Clerk of Works for the Dearne UDC and his wife Jessica (nee Taylor), who had been married in Swinton on 29 August 1921.

On 5 March 1954, however, tragedy would strike the Bishop family when a fire would engulf their home, whereby Dobie would be on hand to rescue his twenty-four-year-old daughter, Patricia, only for her to die some days later.

A hero? I wouldn't go that far.

In early 1960, Robert George Russell Dobie vacated the house at No 12 for the Watson family to move in and took up residence further down the street at 22.

"What I always remember, was lots police coming to our house," my auntie Anne explained. "My dad went crackers as it was absolutely nothing to do with us and everything to do with a man who had lived there before – Dobie."

The police would go on to search the property at No 22 and consequently arrested its owner.

Janice Pauline Noon was a girl two years younger than my auntie who had lived nearby at 44 St Mary's Road, with her parents Tony and Jane (nee Ford). "As kids we were made very aware that we had to watch out for him (Dobie) when we were playing on Goldthorpe Rec," she said. "My mum seems to think that he was hospitalised one particular time, when a group of local men dragged him out of his house after touching up a young girl."

There were certainly worse offenders than him.

Sir Fenton Atkinson QC was a British High Court judge, perhaps best known as the man who oversaw the trial of the Moors Murderers, Ian Brady and Myra Hindley, at Chester Assizes in 1966.

"This crime is almost the most serious known to our law and again and again and again you have committed this absolutely abominable act," snapped the Judge.

Standing a mere 5'1 in height, fifty-four-year-old Matthew Carr Prest had just moved into lodgings on Goldthorpe's Hope Avenue and possessed some insatiable, albeit warped depravity for small boys.

On 15 July 1938, the jury at Leeds Assizes had found him guilty of raping a young boy in Bolton-on-Dearne and indecent assault on another.

Prest had come down into the eastern Dearne Valley from the Easington area of Durham. He firstly settled in Denaby and Mexborough but after the First World War focused his sights on Goldthorpe, and stalked the yards and backings of the village's north-eastern terraces, whilst lodging with Thomas and Maria Davies at 2 West Street between 1932 and 1936 and then over at 6 Charles Street with Herbert and Rebecca Wilcock during 1937.

His father had been thirty-seven years old when he died in the Trimdon Colliery explosion on 16 February 1882, whilst his mother died in the Union Poor House in Houghton-le-Spring just over five years later, with the six-year-old Prest ultimately becoming an orphan.

Judge Atkinson handed him a sentence of seven years, which he unsuccessfully tried appealing.

Prest was incarcerated in HMP Maidstone – the prison that was used as the backdrop for the filming of the 1974 BBC sitcom *Porridge*. Just like Ronnie Barker's character, Fletch, – he would not be on his own as he would eventually bump into someone that had been handed a five-year sentence by Justice Sir Frederic John Wrottesley QC at Leeds Assizes just three months prior. Not only was this man originally a miner from the Durham coalfields, but one who had for the past six years – lived in Thurnscoe.

Armstrong Bell had been one of the influxes of migrant miners that had come down straight after the 1926 strike in the hope of earning a better standard of living for his family, and had, it is quite fair to say, moved about quite a lot within the villages East end. Whether or not this was by choice or because he was forced, is unclear.

He firstly set up home at 18 Hanover Street but was one of the many that were laid off when the manager of Hickleton Main – John Minnikin, made the decision to temporarily close down the Parkgate seam on 11 February 1928. This was something that resulted in the laying off of 460 miners. He also shut down the colliery's brickworks, where a further forty-eight men would be put out of work.

"We have to face the fact that there are too many collieries and too much coal at present," explained the Colliery Manager. "The weekly output of the Parkgate seam is 2,000 tons, and when the whole colliery is in full swing – 20,000, which is a very high output for a single colliery, and under present conditions, too large to be profitably marketed."

This is what happens when manufacture, or in coal mining's case – production, exceeds demand.

The reason why the coal from the Parkgate seam had been in low demand, had been because unlike the coal from the Barnsley Bed, it was a type mined solely for industrial use, such as gas making and the manufacture of steel.

As for the closure of its brickworks, he added: "We have kept hard at it for years, supplying bricks for all the housing schemes – however, all the building work has now come to a standstill."

There was also a problem with the housing situation, which saw a lot of movement of families from one property to another.

"The colliery has an estate of about 1,000 houses, a number of which are at present empty, partly through migration of the colliery population, and partly through a tendency on the part of the company's tenants to move into newer houses provided in the same district by the local authority… or houses with rents at a slightly lower rate."

In just six years, the industrial Utopia that Thurnscoe once was, had changed.

With around 500 wagons of unsold coal on the surface, and little chance of miners being integrated into other parts of the mine, Armstrong Bell, headed for the pits of north Doncaster and spent a couple of years living between Moorends and Dunscroft.

Whereas Matthew Prest was a single man – not that it stopped him from falsely claiming subsistence payments from the Doncaster Guardians during the 1926 lockout – something which saw him slung in Wakefield Gaol for a month, Armstrong Bell was not.

He had married Elizabeth Jane Carr in 1919 and between them they had had four children, the youngest two being born in Thurnscoe.

On his return to the village in 1931, Bell moved between five properties: 21 York Street, 17 Hanover Street, 36 Lancaster Street, 9 York Street and by 1938 – 10 Roman Street.

Hickleton Main and Brodsworth Collieries were synonymous, and not just because they were two of the most successful collieries in Yorkshire nor the fact that they linked underground. Brodsworth had been sunk and developed by a joint venture of the Hickleton Main Colliery Company and the Staveley Coal and Iron Company and in early-December 1911, with both shafts down and production in full flow, Hickleton Main's forty-one-year-old undermanager, John Criddle – who had also been one of the men who had worked on sinking the mine, had been appointed as Colliery Manager at Brodsworth.

Both pits had been sunk away from the actual villages and whereas Thurnscoe East had been borne, so had the New Model Village of Woodlands. This had been designed and built by the architect Percy Houfton and quite unlike Thurnscoe East, Woodlands – as in its name, boasted extensive open spaces and offered many different designs of houses, with living conditions for their time, being described as superb.

Another one of the major plus points of Woodlands, was that it was situated on the Great North Road. This was the main route between Doncaster and Sunderland and therefore a place where the families of Durham miners congregated to alight the stream of buses that went back and forth and provided connections to the mining areas of the densely populated smokestack city – places such as Silksworth, Ryhope and Bishopwearmouth.

In the 1930s there was public transport everywhere – however, a trip into Woodlands from Thurnscoe couldn't be done direct, therefore it was a bus into Doncaster to alight the coach or a 45-minute (or a five and a half-mile) hike up Hickleton and over the backs through Pickburn – the latter of which, back then certainly wasn't seen as being out of the ordinary. It also saved money – especially if they were four of you.

On 3 March 1938 there had been a fatality at Hickleton Main where a heavy fall of coal had dislodged a prop causing it to shoot out and fracture the skull of sixty-two-year-old John Heather of 107 Thornley Crescent. However, on admitting him to Mexborough Montagu Hospital he was pronounced dead. A death underground meant one thing – having the following day off. Therefore, a long weekend was on the horizon, which became quite appealing for Armstrong Bell as his wife was due to visit her family up in Durham with her three youngest children – Eileen, five, Olive, ten and James, thirteen.

With the weather expected to be fine throughout the district a brisk walk over Pickburn was on the agenda. Bell could also make sure they got off okay and if he felt inclined, sink a few beers in any of the nearby local hostelries such as the Woodlands Hotel or The Bomb. Or better still, he could even take in a matinee at the Picture House before his walk home, as it was only a few strides from the bus stop.

I have absolutely no idea where the forty-one-year-old went – however, what I do know is that he ended up at the other side of the Great North Road and in the busy Market Square where a seven-year-old girl had become estranged from her sister. The details are sketchy, but what is known is that he induced the little girl to go with him on the pretence of finding her elder sister. However, that never happened, and the girl ended up being sexually assaulted.

The stories from Thurnscoe, Goldthorpe and Bolton-on-Dearne's dark past may be well hidden and in part forgotten, but they have always been there.

I mentioned the fact that Taylor Street had had its name completely erased in the late-1980s with no real explanation as to why. What is true is that the street had an indifferent history, but more so in recent times. For a while it sought sanctuary to a violent rapist who was also thought to be a serial killer – however that would be me jumping ahead of myself.

Now, it is here where I must tread carefully, not at least where the law is concerned. Therefore, I will present a series of facts to relay the story.

Robert Abraham Duggan was one of seven children, that had been raised in another godforsaken house on Thurnscoe's King Street. It was a property where his parents John and Florence (nee Londesbro) lost their son, Alfred at just two weeks old. This had been just two years after its previous occupants – William and Janet Knox (nee Cowley) – who had also come down from Durham, had lost their daughter Sylvia – aged just three years and six months.

Please note the names – that of *Sylvia* and *Cowley*, as they will become very apparent.

Soon after the tragedy, the Knox family vacated the house at 37 King Street. Maybe it had been perfect timing as they just missed what was a hostile mob of 200 people descending onto the street following numerous fights that had broken out in the village on the Friday night of 1 July 1932. This particular one, had started on Windsor Street and ended up involving PC Joseph France and a thirty-year-old miner by the name of George Hibbert – the latter of whom had a truncheon whipped across his forehead and ended up spending three months in prison for his pain.

Hibbert had lived at 14 Wellington Street, Goldthorpe with his wife Alice (nee Whitehead), and for a short time during 1933, rather strangely had Mathew Prest lodging with them. After Prest was sentenced – Hibbert along with his wife, twelve-year-old son and nine-year-old daughter, would leave Goldthorpe forever and move into a terraced house at 13 Oliver Street, Mexborough.

As for the Knox's, they moved into a recently constructed property at 24 Deightonby Street – the exact same house that my family would move into nearly forty years later, whilst the Duggan's moved into 37 King Street, the last house-but two on the left-hand side.

What **has** to be mentioned, is that, as with the Taylors and Ropers, there are several different families of Duggan's – neither of whom are related.

As for Robert Abraham Duggan, he was born in King Street on 9 November 1945.

At twenty-eight-years old he married a divorcee from the Royston area of Barnsley on 20 April 1974 and eventually moved into a property at 41 Taylor Street. This was the last house on the street and fronted onto what was a compact but unkempt green and the streets three-pronged intersection with School Street and Thornley Crescent. It was also more or less opposite No 34 – the home of his mother.

I had, in fact, been to his house before – on the Saturday morning of 11 May 1985. Robert Abraham Duggan, however, hadn't been there. He had been serving time in prison.

The first thing that struck me is that it was filthy, but certainly no different to some of the squalor that I had seen families residing in on either Brunswick Street or Briton Square. Squalid conditions don't necessarily go hand-in-hand with evil, but 41 Taylor Street – well, that house was at the core of evil.

"My mum used to hear the kids screaming through the walls – it was horrendous," explained their former next-door neighbour, Sancia Miles (nee Frost). "My mum felt guilty for years for not knowing, as the kids used to beg her to sleep at ours. However, she never guessed what had been happening. That was until it all came out."

"Their mother wasn't a full shilling. She was terribly slow and allowed it to happen," added Duggan's niece, Pauline Gadd. "She ended up having all the children taken off her."

Robert Duggan had been convicted of the rape of his three stepdaughters.

He died in Kemple View Psychiatric Unit on Longsight Road in the Langho area of Blackburn on 31 October 2011. The cause of death was Bronchopneumonia – something which had been brought on by heart disease.

A question could be asked of why I would ever have been at this property, which is a fair question to ask. I had been both a good friend and a workmate of Duggan's stepson.

The stains of disgust left by Duggan, unfortunately do not end there.

Robert had a brother by the name of Leonard who was five years older than himself. He had married a woman by the name of Joan Davis when he had been nineteen years old and for a time lived around the corner from his brother at 7 Willow Road on Thurnscoe's REEMA estate. Again, according to his niece, Pauline Gadd, Leonard Duggan ended up being sentenced to 10 years for indecently assaulting one of his grandchildren.

There are worse stories, some of which never got to Crown Court and which when they did, broke down.

It was common knowledge that during the 1950s a father on Tudor Street had been raping his daughter who it was claimed, even gave birth to his child. However, one of Thurnscoe's most high-profile failures culminated in two ladies having to cut a distraught young lad down from a tree in Bolton-on-Dearne after the trauma he endured a child had him try to hang himself.

In my mind, Lindley Crescent, was without doubt one of the best streets in Thurnscoe. Not so much, because of how it looked, more to do with the fact of the people that lived there – two of which included my grandma and granddad (Elsie and Eric Ellis).

Unfortunately, not all were good and that included a man by the name of Frederick Robinson who lived a mere eight doors down from them.

I can't say as I knew him – however, near-neighbours who I am still in contact with now, explained that his wife, Rosemary (nee Hogarth) had been a good friend of my grandma's.

Frank and Rose(mary) were married in 1949. He had been twenty-three and she twenty-two. Between them they had four children within the first eight years of their marriage – Judith, Gerald, Lorraine and Richard.

"He was a vile man," explained John Bailey.

John was a Thurnscoe lad – born in March 1960 to Lawrence and Hilda (nee Robinson) and lived at 58 Derry Grove. "Frank Robinson was my mother's brother."

Note that John refused to refer to him as his uncle.

Frank Robinson possessed a chequered past and had been hauled in by the police after a girl with learning disabilities had been attacked on Lindley Crescent. This had been long before they charged him with just under a dozen counts of sexual engagement and exploitation of a child. It was a case which was widely reported by the local media – the *Barnsley Chronicle* in particular. What made it worse than it already was, was that the said child had been his grandson, who according to John would have been around eight years old at the time.

"He used to take his grandson to parties where men were allowed to mess with him," he added. "One of the houses that he used to get taken to, is a cottage that stands alone, and which is located on the right side of the hill going up Derry Grove."

According to John, this secret stayed hidden right up until they day the young lad tried to hang himself.

"His care team said he had to go to the police and tell them everything. No one in our family had any idea."

For some unknown reason, the trial at Sheffield Crown Court collapsed and Frank Robinson came away with a not guilty verdict and died in the summer of 2006, aged eighty.

As for his grandson, he still lives in the area and resides in one of the new builds close to where Highgate Colliery once stood.

Suicide is understood much more than it once was, and social media is full of advertisements claiming the awareness of the subject. Personally, I feel that this is a contradiction in term, as Facebook, Twitter and the likes, can, more than not, be its root cause.

My family have had a few suicides, though one of them was defined by the coroner as being a Death by Misadventure. This was the son of my great auntie Elsie (nee Carman), who prior to her marriage to Kenneth Kendall in 1952, lived at 4 Welfare View, Goldthorpe.

Her son, Peter – who was of course my second cousin, was killed after walking in front of a train during February 1984.

More recently my cousin, Samantha (Sam) (Durose) – formerly of 60 Ingsfield Lane, Bolton-on-Dearne, lost her teenage daughter, Abbie (Bannister) to suicide. "Behind her eyes and smile, she was so tormented," our Sam had told me.

She was an extremely pretty girl, that is for

sure. *I have eyes that see, and ears that hear,*

But my mouth is shut, And I have lost my words.

My eyes cry tears, caused by words and thoughts,

And my ears can't stop, Although I wish they could.

But neither can my mind. As my mouth can't speak as my mind's too loud,

I could… And my mind would… louder…

It is like I am broken, and I can see the pieces around me, but each piece I pick up cuts me deeper than before.

I don't know whether that was a poem or a cry for help. It was, however, something that our Sam found after her daughter's death that had been written down and which she wanted me to see.

It is such a tragic story. Most suicides are.

I vividly recall staring over at the Marist Sister's bungalow at the point where Goldthorpe's Lockwood Road merges into Thurnscoe's Pit Lane on a very sunny afternoon on the Easter Monday of 1969. I have no idea why, but the nuns were always a figure of interest to me as a child, and I recall asking a series of questions to my mum, whilst my twenty-two-year-old uncle Pete – who back then was a Trooper in the Royal Hussars, had been due to be married to Margaret Dawson at Goldthorpe's Sacred Heart Church.

Their marriage was not one that would last, and as you will see as the story progresses, my feelings for his wife are one of complete indifference.

In the early days of my mum and (step)dad being married, I rarely saw them together as a couple as uncle Pete had been stationed overseas in the Munster region of West Germany, where they had had their first child – Julie.

My recollection of my auntie Margaret is that she was quite a tall woman who had quite an uncanny resemblance to the Ad-fab actress, Joanna Lumley. She had lived opposite my mum's mother – my grandma (Helen) Carman at 47 Ringway, Bolton-on-Dearne.

Her parents were Harry and Theresia (nee Brandl), the former who had been a miner at Barnburgh Main, whilst the latter was an Austrian who had come over to England around 1948.

Harry and Theresia had a son in 1952 by the name or Eric – who, when I had been a young lad owned the keys to an ultra-cool and bright tangerine-coloured Bond Bug, which was a Reliant-built wedge-shaped microcar, with a lift-up canopy and a 750cc lump under the bonnet.

I recall Uncle Pete getting discharged out of the Army and of him and Margaret initially renting a house at 2 King Street, Thurnscoe.

This was another property within the terrace where a baby had lost its life – this time Susannah Williams on 1 January 1907. What a horrible start to their New Year, eh?

Margaret had worked as a ladies' hairdresser for a lady by the name of Mary Wainwright (nee Bright) next-door to where Ivor's Fish and Chip Shop once stood on Thurnscoe's Houghton Road and whose husband, Ted, also owned the garage nearby.

Ted and Mary had been married in 1941 and between them had two daughters – Patricia in 1943 and Glenda in 1945. It was a sad tale whereby Patricia died after eighteen hours, whilst her younger sister died well before her first birthday.

I was told that after the death of both Ted and Mary Wainwright, everything was left to Margaret – which according to my uncle Pete, was the catalyst for her walking out on their marriage and taking her two children, with her – the youngest being a boy, who was named after the father.

Did it happen like that? I am not so sure.

After Uncle Pete left the Army we ended up being their neighbours for a period of just under four and a half years. What was strange, is that although they lived next door, apart from the kids all playing out together, we didn't seem have that much to do with them.

I recall Uncle Pete owning a grey 1964-registered Vauxhall Viva HA, then suddenly both he and it were gone. He had left their newly built house on Bolton-on-Dearne's Flower Estate and had gone over to work in Saudi Arabia, which was in fact the catalyst for Margaret leaving him. According to my mum she had been having an affair.

Their ultimate separation, which came a few years later – possibly 1980, would hit their son particularly hard. Not at first, but certainly later-on. I thought young Peter a wonderful little lad with his long face and sticky-out ears. He was a sharp-witted little *Herbert* and possessed both a chippy personality and a fearless prose. With only a few months age difference between them, he and my younger brother, Joel, were best mates, so much so, they went everywhere together.

"I'm leaving the chuffing country when you two get to eighteen," was Uncle Pete's retort, as every time one of them got up to go to the toilet – the other one went too. They were inseparable. This was something that had me get nasty with young Peter around the spring of 1989. Knowing what I know now, I should have handled it differently, but I did not. My sole aim had been to look after my brother.

At sixteen years old my brother had been living within a poor environment, which is something that I will touch on later. Both my parents were never in. My mum was always at work and my (step)dad often out propping up the bar down at The Fairway. Our Joel's home life was non-existent, and he was let do whatever he wanted. If you looked at young Peter, he had been exactly same. Margaret was in her own relationship with a man by the name of Pete Swallow and as I have already said, Uncle Pete had lobbed-up with Carol French – a woman who would ultimately bleed him dry.

Both sets of parents were much too pre-occupied with their own bullshit to see what their sons were up to.

Joel had been hanging around with young Peter when my wife raised the alarm. At that time, I had been working with Cementation Mining on the sinking of a new mine in Leicestershire's Vale of Belvoir, where my shift cycle only allowed me one day off every three weeks. Therefore, the rot had well and truly set in when I eventually came back up north.

"There's been some fall-out at your mam's and our Joel's left home," said my wife, on me coming into the house one Friday evening. "You need to go get him."

My wife's main concern was that his cousin had been hanging around with him – and it was no great secret that young Peter had recently been introduced to hard drugs.

I asked around and found out through one of his friends that he had been staying at a house on Goldthorpe's Homecroft Road, which I was led to believe belonged to some fraction of the Edmans family. I knew very little about them, although in later years I would find both John (Eddie) and his wife, Julie (nee Hiles), extremely colourful characters. The same could not be said for their son, Josh, however. When he had been just fourteen years old he came to national attention after Magistrate Barbara Marsden lifted reporting restrictions (on a juvenile) so that the media could name and shame him after she sentenced him to a twelve-month detention order. He had blatantly breached a three-year ASBO after thirty-nine separate counts of robbery, violence, and threatening behaviour in and around Thurnscoe.

The last I heard, Eddie had died, and the rest of the family were living on Challenger Crescent.

As for our Joel, I ended up taking him with me on the Sunday night and helped set him up with a job in some wire works factory on the Monday afternoon. I also bought him a bike and told him that he could live in the caravan that I owned, which was sited in some cobbled farmyard in a quaint little village called Ab Kettleby, which was a mile or so from where the new mine was being developed.

Life had been laid out on a plate for him. For quite a few weeks he managed to get up and go to work, whilst on my third weekend I would drop him off at my mum and (step)dad's. That was until young Peter arrived on site and totally upset any equilibrium that existed.

Joel stopped going to work and things begun going missing from Farmyard, which culminated in him losing his job. The farmer who owned the land also wanted them gone. I went fucking apeshit, especially as it ended up with young Peter temporarily staying at my mum's and Joel going back off the rails. I say temporarily, as I went up to my mum's and ended up coming face-to-face with a sixteen-year-old lad whose head and vocabulary was all over the shop and who had a body that was perspiring to such an extent that he was wet through.

"I'm telling you, fucking now," I yelled at him. "Go back to your mam or dad's."

Did he? No. Neither of them wanted him.

The next time I saw him, he was ambling up from The Flower Park towards The Docket on Welfare Road. It was the morning of 28 April 1995 and I along with his father had just picked up a death certificate from Dr Dutta's. It was just a few hours after my (step)dad had died. Young Peter had been conversing through the passenger car window with his dad and sounded like some deadbeat hippie.

Fast-forward twenty years and what he had been left with was a body which no-one wanted near them and one which its immune system had broken down. It was rotten from heroin abuse. Following the death of his mother, he decided to take his own life. It was needless, but that is what he wanted.

I think back with fondness to him and Joel sat at on either knee of my granddad Ellis at the blue Formica table inside 63 Lindley Crescent and all I can do is shake my head.

These were two little lads that could have had everything.

Outside The Whinwood Hotel - September 1992.
From Left to Right. Scott Carman, Joel Rayner, James Durose-Rayner and Pete Rayner

6.   Avalon

My mum's continual wanderlust made sure that we had moved around a bit. During my short twelve year life I had already had one stint at living in Thurnscoe East, moving there in autumn 1970 before leaving in haste for Bolton-on-Dearne on 23 September 1972.

Deightonby, which was a place in the area named in the Domesday book, is the most westerly street in the East end. It runs adjacent to the railway exiting close to the point between Briton Street's confluence with Brunswick Street and Chapel Lane at its northern end and Windsor Street at its southern. Its centre forms a crossroads between Roman Street and what was once a bridge over the Wath Branch Line, of which the steel-built structure, although heavily graffitied and infilled with rubbish, had still been standing when we left.

The valid point of my mum's wanting to move up into Thurnscoe East had been quite simple, and although I never liked it, it made far more sense than the time when we moved back there in 1977.

The house at 24 Deightonby Street had been an upgrade on the house we had moved from, in that it had an inside toilet and bathroom, but that is as much as it did have. It also had a front and back garden, the latter, which to a seven-year-old seemed immense – especially when he had been charged with digging it.

The property had a front room and a kitchen that was separated by a staircase which led to three bedrooms. The kitchen had a sink beneath the front window and three doors at the rear: the left one into a passage that provided access to the back door and the toilet, the central one into the pantry and the right one into the bathroom. A gas cooker sat snugly in an alcove between the bathroom door and the left side of the fireplace, whilst a twin-tub washing machine was situated in the one to the right. A table and four chairs had been placed opposite the fire, with the other décor in the kitchen being a rusty orange coloured hearth rug and a pair of violet curtains.

My mum's idea of colour coordination was enough to drive a person insane.

I can't remember much about the front room, apart from the fact that our rather perplexing coin slot operated television was under the front room window. I say perplexing, as one Saturday morning, whilst my mum and sister had been shopping in Goldthorpe and my (step)dad had still been in bed after coming in off night shift, I tried in vain for over half-an-hour to switch the thing on so I could watch David H. DePatie and Friz Freleng's *Pink Panther Show* in black and white.

"It's easy," my (step)dad told me, after I'd purposely woken him up around 11.00 a.m. "You pull it out and then you turn it."

I still remember him sat there, with his eyes still shadowed from the coal dust, sipping at his mug of tea and laughing at the Pink Panther's adversary and fall-guy – the little white bloke with the moustache, as everything he tried to do ended in disaster.

He never asked for much. His mug of tea and a read of his paper. A shift at work and to come home to his family, have his supper and watch TV. And then on a weekend, to go out for a few pints.

Our house was five doors up from one of my grandma Ellis's dear friends – Beatrice Fish. Her eldest son Jack, had been in the Royal Artillery and had been captured by the Germans in June 1940 and held as a Prisoner of War in Stalag XX-A in Western Poland, along with Airey Neave – the former M19 Agent and Tory politician who was mortally wounded on 30 March 1979 when a bomb exploded beneath his car and took off both his legs.

We lived straight across the street from Tom and Elizabeth Morrisey, which was another house with another grizzly story attached to it – however, its owner certainly hadn't been one of those poor souls who found eternal solace in Thurnscoe's drowning pool.

On 21 February 1936, a sixty-six-year-old miner by the name of Oliver Gilbert went upstairs, put a washing line around his neck, fastened it around the bedpost and hung himself in the larger of the three bedrooms in 29 Deightonby Street.

He hadn't worked for some years as he suffered from heart problems and chronic bronchitis – however, it was said that he had become severely depressed after the death of his seven-month-old grandson, Derek (Bell), who had died in the house earlier that month.

Oliver's was a sad story as he and his wife Lydia had already lost a grandson – seven-year-old Kenneth (Field), just four years prior. The couple had also lost an eighteen-month-old daughter by the name of Gladys, when they had first moved to Thurnscoe and lived at 30 King Street in 1906.

He would, however, miss further heartache when yet another seven-year-old grandson – this time Raymond (Gilbert), died in August 1944.

Oliver's hadn't been the first suicide by hanging on the street, however.

On 29 September 1932, the body of a thirty-eight-year-old miner by the name of Thomas Arthur Steer was found hanging dead by a scarf from a hat rack at the foot of the stairs of 126 Deightonby Street. He too had become depressed – however, his suicide had been purely down to the lack of work at the pit. He left his wife Alice (nee Addy) and a nine-year-old son by the name of Lewis.

An interesting story is the one that loosely surrounds Bertram and Ivy Mullis (nee Littlewood) who lived at 95 Deightonby Street and had an older couple by the name of Aaron and Mary Jane Owens (nee Layte) living with them.

Aaron and Mary had been married at the Holy Trinity Church in Elsecar on New Years' Day 1908. They had a child by the name of Frederick almost exactly six years later who sadly died aged one month old.

My thoughts are, and this is exactly what they are – is that Bertram Mullis was taken in (adopted) by the Owens family when they moved to Thurnscoe in 1924 – firstly living at 2 and 6 Butcher Street and then 13 High Street.

Why? An interesting one, this.

Bertram's mother was thirty-five-year-old Clara Mullis. She was housekeeper to farmer and market gardener Alexander Gibbs and his wife Lottie Clementina (nee Sculthorpe), and had been employed to look after their two children – eight-year-old Alex and five-year-old Muriel.

They lived at 63 Newman Road in the Erdington area of Birmingham – a newly constructed house just north of Rookery Park and Birches Green.

What would happen, however is that Clara would get *caught on*, and on 13 March 1909 give birth to her son, whose father just happened to be the head of the household.

Alexander would end up leaving his wife and children and throwing his lot in with Clara. They moved into White House Farm in Norton Lindsey, where he took up a job as Farm Bailiff. Strangely, their child, Bertram, never went with them and somehow ended up in the Dearne Valley.

Maybe Clara was related to the Mullis families in either Thurnscoe or Wombwell? It is something that I don't really know the answer to. Nevertheless, that is where he ended up.

After he married, Bertram temporarily moved in with Ivy's parents – Ellis and Elizabeth Littlewood (nee Statham) at 4 Houghton Road, but shortly after got the house on Deightonby Street through his employment at Hickleton Main – where Aaron and Mary would join them.

On Friday 23 August 1935, Aaron Owens – who worked as a chimney sweep, had been walking along the bridle path which passed the small woodland of Whin Covert on his way between the end of Peartree Avenue and towards both bridges that crossed the Sheffield – York and Wath Branch Lines into Thurnscoe East, when something caught his attention from behind a fence – namely a sixty-seven-year-man swinging from a tree with a rope around his neck.

Charles Roebuck Godley's family were, without doubt, one of the oldest families in Thurnscoe going back as far as the 1700s. In fact, if you look up George Street, the Godley family are still there now.

He never married and had lived Thurnscoe with his sister and brother-in-law, Anne and Joseph Bartle on an intermittent basis. He had reportedly been involved in a serious accident underground at Hickleton Main and as a result, suffered head injuries which led to fits of dizziness.

When Aaron Owens got to him, he managed to cut him free.

Charles Godley would end up spending some time in Doncaster's Western Hospital on Springwell Lane, Balby – a former union workhouse equipped with several wards for patients with mental illness.

What is unknown was how long he stayed there, but what is known, is that his sister and brother-in-law were injured when Joseph crashed his motorcycle into a wall at the bottom of Chapel Lane on 26 October 1937 and had to be transported to Mexborough Montagu, where it was found his sister had fractured her ankle.

His brother-in-law, Joseph Bartle died at his home at 41 Thornley Crescent on 14 April 1940, whilst Charles Godley died the following September.

As for Aaron Owens, he and his wife lived at 8 Low Grange Road – where they died in 1951 and 1968, respectively – however, what would happen is that their *adopted* son and his wife – who lived ten doors up at No 28, both died on 5 November 1967.

Bertram and Ivy had been driving on the A1 Great North Road close to the Skellow turn-off during darkness, when the vehicle they were in, was hit head on by an articulated lorry – Bertram dying of lacerations to the brain following his skull being fractured.

There have been other suicides by hangings and indeed some failed hangings in the area, and if you wanted to see real misery, then Mexborough or Denaby was the place as there was a time in September 1921 – when a there had been three hangings in ten days.

i) The inquest at the Horse & Groom public house heard how Henry Hopkinson, the husband of fifty-seven-year-old Emma, found his wife hanging off the bedstead with a silk handkerchief around her neck in the bedroom of 25 Elizabeth Street, Goldthorpe on 2 May 1904. She had been in Sheffield's Middlewood Hospital twice – and for some reason, was frightened of being admitted there again. It does make you wonder what happened whilst she had been there.

ii) On June 1909, nineteen-year-old Elizabeth Mason was found in a dazed state in the back bedroom of 12 Cemetery Road, Bolton-on-Dearne, foaming at the mouth and with her face the colour of blue-going-on-black. A skipping rope had been tied around her neck a total of seven times. A failed attempt of suicide brought on by nothing more than sibling rivalry.

iii) Keen angler, Alfred Crofts had been at the Reser fishing, when twelve-year-old John Willian Connor had got stuck in its clay bed, pulled under and drowned in August 1909 and was the one who dragged the lifeless body of fifteen-year-old Thomas Hamilton of 7 Co-operative Street, Goldthorpe out of the pond on the afternoon of 4 September 1914. Alfred had, in fact, dragged three dead bodies out of the drowning pool. The thirty-eight-year-old Alfred married a woman called Margaret Hayes in 1898 and had several children – however, in April 1914 she left him for another man, which according to her husband created much gossip. On 5 July he could stand no more and tried hanging himself in the front room of his home at 3 Whitworth Street, Goldthorpe. Fortunately, the cord broke leaving him unconscious on the floor.

iv) A small triangle of misery in the terraces just east of Goldthorpe's Straight Lane continued on the Tuesday afternoon of 13 October 1931 when a forty-nine-year-old platelayer by the name of George Herbert Smith hanged himself in the large bedroom of 18 Manor Avenue. According to his wife, Dora – he had been a prisoner for nine months during the First World War and often complained of severe head pains – however, it had been the fact that he had been out of work twelve weeks which had led him to do the deed. He had somehow fastened his wrists together and thrown a clothesline over a bed post – the force of the drop, almost cutting his throat.

That wasn't it, however. Far from it.

On 2 July 1927, a twenty-nine-year-old widow by the name of Annie Quinn (nee Jackson) tied the knot with a man two years her junior by the name of Edward Renshaw Gregory. It had been a relationship that had created much gossip as they had been living together under the same roof at 43 Welfare View – albeit with Horace and Elizabeth Newcombe (nee Parkin) – who rather strangely ended up at 16 Manor Avenue, with Horace being the one who cut George Smith down. It wasn't so much the "under the same roof" that had generated the nudge-nudges, however, but the fact that she had had a baby by the name of Kenneth in November 1926 – which died the very next month.

Her first husband, Joseph Quinn – a colliery fitter, had been involved in a fatal accident in the coal preparation and screening plant at Barnburgh Main on 20 October 1925. It was an horrific death which saw him pulled into machinery and had one of his legs ripped clean off. It had been Edwin Drabble of 16 School Street (then Elm Terrace), Bolton-on-Dearne – my nana Durose's stepfather (who would have course been my great grandfather), who stopped the machinery, and who was called as a key witness at the coroner's inquest at the Horse & Groom.

The couple, along with their two-year-old son, George had lived at 48 Lesley Road – part of a row of terraced houses that back onto the railway line that served Goldthorpe Colliery and from the front looks out over the mildly scarping terraces of both Manor and Melton Avenue's, and indeed the eastern Dearne Valley.

Annie and her new husband moved into 10 Manor Avenue, where they had three children. Unfortunately, on 16 November 1931 – they lost two of them, Ronald aged three and Elizabeth aged eighteen months. Earlier that year, eleven-year-old Annie Turner and sixteen-year-old Irene Cox from 24 and 15 Manor Avenue had died too.

The Gregory family left No 10 and moved into No 18 and whilst its new occupants John and Edith Woolley (Gascoigne) turned the house into an illegal bookmakers, Annie gave birth to another daughter on 2 December 1934. Unfortunately, it had been born dead.

The Sharman twins from 6 Manor Avenue had died in the New Year of 1922, aged just thirteen and twenty-five days – a house which on 29 March 1927 would witness more tragedy – not at least the death of thirteen-month-old Ruth Callaghan. There was misery was everywhere, but what made the fact worse that there were all these dead children around, was the fact that Amy Stephens – who lived at 20 Manor Avenue, was one of the village's dark secrets. She was one of those you went to if you wanted to lose a child before it was born.

v)   The cellar of 85 Doncaster Road, Goldthorpe has held a secret for years.

In the early hours of Sunday morning on 15 May 1932, a sixty-two-year-old man, struggling for the last eight years with health problems and unable to work for the past eight weeks due to bronchitis, influenza and neurasthenia, hanged himself from a beam. John Hargate had had enough.

vi)   "I found my father hanging from a bedpost with a clothesline around his neck," explained thirty-one-year-old Ernest Steel to the District Coroner, W.H Carlile. "He must have smuggled it in."

At 6.30 a.m. on Monday 30 May 1932 – in the large bedroom of 23 Butcher Street, Thurnscoe – his sixty-six-year-old father, Ellis Steel, contorted from excruciating pains in his stomach from the degeneration of his spinal cord, had dramatically ended his life.

Ellis would be buried in Thurnscoe Cemetery with his five-year-old son, Clifford who had died in the run up to Christmas 1906.

vii) The presence of a (benign) tumour set the precedence for sixty-year-old Jane Elizabeth Daykin to hang herself in the front room of the Old School House, on Cemetery Road, Wath-on-Dearne on 17 February 1938. Yet, another suicide.

viii) Jim Leech was an ex-miner who had worked at Dearne Valley Colliery and who had been bedridden due to bowel cancer. The seventy-year-old lived at 8 Vaughan Terrace, Great Houghton with his wife Elizabeth and around 4.00 p.m. on Tuesday 15 March 1938, was found hanging by his neck from a cord in the alcove of his bedroom with his feet six inches off the floor.

ix) On 6 June 1942, twenty-five-year-old Vincent Murray of 159 Furlong Road, Bolton-on-Dearne was cut down in an unconscious state after trying to hang himself off a water cistern in the toilets in Barnsley bus station. He was revived after being given artificial respiration and was taken to hospital. Vincent had been discharged from the Army in February after being described as being medically unfit and had become severely depressed – and at times, he was inclined to become very violent.

x) Eighty-one-year-old Elizabeth Jane Carrington was found dead by her brother-in-law in the bedroom of 19 Chapel Street, Bolton-on-Dearne on 19 January 1956. Suffering from ill health for several months and more recently with a bad bout of flu, she had tied a washing line around her neck and hanged herself from her bed. There had been suicide's in her family before. At 11.30 a.m. on 8 February 1913, Elizabeth's thirty-six-year-old brother-in-law, George Ernest Carrington was found drowned in the brick pond. He had been missing all night. He had suffered from the repercussions of an operation on an internal problem that he had had some six years previous and had become extremely depressed. Having his nineteen-month-old daughter, Mildred die exactly two years earlier and a fifteen-month-old daughter by the name of Marion pass away in April 1907, cannot have helped his state of mind, either.

Some eleven months earlier Elizabeth's fifty-three-year-old near-neighbour up at No 23, Stewart Vincent Ward, had hit the national headlines after he had thrown himself in front of a train. The reasoning behind his suicide – according to his wife Olive (nee Watson), is that he expected promotion with the Yorkshire Electricity Generating Board and never got it, was demoted, and offered a menial job some nine miles away.

xi) On 9 July 1956, seventy-five-year-old William Jenkinson left his home at 15 Peartree Avenue, Thurnscoe with the intention of going for a game of cards – however, he never returned home. Depressed due to his failing health – namely appendicitis and the occasional blackout, he was found on Clayton Lane two days later. He had hanged himself from a tree.

xii) And so as to not leave Denaby out, on 14 August 1958, the body of seventy-year-old Martin Fahey had been found hanging in an allotment shed. According to Pathologist, M.D Innis, Fahey, a former patient at Stanley Royd Mental Hospital in Wakefield, had been dead five days.

Possibly the most haunting story took place in West Melton on the Monday afternoon of 3 August 1936.

The property at 3 Stokewell Road is still standing, but which I am (rightly or wrongly) assuming was part of a post-war renumeration, when further properties were built at the end of the street, which saw the numbers of the houses changed.

Its occupiers were Robert (Bob) Alderson and his wife Ruth Emma (nee Cunningham), who had married in 1926 and had two children – Peggy aged six and Peter aged nine.

At 1.30 p.m. on that fateful day, the thirty-seven-year-old husband complained that he didn't feel too well and told his wife that he was going to go to bed for an hour. With the children on holiday from school, Ruth said that she would take them out for a walk and did so, taking the back-door key with her. On returning to the house at 4.00 p.m., she found the door bolted. She did no more than have her son climb through the open window and unbolt the door and made tea for both kids before clearing away the pots. Around 5.00 p.m. she intimated to her son to go wake his father. "Go and have a lie down on the bed with your dad," she winked, knowing full-well that this would get him out of bed.

Peter took up her advice – however, as he approached the staircase he was met by the horrific sight of his father at the top of the stairs – eyes bulging and hanging by the neck from a rope in the loft. His feet were about two foot off the landing floor.

During the inquest at Wath Town Hall, next-door neighbour Daniel Bullen described what he saw to the Deputy District Coroner A.M Connell. "On Ruth telling me that Bob had hanged himself, I took a knife and on reaching the landing I saw him, hanging with a rope around his neck from a clothes prop that had been anchored in the loft. I, along with Ernie Spencer from the next street (Oak Lea Avenue) cut him down and Ernie tried to give him artificial respiration. Unfortunately, we were too late. He was dead."

Life goes on however, and Ruth married a man two years later by the name of Septimus Parker – both of whom lived out their lives on Wombwell's Bartholomew Street.

Never think that the Thurnscoe connection goes away – because it does not.

What is interesting about this from my perspective is that Ruth's parents lived at 15 Welfare View, Goldthorpe, just five doors up from my great grandparents, Joseph and Elizabeth Carman.

What is interesting from a Thurnscoe perspective is that on 2 September 1929 at Hanover Street's St Hilda's Church, Ruth's younger brother Edmund, married twenty-three-year-old Doris Hanson, and in doing so would help create an East end legacy that is still going strong.

Remember, the story of the rioting in Thurnscoe during the early hours of 21 November 1984?

They had a daughter in 1932 by the name of Doreen who would go on to marry Frank Tutin in 1953, who between them had eight children – one of whom was Colin.

Now, I hadn't known Colin on my first move up into Thurnscoe East – I had, however, certainly known his cousin – John Cunningham.

In 1912, Thurnscoe UDC began the construction of a new housing development between High Street and what was then Back Lane (Houghton Road), which was flanked at either side by Kingsway and Chapel Street.

These were eight banks of terraced houses, forming four streets with twenty houses on each. These were affectionately known as *The Avenues* during their early years and more cynically as *The Dolebacks* after the construction of both new model villages at either side of the colliery in 1926 and 1954.

As with most street names, they took the rather grand names of Earls or Lords: Halsbury, Salisbury, Marlborough and Landsdowne – the latter of which strangely had a 'd' too many.

During the late-1960s, a lot of these properties were becoming both empty and derelict, and Barnsley MBC, who had already begun undertaking massive slum clearance exercises, had pencilled these, along with parts of Chapel and Church Street, for demolition. The Avenues were finally brought down in 1973.

What is strange about this, is that the hardwearing bricks and mortar of Thurnscoe's Avenues only lasted sixty years – which is fifteen years less than the Jerry-built and gawdy-coloured prefabs that were erected off Bolton-on-Dearne's Ringway estate after the war – and they are still standing.

We had lived on the very top avenue that ran behind the rear of the shops on Houghton Road. The rear of 14 Landsdowne Avenue was directly opposite a dark, tight, and unevenly floored ginnel that provided access onto the busy road. The commercial premises with the mock-Tudor frontage and their nine Dormer-style windows to the right and the conventional stone-fronted shops to the left – one of which included a bakers (now Cooplands), of which its huge front window boasted flaky pastry cones full of piped fresh cream and chocolate éclairs, whilst at the back of the counter, warm loaves of bread with their burnt crusts filled the shelves. Houghton Road had every conceivable shop imaginable – however, either end of the avenue could not have been any more contrasting. At one end of the backings was the Emmanuel Pentecostal Church with Lloyd's Fish and Chip Shop next door and at the other, the Thurnscoe Social & Memorial WMC (The Clog) with Norman Grundy's bookmakers conveniently sited next to it. It was a marvellous place. There was Betty Addy's beer off, a newsagent, two butchers, Scarrott's haberdashery shop and Lloyds DIY, a busy greengrocer, Webster's gents' outfitters, and the Co-op mini supermarket, which employed a man with down syndrome by the name of Royce. And there seemed to be sweet shops everywhere – not at least Harry Dainty's at 143 Houghton Road and Mabel Spencer's over the road at the end of Clifton Terrace – No 124, where Sweeney Todd's Barbers once stood.

My place of learning was just around the corner – Houghton Road junior and infant school. It was a huge, red-bricked building, which in spring had cherry trees blossoming on its frontage, whilst inside, there was always that continual smell of hyacinth plants in bloom.

Opposite the school stood the huge flat roofed Broadway building, which when I lived in The Avenues, housed Stones' garage. There was a steel Michelin map of Great Britain on its outer wall, which was rusting away around its edges, along with two oblong-shaped fuel pumps with a plastic Shell logo on top that no longer pumped petrol.

With the most of Church Street flattened, The Avenues and part of Chapel Street ready for demolition and Gooseacre school in pre-construction, the landscape of Thurnscoe was beginning to change.

The feelings that had on my first day at Houghton Road school and going back to Thurnscoe nearly eight years later in 1977 could not have been anymore contrasting. I remember in vivid detail, of my mum taking me through the front gates of the infant school and walking me around to the first of its two rear entrances and directly opposite what I remember as a Terrapin modular building (annexe). It was here where I was met by two young five-year-olds – both of whom were sat on a wooden trolley, and who I would come to know as both miners and men. Andy Moore and Andy Roper.

As I would be starting my First Year in the infants – John Cunningham would have been starting his Second Year in the juniors. However, when I really took notice of him was when I had actually started junior school – as by then he had been in his last year. He appeared quite a big lad who always had loads of mates around him, and I vividly recall him strutting around the playground in a red jacquard tank-top: The Cock-of-the-School.

"A tank-top," shrugged my (step)dad, whilst he was engrossed in watching *The Virginian* on TV. "What does he want a tank-top for?"

"Oh – and it's got to be red," said my mum.

I remember it like it was yesterday as for some reason the TV had been in the kitchen... and a week later, we left for Bolton-on-Dearne.

Thurnscoe East was rough and unappealing – even on my first move there, but in 1977, there had been nothing short of a hateful feeling about the place.

Throughout my brief stay in Bolton-on-Dearne, I would often come back – whether it was to my see my grandma and granddad or a family that my mum and (step)dad had befriended whilst we had lived down on The Avenues.

Barry and Carol Oldfield (nee Austin) had lived at 12 Chapel Street and were people who I had always known as my *auntie* and *uncle*. They also had a young daughter by the name of Debbie, who in my mind was nothing short of brilliant – and possessed a sparking personality and a smile you could die for. There was possibly a reason for that, as in my mind, her mum was an angel.

Carol cut a petite, albeit buxom figure with a small, pointed nose and a lovely demeanour, whilst in sharp contrast, Barry was a small, vociferous and an extremely humorous man. If I could have hand-picked an auntie, uncle and cousin, then these would have been it. I loved them all and I vividly recall being distraught at the news of them leaving and moving up into Thurnscoe East and on to 4 Briton Street.

I remember having my sixth birthday down at The Avenues and Our Debbie, not yet two years old, singing *Happy Birthday* to me. And then I at hers a couple of months later, being the only little lad amongst nearly a dozen young girls, including her auntie and her mum's sister, who was strangely only one year older than me at school.

Tracy Austin was a girl that was the spitting image of her and Carol's mum. Lillian (Lil) (nee Wright) was a lovely white-haired woman who lived at 17 Briton Street.

This street ran from Roman Street and provided access to not only its cul-de-sac of the same name, but to Hanover, Cromwell, Brunswick and the end of Deightonby Street – which was the street it ran parallel with, before connecting with the western end of Chapel Lane.

The only way you could get to live in one of these colliery houses is if one of the family worked at the pit itself – however, since the privatisation of the coal industry in 1947, things had long since changed. If a man terminated his employment with the colliery, be it his dismissal or just a case of him throwing in the towel, unlike what happened during the Denaby Main evictions – ex-miners from the colliery, could keep their house.

Barry and Carol's neighbours, and some of their near neighbours, were the epitome of the darker side of East end life – but that said, it certainly didn't make them bad people.

Around the time of the coal board's nationalisation, Harold (Sonny) Fryer had married Minnie Barthorpe and between them they had seven children and lived at 6 Briton Street, whilst in 1953, Donald Frost had married Joyce Gwendoline Jones and they, like the Fryer's, also had had seven children and lived at No 2.

On 24 April 1937, the-then twenty-one-year-old Sonny, who back then had lived at 40 Lancaster Street, had been sent to prison for theft. As for the Frost's, they were even more colourful.

There is no denying, that even after the Second World War, times were hard – no more so, in a pit village, and nine people living in a three-bedroomed house and trying to survive on one pit man's salary – which contrary to popular belief, was never that good, brought with it a certain poverty.

Whilst we had been down in The Avenues, we had literally nothing. At first, I had moved into the house with just my mum, therefore the fact that she had to look after me, meant that she couldn't work. On both meeting and then marrying my (step)dad on 4 January 1969, as she had been pregnant with my sister, Joanne, things became slightly better. On his discharge from the Army my (step)dad had got a job with ICI over in Huddersfield, which although it meant him catching one of the chartered Hanson buses on Houghton Road at daft o'clock in the morning and coming home late in the evening, it did mean that my mum didn't have to hide from the rent man on a Friday.

That train of thought soon changed after she had had the baby, as the conundrum, which was my mum, suffered badly with post-natal depression. This, she said, was mainly down to the fact that my sister had been continually bawling. I however, solely put it down to the fact that my mum was just being my mum. It would be something that forced my (step)dad to pack in his job, fearing that she would strangle his daughter.

Was she capable of doing such a thing? My mum was very capable of doing such a thing.

My (step)dad packing in his job, brought with it its own hardships, which were, from my point of view, temporarily offset by me having a wonderful grandma and granddad, and later on, by him getting a job closer to home – and becoming a miner at Hickleton Main.

I knew a few kids from within the Fryer family – most notably those around my age such as the lurch-like Karl who was two years my senior, along with his younger brother Dean and his sister Karen. Their father was an amiable enough bloke, and in my mind possibly remembered most for always being seen around the pit estate pushing a wheelbarrow around.

Back then and certainly unlike now, being on the dole brought with it its own hardships, but for large, overpopulated families, there wasn't that big a difference whether you brought home a wage, or you didn't. Therefore, to certain families, it made fiscal sense not to work.

Don Frost was part of a huge mining family and was a very well-liked guy – especially by my (step)dad. As for me, I found his kids extremely confrontational, none more so than Jimmy and his elder sister Lorraine, both of who were the only people that I had ever met who could use the F-led superlative and adjective two or three times within the same sentence. They both swore like navvies, and Jimmy – well my first impression of him frightened the life out of me.

With the unkempt blond hair, goggled-eyed expression, and vicious tongue, he always appeared aggressive and it would be something that would only get worse on us moving into Thurnscoe East in 1977.

However, there is a story here that should be told and that is of his younger brother Robert (Rob). He was both a year younger than Jimmy and I and was a lad with special needs. For as much as Jimmy was confrontational, Rob was not. He did, however, swear like a trooper and to make matters worse he had a loud booming voice which amplified the fact ten-fold. I found him a truly wonderful lad, and it would be here, and as time went on, that I would see a completely different side of both Jimmy and Lorraine.

In the 1970s, children such as Rob, were being accepted, although I would use the word *tentatively* in there, as there was still quite a lot of stigma attached.

I found that there were always the whispers, the nudges and at worst the piss-take, that followed Rob around. Sometimes it became quite hurtful and I remember seeing him once or twice, sat deep in thought and much like a scalded child, after certain things had been said.

Jimmy and Lorraine were often tasked with looking after him – maybe voluntary, maybe not, but whatever it was, they did it and in later life it did have me thinking. Jimmy and Lorraine weren't being confrontational – they were just very angry kids and nothing more.

Whereas Jimmy caused me trouble on my second coming, the opposite could easily be said of Lorraine.

There is a story which perhaps Jimmy and Lorraine didn't know.

Their great grandmother was a lady by the name of Eliza Frost (nee Wood), who for a time lived on Alma Street over in the Dodworth area of Barnsley. She was a lady who had been committed to Sheffield's Middlewood Hospital (then South Yorkshire Lunatic Asylum), a couple of times whilst in her thirties.

There was, perhaps some reasoning behind this. Her husband and therefore Jimmy, Lorraine's and Rob's great grandfather, Charlie Frost, was the quintessence of what could be described as a colourful character. Whilst still married to Eliza he became the subject of an acrimonious and rather much-publicised divorce – being labelled in court by Justice Gorrell Jones in the spring of 1901 as the co-respondent – the problem – and not least, *the wicked adulterer.*

Charlie, who was originally from Stoke-on-Trent and who worked at Dodworth Colliery, both as a miner, then later on at its Coking Plant, had been having a torrid affair with a young married woman by the name of Martha Cronkshaw (nee Townend) – the wife of Jimmy, who was a joiner at Hickleton Main.

Although the thirty-eight-year-old Charlie Frost lived in Dodworth, his younger cousin of three years – Jimmy Frost did not. He lived with his wife Mary on Goldthorpe's Elizabeth Street and it is here one could suppose how he met Martha.

What is known however, is that during this tumultuous affair, Eliza Frost was committed to Middlewood Hospital on 14 November 1899 for near on six months. This was after trying to commit suicide by drinking ammonia. On her release, things would be no better as she found that Jimmy Cronkshaw's estranged, and now heavily pregnant wife, was temporarily living with her husband's mother Ann, over at 13 Wilson Street in Dodworth.

What happened, is that Charlie left his wife and he and Martha moved to South Elmsall, where they had a baby girl by the name of Amelia, who sadly died shortly after. It was here that Martha was served divorce papers by her husband's solicitor, Mr Dunlop Hill.

What is unknown – by me that is, is what happened to them as a couple.

What I do know is that Charlie would be at his wife's bedside in their home at Alma Street when she died in 1906. At thirty-nine years of age she may have won back her husband, but she had lost her longstanding fight against tuberculosis.

If you want another connection, Charlie Frost had another relation of a similar age by the name of George Frost who had come up from Staffordshire with his family who for a time lived in Thurnscoe, where he too would be committed to Middlewood Hospital.

After the first half a dozen times of me being spat at, name-called, pushed kicked and thumped whilst waiting to get on my bus at Hanover Street, I decided to alleviate the problem and walk, which meant a journey over Pit Lane, which back then looked completely different to how it does now.

Pit Lane has been reprofiled several times throughout its history, but all I can tell you is both how it was when I was a child and how it is now.

The graffitied red-bricked wall was always the first thing that greeted us on exiting the pit baths to go down the mine. *Vote Briscoe, Not Scargill*, read the white painted scrawl on the rear of the wall that separated the colliery from the terraced houses on Lidget Lane's Hickleton View.

That act of erudition and foresight had most likely been daubed around the time of the Yorkshire Area Presidential elections in the mid-1970s.

The walk past the pit baths and down the lane and beneath its array of bridges and steaming pipes – thirteen in all, unlike today produced a sweeping left turn at its end, with its then its uneven concrete causeway and pebble road snaking its way to the right and all the way up to the Marist sister's bungalow on Lockwood Road.

By the 1970s, Pit Lane – just like Thurnscoe's East end, was looking tired and in need of replacement and come 1978 with its substructure subsiding and with it being heavily overgrown in places, that is exactly what happened. As part of an investment that must have cost hundreds of thousands of pounds, the colliery spoil heap was reprofiled. With its transformation, a deep crevasse that contained a lake-cum-slurry pond was created, which was the new discharge point for the mine water, along with a peripheral fence and a new tarmacked lane, taking the lane over the opposite side to where it once was.

I, along with a new school mate and near-neighbour – a bespectacled lad by the name of Richard Clements-Pearce, would be the first ever people to walk over this newly completed structure.

I never fully appreciated Richard, nor indeed his family until I became much older, which is a shame as they were such lovely people. Looking back at it, I was no dissimilar to Jimmy and Lorraine Frost – a child that had become angry.

Like Tim's family, Richard's had come together as two different families under one roof. This had been due to the marriage of his father, Ernest – which was most definitely his *Sunday name* as "Clem" is what he preferred to be called, and a lady by the name of Rita Husband (nee Sanderson). And by calling Rita a lady, that is not understating it as she was exactly that.

Clem was a charming albeit boisterous and booming fellow from the East Lindsey district of Lincolnshire and came to the union with the elder two of his four children – Richard and his sister, Sharon, who was one year older than us and therefore in the same year at school as Lorraine Frost.

Rita was a Thurnscoe girl through and through and had married a man by the name of Roy Husband, and came to the union, with their only daughter Karen, who was three years older than me.

There is quite an unsavoury story that Rita often told me and Richard, about his mum and the other two children – and the reasoning of why Clem had left her. That, however, is Richard's story to tell, and certainly not mine.

Richard, like myself, had already had a taste of Thurnscoe and indeed its younger population and had joined me at Dearneside Comprehensive at a similar time of us moving into its East end and it would be on the build up to the Queen's Silver Jubilee, through a succession of fundraising for both a street party and a coach trip to Cleethorpes, that I got to know them well.

What is strange is that they had firstly lived at 57 Lancaster Street – a four-bedroomed property, before flitting next door to No 59, which only had three. I found it interesting watching the house move and to see everything going out of the back door, over the fence and into the other house.

They were some quite nice times and I remember us both setting off to Cleethorpes on our bikes in the early summer of 1978 and Clem and Rita's five-year-old son, Kevin – who Richard absolutely adored, waiting at their gate for our arrival back into Thurnscoe that evening.

I would get to know Clem as a belt maintenance fitter down the pit, and one of the instances that I recall was when the colliery's East Side cable belt had snapped, during one afternoon in early 1983 – as he had been tasked with its repair.

The cable belt was a huge structure – possibly over two miles long and was much different to the other conveyors in the mine, as has its name suggests, it was carried by two steel cables at either side that ran on a series of heavy rollers. It passed through some of the most intricate mining that I have ever seen – and to put this into contrast, I have been involved on some very high-profile jobs, not at least huge three-stage junction / gallery works that were nearly forty-feet in height as well as state-of-the-art circular concrete tunnelling.

There had been three sections of roadway constructed in a wooden herringbone pattern – quite unlike anything I have ever seen. It had been something that I would marvel at, in that I would have loved to have seen how it had been built.

"It always fascinated me too," explained Phil Atkinson – the Official whose job it had been to oversee the East Side roadways. "I was told by Billy Hayes's father – Dick, that it had been constructed during the Second World War when there had been a steel shortage. It was precision timbering in ground considered to be stable."

The longest section had been around 120 yards with the two shorter sections once forming part of a back rip.

Although the belt itself, was an extremely smooth ride, it was forbidden for men to travel on it, not just due to the low roadways that it passed through, but more to do with the fact that miners had both damaged, and in some cases lost their fingers, getting them caught between the cables and the rollers. Just prior to it snapping, Darren Eades had done exactly that and had had his fingers crushed.

If you want a connection, which will go some way to show how close-knit these mining communities were, I will give you one.

As stated, Clem's wife had previously been married to Roy Husband, who was one of around thirty men who had been injured on a runaway paddy train at the pit on 13 November 1973, whereby the locomotive struck a girder and derailed. By then, Roy had remarried a woman by the name of Mavis Eades (nee Caddick). She had previously been married to Darren's father's eldest brother, Terry.

As for the broken cable belt, it had ripped and parted, concertinaing close to one hundred yards in either direction. It was therefore left to Clem, under the supervision the Colliery Overman – the rotund, volatile and helmet-kicking Dennis Robinson, to repair it, as the two tunnels, which were being driven to access the new Silkstone development, and which I was part of, loaded directly on to it. This would be the only time that I would ever see Clem as a workmate.

The last time I ever saw him as a man was in 2001 and after I had left the area. I had pulled up outside what used to be Vallances (formerly Clays) electrical store on Doncaster Road, Goldthorpe, to call at the Yorkshire Bank. Both Clem and Rita looked the same, but maybe a little older, and the conversation we had, although it was brief, followed the line of many I have had with people that I have bumped into in later life, and to relay its content, would, I am sure, make me sound conceited, therefore I won't.

What I didn't know until this day, was that the blond-haired little lad, who had been the apple of his mother's eye, and who his big brother dearly loved, had recently died, aged twenty-five.

I think back to moments in their kitchen – the openness of Rita candidly giving me and her (step)son, the facts of life, whilst we sat at their table and in front of what was always a blazing coal fire in their cast iron Aga (range), and at our hanging on to her every word. She was such a wonderful lady and Clem a lovely man, and a couple of things spring to mind, which provide a great example to the thoughtful, considerate, and caring people that they both were.

My memory of Clem is in his asbestos-constructed garage, diligently seeking out parts for our bikes, whilst Richard and I huddled around its smoking cast iron stove, listening to the signals, whistles and screeches of music coming from his Topaz-branded MW/LW radio that he had bought with money that he had earned from potato picking. A memory of Rita is of her calling down at our house with a baking tin full of mince pies that she had gone out of way to bake for me.

Although things such as this obviously left a personal lasting impression, it was absolutely nothing compared to the bigger picture.

It was a well-known fact that from time to time Clem and Rita used to take in Foster-children. I recall a couple of brothers briefly staying there – however, it was a little girl that I remember most vividly. A girl who was temporarily placed there and who eventually became a part of their family.

Cyril Swift was a tall, thin, and stooping fellow. He had married a woman by the name of Gladys Jenkinson in 1969 and they had a couple of kids – Anthony in 1970 and Anita in 1975. It would be quite wrong of me to say how their rather frail-looking three or four-year-old daughter came to live with Clem and Rita as I could be wrong. However, what I can say is that Cyril – sometimes with his son, often called to see how his daughter was doing and would appear totally devastated on having to leave her. On the flip side of the coin, I never once recall seeing Anita's mother visit, which maybe goes some way to explain, why the little girl had been placed where she was.

There was a strange story of the houses that they both lived in and vacated, sadly none of which are there anymore, so which cannot provide proof of the thriving hive of activity that we all once shared.

Howard Hopkinson had married Sheila Moody in 1953 and between them they had nine children, with Neil who I have already mentioned, perhaps being the one that I knew the best. Not content with having eleven people in the house – they also had the eldest son's wife living with them, his elder sister's young child – Lyndsay, as well as a lodger, who was a frail old man by the name of *Roy*, who like Cyril Swift, possessed a stoop along with a huge arced nose.

That aside, and as with Richard and his family, they were a family I never genuinely appreciated. Not only were Howard and Sheila lovely people, who I got to know much better in later life, for such a big family, they unlike the other large families in the East end, refused point-blank to live in squalor. They were an extremely close-knit family – and the mother, who could at time appear quite brash if not coarse, was lovingly adored by each and every one of them.

Rita would at times, have me and their Richard in stitches, with some of her tales of the Hopkinson family, not at least with why the lodger was there.

Unlike Neil, his two elder brothers would go on to be miners at Hickleton Main – these were Steve who had been born in 1959 and would marry a girl the following year by the name of Gail Rhodes, and Chris who was two years younger. Steve was a smart articulated lad who I thought was a brilliant bloke and who later left the industry and went on to become a male nurse at Sue Ryder. The story surrounding Chris, however, is far darker.

Chris had survived a horrific road accident when he had been a young boy and being both tall and blond, he grew up into quite a handsome young man. There had however, always been a story doing the rounds about his dismissal from the pit – and to get the sack from Hickleton Main at that point in time, due to the power and weight of the NUM, could have only been for a handful of things. It was said, and quite often, that Chris had been caught breaking into the lockers in the pit baths and stealing from his fellow workmates. Why he did it, I suppose only he could tell you – however, it was a black cloud that would follow him around for years and how he stayed in Thurnscoe's East end was a testament to the strength and character of his family. The upshot was, that his was a family that stuck together, no matter what.

It was Neil and possibly his rather shit stirring nature, that I got to know who all the spitters, the name-callers and the flaggers were, who had created the misery on my second coming to Thurnscoe East. What he negated to tell me, however, was that mob rule was the name of the game – but more importantly, that the majority of these came from large families, which had either big brothers or big cousin's and whatever I was thinking of, I should immediately forget it. And that also applied to my angry and foul-mouthed adversary on Briton Street.

As much as I didn't quite ever know the Frost's and the Fryer's, there was another family situated at the foot of Briton Street and who had a highly contrasting lifestyle, that I did.

My mum's circle of what she termed as *friends* was never huge, of which by the story's end you may well get to understand why, and how she became friends with Mick and Ann Wharton (nee Mellor) is possibly down to the gregarious nature of Barry and Carol – who lived opposite, rather than anything that my mum could have possibly offered.

Mick was huge bear of a man who had a slight resemblance of the actor Jack "Phwaay" Douglas – the actor who had been an integral part of the *Carry On* team during its final years. I always found him to be an extremely thoughtful, and more importantly, a person who would take time out and speak with you and treat you as an equal. In sharp contrast, his wife could often appear both pretentious and aloof. Between them they had three children including a lad who had been in my year at school and was someone who I would come to know quite well. Steve, however, wasn't the natural son of Mick, and at times it could show in that he often had quite a petulant nature towards his stepfather.

I found Steve a clever, articulate and quite an engaging character who at times could possess similar traits to his mother, suggesting that maybe the main reasoning behind his petulance towards his stepfather, was that as Mick was unemployed and he needed someone to blame. This was a shame, as Mick, always talked him up.

I got to know him quite well prior to the final year in school, which was a time when our complete difference and respective outlooks well and truly came to light: his acumen for knowing exactly where his bright future lay and my non-conformity in that I didn't give a shit.

"On the first of September (1980) I'm going into the training office at the pit to get an application form," he explained, with a touch of brashness.

It was his intention to become a craftsman – either an electrician or a fitter.

The irony being that I got set on and he did not.

I never heard this from the horse's mouth, but I understood that he had failed his medical, due to having poor eyesight, which was something that I heard my mum say to my (step)dad, that he had blamed his mother for.

At times and although it was quite different, Steve could come over as angry as Jimmy Frost, who by that time was a kid who I got to quite like, which was more to do with the fact I had thumped him a few times, than me actually having anything in common with him.

Mick's tales of him being a doorman at the bowling alley on Doncaster's Silver Street in the 1960s, were the stuff of legend. Whilst he worked there, he had met Keith Richards, just as The Rolling Stones had become famous, and I recall him describing his spider-like fingers in great detail. As was the story about it all kicking off and him throwing a bowling ball downstairs at some hoodlums.

Looking back at it, they were nice times – however, there was always a silence behind the reasoning of Mick's *being unemployed*.

As I have stated, at some point in time you would have had to work at the colliery to live in a pit house.

Hickleton Main was essentially two pits that you accessed through three shafts.

The Parkgate side of the pit was accessed via No 3 shaft which had the smaller headgear. This passed the Barnsley-bed seam, which had been worked-out to exhaustion during the 1950s and provided access to the much deeper Parkgate and Thorncliffe coal seams and what would be the new Silkstone development down the colliery's East Side.

The Low Main side of the pit was accessed via No 1 and 2 shafts with the large blue headgear and provided access to both the Meltonfield and Newhill seams.

I only ever worked down the Parkgate side of the mine, therefore it would be wrong of me to try and describe the Low Main part of the pit. What I did know, is that unlike Parkgate, coal was hauled out of the No 1 and 2 shafts in mine cars. To haul these, you needed huge powerful diesel locomotives – and working down the Low Main part of the colliery and driving a locomotive is exactly what Mick had done.

What was often said, that prior to the termination of Mick's employment at Hickleton Main there had been a huge crash down that side of the pit involving dozens of mine cars that resulted in hundreds of thousands of pounds of lost production, with its cause being cited as driver negligence.

It was something that had been mentioned on me first working at the pit and it was described as having catastrophic consequences and much worse than Eddie Lockwood's getting out of jail by *nipping for a shit* story.

To access the new Silkstone development down Parkgate's East Side, we had to get there on what was always labelled as a *Paddy* train, which due to the development's long distance away from the pit bottom, was hauled by one of these diesel-driven locomotives.

I recall coming off a night shift in early 1983 and being on the Paddy as the locomotive approached some form of safety gate that was sunk into the floor (as opposed to the standard Drop Warwick (Derek) that was attached to the roof), prior to turning into the tight left-hand bend on its final destination into the pit bottom.

Gordon Weeding was a forty-four-year-old that lived on Thurnscoe's Cromwell Street who was one of the drivers of the East Side locomotive. He had been saddled with the nickname of Gupta, after I.S Johar's characterisation of the engine driver in the 1959 film *North West Frontier*, and was of a Romany appearance, cutting quite a spiderish figure with his long unkempt black hair and small frame. In later life he would become something of a radio ham and a controlling member of Thurnscoe's Citizens Band Radio Club, which ran out of The Fairway one night a week. However, at that time he was merely our genial loco driver.

The Silkstone development basically comprised the construction of two tunnels that were being driven down 1:4 and 1:5 gradients respectively – meaning that for every four (or five) yards the tunnels advanced, they dropped one yard. These steep headings were being driven between what was a huge Concorde-spec rope-hauled Paddy, that at one time provided access into the old East Side developments of the Parkgate seam. These had been heavily mined throughout the 1950s and 1960s – and were where my uncle, Steve Carman had worked with my (step)dad during the early 1970s, both as a young fitter and miner respectively.

Being such a small development, it only needed four tunnellers in each heading, three TPA's that doubled as back-up miners, two fitters and an electrician to cover both drives and a couple of Officials, therefore the Paddy on its outboard journey was carrying less than twenty men, including both the driver of the locomotive and its guard – the latter of who was generally Terry (Tex) Lloyd.

It was another Tex – Terry Rodgers, a moustachioed and sharp-witted miner off Tudor Street, who possessed a broad Barnsley accent, who made initially made the suggestion that we were going rather fast and on him turning to look over at the locomotive, its driver appeared to be slumped over in his cab.

Gordon had fallen asleep at the controls and that being the case, the locomotive was out of control, picking up a pace and trundling towards the safety gate and tight bend.

It was a surreal sight – the carriages rocking from side to side and the sight of the huge locomotive almost bouncing on the rails and narrowly negotiating its way beneath the low frames of the steel square-work supports. In a confined space, everything seems much quicker – and the 20-25 mph that we were travelling at, felt quite off the clock.

Was it not for the quick-witted thinking of Tex and the screaming and shouting of his mate and fellow tunneller Pete Denham, we would have been involved in a very serious accident – me especially, as I cut my conversation short with Jimmy Burke and Pete Duggan and had been debating jumping off.

The demolition of Taylor Street, Thurnscoe c. Rainer Unkel).
Top. Sisters Cheryl Louise and Davina Lily Norris walking hand in hand. These two pretty girls would
have a dark future ahead of them. Bottom. Kids congregating in the front gardens.

7.   The White Lady

The Silkstone development down Hickleton Main, would be driven to form a coal face – however, I would not be there to see it in production. I have contrasting thoughts about various times in my life – and from mid-November 1982 through to the early summer of 1983, that contrast was immense.

There was certainly nothing wrong about the job, as I saw it as the second step in my *career* towards the greater good, even though both my constitution and temperament, did at times, leave a lot to be desired.

The two tunnels were being driven using what is generally termed as drill and blast – but what I first came to know as bore and fire. Even now, I still look back, and in my mind, it is the most honest way of constructing a tunnel, and the satisfaction you get at the end of a shift cannot be matched.

Why is that? Possibly because **all** the miners are continuously working – drilling, spotting, priming, blasting, mucking out and erecting steel supports as opposed to one sitting on a machine and seemingly doing all the work, which is rarely ever the case.

For anyone who has never been down a pit, it is best to consider mining as a series of rectangular blocks of coal. To mine these blocks can be done in one of two ways, but to access them, you always need two tunnels which are generally termed as *gates* – both around 200 yards apart. These are driven to a certain point: as an example, say 2,500 yards.

Generally, the first to reach the 2,500-yard point, will turn and create the 200-yard-long link with the other tunnel, which will on its completion, be installed with supports and a coal cutting machine (shearer) and will therefore form the coal face. In modern times, the direction of the coal face, tended to come back towards the start of the huge rectangular block, which is known as retreat mining, and is much quicker, negating the need for what was always referred to as either main or tail *gate* rips, which are essentially the gradual construction of two tunnels as the coal face progresses in the opposite direction. I may well be wrong, but Hickleton Main – certainly while I was there, only had coal faces that went forward.

As the gases which emanate from deep mining are extremely dangerous, the ventilation of the coal face – and indeed the pit itself, works on the principal of circulated air, whereby air is forced down the main tunnel (gate), through the coal face and then out through the return tunnel (gate).

As the Silkstone part of the mine was a development and no coal face had yet been formed, the main tunnel (gate) was termed as the Intake, where the air was intended to be forced down on construction of the coal face, and the other tunnel was termed as the Return, where of course the air would come out. However, *and to bore you further*, to keep the air flowing in the direction you want it to flow, a series of what are termed as air doors are present throughout the mine, which due to the force being generated by both the intake and return of air, creates a huge air lock within them, that can both cause your ears to pop and which can slam shut. And if you are not careful, take your fingers off.

On me first going underground in mid-1982, I would see a young trainee electrician, have his fingers crushed by one. Andy (Red Legs) Rydelewski, had been a year older than me at school and as his name suggests, was a by-product of the Second World War – something that saw his father – Zbioniew, settle in the country and marry a girl called Joyce Weaver.

Andy was an affable lad who did his bit to cement Thurnscoe-Goldthorpe relations and married a girl that I went to school with, by the name of Kim Lewis. She was the younger sister of a belt maintenance fitter at the pit that I got to know quite well, called Johnny.

Andy's injury was the first I had ever seen – however, in comparison to some that had happened down Hickleton Main, it could be considered quite trivial.

You only had to look around at some of the men who worked on the colliery surface (pit-top) and who had jobs that entailed lighter duties.

Part of my long-drawn-out pit-top apprenticeship to the greater good, was working in what was termed as the *Bag Room*. This was located between the pit baths and the canteen, and although I considered it a *wank* job, handling the miners clean and dirty laundry – overalls, used socks and shorts, cleaning rubber dusk masks and what have you, it would be there that I would see the effects of the darker side of mining at first hand.

Reg Cole was both a very smart and amiable man of around fifty-six years of age, who lived a few doors up from where we had at 36 Deightonby Street. He was also an extremely mobile man, considering the fact that he had lost a leg in a roof fall, prior to his marriage to Beryl Worth in 1962. There was also another man – a frail guy by the name of Kenny Bailey who lived on the REEMA Estate who had a badly mangled arm.

As I recall, none of them really spoke of their injuries and it was left for others to fill you in.

The Bag Room was run by yet another moustachioed man with a slight resemblance to the comedian Bobby Ball. The diminutive Pete Ranskill had got the job by being quite close to the colliery's much-reviled Personnel Manager – Colin Ashworth.

Pete, who lived over in either South Elmsall or Upton, had worked in the colliery's medical centre and there had been some major incident underground where he and the other First Aiders had pulled out all the stops to try and save a life, which was something that must have truly impressed Ashworth.

The story regarding our Personnel Manager was that in times-past, he had been some Undermanager that had been gassed whilst underground, and not only did he look grey and drawn, but he was also extremely ill. I seem to recall that he had a problem with either his liver or kidneys.

Pete was the only person I ever knew at the colliery who spoke highly of him – however, the head of the Bag Room was something of a conundrum and certainly did have his share of idiosyncrasies.

One thing I have always done whilst mining, was to take in everything around me. In one instance I would see Pete having the craic in his broad Barnsley accent, then barking out orders to us. Then he would turn his attention to Kenny and take the piss out of his plastic arm and his going for a shower in the disabled part of the pit baths. Then you would catch him in the canteen around 10.00 a.m., with his T-shirt up around his neck and massaging a hairy chest, whilst at the same time trying to chat up Jenny Conley (nee Cox), the best looking of all the canteen ladies and the wife of the Union man, Brian. He was an interesting guy, that is for sure, and he was absolutely first class at telling a tale.

He had the Bag Room running like clockwork – however, the only days there was any real work was on laundry days. This involved sorting and dumping the bagged dirty overalls into the wheel-mounted steel cages and loading them onto a lorry supplied by the cleaning contractor Sketchley's and then sorting the clean overalls and putting them into miners' lockers with the aid of a load of monotonous work and use of the Master Key. It was, if I am being honest, a position of immense trust.

I had my arse kicked a couple of times, but that was for looking after my (step)dad and providing him with brand new socks and shorts as opposed to the laundered (and used) ones, but that was quickly offset by the fact that I offered to work afternoon shift – a shift that no-one wanted, and which left me both on my own and to my own devices.

Any job is easy once you know how it's done. The first thing I did after afternoon shift went underground and the day shift had come out and been showered was to handle the workload of dirty laundry and clean all the rubber dust masks... and the crème de la crème of handling chitties – the requests for new workwear. I knew only too well how this worked and my (step)dad and my girlfriend's dad were never short of new pit boots, belts, helmets, gloves, socks or anything else that the Bag Room handled, whilst I worked there.

I remember handling the laundry one Friday afternoon during May 1982 and hearing a tape recorder being continually played and repeatedly rewound in the nearby office at the end of the pit baths.

The song: Duran Duran's *Hungry Like the Wolf*.

The repetitive music was being played by a lad a few years older than myself by the name of Gary Barnfield, who just four years prior, had suffered an horrific injury whereby he had had part of his face crushed. This, however, this was not a work-related injury but something that occurred away from the pit, but which went some way to show – even back then, what a decent and considerate employer the NCB were.

Gary had been involved in an appalling motorcycle accident, just outside what was once Waldron's Farm on Shepherd Lane. The scenes were horrendously surreal in that a thirteen-year-old Colin Hunter saw it from John Street and raced down to be one of the first on site, only to see a young lad with the visor from his crash helmet lodged in his face. There was an even darker side to this story which was told by Pete Ranskill, in that he had been due to be married and that post-accident, his girlfriend couldn't deal with the sight of his injury and duly dumped him.

Some of the stories we got told of the atrocious injuries and the deaths in the pit could have quite easily given a young lad just starting out, nightmares – however, as time progressed, you became quite numb to their effect.

Most deaths underground occurred by roof falls.

i)   At 12.30 a.m. on Tuesday 26 April 1927, thirty-one-year-old Joseph Hollins of 35 Cromwell Street and forty-four-year-old Allen Lodge of 21 Shepherd Lane were killed whilst back ripping a tunnel in the Parkgate side of the mine. They were both crushed by a fall of rock weighing around four tons.

     Hollins had been one of the many miners that had their employment terminated at Harworth Colliery and had only worked five shifts prior to him being killed.

ii) Forty-seven-year-old Jonas Mitchell of 16 Butcher Street got crushed in the Parkgate seam of Hickleton Main on Thursday 5 January 1928, when a piece of muck came away and crushed his skull.

iii) Two Goldthorpe lads, who were not only brothers-in-law having married sisters Rose and Alice Deborah Collins from 68 Highgate Lane but were also best friends who both worked together as miners at Goldthorpe Colliery.

     On 7 December 1928, twenty-five-year-old Harry Taylor of 20 Washington Road and twenty-six-year-old Arthur Brammer of 16 Goldthorpe Road – a house opposite the Buxton Arms, had been working in a back rip at Goldthorpe Colliery, when a roof fall occurred and two girders that they were setting came crashing down – one of which killed the latter outright. Arthur and his wife, Rose, had just had a baby daughter, Annie.

     Rose remarried Reginald Thompson in 1933 and eventually moved into a house at 13 George Street, Thurnscoe – but never think that tragedy only strikes once. It would be here in December 1942, where they lost a daughter by the name of Betty, aged fourteen months.

iv) A hero of the First World War, twenty-year-old Arthur Monks had been one of the British troops who liberated Baghdad on 11 March 1917 but on 26 August 1932, he would be deep underground at Hickleton Main and drawing off props on 205 stall with his mate, Isaac Parker of 45 Tudor Street.

     That morning, he had left his wife Beatrice (nee Platts) at their home at 79 Probert Avenue, Goldthorpe for his fifteen-minute walk over Pit Lane with no knowledge of what his immediate future would hold. He had seen plenty of hurt before – not at least with the death of his eight-month old son in October 1921 when they had lived on Goldthorpe's Queen Street, which was something he and his workmate shared – as Isaac and his wife, Ivy (nee Besant) had had two kids that had been born dead.

     At 8.30 a.m. on that fateful Friday morning an almighty bump occurred which was followed by a terrific crash that had miners scurrying for cover. The roof fall had been that bad that over thirty miners were utilised over a period of five hours to finally recover Arthur's body. He had suffocated to death.

v) Just two months later, forty-year-old Robert Sussams of 68 Brunswick Street had been working with Les Hipwell's father, Joe on 206 stall and ended up being completely buried by a massive roof fall. He was another one who eventually died of asphyxia.

vi) In the early hours of Thursday morning on 15 July 1937, twenty-two-year-old John Ascoft of 60 Tudor Street was crushed by a roof fall, that killed him instantly. He suffered a fractured skull, ribs and spine.

vii) William Stephenson of 66 Deightonby Street had only been working at Manvers Main a fortnight when on 28 February 1941, he was fatally injured in a roof fall on 17s tail gate in the Parkgate seam. He died from a fractured skull.

viii) At around 1.00 a.m. on 11 July 1941, thirty-three-year-old John Slee of 104 Deightonby Street had been working with thirty-six-year-old Arthur Hull of 32 Lancaster Street and got caught by a fall of coal on the 278s unit in the Parkgate seam. The fall fractured his pelvis in five places and ruptured his bladder. He died a day later in Mexborough Montagu, leaving a wife and three children.

His wife, Bertha (nee Lockwood) remarried a twice widowed man by the name of George Harvey in 1944 – and had lived at 24 Challenger Crescent before he died on 29 September 1956.

ix) It was a similar tale in the at Hickleton Main on 17 September 1942. Thirty-year-old Bernard Davison of 38 Lancaster Street was working with twenty-four-year-old John Warrington of 24 Taylor Street and twenty-six-year-old Horace Wright of 10 Lancaster Street in the 141s stall in the Barnsley Bed seam when a huge piece of muck dislodged two props and crushed him. Death, it was said – had been instantaneous. Bernard suffered horrendous injuries including a fractured skull, ribs, right leg and spine.

His widow Phyllis (nee Lawson) remarried Robert Usher in 1953 and for a time they lived at 35 Briton Street, Phyllis finally passing away in Dearnelea Nursing Home on 11 March 2008, aged ninety-two.

x) In late-July 1956, forty-three-year-old Joe Batchelor of Mill Street, South Kirkby had been one of three miners that got caught in a roof fall in the Parkgate seam at Hickleton Main. Unfortunately, however, Joe didn't survive the fall and died of asphyxia.

There was a similar one a few years later when on 3 March 1959, thirty-seven-year-old George Baker of 29 Hall Broome Gardens, Bolton-on-Dearne was killed on 105's unit in the Meltonfield seam of the pit. Employed as an Official, he had been priming up to blast the face when a roof fall occurred, and he too got buried alive.

He left a widow, Blanche and two children – fourteen-year-old Beryl and six-year-old Russell.

There were some truly horrific stories.

"A terrible accident at Hickleton Main on 7 November 1934 in which a young screen worker was killed and mutilated by machinery, was inquired into by the Doncaster District Coroner W.H Carlile when he held an inquest on 22-year old Frank Wilson of 62 Deightonby Street," said the *South Yorkshire Times*.

Frank was the son of Henry and Emma (nee Hampshire) and worked in the pit bottom bunker – however, on that fateful Wednesday morning and whilst he had been clearing coal, his clothing became entangled with the screening machinery and he ended up having his arm torn from his body and both legs ripped off from below his knees.

Possibly the worse one I have come across was the death of a twenty-four-year-old by the name of Harry Kilner at the newly sunk Barnburgh Main, on Friday 23 November 1917.

Now, Harry certainly hadn't the nicest of people – that's for sure. He had been one of a dozen *usual suspects* brought in as part of a line-up in the yard of Goldthorpe Police Station on the Saturday afternoon of 8 June 1912, following an incident up near Bella Wood the previous evening.

What should be known is that he resided in an overcrowded terraced house at 81 Main Street, Goldthorpe – a property along with No 85, that the Kilner family would occupy for eighty years.

At nineteen years of age, however, he had followed three young girls into a field, one of who had been Nellie Bailey – the ten-year-old daughter of Edwin and Ellen (nee Beresford) of 88 Doncaster Road, Goldthorpe.

Nellie had been picking flowers with two girls a year younger than herself, including her best friend, Alice Milner – a girl who she would even be Maid of Honour for at Owston's All Saint Church some eleven and a half years later, when Alice married Jonathan Greenbank on Boxing Day 1923.

The other girl had been Annie Watkinson who lived at 16 Orchard Street, Thurnscoe – another house with a dark past – the three-year-old son of John and Winifred Bladen (nee Sharp), Charlie dying there just before Christmas 1945.

The three girls were approached by Kilner, his motive being obvious. He initially tried to corner Alice, but she managed to evade him. Unfortunately, Nellie hadn't been as quick.

All three girls picked out Kilner in the identification – and after the jury found him guilty at Doncaster West Riding Court the following Tuesday, the Chairman J.W Hodgson had no option but to send him to prison.

Harry had worked on and off in the pits ever since he had left school, and on getting out of prison he got another start – this time at Barnburgh Main, where he was eventually employed in some supervisory role on what was known as Eight's Landing.

Harry Kilner was described by many as being overanxious, and was, it was also said, inclined to twitch a bit, if things went wrong, which on that that fateful day is exactly what happened. He had apparently been getting frustrated with some fifteen-year-old haulage hand – a lad by the name of Sam Fletcher off Mexborough's Doncaster Road, as a run of twenty-six tubs had come off the rails. That being the case, he hastily removed the lad from his duty as engine driver.

Obviously, I wasn't an eye witness, but what I do know is that Harry proceeded to try and get the hauler to pull the tubs back on the rails by snagging at them using a succession of forward and reverse pulls. This in effect created a lot of slack rope and formed a loop, which duly wrapped around his neck.

"I saw a kink of rope come off the drum of the engine and looked around and saw that the loop was round Kilner's neck," explained Sam. "The rope drew Kilner into the drum and once there pulled his head clean off."

Robert James Hedley – who would eventually move into a property at 2 Windermere Avenue, Goldthorpe – had been the Official on the district and explained that he had been helping and that all but three tubs had been got back on the rails. "He must have suddenly reversed the drum to get a snatch at the tubs. He was quite competent on the engine, although he drove it a bit faster than I would have done," he explained.

As for Harry, he was the great uncle of Roy and Julie Kilner – both of whom I knew.

As with their great uncle, both were quite diminutive in stature and possessed curly hair, Julie's being the darkest of brown.

Whereas Julie had been in my year at school – Roy had been someone that I would eventually work with – although, certainly not on a regular basis.

Doncaster-based Cementation Mining had mining contracts all throughout the UK's coalfields, one of which was the Parkgate development at Maltby Colliery, where the company were in the throes of constructing a new pit bottom. I had transferred over to the job after the company had completed the second phase of works at the Asfordby New Mine in the Vale of Belvoir in March 1990.

I had initially been pencilled-in to work on the reprofiling of a drift tunnel by under-mining the floor using a Hausherr dinting machine in an area close to where Roy's team had been driving a new heading. It was, however, a job that I would never do. I was thrown in with one of the three-man tunnelling crews employed on the creation of the new pit bottom. It was also a job, where we would be driving huge tunnels through several geological faults and one where I would be underground when the shaft pillar broke. The former culminated in huge falls of rock and saw several injuries, whilst the latter created an extremely eerie atmosphere and one which you could not see your hand in front of your face due to the thick dust, after what was one god-awful fucking bang.

Rather strangely, the last time I saw Roy was in my office some eight years later, along with a bearded man by the name of Gary Bentham – who had been dismissed from Cementation's contract at Maltby Colliery before I had arrived on site following some alleged altercation with the company's Project Manager.

The reason that they had been in my office was that they had been trying to find a way forward for some mining company that they ran called RD Mining.

Roy's sister married a gregarious miner that I also knew, by the name of Alan Kerry, and who both live on Thurnscoe's Crossgate – the street of prefabricated concrete pit houses, which form the entrance into Lindley Crescent.

Looking back, a lot of us formed a part of someone else's family, and that was no more evident than in the rip of the Intake tunnel that formed part of Hickleton Main's new Silkstone development.

Ronnie Whittaker, who was another man who possessed – not so much a speech impediment but who spoke as though he had some form hearing problem, was the brother-in-law of the one-time golden boy of Thurnscoe school football, Gary (Nutty) Kerley, through their marriage to two sisters.

Gordon Elliott had married a girl called Margaret Gadd in 1953 and had five daughters and a son, the latter of who was a kid the same age as me and who had been named after his father.

My only real recollection of him was when had been in Houghton Road Infant School and trying to extract a plastic dagger out of his hand under the watchful gaze of the huge rocking horse in Mrs Gilbert's classroom during the spring of 1970, which is a completely different scenario to that of the little fearless little warrior, that was his cousin, Don.

Out of Gordon's five sisters, four married miners: Ronnie, who always came across as both an amiable and considerate man had married Christine and lived over near the *Bullring*. The highly sociable and often-boozing Gary had married Caroline and lived a few doors up from Lil Austin on Briton Street. Margaret had married an electrician at the pit by the name of Alan Danforth and lived on Cromwell Street. The youngest sister and the one I certainly knew the most had been Kay. She married a fitter at the pit who was a lovely fellow by the name of Graham Brook. Both lived next door to my mum and (step)dad at 53 Lancaster Street.

I remember post-strike, regularly walking around the corner with Gary from Roman Street onto Briton Street to see Caroline standing at their door and waiting for her husband's return from work, as much as I remember the summer mornings at home when I had been a kid and listening to Kay singing along to Radio 1 with their back door ajar.

The Return tunnel had been no different – three of its miners who lived just a few strides away. I could see Pete Denham's house from our room window, whilst directly across the street at 56 Lancaster Street, lived the twenty-four-year-old Paul (Tacker) Tasker. He was a booming character and one of five lads from another large mining family whose father Tommy, was from Barnsley. And right at the very top of Lancaster Street lived the twenty-four-year-old Jimmy Burke, a truly brilliant man, who married Gillian (nee Taylor) – the granddaughter of Willie Taylor, the miner who drowned in the colliery reservoir in 1930.

Jimmy Burke would go on to have a catastrophic accident at Bentley Colliery post-strike, and how he survived the injury was a testament to the strength of both the man and his character.

Whilst working down on the Silkstone development the nearest I got to seeing an accident was James (Jumbo) McNulty and myself at the top of the heading causing one, and Jimmy Burke being one of the lads at the bottom, who had been clambering up into the tunnel's roof trying to avoid it.

Very similar to the situation with Harry Kilner over 65 years earlier, we had been getting frustrated with what was normally a quite capable Pickrose haulage engine, which due to the tunnel's steep gradient and the sheer weight of the steel colliery arches, struts and corrugated sheet supports, had become rather overtaxed.

There were three transfer points which needed manning-up and being that I had been eighteen years old at that time, I was put on three shifts. As that was the case, we generally had a couple lads from the Class of 1981's intake that were still seventeen, billeted down the colliery's East side on a two-shift scenario. These filled in on both day and afternoon shift, whilst the night shift was covered by Robert Abraham Duggan's stepson – Pete, along with George (Judd) Errington.

The only one outside of the Class of 1981 that ever got sent down the East side while I was there, was the rather diminutive and bespectacled grandson of John Fingers Billam and therefore the nephew of Goldthorpe's body in the boot murderer and the master of tall tales that was Big Pinky – a kid by the name of Allan Billam, who apparently owned a helicopter, which he kept in his attic.

Paul was an amiable character whose favourite saying at the time, was as I recall: "Suck my root".

As for Jumbo, his colourful history could have been a lot different. He was a kid with fearless nature and a gritty Scottish accent that arrived one morning at Carfield during 1973. I recall him being chaperoned by a tall gangly kid two years older than us called Paul Mattrick, whose parents Bill and Sylvia had lived in one of Thurnscoe's dark properties at 65 Church Street. This had been a house where Lily and Leslie Smith had perished as babies in 1921 and 1925 respectively, and where eighteen-year-old Fred Brundle had been staying with relatives when they fished his dead body out of the Drowning Pool on the Friday afternoon of 19 August 1910.

Jumbo's father had started work at Highgate Colliery and would eventually be employed as an Official. James McNulty (Snr) had initially come over from Coalisland in County Tyrone and met his mother, Lilian who had been from Bo'ness – a beautiful town, which is situated on the southern banks of the Firth of Forth.

"I remember as a kid, being sat in the car whilst my dad had an interview at Clipstone Colliery," he told me quite recently.

I used to pass Clipstone regularly on my way down into the Vale of Belvoir, with its imposing headstocks, which when they were constructed in 1953, were said to be the tallest in Europe. If you want a Thurnscoe connection – then the winding engines were constructed by Markham & Company – the other half of the joint venture with Davy Mining that sunk the shafts for Hickleton Main.

If you want Jumbo-connection, then it would be the fact that I could have never in a million years have imagined him living anywhere in north Nottinghamshire – which is something that will become very apparent as you read on.

On this particular afternoon, however, Pinky had been on the engine, whilst Jumbo and I had been tentatively tramming the roof supports down into the rip.

I say tentatively, as we knew that the haulage engine had been playing up and that its clutch was slipping. Basically, we were pissing in the wind. Ordinarily we could have waited for a replacement engine being fitted, but that was in the pit bottom awaiting transportation by the sleepy-eyed amateur radio ham that was Gupta – the man who had tried wiping us all out a few weeks prior. Therefore, we persevered with taking the materials down the drift on a series of steel lockers, wooden chocks and sprags, which if the Health and Safety Executive (HSE) would have seen us doing it, would have had a fucking fit. Obviously, the tonnage to N/m2 ratio always dictated what was going to happen, and as we did our best to hold back the runaway train, it eventually beat us. Watching the four lads in the rip of the tunnel trying to scramble around to safety was quite humorous, as was listening to Jumbo relaying his screams of "Get out of the fucking way".

It made a right mess, but there was an upside. Apart from the tubs and trams being scattered all over the place and the safety buffer at the end of the rails getting completely ripped off, all the steel arches had unloaded themselves, and all just a couple of feet from the rip.

John (Dolly) Dolman and George Whitehurst made up the other two of the Intake crew, the former who I perhaps knew the least and who I believe lived on Deightonby Street, whilst the latter for a short time, would become my near neighbour on Briton Square – and one of the things that often puzzled me about George Whitehurst, surrounded a guy that I had once seen sat upon his roof?

Now here is a story.

George Merricks was born on 23 August 1899 to a miner by the name of Robert, who had come up from Staffordshire and for a time lived in an over-populated two-up-two down terraced house on Kenyon Street off Doncaster Road in South Elmsall, with his mum – Sarah, two sisters – Anna and Clara, and six lodgers, most of who worked at the nearby Frickley Colliery.

The reasoning behind his parent's separation, when he was just fourteen years old is unknown. What I do know, however – is that the separation, placed huge hardships on his mother, as his father had not contributed any maintenance for three years – which was an amount totalling £93 and twelve shillings (£10,780, circa 2020), and as a result, his father had been sentenced to three months' hard labour.

From what I can gather, George possessed a roguish nature and during the time of his father's neglect, was in and out of trouble all the time. Whether this was because he had no guiding hand from his father and with his mother working to keep the family's heads above water, he was let loose to do what he wished, was at that time quite unclear – however, as time goes on there becomes a pattern.

He was eventually sentenced to three years in borstal and on being released he was drafted into the hell that was the First World War, coming out as a highly decorated Corporal. By then, his family had moved to Goldthorpe, where on New Year's Day 1923, an elderly and much-wiser George – who by then lived at 11 Charles Street, married Ivy Emma Fairchild at St John the Evangelist and St Mary Magdalene (Parish) Church on Lockwood Road.

Whilst George went to work at Hickleton Main the couple had a son by the name of John Robert, along with a daughter that they named Gladys, the latter who arrived during the early stages of the seven-month pit lockout of 1926.

All the surrounding area suffered tremendous hardships, however, Thurnscoe was nowhere near as bad as other mining communities.

The manager at the pit at the time, John Minnikin, reportedly turned a blind eye to the scavenging of coal from the colliery spoil heap, but even though this kept the house warm and heated the back boiler, it didn't put food on the table. The lack of nutrition caused George to become too ill to work after the lockout came to an end, and to compound things further, hundreds of men had flocked down to the village straight after the strike. These were from the Ryhope and Silksworth area of Sunderland – men who had heard stories of miners earning tremendous amounts of money and who had come down in the hope of getting employment, with thirty of them getting both set on and given the keys to properties on the newly constructed northern arm of Brunswick Street.

The situation up in the Durham coalfields – Ryhope in particular, was dire, with it being reported that miners had been told by the colliery owners post-strike, that all that was on offer was what had been often termed as *starvation wages*, with no miner earning more than twenty-five shillings (£76.60, circa 2020) a week, with the basic rate being a paltry two shillings (£6.13, circa 2020) per shift.

To make things more interesting, around 120 displaced miners from Harworth Colliery had also been set on at Hickleton Main. This was something that had added to the existing tension. It was said that ten miners had broken the strike, which resulted in a police presence at the shaft side on everyone returning to work. I know of three of them – Thomas Thomas of 13 Briton Street, Thomas Margison of 16 Orchard Street and Lewis Simmonds of 34 King Street, the latter of whom I will get to shortly.

Heavily in debt, George needed both money and food, and his experience, gained from pilfering in the period after his father had left home, temporarily saw his family survive the hardship. That was until he got caught red-handed coming out of the back of some lorry at South Elmsall railway station.

Labelled by the press as the human mole, as he had tunnelled beneath a wall to get access to the trucks, he was sentenced to nine months hard labour – however, what he told the judge on his sentencing was quite heart-wrenching. "I was just looking for food for my wife and children."

On his release from prison and after losing his job at Hickleton Main, he relocated over to both Dunscroft and Stainforth for a time, where they had another child by the name of William, prior to Christmas 1928. However, just a month later, he was caught illegally extracting electricity and sentenced to a further two months imprisonment and fined £3 (£190, circa 2020).

A pattern was beginning to form and on 26 February 1932, he was sentenced to a further nine months hard labour. This was for stealing coal from Stainforth railway sidings. This caused a massive uproar, so much so, that his case went before the Home Secretary, Herbert Louis Samuel in the Houses of Parliament, with a view to remission.

It appeared that George, although very much in the wrong from a legal point of view, was fighting tooth and nail to enable his family's survival, something which during the ensuing Second World War, he would be able to do absolutely nothing about.

After serving his sentence at Her Majesty's Pleasure, George along with his son John Robert, got signed on at Hickleton Main and the family firstly located at 5 Hanover Square before moving on to 38 Briton Street, and opposite to where Nelson and Gertrude Frost's grocery store (No 55) and Lenny and Annie Andrews' fruit and vegetable Shop (No 57) were situated.

We could assume that everything was good, and that family life returned to normal. That certainly was not the case. The break out of hostilities had George – a seasoned veteran of the first conflict, drafted into the British Army's Military Corps, whilst his daughter, would get a job at a munitions factory in Doncaster, before leaving after being accepted for new job at a mill over in Bradford.

What history will tell you is that never happened and that her dead body was found on waste ground just off Nora Street – between the Goldthorpe Hotel and The Reform WMC (was Greenfields). After what was described as a fierce struggle that involved half her clothes being torn from her body she was strangled, with some form of ligature.

A telegram was sent to her father who had been stationed in the south of England, requesting his urgent return to Thurnscoe. It had, however, been a message that was vague in its content, and after travelling fifteen hours to the bus station in Doncaster's Waterdale, he realised of the reasoning behind the urgency. George heard some people talking of the murder of a young girl in Goldthorpe and on him inquiring further, he duly collapsed. The man who had fought through the hardships of the 1920s to keep his family from the clutches of starvation, had had his daughter taken from him.

The murder case was headed by Supt. J. Walker of Doncaster, together with a Det. Chief Insp. W. Lee and Det. Chief Insp. C. Marston, of Wakefield.

With Britain at war and blackouts being a regular feature, it became common knowledge of a man that had recently been undertaking attacks on young girls. Two had been approached close to what was another notorious bridge on Straight Lane and there had been similar attacks outside the two cinemas', which were located either side of the Horse & Groom public house.

Regardless of what her mother had said in that she wasn't the type of girl to have boyfriends, everything had pointed to her going on a date.

She had been in a rush that cold Sunday night of 7 February 1943 and according to the neighbour, twenty-three-year-old Edith Crackles (nee Bargh) of 40 Briton Street, she had someone to see. Her dress code, however, certainly didn't strike me as someone going on a date.

The diminutive and fair-haired Gladys had been wearing a blue blouse and skirt, a three-quarter length brown coat, a brown scarf with yellow stripes, and a yellow scarf worn as a turban. The strange thing was, is that she was also wearing blue overall-type trousers.

She left the house at 7.15 p.m. and the next anyone ever saw of her was at the scene of her murder. There were no witnesses that had seen her, which for a Sunday evening in a mining community, was very strange. How did she get to Goldthorpe? The police, who took over 500 statements and interviewed thousands of people, claimed that not one person had seen her on her journey there, nor at her final destination, with the steward at the Reform

WMC (also known as The Nut) – Bob Marriott, stating that he would have certainly recognised any girl entering the club wearing trousers.

The most straightforward way of getting from Thurnscoe to Goldthorpe was, and still is, by walking over Pit Lane. In my mind, she didn't go that way and aged at just sixteen years and ten months and given her appearance, it seems hardly likely that a dance hall or public house would have been her initial destination. So, where did she actually go?

Ellen Barlow was the twenty-three-year-old daughter of Herbert and Mary (nee Burton) and lived at 43 Chapel Lane, which was around 500 yards from the home of the Merricks. The lane itself runs on the periphery of Thurnscoe East's pit estate. This is partly as a one-sided street looking out onto allotments and fields and then as a bridle path as it meandered past the rear of the dog track, colliery brickworks and Lidget Wood, thereby linking the old wooden bridge on the Wath Branch Line with the very end of Lidget Lane – the lowest point of escarpment up into Hickleton.

Ellen had not only recently got married to a man by the name of Douglas Fair; she had also had a baby daughter to him by the name of Mary, who at the time was less than five months old.

Her husband originated from the Attercliffe Road area of Sheffield, which is a long industrial and commercial road that is one of the main arterial routes into city centre and that at one time was filled with steelworks, foundries and armament manufacturers. That being the case it had been both targeted and heavily bombed by the German Luftwaffe all throughout the war with the train lines south of Bolton-on-Dearne's Lowfield Road also being subjected to air raids in their bid to stop coal being transported into Sheffield from the pits in the eastern Dearne Valley.

Tucked away in an indiscreet commercial property, and amongst all this heavy industry, had been James Fair, a repairer of shoes and boots. A cobbler of sorts. It was a profession that his middle son would take up after leaving school at fourteen years old up until his enlistment in the army in June 1937.

With the country gearing up for war, thousands of people were displaced, one of who had been Ellen Barlow, which is most likely the reason of how she met her husband. They married and she moved in with her in-laws above the shop. Ellen, however, was moved out to Eaton Hall in the Gamston area of Retford.

This was a stately home located off the Great North Road, which was owned by Sheffield industrialist Charles Kayser and his wife Katherine (nee Price) – the latter of whom was a County Councillor and Justice of the Peace. It was Katherine who agreed to let the upper floor of the hall, be used as a maternity hospital for soldiers' wives who had been bombed-out of their homes.

It is hard to describe someone you have never actually known personally – however, Ellen's husband it is very fair to say, certainly had his demons.

Gladys, like most girls in the East end of the village, had gone to Thurnscoe Hill school, along with Ellen Barlow's younger brother Fred, who was of course Douglas Fair's brother-in-law. Fred was one year older than Gladys and at the time employed at the nearby Houghton Main Colliery in Little Houghton, or what is often termed as Middlecliffe.

During the early evening of that fateful Sunday, and rather coincidentally, Gladys had been in Edith Crackles' house next door and had asked her to cut out some new soles for her shoes. By coincidentally, I mean that their next-door neighbour was, also like Douglas Fair, a repairer of shoes and boots.

She explained that Gladys often called in and chatted with her. Whilst she was there, she heard the radio programme change at 7.00 p.m. – which just for the record, was an adaption of John Maddison Morton's *Box and Cox* farce, and Gladys immediately became concerned about the time and stated that she "had someone to see".

What is also strange, is that on Gladys's body being found, all she was wearing was a pair of long socks and shoes, although one had come off. The rest of her clothes, including the overalls, had been strung about the place.

The pathologist, Dr Peter Lindsay Sutherland, maintained that although there had been a fierce struggle, no sexual activity had taken place, either consensual or non-consensual. What was not said or confirmed however, was if she had been sexually active prior to her murder.

Interestingly, surviving relatives of the dead girl have said that she was four months pregnant – however, that had **not** been stated in the pathologist's report.

By the late evening of 11 February, the crime appeared to have been solved and the police came in great numbers into Thurnscoe East, entering 43 Chapel Lane and making an arrest. Douglas Fair had made the first move. He had showed his hand and using a technique of deflection had somehow implicated his young brother-in-law, Fred Barlow.

It was said that Fred had been questioned all night at Goldthorpe Police Station, but according to members of his family, he had an alibi. The timing on finding the body made things hazy, with the pathologist stating that the girl had been dead between six and twelve hours – meaning that she had met her fate anytime between 11.00 p.m. and 5.00 a.m. As for Fred Barlow, he could cover either all, or part of that window of time, as he had either been getting ready to go to work or had been at work. Whatever it was, he was ruled out as being a prime suspect. Therefore, the following day the hunt for the killer was resumed involving a new line of enquiry, the only real clue being a khaki forage cap, that had supposedly been left at the crime scene. This had been a similar cap to what John Le Mesurier's Sergeant Wilson character was often seen wearing in the wartime-based sitcom, *Dad's Army*. Therefore, *the serve* was returned to the former prime suspects brother-in-law. It was supposedly Douglas Fair's cap.

The newspapers reported that the police had a difficult task in view of the absence of clues and the **one** puzzling aspect was, that no one had yet come forward who had seen Gladys after she left home and her movements thereafter. That was until her body was discovered.

My theory is quite simple. Gladys was at what is a strange age for a girl, as in the main, they mature much faster in adolescence than boys, which we are often told is all down to physiology and hormones, and as that is the case, they tend to become attracted to slightly older boys. Therefore, the reason nobody saw her is straightforward. She did not want to be seen.

Gladys deflected any suspicion to her mother by dressing down and saying that she would be home by 9.30 p.m. It had snowed quite heavily three days prior, leaving around six inches in places, which compounded by the low temperatures of the following days, had made it turn into ice, therefore taking the edge off that dark February night.

Although he could drive and of that there is no doubt, Douglas Fair had neither a car nor a licence. It is my presumption that the only way he could have really sold a clandestine meeting, was with the lure of them both slipping off to a pub – or better still, the Astoria dance hall. A dance hall, where she had recently told her mother that although she didn't go in them, she often used to look through the doorways at the people dancing inside.

The upshot is that Douglas Fair had more than likely promised her that he would treat her like a grown-up.

As a young lad, possibly too young to go out drinking and too bored to be hanging around the house, I would often take an identical journey with my girlfriend who lived on Chapel Lane. It is my theory that Gladys walked up both legs of Brunswick Street and met up with Douglas Fair at the far-southern end of Chapel Lane before taking a walk up to Hickleton's T-junction with Thurnscoe, and down past Bella Wood and into the far end of Goldthorpe. It was a walk of less than three miles. A walk in which he could assertively sell her his vision of blarney – maybe him leaving his wife and the two of them running off together. Or maybe not. Whatever it was, that walk was the *getting to know you* phase, whereas the part in the dimly-lit waste ground, which was part-sheltered by the huge building that was the rear of the Reform WMC, would be quite something else.

It is my thought that she herself removed her trousers, as why on finding her would the shoes be still on her feet? Was this the prelude for them to go inside the club? "Let me take these off first," she could have said.

Everything about her murder leads you to assume that it was sexually motivated, but with no sex. Maybe he had made his move and that she had knocked him back as it had started to become serious. A married man of that age

77

is quick to pursue an opening and maybe he took it and whilst doing so he got knocked back, therefore pushed that bit harder before getting disturbed. Maybe the ligature was some form of sexual tool that he liked using and one which he had used before on his wife? What is true is, that whatever he did, it resulted in a scream or screams, and maybe not wishing anyone to find out about the clandestine meeting, the answer was to shut her up and what better way than doing that, would be to make it permanent. There are lots of maybes in there that make the theory thin, but the fact that he supposedly lost his cap in the struggle, puts him there. With the genetic profiling and the forensics of today, using DNA, he would have been both tried and hanged. Well, you would think so.

What do I know of Douglas Fair? Quite a lot.

He was born on 17 February 1919, therefore at the time of Gladys's murder he would have been ten days off his twenty-fourth birthday. He was around 5'10 and described as a decent looking man and very neat in appearance. He was certainly the type of man that a plain girl, not yet seventeen years old could easily fall for. And Gladys was exactly that.

The reason that he was living with his wife's family on Chapel Lane is that he had been medically discharged as being mentally unfit for service in September 1941, and as such, went into the pit. He had been court martialled in Aldershot and imprisoned before the outbreak of hostilities and a few days before the Nazi's invaded Poland, for both taking a vehicle without the owner's consent and going absent without leave. From what members of his family had said and by reading between the lines, he certainly didn't want to go to war, as has soon as he was released back into the army, he was imprisoned again for a similar offence. In fact, the whole of his life was a series him being incarcerated for theft.

But to kill a young girl?

George Merricks was no fool. He made his feelings known to the police. He moved heaven and earth trying to force the investigation, but the police – stretched to the limits with wartime crimes, didn't just let him down, they let him down badly. George would become a broken man.

It could be said that Douglas Fair was too clever for the police – however, there was a bit more to it than that. He possessed the split-personality of a schizophrenic and as such, he could quite easily make a downright lie appear as the truth. In short, he was a pathological liar that knew no bounds.

On 3 September 1946, a Retention Order was made on him under Section 16 of Lunacy Act after several similar acts of vehicle theft, one of which involved an incident on Doncaster's Thorne Road, close to where the Royal Infirmary is sited. He had stolen a car from the Market Place and whilst being pursued, rammed two cyclists – Harold Taylor and Sidney Horsfield, dragging their broken bodies nearly a hundred yards in the process. On being taken to court and with numerous witnesses to confirm his guilt, brazenfaced he pleaded *not guilty*. Why not? if he could get away with murder, what's a broken leg and a smashed-up pelvis?

What followed, was twelve months in Sheffield's Middlewood Mental Hospital and on him getting out a similar series of events followed whereby he ended up in Broadmoor.

Senior Probation and After-Care Services Officer, Brian Fellowes, explained that the consultant psychiatrist at Middlewood had told him that he considered Douglas Fair to have a psychopathic personality and that it had proved impossible at Broadmoor to provide the necessary strict supervision that he required.

Ellen Barlow divorced him in 1952 on grounds of cruelty and desertion. Strangely however, he married a girl by the name of Irene Davis, the very same year of his divorce.

Dr Robert McDonald who had been a psychiatric consultant at High Royds Psychiatric Hospital in West Yorkshire made a statement in early 1969 after Douglas Fair had escaped from Middlewood and burned down some buildings at Wharfedale Grange Farm.

The farm was located off the A61 Leeds – Harrogate Road in the village of Dunkeswick, just north of the River Wharfe and west of Wetherby. The consultant's statement said that for years Douglas Fair had suffered from "uncontrollable impulses" and that every two or three months he gets an unbearable feeling of tension which can only be relieved by committing of acts of this nature. However, what the consultant stated thereafter further instils the belief that he murdered Gladys Merricks and said: "Douglas Fair feels a bitter hatred towards all women and told me that he would attack even an unknown woman if given the opportunity. He is quite unable to control his abnormal impulses and expresses the fact that he might kill or seriously injure women."

Glasgow-born Dr Geoffrey Pollitt, who was a Deputy Director of the prison medical service and who was involved as a medical expert in numerous high-profile arson and murder trials in the north of England said on Fair's admission to Broadmoor: "He is liable to over indulge in alcohol and the combination of his uncontrollable urges and the loss of self-control caused by the alcohol result in his committing offences. Fair also states that he is liable to sudden impulses to harm innocent women and children and expresses considerable fear that he may do so."

In February 1959, he had been found guilty of threatening to murder his wife and was sentenced to four years imprisonment and on immediately getting out of prison he was convicted of arson and threatening to kill his wife yet again. He was therefore made the subject of an indefinite Hospital Order under Section 65 of the Mental Health Act.

If you want other angles.

i) Edith Crackles' thirty-three-year-old husband Clifford, who lived next door to Gladys, was committed to Sheffield's Middlewood Hospital – and died there in May 1980. He had to have been sent there for some reason.

ii) The murders of Anne Dunwell on May 1964, and Heather Rata on 28 June 1968, both involved them being strangled in a sexually motivated attack by someone local. And in both murders, the use of one of their stockings had been prevalent as the murderer's tool of choice.

However, if you want his guilt cast in stone.

Douglas Fair confessed to the murder on two separate occasions – on 3 September 1949 and on 30 January 1951.

As for Gladys, her body had been discovered by retired miner, Tom Lockwood at 11.15 a.m. the following day. Tom was the brother of John Lockwood – two lads that had been brought up in a house on Green's Terrace in the Broad Royd Head area of Darton in the western Dearne Valley around 130 years ago. Both would go on to work at Hickleton Main, moving into houses just ten doors apart from each other at 69 and 49 Chapel Street, Thurnscoe.

John was the grandfather of Briton Square's *fiddler on the roof*, who was none other than Eddie Lockwood. Eddie's sister, Elizabeth (Liz), had married George Whitehurst in 1975.

As for George Merricks, he survived his daughter by nearly forty years and died in 1982.

As for myself, I never knew any of the Merricks, although Gladys's nephew and niece, John and Gillian (now Hirst), the latter who is a couple of years older than me, live in Bolton-on-Dearne – one just off the Concrete Canyon and the other on the Flower Estate.

As for Gladys, she lives on in legend as the ghostly presence of the *White Lady* that supposedly roams Bolton-on-Dearne's cemetery.

8.   We Are All Made of Stars

There are two council estates in Bolton-on-Dearne, both of which are located at either side of the interchangeable Thurnscoe Road / Highgate Lane – the road which carries traffic between the junction of Carr Head Lane and the A635 Barnsley – Doncaster Road. Both estates possess two large streets – that of Ringway and that of The Crescent. As a child, I moved between them both.

In February 1968, I recall running away from the place I had temporarily been living – a property at 40 Ringway, and cutting through the middle one of its three eastern side extensions and racing across the road towards the gate into the cemetery and nearly being run over by a Sunblest bread van on its way up towards Carr Head Lane.

To this day, I remember it vividly.

I had been on my way to a property at 9 The Crescent – the home of my grandparents, Sam and Minnie Durose (nee Griffiths).

My nan's house backed onto the cemetery and took up a huge corner plot at the first of the two cul-de-sacs on the street. Totally unlike it looks now, the garden was surrounded by a high hedgerow and contained a huge oak tree (I think). There was also a high wall which ran off the house and as you walked in through the (outer) back door you entered a passage which had an inner door at its end – this time with glass in the top.

My nan always maintained that she had heard faint tapping on the inner back door, but on looking through its window, she could not see anyone there. A couple of minutes later there had been another faint tap. This made her third eldest son get up and have a look outside. And there I was – dressed in just shorts and a T-shirt and standing there freezing. I had only been three years old and I had made the journey to try and find my dad.

"It's our James," exclaimed Uncle Paul.

"I've come to see you," is exactly what my nana told me that I had said.

My nana warmed me up, put me under her coat and carried me all the way back to 40 Ringway, where she witnessed me being throttled by my mum.

"The poor little bugger," she had told her son on her return. "I wish I hadn't taken him back, now. Helen gave him a right good hiding."

My mum had a right to be worried about my whereabouts.

My dad's cousin Les Durose, had been eight years old when he toddled off on the Wednesday afternoon of 17 June 1936, never to be seen alive again. It was said that he left his home at 58 Annerley Street, Denaby to go catching minnows with two of his mates. At around 6.15 p.m. he ended up in the Sheffield and South Yorkshire Navigation Canal at a place close to the Toll Bar at Mexborough. My dad told me that numerous attempts were tried to recover the little lad, but the waterway had been heavily littered with obstructions that in the end the police had to retrieve his body with the use of grappling irons.

Can you imagine how my dad's uncle Bill and his auntie Harriet (nee Hazelhurst) felt standing at the Canalside watching them drag the canal?

It wasn't just in Denaby, as both Ringway and The Crescent and seen some of its children go missing – and some in similar tragic circumstances.

On 11 July 1938, a pair of two-year-old toddlers – a boy and girl who lived at 123 and 125 The Crescent, respectively, had wandered away from their homes. Being inquisitive, they climbed through a broken fence onto the railway embankment close to where the Sheffield – York railway line crosses over Furlong Road via (which was at one time was) a stone-built bridge. This was certainly a structure with an indifferent history, as one or two have used it as an anchor point for their ligatures, before throwing themselves off and hanging themselves.

The little girl, Florence Glasswell, was hit by a train and it was only the sight of the little lad sat on the parapet of the bridge that gave cause for concern.

It was a near-neighbour and the proprietor of the newsagent shop at 139 Furlong Road by the name of Frank Staniforth who went up onto the embankment to bring the boy down. On getting there, however, the sight he saw must have turned his stomach. He found the little girl laid unconscious with her legs severed and quickly raised the alarm, with several women immediately running to the scene – one who was Florence's distraught mother. The little girl was rushed to hospital only to die an hour later.

That little lad? Eric Latham – the uncle of Brian.

Florence's parents – Albert and Doris (nee Margrave) had married at Bolton-on-Dearne Parish Church on what was a blustery Saturday afternoon on 6 July 1935 with Cyril Parkin of 5 Windsor Street, Thurnscoe being given the duty as best man – his second time in seven months.

Cyril had been part of the Parkin-dynasty at Hickleton Main and was employed as a Checkweighman. His father, James had been an Undermanager who was awarded the Edward Medal in March 1923 for his part in the ultimately failed rescue of Arthur Bridges after a roof fall on the Tuesday afternoon of 24 October the previous year, whilst his two elder brothers, Jim and Leonard, had also held the same rank. Leonard was perhaps the more well-known as he lived at 79 Stuart Street with his wife Helena (nee Wood), and who were of course the parents of the ITN newsreader by the same name.

The back end of that dynasty had still been present at Hickleton Main when I had been there. One of the lads from the year above, Dave (Pip) Parkin had been an apprentice fitter on T01's – the unit that was being salvaged and on which my (step)dad was one of the three Officials.

Pip, who last time I knew, lived at 101 Merrill Road, married Denise Birch in July 1988 – a girl that had lived next door to my Grandma Ellis at 61 Lindley Crescent since 1968. She was one of three children to Vicky (nee Ellse) – a gregarious lady who as a child, had lived at a property at 11 Middlecliffe Lane opposite the Dearne Valley Colliery in Little Houghton.

I fondly recall being sat in their house with her younger brother and sister and watching Hanna Barbera's *Lippy the Lion Show* – with Wally Gator and Touche Turtle and Dum Dum.

Vicky remarried Michael (Mac) McKenning in 1977. He was a smart looking lad eleven years her junior, who back then had been serving in the Royal Horse Artillery, whom she had met in The Drum.

Her new in-laws at 33 Hanover Street, however, had what would very much be termed as the black sheep of the family. Billy McKenning was the twin-brother of Jack and the younger brother of Vicky's new husband. Described as a loner, Billy had been responsible for at least two rapes – one in Goldthorpe and one close to where The Plant used to be in Mexborough, as well as an attempted rape behind the electricity substation on Thurnscoe's Lidget Lane, where it was said he stalked a lady off George Street who had been on her way home.

"Nobody wanted to know him after what he did and Mac's family would never talk about him," Vicky told me.

"I cannot help feeling that parents who allow children of this age to run about on their own are running a serious risk," said Doncaster District Coroner, W.H Carlile at the inquest. "Parents have a responsibility, but perhaps they do not realise it."

It came out that Albert had been asleep, whilst Doris had been chatting with her neighbour, Catherine Latham.

Resident House Surgeon at Mexborough Montagu Hospital, Dr Rudolph Stuppel explained that Florence had been admitted to hospital around 1.00 p.m. in an unconscious state. Her skull had been crushed and brain and tissue exposed. And added to that, her left foot was missing.

Never think that any tragedy ends there because it does not.

Albert, who was a Thurnscoe lad, born at 16 Church Street, would leave The Crescent and move into another godforsaken property after the outbreak of war – this time one in Goldthorpe's north-eastern terraces at 12

Cooperative Street. This was a house that had seen the death of two sets of siblings: Jack and Kathleen Ware aged ten months and six years old in 1908; and John and Catherine Barry aged seven months and two years old in 1912.

There had also been similar stories next door at No 14 and down the road at No 29.

Henry and Mary Formstone (nee Roberts) lost two children within the space of nineteen days during the late-summer of 1913 – Doreen aged twenty-one months and George aged four months; whilst down the road at 29 Cooperative Street it was a tragic story. Rowland and Emily Sharp (nee Lee) had eight children, four of who died aged eight to sixteen months between 1915 and 1928.

Why Albert ever made that move, only he and his wife knew the answer. Not only would they have no more children, he would witness the deterioration of his wife's health and her untimely death on 16 June 1955. Doris had suffered from chronic bronchitis and emphysema and died in Montagu Hospital following a heart attack. She was forty-four years old.

Rather strangely, he quickly he got involved with woman a year older by the name of Evelyn Crossley off 3 St Mary's Road who he married on 19 May 1956 – just eleven months after his wife's death. What I can say is that Evelyn certainly wasn't the woman she claimed to be. Maybe this was something that eventually saw him committed to Sheffield's Middlewood Hospital, where he died in May 1967, aged fifty-eight.

Not all missing children suffered the fate of little Florence, however.

On the Tuesday afternoon of 8 February 1949, the police along with a huge proportion of residents off Bolton-on-Dearne's newly constructed circular cross-sectional council estate were out in force searching for a little girl, just twenty-three months old by the name of Vivien Boreham. She had gone missing from her home at 71 Ringway.

Back then, Ringway was an extremely dangerous place, especially as the rear garden of the Boreham's house backed on to the Wath Branch Line, which even though it had been closed to regular rail traffic well before the Second World War, it was still used on and off and was therefore quite an unsafe place for children to play. There was also the Suicide Bridge on Carr Head Lane, which was a structure that was still having people throwing themselves off. And just off the estate, the Hull-based contractor Spooner Construction, were in the process of building the prefabricated houses that would complete the construction of Carrfield Lane, Crofton Drive and Hall Broome Gardens.

Eight policemen had continued their search all through the night and at 9.30 a.m. the following day, and to the relief of her twenty-four-year-old mother Christine (nee Fryer), the little girl was found safe and well. She had fallen asleep in the outhouse of a near neighbour.

Just under three and a half years later a three-year-old lad off Furlong Road by the name of Kenneth McFadden decided to do a bit of exploring and left his friends playing close to the Brick Ponds on the Sunday afternoon of 8 June 1952 and went for a walk. Rather strangely, the infamous bridge at Carr Head Lane was his destination and that is exactly where a milk girl doing her rounds on the following morning found him. Not, so much on the bridge, but laid fast asleep, close to it and clutching his toy engine in one hand and a bunch of flowers that he had picked for his mum in the other.

Over fifty people had been involved in the search with the police having to drag the three brickyard ponds and comb the nearby fields and hedge bottoms.

The sighs of relief had been in sharp contrast to events at 31 The Crescent just a week or so earlier before little Miss Boreham had gone missing, whereby a twenty-eight-year-old mother attempted to murder her two-year-old child before trying to take her own life.

In early 1975, I had been in the Third Year (Year 5) of Carfield Primary School – under the tutorage of a Czechoslovakian-born teacher by the name of Mr (Kurt) Kneissl, when a lad who had come down from Highgate Junior School had been introduced to us and dumped in the seat next to me.

He was an amiable lad, by the name of Paul Ludlam.

I cannot recall the reasoning of his moving schools, other than the fact that he had lived on Bolton-on-Dearne's Caernarvon Crescent, and just a few doors down from my uncle Paul and auntie Anne.

What I did not know at that time, however – was that his father, Tony, had not only known my dad, he had also grown up next door to my great grandfather at 15 Wellington Street, Goldthorpe. Paul's grandparents were Harold and Winifreda Ludlam (nee Howe).

Now, before I go on to explain any further, I need to give you some background.

There were two colourful families who were quite well-known in pre-war Goldthorpe and who were tied into similar families – one of which were the Stanton's who eventually set up shop in Mexborough and who I will fill you in on later.

Albert Smalley and both Jim and Pat Noon were avid bookmakers. They not only indulged in a lucrative track-side business, but also had stakes in unlicensed premises in the village's north-eastern terraces not at least 18 Nora Street, 41 St Mary's Road and both 20 and 27 Main Street. That being the case, they were always in front of the bench at Doncaster West Riding Court.

In fact, Jim Noon's wife, Rhoda (nee Roe) – who often helped as a clerk of sorts, lived until the ripe old age of 101 and passed away in Hickleton's Sue Ryder Home in 2002. I suppose there is a lot to be said of leading an exciting life!

The Noon's nor Smalley's businesses were not, however, quite as lucrative as the one which rival Goldthorpe bookmaker, Joseph (Jim) Morris ran out of 23 Orchard Street – a man who even ran his own professionally printed Football Pools. If you want a bit more background, Jim was subject of a coroner's inquiry in Barnsley on 17 January 1938 after he had both run over and killed some tramp on the A635 between Highgate and Billingley.

Neither were the Noons and Smalleys anywhere near as successful as the street-smart Arthur Beevers (Snr). He and his wife Rose (nee Kemp) had used the boarded-up shop front of their home at 33 Kelly Street to run their business. It was something that saw them invest heavily on the purchases of the said property along with No's 35 and 37 – the latter of which was occupied by a son by the same name. Arthur (Jnr) who was a miner at Hickleton Main, had married single mum, Ethel Hotchins in 1928. She was the mother of a two-year-old lad by the name of Manley Hotchins.

As street-smart as the Beevers family were, there is rarely anything more stupid than a love-sick woman.

On 25 November 1934, Arthur Beevers (Snr) died, aged 65, whilst over in Wath-on-Dearne on 8 February 1937, a forty-eight-year-old lady by the name of Annie Matilda Robinson also succumbed to life.

There was a link and one which saw Annie's husband, Cecil Robinson, publicly issue the threat of legal action on 14 August 1941, stating that proceedings would be taken against any person or persons uttering slanderous statements against his name.

Why, one could ask?

Cecil's wife had been in failing health for some considerable time and it had been implied that he had been seeing another woman. Whether or not this had been while his wife had still been alive, I could not say. The fact was, however, that the suave and sophisticated former insurance agent – a man who had also been secretary of the Sandygate Club, had commenced a relationship with Rose Beevers. It wasn't what you could call a flash in the pan either. On 5 May 1942 he married her, only for his bride to drop dead seventeen days later and leave the fruits of her and her dead husband's graft and guile in his capable hands. This included the house which Arthur (Jnr) and his family lived in.

Her sons must have been livid – especially when Robinson put the three properties up for sale at an auction run by Barnsley-based Messrs C.E. Smith & Son at the Horse & Groom on Monday 14 September 1942. It was something which would see them have to pay £815 (£41,415, circa 2020) to get the properties back in the family. Therefore, not only did they have to chump up for what was rightfully theirs, it is my thoughts that they also paid well over the odds as £600 – was given as a ball-park figure. Robinson appeared a very clever man and it could have been that the auction had been very much rigged.

These bookies had been part of a time where both their back street and under-the-counter activities along with the insouciant way they handled the police and took their huge fines, made them quite popular. In a nutshell, these were people that just didn't give a fuck – therefore, it does make you wonder if Robinson did indeed have any comeback.

What do you reckon?

The Beevers' family occupied two of those houses for many years to come with Manley Hotchins and his wife Mavis Carline – who during the 1970s, I would live across from on the Flower Estate, occupying the house right at the end of the street.

As for the Noon-Smalley connection. This, you would think, could have been further solidified when on 2 November 1946 at Surrey & South Western (Hindhead & Churt) Register Office, Eric Noon married Kathleen Smalley. However, relationships do not always work. Well, this one didn't anyway.

Eric's father, William Henry (Bill) Noon, had initially come to the area with his brother-in-law, John Woolley in 1923. The two of them got a start at Hickleton Main and set up home at that infamous property at 23 Orchard Street. However, around the time of the death of twenty-eight-year-old William McCanaan of 4 Edward Street, Thurnscoe on 3 October 1925 – who was yet another who got caught by a roof fall at the pit, the management had begun discharging a number of men. These were mainly those over a certain age, along with the last-in-last-out – one of whom who was Bill.

For the record, William's elder brother, John McCanaan, also died at Hickleton Main on 6 December 1927.

Bill Noon wasn't one of those who stuck fast. He got a job at Markham Main and had the family relocate to Armthorpe for a couple of years. However, the General Strike followed by the lockout of the miners during the year after hit all these mining communities hard, and on 12 May 1926, Bill had been part of a 300-strong mob, some of who had been armed, who had been stopping the transportation of fish and potatoes between Grimsby and Doncaster on the A18 at Edenthorpe. It was something which saw him convicted under the Emergency Powers Act and sentenced to three months hard labour.

Bill came back to Goldthorpe after a couple of years and he and his family set up home at 27 Victoria Street – however, 1936 was a god-awful year for him as his family was decimated. His three-year old daughter Irene died in late-January, which was followed by his wife – Emma Elizabeth (nee Woolley) on 7 June 1936, aged forty-one.

At just sixteen years old Eric Noon had lost his mum and sister – therefore, his father would have to look after him and his younger brother and sister. And to compound things further, there was a war on the horizon. It would be something that saw Eric leave his job on the haulage at Hickleton Main, join up and get deployed overseas in the far east fighting the Japanese.

There were hundreds of brave lads from the area that had done the same – some of whom became prisoners of war and some who would never come back.

Eric did, however. On 17 March 1944, he was placed in the National Service Reserve "W" list, due to the fact that the United Kingdom was facing severe manpower shortages, and he had a special skill set – that of a miner. There could have also been other mitigating circumstances to his service ending prematurely, say humanitarian or medical – however, I could not say.

At the beginning of the war Kathleen Smalley had been stationed in the Alexandra Orphanage, which was in the Maitland Park area of London's Haverstock Hill – where at nineteen years old she had been employed as some form of domestic. From there she moved to 1 Wolseley Road in Aldershot. How she had got there, again, I really do not know – however, what I do know, is that she would eventually go back.

Did Eric meet her down there or up in Goldthorpe? It is another question that I don't really know the answer to. What I do know is that she was an unmarried mother with a son to a Canadian soldier by the name of Malvin McMellan who had been born on Parkhurst Road in North London on 11 August 1945.

I also know she had been employed as a cook/domestic in the Twizzlewigg War Nursery on Tilford Road in Hindhead, Surrey along with the fact that she was pregnant when Eric married her.

With military personnel being repatriated and the whole country in the process of change – not least with rebuilding its infrastructure, there were huge shortages – not at least for housing, hence why around fifty families, including my grandparents, had been billeted in Nissen Huts down at the bottom of Bolton-on-Dearne's Lowfield Road.

That being the case, Goldthorpe's dimly lit north eastern terraces awaited them.

On 28 June 1947, the recently married Kathleen Noon gave birth to a baby daughter in Mexborough Montagu who she named Audrey. Unfortunately, however, Kathleen would suffer post-natal depression, something which saw them move from his father Bill's house and up the street lodging with his elder brother, Edwin and his wife Elsie (nee Berry) at No 19.

There was obviously a lot more to this.

It could be said that Kathleen was, indeed, high maintenance, but what I don't know is if her depression had been accelerated by her husband's behaviour. Whatever it was, it was something that saw them move out from his brother's then into another terrace – this time, just off Cross Street at 13 Claycliffe Terrace with George and Jane Kerry (nee Longbottom). Yet another house that has the ignominy of a child death – this being a two-day-old lad by the name of John Carroll in 1917.

This was always going to be a lousy marriage and in next to no time, there was another move. This time to Bolton-on-Dearne, with the family residing in lodgings at 31 The Crescent along with Eric's cousin, Tony – who was the son of the bookie, Pat Noon.

Christmas 1948 was when everything came to a head. With just Kathleen and her three-year-old son alone in the house, her intentions had been extremely clear. She set about murdering her child and killing herself. How far she got, how she was stopped or indeed how she intended to do it, remains a mystery. I could easily hazard a guess – gas poisoning most likely, but facts are what count. Kathleen was remanded (twice) until 18 January 1949, pending a psychiatric evaluation.

With none of their family prepared to put them up, Eric went to look at a huge boarded-up and neglected property. It was here where they would stay for a total of thirteen months – as squatters in Thurnscoe's Old Rectory.

With a condemnation order on the property as Jack and Jim Settle of 39 Butcher Street had bought the three-acre plot, no running water, electricity nor indeed heating, two children with whooping cough and a wife with mental health problems and ready for a stint in Middlewood Hospital, an eviction order was served.

The start of the demolition of the Old Rectory commenced on Tuesday 11 April 1950. It was then Eric's family were moved into temporary accommodation at 212 Furlong Road along with John and Mabel Jenkins – a couple who had been married since late-1944 and who, along with their two children, Ken and Patricia, had been one of the other families that had been squatting with them.

It is here, where things become a little clearer as Kathleen packed her bags and along with her son, left for London, eventually residing at 76 Palace Gardens in Notting Hill.

Mabel Jenkins, however, is key to the rest of the story.

She was the younger sister of a man by the name of Harold Ludlam and therefore the sister-in-law of Winifred, who were of course, Paul Ludlam's grandparents. And when Kathleen left, Eric and his daughter, Audrey, who he had custody of, moved in with them at 15 Wellington Street.

And why not – Audrey had three ready-made playmates including their daughter Janet, who was the same age.

On 6 April 1951 Kathleen Noon would give birth to a child by the name of Alan in the Royal Northern Hospital on Islington's Holloway Road – just a hundred or so yards from where she had had her first child, whilst in 1952 Winifred Ludlam would have a son by the name of Brian.

It would come to pass that both these children had the same father.

Eric Noon had abused his friend's hospitality and trust. He had been having an affair with Harold Ludlam's wife. A broken Harold sued for divorce citing his wife's adultery. It was, however, something that he would not get until July 1956 – with Eric rightly having to pay costs.

In 1954, the NCB had just completed the construction of a second new model village and one which spanned either side of Thurnscoe Bridge Lane. Eric moved into one of these brand-new houses with his new family – just ten doors down from my Grandma Ellis at 43 Lindley Crescent. It would be here on 21 February 1955, that Winifred Ludlam would have another child to Eric. Unfortunately, this one had been born dead.

Eric would finally marry Winifred in early 1960, whilst on 30 March 1968 at St Helen's Church in Thurnscoe, their daughter Audrey would marry a twenty-two-year-old miner off Bolton-on-Dearne's Concrete Canyon. Maurice Bainbridge's family had come down from the north-east and settled at 24 South Drive.

Her stepbrother, David Ludlam and his new wife Kay (nee Wilkinson) were best man and maid of honour – however, Audrey's mum, Kathleen, would not there to see it.

On 9 June 1965, she had passed away in St Charles Hospital, Kensington. She had died of Uraemia and Peritonitis – a condition which had brought on internal bleeding – both in her urine and her brain.

The three-year-old boy that she had tried murdering in a house in Bolton-on-Dearne during the Christmas period of 1948, had been at her bedside to see his mum go. However, what she had done, was to take a deep dark secret with her. She had lied to her son. Not just about her trying to murder him and her failed suicide, either. She had told Malvin that his stepfather and the father of his sister and brother, Eric Noon – was dead.

Eric died some twenty-six and a half years later on 20 December 1991, aged seventy-one.

As for the address at 40 Ringway. This was a property that I recall most vividly as it was the house of my mum's mother – my grandma – Helen Carman (nee Gilmer).

As a young child a series of lilac trees adorned its steep frontage, whilst wide-paned glass windows followed suit with every house on the street, sadly however, and solely due to progress, neither of these are evident anymore. As the front door was rarely ever used, access was via a door down the side of the house, which as soon as it was opened, you were greeted by a wind charm and a smell that has never left me. All houses carry their own form of aroma and my grandma's was no different. On entering the kitchen, immediately to the right was a door, with a step down into a pantry that rarely had anything in it apart from condiments, whilst a door next to it carried a long passageway to both the front door and the foot of the stairs. Straight in front was a series of drawers and cupboards and on opening the tallest cupboard you would be greeted by the date of every one of her grandchildren's birthdays. To the left was a gas cooker, washing machine, fridge and sink, where one year there would be a semi-catastrophe as a goldfish went down the plug hole and a panic ensued with my mum racing outside to try and retrieve it before it ended up going down the grate.

The adjoining dining room always seemed full of ticking clocks along with a glass fronted cabinet that housed a mix match of glasses. It would be here as a child that I would recall watching my mum's younger brother playing Ken Howard and Alan Blaikley's rather hauntingly penned *Zabadak* on the record player, and where I along with my grandma, would eat our Christmas dinner of 1980 together.

I spent part of 1967 and 1968 living in that house and sharing a bedroom with both uncles – Rob and Steve. I also remember waiting for the return of them both from Mexborough Technical College on their bicycles, whilst standing on the wall with my elder cousin by two years – the stepson of my mum's sister, my auntie Heather (Greaves).

Our Steve, ever-brash and both chippy and competitive was always the first around the western leg of Crossway and the one who my cousin, Tony would always root for, with our Rob – the more laid-back and therefore the one left trailing behind.

The lounge was the place, where, when as I was growing up as a teenager, I spent many Thursday evenings, drinking cups of tea and eating some form of fruit cake, as that is what my grandma made sure she had in when she knew I was coming to see her.

My grandma Carman was a completely different type of woman to my (step)dad's mum. My grandma Ellis went without to make sure that we were spoiled rotten, and never once did I hear a cross word pass her lips. My grandma Carman on the other hand, could appear to others as being aggressively frugal and very straight talking in that she took few prisoners.

My nana Durose told me in later life: "She was a very hard woman, James."

Maybe so, but not to me.

I suppose I was lucky in that I saw each and every side of the complex lady that she was, whilst growing up, and the one thing that I will always say, is that she never let me lose my identity and the fact of who I was. This for me as a young lad – was a very big thing.

Now here you will get a picture of where this is going.

One of my earliest recollections of 40 Ringway had been around 1967 and it hadn't been pleasant. This had absolutely nothing to do with any of the people who lived there and everything to do with my dad.

The Durose's were a big male-dominated family. There were five sons and one daughter, with my dad being the eldest. He was someone that I always saw as just a lovely man. I wasn't imagining that, because that is exactly what he was. To me, that is.

My parents had been fighting and I, at just three years old, had been screaming as witnessing it had been nothing short of brutal.

In later life my mum told me, that was it not for my screams, she would have lost consciousness and my dad would have probably strangled her. These screams however, had been heard by a near neighbour.

Norman Dunn was the adopted son of Christopher and Mary (nee Walton) who like many, had come down from the north-east to work in the mines and had settled at 45 Lancaster Street. On the breakout of the Second World War, Norman had like many men from the district, left the pit to enlist and married his girlfriend, Daisy Liversidge – a girl from 82 Deightonby Street, the following year.

The battle-hardened Norman who lived at No 44 – the house on the corner of the western-leg of Crossway, had heard the screams and burst into the house, dragged my dad off my mum, pinned him up against the hearth and punched him in the face. My dad always maintained that that didn't happen, but it did. He had a mark on the bridge of his nose for quite a while after that.

It wasn't the first time that I had seen that as a child. On my mum finally leaving my dad, I remember being sat in the pushchair at the foot of the stairs of the prefabricated pit house that we had all shared together at 11 Maori Avenue. I had watched on in terror as my dad beat the living daylights out of her. It was the day we parted as a family. My mum always maintained that she had left my dad due to his physical abuse hence, that was the reason why I had been living on Ringway.

I certainly think there is much more to the story, with **control** being a big part of its mechanics as for the early part of my life, my mum used me as nothing more than a pawn in her continual quest of keeping me away from my dad's family.

I am not quite sure of the timeline of events, but I recall a time that my mum had written him a letter, which was handed to him at the door. His next journey had been to go straight up to Goldthorpe Police Station, which was the first – but certainly not the last time, that I ever saw its white-tiled interior.

Although my dad was granted custody of me on a Saturday or Sunday, my mum made things extremely hard and made him work for it, as like most miners, he worked three-shift pattern – his being in the rips over at Barnburgh Main.

There was one time in particular that things became extremely heated and this was after my uncle Rob – who would have been around eighteen years old at that time, had told my dad on his arrival at the back door of 40 Ringway, that he couldn't see me. The reasoning behind this was unclear.

During my early teenage years my dad recalled the story quite a few times, and that was of a bus journey he'd had immediately after and where he had both seen and confronted his ex-brother-in-law about what had happened. As it was, our Rob had had his mate with him, who ended up taking a good hiding.

"I didn't know what was going on," my dad had told me.

My dad had his idiosyncrasies and jealousy and insecurity were both a major factor into who he was back then. He must have obviously thought my mum was knocking our Rob's mate off.

Was she? That is a question I couldn't answer.

Those days throughout mid-1967 into early 1968, meant spending Saturdays between our old house on Maori Avenue and my nana Durose's on The Crescent.

The house at Maori Avenue was of a similar design to all the prefabricated pit houses that were constructed in the 1950s and wasn't too dissimilar to that of my grandma Ellis's on Thurnscoe's Lindley Crescent. That is, however, where the similarities ended. With my mum gone, the house always appeared cold an unlived in.

You went through the back door – which was at the side and were met by a sky-blue kitchen cabinet with a pulldown cupboard, which doubled as something of a kitchen top. These were all the rage with the working class at the time and very 1960s. The window in the kitchen, always seemed to be full of dead flies and the front room was full of my mum and dad's furniture that appeared ready to be shipped-out at any given moment. It was also the coldest room in the house.

My nana Durose was a well-rounded woman and a total contrast to both my other grandmas. The main difference was that she was **always** overly-affectionate and possessed a broad-Yorkshire dialect – and as such, she spoke in bible-talk, her sentences often being littered with *thee* and *tha's*.

"Tha' were kept away from us, love," is what she said to me in later life – time and time again.

I knew that. I always knew that.

There was a story that concerned events of 24 April 1942, that if things would have been different – then I wouldn't be here.

My nana had been pregnant with her first child – that being my dad and had an appointment at the doctors. As such, my granddad, who, due to the country being at war and being in a reserved occupation, couldn't have a day off, had managed changed shifts. What would happen around 6.00 p.m. was something quite unprecedented in mining. The people of Bolton-on-Dearne, Goldthorpe and Thurnscoe were alerted to something that made them stop what they were doing. Doors and windows on the council estates were opened and shoppers were stopped in their tracks, whilst over on the pit estate in Thurnscoe East, chimney pots were shaken from their houses. The huge bellowing noise of the earth cracking had got everyone's attention. Part of the underground workings at Barnburgh Main had experienced a huge ground movement, whereby an aggressive floor-blow saw the inverts raise and crash into the ceiling thereby cutting off both air supply and egress to an area of around two acres.

"The floor just seemed to come up and hit the roof," explained Matthew Fairhurst of 14 Whitworth Buildings, Thurnscoe. "There were around four of us who had to crawl over one hundred yards along the main plane which was only six inches high in places."

A total of twenty-one men had been caught in the collapse including four who died – two being local lads: Fred Southwell of 147 Ingsfield Lane, Bolton-on-Dearne and Alf Lackenby of 9 Princess Road, Goldthorpe.

It had also been in the Parkgate seam, where my granddad should have been working. It wasn't the first tragedy at the pit, and it wouldn't be the last. On 26 June 1957, there was an explosion at the mine whereby six men were killed.

Never ever think that the miner of yester-year doesn't deserve respect.

My dad once told me that my mum and I were once on the old 29 bus. Its route was Thurnscoe East to Wath-on-Dearne, using Hickleton Main as its Terminus and backing up Tudor Street to spin around for its return journey. During late-1967, I recall my dad alighting the bus at the bottom of Canberra Rise, and although I kept on turning around to see him, my mum kept on making me face the front.

Was that true?

I am afraid it was and that is how I was made to think throughout my early life. I couldn't even mention the Durose's in her company. This was totally different her younger sister by two years – my auntie Heather and indeed my grandma Carman, who, during those Thursday evenings I spent with her, used to relay me tale after tale about my mum and dad. And the thing was, is that she never ever showed any negativity, whatsoever. This was one of the main reasons that I loved her so much.

"I remember them having a right go at each other in the bedroom and me trying to break it up," my grandma chuckled. "I had no shoes on and your dad was wearing some of those brogue-type shoes and I ended up with cuts and bruises all over my feet."

My grandma's non-negative appraisal?

"You can always tell a man by the shoes he wears and how clean they are," she said. "And your dad – he always wore lovely shoes."

Although at the time of my mum and dad's separation, my grandma and my dad hated each other's guts, and of that there was no doubt – my dad did have a huge respect for her and rarely failed to ask of her wellbeing.

My grandma had been brought up in the tenements of the inner-city slums of Glasgow and had lived between Scotstoun and Partick, before coming down to live in the eastern Dearne Valley.

My dad often told me the story of this lady with a strong Glaswegian accent living in one of the aforementioned army huts on Lowfield Road just after the Second World War and going door-to-door selling pegs. She had been pregnant with my Uncle Rob at the time.

Strangely, the only time I ever recall her having a Scottish accent, was after she had had a drink, as in the main, she spoke the Queen's English.

My dad would be diagnosed with stomach and liver cancer at the end of the Miners' Strike and would only survive the disease until 12 December 1985. One of the last conversations I had with him before he died, was of my grandma Carman calling him and of them having an hour-long conversation and one where he apologised to her for how he had been. In my mind, I thought that a wonderful thing to do.

She was without doubt a multi-dimensional lady who like my mum and dad possessed her fair share of demons – however, one thing that always stands out was something that happened one night during early 1974.

As I have mentioned, we had moved to 102 Primrose Close on the newly constructed Flower Estate in September 1972 and all that separated our house from my grandma's was a short walk over the levelled-out old Wath Branch Line and a short cut through Harry Dawson's back yard at No 47 – and with her house devoid of her recently married sons, my grandma was often over at ours.

Uncle Rob had married an extremely pretty and petite young girl by the name of Joy Severn in 1971 and by saying that I am not understating it, as she was like a model and so very *Patti Boyd*. As a couple they appeared very upwardly mobile and did something that none of our family had done. They had bought their own house on Swinton's newly constructed Lime Grove estate, which just a few years early was termed as Birdwell Flats, had been levelled as part of the local authority's slum clearance, whereby the waterworks, pumping station, railway goods shed and several terraces – including part of Charles, Crossland and Carlisle Street had been flattened, and the ground remediated and reprofiled to make way for its construction.

Our Rob always appeared the more articulate of the two brothers and always came over as being very caring and considerate. That is not to say our Steve wasn't any of those things, however.

Looking back at it, Rob and Joy appeared to have a life plan and it would be in 1974, that I saw it flourish, whilst sitting on the settee part-watching *Are You Being Served* on TV.

"Mam, Joy's pregnant," he told my grandma.

I have seen hundreds of emotional scenes throughout my life, but this one still sticks with me. Why? Possibly because it was the only time I had ever seen my grandma absolutely overcome with emotion. She cried her eyes out. I still remember it vividly and afterwards of our Rob driving me up to St Andrews Square and to the top fish and chip shop, as unlike Baker's fish shop – much the better one at the bottom of the Square, it sold haggis – and that is what my grandma often had.

Although our Rob often visited and was nothing short of a brilliant bloke, it was my uncle Steve that I was perhaps the closest to. He was just thirteen and half years my senior, gregarious in nature, possessed the look of a rock star with his long hair, and rode a Triumph Tiger 90 motorbike. And not unlike his elder brother, had married a petite, pretty, sparkly-eyed girl who was the daughter of a displaced Welsh miner and his wife – Elwyn and Brenda Jones (nee Davies).

Whereas our Rob's wife, Joy, appeared the more reserved, Ann was witty and fun, and she and our Steve bounced off each other like you wouldn't believe. An exaggerated "Oo-heck" is what she often winked, when she made out that things weren't going as planned. Not that they ever were, however.

Manchester - July 1995. Left to Right. Ann Carman (nee Jones), James Durose-Rayner, Julie Durose (nee Mason) and Steve Carman.

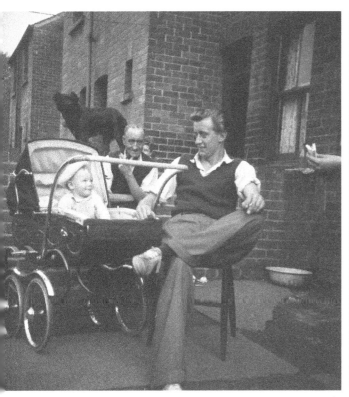

Top Left. Outside 1 Landsdowne Avenue, Thurnscoe - part of the Hudson family (John and son, Arnold) circa 1961. Top Right. Eva McKenning (nee Francis) standing at the back gate of 93 Lidget Lane (Betts Buildings), Thurnscoe, with Saxon Street in the background circa 1965. Bottom Left. Outside 16 Landsdowne Avenue, Thurnscoe circa 1940 - John Pressland with his daughter Janet (now Dodsworth). Bottom Right. Bridget Weddell (now Ryan) standing with her mum, Hilda (nee Hinchcliffe) outside 53 Ringway, Bolton-on-Dearne circa 1961

9.   Pretty Polly

My young uncle and his new wife moved to 17 Broadwater, close to where the old Wath Branch Line once crossed the Green Bridge down at the far end of Bolton-on-Dearne's sprawling Concrete Canyon. The street itself is aptly named as its length follows the exact direction of the River Dearne on its way down past what was once the site of the old paper mill and towards the Ten Arched viaduct that carries the Sheffield – York railway over the river.

The area hasn't really changed since the time I first went down there near-on fifty years ago and still appears as run-down now as it did back then. Not that this ever bothered our Steve and Ann, as you always had the feeling, that so long as they were together, nothing else mattered.

Bolton-on-Dearne's 692-unit prefabricated new model village had been constructed at a similar time to Thurnscoe's and had been built either side of the odd-numbered, red-bricked houses on Ingsfield Lane that had been up since the turn of the century.

"Steam trains from Manvers and Wath Main used to run at the top of Ings Lane football field and you could still see part of an old railway platform," said Colin Meakin.

Colin had been an Official on T01s unit at Hickleton Main, just before I started and by the time, I had been deployed underground in 1982, he had been bossing one of the three shifts on T02s. His mum and dad were the first ever family to move into 102 Ingsfield Lane during 1952.

The football field itself had been heavily backfilled, as at one time, the Lane backed on to a deep quarry and the Wath Main Brick Works – the exact works that supplied the red bricks for the construction of those first eighty houses.

"Neither the road nor back gardens had been finished, and when it rained, delivery vehicles such as the Mother's Pride van had to be shoved out of mud," he added.

As with Thurnscoe, the pit estate was fully completed in April 1955 and was part of an investment by the NCB that saw 20,000 homes constructed – the flagship project at Bolton-on-Dearne being the largest of its ninety-three sites.

In its short time there has been quite a few strange things occur – from the police coming down on the street in numbers during October 1958 and looking for three arsonists that had torched part of Bluff's Farm on Wath Road – to a Peeping Tom in 1955, who was thought to have been twenty-eight-year-old Roland Bateman of 24 Hawthorne Road, Wath-on-Dearne, who had been chased off Ingsfield Lane by several women wielding carving knives – to the much-publicised manslaughter of a sixty-two-year-old lady by the name of Fanny Stone on 2 August 1975. The latter of whom who was a lady that had eventually died of toxaemia – something which had been brought on by her starvation.

Fanny Stone was originally from the Mexborough and Denaby Main area living on both Dolcliffe Road and Annerley Street before moving in with her sixty-six-year-old brother, who although a widower – had been in a common-law relationship with a fifty-four-year-old woman by the name of Gwendoline Dobinson (nee Priest).

Her brother, John Edward Stone, had been an ex-surface worker at one of the pits and possessed several convictions, one of which had resulted in him being sent to prison in October 1959. There had also been one as far back as 1923 when he had been a boy, and which had been subject to a Home Office inquiry after Don Valley MP, Tom Williams had argued against the extremity of a sentence meted-out at Doncaster West Riding Court by E.W. Pettifer, who had sent him to Borstal.

John also had a thirty-four-year-old son by the name of Sam who was mentally impaired.

Fanny Stone would join them in 1972.

It was a neighbour who first rang the alarm bells after noticing a strong lurid smell that had been coming from under the floorboards over a period of a few days. After a bit of head scratching, she put it down to the fact that the smell was coming from the property next door. She wasn't wrong. On Gwendoline opening the door, the smell she was met by, had been far worse. It stunk of rotting flesh. Upstairs in the back bedroom of 75 Broadwater, Fanny Stone had been laid corpse-like in her bed for days.

When the police were alerted, they found her in a hideous condition – covered in sores and laid in her own filth. Her corpse weighed just 5 stone 5 lb.

The couple were charged with gross negligence manslaughter with their trial at Sheffield Crown Court being presided over by Sir Leslie Kenneth Edward Boreham QC – the judge who would later oversee the trials of Peter Sutcliffe in 1981 and the Brighton bomber, Patrick Magee in 1986.

"This is as bad a case of neglect as I have ever come across," he told them.

It was said by John Stone's defence counsel that his client was of low intelligence, partially deaf, almost blind and had no appreciable sense of smell.

As for his dead sister, she had been described as a stubborn woman – with one of her foibles being that she was morbidly anxious not to put on weight, which was certainly not unlike my mum in later life.

That being the case she was left to her own devices. At first, when the couple went for a night out to either the Ings Lane WMC or The Collingwood, she would creep downstairs and make a meal but after a while she began denying herself food.

It was said that John initially made half-hearted, and then no efforts to do anything about his sister's deteriorating condition, whereby she became extremely ill.

"You have been found guilty on clear evidence of gross neglect which caused her death in dreadful circumstances," said the judge.

John received three years – which was later reduced on appeal, whilst Gwendoline got an eighteen-month sentence that was suspended for two years.

As for the Peeping Tom, he was never caught, although on 21 July 1958, Roland Bateman was in Rotherham West Riding Court and found guilty of conduct liable to cause a breach of the peace – staring through peoples windows, and was fined £10 (£243, circa 2020) and bound over for a year.

A stranger story on the street occurred straight after a weekend where Henry Cooper had been stopped by Cassius Clay in the sixth-round of a World Heavyweight Championship fight in front of 46,000 at Arsenal's football stadium and the day after the 1966 Formula One season opened with the Monaco Grand Prix – a race which had won by Jackie Stewart.

In between those events, however – there had been a national media frenzy over in nearby Worsborough Common after three people had sustained gunshot wounds at a property at 13 Mount Vernon Avenue – one of who was a widower by the name of John Ellis.

This followed the two and two's wrongly being put together by journalists who seven years earlier had reported on a story in Wombwell where a man by the same name had strangled his wife with a white suspender belt.

The area around Wombwell Railway Station in 1959 looked absolutely nothing like it does now. Back then, the area that was sandwiched between the western part of both Summer and Hough Lane was a thriving community with a colliery with its three smoking chimney stacks overlooking Wombwell Main Row – a street of almost a hundred houses that comprised three rows of terraced properties which was in essence, broken north-to-south by wasteland. One bank at the northern end at two at the southern, the latter of which exited onto Hough Lane opposite the Foundry with Wombwell Main WMC and a garage more or less opposite – and the recently widened bridge over the Leeds – Sheffield railway line to their right which served both Wombwell West station and the sidings into the pit.

During the early summer of that year a woman had regularly been spotted on Hough Lane being picked up by a man in a Zephyr Zodiac. You couldn't really miss it, with its two-tone coachwork, white wall tyres and twin-spotlights. It stood out as much as the age difference between the two as they danced to Bert Gee & Boys at Mexborough's Empress Ballroom on a Monday night.

It had been the start of a torrid affair borne out of need – and an affair that everyone got to know about.

Grace Ellis was a flighty albeit pretty twenty-four-year-old trapped in a marriage that she did not want. Her home on Wombwell Main Row was hardly squalor but boasted little. In a nutshell, they had nothing.

As she opened the door and clambered into the car, the first thing she had noticed was its clean and plush leather trim interior. It was, however, what everyone else noticed that soon became the problem.

In tight mining communities you cannot have secrets and Wombwell was no different.

Thirty-seven-year-old Jack Caunt was an opportunist who had lived on the street that ran parallel to the row of terraces on the opposite side of the waste ground at 82 Windmill Road, along with his wife Mildred (nee Hallworth) and their three children – Yvonne, seventeen, James, eleven, and little Jack, aged nine.

One of his best friends had been Derek Lawcock – who along with his wife Muriel (nee Newsome) had lived next door to Grace. It was a convenient coincidence and one that he initially used to get close.

Caunt used the car to advertise both his prominence in the community and of course, his wealth. The superficial materialism of a car even now can be a head-turner. Back then – and at a time when few men owned them – especially miners, it was the ultimate magnet in attracting the opposite sex. Quite fucking-mind-blowingly so, in fact.

He made his move on the Saturday evening of 9 May 1959.

Close your eyes and try to imagine the scene in *kitchen sink* black and white.

The noise and smoke emanating from a hundred or so people crammed into Wombwell Main WMC, with glasses clinking and the noise of conversation providing the backdrop to a *turn* on the stage who were belting out a poor man's version of The Four Preps' *Big Man*, with most of the females in the club clapping along. You know the one: *I was a big man yesterday but boy you oughta see me now.*

After the song, two giggling women, neatly tucked their handbags under their arms and temporarily left their table to squeeze through the crowded room and make their way to the Ladies'.

There are people all around. Women sat sipping at their Babychams and Port and lemons merrily chatting away about subjects as rangy as the price of Martlett Pears to the part-exchange, no deposit and easy weekly terms on furniture being offered by Cussins down on Wombwell's High Street, whilst the men – pint pots in hand, maybe a cigarette in the other, were in conversation about the Monday night meeting over at Wombwell's Reform Club – where the NCB's Area General Manager, J.E Longden and the NUM Yorkshire Area Secretary Fred Collindridge had been part of a contingent belly aching about the drop in demand for coal.

At the time, the NCB had pencilled thirty-six collieries for closure and had promised the NUM that it would be reducing its opencast operation – the most profitable arm of the company, by three million tons per year due both the drop in demand and existing stocks of coal at the pit heads.

On one hand it shows the sheer stupidity and non-business acumen of a nationalised industry – closing its most profitable, and on the other how quickly things turnaround.

On 13 October 1954, the NCB's Doncaster Area Production Manager, J Dearden had told the *Yorkshire Post* that they had sunk a 240-yard-deep borehole in anticipation of constructing a new mine in Scawsby – close to the Sun Inn's junction with the A635 and Great North Road. This was supposedly to access the Shafton Seam – however, the quality had not been there. They were therefore looking to sink another borehole close to Old Brodsworth, where they were hoping to build a drift mine to access what was a five-foot coal seam – similar to that of Goldthorpe, and had received no objections from Adwick-Le-Street UDC regarding its proposals.

"There's a few of us on about going to Doncaster Races next Saturday. The train leaves from the Central station at half-twelve. You fancy it, Jack?" asked a man in his early thirties in between sipping at his pint.

Jack's attention, however – had been elsewhere.

He stood up, wiped the froth from his mouth and straightened up his tie. "Two minutes," he said, prior to him leaving the table and pushing through the crowd at the bar to make his way towards the toilets.

"Oh – heyupp!" a girl, drunkenly chuckled on copping sight of him as she came out of the toilets.

It was Grace and her friend.

"You look well," he said, doing his best at trying a bit of flattery. "New dress?"

"It's called The Charmer," she grinned. "From Jax's at Rotherham."

"It looks nice."

"It should do – nearly two quid it cost," she lied.

"Do you fancy nipping outside for five minutes?" he asked.

"Why?" she shrugged.

He responded by looking at Grace's friend in a round-about way to get her to leave him alone with her.

"I'll be two minutes," she told her mate, as the traffic to and from the lavatories went back and forth both cutting in between them and limiting her gaze.

"Come on – let's go outside," he said.

"Outside? I am not going out in the car park with you. Anyway – why d'yer want us to go outside for?"

"What – you don't know?" he winked.

She stood there, trying her best looking good, and flirting, giving quarter- and half-twirls in her colourfully chic dress.

"Fancy going for a drink one night, then?" he asked.

"What, yer want to take me out?" she shrugged.

"Yeah."

"But I'm married. You're married."

With picture houses and dance halls scattered all around the area, there were hundreds of places he could take her. The *Big Country* was on all week at the Majestic in Mexborough, *Peyton Place* down at the Grand in Wath-on-Dearne, whilst over in Goldthorpe the *Room at the Top* was playing until Friday… and that was the film everyone was talking about.

"So, what are you after?" she smiled.

"I want what all the Joes want," he said, trying his best to do an impression of Laurence Harvey's flat-capped characterisation of Joe Lampton in the much talked about film.

"I wouldn't mind going dancing," she told him. "If we can go in yer car."

He had cracked it. Within a month they were going out four and five times a week. She had seen it as an escape from the monotonous humdrum of everyday life. He had been in it solely for the sex.

At 12.21 a.m. on 27 June 1959, a telephone call was picked up at Wombwell Police Station which said: "This is Mr John Ellis of 81 Wombwell Main Row. Will you please come straight away? I have murdered my wife. It is opposite Wombwell Main Club. I will be at home."

John had married Grace (nee Utley) in December 1954 and between them they had two young children – a three-year-old son, Malcolm and a one-year-old daughter, Carol.

Things had come to a head exactly two weeks before.

"Jackie Caunt has been seeing your wife – everyone in the club is taking about it," he had been told.

The previous week they had been seen in the Empress Ballrooms, smooching along to a song that Frankie Avalon had had in the charts at the time and which peaked at No 16.

Venus, if you will – Please send a little girl for me to thrill,

A girl who wants my kisses and my arms, A girl with all the charms of you,

Venus, make her fair – A lovely girl with sunlight in her hair,

And take the brightest stars up in the skies – And place them in her eyes for me.

"You've been seen dancing with him – and to that stupid fucking song that you keep on singing," John had screamed on him getting home.

He certainly hadn't been wrong. It had been **their** song. And to make it worse it was something that she never denied.

"You'll never fucking learn," he snapped.

"I've learned plenty," she bitched.

"So, has he fucked you?"

There was a silence.

"So?" he screamed.

"Yeah, loads of times," she replied. "In his car mainly – down Smithy Lane and the path into the woods off Dovecliffe Road."

She didn't just leave it at that. She had also been very graphic – especially about how he did it and more importantly, what he liked, with a certain white lace suspender belt often being mentioned.

"What, do you mean he bought it for you?" asked her husband.

"For my birthday," she winked. "And he's always on at me to wear it."

The trial at Sheffield Assizes and the murder of a pretty girl, created something of a media frenzy. It was presided over by Sir Richard Everard Augustine Elwes QC – a judge who had a background of handling complex and high-profile murder trials at was a complicated time for judges – especially considering the introduction of the Homicide Act 1957. This law in part, reformed the defence of provocation – diminished responsibility, thereby severely restricting the handing out of the death penalty.

Elwes' greatest mistake would come sometime after, however, when double murderer Christopher Simcox had passed through his court room. Simcox had an extremely violent past – mainly domestic, but violent all the same. He had already murdered his second wife, Hilda in 1948 – stabbing her to death and serving ten years as part of a life sentence.

In October 1963, Elwes had Simcox in front of him on a charge of threatening to murder his third wife, Ruby – this time with a gun. Elwes let him off lightly, slapped his wrist and sent him on his way with a three-year probation order. Eleven days later, however, that gun was used. Simcox shot his wife and her sister – fifty-three-year-old Hilda Payton, the latter who died.

I am not sure if Elwes ever donned the black cap throughout his illustrious career, but he certainly hadn't been averse to handing out life sentences.

Just a month before he had John Ellis in front of him, he had presided over the trial of the double murderer William Alexander Wilkin at Durham Assizes.

Wilkin, a highly intelligent individual who entered a plea of insanity, had killed twenty-five-year-old Dorothy Connor and her two-year-old son Michael in a frenzied hammer attack at their home in Lansdowne Street, Darlington during a botched burglary.

Wilkin was indeed found insane and ordered to be detained for life.

Botched robberies happen. Just a couple of months before John Ellis had hit the triple-nine, one had occurred just six-and-a-half miles away.

On 10 April 1959, eighty-one-year-old chiropodist and hairdresser, Ernest Crapper had been found in his shop with his wrists bound with cord and severe head injuries – his skull had been fractured and home ransacked. He had been beaten over the head during a robbery and died in Rotherham Hospital, just four hours later.

A Det. Insp. Walter Barkby headed the local investigation whilst Det. Supt. John "Monty" Blue of Scotland Yard's Murder Squad handled the forensics after the five-week manhunt had stalled.

It was then the Chief Constable of Rotherham – James E. Cotton, made the decision for mass fingerprinting to undertaken in the town – 30,000 in all – with police still looking for someone 5'7, aged about thirty, wearing a grey felt cap and grey belted raincoat and carrying an attaché case.

According to his younger brother – a retired policeman over on The Wirral, twice-married Ernest had formed a habit of keeping large sums of money in his premises at 24 Greasborough Road, Rotherham – a shop that was demolished during the early-1960s as part of the slum clearance and modernisation of the town centre.

George Jackson of 38 Shaldon Grove, Aston-cum-Aughton, was eventually charged with his murder and on 26 November 1959 at Sheffield Assizes – the twenty-eight-year-old, who I am informed was a miner at Treeton Colliery, was sentenced to twelve-years for manslaughter.

As for Justice Elwes, earlier in the year he had presided over another double murderer – this time twenty-eight-year-old Henry King at Manchester Assizes.

The situation was not unlike my dad's when my mum had left him, in that his twenty-year-old wife, Sheila (nee Bullen) had left their home at Wellesley Street, Blackburn, taking their six-month-old son, David with her and had moved back in with her parents. Whereas my dad had wanted to throttle my mum for whatever reason – being controlling and pissing him about with his parental rights to access, most probably, Henry King did not. He had bought a gun solely with the intention of murdering his wife and child. He only finished half the job as the police arrived on the scene and a siege took place. Tear gas was slung through the back window and the police dogs sent in. It was a mess. Henry King ended up shooting his wife as well as emptying the gun on two policemen – unloading one in the groin of PC Jack Covill and shooting Det. Insp. James O'Donnell in the lower abdomen – the latter who died.

King was sentenced to life on 13 March 1959.

It had been the same end game for twenty-five-year-old Henry Howard Mitchell and twenty-six-year-old George Jones who between them had battered newsagent Augustus (Gus) Roberts to death with an iron bar in the front of his shop on Dock Street, Newport on 19 February 1959.

The four-day trial at Monmouthshire Assizes had created widespread interest amongst the legal profession because of the dilemma it presented under the said Homicide Act 1957.

Both men were eventually found guilty and sentenced to life on 11 June 1959.

John Ellis had therefore, come in front of him at a point in time when big changes in the law were taking place – especially where both extreme provocation and diminished responsibility could dictate a favourable outcome – for the defendant that is, and certainly not for the victim.

He was defended by Peter Stanley Price QC who had been the Crown Prosecutor on the trial of twenty-two-year-old John Bell of Maple Grove, Conisbrough in March 1957. This sad story surrounded events at a New Year's Eve party in Edlington, which ended up with Bell fatally stabbing his younger brother Sidney in the stomach. It had supposedly been a fight over a girl by the name of Jean Lyon.

Whilst John Bell would be found guilty of manslaughter and handed a seven-year stretch, Jean Lyon would marry a man by the name of Geoffrey Williams a year or so after.

As the famous quote from Dutch philosopher, Desiderius Erasmus says: *Women – can't live with them, can't live without them.*

In the case of John Ellis – a former soldier in the Coldstream Guards, the police went to the house and found the body of a woman on the floor.

"I have strangled her," he told them.

He wasn't lying – he had.

The Crown Prosecutor was Sir George Stanley Waller QC. He had been the defence counsel for forty-year-old Sarah Lloyd of Broadlea Walk, Bramley when she was sentenced to death on 5 May 1955. This had been a neighbourly spat that had culminated in Mrs Lloyd walloping her elderly neighbour around the head with a spade after being attacked by her. Waller pleaded the case as manslaughter – which it obviously was – however, the judge overruled.

Det. Sgt. Kenneth York had been the arresting officer claimed that John Ellis had said: "I am glad I have done it. She drove me to it. She had it coming to her."

What the jury would hear, however, was the build-up as to the reason why.

John Ellis had not only been upset at his wife's infidelity but the fact that he was away from both his children. In fact, I would not be wrong in saying that he was absolutely devastated. He and Grace had arranged for a trial separation.

Reading between the lines, my thoughts are is that she just wanted shut.

With nowhere to go, he went to his father, Frank, who although he lived in Ardsley, he owned a butchers shop at 17 Snape Hill Road in Darfield. Frank suggested that his son stay in one of the spare rooms above the shop.

"He came to my shop on Friday 26 June," his father told the court. "He hadn't had anything to eat since Thursday morning and told me that Grace had been having an affair with a man who drove a Zephyr Zodiac. He told me that they had just separated for about a month until she decided which one, she wanted."

Frank explained that he took his son home to his house on Ardsley's Alexandra Terrace – which backed onto the railway sidings which were located just off the busy Stairfoot railway junction, where he made him some supper and they both watched TV. For the record, *Emergency Ward 10* had been on followed by *Take Your Pick*.

"My son started to cry. He said he thought the world of Grace and just didn't know what to do," he added. "He saw the photograph of his baby daughter on top of the television set and just said that he had to go home. He picked up his coat and then left. He was extremely upset and talking about the children most of the time."

Thirty-three-year-old Derek Lawcock had married Muriel Newsome in 1946 and as I have already said, he not only lived next door to the Ellis's at No 83 but had also been a good friend of Jack Caunt.

According to his thirty-year-old wife, not only had John Ellis asked her husband about the affair – she had been in the car with both Caunt and Grace on 29 May when they went to Barnsley. She had not only seen Caunt give her a ten-shilling note (£11.81, circa 2020), which she had bought the item of lingerie with, she had been there when she had actually purchased it.

"She initially told me that she wanted to go into Barnsley to see about buying an electric washer," Muriel told the court. "Jack gave her the money as it had been her birthday."

John Ellis had been distraught and even went to Caunt's home on Windmill Road, hoping that him putting the cat amongst the pigeons with his wife Mildred, would put an end to the relationship. According to Caunt, it did not. Whereas Grace wanted her husband gone, Mildred did not. Caunt – a miner, appeared to be a man in demand.

Grace's mother, Lily Utley of 292 Hough Lane put the blame solely at her son-in-law's feet. "My daughter said she was absolutely fed up and couldn't care less about him. She never had any money to do anything. What our Grace did, she was driven to do by her own husband."

Caunt admitted that he had known Grace Ellis a long time but told the court that he had only been going out with her for around five weeks. "We usually went out alone and riding around," he said, adding that they went into

Barnsley near her birthday and went into a store where she bought the suspender belt – and with the money that he had given her.

He severely underplayed the intimacy of the relationship. There was a reason that John Ellis had flipped – a mechanism that had brought on his killing of her. When Ellis had got home to 81 Wombwell Main Row the house had been both locked and in darkness. He knocked on the back door and after a time, a dishevelled-looking Grace opened it. Her clothes were in disarray and her hair ruffled. This had been something that had been corroborated by a near-neighbour – thirty-year-old Tom Chipchase, who had seen it all, whilst sat having a cup of tea on the rear doorstep of his home at No 89.

He told the court that Caunt had come out of Derek Lawcock's house and sneaked into Ellis's home at 11.30 p.m. Grace had let him in by the back door and within minutes the lights had been switched off.

Meanwhile, Ronald Matthews, who lived around the corner from the Ellis's in The Bungalow on Dovecliffe Road, had seen John walking back from Ardsley and offered him a lift in his car.

"Where are you going?" Ronald asked.

"I've had some trouble at home," Ellis told him. "I'm just going back to try and patch things up."

"Jump in then," he said.

Ten minutes later, John Ellis arrived at the terraced property, which he too noticed had been in darkness and knocked at the back door. Eventually Grace opened it. Her husband immediately suspected that he had walked in on the two – however, Caunt had been nowhere to be seen. He had left via the front door just seconds before Grace had opened the back door.

Caunt admitted to the court of his being there, but that is as much as he did do. He claimed that he had no idea who had been at the back door. He also claimed that he hadn't been fucking her. It was something that her husband knew was a downright lie. More importantly, it was something that the jury knew was a lie.

Caunt was questioned about a sofa in the room and about him having sexual intercourse with Grace on it – however, he flatly denied it.

John Ellis knew there had been someone in the house and that sex had occurred and rigorously questioned his wife about it – so much so, he followed her into the outside toilet – which, without wishing to sound facetious, intimated that his wife wanted to discharge any evidence of Caunt ever being there.

There was a reason that Peter Stanley Walker QC pushed Jack Caunt to the brink on the question of sexual intercourse at that particular time. On a woman being killed the pathologist goes over every little thing. There had been evidence of sexual activity that night.

Caunt admitted having sex with Grace on at least four occasions, but he would not put his hands up to one of those being on the night in question. "She took nothing off, while I was with her," he said.

She had no need to. That wasn't his thing.

"When Grace eventually opened the door, she was straightening her frock and tying back her hair," her husband had told the court.

However, what John Ellis had told the court prior, was how his wife had taunted him with Caunt's obsession with her suspender belt. "She would show it off and say it how lovely it was. Then there was a song which was a favourite of theirs – *Venus, Goddess of Love*. And she used to sing it all the time. She knew it made me fed up and depressed."

The Crown Prosecutor told the jury: "The white suspender belt was an object portraying hatred for Ellis and represented a symbol of his wife's association with Caunt."

In his final speech, Peter Stanley Price QC urged the jury to bring in the manslaughter verdict: "John Ellis had had burdens to bear that he could not endure and had been driven beyond endurance."

In summing up Justice Elwes told the jury: "You are not here to try Jack Caunt and my advice is not to waste your intelligence on him."

John Ellis was convicted of manslaughter and sentenced to five years, whilst Jack Caunt died on 1 August 1971, aged forty-eight.

As for the events on the following Monday of 23 May 1966 – on one hand it could have been seen as just a continuation of several tragedies, yet on the other, part of a dark history that would unearth so much misery.

Like many in that small pocket of Bolton-on-Dearne's Concrete Canyon, just over eleven months earlier, the occupiers of the house at 110 Broadwater had respectfully stood out on the street with hundreds of others as a funeral cortege left the home of their near neighbours – a house whose rear garden had backed on to theirs.

On Sunday 2 May 1965, there had been a horrific crash a few hundred yards away at the bottom of Dearne Road, where two sisters were killed and three other people were seriously injured after a minivan they were being taxied by, collided head-on with a lorry, which I am told belonged to a Goldthorpe man known as Ginger Rowland.

Twenty-one-year-old Dorothy Thompson of 18 Mill View got away with spinal injuries – however the pretty daughters of Joe and Lilian Jardine of 10 South Drive – Marion and Janice, who were seventeen and nineteen years old respectively, did not. They sadly died shortly after being admitted to Mexborough Montagu.

Their *ride* had picked them up from Wath Pavillion (Wath Athletic Ground), which at one time had been located off Moor Road opposite where Tesco now stands and where the two sisters had fifteen minutes prior, been dancing to Joe Loss & His Orchestra's *March of the Mods* with my auntie Heather (Carman) and Jenny Johnson (now Woodhead).

From what I am told, the driver – Chris Anderson, who sustained injuries to both legs and his head, ended up marrying a nurse at the hospital, a local girl by the name of June Lancaster. And if you want a bit more history, the last I heard is that they were living at 11 Kennedy Drive.

As for the Jardine's near-neighbours?

In 1954, a sixteen-year-old girl by the name of Kathleen Elsie Coldwell eloped with her boyfriend. Ted Baines was the younger brother of Elizabeth Exley – the mother of Derek, the little lad who got killed on the Sheffield-York railway at the back of Thurnscoe's King Street and had married Kathleen in Gretna Green. It was a union that would eventually produce five children – Josie (b. 1958), Paul (b. 1959), Diane (b. 1960), Angela (b. 1962) and Alan (b. 1964).

What is unclear, is what led to the events on 23 May 1966 and twenty-nine-year-old Kathleen committing suicide whilst at the time trying to murder both her two youngest children. It had been a similar situation to that of Winifred Shingler (nee Allott) nearly seven years earlier, with carbon monoxide poisoning – gas inhalation from the domestic supply, her chosen way to go. However, the twenty-seven-year-old, Winifred only managed to do half the job and ended up on a murder charge after she had killed her two-year-old son, Barry – however, I will touch on this shortly.

The only thing the neighbours got to know about Kathleen's suicide attempt was the fact that the lounge room window had been smashed after the relevant authorities had tried gaining access the property in their bid to save her and the children. The children survived but Kathleen had been dead on arrival at Mexborough Montagu.

Suicide is never straightforward, and the only people it really affects are those who get left behind – one of who was a brave four-year-old little girl that had been dragged to safety.

It is here, however – where there becomes an ugly twist in the tale.

Angie Baines (now Smith) is not someone that is afraid of the truth. Far from it. "My dad would never say anything about my mum's suicide and that's what makes us all think there was a lot more to why she did it," she said. "According to my mum's brother, my dad certainly wasn't the man that I thought he was."

Her mother's suicide immediately put a strain on her father as he had to pack in his job at Hickleton Main, not that Angie recalled this. "I can only ever remember him working on building sites," she added.

Within a few years her father would begin a relationship with an unmarried twenty-one-year-old, who not only had a son, but had also been pregnant. My assumption is – and that is what it is – is that the connection in how they met, had been due to the family that resided over the road at 135 Broadwater – that of John and Irene Lumley (nee Stamper).

"We would have been put into care if it had it not been for the fact that my dad met her."

Now, this part – solely due to the legality regarding the laws surrounding anonymity in sexual crimes, is like trying to navigate a minefield.

This plump fair-haired girl that Ted had got involved with, was the eldest of seven children to Sam and Elizabeth (Betty) Lumley (nee Hall), a couple that had married in 1946 and for a time lived in one of the Nissen huts down on Lowfield Road. That was until the local authority gave them a house at 55 The Crescent.

Sam had been the younger brother of John Lumley.

"She was always after your dad," my auntie Liz (Durose) told me regarding Sam's eldest child, adding to the fact that her mother – who is of course my nan, had in no uncertain terms, told her to keep away from the house.

Sam had been a belt maintenance fitter at Barnburgh Main and lost his wife to cervical cancer on 22 June 1961, aged just thirty-four. This, I was told, created a situation that had been well-noted by neighbours and near-neighbours alike – that, being the father's unhealthy interest in his daughters. And at fourteen years old, his eldest daughter received the brunt of it.

"Everything was hushed up back then," added my auntie Liz.

It was certainly nothing out of the ordinary. On 22 November 1956, forty-eight-year-old George Day of 6 Sandal Road, Conisbrough had been sentenced to three years for the exact same thing. He had form too. In July 1930, he had been found guilty of indecently assaulting three girls – an eleven-year-old and two seven-year-olds – the only thing keeping him out of prison was him being crippled.

May Noble (nee Gray) had been the shop steward at the English Rose sewing factory off Highgate Lane and had lived at 63 The Crescent for years – as had her in-laws, Bob and Jessie (nee Bodkin), who had not only lived next door to them but also two doors up from the Lumley's. "After I married Dave in 1964, we got the house on The Crescent and there was always a lot of talk about the dad and his daughters," May explained. "One of them had been friends with Dave's sister. She was extremely petite with mousy hair and one of things that you noticed was that she used to try and stay out until her dad went to bed."

This was something that had been verified by his granddaughter.

"I used to think there was something strange about him," added Angie. "However, it wasn't until he died in 1985, that it all came out."

Walt Claydon was a Swinton lad – and had lived at 29 Hatherley Road just off Mexborough's Roman Terrace before leaving school and becoming a joiner/carpenter for Bolton UDC.

Walt had come to national media attention when on the Monday afternoon of 18 June 1956, he helped rescue an eleven-year-old lad – the son of a councillor, who had fallen in the Bowbroom Locks on the Dearne and Dove Canal section of the Sheffield & South Yorkshire Navigation. What made the rescue special was that since being two years old, Walt had had to battle against polio – which at fifteen years of age had seen him have seventeen operations, leaving him partially paralysed in one of his legs. This, however, did not stop him from scaling down a 30-foot high lock gate to just above the water level and sticking out his leg with the calliper on and pulling the boy to safety.

Being employed in the estates/housing repairs office of Goldthorpe Town Hall – Walt had a job which brought him into close contact with a lot of people, not at least on both Bolton-on-Dearne's Council Estates. "Sam said that no other man was going to take his daughter's virginity until he had been there first."

Disgusting as it was, his granddaughter had his number?

"I'm wondering if Sam fathered by stepbrother as it would go some way to explain why my stepmum was always very nasty with him," said Angie.

It had happened before, and it would happen again.

i) On 4 December 1923, sixty-three-year-old labourer, John Drewitt of 16 Thomas Street, Swinton was sentenced to eighteen months imprisonment by Justice Sir Henry Alfred McCardie after being found guilty of incest with his twenty-five-year-old daughter.

The same judge would preside over lots of similar cases not at least one of the most talked about paedophile cases of 1930, which I will touch on later.

On 3 December 1931, Tom Neal of 32 Winterwell Road, West Melton, had been found guilty at Leeds Assizes after being on trial for serious offences against two of his daughters – aged fifteen and seventeen.

On passing sentence, Justice McCardie said: "People generally do not realise the extent and gravity of these cases sufficiently. The pollution of one's own children is indeed repulsive and ugly."

The forty-seven-year-old bricklayer was sentenced to three years penal servitude.

ii) On the Friday evening of 6 July 1934, Albert Rayner (no relation, thank fuck) escaped from the holding cells at Leeds Town Hall after pleading guilty to incest with his seventeen-year-old daughter.

Justice Sir Malcolm Martin MacNaghten, who presided over the case, intimated that he would delay sentencing until later in the day after provisions had been made for the welfare of his four children.

The forty-two-year-old miner was described as 5'4 and had two fingers from his left hand missing, both having been amputated. He had also been dressed in a shabby brown suit, collar, tie, and cap.

A huge manhunt ensued with the police armed with flash lamps, searching Conisbrough Cliffs, Denaby Craggs and fields behind Cadeby Colliery after a sighting was made.

He was later found at his home at 41 Blythe Street, Denaby, where he eventually asked his family for forgiveness. His first words were, however: "For God's sake give me a cup of tea and fetch the bobbies." He had been on the run all weekend.

On the police arriving they found that a huge hostile crowd had assembled around his house. He was sentenced to four years penal servitude.

He hadn't been the only local man to escape incarceration. On 5 January 1973, David Poulson made a daring escape from Wakefield Prison after scaling a 20-foot wall under the cover of fog and spent the weekend on the run, the police finally arresting him and fellow escapee – murderer, Geoff Mycock, in the village of Little Smeaton, just north of Askern.

Twenty-five-year-old Poulson had been brought up with his parents Richard and Sophia (nee Johnson) at 3 Thornley Crescent, Thurnscoe. His younger brother, Willie – a wiry fellow, had been a Market Man at Hickleton Main, my main recollection of him being that he and Howard Hopkinson had spent a week down on the Silkstone development – filling in and doing various remedial works, with one of these being the installation of a Manchester Gate in the Intake drift. Rather interestingly, and to much amusement, they initially installed it the wrong way around, so the safety gate opened downhill.

As for David – he had been serving a sentence of seven years for wounding with intent.

iii) On 30 November 1938, Thomas Maxwell Ireland was sentenced to three years penal servitude at Leeds Assizes after he was found guilty of incest with his fifteen-year-old daughter.

The thirty-nine-year old miner of 21 Queen Street, Hoyland – who along with his common-law wife Annie Robinson, were both branded as liars by Justice Lewis, after Ireland was found not guilty of carnal knowledge with his daughter.

"This is a shocking case," he said. "What makes it worse is that you went into the witness box and told lie after lie and I have no doubt the woman with whom you live also told lie after lie in order to persuade the jury you were not guilty."

According to the court transcripts, even the police had called him a "Fucking liar".

The girl had allegedly been pregnant.

There is a lot more to these stories – however, some things are best left buried deep in the past.

As for Sam Lumley – with all his daughters gone, the forty-seven-year-old would go on to remarry a pregnant twenty-one-year-old divorcee by the name of Lily Bunting (nee Cadman) in 1971.

Lily's first husband, Phil Bunting, appeared a very well-liked lad and lived at 8 Central Street, Goldthorpe. He lost his life at twenty-nine-years old in tragic circumstances. In early November 1977 he had been involved in a haulage accident at Barnburgh Main, whereby he died after being pulled beneath a bogey (tram car).

I am not sure how long the marriage between Sam and Lily lasted – but Lily ended up remarrying John Duerden in 1983 and lived over at 23 Cromford Avenue in the Athersley South area of Barnsley up until her death in January 2011.

Kathleen Coldwell's may have been the first gas poisoning-based suicide on Broadwater, but it certainly wouldn't be the last.

Back before the use of natural gas became commonplace, the gas for cooktops and ovens had been coal gas – something, which was artificially created by heating coal in an oxygen-deficient atmosphere. It was mostly flammable – hydrogen, methane mainly, but contained a small amount of carbon monoxide, Manvers Main being the area's biggest supplier. Suicide victims would breathe the gas in the oven and the carbon monoxide would get into the haemoglobin in their blood – as it does when the poor souls use the exhaust pipe of car and a hose. The haemoglobin binds strongly to oxygen – however, it binds even more strongly to carbon monoxide, therefore, instead of providing oxygen to a body's cells, it brings carbon monoxide, and the person dies from lack of oxygen.

I was often told during my sixty days underground training that after a person dies from carbon monoxide poisoning that their facial features rather strangely, look very healthy. How true that is I could not say.

Now, regarding the case of Winifred Shingler. She had been under a psychiatrist in Sheffield as she had been depressed for some months one of the things being that she had been obsessed with having some undiagnosed heart disorder. She married her husband, Roy in 1953 and had not long since moved into a three-bedroomed property at 24 Worsbrough View, Tankersley with their two children – four-year-old Shirley and Barry, aged two. Roy worked long shifts as a power attendant – possibly at Hunshelf Bank Substation near Stocksbridge, which meant early starts with events on the Wednesday morning of 15 July 1959, being no different. By midday, however – he had received a message at work: "You have to come home immediately."

His brother-in-law, Jack Allott had called around, only to find the kitchen in a state of disarray, and his sister in bed with his nephew, unconscious – and his niece, Shirley totally unaware of what had gone off and happily playing in her bedroom.

"I have gassed Barry," she said.

Jack shouted the neighbours who alerted the emergency services, a Dr Dooley arriving at the semi-detached property and trying in vain to give the little lad artificial respiration. He was eventually taken to St. Helen Hospital in Barnsley. Unfortunately, however – he died at 5.00 a.m. the following day.

"Barry was crying and crying," she told the doctor. "I had a pain in my chest and a headache. I thought I was going to die, and nobody can look after Barry like me, so I was going to kill him."

A Det. Const. James Fenlon eventually arrested her and charged her with the murder of her son.

"Barry started crying and I felt fed up. I put the gas pipe in Barry's mouth and after putting him to bed I came downstairs, stood at the side of the table and did the same, and afterward collapsed, knocking everything over. I then crawled upstairs. I remember writing a note – but I can't remember what it said."

The suicide note read: "Dear Roy. Take care of Shirley. I do not want to live, and Barry is better with me. I have gassed Barry and me."

At Winifred's trial at Sheffield Assizes on 26 November 1959, she was found guilty of manslaughter and given a two-year probation order.

Roy Shingler stood by his wife, the couple having three more children – Trevor (b. 1961), Paul (b. 1962) and Clifford (b. 1964).

As for Barry – he is buried in Chapeltown's Burncross Cemetery.

The last I knew, the couple lived at 44 Newgate Close in the High Green area of Sheffield up until Roy's death in 2004.

Now, back onto Bolton-on-Dearne's Concrete Canyon.

On Monday 11 July 1968, sisters Joan Bell and Lilian Hopkinson (nee Carter) forced entry into a property at 32 Broadwater, to find the latter's husband dead. Twenty-one-year-old Terry was the younger brother of my old near-neighbour, Howard Hopkinson, and had been on something of a downward spiral since Lilian had walked out on the marriage, taking their children with her. Terry had been dead three days.

Lilian, much like my mum, had married when she had been seventeen years old and had left him on Saturday 25 May for reasons that she refused to state at the coroner's inquest. What she did say, however, is that he had been due to appear in court.

"He hadn't worked for a year due to having tuberculosis, which seemed to have been cleared by the time I had left him," his estranged wife had told the coroner.

What was true is that during the forty-four days between his wife's departure and his death, he had often been seen in the Collingwood Hotel and drinking heavily – which for Terry, was quite out of character.

There is, however, a reason behind every suicide.

"We went to the house and found both doors locked, and the curtains drawn," added his wife.

The second-generation prefabricated colliery houses all had the same dated design, which originally included a dining kitchen and what was termed as a wash house that was located next to the back door – a place where the cooker, fridge and indeed washing machine was kept. Rather strangely, however, the sink was in the dining kitchen.

She explained that the access to the wash house part of the kitchen had been blocked by carpets and blankets – and once it was eventually forced open, she had found her husband laid alongside the oven, along with a suicide note and photographs of his children.

What she wasn't telling the inquest, would soon come out, however.

The experience of moving from the high cracked ceilings of the old Houghton Road Junior School into the contemporary environment of Carfield Primary School had been quite an eye-opener. Everything about it felt new. From the great hall to the bright compact classrooms with their huge windows, along with the two playgrounds that were diligently separated by an arced tarmac path, and the slightly elevated football field with the goals at either end. Everything about it seemed, well, very modern.

Part of my induction into the Carfield academia was not only meeting new friends but being introduced to watching TV as part of our lessons. It was a whole new world.

I remember being sat in the classroom with Mrs (Janet) Wyatt as our teacher and at our tables that were identified by being colour coded. Not by paint, but by name – the one I was at, being blue.

"What, you watch telly?" I shrugged on first being told.

I still remember walking down the corridors and through the hall where a moveable and concertinaed screen partially hid the dinner tables from the great hall itself.

"Please turn to page twelve in your blue hymn book," our headmaster Mr (Walter) Cooke would say.

Oh, Jesus I have promised – to serve thee to the end… the song would go.

"And now to page ninety-two in your red hymn book," he would smile.

Gracious spirit holy ghost, taught by thee we covet most…

It was a time I look back to with great affection and how I wish I could nip back into the past to see all those little faces singing at the tops of their voices.

I can still put the page numbers to a lot of those beautiful hymns.

"Come on, children," he would say. "Let the people in the old folks' bungalows (Green Gate Close) hear you sing – let's make the roof of the hall shake."

What a marvellous and caring man he was!

There was a false door to the left of the partition, where we would be guided, and it was here that I would sit in awe and watch the school's programme *Look and Read* at 10.00 a.m. on a Monday. Firstly, it showed the very eerie *Boy from Space* and a bit later on, *Joe and the Sheep Rustlers*. It was all compelling viewing and very interesting to someone such as I. So was the lead up to the Christmas party.

"What, we have to dance with girls?" I asked with some aghast.

All through the December of 1972, our *Movement* lesson was temporarily replaced by dancing – which in my mind was each as rubbish as the next. From prancing around in your vest and underpants to Bach's *Toccata & Fugue in D minor* and Vivaldi's *Four Seasons* to having to old hands with the likes of Voodoo McGoo and Debbie Clapham. I have to admit, there wasn't a great deal in it. The only upside is that it gave you an insight into who you were going to ask to the party itself. As I had been the relative newbie and the rough arse from Thurnscoe, it was a toss between Amanda Metcalfe or Debbie Calladine to do the *Out and In and One, Two, Three* along with the dreaded *Barn Dance* – a nifty number which had you continually changing partners.

What I didn't know at that time was the girl that I would be dancing with on the Monday afternoon of 11 December 1972 had been one of those innocent little faces on the photographs at the side of the gas oven down on Bolton-Dearne's Concrete Canyon.

Debbie's twenty-one-year-old mum had left her husband and ended up shacked up with a man by the name of Alan Calladine, who she married less than a year after her first husband's death. The little girl had been born Debra Hopkinson. It was all extremely sad.

To my knowledge, Debbie's mum and stepfather are still in Bolton-on-Dearne and live at 35 Carrfield Lane. Just around the corner from that property as you walk up into the Ringway estate there is a street that is aptly named Carr Green as it is smartly formed around a central greenspace. That said greenspace was often used by the children of Carfield school to sort out their differences.

I still recall walking through Hall Broome Gardens and Crofton Drive in early-1973 as part of a horde of children intent on seeing a fight. This one was different as no punches were thrown. It was just wrestling, scratching and hair pulling. Debbie and Julie Atkinson (now Link) had had some fall out, and both were being egged on by the masses, intent on watching the two girls tear bits out of each other. As you will find out as you read on. Kids can be extremely cruel, and this was no different. Little did anyone know that just a few years earlier, Debbie had lost her father.

Not very nice, is it?

As suicides go, it has to be said, that there have been some rather macabre ones, two of which did have me shaking my head and both of which a linked to Dearneside's Class of 1981. One also had links to Bolton-on-Dearne's Concrete Canyon – most notably the property at 63 South Drive.

The first, however, occurred on the Tuesday morning of 29 November 1977. A great evening's viewing had been interrupted straight after *Ivor the Engine*, when my (step)dad began switching channels from ITV's *Calendar* over to the BBC's *Look North* and back again searching for some local news story.

On my part there had been some fire at Mr Pugh's barn and the new fire engine got stuck in the snow, with Ivor the Engine, along with Jones the Steam helping sort it all out. My (step)dad, however, also had an interest in that evening's viewing and had been looking forward to watching two of his favourite programmes. *Get Some In* with Wolfie Smith's version of a Teddy boy stuck in RAF training and one of the best, if not underrated sitcoms ever in *It Ain't Half Hot Mum* – the latter of which had had a huge bearing on the piece of news he had been hoping either Mike Smartt or Richard Whiteley would ultimately get to.

Unbeknown to me there had been an incident involving a twenty-five-year-old man from 19 Browning Road, Wath-on-Dearne, who I am led to believe was a second or third cousin to the stepfather of the lad I had jumped on the 213 bus outside Taylor's Shoe Shop in Goldthorpe that same afternoon.

On us moving into the Second Year (Year 8) of Dearneside, Wayne Tansley and I had been thrown together in a form that was made up of several other adolescent miscreants. Our form teacher had been Miss Elizabeth Queening, who was quite a straight-faced twenty-six-year-old lady who just a month or so later, would become the focus of some juvenile gossip following a school skiing trip in the Italian Alps. It had been alleged that she had been seen canoodling with one our metal work teachers – a bearded fellow with quite a nice demeanour, by the name of Mr Ken Dean. It had hardly been a rumour without foundation. They eventually married and Mr Dean, rather strangely, became my form teacher in the last year of school.

Wayne's mum – Sandra, had not only worked with mine during their younger days, but had recently married Terry Bradbury. At this point in time, their family had lived in Great Houghton, but would relocate onto Goldthorpe's Beever Street, sometime later. As it was, it became a regular bus ride home, with Wayne and myself generally checking the proceeds of crime after a visit to Taylor's Shoe Shop – a place where we often bought the Tuxan Red polish for our Dr Martens boots – Wayne's having the high-leg and mine the medium.

What occurred as we were on our way to school is that twenty-five-year-old Gary Bradbury – employed as a fitter's mate at British Steel's Templeborough Mill in Rotherham, would throw himself into a 1,300-degree centigrade furnace.

His father, Jack, explained that he had suffered from ulcers and had been in and out of hospital – but apart from that he had never gave him cause for concern.

Cecil Cutts, a fitter at the plant, told the inquest that Gary had gone into his cabin while he was having a break and seemed very agitated and wound up – something, which he claimed had been very out of character.

Shift Manager Jack Jones, saw Gary jump and explained that the *jump* was definitely a jump and not a fall.

There was very little of the body that remained according to the pathologist, Dr Alan Usher.

The second suicide had some reasoning, behind it, but not much more.

George Pendlebury had married Beatrice Moore in 1953 and between them they had two children – Jean (b. 1955) and Graham (b. 1958), and for a time lived on Bolton-on-Dearne's Concrete Canyon before moving into a property at 220 Wath Road, Mexborough.

At 3.20 p.m. on Friday 16 June 1961, the thirty-one-year-old miner and father of two threw himself down the 2,000 ft-deep No 4 shaft at Manvers Main. The reasoning: he'd had three bets go down at Cyril Norman's bookmakers and lost £46 (£1,046, circa 2020). The following day he had supposedly been due to go on holiday.

"Before anyone could intervene, he vaulted over the safety gate and disappeared down the shaft," said one of the miners waiting to go underground.

I am only glad that I wasn't one of the Onsetters in the pit bottom having to shovel that lot up.

I've not seen occur at death at any colliery – although my uncle Steve (Carman), certainly had.

He had kicked off his working life as a fitter at Hickleton Main and for a time worked with my (step)dad and that being the case – he not only played Sunday football with a Thurnscoe pub side – The Fairway, he also found time to pop in to see us, both when we lived down in The Avenues and after we had made the move up to Deightonby Street.

"Now then, Garth," he would wink before referring to me as a *hooligan*.

In fact, he was instrumental in helping us move up into Thurnscoe's East end and I remember being on the back of his motorbike as we shot under the Sheffield-York railway line and down past Brough's Corner at top speed. Well it certainly seemed like it at the time.

It was during the summer of 1972 that I became a part of their life. For a few weeks, anyway. I'm not entirely sure of the hows or whys surrounding it, but whatever it was, it was quite the eye-opener as their life appeared quite something else. Ann was a hairdresser who had packed in work. I think she may have just been pregnant with their first child – our Scott – however, I am not really one hundred percent on that. Whatever it was, all I saw her as, was the coolest auntie in the world and the template for what *is* the perfect wife.

While I was staying there, she would often take me around to her mum and dad's house at 13 Melbourne Avenue – a street which runs parallel with the bottom half of Canberra Rise connecting with both Princess and Coronation Drive's. It was here that I was introduced to her younger sister, Lynn, who was just two years my senior in age and a further five in maturity. She took time out to diligently explain loads of things that I had been totally unaware of. 1. That Donny Osmond was brilliant; and 2. That our Steve was a Hells Angel.

"What's a Hells Angel?" I'd asked.

"You have to be a Hells Angel or a Skinhead," she had quite rightly pointed out.

In that case I was definitely a Hells Angel.

I think it was around that time that our Steve had thrown in the towel at Hickleton Main.

"I was on P29s down the East Side of the pit working with your (step)dad and they had just fired the rip. It was red hot, there was dust everywhere and I was full of spots," he told me in later life.

Colin Meakin referred to some units down the old East Side as being like *Dante's Inferno* – not at least the P34s unit.

After a few weeks Steve went private contracting in the pits with Barugh-based Amalgamated Construction Company (AMCO) and I am assuming that is where he was working when I spent the three weeks in 1972 with them.

My new auntie had me completely in awe and showed an interest that I had never seen before. From having me and their Lynn in competition, drawing things such as a glass swan ornament that adorned the top of the TV; to taking me around the backings that ran behind Ingsfield Lane and to Mary Roberts' shop, which was in reality a lock-up brick shed and letting me pick some sweets; through to us sitting on the sofa whilst we watched the old *Scotland Yard* series on TV. That was the episode where a woman is found drowned under suspicious circumstances and the brilliant Det. Supt. Reynolds investigates a lawyer for possible insurance fraud and finds the murderer by tracing some invisible mending within his clothes.

Maybe the detective could have helped Mrs Roberts' insurance case as on 25 November 1952 two explosions occurred, which obliterated her outbuildings, sending bricks and mortar everywhere. This, it was said, had been caused by a leaking fifteen-inch gas main which had been unknowingly ignited by her coal fire.

Sometimes in life, things at the time can appear nothing, but their impact can be nothing short of massive. My life would take a similar path to our Steve's, but whereas he had installed the foundations of his life on the proper footings, mine had been built on running sand.

Around six years later, I had been tasked by my mum to drop something off at their house although for the life of me I cannot remember what. I do recall riding down on my bike along with Richard Clements-Pearce and on Ann seeing me her first word were: "Don't go, Steve will be home from work in a bit."

She wasn't wrong.

The next thing I know, he had me drag this old Puch moped from out of his shed and kicked-up its engine. "Go on, then," he said. "Take it over the field."

I raced along the back of Broadwater and over the floodplain of the River Dearne at nearly thirty miles per hour. It was a brilliant feeling, however, what I didn't know until this day was that around that time, he must have been wrestling with quite a few things in his everyday working life.

Back then underground contracting in the mines was much different to how it was when I had been doing it. Contracting has always been a contacts game of who you know, rather than what you know – but back then it was a highly-aggressive profession and littered with what you could term as mercenaries. They came in different guises – foreign nationals escaping conflict, head cases, heavy drinkers, ex-convicts, and men who for one thing or another had been sacked from the NCB – all of whom had one thing in common. They were in it solely for the money, which compared to that the NCB paid, was massive. The jobs that these contractors were therefore tasked to do was extremely varied. Even when I was doing it, that was always the case. You were tasked with what the NCB's direct employees could not or indeed did not want to do. One month you could be tasked with ripping out tunnel supports and reprofiling the structure in seriously high temperatures with literally no ventilation and the next sinking a ventilation shaft in dusty and freezing conditions where the force of the air and its noise continually throws up debris at your face and body, whilst at the same time trying its best to deafen you.

The company our Steve worked for, AMCO, had been constructing a ventilation shaft over at Dinnington Colliery near Rotherham and on an extremely steep +/-1:1 gradient using standard steel arched supports (rings).

"It was the most dangerous job I had ever worked on, boring (drilling) uphill off a scaffold," he told me. "I was working with two Polish lads, Ambrose Černá and Pal (Paul) Kyter and everybody got hurt at one time or another. Just as the job was finishing, they were pulling the bogey off the monorail out of the top of the shaft and it slipped back. So as not to get hit by it, Paul dove off to grab the rings and couldn't hold on."

Pal Kyter was killed after falling down the shaft.

"As for Ambrose, he died in the early 1980s after he got crushed behind a Stanchion leg, whilst constructing a junction at Houghton Main – again working for AMCO."

10.   1982 (Part 1)

As our Training Manager moved us around a bit, I ended up working on numerous jobs on Hickleton Main's surface prior to me going underground and as that was the case, I'd got to know hell of a lot of people and they I. Pit life tended to be like that, which is possibly the only thing the left-wing historians have ever got right. It was a hive of gossip, which after it had done the rounds came back to you in a highly exaggerated form and was absolutely nothing like what it started out as. That was especially the case if a miner's wife got hold of it.

The only miners' wives that worked at the pit were either cleaners in the offices, wages clerks or in the pit canteen, which was a place where the NUM men tended to place their partners. However, there was a woman in there that I remember who lived a few doors down from us on the other side Lancaster Street – a stern looking lady in her late fifties, with a long face by the name of Lydia Oliver (nee Gardner).

Whilst doing a week or so in the Time Office I got to know the pit top security guy by the name of Jim Gibson, who patrolled the colliery's surface – a kind of pit bobby if you like. His being there was solely to make sure that no pilfering was going on. He had a similar broad Yorkshire accent to that of Tex Rodgers and I found it quite enlightening hearing about some of the stories that he reeled off, especially regarding his self-proclaimed brilliance and marvellous success rate.

Just a couple of weeks earlier, whilst Daz Eades and myself were under the direction of John (Quincy) Gwynne, a moustachioed fitter in the old Wagon Shop – a red bricked building which was located at the far end of the colliery (now Harrison's Antiques), our supposed supervisor and mentor picked up what looked like a long tubular pipe from a conveyor system and legged it over Lidget Lane and up to his house on George Street. He like many at the time, was another amateur radio ham and wanted the white conveyor pole to help mount his fifty-foot transmitter aerial.

As for the colliery's sixty-odd year old head of security, he had been nowhere to be seen.

"He tends to embellish the truth," candidly explained Brian Cooper – one of the guys in the Time Office.

On getting back to the Bag Room prior to us being sent underground, I asked Pete Ranskill about the enigmatic Mr Gibson, who as always, filled in some blanks about something that I already partly knew.

There was a young married couple on our street that lived five doors down from us at No 43 and more to the point, opposite the sharp-faced lady who worked in the canteen. Val Bird had married Marlene Crossley – the daughter of our next-door neighbours, Harry and Margaret (nee Duggan), a year or so after we moved on the street.

Val was a rope man at the pit and was an extremely well-liked lad with a gregarious nature. The story was, that he had had his annual fuel allowance taken from them as it was alleged that he had been selling his coal – a concession that we got for free, being that we were employed by the NCB.

It wasn't a hard trap to fall into and I remember a few times after Hickleton's Home Coal lorry dumped a ton of the stuff on the street outside our house of someone knocking on our door and asking if we fancied selling it. If it had been up to me, I would have sold it straight away, as during my early teenage years it was I who had been generally tasked with getting it in. It was an easy way of making £50, and if you had plenty already stocked in your coal house, it was something I couldn't really fault. However, it was said that Lydia was extremely chummy with Jim Gibson, and that it was she that had made sure that Val's coal allowance had been taken from him.

"Aah, I seh, is that Jim Gibson – t'police bobby," I asked over the pits internal phone system, with a broad and much put on Yorkshire-dialect after finally managing to track down the pits elusive head of security.

"It is, lad, ay," he replied in an exaggerated drawl that was just as bad as my effort. "What can a do for thee?"

"It's I that can do summat for thee," I told him. "It's going around t'pit that tha's been tuppin' Lydia from t'canteen – yer know, getting t'owd end away with t'lass and I just want thee to confirm it before I let t'editor of *t'Yorkshire Miner* know."

The bloke went ape shit and even more so when I asked him to clarify the spelling of his name and confirmation of his home address.

As for the *Yorkshire Miner* it was the Union's mouthpiece and as such full of Trotskyite and Socialist drivel. In a nutshell, it was a pile of shite that we, the NUM members, funded. All it was ever good for was starting a fire in the hearth – mainly because of the drawing capability of its large pages.

I may have enjoyed being underground after I had turned eighteen and got myself a decent job – however, at first it was a case of doing twenty days of what was classed as Close Personal Supervision (CPS) and as was the norm, we got put with the two methane boring teams, who were probably the biggest set of dossers and shirkers that I would ever come across. There were two crews – a 5.00 a.m. and a 6.00 a.m. team, and after doing a dozen days with the early-risers, Tim Bright and myself got sent out of the pit.

I have no idea why they were called methane borers as the only time I recall them doing any methane boring was one afternoon shift up on P80s. Every job description had its manager – and the Head of Methane Boring was no different and run a bearded guy off Deightonby Street that had originated from Durham, by the name of Alfie Mullins. If you ever watch Martin Scorsese's 1990 film *Goodfellas* – then look for Chuck Low's portrayal of the rug fitter that is Morris Kessler. He and Alfie could have been twins.

Alfie was a sound enough bloke who it was alleged, had got his job through both how he was and of course, who he knew. He was the underground equivalent of Pete Ranskill, if you like. However, I will give him his due, he put a shift in when he had to.

Daz Eades and myself had been put on the 5.00 a.m. shift, which not only meant that we had to get up in the middle of the night, we got stuck with two brothers, Dennis and Gordon Hopper, and a tall lanky kid with a chip on his shoulder by the name of John, who was that fucking interesting, I've forgotten his surname. Things changed a bit when Tim was brought into the fold. He had had six weeks off work following a motorbike accident down at the notorious crossroads near the Cottage of Content in West Melton and had done his cruciate ligaments. All we seemed to be doing was lifting pipes, mixing hard stop (cement) and creating stoppings. There was no need to have a team of twelve doing it. Two of us could have easily done it all. We were the equivalent of the Undermanager's bitches. Any shit jobs that needed doing, the undermanager just got Alfie on the phone. There was also little bloke by the name of Wilf who was part of the team and who was someone I never ever saw go underground. To be honest, I never saw him actually do anything. All I remember about him is that he wore a brown old-fashioned pit helmet with *Wilf* written on the side. Looking back at it, you could easily see why these collieries were haemorrhaging money. And this was just the tip of the iceberg.

My first day underground was an eye-opener. It was very fucking hot and the districts within the Thorncliffe seam were miles from the pit bottom.

T01s was a face they were salvaging, meaning that all the face supports had to be part-dismantled, dragged off, overhauled and sent on their way to gear up another face. There was a problem in that the tunnel that was the supply (tail) gate to move them down was generally in a poor state of repair and was only twelve or eighteen inches high in places, which meant that not a great deal would travel through them without being stripped down to the bone. Looking back, a lot of what we did made little sense. I'm still not sure what our remit on T01s main gate actually was, as we didn't seem to do a deal and all I remember telling my dad on the phone afterwards was how rubbish it was.

Although it was hot, in comparison to some of the places I would end up working it was nothing.

Being sent out of the pit was interesting as it coincided with a lousy argument at home.

I have already mentioned the failed purchase of the bungalow on Thurnscoe's High Street and the new-build bungalow in Swinton and the probable reasoning behind why they didn't go through and how my (step)dad's getting cold feet was the first step on the path to matrimonial suicide.

My mum was never happy. If my (step)dad would have got her the bungalow she would have only wanted something else. It was just how she was. As I've got older, I can sympathise with how she felt, as I am one of those people that will never settle for anything less than exactly what I want. My wants in the main, however, have always tended to be addressed. The failed house purchase was some way rectified by my (step)dad eventually giving the nod for my mum to call in at Ringway's (now Stoneacre) Ford dealership across the road from the Sun Inn on Doncaster's busy A638 York Road and sign on the dotted line for a new Ford Granada 2.3L. That, however, would be several months into the future.

As good a year as 1981 had been in my home life, 1982 would be the exact opposite.

My parents had started arguing. This was nothing new as I had witnessed some appalling rows and as was generally the case, I was often caught in the crossfire. I loved my (step)dad, but it is fair to say that when shit happened at home, I was always the cuckoo in the nest. I had seen this play out time and time again.

Whilst we lived on Bolton-on-Dearne's Flower Estate, circa 1974, I remember a vicious row between them, which culminated in my (step)dad walking out and taking my younger sister and brother with him.

If the tenants of 102 Primrose Close who followed us in, post-1977, looked closely at the foot of the stairs, there would be a mark bearing the perfect indentation of a 50p piece after my dad had slung all the change out of his pockets in temper. His outage of temper was never one of violence, just the destruction of property. Fucking stupid really, as it was mainly the stuff that he had worked hard to buy. My mum's, however, was most certainly violence.

It's hard to write a story without being honest, but one of the things that let my mum down was the fact that she was physically abusive – not just to me, but at times, to my younger sister. And it could be brutal.

"The thing is with your mam, love," once said my auntie Carol (Oldfield), "is that she just didn't know when to stop."

It was something which was often echoed time and time again by my mum's younger sister, my auntie Heather.

My mum had a problem in that she felt the need to express her anger with her fist or anything heavy that she had close at hand. I can sympathise with her as I know exactly how she felt. I possess the same horrible and destructive gene. However, here is the thing – over time I learned exactly how to manage and direct it. My mum, for her sins, did not. Consequently, we suffered.

My grandma Carman often used to tell me the story behind the bent poker that at one time stood proudly within a black-painted steel sleeve on her hearth and the reasoning why it was deformed at its point. "I bent it hitting your uncle Steve," she'd wink.

Did I believe her?

Knowing what I know now, it is a hard one to call.

I was told something by my mum in later life. It is a horrible story, but it needs telling if not just to give the reader some background into the complicated lady that she was.

I mention her mum – my grandma Carman with an affection. I am not making it up as that is exactly how I saw her. My grandma had a husband who I haven't yet mentioned – Joe Carman.

Every person that I have ever spoken to tends to say the same thing about the person who was my grandfather, in that he was a very smart, articulately spoken, and intelligent man. That is apart from my grandma and the two sons that she absolutely adored.

In the 1950s Bolton-on-Dearne's Co-operative store hadn't been in St Andrews Square as it is now, but on the site of the DIY store opposite The Angel public house at the top of Mexborough Road.

When my mum was around seven or eight years old, she had been tasked with taking the wheelbarrow from 40 Ringway and picking up a sack of coal – probably a half hundredweight bag. What occurred, however, is that the errand she was running took longer than it should have done – in fact, much longer. When she returned her father did no more than beat the living daylights out of her, hitting her around the head and kicking her in the stomach several times. It sounds appalling, I know, but it needs to be said. The reasoning behind her taking so long was that her appendix had burst, and she could not lift or wheel the barrow. Nevertheless, in her father's eyes that had been no excuse.

The upshot, is that my mum got brought up around violence and she carried the tradition on.

"It happened in most houses," my mum explained in later life. "I was just something that no-one ever spoke about."

The first beating I recall receiving from an adult, was rather strangely not meted out by my mum and strangely something I have never really shared with anyone outside my wife and my auntie Anne, the latter of who was nothing short of fuming after I had told her.

I have mentioned Harry Dawson as a man that lived opposite my grandma at 47 Ringway and whose garden we often used as a short-cut. Harry was a small, likeable, albeit horse-faced fellow who I remember as a teenager riding around one of those old Honda mopeds. He was also a person who regularly called in at my grandma Ellis's house on Lindley Crescent – mainly to drop in money for one of several things – a joint of beef most probably, as her youngest son, John (Ellis) worked as an assistant butcher in Jim Sharman's, which was a shop with a sky-blue half circular sign above it that was opposite Brough's supermarket on Shepherd Lane. That being the case, she was always in possession of cheap cuts of meat.

His daughter Margaret Dawson had been a good friend of my mum's when they were growing up, which was something that one could assume would have been further reinforced in April 1969, when she married my uncle Pete. That, however, wasn't really the case.

My dad did not like her and often told the story of Margaret going down to their house when he and my mum had first been married and when we lived at 15 Barker Street in Mexborough along with the fact that she had been instrumental in setting my mum up to go out with her then-boyfriend's brother – which was of course my (step)dad.

"I'm sure she was seeing him while we were married," my dad had often told me regarding my mum and (step)dad.

My thoughts on the matter? It is possible, but unlikely.

As I have already said, a major part of my dad's failings was his insecurity – mainly his distrust of women along with his innate jealousy.

My mum would go on to marry my (step)dad on 4 January 1969, which was a date, some months after she and I had first moved into 14 Landsdowne Avenue.

Between those dates had been a time when my mum and (step)dad were seeing each other – courting if you like. This meant that I obviously had to have someone to look after me when my mum was out. On the day of my mum's marriage to my (step)dad, I had stayed at my nana Durose's house at 9 The Crescent, which is something I still remember vividly to this day, as I do my earliest recollections of my (step)dad's mum – my grandma Ellis.

My grandma Carman on the other hand had refused point-blank to play cupid, which was the main reason for us leaving Ringway in early 1968 and having to temporarily stay with my auntie Heather and uncle Jimmy (Greaves) in their terraced home at 45 Barnburgh Lane, Goldthorpe.

The house on The Avenues was a three-up-two-down and possessed a damp kind of smell that has stayed with me all my life, as did my soon-to-be auntie supposedly looking after me prior to her marrying my uncle Pete – the main reason being that she gave me a leathering that I will never forget.

I recently looked back at some photographs of me around that time and tried to think what on earth I could have possibly done to deserve the beating she gave me, and I honestly cannot think of one. Really. I said the same thing to my auntie Anne, the other year.

As for Margaret, I saw her shortly before she died, which had been the first time in nearly twenty years. "Where's all that lovely blond hair gone?" was the first sentence she spoke.

"I used to babysit for you when you were little – can you remember?" had been the second.

I remembered it vividly and not being able to cry properly as the good hiding I took was so fucking severe.

That beating was well and truly trumped by my mum in 1974 – however, there was at least some reasoning behind this one.

My younger sister had started at the infant school on Priory Road and I was tasked with picking her up, as I often did with having to pick her up from Emily Bradley's dance school – an outbuilding which was to the rear of The Collingwood Hotel.

It was nothing new, as from being four or five years old I had become my mum's personal slave. "Twenty Number Six Tipped," was her most favoured demand and the purchase of that item generally came before anything else. We could have no food or milk in the house, but she would always have a cigarette in her mitts.

Whilst we were up at 24 Deightonby Street in the early 1970s, I was often tasked with seeking out who sold them at the cheapest price. Back then Richard and Hannah Howley had two shops on Lidget Lane – a fruit and vegetable shop and a grocers and off licence, and it was the latter who knocked out her favoured No 6's at 19½p (£2.78, circa 2020), therefore that is where I was often sent.

On being sent for my sister I noticed 10p (£1.15, circa 2018) on the side in the kitchen and I took it without asking. If I would have asked, I would have only been told *No*, therefore it was as simple as that.

On picking my sister up, which was a task in itself, as one of the teachers at school – a sharp-faced lady with a facial mole by the name of Mrs Starkey – claimed that I was too young to be picking her up and initially refused to sanction my sister being taken out of school until she spoke with me at length. That aside, after I had been given the okay, we called in at Pyott's newsagents on St Andrews Square and with the money I had taken, I bought us a Topic chocolate bar apiece.

When we got in, it quickly turned into the Spanish Inquisition. My mum wanted to know where the money had gone as that was money to go towards her much-needed nicotine rush. However, the more she pushed it, the more I denied it. Then it happened. A punch in the face followed by her dragging the Y-shaped rubber hose out of the old twin-tub washing machine. The beating I took was enough to turn your stomach and at one time I thought I was going to lose consciousness as I banged my head. I was black and blue all over, so much so I was kept off school the very next day.

"Jesus Christ, Helen, what have you done?" was my (step)dad's first reaction on him getting in from work.

Was I wrong? Yes.

Was it worth it? To see my sister's eyes light up when I passed her the chocolate bar, most definitely. I would have done it another thousand fucking times.

That was an instance which was followed by many more similar ones, but which ultimately stopped as I got older, though I have to admit, it was not for the lack of her trying. This was one of the reasons whereby an argument ensued during my first few weeks underground at Hickleton Main.

I was unaware of what the problem was at home as I was still only young. However, knowing what I know now – a well-worn cliché, I know – it was all too obvious.

My mum was unhappy. Not with one thing, but with a number of things. Not getting the bungalow played a big part, but it wasn't the only part. The main problem she had with me was how I spent my money, and it was something that she always seemed to be moaning about.

I was given the option of tipping-up and getting spending money, like what families did in times-past or paying board. You must remember that at just seventeen years old I wasn't that behind the door, and I knew exactly what would have happened if I'd have given her my wages. I would have been left with nothing and they would have gone out and got the bungalow.

Really? Yes.

In late-1979 my mum went into business with my auntie Heather and between them they bought a lock-up fish and chip shop on Grove Street in Worsbrough Dale. It was a building that was hidden away beneath Bank End Road and less than one hundred yards from Pantry Hill – the place where Arthur Scargill grew up.

Auntie Heather was no fool and immediately saw that there was a problem and wanted out. She let my mum down gently and sought to paddle her own canoe by buying a similar business on Lunn Road in Cudworth and turning it into a great success. As for the shop on Grove Street, it was nothing short of a lemon – however, with more professionalism and less frugality, it would have certainly done much better.

I was quickly drafted-in as full-time slave with the promise of £25 (£127.79, circa 2020) per week on the proviso that I bought my own clothes. It was a brilliant offer, which I duly accepted. I worked long hours, so much so, I was often falling asleep in school. I thought it was brilliant. However, that soon changed as it was much easier for her **not** to pay me and after five weeks in, that is exactly what happened.

No person could never go into business with my mum and that included my (step)dad. My experience of my mum with money, was enough to kick the idea of her ever being in charge of my wages, well and truly in the head. I initially paid £10 (£43.32, circa 2020) per week board – firstly via bank transfer into a TSB account that I had opened, whilst I'd been at Markham Main Training Centre, which according to my mum was to be used as some form of savings account. This was quite possibly for the bungalow, as after that got knocked in the head the account was quickly emptied. Then it was a case of me giving her the cash.

The receiving of my board was never a very gracious event as she was always moaning about money and her lack of, and the sight of carrier bags of new clothes, shoes and records regularly coming into the house – along with my recent purchase a red Suzuki motorbike drove her to the point of insanity. This was partially offset by her raiding my wardrobe and purposely shrinking my T-shirts in the tumble-dryer so they would fit her.

It was here that we came to an impasse. I was unimpressed about her ruining my clothes – amongst other things, and she was unimpressed that I was using her house as a hotel. She ended up attacking me, putting huge scratches around both my neck and face, before I stopped it dead. Both physically and verbally. I told her that she was a useless mother, pointing to the fact that she didn't give a damn about her kids and that there was never any food in the house, which there wasn't. The upshot was that she told me to get out.

My girlfriend saw the marks around my face and neck and went mental.

Whereas I was just upset, my girlfriend just saw it as a way of getting me further into her clutches. She was an extremely divisive young girl who, like many women I have known, had a divide and conquer philosophy. She saw my mum as an obstacle that needed firmly removing from my life.

Why? Her reasoning was simple, my mum hated her.

Why? For the exact same reason. She hated my mum.

I just saw it as an out and out battle for control – however, my girlfriend was building up the kind of ammunition that could ultimately self-explode, which is exactly what it ended up doing.

My first port of call was to see my grandma Carman.

"Have you been fighting?" she asked, as it must have looked as though I had been mauled by a cat.

I was upset.

"Pull yourself together," she snapped. "And tell me what's been going on."

The man-management skills of my grandma, when it came to me, were nothing short of brilliant, and it is just a shame that the younger members of our family, such as our (uncle) Rob and Steve's kids never saw her at the peak of her powers as she truly was one hell of a woman.

"You can stay here tonight so it can all blow over and I'll speak to your mam in the morning."

It was one of the best nights in I had had in ages. We ate fish and chips and had some great conversation – mainly about me as a kid and my mum and dad, which was topped off with her packing me off for work the very next morning. And as she often did, she waved me off until I was out of sight at the north-western curve of Ringway.

Thankfully, I was on at 5.00 a.m., so very few people saw the mess around my neck and face. Work started with us bumming around in the pit bottom waiting for some heavy apparatus to take up to T02s main gate rip.

A rolling stone gathers no moss – a stopped conveyor means production lost, the sign read in the pit bottom.

It was the most practical thing that could ever be said in a pit. You stopped one conveyor and you stopped everything. The apparatus we picked up could have been anything. To me it was just a complicated piece of steel and pipe, which Tim and myself got tasked with carrying from the pit bottom, under the West Gearhead and through the air doors and on to the Paddy road that served the Thorncliffe district.

We had a few things to do first however, such as lifting and grading pipes as the lads who ran the haulage had been knocking them about whilst transporting materials. It was then we were tasked with carrying the lump of metal. My first argument was simple. "We've already carried the fucking thing miles," I snapped.

The language within the pit, was always as such, with every sentence littered with F-led superlatives, which was strange as neither my mum nor (step)dad used them at home. The first time I ever heard the word used was in a heated debate one Sunday lunchtime at 51 Lancaster Street, when my grandma Carman had come over. I have no idea what the subject had been, but my (step)dad and grandma were sharing a bottle of whisky and my mum said something that my grandma didn't agree with and she cut her dead. "All I have got to say to that Helen, is fuck off," she snapped.

After my grandma had left there had been a furious row between my mum and (step)dad, which saw the latter smashing up some teak and black vinyl chairs as part of a dinner table set that had been bought on hire-purchase from Cavendish Woodhouse in Goldthorpe. At the time this had been an elongated shop that ran across the upper floors of Arndale House, close to where the Rusty Dudley public house now stands. The problem was that my mum had been both outranked and outflanked by my grandma, therefore, she felt the need to bully and my (step)dad got it in the neck. His outlet for anger was simple – he just smashed things up.

There was still the argument of who was carrying the apparatus as the coal face was a right fucking hike.

"We'll do a hundred yards apiece," said one of the methane borers. "You do the first hundred."

Whilst growling a bit, we did it.

Then came the straw that broke the camel's back.

As stated, it is the conveyor that carries the coal towards the pit bottom on a rolling belt principle. As it dumps the coal or stone onto another belt the top side of the belt becomes the underside of the bottom belt moving through a series of drive rollers and loops before it begins its journey back to whence it came.

Their turn. They just carried it past the drive rollers and slung it on the bottom belt and it quickly became our turn to carry it. "We'll do what you did," Tim told the borer.

"You can't, there's not enough room on this belt."

I wasn't happy about it at all and told them all to "fuck off".

That was it. Dennis Hopper phoned Alfie Mullins, and Tim and I were sent out of the pit. On our way out, however, I bumped into a kid from the Class of 1980, who lived just up from me at No 61. Anthony Cooke was a solid kid and quite good looking with a great sense of humour, who at the time he had been courting a girl that he would marry by the name of Vera Charlesworth.

Rather strangely, his younger brother Sam recently contacted me and told me that both he and their Anthony are now living in Australia and are both heavily involved in mining.

"Where are you going?" asked Anthony.

I told him the whys and wherefores and who was to blame – mainly not us.

"That John?" he said. "He's a right wanker. When I was with them and doing my CPS, I was ready for kicking his fucking head in."

Did fighting between miners happen underground?

Oh yes, which is another thing these left-wing historians that pontificate about the Miners' Strike fail to tell you.

Me? During my short and *distinguished* career, I have had some right up and downers, but only twice have I ever belted someone. Once in 1987 and once in 1994, though there were times in between where it could have got very nasty, but didn't, and which is something I'll get on to as the story progresses.

On getting out of the pit we were summoned to see the Training Officer, Ron Lester, who heard our side of the story and gave us a mini-bollocking, before sending Tim on his merry way and keeping me in his office.

"I'm sorry, Ron," I shrugged. "It'll not happen again."

This was an instance and one which rarely, if ever, gets mentioned, and that is how the NCB – especially at Hickleton Main, nurtured and looked after all its young lads (trainees). It was man-management at its very finest.

"I'm not bothered about that," he told me. "Shit like that happens all the time. What I am bothered about is what's been going on at home. I've had your (step)dad in here this morning and he's really upset."

That bit upset me as my (step)dad certainly didn't deserve what he was getting.

"It's part of my job to make sure that everything is alright with all the young lads at the pit – both here and at home."

Ron was a truly brilliant bloke, who sadly died the other year.

"Your mam to your dad, is like your girlfriend is to you," he told me. "It's not nice to speak to her like that."

I eventually went home and saw my mum, who had not only had a day off, she'd also had my grandma on the phone.

"Your dad was really upset," she told me. "It's the first time I've ever seen him like that."

There was a huge problem at home that at the time I was unaware of – however, for the time being, the cracks were temporarily papered over.

Hickleton Main's Silkstone Development circa 1982/3. Top. Fitter, Johnny Brown standing on the curve going into the Intake drift and Bottom - sat on the Concord engine that drives the Paddy into the mines old East Side Workings (c. Geoff Lowther)

117

11.   1982 (Part 2)

In life, you get dealt the hand you are given and use those cards as best you can. Some you keep, some you exchange, some you lose. Sometimes luck plays its part, but in the main, it is how you play the game and skill that dictates the outcome.

My childhood wasn't always bad and there are many people out there, my age, who had far worse starts and who turned out great lads. There are also some lads that had great starts and turned out real shit bags. As I have said, it is generally how you play the game.

My uncle, Steve Carman, once told me: "Life is all about timing."

That is one of **three** things that he told me when I was younger, that rings 100% true.

My mum's reluctance to sign on the dotted line robbed me of an apprenticeship and the first steps to becoming a mining engineer. Never forget those words, life is all about timing, because if that would have happened – my mum signing when I had asked – my life would have taken a completely different path.

At home, even though the rift had been somewhat healed between my mum and myself, the problems were always there.

My mum never seemed to be in and there was never any food in the cupboard, which mirrored something that my mum had told me about when she was growing up. My grandma and granddad Carman hated the sight of each other and therefore their kids got neglected. My mum had hated it. "There were only ever baked beans in the house," I remember her telling me.

During the latter part of 1982, that was exactly how our house had been – minus the baked beans.

It was a situation that was often exasperated by my girlfriend, who since the mauling I had received from my mum, was not only stand-offish with my parents, but callous in her forthright opinion of them. I didn't know what the problem was – however, everyone else did, not least the young girl that was doing her damnedest to take control of me. This was something that my (step)dad had an opinion about.

"You let her treat you like shit," he told me. "You're cunt-struck."

My (step)dad may well have been talking about me, but the reality of it was, that he was sadly describing himself.

The relationship with my girlfriend should have ended after six or eight months, as it had run its course. The fact that it did not, was to create a whole host of problems. I felt that I was being made part-culpable for the situation at home by my (step)dad, which was something that made sure I was at my girlfriend's house much more than I was ever at home. In fact, I was just about living at 9 Chapel Lane throughout the late summer of 1982.

Johnny and Joyce Evans certainly didn't deserve what I was going to bring them, as in the main they were very nice people. It is fair to say that the latter had an inquisitive and opinionated nature, which was often fuelled by things that she picked during her work on the local authority's Home Help scheme up in Thurnscoe East. It was a job which brought her in contact with lots of different people – older people.

One of her clients that she looked after was a sixty-six-year-old woman at the top end of Deightonby Street by the name of Euphemia (Fee) Cowley, who had her two granddaughters living with her – Gail and Helen; the former who supposedly quite liked me and the latter who did not. Of why this was so, I couldn't really say, as I knew neither of them.

Mrs Cowley's husband, Andrew, had been a rope man at Hickleton Main before going to college and becoming an electrician, but at seventy-one years old, he had long since retired.

Joyce loved conversation and at times I couldn't get enough of it. There were other times that I thought her quite blunt in her appraisal and it seemed to be after visiting Mrs Cowley's house that she had begun inquiring about certain things that concerned me.

Joyce's youngest daughter, who was of course my girlfriend at the time, was an extremely testing young girl and often wound me up by frequently mentioning the events of her everyday life. Mainly, who fancied her, along with which lads had asked her out.

When I first met her, she was quite plain-Jane, but the fact that she had hooked up with me had made people very aware of who she was, and as such, she grew up far too quickly. I think she was quite friendly with Helen and it was here that things could have got relayed back to Joyce. I'll make no bones about it, Thurnscoe's East end was a proper little sewing circle.

The Feasts were a huge East end family, many of whom worked underground at Hickleton Main.

There were also many of them a similar age that I knew quite well. Some like Don, Kevin and Frank, I liked – some like Stuart and John, I did not.

John was the third youngest child of Percy and Ann Feast (nee Cliff) and was part of a family that lived in one of the latter odd-numbered properties on Stuart Street. I knew who he was through him being Kevin and Cathy's younger brother. Kevin was quite a big strapping lad with a great sense of humour who ended up being an Overman at Goldthorpe Colliery, whilst Cathy was a very friendly girl a bit older than me, who I often got confused with another Cathy (Smith) that had worked in Irene Ratcliffe's busy Newsagents close to the entrance to the Pit Baths on Lidget Lane.

My girlfriend had told me that John often tried touching her up. Groping her.

Had he? No idea. I just went by what I had been told.

Nowadays, if someone did something like that it would be considered extremely bad, culminating in a charge and conviction followed by several years on the sex register. However, back then it was accepted as the norm and the only way to deal with it was the issue of a threat.

"Tell the bastard, if I see him, I'll kick his head in," is basically what I said.

She obviously did and as I saw him pass on the bus a few days later he gave me the two-fingered salute and called me a wanker through the window. All good fun.

A week or so later when I had been coming off day shift, I collared him outside his house. I had been still caked up with coal dust around my eyes, whilst he was in James Dean-mode and casually puffing at a cigarette. I gave him a finger in the face and issued him a threat which was duly reciprocated by him blowing smoke in my face. I then hit him full-on with the motherfucker of all head butts, which not only knocked out a few of his front teeth but had blood everywhere.

There is, however, a bit of a pattern here.

I recently had a conversation with the Deputy Editor of the *Rotherham Advertiser* – a lady by the name of Adele Forrest, after I had dropped on an article which mentioned Percy Feast's younger brother, David. He had been standing trial over at Sheffield Crown Court for historical sex offences. David had been accused of raping a young relative that he used to babysit as a teenager during the 1970s.

"He got ten years," Adele told me.

David Feast had married Lorraine Ward in 1977 and between them had had two children – Lorraine Andrea (b. 1980) and Tracey Louise (b. 1981) and prior to his conviction had been living at 28 Common Road, Thurnscoe.

"He was found guilty of two counts of rape and four of indecent assault against a girl under the age of ten, when he was a teenager," she added. "The girl's parents testified that they knew about the allegations in the 1970s and 1980s, but there was an agreement within the family not to go to the police."

At home my (step)dad was going mental. The police had been up at the house wanting to arrest me on a charge of grievous bodily harm. I shrugged it off as nothing and stayed at my girlfriends until the heat died down. At work, however, it was a different thing all together. As I have already intimated, the Feasts were a big family that stuck together and whilst getting showered in the Pit Baths I was pointed out by Frank to John's father. "That's him."

I was crowded and jostled a bit, but nothing really happened, although Frank did threaten to give me a good hiding.

It hadn't been the first time I'd knocked someone's teeth out and it wouldn't be the last.

Just a couple of years earlier, some kid from off The Spike had been doing the same and giving me the exact same salute from a bus… and rather strangely in the exact same place as John had… a weird one, that?

Brian Wood may have been part of Thurnscoe's Class of 1981, but he was a kid that I didn't know that well.

In the last year of school, I had been hanging around with Steve Wharton and Billy Coulson quite a bit, which got me into all sorts of scrapes, not at least with the police. I remember telling Steve about this kid *flagging* me and inquired about him. All I got back, was that he was big.

It was quite an understatement. He was fucking massive.

I remember us walking through Thurnscoe's derelict Old Hall and towards its entrance onto High Street during early 1980 and of three lads coming towards us, one of which was Brian.

I must have caught him with one hell of a punch as not only did he hit the deck I also knocked out both his two front teeth.

I bumped into John Feast at my sister's wedding reception in the Halfway Hotel some years later and I must admit – he had turned into a great lad and I totally enjoyed his company. Brian, however, hadn't been quite as receptive when I saw him in later life. An "Uh" was as much as he grunted.

All this stuff however, had been getting exaggerated all out of proportion and continually being relayed to Joyce. "Mrs Cowley said…" began to become part of every conversation that I was privy to.

At home, my (step)dad was seeing how I was dealing with things and it drove him to despair – or that is what I thought at the time. Towards the back end of 1982 he was unhappy and drinking heavily. My mum was always out, and my younger sister and brother were getting severely neglected. As for me, I was feeding myself from either the fish and chip shop or around at Johnny and Joyce's.

What I didn't realise at the time is that my (step)dad hadn't been mad at me with how I was conducting my life, he had been mad with himself.

"Your mam's having an affair with the manager at the sewing factory," explained my girlfriend.

She was, and everyone knew about it, including my (step)dad.

As for me, I had been oblivious.

After my mum offloaded the fish and chip shop in Worsbrough Dale, she got a job as a machinist at the English Rose, which as I've already stated, was a sewing factory that was situated in the shadow of the railway embankment that once carried the old Wath Branch Line across the bottom of Highgate Lane. They knocked out goods to St Michael – the old Marks & Spencer brand, and it was here that she had been fast-tracked to supervisor.

I would not be lying in saying that I felt that everyone was talking about me, not at least my girlfriend's mum and dad.

Miners generally worked a three-shift pattern and as they tended to live in close proximity to one another, affairs were nothing new – especially in Thurnscoe, Goldthorpe and Bolton-on-Dearne.

When we first moved onto Lancaster Street in early 1977, we had had completely different next-door neighbours.

Gerry Crossland was a dark-haired man of Romany appearance who was employed at Hickleton Main as a shaft man / blacksmith. He had come over from the Bradford area with his wife. She was a Thurnscoe girl by the name of Kathleen (nee Probyn), who he had married in 1965. They along with their first-born child Beverley (b. 1967) had moved into the house at 49 Lancaster Street and had had a further two children – Gary (b. 1970) and Nigel (b. 1973).

I thought them an extremely lovely family, especially their kids. I still have fond memories of the youngest lad, with his blond curly hair and snotty nose running around the front garden whilst still in his nappy. Kath would sadly walk out on her husband, shortly after we moved up there, taking all three children with her. For months after, I would often look out of my bedroom window and into Gerry's rapidly overgrowing back garden, which had a five-speed Raleigh Javelin racing bike locked to one of the two concrete poles that held a washing line and which was sadly rusting away. His wife had left him for another man – however, that story certainly didn't end there.

At just over five and a half feet tall, Gerry hardly cut a dashing figure, but there is another old and well-worn cliché in that there is someone out there for everyone. Suddenly, there was activity coming from next door. You could hear hammering and drilling going on. It hadn't been a one-off either – it was happening on a regular basis. When I was first invited into their house it appeared dirty and unkempt. I had seen much worse, but all the same, it hadn't been the cleanest of places. Gerry, however, was doing a full re-fit of what would be his rather sophisticated bachelor pad – brass plates on the wall et al.

The next thing I know is that my (step)dad was hanging out my younger brother's bedroom window late one night, whilst in heavy dialogue some man in the street. "Look, pal, just pack it in and go home," he said.

"That bastard has got my wife in there," the guy shouted up.

Bill Cooper is someone that I will get on to in a bit. For now, he had married a two-time divorcee by the name Rita Chamberlain (nee Cooper), who had been the femme fatale that had been tucked up in Gerry's love nest. Back then, it had appeared quite a heart-wrenching scene but knowing what I know now, Rita certainly had her reasons.

As for Gerry and Rita – they married in 1979 and we had been invited to their wedding reception in The Fairway.

What could be confusing is that Rita's maiden name had also been Cooper, although a totally different family to her husband. She was in fact, the younger sister of George (Judd) – a no-nonsense kind of bloke whose presence was always well-noted. He didn't say a lot, but you always knew he was there.

That night at their wedding I witnessed something that has always stayed with me. Earlier in the evening I recall walking down to the foot of Lancaster Street and seeing Judd and his family – all who had lived on the northern arm of Brunswick Street, standing outside the pub waiting for his newly married sister and her husband to arrive. It would be inside, however, where I would see a different side to Judd.

Rita had asked the DJ on stage for a particular song to be played and just prior to him flipping the disc she cajoled her very laid-back, albeit reluctant big brother, into having a dance with her. If you have ever seen the scene from within Quentin Tarantino's 1994 film *Pulp Fiction*, where Uma Thurman's Mia gets Vincent Vega up to dance, you wouldn't be that far away. However, whereas the fictional characters were coolly twisting away to a rather sedate Chuck Berry number, the real deal did not and set about bopping and jiving to Elvis Presley's *Hound Dog*. And you want to know something? Never had I seen anything like it. They were both fucking brilliant.

Things came to a head in the run up to Christmas 1982, which was a truly lousy time in my life.

One Sunday morning I got up to go out around 11.30 a.m. and my mum kicked off.

Even though I had just turned eighteen, had started working shifts and recently had my board upped to £15 (£58, circa 2020) per week, my mum still expected me to help with the housework. I made my bed, kept my bedroom tidy and cleaned up after myself. In short, I was quite a clean and well-turned-out kid. "I'm going out," I told her.

She slammed the front door shut and attacked me giving me a mauling like you wouldn't fucking believe. That was until I stopped it dead. I remember it as though it was yesterday. I had to pin her up against the wall beneath the electric box. She was clawing away, scratching my face, and screaming like some wild animal. I had seen her flip before, but never like this. She was out of control. Her eyes were the darkest of dark brown, going on black.

I released my grip to leave the house, which had been a huge mistake, as the next thing I knew I had some concrete ornamental pot that she had brought back from Torremolinos smashed around my head. This not only gave me a gaping wound but had blood streaming down my face.

My ten-year-old brother, who was one of the nicest little lads you could imagine had been watching all this unfold. I'd had this all my life, soon it would be his turn.

I went around to my girlfriend's house to get cleaned up and her mum couldn't believe what she saw. "What did you do, love?" shrugged Joyce.

I hadn't done a thing and I told her as much. My mum had a problem. As I have said, she was all about control and with me she had lost it. However, letting Joyce see my mum's handy work had been a mistake, as not only did she know about my mum knocking off – she now knew about the physical abuse I had suffered. Unbeknown to me, I was giving her bullets to fire.

Everyone has secrets, not at least old Mrs Cowley – but first, three stories, one trivial, the others not so.

Brunswick Street's lower numbered and southern leg had a huge mining family that lived in one of its houses.

Tom (Raz) Bradley was the grandson of Ben Sims – the man who committed suicide by self-mutilation in September 1941 and had married a girl called Mary Roughley in 1959. Raz was a powerful and aggressive-looking miner made even more so, by his body being full of tattoos, whilst Mary was another archetypal miner's wife – an extremely chatty lady and full of gossip. I knew her quite well and assumed that she was a good friend of my girlfriend's mum's as she quite often called around – generally on a Sunday morning.

Joyce ran several of what were termed as *Clubs* – where people that she knew could buy goods on credit from the *Empire Stores* or *Great Universal* catalogues. At times, I was mesmerised, as she appeared to handle more money than a bookie, with one of her biggest and most trusted customers being her sister-in-law, Jean Roper (nee Moody). Jean was a lovely woman who also lived on Chapel Lane. She was the sister of Sheila Hopkinson and had married Joyce's elder brother Albert (Pop), and who like Joyce, also had two daughters – Sharon (b. 1961) and Sandra (b. 1965).

As for Mary, she and Raz had six kids – Paul (b. 1960), Carol (b. 1961), Steve (b. 1963) who I mentioned earlier, Graham (b. 1964), Tina (b. 1965) and Nigel (b. 1967).

I knew them all – however, it would be quite right of me to say that it was the four younger ones that I knew the best, especially Nigel, as for a time he had been my sister's long-standing boyfriend after she split from her husband circa 2002.

The Bradley's house on Brunswick Street – just like my girlfriends, linked on to a couple of others, to form a terrace along with a long dark ginnel, that always possessed the heavy smell of Chloroxylenol. That smell of Jeyes fluid along with the deep fishpond around the rear of the house, which housed a huge Jack Pike are the main memories that I have.

During 1982, the eldest son Paul – who I recall being a rope man at the pit – married a girl from Thurnscoe Bridge Lane by the name of Julie Brockhurst. She was the elder sister of Chris, a lad with dark curly hair, who was both part of Thurnscoe's Class of 1981 and an earlier of its intake of lads that had started at Hickleton Main a few months before me.

Both children were the product of Horace and Joyce (nee Simmonds). Horace was in his mid-to-late fifties at the time and worked in the pit baths. His elder brother was Thomas (Tom) Brockhurst who had been one of seven men who had been trapped underground on 10 October 1960, following a huge roof fall in the Parkgate seam.

Paul and Julie would come to live next door-but-one to his parents. Their house, however, would soon become detached, as a subterranean watercourse that ran beneath several properties on its way down to Thurnscoe Dike, had been causing a huge amount of subsidence.

Late one night, I recall walking past their house and there had been a huge argument between the two, so much so, you could hear it out on the street. "Put that fucking poker down," screamed Julie. "Who do you think you are – Superman?"

I think she was vastly over-egging it, but all the same, out on the street you had no idea what the consequences would be inside. He obviously had a metal implement in his hand. So, what was he going to do – hit her with it?

Andrew and Fee Cowley (nee Davison) married in 1935 and had set up home together at 15 King Street, which was one of the first streets to be built in Thurnscoe's East end and which is one that has some truly horrible history. An example: On 30 September 1906, a posse had gone in search of a forty-five-year-old miner from Staffordshire by the name of George Boast. He had raped an eight-year old girl by the name of Ada Etchells, who lived with her parents at No 34.

As for the Cowleys, they would suffer some horrendous misfortune, losing three of their four children in tragic circumstances.

Their second born child, Robert died on 8 January 1944 in Mexborough Hospital, aged three and a half. He had suffered with haemophilia since birth.

On 22 April 1966, their youngest son, John, who had been an apprentice electrician with the Yorkshire Electricity Board, died following a fatal collision on his motorcycle whilst travelling between Thurnscoe and Swinton. His bike was hit by a Mini; the sixteen-year-old suffering horrendous injuries fracturing both femurs and wrists as well as the base of his skull. Consultant Pathologist, Dr G.D. Powell explained at the coroner's inquest that he had also experienced multiple lacerations to his head and body and that his death had ultimately been caused by shock and haemorrhage.

Unfortunately, both tragedies would be usurped when their daughter's life was abruptly ended on 22 August 1968.

Just over three years earlier on the Saturday afternoon of 24 July at St Hilda's Church – twenty-three-year-old Sylvia Cowley married into one of the several sets of Hardman families that lived in Thurnscoe's East end – this being twenty-eight-year-old Ronald (Ron), the son of Herbert and Gertrude (nee Mason).

The Rev Ken Emerson conducted the ceremony on what had started off a sunny day but which after a thunderous crack in the sky, forced the heavens to open with heavy rain forcing everyone inside. Maybe, that was okay as some of the men had one eye on the sport as England had been playing South Africa in the First Test at Lord's. The day before, Geoff Boycott had had to weather a vicious and rather unfriendly onslaught from the Springboks' fast-bowler Peter Pollock and was lucky not to have been both cleaned bowled and caught out with just eight runs on the clock. That morning, however – was a new day, he had started at the crease at eleven not out. Unfortunately, he didn't last long and was caught by Eddie Barlow after a further twenty runs.

In the news, the trial of Henry Burgess had been creating huge interest. In a jealous fit of rage, the spurned forty-one-year-old police sergeant and father-of-three, had murdered his twenty-three-year-old former girlfriend Veronica Baker. This was after he had shot both her parents.

It was also the weekend Great Britain's former World Light Heavyweight Champion Freddie Mills was found dead in the back seat of his car with a bullet through his eye.

It was an ominous start to a marriage that was always doomed to fail.

Sylvia had been born and raised at 4 Briton Street – a property which her parents vacated shortly after their daughter's death, leaving my adopted uncle and auntie, Barry and Carol Oldfield, to move into it in 1970.

Ron and Sylvia had a ten-week old son and two daughters – aged one and two years old respectively and who I have already mentioned – these had been the ones that at the time had been living with their grandmother, Mrs Cowley – Gail and Helen.

There was a reason behind this. Their father was in prison. He had been convicted of killing their mother.

I was told that Ron, like most of the lads at that time, had started work at Hickleton Main, although I don't have any documentation to support this. I knew he had grown up at properties at 5 Norman Street and 68 Brunswick Street and that he had been a bus conductor before becoming a full-time Agent for the Refuge Assurance Company – a job which he had packed in due to it getting him down.

How that was so, I really haven't a clue, as his next move totally contradicted that.

On 21 February 1964, he took over from the previous landlord Eric Jarvis and was handed the keys as licensee to Thurnscoe's Whinwood Hotel – the large, red-bricked building that for over sixty years would proudly sit on Merrill Road.

According to reports, the pair had been a couple three or four years before they married and whilst living together it had been said they had a relatively happy marriage. All I can say regarding that statement is that nobody – and I mean nobody, really knows what goes on behind closed doors.

On the Wednesday night of 21 August 1968, there had been Bingo on at The Docket and Ron and Sylvia had had a night off from the pub – leaving the running of the bar in the capable hands of Sylvia's mother and father.

They had been sitting most of the night with forty-seven-year-old Joe Simpson of 95 Merrill Road – who had been one of Ron and Sylvia's teachers up at Thurnscoe Hill, whilst in the upstairs flat of the Whinwood Hotel, two teenage babysitters had been anticipating watching the latest twists on *Coronation Street* along with the *Enemy at the Gates* episode of *Dad's Army*. The TV viewing for that night, however, had been heavily disrupted by the day's events and the Soviet Union's (Warsaw Pact) invasion of Czechoslovakia took precedence, being flashed across the UK's TV screens all throughout the night.

On Ron and Sylvia getting back to The Whinwood an argument ensued. According to Sylvia's father – there certainly didn't appear to be any friction between the two – however, that is not to say there wasn't any. Ron's in-laws left the premises at 11.40 p.m. and just over one hour later the police were on site – with Ron being arrested for the murder of his wife.

Now, what happened in that window of time may never be known. What is, is that Sylvia's husband had emptied one of the twin-barrels of what was a US-manufactured twelve-gauge shotgun into her face at point-plank range, literally blowing her head clean off.

"It was an accident," thirty-one-year-old Ron told the police. "I had been accusing her of going with other men, knowing it wasn't true. I got the gun to make me look big. It was purely accidental."

"There are only two people that know exactly what happened, and one of them is dead."

Those chilling words came from Audrey Nelson (nee Mason) of 4 Pangbourne Road – an innocuous property whose rear garden once backed onto the Whinwood Hotel, and who was a relation of the Hardman's. Audrey was very old school and one who pulled few punches – especially regarding Ron. "He is nothing but a coward."

Audrey died on New Year's Day 1996, and in the twenty-eight years following Sylvia's death, she never let her guard down in her contempt of the man.

"Ron Hardman was my dad's cousin," said Audrey's granddaughter, Gwen(da) Cole (nee Nelson), who was also one of the girls that I had grown up with whilst in Houghton Road Infants. "After the incident, it split the family in two – some taking Ron's side and some, Sylvia's."

The trial at Sheffield Assizes on 4 November 1968 was presided over by Justice Sebag Shaw QC whilst Peter Taylor QC was Crown Prosecutor and Henry Scott QC defended.

Justice Shaw had been Junior Counsel on the failed defence of Ruth Ellis in 1955 – who was of course the last woman to be hanged in the UK and had more recently, presided over the trial of a twenty-eight-year old man who had been charged with a murder up in Thurnscoe East.

Hubert Adams married a lady by the name of Matilda Tout in 1932 and lived at 31 Nora Street, Goldthorpe before moving to 75 Briton Street sometime during the war.

The couple had a son in early-1940 – Raymond (Ray), who would grow up in Thurnscoe's East end – one of his best friends being a lad in the same year at school by the name of Joseph (Joe) McHugh.

Whereas Ray's life took a similar path to most Thurnscoe lads – leaving school, going into the pits and getting married – his best friends did not.

Joe, whose father worked in the rips at Dearne Valley Colliery in Little Houghton, had signed on with the 16th/5th The Queen's Royal Lancers in 1956. At just sixteen years of age he had left the village for a career in the military, firstly becoming a Bandsman and even attending a twelve-month course at the Royal Military School of Music in Twickenham. Outside of being stationed at the Wathwith Camp up at Catterick Garrison, his eight-year stint involved postings in Sennalager and Osnabrück in Germany and along with its merging with the 12th Infantry Brigade, eventually being deployed to the dangerous situation that had developed over in Aden.

After being discharged, Joe came back to the reality of Thurnscoe, but as is generally the case, those that go away to experience different things, think that the experience gained, racks up the points on life's board – in that when you get back, you are seen as somewhat special. It is something that I have seen time and time again, a great example being my wife's relations when visiting from Australia. They hardly expect the key to the city – just to be looked up to as *we have done it all and you are still here*. Unfortunately, for them that is, that is rarely the case.

"We were all from the ratholes of England and we couldn't wait to get back," said Harry H Corbett's alter ego, regarding his return from the Army in the *Desperate Hours* episode of *Steptoe and Son* that had aired at 9.35 p.m. on Monday 3 April 1972.

Joe's come *down to earth moment* had been a million miles from band stand and hobnobbing it with the likes of Colonel Denis Douglas Pilkington Smyly and his pretty wife, the Honourable Dorothy Margaret Berry – the third daughter of Lord Buckland of Bwlch. He landed in Thurnscoe and ended up with a job as the Assistant Caretaker up at the school.

Meanwhile, Ray had to some extent moved on and seemingly married well.

On 28 January 1961, Ray had tied the knot at Clayton and Frickley's All Saints Church with a twenty-one-year-old girl by the name of Eileen Fox – who lived with her parents in one of the quaint cottages on Clayton's Chapel Hill.

Although still a miner, he had left Thurnscoe and was living in the more salubrious surroundings of Clayton – in a house off Tan Pit Lane at Tea Pot Corner, with his wife and two sons. And this was at a time when much of Thurnscoe still had to nip out into the yard for a shit.

As for Joe – he had been back lodging with his parents in Thurnscoe.

Reading between the lines, Joe wanted what Ray had. Why not? He reckoned he had earned it.

The three-shift pattern that miners had forced upon them, played into the hands of the nine-to-five existence of Joe and he made a play for Ray's wife, which the court heard had been duly reciprocated.

Unlike the case of John Ellis and Jack Caunt, Ray Adams was a person that refused to take any shit.

It was perhaps a chip off the old block. His father, Hubert, was as confrontational as confrontational could be and on several occasions, he had let his temper get the better of him, not at least at work. On 4 January 1934, he beat up an Official by the name of Clarence Simmonds at Goldthorpe Colliery and on 4 November 1941 and absolutely leathered forty-one-year-old Joseph Thorlby – the Head of the Lamp Room at Hickleton Main, knocking out several teeth in the process.

On 29 August 1968, things came to a head when Ray found out that Joe had been having an affair with his wife and using a twelve-gauge, gunned him down on the pavement outside Joe's home at 13 Windsor Street. The blow from the shotgun killed him instantly.

Exactly two months later the jury at Sheffield Assizes found him not guilty of murder – but guilty of manslaughter.

Justice Shaw was extremely lenient in his sentencing and stated: "This is a very special case in every sense."

He handed Ray Adams a two-year suspended sentence, meaning that he walked out of the court a free man.

A crime of Passion? Yes. Extenuating circumstances? Yes.

It was also premeditated in that he went to his home armed with a gun and shot him through the heart. For me it was never manslaughter, but murder in that he meant to do it.

The justice system is heavily flawed – that is for sure.

On 23 November 1960, William Henry Siddons of 62 Elm Road, Mexborough was sentenced to six months imprisonment at Sheffield Assizes by Justice Marshall.

His defence barrister Rudolph Lyons QC had worked out some quid pro quo deal with the Crown Prosecution to plead guilty to a revamped charge of unlawful wounding.

His wife, Kathleen (nee Reynolds) had been having an affair with a man by the name of John Ingham, who after he caught him in the act – and believe me – he really did, loaded up his twelve-gauge and chased him out into the yard. As Ingham, a father of five, vaulted over the back fence, William aimed at him and fired, part of the blast hitting the galloping lothario in the side of the head.

"There is considerable sympathy for you," said the judge on sentencing him. "No one in the court could feel other than a great contempt for Ingham who has violated the sanctity of your matrimonial circle."

So, why did he get six months and McHugh walk free? It just doesn't add up.

Walking into Crown Court is one thing, walking out is another. You just never know what is going to happen. I suppose Ron Hardman felt the same but had to have been encouraged by the lenience show by the judge – the case of Ray Adams being just the tip of the iceberg when it came to his compassion.

Straight after Hardman's trial, Justice Shaw was drafted in as one of the three appeal judges on the alleged mistrial of the Cannock Chase Child Murderer, Raymond Morris – a man who was nothing short of a fucking animal. After an intense manhunt, which was said to have usurped that of the Moors Murderers, he received a life sentence. This was for the murder and rape of three children – Margaret Reynolds and Joy Tift aged six and five in October 1966 and seven-year old Christine Darby in August 1967.

"Mr and Mrs Cowley left the Whinwood Hotel and with no sign of friction between their daughter and son-in-law and within an hour she was dead, having received the most shattering wounds to her head," explained Peter Taylor QC in his opening statement.

"My gran said that her head was all over the bedroom," said Gwen Cole.

At 12.30 a.m. a telephone call came into Goldthorpe Police Station: "Send someone straight away please, I have just shot my wife with a shotgun. Please hurry."

A similar call was repeated ten minutes later. "Have you sent anyone yet? The kids are here. It was an accident."

The police arrived on site at 12.45 a.m. and Ron Hardman met them at the door. "It was an accident. She's dead. We had a bit of an argument. I pushed her and then took the gun off the top of the wardrobe. It just went off."

The police found Sylvia Hardman lying on the floor of the bedroom in her night clothes with the gun on the floor nearby. Her body was laid in a pool of blood, her face unrecognisable and the room splattered with evidence of the terrible force of the discharge of the gun.

Gwen had been spot-on.

According to the Pathologist Dr Alan Usher, the gun had been discharged at a range of less than twelve inches, meaning that Ron Hardman literally had the gun stuck in her face.

He had told the police: "I didn't know it was loaded. I have never fired live rounds in it only half-cartridges – blanks. I must have pulled the trigger."

He had indeed.

126

Ron Hardman was taken to Goldthorpe Police Station to be questioned and made a voluntary, albeit well-thought-out, statement.

"There are only two people that knows exactly what happened and one of them was dead."

Please remember those words, as in a murder investigation such as this, the police hear from one side, and one side only. All they had to rely on was factual evidence and forensics and Ron – well, he never denied killing his wife, he just said that he never meant it.

"On returning to the Whinwood I said to the wife that I would carry the money from the tills along with her up to the flat and she told me that I 'wasn't big enough'. I told her to get some other man, then, and she said. 'There is no one else for me'."

I have trawled through hundreds of court depositions and news reports on murderers, rapists and paedophiles and one thing that always stands out is the macho masking of diffidence within their statements. The *Me Factor* if you like: "<u>There is no one else for me.</u>"

"Me, being jealous, I wouldn't let the matter drop. I had been accusing her of going with other men, knowing that it wasn't true. I got the gun to make me look big."

However, to overwrite what he had just said he went with the *Me Factor* again.

"She was waiting for me in the big Lounge bar when I said that I'd carry her upstairs. By saying that 'I wasn't big enough' she meant that I had put on a bit of weight," he explained. "I told her if I wasn't big enough for her to get another bloke. She told me not to be so silly – '<u>you are the only one that matters to me</u>'."

Ron Hardman stated that he had just been in a sulky mood and that he ended up on the settee.

"A few minutes later, she told me that if I didn't come to bed with her, now, that I would never get in bed with her again. I sat on the settee another few minutes. We were just niggling each other. It was just a silly row. I then went into the bedroom and she was lying in bed. I told her that if I can't get into my bed, then nobody will. I was in between the bed and the wardrobe and told her – then, if that is the case I might as well shoot myself."

He then played that *Me factor* again.

"She told me not to be so silly and said that <u>she didn't mean anything like that</u>."

After describing the shooting of his wife, he rather conveniently became overcome with emotion. And why not – his whole life was at stake.

Whilst being cross-examined he described himself as being over-protective rather than jealous and denied being angry.

"In your statement, you did, however, mention that you were jealous a total of four times and this was a voluntary statement that you had written yourself," said Peter Taylor QC, prior to reading from the piece of paper. "You said: 'I would never have done it, only I was very jealous.'"

A lot of the defence was dependent on the firearm in that there had been a failure in the safety mechanism. The prosecution, however, weren't convinced. To fire the gun, someone had to pull the trigger.

If you have ever been part of a trial at Crown Court, you will know that the story the jury hears doesn't even scratch the surface of what really happened. Statements are both doctored and ripped apart, with the scales generally tipped in favour of the defendant. And why not? Innocent until proven guilty. Most Crown Court cases, however, do not involve an innocent mother of three having her head blown off with a shotgun.

Ron Hardman was sentenced to three years for the manslaughter of his wife.

The Crown Prosecutor, Peter Taylor QC didn't believe him nor did Det. Supt. Stanley Woolfenden.

So, was Ron Hardman lying? Well, he certainly wasn't telling the truth, that much is certain.

"I think he was having an affair and he wanted it to look like an accident," added Gwen Cole.

"We were never questioned by the police," said Irene Bridgen (nee Taylor).

Irene had one of the two babysitters in the Whinwood Hotel that night. The other one had been Ann Marie Peace – the fifteen-year-old daughter of Horace and Kathleen (nee Whittaker) of 3 Briton Square.

So, why should the police have been interested in speaking to the babysitters?

Maybe, because after getting in from The Docket, Ron had walked Ann Marie home and it had been that what the argument had really been about.

Hearsay? Circumstantial?

Not really. After his release from HMP Armley he ended up having three children with her: Nigel (b. 1973), Darren (b. 1974) and Wayne (b. 1977).

Ron died in the spring of 1990, aged fifty-three.

What is strange is that Ann Marie married Clifford Hudson in 1994 – whose younger brother Steven had been the subject of rather hateful accusations from a section of his wife's family and her friends following her untimely death on Sunday 13 June 2012.

The accusations certainly weren't without foundation – however, hearsay carries little weight outside of the facts.

Hudson – extremely aggressive in nature, possessed a history of violence and was a man very typical of a latter-day mining contractor, which was the job in which he was employed.

Steven Hudson had married Jean Goldthorpe at Barnsley Town Hall on Wednesday 9 September 1987.

It was his second marriage. He had previously been married to Elaine Marie Jowett in 1972 with whom he had a daughter by the name of Donna a year later.

As for Jean – she was an extraordinarily beautiful lady with a nice demeanour who had two pretty daughters – Marie, aged eight and Jayne, five. The two girls were from a previous common-law relationship with Garry Weddell – the son of Roy and Kay (nee Greenoff) – a couple who had married in 1954 and for a time lived on Goldthorpe's northern terraces at 1 West Street.

The main facts are that Jean – a retired hairdresser, had collapsed in the rear garden of her home at 29 Marlborough Close, Thurnscoe and was rushed to Sheffield Hallamshire Hospital, where she sadly died.

The fact that there was no coroner's inquest, was highly irregular – especially, given the cause of death and both her medical and personal history.

I cannot cite medical negligence as I wasn't there – therefore, I must again stress, that I can only put over the facts.

According to thirty-three-year-old Dr Veejay Bagga – Jean died of a subarachnoid haemorrhage – a life-threatening type of stroke caused by bleeding into the space surrounding the brain, which he stated was possibly brought on by a spontaneous rupture of a posterior communicating artery aneurism. I say possibly, as back then – and although Dr Bagga had got his PhD Neuroscience in 2005, he had only been in Sheffield ten months – and as a Medical Locum, which is a person who temporarily fulfils the duties of another. In his words he was a "Neurosurgical Trainee with an interest in paediatric neurosurgery, neuro-oncology and spinal neurosurgery."

You want another fact? Then that comes from the General Medical Council's (GMC) Chief Executive, Niall Dickson who stated: "Locum work is risky in the sense that the doctor may not know enough about the hospital where he or she is working. It is also risky in the sense that they may be brought in when the team is under considerable pressure – therefore, it is an area where we have some concerns."

Figures from the GMC showed that during the period from 2011 to 2013, locums working in the acute sector – mainly in district hospitals, were attracting almost twice as many complaints as staff doctors. That amounted to more than 250 complaints each year. The main fact being that the majority of those complaints resulted in formal investigations.

Was this one?

That is a question I do not know the answer to – however, you don't need to be a medical expert to know that the main cause of a subarachnoid haemorrhage is without doubt, head trauma.

So, was that the case here?

You will have to draw your own conclusions, however – the word *Trainee* does not inspire me with confidence.

The alarm bells should have sounded on checking Jean's medical records – however, they didn't. My thoughts are – and that is all they are, is they were **not** checked.

Jean's medical history contained a previous case of head trauma. She had been hospitalised for a considerable time – a fact which would have certainly been logged in her medical records. She took several blows to the head – the ferocity of which had been so severe, the surgeons struggled to quell the bleeding. According to family and friends, Jean had been extremely ill.

"He was always hitting her," said her cousin, Pat Whitmore (nee Rich). "We begged her to stay away from him, but she wouldn't."

"He is nothing but a thug," added one of her friends, Sheila Jow (nee Sims). "One night he beat her so badly – that if neighbours hadn't called the emergency services, she wouldn't have made it."

"When she died, we all blamed him," added Pat.

All the signs were synonymous with a physical abusive relationship and this included what is nowadays termed as *gaslighting*. This is a form of psychological manipulation in which the abuser covertly sows seeds of doubt making the victim question their own memory, perception, or judgment using a tactic of denial, misdirection, contradiction, and misinformation in his attempt to destabilize the victim and delegitimize their beliefs. In South Yorkshire, the term is *playing them*.

"He brainwashed her into thinking that she was always at fault," said Sheila.

Gaslighting in a nutshell.

The facts were that she had a medical history to suggest that in the past she had suffered extreme physical abuse in the home, some of which had resulted in her being hospitalised.

It is easy to listen to gossip whether true or malicious – however, facts don't lie.

Jean was badly let down and another failure of the system.

Proving beyond a reasonable doubt, the connection between an assault and a subsequent death can be difficult, especially if the period of time between these events is lengthy. And I have to hold my hand up, without those records I do not know what the timeframe was between the last assault and Jean's tragic death. I seem to recall that I was once told that it is two years, but that may not be entirely correct.

"Every family has their problems," explained Jean's youngest daughter, Jayne.

Being brought up around violence, I can totally appreciate that statement, but not every mum dies. There has to be accountability and in this case there was none.

There has been a similar situation in Thurnscoe, before – but it was hardly a domestic.

On 1 September 2004, an altercation occurred at the top of John Street during a kickabout with a football. Thirty-year-old Shane Hart took exception to something that had gone down and headbutted a near-neighbour, which fractured his skull.

Thirty-two-year-old Wayne Jose was admitted to Barnsley hospital but released after two days. In fact, the assault wasn't even reported to the police. Unfortunately, he had to be readmitted on 27 January 2005 following a bout of headaches and died the next day – the post-mortem revealing that it had indeed been due to the head injury. Doctors had diagnosed an abscess on his brain, which had resulted from the fractured skull and he died of meningitis.

Shane was initially charged with murder but pleaded guilty to a lesser charge of manslaughter and was sentenced by Judge Alan Goldsack QC to three years.

The period in between the attack and death was nearly five months.

The tragedy, however – was placed firmly at the feet of both the police and the hospital.

Det. Supt. Rob Haworth who headed the investigation said: "There was an initial police investigation and perhaps it was not as thorough as it should have been."

Shane's defence counsel Simon Bourne-Arton QC added: "It was not a premeditated attack although the defendant has to accept his action in part caused the death, but had the appropriate treatment been given to Mr Jose in hospital, in all probability death would not have occurred and he would not have faced this charge of manslaughter."

Although completely different, there were similarities.

Regardless of the timeframe, Jean's family ought to immediately have got a good criminal solicitor involved. They could have requested witness statements, pulled both Jean's medical records and Hudson's criminal convictions from the National Police Computer (NPC) and possibly through a barrister presented it to South Yorkshire Police's Criminal Investigation Department. Statements are the secondary evidence to link the primary – that of facts. A couple of tenacious detectives could have easily added weight to this and if the timeframe was conducive, presented a possible case of manslaughter to the CPS. Sadly, that bird has flown.

To travel from Thurnscoe to Barnsley, however – you do not necessarily need to use the 226. In life, there are always other options.

Back at home, my (step)dad was anything but pleased with how I had spoken to my mum, especially as I'd more than inferred that I knew she was having an affair.

"You're a fucking lousy mother and an even lousier wife," I had told her when I'd had her pinned up against the wall. "You're a fucking disgrace."

He should have dealt with it there and then, but he didn't. He just didn't know how to.

I wanted my (step)dad to shout and scream at me, so we could get it out in the open. His way of dealing with it was to go down to The Fairway and drink it away, which is the worst thing anyone could do. Drinking doesn't solve problems – if anything, it helps escalate them, as I would soon find out.

I was never a drinker and as a rule, didn't go out to pubs – and if I did, I had to be literally dragged there.

My (step)dad saw my girlfriend as someone who made me miserable. "You're a great catch," he said. "You have a job. You don't drink. You don't smoke. And you don't gamble. Why don't you piss her off and get yourself someone else?"

In my mind, taking tips about life from my (step)dad appeared as productive as sticking my head in a gas oven.

As it was the run up to Christmas, most people were in a festive mood and I had been continually badgered about going to the pub, with The Fairway, being the most convenient. I can still remember the songs that kept on being overplayed on the jukebox, and even when I hear them now, it takes me back to being in the lounge of the pub at that particular time. Boy George's *Do You Really Want to Hurt Me?* Tears for Fears' *Mad World*, The Human League's *Mirror Man* and Eddy Grant's *I Don't Want to Dance*. It was a truly miserable time for me.

I didn't have a lot to drink maybe four or five pints of lager – but with me it was a mistake. I should have gone home but I didn't. I took my girlfriend home and went in for a coffee. Johnny and Joyce had been in the Coronation WMC and had come in around the same time.

I loved both her parents and looking back, all they had ever been was nice to me – however, if Joyce had something on her mind then it had to be said. "I saw your mam out earlier but there was no way I was talking to her," she quipped. "I think it's shocking how she's carrying on. She ought to be ashamed of herself."

It didn't end there as Joyce was always a woman who had plenty to say and just as she was about to slag off my mum any further, I kicked back.

"Who the fuck do you think you're talking about?"

I didn't mind expressing an opinion about my mum, but I certainly didn't like anyone else talking about her.

She was taken aback.

"I'm not having you talking to her like that," shouted Johnny, as he got up and pointed in my face.

There was a few more points in the face from him before I cut him dead. I hit him with a head butt and broke his palate and a few teeth. A commotion ensued whereby I was attacked by my girlfriend's elder sister who was wielding a carving knife, whilst the next-door neighbour Graham Evans (no relation) got involved. It was a fucking mess.

I have very few regrets in life – however, this, it is fair to say, would be one of them. Johnny was an extremely nice guy. He certainly didn't deserve me. Neither of them did.

I went home and told my mum and (step)dad both what had been said and what had happened. I got thrown out of the house – not physically, just told to go. My (step)dad just couldn't handle it. "And don't be going down to my mam's," he snapped.

My grandma Ellis would have been distraught if she had known what had been going on, therefore that would have been the last place I would have gone.

I remember being huddled up in one of the entrances of Thurnscoe Hill Infants School absolutely freezing. I had nowhere to go.

Although the money was never great, work was a great outlet and I will give Johnny his due – he never said a thing regarding the incident, although it was obviously seen as the conclusion of my relationship with his daughter. By me that is, not by her.

I was trouble and put in the wrong environment, I was even more so.

Col Hunter said in later life, "You were always an angry kid, J."

He knew me as well as anyone and was right, I was. I possessed some of the same horrible characteristics that my mum had. I apologised to Johnny. I was out of order and I needed to tell him that regardless of what he thought of me.

I managed to get back in at home by the skin of my teeth only to leave on the New Year's Day of 1983. My (step)dad had been drinking in The Fairway and had come home drunk and punched me in the face and was it not for the fact that my mum came racing into the room and put a carving knife to my throat, it would have ended far worse than it did. One of the easiest things in the world is to turn over a drunk. Absolutely nothing had been said. My (step)dad was angry, frustrated and just fancied belting me.

It is hard to gauge how he must have been feeling as what he was going through at the time is something that I have thankfully never had to deal with. Instead of him dealing with the problem he was blanking it out; numbing the pain through drinking and him seeing me, just made things real again. He knew that I knew.

I will fast-forward to 24 March 1990 – which was the only the second time my (step)dad ever poured his heart out to me. His mother, my grandma Ellis, had died. It was the only time that my wife has ever seen me drop to my knees. I was distraught. My grandma was the most selfless woman that I had ever met and ranks up there with the very best.

My mum, all harassed and bothered had been out at work but had returned home in a foul mood. The inconvenience of my grandma's funeral had messed up her day. If it had been up to her she would have turned up at Ardsley Crematorium in her work clothes – if she would have even turned up at all. I recall her grizzling at the fact as she came down the tight staircase at 51 Lancaster Street after a quick change of clothes. My dad was in pieces, my mum hard faced. If ever there had been a time where two totally contrasting emotions between my mum and (step)dad could be seen, it was on that day. She just didn't want to be there. It was disgusting.

Straight after the service she went back to work and sometime afterwards my (step)dad came around to our house. He cried his eyes out. "My mam's dead and she doesn't care," he said. "She should be here."

"Dad, why don't you leave her?" I told him. And you must remember, this is my mum I was talking about.

His reply?

"I love her."

My (step)dad was a truly lovely man whose only act of folly was that he married my mum. He would die just over five years later. My mum was always working, and he was always in The Fairway. Though excessive drinking he ended up with a prostate problem that hadn't been diagnosed quickly enough. It turned cancerous and spread. I was up at their house at 6.00 a.m. on Friday 28 April 1995 and holding him when he died.

His last words?

"Helen."

He was calling for my mum.

He just loved her. I suppose you can't knock a man for that.

Christmas 1981. My (step)dad and mum. In the kitchen of 51 Lancaster Street, Thurnscoe and (quite obviously) just back from The Fairway

12. I'm Mandy, Fly Me

There was an explosion in the distance and the whole backdrop of the northern dogleg of Derry Grove lit up. I had never seen the sky as bright. Although it was late at night, it could have easily been mistaken for a summer's evening or quite even dawn, with the deep orange sun rising, was it not for flames, leaping over twenty- maybe thirty-feet-high clutching, snatching, and clawing for their hit of oxygen. As two young lads ran towards me all I remember was that night sky looking like it was on fire.

I had been sat on the bonnet of a car outside No 30 – the former home of Shirley Amos (nee Peirson), a lady who had been killed onboard a boat in Gibraltar and her body thrown into the sea, whilst engaged in a phone call that had everything to do with my brother.

Then, just as the light began fading, I heard the whoosh of another explosion, which again lit up the night sky. The spectacle was surreal.

I only ever come back home for two reasons and that covered both.

The phone call had been from a Sheffield-based solicitor. My brother had been arrested on some charge of threatening behaviour and had been holed up in the police cells at Barnsley. The root cause, I was informed, had been his wife. That was certainly no surprise.

Fifteen minutes later I received another call. The police had arrested someone for the arson.

The person at the other end of the phone? Remember that property I mentioned at 2 Lancaster Street?

Neil Atkinson had been my brother's best friend since us moving to Thurnscoe East in 1977.

Unfortunately, during the early hours of New Year's Day 2011, that thirty-four-year friendship would end abruptly.

In that instance I received another telephone call from his wife. My brother and Neil had had some altercation, the reasoning of which is their story to tell and not mine. Neil had kicked our Joel in the head and fractured his eye socket. His face was a mess.

I told my brother that he had three choices.

He didn't want the police involved. The reasoning behind that was simple. A court case has the tendency to take over your life and I was certain that he didn't want to spend the next few days being interviewed by the police and for it to come out as to why Neil had leathered him.

His wife wanted me to go fuck Neil up, of which I refused point-blank. Stupid women do have the tendency to be over dramatic and this was a point in case. "I want the bastard shot," she told me.

They didn't have a pot to piss in, so raising the finance for that was certainly a non-starter.

Rather strangely, my other sister-in-law said something similar about her once-troublesome neighbour not too long ago. "Who's going to pay for it – you?" snapped my wife. "Because I'm not… and he is definitely not doing it."

Gangster wives, eh?

That problem was easily solved. I just threatened him via a third-party. Do you remember me also mentioning the property at 47 Hanover Street? Well, its owner was that third-party – my Mr Fixit and one of Thurnscoe's Kings of the Kerb.

As regards the injury to my brother, there was another way and on Neil phoning me I told him that he had to make it right.

I will be honest, although the lad had his idiosyncrasies, and of that there is no doubt, he was as straight as a die with me. He offered money to make things right. In my mind, he absolutely did the right thing.

133

"You have to give him a reasonable figure to aim for," I told his wife. "An end figure."

She didn't listen to a fucking word that I had said and after a month of him coughing up it became very hit and miss. I then had her on the phone to me every other week, pissing in my ears.

"You have to give him that end-figure otherwise he will just stop paying," I told her.

"He will pay until I say he stops paying," she snarled.

I was wasting my breath as is generally the case when you are dealing with some fucking moron who's acting like she is ten ton.

Neil did stop paying. I knew he would. I believe he had coughed up around £1,500.

As for me, I was merely used by his wife. I am only ever any good to them when they have shit that they cannot deal with.

As for the arson, it had been Neil's younger brother who had been arrested. The brief I had paid money to, got both him and my brother off.

I recall a couple of similar instances, one over at Fredrick Street, Goldthorpe and another on Harlington Street in Mexborough – the latter of which I again ended up sitting on the bonnet of my car – but this time outside Bolton Fisheries on Furlong Road, eating a fish patty and chips out of a polystyrene tray.

Exactly seventy years earlier and with Great Britain just ten months into a war that would last a further five years, German bombers regularly flew over the Dearne Valley, on their way to wreak mayhem and destruction on Sheffield, therefore blackouts were the norm.

The people who enforced these, were termed Local Defence Volunteers – the LDV, a body of men that were formed on 14 May 1940, after Secretary of State, Anthony Eden gave his famous radio broadcast: "You will not be paid, but you will receive a uniform and you will be armed."

Although, it didn't quite go like that, Goldthorpe Police Station was inundated with men wishing to join. And why not? To any autocratic power-crazy individual, the situation read like *Pennies from Heaven*. As for fifty-seven-year-old Henry Hough of 15 Edna Street, Bolton-on-Dearne – well, he had been one of the first beating down their door.

There were, however, certainly two sides to Henry.

On 7 September 1908, aged twenty-four, he had been injured in a horrific accident in Manvers Main whereby he suffered two broken legs and a broken arm. Five years before this, however, the nineteen-year-old been the subject of much local tittle-tattle – something which raised its head immediately after he had become the rather despotic Section Leader of Bolton-on-Dearne's LDV.

On the Sunday evening of 19 July 1903, he along with seventeen-year-old Herbert Garbutt had come across a sixteen-year-old by the name of Maria Adsetts. Although she had lived on a farm over in Billingley, her father had died, and she had had to seek employment in Bolton-on-Dearne as some domestic. From what had been reported at the time, Henry and his mate had dragged her into a field and raped her.

There had been frantic scenes at Doncaster Court on the morning of Thursday 30 July with women fighting to get a front seat view, with the *Leeds Mercury* reporting that "These blacklist cases always attract a gallery of women", with the judge having to order the removal of several of them for giggling, before going on to totally lose his cool and completely clear the court.

As for Henry and Herbert Garbutt – although they denied the offence, they were found guilty and sentenced to 18- and 15-months hard labour, respectively.

Rather strangely, Maria Adsetts would not only marry a twenty-seven-year-old miner from Thurnscoe by the name of James Price, shortly after the trial – but would also lie about her age to do so.

Fast-forward to 15 July 1940, and not unlike Mr Hodges, the Chief ARP Warden, played by Bill Pertwee in the popular wartime sitcom *Dad's Army*, Henry Hough had been throwing his weight around – and literally too, as he was described a huge bear of a fellow.

At 10.45 p.m. he had been standing outside the fish and chip shop (now Bolton Fisheries) at 31 Furlong Road, quite drunk and worse for wear, shouting about the ineffectiveness of the blackout – with his focus being on that of the said fish shop. He went home but returned around five-minutes later with his shirt sleeves rolled-up stating that he wanted one of his neighbours as a witness against the owners of the shop – Bill and Margaret Matthews, who he said, were blatantly flouting the blackout laws.

One of their customers had been a thirty-five-year-old Wagon Emptier at one of the nearby collieries by the name of Percy Walton. He refused to have anything to do with him and in no uncertain terms, fucked him off. It was claimed that Henry accosted him, whereby he knocked a parcel of fish and chips out of his hands. In retaliation, Percy did no more that smack Henry in the mouth, the latter of whom, lost his footing and fell onto the kerb. Unfortunately, that blow had been fatal. He hadn't lost consciousness, but there had been quite a lot of blood coming from both Henry's mouth and ears.

One of the main witnesses had been Dr Gervase Brennan Kelly of 2 Furlong Road, who had heard the argument taking place prior to him hitting the deck. He came to the assistance of Henry and asked for his removal off the kerb and for him to be taken home. Unbeknown to everyone at that time, the impact of the fall had fractured his skull and within half-an-hour Henry would be dead.

Henry Hough was described by Crown Prosecutor Richard Linney as a powerfully built and heavy-set individual, both awkward and truculent in nature and someone who had been making a nuisance of himself.

Mrs Matthews had already called the police regarding Henry's erratic behaviour.

All Henry did in response, was tell her to that he "weren't afraid of the Bobbies" and duly flashed his LDV badge. In fact, he flashed that badge a lot.

Percy Walton had tried to get away, but Henry and forced himself on him. "I want thee as a witness," he had said, whilst manhandling him.

"I'm not standing for this," Percy had told him, and duly walloped him.

"He had been outside for nearly an hour shouting and behaving as though he was drunk," Mrs Matthews told the court.

"I punched him in the mouth because he was shoving me about," Percy had said to a Police Sgt. Glasspool when he had eventually arrived at the shop. "I wasn't being ordered about by someone like him."

What was strange about it all, is that although Percy Walton, who lived at 37 Furlong Road, was arrested, and charged with manslaughter, there had been a problem with how the case had been presented.

On 29 July 1940 at Doncaster West Riding Court, defending solicitor Albert Maith stressed that a Prima Facie case had not been made out to warrant his clients committal and Thurnscoe-based Chairman Mark Nokes totally agreed. He did nothing more than dismiss the case, but in doing so created a lot of resentment within the Hough family.

By and large Nokes was a decent man, but he too had his idiosyncrasies – not at least with events surrounding the shooting of a twenty-two-year-old domestic servant, Rachel Robinson in his home at Red House Farm on Thurnscoe's High Street on 5 April 1922. His son was said to have accidentally discharged the gun with reports falsely stating that her injuries were not that serious. Rachel, who at that time lived at 31 Chapel Street, Thurnscoe had taken a gunshot to her hip. It was something that not only made her lame but had her having to walk with the aid of a stick.

I would be wrong in suggesting that he had it all covered up, but being who he was, Mark Nokes certainly downplayed the issue for it to go away.

If you want a bit of local history – Rachel, quite a talented pianist, married William (Bill) Beevers in 1929 and lived at 2 School Street, Thurnscoe right up until her death on 8 March 1979. Her husband did even better – Bill did get his telegram from the Queen.

As regards the result of Mark Nokes' judgement, it was suggested that other forces had been at work. Mud sticks and the indecent assault in 1903 was one of the things that had reared its head. On 17 August 1940, Henry's wife – Lily (nee Hadley), issued a statement in the *South Yorkshire Times*: "Legal proceedings will be taken against any person or persons making slanderous statements against my husband, Henry Hough, recently deceased."

It was a sad, tragic albeit avoidable affair, but it was what it was.

What should be known is that Henry and his wife had lost two children – 15-month old Thomas Henry in September 1913 and Daisy aged five months in July 1925.

"I started working for Bolton UDC in 1962 and was just on my way home to Broadwater on my bike," explained the reluctant hero who had saved the little lad from drowning in the Bowbroom Locks. "I was on Prospect Road just near the tennis courts when a policeman stepped out into the road and asked for my help in breaking down a door."

Henry Hough had a younger brother by six years who lived at 53 The Crescent – the house next door to that of the Lumley's.

"Sammy Hough had boarded himself in his house and social services were extremely concerned as he had become a threat to everyone," said Walt Claydon.

Sammy's wife Isabella (nee Fox) had recently died. They had been married forty-five years.

The policeman and Walt, both shielded by dustbin lids, as Sammy had been throwing things at them, finally entered the house and managed to hold him down whilst Dr Kaye had sedated him. Unfortunately, the loss of his wife had preyed on his mind and although he survived her by just over ten years – he sadly had to be sectioned to Middlewood Hospital, where he died in April 1972, aged eighty-two.

Prior to them being married, Sammy and Isabella had lived at 15 and 9 Furlong Road respectively.

Fast-forward to May 1999, and Paul Bryan Calladine married a local girl by the name of Sally Anne Yates, who moved into one of the properties in between, that in its former life had been a busy Drapers shop – that of No 11.

Sally-Anne had the unfortunate circumstance of being in the wrong place at the wrong time – and on two occasions with the same man.

Nothing seemed out of the ordinary for the Dearne High (formerly Dearneside Comprehensive) school's Fifth Year (Year 11) pupils, whilst slouching about in the ROSLA block on the morning of Friday 22 May 1992.

Some of the girls may have been chattering about last night's telly, where a few of them had been drooling about the lead singer of Ugly Kid Joe – following their debut performance of *Everything About You* on *Top of The Pops*. There was also the twice-weekly *Eastenders* to have a natter about – the episode where Dot Cotton found out that the laundrette had been burgled. The lads, however, were probably more interested in the hero in the string vest that was Rab C Nesbitt, who last night had moved into his own flat with his bestest-buddy ever, Jamesie Cotter. "Hey… Ella," he would say in his exaggerated-Glaswegian drawl.

Unbeknown to most of those innocent faces, a few of the girls, had a major problem coming their way – not at least Sally-Anne.

In the UK, there is nothing to prevent anyone under eighteen being identified in the UK, it is plainly down to the ethical code those concerned – however, the law does change when proceedings become active and in this instance it did. Therefore, under section 49 of the Children and Young Persons Act 1933, which protects the identity of witnesses who are or in this case, have been minors, I must again be vague.

Sally-Anne had been friends with a fifteen-year-old girl off Washington Road, Goldthorpe. Her father worked for S&H Recovery Services – the Doncaster-based vehicle recovery firm that who went into voluntary liquidation on 12 July 2011, whilst her mother I am told, had worked as a receptionist in the doctor's surgery.

The girl had been in a relationship with a twenty-one-year-old man by the name of Richard King, who I am also informed, that due to his appearance carried the dubious nickname of *Bones*.

That afternoon, Sally-Anne's stepsister had been accosted on the school field by the said man.

"He blamed me for his girlfriend splitting up with him and he wanted to know where she and I were," said Sally-Anne. "I had nothing to do with it. She had finished with him because he had been abusive."

He had told the girl that he was armed and was in possession of a .45 Magnum.

"It was a situation that could have been avoided. My stepsister had reported the incident to the school office, but they didn't particularly believe her, and as such we just went into our maths exam."

Bones, however, became unhinged and started brandishing the firearm saying that he would kill himself if he could not see his former girlfriend. The police were called, and the school was evacuated.

"Part way into the exam a teacher escorted me from the hall," added Sally-Anne. "My stepsister followed, and they put us in a storeroom in an art class until the police arrived. We were then led out of school with blankets over us."

Laura Bedford – a girl who had grown up in Bolton-on-Dearne's Concrete Canyon, living at 7 Broadwater concurred: "The incident had everyone in panic and saw some children climbing out of windows."

"Mrs Farrow had her five minutes of fame, though – as ITV's *Calendar* interviewed her," said Sally-Anne.

Pamela Farrow (nee Syngrove) had been the Head of the Fourth Years when I had been there as well as being my Biology teacher during my last two years. Quite a wiry and sharp-faced lady, she had been married to Dr Clifford Owen Farrow – who ran his general practice from the same building on Barnsley Road, as Dr Kaye, and had recently moved from Goldthorpe's Pickhills Avenue over to the more salubrious surroundings of Harlington, where they lived at 21 Fitzwilliam Drive.

I wonder if she mentioned her hip replacement operation as when I was in her class she was always on about it?

It certainly hadn't been the first gun incident at the school. On 1 February 1987, fourteen-year-old Amanda Jayne Moulton had been shot in the face – it being thought that the gunman's intended target had been headmistress, Mrs Jean Rodgers.

As for Sally-Anne, the incarceration of the oddball that was Richard King did little to put an end to her intimidation at his hands. When he got out of prison, he began following her, the last straw being when he was waiting for her beneath the bridge that carries the Sheffield-York railway line on an embankment between Furlong Road and Highgate Lane, and which provides access from the Dearne Miners Welfare football and cricket pitch into the estate that was constructed by Walter Dunk in the late-1960s. When I had been growing up, the first thing you tended to notice was the smell from the public toilets located to the rear of the cricket pavilion, which by then had fallen into a sad state of disrepair, becoming something of a target by vandals.

"He was reported to the police again and warned to stay away from me and thankfully, that was the last I ever saw him," she said.

The immediate area does have a bit of horrible history.

On 23 June 1994, a seventy-five-year-old was arrested on suspicion of raping a twelve-year-old girl behind the cricket pavilion.

John Henry Allsop lived at 49 Welfare View, Goldthorpe and was a regular in the Union Jack WMC (The Comrades) on High Street and one of the people that he used to drink alongside was my dad's uncle – Frank Durose.

Because he was regularly seen wearing a tartan cap, it was assumed that he was Scottish – however, that was most certainly not the case. His mother and father, Thomas and Mildred (nee Ratcliffe) had married at the Church of St Andrew the Apostle, Bolton-on-Dearne on 24 October 1916. She had been a widow with six children living at 30 Station Road (formerly Elm Terrace) – her first husband George Ernest Carrington having died three years earlier.

His father was seven years younger than her and on getting married he moved into her home where they had a further three children – John Henry being the middle child, born on 16 November 1918. He was quite short in stature and possessed distinguished deep-set eyes. On leaving school, he got a job at Manvers Main Brickworks prior to him joining up to fight in the Second World War in October 1939.

He returned to a civilian life of virtual anonymity – that was until he was charged with rape.

The warning signs, however, were always there.

"He was a horrible, vile man and used to say inappropriate and gross things to young girls," said Laura Bedford.

She had also been in the same year at school of the girl who had been raped and further explained that he had used a broken bottle to threaten her.

It is here where I will introduce you to possibly the worst shitbag that ever came from Bolton-on-Dearne – however, there are things in 1976 and 1981 that need to be said.

In both these years I had left my respective schools of Carfield Juniors and Dearneside Comprehensive and I recall the emptiness of everything coming to an end. As much as I didn't particularly like school, those respective years – as I have already said, were quite good.

As a sixteen-year-old in Dearneside, you began being treated as an adult.

What is strange about that statement, is that just a few months before, I along with half a dozen other lads – including Roger (Kitch) Kitchen and James (Jumbo) McNulty had been dismissed from taking part in the school's annual Sports Day. It was the era-post Sex Pistols and Jumbo and Kitch were well into the punk and the swastika's, with the latter of the two being an incredibly talented and artistic lad.

"We were the Mavericks," Jumbo recently told me. "We were in all the top classes and never had to try."

The Head of Physical Education, Mr Fred Hemsley, certainly didn't think that.

We had been dismissed for wearing red Nazi armbands that Kitch had spent literally hours putting together along with drawing Hitler moustaches on our faces.

We just thought it would be a laugh, but he went fucking crackers and marked us all down by giving us a shit report. On my part, I got two D's and an E for Achievement, Effort and Conduct, respectively. It was bullshit. From an achievement perspective I excelled in the majority of sports and even played for the school football team, which just goes to show – if the teacher doesn't like you, he's not going to do you any favours.

I suppose it all boils down to a form of quid pro quo, in that you show the teacher respect and you get it back.

I know that if I would have put my heart and soul into my last year, I would have come out with some extremely good grades, the fact that I did not was therefore solely down to me. Nevertheless, I never took the easy option of leaving at Easter, which due to my age I could have done, and I stayed right up until the very death.

The ROSLA block had been a great place to hang out at break and I felt very privileged to be part of what was a great year. Some of the kids that I went to school with have turned out to be fantastic adults in that they think for themselves and won't be bullied or shepherded into what is that flat-cap herd mentality that our parents had come to trust. The ROSLA was where you could see the different outlooks and artistic tastes in your fellow pupils. It was something that you would have never seen in a playground.

The ROSLA was where Dean Cresswell introduced me to American rock band Lynyrd Skynyrd and their timeless classic *Free Bird*. It was there where Alan Bainbridge told me of John Lennon's murder on the Tuesday morning of 9 December 1980. It was there where Tony Waugh used to regularly talk over the weekends football his favourite quote being that Trevor Cherry of Leeds United should be playing for England. It was there where the sophisticated petrolhead that was Phil Kitchener used to take time out to explain all the great musicians of heavy rock and urged me to check out Hawkwind and their classic – *Silver Machine*. "Lemmy out of Motörhead used to be their bass player and singer," he said.

A great lad, Phil! They all were.

He told me quite recently: "You see someone every day for five years and then you never see them again."

It is quite sad really.

I also recall our Sociology teacher who had come up from the new town of Crawley and who wore these brown suede brothel creepers singing along in the ROSLA to Dire Straits' *Sultans of Swing* that had been playing on the record player. It was quite apt really, as a couple of years later he ended up shagging one of his former pupils and leaving both his wife and job.

My last ever day had consisted of taking an exam in the morning and being invited as a ringer in one of the Fourth Years (Year 10) *Games* lessons and having a great game of football. I say great, as not only had I been a year older, I had also been training with a local pub team and that being the case, my performance was very reminiscent of Pelé (sic).

All the while I played in that game, the girls had been playing hockey or rounders opposite, I can't remember which, but what I do recall speaking at length with one of the girls who were out there on that very last day.

My recollections of Gaynor Mellor (now Coulthard) were of someone who was bubbly and outgoing who metamorphosed from something of an awkward looking little lass into a girl that you would quite possibly want to spend the rest of your life with. At fifteen years old, I thought her quite perfect.

This was something that was recently echoed by her elder sister, Angie: "We must have been really ugly kids, because when my mam died and we cleared out the house, there were absolutely no photographs of me and our Gaynor at all."

Their family were no stranger to tragedy – especially on their mother's side.

Their mum, Maureen Louisa Mellor (nee Butler) had an aunt that she was named after but had never met.

Seventeen-year-old Louisa Margison had worked over in the mills in Halifax until her mother, Sarah (nee Cluley) had been taken ill. Following chronic stomach pains, she had been rushed into Mexborough Montagu Hospital and diagnosed with appendicitis. Unfortunately, it was something she never recovered from. She died on 28 October 1932, aged forty-four.

Louisa, it was said, had packed in her job to run the house at 3 Dane Street, Thurnscoe – however, on the morning of Tuesday 21 February 1933, another tragedy struck.

She had just made her father, Joe, his breakfast, and was standing with her back to the fireplace after taking the frying pan off the hob when the long black ankle-length dress that she was wearing caught fire. The fire was that intense that the smoke it generated, alerted their neighbour Joseph Agar, who between he and the father, did their best to quell the flames.

Louisa, however, panicked, and that hysteria created a major obstacle for the two adults trying their best to put out the fire.

"We wrapped a quilt and a thick rug around her, but I could not do it properly due to her struggling and screaming," her father told W.M Carlile at the coroner's inquest.

The House Surgeon at Mexborough Montagu, Dr Nora McNaughton said that Louisa was admitted to hospital at 10.00 a.m. suffering from extensive burns to the head, neck, chest, arms, the left side of her back and upper parts of the legs.

"The burns were neither deep nor severe – it was the shock that resulted in her death in the evening."

Her father also sustained burns to his hands and arms whilst trying to put out the flames.

As for Gaynor, that had been the last time I ever saw her.

My last days at Carfield Junior School had some similarities.

We were gearing up for what would be a long hot summer, three weeks of which we would spend at my auntie Heather's caravan at a camp site located off North Sea Lane in Humberston. They were great days. I recall listening to Elton John and Kiki Dee's *Don't Go Breaking My Heart* being regularly played on Radio One along with the timeless classic that is the Starland Vocal Band's *Afternoon Delight*. I also remember me and our Tony losing the dog on the Tuesday evening of 3 August. And the huge swarms of ladybirds. Never have I ever seen as many.

I remember the trek over from Carfield to Dearneside and to be shown around like it was yesterday.

Our teachers Mr Bruno Capaldi and Mr Kurt Kneissl escorted us under the bridge from the Dunk houses and through the Dearne Miners Welfare Park where, Roger Kitchen gave some friendly advice to one of the lethargic landscape gardeners that was gainfully employed by the council. "Get thee back into it," he quipped.

The guy went berserk and was it not for Mr Kneissl, he may well have a taken a clout.

What is strange, is that the said teacher hadn't been averse to dishing out a bit of corporal punishment, and one of the two beatings I saw him mercilessly hand out had indeed been to Kitch.

On getting to Dearneside I remember Richard (Bonzo) Holmes hanging out of the window and shouting over at us – and the French teacher Mr Moozer Morris giving him a bollocking. To us, and in sharp contrast to Carfield, the place seemed both intimidating and immense.

You walked on the left, you addressed the teacher's as either *Sir* or *Miss*, the cane was the preferred childhood behavioural device and just to keep you on your toes, there was the off chance that at any given time you could get dragged into the toilets and bog-washed by the elder kids.

Although leaving junior school was exciting, it was also quite upsetting too. I remember Mr Capaldi telling Alan Bainbridge and myself: "I hope you are not going to forget us and that you are going to come back and see me."

How could that not put a lump in your throat?

He did actually call at our house after the summer holidays to drop in a folder of my work that I had knowingly left at school. I never took any schoolwork home whatsoever – the main reason being, that my mum had the tendency to pick fault with it and make me do it again.

It was also upsetting leaving behind all those children that you had grown up with – one of whom was perhaps one of the prettiest little things you could imagine.

"He's going out with one of the Rolfes," my mum had told my grandma Carman, whilst over at her house on Ringway.

"Which one?" inquired my grandma.

"Betty Blakemore's lass – Mandy."

I never really understood the reasoning behind their nudges and whispers. That was until now.

Although she was a year younger than me, she was far more mature than her tender years suggest.

"It's Mandy this and Mandy that," my mum would say, whilst at the same time pulling my leg.

As I have intimated, my mum did have a nice side.

Mandy Rolfe was certainly no ugly duckling, that was for sure.

I recall bumping into her in Bolton Club (formerly Abram Hill WMC) one Wednesday night during 1985.

"Is it James?" she smiled.

I hadn't seen her in years – and for the life of me I cannot seem to recall her in Dearneside, quite possibly because I was too preoccupied with being a dickhead.

Although her pretty features had still been evident, she looked dowdy, downtrodden, and indeed quite weighty. I now know that at the time she must have been about seven or eight months pregnant, which was something that would pave the way for a marriage with a kid much older than us that wouldn't last.

"Can you remember that time in the library at Carfield?" I winked.

"Yeah, I definitely can," she smiled.

That smile. Wow.

It was all innocent stuff.

We spoke for a few more seconds and I never saw her again.

The guy she married was Billy Parr, the elder brother of Carol – the pocket rocket speed queen of Carfield's 1973 sports day.

In the spring of 1975, he along with his younger brother Garry (Plug) Parr, walked themselves into Dearneside folklore, after the teacher's refused to teach them following some assault by their father on the headmaster, Mr Leonard Dickinson. According to one of Plug's best mates – Mick Richardson, his dad had bounced his head off some radiator.

It is here, however, where the story gets murky.

Mandy had an uncle by the name of Ken Rolfe, who during the 1950s was responsible for the rape of several girls in and around Goldthorpe and Bolton-on-Dearne, including the daughter of a policeman.

On 5.30 p.m. 4 April 1957, a sixteen-year-old shop assistant from the Highwoods Road area of Mexborough had been walking down the town's Quarry Lane when she was accosted from behind.

Described as being very shy, the girl who had been a former pupil of Dolcliffe Road School, put up one hell of a fight.

Thirty-year-old Ken Rolfe, who at the time had lived at 6 East Croft on Bolton-on-Dearne's Ringway estate, had waited until she had got close to the entrance to what was a disused quarry before he pounced. He gagged with his hands before dragging her onto some grass where he tore off her underclothing.

As she tried to fight him off, he beat her around the head and face.

"I was screaming and shouting as he kept hitting me in the face with his fist," she said. "He then turned me around and pushed my face into the ground, and then told me shut up because he wouldn't be long."

Rolfe was immediately apprehended – the main thing connecting him to the crime being his motorcycle.

He was charged with attempted rape and indecent assault occasioning actual bodily harm.

The girl, who I am told for a time moved into the Dunk houses at the bottom of Highgate Lane, was left with a black eye, bruising to the left side of her face as well as a broken tooth.

As for Rolfe, he had only been married thirteen months – his wife was expecting a baby.

His trial at Leeds Assizes was presided over by Justice Sir John Percy Ashworth – the judge who oversaw the trial of the murder of John Alan West on 7 April 1964, which led to the last death sentences ever carried out in the United Kingdom.

"This is about as revolting case as this court as ever had to listen to," he said. "You are a man who has done it not once, but several times before. I believe that it is my duty to take steps to stop you doing it again for a very long time."

On 19 July 1957 Rolfe was sentenced to seven years amid his shouting threats of violence toward the family of the girl.

However, it certainly would not end there.

On getting released from prison he relocated to Sale Road, Norwich – as that is where his wife had been from – eventually setting up a business as a travelling greengrocer, hawking potatoes. Possibly an ideal job for someone as predatory perverse as Rolfe? The origin of those potatoes, however, would be the thing that would bring him down.

Heather Rata was the sixteen-year-old daughter of John and Grace (nee Capel) and lived at Northam House – a six-storey block of flats overlooking a church on Cromer Street in the Holborn area of London. Dark-haired and extremely pretty, she had also been a pupil at the Dame Alice Owen School in Islington, but on the Thursday morning of 27 June 1968, she had been at home studying for her GCE O levels.

Her parents had been out shopping and returned home around 2.00 p.m. to find their daughter lying dead on the kitchen floor. She had been both raped and strangled to death with one of her black stockings.

Her mother passed out from shock with neighbours witnessing her husband struggling to carry her down the several flights of stairs to the ambulance.

A Det. Chief Supt. Saxby led the manhunt and had eighty detectives working the case. "This is a terribly vicious and sadistic attack," he told reporters. "There had been a violent struggle. Pots and pans had been hurled about and furniture overturned."

What initially threw the police was the fact that £200 (£3,666, circa 2020) had been stolen, leading them to think that Heather had perhaps disturbed a burglar. Three days after her murder, however, it became very clear that they were looking for a hawker selling potatoes – and one who was getting his produce from The Fens.

Ken Rolfe was arrested at his council house in Norwich on 4 July and duly charged with Heather's murder.

His trial was at the Old Bailey on 19 December 1968, where the court heard that he had a long criminal record for having sex with under-age girls and sexually assaulting young women – all of who had been from the eastern Dearne Valley. He pleaded guilty and was sentenced to life imprisonment. Life meaning life. Ken Rolfe had a heart attack and died in HMP Wakefield on 11 September 1991, aged sixty-five.

Now here is the thing. When Rolfe had been eleven-years old he had lived at 13 Hope Avenue, Goldthorpe. Have you any idea who his neighbour was? The child rapist, Matthew Prest.

Bastards aren't necessarily born like that. Some of the time they can be moulded into who they are.

As for Rolfe's niece. Mandy died on 12 October 2015, aged forty-nine.

I'm Mandy, Fly Me.

That was a song in the charts around the time of our friendship.

I think it was Wayne Cadman who started it. "Mandy," we would say.

"Fly me," she would reply.

Mickleton Main circa 1983. Top. Looking down Lidget Lane. A view of the manager's office and lamp cabin. Bottom Left. A view from the muck bunker - the Reser and Tudor Street in the background. Bottom Right. The colliery stockyard.

13. Cuckoo in the Nest

I was picked up in a Morris Minor 1000 estate and retrieved all my clothes from my mum's. I was to stay with my dad and his wife Paula (nee Newton) along with their children – my other half-brother and sister, Shaun (b. 1974) and Louise (b. 1976). They lived in a three-bed semi at 8 Marquis Gardens in Barnby Dun – which as I was growing up, was a quaint little village situated between the mining communities of Bentley and Stainforth.

"How long do you think that will last?" said my mum.

I said nothing and left.

New Year's Day 1983 had been eventful, but if I needed my life to progress it was here where it would happen.

You could say my dad was the opposite of my (step)dad. He was an alpha male who grafted day-in-day-out, twelve hours a day and seven days a week as site foreman on Roade Aggregates' ash and coal reclamation site off the A19 Toll Bar Road, which was a few hundred yards down, from what was at one time from Dario's restaurant on the three-pronged fork up into Owston Park, Sutton and Askern.

My dad's wife had been a trained typist and secretary who at one time worked at Doncaster's Coal House just off the Waterdale, and International Harvester's (Case) on Wheatley Hall Road, but had finished work since the birth of their children.

My mum, as in most things, was blunt in her appraisal of Paula: "She's built like a brick shithouse."

Paula was extremely nice to me as a young child – however, since she'd had her own two, I felt, and rightly so, that I had again become the cuckoo in the nest.

Is this me feeling sorry for me?

Feeling sorry for myself is something that I have never really had to do as I always had relations such as three sets of grandparents and a few aunties and uncles who could do that for me, so I reckon I was fairly well-covered.

My dad was working as a miner at Barnburgh Main when my mum left him, and he was left to pick up the pieces of what he lost – and believe me, he lost a lot. It was something which he readily admitted to me as I was growing up. He loved my mum but couldn't handle the relationship. He was insanely jealous and perhaps after me seeing how my 1982 had panned out, maybe he had good reason to be.

I remember most vividly of playing out outside my auntie Heather's house at 45 Barnburgh Lane, Goldthorpe one afternoon in 1968 and him walking up to me, his eyes still heavily lined by the coal dust from his day shift underground, giving me a cuddle prior to slipping me a shilling to spend in the shop a few doors down.

These were times I remember, with an affection – not least because I had been living under the roof of my new elder cousin, Tony Greaves.

He knew every kid that roamed the backings, not at least the popular little lad who lived in the beer-off located on Barnburgh Lane's junction at 83 High Street. He was the son of Don and Brenda Ballance (nee Oldfield).

Wayne would be in the same school year as me but would never make it into Dearneside. On 3 June 1973, and whilst in the First Year (Year 3) of Goldthorpe Junior school, he lost his life to peritoneal mesothelioma – a cancer of the abdomen that is generally associated with the ingestion of asbestos fibres.

According to Ann Jones (now Lacey), a dark-haired girl whose parents had the shop shortly afterwards, Wayne had been ill for quite some time – his premature death affecting both teachers and pupils alike.

It was his little bike with the chunky tyres that I had got on to ride from the top of the backings off Frederick Street. It was also his bike that I had crashed on hitting the rear yard walls of Barnburgh Lane at the bottom. There had been quite a lot of blood – mainly from my knees and elbows. "That was brilliant," enthused our Tony.

Wayne didn't think so and was more concerned with his handlebars and seat being twisted.

In one of these houses had lived another lad in our year by the name of David (Bod) Badkin whose elder sister Christine had taken us around to see their dog after it had had a litter of puppies.

For a short time, during the latter months Miners' Strike, I would hook up with a girl who was a friend of a girl that David had supposedly been in a relationship with. It would, however, be quite wrong of me to relay her name – the main reason being that she had been something of a nymphomaniac. It was said that no matter which tradesmen she had call at the house – she made sure that she had sex with them.

"What, all of them?" I asked.

I had seen her just the once and whilst down in Swinton at The Towpath. I seem to recall that she had just done the TV repair man, but I could be wrong. "She just really likes sex," I was told.

If you want a much more interesting story, then that would be of David's father.

Frank Badkin had married Margaret Parker in 1962 and between them they set up home in Bolton-on-Dearne at 17 Vancouver Drive and had four children. Nothing is forever and Frank went on to remarry.

On 30 August 1983 and whilst living at 1 Chapel Street – the house that backed on to the cemetery, he died suddenly, aged forty-two. The tongues were wagging – not least from within his own family. According to his daughter, Christine, she had been convinced that her father had been poisoned.

It certainly wouldn't be the first time.

On 16 February 1968, twenty-five-year-old Adrienne Taylor (nee Drower) had been part of an extraordinarily complex murder suicide.

She had become the figment of obsession of the Warehouse Manager of glass bottle manufacturer, Dale Brown & Sons – a firm that had premises on Whiteley Road, Swinton.

Percy Beevers, a fifty-three-year-old former colliery hewer and professional golfer, lived with his disabled wife, Gladys (nee Cox) – a lady who was five years older than him in one of the eight flats at Highfield House on (4/) Sandygate, Wath-on-Dearne.

He had been part of an affluent family from Brampton Bierlow two of whom had been responsible for the construction of Goldthorpe's Beever Street in 1905 – that being Joe Beevers and his son-in-law, Tom Johnson Snart. For the record, the street was originally named Beevers Street, but sometime later lost the "S".

Totally besotted, he brought a rose into the office each day as a gift for Adrienne, who had been employed as a clerk – however, his affection certainly hadn't been reciprocated. Although married to her husband Robert – a twenty-eight-year-old electrician at Manvers Main, Adrienne had been having an eight-month affair with one of the firm's drivers – thirty-one-year-old Michael McCoy of John Street, Thurnscoe.

Beevers had apparently been distraught at the affair and during the subsequent Christmas period had even sent an anonymous letter to her husband citing the affair, which was something that Adrienne had taken exception to.

According to McCoy – the son of Matthew and Susan (nee Bailey) – formerly of 11 Church Street, Thurnscoe, Beevers had tried everything in his power to separate the two: "I had formed a relationship with Adrienne and often saw her at the factory and on many occasions, Mr Beevers would suddenly appear on the scene. I formed the impression he was doing his best to keep us apart during working hours. Just before last Christmas, the two and had had a huge row, with Adrienne telling me afterwards that he was taking her out of his will."

What would happen however, was that Beevers had got hold of some arsenic from one of the security guards at the factory – a man by the name of Peter Kerr, his explanation being that he needed it to get shut of insects in his garden.

It had been a lie. Over the course of the preceding six months he had administered the poison several times – four of which had resulted in Adrienne vomiting. In one instance, however, it had played in his favour as her leg had become limp, and Beevers – well and truly in Benny Hill-mode, had managed to massage it for her. "Learning all the time…" (sic) Google it!

This had been a short-lived hit of emotion as on trying the same trick again – this time by administering the poison into her flask of mushroom soup – she died, some of her last words being: "I have never felt as ill in all my life – I'm sure that it is the soup I've just had."

"Last summer Adrienne had told me that she had been going out with a man named Mick and that she loved him," explained Irene Kemp, one of the other clerks at the factory. "And that Mr Beevers had become very jealous."

"Adrienne was a beautiful lady," added another one of the clerks – Janet Spencely (nee Brewin). "Mr Beevers was a frustrated man whose head was very easily turned – especially as his wife had been an invalid. What is true is that he tried everything he could for her to show him some attention – then on the following Monday, I was met at work by the police."

Det. Supt. George Oldfield and Det. Supt. Stanley Woolfenden had headed the murder case and the latter had questioned Beevers about his association with Adrienne.

At the coroner's inquest, held by Dr Herbert Pilling, the policeman said: "Mr Beevers told us that on a number of occasions that he had told Mrs Taylor not to be silly (regarding the affair) as she had a good home and a good husband and added that he certainly hadn't been jealous of Mr. McCoy. Beevers also denied having an affair with Adrienne and writing any anonymous letters."

Four days after being questioned by the police, Percy Beevers and his wife were found dead in their home. He had gassed both himself and his wife.

The pocket money that I received from my dad was the template for each weekend that I saw him as I was growing up. He saw me and gave me spending money – and as the years went by, it went up – 10p, 20p, 50p to £1.

My mum made out that he was buying me – guilt money – something that I have heard her say about me many times in her later life.

In my mind, to give something is just as good as receiving, which is one of the many reasons that I love Christmas so much – however, it is the fact that I could, and still can do it, that really riled my mum.

On Mother's Day 1982 I bought her a top of the range electric knife – £14.99 (£58, circa 2020). My (step)dad called me a *snake in the grass*; whether he meant it or not, I don't really know, but that self-same knife made its way over to Christine Walton's house only to be wrapped up as a wedding present for me on 1 February 1986.

I am not averse to the redistribution of gifts, but that was just taking the piss.

Fast-forward to 2002 and Auntie Carol's husband, Barry (Oldfield), had to have a hip replacement in Doncaster Royal Infirmary and as she couldn't drive, she was at my mum's and panicking a little, as it was four bus journeys there and back. I therefore took a day off work and offered to drive her.

Whereas Carol was extremely grateful, my mum fucking hated it. And you must remember this was her best friend. It was even worse after Carol had told my mum that I had sent her a bouquet of flowers. "He buys people," she said to my sister regarding my gesture.

No, I do not. It is just that I never forget the people that had been kind to me as I was growing up and Barry and Carol were two such people.

When I was in Carfield Juniors, the Friday afternoons were brilliant. The main reason being that I would see my dad the very next day and have a full day over at what I considered their brilliant new house in Barnby Dun. For me, it was a completely different world. No screaming nor shouting and one hundred percent attention, by the man I thought was the best person in the world.

"He was only interested in you when he didn't have a girlfriend," my mum had often said.

What was strange about that comment is that I rarely remember him missing a weekend, even when I was a little lad. If there would have been a time, it would be when he left the pit to go and work at over at Immingham in 1969.

"Who is that fat woman looking through the railings?" one of the children had said, a few weeks after I had started at Houghton Road's infant school one playtime.

With my dad working away it had been a time when my nana Durose lost her weekly access to me. For four years I had been their only grandchild and had seen her and my granddad, on a weekly basis without fail. My mum, however, had refused to have any interaction with my dad's parents, therefore my nan had made a trip from Bolton-on-Dearne to the place that she knew I would be.

"Come here and gi' thee nana a love," she smiled.

Her only contact had been cuddling me through the school railings.

It was fucking heart-breaking. My mum should have hung her head in shame. She was just so obstinate and controlling.

My dad and Paula moved around a bit. From a flat at 36 Alexandra Road on Cleethorpes sea-front, to a flat on St Mary's Road in Doncaster's Town Fields area and a short walk from the subway where twenty-eight-year-old Cheryl Louise Camm was murdered in 2008. Then over to 63 South Street a long since demolished row of terraced houses in Doncaster's Hyde Park area, before finally settling in Barnby Dun in 1972.

Getting up on a Saturday mornings to watch the old re-runs of *Champion The Wonder Horse* or *Whirlybirds* and waiting for their red 1300 Mark II Cortina with the registration plate XWC 170F to pull up outside Primrose Close and sound its horn, was a great feeling.

The layout of their house was not unlike ours – but theirs wasn't rented, it had been bought. It was here that I understood the difference of buying and renting. My dad and Paula were very upwardly mobile and appeared to have a plan. I really liked it there and my dad knew that.

"If you lived with us…" he would often retort at my moans and groans concerning my everyday life at home.

Things came to a head after I had mentioned being beaten with the rubber washing-pipe.

His letter to my mum and (step)dad of – *if they didn't want me living there that he'd gladly have me at theirs* didn't really help, it just pissed them off. They obviously saw it as me *talking out of school* and airing their dirty washing. Nevertheless, there was no way that she was going to sacrifice her piece on the chess board. Certainly not when it had played out so well for her in the past.

Before they bought the car, Barnby Dun to Bolton-on-Dearne or Thurnscoe was a total of eight bus journeys for either my dad or Paula. There was no putting me on the bus for my dad to pick me up at the other end, she made him earn his corn and boy did he have to graft. He had to turn up at 10.00 a.m. and get me home by 6.00 p.m. I couldn't understand it back then and I can't understand it now. Even though you have had history between yourselves, you don't persecute the one thing that you made together. I will say it again, to me it just never made any sense.

On my dad and Paula getting the car, which made picking me up, far much easier, my mum had several brainstorms which came immediately after the 1974 Miners' Strike and all of which entailed emigration. Choices one to three were: Australia, Canada and South Africa – and in that order. However, all their applications were rejected.

By (step)dad didn't possess a highly skilled profession as say a mining engineer, fitter or electrician and not having any relatives already placed over there and having a wife and three kids in tow, one of which was someone else's, he stood very little chance of it working out – and as my dad over in Barnby Dun candidly stated: "It's not happening."

"He can't stop you going, if you really want to go," duly explained my mum.

Reinforcements were needed, and my mum had my grandma Carman come over one evening to explain things, if not to just sound me out. She immediately knew that I didn't want to go, so much so, that I told her that if I couldn't live with my dad, I could go live with her, which brought a smile to her face. It certainly hadn't when I'd been seventeen but at nine-years-old, I was a much cuter proposition.

Looking back at it, the chances of us emigrating were always thin – however, there is something that has always stuck with me, which someone said to me in early 1994, and everything about it was just dirty, underhanded and plain nasty.

On my first time up in Thurnscoe East our neighbours on Deightonby Street had been Ronnie and Pat Bilton (nee Wilson), who between them had two daughters, Kathleen and Mandy, both of whom were slightly older than me.

Ronnie was a short and rather strange-looking character whose extended family were not only massive but scattered all around the East end – especially on Brunswick and Lancaster Street. I knew some from Hickleton Main, such as Billy Bilton, who ran the pit's telephone exchange but there were many, many others, one of whom was a tall and quite an aggressive-looking lad my age, who was often at his uncle Ronnie's.

As a young lad, Mick Jacques had a highly confrontational nature, and it wasn't until my second stint up in the East end that his hostility towards me was fully exorcised. It was late-spring 1977 and I had been walking along Windsor Street, and as I walked down the dip, to where the garages were situated on the left and just before its junction with Deightonby Street, two lads walked over to me, one of whom was Mick.

As ever, I was wearing my royal blue jersey, that fully advertised the fact that I wasn't a pupil of Thurnscoe Comprehensive, and which almost always invited confrontation.

Mick had seen the aggravation I was getting at the Hanover Street bus stops and was chippy and antagonistic, deciding to give me a push and a shove. Why not, he had seen it play out a few times after my arrival that February. As soon as I retaliated and gave him a smack in the mouth, he wanted absolutely none of it. From then on, he kept his distance and if he saw me – which he did – he acknowledged me with a nod or an "alright, mate". We were certainly never close, though in later life, I thought him quite a nice kid. The other kid who he was with that day had been Darren Eades.

Mick had a sister by the name of Tina, who I never really knew that well – which was possibly down to the fact that she was a couple of years older than me. She was, however, an extremely pretty girl who married Bill and Kathleen Glover's (nee Tarmey) only child – Kevin.

I knew Kevin mainly through Carl Eades, as post-strike they not only worked together, but lived in close proximity to each other, within the El Dorado for redundant miners, that was the newly constructed residential development off Thurnscoe's High Street – which were generally referred to as "The houses behind The Ship".

Kevin was not only a miner at Hickleton Main, but an extremely affable and good-natured lad. I am looking for a fault, but I cannot see one. He was just a nice, genuine kid.

One of his best mates was a local lad by the name of Mick Wakefield, who had just split up with his girlfriend and who lived opposite Brough's old supermarket on Shepherd Lane. He was a kid who I would get to know quite well.

Mick had been employed as a fitter at Barnburgh Main and who like many others had sold his job for a redundancy pay out and then sneaked in by the back door to work for a private contractor; namely the firm I worked for – Cementation Mining.

He was a tall, smart, and somewhat good-looking kid with long hair and a gregarious personality. You couldn't help but like him as he appeared an extremely nice lad, and as such, I got on with him like a house on fire. However, if you scratched beneath the surface, that really wasn't the case.

Couples split up. It's happened a million times before and will happen a million times in the future, but how he firstly went about it and more importantly, how explained his ulterior objective, was by far, much worse than the deed itself.

He had lots of things in common and considered Tina a much better friend than Kevin. I know that because that is exactly what Mick had told me.

Kevin's neighbours had begun talking well before it became nasty, but as is the case, the man – or indeed the woman, are generally the last to know.

As was often the case, miners arrived at the pithead only to have to deal with some form of industrial dispute, and in most cases, it was one which was rarely caused by the men in question. Kevin returned home only to find Mick in his house, but not so much with his wife, as that ship, according to Mick, had already sailed. In Mick's words he told his mate that he had nipped around to borrow – or to drop off some CDs. There was no doubt about it – it had been a close call.

Whilst the affair had been on-going Tina got pregnant and had twins – however, there was a twist in the tale as Mick wasn't the father. Nevertheless, everything was brought out into the open, and Tina left her husband and threw her lot in with Mick, moving into his house in the Cusworth Lane area of Scawsby. It was bad, however, what he told me in early 1994 was much worse.

Being the father, Kevin had rights of access, but the fact that he had been turning up on a weekend had been pissing Mick off. As Kevin didn't drive a car – he owned a powerful motorbike – he collected his children by public transport and as that was the case, Mick candidly dropped this one out: "I could do with us moving just far enough away, so he gets pissed off and thinks *fuck it*."

Did he?

Of that I do not know as I lost touch – however, what I do know, is what Mick was wanting to do, was exactly the same as my mum had wanted to do in 1974.

Moving to my dad's house in 1983 brought with it its own problems, not at least in how I was going to make day shift through the week. It also brought another in that I came as a package.

After the incident at my girlfriend's house, the relationship had run its course, to the point where it was fair to say that I had been totally excommunicated from 9 Chapel Lane. The relationship with my girlfriend however, had survived; the main reason possibly being the fact that I had finally left my mum's. Or possibly not.

Looking back at it, it was a time that I wouldn't change as I got to know a lot about my dad – yet on the other, it was a time when I was often stressed, if not at my wit's end. The snide comments from Paula along with her underhanded scheming, and the fact that I was often out going backwards and forwards to work and having to handle what was becoming a highly domineering and confrontational girlfriend.

With Paula, it wasn't like that at the start, but it certainly became like that. Her nature is one of interference and being very loud in volume. The sight of how I spent money and how she saw me being manipulated by my girlfriend, drove her to despair, so much so, she was always on mine or my dad's back regarding one thing or the other.

I earned nearly as much money as my dad – however, he had commitments such as keeping a home, a family, and of course the bills that come with it. I of course, had no such commitments and spent my money on whatever I pleased.

It is hard to fault her for certain things as she was a very good mother to my younger brother and sister, albeit a bit over-protective.

Paula was a local girl who was the eldest daughter of Jack and Joan Newton (nee Brown) – the latter of who grew up at 44 Highgate Lane and had married my dad towards the back end of 1969.

She was a woman in sharp contrast to my mum, as my mum would never have put up with certain aspects of Paula's life. Certainly not the *fetch me, carry me* principles that my dad had installed. It is fair to say that Paula was an attentive wife who made sure that there was food on the table when he got in from work and that whilst my dad was in the house, he did nothing. I also wouldn't be wrong in suggesting that she was also very heavily reined. They had had a car for a few years and then they didn't. For Paula, who was the only one of them who could drive, the car had been everything. It had been a freedom of expression that she never had whilst I was there. Needless to say, that when I bought a car, especially the type of car it was, she had a huge opinion about it.

As I have said, I was always a person who continually surveyed everything around me, be it at home or at work. At times and mainly through lack of verbal interaction, it may have looked that I was totally uninterested, but that was never the case.

My mum was a conundrum of several complicated personalities that often blew in different directions, be it up and down or hot and cold. Paula was very easy to read as she hid nothing, least of all how she saw me.

"You're more a Carman than a Durose," she would tell me – obviously meaning that I was more like my mum than my dad.

I knew exactly what she was getting at. I always did.

My grandma Carman, who throughout my early years was the person outside of my parents that I was perhaps the closest to, often said, "I can definitely see your dad in you, but I can also see your mam and our Steve."

Paula had gone to school at Highgate Juniors with both my uncles, Rob and Steve, with the former being in the same year as her throughout school.

She was, however, another who didn't like my girlfriend.

My dad was absolutely nothing at all like my mum had described, and when I saw him – as his hours at work were long – he just appeared extremely laid back, although he did have his moments. Even after he had come home from work, his immediate boss – the Site Manager – always tended to have him on the phone for half an hour. As I have said, Paula always spoke at volume and when she was pissed off, it became louder and louder and louder. I wouldn't call it a fault; it was just how she was. She was just a *nag*. In the main, my dad took the nagging with a pinch of salt – however, there was one time I recall that she was continually riding me. They were going on holiday to Bridlington and I didn't want to go, and she was going on and on and on and on about it. I must admit, she just wouldn't shut up.

"If you don't bloody shut up, I'll end up giving you a backhander," was all he said.

Paula just went the colour of beetroot and stormed out.

I was there just short of nine months and that was the only time I ever saw him lose his temper with her.

I never argued with her and just got on with it – however, the car was a constant bug bear.

On moving in with them, me trying to make day shift – a 6.00 a.m. start, was extremely hard.

In 1956, due to geotechnical and water issues, Thorne Colliery had been winding down its operations and its men were being transferred to different pits in the area, one of which had been Hickleton Main – who took 140 of them on. It was supposedly only going to be temporary, as whilst the pit had been in full production, it had been one of the most successful collieries in the area. That temporary measure was still in force come January 1983 with the Adwick-on-le-Street bus and coach operator Beehive (now Wilfreda Beehive) being contracted to take the ex-Thorne Colliery miners from Moorends to Thurnscoe.

It's strange what goes through your mind when you are young lad, because my thoughts were of some old *trip bus* full of miners in 1950s attire, wearing flat caps and hob nail boots, which was absolutely nothing like it was.

I phoned Beehive's head office and inquired into the route of the bus and asked if it could pick me up. Not from Barnby Dun but from a junction of the A18 top side of Edenthorpe, which was around two miles away, meaning getting up at three o'clock in the morning and a forty-minute walk in the freezing cold. On getting on the bus it was an eye-opener and yet another example of how the NCB wasted its resources. The bus contained just six men, all of whom were in their forties and fifties.

Those dayshifts absolutely crippled me, especially as during January it had snowed heavily and the walk down Armthorpe Lane, which had absolutely no pavements, was nothing short of treacherous.

I thought about buying another motorbike – however, I decided on a car.

This would be a huge turning point in my life.

I had been more or less ready for my driving test when Christine and Frank split up and although Frank urged me to keep with the programme, even though driving lessons with him after he had left were costing £1.50 (£5.35, circa 2020) more, due to him having to travel from Sheffield, I not only thought that money could be better spent elsewhere, I had also gotten bored. I had other things taking up my time.

The idea of me having a car was nothing new, but me saving up a couple of thousand pounds was never going to happen. By February 1983, however, the landscape had changed dramatically and now being eighteen years old I could go to the Yorkshire Bank in Goldthorpe and get a loan.

Once Paula knew I was on about getting a loan, her divisive nature took hold, and she began asking question after question and continually voicing her concerns to my dad.

I still recall a lad off Tudor Street by the name of Ian Beaney buying a green Talbot Sunbeam – the first lad of the Class of 1981 to get a loan for a car, and driving it up and down Lidget Lane at well over 80 mph. There was also a kid who got stripped next to me in the pit baths nicknamed *Squeak* continually droning on to Andy Redlegs about supposedly having the fastest 1300cc on the planet – a Ford Fiesta 1.3S. All the young lads around my age were buying cars.

Many of the lads that had signed on at Hickleton Main tended to be driving, with Ford Capris being the in-thing.

As for me, I have always thought that a car is an extension of your personality. Nowadays, most of my friends drive BMWs, Audis or similar. There is nothing wrong with that, other than they are predictably reliable and very fucking boring. That is definitely not me. I like my white Jaguar sports car with its piercing cat-like eyes, feline prose and a growling V8 five-litre engine that kicks out 400 horsepower.

Back then, however, I fancied an Alfa Romeo Veloce Sprint or an MGB Roadster. A sports car that no one else had and which looked the part.

I remember my dad coming in after a night out at Rockware WMC, which was a works club off Clay Lane West in Long Sandall and asking: "Have you put a deposit down on an MG at some kid's house over in Dunsville?"

I had. I had given him a £50 (£178.23, circa 2020) cheque as a deposit.

My dad knew the lad's dad as he had worked with him, whilst he had been employed at Rockware Glass in the early-to-mid-1970s and he had been saying to my dad that if I didn't get the loan for the car, I would forfeit my deposit – basically that I would lose the £50.

"That's definitely not what was said," I told him.

It wasn't. The loan was a formality – I'd just not had time to go and sign for it as I had been on night shift all week. In fact, I hadn't even gone to Dunsville. The kid had driven the car over from his house on Mulberry Avenue to show me what was his 1976 registered blaze red MGB GT.

I had to hand it to my dad, he didn't like the thought of someone trying to take the piss out of me. He got on the phone and completely switched personality from the laid-back man that I had come to know into a very sinister-sounding guy. "I've just had a word with my lad and what you've been telling me is wrong," he calmly stated. "And I'll tell you now, if that £50 isn't dropped at our house by tomorrow, you'll have me to deal with."

I still wanted the car but in my dad's mind it was a case of father like son and there was no way he would be getting his hands on any of my money. "There'll much better cars out there than his," he told me.

I eventually bought an immaculately restored 1969 registered white MG Midget, YJW 8H – a car which is still running around now, from some motor fanatic over in Thorne. Apart from it immediately needing a new battery it was the most perfect car you could ever imagine. It had the chrome bumpers, stainless steel twin-carburettors, knock on- knock-off wire wheels and every conceivable dial imaginable on the dashboard, along with a black rag top.

As good as the car was, there was to be a few downsides to my £850 (£3,030, circa 2020) investment, one of which was Paula, and the fuss she kicked up about me driving the car whilst not having a full licence was unbelievable. At first, the car was idle whilst I was fast-tracking my driving lessons in a bid to get my test passed, sometimes having multiple double lessons whilst coming straight in off night shift. However, the thought of me getting up at three in the morning and walking the two miles to catch the Beehive bus was too much of a temptation and in the end, I just thought *fuck it*.

Paula's divisive nature saw an opening and she went for it. Even to this day, I don't think me driving the car was the problem, it was me having the car and her not having one, that was really the problem.

My initial thoughts were to let her drive it and she knew that. That line of thought soon changed, however. Was I being selfish? Perhaps I was, but in my mind, if she wanted a car – which believe me, she certainly did – then she should buy one. In fact, there is a story that I had forgotten and one that had been dumped well and truly in the past. I only spent a bit more than half the loan money and one night, I offered my dad and Paula the money for a car, her car, with no strings attached. Obviously, they would pay me back, but I certainly wasn't in any rush for the money.

"It's a nice thought and I'll certainly think about it," said my dad.

He never took up my offer, but it was something that I meant. If I had offered my mum the same deal, she would have ripped my arm off for it.

How I lived my life and spent my money drove Paula to despair. It did with my mum, but my mum had a car as well as her financial independence. Paula had neither and having all day and all day to do it in, can sometimes be a huge burden to carry. I often think that she was more frustrated than frustrating. Frustrated with her life in that she had to ask for everything, frustrated that she could drive but didn't have a car. And she was certainly frustrated about her weight.

"Get lost, you big fat pig," our Shaun once shouted as he ran upstairs after being told off.

I didn't find it amusing, because it wasn't. My dad, however, thought it was hilarious.

It was a touchy subject.

My nana Durose nicknamed her *Butch* due to her size, which again wasn't nice – however, my nan maybe had her reasons. After our Shaun had been born, my nana had put her head in the crib, pram or whatever it was and gave him a cuddle, pinched his cheeks and said, "Ooh, isn't he fat?"

My nana didn't mean anything by it, she just said it out of impulse and as a term of endearment, and of that I know, as she would **never** ever knowingly say something that was hurtful to one of her own.

Paula's retort was not only scathing it was downright childish. "He's not fat – you're fat!"

Our Steve's wife, my auntie Ann, had problems with keeping her weight down after she'd had both kids, however there were compensations – Ann was beautiful, Paula was not.

Paula had many good points, however, being divisive certainly wasn't one of them.

Me having the car blew her mind and she was on at my dad about it all the time, so much so, he pulled me up about going out in it before I was ready for going out. It was one of those conversations that starts off with, "While you're living in this house…"

Was he worried? No, I just think he was being nagged into saying it.

My dad had been a wayward kid, and to a point at that stage in my life, much more than me.

At just turned eighteen years old, apart a few cautions at Goldthorpe Police Station for taking stuff that didn't belong to me and fighting, I had no criminal record whatsoever. I was basically a clean-cut kid that had everything.

My dad had been locked-up in prison for breaking into the old Army Stores that was at one time located on the corner of Market Street in Goldthorpe and smashing up Vinny Matthews' (later Rocky Wall's) café by the time he was my age, and there was even a story of him stealing a horse from a nearby field and riding it through the centre of Goldthorpe that was told to me by some electrician up at North Selby Mine during 1992.

My nan told me many a tale about his exploits – the police raiding their house looking for the proceeds from the robbery of a beer-off or warehouse, which he had buried in my granddad's flower bed at 9 The Crescent and her having to drop him cigarettes off while he had been locked up in the holding cells down at Mexborough Police Station. Even in later life he'd had his moments. Him and a mate had been coming home from the pub in a car late one night, when his mate was pulled over and breathalysed. Being over the limit his mate was arrested and taken to Stainforth Police Station. My dad obviously wasn't arrested and as such was free to go. Nevertheless, they were down at his house at Marquis Gardens the very next day.

"A police bicycle was taken from outside the station," the policeman told him. "Was it you?"

It certainly was. He had ridden down as far as the Fordstead Lane swing bridge and slung the bike in the River Dun Navigation Canal.

And I have lost count of the times he used public transport such as buses and trains without actually ever buying a ticket.

Therefore, to have him allegedly worried about me potentially getting a £10 (£35.65, circa 2020) fine for driving on a provisional licence was both extremely contradictory and made little sense at all. She was *riding* him and to shut her up, he had to say what he did.

That night when I came home, he said little. He had been trying for me to live with him for years and now he had it, he didn't know what to do.

I still remember coming in and seeing him sat watching Monty Python's 1971 sketch comedy film, *And Now for Something Completely Different.* I tried to converse with him – however, he was having none of it and was extremely quiet. He had something on his mind and while I was in bed he came into the bedroom and said, "Tomorrow morning, I want you to leave."

It was something that I would never ever have told any of my children. If you have a problem, you deal with it, you never turn your back on it. Especially when it concerns your kids. Your kids are your everything.

Paula had nagged and nagged and now she had nearly got what she wanted. What she really wanted however, she got the very next day.

I didn't have a clue what I was going to do. My grandma Carman's house was the most logical first point of call – however, I knew only too well that although I was more than welcome on a temporary basis, she was a woman that it was fair to say, liked her own space.

It never got that far. I had too much on my mind and was driving the car too fast and hit a patch of black ice on Marr Drag and spun the car out of control. I was fortunate to survive the accident. I even remember telling one of the motorists who pulled over to drag me out of the car: "I wish I was dead."

Paula had won. She didn't have a car and now, nor did I.

However, as I told my girlfriend at the time: "I can always buy another car, but she'll always be a fat ugly bastard."

That may have been me being both scathing and childish, but it was also me being truthful.

"Perhaps if you'd have been more experienced on the road it wouldn't have happened," she told me afterwards.

Any chance to twist the knife.

I still recall her trying to reverse into a parking space topside of Bridlington Spa on South Marine Drive in the summer of 1975 and her bursting out crying because she couldn't do it. There was a similar instance in the car park of Weston Park Hospital in Sheffield in summer 1985, when she had been kicking off because some other cars had supposedly blocked her in. They hadn't, she was just an extremely poor driver and it was left to the cuckoo in the nest to reverse the car out for her.

Most insecure people refuse to believe their shortcomings and doing someone down is a way to make them feel superior. When men do it, I refer to it as *one-inch dick syndrome*. Men who have been endowed with a clitoris instead of a penis. You will meet a few of these as the story unfolds.

Paula was always after a part-time job and due to her qualifications, her getting a secretary's job was certainly not out her grasp, therefore in her mind that was exactly what she was aiming for. The excuses that she made for not getting one were the most obvious: Someone they know got the job. She was too overqualified. Her age or the hours were a problem. Or she didn't want the job anyway.

However, her fuming and blasting after being turned down for a part-time job at the local bakers, Hagenbach & Sons, explained quite a lot.

My dad was philosophical about the car. "Put it down to experience," he said.

Paula however, felt the need to continually ride me and now the car had gone it would be about something else. It is fair to say that the woman was forever on my case.

"Our Shaun won't be getting away what you get away with," she said, regarding something that my dad had supposedly said.

My brother and sister were a huge plus while I was there. I loved them a lot.

Our Louise was a right missus – a madam, and I remember her kicking off one Friday evening when my dad had refused to let her take her pram and dolly-dolly up to what was the huge Gateways supermarket behind The Pinfold and close to the junction near the White Hart public house. She stamped her feet before doing no more and ramming the pram against the glass paned front door and putting its window through. Now, that did amuse me.

For our Shaun to have a big brother living with him was a bit special.

"I didn't want you to leave," he told me in later life, after laughing about him waking me up after I had been on night shift to take him up on the fields behind the Parish Hall to play football. They were just extremely nice kids who unbeknown at the time were going to have their lives turned upside down.

I remember coming in off one particular day shift to have Paula immediately grizzling in my face.

Our Shaun had been in our bedroom spring cleaning and tidying up all his comics. I had mentioned doing it when I got in – however, my brother beat me to it and was apparently obsessed with impressing me.

"You don't ever tell him to do anything – it's his house, not yours," she sniped.

There were hundreds of similar instances.

I think she looked at me and just saw my mum. There were, however, other things that I picked up on, when her sniping was directed elsewhere.

A family lived directly across the road, Alf and Pam Baker (nee Pigott), who in my eyes were just nice people. I knew one of their sons quite well – Simon, who was a school year older than me and his younger sister Jill, who often used to parade around in her bedroom window in her underwear, which certainly used to have Paula chucking the teddy out of the pram. It was, however, the eldest or second eldest son that I remember her directing her wrath at. He had a brand-new Ford Capri and lived in the Belle Vue area of Doncaster and a couple of times, whilst visiting his mum and dad with his wife and kids, Paula made it plainly obvious about him allegedly flaunting his wealth. I cannot remember it word for word but being "up to his eyes in debt" was mentioned. It was much worse when one of their kids had some squabble with hers. I saw a side of her that I had never seen before and that was her knocking out a foul-mouthed tirade that just didn't make any sense. She growled, effed and blinded, but what I remember most about it, is that she didn't know how to use the words correctly. It was funny, more than anything. She was just saying swear words as part of some nonsensical sentence.

Working at Hickleton Main was becoming a nightmare. Not because of the job itself, just the long haul of travelling and the early hours of plodding down Armthorpe Lane. It was extremely hard, and I even contemplated going on regular night shift, which brought me into contact with the Personnel Manager, Colin Ashworth and Ron Hardman's younger half-brother, Kevin, who at the time was a NUM delegate.

"I'm not having you talking to the lad like that," Kevin yelled at him at mid-point.

It was a right up and downer and I was the piggy in the middle.

"He's a right fucking wanker, Jamie," Kevin told me as we walked around to the Union office. "If we can't get this sorted today, chuck on the club (sick) for a week."

Kevin and Billy Hayes batted my corner and what was mentioned was a transfer to Askern Main Colliery – including the £1,000 (£3,564, circa 2020) transfer money that was allowed at the time. For me, it was a right result. A grand in the back pocket and not as far to travel.

I wasn't the only one that was offered a transfer. The six Thorne lads that I sometimes travelled with were offered the exact same, along with a big framed Thurnscoe lad off the Whitworth Buildings by the name of Keith Brettoner, who I was led to believe had either been fighting at the pit or had threatened one of the undermanager's.

Moving pits was a total culture shock and I immediately understood what the Training Officer, Ron Lester had been doing.

At Hickleton Main I had been nothing short of spoon-fed and handed what was a great job. At Askern it was very much different. The pit was the most northerly of all those in the Doncaster Area and was extremely well ventilated, meaning that it was very cold in comparison to Hicketon – especially in the main gates (intakes). To get onto the two districts – the Main Line and the Union Line – men were hauled inbye, by huge diesel engines. On first getting there I was dropped off in the middle of nowhere and given the job of supervising three or four conveyor belts. It was a mong job that befitted the person doing it. I immediately realised my folly. I knew absolutely no-one there and had jumped headfirst into a pit where I was firmly at the bottom of the list and the last in line for any decent jobs. Looking after conveyor belts meant that that I was in a main gate, and I had gone from wearing minimal work gear and in most instances just a pair of shorts to stood around freezing my knackers off. All the conveyors operated from the surface and my remit was to make sure that they ran freely and unhindered and more to the point, that I cleared up any coal spills. I remember working that job all week, and half the time I was sat huddled in some manhole trying to get out of the wind.

What would happen however, would become a huge learning curve.

The miners at Askern Main appeared much different to those at Hickleton Main as the eastern Dearne Valley – especially Thurnscoe, is a far more aggressive place to live. Askern, although very much a pit village in every sense, especially given the smog and dust generated by the horrible dirty fucking Coalite plant, was often labelled a *Bus Pit*, as men travelled from everywhere to get there. From the Hexthorpe and Balby areas of Doncaster in the south; to Kirk Smeaton, South Elmsall and Upton in the west; and of course, from Thorne and Moorends in the east. And these were broken up by the local lads who lived in the nearby aspiring villages of Sutton, Campsall and Norton. In the main, its miners were perhaps more cosmopolitan and came over as certainly more well-spoken, if not more thoughtful people.

After a week or so, I was given a proper job on what would eventually be the B50s retreat face. However, when I got my docket on my lamp it was just a completed development with no face supports nor machinery and just comprised three tunnels: a main gate and tail gate linked by the tunnel that would form the face. What I was yet to understand was that certain miners worked in crews that did similar jobs all throughout their working life. I had seen the development teams down in the East Side of Hickleton and understood that my (step)dad was regarded as a face salvage Official. Here at Askern, I would be part of the face installation team, which for me was extremely interesting, especially as I was one of only three people in the mine that could operate what was a highly complex piece of kit for the dragging and turning of the hydraulic supports onto what would be the coal face.

What was also interesting was the size of the coal seam. It was little over three-foot in height, which would be a huge point in detail during the forthcoming Miners' Strike and why there was a huge disparity in wages both at different mines and in different coal fields.

155

You can be the best miner in the world, but you can only deal what is in front of you, and if four strips of coal is the maximum you can win during an eight-hour shift and that coal seam is only small, then you're very limited to what you can achieve.

The Official supervising the miners on the face installation was a guy by the name of Dennis Thompson, who could sometimes come across as being both witty and sarcastic. He was, however, someone who took me well and truly under his wing. All the lads did. I was extremely well looked after and there is something that still gives me a lump in my throat that happened immediately after the strike.

I had been at Askern a while and my (step)dad was to be transferred there with a load of other miners from Hickleton Main and I remember being in the canteen, when Dennis and the man who would become one of the greatest blokes I had ever have the pleasure of working under – an all guns blazing Official from Campsall, by the name of Brian Bennett, came over to me and asked: "Where's your dad, James?"

The next thing I know they are shaking hands with my (step)dad and immediately made him welcome. The pride I had in knowing them both at that exact point in time was immense. I had become a well thought of miner, who everyone knew as *James – not Jim.*

I still remember my first meeting Brian when the face installation had been completed and the production team took over and him shouting over the face Tannoy: "Jim, can you turn the picks over for the main machine?"

"You can fuck off," I told him. "My name's James."

I had all the lads on the face pissing themselves, as absolutely nobody dared talk to him like that.

He stormed off the face intent on giving me a right bollocking and all he got was more of the same. "My name's fucking James, not Jim."

He was such a lovely guy and nothing at all like the brash, aggressive if not arrogant façade he often portrayed. I would have run through brick walls for the guy, he was that good.

I still think of those dark days of first getting to Askern Main and the reasoning behind it – however, it is something that I wouldn't have changed for the world.

I remember the installation of the face and one of its miners who would become the very first scab at the pit during the twelve-month strike – a guy with curly hair by the name of Gordon Cufflin. I found him quite an engaging chap to speak with, as he had had a varied career outside of mining and at one time had been a professional diver on the oil rigs. During August 1984 he was in the national papers issuing threats that if any striking miner dare come to his house, they would get both barrels of his shotgun emptied in them.

The strange thing is, is that I never saw him again after the strike.

On the home front things remained the same, but I knew where I was heading. In my mind I wanted a house and the easiest way of getting one was to put my name on the NCB's housing list. That, although, never stopped my looking at other houses, with my real preference being to move to the village of Norton, and why I didn't, I still don't have an answer to as it would have been a move that would have made complete sense. At just a few pounds under £10,000 (£35,645, circa 2020), I viewed a red-bricked house on the village High Street, but even though I had the money for a deposit, I failed to put in an offer for it.

I felt a huge part of the colliery and its workforce, especially as I formed an integral, albeit lowest paid member of the face team, who regularly held the Paddy up by staying until the death trying to cut as much coal as possible.

The face itself had been badly designed, which was something that I would see in mining time and time again. It made you wonder how half these engineers got their stripes. The stage loader that transferred the mineral on to the main gate belt and the belt itself were on the wrong side of the tunnel. Therefore, instead of taking a few shifts to move the entire conveyor belt over the other side of the tunnel, they persevered with it and built a stage loader which comprised a jazz pan in its centre. This took the mineral from the end of the armoured flexible conveyor at the end of the face and which kinked into the direction of the main gate belt. It was a fucking lemon that was forever holding production up, with its flights and chain continually coming out of its runners or off the sprocket, or at worst, fully breaking.

"What's up with the face chain, James?" Brian would yell. "James, what's up with the face chain? James...?"

I'm on with digging it clear to find up what the hell's up with it and all I'm getting on the Tannoy is my name being continually shouted. Still, at least I wasn't being called Jim.

I helped dig that dumb-designed panzer out time and time again. It must have cost the mine a fortune in lost production, just because they wanted to cut corners by saving money on not having to move the main gate belt over to the opposite side of the tunnel. In fact, the only time I ever recall it being of any use was during the Friday afternoon shift on 23 December 1983.

Only a skeleton crew of miners had turned up for work, with the majority of young lads picking up their wages and going into Doncaster in the hope of tapping up some of the girls who worked in factories scattered around the town, such as S.R Gents, that were breaking up for their Christmas holidays.

As for us, we went underground cut off two strips of coal and then had a party.

With the stage loader possessing a kink from one side of the gate to the other it needed to have a bridge for the men to cross over it and that bridge would ultimately have a table cloth placed over it in the form of a tarpaulin and never again in my lifetime would I see a scene underground like it. I remember Brian taking me across the coal face to the bob hole in the tail gate and on our return into the main gate there were a few lads putting out all the food, one of them being Bob "The Rapist" Clark, a loveable rogue of a lad who along with a dozen others, once got falsely accused of raping a girl near Askern boating lake.

"I wish I knew the name of your fucking lawyer, Clarkey," our fitter, Kevin Cottam, used to say, whilst trying to wind him up.

The sight of seeing a total of just over four dozen cans of Long Life lager stacked up on that bridge along with all the pork pies, sausage rolls, pickles and cakes was nothing short of brilliant, as was Brian making sure all the empty cans got thrown well into the gob, which was a pit term used for the old collapsed mine workings behind the face.

I needed to have both my time at Barnby Dun and Askern to progress my life and as I have already said, both were a huge learning curve.

For as much as Paula had her spats with me, what I did like about her, were the tales I was told, which I would have never ever had heard if I hadn't been there – some of which had me in stitches, especially when my dad got involved.

My dad's brother, Uncle Paul, had four children with Auntie Anne. These were our Paul (b. 1969), Tracey (b. 1970), Steve (b. 1972) and Mark (b. 1979).

As soon as my cousins found out I was living at my dad's, they seemed to be at the house every other weekend, which pleased my younger brother, as the lads were great footballers – with our Shaun soon following suit, albeit for a very short time.

Our young Paul is one of the funniest kids you could ever meet, but it's our Tracey that often had me creased. Even at just twelve years old, she was a missus – dry as a bone and saying whatever came into her head, no matter what the consequences.

As I recall the tale, our (auntie) Liz's three kids – Scott (b. 1972), Kelly (b. 1973) and Leah (b. 1976), had apparently been over at my uncle Paul and auntie Anne's and our Tracey in all her wisdom decided that it was time for the middle one to meet her real dad. She only ended up knocking on the said Mr. Keith Spence's front door, which I am sure was a huge shock for he and his wife. According to Paula and my dad, our Kelly thought our Liz's husband, Graham Pettinger, was her dad, and on being told what had happened, our Liz went apeshit.

My nana could also tell a tale or two about our Tracey, one of which involved my uncle Les's eldest child, Donna (Durose) (b. 1970).

They had both gone down to see my nan, and as she always did, she immediately made a point of feeding them. In this instance it had been pie and chips.

"Where's your pie, Donna?" my nan had asked.

"Our Tracey's just ate it," came the reply.

Not only had our Tracey eaten her pie, she had also copped for our Donna's.

"You, greedy little bugger," is what my nan had supposedly said.

Our Tracey's retort after being verbally scalded, involved running off and shouting at my nan, "I'm not coming here again."

"I don't want you to bloody come here again," my nan had stated.

Did she?

Of course, she did. It was her nana.

Paula didn't mind talking about the Durose's – however, she often got touchy when her elder brother, Ron Newton (b. 1948) and his wife Mary (nee Fowler) were mentioned.

I knew Paula's younger brother Russell (b. 1961) and her younger sister Gail (b. 1957), both of whom I thought were extremely nice people. In fact, I remember visiting quite a few of her relations – one set of which, lived in the suburbs of York, who I thought were nothing short of lovely.

Russell was also a miner at Hickleton Main who I would get to know better after the Miners' Strike, whilst their Gail had just been married and had recently suffered a tragedy, losing an infant child, with my dad explaining that the little lad's funeral was one of the most heart-wrenching things that he had ever witnessed. I did say, didn't I?

As for their Ron, I only ever recall seeing him once or twice, but my dad gave both barrels in his astute description one time after they had stayed, in which he relayed several things: the high-handed nature of Paula's sister-in-law; her brother being both bald as a coot and totally henpecked; and the fact that they had a little dog which when they stayed, had pissed all over the bed.

That was another time when Paula went the colour of beetroot and stormed out crying.

As I have got older, I don't mind anyone's opinion about any of my family, and the reality of it is, is that it is not something that is cast iron and one hundred percent, but just what it is – an opinion.

During the late summer of 1983, the landscape changed dramatically and that was after the girlfriend and I split up. It should have certainly ended there, but it did not. My relationship with Paula, however, immediately changed.

"I've never seen you as happy and content," is what I got told.

There was a bit more to the situation than that, in that the housing committee or whatever it was, over at Hickleton Main were ready for dropping me a house, with my thoughts being that it was a house on Crossgate. This was the street at the foot of Lindley Crescent and the exact same street where my Grandma Ellis lived. Jackie Moon had always been a chirpy albeit rotund miner who I had known since I had completed my training. He had been employed on the salvage belt, within the highly mechanised colliery screening plant on the opposite shift to Ernie Hill and had sadly died, aged forty-nine. I was at the very top of the housing list and me getting his house looked like a foregone conclusion – especially as I had made it known to Ronnie Rich, who was on this so-called housing committee that this **was** the house that I had been waiting for. I would soon be a near-neighbour of my grandma's, or so I thought. Life working in the pits, however, was extremely political, especially the committees that were controlled by the NUM. It was always a case of *who* you know.

I had been waiting for a house since a few days after my eighteenth birthday, but what that told you is, is that I was still young, and I could therefore be easily fobbed off.

Now here is the strange thing.

I had been excommunicated from my girlfriend's house up until early July, when I was told that it was alright, for me to be let back in. If the shoe had been on the other foot and someone had done to me what I had done to them, there is no way on earth they would have ever got back in. I don't know why it happened – it just did. There was never any explanation. However, a month or so after I got back in, we had split up.

As I lived in Barnby Dun and worked at Askern Main, outside of my two grandmas and the odd auntie and uncle I visited, I had lost touch with a lot of people in Thurnscoe, even though there had been a steady influx of lads taking the same path as me and being transferred from Hickleton over to Askern.

I got in from work one day shift to find that my girlfriend's mum had phoned, and it was quite urgent, and therefore could I call her back.

I knew straight away that the reasoning behind the phone call was that the people at Hickleton Main Estates office were trying to contact me regarding the housing situation. I rang Joyce and found that a guy by the name of Graham Creighton had been trying to contact me.

I didn't know him from Adam and therefore asked Joyce for a run down on who he was.

She told me that he worked as some Onsetter in the pit bottom, was on the committee at The Docket and also happened to be on this housing committee. "I'm not keen of him," she said. "He comes across as a bit surly."

Joyce was always a hive of information and not unlike Johnny the shoe-shine guy in Zucker, Abrahams, and Zucker's satirical comedy at the time, *Police Squad!*

He had told my girlfriend's mum that there were six properties on offer and that I could have my pick. I wasted no time in mentioning Jackie Moon's old house at 15 Crossgate.

"I don't think that's one of them, love," she said.

I had been continually telling my grandma and granddad that it was a nailed-on certainty that I would be moving near them, and I was now being told that wasn't the case.

I shot over to Thurnscoe to catch this Graham Creighton – however, he wasn't at the pit, but at his home at 6 Briton Square, where he duly handed me the list of six houses – one of which was directly opposite his at No 16.

The last thing that I ever wanted, was to live back up in Thurnscoe East. I wanted the house near my grandma and granddad.

"Where's the house on Crossgate?" I said, looking at the list. "Jackie Moon's old house?"

"That one's been taken," he told me.

I was anything but a happy fucking chappie and went mental. I had had eight months living on my wit's end and keeping my mouth shut until my number came up and all I saw, was that I was being coaxed by some bald bloke with a chisel chin and glasses into some fucking rat hole opposite his.

"There's nowt up with Briton Square," he told me. "It's a good street."

All I saw was a square full of noisy kids and Freddie Bevins sat on the step at No 13 having a mug of tea.

The other five houses on the list were a right assortment of potential fucking demolition cases, including one on Hanover Street that had recently been the scene of a hanging.

I did quite like Freddie Bevins, however. He had been one of my (step)dad's old workmates who I had last seen underground at Hickleton Main, grafting alongside an old collier by the name of Tommy Chapman in P80s tail gate bob hole. They don't make people like that anymore. He was a very genuine man.

I had spoken to Graham like shit and all I wanted to do was go down to the housing office and leather someone, mainly the person who had done the back-door deal to get a guy by the name of Frank Nicholson in. Graham told me that the committee man had been reprimanded, but that didn't make it any better. The whole situation stunk. The guys father lived a few doors away at 11 Lindley Crescent and obviously knew someone who knew someone, and his son, being ten years older than me and just recently married to a woman by the name of Nora Chandler, ended up moving there instead of me. Or that is what I was told by my grandma Ellis, when I had gone down to see her.

My grandma knew everyone, including Freddie Bevins, the latter of who had even invited me over for a cup of tea and confirmed to me exactly what Graham had said, in that Briton Square, was quite a good street. I had to admit, at the time I was livid, but as time would pass it would be a decision that I have never regretted.

As for the house on Crossgate, it was a godsend not getting it, as the short cut from the bottom corner of Lindley Crescent into Thurnscoe's East end, would make all the national media outlets, including the front page of *The Sun*, whose sensationalised headlines were enough to make a person throw-up.

There is a snicket in the bottom corner of the crescent that takes you via a low underbridge beneath the Sheffield-York railway line. At one time there was only two footpaths after the bridge – one up the side of the railway track or the one up a huge scarp – both of which led onto what was at one time the old Wath Branch Line, but what in my lifetime has always been The Drum playing field.

Since the reprofiling of Pit Lane in 1977, however, a third footpath had been made, which directly connected the crescent with the pit, and just a couple years after I had been rebuffed for the house on Crossgate, the South Yorkshire Police had been out in force. They had set up a crime scene and were thoroughly combing the area. A sixteen-year-old girl had been bound, gagged, and raped at knifepoint just off a disused railway track.

Even after it was reprofiled, Pit Lane was still a dark inhospitable place with a horrible fucking history. And it certainly wasn't the first rape there as the family of Agnes Oldfield would testify.

The twenty-eight-year-old from 46 Church Street, was subjected to a malicious wounding, robbery and attempted rape by two men on 20 October 1902 – one of whom was sentenced to fourteen days imprisonment, after pleading guilty to a lesser charge.

As regards to more recently assault, a few miners from the Class of 1981, were questioned, with it being suggested that the rapist was a local man. The police were right. He was.

What I was to know immediately after the event, is that it was a girl that I knew extremely well. A girl that had called at my house on Briton Square many a time, along with her best friend who was my younger sister, Joanne.

Most rape cases have a lifetime anonymity for the victim, in that the names are kept secret, unless that anonymity is of course waivered, therefore it would be both quite wrong and indeed illegal for me to name the victim of the crime, even though it was well-known locally. I can, however, bring the world down on the rapist.

In September 1972, I moved from Houghton Road Infants and into its junior school. I remember the very last day in the infant school like it was yesterday because something very different had been happening. A new junior school had been built off the north-western corner of Merrill Road and nearly half our year were moving there, and those that were staying, had to sing to those that were leaving. It was quite emotional, as in my last year, I had made some great friends. There were two wooden annexes (Terrapins) within the infant playground that ran up the rear walls of Taylor Street and which housed the classrooms of both Mrs Wheeler and Mrs Follows, and we were all sat opposite them, whilst singing to the other children. However, what was happening in our year, was also happening in the first three years of Houghton Road Juniors, and children were leaving – one of who was a Third-Year pupil by the name of Alan Conner.

He was the cousin of a snotty-nosed kid in my year who once raised the roof in my very first year of the infants when we were stripping down to our Y-fronts for a lesson that was always dubbed as *movement*. The lad got lost in the moment and the next thing we all know is that he had taken his vest and underpants off and as such, was completely naked. Whilst everyone was laughing, the lad had been distraught.

Our teacher Mrs Gilbert tried to make light of it. "Poor Trevor," she smiled. "I bet you thought that you were getting ready for bed?"

Harry Conner had married Margaret Rose Hopper in 1957 and between them they had had three children – Steve (b. 1958), Sandra (b. 1959) and Alan (b. 1961) – the latter who had been born in Kenya.

The lad in my class had been Trevor Cattell, whose elder brother Brian had married Sandra Conner in 1980, and who for a time lived at 3 Merrill Road – which in days past had been the old Gooseacre Lane that had once meandered up into the old tree-lined Whin Wood, but which after its construction formed the entrance at the topside of the Big Lamp up into the huge sprawling council estate.

My connection with Steve Conner is slightly more interesting, as he married a girl in my year at Dearneside Comprehensive by the name of Julie Londesbro, who was not only a very nice girl, but along with her cousin Donna, became a good friend around 1980, which I'll explain a bit more as the story progresses.

The elder brother and sister never left the locality, with the former still living at 8 Co-operative Street in Goldthorpe and the latter remarrying Bert Butler in 2001 and moving to the other side of Thurnscoe's Big Lamp – over at 6 Horsemoor Road.

I always believed that Alan Conner was a face that I had never seen – however, that certainly wasn't the case. People can sit in the background and go unnoticed all their lives, however, this one certainly wouldn't. Neighbours told the police that he was a quiet lad, which gave slight indication to why the *penny* never dropped straightaway.

During my early senior school years – perhaps 1978 – his was a face that I along with Richard Clements-Pearce had sometimes sat across from, after boarding the 226 opposite Liptons (Brough's) supermarket, as he, just like us, went to Dearneside.

Maybe, Richard has a better recollection of him, but from what I can recall, he was a normal looking lad, who to say he came out of one of the shit holes on Taylor Street, made out that he lived some Fantasy Island existence and came over as extremely boastful. "Uh, it's that wanker, again," Richard would whisper.

Although it was nothing to compare with the horrific experience that her friend had been though, my sister had been devasted. They had been best friends for quite some time and had even been in the Thurnscoe Drum Majorettes together – an annoying body of baton-twirling and kazoo blowing young girls that are synonymous with many mining communities in the north of England – the treasurer of whom, had been none other than my grandma Ellis.

Conner, who was suspected of committing eight rapes and serious sexual assaults in the Dearne Valley area, between 1983 and 1986, was caught relatively quickly and handed a six-year sentence at Sheffield Crown Court, which for me, wasn't nearly enough. After serving four years he went out and did a copycat rape of an elderly magistrate coming from Midnight Mass in the early hours of Christmas Day, 1992, before creating his pièce de résistance some nineteen months later, whereby he raped and murdered a twenty-two-year-old chambermaid, before committing suicide by hanging himself.

My thoughts are is that the horrible piece of shit did away with himself nine years too late.

During the last couple of weeks at my dad's it felt like that my life was moving forward which for me, was a great feeling. I had put pen to paper for the house on Briton Square and had put in a request up at the Estates office on Briton Street, to give it a minor upgrade.

I bought a Tricity Contessa ceramic hob cooker from the Danum Co-op store for £449 (£1,600, circa 2020) on a two-year credit agreement and a £262 (£934, circa 2020) Zanussi washing machine from Vallances (formerly Clay's) on Goldthorpe's Doncaster Road on a twelve-month interest-free one, whilst for months upon months I had been stashing stuff for the house in the front bedroom of my grandma Carman's house on Ringway.

The big surprise was that my dad and Paula had bought me a £250 (£891, circa 2020) double divan bed as a going away (and don't come back) present from Barker & Wigfall on Doncaster's Hallgate, of which there is a story attached, but which, now is not the time.

This was a time in my life when I appeared happy and in full and total control of everything around me. However, there was to be a slight twist in the tale.

14. Motherfucker

"She's really missing you, you know," is what I was told by her mum.

My life has always been one of two steps forward and one step back.

Am I sure that I didn't mean that the other way around?

No. I was always destined to move forward, it is just that when I make the move, something tends to drag me back and this was one such instance.

I passed all the exams to progress being a mining engineer and ended up as a miner.

Like I said, two steps forward and one step back.

I would have no hesitation in saying that I got on with my girlfriend's parents much better the second time around than I did the first, although that could not be said about the elder sister, Ann. What could be also be true is that she hadn't liked me that much the first time around – however, that would be something that I could put down to the *elder sister syndrome* and something that I would certainly never lose sleep over.

Joyce moved mountains for me to get moved into Briton Square and was always on the phone, whilst I was over in Barnby Dun. She worked extremely hard sourcing me this, that and the other and wanted nothing more than to see me in the house, so much so, I was being invited for tea even though my relationship had terminated with her daughter. Admittedly, it wasn't new or top range stuff that my wife and I provided for my son or daughter with a swipe of a Debit card when they moved into their houses, but back then times were much different, and you can probably see that from how much things cost, compared to those of today.

She got me a second-hand Axminster stair carpet courtesy of Mary Bradley for £30 (£107, circa 2020), a huge room rug from one of the old ladies on her Home Help round for £10 (£35.65, circa 2020) along with a load of curtains from her elder sister, Elsie Watson (nee Roper).

I had also commenced dialogue with my mum and (step)dad and that too was much better this time around, although with my mum, it was always going to be something that was temporary, and something she would never be able to keep up, which was a shame because when she was good – she was very good.

Grandma Ellis offered me the refrigerator that all the grandkids had grown up loving, which often had an ice box full of frozen Mars Bars. It was an American design and not too dissimilar to the repro models that the Italian electrical manufacturer Smeg knocked out a few years ago – however, hers was a standard refrigerator as opposed to a fridge-freezer.

Did I take up her offer?

No, as much as I loved it, that was my grandma's fridge and would have never looked right in my house. Therefore, she did no more and whipped up another fridge from somewhere else along with a black and white TV, kitchen table and two armchairs – the latter of which were from Shackleton's, *you know* (sic the 1980s advert).

My grandma raised funds for the majorettes by doing jumble sales and bought me the TV for a nominal £1 (£3.65, circa 2020).

It may have taken around three weeks to warm up when you switched it on, but that TV had a great picture and looked very retro.

That house on Briton Square was the scene of pure happiness and little did I know while I was sat in one of those high-back armchairs in front of the cast iron fireplace and oven, that exactly ten years later, I would have lawyers from Nabarro Nathanson, who were representing British Coal (NCB), camping outside its front gates trying their damnedest to serve me with a high court writ, which is certainly something that I will elaborate on as the story progresses.

Life back then was simple, but taking the girlfriend back was always going to complicate things and that is exactly what it did. She immediately began questioning things, most notably: why I had bought an 800-rpm washing machine and not one that spun at 1100-rpm, and why my dad and Paula had bought me a standard double-bed divan, but without the drawers.

My mum and (step)dad had been back and forth dropping stuff off, but as soon as they copped sight of her, that was it. They stopped calling down.

I had also been taking our Shaun backwards and forwards between Barnby Dun and Thurnscoe, which was something that he really liked as he got introduced to a lot of people. On getting the girlfriend back in tow, that stopped too.

I have always considered myself a strong-willed kid and looking back at it, I could perhaps see why her mum wanted the relationship *back on*. I was perhaps the only one who could handle her overly complex personality.

Getting backwards and forwards to work at Askern Main was made easy, as by that time, around eighty lads had been transferred from Hickleton Main, therefore it was a case of a thirty-five-minute journey by bus, which picked us up outside The Fairway.

The plus side was that there was that a lot of lads my age who had been transferred such as Tim's cousin – Gary Bright; the lad who was turned away when I was signing on at the pit – Dave Helm; one of the lads who had worked nightshift down the East Side at Hickleton with me – Pete Duggan; one of Thurnscoe Comprehensive's extremely gifted schoolboy football players – Kevin Turner; Malcolm Hudson – the blond-haired lad that I'd grown up with down in The Avenues; along with one of the nicest kids you could ever wish to meet in Billy Coulson.

It was a time in my life that I totally embraced, as everything was **that** good.

Looking back, there are things that you remember that are trivial, however, if you think about them there always tends to be some reasoning.

I always remember getting up one morning in October 1983 and looking in the fridge to see what I could make for dinner when I got in. I was on Afternoon shift, and thought, *I fancy something different*. I nipped over Pit Lane to what at one time was the Supersave supermarket within the old Empire Picture Hall building in Goldthorpe and bought a packet of two Plaice fillets in breadcrumbs. It was nothing, but it was something. Suddenly I had choices in my life. I didn't have to eat what was put in front of me, I didn't have to go to bed when everyone else did and I could stay out until whatever time I wished. I had freedom, which was something that my grandma Carman explained to me when I saw her. "That's why I love it on my own," she told me. "You are beholden to no-one – you're your own person."

I felt that my job was the best ever, mainly because I was made to feel important, and not just by the Official in charge who was of course Brian Bennett, but all the senior staff at the mine – including the Undermanager's, all of who knew my name. In my mind, I felt that I was a somebody.

The only downside was that I had still been paying for the car that I had written off, which at times was something of a bug bear – especially when I had to use public transport to get to either Doncaster or Barnsley. However, looking back at it now, it was a blessing in disguise as I am certain that if I had still had it, my life would have taken a much different path.

I still remember the day I finally moved out from my dad's over at Barnby Dun and of Paula sat on the chair opposite me. "I really wish your dad was here to see you off," she said.

She was quite emotional.

"We all got on quite well, didn't we?" she added. "Apart from the thing with the car."

My dad had been at work when I left.

The man who loaded up the car for my life back in Thurnscoe was the self-same person that I had assaulted and turned his and his wife's world upside-down nearly nine months earlier, which says everything about the man. He was not unlike my (step)dad, in that he really deserved much, much better than he got.

The car was at best a superficial asset, which I am sure would have made my life easier – especially, during what would be a mad six-months straight after the miners' strike. However, here's the thing: Although I don't like aggravation, I have always tended to operate at my best when things are against me, although it is very true to say, that at the time, I certainly didn't know that.

I suppose Billy Coulson was the person that I was closest to at the time. We may have been totally different people, but we found ourselves in similar situations and had similar interests.

I was in the Mrs Wheeler's class with him in Houghton Road Infants, with the teacher being an elderly grey-haired lady whose favourite saying was, "By Jingo."

I remember us doing some clay work one particular day in 1972 and Billy forgetting to put his watch back on and leaving it at school. The very next day the teacher handed it him back, after asking whose watch it was.

"I bet your mam gave you a right telling off for losing it, eh Billy?" said Mrs Wheeler.

"Yeh, I got sent to bed," he claimed. "I climbed out the window and my mam was waiting at the bottom of the drainpipe with a frying pan."

The fibs that kids spin, eh?

My favourite yarn whilst in the infants, had been whilst in Mrs Gilbert's class.

Andy Roper was a kid that always seemed to swim in my slipstream throughout my mid-twenties-to-thirties, but back in 1970, he was just a cute little blond-haired lad who once amazed the teacher and all the class with his rather tall story of him hatching a chicken from an egg with the use of a couple of blankets.

As for Billy, he had been a good mate of Steve Wharton's through the latter years of school and it was through Steve that I had initially got to know him.

Billy lived at 67 Derry Grove with his mum Nora and his elder brother Eddie, the latter of whom I remember hitting with a needle on a cork. This had been shot from a homemade blow pipe that had been hand crafted by Steve from a piece of 15 mm copper tube.

Whilst knocking about with him we got into all sorts of scrapes, not at least breaking into one of the lock-up shops down the side of Thurnscoe Market only to find out that it was some form of hosiery, knicker and sock shop. I flogged my proceeds of the haul on the school bus the very next morning, as the Globe-owned coach that shipped us to Barnsley Technical College was half full of girls who were doing typing and shorthand courses.

As we had fled, a glove had been left at the crime scene – however, it wasn't the DNA that brought me in front of a detective at Goldthorpe Police Station, but the fact that our ex-breadman Ray Scholey, who at the time was renting a house on Shepherd Lane had seen me with the two other lads and had grassed me up.

My mum was adamant it wasn't me. "That's definitely not his glove," she said.

She was right, it wasn't – it was Billy's.

The thing that I recall during the period when I was knocking about with him, was that he and Steve were continually being bullied by a certain group of lads from the Lindley Crescent area, two of whom were Paul Cook and Graham (I think) Hope, both of whom were quite big lads, but a year younger than us. With me, the only time I ever really took a crack, was from four categories of bully: lads in a group, lads older than myself, lads who were handy themselves, or all three categories at once.

These were neither and I immediately fronted them up on Billy being threatened.

None of them wanted it – however, the girl they were with certainly did.

Tina Bradley was a pretty, headstrong girl off Brunswick Street, who as I have already said, was both the daughter of Mary and a year older than me. She did her best to egg them on to both have a go at me. "Go on, hit him, Paul," I recall her saying.

Girls eh – who says they don't cause trouble?

That, however, was the catalyst for a whole host of trouble, which first started with my knocking Brian Wood's front teeth out and then one evening being confronted by around twenty kids in the Market place, who were headed up by some ginger-headed kid, who from a distance seemed well over six-feet tall.

It was Steve Wharton who told me: "Run."

All the lot of them headed towards me, with their leader ripping off his coat or jumper. "Come on then," he screamed.

I took Steve's advice and shot off down the back of Shepherd Lane – however, this kid was like some fucking gazelle and was always in my sights and was it not for me wrapping the stem of a yard brush I was carrying around both his shins, I'm almost sure that he would have caught me.

That lad?

A Barnsley schoolboy's 100 m sprinter – the affable and very funny lad that is Brian Moffatt, who told Steve the very next day: "I've got have a fucking race with him."

In early 1997, I remember being stood with my wife in the rear garden of a huge empty house on Thurnscoe's affluent High Street and watching both our kids playing, while we spoke about the possibility of us buying the house. It was Brian Moffatt, however, who got in there before us. He is a good kid, Brian. I always liked him.

One evening the very next week we had gone to Thurnscoe Comprehensive to listen to a talk on sexual hygiene and contraception, that we thought might be good for a laugh and which had both Fourth and Fifth Year (Years 10 and 11) students there. These included some huge, brash big-mouthed lad, who was trying to be the centre of attention by asking idiot questions, much to the amusement of his underlings, one of whom was a lad who I'd been in the infants with – Don Elliot.

As was the case with Brian Moffatt, I always liked Don. He was an exceptional, albeit predatory schoolboy football player and was an extremely humorous lad. He was also a very handy kid.

As Steve and I left Billy to go home via Kingsway, I was jumped by two lads outside The New 'Un. It was Don and this big kid as supposed payback for me knocking Brian Wood's teeth out.

There's no shame in taking a pasting – however, the big lad was like a fucking animal and continually kicking and stamping on me after I was dragged down in the bus shelter. I just could not get away. I think it was Don who ended up pulling him away. "Come on, he's had enough," he said.

The kid was having none of it and was just screaming at me whilst laying in the boot.

The very next day I couldn't get out of bed and my mum ended up taking me to Mexborough Montagu Hospital for X-rays. She thought that my ribs had been broken. As it happened, they had not, they had just been badly bruised.

You do things when you are young kid that you wouldn't do as an adult and I have never sought payback or retribution with any one for what was done in what was quintessentially another life. I refer to it as *kid's shit* and nothing more. This one however, was different.

The Thurnscoe Cinema Company owned a huge red-bricked building between the Market Place and the Sheffield – York Railway Line, which I recall my (step)dad once telling me that he and his younger brother – my uncle Pete, were taken there by my grandma and granddad Ellis to see *Seven Brides for Seven Brothers* on New Year's Eve 1955. However, during my lifetime it was never a picture house, but a bingo hall before becoming a snooker hall-cum-public house.

When the Top Spot first opened its doors to the public it was as plush and upmarket as any snooker hall in the country – it was that good. However, with Thurnscoe being the volatile place it is, it has never really been a place to endear something new, and as with The Bomb at the foot of Stuart Street, which underwent an expensive overhaul and refurbishment around a similar time before being rebranded as Harvey's, it immediately attracted a younger clientele and began to gain a reputation – especially for violence.

One Saturday night in December 1989, a triple-nine call went out from the Top Spot and a green army ambulance (the normal ambulance men had been on strike) had been on site with paramedics trying to resuscitate a twenty-five-year-old man. He had been laid-out unconscious for twenty minutes.

I had seen him out a few times and he had never bothered me. However, this night in question, Andy Roper had been winding me up about him while we had been in The Galleon fish and chip shop, just around the corner on Shepherd Lane and I just thought *Fuck it*. I went back around to the snooker hall, sought him out and tapped him on the shoulder.

"Remember me?" I asked.

"Yeh, I know who you are," he replied.

He certainly did. I knocked the fuck out of him.

The kid? Steve Davies – the brash big-mouthed bully.

There is an old adage that states the apple doesn't fall far from the tree and here is where I can give you a bit of background regarding the kid, and something which goes all the way back to 4 November 1954 – a time when his grandfather murdered his grandmother.

His grandparents were John Robert Davies and Mary Ellen Gallagher, who resided just off The Avenues at 11 Church Street.

His grandmother was the daughter of Jim and Emily Ball (nee Clevelet), the latter of whom had made the same journey as my Nana Durose's parents and had come up from the Cinderford area of Gloucester to where the mines were being sunk, with Mary being born in Denaby.

She had already had a child before she married a man by the name of Martin Gallagher in 1925 – however, he deserted her after three months whereby she threw in her lot with John Robert Davies eventually settling at 36 Church Street, where between them and although they were never married, they had seven children: John (b. 1928), Charles (b. 1931), Mary (b. 1935), Robert (b. 1937), Jean (b. 1942), Danny (b. 1946) and William (b. 1948).

Shortly before 6.15 a.m. on that fateful day, Police Sgt. Harry Dixon was awakened by a continuous rapping on the letter box of the police house, which was located on Thurnscoe's High Street at the foot of Derry Grove.

"What's the matter?" asked the policeman, as he came downstairs.

"Can I see you a minute?"

It was John Davies.

"What do you want?"

"I've done our lass in," he replied. "I've strangled her."

What the policeman saw when he opened the door was a man, wearing a blood-stained neck scarf who was in what he described as being in a "fairly composed state". However, when he asked him if he would go back to the house with him, he replied, "Am I fuck – I might as well go on a fucking rope as live with that woman."

Sgt. Dixon called it in and went to the house with Chief Insp. Robson to find the dead body of Mary Ellen Gallagher, whilst Davies was cautioned and removed to Mexborough Police Station.

Church Street was much like Chapel Street next door and comprised two long rows of over forty terraced houses, which ran along either side of the street between Houghton Road at its top and High Street at the bottom, with Davies's house being the sixth house up on the left-hand side.

It is fair to say that the home was both cramped and in a squalid condition. A two-up two-down, with nine people living under its roof and no bathroom facilities, bar the outside toilet at the end of the yard, with the front room being utilised as a bedroom.

Davies had been getting agitated. "Can we get on with the fucking job now and get my statement written up?" he had asked the policeman, before his removal to Mexborough.

166

Dr David Ernest Price, a registered pathologist to the Sheffield Regional Hospital Board who was attached to the North Eastern Forensic Science Laboratory at Harrogate, had the body removed from Church Street at 8.40 a.m. It was then taken for a post-mortem examination at the mortuary, which was located close to the Brick Ponds and to the rear what was known as the Packey's Puzzle at Bolton-on-Dearne – a part of part of Furlong Road that had originally been built in the late 1800s to house the workers in the brick yards. For the record, a Packey was what the locals used to call rent collectors.

"Death was asphyxia due to suffocation of the type we call smothering," he explained. "I thought the findings of the lower part of the face that something had been pressed on the mouth, which could have been the bloodstained piece of sheet."

There had indeed been bloodstains on one of the sheets, which were also stained with saliva, whilst the bed, clothes and mattress beneath the body had been saturated with urine, the latter of which often happens when you lose consciousness due to strangulation.

Over at Mexborough Police Station, both Det. James Colin Craggs who was stationed at Goldthorpe and PC John Edward Barley had been speaking with Davies, both of whom stressed that the man's relationship with his wife was anything but normal, with Craggs remarking that he had made a number of derogatory remarks about his wife.

"She's the worst fucking woman in Thurnscoe," he told them. "The fucking rope won't frighten me – not for that cow. She's boozing all day in the Butcher's Arms and then comes in fucking and blinding in front of the kids. Boozing, horse racing and shagging – that's all she's bothered about."

There was, however, much more to the story, much more, and it had everything to do with the second eldest son Charlie Davies – the father of Steve Davies, the bully.

"Her own son has been shagging her," he snapped. "I've chucked him out two or three times. She's better off dead. They're all better off without her."

It was true that he had kicked him out. He had been living with an aunt at 24 Church Street for around six weeks, but he denied any wrongdoing. His father, however, went into far more detail during his interview.

"She was round at the Butcher's Arms last night. She wasn't drunk when she came in, but she'd had plenty. She started getting on at me after the kids had gone to bed and then set into me again this morning. She was fucking and blinding at me all the time. I couldn't make owt of her and I just told her to shut up."

He was then asked why they had the argument.

"When she got on to me this morning, she was playing hell because I had turned one of the lads out. This was our Charlie. It was because about six weeks ago I woke up and caught him slorming about with the missus. He was kissing and cuddling her in the kitchen. They thought I was asleep, but I woke up and caught them at it. All Thurnscoe knows about it. This morning I told her to keep away from him and she said that she wouldn't. They've been going out together. I got in a temper and strangled her. I did it with my hands around her throat and gripped her. She started kicking and trying to get out of bed, but I held on to her and she started frothing at the mouth. I then knew she was dead. She's better out of the road."

PC Harold Parsons who was stationed at Thurnscoe was at the murder scene with his sergeant and took a pair of knickers which had been lying close to the left foot of the woman on the bed, which according to the policeman, appeared bloodstained. However, on the post-mortem, Dr Price found something else. Semen was found inside the dead woman.

"I took swabs from the vagina which showed no signs of injury – however, there was semen found, although it is not possible to say whether intercourse had taken place before or after death."

Dead or alive, one thing is for certain – the sex certainly wasn't consensual.

Davies was formally charged with murder at 1.40 p.m. that day and he was remanded in Armley Gaol pending trial.

Davies, who had been a former surface worker at Hickleton Main turned manual labourer, was ill, and had been brought home from work in early September. According to his family practitioner Dr Francis Joseph Boyle, he was being treated for stomach ulcers – something which was making him lose weight. It was also alleged that the doctors at the hospital had told him that he only had six months to live.

(Sir) Rudolph Lyons QC of Park Square, Leeds defended Davies – however, whilst on remand he had been hallucinating and had thrown himself head first into a wall and attacked other inmates for no known reason and was therefore declared as unfit to plead by the Principal Medical Officer at the prison, Dr J.L Walker.

He was detained indefinitely.

John Robert Davies certainly didn't have just six months to live. He died in Sheffield's Middlewood Hospital on 3 June 1983, aged eighty. But what is even more strange is that he is buried in Thurnscoe Cemetery alongside the woman he murdered. As I said – very strange.

As for Charlie Davies – he had been a twenty-five-year-old Signalman in the Royal Signals when he married twenty-two-year-old Alfreda Astbury on 20 July 1957 – being discharged from duty and going into the mines thereafter. They had their son, Steve on 14 March 1964 whilst at 10 Wensley Street, Thurnscoe.

The Class of 1981 was not unlike its predecessor in that it did have its own bad eggs, although they were very far and few between – and to my knowledge, absolutely none, were working in the pits.

One of them had been in my form in the very last year (Year 11) of Dearneside Comprehensive and who for a time had lived at 37 Briton Street – a house opposite the old NCB Estates office and close to where Gladys Merricks' family had lived.

Bryan Frederick Robinson could be described as a loner and to my knowledge had very few friends, if indeed he had any all. This was something that his former neighbours from No 39, David and June Riley (nee Williams) further confirmed after Judge David Tremberg sentenced him to eight years in prison, when they described him to local reporters as being a strange, scrawny person with several front teeth missing. To add to that he was a man that was always scruffy, smelly and unkempt.

Robinson had worked as a carer for Sue Ryder – which operates the Hickleton Hall Care Home, that is located immediately to the rear of St Wilfred's Church, for twenty-four years.

In 2008, the-then forty-four-year-old, whose wife Patricia (nee Collier) also worked at the facility, was caught in one of the rooms with his trousers around his ankles, while he was supposedly tending an elderly patient – who was not only semi-naked, but in the final stages of Huntington's disease – a condition which had left her unable to talk or walk and doubly incontinent.

His employers immediately suspended him from duty and as he hurried home to pack a suitcase the police were already on Briton Street waiting to arrest him.

Det. Chief Insp. Mark Monteiro commended workers at the home for the way in which they handled everything, stating that the speed at which the incident was reported enabled detectives to quickly arrest him, gather vital forensic evidence and interview all the witnesses.

Robinson was found to have significant amounts of the dying victim's DNA on his body and during the police interviews he claimed that this must have been transferred when he was changing an incontinence pad. He did, however, admit to inappropriately touching himself (having a wank) in the patient's room. He was subsequently bailed, but after a three-day trial, in which some of the jurors were both visually and emotionally troubled, he was found guilty of rape.

I suppose it would be hard to top that with a worse person from the Class of 1981.

During the long summer of 1977, I spent a big part of that knocking about with several kids from Brunswick Street or jumping on an open-backed truck close to the pit gates which was driven by a red-faced bloke by the name of Rueben that had taken us pea picking. It would be during the latter where I would bump into a ginger-haired and freckled-faced kid by the name of Mark Williamson. He was an amiable lad with a great sense of humour who I would often see whilst we were on a night out in Thurnscoe. My last few recollections of him were in Harvey's, which was of course at one time The Bomb, and which was located at the foot of the road he lived – that of Stuart Street and whilst in The Fairway, which was conveniently located at his streets end. And as such he regularly moved between the two.

Mark always came over as being the ultimate party animal. That's just how he was. Very harmless and quite fun to be around.

It could be said, and quite rightly so, that he had a problem in that he liked a drink and as such he drank heavily, but that didn't take away any of his nice points, because unlike some, he was rarely ever nasty with it. Very fucking argumentative but never nasty!

"This lad," he'd slur, as he aimed some dialogue towards my wife, "is just a great fucking lad."

"Do you want a beer, Mark?" I asked.

"What did I tell you?" he further slurred. "A right fucking lad."

It would be in The Fairway however, where I would get chance to speak with him, as one of my neighbours from 14 Briton Square used to call around during the week to ask if I fancied nipping to the pub with him for a couple of beers and a game of pool.

You could only ever describe Jimmy (Smurf) Ridsdale as being a lovely man. Diminutive in stature, with a bald head and Zapata moustache, he was everything that was good about living up in Thurnscoe's East end and was a throwback to times-past, when neighbours would do anything for one another. He had married a woman by the name of Shirley Weeding in 1973 – the younger sister of the sleepy-eyed East Side Loco Driver, Gordon, who not long after the birth of their son Jonathon in 1982, had walked out on him and their five children – the eldest who wasn't even his. As such, he had had to pack in his job at Hickleton Main to look after the children and supplemented his DHSS payments in a similar manner to that of Sonny Fryer, by doing remedial tasks, such as getting people's coal in and gardening. Jimmy was a truly marvellous fellow, therefore, even though playing pool was something I was never that overly bothered about, I rarely turned his offer down.

Mark was always a regular face in the pub during midweek – however, as we generally went out early-doors, he was relatively sober – possibly as he had only had time to shift about seven or eight pints.

Around this time his younger sister Cheryl had been in a relationship with a kid out of our year who I had met around the same time as Mark. He was also someone that I knew extremely well, with my very last line of conversation being: "What the fuck was she doing with him, Mark?"

All he could do was shrug his shoulders. "I've no idea, mate."

Alan Robert Cook was born at 71 Brunswick Street to John and Sandra Joyce Cook (nee Scrimshaw). He had an elder sister Jackie (b. 1963) and three younger brothers – Terry (b. 1968), Stewart (b. 1971) and Nigel (b. 1973).

He possessed long brown hair and had eyes to match. He was also a kid that you could never turn your back on. That is not to say I never got on with him, for in the main, especially in the early days of knowing him, I did.

At first, he appeared an engaging kid with loads of tales to tell, but like most things, when you scratch the surface there is much more underneath. With his mum being from the huge Scrimshaw family, he had lots of similar aged relations that I grew up with. Cousins such as Owen – who had lived on Bolton-on-Dearne's Stumpcross Gardens, with his dad Tony (according to his son), at one time owning a rather stylish Russian-built Moskvitch motor car. There was also their Donna, who lived in one of the earlier odd-numbered houses on Goldthorpe's Hope Avenue and who was one of the nicest girls you could ever wish to meet. During the latter years of school, she'd had a best friend who was another relation of his – this time through his father's side of the family, who I recall had moved back into the area, from Bolsover. Julie Londesbro was not only his cousin, but as I have already said, also the sister-in-law of Thurnscoe's very own black sheep – the serial rapist and murderer, Alan Conner.

Donna was without doubt one of the most obsessive young girls that I had ever met and used to drive my (step)dad berserk, due to her incessantly ringing up the house. Around that time a person could hang up the phone, but if the person at the other end didn't want to put their phone down, then the line would be continually engaged. And that is what happened – and on a regular basis.

"Will you tell that lass to stop pissing phoning," he'd snap at me. "She's getting to be a right pain in the arse."

She wasn't really. My thoughts now, are that at the time, she was going through quite a rough period, as her mum Jean (nee Clayton) had recently walked out on her dad. That, however, is Donna's story to tell and certainly not mine.

He also had couple of other cousins our age who lived in Thurnscoe East and who I didn't know that well. One was Robert (Snag) Stringer – a witty lad with the face of an old man who had lived on the northern arm of Brunswick Street and another, who was Ian Hughes. Ian was one of those music loving petrolhead's who signed on at Hickleton Main just a couple of months after me, and whose father Joey – just as with Jimmy Ridsdale, was another first-class bloke and who is someone that I'll definitely get to.

I had first noticed Alan during the build up to the Queen's Silver Jubilee. We were supposed to have a series of street parties, but the weather never held up and it ended up pissing it down. Barnsley MBC, therefore, let us have the use of Thurnscoe Hill Infant School for a few jumble sales and a bit of a party prior to us topping off the celebrations with a coach trip to Cleethorpes. Due to my popularity (not) of being from Bolton-upon-Dearne and going to Dearneside, he certainly knew who I was. He was one of those kids that continually looked you up and down and someone you could never ever read, and at times, it would be fair to say, that he came over as very dark. I got speaking to him at the beginning of the school's six-week holidays and I thought him a fascinating kid. The stories of his dad loving the old Rock 'N' Roll music – in particular, the Big Bopper, and of his uncle Joey (Hughes), who he often described as the hardest man in Thurnscoe, had me enthralled. As was his description of the pecking order of the best fighters in what would soon be the Second Year (Year 8) of Thurnscoe Comprehensive. He was a good kid to know, or so I thought. The truth was is that there was an underlying motive and he had purposely attached himself to me, like he would with another one of the Class of 1981. He was like one of those snakes – just measuring up his pray before he made his move to both squeeze the life out of it.

I had a list drawn up in my head of all the kids who had caused me grief since February that year, something which Neil (Hopkinson) had helped me compose and which I had already done a bit to rectify. I had beat the living daylights out of both Jimmy Frost and Tony Taylor, the latter of who was the younger brother of my uncle Pete's common-law-wife, Irene Bridgen and therefore the grandson and great grandson of Willie Taylor – one of the many poor souls that sought eternal solace in Thurnscoe's Drowning Pool. To some extent, Tony – bless him, got some form of recompense while I was on the southern arm of Brunswick Street and mucking about outside the home of Granville and Jean Bilton (nee Saunders). I looked up, only to see a posse of around a dozen kids, one of who was Tony. He was being led by this much elder lad who had a huge squarish head and whose eyes appeared set unusually wide apart. Not only did he also possess a strange face, he had hands like fucking shovels, which he duly clenched into a pair of fists before giving me a right couple of winders around either side of my head.

"That was Phil Stringfellow," explained Alan. "He's two years older than us."

I last saw Phil at our Donna's (Durose) wedding reception in May 1991. He was still as handsome (sic), but nevertheless, quite a lovely lad. He was also the cousin of Martin and John Finbow, the latter of who was another that had drowned in The Reser back in 1963.

Alan not only seemed to know everyone but had also had a fight with everyone too – including both Phil and Martin.

What would happen however, is that his life on Brunswick Street would shortly come to an end. His family would have to uproot and do what was termed as a *moonlight-flit*, prior to the bailiff's entering the property to seize what furniture they did have for non-payment of rent. It was the first time that I had ever heard of anyone being kicked out of their house. I felt sorry for him, especially as the temporary accommodation that he would be moving into was some dirty static caravan sited directly on what was part of the old Wath Branch Line sandwiched between the rear gardens of Goldthorpe's Probert and Hope Avenue's.

You can end up putting a series of two and two's together and never end up with the right answers.

I seem to recall that his father had finished or been finished from the pit. I cannot recall his mum being around at the time, although I could be wrong. What I do know is that things were extremely bad with the family at that time. It had been mentioned locally – possibly via the Hopkinson family, that one of his younger brothers was blind or partially blind and that the problem could be perhaps be rectified by some state-of-the-art surgery in Russia.

It hadn't just been idle gossip – Alan's younger brother Terry had been extremely poorly. He would never reach adulthood and died in Sheffield's Children Hospital on 8 January 1985, aged sixteen. He had been fighting against what was termed by Dr J Wales at the hospital, as a Malignant Astrocytoma – a type of cancer that forms in the brain or spinal cord. It was all very sad.

I'm not sure of the exact timing, but not too long after Terry's death, I recall that another one of his younger brothers had been one of the three teenagers who had supposedly been convicted following an arson attack on Goldthorpe Library. It was a fire that had been so intense that it melted the UPVC windows on some of the houses on Goldthorpe's Queen Street and which ultimately saw the building demolished.

Whilst they had still been in Thurnscoe, I had also regularly noticed Alan's elder sister Jackie.

She possessed a striking similarity to Sissy Spacek's characterisation of *Carrie* in the 1976 film of the same name. She always appeared to have her hair in pigtails, wore a headscarf and rarely smiled, if ever, which was something that would be duly explained to me – not by her brother, but by a female member of the highly knowledgeable (sic) Hopkinson family.

A couple of years earlier and whilst she had been playing with her friends on Brunswick Street and skipping, the rope made contact with her head and knocked off her headscarf, which had been attached to what was a wig that revealed a head with very little hair. This created not only gasps of disbelief from the other children, but also fits of laughter. I was told that Jackie was distraught. She had suffered from severe alopecia from being a young child and the insecurity it must have created whilst growing up, one could only imagine. Jackie was a nice kid. She never ever deserved that.

All things considered, they were a family that had had it hard – however, Alan's sudden hatred towards me, was something that I could never ever fathom. As I have said, you never ever knew what the kid was thinking and whilst out walking the dogs on the huge field off Chapel Lane, he attacked me with a flurry of punches for no reason whatsoever. It was something that happened a further three times while I was twelve to fourteen years old – the most severe being on 31 October 1979, whilst on Hanover Street waiting for a bus. I had been destined to go to some Halloween party at Dearneside and whilst completely side-tracked and in conversation with Neil Hopkinson, he along with two others jumped me – the others being Wayne Tansley and Jimmy Frost, the latter who I don't think actually did anything. It could have easily happened another four or five times in between, was it not for the fact that I could outthink, outpace, or outmanoeuvre just about anyone my age.

Wayne had been not only my nemesis through senior school, but he had also been part of a huge mining family in the East end. Physically, he developed much quicker than I and the fights we had, especially when I was around sixteen and seventeen years old, he had always tended to get the better of me. There was, however, a time on Hanover Street during spring 1982, when this hadn't been the case. I had just called in at the Yorkshire Bank in Goldthorpe on my way home from work and disembarked the 213 bus, whilst he had been in the opposite bus stop talking with the girl who would become his common-law wife – Jacqueline (Jackie) Murray. I slipped the blue cheque book into my back jeans pocket walked up to him and gave him one hell of a right-hander, putting him firmly on the floor before duly stamping on his head. The sad thing about it all is that I really liked him and thought him a wonderful lad. As I said – it was all just *kids shit*.

Prior to him meeting Jackie, he had suffered the same fate as I had, and had **let** Alan attach himself. Wayne was nowhere nearly as quick as me and would suffer much worse.

Jackie sadly died on 11 January 2006, aged thirty-eight, which was something that Wayne must have taken extremely hard. The last time I ever saw him was one Christmas Eve a few years after her death. He had been stood alone at the bar in the Golden Nugget WMC (Pigeon Club) on Goldthorpe's Co-operative Street and was barely recognisable from the smart, albeit highly confrontational kid with the volatile persona that I once knew. He survived his wife by just eleven years and died in 2017, aged fifty-two. One thing I will say about Wayne is that he dearly loved Jackie.

As for Alan, you just never knew what was going on in his head, therefore the best thing all around was to take two steps back and keep him at arm's-length, which is exactly what I did one night in The Fairway a good few years after.

There had been talk that he had been handed some jail time following a volatile domestic incident with Mark Williamson's younger sister, Cheryl. Thurnscoe, however, is one of those places where you have to take things that are said with a pinch of salt, even from the guy who was saying it – in this instance, her brother. One thing for sure, though, is that he went missing for a period of time and she ended up moving away from the area.

On reappearing from his absence, he had been sat on his own in the right side of the lounge, looking vastly overweight and both dishevelled and drunk. As I walked through the front doors and into the pub, he immediately acknowledged me like some long-lost friend and tried to make chit-chat. That, however, was never going to happen. It is a shame as nowadays he appears content amongst what I am sure is a lovely family.

"I'm not like that anymore," he recently told me over social media.

The thing that I never knew until recently is that Alan and Cheryl had had a child, Sam, who died in July 2004, aged eighteen years old.

No-one deserves that kind of hurt.

As for Mark, his heavy drinking had caused him to suffer from cirrhosis of the liver and chronic pancreatitis, which culminated in heart failure instigating the loss of his life at just forty years old. What was even stranger, however, were the circumstances surrounding his death.

Mark never strayed far throughout his short life and had lived at 61 Stuart Street with a twice-married woman from Thurnscoe who was fourteen years his senior, by the name of Sylvia May English (nee Hart), who rather strangely died straight after, with both their bodies being found on 5 February 2005.

Assistant Deputy Coroner, Donald Coutts-Wood recorded an open verdict stating: "I cannot ascertain who died first although the more likely one is Mark Williamson."

It is believed Sylvia had found Mark dead in their bed and died afterwards, possibly from hypothermia, as her body was found fully dressed on the bathroom floor.

"I personally think Sylvia, who had slight liver problems consistent with effects of alcohol and anti-depressants, which were found in her blood, became upset and distressed at having found Mark dead and in whatever condition she was in had thrown things around," explained Det. Sgt. Karl Saxton. "If there is a condition for a broken heart, I would suggest that, as the couple were said to be extremely devoted to each other."

Home Office Pathologist, Dr Ken Shorrock had described Mark as being "severely emaciated" and around six stones (38 kg) in weight. "He hadn't died of alcohol intoxication, it was a combination of liver disease, pancreas disease, with his muscles wasting away and it was one of those in his heart that ultimately caused his death."

If you want another bit more of Thurnscoe's horrible history, you don't have to look that far.

When he had been forty years old, Cheryl and Mark's father – Colin Williamson, a Pan Turner at the colliery, had lived at 6 Dane Street North with his first wife, Ethel (nee Bladen). On 17 January 1957, he had been committed for trial at Sheffield Assizes after being charged with five offences of indecency against three girls when they had been between ten and fifteen years old. The offences had occurred between 1946 and 1955, when Ethel had been in hospital.

I'm not sure of the sentencing or how much time he served, but I do know that his wife eventually passed away in July 1960, aged forty-two. He remarried Rowena Lee a woman who was seventeen years his junior in 1964. She was of course the mother of Mark and Cheryl.

As for the bullying, I have played both sides of the fence – both physical and mental. Kids can be cruel, of that there is no doubt, but it can be dealt with. It is a simple case of how much you love your children and of course how far you wish to go.

I kept a lot from my mum and dad as I dished far more out than I ever got back, but the stuff they did get told, they had been worse than useless at dealing with it.

As a father, I had a problem to deal with when my fifteen-year-old son came home with a fractured cheekbone. Luke Storrs had been a kid that had been local to me. He had been at the scene and confirmed that my son had been hit around the face with a hammer. Nowadays, he is a popular scratch musician who uses the pseudonym Franky Wah and who was someone that I got to know quite well due to us both owning gyms. He told me that there had been three assailants – two of whom had held him back, the other who dealt the blow.

My wife made the phone call to one of the parents, of which the reply immediately took her aback.

You know the one: "How dare you. My child would never do that etc., etc."

My telephone call was much, much different.

"I've got a lad on the firm who will come through and put some steel in all three of them," is what I got told.

I could never hurt a child, never mind target one. Also, having someone knifed up is not really my thing – although, I must confess, it is something that I am not a stranger to.

Now, here is where I must again be vague and therefore use that play on words.

It is a route that I had gone down before. It was also a job that went badly. The target had been an active paedophile who fled the area. Generally, it takes less than five minutes to find someone, but in this case, it took me quite a few weeks to track him down as these people are extremely underhanded and shifty. I ended up finding him in the Liskeard area of Cornwall. The reasoning as to why the job went badly. He survived. I really can't be any blunter.

In the case of my lad, all three sets of parents were targeted, and the emergency services were fucking everywhere. If you are going to do something it always best to do it right. What I didn't envisage was the tenacity of the police in trying to track down my son. They wanted their first building block. Hearsay is no good. They wanted that written statement of motive.

My wife had rushed him over to the A&E at Doncaster Royal Infirmary – the X-Ray of which confirmed the fracture to his face. The police had gone in the opposite direction and shot through to Scunthorpe General. By the time they had got to us my son was with his sister. There was no fucking way on earth they were turning this around and putting it at my feet. Rule number's one and two: do not let yourself be bullied and never ever give a statement.

After the carnage – and believe me when I say it – that is exactly what it was, the police rigged up discreet high visuality cameras in the house directly across. These were supposedly to focus on my movements, which after some rather finger-in-the face dialogue from my wife to our halfwit of a fucking neighbour, she got removed the very next day. The damage, however, had been done. The story made the front pages of the local media on two consecutive weeks. Two sets of parents – the same job. I will tell you what else happened. The parents of the boy who had dealt the blow sincerely apologised to my wife. My wife was also quite reciprocal in her dialogue. She said that she was very sorry to hear that her business had been burned to the ground.

As for Mark Williamson, he died far too early, as could be said of another lad from the Class of 1981 – and one who had started alongside us in the pits.

I still have fond memories of Malcolm Hudson riding around The Avenues on his tricycle – a contraption that he wouldn't let any other person use.

The son of Dennis and Doreen (nee Eyre), he had lived at the end house on the second row of Landsdowne Avenue, which I am surmising was number one. Whereas our front garden possessed a scorched piece of earth from the previous Bonfire night and elsewhere was overgrown with weeds, along with what looked like some broken-down 1930s Armstrong Siddely car two doors up, his was extremely well looked after. It also had a strawberry patch that had been tenderly planted by his father.

He was the lad that I grew up with, not only in The Avenues, but through Houghton Road Infants. Whilst out of school we patrolled every inch of those streets, whether it be checking out the interiors of the fast-emptying houses or scaring ourselves shitless by telling each other tales of ghosts that haunted the Emmanuel Pentecostal Church (Tin Chapel) on Chapel Street. This was a building that is no longer there and with its high frosted glass windows, once backed onto the rear backings of Landsdowne Avenue's even-numbered properties. Time and time again we tried to peer through those rear windows trying to make out what *evil* deeds were being done inside.

A trip up the snicket between Lloyds DIY shop and the fruit and vegetable shop, took us onto Houghton Road where there were shops in abundance, with a Wrigley's chewing gum machine outside the Co-op supermarket being a great source of intrigue, especially one day after it had been refilled and not properly closed-up. The fruit and vegetable shop (now D.J Foods) had a broken down Commer or Thames van parked up in the rear yard, which was full of old boxes, the fusty smell of which I still remember like it was yesterday. As with the old car on next-doors front garden, we took it in turns to pretend to drive it.

I still remember my mum coming out onto the street, soap suds up her arms looking for me and the dog, the latter of which I was supposed to be taking out for a shit. I, however, had been more preoccupied bobbing-down in the old broken-down car and trying to stop it from barking as it had copped sight of its owner.

I remember going back home five minutes later wondering why she had been looking for me.

"That *Dick-a-Dum-Dum* song was on the radio," she told me.

I have always remembered it as *that song*, but I could never recall the tune or who indeed sung it, until I looked it up. Even the iconic 1970s footballer Alan Hudson said he had never heard of it and he used to be regularly boozing down King's Road, which was the other part of its title.

If you don't overplay them, certain songs always take you back to some era in a person's life and the song I most recall that was on the radio whilst living down in The Avenues was Esther & Abi Ofarim's *Cinderella Rockefella*, which places me there in spring 1968. This is much the same as me hearing the Bee Gees' *Massachussets*, which places me at my auntie Heather and uncle Jimmy's at 45 Barnburgh Lane in autumn 1967.

Back then, there seemed to be a radio playing in every house.

The song that always takes me back to the earliest time at my grandma Ellis's was hearing The Seekers' *Georgy Girl*, which would make it around spring or summer 1967 – however, the one I recall the most vividly was Scaffold's number one hit, which still as me smiling as I recall my (step)dad singing it and purposely changing its chorus: *Lily the Pink, the Pink, the Pink, she made a big stink...* This was something he always did with my daughter and which always had her giggling. Just imagine *Postman Jake with his Eight Foot Rake (Postman Pat with his black and white cat).*

On immediately arriving at Landsdowne Avenue, I was placed in pre-school in the old red-bricked Thurnscoe Central Hall Methodist Church opposite the junior school with two of my main recollections being that there was a great sandpit to play around in along with a kid who was strangely labelled *Diddle-Diddle-Dumpling, my son John* that in one instance had shit himself.

For a child, The Avenues and surrounding area were a place of adventure and us leaving would come straight after a storm. My mum explained that it had been thundering and lighting, which was followed by a torrential downpour of rain. Our house always had that old, damp, fusty smell and on her getting up during the night and going downstairs, she heard noises and turning on the room light, she found the carpet to be crawling with black clock beetles. "You've never seen anything like it," she told me. "There were hundreds of them, and your dad was running around and hitting them with the poker."

We weren't the only house on The Avenues that suffered from them, I think every house did.

If you stand in what is the now the car park of the ASDA supermarket on Houghton Road and look over at what is now is some Community Centre and sheltered accommodation for the elderly, it is hard to envisage the noise of the hundreds of children that once filled those two huge playgrounds behind its infant and junior school.

I still recall around two dozen or so young lads walking arm in arm around the playground shouting "Anybody in my way gets a kick!" to the numerous games of marbles we had in the holed-out tarmac close to its peripheral walls, with a kid by the name of Shaun McLaughlin being the undisputed champion of champions. I do, however, once remember Col Hunter throwing a marble from close to the Annexe where Mrs Follows taught class and over to an holed-out piece of tarmac near the coal bunkers, a length of which at that time seemed immense, and getting a hole in one and Shaun absolutely refusing to give him his marble as he was supposed to be playing me.

Malc was the more laid back of us all and never ever kicked off during our games of Cowboys where Dean Naughton and Shaun Hufton always wanted to be Hannibal Hayes and Kid Curry out of *Alias Smith & Jones*. As for the rest of us, we were designated with the leftovers of what was the cast of either the *High Chaparral* or *The Virginian*, with me often refusing point blank to be fucking Trampass again. Poor Andrew Hyde – he always drew the short straw. Andrew, the son of Les and Iris (nee Taylor), was a portly kid that had moved into my grandma Ellis's mum's house after she had died and who was often saddled with being one of F-Troop.

My great-grandma Hampton (Sarah Elizabeth Cowen, nee Hunt b. 1886) died in December 1971. I remember her often sat in a rocking chair in the kitchen of my grandma Ellis's at 63 Lindley Crescent and on the odd occasion of my grandma taking me to her house at 13 Garden Street, being mesmerised by an ornament on a Welsh Dresser that constituted both God and Jesus up in heaven. A widow herself, she had married William Hampton in 1959 and had moved into the house he had shared with his wife Ann, who had passed away some seven years earlier.

What is strange is that Andy still lives in the very same house!

Towards the back end of 1983, Billy Coulson had been deployed underground quite close by to the district where I worked and as such, we travelled inbye together. Firstly, on one of the huge diesel-hauled Paddy trains and then on a low rope-hauled Paddy which took us closer to the coal face.

The one thing I recall is the timing of us changing from one train to the other, which was a time when the day shift bumped into the afternoon shift and vice versa and Malc Hudson shouting: "It's pissing it down outside."

It wasn't, it was just a case of piss-ball and somewhat displaying his displeasure at having to go underground, whilst we were all travelling towards the surface.

Those would be the last words I would ever hear him speak, as he lost his life on 18 May 1985. He was killed in a car crash around one and half miles along the same road from where I had lost control of my car.

Their car had been driven by Steven (Ribby) Wray. He was around eight years older than us and the younger brother of Kenneth – a man that had been convicted of the manslaughter of three-year-old Shaun Lewis Meredith of 61 George Street, Thurnscoe on 16 April 1973.

It was said that Kenneth Wray had kicked (or punched) the little lad in the stomach. It was a severe blow which a ruptured his duodenum, thereby poisoning his bloodstream. He had been dead on arrival at Mexborough Montagu Hospital.

I have heard different stories, but it is rare that you will ever get to know the truth in cases such as this. As already astutely stated by Gwen Cole's grandmother – it is a situation where the only person left to tell the tale is the killer – and they will lie through their fucking back teeth to plead their innocence.

As for Malc Hudson, he had been in a vehicle that had been travelling much too fast and which was over cramped – with Kev Turner, Steve (Chalky) Whyte and Paul Unsworth being its other passengers. And as a vehicle pulled out of Blacksmiths Lane onto the A635, the driver braked, before losing control and ploughed into a lamppost just outside what would eventually be Marr Lodge. It was tragic. Malc was just twenty years old.

Gary Bright was planning on travelling with them, but he told me that he had been playing cricket.

Gary was and always will be a very colourful character, and inside that loud, brash façade beats the heart of an extremely nice and very honest lad. Too honest.

Although we went to different schools, I always knew who he was. You couldn't miss him. Not just because of his size, which was nothing short of fucking huge, but because he was always talking, yelling, shouting and pointing.

Their Tim (Bright) could easily be described as a good and dedicated sportsman, whereas Gary could be described as a brilliant and undedicated sportsman, and there in a nutshell I suppose, you have the parallels between the two cousins.

Tim always appeared to be quite meticulous and serious in how he dictated his life, whereas Gary appeared a kid who just didn't give a shit, which if I'm being honest, is nothing at all like either lad.

As a young kid, Gary was often labelled as Thurnscoe's next Jackie Hampshire, his vocation to be an opening batsman for Yorkshire. He really was that good.

On starting out at Hickleton Main, he tested Ron Lester's patience time and time again and I think in the end Ron just gave him up as a bad job. He stuck him under the guidance of Sid Calderbank – an Official who deployed a load of lads on what was Belt-Clean Up – another Mong job shovelling shit and clearing coal spills.

On his transfer to Askern Main he was given the responsibility of manning some transfer point out in the middle of nowhere, but even then, he got himself into bother.

As I have mentioned before, as a conveyor belts take mineral outbye and towards the pit bottom, the opposite can be said of the bottom belt, which can be used to transfer tackle inbye and towards the coal face. Rumour had it that Gary had been fined by either the Overman, Undermanager or Manager for some minor indiscretion – something which at the time his angelic deportment had emphatically denied.

A transfer point involves the operation of a conveyor to dump mineral onto another, which someone else is obviously operating – however, Gary was getting restless and needed a shit. It happens. Every miner would have needed to have knocked one out at some time or another, and as this was 1983, there was no Health and Safety regulations to state that there needed to be toilets scattered around the mine. In fact, I once recall being part of a crew sinking a ventilation shaft in December 1993 and a lad from Tarmac Construction who was supposedly showing us how to line the structure with steel reinforced concrete asking: "Where are the toilets?"

"There isn't any," I said.

He couldn't believe it.

"Just dig a fucking hole and do one," I told him.

"What do you think I am – a fucking animal?" he snapped.

As for Gary, the last thing he wanted was to smell his own shit, so legend has it – and I stress legend – is that he stuck is arse over the main structure of the belt he was operating to send his excrement inbye on the bottom belt and let the other Transfer Point Attendant (Button Man) deal with it. Little did he know however, that some Belt Maintenance Fitters had sent their bag of tools inbye at a similar time and when they got to the plough, which had a dual purpose of screening the coal fines and stopping them going around the return roller as well as sliding equipment off the bottom belt, they found their tools to be absolutely covered in shit. And as Gary must have weighed in at nearly 20 stone at the time, it is highly unlikely that it would have been a small deposit.

As we all used to travel to work together, there became quite a nice atmosphere – especially on Afternoon shift, with Gary being absolutely obsessed with *Auf Wiedersehen, Pet* and Tim Healy's bit on the side that was Dagmar. As such he used to continually knock Geordie phrases out, much to the dismay of a few of the lads who liked listening to Simon Bates's heart wrenching *Our Tune*, which started to play around the Redhouse turn off at Junction 38, before we cut across the A1(M) on our way over to Askern.

In fact, as Christmas 1983 approached I remember the DJ playing Bruce Springsteen's extremely cringeworthy version of *Santa Claus is Coming to Town* and Tex Rodgers candidly stating: "All this fucker wants, is some lead in his ear."

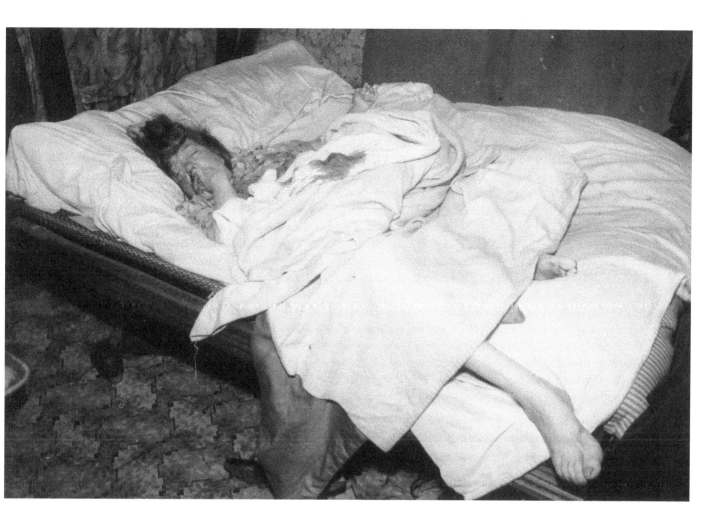

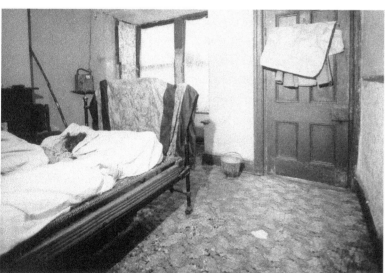

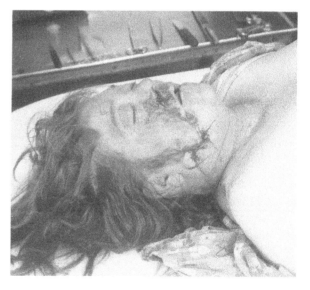

The murder of Mary Ellen Gallagher of 11 Church Street, Thurnscoe (c. DPP / National Archives)
Top. John Robert Davies strangled his common-law wife to death on 4 November 1954. Bottom Left. The bucket, is a statement of the toilet being out in the yard... the state of everything else - the squalor. Bottom Right. The deceased inside the mortuary near Bolton-on-Dearne's Brickyard ponds.

15. Roy of The Rovers

I loved football and I loved playing football. I think a lot of that came via our Tony (Greaves), who was the Carfield school team goalkeeper and who as glory boys often did, flitted between supporting the in-teams at the time. In our Tony's case it was Manchester City and then Tottenham Hotspur – who at the end of the 1960s and early 1970s were both quite brilliant teams. That was until Manchester United bounced back from being relegated and started imposing themselves in the top tier of football. Anyhow, I'm digressing. The first game I remember playing was in the first year of the junior school at Houghton Road. A 2-2 draw in which Andy Roper poached our two goals. From then on, I was hooked, and everything revolved around it. On moving back to Bolton-on-Dearne and starting at Carfield – and with our Tony being a couple of years older, I got introduced to a lot of older lads, some of who played in the school team – and at mid-morning and dinnertime break, or playtime as it was then known, there was always a game with some form of ball. Be it a cheap and nasty lightweight vinyl one that tended to float anywhere and everywhere or a tennis ball, it didn't matter, there was always a game of football. One of my first recollections was in the autumn of 1972 in the larger of the two school playgrounds that run parallel to Highgate Lane and playing away from the entrance from the main road towards the school, which doubled as the smaller nets I scored a goal. A snapshot which flew over the goalkeeper to make it 1-1.

"That was over," I remember someone on the other side arguing.

Johnny Loraine was having none of it and dutifully explained that the shot was dipping, and it was indeed a goal. Johnny was one of the coolest kids in Carfield. He played in the school team and more to the point he wore white Alan Ball-type boots. He was an extremely nice kid, who lived on the Flower Estate and who immediately on leaving school would marry his childhood sweetheart, Kim Battersby – the cousin of Glenn.

Carfield school team circa 1972/73 played in black and yellow striped football jerseys and my life's ambition at the time was to wear one. There were two players in my year that you could say were better footballers than me – Gary Salkeld and Alan Bainbridge.

Gaz was the better of the two and owned a Brazil 1970 shirt, and as that was the case, he reckoned to be Jairzinho. He was a fantastic player with brilliant ball control, so much so, you would have thought that the ball was glued to his feet. However, he was never the quickest of players.

Alan was a totally different type of footballer and was more of a team player. The thing which set him apart from everyone else was that he was not just an intelligent little lad, he was also naturally left-footed.

Strangely, Alan had been the goalkeeper who my dipping shot had beaten. Not because he was a goalkeeper, but because at that time he didn't know any of the big lads – and the little kids or the shit players generally got shoved in the nets.

One year on, however, it would be Alan, walking into the last lesson of the day dressed in the famous yellow and black striped football jersey. I remember it vividly. We were all seated on the wooden floor in the hall that was the central and focal point of the school watching him proudly walking in with the number eleven sewn into the black shorts. A second-year junior playing with all the big lads in the school team. I couldn't wait for my time to come – however, it never would.

The school team was run by the Czechoslovakian-born Mr Kurt Kneissl – one of the last of the dying breed of truly disciplinarian schoolteachers. His run-of-the-mill punishment was *automatic five pages*. He appeared a smart, heavy-set man with a receding hairline and was someone that it was fair to say, did have his demons. He would become our form teacher in the Third Year (Year 5) of Carfield and it would be here that I would see the two sides of the man who was known to the elder lads who he had taught, as *Hitler*.

I thought him a quite a good teacher and there was a very good reason for that – however there were some that didn't. Although throwing a five-page essay at some kid for a minor indiscretion was his thing, he wasn't averse to beating a child and on two occasions I saw him lose control and beat the living daylights out of both Roger Kitchen and Stephen Tomlinson – and for what, I really cannot remember.

Kitch was an extremely funny kid who lived at 151 Ingsfield Lane – the long street which separates the geographically named concrete pit houses on the hill that are centrally split by Canberra Rise and the low-lying concrete pit houses within the Concrete Canyon.

During the mid to late 1970s Kitch had a place in Carfield folklore where younger kids would come up to him in awe just to shake the hand of the lad whose huge red bogey was present in the latter pages of Frances T. Humphreville's novel, *Top Flight*. It was the sort of infamy which would last a lifetime and even now I remember opening the pages and having several secret looks at what was an artistry unparalleled. As I have already said, Kitch was very artistic (sic).

As for Steve Tomlinson, he was a kid who had been in foster care with the Grocock family that lived just off Commonwealth View – in one of the last houses on Carr Head Lane close to where the Wath Branch Line once passed beneath the infamous suicide bridge. It was a structure that had claimed many lives, with one of the last being an eighteen-year-old by the name of Francis Bernard Davy from York Road, Doncaster during 1944. As for Steve, he was later adopted.

A recollection of him, bar the beating he received from Mr Kneissl, was of us all singing *Praise, my soul, the King of Heaven* in the Hall and him nearly bursting his lungs trying to sing the chorus: "Praise him, praise him, praise him, praise him; Praise the everlasting King."

It was Mr Kneissl who taught me how to do fractions. I had got by, from copying off a couple of girls on our table – and although they got a few wrong, they also got a few right, which meant that I had sailed beneath the teacher's radar for quite a while. That was until they had stopped letting me copy. It was then that he copped onto the fact that I couldn't do them when I got none out of twenty. It took him ten minutes to show me how they were done and the next test we had, I got a perfect twenty. I was clever enough, but my main problem was, if it didn't interest me, which Maths certainly did not, I tended not to listen.

As for football, I loved it and Mr Kneissl knew that, so much so, that after the school team got knocked out in the semi-finals of the Totty Cup against Rawmarsh Monkwood, he prepared the blueprint for what would be the following season by putting together a new first-team devoid of any Fourth Year (Year 6) pupils and arranged three home fixtures to see out the season. These were against Bolton-on-Dearne (Lacewood) Juniors, Goldthorpe Juniors and Thurnscoe Gooseacre – with me wearing the Number 10 shirt.

Strangely that season, Carfield had worn a brand-new blue strip, of which possessed a red and white diagonal sash across the breast of the shirt and being in Mr Kneissl's class we were told the reasoning behind why there was a much larger number five shirt and shorts. These were to be worn by Neil Brearley aka Tea bags. A rather rotund lad with a high-pitched voice.

As for the three games – we absolutely hammered Bolton Juniors 7-0, beat a brilliant Gooseacre side 3-2 and drew 1-1 against an even better Goldthorpe side – the latter who were littered with some very good young lads, and who the very next year would reach the final of the Totty Cup – beating none other than Gooseacre 3-1 in the semi-finals.

Even though they were at full-strength, Bolton Juniors were a notoriously weak side and only possessed one decent player, that being a dark-haired kid by the name of John Grierson. As this was the case, I remember a few different faces in our team, one of which was, Anthony (Horlicks) Allsop a brilliant lad who in later life would unknowingly help me prepare for a huge career change.

One of two main recollections of that game, was of John Weddell being upset at being substituted at half-time and on me walking off the pitch, thinking that, although they knew I was playing, neither my mum nor (step)dad had bothered to come and watch me.

As for the game itself, how I never scored, I will never know as I made three or four of the goals. The game against Goldthorpe was a bit special as it was me who hit the opening goal – a left foot shot from outside the area

179

after Gaz Salkeld had had his shot blocked by a defender. All I really remember about it was beating Goldthorpe's argumentative and aggressive right-back to the ball and Eric (Eggs) Francis jumping on my back after I had scored.

Just for the record, their right back that day had been Shaun Hill – who is definitely someone you will get to know as the story progresses.

The game against Gooseacre was even better as I played against kids that I had been in Houghton Road Infant School with, and although it was hardly as one-sided as the game versus Bolton Juniors, the score certainly didn't give a true reflection of the game. We played at what I would have called – full strength, with our three goals coming from a hattrick courtesy of Gaz, with the winning goal itself being a penalty. Their two goals had been poached by Don Elliot.

The lad who had kept the scores down, however, was Gooseacre's red-shirted goalkeeper, Mick Whitehurst – the younger brother of Billy, the ex-Newcastle United and Stoke City centre-forward.

Mick had turned in a performance of cat-like agility. He had been nothing short of outstanding, turning several shots onto the post – one of which was from me and even denied Gaz a further two or three goals. He even nearly stopped Gaz's penalty – getting a hand on to it and palming it onto the upper inside of his left-hand post.

The game went 0-1, 1-1, 1-2, 2-2 and then 3-2.

Another recollection of that game was seeing the gazelle-like Neil Lacey of Gooseacre, shoulders-high and racing through on our goal at the end of the game to hopefully secure an equalizer, only for the blond-haired Mick Crook to dispossess him as though he was coolly picking his pocket and play the ball up to me.

We had what looked like a great side. It started off with Owen Scrimshaw as goalkeeper – however, Owen had been dropped after a couple of errors and Paul Lockyear ended up taking over.

Dean (Dino) Newcombe and Darren (Daz) Hughes played at both right and left-back respectively, both of who, in my opinion were head and shoulders above any full back that I had ever played against as a kid, whilst Mick Crook and Graham Freeman were at centre-back.

Dino was the grandson of the man who cut down the man that hanged himself in 18 Manor Avenue in 1931, whilst Mick was the son of Albert and Miriam (nee Grainger) and the younger brother of John Crook – the most *famous* butcher in Goldthorpe. With his long blond hair, he possessed an uncanny resemblance to the front man out of rock band *The Sweet*, and as such was perhaps the coolest ten-year old you could ever meet. In fact, in 1988 he married a very pretty girl a few years younger than us by the name of Julie Simpson and between them they had four kids – two of whom are Kieran and Brandon – the front man and drummer with the indie band The Sherlocks. I bet their dad never told them that he used to like Gary Glitter!

Graham possessed quite an explosive shot and was the exact opposite of Mick. He was the son of Ray and Jean (nee Murray) and had an elder brother and sister – Nigel and Lorraine, all of whom had moved from 140 Smeaton Road, North Elmsall onto 14 East Croft. This is the cul-de-sac off the eastern leg of Crossways that backed on to St Andrews Square. They all possessed quite a broad accent but the most notable thing about them – with the exception that they had a very generous auntie who owned a sweet shop down near the Cross Daggers public house, was that they were all extremely tall.

His elder brother was not only the Head Boy (prefect) at Dearneside when I arrived at the school but a straight 'A' student with an IQ that was through the roof. What was strange is that he never hit the heights he should have.

I remember reading either the *Dearne Valley Weekender* or the *South Yorkshire Times* which explained that a Nigel Freeman, who had been the Treasurer of The Comrades WMC, had been arrested, charged, and eventually sentenced to prison for embezzlement.

The midfield was made up of John Weddell and two great lads from a year below us – the long-haired Eric Francis and the ginger-haired Graham (Davish) Davis.

John was a very smart, albeit very spoiled kid who lived across the road from my grandma Carman's on Ringway. His dad Joey was Training Officer at Manvers Main and his mum Brenda (nee Hinchcliffe) – a schoolteacher at Gooseacre.

I have quite a few recollections of John as a kid. The first was of him being a Page Boy at my uncle Pete (Rayner) and auntie Margaret's wedding at the Sacred Heart Church and of us playing Jack, Jack, Shine-a-Light in John Pugh's back garden at 38 Crossways and us all going home absolutely filthy as we had been playing on the coal heap.

As for football, I remember us playing some four- or five-a-side game, just off Ringway's junction with Crossways, us all in our scruff and John the total opposite. He was decked-out in a white Leeds United kit, with both a Number 8 sewn on the back of his shirt and a flapping Number 8 sock tag. It was also his ball, therefore we all had to do what he said, which meant his side winning no matter what. This was to be a trait that followed him all the way through school. I remember Tim telling me the tale of a cricket game on The Rec in the latter years of senior school, whereby he was given out – and as the cricket gear – i.e. the bats, ball, pads and wickets were all his, he stomped off taking all the gear with him. Being spoiled aside, I always thought that he was a very tidy football player.

As for Eggs and Davish, they were extremely talented players for their age, as were quite a few of the younger lads in Carfield at that time such as Andy Mangham and Darren Scothern, both of whom were two and three years younger than me respectively, and both of who could have made a living out of football if they had had the breaks.

Eggs was a brilliant young player, whilst Davish was the more industrious. To complement that midfield was Gaz Salkeld, who was given a fee-role to either pick up the ball in defence or bomb forward in attack, whilst Alan and myself played up top – well we did in that final game against Gooseacre.

Were Andy Mangham and Darren Scothern as good as Gaz and Alan?

Gaz was extremely confident, had an outlandish brilliance and was by far more skilful – however, a lot of the time, and like most young lads do at that age, he tended to play for himself. Alan was a totally different player and being heavily left-sided he could be left out of the game if the play was on the other wing. He could also be bullied, something that Gaz would never ever let happen. The upshot being that Gaz could carry an average side and Alan could not.

The answer to the question is that at their respective ages, Darren Scothern was perhaps the best footballer of them all and possessed similar traits to a similar aged kid over in Thurnscoe East by the name of Garry Till, who had a similar kind of unflappable elegance. In the year above us, I thought both Gary Moody and Dave Kelly quite brilliant, but Darren I have to say, was very special.

I couldn't wait for the following season – however, what happened during the summer holidays made sure that I would never play for Carfield again – although whilst in the First Year (Year 7) of Dearneside, I did actually play against them in a Friendly match on 13 October 1976, with me scoring the second goal in what was an easy 3-1 win. I remember the date as I got home half way through *Striker*, which was a hugely popular TV series for kids at the time which had been penned by the man who played the ghostly Marty Hopkirk – and of watching *Carry On Cabby* straight after *Nationwide*.

I recall the summer of 1975 starting off with me bumping into Alan whilst on a two-week holiday with my dad and Paula down in St Ives, Cornwall. We were staying in some huge static caravan in the grounds of Carbis Bay Hotel, whilst they were down for just over a week and staying in some hotel in the Trelyon Avenue area of the town. On getting back to Bolton-on-Dearne, the landscape was beginning to change and what was once an acre or so of waste ground that separated the 120-unit residential development that was the Flower Estate and Carrfield Lane, now had a fenced compound within its bottom right-hand corner. This contained both the site offices and stores for what would be Phase 2 of the development – something which would see the construction of both Beckfield Close and Grove.

From me arriving back in the village in late-September 1972, that waste land, which contained two huge mounds of earth along with the flora and fauna that grew wild such as the oxeye daisies, dandelions, meadow buttercups and cow parsley (mother die) had been playground to all the kids that lived there. It would be quite unheard of today with children content at making dens and catching butterflies and bees. That, however, is exactly what we did do. There had also been the waste ground opposite Billingley View, where a new school called Heather Garth was being built – and where in time, Mr Kneissl would become its headmaster. Times were changing.

I still recall about twenty of us playing a game of cricket on the waste ground opposite Billingley View one Monday evening during summer and afterwards getting a bath and sitting down with my brother and sister to watch *The Waltons* on TV.

Opposite us and in the bottom house of Broom Close, lived Patrick and Ida Thomson, along with their youngest son, Karl, who was a bespectacled lad two years my senior at school.

Patrick had been born in the north of Liverpool and had been a widower prior to marrying Ida Bagshaw a couple of years after the Second World War. His first wife Margaret (nee Farrell) had died and had left him with two sons to look after – Pat and (John) Inky.

"I arrived in Bolton-on-Dearne on 2 January 1949. I had come down by train from Liverpool along with my brother, Pat," explained Inky. "I remember my first sight of the Nissen huts at the bottom of Lowfield Road as we left the railway station. At eight-and-a-half years of age It was a vivid memory. The only pictures we had seen had been in the newspapers."

I certainly knew Pat, as he was one of my dad's best friends and had a lovely wife by the name of Rose (nee Depledge), who he had married in 1960. They were best man and maid of honour at my mum and dad's wedding on 13 November 1963.

My dad had a photograph of him as a teenager dressed in military uniform – a paratrooper. Pat and Rose would initially set up home in Thurnscoe's western terraces – at 23 Orchard Street and go on to live at 47 Stuart Street. He also worked down the Low Main part of Hickleton Main, where just before the Miners' Strike, he would be voted-in as one of the NUM representatives.

Inky picked up his nickname following some spat with a fellow pupil on his first day at Mexborough Technical College. "We were waiting for the school bus when Les Wilcox and myself got into a scuffle. I swung out with my satchel, which struck him. Unfortunately, it had a bottle of ink in it that spoilt all the new text and exercise books that we had just been issued with that day," he told me.

"The very next day the Headmaster, Mr Tom Horncastle, led me by the ear onto the stage at a mixed assembly and introduced me as Inky Thomson – the lad who had destroyed expensive educational materials and the name stuck."

Inky took a similar path to his brother – however, he was far more ambitious and picked up certain socialist traits from his (step)mum, Ida. It would something that not only served him well, but which generated a huge respect from a lot of people – one of whom is me.

The main recollection I have of Inky was him driving to his parents' house and parking up his Mark IV Ford Zephyr 6 in front of the garages that separated the two Close's, and him getting out of the car looking like Rod Steiger's Komarovsky character in David Lean's adaption of *Doctor Zhivago*, with his pointed beard and piercing eyes.

As for Inky, their Karl was in awe of him, and quite rightly so. He had married a girl by the name of Christine (nee Bull) in 1963 and became a senior NUM official at Highgate Main Colliery and who was extremely active in the Miners' Strike. He later became the deputy leader of Barnsley MBC.

Old Pat and Ida also had two daughters: Marie who I rarely saw, and Christine, who I did.

As for Karl, he looked remarkably like his two half-brothers and wearing NHS glasses, often with a plaster holding them together, he was of a more studious appearance. He was also a person who at times wore his erudition a little bit too highly in that he often came over as being a self-proclaimed expert of both everything and anything. One nice recollection of this extremely engaging young chap came after a heavy snowfall in January 1977, which forced an early closure of Dearneside Comprehensive, and of us walking home across The Rec opposite Carfield school. It was here that he educated me on police techniques in tracking footprints. I was mesmerised. He explained that although he and Alan Johnson – a kid in his form, who in later life would go on to manage Ings Lane WMC, both had the same type and same sized shoe, they would be able to tell whose footprints they were, by the depth of the imprint as Alan was slightly taller. There was no doubt about it, he put himself over as being quite clever. He was also quite devious, and nearly four years earlier during the summer of 1973, he had lied to his mother after being involved in a fight with me on the old railway embankments off Ings Lane's football field.

He had received a burst nose after Brian Taylor – his next-door neighbour-but one, who was around four or five school years older than me, along with his mate, had got us to fight each other. It was cruel, but the fact was, it is what kids did back then.

As for Karl, he had said that Brian and his mate had held him down whilst I had hit him and as a result, I received a good hiding with the belt from my (step)dad. This would be the first of the two times that he ever hit me. It was also something he apologised for in later life.

What is strange, is that I bumped into Karl at the bar in the Top Spot snooker club around 1990, and in a round-about way he brought this up. I say strange, as he remembered *his* story and not what really happened. My wife immediately took a dislike to him and asked afterwards why I just didn't give him a smack in the mouth? I couldn't really answer that, as I had handed out beatings for much less.

Karl had two relations that were brothers, both of whom were as different as chalk and cheese and both who would have totally contrasting lives.

Their mum Pauline (nee Hurst) I seem to recall, was quite pretty and during the said period drove a relatively new Volkswagen Passat. The story was, that she had been previously married to a guy called George Miller and they had had a son called Paul who was four years above me in school. She had then left her husband and hooked up with a man by the name of Harry Baxter and had both Nigel (Biddy) and Adrian (Ady) in quick succession.

Harry Baxter had lived at 75 The Crescent and was someone who had been a very colourful character. On 22 January 1957 at just nineteen years old, he and Terry De Carolis of 111 Ringway had been found guilty at Rotherham Quarter Sessions and sent to Borstal for stealing cigarettes. It sounds extreme, but there was a lot – 39,000 to be precise.

Although that was a decent haul, it was easily usurped by a near-neighbour of two sets of my great grandparents on School Street – the Griffiths's and the Drabble's.

On 28 July 1949, Jack Hirst had stolen 170,700 cigarettes and 3 lb of tobacco from a goods train at Colwick Sidings, East Markham, which had been valued at £1,359 (£49,810, circa 2020).

Described as a motor repairer and wrecker, the thirty-eight-year-old lived with his wife Lily (nee Eaton) and their three children – Jacqueline (b. 1935), John (b. 1937) and Michael (b. 1944) at 24 Station Road, Bolton-on-Dearne.

He was sentenced to five years at Nottingham Quarter Sessions on 11 October 1949.

Aside from being vociferous, Adrian was absolutely nothing at all like their Nigel and was just a kid that everyone liked.

How they were supposedly related to the Thomsons I didn't know, but Ady was a regular visitor up to the Flower Estate during the summer of 1975. I thought he was a great lad and he quickly became a good mate – his first request to me being, to step in and stop a fight between his so-called cousin, Karl and Paul Gundry – the latter of whom was not only my next-door neighbour but had been five school years younger than Karl.

It had been a fight of contrasting styles. Paul was a lovely kid, and for his age was quite fearless. He had a one-dimensional style of fighting – head down and windmill-style. His more senior opposition was, according to the man himself, an expert in Judo, and possessed a rather strange kind of Frankenstein type of arms stretched-out strangulation technique that may well have worked if it hadn't for the flurry of punches that he'd been receiving. In the end Ady and I broke it up, but I have to say, the crowd which had gathered around all thought Paul had come out well on top.

That aside, the main thing we did whilst Ady was around, was to race around the waste ground – either on our bikes or running, the latter of which created something of an alarm a few weeks into the school holidays.

The course started from behind the four garages that separated Primrose and Broom Close moving towards the rear garden of Harry Dawson's house at 47 Ringway and then down past the old detached garages towards the old railway bankings on Carrfield Lane and then around the site offices and compound towards where the new school was being built on Billingley View. Ady being Ady wanted to do race after race after race and on his fourth time around, he collapsed.

His mum was in panic and on arriving at the Thomson's she was of course nothing short of distraught – however, Ida, bless her, did try her best to calm her down. The upshot being that he had fainted, and as that was the case, under no circumstances whatsoever, his mum had told him, could he race again. We didn't. We went over what was termed at the time as *The Seven Fields* towards the old quarry up near Billingley and after getting jolted on a couple of electric fences, we decided to steal the two energisers that charged them. Not content with that, we then climbed beneath the mesh fencing of the site compound on the waste land and stole a load of gas regulators or timers, which were to be put into the new homes that were about to be built and which were of no use at all. It was all exciting stuff, so much so, we ransacked the a few gardens in a couple of allotments. Those that ran parallel to the bankings off Carrfield Lane and those to the rear of Green Gate Close and in the shadow of the embankment that carried the Sheffield – York railway line.

One afternoon, however, I recall us coming back from a family shopping trip in Goldthorpe and as my mum pulled the car up outside our house, a bearer of bad tidings was evident. In this case it was our neighbour, Jack Gundry. He told my mum that the police had been around to our house as me and Ady had been stealing from the site compound. It was obvious what had happened. His son Paul had grassed me up and someone had called the police – Jack most probably. It hadn't been the first time Paul had grassed me up. A year before, he let it be known that I had set the waste ground on fire, which was something that attracted a large crowd along with two or three fire engines to put it out.

My penance for the stealing? As well as being grounded, I was banned from playing football for the school, which was a shame as Carfield were absolutely dire the following season, getting knocked-out of the First Round of the Totty Cup – 5-0 against Rawmarsh Sandhill.

As for his elder brother, I last saw Nigel Baxter in Barnsley Magistrates Court in early 1991, looking angry, pale and gaunt. I was in the first stages of trying to defend some charge of grievous bodily harm.

As for Biddy, he had been involved in some complex drug-related case that I didn't really understand and had been livid after I let him know that I had seen the court usher just inform the police that he had absconded.

Prior to that, the last I had seen of him was outside Bolton Club one Wednesday night a few months after the Miners' Strike. He had just wrapped a tyre iron around his ex-girlfriend's father's head. I saw it happen and what I saw, was nothing short of brutal – his victim was absolutely covered in blood.

"What the fuck, Nige?" I said, after running between them.

I didn't exist. All he had was a vacant look in his eye as he threatened not only his near concussed ex-common-law father-in-law but also the man's daughter and his eighteen-year old ex-girlfriend – a blonde-haired girl by the name of Tracey Marriot (now De Carolis).

Notice a link?

Col Hunter was with me at the time. "Don't get involved, J."

It was good advice. I didn't.

Nigel also looked totally unlike Ady. He hardly cut the most handsome of figures and possessed a long horse-face and a skinny frame. He was, however, someone that did grow on me. He had a big mouth but was extremely funny. A colourful a character if you like, and one of the things I recall was during the Fourth Year (Year 6) of Carfield and preparing for a school play that was due to be aired in Assembly about bullying and him playing the part of the bullied kid. His brainwave was that he needed to make himself look even more downtrodden and poor, therefore he took some already ripped red T-shirt and went over to the flower beds behind the teacher's entrance to try and cover it in dirt. As he was doing it, one of the teachers, Mrs Florence Gibbons arrived at school, saw him both covered in mud and damaging the flower bed and went apeshit. "What are you doing you horrid little boy?" she shouted.

Mrs Gibbons bless her. She was a fiery albeit diminutive stone-faced lady, who the last time I saw her had been during the late 1990s. This was after I had come across her in the car park at Goldthorpe Market, where she commenced giving me a bollocking for parking my car too close to hers. That was until I gave her the respect that she deserved and told her what a lovely teacher she had been.

I wasn't lying. She was. Quite hard, but fair.

"I certainly remember your name," she said.

"So how are you doing?" I asked. "And how's your daughter – Cathryn?"

That was it. I never realised what a great conversationalist she was. I was stood there a good twenty minutes listening to her, whilst at the same time keeping an eye on the traffic warden who was hovering around like some vulture over a corpse.

She had married former headmaster of Carfield – Mr Walter Cooke on 23 August 1979, who sadly passed away in 1995. As I have already said, he was a truly lovely man who played the piano nearly as good as Les Dawson.

"Come on children, I'm not very good on this so you'll have sing louder to cover up me playing all the wrong notes," I once remember him saying, after he had stood in for the regular pianist, Mrs Webster, during one assembly.

Mr Cooke was originally a Thurnscoe lad – born 8 September 1929 and brought up at 73 High Street. He was the son of Henry Cooke – a Grocery Branch Manager of the Co-operative store. The thing I didn't know, however, is that while he was headmaster at Carfield – he had lived at 30 William Street, off Highgate Lane.

As for Nigel, his life would end in the grizzliest of circumstances.

He had been living with a thirty-one-year-old woman at 15 Avenue Road, Wath-on-Dearne by the name of Wendy Freeman along with her two children – a girl of twelve and a boy of nine, when on 4 November 2000 she couldn't take any more abuse. In a frenzied attack, she stabbed him a total of eighty-nine times, stuck his body in a black bin bag and dumped it in the cellar.

The world of drugs is one that is often glamorised onscreen, however, the reality of it couldn't be any more different – especially when that drug is heroin. It is a dark, filthy existence that creates grey bodies which reek of sweat and which will do anything to maintain that flow of capital to fund their habit and stave off the aggressive symptoms of the chemical's withdrawal. It is an extremely vicious circle and one which no person in their right mind ought to get involved in. It is that bad.

Nigel and his partner were both heroin users, with the latter explaining during her trial at Sheffield Crown Court, that Nigel had forced her on the stuff in a bid to have more control over her.

He was certainly capable, but whether that is entirely true or not, only she would know.

What was true is that Nigel had numerous previous convictions for violence and drug-related offences and was using the house to deal – however, here is where the reality of a being low-level heroin dealer and user shows itself.

On the morning of that fateful day, Nigel had used his partner's bank card to withdraw £40 from her account and on returning home he dragged her from bed and demanded to know where she had hidden the rest of the money that he knew she had been putting away for Christmas. This wasn't anything new. Hard drugs and violence go hand in hand.

She had once fled to a women's refuge and had an injunction served on him after he had beat her. All he did was find her and tear it up. It was a similar story after she had left him, only for him to find her at her parents, who he duly assaulted.

Wendy's barrister, Jonathan Hall QC told the court that she had tried to placate him, without success, and that Nigel had punched her in the face before he began inflicting serious wounds to her legs with a knife. He also said that after he had killed her, he was going to do the same to her children, who were there watching him, if she did not tell him where her money was hidden.

According to police interviews the children later told detectives how they saw Nigel first punch and then cut their mother, while he told them: "I'm going to cut her up nice and slowly, and then I'm going to do you two."

Mr Hall stated that Wendy panicked. She bit Nigel's hand, so he dropped the knife, which she then grabbed and used to stab him repeatedly, then afterwards got the children to help her put his body in a bin bag before placing it in the cellar.

"Wendy Freeman had been the victim of previous assaults by Nigel Baxter but that morning he took things further and after punching her in the face and began torturing her by cutting her legs and demanding her Christmas savings so he could buy heroin," he said.

"The stabbing was a desperate response to his behaviour, after she had been worn down by years of mistreatment. She had acted when she was depressed and terrified for her family."

It was Wendy's parents that had called the police after she had told them what had happened.

Judge Justice Holland QC, who presided at the trial, said that **if** her frenzied stabbing of Mr Baxter and her involvement of the children in moving his body reflected the **only** facts in the case, she would have received a very lengthy sentence, but the full circumstances put a different complexion on the case. He was satisfied Nigel had acted in an aggressive and bullying way towards her and her children, possibly aggravated by his withdrawal symptoms from heroin.

"Had the use of the knife at that stage been no more than required to defend yourself and the children, then no offence would have been committed, because you would have been acting in lawful self-defence," he explained.

"Your use of the knife went far beyond that. It wasn't just one blow, it was eighty-nine (89)."

The judge said there **had** to be a jail sentence, but in the exceptional circumstances he could keep it short. Wendy admitted to manslaughter on the grounds of provocation, which was accepted by the prosecution, and she was jailed for eighteen months.

As I said, the world of drugs is a dark, ugly world.

A nice recollection of Nigel would be one Saturday morning in spring 1976, when Carfield held a Chess Tournament. I had taken my sister into school as Wayne Cadman had done with his younger brother, Ian, as it was a competition open to any of the younger members of the family who could play. Nigel didn't play but he came on his bike to watch. It had been Nigel who offered to take my sister down to where the orange squash and biscuits were being handed out. It was an offer of kindness that resulted in my sisters' photograph appearing in the *South Yorkshire Times*.

He wasn't always a bad lad.

Another drug-related tale. On the Sunday evening of 28 September 2014, and for no apparent reason, a twenty-nine-year-old by the name of Steven Watkins attacked a man outside McCabe's funeral directors on Thurnscoe's Houghton Road – whereby his thirty-three-year-old victim suffered stab wounds.

"We had been in The Clog at the time and I had just taken my mother in law home," explained Caroline Jones – a lady who lived on Cumberland Way, Bolton-on-Dearne.

However, on returning for her husband, the alternator on their Suzuki Swift had been playing up and the battery became flat.

"I was sat in the car watching my husband fiddling about with the wiring to the battery when I saw a man approach the car. I thought that it was someone who my husband knew and that he had come to help us as my husband greeted him with the words, "Alright mate?"

I was totally shocked when he the produced a knife and said: "Do you want some of this?" before proceeding to nick my husband's neck with it.

My husband pushed him away and then locked the door. I was screaming my head off and trying to phone the police."

Watkins' movements were highly erratic. They bore all the hallmarks of someone on drugs and after walking away came back again, whereby a struggle ensued and Caroline's husband ended up getting stabbed – the knife just missing his liver.

"It was just a case of us being in the wrong place at the wrong time," added Caroline. "The irony about it is that my husband never even wanted to go out that night."

Officers from South Yorkshire Police undertook something of a half-assed manhunt and carried out searches at addresses in Thurnscoe after several sightings of the assailant – most notably in School Street and Tudor Street.

Watkins had been on the run fifty-nine days before they caught up with him around 11.00 p.m. on 26 November.

He was sentenced to seven years and ten months at Sheffield Crown Court.

During the time my time on Landsdowne Avenue, my dad would pick me up on either a Saturday or Sunday, with the latter being the day I remember the most, as a big Ford Zephyr would make its way along the backings which was operated by a driver from Bagnall's Taxi's down Lowfield Road.

On the Saturday's he picked me up, we would often catch the old 23 bus back from the old Mansion Park bus stop, which was a concrete structure located close to Wath Road's intersection with Dearne Road and which for years had the words *Segovia* graffitied on its inner wall. (Andrés) Segovia being of course, one of the greatest classical guitarists of our time.

Straight opposite the bus stop had been a shop that was part of West Avenue, which is a row of houses that run both parallel and to the rear of Dearne Road. The shop, which had some indifferent history – not least on 19 July 1949, when following de-rationing its owner, sixty-eight-year-old Amelia Wilkinson (nee Ward) was fined £3 and six shillings (£121, circa 2020). She had been selling food unfit for consumption – mainly chocolate that had been infested with hundreds of insects with elongated snouts – weevils.

The shop itself has long since gone, but if you look closely, you can see a slight imprint of where its front window, which once displayed jars upon jars of sweets, once was. That sweet shop was part of the treat of my dad taking me back to Thurnscoe, with him often doing his version of the end of the 1950s children's television series *Andy Pandy*, and singing: "Time to home, time to go home."

Little did I know at that time, that I would shortly be invited into the said property, which during the early 1970s belonged to two good friends of my auntie Heather and uncle Jimmy.

"You can have some chips when your dad comes in, or have a cup of tea with me," are the only words I can ever recall the lady who owned it, saying to her then-four-year-old son.

James (Jimmy) Woodhead had married Jennifer (Jenny) Johnson in 1966 and four years later they had a child by the name of Tyron, who on 20 September 2011, was gunned down on his doorstep at 45 Doncaster Road, Wath-on-Dearne.

The murder and robbery along with the torching of a garage he owned, had all the hallmarks of it being drug-related, which was something that was confirmed by Det. Supt. Matt Fenwick. He had been dealing crack cocaine from his home.

A twenty-three-year-old from Rotherham by the name of Nathan Wingfield and thirty-year-old from Thurnscoe by the name of Stephen Rodgers, were part of a three-man team, all of who had been armed, and who went to his home with their sole aim of stealing drugs and money.

This was less than a hundred yards from the spot where Nigel had been knifed to death.

Both were found guilty and Judge Roger Keen QC said that here had to be a deterrent element in the sentence. He sentenced Rodgers to a twenty-one-year term for manslaughter, while Wingfield was jailed for twenty years for manslaughter and a further five years for robbery.

On me getting to Dearneside, not only did I get to rub shoulders with some very good young footballers as each year had an intake of between 250 and 270 pupils from not only Carfield, but also Goldthorpe, Highgate and Bolton Juniors, I also got to see how many an enthusiastic young lad got passed over.

The Head of Physical Education (PE) was of course Mr Fred Hemsley. To a young kid, he could come over as both brash and a bully and knew little of the boys he taught.

We had a half an hour lesson of PE once a week – in which he was the teacher and which took in any number of sports, including football, rugby union, wrestling, gymnastics – including both the wooden horse and the parallel bars, along with various assault courses and cross country. Then once a week we had an hour lesson termed as *Games*, which comprised football from September to Easter and then cricket and baseball thereafter. This was taken by both our Drama teacher, the bearded and vociferous Mr (John) Naden and the moustachioed albeit much milder-mannered Mr (John) Watson.

A lot of PE lessons were taken in the old gymnasium, which back then was located to the rear of the school and which ran parallel with the Buxton Arms public house which at times were okay, but nothing at all like *Games*. Mr Naden and Mr Watson were extremely enthusiastic teachers and rain, hail, wind or blow we tended to have a game of football. It would be here that I would come up against two of the most gifted eleven-year-olds you could ever imagine.

Andy Womack and Ian (Willy) Wilcock were exceptional football players. Andy was a clean tackler and a beautiful passer of the ball, whilst Willy glided through games like a young Denis Bergkamp. They were both highly technical players and very cool and composed. What set them apart from the likes of Gaz Salkeld and Alan Bainbridge, is that they always seemed to have time on the ball, were never greedy and always looked to pass. Looking back at it, if a proper football coach could have got hold of these two at that moment in time, they both would have made it as they were that good.

In comparison, I was one-dimensional relying solely on speed and aggression. That said I did used to hit goal after goal after goal in every game we played. However, what was said by Mr Hemsley at the start, was that the manager of Dearneside First Year (Year 7) football team only wanted players that had represented their schools, and in my mind, that had immediately ruled me out.

Many a time Mr Watson would shrug his shoulders and ask the question of why I wasn't in contention for a place in the side?

In the Second Year (Year 8), we had a new PE and Games teacher – Mr (Jack) Taylor. He was a slight young man with a Tom Sellick-styled moustache, who was not only football through and through, but was also one of the new style of teachers in that he was very articulate and praiseworthy – certainly to those who deserved it. We also liked similar music to each other.

In the old gymnasium we played five-a-sides whilst in *Games* we continued what we had been doing whilst in the year below – however, Mr Taylor immediately singled me out. "You should be playing for the school," he told me.

In PE we always shared the lesson with another form from the same year and in this instance, it was the form that Shaun Hill – the school team's inside-forward was in, and Mr Taylor rode him like you wouldn't believe.

Much to the amusement of the teacher, Shaun being of an aggressive nature, used to flip his lid big-time at some of the jocular comments he had aimed at him. I always remember a football game in PE where our side were playing towards the goals in front of the Brick Ponds. I had raced onto a through ball and flicked it both past the goalkeeper, Alan Davies's left hand and into the corner of the net from just outside the penalty area, with Mr Taylor asking straight after, why I hadn't taken the ball further and rounded the goalkeeper instead?

"After running forty yards for the ball it seemed daft running another ten to get around him just to tap it in," I answered.

"You see, Hilly," he told Shaun. "He knew what he was going to do even before he picked up the ball."

It didn't end there. From a corner I blasted a header past the goalkeeper and into the top corner which immediately had Mr Taylor on Hilly's back. "Did you see that?" he grinned. "That was a right header."

Hilly kicked back and told me if I scored again, he'd kick my head in.

What happened? I scored again. Did he kick my head in? No. All he did was chunter at Mr. Taylor all the way back to the gym.

Shaun's aggression was merely a front, although in the Fourth Year (Year 10) he did give me a dig in the ribs whilst we were wagging dinner's around Frank Wells's pond after I refused to give him some of my chicken-flavoured Smax. These were an oval savoury biscuit that were quite popular around 1980. What really flipped him was that I let Andy Burton have a couple! Just for the record – he immediately apologised and smoothed things over by giving me the saddle off some racing bike that had been dumped in the Brick Ponds.

At times, I can't believe some of the shite that I can remember!

In Five-A-Side football and within a small and compact gym I could never utilise that speed – therefore I played in goal and it would be here that I would make my mark, as I very rarely got beat. I remember one particular lesson where we stayed on the court and went around twenty games unbeaten and Mr Taylor raving on about me. "I can't weigh up what your best position is," he said.

I could, and it certainly wasn't a fucking goalkeeper – however, during some test whilst in Mr (Len) Nuttall's English class, I was called out by my former First Year (Year 7) Maths and Second Year (Year 8) History teacher, Mr (Ian) Fieldsend.

He was a young teacher who rather strangely possessed a head of grey curly hair and who wore highly fashionable gold rimmed spectacles. He like Mr Taylor, was one of the new breeds of teacher who heaped praise on those who deserved it.

As for me, he said that Mr Taylor had been raving on about me and would I like to play for the school?

"No problem," I told him. "What position?"

It was as goalkeeper.

"Mr Taylor tells me you're really good," he added.

"Yeh in Five-a-Sides," I told him.

The difference in playing in the gym and out on a field is massive, as are the goals (nets). If you want a comparison stick a good pool player on a snooker table, as that is the learning curve I would have to endure.

With Mr Fieldsend being quite a laid-back teacher, the team tended to pick itself – however, what I would see would be a team that was built around the Goldthorpe Juniors Totty Cup Finalists of 1976 and of which the set up was all wrong.

My first two games were away against Charter Comprehensive and away against Broadway Grammar School, which during the restructure of the British education system in September 1987, along with Holgate Grammar, had been amalgamated to become the new Kingstone School.

In the first game, we played on a field that overlooked the M1 motorway and drew 4-4. I played shit and the thing I vividly remember apart from having a penalty scored against me was the fact that one of our central defenders, the brash and lanky Nigel (Nigger) Coulson screaming at me for giving him the ball. This was a contradiction in terms as in *Games* or PE he always wanted the fucking ball and very rarely ever passed it.

We won my second game 4-3, which was another game I failed to save a penalty, but which was a game I felt I played well in.

My third game was the ultimate eye-opener. A home game against Thurnscoe Comprehensive.

These were a machine-like team in the mould of Don Revie's Leeds United. A hard, aggressive, calculative, and extremely skilful unit that demolished all that was in front of them.

I remember most of the players they had that day, but not them all.

If I hadn't been in the nets, they would have put twenty goals past us, they were that good, but here is the thing. Man, for man, there wasn't much to separate the two teams, it was just that their balance was right and ours was not.

Dearneside Comprehensive rarely got beaten, but these were head and shoulders above everyone and the one thing I remember is that they always played as a team and they were always talking to each other, whereas the lads who played for us, did not.

"Andy's ball", Andy Moore would shout.

"Don's ball," Don Elliot would shout.

"Brocky's got it," Chris Brockhurst would shout.

"Kev's free," Kev Turner would shout.

And how they used those fucking wings.

Neil Lacey as always, was like some gazelle who turned an out of position Andy Lee inside-out, so much so, I'm surprised his underpants were still on the right way around by the end of the game.

They played out from the back like the Dutch national side and had the best central defender in school's football in Andy Moore, who went for trials with Arsenal along with the most predatory striker ever in Don Elliot, the latter of who was continually snapping away at the loose balls within our defence like some fucking bloodthirsty jackal. I am not 100%, but I think Don went for trials with a top side.

Put Chris Brockhurst in the engine room and boy, did that machine tick. However, what I will say is that possibly one of the most skilful midfielders of their year never ever played, which to me was strange.

Darrell (Coop) Cooper was a stocky lad off Brunswick Street and of course the nephew of Rita, who left her husband to marry our next-door neighbour at the time – Gerry Crossland. Due to his stature, he was both nimble on his feet and a fantastic passer of the ball who rarely if ever, gave it away cheaply. His style reminded me of Glenn Hoddle – he was that good.

We got beat 5-1 and I remember Mr Fieldsend telling me that I had played great. "You're improving every game," he said.

"Yeh maybe," I said, "but our defence is wank."

That comment certainly took him aback.

Both Dean Newcombe and Darren Hughes should have been at right and left back as Andy Lee was never a full-back. Phil Kitchener and Nigel Coulson played in central defence, but as I've said, Nigel was too greedy, and Phil could get caught out with pace, and someone as cute and clever as Don always had the legs and know-how to outdo them both.

At the back end of my tenure at Dearneside I would have *Games* or PE with a kid by the name of Ronnie Dodds, who was as a colourful character as you could imagine. When you played against Ronnie you knew you'd been in a game and I reckon if you would have stuck him on Don Elliot – Don would have been sent off within ten minutes – quite possibly for thumping him.

Although he certainly didn't look it, Ronnie was one of the cutest players ever and was always most apologetic after he had fractured your leg or done your cruciate. It was just how he was. You couldn't help but love the lad, and as with Daz Cooper over at Thurnscoe Comprehensive, how he never got involved in the school team setup was a mystery. He was hardly as gifted as Andy Moore, but you knew you were playing against a lad who could handle himself, head the ball, bring it down, control it… and when in doubt, hoof it out. If we would have put the right player alongside him, he would have been exceptionally good.

Our midfield was exceptionally gifted and comprised Goldthorpe Juniors' golden boy Andy Burton, who I remember being linked to Southampton on our leaving school. Then there was Tony Waugh and the highly-skilful Gaz Salkeld – who at the time I thought was a dead ringer for the front man out of the pop group *Madness* – Graham McPherson, who is of course better known as Suggs.

Gary was from a big Mexborough mining family, his great grandfather, Vernon, witnessing what was possibly one of the most drawn out, torturous and horrific deaths ever at Manvers Main Colliery, when on 10 January 1910, a forty-year-old dataller from 127 Queen Street, Swinton by the name of Robert Barnard was killed.

Some misunderstanding had taken place with the signals in the shaft, which caused the cage to lift dragging him upwards from the pit bottom for a distance of seventy yards and not only crushing his thigh and creating a compound fracture, but tearing all the muscle from around the bone as well as completely crushing his arm, leaving him hanging and suspended, both dangling and face down for a total of four hours.

Gary was a kid who could not only play with the ball at his feet but was one who could well and truly handle himself and I suppose it is the latter where I could give you story upon story – however, for the time being I will give you just two.

He was fearless, and nothing fazed him. Not the bigger kids, not anyone. I had only been at Carfield Juniors a few weeks when he had some argument with a lad two years older than us and who lived close by on the Flower Estate by the name of Stuart Horner. I don't know what started it, but I have to admit, I had never seen anything like it. The ginger-haired Stuart was much taller – however, Gary possessed lightning reflexes and seemed to throw punches from every conceivable angle, every one of which hit its target and even when it was being broken up Gaz was still belting him.

Fast-forward three years and Gaz, Wayne Cadman and I were walking home from school and following part of the route up the old Wath Branch Line over Carrfield Lane and up towards where the Suicide Bridge once stood. Then, just as we reached the top of the path into the Flower Estate, a lad two years older than us by the name of Mick Johnson started throwing his weight around and pushing and shoving us. He was just another bully. What I remember is that we must have been to Thurnscoe Baths that day as I recall Gaz having this towel in his hands and on Mick shoving him, he turned around and said: "If tha does that again, I'll black thee eyes."

The next thing we know is that Gaz has got him down on the tarmac and beating the living daylights out of him.

As I said – fearless.

In local amateur football he became one of the best central defenders in the area and looking back at it, not only should he have been made captain, he should have played alongside Ronnie, completing what would have been a brilliant defence. It would have also given Andy Burton and Wuffy more freedom to work as they always seemed to get in each other's way – certainly against the better teams. And Phil Kitchener could have possibly been involved in midfield as its anchor man.

I would have certainly had Andy Womack in the midfield somewhere – however, as we got older, I noticed certain things with Andy, that happened to quite a lot of lads in that they lost confidence when up against the much bigger lads. I reckon that would have been drilled out of him if he had played more regularly.

Up front however, we were very lightweight.

Alan Bainbridge was a lovely junior school player but was beginning to carry a bit of timber – not because he was fat, because he wasn't. He just that he seemed to have got tall over a short period of time, and although he could still play, he had lost the bit of speed he once had – although I once remember him filling in at left-back in a game against Holgate Grammar School and having the greatest game ever.

I would say Ian Wilcock was my favourite player. He was someone who could come over at times as being moody, but all the same, his poise was exceptional and his finishing clinical. He should have really played as a deep lying forward.

As for our other starlet (sic). He had been the full-back who had played against in the late-spring of 1975. Shaun Hill was a lovely lad who was both quick and aggressive and whose one failing was that he would never pass the fucking ball. That was just in case he made the other player look good.

We were once playing a game over in the Carlton area of Barnsley – Outwood, I think, which was another game I failed to save a penalty. It was an icy windswept Saturday morning and therefore Shaun decided to wear gloves. Not just gloves – gloves, but these great fuck off motorbike gauntlets. I had the tendency to use the space outside my eighteen-yard box – I would say it was to keep the play flowing but, on my part, it was more to keep involved. I had taken a ball off one of their forwards, looked up, saw him free, and lumped the ball up to him. As for Hilly, he just hit the ball blind from around thirty yards, and lo and behold it went screaming into the top corner. If he ever mentions that he meant it, tell him he's a liar. He just booted the ball, and the wind took it in. The next thing I see is his arms aloft and that he is waving over at me. "Gyate ball, Yayna," he shouted.

Shaun, bless him – he couldn't pronounce his R's properly!

School football always tended to be on Saturdays and I often remember Globe of Barnsley – the bus company that was contracted to our school, parked up outside Daz Hughes's house on Prospect Road, with Mr Fieldsend either trying to knock him up or drag him away from Noel Edmunds' *Multi-Coloured Swap Shop*. Daz was a firebrand of a character and one of the loveliest kids you could ever wish to meet. How I miss them all.

My favourite time playing school football was during a Five-A-Side tournament of which the venue was at Thurnscoe Comprehensive's state-of-the art indoor sports hall. We had three games and as our names got drawn out of a hat, we were put up against Darfield Foulstone, Darton and some other Barnsley school that I forget.

Darfield had their own schoolboy hero, who the last time I saw him had a carpet shop – E & S Carpets and Furnishings, that was located in Great Houghton and who fully fitted out our offices in 2003.

Ernie Heseltine was the schoolboy equivalent of *Roy of The Rovers* and such a lovely lad.

Darfield were a brilliant side who drew parallels with Thurnscoe Comprehensive, although Mr Fieldsend said that in his humble opinion, the latter were the much better side.

As we had three games the twelve outfield players that we took alternated and were spread across each game, with the weaker five being put up against Darfield, who easily beat us 3-0.

The second game was much different – a 0-0 in which I saved everything that was thrown at me, including a penalty. That was perhaps, the best feeling I ever had playing school football, with everyone patting me on the back – including Ian Wilcock, who was a player who was made for Five-A-Sides, making the biggest fuss of all, which was most unlike him.

In our next game, we walloped Darton 3-0 – however, as Darfield had thrashed everyone it had been they who progressed to the finals and not us, which I recall was to be played at some other date. I still think if we had played our strongest side all the way through, it would have been us who would have progressed.

I recall a great game against Darfield Foulstone one Saturday morning in January 1980 and us getting thumped 7-3, of which the score line certainly didn't reflect the game itself, as that could have ended 15 apiece it was that open. I remember Ernie racing through on goal at the death and him trying to slip the ball down my left side and thinking he had scored with me clawing the ball back. I also brought him down for a penalty, which I totally blame Daz Hughes, for even though he was still in bed. Our stand in left-back that day had been John Weddell, who had failed to put a tackle in. Although John was a nice player, at fifteen years old he was far too lightweight and was easily bullied off the ball.

Left. Me with my parents - Jim Durose and Helen Carman outside the Buxton Arms, Goldthorpe in 1967.

Right. June Darby (nee Bradley) with her son, Darren.

During 1980 I was once wagging (truant) dinners and thought that my mum had seen me. She hadn't. I had confused her with Darren's mum as from a distance they looked very much like one another.

16. **Voyage Libre** (The Strike – Part 1)

I remember us being sat in *Bolton Club* around late lunchtime on New Year's Day 1984 – me, my girlfriend along with Tim Bright and his, a girl by the name of Dawn Bryan – off Sheffield's Parson Cross council estate, knowing that at some point in the future, that we would be going on strike. It was always inevitable. Always.

I had set up an account with the Abbey National Building Society sometime prior, but during November I had applied for a mortgage to buy 16 Briton Square, which had been duly accepted, whilst all the groundwork and the searches were being conducted by Brian Emmet of Emmet & Co Solicitors (now Taylor Emmet LLP) of Thorne Road, Doncaster.

I never really minded strikes, as in my head I just thought of them as rest days or holidays. A day or week off to do whatever you please – however, people were talking about the next one being three to four months, and by the time the end of January came around I would be due to sign all the documentation to complete the purchase of the house.

At just £4,400 (£14,994, circa 2020) it looked an extremely sound investment.

I had listened to what a lot of people were saying – my grandma Ellis in particular, and surveyed all that was around me, waited a couple of weeks and then gave back word. At just turned nineteen-years-old I had made what was to turn out as one of the smartest decisions in my lifetime and one which would make the difference between survival and starvation. I look back and remember some of the immature things that we both say and do when we are that age, but this, I had to say, had been a very mature and thoughtful decision, which had been fully backed by my girlfriend's parents – especially her mum, Joyce. "I really think you are making the right decision," she told me.

Was I scared? Not especially. To me the future looked… well, interesting.

I remember going into work on Tuesday Night shift on 28 February 1984 and the chock fitters walking out over some dispute. At Askern Main, we were all out days before the actual strike in Yorkshire had been called. I had £6 (£20.45, circa 2020) in the ash tray (not that I smoked) on the mantlepiece, £110 (£374.85, circa 2020) in the building society, a week's wages due on Thursday and a coal house stocked three-quarters full of fuel. I knew that I could easily ride out a couple of weeks, or even a month on strike.

On the works bus dropping us back off in Thurnscoe, Billy Coulson, Dave Helm and myself thought it would be a decent idea to go for a bike ride around Hickleton, High Melton and Cadeby, which is exactly what we did. I remember the route, the conversations and on them calling in at my house – Billy dropping me off a composition of songs on a tape cassette that he had made of his favourite rock band, Led Zeppelin.

It would be the start of a year that would see me lose everything, whilst at the same creating what would be a completely new life. This strike needed to happen for my life to progress, but like most things, I just didn't know it back then.

After a couple of weeks on strike my girlfriend's mum advised me to create something of a siege mentality. "Freeze the HP payments on your loan, cooker and washer and fill in a form down at Goldthorpe Town Hall (Goldthorpe is a village) for a rent and rates rebate," she told me.

Her parents, like most of the older end of the East end of Thurnscoe, had been through the strikes of 1969, 1972 and 1974 and knew exactly what to do. All I could do after I had written to the credit companies and filled in all the forms down at the Town Hall, was to wait and wait and wait until all my money ran out and it was then, that the reality of the situation hit home.

I have read many things about the 1984/85 strike, some of which have been written by journalist's, and on a few occasions, I have seen the words "Strike pay" mentioned, therefore let me put this straight. There was **never** any fucking strike pay. **Never**.

I spent the mornings listening to Radio One – Simon Bates and his *Our Tune*, which continually reminded me of travelling to work on the afternoon shift, which was followed by Mr Young, Free and Single himself – *Ooo* Gary Davies, *Ooo* Gary Davies… *on your ra-dio-o.*

I had absolutely nothing, yet Tim was getting around £27 (£92, circa 2020) per fortnight, as he had made the course for that of a mining engineer and as such, he was getting some form of DHSS payment for going to Barnsley Technical College once a week, whilst my mum, as I've already said, had held my application back. It was something which burnt a hole in my soul throughout the first six months of the strike, not because, he was getting money and I was not, but that I thought he often flaunted the fact.

I have always regarded Tim as a brother. As kids we did everything together – however, he has always had a competitive nature about him – call it a kind of sibling rivalry if you like – and it has always been a case of him trying to *one-up* me.

Is that the reality of it, or is it just in my head?

I am sure you will be able to draw your own conclusions as the story progresses.

Tim and I had been going to the soup kitchen at the Welfare Hall in Goldthorpe, where you showed your brass pit check, tipped your hat and thanked god for three fish fingers, peas and chips. It was demeaning, and I hated it. I hated the fact that my life hadn't just stalled but had gone backwards. I looked in the pantry at home and there was nothing. It was like being back at home during those dark days of late-1982.

My girlfriend helped with a carrier bag of shopping from time to time, but she was buying all the wrong things. A siege is built on a regular supply of potatoes, eggs, meat, bread, and coffee, not things such as a Mr Kipling sponge sandwich and a six-pack of crisps.

"What's all this shit?" I remember saying. "I'm not here having some fucking tea party."

A true story that is.

As was the time she called in from work one evening. "I was going to buy you some food shopping, but I got you this instead," she said.

She had bought me a grey V-necked jumper, which believe me when I say it – nearly tipped me over the edge.

It sounds ungrateful, but at times I was close to starving, and it was in early-April when I started to become depressed. There was, however, some form of minor salvation around the corner.

My due diligence in not buying the house reaped its benefits as I suddenly began receiving a rent rebate through the post – a cheque from Barnsley MBC for £8.75 (£29.82, circa 2020). It was highly unexpected, and I spent the next few days looking at it until another one arrived the following week. I honestly thought there was some mistake being made as I had anticipated the local authority paying the monies directly to the landlord, which was of course the NCB.

I immediately put it in the Yorkshire Bank to draw it straight back out again and went on something of a mini shopping spree in GT Smiths supermarket opposite.

I mentioned this to the Co-op milkman who was doing his rounds one morning and he told me that he would gladly cash the cheques for me and that is what happened almost every Friday. With my new-found wealth, then came the decisions of what do I purchase – a pound of sausage or some soap and deodorant? Four tins of beans or some washing-up liquid and bleach? These were choices, that to me, were nothing short of huge at the time.

I remember going down to the old Co-operative Store on the junction of John Street and Houghton Road, which was at the time nicknamed *The Tin Man*, possibly due to the way the store had been set out with boxes upon boxes of canned foods stacked on the shelves and buying some shopping but coming up thirty or forty pence short. It was embarrassing as I had always had money. Fortunately, it had been Sheila Denham (nee Grimshaw), the wife of Pete and the mum of Andrew and Paul, who had been on the till and she let me take home my shopping and drop the change in later. It was a continual case of robbing fucking Peter to pay fucking Paul.

I was on my own and it would become far worse before it got better.

The fact that I had fuel in my coal house was a plus – however, that wouldn't last forever and that was much sooner than I thought, as my girlfriend's dad called down one day. "Have you got plenty?" he asked.

"Plenty of what?" I asked.

"Coal?"

"I've got some," I said.

He opened the coal house door and what he saw was the fact that I did have some – less than half a dozen barrows.

"Take some if you want," I shrugged.

"Are you sure?"

He didn't want to, but I let him. He had a family and needed a constant supply of hot water, whereas I could get by just switching on the kettle or boiling up a few pans.

It was Tim that gave me some form of sanity, but even then, the thought of him spouting his wealth and publicly counting his twenty-seven doubloons really pissed me off, especially when he chucked £6.50 (£22.15, circa 2020) on some trendy haircut at some Italian hairdressers in Barnsley and pontificated somewhat, by giving me the over-elaborate description of the fifteen-minute chat he'd had with some knob called Mario that had preceded it. That money was nearly three quarters of the money that I had been surviving on, and which had included weekly payments towards my water and electric.

The disparity of wages between miners had always been a constant bug bear, and no more so than during the strike. I had a house to keep and was having to spend my rent rebate solely on my survival, knowing full-well that at the strike's end, if indeed there was an end, that I would be heavily in debt. Like I said. I was continually robbing Peter to pay Paul.

It was towards the end of May that the rot really set in and when my girlfriend in her wisdom, packed in her job at the Two Steeples sewing factory – a huge green flat roofed building located off Rotherham's Tenter Street.

"What the hell did you do that for?" I asked.

The reasoning behind it beggared belief, however, the fact was, that nothing she ever did would have ever surprised me.

I then had her down at the house all the time, which meant that the money that I had been surviving on was now being stretched between two people.

As I have got older, I have always regarded myself as someone who possesses a nil constitution for bullshit, but looking back at it, I must have put up with a hell of a lot, which was something else that would get worse.

After the experience of being jilted by Steve Hollis a few months before her wedding in 1981, her sister had worked hard on wanting to put *right* what she obviously saw as some huge *wrong* and had diligently cornered her prey, and just in case *it* changed *its* mind, she was fully focused on having him marched up the aisle at the earliest convenience possible.

This was to a striking miner with the wedding being fully funded and not match-funded, by her striking father. My thoughts then, were exactly as they are now – it was a very selfish act from a very selfish girl, whose piece de la resistance was to put me firmly in my place by banning me from her wedding.

The lad who she was to marry had been twenty-four-year-old Derek Harnett, a miner from Great Houghton, whose grandfather's cousin, Arthur, rather interestingly, had been sentenced to death at Leeds Assizes on 22 July 1927 and executed by Thomas Pierrepoint in Armley Gaol some forty days later.

It was said that there was insanity in the family – Arthur's grandmother had committed suicide and his grandfather had died insane.

I am certainly not suggesting that this was the level that Ann was working at in her bid to snare a husband, just that there were several facts at work that were put forward by the counsel for the defence that could have saved

Arthur from being hanged. The other was that he had contracted Malaria and Sandfly Fever whilst he had been over in Iraq with the Durham Light Infantry after the war, which gave him massive head pains and caused his eyes to look like they were popping out.

Arthur Harnett had been drinking at the Bluebell Hotel in Hemsworth and called to a property at 2 Westgate, where he slit the throat of a woman by the name of Isabella Moore whilst her husband had been on afternoon shift at South Kirkby Colliery. It was said that Arthur and the husband had been friends – however, the friendship had ended abruptly when he suspected they were having an affair.

Arthur was arrested and charged with murder at Hemsworth Police Station.

Trivialities aside, weeks prior, Ann had tried forcing an argument over something that didn't make any sense – a bowl or some Tupperware dish that I had supposedly borrowed and not returned – and the fuss she had kicked off about it was nothing short of unbelievable.

"I've not got your fucking bowl," I remember telling her. Numerous times.

I have encountered many a spoilt bitch throughout my life, but hand on heart, never had I ever come across one like this and I said as much to both Tim and her sister at the time, in that I pitied the poor bastard that she was marrying. Steve Hollis had been clever. He'd had a right fucking escape.

The fact that she wanted to put me in my place was fine – however, the fact that my girlfriend didn't kick off about it anymore than she did, said it all. Six months prior she would have panned her elder sister's face in – now it was a shrug of the shoulders and a "What can I do about it?"

The writing was on the wall and exactly a month later the relationship ended.

I wasn't stupid and was well-aware of the reasoning behind it.

A lad a year older than me who also worked at Hickleton Main, had been trying to tap her up a week or so earlier and had obviously turned her head.

23 June 1984 was the day it ended.

Am I that sad that I remembered the date? Hardly, I thought it was much earlier.

We were at Billy Coulson's house and sat with him and his girlfriend – a girl by the name of Paula Hole (now Davy) – drinking coffee and watching clips of *Frankie Goes to Hollywood* from the two-day New Brighton Rock pop concert, which had been held one month earlier and which was to be shown later that night.

I remember the parting of the ways like it was yesterday and walking up the side of Thurnscoe Baths, past the corporation depot and along the Sheffield – York railway line on my way home. In the past we'd had arguments and fallen out, but the next day or the day after, it was generally all forgotten. It had been a highly volatile relationship that had kept on surviving when time after time it should have been cut dead.

I remembered a time shortly after that, when all I had in the pantry had been a can of beans and of me trying to eat them without any bread. I ended up slinging them across the kitchen, before going into the room, tipping this orange and brown striped sofa on its head, which had been kindly given to me by Tim's nanan (Nellie) Wright (nee Sanders), and ripping off the lining from its base with a Stanley knife and trying to root out coppers or silver.

That had been my lowest point thus far and if I am being honest, I had never felt so alone in all my life.

I remember telling my son a few years back – never think it's the end of the world. Things might look black at the time, but they are not, really.

I was nineteen years old and had seemingly lost everything, but the irony was that I always kept telling myself that it was only temporary.

The problem that I had made for myself, is that I had always neglected a social life for my private life. I had a girlfriend, and in my mind, I didn't need anything else. Lots of young people at that age think the same and it is one of the biggest mistakes they could ever make. A person always needs other people around them. Always.

I remember having a conversation with Tim's mum, Jill, around the same time. "You should go see your mam and (step)dad," she told me.

She was not only very caring – she was also very right.

With the girlfriend out of the way it opened the door for my mum and (step)dad, both of whom would try their utmost to both salvage and reconstruct a relationship with me and undo the bad feeling of my leaving home. I had absolutely nothing, had lost weight and on my arrival at their door I was immediately fed and watered and sent back down home a few hours later with a carrier bag full of food and toiletries. It would be a time in my life when my family would hold my life together and I don't say this lightly – there had been some very dark days.

One thing sticks in my mind around that time and that is of a Fitter from Askern Main banging on my mum's front door. "There's been a kid called Steve Shaw here looking for you," my (step)dad told me.

Steve was a Thurnscoe lad who had been four school years older than me and who had been transferred to Askern from Highgate Main Colliery a couple of months after me. On B50s becoming operational as a retreat face, he had been the seconded as the second fitter on the district. At first glance I found him to be quite underhanded and something of a shit-stirrer. He played pub football with The Fairway alongside Mick Robinson, a lad some eight years older than myself who had not only grown up on Briton Square, but who was engaged to a girl by the name of Tina Cotter, who at that time had been the best friend of my ex-girlfriend's sister. Therefore, it is fair to say, that not only did he very much know who I was, he was also privy to a one-sided version of the volatile relationship with both the ex-girlfriend and of course her parents.

"What did he want?" I asked.

"He said that you need to go and see a man called Pat Hewitt at your pit about having regular food parcels dropped off."

I got down home to find that Steve had dropped off two carrier bags of food. To say that I was overcome with emotion is a massive understatement and even now that self-same memory still puts a huge lump in my throat. I thought I'd been forgotten about and left to rot.

The emotion wasn't any less after I had finally made my way over to the NUM office at Askern Main.

"We couldn't find you," Pat smiled, as I was asked to fill in some form, docket or whatever.

If I rightly recall, the NUM thought that I still lived over in Barnby Dun. From that day onwards I had a food parcel dropped off every week.

What I didn't know is the bigger picture of what was actually happening at the time.

I'd had *invitation to scab* letters drop through my letterbox a couple of times and I just thought that everyone was getting them. They weren't. I had been targeted. The NCB were utilising its propaganda and had been highlighting all the weak links, and a young miner living on his own and well away from the colliery he was employed at such as myself, was a prime target to scab.

Did I ever think about going back to work? Yeh, of course I did. I think every miner thought about it at some point.

The historians of the strike mention the hard left, the left, the moderates, the right, the far right and try to categorise everything, so that everything fits nicely into place and so that everything can be easily explained, which is not only wrong, it's fucking pathetic.

I come from a working-class background, but it doesn't mean that I followed the left-wing rhetoric of what was around at the time. As much I liked listening to Scargill – and I did, most of the time I found the man extremely frustrating, and what is almost a nailed-on certainty, is that most of the great orators of socialism wouldn't have a clue how to run a fucking business, Scargill included.

What stopped most of men scabbing, certainly in the Doncaster Area, was nothing to do with left or right, but was plainly down to a fear of reprisal.

Thurnscoe is a place that doesn't easily forget, and it was a well-known fact at the time, that men had been seen patrolling the streets during the early hours, checking to see which lights were being switched on. There is fuck all political about that.

The fact that my rebate was still being cashed, I was being fed at my mum's and I had a regular supply of food parcels turning up at my door made everything far much easier, and one thing that I will always say is that the NUM at Askern Main looked after its members a lot fucking better than it did at Hickleton. Bar the odd tin of chicken *on the bone* that had been shipped over from Russia, my food parcel contained little rubbish. It was a time that the strike and my fortunes began to turn, and Tim being summoned to the NCB's Area Head Office at St George's would give him something of a reality check to the situation that I had been saddled with since day one.

I went through to Doncaster with him only to hear screaming and shouting from behind the closed door. He had been missing days from his mining engineering course at college and one of the Area Directors – not sure which, did no more than cut it dead and duly kicked him off the course. And with that, his fortnightly payment of £27 had gone.

His dad went apeshit. He had reason to. Pete – just like me, had put up with having nothing for months.

If that would have been me, I would have held on to that course for dear life.

I remember going down to his nan and granddad's house, which was situated opposite the entrance to Bolton-on-Dearne Railway Station and spending a sunny afternoon creosoting their fence. I had already turned over the front garden for my Grandma Ellis and painted the unused outside toilet for my grandma Carman, both of whom had each given me £5 (£17, circa 2020) for my efforts. That was certainly not why I did it, however. I had done it because I wanted to, as from a personal view I needed to feel useful.

Tim's nan, Florrie (Beaumont), gave us both a fiver, but I gave mine back.

"Take it," she said.

"No, I'm good," I told her.

Florrie and Joe were extremely nice people who during the 1970s had had their number come up – or eight rather, as they'd had what at the time was a huge win on the football pools. Five pounds was nothing to them but everything to me, yet I handed the money back.

Both my grandparents had nothing in comparison, and I had taken their money, so why not Florrie's?

Maybe someone can explain that to me as I still don't know why I did it.

That night we had tea at their house and Tim's granddad's brother (Bill Beaumont) came over and we spent the night playing cards – a game called *Queenie* for small stakes. The long trips inbye on those diesel-hauled Paddy trains over at Askern Main must have played dividends as it was a time that we regularly played a card game called *All Hearts*. I wouldn't say I was good, but playing against some of those miners, you quickly learned how to set up your hand and I ended up clearing the table. I went home with around £18 (£61.34, circa 2020) in my pocket including part of Tim's creosoting money. It had been a great night, made even more so as Tim's granddad had continually been haranguing him about not working.

It would be shortly after this, that going down to Cambridgeshire to work in the fields and orchards was mentioned.

My dad's brother, my uncle Graham (Durose), had lived life to the extreme and had died of heart failure in 1980, aged just thirty-six, with the majority of his short life being spent in Wisbech.

Moving backwards and forwards between mine and Tim's house at 178 Furlong Road, I had dropped on my auntie Anne (Durose), who had alighted the bus outside Goldthorpe Junior School. If I recall the conversation, my uncle Paul had been down to Wisbech and come back north with Graham's daughter, my cousin, Samantha – and that I think, was the catalyst for me thinking: *Wisbech could be good for some cash in the hand work.*

My dad had been down to Wisbech numerous times, the last of which was probably to bury his brother – however, whilst I had lived there, he had told me hundreds of tales about the place, not at least the huge amount of work that was available. Therefore, I thought it prudent to go over to Barnby Dun to get the inside-track.

What was unknown to me at the time is that my dad's life would soon be coming to its end, but during the summer of 1984, he still looked as big, powerful, and as fit and healthy as he always had. However, what is true is that he had started complaining about his diet and of certain foods not suiting him – especially foods with a high cholesterol, such as bacon and eggs.

"I'd love some with you, but they'd cripple me," he had once said, on calling in on me at Briton Square. This had been during a dual visit, on which he had also dropped in at his auntie Jess's (Smith nee Durose) down at Thurnscoe's Togo Buildings.

My dad had a bit of the entrepreneur about him and before I moved in with his family for those eight months, he had bought an acre of what was quintessentially scrub land at the side of the River Dun Navigation Canal, off Bramwith Lane, which in times past, had had two or three planning applications for the construction of a bungalow, knocked back.

Whilst I had been living with him, a lot of conversation between him and Paula had been how best to utilise his £1,600 (£5,452, circa 2020) investment – however, his wife's angle was as unassuming as it was one dimensional. It had been a simple case of her continually nagging him to get shut.

There was a bit more to it than turning it over for a quick profit as it had been used as some form of ash tip, and as the firm that he was employed by were an aggregate and recycling specialist, he felt sure, they would remove the several hundred tons of ash in return for some form of cash backhander.

My dad had sat on that land until the timing had been right and when I went over to see him, he took me over to see what was a newly levelled and remediated piece of land that he had temporarily turned into an acre of allotment. This was something that wasn't entirely new to him as when he had been married to my mum, he'd had one of the allotments off Mexborough's Adwick Road – a place which has borne witness to murder, suicide and rather strangely, something that was apparently quite popular at the time – voyeurism and is something that I will fill you in on shortly.

From me being a young kid however, my dad had always been fascinated with the thought of owning some form of small holding and living off the land. He was also highly experienced when it came to hunting game and I often remember watching him set snares and traps in the woods close to the Doncaster Golf Range off Armthorpe Lane, along with the black art of skinning rabbits, without damaging the meat.

I look at my son, Jamie, now, and the similarities are uncanny as he's my dad's double in how he goes about his life. Yet the irony of this is, is that it's solely genetic as they never actually met.

I probed my dad about the whys and wherefores of the situation down in Wisbech as he plucked vegetables from his land for me to take home with me, before he completely changed the subject. "That's what I meant to ask you," he said. "Do you know a girl by with the surname of Neal?"

I nodded and told him that I had been at school with both Debi and Dawn, although the latter was some four school years younger than me.

"That's her," he said. "Debi."

"What about her?" I shrugged.

"She's been in the 'papers and won some modelling competition," he told me. "If it's the same lass – I went to school with her dad, Arthur."

It was the exact same family.

Like Mandy Rolfe, she had been a girl who I had been quite close to in my last year at Carfield, as during 1975/76 they had mixed some of the brighter Third Year (Year 5) pupils with the Fourth Years (Year 6), possibly in anticipation of the elder children bringing the younger ones on – one of who was the blonde-haired and saucer-eyed Debi.

Mr (Bruno) Capaldi had a drive and eccentricity about him, which in my opinion was unparalleled by any teacher that I had ever known and who was in short, a wonderful man who I am quite sure was well-respected by every pupil that he ever taught. Born in Liverpool and from Italian descent, he had quite a charming nature about him, especially when in the company of the other sex. One of the things I remember was my being taken to the dentist, which back then was in some clinic located down a snicket opposite Dearneside, that was sandwiched between the rear of the Welfare Park and the back gardens of Washington Road. As my appointment was late morning, my mum had had to go to Carfield to pick me up. On her coming into class, our wiry thirty-nine-year-old teacher, whose hairline had long since receded and was at that time cropped to the bone, suddenly transformed into this suave and sophisticated fellow, much to the disdain of a couple of girls in class – one of who was Michelle Thacker, a blonde-haired girl who lived in the early numbered red-bricked houses on Ingsfield Lane. "Your mam must put a pint of mascara on," she bitched.

Even at an early age, kids had a cynical view of how parents appeared.

Often, the young lads would converse as to who had the best-looking mum, and I will tell you now, it wasn't mine.

I remember being in Goldthorpe one Saturday morning during early 1976 and whilst coming out of D&D Traders with my mum I saw Debi with hers. If you ever wanted to see a picture-perfect family, then hers would have been it. Her mum Barbara (nee Johnson) was nothing short of beautiful as were all her three young children, all of whom had a very Scandinavian appearance.

During the early days of the strike I often remember being at Tim's house and seeing both sisters walk past, Dawn more so than Debi, on their way down to their home at 25 Kennedy Drive.

My dad then went on to tell me the story of their grandfather, Sam Neal, who as a child had lived in the terraced houses that formed part of Furlong Road's Packey's Puzzle, which during my tentative school years throughout Dearneside, possessed two shops. Old man Hayes's somewhere in the middle and Bernie Blakemore's at the far end, both of whom who candidly showed their business acumen. They willingly catered for the needs of their eleven to sixteen-year-old customers who couldn't afford packs of ten's and twenty's, by selling cigarettes individually priced at three pence apiece… and with a match tucked into their ends.

It was nothing new. On 7 July 1957, forty-eight-year-old Hannah Oxley, who had the exact same shop at 226 Furlong Road, had been in front of Doncaster West Riding Court after being caught red handed, doing the exact same thing.

Could you imagine the outrage if shops did something like that now?

Packey's Puzzle backed onto the old clay pits, which at one time had formed part of the brickworks, that had not only provided the bricks for the carcass of the house that Sam had lived in, but most red-bricked houses that had sprung up during the sinking and development of Hickleton, Goldthorpe and Barnburgh Main collieries.

By 1929, the manufacture of bricks had ceased, and all the three pits had been filled with water to form what is known known locally as the Brick Ponds, with pond No 1 being up to sixty feet deep at the point where the Far Moor Dike exits the culvert at the periphery of Dearneside's playing fields.

During late-June that year, temperatures topped eighty-three degrees and with up to fifteen hours of sunshine it created something of an attraction down at the ponds, as people began bathing, which back then was not uncommon – nor was children drowning.

On 18 June, an eighteen-year-old off The Crescent by the name Allen Blessed – who was also the uncle of the actor Brian – had been walking around the ponds and had to go into the water to retrieve a five-year-old boy by the name of Tommy Fitzpatrick who lived at 136 Furlong Road – the house directly opposite what is now a Chinese takeaway, and had to give him artificial respiration.

Just a day before, Ernest Limb of 10 Ladycroft – the row of terraced houses that at one time were located at the bottom of Station Road opposite The Collingwood – had had to go into the water to rescue a ten-year-old lad by the name of Ralph Parker, whose legs had seized due to cramp.

It was on 21 June, however, with the temperatures still in the summit, that Debi's grandfather would save the life of six-year-old boy by the name of Leonard Fowler. Aged just fifteen and whilst fully clothed, he dove into the very deepest, darkest part of the pond to rescue the little lad from drowning.

"Bolton-on-Dearne is proud of one of its boys," wrote the *Leeds Mercury*. "Samuel Neal, son of Mr Arthur and Mrs Elizabeth Neal of 246 Furlong Road who saved the life of Leonard Fowler from drowning in the Brickyard pit has been presented with a silver watch from Mr Pownall – the Headmaster of Bolton Council School on behalf of the teaching staff and a Certificate of the Royal Humane Society by Mr George Probert, Chairman of Bolton UDC."

Sam was a hero and deservedly so, as all one needs to do is to look around to see that his selfless actions preserved several generations of the Fowler family.

Leonard Fowler would marry Elsie Mountford in 1943 and between them they would have four children – Kay (b. 1945), Lenny (b. 1949), Russell (b. 1951) and John (b. 1953) – who themselves would all marry and have children, some of whom are still living in the area with their children. One of these is Leonard's grandson and namesake, who at one time was living off Bolton-on-Dearne's Ringway at 12 Brow View. He moved and took the short journey down Lowfield Road, over the Milky Stream that cuts through the Adwick Nature Reserve on its way to the River Dearne, and into the neighbouring village of Harlington, and who now resides at 71 North End Drive.

The strange thing is that Sam's grandson and Debi's younger brother, lives just over the back from him and in the very next street at 25 Cambridge Close.

I wonder if they know each other?

As for my dad, he would eventually sell his acre of scrub land at a huge profit and end up paying off his house – however, that would be something that he would never ever get to enjoy.

I look back at 1983 and 1984 and of the things that I went through and what I learned.

"Put it all down to experience," my dad had often told me.

He was very rarely negative, but I have to say that Wisbech was to be an experience that I would never wish on anyone.

What happened whilst the preparations were being made to go down there, was something quite out of character. I was never a drinker in the sense of being a regular pub goer. Back then it just wasn't me. I did go out, but it was certainly very sporadic. Since New Year's Day I had been to the pub once – The Carousel in Chapeltown around mid-April with Tim and his girlfriend – and that had been something I hadn't really wanted to do, as I thought it was a waste of money that I had not got. That being the case, it had been my girlfriend who had coaxed me in and had coughed up for my three pints of lager along with a couple of songs on the jukebox – Steppenwolf's *Born to be Wild* and Status Quo's *Pictures of Matchstick Men*. What a memory, eh?

I wouldn't say that I was going stir crazy, but at nineteen years old and being a month without female companionship, I felt that I had unknowingly been forced into some corner that I didn't want to be in. I was already in one, which was certainly not of my own making with the strike, so to be in one, solely through a lack of my own social cohesion was quite unacceptable.

I look back at going out with less than a fiver in my pocket and just shake my head, as nowadays I can't go into a pub with less than £200 in my wallet.

Due to its locality, the Dog End (Tap Room) of The Fairway had been the obvious point of call, however, the ex-girlfriend finding out I was in made our stay there relatively brief.

"My mam wants to know if she can have her casserole dish back," was her opening gambit, post-her entering the male-only environment amidst nudges and whispers to interrupt our game of pool, and whilst wearing the shortest dress imaginable.

If it wasn't a fucking Tupperware dish belonging to her sister, it was some other dish belonging to her mother.

"I'll look for it," I told her.

Tim didn't particularly want to drive around, especially as his money had been stopped. I, however, didn't fancy hanging around Thurnscoe, whilst my ex-girlfriend tugged at the strings in her bid to orchestrate more fucking misery on me, therefore I mentioned driving down to Wath-on-Dearne, where some old church had recently been converted into a public house.

We had only been in the Church House less than fifteen minutes when I got talking to a couple of girls.

Getting a girlfriend was never a problem it was keeping them interested that was the tricky bit, as a life without work or money is basically a life of nothingness. The one thing it did, however, was to immediately exorcise the ghost of the ex girlfriend.

Without wishing to sound dirty, having a regular girlfriend at that age boils down to two things. Having regular female company on your arm, in that you are not the odd one out, and getting regular sex. You move on and it becomes very much the same, but with the difference in that it's all a completely new environment.

Rachel Wilson was the second youngest of four daughters and lived on Newsam Road, which is a street in Kilnhurst that is located off Highthorn Road, which runs between the end of Swinton's Lime Grove estate and an area of Wentworth Road, where it crosses over the North Midland Railway line close to the River Don.

What would be strange is that like a lot of girls that I would come to know, she would already have some soon-to-be ex-boyfriend, which was something that I certainly didn't know as we chatted to each other on our journey over to Swinton.

I remember being in The Towpath public house that at one time was located directly opposite E.W Waddington's boat and timber yard alongside Swinton Lock No 4 on the Dearne and Dove Canal – and which during the mid-1980s was a busy, bustling pub that attracted hordes of young people, with its loud music and dimly lit interior.

Growing up in Thurnscoe's East end, confrontation was certainly nothing new, and on her boyfriend aggressively introducing himself – not to me, but to her, my first instincts were to smack him in the mouth. However, the fact that the pub had two bouncers less than six feet away and was too packed to move, let alone throw a punch, it stopped anything untoward happening. That aside, Tim certainly wanted none of it. "We don't know anyone down here," he said. "Well end up getting our heads kicked in."

As it transpired, that never happened and the last I ever saw of her boyfriend, was of him and his mate throwing bricks at Tim's car as we drove away with his girlfriend in the back seat.

I had a two-week relationship with her prior to us heading down to Wisbech and I quite liked her family, not at least her elder sister, who would go on to marry a lad who would not only become a great friend of mine in the early 1990s, but who was also the step-brother of the man who had jilted my ex-girlfriend's elder sister prior to them getting married – Steve Hollis.

Small world, eh?

Her father, John, was a sinewy fellow with a moustache who had originally been from Thorne and who I recall was wearing just a pair of denim shorts and fitting a patio door, when I first saw him. Although he certainly worked in a mining related industry, he wasn't a miner and was employed at Smithy Wood Coking Plant. This was located between Ecclesfield and Chapeltown and was a place where coal was converted into coke for the city's blast furnaces. His wife Connie was a lovely lady, who, having four other women in the house, certainly wasn't behind the door regarding certain subjects, and I wouldn't be wrong in saying that there was always some healthy tongue-in-cheek dialogue bouncing around, along with the odd nod and a wink.

It was however, never going to be a relationship that would prosper.

"Look, I have to go and find some work down in Wisbech," I told her. "We can end it here or continue it when I get back – it's up to you."

She wanted continuance, however, Tim's fiancée did not.

Their relationship ended abruptly – firstly with him losing the right to his £27 *scab payment*, which stopped him putting petrol in his car, and then with him totally out of the way in Cambridgeshire, it had been a case of her going out every night.

I once remember Tim's dad telling me: "That Dawn he was going out with was the ideal lass for him. She was a bit rough around the edges, but they suited each other."

The venue for that statement – the day of Tim's second marriage. 11 May 1996.

I thought the exact same as Pete, in that Dawn was a nice kid.

The strike killed many a relationship.

I had been engaged to my ex on a sort of *on and off* basis. I think she slung her engagement ring about four or five times throughout our tumultuous two-and-a-half-year relationship, and although no-one wanted it – least of all both sets of parents, our getting married was thought as being something that was inevitable. The truth was, that she had pushed to live with me on a couple of occasions whilst I'd had the house, but it was something that I neither wanted and nor could afford.

The reason being?

It was at a time that I was a two and four months into what would be a twelve-month strike.

Tim was quite philosophical regarding his relationship ending and in truth discarded Dawn like some old boot. "If what she wants to do is go nightclubbing, then fuck her," he said.

Tim partly blamed himself for the relationship with my ex-girlfriend ending. That's not me saying it, that was what he said at the time. His presence at the house had upset the equilibrium somewhat and she felt threatened, which looking back at what I have just said sounds really fucking gay. It was, however, one of the reasons that she had packed in her job. She had a divisive nature and was jealous. She had packed in her job, so she could be with me, or that is what she told me.

Like I have already said, nothing she ever did surprised me.

The thought of driving away into some new experience was one of excitement – however, me bumping into Tony Waugh outside Heppenstall's florists on Goldthorpe's Barnsley Road, gave me some food for thought. "We've just come back," he told me. "There was no work."

Tony had been set on at Hickleton Main in one of the last groups from the Class of 1981's intake and was a kid that was very level-headed, and if this is what he was saying, then I had no reason whatsoever to doubt him. In short, he was a very good kid.

He had however, gone down in a large group and they knew nobody down there. There were just two of us and my dad had given me several addresses in nearby Walsoken who to contact.

I vividly remember leaving Rachel's the evening before we left for Wisbech, and whilst on the 273 bus back home to Thurnscoe passing Tim's house, to see him packing a huge camping stove that he had borrowed from a neighbour, into the boot of his car, and the reality of our decision hitting home.

The washing machine that I had bought from Vallances on Interest Free Credit had £109.16p (£372, circa 2020) outstanding, and my thoughts were to try and earn the money to get it paid off. I had made a few payments at the beginning of the strike until my money ran out and then had to write a letter to put the remaining payments on hold. With the cooker, I didn't mind so much, as that was purchased on credit through the Co-operative Bank on Balloon Street in Manchester with an APR of 28.5%, whereas Vallance's credit facilities had been self-funded by the store. I had also known the shops General Manager, Alan Hewitt since I was a young kid back when the shop was Clay's – my earliest recollection of him being at my grandma Ellis's house and of them chatting about politics. There was a kind of loyalty to my thinking.

After calling in at Billy Coulson's and dropping off a key, so he could check on the house, I went home and packed up a bag of clothes and some toiletries along with some purpose bought provisions – such as a 52p (£1.77, circa 2020) bottle of St Ivel Five Pints dried milk and a 63p (£2.15, circa 2020) bottle of Timotei shampoo and whatever tins I had left in the pantry.

We went down on the Sunday morning of 19 August 1984.

My mum had given me £10 (£34, circa 2020) and I had what was left of my rent rebate, although that had been partly spent on the four gallons of petrol to get us down there and if unsuccessful in our pursuit of work would be needed for the four gallons to get us back home, which at £1.75 (£5.96, circa 2020) per gallon, worked out at around £14 (£47.71, circa 2020). Therefore, from a financial point of view, we knew what to expect.

On getting there we immediately set about knocking at the doors of each of the addresses I had been given, and we were told exactly what Tony had said – nothing doing. On being knocked-back we never showed any real sign of panic, with our initial thoughts being to ride out the first few days and to see what happens.

Wisbech was a sharp contrast to the surroundings that we had left, with students sat out on the lawns of St Peter and Paul's Parish Church and families walking around its marketplace on what was a beautiful sunny afternoon. In comparison, the eastern Dearne Valley – especially Thurnscoe, seemed dirty, run-down and full of unhappy, angry people – two of whom, after getting our bearings, called in at the old Victoria transport café on Lynn Road in Walsoken where we ate a late-Sunday lunch of fishcake, chips and peas.

The café would provide us with one of four bases, as it had decent toilets, provided cheap food and had a concrete hardstanding around the back where we could kick the football around whilst listening to Radio Caroline on Tim's silver TR-7 branded transistor, which we regularly placed on the black vinyl roof of his car.

On driving around a bit, we found our main base, which would be our place to sleep. A grassy piece of land on some sharp bend on Broad End Road, which was some country lane just over one and a half miles from the café – a base which had orchards scattered all around it.

When you need a job, the most obvious place to go is the Job Centre, who had a card in the window stating that Smedley's wanted night shift operatives for their canning factory. This was a building located relatively close to the café on Lynn Road. We were welcomed with open arms by the General Manager and filled in all the forms for a start that night. That was until he realised that we were striking miners who still happened to be employed by the NCB.

"The only way I can see around this, is if you terminated your existing employment with the 'Coal Board," he told us.

I hadn't been on strike nearly six months just to uproot everything and spend the rest of my life on night shift in some town a million miles away, fucking about ramming peas and carrots into tins. Not for £75 (£255.88, circa 2020) a week, anyway.

We went back to the Job Centre and told the manager our problem and who immediately went in one of the drawers and handed us the address of a company that ran its operations out of 2 Victoria Street. This was just a short walk from the marketplace.

Nowadays, Fred Bassett & Sons are labelled as a firm that supply labour – mainly Eastern European migrants – but back in 1984 they regarded themselves as gang masters. The company had been going since 1930 when they had been employed sort of ad-hoc by farmers – primarily picking and planting potatoes, sugar beet and daffodils. However, when we saw the heir apparent, a lad some four years older than us and who bore the same name as his grandfather and founder of the company, the landscape had changed somewhat.

I was under the impression that we would be clearing orchards or maybe picking hops, but it was a case of us weeding between rows and rows of cabbages and on one particular day – filling crates of blackberries, the latter of which was both piece work and provided us with a set of hands that for the life of us, we couldn't get clean.

The money we would have earned at Smedley's would have been subject to taxation by the Inland Revenue – working for young Fred however, it was not. £15 (£51.12, circa 2020) per day cash and £13 (£44.30, circa 2020) on a Friday, as we would be knocking off an hour early.

Our idea was to live as cheaply as possible and that line of thought was firmly backed up when I saw some of the culinary delights that Tim's nan (Florrie) had packed him up.

"Fucking Toast Toppers?" I shrugged.

"Yeh, they're alright," Tim told me.

They were on par with the tin of Saucy Spuds and cans of Tip Top evaporated milk that she had given him.

In my humble opinion, all Florrie had done was emptied all the shite out of her bottom drawer and given it to her grandson for us to recycle down in Wisbech.

Back then, some food could be considered as being expensive compared to that of today – especially if you were a tea or coffee drinker. A 200 g jar of Nescafe was £2.35 (£8, circa 2020), whereas nowadays you can buy the self-same jar for £4 in Tesco. A box of eighty PG Tips Teabags was £1.08 (£3.68, circa 2020), whereas now you can get them for £2 from Tesco – or if you are really bargain hunting you can buy Tesco's own brand of eighty Tea Bags for just two-pence more than the 1984 price. The same applies to a 1 kg bag of sugar, which back then was 44p (£1.50, circa 2020) and is something you can buy with a branded label, such as Tate & Lyle, some thirty-six years later for just 69p.

Our diet was to be simple. Coffee and beans (or similar) and toast on a morning, with the dried milk or Tip Top utilised as our milk, a full loaf of bread and Jam or spreadable cheese, which would be shared during our lunch break in the fields, and a Pot Noodle for dinner, all of which sounded completely do-able – that was until you actually fucking did it.

Tim had introduced me to the quick easy snack, which around the time had been intensely marketed by Golden Wonder with Ray *I'm the fucking Daddy* Winstone as its poster boy and which back then retailed around 38p (£1.29, circa 2020) per pot. That being the case we bought two dozen of them in various flavours to take down with us and if you want the honest-to-god truth, I have never eaten one since. Other people must have also grown wise, as you can now buy a chicken and mushroom flavoured Pot Noodle from Tesco for just 50p, which is about ten-bob more than the horrible fucking things are worth.

On the upside, Wisbech is a place where you could never ever starve as the surrounding fields were packed full of fruit and vegetables, which was something we immediately cottoned on to and after a day or so of sticking to our rigid diet, I threw in the towel. It was then I waded out into one of the orchards and came back with a carrier bag full of apples, which I finely sliced and then covered with Tip Top. It wasn't great, but not only did it give us our daily shot of Vitamin C, it also got shut of the aftertaste of those noodles. That was until next morning when the remnants of the Tip Top had begun to curdle in your mouth.

We had a dessert every night, with me staggering it a bit, alternating between Granny Smiths, Golden Delicious, a Russet type of apple, and a couple of times I remember us having pears with me often adding wild blackberries or raspberries to the dish.

Our breakfast habits also changed over the first few days, which was mainly due to the lack of us not having a fucking industrial dishwasher on site.

Although the unwritten rule was that we shared everything equally on a 50:50 basis it was never really the case. We had all the plastic plates, dishes and cups along with a knife, fork and spoon apiece, which were easily cleaned by boiling up water and washing them in a washing-up bowl with some Fairy Liquid that I had taken down. The stove we had borrowed, however, came with a proper camping saucepan and just happened to be the total opposite of non-stick. After the second time of using it – I think there had been two 29p (£1, circa 2020) cans of Heinz Ravioli in the pan at the time, I refused point-blank to ever use it again.

The upshot was, that we still had a good few tins of beans and spaghetti left in our supplies, which I ended up writing off, as unlike Tim, I couldn't eat them cold.

Our morning ritual was to get a wash and clean our teeth at our third base – the municipal toilets in the Town Hall car park – with me making sure that the council offices would always be two pints of milk light each morning.

The work in the fields was as mundane as it was boring, but at least we were doing something.

I envisaged seeing fields full of students from college or university happily working away, but that was never the case. Most of the people I worked alongside seemed gypsy-like and very rough around the edges.

The evening ritual was to go to our fourth base – Wisbech Leisure Centre – where we could get a shower and wash our socks and underwear, before having a swim in the baths for an hour or so. To say that we slept in the car for fourteen nights, we kept ourselves extremely clean.

The hardest part I recall was being down there on a weekend, when there was no work.

Generally, a person enjoys their weekends off, but I hadn't come down to Cambridgeshire to enjoy it; I had come down to earn some money and not fritter it away on trivialities, which is what Tim accused me of when we called in at a supermarket next to The Duke's Head public house opposite the church on our first weekend off.

"I'm not putting half to that," he snapped.

"I'm not fucking asking you to," I told him.

I had eaten shite all week and I needed to taste something different.

Back then supermarkets didn't stock the high-grade and cosmopolitan foods that they do now. All they tended to supply were the everyday essentials and the furthest they pushed the boat out was to stock things such as continental wines, cheeses and fruits, along with the recently launched frozen foods such as a 59p (£2, circa 2020) pack of four Findus Crispy Pancakes or a 78p (£2.66, circa 2020) pack of two Birds Eye Grill Steaks. You have to remember that in 1984, Pot Noodles were considered as being somewhat exotic.

I had spent 19p (65p, circa 2020) on some Jacob's Cream Crackers and 38p (£1.29, circa 2020) on some Hayward's Piccalilli, and the fuss he kicked up was quite unbelievable. And this was the person who had been trying to get me to cough up a similar amount of money to go the local cinema and watch Darryl Hannah as a mermaid in some pile of shite film titled *Splash*.

As I recall we spent half a day not talking, but I will tell you this much – the greedy bastard helped me eat those crackers and piccalilli.

During the silence I used the phone box in the marketplace that was located outside The Muppet Inn public house to phone my dad. He was well impressed that I had made it down there and that I was working and who told me that he had often used the transport café that we had been using. I also phoned my mums and had my (step)dad telling me that there had been miners returning to work in the Doncaster Area – with both Markham and Askern Main being mentioned.

Tim also phoned home – however, his conversations were a bit more heated than mine in that his nan and granddad were still on at him. And of course, he phoned his soon-to-be ex-girlfriend, who hadn't been at home the previous half-dozen times that he had called.

In comparison, my life had begun to have shape and meaning, whereas his was seemingly falling apart.

It wasn't actually said, but I thought that Florrie and Joe would have liked to have seen him on one of those heavily armoured buses that had been regularly seen on the *News*, speeding through the picket lines – as when I saw them, they were continually on his back for not working and that would become much worse when we eventually got back from Wisbech, with Tim snapping at both of them in reply: "Well, I'll scab then, shall I?"

"I'm not saying that," his granddad told him. "You should have stayed down there."

What his granddad was saying had logic. However, it wasn't Joe who had been living like a tramp and surviving on junk food and the fruit that we'd been pilfering out of the fields.

It was a hard two weeks and the only time I could ever recall us enjoying ourselves was a few days before we came home. We'd had a break from weeding the cabbage fields and had been clearing some fields of onions, some of which went quite well with our spready cheese sandwiches during our lunch break.

That evening we'd had a bath and done our laundry in the Leisure Centre and then went to its bar and copped a pint of lager, which was followed by half a dozen more, which resulted in me throwing up and us having to sleep in the Leisure Centre car park. I told you I wasn't a big drinker!

The last day in Wisbech was, I have to say, certainly the most eventful.

We had been switched from the fields around the Walpole St Andrew and Tilney St Lawrence areas and closer to Wisbech where we were utilised in some huge, gated grove containing what was literally hundreds of rows of blackberry bushes. We had to fill a 2 kg flat crate to earn £1.30 (£4.43, circa 2020). I must have eaten the first two crates as I always seemed to be half a crate behind Tim, up until the last one, when Fred – bless him, accused me of trying to do him.

"Two kilograms," I told him. "I've just fucking weighed it."

I had. One of the other field workers had been taking handfuls out of the crates that had already been weighed to fill up theirs.

I must admit, there were some very dodgy characters employed working the land, so much so, we had our valuables on us, wherever we went.

That afternoon we stayed until four o'clock, made £15.60 (£53.16, circa 2020) from picking blackberries and a further £2 (£6.82, circa 2020) apiece for helping load up the lorry. The only downside was that come bath time, we just couldn't get our hands clean.

I went straight into the marketplace and bought myself a pair of black Adidas Kick trainers at £12 (£40.89, circa 2020) and a LP record titled *Now, that's What I Call Music 3*, for the girlfriend.

On getting into the Leisure Centre swimming pool, we had the manager threaten to throw us out as our hands were heavily stained from the blackberries and even a scrub in the showers and all the chlorine in the water couldn't shift it.

"They're not dirty," I told him. "They are stained, and it won't come out."

That night had been planned since the day we got down there, our remit being to fill the car with as much fruit as possible and take it back home. What was also planned, was to siphon off the petrol from some car that had regularly been parked up on nearby Black Bear Lane, and as such an eight-foot piece of flexible hose had been purchased for the job.

The idea we had was to go into the orchards and fill up all the sacks and carrier bags that we had on us and leave them close to the roadside and pick them up one after the other, prior to our trip back up north.

What was true is that we brought back nearly half a ton of apples with a market street value of around £300 (£1,022, circa 2020), however, things certainly didn't go to plan.

As kids, we were always up in either Clayton or Hooton Pagnell raiding orchards during the summer school holidays and one thing which was immediately noticeable, was that the apple trees in Walsoken had been commercially grown to be easily farmed and to produce as much fruit as possible and therefore the trees were quite short and extremely full.

We hit orchard after orchard after orchard from late evening all the way into the night until it got too dark to operate as quickly as we would have wanted. It was then, whilst in an orchard on Wheatley Bank, that either Tim or myself hit some form of tripwire, which a short time after culminated in the high beam of some Land Rover picking up our shadows and driving hard at us. I remember bumping into Tim as we zig-zagged through the trees during our effort to get away, which produced some levity after we eventually found a gap in the hedge row at the orchard's southern periphery. However, that levity was short-lived after I refused to siphon off the petrol from the car that we had targeted. "I'm not doing it," I told him. "I've got a bad feeling about it."

He accused me of being both gutless and a hypocrite.

In my mind I was neither.

The easiest thing in the world is to empty a tank of petrol using a siphon. I was around twelve years old the first time I had been shown how to do it by our science teacher Mr (Rod) Bramall, and I had perfected it to something of a fine art. As such, to stick a tube into some petrol tank and empty its contents would have been relatively simple. The truth was, however, is that I **did** have a problem with it.

At this juncture in the strike it had been common knowledge regarding the theft of coal from out of one of the stockyard's close to Bolton-on-Dearne's ten-arch viaduct, where the Sheffield – York railway passes over both Mexborough Road and the River Dearne and which during the strike crudely misinformed the public that *PC Ian Dodds Sucks Dead Dog's Dicks*. The coal hadn't been stolen out of necessity, but on a commercial scale and for personal gain. It was being stolen to be sold at one hundred percent profit.

The thought of us making money from the fruit we had pilfered never crossed my mind once. Never. My idea was to spread it around and give it away to those who needed it and that is exactly what I did. "Is it okay for me to take some round for Alan Greaves," asked my (step)dad the very next morning.

"Yeh, course it is," I told him.

Alan was the striking brother of my auntie Heather's husband, Uncle Jimmy, who lived at 24 Cromwell Street and was someone who my (step)dad often went riddling for coal with on the site of the old Lidget Wood.

Stealing petrol however, would be for personal gain and dependant on just how much juice was in the tank, could have been very much Tim's personal gain and knowing this, he must have seen it as me taking money out of his pocket, and as such, he became quite confrontational.

"We've had a good run," I told him. "Leave it."

As I have already said, I had been battling away for the past six months, stretching what money I could get hold of, eating garbage and poncing off my family for hand-outs, which was something that had never been me. As for Tim, the experience to him was new and the money he had earned – and believe me when I say it – he had truly earned it, he just didn't want to waste on petrol.

On us driving into Thurnscoe around 2.30 a.m. on the very first day of September 1984, Tim had been under the impression that he would be dossing at 16 Briton Square – however, I cut that line of thought dead. We had done well to stay the course and bar the odd argument, we had got on well.

I had done what I had set out to do and had not only come home with more fruit than you could ever imagine and around £119 (£405.52, circa 2020) in cash, I had opened my door to be welcomed by two food parcels on my kitchen table along with a couple of envelopes containing rent rebate cheques totalling £26.25 (£89.45, circa 2020).

This was the most affluent I had ever been during the strike.

Top. A heavy picket at Edlington's Yorkshire Main - September 1984 (c. John Sturrock) Bottom. A picket at Harworth Colliery - James (Jumbo) McNulty, Carl Eades and Colin Hunter peering through the railings (c. Newsline)

17. Dark Side of The Moon (The Strike – Part 2)

I couldn't wait to get back home. I had money, I was tanned from working in the fields and I had a girlfriend to come home to – however, all of that would be temporary.

That Saturday morning, I went up to my mum's and dropped in several carrier bags of fruit, walked over Pit Lane to Goldthorpe, where I paid off the washing machine in full and then made the journey down to Mexborough to meet the girlfriend.

My mind was in overdrive and the thought of earning more money was at its forefront. Wisbech was an experience, but it wasn't one that I enjoyed – however, when you're skint, you will do almost anything to turn that situation around. The fact that it was rumoured the strike would soon be at its end as conciliatory talks between the NCB, the NUM and ACAS had been planned, was something that I recall feeling quite optimistic about and as such no real concrete decision had been made to go back down.

What was true, is that the girlfriend I had left was a totally different girl to the one that I had come back to and I remember walking alongside the Dearne and Dove Canal, whilst we watched on as some kids jumped off a pipe bridge into the water and thinking, that here I was, doing something that I didn't want to do and being somewhere that I didn't want to be.

I was firmly planted in the middle of what would be the biggest and most violent industrial dispute the country would ever witness – with the purchase of my own home, along with my life itself firmly on hold and I here I was stood around wasting my time.

I went up to my mum's the very next day, made the phone call and duly dumped the girlfriend.

With her out of the way the second visit to Wisbech was planned, with me calling the gang master just to make sure that there was still plenty of work about – however, when my mum, quite out of the blue asked if I fancied going with them in their newly purchased mobile home and touring the south coast for a week, I jumped at the chance.

Tim went apeshit. "What about us going down Wisbech?" he snapped.

Fuck Wisbech, I thought.

In my mind, it was a last chance to go on holiday before we went back to work.

I remember us calling in to see my grandma Ellis's sister-in-law and (step)dad's auntie Kay (Smith, nee Rayner) down in Luton and having a meal in their house before heading down the M3 towards Southampton. What had always seemed strange was people's perception of Arthur Scargill outside mining communities. My (step)dad's cousin and his auntie Kay's daughter, Patricia, apparently hated the man and was extremely forthright in her views, which was something that had been mirrored by some of the people we had come across in Wisbech.

One of the things that happened on the evening of 8 September 1984, is that my (step)dad's auntie gave him an old steel pencil box which was full of his grandfather's medals and I remember him diligently looking through them whilst in the motor home. "I'm going to get these mounted," he told my mum.

Did he?

No, I did.

On our way to the south coast we parked up in Winchester and whilst my parents went shopping with the kids I opted to stay in the camper van and wait for the BBC News to come on over the radio. I remember it like it was yesterday. Looking out into the Colebrook Street car park and over at the city's huge cathedral I was confident that the strike would soon be at its end. There had been a meeting that had rumbled on since the day before and which had relocated itself to British Ropes' (Bridon International) headquarters at Warmsworth Hall, off the A630 near Doncaster. On hearing the news, my heart sank. Both parties had walked away from the negotiating table.

I had lost everything, fought back a bit, and rode my luck and had a few things drop in my lap, which in reality had presented something of a false image of my life getting back on track. It would be here during 1984 however, where I would be at my very, very lowest. Both my parents knew how I felt. I wanted nothing more than to get back to work and put everything behind me. However, to turn your life around and bounce back, there is no better place to start than at rock bottom.

Portsmouth, Brighton and Hastings were all beautiful places and I recall sitting on the sandbanks at Shoeburyness towards the back end of that week and watching the ships sail in and out of the Thames Estuary. Like Wisbech had seemed, it was all a million miles away from the dark, miserable fucking place that was Thurnscoe.

My sister Joanne was always asking if I was alright and tried to engage me in conversation by quoting snippets from her *Smash Hits* magazine, which was a publication that at the time covered the eighties music industry from a teenage girlie perspective, as well as regularly asking me about the music which was being played over the radio such as Lloyd Cole's *Forest Fire* and David Bowie's *Blue Jean*. All week, that young girl gave me sanity. I can't thank her enough.

On getting back home, Tim tried to resurrect the idea of going down to Wisbech, but my thoughts were as crude as they were cynical. *Fuck Wisbech.*

On 17 September I remember walking down Windsor Street and over Lidget Lane to the NUM office and asking some delegate who was sat behind a desk: "I'm wanting to go picketing – how do I go about doing it?"

For months I had seen the violent confrontations between miners and police on both the BBC and ITV's *News* and never once did I fancy being a part of it and even now, I don't really know what ever made me take that decision. Maybe I had just had enough and if I hadn't taken that route, maybe I had have gone down the other route – the dark route – the route which you don't ever come back from. I just don't know. What I will tell you, however, is that the decision I made provided me with an outlet for a violence and anger, which was not only quite unprecedented, but which is something that has been buried deep within my soul ever since. If I am being honest, it is also one which at one time I found extremely hard to manage but is one that I can now take out and use whenever I feel the need. You are who you are, and I have never hidden that fact. I had been extremely pissed off and I wanted nothing more than to go out and hurt someone.

The fact that I didn't know how to go about going picketing, perhaps told you everything you needed to know about the NUM, in that it was a body that over time had become estranged from its members. As I have already said, I was never into politics and it is only recently and since the referendum on Brexit and the Rotherham child abuse scandal that I have become the one thing that my grandma Ellis would have hated me being. That is a lad from a working-class background with certain far-right ideals. However, what has often been said is that the political spectrum is not linear, but circular and that the extreme left always ends up rubbing shoulders with the extreme right.

Think of it as a clock face. The left arm goes anti-clockwise and the right clockwise. At half past six these two arms on the clock may well profess to possess completely different ideologies, but it is the same end result. Project Fear and one leader in total control. Joseph Stalin and Adolf Hitler.

The leaders and opposition that we have had since Tony Blair are nothing more than twelve o'clock politicians – the government stifled by the House of Lords and woke-led, blame culture agendaists whilst its opposition is in no-man's land and unsure of what it actually is.

One could suppose that Priti Patel and Diane Abbot are at the extremities of either party. The former is supposedly an advocate of the death penalty whilst the latter – if she was let loose to do whatever the fuck she liked, would most probably usurp Robert Mugabe and have the white upper and middle classes living in fields after seizing their property and letting it to Eritrean and Somalian immigrants.

Socialism is a fantastic concept, and I would like nothing more than to see every person in the country in employment. However, where socialism falls down is that its advocates tend to promote a lethargy and idleness as part of some insurmountable Utopia where four or five people are utilised to do the self-same job and where they all earn the same. My thoughts have, and always will be, that the harder a person is prepared to work, the more he or she should be rewarded.

I never saw the NCB as the enemy and one thing I vividly recall is browsing through the company's monthly newspaper – the *Coal News*, as I often did with both the NUM's red rags, *The Miner* and *Yorkshire Miner*, with the latter's only real use being that it came in handy for lighting and drawing the fire. However, I have said that already. The *Coal News* was partly interesting as from time to time it contained advertisements for home improvements along with finance packages for its employees. "Get a new central heating system installed," it read. "A new stone fireplace and eight radiators all for £1,600 (£5,452, circa 2020) – and all at just 4% APR."

Remember that. Just four percent.

I forget how much my NUM contributions were prior to the strike, but I wouldn't be far out if I stated that it was just over £1 a week, meaning that a union with 170,000 members turned over around £8.85 million (£30.16 million, circa 2020) per annum. This could give you some idea of not only the financial clout that they carried, but why a reduced workforce was something that it felt compelled to fight against and why straight after the strike it went the way of its nemesis – by offering goods that could be paid for on a weekly basis.

The NUM would open what was termed as *Pit Shops* within the colliery grounds, selling things as wide ranging and diverse as Donkey jackets to ladies' hair tongs and heated curlers along with vouchers that could be spent at Fenning's DIY shop and Kwik Fit – all of which could be taken off your wages at anything up to £20 per week.

I remember getting a £100 (£340.78, circa 2020) voucher for Kwik-Fit, which was to be paid off at £10 per week. I went in after eleven weeks to ask why they were still taking the money out of my wages. It wasn't any mistake, it was interest – 15%.

And always remember that. Fifteen fucking percent.

We turned up to go picketing and it would be here that not only I would see how the NUM operated, but the animosity that having no money created between miners, not at least with myself and Tim. Our destination was Carcroft Workshops, which was a place located close to where my dad used to work with Roade Aggregates – just around the corner from the huge Asda supermarket and the place where Tim would park up his car.

The money was handed out by a NUM man by the name of Les Hipwell. Tim, being the driver of the car received £6 (£20.45, circa 2020) and passed £1 (£3.41, circa 2020) to both myself and the other passenger, who was Daz Cooper, whilst keeping the £4 (£13.63, circa 2020) to himself.

Just over seventeen miles at £1.75 per gallon, that was 87p for the petrol and £3.13 (£10.67, circa 2020) to go in his pocket.

When you have little or no money, you notice every fucking penny.

The picketing itself was nothing special and apart from turning a police car over and me kicking a policeman on the thigh and someone else getting arrested for it, that was about it. What it did do however, was reintroduce me to a lot of lads that I had not only worked at Hickleton Main with, but some who I had been with at Houghton Road Infant and Junior school. People such as Carl Eades and Colin Hunter, the latter of who I had noticed had been recently driving onto Briton Square in some sky-blue Mark II Ford Escort and going into an empty house.

As you do, I enquired as to how much these miners were getting for picketing and as was the norm it was between £1 and £1.50 (£5.11, circa, 2020), dependent on how many lads were in the car and how much the driver wanted to give you, and that being the case I was immediately on Tim's back and wanting an extra 50p (£1.70, circa 2020).

The amount seems nothing, but I vividly remember tearing open the base of my orange striped sofa during the dark days of July 1984, and of my elation after I found 6p (20p, circa 2018), which was enough to put towards the

8p I had left from that week's rent rebate to go out and buy a 14½p (48p, circa 2020) packet of custard cream biscuits.

The hardship of the 1984 strike was nothing compared to the hardships of 1926 and 1912, but even knowing that it still didn't make it any less hard.

I think we had been out around three or four times when we were tasked with an £7 (£23.85, circa 2020) picket over at Allerton Bywater Colliery near Castleford and to get as much money as possible out of the picket, there were just three of us travelling in the car, the other of who was Billy Coulson. I remember us driving out of the pit yard and Tim heading the wrong way and then pulling the car into a layby that was at one time opposite Bella Wood.

"What's up?" I asked.

"The car," he shrugged. "There's something wrong with it."

In my mind, there wasn't anything up with the car – he was just like a lot of miners at the time, in that he was depressed.

I look back at that time and what was to follow. It was another watershed moment that had me think, *Fuck this*, and later that afternoon saw me walking around the corner on to Briton Street and knocking on Carl Eades's door at No 27 and on me telling him what had gone off, he said: "Me and Col will use both cars. Just jump in with one of us."

Carl was a lad with an acerbic wit which could be heavily misinterpreted by the person on the receiving end, which was something that often masked the caring and considerate nature the lad actually possessed. He was also someone that played to the crowd with his number one fan and sycophant being John Gratton. He was a lad from 9 John Street – which was the most easterly of the three accesses onto Thornley Crescent and into the Reema Estate, and another one of the Class of 1981 that had been signed on six weeks before me.

As with Tim – Carl, Col and John had all made the mining engineering course, however, all of them had felt the effects of the Government's heavy-handed approach in dealing with the strike.

All three lads had been out picketing since the early days of the strike, with John getting arrested at the ultimate blot on the landscape that was Harworth Colliery. As I understood it, part of the conditions of his bail, banned him from actively picketing, therefore he flew beneath the radar somewhat and did the morning's run out of Highgate Main Colliery which covered the Power Stations on the River's Aire and Ouse, in that he picketed both Eggborough and Drax. The downside, however, was that he had been temporarily kicked of his college course until the outcome of his trial, which of course meant that his DHSS payment had been stopped.

By September 1984 however, and with the NCB hard at work and actively pushing for miners to return to work, the Government did no more than stop every DHSS payment, meaning that we were all in the same boat.

What was interesting is that all three lads had completely different lives, yet at times they entwined perfectly with mine, Billy and Tim's – that was until Tim became sick of Carl's caustic comments and John's continual pontification in backing them up. You really had to possess a thick skin to deal with the humour and take the insults, but the reality of it was, that it wasn't really meant and was just what it was: piss take. My personal view, although I could be wrong, is that Tim refused to allow himself to mix.

The brunt of the humour, however, was never really directed at Tim, but Col.

Colin had a dark underside in that he was extremely manipulative, which due to the gregarious façade he carried, often passed unchecked. That's not a put down, but my pure admiration of the lad. Colin certainly may not have looked it, but he was the ultimate alpha wolf, whose predatory instinct for survival was quite unmatched. He was also very thick-skinned, therefore nothing that was said – and I mean nothing, ever seemed to get him down.

"The sneaky little bastard" and "The selfish little cunt" were continual three-barbed superlative-cum-adjectives that Carl often referred to when describing him, with the common denominator being that he was small. This was strange, as although he was much shorter than me, he was a similar height to Carl. I think that stemmed from their time at school, when Col – like another one of the Class of 1981 who went to work at Hickleton Main, Pete Hill – were extremely small in stature in comparison to the other kids, with the latter's favourite saying at the time being "Eh?"

Col had married a girl from the Crystal Peaks area of Sheffield by the name of Joanne Wild and shortly after they had a daughter by the name of Nicola, with the idea being that 8 Briton Square would be the place where they could start the rest of their lives. However, nothing back then was ever straightforward, and the child spent a huge amount of time in hospital, with what I was to understand was some heart problem. During the early days of his marriage, Col had lived with his wife under the same roof as her parents, but the strain of him not working and her father putting pressure on him to return to work after his DHSS payment stopped, resulted in him living back in Thurnscoe, and as Col's (step)father was on strike, it was a case of him having to temporarily doss at Carl's.

Mine and Tim's relationships with our respective partners had both ended and Col's would soon follow suit, though it was not for the lack of him trying to hold it all together. I still remember him buying a pack of 29p (99p, circa 2020) nappy liners from the chemist shortly after some mini riot over at Edlington's Yorkshire Main Colliery, where around 2,000 of us witnessed James (Jumbo) McNulty fighting with a few policemen, before getting arrested and slung in the back of some meat van.

It was something I could never understand, the way some miners openly courted confrontation at the very front of the picket lines. I had already seen Kevin (Bud) Green get arrested on my very first picket for doing the exact same thing.

As we had jumped in with Col and Carl, our eating venue immediately changed from the soup kitchen's at Goldthorpe's Welfare Hall to that of The Docket on Thurnscoe's Welfare Road, which I had to say had a certain amount of déjà vu about it. Between 1969 and 1972 I had often made the journey with the exact same lads – walking both hand in hand and in crocodile procession from Houghton Road Infant School, down Welfare Road and past the huge red-bricked Broadway building that back then was Stones's garage and to a place directly opposite, where huge cream Army-type huts provided the setting for our school dinners.

I still remember playing out on the lawn, which backed on to the rear of the New Un' public house, prior to us going inside and a lad by the name of Paul Waite stood on some elevated manhole shouting, "I'm the king of the castle and you're all dirty rascals" and me ripping some flowery elasticated tie from around his neck.

Paul Waite – bless him. I still have a lump of lead above the knee where he rammed a pencil into my right leg shortly after. The last time I saw Paul, he had car painting and body shop working out of Ken Brown's old premises on Furlong Road, which during the strike had been a motorcycle showroom. He had just repainted my car after some shitbag had run a key up the side of it.

The Docket not only provided much better food, but unlike the Welfare Hall it was a working men's club. This meant that it had both a pool and snooker table and served drinks at a much-reduced rate – with half a pint of what was termed as *Jungle Juice*, being just 9p (31p, circa 2020); a drink that was basically a combination of water mixed with dilute orange. More often than not, we were in there well before ITV's *News at One* and got chucked out around 3.30 p.m. Suddenly my life began to have a structure and rigidity about it and the one thing I wasn't – was on my own.

During late-September there were violent clashes on the picket lines, not at least at Maltby Colliery, Brodsworth Main and Kiveton Park Colliery, but very few would ever compare to a night picket over in Thrybergh, which was described by outlets of the national media at the time of being the worst during what was then, a twenty-seven-week old strike.

We had only been travelling together for a couple of days, when on the afternoon of 27 September, Carl called at my house to let me know it would be a midnight picket, with me immediately thinking that it would be some long drive to a faraway pit. In fact, I even remember making up a flask.

Silverwood Colliery was the exact opposite of being a long drive and was only a short journey through Mexborough and Conisbrough, with both cars parking up in some elevated car park, top side of the pit on Hollings Lane.

Orgreave readily sticks in the mind of the public and historians alike as it had been a mass picket that had been heavily televised – however, the reality is that it was very much coordinated and man-managed by the police and as such, something of a farce. There were certainly clashes, but in the main, miners offered themselves up to be shepherded into some field, whilst the president of the NUM, Napoleonic in stance and loud hailer in hand, failed miserably before being arrested as he tried to recreate his Saltley Gate.

The huge numbers of miners, a sunny day, along with the huge number of police and the television cameras made it a spectacle to be remembered – however, the real irony was that it centralised the problem and took pickets away from the pit heads, therefore allowing more men to return to work.

Bryan Robson, who was a senior NUM official at Hatfield Main during the strike, and who became someone that became a good friend in later life, said regarding Scargill that day. "The man was a fucking idiot – he helped do the police's job for them."

Ask any career criminal when they feel it is best to operate and they will all tell you the same: during the night.

At Silverwood, it was dark and damp, and miner upon miner began converging outside the pit gates and within the hour quite a crowd began to swell.

My recollection was that the initial trouble had been started by the arrest of a man who was both drunk and abusive, and aimed his insults at one of thirty or so police that had been visible. "You're nothing but Thatcher's fucking puppets," I remember him shouting.

After ten minutes of listening to his ranting, more police came out from behind the pit gates and it soon became obvious that he had become a target, and with the assistance of two or three of his colleagues, the police man who he had been hurling insults at, duly dragged him out of the crowd and arrested him. What is true is that I was one of the miners trying to obstruct the police as they arrested the man, and I duly took a punch in the mouth for my efforts.

I was livid and immediately looked around on the floor for something to throw, however, the missiles had already started being slung, with the lads from Thurnscoe doing all the throwing – the worst offender being Billy Coulson. Once it started it had a kind of knock-on effect, and it didn't take long for the police to retreat into the pit yard amidst a hail of stones and bricks before deploying the long shield unit and calling for more reinforcements.

I remember calling at Billy's house after my first picket at Carcroft and asking him if he fancied coming along. His mum Nora (nee Lampard), who was part of the huge influx of families from Durham that had migrated to Thurnscoe in the late 1950s – early 1960s, was around fifty-five years old at the time and the last thing she wanted him doing, was going picketing.

Billy was the youngest of six children, and it would be fair to say that Nora or *Mrs C* as Paula Hole often called her, did spoil him quite a bit. There is, however, a story in that she had already lost a son by the name of Alan, who would have been Billy's younger brother by just three years, and just a few months after he was born. As such, and with nothing other than her pure concern for his safety, she told her son that she would prefer it if he didn't go. She had a point. He was the worse one out there that night – a right fucking animal.

The police movements caused a split in the picket lines – some going towards where we had parked the cars and the others, including Billy, Col, Tim and myself going up the hill towards some terraced houses opposite a wooded area, where we began dismantling front garden walls to provide us with aggregate to throw.

The national media, including the ITV and BBC News, suggested that there were around 700 miners that created a road blockade, which formed the catalyst for an ambush. As I recall, that was never the case. There were around half that number of miners who were a part of our group, but their attention was solely on the police with the long shields down at the colliery itself and who they were throwing missiles at. What happened, is that the initial altercation had obviously been called in and buses upon buses of police were driven down Hollings Lane from the direction of The Cavalier public house, which one could assume had been based off either the M18 in Hellaby or over in Mexborough. Wherever they came from, they hadn't been prepped on the size or mood of the picket, as the buses – none of which were armoured, drove straight into the rear of the huge group of miners, whose focus had been directed elsewhere. Suddenly, to our amazement, we had standing targets to hit and as such, everything was thrown at the vehicles. There were windows upon windows being smashed as the driver of the first vehicle tried to crawl his way through the carnage at snail's pace. The main reason, however, of why there had been a hold up, is that the police motorcycle which was being ridden behind the few police dog vans which led the way had had Billy to deal with. He had ripped a steel gate from one of the front garden walls and had run into the road and wrapped it around the front end of the bike. How that policeman stayed on the bike was either a testament to his skill or just a case of fear keeping him upright. The gate got fast in his wheels, and with sparks flying from metal on metal and metal on roadstone, all the buses behind had to stop. Billy had caused the delay and the crowd, obviously pumped up with adrenalin, went into a frenzy. Never had I seen anything like it. It was a madness unparalleled and the terror that those policemen must have felt must have been something else – as for a minute or so, they were all completely trapped. Every single vehicle got hit.

The construction of the barricades came shortly after, when half the wooded area was dragged out into the road. This was something that was intended to stop or slow down the bus that we understood would be bringing the two scabs into work.

I have read articles from journalists and heard people within the Government at the time say that the mass pickets of 1984 were coordinated as per some amateur paramilitary movement. That was never the case. Nobody told you what to do and there was rarely anyone enticing the violence. Most of the time the violence flared ad-hoc, mainly after the scab bus had gone in and when the miners refused to move on. Then as soon as the short-shielded police were deployed, that is when the real trouble started, although it would be a total lie to state that we were all innocent, because we were not. "Stop throwing stones from the back," was the regular call that was made by the miners at the front, prior to any riot.

We had no idea what was happening elsewhere, although we heard later that a couple of police dog vans had been turned over with dogs running free and, in the confusion, attacking police and miners alike and that and some police man had been hit around his head.

What we did know is that a huge number of police were now at the colliery and who we knew would be shortly making their way up the hill – however, what I will say is that I can't ever recall seeing the scab bus that morning. Within an hour there were police everywhere, especially outside The Cavalier public house, where Hollings Lane intersects with both Moor Lane and Braithwell Road – a good few of which that were mounted on horseback.

I had already seen the mounted police in action, but at that time had never been up that close to one, although that would soon change.

As it had been a night picket and the temperature had dropped, I had been wearing a sleeveless royal blue padded coat over a faded Wrangler denim jacket, which, with me having different coloured arms, sort of singled me out from the crowd. Therefore, as we were being forced off the road, the most senior police officer on site up at the junction, who was holding some halogen flashlight in his hand, pushed me in the back to move on. Obviously, I'm not going to admit that I duly spun around and smashed him in the face, but I felt that I needed payback for the crack I had taken earlier.

Col told me that he couldn't believe what he saw. The officer hadn't gone down, but he had staggered back a bit and dropped his lamp. Straight after there was one hell of a commotion, with the flashlights following my every movement towards the rear of some bungalows off Braithwell Lane and mounted police on horseback trying to part the crowd.

"Take your jacket off, kid," said one of the pickets, as we got down behind some privet. "You stand out like a sore thumb."

As I did, I got talking to a few young lads from Dinnington Colliery who had witnessed what had just happened. It had been one hell of a night, which was capped off by Carl flooring his Ford Capri through Denaby and nearly totalling it near Mexborough Power Station on our way back home.

"For almost twenty-five minutes the police came under a barrage of bricks, stones, pieces of timber, and chunks of metal machinery hurled through the darkness," wrote Peter Davenport of *The Times*. "Eight officers were injured, with five taken to hospital for treatment and two police vans overturned as pickets completed a pincer movement to attack the beleaguered convoy from the front and rear."

Supt. Peter Lodge, who oversaw the convoy, described the situation as a carefully planned ambush. "It was very frightening, the worst situation I have ever found myself in. It wasn't picketing. It was just hundreds of men out to injure police officers and damage police vehicles. It was entirely unprovoked and the most diabolical incident I have seen during the strike."

The article read further: "The attack began in darkness shortly before 2.30 a.m. as Mr Lodge in a police Range Rover led a convoy of nine dog vans along Hollings Lane towards Silverwood Colliery, near Rotherham, where two men have been defying the strike for several weeks."

Supt. Lodge had already seen Orgreave, now he had seen Silverwood, and had described it as being the "most diabolical incident he had seen during the strike" and "The worst situation he had ever found himself in".

There you go, mainstream media: **Orgreave was a myth**.

What of the other news reports?

The supposed paper of the people, *The Sun*, was intending to run with the headline "Scum Miners" in its 29 September edition, however, the print workers downed tools and refused to work, and although the story depicting the events at Silverwood would be lost in time, the fact that the Saturday's edition was not published, is pure testament to the violence that went on that night.

This was to be the start of a crazy couple of months.

As Carl and I (and his lodger) were living just around the corner from each other, it became customary to breakfast at each other's house – nothing much, just toasted bread and coffee – however prior to that and straight after the riot at Silverwood, I was asked by Carl if I fancied a Saturday afternoon picket, with him and John Gratton over at Drax.

As I have said, I had only been picketing with Carl a few days, but what I immediately noticed is that he spread the money around and for the trip out to Drax, he said: "I can give you two quid."

"Yeh, sure," I replied.

The picket to Drax was a £12 (£41, circa 2020) run – £2 (£6.82, circa 2020) each, plus £6 (£20.45, circa 2020) for the tank, which for a fifty-minute drive each way and with Emerson Fittipaldi's idiot brother at the wheel, I thought could be stretching it.

"Come around about one," he told me.

It had been the first time I had ever been invited into his house and what I didn't expect was for him to be cooking a pan of chips in some kitchen that made mine look like something out of *Homes & Gardens*.

Briton Street along with its Square of the same name, had been built in the mid-twenties, and as such, the style of its houses were considered old-fashioned in comparison to the prefabricated concrete structures that had been constructed as part of the Derry Grove and Lindley Crescent developments in the 1950s; the latter having their bathrooms and toilet located directly at the top of the staircase.

All the three-bedroomed houses up in the East end were of a similar design, with the kitchen possessing not just a fireplace and sink, but access via three individual doors into a bathroom, pantry and toilet, with the only difference being that my house at Briton Square rather strangely had its rear door access at the side of the house and not at the back, meaning that my pantry was where a back door should have been. I have no idea why it had been built like that – it just had.

27 Briton Street was where Carl's family had moved to during the 1970s, and with his parents splitting up and moving on, he along with his girlfriend, Maxine Swift, a girl from up the street at No 73, had opted to buy the property from his father, which if I recall, was at a price that was around twice more than I would be paying for mine. That was when or indeed if, we eventually got back to work.

I was mesmerised and looking around it resembled some scene out of the TV series *The Young Ones*. His cooker was lodged between the fireplace and sink and just about under the front window and as such, the heat from the chip pan was steaming it up, whilst at the other side of the fireplace was a tall refrigerator which housed a black and white portable TV on its top, with the focal point of the room being some settee and chair with piles and piles of magazines rammed under and down the sides of each of its cushions. In fact, there seemed to be magazines everywhere.

The pièce de résistance of this homely surrounding was some fearsome and stinky hound with a penchant for shitting in the house, which is what it did most of the time after Carl's dad had banned him from keeping it down at his allotment. This was after it had wiped-out out half his livestock and put some goat he owned into early retirement. Most of the time it was kept in the short passage between the toilet and bathroom that both gave access to the back door and which that day had been shut off by one of several inexplicably coloured doors.

"After our old man and my mam split up, she ended up coming back for a bit and the only thing I ever remember her doing whilst she was here, was painting all these doors some shitty brown, prior to her fucking off again," Carl explained.

Please note: The colour of his kitchen doors and architrave were the exact same colour as his Ford Capri!

John had already been at the house when I arrived, and like Col, was a kid that I had known whilst going through infant school. A nice recollection of the lad would be after we had been taken down to the Old Hall on Thurnscoe's High Street, which prior to The Avenues being built and the creation of the shopping centre on Back Lane – which would of course be reprofiled to become Houghton Road, had been the main thoroughfare through the village. It had been a kind of nature walk where Mrs Wheeler had pointed out the rookeries in the trees and on us getting back to class, John had been praised for the fine detailing of the twigs that formed the bird nests that he had drawn.

John was the youngest of three children to Douglas and Margaret Gratton (nee Batram), the latter of who along with his mum's brother – his uncle Billy, he still lived at home with.

John had had an elder brother by the name of Douglas who had been born dead on 23 April 1963.

I can recall both his parents as a kid, as on the odd occasion I used to call down for him on my way to school when I had lived on Deightonby Street, although he would lose his father whilst he was in his First Year (Year 7) at Thurnscoe Comprehensive. He sadly died in December 1976, aged forty-eight.

Douglas's parents George and Gladys (nee Hawkins) had originally lived at 61 Barnsley Road, Highgate, with his wife's family – however after the birth of Mary (b. 1911) and his elder brother Samuel (b. 1922), they moved over to 25 Cross Street in Hemsworth, where his father worked as a Fireman in the colliery boilers. Douglas, however, would lose his mother when he was just eight years old. Gladys died in 1936, aged forty-seven. Strange?

Margaret had been brought up with her aunt and uncle, Fred and Martha Batram (nee Denton) in an overcrowded two-up two-down on 20 William Street in Highgate and would marry Douglas in 1954.

If you want an interesting story, the family of John's grandparents and great grandparents were in Highgate at 2.20 a.m. on 26 September 1917, when the area was subjected to an aerial bombardment from a Heer LZ 93 Zeppelin. The raid, in which several HE bombs, and incendiaries were dropped, managed to take out part of the bridge that carried the Wath Branch line over the bottom of Highgate Lane, along with some nearby telegraph wires and windows of several properties on both George and William Street.

Cruising at an altitude of over 10,000 feet on a pitch-black night and with low lying clouds, the huge eerie presence of the 650-foot long by 75-foot wide airship was never seen and only the distant humming of its engines could be heard. It had crossed the North Sea with the intention of hitting the Parkgate Iron and Steel Works, north of Rotherham and moving in a north to southerly direction picked up the line of the Sheffield-York railway where between Thurnscoe and Bolton-on-Dearne it dropped a series of bombs in a straight line, four of which failed to explode.

The first exploded between Clayton and Thurnscoe, three exploded at Highgate and four were dropped on Bolton-on-Dearne – one of which exploded close to the area where Carfield school would eventually be built, of which the impact blew out forty or fifty windows. Another was dropped on the grounds of the vicarage close to St Andrews Church and another exploded at the crossroads with Wath-on-Dearne, before it crossed the River Dearne to wreak havoc in Mexborough and Swinton where it dropped a further eight HE bombs and three incendiaries, before focusing its wrath on Sheffield.

The only way I could describe Margaret would be as an extremely lovely lady and the consideration she often showed, especially after I was married, is something that still puts a lump in my throat. A genuinely nice woman. John carried the self-same trait and some of the selfless things he did, made you realise exactly who he took after. Both his elder sisters, Pauline and Julie, had a similar manner, although it would be fair to say, that unlike John and his mum, I didn't really know them that well.

We all have our petty foibles, downsides, shortcomings or whatever, and John's was, that at times he could come over as being rather sanctimonious with his ultimate delivery being to *know thy place*. During the strike it reared its head several times, but the fact he was such a lovely lad temporarily masked over any minor defect that he may have had.

He was in a relationship with someone I knew quite well. Tracy Greaves was one of six children and the daughter of Alan and Rita (nee Hunt) and who was, therefore, the niece of my auntie Heather and uncle Jimmy.

I had known Tracy since we were kids, with the first thing you noticed being her smile, and although we weren't related as such, it made her a cousin of a cousin. If you want a story – both mine and her cousin – our Jonathan (Greaves), once nearly killed her. Tracy had been sitting on the windowsill of one of the bedroom windows in their house on Cromwell Street and for some unknown reason our Jon pushed her out of the opened window. According to Tracy, the honeysuckle plants in the garden broke her fall and she was able to get up and walk back inside the house.

Thurnscoe is full of similar connections and if you want a rather sinister example, one has to look no further than Carl, who through the marriage of his dad's sister – his auntie Mary (Eades) to Peter Cattell in 1957 – links him to Thurnscoe's Pit Lane rapist and the murderer of Sandra Parkinson, through their son Brian's marriage to Sandra Conner in 1980.

Maybe Carl should have slung that fucker out of a window.

I can briefly recall stopping at Tracy's house when I had been around five or six years old. I'm not sure the reasoning or much else about it, only that I had cornflakes for breakfast and there seemed to be kids everywhere, one of who was a toddler who bore the same name as her mum. Rita was born in 1968 and tragically died of silent pneumonia some seven years later.

I keep saying it, but I can't think of anything more tragic than losing a child, and one of the things I always noticed about Tracy's family, is of how close they all were.

Although I had worked with both John and Carl down the Silkstone development, when both lads filled in one afternoon shift manning one of the main Transfer Points that loaded onto the East Side Cable Belt, it would be fair to say that as young men, I didn't know them all that well. However, they certainly appeared to know a lot about me.

I had always tended to court confrontation and whilst growing up in Thurnscoe's East end I had seen more than most; in fact, a lot more than most and instead of keeping my head down and shutting my mouth, I tended to kick back.

Tracy's brother Steve, who is a year older than us, had married young. His wife Joanne had become pregnant when she was sixteen years old and Steve had done what he considered the right thing to do and married her. Just like Tracy, I thought Steve was a great kid, although at that time, the jury was certainly out on his wife.

Joanne was the middle child of Mick and Carol Russell (nee Green), whose family had relocated from Thorne and who had moved onto the northern leg of Brunswick Street during the mid-1970s along with her sisters, Mandy and Michaela. She was an extremely pretty girl, who was a school year younger than me, and who my mum once exclaimed after first seeing her: "She's the spitting image of your auntie Elizabeth (Durose), when she was a young lass."

My auntie Elizabeth was the one who became *Miss Pears Soap* sometime in 1961.

When I was around fourteen years old, Joanne became my girlfriend. I was well-impressed as her appearance far exceeded her age. As I said, getting a girlfriend was always easy – keeping them interested, however, was not.

It was during the early summer of 1979 that she asked me to go out with her and I recall going around to her house and being introduced to all this music, that I had never heard before, some of which I thought was good and some of which I did not. *Touch of Velvet, String of Brass* by The Mood Mosaic, *Skiing in the Snow* by Wigan's Ovation, *Jimmy Mack (When are you Coming Back)* by Martha Reeves & The Vandellas and *Reunited* by Peaches and Herb.

She and her elder sister were into what they termed as Northern Soul and as such, they made sure that they went out anywhere they could to listen to it, whether it be Middlecliffe WMC in Little Houghton or some dimly lit night spot tucked away on Doncaster's Silver Street called Zhivago's. As for me, I was still riding a bike, nicking apples, fighting, and doing all the other shit that lads at that age do. I could never compete with that. In the end I jacked her in and called her a *slut*, which was wrong of me, especially as I know the lovely woman that she grew into.

Her mum was like the fucking Terminator and pulled me up early one morning on Windsor Street, whilst I was on the way back from my grandma Ellis's. Carol then gave me the finger in the face and informed me in what I could only describe as quite a sinister voice: "I'm sending Mick around to your house to go and beat your (step)dad up."

Mick was a monster of a man.

Did he hit my (step)dad? No.

The last I saw of Mick was after a riot outside Brodsworth Main Colliery in October 1984, when I had become separated from Col and Carl during the confusion, and on seeing me stranded and walking back towards Pickburn's five-lane ends, he stopped the car and duly told me to jump in. Mick was a great bloke.

As for Joanne?

Her husband's uncle and mine – my uncle Jimmy – worked in the estimating department of some scaffolding firm over in Leeds. He had been part of the crew that erected the scaffolding on Sheffield Wednesday's cantilevered North Stand and more interestingly the huge cooling towers at Ferrybridge C on the River Aire – the self-same ones that collapsed on 1 November 1966.

Jimmy's great tale was the fact that he had walked heel-to-toe and without any safety rail or harness around the very top of those self-same cooling towers, telling me in much later life, "I must have been fucking mad."

Jimmy got her husband and his nephew a start at his firm – however, one thing that was hidden, whether purposely or not, was that Steve suffered from a type of epilepsy and was therefore subject to having fits. The closest I had ever been to seeing anyone have a fit, was one time in Dearneside Comprehensive around 1978, when Paul Ludlam – the lad whose gran ran off with Eric Noon, collapsed in assembly and went into some violent spasm. Very fucking scary.

Whilst working up on the North Selby Mine in Escrick, Steve had something similar whilst at height, which caused him to lose his footing and tumble. Although he survived the fall, he was in a very bad way and all through

Steve's long recuperation and pain-staking rehabilitation, Joanne never left his side. In short, she was one hell of a wife. The last I heard they lived at 25 Lindley Crescent.

John was well-aware of the stories that surrounded me, as was Carl, both of whom – not so much brought up the subject of my ex-girlfriend, but the fact of who she was now seeing along with as much other information as they could generate. This was just to see how quickly I got pissed off. And they say kids are cruel! Grown-ups can be just as fucking bad.

Working in the pits was no different to life on its surface within the mining community, in that everybody tended to know bits of everyone's business and more often than not, certain aspects of it tended to get exaggerated the more it was passed around, with the upshot being that it was hard to decipher what was the truth and what wasn't.

"She's seeing Richy," was Carl's opening line, as I got passed my plate of chips.

I knew who she was seeing. I didn't need anyone else to tell me.

The Cooper children in the front room of 78 Brunswick Street, Thurnscoe, with Daz - central, holding the baby.
No idea, where Jimmy - the eldest is !

222

18.   The Girl With The Sun in Her Hair (The Strike – Part 3)

It was a cold Wednesday night on 10 October 1984, when I remember being part of a picket outside Thorpe Mash Power Station. This was a huge electricity generating complex on the banks of the River Don that was located just outside the village where I had spent eight months living during the previous year. A hundred or so miners had converged at its gates around 10.00 p.m., along with a dozen or so local lads, the latter of whom I am sure were there to add a bit of menace to the picket, which we were informed had been deployed to stop the lorry movements of coal that had supposedly been planned. It was a bluff. A senior policeman turned up from inside the gates and told us that there would be no movements of coal and could we all go home.

Silverwood had blown everything away. The violence, the terror, the excitement. Every time I went out, that is what I hoped for and a night time picket in a place that I knew well had been more than welcomed. I expected everything and got literally nothing. £1.50 in the pocket and not one brick was thrown.

"You've not seen owt," John would smugly retort during dinner. "We were down in Nottinghamshire during the early days of the strike. I saw it every day."

In my mind he hadn't. I just saw him as someone who kept out of trouble going backwards and forwards to Drax with Tracy's elder brother, Alan.

Carl, Col, Tim and Billy were always up for it, the latter of whom at times I thought needed either gently coaxing onto a chaise longue or an injection in the temple prior to being zipped up in a straitjacket.

On 11 November 1983, Billy and myself, along with another one of Thurnscoe Comprehensive's Class of 1981, Dave Allott, had had a couple of hours sleep off night shift and had jumped on the Friday afternoon shift's pit bus to take us back through to Askern Main. The idea had been, so we could pick up our wage packets and stick a Rest Day in for that Friday night. My reasoning had been simple. There was a great night on TV. The *A-Team* was on at 7.30 p.m. along with the first ever showing of *Auf Wiedersehen, Pet*, which Gaz Bright had been blagging everyone's head about all fucking week and had been nagging the Bob Carolgees lookalike that was Pete (Houdi) Errington to tape it for him. And to round off a great night, Marvin Hagler was due to fight Roberto Duran straight after the *News at Ten*. And if that wasn't enough to whet one's appetite, *Bananaman* was on at teatime.

"This is 29 Acacia Road. And this is Eric, the schoolboy who leads an exciting double life. For when Eric eats a banana, an amazing transformation occurs. Eric is Bananaman."

From the sound of Eric's accent, he could have easily lived somewhere on Bolton-on-Dearne's Concrete Canyon.

I remember going, like it was yesterday – it was the coming back part, that I have completely forgotten.

Getting to and from Askern, was two bus rides with the short interchange being to jump from one bay to another at Doncaster's North Bus Station, and where only the week before I had seen Billy stood outside the newsagents and draped over its galvanized railings, with his head in his hands. Just thinking about it I've got the smell up my nose, exactly as I had back then – mainly the stench from the adjacent toilets.

When I had enquired to what he was doing he told me that his girlfriend had got the hump and had just stomped off back down the subway into the Arndale Centre.

"I can't understand it," he shrugged. "Why would she leave a handsome bastard like me?"

He was a character.

As we came into the bus station around midday it was Billy's idea to nip to Fox's record shop and mine to call and have a drink thereafter. Therefore, on walking out on to St Sepulchre Gate it was a toss-up between the dark seedy dog hole that was The Nag's Head or some trendy new bar with a video jukebox that showed female mud wrestling called The Yorkist. After watching David Bowie put on his red shoes and dance the blues a couple of times, that was it. The next thing I know, I'm in bed and hearing banging on my door. On opening it, there was Billy telling me that we had nearly been arrested for being drunk and disorderly in the Arndale Centre – with some detective having to show us his badge and ID card, and that Dave Allott had told him to "Fuck off". Oh yeh, and that I had been continually complaining about losing my cheque book.

"Where is my cheque book? I asked him.

"You lost it," he said.

"Where?"

"How do I fucking know," he shrugged. "It wouldn't be lost if I knew where it was."

Aside from the bike ride in late-February, the last time few times I had been out with him prior to that had been quite eventful.

i) I had stopped him getting bullied in the Old Hall and had to knock Woody's teeth out a day later.

ii) I had been chased down the back of Shepherd Lane by some marauding mob led by some carrot-topped giant, the day after that.

iii) I had been rolled over in the New 'Un bus stop by Don Elliott and the son of the *alleged* motherfucker off Church Street and had my ribs kicked in a few days after that.

iv) I had spent two hours in Goldthorpe Police Station whilst two detectives were trying find the whereabouts of around two hundred pairs of stockings and a nightie that he had pinched for his mum the week after.

"A right afternoon that was," he told me.

Every time I went anywhere with him there was a skirmish. He ought to have gone to Thorpe Marsh that night. The reason why he didn't? He was still living with his mum and she went out on a Wednesday night, and of course, that being the case, he and his girlfriend had the house to themselves.

I recall being in Carl's car, whilst Col followed on in his. Generally, we had three bodies in each vehicle, although for the life of me I can't remember exactly who was there, just that one of Col's passengers was his younger brother. I had known Andy Hunter for as long as I had known their Col. A good-looking, smart, witty kid who was the loudest of the loud. He was as gregarious in nature as his elder brother and with the heart of a lion to match. The lad would do anything for you.

During the pit strike he went picketing out of Highgate Main Colliery with his dad, Roger, however, the strange thing was, that he wasn't a miner. He was part of the three million unemployed, who due to the strike, couldn't work. The mining industry sustained lots of other businesses, not at least its private contractors, some of whom, like I have already said, dealt with the freshly mined spoil and the reprofiling of the tips. The strike not only affected companies such as these from a financial point of view, but its temporarily idle workforce, and Andy – well he was one such kid.

Fast forward twenty years later and Andy was some solitary figure propping up the bar in either the New 'Un, The Clog or the Butcher's Arms – vastly overweight and looking somewhat dishevelled in appearance, and who for most of the time was drunk. On Friday evenings after work I would often leave the office and call in at one of the three pubs and if he wasn't in, ask his whereabouts. What I always did and now know that I should not have, was to leave him five or six pints which were paid-on behind the bar after I had had left. Andy was always grateful, but as for me, I thought I was helping him, but I wasn't.

In March 1989, Andy had been on a stag do in Amsterdam and had been hit by a tram. According to their Colin, they had no idea where he was, and as such Interpol had been drafted in to conduct a search. He was later found in the Intensive Care Unit of Amsterdam Hospital and in a coma. After he eventually came out of it, the surgeons found that he had suffered some form of head trauma. He was never the same lad again.

There are huge comparisons with Andy's accident and that of Steve Greaves – however, Steve had Joanne by his side – a woman who was extremely devoted and ever-loyal. Andy did not. He had married a girl by the name of

Tracey McGeever and had a daughter shortly after by the name of Gemma. They had set up home on Bolton-on-Dearne's The Crescent, before relocating to a house on Thurnscoe's Reema Estate. According to their Col, both Andy and Tracey had been having issues, and as such, she ended up moving back into her mother's and taking their daughter with her.

"I'm not sure if our Andy started drinking more because of the marriage troubles or it was the drinking that started the troubles," Col explained. "The latter is what she always blamed it on."

On Andy coming out of coma, Tracey appeared to give their relationship another shot – however, according to his family this certainly was never the case. Their Col intimated that her reasoning for having him back could have been solely financial, and possibly due to Andy receiving a pay-out, as there was very little love there, which is something that his mum, Iris certainly saw on her visiting him one day.

Still heavily in recovery and with brain damage, Andy was the constant butt of jokes between Tracey and one of her mates.

"They were taking the piss out of him," Col told me. "My mam thought it was disgusting and ended up bringing him home."

As for Tracey, she did no more and went and chucked her lot in with another one of Thurnscoe's Class of 1981 – Mark Taylor.

Due to Mark's uncanny resemblance to Paul Michael Glaser's character in the mid-seventies American police action television series *Starsky & Hutch*, in which he was one of the two main protagonists, he was given the nickname, *Starsky*.

"I found it hard to dislike him," Col explained. "He was extremely good with Gemma."

As for myself, I quite liked Tracey and obviously had no idea of the stress she was under, but I still can't help thinking that what she did was wrong.

It was summer 2005 when I received the phone call from Col: "Our Andy's dead, J."

For twenty-three days and at just thirty-nine years old, Andy had been sat in a chair in his local authority-assisted bungalow on Thurnscoe's Pear Tree Court, waiting for someone to find him. The tragedy wasn't so much in his death, but the fact this lovely kid who had the world at his feet straight after the strike, had died alone. It was as though he had become an encumbrance, a burden, been pushed in a corner and forgotten about. It is true that things move on and that we all have our own lives to lead, but as for Andy, he lost his, the moment Tracey left him.

One memory that will always stand out was in Cortonwood WMC on 1 February 1986 – the night of my wedding, with Andy along with Paul Rice and Andrew (Mano) Makings running around the dance floor with a black mock coffin on their shoulders that was inscribed *R.I.P Ian McGregor*.

Andy was a great fucking lad. I do miss him.

On our way back from Thorpe Marsh the two cars diverted through Bentley and past C.F Booth's scrapyard and metal recycling plant with its two rail-mounted cranes and beneath the two steel bridges that carried the East Coast Mainline over St Mary's Roundabout, before making our way down the A638 York Road and passing the old Roodhouse Fiat dealers that once stood on its Sprotborough junction. It was then we reached our destination and pulled into the petrol station opposite the flood plains, which is where Morrison's supermarket now stands. It was also an area I recall very well, as during the summer of 1971, I nearly got run over by a car in the exact same spot.

As seven-year-olds, I along with another one of the Class of 1981's intake into Hickleton Main – Andrew Gardner, had made our journey on our bikes into Doncaster. He was on his purple Raleigh Vanguard with its cool sloping crossmember and I on my red Raleigh RSW 14 that my grandma and granddad Ellis had bought me the previous year, which had some pissy-off white storage box at the back that kept on falling off.

Andy's dad Henry was a Shaft Man at Hickleton Main, and to my knowledge, his wife June (nee Prescott), still lives in the same house as they did back then – 4 Deightonby Street. Henry, however, sadly died just recently.

Whilst filling up the cars, Col asked if I fancied going out Friday night. "Come on, J – me, you, John and Bri Latham," he said.

My rent rebate was still being cashed and I had the £7.50 (£25.56, circa 2020) a week money that I was earning from picketing, plus the money from the weekend run over to Drax, the latter of which was to become a regular feature of what would become an extremely violent run up to Christmas. Therefore, even though it went against the grain somewhat, I gave the idea the nod.

At that time and although we regularly saw each other, it was a bit sporadic in that we all seemed to be in different places at different times. John spent the mornings up at Drax Power Station, whilst we were all outside some colliery in South Yorkshire, although on one occasion during this period I remember us being chased by the police around Langold Lake after we had been turned away from Shireoaks Colliery in North Nottinghamshire. The fact that Col and Carl attended their courses at Barnsley Technical College on Tuesday and Wednesday's respectively, also created something of a hole – as did the fact that Tim appeared to have some problem with Carl and/or John, which undermined the structure of the overall friendship. As for Billy? Well, he was just Billy, and like Col, you just couldn't help but love him.

The soup kitchens down at The Docket appeared to be the only time we were all together and come Friday 12 October 1984, we were all caught on TV in during a morning's mass picket at Brodsworth Colliery, which was unfortunately overshadowed by the fact that the IRA had made an attempt on Margaret Thatcher's life and had tried blowing her up in some hotel down in Brighton, killing five people and injuring thirty-one.

All the mornings were becoming dark and my memory is that it was just damp and miserable rather than cold, with that autumn smell of falling leaves and earth being farmed being all around us. As with most places, Brodsworth Colliery looked absolutely nothing like it does now and back then was situated on the outer edges of the Woodlands pit estate near Adwick-Le-Street, with its strangely designed early-twenties art-deco houses along with its inner-Bullring, meaning that the houses on The Crescent and East Avenue backed on to it, rather than faced it.

Carl generally parked up on Green Lane, which I remember well as he bollocked me after I had opened the passenger door and got it stuck in some unusually high grass verge between the road and the pavement, and on pulling back the door it gave a rather aero-dynamic feel to his car.

"I'll have to park the fucking thing the other way around next time we come so you can balance it out," he snapped.

The lad had some bad luck with that car. I remember us walking back after an extremely violent picket in Brampton Bierlow a month later and watching on as some and some great filthy Barnsley MBC dustbin lorry made its way up Dearne Road towards its junction with Chapel Avenue and scraping through a seven-foot gap between the cars with its seven-and-a-half-foot cab. It was quite surreal, as just behind us was the aftermath of a riot, with bricks and glass all over the floor, a burned-out portacabin with police everywhere and here was Carl growling at the dustbin man with no copper prepared come over and confirm what had just taken place. What is true is that although they exchanged details, Carl never got paid out for that.

Brodsworth Colliery was located on Long Lands Lane and opposite open fields, with the only thing in sight being the Markham Grange garden centre and nursery some way down the road along with some allotments at the other side of the field. What I didn't know at the time was that one of the scabs that were being ferried through the picket lines, was someone that I would end up working alongside some five years later.

Mounted police on horseback were always a feature of the Brodsworth pickets due to its vast open spaces and as the crowds began to swell and the dark began to turn into light, the odd stone began being thrown along with some pushing and shoving, with the mounted police trying to keep order by holding back what was starting to become an aggressive crowd. I noticed one officer on horseback who had his visor raised, whilst issuing orders to miners who were refusing to get off the road. I was maybe ten feet from him when a half a brick struck him full-on. Within seconds there was blood streaming down his face. Like it always was, once one starts, they all start and as soon as missiles started being thrown, the police lost control of the situation and miners who had been pinned back were now running anywhere and everywhere, with the open fields, with its readily made supply of ammunition of limestone and sandstone cobbles being gratefully accepted.

The police were getting hit from every angle. Whereas Silverwood had been described as an ambush, this was a full-frontal assault, with all the police having to retreat into the colliery entrance. All it had taken was a few keen lads within a huge crowd to start the melee and what followed was carnage.

I look at the 1968 film *Planet of the Apes*, when the gorillas on horseback are chasing the humans through the fields, and in my mind, and bar the fact nothing was growing in the field opposite, that is exactly what it resembled.

It would be here that I became singled out by one of the mounted police. It is hard to describe what is happening all around you when your sole aim in life is to escape from a fucking some huge galloping and snorting animal carrying an ape which appeared just as big, being bulked up with padding and a crash helmet and who was gleefully swinging some big stick at you. The horses are very quick and only my zigzagging over the field held it off, and even then, the thing managed to tread on my heel, ripping off one of my boots in the process. However, as I hopped around whilst trying to reclaim it, I then came entangled with the horse, the ape, and more importantly his big stick. The upshot being that he was trying to beat me with it, and I didn't want to be beaten, therefore I refused to let go and held on to it for dear life. The horse moving around and me grappling with the stick must have unsettled him in his seat, and as I was just about pulling him off, a couple of miners grabbed hold of him and dragged him from his mount. It would be here I would see the difference between me – a kid not yet twenty years old, and some well-developed miner maybe ten to fifteen years my senior. Whilst the policeman was on the floor my kicks and punches didn't seem to do anything against all the padding. His did though. The miner held him down by the inner roof of his helmet and was smashing him in the face. It was only brief, but it was something that has always registered.

"You okay, kid?" he asked.

I was.

The strange thing is, is that I had no idea who the miner had been, as I never saw him again.

By the time the police restored some form of order it was light, and even after the bus with its meshed armour drove through the colliery gates, the crowd refused to disperse. I would see this time and time again. "Scab, scab, scab", would come the shouts. It made no difference, they always got through.

All the NUM was doing was pissing its money away on mass picketing – a 1974 solution to a 1984 problem. It was never going to work. Time progresses, and things change, yet the people at the top of the chain acting on our behalf were running blinkered, and only saw one thing. I knew it back then as I know it now and I often recall being at Carl's and airing my thoughts. "Whoa, that's scab talk, that is," he would candidly state.

Any sign of dissent was always seized upon and I often remember Col being singled out from certain people down at the NUM office as being a *mole*. I have absolutely no idea why – maybe the trips backwards and forwards out of the area and into Sheffield. To be honest and looking back at it, I found it strange, but back then people were both angry, paranoid, and needed scapegoats.

There was the Hickleton Main's NUM treasurer Les Hipwell, handing out the money as though it were his own and talking down to you. Everything about it fucking stunk.

I remember my father-in-law telling me the tale about a high-ranking NUM official at Cortonwood Colliery by the name of Mick Carter: "All throughout the strike I was always short of cigs, but one thing I always remember, was that every time I saw him come out of the shop, he always had a pack of twenty on him."

Do I think certain aspects of the NUM money was being skimmed? I fucking know it was.

227

This is something that goes back to 2 July 1924, when Thomas Mullens, the Secretary of Goldthorpe Colliery's branch of the Yorkshire Miners' Association (later NUM), was dragged in front of Doncaster West Riding Court.

Mullens, an active member of The Communist Party, who lived with his wife, Ethel (nee Smith, was Boyle) at 9 The Green, Bolton-on-Dearne, had allegedly falsified the accounts thereby scamming £227 (£13,841, circa 2020) from the Union's coffers.

His case went to Leeds Assizes on 25 July in a trial that was presided over by Justice Sir Rigby Philip Watson Swift KC and although, C Paley Scott defended, Mullins was found guilty and sent to prison.

There were numerous stories doing the rounds, more so after the strike, of miners rifling through the money collections and pilfering silver. If you are starving and your family are going without, it is only human nature to do what you can to try and alter that situation.

The NUM had thousands of pounds in cash going to its branches every single day. To take twenty or thirty pounds from that would be the easiest thing in the world. Just move some figures, pencil in a few more cars, add a few more bodies. The same goes for the food parcels. Are you telling me that the NUM officials, those who were first in line, weren't looking after number one and creaming the best bits for themselves and their families?

Les appeared very self-righteous and I once remember him speaking to Col in a very high-handed manner. This was a lad who was estranged from his wife through no fault of his own, with a baby in hospital and with a rickety car with a blowing exhaust and a ruptured suspension, who at the time needed some finance to go towards the cost of an elliptic leaf spring to take it through its MOT. The lad desperately needed that car.

Here comes the well-worn adage, the cliché, in that *I wish I knew back then, what I know now.*

We were young, therefore we put up with shit. If it were now, I would have dragged him over the table and beat the living daylights out of him… and in front of all his fucking minions. We were all in the same boat, yet some were not. That is fucking Socialism for you.

"We all need to be the same… just as long as I am in charge."

Carl once had a similar problem with Les and unlike Colin, flatly refused to be subservient to the master. "I'll tell you what I'll do then – when I leave here, I'm straight on the phone to the Coal Board and I'm going to ask them to sort me a bus for Monday."

Out of all of us, it was Carl who took the least shit.

"You ought to have seen the useless cunt's face," he grinned afterwards.

After our refusal to disperse, the mounted police moved in, followed by the police with the short shields. All we had to combat that with was lumps of concrete, bricks, and stones, along with the hasty speed of retreat.

Being young wasn't the encumbrance on the picket lines that it was in life, as I saw men get arrested, just for being old and therefore slow. It was rarely the so-called hot-heads, the trouble causers and stone throwers that got arrested, just the less-mobile. I always remember seeing Kay Bastow's dad – John (Jock) of 66 Tudor Street get arrested – not at Brodsworth, but outside Goldthorpe Colliery. The man did absolutely nothing wrong. He was just there. The same goes for one of my ex-neighbours at 23 Deightonby Street – Neil and Julia Falkingham's father, Keith.

Good honest hardworking men with families on the breadline, being dragged by the scruff of the neck and slung into the back of some meat van. It was fucking heart-breaking to see.

We held our own for a time and I recall a photographer from some red-rag publication titled *Newsline* taking shots of us breaking up concrete, prior to James (Jumbo) McNulty threatening to break his jaw. "I'm on your side," exclaimed the man with the camera.

He wasn't anyone's side, least of all ours. He was just there, feeding on the scraps. These people were everywhere. A strike used to be called at local level and a quarter of an hour later you would have people outside the pit baths trying to flog you copies of the *Socialist Worker*.

I once recall a miner off Thurnscoe's Chapel Lane by the name of Johnny Holliday, calling them "Scum" at their delight in what was our suffering. He was right. They were bottom feeding off our misery.

The flashing of lights and the screaming of engines from the police's Transit vans moved the confrontation into the Woodlands pit estate. There were miners being pounced upon and arrested everywhere. There was some retaliation, but not a deal. Everyone was now on the back foot.

One of the things I remember was seeing Col being chased with some bobby trying to hit him around the back of the head with his truncheon several times, whilst charging across the inner-Bullring, and whereas Col, due to his size, moved freely beneath all the washing lines the police man did not and became entangled, which obviously slowed down the chase. It was pandemonium, but what we were to see was one of the funniest, if not most heart-warming moments of the strike. "Come in here, love," shouted this white-haired old lady from the back door of her house. "Over here."

Col and I shot over and dived through that opened door. It was like the milkman scene from *Monty Python's Flying Circus*. Here was this little old lady picking up miners off the street like the scantily dressed collector maniac that had amassed the milkmen. There were around thirty of them laid out on her kitchen and room floor and here she is, locking the door before pandering around them all and making them all cups of tea. It is a memory that still puts a lump in my throat. You can't beat real people.

From around 2004 to 2007, I had a photographer freelancing for me by the name of John Sturrock, who had worked for the SW1 (Socialist Worker) agency and who had taken thousands of photographs during the strike, the majority of which, during the early days of our working relationship we went through at my kitchen table. "That's Brodsworth," I told him.

"I took that shot from off the top of a haystack," he said.

There we were, Col, Tim and me running from the police and around some stationary Ford Fiesta and towards the pit estate.

At first looking at the photograph, it was hard holding back the emotion, as we were just nineteen-year-old kids who were pawn's in a game of chess that we all knew we would never win. All we had was each other.

My relationship with John, if you can call it that, had commenced during the weekend picket to Drax, where I travelled shotgun and alongside Carl, with him sat across the back seat, continually probing, asking question after question and for every answer I had given, it had been immediately seized upon by the driver, who turned it upside-down, back-to-front and inside-out to find some flaw. It was how they both operated.

John was humorous, but nowhere near as quick-witted as Carl. If you get time, watch the 1983 film *Trading Places*. It is the one where Winthorpe, the snobbish Wall Street investor played by Dan Ackroyd and Billy Ray Valentine, the low-rent con artist played by Eddie Murphy, find their positions reversed. In it, there is a scene early on, where the latter is in the police holding cells being aggressively questioned by two big black guys over his bullshit "karate expertise" and "where's my bitches" comments. That was Carl and John in a nutshell. One (Carl) pulls you up on everything, whilst the other (John) just growls, "Yeh".

My ex-girlfriend had always been the major source of intrigue. It was hardly a case of her progressing her life – just moving from one striking miner to another.

At that time Terry Rich was just a name – a kid who I had heard of but knew very little about, with the exception that his elder brother Ronnie lived opposite, but some way down the street from my mum and (step)dad on Lancaster Street.

"He's got a car," grinned John.

He had. A black Mark II Capri, with mock tiger skin seat covers.

I'd had a white 1969 MG Midget which had been a thousand times the car, but which I had unfortunately written off on Marr Drag the previous year. That was it. I had given them more failure to feed on. They were like a pair of velociraptors in their unquenchable thirst for blood, and although it was at my expense, I thought the humour dry and funny. What I had to kick back on however, was the difference between **fact** and **fiction**. Being that my ex had worked at the exact same place as Tracy (Greaves) for seven months, it gave John something of a supposed inside-track on my life. "She said that everything that is in your house, she paid for and that you both split up because she was sick of paying for everything," he grinned.

I couldn't believe what I was hearing.

I was glad when Tim was present during that week, and I immediately asked John to repeat what he had said, and credit where credit is due – he did.

"She's a right lying bastard," Tim told him, before directing his gaze at me. "You want to tell 'em about the ring."

"No, I don't want to tell them about the fucking ring," I grimaced.

"Er, what about the ring?" asked John.

They were like a set of washer women at times.

The story of the ring was a trivial and irrelevant part of our final days together. We had been sat in the lounge of 178 Furlong Road along with Tim and his then-girlfriend Dawn, with my ex continually bragging about one thing another – mainly this Eternity ring she'd had on her finger, both regarding the make-up of its paste, but more importantly – to her that is, its alleged price tag.

"It cost one hundred and ninety pounds," she told them.

"No, it didn't. You paid twenty-seven quid for it from Robert Anthony's second-hand jewellers in Waterdale," I told her.

It was then she flipped her lid and attacked me.

Both Dawn and Tim had been aghast, but it was nothing new. When I said our relationship had been volatile – I meant it.

Tim had a lot more stories to tell, but in my mind, I hated it, as all it ever did was make me look stupid. Now it was Terry's problem and how he suffered. I knew she would be far too headstrong and aggressive for him. She treated him disgracefully and he certainly never deserved what he got.

I remember Debbie Davidson (now Howell) telling me the story of an altercation just off Dane Street's Bullring, and her beating him around the head with some handbag. I would say that was nothing as I'd had a pair of scissors rammed into my arm, but compared with what Terry got, that is certainly not the case.

I remember walking down from my mum's and onto Briton Street during the summer of 1986, and Carl banging on his window before coming out to see me. "Have you heard?" he grinned.

"Heard what?

"Your ex got married the other day – everyone's been on about it."

It was common knowledge that their wedding had taken place at St Hilda's Church on Hanover Street a week or so prior.

"She refused to get married and wouldn't go into church," he said. "Her dad was going mad and had to literally drag her up the aisle. Richy was distraught."

As I have said, nothing she could have done would ever surprise me.

Over the years I have got to know Terry quite well and there was a story of me and the wife going into The Ship on Thurnscoe's High Street, on New Year's Eve 1996. I recall us being in a group of people along with Dean and Dawn Carter (nee Rogerson) and of Terry standing in the doorway. As you do, you shake hands with the man and the woman gets a peck on the cheek, and on my wife receiving one, I quipped, "Fucking hell, Terry, you're not after this one as well, are you?"

I don't think he knew what to say as he was such a lovely lad, but as nice a kid as he was – his family, like most up in Thurnscoe East, do have some dark history.

Terry's father John had been brought up at 10 Dane Street South on the opposite side of the street to the Crooks family who lived at No 3. John's younger sister who would be Terry's auntie Elsie married a man by the name of Arthur Crooks, whose grandparents, Charlie and Emma (nee Mear), had lived at 4 King Street.

Charlie and Emma had married on 23 January 1886 and rather strangely at the same church as my great-great granddad, Samuel Durose – the St Leodegarius Anglican church in Old Basford. Just like the Durose family he had come to the area by way of Denaby Main.

Charlie was another colourful character who, reading between the lines, quite liked a drink. This was firmly backed up by his criminal record, which partly comprised court appearances for being drunk and disorderly, street betting and thrashing his wife. In fact, during the autumn of 1911 his wife had left him. She had temporarily moved in with their daughter Lily and her husband Arthur Allington, just over the road at No 9. The reasoning behind this, had been put down to, not only her husband's drunkenness, but his innate jealousy.

There had been a foundation for the latter, however.

His wife Emma had been part of a street betting circuit run by Sam Williams of 11 King Street – Emma being one of the four lookouts that had been consistently posted on Lidget Lane. That was until they had been caught and fined. There had been more to the relationship as Sam's wife Florence had not only accosted Emma in the street but had also told Charlie what had been going on, mainly, that she had caught her husband shagging his wife down the backings.

Charlie had been both downhearted and depressed and on the Saturday night of 18 November he had seen his wife with two of her friends in The Goldthorpe Hotel and said, "Look at the whore", before running up and booting her.

As Christmas approached, Emma returned home, however, the quarrels between the pair continued, something which was exasperated further, the day before Christmas Eve. That Saturday, they had been out drinking in the Horse & Groom in Goldthorpe and rather strangely they ended up returning home around 10.15 p.m. along with a woman by the name of Annie Simpson. It was said this woman had been waiting for a daughter, who never turned up and therefore had nowhere to go.

The Crooks' house at King Street, which incidentally still stands today, was a standard two-up two-down, four-roomed terrace, with a toilet in the back yard.

It is hard to gauge what really happened on them getting home – however, what was made public was that Charlie went into the coal cellar and brought up some drink and that he and Mrs Simpson continued drinking, with all four children – Charles, nineteen; Jesse, eight; George seven and Annie four, being upstairs in bed.

Charlie's wife Emma, fell asleep on the sofa only to wake up to find her husband and the woman in what was described as an *embrace* with them kissing. It could, however, have been that it was much more, as the *Yorkshire Telegraph & Star* would go on to report it as "A Drunken Orgy" with the intricate details of what was within the police statements having been left out on its publication, making what really occurred rather sketchy to say the least.

What we do know is that when Emma remonstrated and confronted her husband. He ended up dragging her around the room, before repeatedly stabbing her.

Hearing his mother's screams, young Charles ran downstairs to see his father inflict around twenty individual wounds around her head and neck. His son went out into the street for help, however, when the police arrived, the house was in disarray and there was no-one in. Emma, who when the police found her at her daughter and son-in-law's, had collapsed and was an exhausted state with almost all her body covered in blood, with the wounds around her ears described by Dr Charles Macolm as being the most severe of her injuries.

As for Charlie, at 2.10 a.m. on Christmas Eve he was arrested by PC Joseph Statham who lived nearby at 28 Hickleton Terrace, and was alleged to have told him: "I can't rest – I've being thinking about doing her in for a while."

Charlie was subsequently charged with attempted murder and remanded until his trial at Leeds Assizes on 12 March 1912, where he broke down in tears whilst admitting to a lesser charge of wounding with intent to cause grievous bodily harm. He was sentenced by Justice Sir Horace Edmund Avory to 15 months' hard labour in Wakefield Prison.

It would be here he would be joined by two rapists from Mexborough a few days later – twenty-three-year-old William Mickleboro of 67 Schofield Street, and nineteen-year-old Richard Thomas Hudson of 8 Wilson Street, who on Christmas Eve 1911, had violently attacked a young woman off 31 Clayfield Road by the name of Mary Ann Smith. As penance for their crimes, they got handed sentences of eighteen- and twelve-months' hard labour respectively by the self-same judge.

As for Charlie's son-in-law, Arthur Allington, who was part of another huge East end mining family – he would take his family the short way across the backings and move into 5 Queen Street (a house that is also still there) before leaving his family to sign on as a reservist with the Second Battalion of the York and Lancaster Regiment to fight in the First World War. He had initially joined up as a nineteen-year-old lad at Pontefract Barracks on 13 October 1902 and had served in India but had left to come back to Thurnscoe and married Charlie and Emma's daughter, Lily in 1907.

He was shot by a sniper on the North Western Front outside the Ypres Salient on 15 February 1915 whilst leaving the trenches for his rations and was buried at the Ploegsteert Memorial in Belgium.

As for Lily, she would remarry on 13 October 1915 – this time, a twenty-two-year-old miner by the name of Samuel Bevins who just happened to be her lodger. They would go on to reside at 11 Lancaster Street right up until her death in February 1952.

As for one of Charlie's other sons, Jesse, he was the father of Phil Crooks – an Official at Hickleton Main who had lived around the corner from my mum at 71 Chapel Lane. He would be someone who as I grew up, I would have quite a lot of respect for.

Rather interestingly – Charlie Crooks, his grandfather, was described as possessing a dark complexion and small build, which was not too dissimilar from that of Phil.

I had been thinking about crying off that Friday evening, as all I had in the house was £4 (£13.63, circa 2020) plus a few coppers. I did, however, know that a rent rebate cheque would drop through the post the next morning and that Col had pencilled us in for the midnight to 3.00 am picket over at Drax the very same night. Still, what do you do? Either buy a pound of bacon (£1.34 – £4.57, circa 2020), a pound of sausage (77p – £2.62, circa 2020), a dozen eggs (67p – £2.28, circa 2020) and a tin of Heinz beans (21p – 72p, circa 2020) or four pints of lager, which amounted to the exact same money? To me, that was three or four meals.

Those Friday nights would be the start of something of a ritual and was something I recollect John Gratton reminiscing about nearly twenty years later. "I still remember us calling around for you during the strike and coming through the back door (at the side of the house) to see you sat at that table with the hair dryer along with that long mirror you always had propped up against the wall," he had said.

I had often read about the success of the strike being reliant on a cold winter and of the NUM's dismay at it being mild. I don't know where they got that from as my house was always fucking freezing, and six saucepans full of boiling hot water along with a few kettles – which was generally enough to fill the bottom of the bath, had steam everywhere, with me having to continually wipe condensation from that said long mirror.

"Fucking hell, J, it's like a sauna in here," Col would often say.

I remember that night well, as John was supposed to call around at 7.00 p.m. and didn't, us ending up getting flashed by his car outside The Gate, which is a public house at the far end of Golden Smithies Lane in Swinton. "I thought you were calling around," Col asked, as he wound down the window.

"I did call 'round," he replied. "Nobody answered."

"What did you knock on the door with – a feather?" was Col's retort.

I remember telling John that he should have just come in. "I didn't like," he said.

What was strange is that he didn't mind ribbing the hell out of you and making out that you were a complete and utter dickhead, yet he had the manners not to come in, unless invited.

Col had called at the house with Brian Latham, the latter of who I had known since I was around seven-years old. He used to live on Windsor Street, at a point close to its junction with Deightonby Street. He had two younger sisters – Caroline and Susan – and an elder brother by the name of Keith, who was not only one of the nicest kids you could ever wish to meet, but in my mind was a dead ringer for Stevie Marriot – the man who had fronted the stylish mod rock band, The Small Faces.

During the strike Keith had been living at the bottom end of Lancaster Street, with a girl from Dearneside's Class of 1981 by the name of Cindy Riley – the girl who Roger Kitchen of *Top Flight* fame had crudely nicknamed *Voodoo Magoo* during the middle years at Carfield school. I could cringe looking back at how cruel we were, as Cindy was a quite a nice girl. The last time I saw her, I think she had married Ray Finbow and was running the Unity (Dearne) Club on Goldthorpe's King Street.

Ray's grandfather, Walter, had set up home on Thurnscoe's King Street – at No 35 directly opposite where eight-year-old Ada Etchells had been indecently assaulted by the jobbing migrant miner, George Boast, some twenty years earlier and the exact same house were Charlie Crooks had died on 19 March 1936.

As for Brian's family, they had long since relocated from Thurnscoe East and on to The Green in Bolton on Dearne. These are two cul-de-sacs that are intersected by Prospect Road and which its centre is filled by Tennis Courts within its northern segment and a crown green bowling pitch within the southern part.

It was an area I knew extremely well as my nana Durose had moved from 9 The Crescent to live within its northern segment at No 26, after the local authority had undertaken a huge renovation project during the mid-1970s. This saw the modernisation of all its properties – with all the downstairs toilets and bathrooms moved upstairs. It was something which saw a lot of people displaced and relocated to different houses within the council estate – not at least my auntie Heather and uncle Jimmy who moved from No 12 to No 99. Thinking back, I can remember our Tony (Greaves) mapping out some false expedition around the back of my nana's house while it was under renovation and me ending up going down some open manhole he had disguised using a capping of cardboard with an overlay of grass. Thinking about it, I was quite fortunate not to break my leg.

Brian's house was a few doors away from the house which was once occupied by a sixty-year-old ex-miner by the name of Bill Lunn. He was one of many who slung himself off Carr Head Lane's infamous Suicide Bridge. His horrific death came in 1934.

Interestingly there are a couple of connections.

The first one concerns two brothers – forty-two-year-old Albert Lunn and thirty-three-year-old Eric Lunn of 1 and 30 Crofton Drive, Bolton-on-Dearne, respectively. Both men committed suicide within two and a half years of one another – Albert on 8 April 1968 and Eric on 1 October 1970.

The first it was claimed, had been part-catalyst for the second, with Eric's wife, Kathleen (nee Hirst), stating that he had become severely depressed since his brother's death.

Eric had been discharged from hospital on the Wednesday and after a search of the fields and waste land off Carrfield Lane, he was found dead just after midnight on Friday. He had slashed his throat and both his wrists. According to the District Coroner, Kenneth Potter, Eric had a history of anxiety and depression and had been in hospital the two weeks prior having treatment.

"His condition had deteriorated over the past few months," said his wife. "He had begun to worry about the trouble in the mining industry – both with the strikes and over his wages."

It was PC John Lineham who found his body which was uncovered close to a hedgerow just off the bankings which once carried the Wath Branch Line.

The second is David William Jones, who gassed himself in his home at 22 The Green.

Veronica – the wife of the thirty-three-year-old steelworks labourer, had left him on the Saturday night of 5 May following some domestic, whereby he had tried to strangle her. He had been drinking heavily and regularly staying out late.

On Wednesday 23 May, she had called at the house to find a note on the dining room mantlepiece, stating that he intended to do away with himself.

PC Dennis Nappy told the coroner's inquest at Goldthorpe that he found Jones lying on his side near the cooker with an unconnected gas pipe in his mouth and a rag wrapped around his head. The gas tap had been turned on but the supply exhausted. He had died of carbon monoxide poisoning.

It was a similar situation to that of James Clarke of 87 Doncaster Road, Goldthorpe.

On 23 April 1959, the sixty-seven-year-old colliery magazine (explosives) attendant had gassed himself and left a similar note.

As suicides go, it did appear quite a popular way to go.

George Herbert Bates was found gassed in the property at 9 The Green on 5 August 1931. He had been a sanitary inspector with Bolton UDC and had suffered from the aftereffects of Malaria which he contracted in the First World War.

Rather interestingly, this is a property where two high-ranking Union officials had made their home – one disgraced and one revered. Thomas Mullens had lived there in the 1920s whilst Inky Thomson lives there now.

As for Brian Latham, one of the things we used to rib him about was not so much the fact that he drank much more than we ever did, but come 10.00 p.m. he generally did his pumpkin-act. It wasn't so much a case him of him *turning Jekyll*, but the other way around, in that you would often get an arm around you along with some slurring dialogue that no one bar Brian could understand. We used to call it his *Charley Says* act – you know, the cat from the public information films that used to run on the TV during the 1970s? *Charley says, don't play with matches* or *Charley says, don't go off with paedophiles*.

It was me who had suggested that we go to Swinton that night. Not so much because the pubs were always heaving, more to do with the fact that I just didn't want to be in Thurnscoe. As for Colin, as soon as he saw the difference between somewhere like The Towpath compared to say the New 'Un – the pub he had frequented straight after leaving school, he had been hooked. Although Swinton was essentially a mining area that is situated on the western bank of the River Don, its slums had long since been cleared and there were new houses being thrown up everywhere, with the main source of industry being Morphy Richards and the glassworks.

I can still remember us parking up the cars outside some cottages on Broomville Street alongside the lock of the canal, where straight opposite you could see The Ship – a strange white elongated public house, which like The Towpath at that time, was always rammed.

The first and only time I had been here had been with someone else's girlfriend. This time would be no different. On us going into The Towpath, who should I see but Debi Neal.

"I can't believe I've seen you," I told her. "My dad was only on about you the other month."

She was with a friend that had been tied to her hip all the way through school – a girl by the name of Sharon Hill.

After nearly spilling a drink all over her, as not only were there people everywhere – I had already had half my night's quota of sniffing the barman's apron, she asked what I'd been doing since I left school. I certainly knew what she had been doing and that was posing in some swimsuit, the photographs of which had been published in all the local papers. Even my dad had seen them in the *Doncaster Free Press*.

"That's really embarrassing," she grinned.

"Yeh, I bet," I winked.

Debi had been in a relationship with Lee Scaife, a kid who when I was thirteen years old handed me a heavy right-hander as I was running up the stairs between the landings of Dearneside's ground and upper floors. To this day I still have no idea why. The amount of blood that it chucked up had been unreal, causing people to think that my nose had been broken, which after an X-ray at Mexborough Montagu I found that it had not. He could have thrown that punch another ninety-nine times and it wouldn't have had the same effect. It was one of those where the arrow and its target had met with the perfect trajectory. Did he mean it? Of course, he fucking meant it, but I'll say this for him, he was as apologetic as hell straight afterwards and more importantly, sometime after the strike when I was in Goldthorpe's Cross Street WMC with a group of six or seven lads from Thurnscoe, one of who was the Fixer himself – Neil Gollick.

My nose has always tended to bleed at the merest tap. What is strange is that as I got older that was never really the case and believe me when I say it, I have been involved in some nasty rucks with some very big lads. My grandma Carman told me that my uncle Rob, had been the same. "You only had to tap the top of his nose and it would be streaming with blood," she said.

She also said a bit more, more than intimating that our Rob's nose bleeding had been the catalyst for my granddad Carman walking out on the family, which was something that both my uncles Steve and Rob added weight to.

My grandma was an excellent narrator of a story, whereas our Steve isn't one to dwell on the past and has said as much. Even so, they both told the exact same story in that my granddad hit our Rob in the face and burst his nose. Our Rob, not one for saying things he didn't mean, just looked up at him and said: "You ever do that again and I'll kill you."

Our Rob has such a great demeanour and is not only the more mellowed of all my grandma's four children, he is such a lovely man, so for him to have issued a threat, it must have been bad.

With me, my mum liked to know what she was aiming at. "Stand still while I hit you," she would say.

You think I'm joking?

The amount of punches in the face that I had taken from her whilst growing up had been unreal, but all beating a child does, is make them resent the person handing them out.

I once saw my uncle Jimmy beating the living daylights out of our Tony around November 1972. Not only was it vicious, he had also done it with a walking stick, as around the time he had been involved in some major car accident. His mate, Brian (Bull) Davis had been drink driving and had piled up his car with Jimmy nearly losing his leg. I can still see it now. It was at the bottom of the path leading up into the Flower Estate.

I saw our Tony in Morrison's supermarket – strangely, the one on Doncaster's York Road circa 2001 – and you know what his first words to me were after our initial "Hellos"?

"Is Jimmy dead yet?"

My grandma Carman despised him and told me as much. "Horrible man – a big head," she would say.

I think a lot of that stemmed from the fact that at the time she said it, she had been helping out at his and my auntie Heather's fish and chip shop in Cudworth, and I remember her saying that he was always bragging about the money he was making.

The strange thing was, that I always liked him. That was until the day I didn't.

A story of his and my grandma's fractious relationship was perhaps best described by the man himself. Jimmy told me that there had been some particular argument between the pair. I can't give you either a timing for the fall-out or even a specific venue, all that I know is that my grandma had told Jimmy. "If you want to hit me, then hit me," fanning the flames further by adding, "Come on then, hit me."

Jimmy did no more than headbutt my grandma in the face and burst her nose.

When my auntie Heather died, Jimmy sold up and moved out to Cyprus to live in a rented apartment close to his daughter (and my cousin), Justine. A short time after that, I got a place above him and in the couple of years that followed I watched on as both his health and mind deteriorated, to such an extent, I had his youngest son, our Jonathan, on the phone after he had spewed out some rather aggressive diatribe towards me.

"You can't have him talking to you like that," said our Jon. "You should have thumped him – I would have."

We had taken our Jonathan's fourteen-year old daughter to Cyprus, so she could stay with her granddad – however, what I hadn't been prepared for the divisiveness of the young girl. Certainly not with us as she was great, but playing her mum, Melanie (now Randerson) against her granddad. She wanted to stay, and her mum said she couldn't. Totally unaware of what was going on, I explained that as we had all flown over on a scheduled Cyprus Airways flight – that I had paid for I may hasten to add, her ticket could be changed, and her stay extended for just a few pounds. All that happened, is that I got caught in the crossfire and ended up having the impossible task of trying to explain something to someone who had become estranged from everyday life and who just wouldn't listen. His only way of communication being to mutter insults whilst walking away.

I had been trying to get our Jonathan on the phone for the past fifty minutes and by the time I had managed to get him to pick up, I was at the check-in at the old Larnaca Airport. I hadn't wanted to belt him out of respect for our Jon, so for his son to give me the green light, I knew exactly what I was going to do. However, by the time I returned to Cyprus I had calmed down, with my wife telling me: "You can't go hitting him – you'll end up killing him."

I couldn't let it go and ended up climbing onto the roof of the block of apartments and duly emptied two kilogrammes of finely powdered garlic into his water tank. I will tell you something – that apartment he lived in stunk fucking rancid for months afterwards. All his clothes, bed linen and what have you had all been going through the washing machine with the water from straight out of the tank. You could taste the stale garlic as soon as you got out of the car in the basement.

"That fucker was for my grandma," I told my wife straight after.

It hadn't really. I had just been mad. Here was a guy that I thought the world of who had spoken to me like shit and for no other reason than some little girl had been playing him. Very sad.

What is true is that Jimmy was brash and very loud. One thing I remember him doing was down at my uncle Steve's during some Christmas family party and of him purposely smashing one of their plates against the taps on the sink and laughing about it, before slumping on the sofa and gorging at a great bowl of peeled prawns. If anyone had purposely done that at my house, they would have had my foot up their arse.

Then, there was the other side to him, very caring and very genuine, which was something that I saw time and time again.

Our Steve once hit the nail on the head and mentioned a sign in his garden that he had stuck in his lawn, when he lived in one of the prefabricated concrete pit houses on Ingsfield Lane and which stated: "If you've not been invited, then piss off!"

The brashness was a façade; a mask to hide his social shortcomings; his awkwardness.

I told my wife: "What is sad about it all is that the guy had so much to offer."

My dad described Jimmy as a young man, of him being something of a loner – however, there could have been much more to it than that.

My auntie Heather had been his second wife. Jimmy had married his first wife – (Patricia) Ann in 1958, when they had just turned seventeen years old. Ann had been the eldest daughter of Anthony (Tant) and (Dot Guest (nee Young), who when they were first married, lived at 77 Cowper Road in Mexborough. This was just up the street and around the corner from where a man cut off his eldest daughter's head some ten years earlier and which is a story that I will touch on later. Although, when I knew them, they had lived at 25 Hope Avenue, Goldthorpe.

Their daughter had died in Doncaster Western Hospital on 19 May 1964 in rather tragic circumstances. This was from a combination of pelvic vein thrombosis, a pulmonary embolism and haemangiomas of the uterus, the latter of which is a rare benign tumour usually associated with pregnancy-associated complications.

Ann had been just twenty-two years old and had left her husband and an eighteen-month-old child.

"I killed my mam – it was having me that killed her," I remember our Tony telling me when I was around nine years old.

Kids pick up pieces of conversation that they should never ever hear.

My dad said that Jimmy's in-laws Dot and Tant, used to regularly frequent Highgate WMC and described them as being genuinely nice people. This is something that Jimmy's niece, Tracy (Greaves) added weight to when she explained that he absolutely adored them. She also added that this was also something that had caused friction between him and his parents – Joe and Helen Greaves (nee Foster) – who had initially lived at 34 Queen Street before moving to the more palatial surroundings of 11 Cromwell Street in Thurnscoe East.

Jimmy had married my auntie Heather in 1966. She had been pregnant at the time, but sadly the child didn't survive. The exact same thing happened a year later. Fate had conspired against them, with Jimmy heavily weighed down with the burden of bad luck.

I remember me and my mum lodging with them at 45 Barnburgh Lane for a short period of time between Ringway and The Avenue's and all I ever had was nice thoughts of them. However, there is something that I recall and which was around mid-1971, when my auntie Heather briefly left him to come and stay with us at 24 Deightonby Street – part of which was photographed. My dad had picked me up one weekend and we bumped into Uncle Jimmy and our Tony and ended up playing on the swings in the Dearne Welfare park and sitting outside the Horse & Groom public house, with a bottle of fizzy orange and a picket of Smith's ready salted crisps apiece. Unfortunately, only part of those set of photographs survived, which is a story that will unfold as you read on.

As for the night out in Swinton, a taxi was due to pick up both girls around 10.30 p.m. where it would ferry them over to the Halfway Hotel, and where of course their boyfriends would be. However, that certainly wasn't a foregone conclusion as Debi was wanting to come back to Thurnscoe and she said exactly that to her friend.

As I have said, getting a girlfriend is the easy bit. It was the hand that I was dealt and the limitations that I had which would cripple me. And with no money coming in, no immediate future and a pile of fucking bills you could choke a donkey with, what could I possibly bring to the table?

My life at the time was also on the first few steps of madness and which would be totally out of control, come the end of November.

I wasn't averse to having a girlfriend, but even if I could keep her, to drag her in to **my** mess would have been selfish and very wrong. If I had to get a girl, it would have to be someone that I wouldn't get attached to and someone that I could easily walk away from. Debi certainly wasn't that kind of girl. She was bright, bubbly, blonde and beautiful along with a personality to match – her only flaw being, that she was with me. I knew the timing was all wrong and whilst I saw her in debate with Sharon, that is exactly what I thought.

As it transpired, Sharon didn't want to go to Thurnscoe. Why would she? She had nothing to go there for. Unlike Debi, she was happy with her boyfriend. I could have easily angled it to go my way, but I didn't. I did the right thing.

I remember seeing her off in the taxi and telling her, "Perhaps when this is all done (the Miners' Strike), maybe we will bump into each other again."

We never did. I never saw her again.

On the Thursday afternoon of 19 October 1989, I remember being underground during the shift change – a time where the afternoon shift takes over from the dayshift. I had been working on the huge mine development project deep beneath the Vale of Belvoir in Leicestershire. I had just climbed under the mini conveyor at the rear of the road header when I heard one of the Yorkshire lads from the other shift saying that someone who worked for the firm that we were working with at the time – Cementation Mining, had died over at Maltby Colliery.

"Who are you on about?" I remember asking.

"A bloke called Arthur Neal," said the lad. "Do you know him?"

I obviously knew **of** him, but it would be a lie to say that I knew him.

"I know his daughter," I said.

Debi's dad had had a heart attack between the air doors and sadly died, aged forty-eight.

My first thoughts were obviously of Debi. Not of us stood in some dimly lit corner in some pub down in Swinton, but of something that happened years before that – and that was of Mr (Bruno) Capaldi having us do some drama lesson the day after I had been to the dentist.

"Debi, you be the dental surgeon with all the pliers and drills," he said, before adding a bit more to the scene. "Your patient though, is really dirty and has bad breath."

Was I in the chair? No, thank god. I think it was Philip Wakefield, although I am not one hundred percent.

I was the one who had to say how good the acting was as I had just been subjected to a real dentist who had plied me with gas before ripping out three of my teeth.

Debi did no more than commence the careful preparation of her imaginary tools, when she suddenly stopped, sniffed a bit, before taking two steps back and wafting her hands around like she was swatting flies. All the class were in hysterics, with the teacher shaking his head and telling her: "You can't go making it that obvious."

There she was, just turned ten years old with her hands on her hips, smiling because everyone thought it hilarious. That is how I always saw her. The template of what I considered to be the perfect girl.

Debi would go on to marry some distant relation of Maxwell Everton – a grandfather's *cousin*, and a man who had lived at 51 Charles Street, Swinton and who for forty years would be incarcerated – later dying in Sheffield's Middlewood Hospital, aged seventy-two.

At 5.00 a.m. on 7 December 1932, the thirty-two year had attempted to murder his wife, Gladys (nee Woodcock) and their eleven-month-old daughter, Elizabeth. He had stabbed his wife in the head and face.

His trial went to the Leeds Assizes and on 8 March 1933, he was ordered to be detained at His Majesty's Pleasure. According to the prison doctor at Armley Gaol, a Dr John Humphrey, Everton was found insane and unfit to plead.

What was never said at the trial, is that his wife had been pregnant with a son, Arthur – who, if the standard forty-week pregnancy cycle is adhered to – had been conceived a mere three days before his incarceration.

As for Debi's dad, he was not only the son of the schoolboy hero Sam but also the grandson of his namesake, Arthur who was the son of an agricultural wheelwright, by the name of George Neal. He had lived in a cottage at 26 North Street in Winterton, but who on all the pits being sunk came to work in the eastern Dearne Valley. There he would meet a girl by the name of Lizzie Pearson, another from a big mining family. She had been stopping with her aunt and uncle – Sam and Florence Broadhead over in nearby Barnburgh and who after marrying her, would set up home at 1 Furlong Road in Bolton-on-Dearne. This was a house next to the Collingwood Hotel and opposite what would become A Brown's butchers, but one which is sadly no longer there.

Debi's dad had followed the family tradition of being a miner and at the time I had been speaking with her, was an Overman at Wath Main.

As for Debi's great grandfather on the other side of the family – well, he was a character.

Sam Neal had married Ada Kitchen of 43 Dearne Road in 1940. Unfortunately, however, her father, George hadn't been there to see it. The forty-six-year-old had been in Armley Gaol after being sentenced to twelve months at Doncaster West Riding Court on 16 May 1939.

238

George, along with James Depledge of 12 Butcher Street – who was Pat Thomson's father-in-law, had been found guilty of breaking into both Parson's Mill, Bolton-on-Dearne and the Goldthorpe Employment Exchange (Dole Office) on 15 April and 6 May respectively – and cracking both their safes.

At the trial, a Det. Insp. Lee stated that George had twenty-three previous convictions – seven for larceny, and James Depledge eight.

That weekend, I did two weekend runs to Drax – one with John and Carl, the latter who was trying to run over rabbits on his way back, and one with Col.

What I noticed is that my credibility with the two lads had spiked after Friday's night out, but what I wasn't prepared for was Colin's honest and forthright assessment of the state of his marriage.

"She told me 'You just don't get it, do you? Don't you understand that I don't want you?'" he told me.

From that day on, Col's marriage was over.

Left. Elizabeth (now Pettinger), Les and John Durose in the front garden of 9 The Crescent, Bolton-on-Dearne circa 1968. Right. The cropped photograph taken outside of the Horse & Groom, Goldthorpe in 1970

Picketing at Brodsworth Colliery on 12 October 1984 (c. John Sturrock). Top. Me (in the light jacket), Tim Bright and Colin Hunter (in front of the Ford Fiesta) running for cover. Bottom. Short shield police being deployed in the Woodlands pit estate.

19.   The User (The Strike – Part 4)

Having closure is a strange thing. I know, as I had recently been there. My relationship had been much longer than Col's – however, one thing that I didn't have, had been a baby daughter.

"Three quid alright, J?" he asked, as he divvied up the picket money.

His wife had just told him that she wanted out and here was the lad acting overly concerned that I wouldn't think the £3 (£10.22, circa 2020) that he was offering, was a fair distribution of assets.

"I'd give you more but I'm having to run backwards and forwards to Sheffield," he said. "I suppose I won't be doing that as often now?"

He said what he had to say and never broke, although it was plainly obvious that he was hurting like hell. I remember stopping at The Black Lion public house over in Snaith on our way over to the power station, having half a lager before they called last orders and that David Bowie's *Starman* had been one of the songs that had been playing on the jukebox.

The one thing that I can say, is that his wife pushing him out, was without a doubt, the biggest bollock that she would ever drop. I had never met her. Very few people had, bar Col's parents and Carl, and none of them had been overly lavish in their appraisal.

Drax was a place where you would just park up the car and let the NUM know if there were any lorry movements in or out and if there was, for us to try and persuade them to stop, which would have been a bit hard seeing as that around 1.30 a.m. Col had slipped out the car and was in the middle of some field with a spade and a hessian sack, digging up potatoes.

"There's another sack in the boot, J," he told me, as I went out in the field to assess the situation. "Go get it and I'll fill it for you."

The next couple of weeks would see us backwards and forwards between Brodsworth, Yorkshire Main and Kiveton Park Collieries along with us having the police turn up in numbers on Briton Square one afternoon. We had supposedly threatened some fifty-one-year-old over in Middlecliffe, who just happened to be some scab Winder at Houghton Main Colliery.

"The Cozzers have been here looking for you," a concerned-looking Freddie Bevins told me. "There were loads of them. It was like something out of *The Sweeney*."

They certainly weren't looking for me. It had been Col's registration plate that had flagged up.

Bob Copping was the nephew of Arsenal and Leeds United's ex-20 cap England international, Wilf – a man who was often described as the hardest man in English football. He was also the most successful of any sportsman from the eastern Dearne Valley, winning two League Championships, one FA Cup and two Charity Shields.

His nephew had been all over the news from day one of the strike. Both rotund in body and hard in face, he had already had his car turned over on his drive and all his windows put through, so threats to him were nothing new. Strangely, I don't recall threatening him, just us calling him a "scab bastard". In fact, directing violence at the homes of scabs was not something that I ever thought about doing – ever. Nor was damaging property belonging to the NCB. The police, however, were always fair game, although we certainly never gave that impression when they returned a short time later.

"You both look like nice sensible lads," said the senior policeman. "Don't go doing anything like that again."

Yeh right.

At Kiveton Park Colliery these two nice-looking sensible lads along with lots of other sensible lads were party to some of the heaviest violence seen in the strike thus far.

The site of the colliery is nothing at all how it looks now and was accessed from two points, via a long lane from the railway bridge – Pit Lane, with the other access being that of Hard Lane. As winter approached, each morning was getting darker, but for some reason the mass pickets to Kiveton were always very early morning runs from Thurnscoe – setting off at either 4.00 or 4.30 a.m. I also seem to recall us going through Thurcroft to get there. Maybe there was something in that, as we rarely travelled via motorways if we could help it.

The colliery was said to have had the unhappy distinction of being the first Yorkshire pit to have returned to work in 1926 and the same was true in 1984, with miners drifting back to work after just six months out.

As I have already said, historians and journalists that have written about the strike seem to do nothing but try to categorise things to help them understand and explain the difference in the attitude of the miners in the coalfields – especially those in Yorkshire and Nottinghamshire.

I would state that most of the Class of 1981 owed our being here to migrant miners from other coalfields. My granddad's family – the Duroses – were a huge mining family that came into South Yorkshire from Nottinghamshire in droves, settling in the Dearne and Don Valleys; as were my nana's – the Griffiths – who had come up from west Gloucestershire and whose Welsh heritage spans back to the early 1800s, living in not only the same street, but the same stone-built cottage in Yorkley for well over a hundred years.

My granddad's grandfather was Samuel Durose (b. 1848). He lived in Kirkby-in-Ashfield and is not to be confused with his elder cousin and namesake who also lived in the same village. His cousin spent large portions of his life doing penal servitude and hard labour in Derby's New County Gaol (Vernon Street Prison). This was for his part in The Brinsley Stabbing Case of 1876 and the malicious wounding of an off-duty policeman, by the name of Insp. John Cowley two years later – which he received sentences of twelve months and five years respectively.

Whereas my great-great-granddad Samuel Durose married Ann Smith at St Leodegarius Anglican church in Old Basford on 21 July 1874, his cousin had married Mary Oxley at St Wilfrid's Church in Kirkby-in-Ashfield on 2 April 1866. My great-great-granddad died of kidney disease at just thirty-seven years old on 31 March 1886, whilst his more colourful relation migrated into the Doncaster area, living at 63 Adwick Lane in Bentley Toll Bar, where he survived his wife by twenty-four years. Mary had committed suicide on 23 April 1900, aged fifty-two. She had taken an overdose of laudanum (opium).

"Me and my knife and my dog can lick any man," the older Sam was quoted as saying after he had beaten a fellow collier from Kirkby-in-Ashfield by the name of Edward (Neddy) Ghent senseless, and to such an extent that he was unrecognisable. It was then he stabbed him several times, leaving him for dead. He was also given two months hard labour for wrapping a poker around the head of PC William Garner in Broughton's Beerhouse some years earlier.

Rather strangely, whilst he had been serving part of his five-year sentence for the assault on Insp. Cowley, his wife had been indecently assaulted by an ex-policeman by the name of James Williamson.

I wouldn't be wrong in suggesting that Samuel Durose appeared something of a *cursed* name. My great-great-grandfather had just had a son prior to his death – who was named after himself and who would die of tuberculous on 8 March 1887, aged just seventeen months.

My great-great-grandfather's eldest son, who was of course my great-granddad, Frank Durose, had married Elizabeth Sarah Bucknall at St Wilfrid's Church in Kirkby-in-Ashfield on 20 May 1899 and who ended up moving to 13 Wellington Street, Goldthorpe. They had seven children one of which included my granddad Samuel Durose (b. 1920). The strange thing being, that he had an elder brother who was also called Samuel (b. 1904) and who was someone he never met. The elder Sam had died of exhaustion on 19 November 1911, aged just eight years old. This followed some torturous six-day intestinal obstruction or atresia.

The other children were: William (b. 1900), Sybil (b. 1902), Daisy (b. 1906), May (b. 1911), Frank (b. 1913) and Jessie (b. 1917) – with Frank and May, still living in the same house on Wellington Street well into the early 1980s, and both of who died in 1986 – with my great uncle Frank being something of a character who regularly drank in The Comrades.

My ancestral relatives were therefore from the exact same place that was being dubbed by Yorkshire miners as *scab central.* "The only good thing to come out of Nottinghamshire is the fucking A1," was one of the things that was often heard said.

One of my (step)dad's favourite statements was that Robin Hood was really a Yorkshireman, and which if you look at the real history – the York Assizes and the financial records maintained by the English Exchequer between 1226 and 1234 – you will find that his comments, although jingoist and very pro-Yorkshire, carry much more validity than that of Errol Flynn swashbuckling in his tights down in Nottingham Castle.

John Gratton's grandfather George Gladstone (b. 1888) was from Leicestershire and Carl's great-grandfather William Eades (b. 1862) was from Staffordshire, which although certainly not in numbers, had a larger proportion of scabs than those in Nottinghamshire – especially the former, as just under three dozen miners stayed out all the way through the strike.

Carl's great-grandfather had come up from Oldbury and had worked on the development of Hickleton Main eventually settling at 78 Highgate Lane – and just a few houses up from where the air raid by the German Zeppelin damaged the bridge carrying the Wath Branch Line in 1917.

However, there was much more to the Eades family, as Carl's grandfather's elder brother, Jack (John) Eades was killed during the Goldthorpe anti-German riots of 1915. However, before I explain further, you need to understand how Goldthorpe is geographically set up.

My thoughts were, and wrongly so, that the place where the village's High Street intersects the old A635 is what separates both Barnsley and Doncaster Road, with the police station on the former and the infant and junior school on the latter. That isn't the case and never has been. Not only does Doncaster Road separate from Barnsley Road at the Lockwood Road junction, but it also changes its numerical arrangement, thereby switching the odd and even-numbered properties to either side of the road. Why this is so, possibly rests at the fact of Lockwood Road's importance during the time of it being the original route from what was once dubbed Goldthorpe Lane Ends (Police Station and Horse & Groom) to the newly sunk Hickleton Main and what had been the first few phases of construction of Thurnscoe East.

As for Carl's great uncle Jack, he was one of several people amongst a crowd of 5,000 who were shot by John Roberts Bakewell – the latter of whom owned the London Tea & Drapery Stores. This was an extensive block of business premises on Barnsley Road, which are the set of shops (now Fulton's Foods and Tote Sport bookmakers) immediately opposite the entrance to Lockwood Road and where the National Westminster Bank once stood.

This was on the second night of rioting on 12 May, whereby £3,000 (£349,021, circa 2020) of damage and looting of goods was undertaken and which followed on from an attack on Fred Shonhut's Pork Butchers – a shop on Doncaster Road, where Laws and GT Smiths supermarkets once stood during the 1960s and 1970s and which was just around the corner from a similar business owned Thomas and Emma Exley at 5 Lockwood Road.

Jack, who not only worked at Hickleton Main and played centre-half for its football team, lived at 27 Jackson Street with his wife Helen, was immediately taken to his brother Alf's house a few doors up at 25 Doncaster Road, before being moved onto Mexborough Montagu Hospital, where he never regained consciousness. He died from internal haemorrhaging that had been caused by his abdominal wound.

It had been a premediated attack on the stores, something which a rope man by the name of Fred Carnley of 23 Main Street duly admitted to the coroner, explaining that it was a well-known fact that the stores were going to get hit and ransacked – with Shonhut's Butcher's suffering £1,300 (£151,242, circa 2020) of damage and theft the previous day.

John Hurley of Hall Street, Goldthorpe received a bullet wounds in the scalp, side, and chest, whilst another miner, Samuel Kilner of 61 Main Street, got shot in the arm. There were, however, two others that took some friendly fire – one of whom was John Carroll, an on-duty police sergeant and local wrestler, who was accidentally shot in the leg, as was seventeen-year-old Albert Watson of Bolton-on-Dearne, the latter of whom had been working as an assistant in the shop.

Thirty-nine-year-old Harold Tabner of 34 Queen Street, Goldthorpe who was smashed around the head with a truncheon on the second night of the riots and forty-nine-year-old Robert Owen Milner of 28 Beever Street were described as the worst offenders by Justice Sidney Arthur Taylor Rowlatt at Leeds Assizes. Tabner had been seen on the first night smashing the windows of Shonhut's Butcher's and throwing hams, bacon, and loaves of bread out to people in the street.

Tabner had a total of twenty-nine previous convictions against him, whilst the more angelic Milner had just twenty-three. As such, Justice Rowlatt sentenced them both to fifteen months hard labour – with Bakewell rather strangely being cleared of the murder of Jack Eades.

This hadn't just been happening in Goldthorpe, it was happening all over the country.

Conspiracy theories point to the fact that the Lusitania was deliberately placed in danger by the British government, to entice a U-boat attack and thereby drag the United States into the war on the side of Britain. To back that up, a week before the sinking of ocean liner, Winston Churchill, who had recently been First Lord of the Admiralty, wrote to Walter Runciman, the President of the Board of Trade, stating that it was "most important to attract neutral shipping to our shores, in the hope of embroiling the United States with Germany".

A total of 1,198 people died on the liner including both women and children, and the press went to town on it, part of which included the publication of horrific photographs of the dead children and the hundreds of coffins being put into the ground.

There is something however, that the historians that have covered the Goldthorpe riots have never mentioned, and it surrounds the character of John Bakewell.

Being the Chairman of the Bolton UDC, it could be said that he was extremely well-connected, which was something that maybe helped him during his trial or trials rather – however, there was the fact that he just wasn't that well-liked.

It is claimed that not only was he an Austrian Jew, but that he had said that he would like nothing more than to "wash his hands in British blood". This was something which he vehemently refuted in court.

The first claim made little sense as he had been born on Chapel Street in the village of Kilburn near Belper in Derbyshire and his first marriage to Edith Mary Newton was blessed at Osmaston Road General Baptist Chapel in Derby. The second claim was purely hearsay.

On 25 August 1905 however, he had been charged with malicious wounding with intent to cause grievous bodily harm after shooting at (Enoch) Robert Taylor and his wife Clara, both of whom lived at 33 Elizabeth Street after some dispute arose over chickens (fowls) being present on a vacant plot of land off Whitworth Street – the place where a car park now stands.

Bakewell took his gun and shot Mrs Taylor in the arm and killed fourteen of their fowls, with one of the seven witnesses to the shooting being none other than Harold Tabner. As for Bakewell, his defence made out that there was a certain conspiracy against him and after six-and-a-half hours the case was thrown out of court and all he received was a caution by the magistrate, George Bryan Cooke Yarborough.

Bakewell retired to live at the rest of his life at Hudson Street in Whitby, and died in 1932, aged seventy-two. He left a will of £6,444 (£441,976, circa 2020).

Fast-forward nearly seventy years, and the wilful damage of commercial property and looting would happen in Bolton-on-Dearne's St Andrews Square when on 1 December 1984, AJ Moody's chemist got targeted. This followed some animosity directed at miner's off Ingsfield Lane, that had returned to work.

Whilst I had been gainfully employed as my mum's personal slave and living on the Flower Estate, I had often been tasked with going to Moody's with a box of Tampax, Fam-Lax or indeed the wonderfully tasting Brook-Lax being her most regular request, with the latter causing some interest out on the street, when Brian Taylor's six-year-old sister shit herself after I had handed a few out.

I had already tried one, which had led to me sitting out the afternoon matinee along with Alias Smith and Jones in the downstairs toilet after getting caught short during Jimmy Savile's regular Sunday afternoon slot on Radio 1.

As for Arthur Moody, he appeared a tall studious fellow who was always smartly dressed in a collar, tie, and a crisp white smock and shuffled around in some Croc-styled sandals, and on reading my mum's note always diligently bagged up the product.

The looting was blamed on local youths as opposed to striking miners, which was something that Walt Claydon confirmed after being asked by the police to board up the windows.

Unfortunately, there had still been several youths inside – one of whom was my former fellow school pupil from Carfield, Stephen Grocock (Tomlinson). Walt ended up on the receiving end of a broken jaw.

Prior to that, things had been intensifying as the return to work was getting closer to home.

Kiveton Park Colliery witnessed several violent clashes whilst I was there, the worst being after the short shield police had been mobilised straight after the mounted section had dispersed us. These were termed locally as *snatch squads*, their remit being solely to wallop and arrest anyone they could. Amidst a hail of missiles, they dispersed us into some field of which had a land drain running around its periphery, with Tim ending up thigh-deep in water and sludge after his jump across fell short after he collided with another leaping miner. It was during this fracas where I would be singled out by some young miners from Goldthorpe Colliery after it was suggested that I had possibly broken the neck of one of the policemen carrying the short shields. It had been alleged that I had wrapped a four-foot-long by six-by-five-inch-thick lump of wood around his head.

He certainly fucking staggered a bit, but it's highly doubtful if his neck had been broken.

During the latter days of October and as my friendship with Col, Carl and John bonded further, the one I had with Tim, not so much deteriorated, but stalled. He had started going picketing out of Goldthorpe Colliery and passing on the chance to eat at the soup kitchen down at The Docket.

Carl and John had continually ribbed him, whether it be about his uncavalier approach on the snooker table. "Not another fucking safety shot, you pussy?" John would grimace, or the fact that his stylish haircut from Mario of Barnsley was well and truly growing out, which according to Carl made him look like a bit of a chip-pan head, and reminiscent of the hurricane snooker-pro that was Alex Higgins. It may sound cruel, but it was never ever meant and just plain banter.

We could all intermingle with each other, which from a being-friends point of perspective was great as throughout the day not once was any one of us really on our own – however, spending nights at home in a freezing cold house, hadn't been much fun and was something that I felt, needed rectifying.

I loved Carl's outlook on life and his candid no holds barred humour, as I did John's conversational skills outside the piss-take, mainly the fact that he had a great acumen for music and when on his own with you, he was just a fantastic kid. However, nothing and I mean nothing, could compare with the alleged selfishness and manipulation of watching Col at work. For all his idiosyncrasies, he was without doubt my uber-hero.

Carl often told the tale of them both nipping down to see another one of the Class of 1981 around this time. Stuart Keen was the only child of Kenneth and Enid (nee Watts) and was a kid you either liked or you didn't. He had always lived right at the bottom of The Avenue's in the terraced houses opposite The Ship.

As a six-year-old kid, I remember watching him sailing a boat around in barrel full of water in the back yard of 112 High Street and recall some altercation in Mrs Gilbert's class, with him bursting Andy Moore's nose after kicking him in the face. This had been nothing too cynical and just a case of them both kicking out at each other with Stuart sat on the floor and Andy on a chair.

I had lost contact with him, although it would to true to say that I had certainly both seen and indeed heard him.

On several occasions whilst I had been at my ex-girlfriend's house on a Friday night and sat watching either *The Fall Guy* or *In Loving Memory* on TV – the latter of which starred Thora Hird as Ivy and Christopher Beeney as her gormless nephew Billy, there had been some action out on Chapel Lane.

"They're at it again," Joyce would say, on getting up to the window.

At that point in time he was in some relationship with a girl our age just a few doors down from where my ex-girlfriend lived and to say it was acrimonious, was an understatement. They were always at each other like cat and dog.

The Shillaws were one of several families such as the Davisons, the Parhams and the Cowleys, that had migrated down from the Sunderland area of County Durham straight after the 1926 strike. They had settled in at 13 Briton Street in Thurnscoe's newly constructed East end and next door to Col's grandparents Ellis and Ivy Fletcher at No 15, with Lynda being the granddaughter of Thomas and Ellen (nee Wallace) and daughter of Tom and Brenda (nee Williams), and therefore part of the future second generation.

If you want a story about the Shillaws, then I have quite an interesting one. Lynda's grandfather's sister, who was of course her great-aunt Elizabeth, through no real fault of her own got dragged into a very public bigamy case in 1947.

On 27 December 1930, she had married a soldier by the name of John Seabury at St Helen's Church in Thurnscoe and had a child by the name of Iris just two years later. The story was that she hated the sight of him and after several break-ups, dumped him on his return from the Second World War. He claimed that he had asked for a divorce and she declined, therefore he did no more and went out and married another woman at Kilcronaghan Parish Church in Mormeal, County Londonderry.

As for Col, on Carl taking him down to Stuart's house, his mum Enid had asked them both how they were and Col being Col immediately made his presence known. "It's been a really cold out… and I haven't had a thing to eat all day."

The next thing that happens is that a rather gobsmacked Carl sees Stuart's mum cooking up Col some bacon, sausage and eggs and minutes later sat at their table tucking into a full English breakfast.

This was exactly how he operated, and I saw it time and time again. Whilst you were being mesmerised by the steady façade of his left hand, his unnoticed right was orchestrating the situation to suit his needs. Col was a born survivor.

As for Stuart, I saw him as both loud and brash. A poor man's Vince Pinner, if you like.

Carl appeared to have plenty of time for him, however, this was possibly down his churlish and very non-PC humour, as in a nutshell, he just didn't give a fuck what he said, or indeed who he said it to.

"Don't you hate it when you're driving along, smoking a cigarette, and you flick your cigarette out the window, and as you drive on for a couple more miles, you suddenly smell something funny and on looking over into the back seat… sure enough, grandma's fingering herself again."

That's off his Facebook page.

I am not sure if he meant his grandma Keen who lived at 19 Probert Avenue, Goldthorpe or his granny Watts who lived at 4 Low Grange, Thurnscoe? Whichever or whatever, that comment could only be described as *pure* Stuart Keen.

I once recall Steve Wharton raving about the kid's artistry during 1980. Steve had this green quilted waistcoat-cum-bodywarmer – the type which almost every teenage kid had at that time, and he explained that Stuart was going to paint it up with the logos of rock bands such as Motörhead, AC/DC, Rainbow and ELO, which of course he did.

He had made it into Steve's confidence, so much so that Steve dragged out some vibrating dildo at their house at 9 Briton Street and showed it Stuart, duly explaining to him that it was his mum's, which she used for massaging her neck. It was a massive mistake. Stuart ended up telling anybody and everybody and even though I had not seen him for almost ten years, I still ended up hearing the tale.

I wouldn't see Stuart to speak to until 2 November 1984.

Carl had tentatively asked if his mate could tag along with us one Friday night. "Their lass has just finished with him and he's got no friends to go out with," he explained.

After being out with him ten minutes I could fully understand both parts of that sentence.

"How's your herpes? he'd shout across the pub, and whilst you were in conversation with someone.

At first, I found it quite humorous; after the tenth time however, it wore a bit fucking thin.

My thoughts were, that with him being the only child, he had been spoiled and was obviously used to getting whatever he wanted, something which was firmly echoed by Carl and rubber-stamped by John.

I found him extremely awkward in the company of people that he didn't know, therefore, to counteract that, he came over as loud, brash and abrasive. He couldn't handle just being a peripheral figure and always craved to be the centre of attention, which of course he never was.

There is a story which happened a month or so after the strikes end. Carl came around to my house one Friday evening and said that he and Maxine had been invited over to some party somewhere off Beckett Road in Doncaster's bedsit-land and did I fancy tagging along? "Just take a few cans of lager or a bottle," he said.

No problem, I thought.

However, there was a catch. "Oh, and Stu's on about coming," he told me.

When in his comfort zone, Stuart played to the masses with his "look at me I'm dead funny" act. In this instance, he knew absolutely nobody and absolutely nobody knew him, therefore he couldn't tell his mong or window licker jokes to get a laugh. The reality was that he was a duck out of water. He had little social cohesion, if any.

As the story goes, it had been quite a party and there were people in and out all night long. The front window got put through at around 10.00 p.m., which culminated in us having the police both inside and outside the house, which was followed by some flash black kid wearing shiny painted red leather shoes and a kaftan getting slug down a flight of stairs. As the revelry started to subside, I found myself sat on some settee with this girl and the next thing I know I am having half a bottle of sherry poured over the back of my head by Stuart who thought it hilarious.

"That's fucking it," I snapped, with my first instincts being to bang him.

I grabbed the bottle from him, however, Carl cut into the middle of us, and stopped anything untoward happening and the next thing I see is Carl dragging him into some corner and giving him *the finger the face*, whilst his girlfriend Maxine is dutifully padded me down.

"What, I haven't done owt?" Stuart innocently shrugged.

"You're being a fucking dick," Carl snarled at him.

And there is the four-lettered adjective that summed the kid up.

Whereas the weekday nights were cold and boring, the days in comparison were great.

I recall Carl coming around one morning. "Some lads have cut into a coal seam on the bankings," he said. "Do you fancy getting a few sacks of coal?"

Uncovering coal seams in our area was nothing new. They were everywhere and my first recollections of seeing one was during the early-1970s whilst on the old 13 bus going up the hill through Barnburgh, where just after Doncaster Road's junction with Fox Lane, some houses were being built that possessed basement garages. It was there that a twelve-inch-thick black vein of coal had been evident.

"Can you see that coal seam?" exclaimed my dad, pointing through the window as the bus trundled up towards the Coach & Horses public house and the infamous Cat and Man (St Peter's) Church, where he had often told me the tale of the valiant knight – Sir Percy Cresacre.

In 1455 he had been returning from a meeting at Doncaster, with either the Knights Templar or Grey Friars, when just as he was approaching Barnburgh, a wildcat sprang out of the branches of a tree and landed on the back of his horse. This threw its rider to the ground and the horse fled. The cat then turned on the knight and therein followed a long, deadly struggle between the two which continued all the way from Ludwell Hill to Barnburgh.

After fighting the cat, the knight attempted to seek sanctuary in St Peter's Church. The fight had been so fierce, however, that Sir Percy fell dying in the church porch and, in his last, dying struggle, stretched out his feet and crushed the cat against the wall of the porch – the blood stains of which are still there now. I know that to be true as my dad showed them me. My dad could always tell a brilliant story!

As for the coal seam, there were several lads who had cut into the furthest embankment of the Sheffield – York railway line, which ran almost parallel with the rear of the houses on the northern leg of Deightonby Street.

My fireplace had had nothing in it since summer, with the last thing I had tried burning being some small bits of tree trunk and half a sack of ash-type clinker that my (step)dad had let me have, which didn't burn too great, gave out very little heat and left a mass of horrible iron-like residue in the grate.

The seam we walked over to was around eighteen to twenty-four inches thick and was the blackest of the black.

Although I was a miner, digging or hewing for coal was not something I was that au fait with. And nor was I that good at it, which immediately gave you an indication of the brilliant hardworking men during the early part of the century, whose dangerous toil in cramped conditions miles underground had helped create the village we lived in. Never forget your past as the people in it deserve remembering!

I was swinging a pick and shovelling coal with the great-grandson of one of the first people to work at Hickleton Main, and I have to say, by god did we work. Indeed, we had to before the British Transport Police got wind of what we were doing, and both closed the operation down and had us arrested.

You could generally tell who worked at what pit in the eastern Dearne Valley by the shape of the coal that got dumped on the pavement outside their houses. Coal from Barnburgh Main always appeared huge circular and thick, whilst the coal from Hickleton Main was small in comparison and easy to shovel. With me working at Askern Main, no one had seen the make-up of my fuel as I paid the £1.83 (6.24, circa 2020) a week to have it delivered in bags and slung directly into the coalhouse.

The stuff we dug out of the railway embankment was extremely high-grade and decidedly volatile, so much so, it nearly melted the grate in my fireplace before burning down to the finest ash you could ever imagine, and heating up my kitchen and boiler in the process. I took some up to my mum's and my (step)dad had to blend it with the shite he had been digging out of the old Lidget Wood to make its embers last a little bit longer.

"It's bloody good stuff, that," he told me, whilst shaking his head. "It just burns too quick."

I think Carl and myself pilfered about half a dozen sacks apiece before the South Yorkshire Police closed us down – mainly for fear of us destabilising the embankment and derailing a train.

As I said, the nights were the worst as I just sat in on a night, listening to Radio 1 – Janice Long or John Peel – or playing music on my Hi-Fi. I recall at one time I borrowed an electric fire from my mum's but after watching it gobble electricity like some mechanical gannet only to generate two bars of heat that couldn't melt a fucking Milky Bar, I chucked it in the upstairs lobby hole. Bed was the only place I felt warm and I put that down to the dark pink hot water bottle that my ex-girlfriend's mum had given me during my first winter there.

Now, the next thing I am going to tell you is something that I am certainly not proud of. It is, however, a story that was borne out of necessity and one that needs telling.

I wasn't yet twenty years of age and I needed somewhere warm to go on a night. The answer was completely obvious. I needed someone to see and a place to go to get me through the cold winter months and past Christmas. However, I needed someone that I wouldn't get attached to. It would be one of the most cynical things that I have ever done in my life and the hurt I would go on to cause, I never ever envisaged. I didn't really want to name names as my actions nearly split a family apart and a lot of what I saw happen, although none of which was entirely my fault, should remain private. However, without a name, what I am going to say would appear fiction – and this I have to say was pure fact.

I watched how Col operated and how he got what he wanted. It may have driven Carl to despair, but I loved his laid-back approach and manipulation. In my case, I needed to attach myself to someone, give them the patter, and just keep giving it, and hope that we would either get back to work or until I had got both Christmas and New Year out of the way. The strike's end, however, looked the most unlikely as it ever had been through the strike – even though by 8 November 1984, the first scabs had started returning to the pit that kicked everything off – Cortonwood Colliery.

Barbara Howe was a Sixth-Form student who lived in the far recesses of Swinton's Lime Grove estate at 10 Muirfield Avenue. She was of dual nationality, having been born in Australia to English and Irish parents, Keith and Ann (nee McMahon), and had two younger sisters, Lorraine (b. 1969) and Joanne (b. 1972). She had an uncanny resemblance in appearance to Joanne Page's characterisation of the female lead in the TV series, *Gavin & Stacey* and even more strangely possessed some of the same annoying traits.

My idea was to never let myself get too close or get involved and bar one time in late-November, I did exactly what I had set out to do. It was the start of a period in my life where I would treat every girl that came into my life disgracefully. I had no real regrets of doing this as my motive was survival.

I first bumped into her in the same place I had bumped into Debi Neal, in Swinton's busy Towpath. She had been out with a friend by the name of Gaynor, whose surname eludes me, but who was fun and flighty. Barbara on the other hand, appeared dippy, and if I am being brutally honest quite drab and dowdy – and as though it had been her that had been on strike for over thirty weeks and not the other way around.

Looks-wise there wasn't a great deal to choose between them, however, the fact that Gaynor was here, there and everywhere and that Barbara's downfall was solely superficial and could easily be rectified by slinging on some make-up and wearing some different clothes, made the latter appear the obvious choice. As I have said, getting a girlfriend was easy, the hard part came in trying to keep any relationship alive.

Before I had gone picketing it had been a case of: What have you been doing today? Nowt. What did you do last night? Nowt. What have you got planned at the weekend? Nowt. As I have already said, mine had been a life of nothingness.

I couldn't even talk about a specific TV programme as I daren't turn the fucking thing on due to me not having a licence, with Andy Hunter informing everyone that a white Leyland Sherpa television detector van had been seen patrolling Thurnscoe's streets and which had been duly bricked.

Now, however, I had a daily life that consisted of violence on the picket lines, a communal breakfast, watching TV up at Carl's and maybe hewing for coal in the mornings along with The Docket, snooker and music in the afternoons, all of which I could relay. Interaction with a girlfriend and her family would be a piece of cake. Or so I thought.

As for Col, I had no idea where he went on an evening although I do recall him going down to see Paul Rice's brother-in-law on several occasions. Mark Beech was a dark-haired lad, who whilst growing up had lived on Bolton-on-Dearne's Concrete Canyon and not unlike Colin, he had an avid interest in music. He was also a Fitter at Highgate Colliery and one of the headcase's on the picket lines.

I still remember Col picking me up from Swinton and a tape playing in his car.

"What's this?" I asked, on getting in.

"The Psychedelic Furs – Forever Now," he told me. "Beechy taped it for me."

Even now, I still think it is an awesome album: *This policeman is just sitting down, in sunglasses and dirt, undercover now at least, so nobody gets hurt…*

As for Paul Rice, he was a right livewire in every sense. In fact, it wouldn't surprise me if it had been Paul who had been terrorising the TV detector van! He was the youngest of seven children to John and Glennis (nee Needham) – a couple who had married overseas in the Episkopi area of Limassol, Cyprus in 1957.

If you want a bit of Thurnscoe's dark history, you need look no further than Glennis's mum and Paul's grandma, who when she was thirty-two years old had been sentenced to eighteen months in prison.

Ivy Mary Needham (nee Yarranton) was Thurnscoe's very own Vera Drake – an accomplished abortionist who had come up from Tenbury in Worcestershire to live at 60 Thornley Crescent, and only got caught out when one of two married women from Worsbrough Dale and Bolton-on-Dearne had blown the whistle on her in 1944.

There was a lot of competition at the time and Ivy Needham – well, she was the best of the best.

As a young kid you knew to give her a wide berth.

"If Mrs Needham catches you in her garden, she will kill you," was the saying.

"It is common knowledge among medical practitioners that a great deal of abortion is practiced in Thurnscoe," exclaimed Dr Francis J. Boyle in the *Sheffield Independent* on 8 August 1935. "It is the cause of many mother's deaths and at the moment we are completely at the mercy of these abortionists."

It is widely assumed that when Paul's grandma was first starting out in the game, she gave an illegal abortion to twenty-eight-year-old Marian Dunbar in 1932 – a woman who lived on Thurnscoe's York Terrace who they ended up rushing into Mexborough Montagu Hospital suffering from acute peritonitis due to the abortion being incomplete.

Marian (nee Cutts) had grown up at 57 Whitworth Buildings – her husband Ernest living just up the road at 8 Vincent Terrace. They had married in 1922 and between them had three children – Gwendoline (b. 1923), Horace (b. 1925) and Beatrice (b. 1929).

The link was that Ernest's mother and father lived across the street and just a few doors down from Ivy at 33 Thornley Crescent.

During the war, she had been a godsend to struggling families – especially in Thurnscoe.

The topography of Briton Street is one where its surface water system discharges down the hill and onto Roman Street, and where during the early-1950s, parts of several unborn children's skeletons were uncovered by street workers from Thurnscoe UDC. This followed complaints about the drains continually backing up. These were what had been termed as *War Babies*.

Some abortions were undertaken in rather spurious circumstances.

Jim Fowler, a general labourer who still lived with his mother and father Tom and Selina over on Thurnscoe's Edward Street had been twenty-six years old when he got his seventeen-year-old girlfriend, Evelyn Wagstaff pregnant. They quickly married and moved into the house next door to where I would live on The Avenues and where between them they had two children in quick succession – Rita and Raymond. However, on 16 July 1941, something went drastically wrong in their home.

There were many who dabbled in the dark art but so as not to be exposed used pseudonyms. Charlotte Clifford and her husband Bill lived on the long-since demolished Sarah Street which was located immediately to the rear of Mexborough's High Street. She used her previous married surname, which was Chambers.

It had been Mrs Clifford who had called to 16 Landsdowne Avenue that summer's day in the hope of terminating the pregnancy of twenty-year-old Evelyn Fowler.

What was not said, was whether or not it was her husband that had been the father of the child as like many others, he had signed on to fight in the Second World War.

Complications set in and Evelyn, like many others, eventually died of peritonitis following an incomplete abortion after being rushed into Mexborough Montagu Hospital. She was buried in Bolton-on-Dearne cemetery.

It hadn't been the first time that her handywork had resulted in a death. On 22 March 1932, Lilian Frost (nee Kent) of 43 Garden Street, Mexborough was another who died of septic peritonitis following an illegal abortion.

Charlotte Clifford was charged at Goldthorpe Police Station with using an instrument to procure a miscarriage and sent for trial at Sheffield Assizes.

As for Evelyn's husband – he remarried Winifred Iles (nee Swiffen) and became the grandfather of Terry and Tony Illes, the latter who had been around three yards away from me at Kiveton Park when I was alleged to have wrapped a plank of wood around the policeman's head.

It wasn't just Ivy Needham and Charlotte Clifford who were at it. In 1939, a thirty-one-year-old by the name of Albert Oliver Tuffrey of 86 Daylands Avenue, Conisbrough had tried giving his girlfriend and local barmaid Edna Brown an illegal abortion and succeeded in killing both her and their baby.

Justice Sir Roland Giffard Oliver said on handing out a sentence of twelve months imprisonment: "People such as yourself who are ignorant and know nothing about what they are doing are taking enormous risks when they embark on a thing of this sort."

As for my superficial girlfriend, she was doing her A-levels through the week and worked on one of the tills at Hillard's supermarket on Mexborough's High Street on a Saturday, therefore her days bar Sunday, were well and truly taken up – or so I thought. In the beginning everything followed my parasitic blueprint and went totally to plan. I honestly thought I had cracked it. Both her sisters liked me and as for her mum, Ann – she regarded me as some long-lost son, dutifully feeding me up on every occasion she could, whilst continually asking me question after question after question. I thought her to be a lovely woman. As for her father, Keith, he could blow hot and cold, but we could interact socially, mainly due to his love for football and Sheffield Wednesday. However, nothing, and I mean nothing, is ever what it seems.

She had an ex-boyfriend who had dumped her but was now going to kill me. That was until he saw me. His modus operandi then changed somewhat, and he was then going to kill me if I did anything wrong to her. As soon as I saw him, it then became clear how easy my initial mission to interact with her and her family had been. He was basically just some weedy, weasel-faced lad off Mexborough's Belmont Street and absolutely nothing like I or any of my friends.

I stuck to the plan but immediately got hit with another problem that she needed to share with me – some *dark secret*, which culminated in her both pouring her heart out and then bursting out into tears, the latter of which she could have been a fucking world champion at.

I had to be honest, the warm house, their colour television set and the half a dozen pancakes and gravy or fishcake and chips I was getting served up on a regular basis, started looking less and less appealing. The girl was an emotional fucking wreck. "I had to tell you," she said. "I bet you think I'm a right slag now, don't you?"

You want to have a guess how many times I have heard that said to me that throughout my life? A fucking lot.

Did it bother me? Absolutely not. My aim was purely subsistence, my remit being to continue with the bullshit and never to get too close.

Ann had been a bookkeeper of sorts, whilst her husband Keith worked in the steel mills over in Sheffield. Just exactly doing what, I had no idea.

As I got to know them all better, I picked up on several things. The father fermented his own wine and always seemed to be sending his daughter out to the off-licence for a four-pack of Guinness. They also had a car in the garage – a 1979 Mark II Ford Escort, that was never driven, and which I was duly informed was solely down to the fact that Keith was serving an eighteen-month ban for drink driving. Therein was the common denominator. The man liked a drink.

As for Ann, she was well-aware that I knew about her daughter's dark secret, which drew her closer to me, and the conversations we had, especially about the picket line violence, miners returning to work and in particular Arthur Scargill, were extremely interesting if not forthright, with "Money talks" being her favourite saying ever.

Just over four years earlier and at a time of rising energy prices, a deepening recession and an overcapacity in the steel industry, the UK's steel workers tested the government's resolve by demanding a pay rise prior to them coming out on strike. My main recollection of this as a fifteen-year-old lad was of our French teacher, Mr Hinchcliffe – who also doubled-up as Careers teacher, explaining to us exactly what was happening along with the fact that my uncle Rob – who strangely lived just around the corner from Ann and Keith, at Calcot Park Avenue, was one of those who had been on strike.

Our Rob had worked at Manvers Coking Plant and when it shut down, some of the fitters and electricians got a transfer to the Shepcote Lane steelworks near Attercliffe – him being one.

During the strike, my grandma Carman regularly fed them, whilst my mum and Auntie Heather, both who ran fish and chip shops at the time, took them groceries. I still remember loading a sack of potatoes into the boot of my mum's red Ford Granada for them.

For fourteen weeks, the BBC's *Look North* and ITV's *Calendar* continually covered the strike – in particular Hadfield's East Hecla Works in Sheffield – as the workers at the privately-run plant, were the ones that broke the strike less than halfway through. This saw major picketing and quite a few arrests. After a car crash of a deal was struck, the government duly appointed Ian MacGregor as Chairman of British Steel, who history will tell you, absolutely ravaged the industry.

That aside and after a few drinks one evening, Keith lost some of his inhibitions, got brave and let the cat out of the bag. He told me that he had scabbed through the steel strike. "It broke my heart having to cross a picket line," he said.

"Money does talk," his wife nodded.

I said little, but took everything in. However, here comes the twist in the tale.

The very next evening when I arrived at their house I was immediately ushered away. Under no circumstances was I to be let in. I just gave a shrug of my shoulders as to why? I certainly knew I hadn't said or done anything untoward. "Please," she said. "I'll tell you later."

My first instinct was to walk away and not come back and I said as much.

That certainly wasn't happening. It was then that I was given the edited highlights of what had occurred the night before. Her dad had beaten the living daylights out of her mum.

"Where's your dad now?" I asked.

I was told he was at the Sportsman Inn up on Swinton's Fitzwilliam Street.

"And your mum's inside?" I inquired.

She was. She was sat on a chair wearing a pair of smashed spectacles that were held together by tape and sported two black eyes and a cut on the bridge of her nose, whilst opposite on the sofa, both her other daughters were sat in silence.

"Are you sure you don't want me to stay?" I asked.

This **was** the closest that I ever let myself get. I felt extremely sorry for them all.

As for her husband, he liked a drink, but he couldn't handle having one and became highly confrontational.

As for the reasoning behind the fall-out?

It was possibly brought on by my conversations with his wife about the Miners' Strike and watching the daily footage on TV at their house along with my candidness surrounding the violence that I was regularly partaking in with the main contributing factor, I think – being his admission to scabbing along with her continual "money talks" diatribe. I truly think that this had created the tension – with my feelings being, that maybe she had forced him to scab during 1980, and that after a drink, things had come to a head.

Her mum had read my thoughts. "It's nothing to do with you being here," she told me.

In my mind, however – it had everything to do with me being there.

Through the years ahead, I would come to work alongside hundreds upon hundreds of scabs and you know the **one** thing that all these fuckers had in common? Not one of them ever openly admitted that they were a scab.

Then, things began to change, and it wasn't a case of me going down to her house, it became the other way around, which fully defeated the object of my plans. And not only was she arriving at my house at night, she was also missing lessons and claiming to have free periods and coming over during the day, which brought some dissension in the ranks as girlfriends – or in my case, *superficial girlfriends*, played absolutely no part in our lives throughout the day.

I had been telling her what she wanted to hear to keep the relationship ticking over so that I could be kept both fed and warm, however, all that I had done, was create some blonde-haired Frankenstein that became as clingy as hell. The more I pushed away the more she held on, with everything she did – from the way she positioned the ironing board on the lowest level possible to her dumb idea of trying to act cute by putting her finger in her mouth, driving me to the point of fucking insanity.

"I've got to get shut," I remember telling Col. "She's doing my fucking head in."

I tried forcing the blame on her dad, which was not only wrong, it was also a downright lie.

She must have told him what I had said, and I remember him coming racing out of their house and trying to catch up with me, to try and smooth things over and make things right – however, my mind was already made up – I wanted out.

It was then my (step)dad became my social secretary, having to handle phone call after phone call after phone call. "I've had that lass on the phone again, bawling her eyes out," he told me.

"Yeh, I've dumped her."

"What for?" he asked. "She was a nice lass."

"Then you fucking go out with her," I told him.

True story, that.

Because I wouldn't take her phone calls she was then turning up at the house and showing me in person, that she really did love me and crying her eyes out at the back door. I fully expected coming in one day and finding her in the house and draped over the settee with her wrists slashed. It was a right fucking drama, and as I had made out that it was her father that was the cause of my wanting out, then came the obvious solution to the problem: "I'll come and live with you then."

That was the fucking last thing that I wanted. However, then came something that I truly wasn't prepared for.

I was up at my mum's when my (step)dad took the phone call – again. "It's that lass's mam," he shrugged.

I picked up the phone and all I got was her mum desperately pleading with me to go back out with her daughter. However, never in my life would I hear something such as this again. It was something that left me literally flabbergasted.

"I'll leave Keith," she said. "I'll leave Keith if you go back out with her."

The likes of Carol Russell, Yvonne Davidson, Joyce Evans, nor the lovely woman that would become my mother-in-law, would never have stooped so fucking low and said something as gutless as that. However, these ladies were different. These were wives of miners. Ann was the wife of a scab.

My aim had been carried out and I kept the relationship fluid from a few days before Halloween to the first Friday in January 1985 – the day of my mum and (step)dad's sixteenth wedding anniversary. It was the worst experience that I have had ever had with any female and it became as scary as hell.

20. Anarchy in the UK (The Strike – Part 5)

The first miners returning to work at Cortonwood Colliery brought the reality of the situation home. *The Alamo?* Hardly. By the strikes end there would buses upon buses being charted by the NCB to ferry the men through the picket lines. This pit had been the catalyst for getting all the men out in Yorkshire, yet by my (step)dad's birthday – 9 November – thousands of striking miners had assembled at the northern edge of Brampton Bierlow, and there were scenes that morning that could only be described as pure carnage.

The village itself, was a place I would come to know well.

Although on my travels from Thurnscoe to Barnsley whilst using Yorkshire Traction's 226 service, I had regularly passed through it, with one of my memories being that there was some outlandish Spanish looking mosaic artwork across next to Cortonwood WMC, I had only ever been there once before. This had been in early 1972 when I had visited the village's fire station as part of some school trip, and whereby two firemen – a Mr Ellis and a Mr Johnson – gave our class in the last year of Houghton Road Infant School a guided tour, with both men showing their acumen, by sliding down the silver fireman's pole. Little did I know that some twelve years later, I would be part of an angry crowd pinning back police lines with a hail or bricks that filled the dark early morning skies, before ramming some torched portable site cabin at them and forcing a Range Rover in, having to crash head-on into it.

Rather than me tell the tale, there is an extremely good piece that I found in the *Sunday Times's* insight publication *Strike*, which was penned straight after, by journalists Peter Wilsher, Donald Macintyre and Michael Jones.

Cortonwood men had come to see themselves as the strike's natural standard bearers. Their operational headquarters on the first floor of Cortonwood WMC and their makeshift picket hut, with its defiant sign – The Alamo, appeared on television screens and front pages of tabloid newspapers as symbols of unbreakable resolve. Week after week they dispatched delegations, demonstration parties and flying pickets to stiffen morale among strikers in other less united communities. But at home in the shack with the battered leather armchairs, the chip pan, the scrawled slogans, and the cast-off TV set, they kept barely a token force. Even the police thought it unnecessary to pay more than an occasional call.

Peace lasted, unbroken, through the spring, summer, and most of the autumn of 1984. Just occasionally there was a faint hint of division – a rumour, quickly denied, that seventeen miners' from Cortonwood had been seen at one of a series of secret meetings that had been chaired by Chris Butcher – who was known nationally as The Silver Birch and that Jack Wake, the NUM Branch Secretary, had been regretting a lack of democracy in some of the national executive's decisions. But nobody suspected, even when the NCB began to step up its pre-Christmas campaign, that at Cortonwood, of all places, there would be a serious rift in the ranks. When it came, it was greeted at first with disbelief, then with fury. The eruption took two days to build to its climax and it was almost a week before the village returned to a state of shocked and suspicious peace.

The first strike breaker was a young man of twenty-three, married with two small children. His normal job was driving one of the colliery's underground trains (Paddy's). Typical of those tempted, whether by frustration of financial hardship, to risk breaching the picket lines, he had worked only a short time at the colliery and lived away from the village in Hoyland Nether. Originally, he had agreed to go in with a mate, but at the last minute his companion had backed out. He was picked up at his home three miles away in the small hours of Thursday 8 November. At 7.30 am, with an escort estimated at some sixty police vehicles, he was driven at high speed through the colliery gates.

It was a full hour later, when the news spread, and some 700 people had gathered, that the first serious clashes began. Milk bottles and stones were thrown, police horses were unloaded from transporters to break up the crowds. And the old age pensioners waking in the bungalow estate that overlooks the pit workings had their first sight of officers with riot shields and protective helmets chasing miners through their allotments and gardens. Deep hoofprints in the pocket-handkerchief lawns showed where the horses had passed. Two policemen were injured, and three arrests made.

That was absolutely nothing compared the very next day, when over 3,000 miners descended on Brampton Bierlow – however, they had been outsmarted in their primary objective. This time the working miner was brought in at 3.30 am when there were only thirteen token pickets on the gate. To pass them, though, he had been provided with an escort of at least 1,000 police.

As new waves of pickets arrived, they refused to believe, or chose to ignore, assurances that they had missed their target. Milling around in the early morning fog both sides put the worst interpretation on every movement and an unmistakable menace hung in the air and at 6.00 a.m. tempers frayed to breaking point.

The police that day were headed by Chief Supt. John Nesbitt of the South Yorkshire Police – the man who had had to deal with a mass picket of 6,000 miners and rioting at Maltby Colliery on 21 September.

The police say that it was a hail of stones and ball bearings, fired from large catapults, that provoked them into mass retaliation and within minutes, all hell had broken loose. Three lamp standards, a length of wall and a concrete bus shelter were demolished to provide one store of instant weapons; a hijacked milk float produced another. As the bottles flew a river of milk ran down the gutters and the street was a carpet of broken glass. A portable site cabin was torched and set rolling down the hill towards advancing police, until it was rammed into the roadside by a police Range Rover. Another followed, and two official vehicles, with their anti-picket mesh windows, crashed in an effort to intercept it. A senior officer was heard shouting: "Some clown is firing an air gun."

The struggle waxed and wavered for at least three hours.

Gradually the disciplined and heavily equipped police established the upper hand. Using dogs as well as horses and driving their vans like sheep dogs to break up the pickets into small manageable groups, they started to force them away from the colliery and into the narrow streets of Brampton Bierlow, which were soon littered with half bricks, rubble and heaps of burning material. When the headmistress of the infant school arrived at 8.10 a.m., she found her playground being used as a redoubt, from which bricks, torn out of the wall of the Methodist chapel opposite were showering onto the police massed outside. The flaming huts, still smouldering, were now safely behind police lines and it was the regular local fire brigade that finally arrived to extinguish them. In the final tally, thirteen police and a number of pickets had been seriously injured, but only four men had been arrested.

Chief Supt. Nesbitt said it had been the **worst** day of the dispute so far – and he was another who had witnessed the **TV sideshow that had been Orgreave**. He had even arrested Arthur Scargill there.

The NCB was committed to a policy of getting men back to work wherever possible, the police to providing the necessary protection for this to happen, and the striking miners to defying them by any means in their power. By Monday morning four men were ready to run the gauntlet into Cortonwood Colliery, and the resulting convulsion, though it did for the moment clear the air and force everyone concerned to stand back and take stock, left a lastingly bitter taste.

Again, the escort convoy roared through the pit gates at 3.00 a.m., but this time in a change in tactics, the police had to deal with not picketing miners, but **unemployed youths** *from the area. At the height of the renewed clashes a petrol bomb was thrown at one of the police Land Rovers, exploding in a Belfast-style flare that lit up the night sky. Soon afterwards a whole crate of homemade Molotov Cocktails – petrol-filled milk bottles – were found in an alleyway. Police and rioters played a grim hide-and-seek through the back entries of tiny gardens while barricades were set on fire behind a long-abandoned building that had once been the Co-op store and the heavy roller from the village cricket ground was manhandled onto the village's Knollbeck Lane and propelled towards the advancing police. It was around 6.00 a.m. before the dozens of specially strengthened Transit vans that had been riding herd round the back streets were released from duty, so that the Police Support Units, brought in from as far away as Norwich and Canterbury, could fall into them and get some belated sleep.*

The *Liverpool Echo* ran with the headlines "A Night of Fire and Fury" and quoted comments from the Chief Constable of South Yorkshire Police, Peter Wright that this violence could lead to deaths, whilst The Guardian ran with similar headlines which stated: "Police Meet Petrol Bombs in Worst Pit Violence" with journalist Malcolm Pithers adding that over in Thurnscoe, miners donned in balaclava's had attacked vehicles belonging to senior management outside Hickleton Main's administrative offices. Everything was coming to a head.

It was to be the catalyst to what would be a strange month and one where I would end up being arrested in Goldthorpe, but rather strangely not for violent disorder, although it was not for the lack of the police trying.

At Cortonwood Colliery, I had been present during all three days of the violence and there were **two** things that I feel the three *Sunday Times* journalists got wrong.

To take the blame away from miners and put the culpability on to unemployed youths was just lazy journalism. There were always non-miners on the picket lines – the same as outside the pit baths when a strike was called at local level, where, as I have already stated, we had the communist parasites flogging copies of the *Socialist Worker*. Unemployed youths didn't know when pickets were being arranged or where they were heading to. The majority of these would have been probably in bed after watching late night TV – re-runs of *Prisoner: Cell Block H*, or whatever.

The non-miners on the picket lines were the people that **always** got tipped off by the NUM. These were fucking anarchists and they were everywhere. They didn't actually do anything. They just stood there waiting, watching, and taking stock in the hope that when the time came, they could plant the seeds that incited violence. Striking miners didn't have the money to waste on making petrol bombs and nor did these so-called *unemployed youths*.

Metaphorically speaking, I or anyone else could have thrown thirty or forty during all three days as there is nothing easier than to throw an object at a huge standing target, whilst hidden within a large group of people. Yet rather strangely, only one was supposedly thrown and although it exploded, it had somehow completely missed. This beggared belief as you just could not miss. Then, the police somehow found a crate of them all readily made up and good to go? This, like a lot of things, just didn't make any sense. In my mind the petrol bombs were put there to be found. For the tabloids to sensationalise a strike that was becoming out of control, they needed seeds of incitement, and in part, it worked. Petrol bombs had never been used before – however, on 14 November, the day of my twentieth birthday, one would be thrown at Goldthorpe Colliery.

The other thing that was wrong in the report was the fact that it wasn't police dressed in riot gear chasing miners through the old age pensioners bungalows, it was the other way around, and nor were these dressed in riot gear. I know as Col, Tim, Billy and myself were part of around twenty or thirty lads that were involved in that particular melee.

The strangest thing I ever witnessed on the picket line, however, had been at Cortonwood and it was something that I have never seen reported. As we assembled to go head to head with the police, a fight broke out between two miners, none of whom I knew, with the bigger of the two slinging the smaller one over his shoulder before kicking him in the head a few times. Why this happened, I really had no idea.

For me, it was an exciting time as I had a freedom to do whatever I wished, with the morning's violence acting as some form of novocaine for the soul.

Whilst hewing for coal, I moved around a bit. I worked with Carl and then with Col and on the odd occasion, with his younger brother, Andy – however, what our actions would do, would form the catalyst for, what was perhaps one of the most tragic events to occur during the strike.

Carl had the tools – the picks, shovels, barrow and what have you – and with both lads alternating Tuesday's and Wednesdays at Barnsley Technical College, I seemed to be grafting with either one or the other.

With the police now patrolling the site of our freshly tapped coal seam that ran parallel with Deightonby Street, our prospecting took us to another railway embankment and close to a place, which had just as much a macabre history as Bolton-on-Dearne's infamous Suicide Bridge. This was a similar steel structure that took Straight Lane over two railway lines within a deep cutting that ran in and out of Goldthorpe Colliery to connect with the Sheffield – York line.

Depressed and in a poor state of mind, a fifty-four-year-old miner by the name of Thomas Gregg who had lived at 18 Sankey Square, Goldthorpe had committed suicide by throwing himself off the bridge in April 1929, with the effects of the forty-foot fall both crushing his skull and breaking his neck.

In early December 1938, twenty-seven-year-old Ernest Stocks, who lived at the house at No 35 on the same lane as the bridge itself, finally accomplished what he had failed to do, three years earlier, and whilst involved in a violent struggle with people on the bridge trying to stop him, he managed to free himself and finally fall to his death.

Both men had worked at the local collieries. The first had been a miner who had been unable to work for weeks due to illness, whilst the second had been a surface worker who had been out of work for five years.

As for the coal seam, it ran at either side of the bridge and along the embankment below two sets of terraced houses that overlooked the railway – Dearne View and Railway View. The coal certainly wasn't as hard nor as flammable in content as the stuff we had recently mined in Thurnscoe. Saying that, I don't think anything was. It possessed several bands (or veins) of a soft greyish muddy shale that ran through it, which although it didn't burn that good, it was very easy to mine, and I recall Carl and myself filling half a dozen sacks in no time at all.

A day after my birthday – 15 November – I had gone with Col, my remit being to double the previous days output, nip to the soup kitchen at The Docket and go down to see my elusive best mate, who I had seen sulking whilst doing a particularly aggressive mornings picket outside Goldthorpe Colliery.

We had succeeded in doing what we had planned, and I had carried the last of the first six sacks to the top of the embankment prior to moving the mineral around to where the car had been parked on Leadley Street. It was here where I was met by around a dozen people in dark blue boiler suits. How they were dressed, however, threw me, and no immediate alarm bells rang – that was until one of them grabbed a hold of me.

"It's the police!" I shouted down, fully expecting the thirty or so miners who had been gleefully digging away, racing up the bankings to drag me to safety. That certainly wasn't happening and all I saw whilst I was grappling with two or three of them was Col three yards or four yards in front of the pack in the bottom of the cutting, scarpering like rats from a sinking ship and racing towards the old demolished bridge that once took the disused Wath Branch Line over to Hickleton Main.

I kicked and squirmed as I was firstly dragged into a Ford Transit, then leg and a wing-style into Goldthorpe Police Station, whilst a crowd of women watched on whilst making their feelings known, by hurling abuse and shouting things such as "You ought to be ashamed of yourselves" and "He's only trying to keep warm".

There was one lady that stood out. A young mum with a child in a buggy, who I had often seen down at the soup kitchen with her husband at Goldthorpe's Welfare Hall, during the early days of the strike. She was small in stature and possessed a peroxide-blonde highlighted hairdo, very reminiscent of Bananarama – a girlie pop trio that had been quite popular at the time.

It wasn't the first time I had been to the police station and it certainly wouldn't be the last, however, what no-one expected were the events a couple of days later.

National TV and media outlets had already covered several scenes in Goldthorpe – one being the surreal sight of hundreds of long shield riot police standing around the periphery of its police station after it had been attacked with missiles. This, however, would be much different.

Not only had our opencast strip mining helped destabilise the steep embankment, but it had also severely undermined it, and whilst three young teenage boys were digging for coal a landslide occurred whereby, they were buried under several tonnes of earth.

Paul Holmes, fifteen, and his brother Darren, fourteen, both off Probert Avenue, were killed, whilst their friend, fifteen-year-old Jimmy Rawson – the son of Jim – a striking miner and his wife Linda (nee Wassell), was severely injured with fractured ribs and a broken leg.

The father of two of the boys, Trevor, along with several striking miners, mainly from Highgate Main, dug frantically through the tonnes of shale and wet mud and after half an hour and managed to pull all three boys out, with the two brothers dying on their way to Doncaster Royal Infirmary. Trevor was reported to have said that his lads had burrowed nine feet into an exposed seam of coal in the railway embankment. That was untrue, they hadn't. I had been there on the Thursday and the seam had already been well exposed by miners, whose eagerness in trying to both dig for fuel whilst avoiding arrest, had failed to support the bank by chopping off the overhang.

The collapse itself, was blamed on the wet November weather, however, any miner will tell you that if you don't support the ground, the surrounding area is always prone to failure.

Throughout the strike, several people had been both injured and killed digging for fuel, including two during that week alone – however, the fact these had been children had made it much more newsworthy and the death of the two boys was reported nationwide and through every media outlet.

My thoughts back then, were exactly as they are now in that it was a tragedy, but one which could have been avoided. However, if you put sentiment aside for one moment, it exposes what is the stone-cold truth – and sometimes the truth is **very** fucking hard to take.

The two lads weren't digging for coal to keep warm, they were in fact, digging it to sell. According to the dead boy's father – who wasn't a miner, but unemployed – they had found a niche in the market, where they could sell a sack of fuel for £2 (£6.82, circa 2020). Therefore, they, like their father, who was also on the embankment digging, were doing nothing more than profiteering from the misery that the strike had created.

Is that me being harsh? Yes, it is. However, it is also me being honest, and unfortunately, here comes the next bit.

We had been mining the embankment beneath Dearne View the previous weekend and I recall some kids being present and getting in the way, whilst trying to carry coal past them and that some miner (or miners) had told them in no uncertain terms, to *fuck off*.

"They've as much right to be here as any of you," argued some guy.

I am not one hundred percent on this, but my thoughts were, that these were possibly the same kids and that the guy that was arguing their case, was their father.

Remember that: "They've as much right to be here as any of you."

Do you want a couple of coincidences?

During the 1926 strike, two Goldthorpe miners – twenty-one-year-old George Phelps of 23 Beever Street and thirty-three-year-old Bill Swift of 10 Cross Street – had been caught hewing for coal in the same embankments and it was said that their actions caused considerable damage, estimated by the colliery owners to be around £250 (£15,319, circa 2020). Both were fined ten shillings (£30.64, circa 2020) apiece.

Just five years before that two brothers had come to Goldthorpe from the Eckington area of Derbyshire and residing at a place that not only backed on to, but which was just 500 yards down the line from where the tragedy in 1984 occurred. That of 93 Frederick Street.

They had both been employed on the haulage at Barnburgh Main and the younger of the two – sixteen-year-old Joseph, had been complaining about an oil lamp of his that had gone missing and according to his twenty-year-old brother Victor (Albert), he had gone to find it. His younger brother was later found dead, having been gassed in some exposed cavity. Their surname? Holmes.

As for me, I was fully processed at Barnsley Police Station and dropped back off home by the arresting officer, who said. "If you see us again – just run. The one thing we won't do is go chasing you."

That could have been construed as a bit of a white lie as the very next day he appeared at 16 Briton Square looking all sheepish in apology. He had bollocksed up the taking of my fingerprints and kindly asked me if he could take them again – and in full view of Carl, Col and John, the latter of who said: "You should have just told him to shove his inkpad up his arse."

I would be fined £40 (£136.31, circa 2020) for trespass and £10 (£34.08, circa 2020) for theft – which were another set of bills that would have to be paid for after the strike.

I wonder if the father of the two dead boys got fined for trespass and theft?

I recall hearing the rattling of my front door a few days earlier at around 11.00 a.m. It was the day of my twentieth birthday. Malc Hall was a twenty-five-year-old miner who lived across the road from me at No 3 and who worked as a Paddy Driver down the Low Main part of the pit.

His wife Wendy (nee Davies) had worked at the same place that my ex-girlfriend had when she had first left school – that place being Michael Mayes (The Albion) sewing factory. This was a huge low-level building off Lidget Lane. Wendy was your archetypal miner's wife in that very nosey and very opinionated with *keeping up with the Jones's* paramount in her make up. After I had first moved in she had come around unannounced to see Joyce hanging some old net curtains and took solace from my assumed poverty. It was nothing malicious and just a case of Wendy being Wendy.

"There's a scab gone into work at Goldthorpe," Malc explained. "There's a load of us going up there now."

I remember it as though it was yesterday.

Malc was the youngest of three children to Bill and Alice Hall (nee Simms), both of whom grew up a few doors from each other on The Spike at 96 and 102 George Street respectively.

If you want some dark history regarding the Hall family then I certainly have it.

Fred Hall was a forty-eight-year old miner that had lived at 16 Norman Street, along with his wife, Jane (nee Spiby) and family – five of who had still been at school.

Fred had been unable to work due to ill health. He had been diagnosed with a duodenal ulcer and had become severely depressed. On the Saturday evening of 18 February 1939, he left the house to go down to the cinema next to the Market Place and never returned.

After an all-night search, his body was found on the Sheffield – York railway line just topside of a bridge, known locally as The Girder – a structure which carries the footpath from the north end of Chapel Lane over to Clayton.

His body had been discovered early the next day by a Foreman Platelayer who had been working on the line. George Barnish of 10 Monsal Street, Thurnscoe had initially been alerted by a man out walking who had noticed something odd – mainly body parts scattered around, including a boot and part of a leg, and on him going to the location he found that it was Fred's body. It had been completely severed in two.

According to the District Coroner W.H Carlile, Fred had just laid across the line and let the train do its job.

This, I am assuming, is where the legend of the ghostly Ragarm was borne.

By the time I had got to Goldthorpe a huge crowd had begun to assemble outside The Goldthorpe Hotel and opposite the colliery, where since the late 1950s, its iconic rapid loading bunker had formed an integral part of the eastern Dearne Valley's skyline.

The mine itself possessed an indifferent history, perhaps more so than neighbouring Hickleton Main as just twelve years after the first ground had been broken to sink its two shallow shafts, the pit was temporarily closed as no market could be found for the type of coal it produced. It also had a huge problem with water and just a year earlier, it had been stated by the colliery owners during a local strike that if the pumps were shut off for forty-eight hours, it would render the pit totally unworkable for twelve months. Those problems reared their head after the lockout of 1926, when on 23 May 1927 the *Sheffield Telegraph* was quoted as saying that Goldthorpe was the worst performing colliery in Yorkshire.

It was also often referred to as the smallest pit in Yorkshire, whereas Hickleton Main was without doubt the biggest, employing around 3,200 men straight after the Second World War. It is strange how things turn around. When we had been doing our training over in Armthorpe, we had several lads from Goldthorpe Colliery on the same course, whose weekly bonus – tonnage per man incentive payments, made ours at Hickleton Main look extremely poor in comparison.

As with most mines, Goldthorpe Colliery did away with the labour-intensive pillar and stall working after the war whereby its coal faces went the way of longwall, which became fully mechanised in 1960. The increased productivity proved the coal winding capacity of the 14'1" and 11'8" diameter shafts to be completely inadequate. Therefore, a new drift tunnel was driven from the surface to the Shafton Seam between 1956 and January 1958 and some eight years later the pit was linked underground with Highgate and began winding all the latter's coal.

If you want a bit of dark trivia, then the first person to lose his life at the colliery was a fourteen-year-old lad off Highgate Lane by the name of Joe Lunness in January 1917. If you want the most ghoulish death, then that would probably be an electrician's mate – a twenty-eight-year-old man by the name of Fred Yates, who didn't actually work for the colliery, but for the Yorkshire Electric Power Company. In April 1928, he and the engineer in charge, a man by the name of Lewis Loukes, had been working within a transformer chamber at the pit and Yates's head had somehow touched the transformer thereby sending 11,000 volts through his body. He was so severely charred that the District Coroner, W.H Carlisle, ordered an immediate burial.

Throughout my early life working in mining I never came across many deaths, never mind one by electrocution – however my uncle Steve did tell me that one of his best mate's elder brothers – Brian Wilson, had died after being electrocuted at Barnburgh Main in 1969. He was just twenty-eight.

His younger brother was Steve (Willa) Wilson – the latter of whom had just started out at the colliery as an apprentice fitter and would marry Jackie Blakemore a year after his brother's death, setting up home at the top of Bolton-on-Dearne's Canberra Rise. He was to become someone that I bumped into during the latter end of the strike and someone I would see on my **last** ever day of mining – and who a few days later would be stood in the kitchen of 16 Briton Square along with none other than Mick Wakefield – the man who Tina Glover threw her lot in with.

A man-mountain of a man in every sense, I thought Steve such a brilliant lad, although in later years very much deaf as a fucking post. He had a reputation that preceded him and according to those who took a belt off him, quite the killer punch – one of whom was the Foreman Fitter on my very last shift underground – Glenn Haigh.

"He was being smart," Willa told me. "He knew I'd run out of money."

As I recall the tale, it was kicked off by a game of Three-Card-Brag in the Dog End (Tap Room) of Ings Lane WMC and Steve knowing that he had the beating of him, wanted Glenn to show his hand. This had been after a huge amount of money had been put on the table.

Three-Card-Brag is what it is – a case of poker-faced bullshitters blindly raising the stakes and was a game that had been banned by the former landlord of The Fairway, Eric Scarrott, around 1980. This was after fights had broken out following heavy losses, as with no set limit, it becomes the man with the most money that wins.

"I know my hand beats yours," Willa had snapped.

"Well go borrow some money, then," Glenn replied.

"If you don't show me your hand, you're going to get hurt," said Steve.

Well, I'm sure you know how the rest pans out.

"I never knew much about it, Jamie," Glenn told me afterwards. "He knocked me clean out."

The thing about it is, is that they were both great lads, both of whom possessed a few demons. Even on my first bumping into Glenn – on Cementation Mining's mine development job at Maltby Colliery in March 1990, he had been standing in some tunnel, whilst at the same time, threatening to leather some fitter from Sheffield.

"Hey Jamie, can you remember that time I was giving Mick Concannon that bollocking when you came on site?" he would often wink, when he wanted me to relay the story to a crowd.

"Glenn was a right nasty bastard with him," I would tell them. "The bloke fucking shit himself."

In fact, he even asked me that in the Dearne Hotel, which was the last time I ever saw him.

Glenn, bless him. The last I knew, he was living in a bungalow on the Barratt Homes development opposite Carfield school.

As for Willa, one of the tales I was relayed, was by the guy who had been the Best Man at his and Jackie's wedding – my uncle Steve – and one which occurred at Bolton Club during the late-1970s.

"There was a team of lads that had come down from Thurnscoe looking for some other Bolton lads – namely Nigel Pugh and his mates," our Steve explained. "It was to do with an earlier altercation up in Thurnscoe, which we didn't know about."

Nigel had married Agnes Naylor in 1970 and to my knowledge had lived at the far end of Maori Avenue, between them having a daughter by the name of Patricia a year later.

"As there always was, there was our two tables in front of the stage where all the football lads and their wives sat every weekend along with Nigel's two tables next to ours," said our Steve. "The night had got to about 10.15 p.m. and Willa came back from the toilet and said: 'Get ready I've just dropped one them in the toilet'. Then it all kicked off. There wasn't a table standing in the bottom half of the club and there was glass all over whilst people stood round the perimeter looking on. I hadn't seen anything like it on that scale. As for Willa, he was knocking them all over the place and would have still been there now if I hadn't said: 'Come on, the bobbies will be here'. I remember we had a good laugh about the weekend after as Nigel had been complaining about the fact, that he was still taking glass out of his backside. It was certainly Willa's night. As for the Thurnscoe lads – we didn't see them again."

More recently, our Steve told me about him walloping some bloke in the foyer of Bolton-on-Dearne Ex-Servicemens Club (The Legion), him being barred and emphatically denying any wrong-doing. This was even though the clubs CCTV footage caught him knocking the guy around five yards, both through the doors and onto his arse.

Don't ask me the reason why, I was too busy laughing.

The last time I saw him was at our Sally's (Carman) wedding at the Methodist Chapel on Furlong Road and the first thing I told my son after giving Willa a hug was, "This lad can knock 'em out", to which I received a playful dig in the ribs. Steve Wilson – a truly brilliant lad.

It is hard to explain what was happening at the time as you as a person can obviously only be in one particular place at any one time – however, what could be said is that I covered more ground on that day and moved around much quicker than I had ever done in my life. The events in Goldthorpe on the day of 14 November 1984, weren't truly highlighted by any TV crew, media outlet or indeed amateur video enthusiast, the latter of which managed to briefly pick me out outside the Goldthorpe Hotel, wearing the grey V-neck jersey that my ex-girlfriend had rather stupidly bought me along with the black Adidas training shoes that I had brought back from Wisbech.

Looking back at the scenes that day, it still puts a lump in my throat.

Goldthorpe like Thurnscoe was a place that tended to police itself. Remember what I told you about first moving up into its East end in early 1977 and of me kicking back at all the animosity along with all the falling outs and fighting. In the end, you just fall in line and become one of them. Many kids that I had grown up with and who I'd had issues with were here, as would be the case in Thurnscoe one week later.

"We live here, you fucking don't!" were the words that I heard most said to the police that day.

The scenes were surreal and something that you could never ever comprehend happening, even though they were. The amount of police in the village that day was obscene. Up at the colliery gates they were decked-out in full riot gear – both long and short shield – as they were outside the police station, whilst in between they were patrolling up and down the Doncaster – Barnsley Road in armoured Ford Transit's with sirens blaring and lights flashing. The police were extremely coordinated and knew exactly what they were doing. Up at the colliery gates they even had their own photographer who was continually snapping away and monitoring the situation, and which was the first time I had ever seen such a thing. However, following the rioting in Thrybergh (Silverwood), Maltby, Kiveton Park, Woodlands (Brodsworth) and Brampton Bierlow (Cortonwood), it made complete sense for the police to undertake surveillance, as the majority of rioting had been undertaken by miners from Goldthorpe, Thurnscoe and Bolton-on-Dearne – the major point being that there had been absolutely no scabs back at any of our pits.

The targets to hit were numerous. I remember racing between GT Smith's supermarket and The Goldthorpe Hotel, darting in and out of people out doing their shopping and in one instance running into the middle of the road and aiming my anger at some police car – a Ford Cortina, with a half-brick rebounding off the windscreen and nearly taking my head off in the process. It is weird what you think of at the time as the thing I most remember about the brick coming back off the car and me dodging it was seeing a women's clothes shop in the background by the name of *Mary Berry*. There were missiles being thrown from every conceivable angle in the area around Doncaster Road's junctions with East Street and Beever Street. Although I didn't see it, I heard that a petrol bomb had been thrown, as Andy Hunter told me that it had set the idiot alight who had slung it.

It hadn't been the first time the police had been dispatched to Goldthorpe Colliery. Just over eleven years earlier and during mid-August 1973, the mine hit the national headlines and had seen a team of police headed by Det. Insp. Terry Addis from Rotherham CID at the pit and questioning around thirty miners. This was after three acts of wilful sabotage had been undertaken on the colliery's 19s district – one of which involved hacksawing half way through a haulage chain on the coal face, which a horrified Area Director, John Mills said could have ended up with fatal consequences.

"A weakened haulage chain is practically one of the most lethal things imaginable. While this has cost us a lot of money in lost production these considerations pale to insignificance beside the thought of the appalling danger to which the men on the coal face were needlessly and deliberately exposed," he said. "It is half an inch thick and runs along the whole length of the face. If it snaps it is quite capable of cutting a man in two with the tremendous backlash."

When you are a young, fit lad within a large crowd you can do almost anything you want as you can stay well-hidden – and even if things come *on top* you can quickly intersperse, therefore leaving the police to drag out the weaker and chase after the slower. As the crowd began to be pushed back by the long shield police topside of The Goldthorpe Hotel, I had been with a few other young lads further down the street and directing our anger at several police vehicles, one of which targeted me.

At that time, I knew could outrun any policeman with or without their riot gear – however, a heavily armoured Ford Transit screaming down the street in first and then second gear, with sirens still blaring was a different proposition altogether. It had singled me out, outside DC Cook's motorcycle showroom on Doncaster Road, obviously assuming that I was the main one that had been throwing missiles into the road. It immediately laid chase as I zig-zagged down East Street and on to Main Street at full pace. Never had I ran as fast in all my life. I was shifting across the tarmac and over the pavement like some whippet – however, that Ford Transit never had me out of its sight. I left Main street via the northern leg of Central Street and ran on to its backings, as I passed West Street. This was the street where the pretty thirty-five-year-old Lucy Jones would be murdered by some shitbag some thirty-two years later, and onwards towards St John and St Mary Magdalene Church, with both my lungs ready for bursting. As I fast approached the entrance onto Lockwood Road the van mounted the pavement and took me out, thereby rolling me over onto the grass outside the village hall adjacent to the church. All I can recall was hearing the van brake hard and its rear doors swinging open with cries of, "Out – out – out – out – out!"

I got off the grass and clutching my left hip ran towards the rear of the church, with the traction of my shoes on the paving slabs being virtually non-existent, which was merely down to the amount of leaves that had fallen. I could hardly breathe, and if I am being honest, I was ready for packing it all in and letting them arrest me. That was until I saw some huge dustbins within an ivy-covered cavity and I duly dove inside and hid behind them as several riot police ran past seconds later.

"Where's he gone?" I heard one ask.

They scoured all the church grounds, whilst I tried not to breathe so loud and heavy, which was a task in itself, as my heart was beating like some out of rhythm big bass drum.

I wasn't, but at the time I seemed to be there ages, when from out of nowhere some policeman spotted me in the undergrowth.

"He's here!" he shouted.

Now here is the thing. This was a young policeman who was on his own and as such, he didn't quite fancy climbing into that cavity without the back-up of his mates, who I recall were being heavily remonstrated to by the vicar – God Bless him.

As soon as the policeman's back was turned, I bolted over the front lawns of the adjoining vicarage past the Sacred Heart Catholic Church opposite and down the first leg of Pit Lane and therein to safety. This would be the closest that I would ever get to being arrested for violent disorder.

We were living in what we thought were strange times. Three million people unemployed, well over one hundred thousand miners out on strike and riots almost every day – however, as strange as these times were, events such as murders in the area were quite isolated and certainly nothing like they are now.

The mines close and there is nothing there to stay for. The older end retires before passing away, whilst the young often move on to live elsewhere, therefore, leaving voids in the once new model village to be filled by strangers.

Lucy Ann Jones was a girl from Bolton-on-Dearne, but one it is very fair to say that I didn't know. That said, I certainly knew her half-brother, who had been a year below me at school and her half-sister's common-law-husband, who not only lived a couple of doors from up where Tim had during the strike, but who had also been part of Dearneside's Class of 1981.

When younger, Lucy's mum had possessed an uncanny resemblance to mine, and I don't say that lightly. They could have easily passed as sisters. To my knowledge she currently lives in what was Phase Two of Bolton-on-Dearne's Flower Estate – Heather Court.

Did I know her? No.

June Bradley originated for the Sheffield area and had married Ray Darby in 1967, but by then they had already had two children – Lee (b. 1964) and Darren (b. 1966) – the latter of whom is the one I knew the best, before they had Kelly Louise in 1969. Then after meeting Keith Jones she had Kale (b. 1979) and Lucy (b. 1981) and lived at 28 Canberra Rise – just two doors down from Jimmy and Jenny Woodhead, whose only child Tyron – as I have already said, had been gunned down on his doorstep in 2012.

As for Lucy, she had been found on the morning of 8 October 2016 after police responded to a call reporting to concerns for her well-being. She had previously been in a relationship with a twenty-nine-year old by the name of Liam Fletcher who lived on nearby Elizabeth Street and who during a sustained violent attack had beat her senseless and left her to die.

Det. Chief Insp. Steve Ashmore oversaw the murder investigation and explained that Fletcher had shown absolutely no remorse for what he had done and had continually denied his guilt throughout the investigation.

After several post-mortems, which put the laying of Lucy to rest on hold, he was committed to trial at Sheffield Crown Court where Judge Julian Goose QC presided over the case.

The judge himself had acted in several high-profile criminal court cases and prosecuted the Dewsbury pair, Karen Matthews and Michael Donovan for the kidnap of Karen's daughter Shannon Matthews in 2009 as well as prosecuting paedophile Ronald Castree, who sexually assaulted and killed an eleven-year-old girl, after letting an innocent man serve sixteen years in jail for her murder.

After hearing the evidence at the two-week trial, whereby Lucy's immediate family heard the harrowing details of the fact that she had received over individual ninety injuries to her body, Fletcher was handed a life sentence, having to serve a minimum of twenty years.

I am sorry, but it is not nearly enough.

Rioting at Brampton Bierlow (Cortonwood Colliery) 9 November 1984.
Top. Throwing missiles at a police Range Rover outside Dil's supermarket and off licence on Knollbeck Lane. (c. John Sturrock)
Bottom Left. A mobile Portakabin set alight and rammed into the police lines (c. John Sturrock). Bottom Right. The surreal sight behind the police
lines as night becomes day (c. Rotherham Advertiser).

21. The Lover's Lane Murder

I need to tell you the first part of this story for you to understand the second, before you get a wild link to the third. Are you sitting comfortably? Then I'll begin.

I remember being sat in the common room of Dearneside's Fifth Year (Year 11) ROSLA block one dinnertime during late-April 1981 and reading a magazine. This had been put together by the writers of the TV series, *Not the Nine O'clock News*, with its parody advert on the rear cover for coal which also advertised the Welsh nationalist group Meibion Glyndwr: *Come home to a real fire – buy a cottage in Wales*, when I wasn't so much interrupted, but had the seat opposite me taken up by a blonde-haired girl by the name of Joy Parker (now Burton).

The ROSLA itself was a flat roofed building at the end of the road and which at one time backed onto the school's playing fields. It took its name from the abbreviation of the *Raising Of the School-Leaving Age* and was a place which also possessed a couple of classrooms, a tuck shop and a locker room, the latter of which had a heavy, slow rolling pool table with tight pockets sat in the middle of it. This had been built from scratch by one of the woodwork teachers, a man by the name of Mr (Norman) Wheeler, who used to drive to school in what looked like some armour-plated security van.

As for Joy, I knew her, but not very well. I had gone a different route to the majority of lads in my year, and was one of only three who had picked Domestic Science as an O Level (GCE) subject, therefore I knew quite a lot of girls, as I did by travelling to Barnsley Technical College on a Friday morning.

Joy's sole remit was to ask me a question.

She had a boyfriend at the time who was a year older than us by the name of Colin Sanderson, who had a sister in my year by the name of Margo. He was another I knew, but again – not very well. According to Joy, her boyfriend's younger sister Tracy, had asked her to ask me if I fancied going out with her sometime.

"Younger sister?" I shrugged. "How old is she – I mean, exactly?"

"She's really pretty," Joy told me.

I didn't doubt it, but the fact that she was two years younger than me was, if I'm being honest, quite a big thing.

To spike my curiosity, I followed Joy outside and over the road where I spoke to the girl through the white railings, which bordered the periphery of the girl's playground. What was strange is that even though I had always generally observed everything around me, I had never noticed this girl before – and believe me when I say it, Joy's statement was nothing short of an understatement. She was extremely pretty and more so than the majority of the girl's in our year.

As with her elder sister, she had dark brown hair, but whereas her sister's hair was quite short, hers was in a bob style. And whereas Margo had big eyes, Tracy did not.

I only remember a few things about the relationship as it was quite brief. The main things I do recall is that I was her first ever boyfriend and that she couldn't really go out through the week as her parents made sure that she studied for her exams. And even on a weekend, there needed to be a place where she was going to. In short, the last thing her parents wanted, was her roaming the streets with some rough-arsed kid from Thurnscoe East who was two years her senior.

"We could go to the youth club," she shrugged, whilst stood in the heavily graffitied bus stop directly outside Taylor's Shoe Shop on Goldthorpe's Barnsley Road. "My mum will let me go to the youth club."

I was ready for leaving school and starting work; therefore the youth club was the last place I fancied going.

"Or there's a talent show at school," came her second idea.

"Yeh okay," I said.

Nowadays, the thought of watching some amateur talent show is about as appealing as having my teeth pulled, but during that time my options were extremely limited.

"A fucking talent show?" Tim shrugged, on me telling him.

As I said, back then my options were limited.

I found both parents extremely nice – however, on first calling at their house at 99 Probert Avenue, which was a house that backed onto the Sheffield – York railway, I recall being immediately shipped straight out into the back garden and ended up being sat with her on the rail embankment talking, whilst her mum played gooseberry at distance and watched on through the kitchen window.

There was obviously some common ground between us as there was with just about every girl I had ever met while I was growing up.

"I'm told she's really pretty," my mum had said.

She was – however, I was immediately hit with lots of do's and don'ts.

It transpired that my mum was being kept firmly in the loop, and by none other than Tracy's mum Joyce (nee Davis), who had not only gone to Dearneside with her, but also worked with her at the English Rose sewing factory. She had also married her husband Denis around the same time as my mum had married my dad.

As for this so-called talent show, there were a few people in the line-up who I knew, one of whom was James (Shep) Shepherd. He was a kid that I'd always had lots of time for and who lived on Dearne Road, which was the main thoroughfare out of Bolton-on-Dearne and which runs along the periphery of the Concrete Canyon before going over the river towards Wath-on-Dearne. Although he was as straight as a die, he had a certain femininity about him, not at least within his voice. He was also an extremely talented guitarist.

However, the act everyone was anticipating, was a four-piece line-up from Highgate who were supposedly going to take off the Sex Pistols. John Farmer was much younger than me and around the same age as my sister, but someone who I totally identified with. He was a complete tearaway, but an extremely respectful kid that oozed talent.

I remember bumping into him a couple of times in later life. The first time being in The Royal Oak in Wombwell where he was banging away on the drums like some maniac, with a band that he played with at the time called Captain Blood.

"What do you reckon, James?" he asked.

"Fucking awesome, mate," I told him.

You could have framed that smile.

"We're playing in Goldthorpe next week," he told me.

He was. I called in and saw him. Great lad, John!

As for the Sex Pistols at the talent show, they along with their enigmatic drummer failed to show.

"I have to be in by half-past nine," she told me, as we sat on a bench outside the fire station at the end of Homecroft Road – her attention fully focused on something that had obviously been irritating her.

She had borrowed a cream box jacket from her elder sister, which had just come back from the dry cleaners, and she had sat through the torturous *Dearneside's Got Talent* contest, with a safety pin and a piece of card stuck in her neck. I had to admit, when I saw her, I found her extremely humorous, but seeing her one night through the week and maybe the odd Saturday or Sunday, it was never going to last.

On 16 May 1981, my parents went away for the weekend, which obviously meant that I had the house to myself, which was something that Tracy's mum immediately picked up on when I had called for her that Saturday morning.

"So, where are you both off to?" she inquired.

"He's taking me to see his grandma," she told her mum.

I had always seen my grandma and Granddad Ellis on a Saturday. It was something of a tradition – a ritual, and one of those parts of my childhood that will always stick with me.

At that point in time, my granddad would have been fifty-five years old and less than two years away from the end of his life. He'd had his first heart attack in 1979, which was followed by several more and although he was well over six feet tall, he was beginning to look quite frail. However, his diet certainly couldn't have helped. I remember my sister giggling about his Sunday lunch habits being reminiscent of *Christmas with the Cratchit's* and of my grandma dishing him out one carrot and two sprouts. "Aw, come on, Eric, you've got to have more than that," she'd snapped.

My uncle Pete (Rayner) recently told me that he and my granddad never really hit it off, which came as a bit of a surprise as I always thought him the most amiable of fellows, which was another thing he put me right on. "He was a handy bloke," explained our Pete. "When we first moved to Lindley Crescent, I once had Cyril Noakes give me a belt around the ear for hitting his son and of your granddad coming out of the house and giving him a right good hiding."

Like my (step)dad, Pete wasn't my granddad's biological father. He had been born in the summer of 1946, which was two years after my grandma's first husband (Granddad Rayner) had fallen at Monte Casino and five years before she married my granddad Ellis, which made him my granddad's stepson.

My mum maintained that he was my granddad's natural son, but he wasn't.

"He pleaded with your grandma to tell him who his dad was just before she died," exclaimed his common-law wife, Irene (Bridgen). "But she refused to tell him."

My grandma was obviously protecting someone, with that someone most probably being a married man.

My thoughts are, and I have said as much to Uncle Pete, in that bringing up someone else's child is not the easiest of things as it is a constant case of treading on eggshells to maintain the equilibrium. My grandma and granddad treated me as their own and the fact that I hold them up how I do, tells you absolutely everything about what kind of people they were. Very loving and very selfless.

"I should have done more for her," I told Uncle Pete, just a few months ago. "They gave me everything and I gave very little back."

"You were just a young lad," he told me.

"I wasn't that young," I replied.

Grandparents are a commodity that are rarely around when you begin to both think and act like an adult and should therefore be cherished whilst they are there.

I still remember my granddad teaching me to ride the red Raleigh RSW14 they had bought me, which he had attached two wooden blocks to the pedals and having me riding from the top of Lindley Crescent and him stopping me just outside their house before I hit the crescent's mini-Bullring.

They were both great conversationalists in that they covered a wide range of subjects, but whereas my grandma's forte was politics, my granddads was sport and Saturday was always, and I mean always, Dickie Davies and *World of Sport*. On the Ball followed by ITV 7, the wrestling, and the results.

As for Tracy, I must have thought quite a bit about her as I had never taken anyone to my grandma's before and I remember us sat at their blue Formica table as ITV 7 showed racing from both Thirsk and Newmarket.

Now and again my granddad used to have a bet with the grandkids on the horses.

"Which one do you think will win this one?" he'd often say, to which the kids would point to the white one or the grey one or the number seven, five, three or whatever.

At sixteen years old I wasn't behind the door when it came to studying form – whether it be football or racehorses, as research and statistics have always been my thing, so a look at Bouverie or Newsboy's selection in the *Daily Mirror* along with their last five placings made picking out a winner in a nothing race relatively easy – even though outside of an extremely rare day at the races, I have never ever gambled on horses.

"Say Primula," I told him.

At 5-1 the horse romped home.

My grandma had offered to feed us, however, my mum had left some pork chops out at home, so that is where we were destined. If it had been over twelve months later, that would never have been the case. For as good as 1981 was, and it was, the following year had been the exact opposite. But I have told you that already.

I remember sat on the bed whilst she rummaged through my fast-escalating record collection nattering away and of us listening to The Beatles' *Hard Day's Night* LP and taking her home just before the start of *Cannon & Ball* and later-on watching Charles Bronson in the ultimate vigilante film, *Death Wish* on my return.

When my mum got back from wherever they had been she asked what I'd been up to and I told her. "We went to my grandma's, we came back here had chops and chips, listened to some records and I took her back home," I shrugged.

"I don't think her mam would have liked that," said my mum.

She then said something which back then didn't make much sense, however, I suppose now it does.

Her brother Colin had just started driving lessons – possibly with my first driving instructor, Frank St. Clair, although I'm not one hundred per cent on that, and one of the things she had told me was that his dad, Denis had sat in on them.

"Don't you find that strange?" she asked me.

Maybe, but certainly not as strange as beating the living daylights out of a defenceless little kid with a rubber washer pipe.

I was held at sort of arm's length for a while in that she couldn't come out for reasons that I never really knew, with the excuse most probably being school-related – homework, studying for exams, although, her coming to our house when there were no appropriate adults present was mentioned, and as such, doing it again, was definitely out of the question.

I felt extremely restricted, however, it was nothing new. I had spent the majority of my sixteen short years being grounded.

"You need to go and see Tracy," my mum told me out of the blue some days later. "Joyce has told me to tell you that she's been in some accident and that she wants to see you."

Looking back at it, I never ever recall phoning her as everything was either pre-arranged or sent via *Jungle Telegraph*… through third parties. Maybe they didn't have a phone? I don't know.

The way my mum had described the accident I expected her sat in some wheelchair and attached to a drip when I made it over to Probert Avenue, which certainly wasn't the case. If I rightly recall, I think as a young child she'd had some problem with her legs and in this instance, she had fallen, but thirty-eight years is a long time and all I seem to remember is a kind of jaundiced bruising around her face.

I didn't stay long as I was told that she couldn't go out.

We broke it off on 6 June, straight after England had beaten Hungary 3-1 in a World Cup qualifier at the Népstadion in Budapest.

We had prearranged to go to see John Belushi in *National Lampoon's Animal House* at the Gaumont on Doncaster's Hallgate and we ended up walking down past The Salutation on South Parade (my favourite Doncaster pub) and around Elmfield Park as she was feeling ill, which in my mind was a right result, as I was worried to death that I didn't have enough money for us to see the film.

Now the second part of the story.

Tracy's dad had an older by the name of Donald who had married a girl called Mary Overton a year before he and Joyce had tied the knot and between them, they had three boys, one of whom had been in my year at school.

"Yeh, he's my cousin," she grizzled, after I had asked her about him.

If you have ever read the *Beano* and come across *The Bash Street Kids,* you will have noticed several highly non-PC characters. The dim-witted Smiffy, the short-sighted Erbert, the acne-ridden Spotty, the serial glutton Fatty, the no-necked Wilfred and of course the devilishly handsome (sic) Plug, the latter of who was a tall gangly kid with what is termed as a huge overbite – mainly an exaggerated top lip.

Richard (Urchy) Sanderson wasn't exactly Plug but he certainly had similarities. He was a tall kid with a stoop and possessed a top lip which considerably overhung his bottom one, whilst due to the darkness of his hair, it could appear greasy.

What is strange is that although his younger cousin may have had a look of either Audrey Hepburn or Nancy Kwan, Richard could have had a starring role alongside Fred Gwynne and Yvonne De Carlo – hence the nickname he had been saddled with since he had been a young lad. However, here is the thing – if you knew where to look, you could tell that they were related.

Like most people that knew him, I found him to be a genuinely nice kid, but bar an "Alright Urch" or an "Eyupp Richard", it would be fair to say that I didn't know him that well.

He was the middle brother of the three sons. Robert was two years older and John five years younger, with all three of them living on Goldthorpe's Dearne View – the street to the left of Straight Lane's suicide bridge, that overlooked the rail embankment where we had dug for coal. Richard at No 19 and his two brothers three doors down, both of whom were still living with their ageing mum.

In July 2014, both Richard's two brothers went on trial at Sheffield Crown Court, with Judge Peter Kelson QC presiding.

It transpired that Robert was a convicted sex offender, for what offence I'm not exactly sure, however, he was someone who the police had been continually monitoring and had therefore attended 13 Dearne View as part of their regular checks.

What they found were indecent images of children and bestiality along with extreme pornography amongst both brothers' extensive collection, which totalled over one million images and videos.

They were both depicted as having all the characteristics of people in social isolation, with their barrister explaining that neither had ever been in a relationship with a female and both of whom, had lived "in their own little world".

Contributing factors to how the two lads lived their lives could have been that they may have possibly been embarrassed by their appearance or personal characteristics, such that they isolated themselves to avoid social interaction out of fear of having people take the piss. Or maybe it was something else entirely, such as a **controlling parent** or **parents** – something that I had seen all through my life. Firstly, through my mum as a kid, and later through the parents of various girls that I have seen. Ring any bells? An important element of this type of psychological control is the isolation of the person from the outside world and controlling their social activity: who they see, who they talk to and where they go, whereby the controlling parent exhibits an insecurity and reactive jealousy.

The judge in his wisdom, sentenced them to undertake three years on the Northumbria Sex Offender Groupwork Programme (NSOGP), which is partly aimed at changing previous dysfunctional behaviours attributed to sex – the latter of which I have an interesting story about.

As already stated, on my first real date with Tracy we had sat on a bench at the end of Homecroft Road and close to its junction to Straight Lane. Opposite were situated two shops, both of which were frequented by children on their way to and from school. On me last seeing her, I had watched England play in a World Cup qualifier over in Budapest. Now here is a rather wild, but dark link between the two.

During my early time at Dearneside Comprehensive I recall the head of the First Year's (Year 7) – a Mrs Venables taking us for one of the three Humanities lessons and at the beginning of the school year her reading out from the register.

"Shelley… er Royce… Rumble?" she asked before checking again. "Is that right?"

"Yes, Miss," said one of the kids. "She's on holiday."

"What kind of silly name is that?" she grimaced.

Not nearly as half as silly as her grandfather's, which was a right mouthful: Laurence Mercury William Frederick Rumble – or Laurie to those who knew him.

As for Mrs Venables – she had never been shy when it came to talking down to children. Ask the classmates of the Pit Lane Rapist – Alan Conners. It was said that she used to rip him to shreds about his shoddy appearance.

That aside, have you ever watched the children's television programme *The Magic Roundabout* along with its numerous loveable characters, one of which a pink, posh talking cow by the name of Ermintrude?

In my mind at the time, Shelley completely epitomised the character. She appeared large in frame and was extremely well-spoken – maybe as though she had been to elocution lessons. Am I being cruel? Perhaps I am, but it certainly wasn't meant like that, as the reality of it was, is that I thought her a very nice girl.

It was Shelley's family who ran one of those two shops off Homecroft Road during my time at Dearneside.

Shelley's parents had married at Bolton-on-Dearne's Parish Church on 27 June 1964, on a day when temperatures topped thirty degrees. Her father was an eighteen-year-old miner by the name of Michael who at the time lived one street up from my mum and dad at 18 Spencer Street, Mexborough along with his grandparents, Mark and Beatrice Thompson; whilst her mum, Pamela (nee Fudge) had lived at 167 Ringway and close to the snicket over to Bolton-on-Dearne cemetery, and who was just sixteen years of age.

The main reason they married so young was that Pamela had been pregnant with Shelley.

The main reason Michael had lived with his grandparents was that his mum had been brutally murdered some fourteen months earlier.

Doreen (Dolly) (nee Thompson) and her husband Laurie lived in a stone built terraced house off Mexborough's Roman Terrace at 14 Oxford Street and between them had four children: Paul who was born a few months after their marriage, Michael (b. 1946), Sandra (b. 1948) and David (b. 1953).

Laurie was a well-paid scaffolder, whilst Dolly was employed more locally down at the GEC (General Electric Company) (now Morphy Richards) in Swinton. Between them, they appeared to have quite an affluent lifestyle, which was made more evident by the fact that they also owned a relatively new green Ford Consul car.

Whilst working at the GEC, the rather foolish Dolly became friends with a twenty-nine-year-old male co-worker who was one of many migrants that had fled the Hungarian Uprising of 1956 – the nationwide revolt against the Marxist-Leninist government between 23 October and 10 November 1956.

It could be said that József Kugler was a man of strong sexual power and performance and at around six-foot tall and weighing in at thirteen-and-a-half stone was physically a strong man. In fact, those were the exact words that were used to describe him by Justice Sir Charles Rodger Noel Winn QC.

Kugler had left his first wife and children over in Hungary and on entering the UK set about inventing a new life. The first part of which he spent working down the mines, which was a job he detested as was living at the Miners Hostel on Mexborough's notorious Adwick Road, where he met a woman nine-years his senior by the name of Piroska Bago – a lady who had entered the UK on 25 January 1957.

It was widely interpreted that between them they had had a son, who she named József – not so much after Kugler, but after her father. By 20 September 1963 however, she would have completely scrubbed his name clean. What was true is that Piroska was already pregnant with her son before she arrived in the UK and had him at Mexborough Montagu Hospital on 5 July 1957.

Kugler portrayed Marlon Brando's characterisation of Johnny Strabler in the Hungarian director László Benedek's 1953 film, *The Wild One*. He bought a motorbike and accompanying leathers and made the eastern Dearne Valley his home, eventually leaving the mining industry and going to work at the GEC where he met Dolly in August 1962.

The thirty-five-year-old Dolly became besotted by him and they began having an affair, whereby it is widely assumed that Piroska kicked him out and he moved into a house on one of Darfield's long-demolished terraced houses – that of John Street, which was located just off Snape Hill Road.

Both being mobile, he with a motorcycle and her with a car, carrying on an affair was relatively easy. They clocked off at 4.30 p.m. and as her husband Laurie didn't get in until turned 6 p.m., it left a ninety-minute window each day to get acquainted, which along with certain weekends, is exactly what they did.

Everyone knew about the affair except for the husband, which is almost always the case. Even her children knew, not at least her fourteen-year-old daughter Sandra, who during the final days of her mother's life would become something of a go-between.

Kugler claimed that he was trying to salvage his relationship with Piroska but the facts state otherwise.

If you ever travel between Mexborough and Bolton-on-Dearne and approach Sticking (Lane) Hill's Harlington Road junction into Adwick-on-Dearne, just look directly opposite. There is a footpath, which at one time provided a second tracked access. This is Lousy Busk Lane which takes you around the back of Mexborough and eventually links up with Highwoods Road off Roman Terrace. In between however, there is another isolated track that leads to Field House Farm – that of Hoy Lane.

As a very young kid I can remember my mum and dad pushing me in the pram or pushchair along the exact same lanes and over to Roman Terrace on our journey back to 15 Barker Street, with one of my earliest recollections being some burst pillows that someone had dumped at its entrance.

Hoy Lane and Lousy Busk Lane were described as a "Lover's Lane" and it was here where both Dolly and Kugler would meet for the very last time.

Kugler explained that during the dark winter nights they had used Dolly's car for sex along with the odd hour at his home in Darfield – but it was Hoy Lane, a place which back then you could drive up, that was their preferred venue.

"Dolly told me that she would never leave me and would do anything to prevent losing me," Kugler boasted. "I am the only one who can satisfy her sexually. Her husband has not touched her for the last two years because he is sexually impotent."

Those words were said during his trial at Sheffield Assizes on 24 and 25 July 1963 – and whilst her husband and children were present.

"Doreen was in love with me and I enjoyed sexual intercourse with her. I enjoyed her as often as I was able."

As were those. Notice the *Me factor*, again?

Kugler was an extremely manipulative and selfish individual – a boastful parasite of a man, who was continually playing with her affections. Strangely, at the same time he had supposedly been yearning to get things *back on* with Piroska Bago, who subsequently had the police arrest him after some domestic incident during a failed reconciliation.

Dolly, who was described by the *Daily Mirror* as "attractive", had heard rumours of this reconciliation and according to Kugler was apparently distraught. "Dolly asked me – if your wife comes back are you going to finish with me?" he said.

He also claimed that he had tried to break it off with Dolly three times before and she said that if I finished with her that she would kill him.

According to Kugler, he was a man in demand, and he loved it. He was untouchable. Or so he thought.

On the run up to the Easter holidays he also made claims that they as a couple were to go to a hotel in Scarborough. "For some fun" as he put it, and further explained that Dolly had even booked and paid for the hotel.

That certainly was never the case. Dolly went with her husband and not Kugler, which was something that he claimed was solely his idea, the reality being that this must have tipped him over the edge. He had to spend the weekend at home and with little or no money as he had recently received his P45 from the GEC after directing obscene language at one of the company's senior management.

On Dolly and Laurie getting back into Mexborough on the evening of Easter Monday, 15 April, he turned stalker and followed them both to Mexborough's Main Street WMC, which was around 700 yards from the Rumble's home on Oxford Street and solely to get him off her back she told him that she would see him the very next day.

That never happened. At 9.00 a.m. on Tuesday he received a phone call from Dolly via Mitchell & White's Vivo Store at 78 Snape Hill, Darfield, who told him that her car had broken down.

What did happen however, is that on the same afternoon he had a visit from Dolly's fourteen-year-old daughter at his home in Darfield who let him know that her father had found out about the affair, so much so, when Kugler moved to surprise Dolly by meeting her outside the factory gates on late-Wednesday afternoon, Laurie was stood there waiting for him.

Kugler claimed that Laurence Rumble threatened to kill him and throw him in the River Don if he didn't leave his wife alone.

However, Kugler wasn't done.

On the very next day he changed his approach and went to the factory gates, not at clocking off time, but at dinnertime, where Dolly completely ignored him, forcing him to whistle her to get his attention. This however created something of a spectacle and one of the co-workers at GEC, a lady by the name of Margaret Johnson heard Kugler tell Dolly: "I want to see you – I have something important to say."

"Well, tell me now," Dolly replied.

"No, I want to see you," he was heard say.

"What about Laurie?" she asked.

"Never mind about Laurie."

However, that wasn't the case. He certainly **was** bothered about her husband, just as much as he was about losing his regular access to sex.

Between 10.30 a.m. and 11.30 a.m. on the morning of Thursday 18 April 1963, Kugler walked into a local household goods and electrical store belonging to a Raymond Parry and purchased a knife.

"I bought the knife for the sole reason of having some protection against Laurie Rumble as I thought he would maybe cut my throat," Kugler claimed, during an interview at Armley Gaol.

What happened next is just Kugler's account, as there were no witnesses to say otherwise.

Shortly after 4.30 p.m. he met Dolly close to the factory – he on his motorcycle and she in her car. They drove away and parked up in one of Mexborough's side streets whereby he got in the car, a couple of kisses followed, and they arrange to meet at one of the places they regular had sex at – that of Hoy Lane. However, she had to go home first to check that her husband wasn't home, a fact which was verified by her youngest child along with a girl by the name of Sylvia Mansell.

Kugler rode close to the rendezvous and parked up off Sticking Hill, whilst minutes later Dolly arrived. Kugler immediately got intimate – however, they were disturbed, or so he said, when a red Yorkshire Traction bus passed them. He emphasised the fact that they harmoniously walked hand in hand a couple of hundred yards down the lane and that they had consensual sex together, whilst both standing.

What happened next was horrendous.

Doreen Rumble suffered sixteen individual stab wounds, three or four of which could have been fatal. The main one had been a wound that went through her five layers of clothing before penetrating a further four inches through her chest, a little off the mid line of the body, entering the plural cavity and striking the heart, whilst cutting off two main arterial vessels in the process. It was a blow which had been generated by an extreme force.

Kugler tried to lay the attack at the hands of Doreen and to make it seem logical, he stabbed himself in his right leg just above the knee. However, the police weren't that stupid. They knew the majority of the wounds were conversant with a person defending themselves against a frenzied knife attack. This was a fact that had been verified by several medical crime scene experts at Kugler's trial as being "Typical defence wounds" which had been inflicted by someone much, much stronger than Dolly.

But even then, Kugler was in denial. "I am taller than her, but I doubt that I am stronger," he said.

After killing her, he put his plan into action and rather strangely handed himself in at Wombwell Police Station. I say strangely, as it was around five miles away from the scene of the crime, when Mexborough had its own station just over a mile away on the banks of the canal. He had thought it through and as he travelled through Brampton Bierlow, he dismounted his motorcycle and threw the murder weapon into the Dearne & Dove Canal.

After taking the police to the scene of the murder he was cautioned, arrested, and remanded at the station but even then, he still wasn't done. He hung on to his version of his events all the way through the process being granted legal aid and getting Justice Sir George Stanley Waller QC to defend him.

That was until the verdict didn't go is way and then he appealed his conviction and dumped his original solicitors – Messrs Stephen Kendrick & Co for Leeds-based Bromley & Walker insisting that he wanted Sir Rudolph Lyons QC and the very up-and-coming junior counsel Donald Herrod, who would go onto be lead defence council in the Poulson case of 1973 to represent him. This was John Poulson, whose rather gratuitous acts led to the downfall of the Home Secretary, Reginald Maudling.

Kugler's case was a blueprint for many an Asian criminal trying to get off with a capital crime as his appeal was founded around his caution at Wombwell Police Station, whereby through his legal team he played the *Language* card.

"Whilst Kugler could understand what one says to him, and he in turn may know what he is describing when talking, he may not be able to use the proper words denoting in the English language what he really wants to say," explained his brief during his initial appeal.

The prosecution was led by Justice Stephen William Scott Cobb QC who chaired the committee looking into physical violence against patients at Storthes Hall Hospital on 11 March 1968, whose case the jury duly accepted.

It took them just two hours and ten minutes to return a verdict of guilty. Kugler was jailed for life.

An interesting fact was that Georgina Penaluna, who was a near-relative of Lewis Penaluna – who along with his wife Cynthia (nee Gosling) ran Lewis & Co. Estate agents at 97-99 Houghton Road, Thurnscoe during the 1980s and 1990s, was one of the people handling the depositions during the two-day trial.

As for Laurence Rumble, sadly the whole affair had been extremely damaging, not just the loss of his wife but also from an embarrassment point of view. Kugler had candidly dragged his name through the mud whilst he had ducked and dived to avoid prison. Laurie had to make a fresh start and he did just that. He and his youngest son David moved over to Merseyside, where he remarried a lady by the name of Yvonne Miles in 1969.

As for his oldest son – the eighteen-year-old Paul Rumble. He had recently married a girl by the name of Carol Croydon prior to his mum being murdered, who between them had three children the middle one being Gary Rumble. He was one of Mexborough's Class of 1981 and who in May 2016 was handed a four-year sentence at Sheffield Crown Court after being found of sexually assaulting a seventeen-year-old girl in Conisbrough.

The influx of eastern Europeans into the Dearne Valley had already created much unrest, therefore the murder of Doreen Rumble didn't do much to heal the divisions – neither did a vicious assault that occurred in Royston less than five months later.

On 2 September 1963, a Hungarian by the name of Sandor Molnar had attacked a young woman and was charged with maliciously wounding with intent to cause grievous bodily harm.

Eileen Thurman had lived with her mother and stepfather, Mary and Jim Baines on Newtown Avenue in Royston and had a two-year-old daughter named Gillian, who Molnar was supposedly father.

It was an acrimonious relationship, which had been on-and-off for quite some time – with Molnar spending some time in prison, but for what offences, I am not really sure.

On the said night, the Hungarian had followed her to the Ship Inn on Midland Road, where he attempted to sit next to her. He was eventually ordered off the premises by the licensee after he began to annoy her. She had been dancing and Molnar – well, he didn't like it.

Molnar left – bought some beer from an off-licence on Midland Road and waited for Eileen to return home. When she did, he did no more than break a beer bottle and ram it in her face and neck, also slashing her arms as she tried to defend herself.

On his arrest Molnar said: "I did it with bottle. She showed me up in the pub. She shoved me away and danced with another man."

I know he was sentenced at Leeds Assizes – however, I am not sure how much time he got.

As for Eileen – she married Jeff Thorpe in 1968 and the last I heard was living on Tollgate Close in the Shafton area of Barnsley.

It wasn't just Hungarians that were creating a resentment.

The body of thirty-one-year-old Mary Hannah Price was discovered under a straw stack on Hampole Road near Hooton Pagnell on 7 January 1956.

There were certain similarities with the Lover's Lane murder in Mexborough in that the dead woman was known as Molly and that her murderer – Jan Mocxygemba, rode a motorcycle.

Molly had been separated from her husband and had lived with twenty-nine-year-old Mocxygemba at her home 4 Victoria Street, Hemsworth.

With Mocxygemba being employed as a miner at Markham Main Colliery, they, along with her three children – Neil, nine, Gillian, eight, and Andrea, six – had temporarily relocated to a property on Lowther Road in the Wheatley area of Doncaster.

Molly had been dead several days with the pathologist believing that she had been murdered on 3 January, and the police – the murder case being handled by Chief Supt. L.D Lowry and Chief Insp. C Lodge, believed that she had been murdered in one place and the body moved some days later.

She had been strangled with a leather pit belt, a farmworker noticing one of her feet sticking out from beneath the straw stack.

Justice Sir Geoffrey Hugh Benbow Streatfeild presided over the trial at Sheffield Assizes and on 1 March 1956 – donned the black cap and sentenced Mocxygemba to death with a provisional date for his hanging at Armley Gaol being 22 March.

The murderer – dressed in a dark blue suit and polo neck shirt, showed no emotion, and was duly taken down. However, the twist in the tale is that he was reprieved.

As for Tracy Sanderson, she married a lad by the name of David Hebden in August 1988.

I am not a genealogy expert by any stretch of the imagination therefore I tend to get lost after the second or third cousins, and I certainly don't do the twice removed kind of stuff – so, here goes.

David's great-grandfather's brother's son was George Hebden. He had married a lady by the name of Margaret Bowden in 1911 and between them they had five children – one of whom was John Robert.

On 29 November 1962, seventy-one-year-old Margaret was committed to Sheffield's Middlewood Hospital after being cleared of murdering her husband.

The jury at Leeds Assizes heard that George had been a retired miner who after a series of strokes had become paralysed down one side of his body.

Their son John, who was also a miner, had found his father in bed in the living room of his parents' house at 17 Richmond Road, Moorends near Thorne on 27 August with his throat cut and his mother upstairs with a razor in her hand.

It was said that although she had dutifully cared for him, the strain of the task had become too much.

On her arrest she had told Det. Sgt. Alcock: "I thought it was the best way to put him out of his misery."

Malc Russell flanked by his two sons - Brian (Left) and Paul (Right).
The photograph was taken whilst digging for coal beneath Hoober Stand during the 1984/85 Miners' Strike.

I only had around twelve weeks directly working with them, but Malc's two sons were possibly the most honest,
enthusiastic and hardworking lads I have ever come across whilst working in the mines - and I do not say that lightly.

22.   El-Mana-Mou (The Strike – Part 6)

I remember walking down Swinton's Lime Grove one dark evening and towards the house of the girlfriend that I didn't want, to see a man dressed in a suit get out of his car and walk through a front door and into one of the bungalows. Through the large front window, I could see him being met by both his wife and two children, and as he removed his jacket, his wife gave him a peck on the lips. The inside of the house appeared bright and clean and a well-dressed Christmas tree stood proudly in the corner. It was reminiscent of a story that my wife once told me about a book that her nanan. (Edith) Wattam (nee Totty) had once read to her when she had been a child, and one which she had been enthralled in. That of *The Little Matchstick Girl*.

Most people fantasise about wanting great things in life, which helps blot out the misery of the everyday grind, and I was no different. I was fast nearing ten months of having nothing and my thoughts at that time were: when would it become my turn? I wanted a wife, a family, along with a new house and a car, but at that point in time the nearest I had ever come to it was never. It all seemed a million miles away.

My mum had been on about getting one of these self-same bungalows in the self-same village, just before those god-awful days of 1982. Two years on and those days were still as horrible, however, this was nothing to do with my parents nor even me, but everything to do with the situation I was in. I looked at my dad and Paula and from the outside looking in, they looked like they had cracked it, but even that had never really been the case.

I remember a time around 1974, that my dad and Paula had been talking about leaving Barnby Dun, with my dad's intention being to move back home to Bolton-on-Dearne. Around that time the Manor Farm buildings at the end of Lowfield Road had just been demolished to make way for both the Calder Road and Sheaf Crescent developments, and it was their idea to sell up and purchase one of these new-build bungalows.

Whilst I had lived with them, I may not have enjoyed the situation I was in, but I certainly liked Barnby Dun. The affluent village had been built around the River Don and the Dun Navigation Canal and had several new developments, none of which I thought I would ever be able to afford. It was a million miles from the smoking chimney stacks of Bolton-on-Dearne's sprawling pit and council estates and even at nine-years-old I thought it quite a strange move. One of my dad's pieces of logic was that he would be able to see more of me, which was something that my mum immediately baulked at when I told her. The reality of it, was that all his family were there, and one thing he loved was his family. That was that bit that I could understand.

Why the move never transpired I don't really know, but at the time they both appeared infatuated with the idea moving into a bungalow. My thoughts are – and this is solely through experience – that when things are bad or just look that way, you look for some form of comfort blanket, and moving back to a place and people that you're familiar with is exactly that. Maybe something had happened in his everyday life to warrant that line of thinking – I don't know.

"Why was my dad different to all his other brothers?" I once asked Paula.

"Because he moved away," she told me.

Experience also tells me that her comment, although very anti-Durose, wasn't that wide of the mark.

Other people you are close to rub off on you, and quite often that happens in a big way.

The Duroses were a family that spent the majority of their life outside of work in the pub and I remember two of my auntie Ann(e)s (as I have three) calling in The Collingwood, not only see both their husbands – which was both my uncle Paul and uncle Les – but also because they knew my dad was in the village. At that time, I could have called in almost any pub in Bolton-on-Dearne on a weekend and one of my dad's brothers (my uncles) would have been in there. I think it was this that Paula had been referring to when she said that by them moving away it had created the difference in my dad.

As I have already said, I had been kept at arm's length from my dad's family, which is something that in later life I could kick myself for letting happen. As a child it was out of my control, but as I kicked back throughout my teenage years I could have done more. Much more.

During the Fourth Year (Year 10) of Dearneside there had been a purge on the problem pupils – the tearaways, if you like – and a whole bunch of letters – thirty as I recall – went out to parents. Mine never got a letter as I had been expelled indefinitely. It was quite a strange time as I had an interview with the Headmaster of Thurnscoe Comprehensive – a lovely man by the name of Mr (Denis) Owen and it looked like I would be moving schools. This was something, which somehow brought an end to all the violence and hatred that had been directed towards me.

"Are you coming to our school?" asked Tony Taylor.

"I think so," I told him.

"You'll like it a lot better than Dearneside," he said.

I even had a girl that I didn't know pull me up in Thurnscoe's marketplace to ask me the same question.

Mr Owen was very much open to me going to Thurnscoe Comprehensive, so much so, I had even chosen my subjects. I had dumped Physics for something that I could actually understand and changed my Electrical Engineering course at Barnsley Technical College for that of Photography.

I was so close to the move, yet it never happened. I think the Headmaster at Dearneside, Mr (Leonard) Dickinson had offered me a way back in and I took the easy route. One of the stipulations was, however, that I had to vacate the school's premises during dinnertime as this and been one of the main problems.

Whilst supposedly having school dinners a gang of us would leave the school grounds and roam the streets of Goldthorpe and get into all sorts of trouble. A caravan was broken into and robbed of all its contents up near Cross Street WMC. The old Goldthorpe Library, the one which was burned down in 1985, had LP records and books continually go missing, whilst every Newsagent in the village was getting pilfered – most notably Drabble's, which was a shop located on Hall Street's junction with High Street. And the stocktaking was definitely down at Duffield's, which was one of three record shops in Goldthorpe that occupied a building on Doncaster Road and was just a few doors down from where The Rusty Dudley public house now stands.

My mum's brainwave was for me to travel to my grandma Ellis's for dinner each day as the Goldthorpe – Thurnscoe bus services served the residents of Lindley Crescent, much better than it ever did the East end. The 213, the 275 and most notably, the 226, gave me a flexibility to go home for dinners and for me it would be a time in my life that I wouldn't have changed it for the world. It was that good.

My grandparents had a set pattern and routine that you could have set your clock by. I would arrive as my dinner was being put out on the table and while the Australian wartime drama which was *The Sullivans* was being shown on TV. The opening of *News at One* would then chime and by the time Peter Sissons or the Thurnscoe-born broadcaster Leonard Parkin had done pontificating half-way through, I had eaten up and was reading through numerous comics or newspapers that were always laying around.

My uncle John (Ellis), who was not only my grandma and grandad's only child between them – but the surviving child of a set of twins, worked as a butcher at Sharman's up in Shepherd Lane's compact shopping centre. As that was the case, he also had his lunch at my grandma's, although he both arrived and left some twenty minutes before me.

Chips and sirloin steak on Monday; a ham salad on Tuesday; chips, minced meat and onions on Wednesday; fish and chips or a mixed grill on a Thursday; and on Friday it was around 1 lb of tripe and vinegar, along with a full uncut crusty loaf and butter, which had been bought fresh off Thurnscoe market that morning.

"How you can you eat that rubbish, Jamie, I've no idea," our John often exclaimed.

John had been a great schoolboy goalkeeper and had turned down trials at Arsenal. As part of his penance he had worked at Sharman's since being fifteen-years-old and had been hacking up animals' carcasses for the past fourteen, therefore his palate when it came to food – especially meat, wasn't quite as varied as mine.

"He was a really, really nice lad and that Noreen Sharman (nee Dunphy) was absolutely horrible with him," Joyce Evans once told me. "She used to speak to him like a dog."

Whilst travelling back and forth from my grandmas on the 1.35 p.m. bus back to school, there was suddenly a face in the seats that I recognised. "Is that our James?" it asked.

My uncle Les (Durose) was without doubt one of the most fascinating and colourful characters that I would ever come to meet. He had a Mediterranean look in that he could have easily passed as a Greek. The dark hair and those dark eyes, both of which were complemented by some Zapata moustache. "I thought it was you," he smiled. "Get yourself over here and come and have a natter."

It was the start of a few months in the late spring of 1980, which made my going home for dinners even better than they already were.

At twenty-nine-years-old, our Les had got a start at Hickleton Main and had been working on day shift down the Low Main part of the mine. As that was the case, he was on the first draw of the cage and through the showers and outside Sharman's to jump on the 226 bus. As for me, I was waiting up at the next bus stop.

His stories were not unlike my dad's – however, my uncle Les was much more adult in his delivery and treated me as an equal. He was an awesome bloke if I'm being honest.

"I always liked your mam, James," was one of the first things he told me.

How could you ever knock that?

The second was about this woman turning up at his door on Bolton-on-Dearne's Coronation Drive, with a kid he had supposedly sired. "I buggered her off straight away," he told me. "Your auntie Ann (nee Burgess) went barmy."

This street was one that had been full of characters – not at least old Bill Parr and Barry Oliver, the latter of who is a giant of a man and someone that I could listen to all day long.

"Let me tell you a story about me and your dad," he told me.

In 1969, they had both upped sticks and moved away, getting employment as contractors on the construction of the infrastructure that formed part of the £50 million (£488 million, circa 2020) Humber (Oil) Refinery – a project that was being built by Power-Gas Corporation, a subsidiary of Sheffield-based Davy-Ashmore. Notice that name again – Davy?

"Your dad was stood at the bar in the County Hotel in Immingham and in some argument with a few blokes – one of who was this big, horrible trouble causing bastard from Scotland. As soon as I heard your dad talking, I knew he was a Bolton (-on-Dearne) lad," explained Barry.

After the introductions, Barry told him: "I'll do these, and you get stuck into the others."

Between Barry and my dad, they knocked fuck out of them all – however, this was nothing new. Barry, a few years younger than my dad, had a reputation that preceded him and had well and truly served his apprenticeship on the cobbles.

"I used to come in covered in cuts and bruises with a pocket full of money," he told me. "Our lass often asking me – 'Where did all that come from?'."

Whilst living over in Immingham, Barry had frequently been engaged in bare knuckle fighting.

He is a character, that is for sure. The last time I saw him was as Landlord of Bolton-on-Dearne Ex-Service & Social Club, at a time just after the Miners' Strike when I had played centre forward for their all-conquering (sic) football team in the Mexborough & District Sunday League – which had been managed by the affable Johnny Bailey.

As for my uncle Les, one of his many other stories was about him and my dad going to see an aged country and western singer by the name of Jimmy Driftwood.

"Here's this bloke on stage who had to be about one hundred fucking years old warbling away with some daft guitar in his hand and there's loads of people yacking in the background," our Les explained. "The next thing I know is that your dad stands up and starts threatening people and telling them to shut up."

All my dad's family had been brought up around country and western music, not at least the 1960's poster-boy that was the *King of the Road*, and it is here where I suppose there is a story.

My dad owned a record collection, which to me at the time appeared vast. It wasn't really – it just seemed that way. This, however, was a thing which had always fascinated me. Ask anyone who knew me through my teenage years, and they will all tell you the same. The main thing that I always asked to see was their records, as a record collection tells you everything about the person that it belongs to – much like a car, if you like.

My dad's collection wasn't something a young lad such as myself would have entertained as it was one hundred per cent country and western, so for me, it was just pure sentimentality. I liked the records that reminded me of the weekends I'd had at his house when I had been a little lad and three LP's stood out, one of which was by Roger Miller. Just prior to my journeys between school and my grandma's, my dad had made space for more music by offloading over a dozen albums by the artist, which was something that I happened to mention to my uncle Les. "So, your dad's given you all his Roger Miller records?" he inquired.

I nodded.

"You lucky bugger," he said. "I would have had them."

It sounds a nothing story – however, that's not the case.

Obviously. I had told my dad about seeing his younger brother and he told me that if I wanted, I could give them him, which was something that I said that I would do   both to my dad, but more importantly to my uncle Les.

For a whole fortnight he had been dashing through the showers and making the bus only for me to let him down – as humping a load of old records around all day if he didn't make the bus, wasn't something that I wanted to do, and I told my dad as much.

My dad's idea was simple. "Go down to The Hollies on a Saturday afternoon and just ask for him at the door," he said. "He'll definitely be in there."

The Hollies WMC was huge public house on Wath-on-Dearne's Doncaster Road and one where its club steward – forty-five-year-old Cyril Dickinson, put a bullet in his temple on 29 June 1940.

Nowadays everything has changed and the main road, the club once stood on has been completely reprofiled. As such, the building is now situated on quite a large roundabout and has a dual purpose, being occupied by Arncliffe Veterinary Surgery and Rotherham Insurance Brokers. Back then however, a tight humpbacked bridge took what was Station Road (now the A633) over what was left of the Dearne & Dove Canal and to a staggered four-way junction. What I most recall about that junction is that there was a bus stop directly on it – and at either side, which always created a bottleneck of traffic.

As for my uncle Les, my dad was true to his word and he along with my uncle Paul, uncle John (Durose) and my grandad Sam (Durose) were in there, drinking beer, playing cards and watching the horse racing on TV.

"There's some kid here for you, Les," said one of the barmen.

You ought to have seen his face when he saw the carrier bag full of records I was holding. He was elated, and even more so come chucking out time.

That Saturday afternoon on 5 July 1980 was a complete eyeopener for me and was something that I learned from. I saw all four traits of the Durose psyche, and my dad wasn't even there. Loyalty, generosity, happiness, and family. I was immediately taken in as one of their own, which of course I was. It was here where both my granddad and uncle Les told me how to work out the handicaps for the horses taking part in each race and it was here where

I was shown the protective nature of the family – with our John making sure I was okay after seven half pints of Mackeson milk stout and Uncle Paul making sure I never lost any money whilst playing cards.

"He's fine," said our John when the barman came into the toilets to see me washing my face. "He's just waking himself up."

As for Uncle Paul, there had been fourteen of us playing a card game, using just three cards. It was a game known as Stop the Bus. The rules were simple in that you had to change one card or all three and after the game had moved around all the players, on the second pick up someone could halt the game by saying "Stop the Bus", before it came around to him again. The good thing about the game is that each of us had three lives at 10p a piece. After an hour or so there was just Uncle Paul and I left in the game and on him changing his card and throwing in the middle he duly stopped the bus. My hand was naff, but what he had done was make the three cards in the middle a bit special. It was a Queen, King, Ace (Aqua). He knew what he was doing, and I left the game with £4.20 (£21.47, circa 2020) in my pocket. It may seem nothing, but to me – a fifteen-year-old kid, it was everything.

Last orders were at 3.00 p.m. and all the family had left by then – however, my uncle Les had gone around to the bookmakers and put £25 (£127.79, circa 2020) on a horse which was running in the 2.55 p.m. Coral Eclipse Stakes at Sandown Park and we were left sat in the club watching the race on ITV, with very few people around. This was quite a wise decision as I have never seen a person's demeanour change as I had in those two minutes.

"El-Mana-Mou will win this," he winked. "It better do, or we'll be fucking walking home."

The horse started the race like some seaside donkey trailing at the back before bursting through the pack and nosing the finish line at 5-2. My uncle Les had just had a return of £87.50 (£447.25, circa 2020). That was £62.50 (£319.46, circa 2020) profit.

To say he was ecstatic was an understatement. He was literally bouncing off the walls and wouldn't shut up about it all the way to him getting off the bus opposite the shop at Bolton-on-Dearne's Mansion Park bus stop.

Fast-forward twenty-two years.

On 27 December 2002, I remember calling into The Dearne Hotel in St Andrews Square with a carrier bag in my hand and to have a few beers with two of my uncle Paul's kids – my cousins Paul and Steve (Durose). As it happened their mum (my auntie Anne) had called in to see me while I was there and had an orange juice.

Remember the Collingwood story and all the family calling in to see my dad?

"Uncle Les is coming up," our Paul told his mum.

"Good god, does he have to?" grizzled my auntie Anne.

Our Les came in and immediately copped sight of me.

"I've got something for you," I told him.

I had. We had just come back from New York and whilst I had been there, I had picked him up a CD boxset of Roger Miller along with a bottle of Wild Turkey Kentucky bourbon. "Can you remember that day when Ela-Mana-Mou won that race?" I winked, whilst passing him the carrier bag.

His bottom lip went, and he spent the next five minutes sat at the table in silence with a lump in his throat and browsing through this Roger Miller collection and just shaking his head.

"That's the quietest I've ever seen him," whispered my auntie Anne.

"I'll drink this tonight," he said regarding the Wild Turkey.

What was strange is on 12 November just two years earlier I had been sat in the exact same seat with my auntie Anne and my uncle Paul.

"It's our James," he tried to say as I walked into the pub. I say try, as he had contracted throat cancer and had already lost part of his tongue.

My wife had told me that I needed to see him. She was right, I did.

I remember the day well as there was some auction being held by members of the Bolton-on-Dearne Cabbage Club (allotment holders) and they were bidding on things like sprouts, carrots and other vegetables. Bar one bid – for flowers I think, I ended up buying the lot and giving them to my auntie Anne.

"You've never made as much money," Uncle Paul tried his best to shout over whilst doing a bit of boasting. "It's our James that's made you all that."

He was right. My presence had interrupted all the highly structured and peaceful bidding.

That was the last time I ever saw him, which was such a shame.

Cancer eventually got my uncle Les – however, whilst he had it, it never really took the edge off his rather colourful life. At over sixty years old, still defying death and part-immobilised, he still managed to drive from his sheltered accommodation at Highgate down to the end of Bolton-on-Dearne's Chapel Street on his mobility scooter and hurl a brick through his ex-girlfriend's window. Unfortunately for him he was arrested outside some commercial properties opposite the Methodist church – most notably the local undertakers.

That building at 45 Furlong Road had seen dead bodies long before it became a funeral parlour. When I had been a child, I remember a couple of shops being there – that of Allott & Spencer's, which provided school uniforms for Dearneside and Trevor Plane's butchers, the latter of which is still a business, but which now operates out of Doncaster's indoor market as Plane & Armstrong.

Long before that, however, the end building was an extraordinarily successful bakers and confectioners that was part of a huge plan and which was being run by a mother and daughter – Annie (nee Bashforth) and Doris Turnbull.

Now here is a story about family and which bar a tragedy, could have put Bolton-on-Dearne, well and truly on the map.

Doris, who was twenty-nine years of age, was one of five children from an extremely well-educated family from Wombwell, that through her mother and father's endeavour and to an extent through marriage, would become part of a business, which nowadays has an annual turnover of well over half a billion pounds and that forms part of something of a national tradition.

Doris had been seeing a man by the name of Peter Creighton who was both five years her senior and who would eventually go on to run a stone-fronted butcher's shop at 121 Furlong Road.

Creighton was a well-known local athlete, competing at various levels as a successful sprint cyclist and as such, was regarded by many as possessing quite the ego, which was something that was picked up on by the Editor of the *Green 'Un*, who had widely reported his conceited attitude.

"I advised her to have nothing to do with him," explained her mother.

It was sound advice, but advice which wasn't taken.

Doris had secretly been seeing the butcher for around three-and-a-half years and had become pregnant. He was informed of her situation and wanted absolutely nothing to do with it.

Around 4.30 a.m. on 23 April 1926, she wrote a short note before going downstairs into the bakehouse, where she duly stuck her head the gas oven.

Her shame at disgracing her family had been too much to bear.

"Peter knows all," the note read. "Ask him. I am sorry for Mother."

Peter certainly did know all and at a heated inquest into her death led by District Coroner Frank Allen, he flatly denied that they had ever been a couple.

The coroner had been furious at Creighton's shrug of the shoulder attitude and his one-word answers.

"So, I ask you again, have you been meeting her?" he stormed.

"Occasionally," he shrugged.

"Did she tell you that she thought she was in trouble?"

"Yeh, on Wednesday morning."

"Why did you not go openly to the girl and if you wanted to marry her, say so?"

"I didn't want to marry her."

"Is that all the explanation you can give?"

"I think she had been out with other people," he mumbled.

"That is always the tale," snapped the coroner.

Creighton just gave another shrug of his shoulders.

"That's a lie and you know it," fumed the coroner. "You've just admitted that she was a respectable woman."

Creighton said nothing.

"I don't propose to express my contempt for him," the coroner told the room. "I consider that he is directly responsible for this unfortunate girl's death and I am not going to waste any more words in expressing my opinion on such a man."

He then turned his attention to Creighton. "Go away I don't want anything to do with you."

Peter Creighton, however, had probably made the worst mistake of his life.

The Turnbull's had been one of those families that had been heavily reliant on the local mining industry and looking in from the outside appeared quite well-to-do. Doris's father – William, had been a tailor and gent's outfitter on Barnsley's vibrant Cheapside before setting up his own business at 7 Station Road, Wombwell. It was here that he accumulated just over £241 (£28,228, circa 2018) of debt before a bankruptcy order was taken out on him.

He explained that the crux of the problem had been trying to pay huge overheads, part of which was his rent at £28 and 10 shillings (£3,336, circa 2020) per annum at a time when cheap rail travel to Barnsley and Sheffield was taking the trade out of town.

I don't really think that was the problem – more of an excuse, as he was a man that apparently possessed too good business acumen and had surreptitiously moved his money through various channels, one of which was his wife.

His business whilst in Cheapside had folded prior to him moving to Wombwell. After that went belly-up, he set up yet another gentlemen's outfitters – this time at 54 Melton High Street, Wath-on-Dearne. This was a stone-fronted terrace shop near-opposite the Dearne Valley Christian Ministries Chapel, that has long since been demolished to make way for unsupported housing accommodation for the elderly.

All five Turnbull children followed his lead and set their stall out to become their own people – however, one could suppose it was with second eldest child, Elizabeth where the story is unearthed.

She and her younger brother Denis became school teachers – however, whereas the brother would go on to marry a teacher and become headmaster at a school near King's Lynn she would eventually change careers.

Her elder sister Harriet had married a baker by the name of Wilfred Crowcroft and opened a bakery in Conisbrough, whilst her other brother Arnold opened a pork butchers and bakery on Cranmer Street in Nottingham. As with Doris and their mother, there was a pattern emerging.

On 10 August 1919, Elizabeth had married a man who lived at 149 Doncaster Road, Wath-upon-Dearne by the name of Francis Elliot Warburton, who had been privately schooled yet worked underground in the mines as a qualified electrician. That, however, was just a trade for Francis to fall back on, as his intention was to become a master baker and that is exactly what he did. He and his wife then opened a bakery at 71 Barnsley Road, which is a building that still stands on the town's junction with Melton High Street.

What needs to be known is that his father's uncles were none other than Thomas and George Warburton – who were the founder and financier of Warburton's bakery over in Bolton. It was around the time of Doris's tragedy that the company were expanding its operations outside Lancashire and taking over several shops, and it is therefore very little surprise that one of those was none other than Crowcroft's Bakery in Conisbrough – and prior to Doris's suicide – the one at Bolton-on-Dearne.

It was around December 1984 that a bakery on Goldthorpe's Barnsley Road became targeted by the NUM.

It was a time of mistrust and mayhem.

The NCB had enticed a couple of bodies through the gates at the local collieries, with the mood in Thurnscoe being extremely tense.

Hickleton Main had had scabs working at the pit towards the end of the lockout of 1926 – however, fifty-eight years had passed and the village, had not so much become tight, but very well policed and not by the fucking authorities either. Bolton-on-Dearne wasn't a village with its own pit per se, but it was certainly very well placed. Wath Main was located on the periphery of its Concrete Canyon; Manvers Main was at the other side of its ten-arched viaduct on Mexborough Road; Highgate Main Colliery was just over half a mile's stride from Carfield Primary School; and Barnburgh Main and Goldthorpe Colliery were both in walking distance.

It was around this time that a few dozen lads had been marshalling the gates at Hickleton Main when a relatively new Lada Riva drove past the bottom of Tudor Street before screeching to a halt outside the colliery's administrative offices. Some of the lads had been hurling abuse as it had been driven past. The next thing I know is that a few of them began charging at it and throwing a volley of missiles at the vehicle, with a half-brick completely taking out the back windscreen.

"Who was that?" I asked, as the driver of the car obviously had a change of thought and sped off.

"Mickey Ryf," Col Tutin told me.

"A fucking scab deputy," another exclaimed.

At that time, he was just a name and therefore a person that I didn't know.

I had heard that he had offered to cross the picket line early in the strike, but for what reason I don't really know, other than his complete arrogance – as being an Official, he was a member of the NACODS Union and as such, getting paid his basic salary.

If you ever look at the 1960s band Manfred Mann, just check out the keyboard player who was both the group's founder and who it is named after and that will give you an idea of what the man looked like. Tall and lean with glasses and a beard. More importantly however, he wasn't a local lad. He had been born in suburbs of Bromley in Kent and had worked in the mines out in South Africa, before coming back to the UK and getting employment at Hickleton Main. That being the case he had little or no idea of the setup of the village, nor how its East end worked.

I would get to know him just before I left British Coal (NCB) and for my part, I thought him quite an engaging chap. My last recollection of him was of him spotting for me and watching the exposed tail gate rip, whilst I had been changing the oil in the return sprocket of an Armoured Flexible Conveyor on B47s face at Markham Main Colliery.

Around that time, he had lived on Thurnscoe's Shepherd Lane and drove a Reliant Scimitar. One story I recall was him telling me about this restaurant which was located close to Whitely Bridge that he and his soon-to-be wife, Janet (nee Copeman) often went to.

As stated, during latter months of 1984 there was a lot of bitterness and resentment around.

Two houses got badly damaged on Ingsfield Lane and it came as no surprise that I knew people within both of them. Paul Dyson and Darren Mitchell – part of Dearneside's Class of 1981.

"The police are appealing for witnesses to two incidents at a working miners' house at Bolton-on-Dearne," wrote Malcolm Pithers of *The Guardian*.

"It was attacked, and a brick thrown through one of its windows late just before midnight (1 December) and just after, an upstairs bedroom in the house was set on fire. Paint was also splashed on the outside walls and more windows smashed. The miner and his family have left to live with relatives."

"A working miner's family were moved out of their home today and extra police were drafted in after violence erupted in a pit village," stated the *Liverpool Echo*. "South Yorkshire Police said the miner – they have not named him, had already moved out because of threats."

What was strange is that just before all this occurred, I remember walking from Thurnscoe and down to my grandma Carman's and whilst I was walking off Highgate Lane and up on to the old railway embankments that once carried the Wath Branch Line, I saw a bus with mesh covered windows pull up and some guy, disembark and run up the embankment straight past me.

That person, I was told, lived at 58 Ingsfield Lane. The house that had been hit.

It was the closest I had ever been to a scab, although within five years that would certainly change.

It is fair to say that no-one trusted anyone and even some of the innocent were getting ostracised.

F. Brown's was a bakery and confectioners that had been in Goldthorpe for as long as I can recall. As with Peverelli's on Thurnscoe's Houghton Road I used to love the smell that emanated from the building, and even more so, whilst I was inside. For me, there is nothing like an uncut loaf of bread with a burnt crust, and Brown's did them to perfection.

I look at the mass-produced bread and pastries that are on sale from outlets such as Gregg's, Cooplands and Fullers and there is just no comparison. Mass marketing has a lot to answer for.

Brown's had been contributing to the NUM all the way through the strike – to both the soup kitchens and food parcels, and then out of the blue they said that they couldn't contribute its quota anymore.

The NUM's argument was simple. Do it or you will lose your business and notices went up urging miner's and their families to stop using Brown's. It was nothing short of a mafia type shake-down, which in my mind fucking stunk.

The bakery wasn't a bottomless pit where it could just give unlimited produce away, which was a fact that the Trotskyites at local level could never get their head around.

Bryan Robson, one of the senior NUM delegates at Hatfield Main, once told me in later life: "You shouldn't have to pay for anything. Everything should be free. You should be able to go and get anything you want."

How that fucking works I have no idea and I told him as much. However, it was a statement that was mirrored by one of these smartly dressed and articulately spoken left-wing anarchists Tim and I had bumped into outside Carcroft Workshops during early autumn.

"We should just be able to go out to work, oil a few cogs and everything should be free," he told me.

What a fucking moron.

The NUM had no idea of checks and balances and you only had to see that at the very top level – therefore, hoping for someone with some sort of business acumen further down the line was a definite non-starter.

I get that fact that the business was built around the self-sustaining mining communities of the eastern Dearne Valley but the answer itself is in that sentence. F Brown's wasn't there as some charity, it was a business.

"Just give what you can, and we'll always be grateful," would have been the best course of action.

It was around this time that Col had had some sort of brainwave.

Even though he had left me to get arrested in Goldthorpe, he along with Carl and John had kept me fully-focused, and my mind occupied, whether it being from hewing coal out of some embankment or railway sidings, going down to the soup kitchen at The Docket, or just going backwards and forwards to Drax Power Station on a weekend. They were all great lads.

Col had managed to throw on the sick.

"How can you throw on the sick?" I asked. "We're not even working."

"Half these fuckers who go down the soup kitchen are on it," he told me.

At that point in time I had never been on the sick – ever.

Col was under the doctors at the Welfare Road practice opposite The Docket. My downfall, however, was that I'd had to register with the doctors when I lived in Barnby Dun, as I'd managed to pull my back after working on some dint on Hickleton Main's P81s after I had switched shifts.

Col had managed to swing it with depression.

"How's that work?" I asked.

"I just told them about me and Joanne splitting up, having no money to see the kid and that I'm really down."

"You told them you were suicidal?" I inquired.

"No, fuck that – just depressed."

"So, how much do you get?"

He told me he would get £27 (£92, circa 2020) a week after standing the first three days.

To me, that was a monumental amount of money – however, there was a downside. As I have already stated, Barnby Dun was absolutely nothing like Thurnscoe – and that included its doctors.

As I was in Barnby Dun, I called at my dad's and informed him of my plan of action and Paula's retort had been exactly the same as mine. "How can you throw on the sick when you're on strike?"

Getting that sick note was the hardest bit of graft that I had ever had to do. It was a very professional-looking female GP and would she fucking hell sign it. "I hear what you are saying – but I can't see how me giving you a sick note will help when you aren't working."

I obviously didn't like making out that I was being no different to some fresh off-the-boat parasite and said everything I could without mentioning the fact that I'd be getting money.

After being finally handed the note, I felt like my uncle Les had after Ela-Mana-Mou had nosed past Lester Pigott's Gregorian into first place over four years earlier. Ecstatic wasn't in it. We would be eating turkey at Christmas, Mrs Cratchit!

The first thing on my agenda was to deposit the note at the DHSS office next to The Comrades in Goldthorpe and nip down to the Welfare Road doctor's surgery to register with someone more gullible than the rather assertive female doctor who had examined my eyes, ears and throat, and taken my blood pressure before insisting on a polygraph test.

"Who do you want to be registered with, love? Doctor Dutta or Doctor Dehadray?" asked the woman behind the glass partition.

"Who's the best?" I inquired.

She just looked at me. Rather blankly if I'm being honest.

"Doctor Dehadray's very good," she shrugged.

I made sure that the next time I visited that I would ask for Dr Dutta, and that is exactly what I did.

The run up to Christmas was strange in that there was nothing really to look forward to – however, once the sick money started coming in along with the weekend pickets and the weekly rent rebate, I wasn't that bad off at all, and at times I was getting nearly £50 (£170.39, circa 2020) a week.

I had gone from near starvation to not being frightened to answer the door.

During early summer I'd had a bailiff call at the house. He had been instructed by the Co-operative Finance at Balloon Street to see if my circumstances were as I had told them, and to itemise the other contents in the house that I actually owned, including the quid television set my grandma had bought me from the jumble sale. To a wet-behind-the-ear nineteen-year-old kid that had never had to duck and dive from anyone who wanted paying, it was as scary as hell.

The weekend pickets at Drax were interesting as Carl had given me something to think about with his mention of the *Unhappy House*, which was a large boarded-up property on the Main Street of a village called Pollington that we regularly passed through.

I remember it vividly as just prior he had been moaning about these so-called new "trendy groups" whilst The Smiths' *How Soon is Now* had been playing on late-evening radio: *You shut your mouth – How can you say – I go about things the wrong way?*

"Unhappy house?" I shrugged.

"Yeh, some bloke killed all his family in it," Carl explained.

A mere fourteen days into the New Year of 1984, firefighters had broken into the blazing home of thirty-nine-year-old David Cook only to find that he had murdered his family. He had killed his wife Pauline (nee Sykes) and two children – twelve-year-old Ben and ten-year-old Nathan with a shotgun. What made it more macabre than it already was, was the fact that the children's cries for help could be heard by neighbours.

After wiping out his family he had set fire to the property before turning the gun on himself.

Why he did that, I have no idea. In my mind it smarts of selfishness and cowardice. It was mentioned that he had just been made redundant – however, a story came out about six months down the line that suggested the murderer had a link with a woman down in Stratford-on-Avon.

Remember my mention of Mexborough's Adwick Road?

Well that is a place you could take your pick of numerous macabre incidents, but I suppose the one that stands out is something very similar to the events at Carl's *Unhappy House*.

Around 350 yards up from the A6023 Doncaster Road roundabout and on the same side as Mexborough Montagu, there are five red bricked villas which are formed in two blocks and all of which possess small front gardens. Nowadays, they are numerically identified – No's 41 to 47 – however, when they had originally been built, they were identified solely by their names – one of which was Scarrington Villa.

Its occupiers were a couple just into their thirties, that had moved to the area from Barnsley.

Walter Henry Trubshaw had married (Annie) Beatrice Dobson in 1899, when he had been a Cashier and Commercial Salesman at her father's glass bottle manufacturing company J W Dobson (Limited). He was also a Sergeant with the Barnsley 'C' Division of the Queen's Own Yorkshire Dragoons – a yeomanry regiment of the British Army who were based at Nether Hall in Doncaster. A 1900s version of the Territorial Army, if you like.

He moved to Mexbrorough after Beatrice's father's company ran into financial difficulties and before it eventually amalgamated with Jabez Nall & Co (Limited) to form Dobson and Nall (Limited). It was here that he was given a similar role as both Clerk and Commercial Traveller, in the employ of Messrs. Peter Waddington and Sons at the New Don Glass Works down on the town's Cliff Street.

He had come up to the area from Napton-on-the-Hill in the Southam area of Warwickshire along with his elder brother by six years – Howard, who for a short time was employed at Mexborough's Pitt Street School (now New Pastures Primary School).

He and Beatrice had two young sons, who it was said they adored – however, nothing is ever like it seems.

Around 3.00 a.m. on Tuesday, 15 November 1904, their fifteen-year-old domestic servant – a girl by the name of Ethel Hill – was awoken by screaming coming from the landing, whereby she jumped out of bed to see Walter, his arm raised high and ready to smash his wife around the skull with some form of heavy cudgel. On him seeing the domestic, he dragged his wife into the front bedroom where Ethel heard what she later described as "horrible thuds" as the husband and father battered in the heads of his wife and two children – Gordon and Walter Kenneth – who were aged just four years old and ten months, respectively.

The screams and noise caused by Trubshaw's deadly work was heard out on the street, with the haunting cries of "Don't, Daddy, don't" and "Die, Beatrice love, die", awaking neighbours Bill and Lily Ellis.

Realising that something serious was happening, Bill and his wife hurriedly dressed before hearing knocking on their door. It was Ethel Hill, who was totally in shock and unable to give any account of what was happening.

The couple proceeded next door and on them going up the stairs they saw Beatrice lying on the floor, with her head both severely battered and covered in blood, whilst on the bed the eldest child laid unconscious, he too in a pool of blood. As was the baby in an adjoining cot. All three were still alive and struggling for survival – however, the husband was nowhere to be seen. That was until a they heard a loud thud.

Bill Ellis tried to force open the bathroom door – however, this was kept shut by the body of the murderer, who had collapsed on the floor. When entry was eventually made, he was found with a huge cut down the left side of his throat, and a blood-stained razor lying beside him.

When two doctors arrived all the victims were breathing but unconscious, each of whom had had their skulls fractured, and were sadly beyond human aid, with the last dying about 5.20 a.m.

Trubshaw had been described as both a loving husband and an affectionate father as well as an expert swordsman in the Dragoons. His social life was taken up by being actively involved with the church and he was even the warden's assistant at the Parish Church of St John the Baptist down on the banks of the Dearne & Dove Canal. The only explanation anyone could offer was that the man's health had been failing for several months and his children had suffered from sickness, with the elder one of the two having to undergo an operation for tonsillitis. It appeared that this had preyed on his mind and he had become depressed. But to murder your wife and two children and then commit suicide in some sudden paroxysm of insanity – just because you're a bit pissed off?

It had similar hallmarks to Harold Marsden murdering his daughter before trying to commit suicide. Harold, however, had witnessed the horrors of the First World War and had come back suffering from shell shock. The closest Walter had got to war was being Master of Ceremonies for various officers' bashes that he had helped arrange.

Harold had been a distinguished soldier who had served in The Royal Army Medical Corps (RAMC) and had been heavily involved in the Battle of Delville Wood (Bois d'Elville), which was a series of engagements that made up Battle of the Somme during the summer to late summer of 1916. Two years later he had been badly poisoned during a chemical attack and following a bomb blast in August 1918, suffered shell shock, whereby he ended up being hospitalised for ten days.

Born on Sandymount Road in what at that time was the Fulwood area of Sheffield in 1891, his family relocated to the Mexborough area as his father Luke, got a job as a miner at Denaby Main. Harold followed in his father's footsteps and started out at the colliery, firstly as a Pony Driver and then as a Fitter – however, a few things must have given him reason to enlist in the Army on 20 February 1913.

On 9 July 1912, and in the midst of all the unrest, the country witnessed yet another mining disaster – this time at Denaby, following two separate explosions at its relatively new Cadeby Main Colliery, which ultimately caused the death of ninety-one miners.

It is hard to imagine hundreds upon hundreds of people in an area that you know, swarming down from the rows upon rows of terraced houses and gathering at the pithead, either in a bid to help or just waiting for news of a loved one. And afterwards the sombre and grave sight of all the horse-drawn hearses moving through Mexborough, Denaby and Conisbrough – with the main procession headed by the Denaby Band of the St John's Ambulance Brigade playing the rather haunting Dead March from Handel's *Saul*.

For one man, thirty-three-year-old Frank Wood of 2 Braithwell Street, Denaby, it all became too much, and he committed suicide by throwing himself in the River Don – leaving behind his wife Eva (nee Caton) and two daughters. Frank had helped bring the bodies to the surface, one of which had been not only his sister's husband, but his best friend – Ben Ward of 1 Tickhill Street, Denaby.

My wife's great grandfather, William Breedon would marry the widow of one of the victims of the disaster – Annie Stribley in 1925 – a man who would die in 1933 after fracturing his spine following a roof fall at Denaby Main Colliery.

Her great grandfather had had a hard life and had already lost his wife Mary Ann (nee Masters) at thirty-two years of age along with two of his daughters – Elsie at twelve years old, and Ethel just two months before her second birthday.

As for Harold Marsden, he became heavily involved on the Western Front and whilst on leave from the trenches on 16 April 1916, he married a girl from 6 Northcliff Road, Conisbrough by the name of Ada Farmery, who was some five years older than him. Between them they set up home across the road from Harold's parents at 3 Pitt Street and had five children – Mary (b. 1918), Nora (b. 1920), Ada (b. 1922), Norman (b. 1924) and David (b. 1927).

On being discharged from the army, some years after the Great War in March 1925, he went back to work at Denaby Main, where shortly after he suffered a serious head injury, putting him in hospital and keeping him off work for several weeks. This was something that gave him a five-inch scar across his head. He then began having major problems with his vision, so much so, on 30 July 1928 he went to see Dr John James Huey at his Ash Mount surgery on Doncaster Road and duly collapsed, having what the Irish-born physician described as some form of violent paroxysm.

Just a few days later at around 3.55 a.m., the majority of Pitt Street were awoken by screams of "Help – get us out – he's gone mad!"

Harold had got out of bed to go downstairs and get some Andrews Liver Salts. He never returned to the bedroom where his wife and youngest three children were sleeping and instead went into the back bedroom where his eldest two daughters, Mary and Norma had been.

On his wife hearing a commotion she got out of bed to investigate and what greeted her was nothing short of horrific. Her husband had completely severed the head of his eldest child, Mary from her torso with a cut-throat razor before proceeding to do the same to himself by slitting his own throat.

His wife struggled with him, managing to retrieve the other child from the bedroom, whilst suffering slashes to her left wrist and began screaming and banging on walls. This alerted not only her mother-in-law Florence (nee Fletcher), who still lived opposite at No 2 but her next-door neighbours who managed to break down the door.

Harold's wife, bleeding heavily, both dazed and confused and in a state of semi-collapse, managed to get the surviving children downstairs whilst neighbour Reg Atkinson helped remove them around to his house.

"Oh, Harold what have you done, love?" exclaimed his mother on looking at the sight of the blood drenched sheets and her son who was by now rocking on the edge of the bed with a gaping Y-shaped wound in his throat. He had also been mumbling senseless gibberish and chewing his tongue, saying that he had been stabbed three times in the chest, before putting his arms around her and inconsolably groaning. She put a pillow on the floor for him to lie on and it was then she noticed the truly horrific sight of her decapitated granddaughter, Mary.

By the time the other neighbour, Ernest Robbins got to the bedroom, Harold was in a state bordering on collapse and had been both incoherent and weak from the loss of blood – however, he tried to revive him by throwing water over the gaping wound in his throat. This managed to bring him around somewhat and he made a fearful noise before saying: "Over the top boys and the best of luck."

The police were soon on the scene and duly arrested him.

The strangest thing about the events on 3 August 1928, was that according to his wife, she and her husband had never had a cross word between them and locally it was well-noted that he was an extremely good father and doted on his children.

Dr Hugh Grierson, the eminent psychiatric specialist, who was instrumental in the high-profile case of Neville Heath, the man who was hanged by Albert Pierrepoint for the sadistic murders of Margery Gardener and Doreen Marshall in 1946, told the court that Marsden was suffering from melancholy-depressing insanity.

Harold looking both grey and drawn, was sentenced at Leeds Assizes on 4 December 1928, where he was found guilty of murder, but insane – and was ordered to be detained at His Majesties Pleasure.

I suppose you can mend a broken leg, but when the problem is in your head?

"How can you be fucking depressed?" was John's response regarding my following Col's lead in his ultimate bid for survival.

John was the one who questioned everything.

It had seemed an age since the dark days of summer and that horrible afternoon sat in my parent's camper van down in Winchester. That had been the point when I had been at my lowest. So, who was John to say what I was and what I wasn't?

"It's no different than being a scab," he candidly added.

And this was a kid who had been getting fortnightly payments from the DHSS for being on his mining engineering course.

Did I kick back and argue? I always kicked back and argued.

During December he asked me if I fancied going with him on the morning picket run to Drax Power Station, as Tracy Greaves' brother, who he generally travelled with, was having a week off. To me that was £3 (£10.22, circa 2020) per day, which added £15 (£51.12, circa 2020) to weekly my earnings, so of course I wanted to go.

This was one hundred percent John. Argumentative, condescending, sanctimonious and often aloof but the reality of it was – he could be a very good lad.

I can still recite all the songs on the tape cassette that he played in his beige Morris Ital, which he had compiled himself whilst listening to Radio One – the main reason being, that he sang along to every one of them.

He was an interesting kid in that being a bit of a petrolhead he had seen loads of live acts – mainly rock bands such as UFO, AC/DC and Thin Lizzy, but he had actually gone to see Wham at Sheffield City Hall. He told me that after the tenth time of listening to his rendition of Careless Whisper!

"Wham – what were they like?"

That was a fucking mistake.

"Let me take you to the place, where membership's a smiling face, brush shoulders with the stars… where strangers take you by the hand and welcome you to wonderland, from beneath their panama-a-as…" he sang.

I just gave a shrug of my shoulders.

"Me and Tracy went the other year," he said. "They had a DJ to support them."

I remember a Fifth form (Year 11) teacher – Mrs Foster, telling me that she had seen The Beatles there in 1964 and I told him as much.

"Don't you like 'em?" he asked.

"Who, Wham? No, I think they're shite."

"Club Tropicana, drinks are free, fun and sunshine, there's enough for everyone," he continued.

He had a great voice, but I had to admit it wore a bit thin by the end of the week.

Col was the same – however, his repertoire was much more bearable: "Stab a sorry heart, with your favourite finger, paint the whole world blue and stop your tears from stin-g-ing."

Maybe I was depressed.

December was a strange month, as we knew everything was coming to an end. All the violence had been meted out during those heady days of October and November – and the fact that we now had a scab at Hickleton Main meant that we weren't really getting sent out to any other pit. Perhaps it was a blessing in disguise as looking back at it, someone could have been killed as things had got that out of hand. Well, someone nearly did get killed.

Exactly fifteen years earlier – December 1969 – I had been a blond-haired sparkly-eyed little lad amongst many other similar kids in my class in Houghton Road Infants, when I witnessed one of the most tender of moments.

I vividly recall two elder girls coming into our classroom – I think one was Francesca (Frankie) Barwick's sister – Jackie, however, I could be wrong, and our teacher Mrs Gilbert asking us to quietly sit down on the wooden floor close to the big rocking horse. The two girls sat on two chairs and sang to us, and after they had completed their song, Mrs Gilbert told them how beautiful they had sung. She then went on to meticulously explain what the song had been about. I remember it like it was yesterday. There wasn't a dry eye in the class. That song? Rolf Harris's *Two Little Boys*.

Half those little lads sat there listening would go on to work at Hickleton Main and half of those were the ones fighting with police outside The Pit Shop on the morning of 22 November 1984.

Everything we did or had done was born out of frustration. Frustration with Thatcher, frustration with McGregor, frustration with Scargill, frustration with the scabs and frustration with ourselves. Just frustration.

My home at 16 Briton Square had a revolving door where people came and went, and due to the fact that I could now afford necessities like bread, tea and coffee and of course due the amount of coal we were hewing which meant that there was generally always a fire in, I always had company.

Col finally ended up with my orange striped settee as my mum gave me her Dralon upholstered three-piece suite. I say finally, as that orange suite had nearly more miles on the clock than John Gratton's Morris Ital. It had travelled from a bungalow on Green Gate Close in Bolton-on-Dearne – to my house – then up to a house on Cromwell Street that John and Tracy were supposedly going to move into – before going down to No 8 across the road. The reason being? John had been ceremoniously dumped.

"Her dad was great about it," John explained regarding the break-up with Tracy. "He just came over and said 'Look, she doesn't want to be with you anymore'."

How that was "being great" about it, I have no idea. I suppose you would have to ask John about that one.

It was the first of many times that Tracy would want out, which was a shame, as whilst she was with him, he was a lot better kid than when she wasn't.

There was an upside to his getting the elbow in that I went into the house and removed all the double sockets and put them in mine. In fact, it was around this time when I began to start thinking of taking more of an interest in the house.

My (step)dad came down and Artex-ed the kitchen, which was one of the stupidest things I ever did, as when I found out how easy it was to apply – nearly everything got splattered with the stuff. It wasn't as bad as over at Debbie Davidson's house, however – her dad had even done the doors, to such an extent, they must have weighed a fucking ton.

Nevertheless, the house began to look quite homely and on the Friday afternoon 21 December 1984, Carl, Col, John and myself sat down at the table in my kitchen and ate fish, chips and peas and downed around four cans of Kestrel lager apiece. "I wish Margaret Thatcher could see us now," grinned John.

Yeh, I bet she'd be right jealous, I thought.

The thing was – he really meant it.

It had been a strange year and so full of change. For me that is. For my (step)dad however, it was a case of more of the same.

I called at their house two days later to see him both pissed out of his head and stumbling about the kitchen. "He's a right drunken pig," grizzled my sister. "He's drunk a full bottle of whiskey down at my grandma's (Ellis) and nearly got run over by the 226."

I carried him upstairs to bed where he began rambling with one of the things he said, being: "And she's been with him again. I've seen them."

Unfortunately, my sister overheard him. "Is my mam having an affair?" asked our Joanne.

"No," I lied. "He's just drunk."

This would be the **only** time I would ever hear him mention it.

He had bent over backwards to give her what she wanted. A new car, a mobile home, a new three-piece suite.

"I always thought him a bit thick," my auntie Ann (Carman) said regarding my (step)dad, after I had first left home.

Maybe she could have chosen her words a little better, but sometimes women, especially the wives of miners, can have a brutal honesty about them.

The return to work at Markham Main, Armthorpe (c. John Sturrock)

Top. A post woman makes her way across the debris during the aftermath of the rioting at Brampton Bierlow (Cortonwood Colliery) on November 1984 (c. John Sturrock) Bottom. Behind the police lines outside the entrance into Cortonwood Colliery (c. Rotherham Advert

23. 1985

I spent the early hours of 1985 in Doncaster Royal Infirmary waiting for my (step)dad to have his head stitched up. The bitterness and resentment in the village had escalated to such an extent, that the Hickleton Main Official's Club (The Spit & Whisper) had been daubed with graffiti a couple of weeks prior to Christmas and on New Year's Eve several uninvited striking miners entered the building and an altercation took place. From what I was told, my (step)dad had tried to get between a striking miner by the name of Kevin (Bud) Green and Phil Crooks – the grandson of Charlie – the man who attempted to murder his wife on King Street in 1911, and ended up getting kicked in the head. It was nothing more than a superficial wound, but one which would dearly cost the miner. Not only would he be sentenced to twelve months in prison – he would also lose his job. It was a very stupid act by a very foolish person. I had seen him get arrested on my first day picketing. He was a livewire that is for sure, but that is all he was.

I recall after his release and of us training with Hickleton Main FC in the summer of that year and of him being on the opposite side. "I thought we were supposed to be playing fucking football," he snarled at me, after I had put the ball between two cones, which had formed the goals… and from a rather outrageous distance.

"Watch him," Andy Moore had whispered to me afterwards. "I've heard him say that he's on about doing you."

Did he? Nope.

That New Year's Eve I had been tasked to act as minder of sorts up at my mum and (step)dad's house as my sister had wanted to have a party and the only way that party happening was on the proviso that I was there, therefore I never had a drink. This was quite a good decision as I recall having to take some fifteen-year-old lad by the name of Glen Freeman back his mum and dad's – Ray and Maureen (nee Cutts), after he'd had too much to drink.

His dad was brilliant. "Come on, lad," he said, as we tried to take him into the house.

All Glenn wanted to do was sit down under the back window, whilst all his mum was doing was giggling at her son, who was continually talking gibberish.

"How much has he had to drink?" his dad asked me.

"Not much – about two or three cans of lager."

Our future, eh? But what a lovely family.

I got back from the hospital in the early hours to see four not so-wise monkeys sat on the stairs – my sister – two of her mates along with the girlfriend that I never wanted.

"What's up?" I asked.

"You don't want to go in there," whispered the latter, as regards me not going into the room.

My mum's idea of a lovely house would never had made the pages of *Homes & Garden*, that's for sure. It certainly wasn't the worst house I had been in, however, it certainly wasn't the best. With NCB houses you were always limited. You can knock them through, stick the bathroom upstairs and pay a fortune for a new kitchen. However, no matter how you try to modernise them and how much money you chuck at the project, just looking through the window and over at the neighbour's tells you what a futile task it is. You can put a pig in an Armani suit, but it'll always be a pig. The upshot is that it will always be a pit house. Is it a snobbishness or pretentiousness on my part? It could be seen as that, but it's not. I spent a huge part of my life and have watched my children grow up in a pit house. The reality is that I have never forgotten where I came from. I am like many ex-miners of my age in that I have just moved on. Strangely though, out of our so-called *strike clique*, the only one who still lives in a pit house is Tim. His is a prefabricated structure with the self-same design as those in Thurnscoe and Bolton-on-

Dearne and which was once part of Toftshaw Moor Colliery's new model village in the Tong Road suburb of Bradford.

"He's got more nests than a bloody cuckoo," his granddad once told me.

Joe wasn't wrong.

I say strangely, as Tim once spoke quite out of turn about our respective situations after British Coal's lawyers from Nabarro Nathenson had been camped outside my house on Briton Square trying to serve us – us meaning he and I – with a writ.

"I've got more to lose than you," he told me.

This was a snide reference to the fact that I lived in a pit house and he at that time did not. There is, however, certainly more to that story.

As for my mum's house, not only was the house held together by Artex, the colour coordination was also enough to drive a sane person well and truly over the edge. I suppose you could partly blame the era that we lived in, but it wasn't just that. My mum's idea of style was never something that would catch on. As kids, half the time she dressed us like dorks.

"What are you wearing – a suit?" asked one of the younger kids off Primrose Close, whilst we were playing on the waste ground off Billingley View.

My mum had made me wear a bright orange two-piece number that she had previously bought me for a family wedding – Uncle Rob or Steve's, not sure which. It was an orange waistcoat and trousers combo, the latter of which had twenty-five-inch flares. Stick a white polyester polo neck on to compliment it and I looked like some fucking extra from Jason King's *Department S*. I would certainly never have been run over in it, that's for sure.

Three splash-Artexed walls were coloured buttermilk, whilst the wall where the open fire stood had been roughly Artexed and painted brown – or scorched earth as my mum candidly described it. The fireplace was a mixture of beige and off beige varnished bricks which was completed by a dogshit-green slate fireplace which one of the outer tiles tended to come off whenever the room got vacuumed, which seeing as they had two dogs and a menagerie of stray cats was at least four or five times a day. Since I'd had the beige Dralon three-piece suite handed down to me, my mum had procured a new one, which could only be described as being an off-pink, whilst the carpet was an array of what seemed like a hundred different colours. We didn't have a room door, my (step)dad had created an arch – again using Artex, and the curtain rail was extended from the front window and over the arch for the heavy brown curtains to create something of a door. It was behind that so-called *door* where all the activity had been coming from during the very early hours of 1985.

I pulled curtain back to see Col on my mum's new sofa and with one of my sister's not yet sixteen-year-old friends – Helen Atkinson.

It was the start of a great romance. That was until her dad found out.

Helen was the daughter of Charlie and June (nee Hillman) and was a lovely young girl. They lived on Rectory Lane – the last street as you leave Thurnscoe for Great Houghton. She had an elder brother by the name of Chris, who was either an electrician or fitter at Hickleton Main and who had once told my (step)dad the story of someone going around to their house to borrow her dad's shiny new ladders.

"Who was it?" her dad had asked.

"I don't know," Helen replied. "Just some man."

Charlie never did see those ladders again.

In my mind it was Helen who helped Col exorcise the failure of his marriage, even though it kept on getting brought up – especially by her dad.

"He's an alright bloke," Col explained. "He offered me a beer, told me that he knew I was married and asked if I minded not seeing his daughter again."

That wasn't all he said – it was just the edited highlights that Col furnished me with.

He had managed to see her a couple of weeks before it ended, which by that time, I had finally dumped my unwanted girlfriend, even though she had completely refused to accept it.

It was around this time that my ex-girlfriend made a fleeting reappearance back into my life and wherever she appeared there was generally some sort of fucking drama. Needless to say, that is exactly what happened.

Although I was generally hanging around with Col, Carl and John – or each of them individually, I still saw Billy and one particular day, he came to the house with his girlfriend, whilst the other three were in the empty big bedroom upstairs strumming an electric guitar Carl had managed to borrow of Stuart Keen. You could tell that there was some tension between them, but that was nothing new, as the *handsome bastard* had once candidly told me in Doncaster's North Bus station.

Paula Hole was the daughter of Stuart and Pat (nee (Smith) and lived at 15 Richmond Road – a well-kept semi-detached property topside of the Big Lamp. At just seventeen-years-old she had either completed or was ready for completing her 'A' Levels and from what I understood, ready for starting work at a bank. She was certainly getting restless – that is for sure, whilst her boyfriend – just like the rest of us, was on a road to nowhere and trying his damnedest to hold on to her. It was something that I had seen time and time again – more recently with my son and one of his ex-girlfriends.

"I told you – I want to go home," she had told him on their arrival.

"What's the matter?" I asked.

"I haven't had anything to eat," she moaned.

"No bother," I said, and I set about making her some scrambled eggs and toast, whilst Billy shot upstairs to be with the others.

I was getting mixed signals from her as she ate and one thing that I did pick up on, was that Billy's days with her were well and truly numbered.

"You didn't do anything with her, did you?" Billy asked me afterwards.

It was a strange question to ask, but one that it is fair to say that I had been asked a few times.

I thought her a nice, highly intelligent and witty girl, but the girlfriends or former girlfriends of any of my friends, especially best friends, are totally off limits. Was there something in what he said, or did it all boil down to his insecurity? I could not say. What I will say is that I have never ever let myself be put in any position for any mate to suspect that. Read on.

When we went out on Friday nights it was a case of us going to Barnsley and then back to Swinton – however, the last place I wanted to be was somewhere where I could be stalked by some deluded and recently dumped girlfriend, therefore we came back to Thurnscoe, where I would be stalked by a deranged ex-girlfriend. The irony about it, is that we rarely went out around Thurnscoe – if ever. What it did do however, had put us all in the proverbial shop window. Everyone knew who we were, although very few had seen us out before.

The nearest I had come to a night out in Thurnscoe had been in the Dog End of The Fairway during the previous July and nipping down to The Docket for a game of snooker with John, who introduced me to his favourite tipple, Lager Snakebite – and what a drink that was. Four of those and I made as much sense as young Glenn Freeman had.

For some reason Billy had tagged along with us that night. It was an eyeopener for him and it certainly wasn't a one-off either. I have often found that when you mention Barnsley outside of Yorkshire everyone sneers at the thought of the northern mining town as being some spit and sawdust kind of place, which is so far from the truth. Back in 1984, even though half its men were on strike, it was such a lovely vibrant place. No-one was up their own arse and you could get along with almost everyone. I would put it head and shoulders above anywhere in the country, it was that good.

On getting into The Fairway, I was immediately approached by my ex-girlfriend who not only wanted to know where I had been, but more importantly who I was with.

Whilst I had been with her, she had used her philosophy of divide and rule, so I was kept away from anyone I could get close to. "You've got to come back to our house – my mam would love to see you," she said.

"Yeh, I bet," I told her.

What was strange about this, is that at the time she was seven months into a relationship with Terry Rich.

With her gone, I was now a completely different person. I had a life. However, for her to judge how far she had progressed, she needed me as some pathetic yardstick – you know, to show that it was she that had moved forward and I who had not.

I am sure she expected me to collapse after we parted, but that wasn't the case. I had felt very alone, that's for sure, but that's as much as it was. Things might seem black, but they aren't really. Stick some time and a bit of tarmac in between and you will get to where you want to go. However, me not taking her on that night created a huge problem for Billy. To try and get my attention she hit on him, and he took the bait.

"Fucking hell, J – you see that?" Col gasped.

I saw, but I just shook my head.

"I'm definitely fucking taking her home tonight," a rather bullish Billy grinned, as he came over.

Col looked at me, but I said nothing.

Billy was playing with fire and was well and truly out of his depth.

As for me, I had to show him that it was I who was the one calling the shots and that I couldn't have anyone taking the piss. I could have hit him, which I was more than capable of doing – however, that would have been a huge show of weakness, therefore that could never happen. It was a case of me biting my bottom lip and moving to take everything from him, which was something that I have done many times throughout my life. Rule one: Someone moves to *hurt* you – you take everything off them.

I made the move and ended up taking my ex-girlfriend home, which really pissed Billy off. However, that wasn't it. That was nowhere near it.

A few weeks later I would do the exact same with his girlfriend, which would be something that would see him refuse to speak to me for the next fourteen years. It is fair to say that my actions literally broke him. To see a twenty-year-old lad that I had grown-up with, leave my house in tears after calling me a bastard, is not something that I will ever forget. It was he, however, who made the first move and not I. Paula had not only told him that I had taken her home, she had also given him a vivid and detailed account of all the events into that night… and the few days afterwards, before hitting him with the big one – in that she was pregnant, and it was mine.

Was she?

No, she had been lying.

It is conceited of me to say that the lie had dual purpose – to both rankle him and to try and keep me interested – but that is exactly what it was. With me, she not so much pushed, kicked, and screamed to try and get what she wanted, she went about it quite differently. She was extremely bright and as such, both calculative and constructive in her approach. Young girls can be extremely manipulative in trying to get what they want. As for me, I just exploited that fact, solely to teach Billy a lesson.

I told Col only recently that I couldn't believe what a using bastard I once was.

As for Billy – he died just the other year, which is so sad. He was such a lovely kid.

Col had seen all this pan-out, but it was only the start. Life was moving at such a pace it became a blur and, on the strikes, end and getting back to work a huge rock star lifestyle awaited us. You think I am kidding? I'm not. It was fucking mad.

I needed someone to slow me down as I had become that out of control. I don't think there was anything ever labelled as post-strike syndrome, but if there was, I certainly had it during the first four of five months after its end and how I ever fitted in going to work was something that I will never ever know. I wasn't the worst one affected by it as you will see, but I was affected. My grand plan had always been a nice wife, a nice family, a new house, and a new car. Fuck that. On getting back to work, the back tax on top of the holiday pay and wages put me on a staggering amount of money – however, solely down to my immaturity at the time I wasn't thinking straight. I was getting in from work to bills upon bills upon bills.

Being on strike was simple. Nobody paid anyone.

The cooker plus interest still needed paying. Twelve months' rent needed paying. A crisp new rates bill for 1985 had dropped through my letterbox along with a letter from the Yorkshire Bank regarding my unpaid loan and of course the interest along with my fine for helping destabilise a railway embankment. In total it worked out at around £1,700 (£5,517, circa 2020) – which for a twenty-year-old kid was quite a staggering amount to cough up. My first thoughts had been to divvy up my wages and start putting together some form of payment plan – however, Col was always going to be a bad influence. "Fuck that, J – just get another loan."

At that time in my life, the end of the strike was the greatest feeling ever, but as a person I had changed. Really changed.

The strike tested my resilience, brought me in contact with great friends and provided an outlet for my anger. I'd always had a volatile personality, but with the strike ending, I had finally got what I wanted – or at least I thought I had. There had, however, been several watershed moments throughout its tenure, which helped change the direction that my life would take.

As for going back to work, it was a pathetic climb-down. There's enough been written about the strike from both sides of the fence to last a lifetime, so I'll not bore you with it. The truth was, that the government had to win. What is now known is that the strike cost the country billions. However, for the government to lose it would have put a huge risk on the security of the nation's power. I certainly know that now, but I didn't back then. For me back then it was solely a case of them winning and us losing. The reality was that to have Scargill defeat the government would have been tantamount to a disaster. He refused to accept economics. He refused to accept the capitalistic nature of the marketplace. He refused to negotiate. His sheer delusion and hard-nosed principals along with his refusal to bend, had not only near-bankrupt the NUM, but had completely split it in two and accelerated the government's pit closure programme. Scargill was a man that always divided opinion. You either liked him or you didn't. The failed negotiations along with the end result was nothing more than a prime example of his character. If it can't bend, it will break. Some left-wing Union men will say that it wasn't just Scargill that prolonged the strike and that there was an Executive who voted. That much is true – however, the Executive were nothing more than a series of Yes-men – an idiom of the story that is the Emperor's New Clothes – a set of patsies controlled to raise a hand at the flick of a switch by nothing more than a megalomaniac.

On news of the strike's end there were NUM meetings at almost every pit. As for me, I went to the ones both at Hickleton and Askern Main – which, as I recall, was the first ever time that I had ever attended a meeting.

The one at Hickleton took place in the Coronation WMC.

The last time I had been in the club prior to that had been on the Boxing Day afternoon some fourteen months earlier at what was known as the Christmas Free 'N' Easy disco. Both times the place had been packed to the rafters – however, it would be fair to say, that you couldn't have had more contrasting atmospheres. A lot had happened in the time between. As I have already said, I had become a completely different person – worldlier, angrier and in-part, completely numb to other people's feelings outside my own circle of friends. I think they refer to the latter as being a selfish cunt.

The meeting itself, started off as a sombre affair, with the senior NUM delegate speaking of the death of a couple of colleagues – one of whom was a forty-five-year-old Official at the colliery by the name of Joe Mellor, whose recent passing had been nothing short of a shock, which could have been put down to his relatively young age.

"He wasn't like most of them," said Brian Conley. "Joe was a good bloke."

I knew who he was, but it would be wrong to say that I knew him. His parents had lived at 28 York Street and his grandparents – who had come to Thurnscoe from Ashton-under-Lyne, had lived at 7 Vincent Terrace. Joe was the eldest of seven children and had lived with his wife Eliza (nee Seel) at 39 Taylor Street. I knew his youngest brother Dougie a little bit better, but not much. He married a girl by the name of Hazel Jefferies and had lived opposite Carl's house on Briton Street in the late-1970s. I knew that, as for a time, Joanne Russell (now Greaves) used to babysit their two children.

Brian Conley then went on to firstly explain to the packed concert hall of how we were to go back to work – assembly-style and behind a banner.

"What about those lads who have been sacked?" asked Mick McGrevy.

Mick was an extremely eloquently spoken man and the father of one of my sister's best friends. He, like my (step)dad had been in the forces, married his wife Jenny in 1967 – who incidentally was the elder sister of a miner off Chapel Lane by the name of Johnny Holladay, and like his brother-in-law, went on to work at Hickleton Main. It is fair to say that Mick was very left-of-centre but not the archetypal red-ragger. Personally, I always found him very sincere in his appraisal. "A miner is not a political animal," he once told me. "All he wants to do is go to work – maybe get a Saturday or Sunday in, look after his family and have a fortnight's holiday each year."

I liked Mick. However, unbeknown to him then, his family would go on to suffer nothing short of a tragedy.

In May 2007, a Renault Scenic carrying his seventeen-month old granddaughter Alicia and his twenty-nine-year-old daughter-in-law, Clare Helen Lane, and which was being driven by his son Brian, had been involved in a horrific head-on crash with a lorry on the A635 at Marr Drag. It had been in the exact place that I had crashed my car just over twenty-four years earlier. Whereas I walked away, Clare did not. She was killed outright and his son – who suffered multiple head injuries, had to be airlifted to Rotherham Hospital.

Although Mick's granddaughter survived, his son would be hospitalised for several months and on the inquest being heard, would, it is quite fair to say, be made culpable for the crash.

I got to know Brian from the fact that around ten years earlier I briefly employed him. I had been urgently in need of someone on a short-term basis and he ended up coming in for two interviews. One via a job advertisement that I had posted in the *South Yorkshire Times* and one via the Job Centre who failed to let us know exactly who the applicant was. I thought him a bad fit, and although I never said as much, I certainly implied it. I ended up giving him a trial and letting him go after a few days.

As I have said, the pits had been a great place for sixteen and seventeen-year-olds to be nurtured. As part of the Class of 1981 – over 100 lads, no different to Brian, had been set on and it had been like that for years. Since 1982, however – there had been none. There was no other industry I know that had been capable of giving a young lad time to grow. Mine was a private enterprise and I didn't have the time to deal with some gormless and lethargic teenager. This was in essence what the strike had all been about. The preservation of the mines and their communities.

"I could see that he [Brian] had one hand on the steering wheel," said the HGV driver for Rawmarsh-based Needham Transport, Keith Taylor. "All of a sudden it was driving straight at me. It didn't brake, it didn't waver, it just kept on coming. The driver's head was twisted away as if he was looking in the back seat. I tried to get out of the way, but there was nowhere for me to go and the car smashed into the front of my lorry, which I ended up running off the road before hitting a tree."

The lorry driver's version of events had been sadly clarified by a Darfield-based joiner by the name of Steve Woodson who had been following Brian.

At the inquest, South Yorkshire Police confirmed that there were no mechanical defects that could have caused the car to veer off course and Deputy Coroner, Fred Curtis recorded a verdict of accidental death.

It was what it was. A tragedy.

"We will do what we can," Brian Conley replied, on getting on to the subject of striking miners who had been sacked. "However, there are miners such as the ones who have vandalised the cameras on the offices [Dave Hollis] and those who were involved in the incident at the Officials club [Bud Green] who we know won't get their jobs back."

"So, what have we been on fucking strike for if we are going to go back without a deal?" grumbled part of the supposed hard-left element.

"Because that's what we've been instructed to do," shrugged Brian. "It's what we'll all be doing."

"Twelve months out – and for what?" came more grumbles.

Then it happened.

"You've always been a fucking Yes-man Conley," shouted a lad from the Class of 1981. "You're all a set of wankers."

Everyone turned around to see James (Jumbo) McNulty stood up and pointing over at the NUM men sat on the stage.

He was right, but he was also wrong. Brian Conley certainly thought so and had him forcibly removed from the room, which I personally thought was very wrong. It was supposed to be a democratic process, but once again, it showed that if the NUM wanted to do something – it did it regardless. He had an opinion, but they, the NUM didn't want to hear it.

I think Jumbo suffered post-strike syndrome more than most.

Like most of the lads from the Class of 1981 our parents had grown-up in an era where The Easybeats' *Friday on my Mind*, The Vogues *Five O'clock World* and The Who's timeless *My Generation* – broke certain taboos whilst at the same time *sticking it to the man*.

We had not.

Our upbringing in part, had been dark. We had just come out of a period where The Sex Pistols' *God Save The Queen*, The Clash's *White Riot* and Elvis Costello's *Olivers Army* had courted controversy, and in a kind of head-rammed-through-a-window scenario, smashed certain taboos. Even The Police had dispensed with their Do Do Do and Dah Dah Darring to reveal the state of Thatcher's Britain with their *Invisible Sun*. As had Birmingham-based UB40 with its politically apt *One in Ten*. And nothing depicted the shallow and selfish greed of the era more than PIL's very in-your-face and aggressively contrived *Public Image*.

The Class of 1981 had been drip-fed on cynicism and Jumbo had been one of its poster boys.

I had been with him whilst hurling bricks at the police, seen him threaten news reporters at Brodsworth Main, get in to hand to hand combat with riot police outside Yorkshire Main before getting arrested, breach bail after being told to keep off the picket lines and still turn up the very next day. In his mind – and this kid was no idiot, far from it – he perhaps saw what I had seen – and more so, since he had been at it since Day One. A condescending body of men sat on their arses over in the NUM office pontificating on how to distribute goods and money. The sad thing was that Jumbo loved his job and ended up being dismissed in rather acrimonious circumstances after we all went back to work. I really felt for the lad.

The meeting at Askern Welfare WMC was far more reserved. Much the same was said as regards the return to work, but the senior NUM delegate Pat Hewitt heaped praised on every miner at the pit who had stayed out.

"Our pit has been second to none," he told the packed concert hall. "Out of nearly two thousand men, we've only had just over twenty return to work. Cortonwood – the pit we supposedly all came out for, have had over one hundred and twenty scabs. You have to look at each other and respect what we have all been through. I think you've all been nothing short of fantastic."

How could words like that not put a lump in your throat. The pride I felt at the time was immense.

Whereas the meeting at Thurnscoe had serious undertones of discontent, the one at Askern had not. You put someone who cares about the other's wellbeing before his own in the chair and it generates respect. Scargill was a man who could never get that. He was a man who was always fucking right – even when he was wrong.

The government had a hit list of seventy-two pits. He was told that information, as the colander that was the NCB's head office at Hobart House in London had gladly relayed it to him. Why not? It was also their jobs that were on the line too.

The government emphatically denied it. "Twenty uneconomical pits at worst," was their stance.

They were lying as the documentation and of course history now proves. Scargill's problem was that although he was right, he just couldn't sell it. The reality was simple. No fucker trusted him.

Since getting in office, all he seemed to want to do was go on the offensive. He despised Margaret Thatcher and all she stood for. However, she alone wasn't the problem. The industry was an old one which still had much of its aged infrastructure in place. Cortonwood Colliery was nearly 110 years old, Hickleton Main, ninety. Times had changed. Scargill and his Executive needed to address the ever-changing landscape and deal with the problems that the marketplace had created for what was an overstaffed, out of date and badly run industry. Indeed, with the government's well thought out 1980 Coal Industry Act, which stated that the NCB would have to become self-financing, the writing was always well and truly on the wall. This meant that by 1984 there would be no subsidised mining in the UK. But it wasn't just that either. The energy industry had recently been privatised and in a huge corporate multi-billion-pound business such as electricity, it is the shareholders that come first. That bottom line counts. Coal was not only dubbed as being overly expensive to mine, the electricity companies were extremely fearful of the man orchestrating the will of the miners digging the fucking stuff, and them removing all the eggs from one basket seemed the most logical and practical way forward. The value of GB sterling and the security of the nation's power supply could not be held with a gun to its head. This was the main reason that the government prepared for the strike and invested millions upon millions in waiting it out.

Would a different man in charge of the NUM have changed things? In my mind it is highly doubtful. The set up at NUM level was as out of date as that of the NCB. It was cliquey to the point of being cancerous. A strike is basically a case of walking away from responsibility because you don't agree with what is being offered. But as stated, you also have to look at the people running the collieries – the managers, deputy managers and under managers. It was always a case of the master and servant – which was something that severely needed addressing. They appeared like demi-gods who the mineworker knelt, grovelled, bowed, and scraped to. "Yes, Mr Woodley" or "Yes, Mr Hodgetts" one would say. It was part of an out of date process that had been passed on since the early days of mining. I am all for respect, but since leaving the mining industry I have never addressed anyone as Mister, ever – and I always pull anyone up who refers to me by the same… or at worse, sir. We are all gifted with Christian names and as people, we, or so we are told, should all be treated equally.

Scargill coming into office just accelerated a problem that was never going to go away.

Area Vice President of the Welsh NUM, Terry Thomas hit the nail on the head. "If we had ninety-nine percent of what we wanted on the table, it would not have been enough. It was a case of no compromise – no move at all. That was the philosophy Scargill had."

In time, I would be invited to meet with Arthur Scargill, but prior to that I would speak to a few of his Executive – mainly about the problems I was encountering within the industry. I was a Yorkshire lad who had worked alongside scab labour in both Leicestershire and Nottinghamshire. For me I was amazed at how little they all knew about the people that they were supposedly representing. I remember sat on the foot of the stairs at 16 Briton Square talking at length with Scargill's right-hand man all the way through the strike – the NUM's General Secretary, Peter Heathfield. He was on the phone to me for around ninety minutes and I don't say this lightly, he came over as a genuinely nice man. I had a similar conversation over the phone with the Area General Secretary of the Nottinghamshire NUM, Henry Richardson and actually met several times with Jack Jones – the Area General Secretary of the Leicestershire NUM, the latter of who, if I'm being brutally honest, I thought was nothing short of a bumbling old twit.

Around this time, I had been left the employ of British Coal several years and had moved into the private sector and due to falling wages and the fact that I was having to pay contributions into the UDM (Union of Democratic Mineworkers), I was looking for guidance. The NUM, however, could offer no help whatsoever and were oblivious to what was going on in the mines. Scargill's desire to meet with me had been somewhat different. He had found out that I was the main driver behind an a highly popular albeit very in-the-face and unsettling monthly tabloid distributed on subscription around the coalfields of the United Kingdom and British Coal's lawyers were eager to silence me, by having their lawyers, serve me with a writ.

I was told that there is a letter from me addressed to Peter Heathfield in the NUM offices on Huddersfield Road in Barnsley, that had supposedly been preserved for posterity. How true this is I have no idea. It was Scargill's Press Secretary Nell Myers, who phoned me during 1995 to tell me that, as whilst moving from the NUM's head office in Sheffield, they had come across correspondence between us.

However, that would be in the future.

"Did you manage to get underground?" Carl asked me on my first day back at Askern Main.

He along with the rest of the lads at Hickleton Main had literally been locked out. Miners from the Kent coalfield had done their damnedest to stop everyone marching back to work and had set up pickets all around the Yorkshire area.

At Askern however, we were led in by Pat Hewitt and amidst angry scenes from miners who had been out over twelve months, he asked them to remove the picket. It was an extremely emotional event, and it would be the first time outside of my personal circle of family and friends, that I would see a grown man cry. The Kent Area had strongly voted against a return to work. They knew that on going back without a deal, they were going be hung out to dry.

"We've been told by the Union to go back," I recall one of the methane borers saying. "The strike is over."

He was right, it was.

Scargill had walked with the miners returning to work at the 112-year-old Barrow Colliery in his home village of Worsbrough only to be stopped at the gates by pickets from Kent.

"I will never cross a picket line," were his words.

A man of high moral standing?

At Askern, Pat got the Kent miners, some of whom were from Snowdown Colliery – one of the first six pits on the governments list to close – to stand down, and we finally managed to walk into work.

That night on the BBC and ITN News, I saw contrasting scenes of the return to work – mainly miners being turned away by pickets from Kent. There was, however, one scene I saw, that will always stick in my mind and that was of one of the pit managers in South Wales standing at its gates and embracing the men as they returned to work. In my mind, I thought that was such a lovely thing to do and was an act of pure class. There was, however, none of that at Askern Main.

"I've been told that we are to offer you gainful employment until a full safety audit is carried out," said the then-manager of pit, whilst we were sat in the canteen awaiting our instructions of what to do next. "I'm told that all three coal faces have suffered relatively little damage and that within a few weeks we should be working normally."

One miner stood up to ask a question and was immediately shouted down.

"Shut your mouth," snapped the Colliery Manager. "You've had all your fun and your silly marches. It's now my job to find you work until everything can be assessed."

The atmosphere was extremely caustic.

"One of the problems is that the pit baths won't be functional for a while as we need to get the boilers back working," he added, whilst at the same time aiming a dig at some of the striking miners who had vandalised the building, of which several windows had been put through.

He also raised the issue of the scabs at the pit. Any act of aggression towards them and it was a case of immediate dismissal.

My first day underground would be the second day after the strike had ended. I was part of a twelve-man crew being closely supervised by an Official, cleaning beneath the conveyors that fed into the bunker in the pit bottom. As I have already mentioned, Askern Main was a well-ventilated colliery, and the cold wind roaring from the downcast shaft made the conditions highly uncomfortable – especially bearing in mind that my last job prior to the strike was at the end of a highly productive coal face, where solely due to the heat, all I tended to wear, was a pair of shorts.

It was a lousy week of shovelling shit in the wind, before I got to back to the end of B50s face and the place where we had spent the remaining hours of that afternoon shift on 23 December 1983, when we'd had that Christmas party. Nothing would ever be the same again.

Dennis Hudson, his father, John and brother Arnold sitting outside 1 Landsdowne Avenue, Thurnscoe circa 1961

24. Angels With Dirty Faces

The NCB had contracted the private hire company F Brown to bus us between Thurnscoe and Askern and had several pickup points within the village, of which my embarkment point was at the bottom of Lancaster Street and opposite The Fairway Hotel – a huge imposing building that is sadly not there anymore. I think we were all happy to be back at work for the time being – however, as time would tell, a lot of young lads became disillusioned, dropped out of mining and would seek employment elsewhere. I remember during the early days of us being back at work at Askern, that the management at Hickleton Main were having huge problems getting its manpower fully utilised and working normally. I vividly recall being bussed to work on one afternoon shift and seeing Hickleton Main's very own NUM troika – that of Brian Conley, Billy Hayes and Les Hipwell stood in dialogue outside the red-bricked colliery administration offices opposite the entrance to the colliery, where the graffitied yellow and blue NCB sign read *Mac fucks Thatcher*. I don't think that was true. They certainly fucked the miners, but I'm sure they didn't fuck each other.

"See no evil, hear no evil, speak no evil," laughed Tex Rodgers, as we passed them on the bus. "The three wise fucking monkeys."

The exact same thing had happened straight after the 1926 strike at Hickleton Main as was happening then. History always tends to repeat itself no matter what subject you cover. Not only had there been huge problems deploying the manpower, there had been other similarities as with the cases of Joe Mellor and Mickey Ryf: the untimely death of a well-respected Official at the mine – not at the strike's end, but prior to it starting, as well as the violent assault on a so-called scab Official.

Fifty-nine-year-old Arthur Ash had lived at 7 Kathleen Street in Goldthorpe – just around the corner from the spot where Gladys Merricks had been murdered some seventeen years later. He had been in the wrong place at the wrong time and been hit by a runaway tub which crushed him against some stationary tubs. He was taken to Mexborough Montagu Hospital where they amputated one of his legs. However, all was in vain. His lungs had also been severely punctured, which at that time, made his death inevitable.

Arthur had seen military service, joining up at eighteen years old and serving in the Boer War before settling at 14 Chapel Street, Thurnscoe along with his wife Mary (nee Hall) and eldest child Phyllis. There they would have a further four children – with only Lily staying in the area. She married a miner by the name of Albert Hobson in 1924 and set up home at 9 Furlong Road, Bolton-on-Dearne.

As for the assault on the Official, this occurred on what would be the precursor to the 226 (23) bus: a tramcar travelling from Wombwell to Thurnscoe and involved lads – two of them anyway, that were synonymous with Thurnscoe – the Hardmans. Hard by name, hard by nature? Maybe.

Three miners – brothers Harry and Bill Hardman along with Edwin Blackburn – were sentenced to two and one months in prison respectively, after it was alleged, they had beaten up a shot firing Official at the colliery by the name of Lewis Simmonds.

"You're a fucking scab," snarled Blackburn. "All your family are scabs."

There may have been some truth in that statement as all three brothers were originally from the Wales Bar area of Sheffield – however, there was much more to that. Much more.

Lewis had signed on with the Third Reserve Battalion of the Oxfordshire & Buckinghamshire Light Infantry to fight in the First World War and whilst on leave had married his sweetheart, Alice Gilthorpe, at the Parish Church in Handsworth Woodhouse on 20 May 1918.

After the war he followed the path of his father and went into the mines.

His father William was the great-grandfather of one of the Class of 1981 – Chris Brockhurst. He had died in the nearby Waleswood Colliery when Lewis had been just eight years old. This was after a roof fall in the South

Level of what was known as the Hardpit, prior to him setting props. His mother, Sarah (Chris's great-grandmother) remarried a Nottingham-born miner ten years her junior by the name of John Green. It was after that they moved from the set of terraced houses on Waleswood Row, directly opposite the colliery, and to 108 Wales Road in Kiveton Park – a property which is still there, and which has more recently been a PC repair shop.

It is hard to imagine, but unlike the rest of the country coming back from war, Thurnscoe was a place of great progress.

As Hickleton Main was continually breaking records – in one instance, hauling 324 tonnes of coal in one hour, its owners set about work on the construction of the 820-yard deep No 3 shaft to access the Parkgate seam along with the sinking of the associated 250-yard deep ventilation shaft.

In the village itself, the local authority was undertaking the work on the construction of 218 houses on a twenty-acre site known as Garden City to the rear of Houghton Road School.

This was land donated to the Thurnscoe UDC by the Rev Thomas Thornley Taylor and would form Thornley Crescent, Taylor Street and John Street.

This followed on from the gift of two parcels land in 1914 – one of which was used in the construction of workmen's houses, which was of course The Avenues; the other for council offices and a public library.

As with hundreds of other like-minded people, Lewis and his two brothers James (Jim) and Lawrence moved to Thurnscoe, with Lewis and his wife moving into a house on King Street where they had two children – Margery (b. 1920) and Albert (b. 1925).

After being called a scab, Lewis had been punched to the floor by Harry Hardman, whilst his brother and Edwin Blackburn set about him, which resulted in him receiving several blows and kicks to the head and face. It was by all accounts, quite a nasty assault.

The scab question was back then, as it was in the mid-1980s. Why would someone run the gauntlet of violence and intimidation when they were living amongst the very same men who would be meting it out? One of the first rules you learn as you approach adulthood, is to never shit on your doorstep. Thurnscoe was a place where everyone knew everyone's business. Even now, you could give me a name from the village and it's an odds-on certainty that I will know or get to know something about them. It's just how these mining communities were.

For Lewis to break the strike at Hickleton Main it would have been noticed, so the question has to be – why?

The fact that he came from the Kiveton Park area, which was right on the border of the Derbyshire coalfield could have had a bearing on it as it is well-noted, that during 1926, it had been the first pit in Yorkshire to break the strike, and it is therefore quite fair to say that was partly where Edwin Blackburn's comments had come from. "All your family are scabs," he was heard say.

All Lewis's family, bar his two brothers, still lived in the area, most of who were miners and by the end of August (over three months prior to the calling off of the strike), it was made common knowledge via the media at the time, that Waleswood Colliery was working at full-strength.

There was, however, another reason.

Like many others, Lewis's son had been born into a world where a lack of money dictated life or death and the baby struggled for survival.

I never had any dependants during my twelve months out, but many did. The question is, how would I have dealt with having a poorly baby whilst having no money? I would have done things differently, that's for sure.

I see people pontificating and opinionizing on a whole range of things through social media, some comments of which are nothing short of churlish and pathetic.

The truth is, is that you don't really know what you would do until it happens to you.

Their little lad, Albert Edward Simmonds, managed to stay alive to see out the strike – however he died aged just twenty-five months old and around the exact time is father had been brutally assaulted.

Sometimes in life, things don't get any better, just worse. Tragedy struck again, and Lewis's wife Alice died in February 1930, aged thirty-six.

Their house at 34 King Street had been the scene of tragedy after tragedy after tragedy. It was also the exact same house where little Ada Etchells had alleged that the migrant miner by the name of George Boast had sexually assaulted her in 1906. Maybe it was cursed. Who knows?

As for Alice, she is buried in Thurnscoe Cemetery along with her little boy.

Just like Mickey Ryf had, Lewis ended up leaving the area.

Whereas Mickey had taken a transfer to Markham Main and moved into a house off Doncaster's Wentworth Road, Lewis had got a job as a Shotfirer at Thorne Colliery – married a widow ten years his junior by the name of Letitia Hallett (nee Gorey) and moved into a house at 22 Bloomhill Close, Moorends.

His elder brother James (Jim) lived at 79 Thornley Crescent with his wife Elizabeth (nee Heath) who as I have already stated, were the grandparents of Chris Brockhurst.

They themselves would also suffer a tragedy when their twelve-year-old daughter, Daisy Edna (who would have been Chris's aunt) died in 1934 from peritonitis, which resulted in a much-publicised inquest into the girl's death had been something that both Chris's grandfather and the general practitioner – a Dr McColm got dragged over hot coals for by the Doncaster District Coroner W.H Carlisle.

There were always child fatalities – the local cemeteries are full of them.

Back then there was little or no health and safety awareness or British Standard (BSI) Kite Marks on clothing and just two months later in March, a ten-year-old girl from 7 Landsdowne Avenue by the name of Ada Francis had her nightie catch fire and died of burns. She would have been the auntie of a rather heavily set girl by the name of Tina Francis who had been in my year at Dearneside.

Up in the East end and at a similar time, a twenty-month-old girl by the name of Constance Taylor had been crushed under the wheels of a lorry, whilst playing with her sister outside her home at 47 Tudor Street. The details of the latter were somewhat confused as one of the witnesses to the tragedy was a thirteen-year-old girl by the name of Gladys Shortt from 55 Chapel Street, whose baby nephew would also die later that year – however, that is another story completely.

Gladys's evidence had pointed the finger firmly at the negligence of the driver of the vehicle and manager of the Wombwell Furnishing Company, Charles Wordley – something that the coroner at the inquest refused to believe.

As for Harry and Bill Hardman, they were part of a family that were the first people to move into one of the newly constructed houses at 72 Brunswick Street, and who were still there when we made our second move into Thurnscoe East in 1977. They were also the elder brothers of Tom, who married Irene Dixon in 1948 and who was the father of one of the lads a couple of years older than us at Hickleton Main.

I first saw Phil Hardman during my early days, whilst working on the colliery's surface and running errands between the Time Office and the pit's administrative offices across the road, the latter of which also housed the surveyor's office. I remember it like it was yesterday. His build and dress were not unlike my own – however, he possessed hair that had been streaked with blond highlights and was far more gregarious in nature. There he was dressed in his purple V-neck knitted jersey with its two grey hoops – which was a popular style that at the time and which had been well-stocked by Ken Ellis' Tailors on Goldthorpe's Doncaster Road, in dialogue with a couple of other lads, whilst etching stencil marks on some draughtman's board.

I had got to know him quite well straight after the strike, as between us we had quite a lot in common, not at least the fact that both our respective relationships had broken down during those twelve months. One thing that sticks in my mind was calling down to his house on Butcher Street to retrieve a brown stonewashed leather jacket that he had borrowed, only to see him outside his house jumping up and down on some squeaky foot pump and trying to re-inflate four flat tyres on his Mark III Cortina. "Fucking Eddie has done this," he told me.

Had he? No idea. Ask Eddie Lockwood.

Prior to me getting to know him, Phil had been seeing Tim's elder (step)sister, Linda Kirk (now Caunter), which had been a relationship that Tim's dad, who was of course, her stepfather, had apparently been against.

"He was a right horrible bastard with me," I remember Phil once telling me. "He was screaming and shouting at me down the phone."

It was hard to imagine Pete ever getting that angry. I had certainly heard him sound off at his son after he had been kicked off the mining engineering course during the strike and he had bollocked us after catching us smoking some (Consulate) menthol-cigarettes in his bedroom when we were around fourteen years old, but that was about the sum of his anger. In short, he was lovely bloke.

As in the song, Linda was the archetypal *Real Wild Child* and as such was extremely popular with the opposite sex. I still recall motorbikes turning up outside her parents prefabricated house at 38 Carrfield Lane during the summer of 1979 and of their Tim telling me about the time they returned home off holiday early to find the house bearing the evidence of the aftermath of some wild party. "The house was a right mess – every bed had been slept in and our Linda was nowhere to be seen – my dad went mental." he said.

Linda's best friends were two lovely girls – the dark-haired Rhona Napier and the doe-eyed Julie Ball. Both had been in the last year of Carfield school when I first went there.

Rhona lived at the summit of Bolton-on-Dearne's steep Canberra Rise and who when she left school, became a well-known hairdresser in the village, having a salon on Furlong Road. As for Julie, she had lived opposite me when we had lived on Maori Avenue with her parents Alf and Nancy (nee Thompson) and elder brother Stewart – a lad that tragically died on 9 April 1980.

The story I was told was that he came off his motorbike and hadn't been wearing a crash helmet. He had been in Skegness and was said to have been pulling wheelies, before falling off it and hitting his head on the edge of the pavement – later dying after being airlifted to Derbyshire Royal Infirmary. He was just twenty years old.

If you want to distinguish the difference between truth and legend, now here is your chance.

The reasoning behind the street names of the eastern Dearne Valley prior to the First World War was very much self-explanatory.

Royalty: King, Queen, Princess, Albert, Edward, William, Charles, Elizabeth, Victoria and Mary.

A patriotic outlook: Hope, Prospect and Welfare.

Geographical: Main, South, Central, East and West.

Locational: Railway and Station, Church, Chapel and Cemetery.

Angular: High and Low, Straight and Furlong.

However, outside of those one could ask why one would call a street something such as Leadley, Kelly, Sankey or indeed the patronymic Welsh name of Probert?

Stewart and Julie's grandfather had been a man by the name of George Ball. He was not only born in Outwood near Wakefield, he was also the adopted son of Bill Probert – the uncle of George Probert.

As with the Eades family, the Proberts had been a big mining family that came up from Staffordshire to work on the development of Hickleton Main, initially settling on Goldthorpe's Main Street.

It is also fair to say that both men were quite upwardly mobile. Bill was a leading mining contractor, whilst George was a colliery Official – the former noticing a highly lucrative trade outside of hewing coal, and going on to set up his own business as a coal haulier (carter). Reading between the lines he appeared a rather colourful character, who it is fair to say, was not too far away from the centre of the action during the Goldthorpe Riots of 1915.

George too, was hardly behind the door, and as with Mark Nokes, he not only became a colliery Checkweighman, he was also appointed Chairman of the Council. Whereas Nokes had headed-up Thurnscoe UDC – George did likewise with Bolton-on-Dearne's.

The two local authorities invested heavily in its villages – however, Bolton UDC didn't have a Lord of the Manor and benefactor as Thurnscoe had in the Rev Thornley Taylor, but nevertheless, praised was heaped on it through the media for what was termed its wonderful progression. Those comments had been aimed at the construction of The Crescent and The Green in Bolton-on-Dearne and both Probert Avenue and Sankey Square in Goldthorpe – of which a further seventeen acres of land had been purchased by the council in February 1919 for £120 (£6,875, circa 2020).

The schemes had been predetermined some years earlier and had been designed by Pontefract-based architects Messrs Garside & Pennington – however, the outbreak of hostilities in 1914 forced the Treasury to put the scheme on hold – the contract being valued at £70,000 (£8.14 million, circa 2020) for the construction of the first phase of works.

As the housing was being built and due to the shortage of materials – the council not only purchased the land for the Bolton Brickyards – it suspended the rebuilding of The Hippodrome theatre on Barnsley Road, Goldthorpe, which had been part-destroyed following a fire in the early hours of 3 August 1914.

As Thurnscoe UDC had its newly constructed Thornley Crescent and Taylor Street rightly named after its benefactor, Bolton UDC opted for its crescent-shaped street to be named after its leader – George Probert and its small square named after Justice John Sankey – a man who not only possessed similarities to the Rev Thornley Taylor, but who also oversaw the Coal Industry Commission Act 1919, which considered the nationalisation of the industry and also the issues of working conditions, wages and hours.

As for George Probert's adopted son George Ball, he was a highly skilled man who was employed by the council as a builder – and worked on the construction of Probert Avenue in 1919, whilst his other son who had been named after him – went on to run the Buxton Arms Hotel with his wife Olive (nee Owen). If you want another connection – George Ball's son and Julie and Stewart's dad Alf, was born at 143 Probert Avenue!

As for Stewart, his epitaph was not unlike the story of twenty-six-year-old Kevin (Spuggy) Spruce, who came off his machine whilst riding up Mexborough Road (Abram Hill) and past the place where Bolton Club once stood. The details regarding his death, however, are extremely hazy to say the least.

It would be a lie to say that I knew the lad as I didn't. All I know of him is that he lived on Bolton-on-Dearne's Chapel Street and that he was a cousin of Debi Neal – her mum being the elder sister of his mum, Patricia (nee Johnson). Kevin died of severe chest injuries – however, there are hugely conflicting views to what exactly occurred that day. As I keep on saying, to lose your child is without doubt to worst nightmare of any loving parent and as human beings, we all need some form of closure. From what I am told, I don't think Kevin's parents ever really got that.

The worst motorbike accident I saw was on 5 May 1996.

Graham Baxter, a lad a year older than myself off Broadwater had been one of a few motorcyclists including my sister's ex-common-law husband, Steve Roebuck, riding up towards the old railway embankments that once carried the old Wath Branch Line over Highgate Lane, when after coming over the brow of the hill, they met a car coming in the opposite direction which decided to swiftly turn into the industrial estate which housed the English Rose sewing factory. It was a crash that took six riders out, Graham breaking both his legs and arms, and one which Gareth Jackson nearly died.

Graham's Yamaha YZF750 – a machine capable of doing over 160 mph, was absolutely totalled.

The scenes looking down from the top of Highgate Lane were strange. I honestly thought it was some May Day celebration as everybody – and I mean everybody was out in the road, with the highly colourful wreckage all around. It was a truly surreal sight.

"I was on my thirteen weeks' notice from Goldthorpe pit as it was shutting," Graham told me. "I broke my femur and had pots on both legs. It certainly wasn't my best day."

When I was at Carfield, my journey's to and from my place of learning had involved cutting through the scrub land where the Feast used to set itself up once a year and where Barratt Homes' Meadowgates development now stands. More or less just down from where Graham had his accident. I still remember watching the fairground workers arriving on site and digging out the standpipe during the summer of 1973 and which rather strangely, was directly where Glenn Haigh's bungalow now stands.

From there it was over the bankings or through the allotments to the rear of Crofton Drive. An alternate route and the quickest way home, however – tended to be through Hall Broome Gardens and onto Carrfield Lane.

My adversary at Carfield had been a lad in the year above – Ian (Barney) Barnish. On leaving Houghton Road School, I immediately became our Tony's (Greaves) protégé, with him having a dual role as my elder cousin and fight promoter – a ten-year-old Don King of sorts.

The school itself comprised a dinner and assembly hall separated four legs of gently sloping, flat-roofed buildings, which housed eight individual classrooms. From an aerial view it could quite easily appear the eerie shape of a Nazi swastika.

The fights he penned me for always tended to be against elder opposition and Barney had been one of the first dozen or so of these. The kid possessed a huge square head with menacing eyes set wide apart along with a mouth that had the appearance of him having no teeth. He was a scary looking kid, if I'm being honest. We had a fight in the playground closest to Thurnscoe Road and I came away with a burst nose. As stated, it was nothing new. I could get up too quick and my nose would bleed. However, that burst nose and the fact that our Tony beat him up straight after, would serve for his continual bullying of me the rest of the way through Carfield, even though no other punches were ever thrown.

Personally, I thought him an extremely interesting kid, as he was as equally as foul-mouthed as Jimmy and Lorraine Frost. On our way home from school he also told me that my mum and dad would have had to have done some rather depraved and disgusting acts together for them to have had me and that Father Christmas wasn't real. I was distraught – not at least about Father Christmas. I did have my doubts, however.

During the run up to Christmas 1971, when Clive Dunn's song *Granddad* had topped the charts, I had spent hours in my Grandma Ellis's front room trying my hand at wrapping some presents. These were mainly for my best mates at school – Malc Hudson, Col Hunter and Shaun Hufton (all miners as part of the Class of 1981) along with our Tony. My grandma had told me that Father Christmas both took and delivered presents, no matter where they were. Therefore, I left them on the hearth where most of the year a wooden-mock draw-tin with a silhouetted picture of the Blue Peter galleon, had part blocked the fireplace.

Come Christmas Day I was left scratching my head. Although Father Christmas had made a drop off at 63 Lindley Crescent – of that there was no doubt, as a huge metallic black spring-loaded rocking horse had appeared, which was for my sister and certainly not me – not one of my carefully wrapped gifts had been picked up. I remonstrated with my grandma whose reply was succinct as it was matter of fact. "I wondered where my ball of string had gone," she said.

I bet Shaun Hufton was dead disappointed with not waking up to that on Christmas morning.

As for Barney, his threatening presence was always there.

"Have him another fight," Gaz Salkeld told me. "I beat him up, easy."

At that time Gaz was primed for greatness and was a kid who would fight anyone – me included. However, Mick Crook had also said the same, the latter of who I had a great fight with whilst in the Second Year (Year 5) at Carfield. It had been very reminiscent of me and Wayne Tansley having a go at each other in the Pit Shop when we were mouthy seventeen year-olds. This time we weren't knocking racks of birthday cards over or ramming one another head-first into counters or refrigerators, it was done straight in front of the teacher's desk and while the teacher was there.

A student teacher by the name of Mrs Will had been standing in for our proper teacher, Mrs (Barbara) Holmes; the latter lived on Thurnscoe's High Street, close to Dr Boyle's Corner, and she had struggled like hell to part us.

As for Stewart Ball, he would have been in one of his final years at Dearneside, when I bumped into him in the snicket near-adjacent to the access into Hall Broome Gardens.

At that time, one of my schoolmates, Wayne Cadman – who rather strangely now lives at 27 Probert Avenue, was one of Stewart's near-neighbours and back then had lived at 1 Maori Avenue, whilst Stewart lived further down the street at No 26, and as such, we all got talking.

Stewart was Wayne's uber-hero – and why not? The one thing I recall is that he spoke to us all as equals. Unfortunately, Barney was also from *his manor* and caught up with us, before craving a bit of attention – mainly via his mental bullying process. "I'll count to ten," he told me. "If you're not gone by then I'll kick your fucking head in."

As it was, Stewart stepped in and candidly told him to pack it in.

The last I saw of Barney was in the Dog End of Ings Lane WMC during the mid-1990s. As I seem to recall, he had just been in the *South Yorkshire Times* regarding some illegal fly-tipping – not him doing it, more to do with him clearing it up and trying his utmost to stop it.

Whilst he was getting served at the bar, I went over and tapped him on the shoulder – however, unlike Steve Davies some years earlier, it didn't result in paramedics arriving on the scene, although I had to say that he was somewhat at a loss.

"I saw the article in the paper," I told him. "What you've done is really good."

He still possessed the same square head with those menacing eyes, along with the mouth that had the appearance of him having no teeth – he was just twenty years older.

The last I heard he had got married and was living next door to his parents – Barry and Shirley (nee Wright), in the red-bricked houses at the top of Ingsfield Lane close to where the Green Bridge once stood. He was a character, that's for sure. One memory I have of him is whilst in the last year of Carfield and of him proudly sporting these *supposed* red and white striped trainers that rather strangely possessed a two-inch heel. It's weird what you remember!

As for the school route home through the allotments, how we never had the committee of the Cabbage Club ban us from travelling through them, I have no idea, as quite a lot of pilfering went on. I still recall dropping our *supposed* dinner on the kitchen floor of 102 Primrose Close in February 1974. It was a live hen that I had lifted from out of one of the allotments.

As stated, when we first moved into the house at Bolton-on-Dearne, money appeared tight and as with those dark days of 1982, there was never any food in the house, therefore, in my mind, I had put food on the table. "Get it taken back," snapped my mum.

I think if I had brought it back both dead and plucked – or better still, in fillets – she would have held on to it as she hadn't been averse to other stuff being dropped on the table such as the turnips, that I had ripped out of the field at the foot of Billingley View during the previous autumn. They had initially been for us to make jack-o'-lantern's, but my mum had a brainwave and tasked me with getting half-a-dozen of them one dark Friday evening, which I did. It was the only time I ever recall my mum asking me to steal food, but the point is – she did, which obviously set a precedence for me to make the decision to take the hen.

The timing obviously also had a lot to do with it.

My (step)dad was a few weeks into the 1974 miners' strike. It was a time, when all the power went off and the candles got brought out. I also recall the strike of 1972 and my mum sending me out onto Deightonby Street to scour the road and pavement for cobbles of coal. As I have said before, times were nowhere near as severe as they were in 1926, but it didn't make my mum and (step)dad's plight any less harsh.

My grandma Ellis was one of life's survivors and made sure that through her connections at Sharman's butcher's and the fact that my granddad helped out at Waldron's Farm during both disputes, that there was always a cheap cut of meat in the oven on Sunday's along with some vegetables. I even remember my nana Durose sending us up a couple of rabbits, which was strange as her and my mum supposedly hated the sight of one another. The food situation, even outside the strike's, always seemed dire. My mum wasn't a bad cook per se, she just seemed to continually economise when it came to the table. I had to hand it to my (step)dad – he rarely grumbled about the shite he had to eat.

Those allotments were a source of food all throughout my time at Primrose Close.

"Where did you get that?" my mum would ask on me dropping off a cabbage, a couple of stalks of sprouts or half-a-dozen sticks of rhubarb.

"I found them," I would lie.

Outside of lifting food or chasing livestock around there was also other things to do down there.

At the entrance near the school, there had been a raised manhole of which the corroded concrete had left something of a bob-hole just wide enough for a child to crawl inside. This accessed the final leg of the surface water sewer that carried flows of storm water from the surrounding streets into Carr Dike – a watercourse, which has long since been culverted, prior to the construction of the Meadowgates development. This was somewhere the kids off the Flower Estate spent hours investigating. I still recall myself and Paul Gundry crawling literally hundreds of yards through the sewer towards a little speck of light at the far end of the pipe. How we survived the journey and never died of asphyxiation from the vaporised water coming off the highly sulphurous disused railway embankment, I have no idea.

It was something that had certainly happened before, however.

On 28 September 1997, an eighteen-year-old lad who lived at 6 Houghton Road had been coming home from a night's fishing, when he thought it may be interesting to investigate the interior of what was often referred to as the Monkey Tunnel. This had been a boarded-up hole opposite Lidget Wood that ran under Hickleton Main's colliery tips and *supposedly* served as some form of ventilation for the mine – although I have no idea how that worked.

My dad had often told me that at one time you could crawl through it and exit through a bob hole near Bella Wood, although I certainly wouldn't like to have tried it. Robert Ascroft did, however, and never came out alive.

With the pit long since infilled and therefore no ventilation being forced through it, water seepage from the colliery spoil that produces poisonous gases just hang around thereby displacing any breathable air.

I remember ringing up Goldthorpe Police Station in July 1994 after I had seen some of the boarding pulled away. "You get any kids go in there and they will die," I told them.

Thyssen GB subsidiary T Bridges had been infilling the shafts and undertaking the reconstruction the peripheral stone wall as part of a remedial works scheme at the time and boarded it up the very next day. Ideally it too should have been part infilled and capped as well, as it served no purpose. If that had been done, then Robert would still be alive today.

Kids had very little fear of their surroundings and back then there was still a lack of awareness even though it was being relayed through school and on TV commercials. There were never any safety signs around and open pipes, building sites and especially colliery sidings appeared great places to play, no matter what the danger was, as is what happened to a seven-year-old boy by the name of Willie Hatton of 26 King Street. He had gone into Hickleton Main's busy sidings in April 1929 and after releasing the brake bar of a railway wagon, somehow got caught beneath its wheels and had his right leg and left foot taken clean off.

Back on point and during the summer of 1979, I vividly recall being part of two groups of teenage lads standing at a distance on the two railway lines which carried the Sheffield – York trains beneath the steel girders that formed part of the substructure of the bridge (The Girder) which carried the path at the end of Chapel Lane towards

Clayton. There we were hurling stones over the top at one another and whilst part-unsighted, a lad a year older by the name of Neil Jackson ended up getting his head split wide open.

Neil was the youngest son of Arthur and Clara (nee Gibson) – the latter of whom was a classmate of the murdered girl, Gladys Merricks. She lived at 66 Lancaster Street – the house directly opposite where she and her husband would raise their family, before moving into a house at 7 Hickleton Terrace. This was three doors down from where the rather haunting figure of a three-and-a-half year old child by the name of Alice Maud Parks was seen running out into the middle of Lidget Lane after setting herself on fire on Christmas Day 1906 and therein dying shortly after.

Neil possessed an uncanny resemblance to Pete Tork – the daft one out of the iconic 1960s TV-pop band, The Monkees. As I had started at Hickleton Main, he was building firmer foundations and doing the groundwork at Barnsley Technical College, for what would a hugely successful career in civil engineering.

He was ten years younger than his brother, Roy – who during the late-1970s of Thurnscoe Mob rule, held legendary status as a barber. He worked in Clark's – a men's hairdressers on Lidget Lane that was sandwiched between where Richard and Hannah Howley's two shops (Off Licence and Grocers) once stood. Pre-punk spiked haircuts for the adolescents and 'something for the weekend for the older lads', led to a popularity that will never again be witnessed in the village and which was something that forced Roy to down-scissors and walk away for a life underground.

"I'd had enough," he told me whilst riding inbye on Hickleton Main's East Side Paddy during mid-1982. "I was getting there at eight o'clock in the morning to see them queuing halfway down the street and not leaving the shop until seven."

He was right. I remember sweeping up for him late one night when I was about thirteen years old. Me and my brother had been sat in the crowded shop since 4.30 p.m. and waiting close on two hours for a haircut, whilst watching the coal fire in the shop petering out. Roy was always too polite to lock the door before 5.00 p.m.

When Clark's shut down, it was replaced by a trendy 1980s unisex hairdressers called Unique, which was advertised by a sign above its window.

The shop was basically two rooms, which as soon as you opened the door there was a smell that hit you that was maybe a mixture of hydrogen peroxide, hair conditioner and shampoo. Once inside there was a waiting room on one side of the partition with its framed monochrome photographs on the wall of both male and female's modelling hairstyles and the actual salon on the other, with its numerous sinks and seats. The place itself employed a pretty girl a year older than me, by the name of Margaret Hole who had married a lad of a similar age by the name of Paul Waite. There were two Paul Waites in the village – the one that rammed a pencil into my leg in 1971 and who married Samantha Gething in 1990, and another one. I knew them both. Margaret had married the other one and had set up home on Deightonby Street, before having two children – Amy (b. 1986) and Oliver (b. 1990).

During the last few weeks of the strike and around seven months after her marriage, she became part of a conversation and the sudden object of desire, after John had been ceremoniously dumped by Tracy. "I'd love a great-looking lass with a nice personality," he told us. "Someone like Maggie Hole."

"Margaret?" I shrugged. "She's married to Waity."

"I'm not fucking saying her, am I?" he snapped. "I'm saying someone like her."

In her appearance and more so with her stature, she possessed a slight similarity to the actress Fiona Fullerton and that, along with the fact that everyone knew her, made her extremely popular – especially with the lads who were a similar age to me.

However, Thurnscoe being the place it was and with Margaret being in the shop window, so to speak, it must have created something of a problem in her and Paul's relationship and their marriage sadly broke down and although I am aware of certain details, it is their story to tell and certainly not mine.

What I can say is that Margaret made a numerous amount of lousy decisions including going on to stalk one of the Class of 1981 and none other than the lad who could defy science by hatching eggs under a blanket.

Her pursuit of Andy Roper was in my eyes a move which bore all the hallmarks of her plunging into the depths of desperation – the outcome being a bit like being coaxed into the Mercedes dealership and being sold on that new SL only to find out when you leave that you've been duped into driving home some red Cortina.

I had known Andy most of my life – however, there are two Andys. That insecure blond-haired little lad who would give you the shirt off his back and the other one. That is the man's man, the ladies' man, the ultimate schemer, the man that every man wants to be, the biggest swinging dick in town. Unfortunately, the latter is just a façade.

Andy had been there on my first day at school and later-on sat cross legged in class in the run up to Christmas 1969 with all the rest of us listening to the two girls sing us *Two Little Boys*. He had been a play mate down in The Avenue's, where I recall both of us playing in the barn of Dobson's Farm. Then, during the bad winter of 1981, amidst the smell of diesel, stood around a blazing fire in some oil drum over in the stockyard of Hickleton Main and freezing our bollocks off, with Andy informing me that a showing of *HR Pufnstuff* was on TV that day, which was obviously a surreptitious reminder of the fact that as a kid, I had been frightened to death of it. Too true. I could never understand why those two idiot policemen never arrested that horrible witch.

I re-engaged with Andy straight after the strike. His overworked underpaid public relations guru had been John Gratton. He was as sanctimonious in his appraisal of Andy's alleged brilliance as he was in publicly addressing mine or anyone else's shortfalls. There was little malice. John was just being John, but if you knew how to do it, as Andy obviously did – John could very easily be easily conned. Andy had matured faster than most fifteen- or sixteen-year-olds and became an old man long before his time, so much so, he looked a good ten or fifteen years older than us on leaving school. It happens. Some lads who were nothing suddenly became something, which was solely down to their sudden growth at that age. The fearless and ultra-talented, Gaz Salkeld in Dearneside and Don Elliot over at Thurnscoe Comprehensive went up to their respective big school's as being untouchable – both on the playing field and out *in the yard*, but by its end they were stood in the shadow of these so-called bigger lads, who did nothing apart from make use of their size.

Les Wall was a great example of this in Dearneside. He was a lad with dank brown hair and a freckled face who suddenly realised his growth and ended up offering Gaz out for a fight down at Bolton feast. With Les being over a foot taller, Gaz sensibly declined and Les's legend was borne. Unfortunately, as it does, both a petulance and an arrogance followed, which wasn't really Les at all, as in the main, he was a good kid.

If you want a story, Les signed on at Hickleton Main as an earlier intake as part of the Class of 1981 and during the year after we had been deployed down TO2s main gate shovelling shit from under the conveyor belts close to the transfer point where the PO2s development mucked out onto the belt. I hadn't been off my CPS (Close Personal Supervision) that long when I followed streams of lads out of the pit by illegally riding the conveyors. After jumping off the legal man-rider at the Bottom of No 3 where Eddie Lockwood operated the belt, everything was new to me. It was my first time riding the belt up towards the next transfer point, which due to it being a low point, collected groundwater and was therefore known as The Swilly. The next conveyor, however, ran both at speed and close to the crowns of the arched supports which meant the person illegally riding it had to lay as flat as possible, so as not to have part of their head or face ripped off. It certainly wasn't the most precarious illegal ride on a conveyor that I had ever undertaken by any stretch of the imagination, but being my first, I missed the disembarkation point – one of a series electric cables that powered the West side of the mine. As I trundled towards the West Gearhead it had been Les who had locked-out the belt and saved me from an uncomfortable trip through the chute and onwards to the bunker.

The last time I saw him was around 1993, whilst in the-then Fina filling station close to Highgate WMC. I had just pulled in for some petrol and he gave me a "Hey, James. You alright, mate?"

The last I had heard was that he had married a girl by the name of Denise Swallow and was living on Thurnscoe's Horsemoor Road.

As for Andy Roper, he was one of these big lads, but a kid that was never arrogant – more aloof and standoffish. In his eyes this was perhaps a sign of cool. The reality was, however – is that he was a lad who sat on the periphery, not wishing to get too heavily involved, just in case he got found out, as some often did.

I think him-being John's uber hero stemmed from school. He had been part of a clique of those sophisticated petrolheads that were part of the upper echelons of Thurnscoe Comprehensive's academia who were heavily into fast cars and rock music, and anyone that dared listen to anything else was well and truly beneath them – me included.

An "Oi, leave him alone" was all it ever needed, and I think that's what happened. At some point Andy had watched John's back. As for my back, all Andy ever did was try and piss up it.

With him being John's uber-hero, it was inevitable that I would eventually re-engage with him. His first lines of conversation covered all the facts that he obviously wanted to put over. He was a lady's man, first and foremost. He made no secret of the fact that he had walked Carl's girlfriend – Maxine Swift home one Friday night when Carl had apparently been down the hole on nightshift, and had had some wild fling with Julie Trueman (nee Platts) – who at the time had been his best mate's wife and was something, which he milked time and time again. "I've no scruples," he used to grin. "I'm a free spirit, me."

I had been down that route, but my actions had been solely reactive than proactive. You start doing shit like that without valid reason and things will always come back and bite you in the arse.

Since school, he had been in a relationship with a lovely girl by the name of Della Ramsden. She had been in the same year of school as us. Her parents were Bob and Janet (nee Riley), who my mum had known since we had lived down in The Avenues and who the last time I heard, had been living on the Manor Road part of the Whinwood estate. Between them they'd had two other daughters – Debbie, who was at that time seeing the bespectacled lad that Ron Lester had turned away on the day I signed on at Hickleton Main, which was Dave Helm – and the youngest, Coreen, who at that point in time, was a good friend of my sister.

Della had got pregnant during the strike and between her and Andy they had set up home in a row of pre-First World War terraced houses off Thurnscoe's Togo Street and ended up having a child by the name of Robert, just before its end.

What is strange, is that all throughout his life he has barely moved more than a few hundred yards from the house where he was born – that being 37 Butcher Street.

Della's father owned a local mini-bus and taxi firm, and it would be here where Andy had both supplemented his £27 DHSS payment throughout the strike and made claim to his legend.

"They all think I look like Rod Stewart," he said, after relaying the tale of him ferrying girls from the sewing factories backward and forward to the Wakefield Theatre Club (Pussycats) or to some hen-do over to Blackpool. "It's always 'Rod, Rod, Rod – come and talk to us, Rod'."

I think the catalyst for his comments came from the fact that around that time Col, John and myself were here, there, and everywhere and he wasn't.

It would happen that I called at their house one Saturday evening quite unannounced as he had been making claim that the brother of the best mate, whose wife he had had the fling with – Joey Trueman, had access to some knocked off Triumph-branded Hi-Fi systems, which were being knocked-out at £50 (£162.27, circa 2020) a pop, only to find out that the reality of the image that he had portrayed of himself was somewhat different.

I remember it like it was yesterday. Della had been in the kitchen cooking bacon, sausage, egg and mushrooms for their tea and the first thing I noticed was that Andy appeared somewhat uncomfortable by my presence. I have known the kid almost fifty years, and in that time, I have been to his house twice – April 1985 (as mentioned) and exactly thirteen years later when he lived almost opposite at 2 Bateman Square – whilst on the flip side he had called out ours literally dozens of times.

I certainly posed no threat, but I was kept at the door for all the time I was there, which was around five minutes. The second thing was the reasoning behind it. As with both her sisters, Della was extremely polite and continually smiling. An extremely nice lass if I am being honest. Although she was a pretty enough young girl – and I hate fucking saying this – she had severely ballooned-out after her pregnancy and in my mind, that was what he hadn't wanted me to see. He wasn't ashamed, why should he be? He just didn't want me to witness the reality of the legend.

As overweight as she was, Della would soon after leave Andy and throw her lot in with none other than Joey Trueman. Crazy world eh?

Fast-forward four years and all our lives had changed – apparently.

I had not so much left mining but had left the employ of the re-branded NCB and was firmly, albeit unknowingly, on the path that would dictate the rest of my working life, when I recall being out in another heavily re-branded part of the village one particular weekend.

Thurnscoe Memorial WMC (The Bomb) had been a huge, red-bricked building at the foot of Stuart Street opposite the Coronation WMC (The Corra) where newly built sheltered accommodation now stands. It was built on land owned by two Thurnscoe butchers – Arthur Pearson and Edward Bingham and costing £11,000 (£291,215, circa 2020) to build, it had opened its doors during the Doncaster Race Week of 1956. In its former glory I had been in it just once – one Boxing Day, where I had witnessed a few old women chewing the cud over a few drinks whilst eating pickled onions from a jar. It was both run down and dated, but even though I had never really used it, it did hold some happy memories from when I had been a child.

My auntie Carol's (Oldfield) parents, George and Lily Austin, used to frequent it, with the former possibly being on the committee, which meant that as kids we always went on the annual club trip to either Mablethorpe or Skegness. I thought Lily, just like her daughter, a marvellous woman. She had white hair and a gravelly voice and grew masses of wild mint in their back garden.

"Hello James, love," her voice would grate, on her seeing me.

The house I lived in at Briton Square was previously the home of Lily's brother and sister-in-law Tommy and Gwen Wright (nee Thomas), both God-fearing people with not one bad bone in their bodies.

I remember when we lived on The Avenues, of us waiting for the trip buses with their growling diesel engines and whistling hydraulics and standing outside Peverelli's bakers and looking on the opposite side of the road at Mick and Billy Whitehurst's family doing the exact same – and one year later, of the radio playing on the bus and everyone singing along to Middle of the Road's *Chirpy, Chirpy, Cheep, Cheep.* You know the one: *"Last night I heard my momma singing this song – Ooh wee, chirpy, chirpy, cheep, cheep – Woke up this morning and my momma was gone."*

Great days. Great memories.

The Bomb closed its doors a couple of years after the strike and reopened them as Harvey's – the same exterior but with a heavily revamped and far plusher interior. By 1989 however, the times along with the village's population were changing. It was inevitable. Thurnscoe still had its clannish aggression, of that there was no doubt. I still remember the shutters on the bar being hastily dragged down as Steve Hudson and a few of his mates kicked the living daylights out of some young lads on the dancefloor amid beer glasses being thrown. It hadn't been that long after that when a few of us saw him doing the exact same thing to his wife outside The Docket.

The younger end hadn't had the privilege of having a heavy industry on their doorstep where they could fall out of school, get nurtured into adulthood and respect the pecking order – something which had been passed down the line for generations. The village was dying.

Rather strangely, Chris Brockhurst had been in the pub that night. Like a few lads before him, Chris had become disillusioned and had recently walked away from mining and had gone to work for ICI.

I say strangely, as you have to watch where this is going.

Andy Roper had been stood at the bar along with his wife, Julie (nee Jones) and had immediately copped my presence. At that time, I knew very little of her, bar the fact that she was twenty years old; that her best friend was the niece of one of my neighbours; and that she worked as some shop assistant. They had married just over one year earlier on 7 May 1988.

He had still been working in the pits but earning less than a third of what I had. Ours had been a changing role. Andy had never had to fight the way I had, to get what I wanted. Like Carl, John, and Col it is quite fair to say that their mining career – if career is the right word, had been handed to them on a plate. It was nothing malicious, more a case of them being in the right place at the right time. Andy had been one of the first of the Class of 1981 to get on the 120-day face training courses, thus copping for the highest basic wage, whilst I had scuttled about amidst the transferees from other pits trying to work out the best way to provide for my family. I had. Come 8 December 1988, I chucked in the towel after finally being offered everything from British Coal (NCB). As with Chris, I had become disillusioned – not with my job, as I loved it – but with the whole system. It was wrong.

I had a deep mistrust of both my employers and the NUM that supposedly represented me. I'd had to fight my way onto the coal face via the fitting staff and three or four days before my leaving, I was handed the forms by one of the Shift Charge Engineers. Supposedly, they had come from the colliery's Chief Mechanical Engineer and were something that would ensure my right to receive the money I knew I was worth. A two-year course at Doncaster Technical College that would see me evolve into a Grade 1 fitter. It was something that I had been promised for well over six months and it wasn't until one of the directors at British Coal's Area Headquarters on Doncaster's Thorne Road had been contacted by Cementation Mining, that my employers made the offer. I couldn't afford to wait a further two fucking years. I owed it to my family to get out and move forward, and that is exactly what I had told Andy Roper on seeing him.

I had spent six months working on a mine development scheme down in the Vale of Belvoir and was earning between £800 and £900 (£2,271 and £2,555, circa 2020) per week gross. It was a staggering amount of money and Andy wanted the same. It would be one of the worst mistakes of his life.

There is more to life than money. Money is an enabler that can give you both comfort and materialism. I know that as it was the sole fucking reason that I went after it. It does not, however, give you a happy home life. It is you as a person who does that. Andy and I are completely different animals. I know who I am and accept my flaws – and believe me when I say it, I have thousands of the fucking things. Andy is different. His idea of himself has always been the same.

To give you some background, Andy is the product of a consanguineous relationship. His mother and father, Rosemary and Harry were first cousins.

James Thomas Roper and Marion (nee Goldie) had his mum, Rosemary, in 1928 whilst Ernest Roper and Elizabeth (nee Hague) had his dad, Harry Roper, in 1915.

Both James Thomas (b. 1881) and Ernest Roper (b. 1885) were brothers.

Inter-family relationships within Andy's family weren't anything new as you only had to look at the Ropers and the Hagues, where at least two sets of in-laws married each other.

This one however, is slightly different. Andy's great-grandfather William Thomas Roper had come up from Darlieston in Staffordshire with his elder brother John to work in the pits – the former as a development worker, who initially settled in Stanley-cum-Wrenthorpe before coming over to Thurnscoe and the latter who was a colliery Checkweighman at Denaby Main and who settled in Conisbrough.

William Thomas had married a lady by the name of Rose Greenaway in 1875, whilst John had married Mary Ann (Polly) Pickin in 1878. Unfortunately, within a year, two of their partners had died. John Roper died in 1897, aged forty, whilst Rose Roper died after giving birth to a child by the name of Albert in 1898, aged thirty-nine.

One year after, Mary Ann moved in with William Thomas and eventually resided at 33 Station Road, Thurnscoe – the terraced house set right against the underbridge which carries the Sheffield – York railway over the B6114 and the one which made national headlines on 21 November 1984.

As a point of interest do you want to know where both Andy's grandparents lived?

James Thomas Roper lived at both 3 and 7 Togo Buildings, whilst Andy's other grandfather, Ernest Roper, lived at 4 Bateman Square.

As for Andy, I helped get him the job and we initially travelled together. We were the only two Thurnscoe lads on what was a mega-project and on the promise of the vast amounts of money being thrown at the job, he did exactly what I had done and immediately bought a new car. However, when I went on my fortnight's holiday to Cyprus, I returned to find out that he had written his vehicle off. Whilst travelling back off nightshift he had fallen asleep at the wheel as he came off the A1(M) slip road at Marr. I hadn't been there to stop it.

It was the first of a series of things that would see him affect my work life, lose his wife and then his job.

My attendance at work at been flawless. The thing that I was told right at the start was, "You miss a shift and I'll sack you."

There is no wiggle room for bullshit with a statement such as that and therefore the parameters were immediately set. In my mind, that is how it should always be. You know where you stand.

On me getting back to work, however – two things happened. As we shared the ride in each other's vehicle the equilibrium suddenly changed. Mine was new and intact – as for Andy, he never truly replaced his and drove a succession of pile of shite motors including a white 1.4L Hyundai Pony and some 3.0L Ford Granada. The former could go from 0-60 mph in just over ten minutes and possessed a continual radiator problem, whilst the latter was reminiscent of *The Sweeney* and had a very dodgy engine and a speedometer to match, the latter of which recorded speeds of well over 70 mph when we were following the milk float down Windsor Street. I missed three shifts whilst Andy was there. He also got hurt in one of the headings one night, which resulted in me having to take him to the Nottingham City Hospital and lose another shift. The rot was there for all to see, which saw our respective shift patterns altered. It wasn't said, but he had become a bad influence on my attendance, and we were split up.

Whilst this was happening there was another problem. He suspected his wife of fifteen months of having an affair.

"You are fucking joking?" I said.

He wasn't. He even told me who it was. It was a kid that I didn't know at the time, and who had signed on at a similar time as part of the Class of 1981 – Paul Braisby. I tended to know or know of, everyone my age, so how this lad had passed me by unnoticed had been quite strange. "I've never fucking heard of him," I said.

He did, however, know me.

My solution was a simple one: "Wrap a fucking hammer around his head and sling her out." And that is exactly what I told him.

Andy's actions were exactly the opposite of what people such as John would have expected him to do. When a man works hard to provide for his family – and believe me, that is exactly what we were doing, he expects a certain degree of loyalty in return. It is not a great deal to ask.

I'm not a male chauvinist pig by any stretch of the imagination – however, I had already witnessed two out three of the most complex women that I would ever meet, both as a mother and ex-girlfriend, and had successfully survived them. Therefore, it is fair to say that I would rarely take shit from any woman.

Andy's idea was to monitor his wife's movements. It was nothing short of pathetic.

I recall picking him up prior to an afternoon shift and of us driving down the A614 Blyth Road towards Ollerton roundabout and him asking me to pull the car over outside some red telephone box, which was strangely positioned in the middle of nowhere, and just past the junction for the village of Perlelthorpe and Thoresby Market.

"I'm going to phone Nelly (Falkingham) to see if he's [Braisby] at the house," he said.

I recall sat in the car whilst watching him over on the phone and just shaking my head.

Nelly Falkingham was a heavy-set lad in the year above, that had lived across from us on Deightonby Street during the early 1970s and was someone who Andy had obviously befriended. During my second stint up in Thurnscoe's East end I had come across him as he had been the dark hobby of both Graham (Raz) Bradley and Anthony Cook – both of whom had continually bullied him. In fact, according to Neil Jackson, some of their victimisation had been quite brutal.

The last time I had seen Nelly prior to him being mentioned by Andy, had been late one evening whilst underground at Armthorpe's Markham Main and of him trying to unblock some grout filled three- or four-inch bagging close to the air doors that separated B51s Main Gate from the return airway. He was a harmless enough lad, but to me he was always that fat kid from across the street.

He had hooked up with a pretty girl from Highgate's William Street by the name of Tracey Mellor (no relation to Gaynor), who had been both a year younger than me at Dearneside and who possessed quite a startling resemblance to Debbie Harry of the rock group Blondie. Rather strangely he ended up marrying her and going on to live at 25 Cromwell Street.

My wife's appraisal of him was far blunter. Remember Zucker, Abrahams and Zucker's 1980 American satirical disaster film, *Airplane*, where the traumatized ex-fighter pilot Ted Striker, bores people senseless to the point of suicide? Well, there you go.

"He has to be the most boring person that I've ever met," she grizzled, after he had captured her at the bar of some pub we had been in before whining on to her for forty-five minutes about the intricate details of driving a lorry along with his failing marriage. "No wonder she fucking left him."

It always surprised me how he ever got with her in the first place – hence the adverb *strangely*.

As for the phone call, it was the start of a series of similar set of circumstances where he became severely depressed and which culminated in him jumping out of the car on Houghton Road's junction with Garden Street and confronting the problem face to face.

"Did you bang the fucker?" I asked.

He did. Unfortunately, the said fucker banged him back.

"You what?" I shrugged.

Andy went all Laurence Olivier and dramatically began clutching at his chest. "It's my lungs," he said.

At the time, I had no idea what he meant. Had he perhaps suffered some form of panic attack? I don't know but it was a possibility.

Dr Peter Corry at Bradford Royal Infirmary openly stated that babies born in cousin marriages can suffer what are called 'recessive' genetic disorders, associated with severe disability and even early death.

Nevertheless, in my eyes the problem was a simple one. Hit him hard and kick her out. He did neither and of course, the misery continued. He was a gibbering wreck of a lad.

I spoke to Paul Braisby some years later when I was working up in the Selby Coalfield. He was as forthright about the affair as Andy had been pathetic. What I do recall about him is that although he was quite engaging to speak with, and he was – he was both opportunistic and predatory, but more to the point, he was a loner. Opportunistic and predatory, not so much because he had exploited the weakness of a naive young housewife, but at the time he was homing in on another girl in similar circumstances. As for being a loner – he like Andy, had very few friends.

If you want an example, Andy's best man at his wedding had been his wife's brother.

In my mind it was like someone owning a red Cortina and getting shut of it for another red Cortina. There has at least got to be some form of progression – however, in this case there was none. His wife's move made little sense.

"I used to wait near the war memorial at Hickleton for your XR3 passing," Braisby smirked. "As soon as I knew you'd gone to work I went down to their house."

There was, however – much more to the story.

Knowing Andy as well as I did, I knew he had his demons, which is something that I can sympathise with him, as I have them too. However, I know where mine come from and to an extent I have learned how to deal with them. His were – even to someone such as I, quite fucking strange to say the least.

Getting dressed up in combat gear, donning a balaclava and walking the streets in the middle of the night with a rifle in your mitts and shooting-out streetlamps is not the actions of a normal man. In fact, it is about two or three rungs down the ladder from setting up a machine gun opposite a school playground.

I also recall him creeping up behind me with some great fucking gun and letting off a series of shots in my face. "I know what you're thinking: 'Did he fire six shots or only five?' Well, to tell you the truth, in all this excitement, I've kinda lost track myself. But being this is a .44 Magnum – the most powerful handgun in the world, and would blow your head clean off, you've got to ask yourself one question: 'Do I feel lucky?' Well, do you, punk?"

"You fucking dickhead," I snarled at him.

"There's no bullets in it," he innocently shrugged.

It may have frightened the life out of me, but I had to admit, it was one hell of a gun, which he candidly informed me was often used to assassinate livestock down on some allotment that his dad had. According to John Gratton, it was hen's, mainly.

Whether it was macho-bravado, brought on by the fact that I had been very matter-of-fact in voicing my opinion regarding a solution to his problem, I do not know – but what he told me next was that he had laced the marital bed with broken glass before he had gone to work. "They both jump in it and they get cut to bits," he grinned.

The other thing Braisby had candidly told me resembled something from Dennis Potter's banned TV series *Brimstone and Treacle* and is therefore not really something that I am prepared to share.

As for Julie, she and Andy eventually parted, and she went on to marry none other than Chris Brockhurst.

What was even more strange, is that the wife of his one-time best friend [Julie Trueman], ended up becoming John Gratton's common-law wife… and who would become their neighbour? None other than Andy.

However, that would be several years into the future and well after I had left the area.

At the strikes end, my dad had called in to see me – however, I hadn't been in, therefore he dropped an envelope through the door with £30 (£97.36, circa 2020) enclosed and a note written on its front: "I'm down at Aunt Jess's – I'll call up to see you later – Dad."

My dad's aunt Jess (nee Durose) was one of Andy's near neighbours. She had been born in 1917 at 32 Cliffe View, Conisbrough and married Uncle Fred (Smith) in 1951 and had lived in Thurnscoe's Togo Buildings for as long as I could remember.

I have very few recollections of her apart from her falling out of one of the hearse's carrying the cortege at my grandad (Sam) Durose's funeral in 1996 and nearly ending up in the hole with him. However, there are plenty of stories – not at least the story of her giving Uncle Fred what is termed as a *Glasgow Smile*.

She was obviously fully conversant in the kitchen as before marrying Uncle Fred she had worked as a cook for the one-time Chairman of Rawdon UDC and chemical tannery owner Thomas E. Gate and his family on Moor View Terrace, which quite close to where Leeds Bradford Airport now stands. However – and this is a big however, she could at times possibly be described as quite absent-minded if not a bit scatter-brained. The majority of miners took what is termed as *snap* to work as whilst working for the NCB (British Coal) we had twenty minutes downtime, when we ate what food had been packed-up for us – which was generally sandwiches. Uncle Fred, I was told, had quite a liking for Pek chopped pork therefore, for most of the time, that is what he had. Aunt Jess had this penchant for taking it out without breaking it, which meant opening the tin at either end, and fully pushing it out unmolested, before thinly slicing it circular from top to bottom so as to fit perfectly on the bread roll. Unfortunately, she put the last slice on that included one of the lids, which during this particular snap time ended up giving him a face that resembled Cesar Romero's *Joker*.

My dad had finally sold the land that he had sat on and had made a hefty profit. He had both paid off and part-modernised his house in Barnby Dun – part of which had involved having gas central heating installed, and as for the money in the envelope, it was a present – a gift, which was gratefully received. It would have even been more so, if it had landed in June or July when I had really been on my arse.

On him getting to the house around 5.00 p.m., he appeared hot and bothered and the first thing he wanted was a drink of water and to wash his face. He should have been happy, but looking back it, he wasn't. His trousers were hanging off him and his shirt seemed baggy. He had lost quite a lot of weight since the last time I had seen him. From what I remember, he complained about some pills that he had been prescribed and turned down having some tea – a fry up of bacon, sausage and eggs, which was most unlike him.

I recall holidaying with them in Cornwall in the early summer of 1975 and on the first day there, of him coming into the caravan laden with a tray of eggs. "We'll have a big fry-up every morning," he smiled. "This is what holidays are all about."

On me offering him one. "I'd really love one, but it'll cripple me," he said.

However, I have told you that already.

To change the subject, I mentioned the fact that I still had Stuart Keen's electric guitar and amplifier upstairs, which Carl had brought around a month or so earlier and which Stu hadn't taken back. "It's a Gibson SG," I told him. "It's a cracking guitar."

My dad loved to strum along to his Country & Western records and a few years prior had restrung his US-styled 1960s acoustic guitar which possessed a pair of classic-shaped f-holes and which he'd had on the top of the wardrobe since I had been a little lad. He had even bought a book of chords for some popular 1960s songs.

Although he was quite capable of playing the guitar, it was the first time that he had ever picked up something of this magnitude, and to say he was overwhelmed… well he was overwhelmed. He sat on the edge of the double bed that he had bought me in the middle bedroom of my house and played that guitar for nearly an hour. Whilst strumming his version of Creedence Clearwater Revival's *Proud Mary*, I had little idea that he was a mere ten months from the end of his life.

"Left a good job in the city – Working for the man every night and day, and I never lost one minute of sleeping, worrying about the way things might have been – Big wheel keep on turnin', Proud Mary keep on burnin' – Rollin' – Rollin' – Rollin' on the river."

All he spoke about afterwards, was that guitar.

As for Stuart, the last I heard of him is that he was living on 130 Houghton Road and employed in the fire service, whilst moonlighting as a bass guitarist in some Doncaster-based punk band, by the name of *Dog Rocket*.

I wonder if he still has that guitar?

Top. Short shield police checking developments on Thurnscoe's Lidget Lane during January 1985 (c. Alamy) Bottom Left. "Mac Fucks Thatcher" - The headgear overlooking the joiners workshop at Hickleton Main in January 1985. Bottom Right. The Dyson's or Mitchell's ho on Ingsfield Lane, Bolton-on-Dearne which was firebombed on 1 December 1984 (c. PA Photos / Alamy)

25. Real Wild Child

The money I had in my first wage packet on getting back to work was unreal. I had received a massive income tax rebate, along with a year's holiday pay and all my Rest Days paid up on top of my basic wage; the latter of which was, truth-be-known, a disgrace to any man venturing underground to earn a living. You take the incentive payments away and you were left with a flat rate that was nothing short of an embarrassment. However, after having months of nothing, a social life that blew everything I had ever experienced away, I was at the happiest point in my life thus far. My new neighbour across the street at No 8 was my best mate and how the lad had looked after me, I couldn't begin to say. I had never had anything like this before. It was the start of six months – half of which, I struggle to remember, it flew by that quick.

All my close friends I had at that time I saw as being special. If you have ever watched the highly popular TV series created by Franc Roddam and penned by Dick Clement and Ian La Frenais – that of *Auf Wiedersehen, Pet*, that is how it was. Not so much in the characters, but in the fact that any one of us could associate with any one of the others – either all of us together or individually. That's just how it was. However, the strike ending forced certain changes in people's attitudes, the first of who was John. We had never lived in each other's pocket, but we were close. With his relationship with Tracy terminating during the latter couple of months of the strike, I wouldn't say that we had become inseparable, but very good friends – especially when the weekend came upon us.

I had wanted to knock going down to Swinton in the head for fear of getting stalked by some suicide blonde that had been harder to get shut of than a dose of chlamydia, therefore, for a time, and just like the 226, we moved between Thurnscoe and Barnsley with one of the places we began regularly ending up at, being some supposed trendy late-night bar on the latter's A61 Wakefield Road called Antonio's. Inside, it was a mixture of ultraviolet lights, huge mirrors, and loud music. At 2.00 a.m., when the main lights went on prior to everyone getting turfed-out, the surroundings appeared somewhat different. Its manky carpet was gammed up with an assortment of chewing gum and dog ends whilst the small bars and mirrors that we had been leaning against were daubed with hand marks, lipstick and god knows what.

I suppose it's a similar feeling when you walk in a pub or club just before opening time and you get that sudden cold emptiness along with a *hit* of stale beer.

We could easily go out on less than a fiver a night – well Col could, as he was generally the designated driver who was easily fuelled by two halves of lager and half a dozen jungle juices. This place however, had a charge at the door and the drinks were much more expensive. I wouldn't say it was a great place, because it wasn't. It just kept us out longer. What is strange, is that after the strike, I can never recall us going there again. However, lots of things changed straight after the strike.

John's ambition on getting back to work never exceeded the purchase of an Opel Manta and getting a dog – a Siberian Husky, who he was going to name Khan.

I had often walked home from Swinton in the early hours during December, whilst I had been seeing the girlfriend that I didn't want and I recall telling him that there was a garage off Mexborough's Hartley Street Roundabout that was tucked alongside the embankment, which carried the Sheffield – Doncaster Railway Line that was a registered Opel dealer and further explained that there was both a red and black Manta on the 1984 'A' plate at just under £4,400 (£14,994, circa 2020).

"I could never fucking afford one of them," he snapped.

I never said he could – I was just making conversation.

It was a similar story after I had dumped the said girlfriend whilst moving around between other different girls.

"Not fucking cool," he'd snap. "I thought you were okay, but you're a cunt."

"You say things when you're younger that you wouldn't dream of saying to people now," Col had said in later life.

The problem he had, was that Tracy had gone from his life. Well for the time being anyway and any mention of her had him *flip a moody* and John being John, he could make it last.

Tracy had an elder sister, by the name of Jill who had been in a relationship with another striking miner. John Hollinshead was one of the pit bottom lads at Hickleton Main – possibly an Onsetter – the person in charge of signalling to the Winder for the movements of the cage. He was extremely outgoing to the point of being brash and possessed dark hair and a Zapata moustache. He was a nice kid if I am being honest. As their relationship petered out so had her younger sisters. Either rightly or wrongly, John in part, laid the blame at Jill's feet, brutally inferring that she was a bad influence on Tracy. "She's a right evil fucking witch," he would often say.

Personally, I think he missed the close-knit community and togetherness of Tracy's family as much as he did the girl herself. John didn't have that. Even though his mum was an extremely lovely lady – an *Angel* in my eyes, the set up a 9 John Street was nothing like up at the Greaves's. Very few places were. His mum Margaret was very caring and considerate and not unlike my auntie Carol (Oldfield), Tim's mum, Jill (Bright), Richard's (Clements-Pearce) mum, Rita, and Steve (Chalky) Whyte's mum, Agnes. These Angels were everywhere, and every mining community had them. They were women outside my immediate family, that I felt were always watching over me and looking out for my welfare. Beautiful ladies with hearts of gold. Angels to the last. The strange thing was, I don't think John ever knew how much his mum did for me, especially when I had first been married.

The Greaves family were very tight-knit and a family that he adored. Tracy's absence in his life had created a bitterness. John always had the tendency to talk down to you, hence why I sometimes refer to the adjective, sanctimonious – however, it became worse to the point of continual condescension and then complete ignorance.

"I can't understand what I have done to him?" I remember telling Col.

During the last few weeks of the strike, we had called into Benders – a tacky theme pub in the Measborough Dike area of Barnsley opposite where the Slazenger factory once stood and where St Joseph's Gardens now stands. It was there we had picked up three female passengers.

We had gone out in John's Morris Ital, but the fact that one of the females – Jimmy Frost's elder sister – had paid him some attention, Col got handed the keys to become the driver.

Lorraine was unique. As vulgar as she was pretty and as coarse as she was blonde, John wouldn't shut up about her. Lorraine was a character, that is for sure. The bad girl with the foul mouth and the pretty face. Little Miss Thurnscoe. The Dorothy Shortt of 1984. Lorraine was the opposite of John. Extremely funny, certainly not behind the door in voicing her opinions and one hundred miles a fucking hour.

"She's fucking great," he said.

Yeh. Lorraine had that effect on people.

She had gone out with Wendy Fereday, who was an extremely pretty girl in the same year as Lorraine, therefore a year older than us, along with a girl our age, who lived on West View Crescent – a street that formed part of the subsidence-riddled estate at the foot of Highgate Lane that were dubbed the *Dunk Houses*.

I had met Wendy before as she had been a friend of my ex-girlfriend's elder sister, Ann.

I still remember her sat at their kitchen table both barefoot and in some 1980s gypsy-skirt whilst quizzing me about her ex-boyfriend.

"Tony Parks?" I shrugged. "Wap?"

She nodded.

At that time, I knew of him, but that was as much as I did know.

Now, with what I am going to tell you, it wouldn't be right of me to name the other girl, therefore I won't.

I knew her well enough as I had gone through Dearneside with her, not at least in the last two years when we travelled to and from Barnsley Technical College on a Friday morning. I also shared the same table in Domestic Science-stroke-Home Economics.

Although she wasn't ugly – far from it, it would be fair to say that her vibrant personality certainly outshone her looks, her small turned-up nose, perhaps being her most striking feature.

Through senior school she had gone out with a lad three years older than us from Bolton-on-Dearne, and when she was twelve or thirteen years old, she had got pregnant. It was no secret. Her boyfriend and I had shared the same classroom at different times as well as the self-same wooden desk, the latter of which he had announced his unfrequented love for her and heavily graffitied its wooden lid with two-inch scrawl. In capital letters it read: "******* HAD AN ABORTION."

What a wanker, eh?

Although John and I were quite alright with the female passengers we had on board – Col wasn't overly impressed. We also had another problem in that we had an odd man out in Brian, who was sat in the middle of us. It happened quite often. It was always a case of one too many or not enough to go around. You could never please everybody – however, it would be here when John kicked back.

Our remit was to drop them off in Barnsley Town Centre – however, both Lorraine and Wendy I am sure, would have tagged along all night if we had asked and John knew this. As I went along with what Col and Brian wanted, I got tarred with the same mucky brush, and more so, as John knew that if I would have put my foot down and moved to appease Wendy, then he could have quite easily copped-off with Lorraine.

"You're fucking selfish!" he stormed.

He may have been aiming his barbed comments at Col, but he meant me.

It was the start of several weeks that would see him be quite off handed with me. Nothing malicious, just snide.

He would buy his red Opel Manta and get his dog. The former of which was perhaps the most gutless vehicle in its class, and the latter which got run over whilst supposedly under his uncle Billy's supervision.

His uncle Billy (Batram) had been an amiable enough fellow but tended to go out for a drink on an afternoon, and as such, when I had bumped into him, he always seemed slightly worse for wear. Certainly not a pisshead, but you could certainly tell that he'd had a drink. The story I got told was that Billy had been drinking when in charge of the dog and that John had flipped and threatened to kill him. Just how much truth there was in that, I couldn't say as John would categorically deny it and Billy is sadly no longer with us. He died in 2006, aged seventy-four.

I think Lorraine would have made him a great partner, which I am sure would be another thing he would deny. Nevertheless, I would have loved to have seen what John's mum and his sisters would have made of her. Lorraine – as with their Jimmy, were a throw-back to both a time and place that we will never see again and were just great kids.

Thurnscoe, Goldthorpe and Bolton-on-Dearne has always had its characters.

When I first landed at Hickleton Main during the heavy winter of 1981, I seem to remember an old guy on the surface by the name of Eric Waldron who appeared a big, brash, burly bloke, possibly in his early sixties, who had both a receding hairline and who wore glasses. I seem to recall that he was Head of the Pit Baths, prior to his retirement, although I could be wrong.

Eric was the son of William and Florence (nee Spencer) and got brought up at 12 Barnburgh Lane, Goldthorpe near opposite the house which I spent several months living during early 1968 after my mum and I had left my grandma Carman's.

Eric had been quite a gullible lad and nothing like the bear of a man he was in later life.

In 1935, whilst just seventeen years old – the self-same age I was when I first bumped into him – Eric got involved with a young girl from Thurnscoe's 55 Chapel Street by the name of Dorothy Shortt, the elder and much more worldlier sister of Gladys. She had been the girl who claimed to have seen an infant child by the name of Constance Taylor get crushed under the wheels of a furniture lorry on Tudor Street just a year earlier.

Dorothy was the eldest daughter of Herbert and Hilda May Shortt (nee Platten) and blew the notion of the archetypal *real wild child* completely out of the window. She was a girl that could not be tamed.

Her father was a Sheffield lad, born on 27 January 1884 and brought up in the Old Street part of the city, which was a row of terraced houses on a steep hill, sandwiched between Park Square and what would become The Manor. As a young lad he moved around the Barnsley area lodging with his relations – firstly at Three Street in Grimethorpe, then on Worsbrough Dale's Ebeneezer Square, whilst working in the pits – firstly as a Pony Driver then as a Trammer.

Her mother was born in the Norwich area on 15 March 1891 and was brought up as a Roman Catholic. Around 1911 she lived as an inmate at the Cheltenham Female Refuge on the city's Winchcombe Street, a place which was later renamed as the North Parade Home for Girls (Fallen Women) before it shut down in 1934.

The reasoning why she was sent away is unclear – however, with it being a place for seventeen- to twenty-five-year-old fallen women, with a minimum stay of two years, it could very well be that she had been an unmarried mother. To add weight to that, while she was at the refuge, a little girl was born with the exact same name as her – Hilda May Platten, and who was brought up by her elder brother George and his widowed wife, Mary Ann (formerly Warminger, nee James).

As with many, Herbert had been a soldier in the First World War – serving as both a Private and Lance Corporal and fighting in both The Battle of Loos and The Battle of the Ancre with the 10th Battalion of the York & Lancaster Regiment, prior to ill health forcing his discharge on 16 May 1917.

He had married Hilda May in 1914 and the following year they had Dorothy who was followed by another three daughters – Olive (b. 1918), Gladys (b. 1923) and Joyce (b. 1924)… along with a rather 'unexpected' younger brother – Ronald (b. 1933) who his mother gave birth to, aged forty-two.

To have a child at that age back then, was fraught with problems – and to add to that, the father, who by then had been a bricklayer, who had worked on both the construction of Thornley Crescent and Thurnscoe's East end, would have been touching fifty.

Their eldest daughter, however, was an extremely wayward and out-of-control girl – something which was readily admitted by her mother and later hammered home by her father.

Around that time, Dorothy would have been seventeen or eighteen years old and had not only left home, she had been freely moving around several lodging houses in Barnsley and continually getting into trouble – theft mainly, but there was always some form of man trouble, which was something that would follow her around for years to come. It was well-noted that she already possessed several convictions for theft – however, the final one culminated in her serving a six-month sentence, arriving at Strangeways Gaol in a dense December fog, just as forty-seven-year-old William Burtoft was being hanged for the murder of Frances Levine. The prison was also where on 31 March 1934, she gave birth to a boy, who she took it on herself to name Roy Roland Shortt.

This was around nine months after the birth of her brother, Ronald.

Shortly after her release in June 1934, Dorothy met Eric Waldron. He was seventeen, she eighteen.

His parents, William and Florence (nee Spencer), opposed any relationship and they warned him against it – the obvious fact being, that not only had she been in prison, she also had a new born baby to look after.

Eric was employed underground as some form of coal cutter, and although his job required a certain amount of nous, he was described as not the most intelligent of fellows. This may or may not have been true as it was used in his defence after the pushy unmarried mother forced him into marrying her on 30 July 1934 – where he not only lied about his age – he also handed the Rector of Thurnscoe – the Rev Daniel E Hughes, a forged letter of parental consent.

The marriage it was said, was nothing short of a fiasco – a sham – and whilst trying to get it annulled, Eric told the police that he had been forced into it, and whilst only seventeen years old, he had falsified his father's signature on the letter of consent.

It was a big thing at the time, which was made even worse, when on 30 September – just two months after her marriage, she not only left her husband, she also left her mother with her seriously ill baby, stole a bicycle and rode off to Barnsley.

Her mother had been at her wit's end, reported the theft to the police and they arrested her a couple of weeks later. However, when they asked of her baby, she replied: "I expect it will be dead when I get back."

She was nearly right.

On 14 October 1934, just a couple of days later, Dr John Livingston McColm of 91 Houghton Road – the building which has long since been Dennis McCabe's funeral home – was called to her parents' house on Chapel Street and pronounced the child dead. There was no postmortem as the child had been suffering with tubercular meningitis.

As for its mother, Dorothy, she was duly charged with the theft of the cycle and a pair of boots from a Town Centre shop, and possibly due to her past convictions, was sentenced to three months in prison, with the Chairman at Doncaster Magistrates Court, a Mr H Woodhouse, appealing for her to pull herself together. "If you carry on the way you are going, lady, I can see nothing but a life of wretchedness and misery in front of you," he had snapped, prior to sending her down.

He was right. On her husband being tried at Leeds Assizes for perjury she tried to claim maintenance for his desertion. Whilst he got off with nothing more than a slap on the wrist, she received an order for the princely amount of sixpence – 6d (£1.80, circa 2020) per week.

It was a slap in the face, but one could suppose it was nothing more than she deserved, and which was something that her father got dragged in front of Leeds Assizes for on 29 March 1936 – possibly the day when Eric Waldron last saw her.

At fifty-two years old, Herbert Shortt had finally had enough and had given her a back hander.

His eldest daughter wasted no time in having him arrested and charged. However, after hearing the details of the case it was thrown out of court.

Dorothy may have fallen-out with her father, but not so her younger sister.

Olive Shortt was seeing a man from the Heeley Bridge area of Sheffield that she would marry some eighteen months later. Bertie Bradshaw lived at 18 Well Place, which was in walking distance and just a few hundred yards from 59-61 Back Chesterfield Road – a property which was located on the junction of both the A61 and the city's Valley Road. It was also the temporary residence of her elder sister and her lover – a lorry driver from Barnsley by the name of Lionel Henry Kipling.

One could assume that Dorothy was a decent-looking girl. Why not, she had no problems whatsoever in attracting the opposite sex, no matter who they were or where they came from… and Kipling – well, this guy was fucking depraved.

He would marry a total of three times during his life – four if you counted another sham marriage with the already married Dorothy Waldron (nee Shortt). However, that is not entirely where the comment *depraved* comes from.

On 21 September 1936, a marriage of sorts took place between the two at Barnsley Register Office and just nineteen days later, a quarrel occurred between them of which the outcome was that she told her new husband, that she was already married. Her mother had tried to stop the marriage – however, she had arrived too late. Dorothy would be arrested on a charge of bigamy and sentenced to fifteen months in prison. Not so much for the offence in question, but for breaching bail and theft.

It was a big let off as Kipling, people would find, was no fucking good.

In 1943 he was sentenced to five years in prison for the attempted rape of a thirteen-year-old girl in Hoyland Common – however that doesn't even scratch the surface.

It was said in court that he had ten previous convictions against him for similar offences on females – four of which were on little girls; one who was an eleven-year-old that he had indecently assaulted at Barnsley during the early stages of the Second World War.

Rather strangely, he was married to a lady at the time by the name of Kathleen (nee Rothery) – a union in which three children were born – Katherine (b. 1940), Terence (b. 1943), who currently lives in the Wadsley Park area of Sheffield, and Margaret (b. 1947).

As for Dorothy, no matter how she tapped those ruby slippers, there was no way back to Kansas for her, and the last I can find of her is living on 38 Church Street, Royston, with a miner nine years her senior by the name of John Morley. She did have children however – Kathleen (b. 1943) and Christopher (b. 1946) – the former who lives in the Cowley Hill area of Sheffield and close to Thorpe Hesley Cricket Club.

As for a current Thurnscoe, Goldthope or Bolton-on-Dearne connection?

After Stones's garage shut down and the Broadway Buildings had been demolished, Welsh-based supermarket chain Kwik-save eventually moved into Thurnscoe and redeveloped the ground where both it and Houghton Road's school kitchens once stood.

Whilst we still lived in Thurnscoe, it was one of the places we regularly shopped – that was until Netto opened its doors on Wath-on-Dearne's High Street, which was something that saw a flurry of shoppers leave one discount supermarket for another, even though that supermarket was four miles away.

The downside with Netto was that it wouldn't accept personal bankers' cheques, which was something that Kwik-save, still did. Therefore, when I first started out in business – and to create something of a Robbing Peter to Pay Paul scenario, we stopped shopping at Netto and recommenced our shopping there.

One of the things I remember was the effervescent smile of one of the young girls who worked on the cashier tills. I knew her, yet I didn't. She possessed dark hair and dark eyes and at that time was possibly one of the prettiest girls around. What I did know about her is that she was around six years younger than myself and that she lived on Bolton-on-Dearne's Ringway estate – right next to the snicket that leads onto Thurnscoe Road, and very close to the place where I nearly got run over by the Sunblest bread lorry in early-1967.

She was also the younger sister of a girl from Dearneside's Class of 1981 – someone who used to travel the same journey to and from Barnsley Technical College with me on those Friday mornings – along with the girl from the Dunk Houses, with the turned-up nose.

Tricia Kay Robinson (now Cherry) had two elder sisters, Tracy and Tanya, the latter of whom had long dark hair and possessed something of a Colgate smile, along with a father-in-law by the name of Ronald, who not only lived on up on Goldthorpe's Manor Avenue, but who was (said to be) the younger brother of Thurnscoe's very own Real Wild Child – none other than Dorothy Shortt.

History is a series of dots that keep on connecting.

I had been back at work less than a month when all the bills started landing. Being back at work gave you money, but most of it was spoken for. Well mine certainly fucking was. The first couple of weeks' wages were just a façade to mask over the misery to come.

"Fuck me, J – you're paying it off over a year?" gasped Col.

I had gone into Yorkshire Bank on Doncaster Road and stuck all my bills in one basket to be paid off over twelve months. I would struggle, but it was do-able. My loan was for £1,706 (£5,536, circa, 2020), which with interest worked out at just over £40 (£129.82, circa 2020) per week.

Col had refused to be pressured and stretched out his repayment – which outside of child maintenance was much smaller than mine, but over a much longer period.

As for me, when each payday arrived, I felt worse than I had on strike. After paying the rent I was left with less than £35 (£113.59, circa 2020) in my pocket and that had to cover my shopping, water and electric bills along with the annual goosing of £220 (£714, circa 2020) for the rates. It was a miserable situation to be in, which was compounded by the fact that everyone around me seemed to be getting on.

Within a couple of weeks, not only had my (step)dad, but Col, Carl and John been transferred to Askern Main Colliery, which meant transfer payments of £1,500 (£4,868, circa 2020). Not only that, John had followed Col into the Personnel Manager's office to inform him that they were on the mining engineering course – and that being the case, they asked when could they expect to commence their face-training?

I have never been one to wish bad fortune on anyone, as whether they have it good or bad it doesn't alter your circumstances. It is you who does that – that is of course when you are in control of the situation.

Our industry was one that was a huge nationalised conglomerate that with government intervention, had just faced-off the biggest industrial dispute of modern times – and which was heavily in debt with half its infrastructure either knocked-out or in a bad state of repair. I knew this and was just thankful for a job. Col was, and to an extent, still is, one of life's chancers and a kid born to succeed. Put him in any environment and he would prosper. As for John, he had saddled up alongside him and come out with a red stripe on his helmet. "I've got to say, it's the greatest thing that's ever happened to me," he grinned.

Obviously, Tracy Greaves had known his limitations.

The upshot was, that if I thought him smug and self-righteous before – now it would be much worse. I was wrong.

Col had some brainwave that involved us going away to Blackpool for three nights, over the Easter holidays, which was something that I had thought about, but which was something that I didn't take on. The reason? I knew I couldn't afford it.

During the first couple of weeks after the strike I had been living the life of some rock star outside of work and suffering the consequence whilst in it. I still recall our Official, Brian Bennett crawling through the coal face one Monday afternoon shift after all the outbye belts had stopped to see what the problem was, and on climbing out into the Main Gate seeing me sparked-out across the gate-end box. "Aw come on, James – on fucking after's?" he grimaced.

"I haven't been to bed since Friday morning?" I told him.

He thought about it for a minute then asked, "Why – where were you on Friday night?"

"I was here with you on fucking night shift."

I couldn't account for one of two days, as it had been a blur, but that morning I hadn't got home until 8.00 a.m. I had gone back home with a pretty young girl who was the elder sister of Stafford Garner. He was a lad who had been discovered unconscious by paramedics in his home at Monsal Street at 4.40 p.m. on 2 April 2020, and who died in hospital three days later – his death being the subject of an ongoing murder investigation.

Det. Insp. Rob Platts, who was overseeing the investigation said that he had died from fatal head injuries, which is something that I will touch on in a bit.

As I said, back then, I never considered myself a drinker – however, the strike ending changed all that as did my meeting with one of the Assistant Manager's at the bank along with all the facts and figures he had given me. It was something of a reality check. "Are you sure you can afford this?" he asked, prior to me signing on the dotted line for the debt-busting loan.

"Yeh," I nodded.

All the way through the following twelve months, all I ever thought about was what I was going to do when it was all paid off and there were times when I was wishing my life away, just to get to its end.

What would happen, however, did give me some respite.

There were rumours that the new influx of miners from Hickleton Main who had come in quite uninvited through the front door, were at Askern Main just as some form of stopgap, and were expected to get thrown out of the back door within the next couple of weeks.

"I've been told that you can either stay here or be transferred to Markham Main with all the rest of the Hickleton lads," explained the NUM Official, Pat Hewitt, after a docket had appeared on my lamp.

All I thought about was the £1,500 transfer money, as in theory that would wipe out all my debt, therefore I gave him the okay.

I say in theory, as little in life is what it seems. Especially when either the NCB or NUM were concerned. The money was quite a lot, but it was a staggered payment over a year. One immediate payment of £750 (£2,434, circa 2020) followed by three payments of £250 (£811.36, circa 2020) every four months after that. Not only was it paid per quarter – it also didn't come as a cheque. It was part of your weekly wage, which meant that it was subject to PAYE, and after it was heavily taxed it didn't look quite as appealing. Still, it gave me some wiggle-room as I knew I was due a big wage after the Easter holidays – however, Col was still selling me the concept of Blackpool.

Whilst knocking around with him, certain things we did, rubbed off on one another – both in good ways and in bad.

As he had a house, he had set about tarting it up. Nothing major – a bit of Artex and a paint job. I had followed suit and done the same and what had been a tidy house with a rather old-fashioned décor that I had not touched since moving in, became very white and therefore looked exceptionally clean.

I still remember us all sat around dossing in his room as he diligently Artexed over the fireplace wall and covering up some of the obscene graffiti which had mostly been penned by Carl and John after I had set him on his way, by both mixing the plaster and applying the first batch. The thing with Col, is that he sat back and took five minutes to think about what he was going to do. As for me, I just did it regardless and time and time suffered the consequences. "You're too impetuous, J," he would tell me.

Tim had added weight to that statement well before. "You really have an erratic personality," he said. On numerous occasions.

An unpredictable hothead?

They may have both been referring to me, but they were also describing my mum.

Stewart Longden was one of Thurnscoe Comprehensive's Class of 1981 and a kid that I just could not take to. The youngest child of Charlie and Jean (nee Wood), he had lived right on Windsor Street's junction with Deightonby. I saw him as conceited – just some kid with a surly attitude.

The other year I posted some local history on social media which created a huge interest, that not only divided opinion, but which he duly responded to: "He's an arsehole – he acts before he thinks."

Although, I think his comments came from the fact that when we were kids I had dragged him off his bike between the two legs of Deightonby Street and kicked him in the head a few times, he may have had a point.

I am often quite spontaneous – however, the one thing I always do is think.

Maybe Stewart took his time and put immense thought in making the decision to leave the village and move forward with his life, and somehow he feels that this has reaped dividends. Maybe he can sit back at night in his favourite chair, take a deep breath, look around and feel a huge satisfaction in what he sees. I say maybe, as I know exactly what he is looking at and that is failure.

Sanctimonious comments carry little weight when they come from one of life's bottom-feeders. Unfortunately, ex-mining communities are littered with them. These are people who look up from the recess of life with nothing more than scorn.

It is sad, but it is what it is.

On Thursday 3 April 1985, we broke up off day shift for the Easter holidays – the idea being that we would meet in the Dog End of The Fairway that evening to have a few games of pool, as John Smiths bitter was being sold at a slightly subsidised rate of 60p (£1.95, circa 2020) per pint.

You had to take your hat off to the landlord, Percy Thompson. He had struggled all the way through the dispute running the place on nothing else but good will and coppers and even afterwards he never ever took the piss. I was told by my (step)dad that he was from the Dunscroft area of north Doncaster – a shithole pit village linked to Hatfield Main, that was basically a long street which possessed the name Broadway. He had married his wife Joyce (nee Cherowbrier) in 1961 and had two kids – Pete and Miley.

Percy did have his demons however, and although I never saw it, rumour had it that he attacked one of the Errington family with a pool cue, and duly clattered him with it. Whatever the reason, I thought him an extremely nice bloke. He left the pub a couple of years after and sadly died in 1992, aged just fifty. As I said, a genuinely nice bloke.

That evening started off with Carl and I playing pool.

"I'll lend you the money," Carl exclaimed. "In fact, you're the only person I would ever lend any fucking money to!"

I had the money in the bank, but at the dayshift's end when the bank was open, I wasn't going to Blackpool. By 5.30 p.m. when it closed its doors, I was wavering. Thankfully, back then I never had a mini bank card, therefore I still wasn't going. Col's acts of persuasion, however, were legendary. You don't get on in life if you don't have the gift of the gab and Col – well he had it in spades. "You can't stay here all weekend on your own, J," he told me. "You'll have a great time, and you won't spend much – just a few quid."

That line of conversation was all geared towards me.

It was the start of a good night. Even my (step(dad) came in. "Your dad phoned earlier," he told me. "He wants you to ring him back."

I acknowledged the fact – however, John coming in side-tracked me somewhat, especially as he had a smile on his face. "I know we have different views on different things," he said, as he pulled me to one side. "But we've all been through a lot and it seems stupid to fall out."

All through the years I have known John, this is how he was. One flick of a switch and you would turn some pontificating arse wipe into the greatest kid in the world. The reason? He had been in the other end of the pub, with the Greaves contingent and he and Tracy were back on – well, sort of.

They had fallen out. He hated me. They were back on. He liked me.

I never understood John as he was ridiculously hard to read. There is, however, something that was said in later life by Tracy to my wife regarding me, that maybe I wasn't meant to hear. "…I told him," she said. "I've always thought of James as a cousin."

Draw your own conclusions on that one. People can be strange.

That was followed by Col coming into the bar, along with their Andy and flashing cash around like Montgomery fucking Brewster and on me telling him that I would make one for Blackpool his face was a picture. You had to hand it to him. His presence always brightened things up.

Carl was going to lend me £60 (£195, circa 2020) and I told Col as much. Col did no more than pull me to the side and dropped me £90 (£292, circa 2020) on the spot. "I've got plenty in the house – just give it me back when you've got it," he said.

I had got it. I just couldn't get at it until Tuesday.

26. Angelic Upstarts

Nowadays it is hard to imagine the huge concert room of a working men's club absolutely packed to the rafters with young people on a dull Monday afternoon. However, at Bolton Club on 8 April 1985, that is exactly how it was.

Back then, Bank Holidays weren't a case of nipping to the retail parks to browse around the likes of Matalan, TK Maxx or B&Q – you either braved both the traffic and the elements by driving to the coast or you donned your best rags and went to the pub.

I look at where Bolton Club once stood, and it is just another faceless residential development of three-storey lumps of breeze blocks and brick facing. It is better than most. Half of Thurnscoe and Goldthorpe has been pulled down to make way for an unlimited amount of these brick-built Wendy Houses, which form part of some obscene land-grab by developers aimed at making more money by producing more and more of what they term as affordable homes.

They call it progress and perhaps it is. Maybe it is me looking through some sentimental lens at what has passed that makes me think that it is not.

I would love to nip back in time, just to confirm what it was really like. Is it just sentiment or was it real? A huge room crammed with around 200–250 young people, dancing around to songs as naff as DeBarge's *Rhythm Of The Night* or Dead Or Alive's *You Spin Me Round (Like A Record)* – with the bar area four, five or maybe six deep, with people just waiting to get served. And on a Monday afternoon.

Nowadays, pubs are virtually empty, but I have often seen people out in their threes and fours, and one of the first thing I have noticed is that they don't talk to each other – they are on their mobile phones, trawling through Facebook or whatever. Where is the fun in that?

"Hiya, where have you been?" I was asked as soon as I walked into the club's concert hall. "I've not seen yer for ages?"

"I've just got in from Blackpool," I replied.

"Who have yer been there with?" she smiled.

"Your ex-boyfriend for one."

"Uh, him?" she grizzled.

Wendy Fereday was a girl who was part of my life's timing – be it good or bad. I thought her a truly lovely girl, but as I have already said, life is a series of sliding doors, and I pulled this one shut myself. I'd had the chance before, yet at that time I was still on strike and from a finance angle, I knew my limitations, as I had with lots of girls – Debi Neal included. It was just bad timing. Now it was not. It was something completely different.

Eight of us had gone to Blackpool and had driven over there in two cars and stopped in two adjoining boarding houses on Alexandra Road – a street just off The Promenade. One of those lads however, had been Tony (Wap) Parks – a kid a year older than myself and someone who I had got on with extremely well.

I had made the mistake with Billy Coulson's ex-girlfriend. I wasn't going to do it again – no matter how good she looked – and believe me when I say it, Wendy was an upgrade on Billy's ex.

Her parents Ralph and Nora (nee Gallagher) had had her quite late in life – at forty-three and forty-one respectively – Wendy therefore being the youngest of three children. I found her very pretty, highly intelligent and someone who was always several moves ahead of you. The thing is with girls of this ilk, is that they are always drawn to the bad lads. Always.

Her parents had lived at 3 Halsbury Avenue during the late-1950s and early-1960s – which was right at the end of the very bottom street of The Avenues.

"So, what are you doing afterwards?" she asked.

I certainly wasn't intending falling-out with any more friends.

As a kid I had been to Blackpool once – possibly during the early autumn of 1971 as part of some club trip to see the illuminations. Nowadays, it is a tacky succession of gift shops and eateries made even more so by the people it attracts – namely stag and hen-dos. However, as a kid, you're in awe of the place. It wasn't much different for me at twenty years old.

I travel the M62 on a regular basis, and every time I pass Hartshead Moor Services between junctions 25 and 26, I still manage to raise a smile and think of Col needlessly feeding coins into the gaming machines in the services' mini-amusement arcade, whilst on our way over there some thirty-five years ago.

It is the same with picking Darrell Cooper up and of him having a brown leather case in his mitts.

I had known Daz several years, although he had been someone that I had never been that close to. This could have been solely down to the company he kept – mainly Jimmy Frost and Kevin Chambers, two kids that had helped make my second homecoming in the East end, initially a living hell. Daz however, was different. He was a very generous and an extremely humorous lad, who tended to give quick-fire replies to anything or everything that was said. Coopisms, if you like.

Generous: Whilst in Blackpool he leant me £20 (£65, circa 2020) as I had run out of cash and he just told me – "Give it back when you've got it."

Humorous: I remember waking up in a double bed and finding him in the middle of me and Col. All he had got in with us for was so that he piss us both off by having a fart.

He was short, stocky, strong as an ox and possessed some resemblance to Scaramanga's diminutive sidekick in James Bond's *The Man with the Golden Gun*, which now I've said it, does him absolutely no justice whatsoever, as the reality of it, is that he was an extremely smart-looking lad.

Throughout 1985 and 1986, he would play a huge part in my life and all I repaid him with at the end was a couple of broken promises, which were partly of my doing, yet partly not.

Hickleton Main had felt Margaret Thatcher's culling of the coal industry with almost immediate effect – Daz being one of the first lads transferred over to Armthorpe's Markham Main, the place where I had first seen him underground during late-November 1981, and a place where I would bump into him again a few weeks after we had been to Blackpool.

When I had first seen him, he had been part of a class of a dozen or so seventeen-year-old lads hurling tubs down some mock roadway in the colliery's underground training galleries, with him at the bottom of the slightly-graded drift, ramming steel lockers into their wheels. It was a scenario that every young lad would experience as part of their sixty days training.

You look at kids of that age now and you have to ask yourself – what have they got? What can they do?

Markham Main (as with Manvers Main) had hundreds upon hundreds of lads from Thurnscoe, Goldthorpe, Highgate and Bolton-on-Dearne pass through its training centres each year, all of whom were taught the basic principles of mining and safety within it, whilst being primed for a life underground.

Now there is nothing like that and nor will there ever be.

"Make sure you put the swan-neck coupling block on before you hook up that tub," I once remember being told.

Outside of those galleries I never ever saw a swan-neck coupling block!

I had mixed feelings of my transfer over to Markham Main as my sole reason for going was the transfer money.

I remember Tony Parks telling me whilst playing pool in the boarding house over in Blackpool that it was a great colliery. "A super pit," was his exact terminology.

There was nothing super about it whatsoever. To me it was just another pit made worse by the fact that all the names of the young transferees had been slung into some hat and had drawn different jobs – some good and some bad. As for me, at twenty years old I would eventually be back doing the job that a seventeen-year-old kid should have been doing. However, if you looked at the bigger picture – there were no seventeen year olds in the mine. We were practically the youngest. Not only had the strike and government policy robbed the industry of dozens upon dozens of fresh intakes of lads, the latter would have hundreds upon hundreds of other miners transferred to the colliery from pits under the threat of closure and jockeying for the self-same jobs that I was. It was soul destroying – not just for me, but for other lads my age. It was a time when a lot of us began to look for work elsewhere.

Col's being in the right place at the right time not only got him and John on their face training but had them docketed on a completely different shift to me. As for Carl, he was on the other shift. The three lads that helped me come through the final five months of the strike were all on different shifts. We had been spilt up.

As for Tim, I wanted him to come to Askern Main, but all he probably saw was Carl and John going there and had therefore opted to be transferred to Edlington's Yorkshire Main – a colliery where the vultures had already been circling.

All through the strike I couldn't wait to get back to work. There was no-one happier than me on climbing onto the cage and being lowered into the pit a day or so after its end. It was a feeling like no other. Six weeks later however, everything seemed a mess – the only good thing about it was that Daz Cooper – and get this, Kevin Chambers were on the same shift.

On the Saturday morning of 13 April 1985, a van had been over at Col's house – the result of which had been some brown semi-shag pile carpet that had been laid in his front room. To me it had been a total transformation. His house now looked like a home.

As for me, I still had wooden floorboards to complement my white interior – along with half a kitchen I had not yet had fitted and curtains that I had not yet hung. "Seventy-five quid from Carpet Warehouse," he told me. "I'll run you up for one if you want?"

Only recently, Col told me about a time when he had been a little lad and his mum and (step)dad – Iris and Roger, had had their first carpet laid. "I came in from school and it was just something else," he said. "We must have been the first ones on the street to get one. All we'd had before was lino on the floor. That carpet along with the blazing coal fire made everything look great."

Bless him.

The building that Carpet Warehouse occupied, was at 44 Barnsley Road, Goldthorpe. It had been built by the owner of The Goldthorpe Hotel – the-then thirty-nine-year-old Sidney Hamilton, and opened its doors around Christmas 1910 as The Hippodrome. However, throughout its lifetime it had been a series of theatre's, picture houses and bingo halls until its closure in the early 1980s.

Remember what I said regarding street names: Sidney Hamilton was a building contractor who became a licensed victualler and publican, who not only built The Goldthorpe Hotel but also the streets around its periphery. Hamilton Road along with Kathleen Street, Nora Street and St Mary's Road. Hamilton is self-explanatory – however, the latter three were the Christian names of his three eldest daughters. And if you want some more history – Sidney's firm also built the Cross Butcher Street WMC in Thurnscoe in 1898 and the parents of Dennis McCabe, used to run the club, when their sixteen-year-old son was just setting out as an apprentice joiner (coffin maker).

I remember measuring up my room – six yards by four yards – and Col taking me up Goldthorpe. We entered the building via a thin passageway which was filled with stacked rolls of vinyl flooring and cheap hearth rugs on one side and some tight glazed office where you paid for your purchases at the other. "Cheque's only accepted with a valid banker's card", read the sign in the window.

From the passageway you entered a vast auditorium with its gently sloping floors and circle above. It had been the first time that I had ever been inside, and even now, I thought it one hell of a building. Back then the hall was filled with rolls upon rolls of carpets along with off-cuts and remnants and that even included the stage. Even so, you could easily image what it must have been like in its heyday.

On a wet Monday evening on 22 September 1913, with a full house expected, people would have been queuing halfway around Kelly Street waiting to get in. With war on the horizon and just ten months away, hard-working men who had spent the morning down in bowels of the earth, deep beneath the periphery of Thurnscoe and Goldthorpe, the majority of who lived in damp, overcrowded houses nearly half a mile above, had come dressed in their best attire along with their families, in a bid to escape their dreary surroundings to be entertained.

Dependant on which review you believed – the 600-strong audience were about to witness an act who many described as being Britain's greatest horizontal bar comedians. The world's greatest comedy triple bar act – clever gymnasts and humourists of ability – a comedy trio who executed a clever knockabout comedy act, their encore generally being a mock boxing match. "Ladies and gentlemen, boys and girls, here they are – The Three Eltons."

There were people locked-out, late arrivals and people who couldn't get tickets. But that didn't matter – they were on again the following Monday.

However, quite a bit can happen in a week. A sixteen-year-old lad off Thurnscoe's Garden City somehow survived after being crushed underground by a series of runaway tubs down Hickleton Main, whilst up on the surface, a gas explosion completely wiped out Wrights Stores – a grocer's shop run by Albert and Mary Brameld (nee Braithwaite) at 85 Whitworth Buildings. The tragedy would not end there either. A few years later they had a son by the name of Edward who sadly died as a baby.

As for me, I had been oblivious to its past. I was solely there to pick out a lime green remnant of a similar style to what Col had bought, mine being slightly more expensive at £80 (£259.64, circa 2020) plus a £15 (£48.68, circa 2020) mock sheepskin hearth rug, which was around £15 more than it was worth.

There was initially a bit of humming and erring surrounding a fitting date – however, my pressuring got the deal over the line. "We'll get it fitted for you today, kid," said the manager.

It was the day of the FA Cup Semi-Finals, the results of which had passed virtually unnoticed as I peered out of the room window as BBC *Look North*'s regional news and sport was about to come on.

I had grown up watching Michael Cooke and Eddie Waring's five or ten-minute cameo as they ran through the local results, whilst waiting to leave my dad and Paula's on a Saturday afternoon, often missing *The Basil Brush Show* and *Dr Who* and not getting back home until *The Generation Game* had been on. And who could forget *The Two Ronnies* mini-series – *The Phantom Raspberry Blower of Old London Town*? Saturday nights back then, eh?

It had been the same window that Col and I had crouched beneath after seeing the police arrive in numbers after what they had obviously seen as an attempt on one of their superior's lives, after the concrete railway sleeper had been hurled off the underbridge some four months earlier. It was also the window, which felt as though I had spent literally half the strike looking through – mainly in fear of the TV detector van turning up outside the house.

I had resigned myself to being let down, but as *Look North*'s intro came on screen, two lads pulled onto the Square and dragged what looked like a crumpled-up piece of rag that had been lifted from some skip, out of their van.

Armed with their stainless-steel knee kickers, Stanley knives and industrial staple guns they entered my humble abode and after five minutes of banging, cutting and nailing, they left me with a new green floor, which after picking up the off-cuts and hoovering up the bits, not even Wembley could have surpassed.

I remember sitting back on the settee as *Robin of Sherwood* came on TV and staring around in wonderment at what I had achieved. Since I had got the house in September 1983, I had gone through nothing short of hell, just to get this far. Never underestimate the little things in life, no matter how trivial they may seem at the time. They are part of a series of dots or the pieces of a jigsaw that link the bigger picture together.

I still recall the elder sister of Stafford Garner calling around and clocking the new green carpet. "Wow – it looks ace," she said.

Much like Wap's ex-girlfriend, Sarah was very much part of my life's timing in that we were in the wrong place at the wrong time.

I thought her mum – Gail (nee Hatton), a truly lovely person. She was queen of the one-liners and extremely witty, that is for sure – so much so, she used to have me creased. She also had a certain nous about her in that on the few occasions when her daughter did come up to the house, she generally had to have something with her. In one instance a little ball of fire running around my kitchen that was her big-eyed, baby brother, Shaw – and in another, some daft mongrel dog, that after I had managed to tie it up, had tried dragging my kitchen table into the room.

"I didn't know you had a dog," I shrugged, after the nineteenth time of shoving both it and my table back in the kitchen.

"We didn't," she said. "My mam said that I should bring it with me."

As I said – a certain nous!

The family were extremely close and after the tragic and untimely death of his elder brother, the said saucer-eyed little lad couldn't come to terms with what had happened and became terribly ill, to such an extent that he too sadly died. Shaw was forty years old.

The murder inquiry, of which I have already stated, is being led by Det. Insp. Rob Platts has allegedly hit a brick wall, even though two men – a twenty-eight-year-old and a forty-one-year-old were arrested on suspicion of murder.

I don't know if they were remanded or even charged, just that they were there.

From a legal stance it is not something that I nor anyone can really pursue as it is an ongoing murder investigation, even though it should be relatively easy to get to the bottom of.

My thoughts are that the police just see it as some assault gone wrong and have washed their hands of it. If a weapon – say a knife or certainly a gun had been used, then Gail and her family would have possibly seen a more rigorous investigation.

It must be frustrating. Someone must be made accountable, and although it won't bring either of the two lads back, the family need some form of closure. No matter how old your children are, they are still your babies.

A family in limbo, all because the South Yorkshire Police are either too useless or too lazy to aggressively interrogate a suspect further than they feel is necessary. And they wonder why people take the law into their own hands.

Markham Main was different to the other two collieries that I had worked.

My first few weeks were spent as some form of Market Man – getting off the cage, walking through the air doors and waiting outside some Official's underground cabin for some Colliery Overman to deploy you onto a district with a specific job.

What is strange, is although a pit is a pit – you didn't have a clue where anywhere was.

"Forty-Sixes (46s) tail gate," I would shrug. "Where the fuck is that?"

Markham Main, however, had one big thing in its favour. Unlike Hickleton, which had exhausted its initial seam of coal in the 1950s and were developing other thinner seams, Markham was still mining within the Barnsley Bed – a seam that was around six-foot thick. This meant that the four strips of coal from the three-foot seam, which the all-conquering B50s retreat face at Askern Main had been turning out on a regular basis, was nothing. Less graft in less cramped conditions along with twice the output without breaking sweat, earned miners twice the bonus they had been dragging at Askern. It also meant more profit, which opened the door to overtime.

"Do you fancy stopping over?" asked a thirty-eight-year-old District Overman by the name of Tony Sivorn.

"Sure," I said. "What doing?"

It was a standard task of moving a couple of trams full of rings up to the tail (supply) gate rip (lip)… a total distance of around 250 yards… and by hand.

This was somewhere where nationalised industry fell flat on its face.

Grafting, whether it be underground or on the surface is straightforward, as was carrying the numerous three-sectional steel supports. Yes, they were heavy and uncomfortable, and the terrain you were walking over both uneven and wet, whilst solely due to the floor blow, the crown of the roof was also quite low in places – but it was do-able. No-one has ever requested me to do a job that I wasn't able to do. Dangerous to the point of being fucking downright stupid – yes, but never not do-able. Everything is do-able. Never, ever, think that it isn't.

As I have said previously, the NCB (British Coal) – helped on by the NUM, made its own problems, with its scaled pay grades of U, C, B and PLA along with having different bonus incentives at fifty, sixty-five and one hundred percent, and hard work, such handballing steel up to the face was billed as PLA work and basically "not our job". And this – well, this happened a lot.

In private contracting the only thing that separated miner from miner were the incentive payments, which were very easily understood. You all got the same rate (PLA), but the men at the back got seventy-five percent and men at the front one hundred. There was far more parity between the workforce, therefore as a miner, you would run through a brick wall if asked. It was how it should have been with the NCB, but it wasn't. You treat your men right and you will rarely have a problem. You pay your men right and you will **never** have a problem. You also get a far more flexible workforce.

Between the two parties they had created not just a vastly overstaffed workforce, but one with an indolence quite unparalleled.

Did we carry the three-sectional rings to the face? We did.

Tony Sivorn promised we would get paid accordingly, threw a ring leg over his shoulder and carried it up to the rip and said straight after, "If I can do it on my own, then I am sure you can do it between you."

What a great bloke.

A great rule in mining: Never ask someone to do something that you cannot or would not do yourself.

Did that happen? Some of the biggest wankers I have ever come across worked in the pit, so yes, it happened quite a bit.

On Daz Cooper being transferred to Markham Main, unlike me, he had been immediately docketed with a regular job.

Was it easy? Yes.

Would I have wanted it? No fucking way.

He had been lumbered with possibly the worst job in the mine. It was termed as X2 – 'X' of course meaning *crossing*.

A conveyor belt from both B51s and B46s main gate's loaded via a chute onto an elevated Armoured Flexible Conveyor (AFC) or Panzer type chain, which took the coal that was being mined past a series of air doors so that men along with transportation vehicles such as tubs and bogeys could travel beneath the continual movement of coal.

Daz's remit was simple: To make sure that when the outbye belts both stopped and started so did his. He was also responsible for operating the two main gate conveyors. It was a busy junction made worse by the heavy dust that continually needed supressing with water, which of course made everything wet. And the noise… well, the noise was fucking unbearable.

Not only was it a lousy job it was one that, with a bit of foresight, could have been wiped out. There were hundreds of similar jobs at this pit as there was at other pits. They were both low paid and needless. A badly designed mine is not just an unproductive mine – it is an unhappy mine.

I remember some three years later, working with a fitter on the repair of the said AFC after it had snapped and Kev Chambers' elder brother Mick being on the job, which had changed slightly, as by then, B46s had been decommissioned and a new face – B47s was being kicked up.

"Have they got you on this regular?" I asked him.

"It's doing my head in, James," he told me. "I've got to get off it."

It was that bad.

The first couple of months at Markham were great. The money I was earning easily paid off my loan and I had enough to get out a few nights a week.

Monday was the Darfield Road WMC in Cudworth; Tuesday was The Fairway; Wednesday was Bolton Club; Thursday's was The Church House at Wath-on-Dearne and Friday, Saturday and Sunday were generally a case of nipping to Barnsley, Doncaster or Swinton and then back home to The Fairway.

We didn't do every one of them each week, everything depended who was around at the time. However, everything comes to an end.

I remember coming out of work one Monday dayshift and having a docket on my lamp and on opening it, my fears were immediately realised. They had found me a regular job at the bottom of B36s main gate… as some fucking Transfer Point Attendant. I had spent eight or nine weeks happily grafting up in the rips and then this. It was the ultimate come down. I wasn't on my own either. A lot of the Thurnscoe lads had been docketed on similar jobs. However, as I have said before, other people's shortfalls in life didn't make mine nor anyone else's situation any better. All I saw in front of me was a basic rate of pay along with fifty percent bonus and a fucking struggle to pay my bills.

"Do what I do," Col told me. "When we go out, just have a couple."

I couldn't drink two halves of lager then go on pop. To me, that was like going into a fish and chip shop and ordering a bag of scraps.

I remember all the way through the strike of public opinion being against us and of several media outlets claiming that we were on three, four and five hundred pounds a week. On being docketed to that regular job, I rarely took home more than £90 (£292, circa 2020).

Fortunately, the Officials on the district, including an Overman with a broad Scottish accent by the name of Bob Donnelly pulled me up after a couple of times of seeing me. "I can't believe they've got you on this job. Give us a couple of weeks and I'll have you off it."

After the strike, the only thing that moved quick was the infilling of the mines.

As for Markham Main, it was getting all the miners from other pits and having them filling the jobs that such as I would have wanted. In part, it was soul destroying. It was a time when I was regularly in hock with the Yorkshire Bank. My loan payment came out and it not only emptied my account but often put me in arrears at the end of the month – sometimes up to £70 (£227, circa 2020). It wasn't just me either. I recall waiting to see one of the assistant managers in these so-called private booths in the Yorkshire Bank one Friday evening and catching a conversation between one of my near-neighbours off Roman Street and the manager – as he, as I was, had been substantially overdrawn.

At just thirty-nine years old, Robin Bolstridge appeared a tall, quiet, and unassuming chap. He possessed longish dark hair and face to match, who when I was at Hickleton Main, had been an Official on T02's, and as such, would have been paid his basic salary all the way through the strike. Even so, that evening in the bank things became quite heated – which was something that was no doubt fuelled by his rather argumentative wife, Sylvia (nee Wilson), who candidly refused to shut up – hence why I was unwillingly privy to their conversation. "I'll explain when I get home," he kept on telling her. Numerous times.

Robin's great-grandfather, William Bolstridge was a Checkweighman at Nottinghamshire's Babbington Colliery – the scene of a violent confrontation of around 2,000 pickets which culminated in more than sixty arrests and seven police officers sustaining injuries on 9 April 1984. His great grandmother Sarah, who was a dressmaker, committed suicide by hanging herself off a bedpost at their home at 16 Napoleon Square, Cinderhill on 21 July 1878.

After losing his wife, he remarried a girl by the name of Harriet Starr who was thirty years his junior at St Leodegarius Anglican church exactly six months later and exactly four and a half years after my great-great-grandparents Sam and Ann (Durose) had married there.

If you want another connection between our two families – I do have one.

For a time, Robin and Sylvia were friends with Barry and Carol (Oldfield), therefore that brought my mum and (step)dad into their company. During the summer of 1972, I recall being in their back garden and playing with their eldest child, a boy by the name of Michael (or Shaun Michael), and of him playing with a big box of toy cars. I recognised them instantly. One was a Corgi manufactured sky-blue Ford Anglia Ice Cream Van along with a white Matchbox Superfast-type De Tomaso Pantera with a No 8 on the bonnet. All the cars he had been playing with were mine. My mum had given them away. It was something that I could never understand at the time.

"You were too old for them," she told me.

I was seven years old.

The real reason was, that all the cars I had, had been bought for me by my dad. It had been just another case of her getting back at him.

Is it possible that I am reading this wrong?

Not really. She had done the exact same thing with one of those TV football-stroke-tennis games that he had bought me for Christmas 1978. In that instance, it got given to Mick Lowe's eldest kid – Gary.

As for Robin Bolstridge, he sadly died in 1999, aged fifty-three.

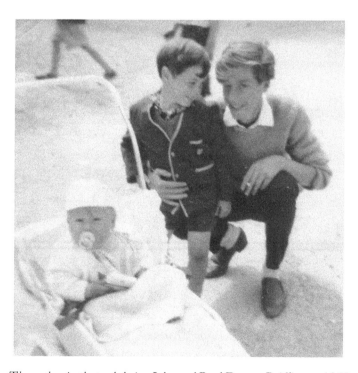

The author in the pushchair - John and Paul Durose. Bridlington 1965

Top and Bottom Left. Chopping out and riddling coal in Hickleton Main's railway sidings during January 1985 (c. Alamy) Bottom Right. The perils of inexperience. The funeral of two teenagers buried by a landslide just off Straight Lane, Goldthorp during November 1984.

27. Wogger

I had recently been told by my (step)dad, that I was becoming both thoughtless and selfish. I was a few things in life – however, selfish is not something that I had ever been. However, at the time of the strike's end he had been spot on. Outside of my immediate friends, I didn't give a damn whose feelings I hurt – especially the female element. However, whilst concentrating on my own personal growth, I suppose I had forgotten to ring my dad after being told by my (step)dad that he wanted to speak with me. That wasn't totally true. I thought it could wait until after I got back from Blackpool. Then I thought that it could wait until after I had been to Bolton Club. Then, I thought it could wait until the weekend. However, by then a note had been dropped through my letterbox from one of my dad's best mates and the brother of the senior NUM man at Highgate Colliery – Pat Thomson. "James, can you go and see your dad – Pat."

It is hard to describe something that you don't understand. At twenty years old I had been through a hell of a lot, but in reality, I didn't really know anything. At that age, you just think that you do.

John (Gratton) had called at the house, which at that time was full of boxes containing a mis-match of unfitted cheap kitchen units from MFI along with some tacky portable bar on wheels which had been salvaged from his (and Tracy's) house on Cromwell Street a few months prior and kindly ran me through to Barnby Dun. I say kindly, as what met me was a red-faced verbal tirade from my dad's wife Paula, and in all fairness, it was something that he should never have witnessed. "You were left a message to call your dad over a bloody week ago," she snarled.

I recall little else about it as I couldn't make out what she was saying due to the high-pitched screeching of her voice.

My (step)dad had relayed the message for me to call, but I thought it could wait. Did I know what the message was? No.

All Paula ever did was wind my dad up, and that is, of course, exactly what happened.

"I'm dying of cancer and you couldn't even be bothered to ring me," he said, as he came down the stairs. "Go on, get out – I don't want to see you."

Paula was extremely loud, and both very full-on and in-your-face – however, immediately afterwards, my dad realised that he had made a mistake.

On me getting into John's car, I was incredibly quiet.

"She's a right fucking idiot," he told me.

I just sat there shaking my head.

"I can't believe how you let her scream at you," he added. "You didn't do a thing wrong."

I had. I hadn't responded to the message and the longer that I left it, the easier it became.

I went up to my mum's that night and both she and my (step)dad were concerned, not just with the words that had been aimed at me, but with the situation. My dad hadn't just been a part of my life, he had also been a part of theirs, be it good or bad. As soon as I had left my dad's house, Paula had been on the phone and it was my (step)dad who took the flak. He had done nothing wrong whatsoever. He had done what was asked and passed on the message, be it vague or whatever.

"Me and your dad have had our ups and downs, but I wouldn't wish cancer on anyone," my (step)dad told me. "As for *that* [Paula] – she's fucking pig-ignorant and she should know better. You're just a lad. You don't know how serious these things are as you've never seen it before."

He was right. At that point in my life, the nearest I had been to death was going to my granddad Ellis's funeral the year before, and that, if I am being honest, absolutely crippled me.

I had been on nightshift a few weeks before the start of the strike, when I had been awoken by knocking at the door – twice. On the first flurry of knocks around 10.30 a.m., I looked out of the window, only to see my eleven-year-old brother [our Joel] obviously bored with trying to wake me and walking off Briton Square. Therefore, I went back to sleep, only to be knocked up an hour or so later – and I mean knocked up. This time it was my ex-girlfriend's mum, Joyce's turn. "James!" she shouted through the letterbox, whilst rat-a-tat-tatting. "You need to get up, love."

I let her in through the back door (which at that time was at the side of the house), and still dressed in her local authority Home Help smock, she relayed the news. I remember it like it was yesterday. "Your granddad Ellis died last night," she told me. "You really need to go see your grandma."

Now, that is how an adult should relay a message. She was very forthright but more importantly, concerned. As I recall, it was either his third or fourth heart attack – the last one being fatal. He was just fifty-seven years old.

Throughout my life I'd had very few bad words aimed my way from my dad. With Paula however, I was always someone that she could aim her snide remarks at, but more importantly, I was someone that she could apportion blame. As I have said before, she did it all the time and it wasn't just me.

I had to admit, that was a low point.

My way of dealing with it was to chuck a few clothes in a bag and jump on a train to Birmingham. I had met a girl on our weekend jolly over in Blackpool and we had kept in contact.

"I can't believe you're going down there," snapped John, on me telling him my plans. "It was what it was – just a fucking holiday shag."

In fact, he didn't say it the once, he wouldn't let it go and said it numerous times.

Now here are the two sides of John: The caring John and the sanctimonious John.

He never approved of how I was, or indeed who I was. I did what he could not. I picked up girls both as quickly and easily as I discarded them. I was both selfish and inconsiderate, and as I would find, it would be a hard thing to shake off. Out of all my friends, Col was the one who understood me the most as he had been there at what in my life at that time was, I suppose, another watershed moment. The night after the riots at Brodsworth and the Brighton Bombing: Debi Neal – the girl I had let walk away.

We always spoke at length, be it any subject – and I could always be honest with him.

He certainly never encouraged me to become selfish and inconsiderate, more intimated it. I watched how he ducked and dived to get what he wanted, and I suppose it rubbed off. "Fuck 'em, J," he used to say.

On me telling him about the situation with my dad his answer was simple: "Just get away for a few days."

Col was as pragmatic as he was sincere. With me that is. My advice to anyone else about the lad himself, is just as pragmatic and sincere: Don't ever cross him – as you will find out.

It was Col and Brian who had dropped me off at Doncaster railway station.

We had been inseparable since that evening on 12 October 1984 – however, the fact that we had all gone back to work had unlevelled the playing field to what was an incredible extent. Throughout the strike there was something of a parity as neither of us had fuck all, including Brian. However, whilst we were in Blackpool the difference had been immediately noticeable, with Brian running out of money and unable to afford to stay the last night – something which the owner of the establishment turned a blind eye to, and which was something that had been a task in itself as the police got called on to Alexandra Road.

"Come on, lad, get down from there and stop shouting," said the policeman.

Brian had been standing on a wall outside the boarding house with a can of lager in his hand firstly singing and dancing – mainly, his impression of Simple Minds.

"Hey, hey, hey, hey – Ooh who," he sang. "Won't you come see about me? I'll be alone, dancing you know it baby… Tell me your troubles and doubts, giving me everything inside and out and…"

And then candidly voicing his opinion towards some lads from Staffordshire, some who it was assumed that had worked during the strike. Well that is putting it mildly. "You're all a set of scabbing fucking bastards," he shouted.

The thing is, Brian had never ventured underground. Some of his family certainly had, however.

"Miners unit-ed – will never be defeat-ed," he sang, after the police had managed to coax him down off the wall.

"Can one of you lads look after him and get him inside?" the policeman asked.

"Don't you – forget about me…" he began singing again.

I had to admit, trying to console him was hard work and even inside the lounge of the boarding house, he was something of a livewire, which was most unlike him. A one-penny slot machine eventually took up his interest after he found that if you kicked it hard enough after releasing the arm, it paid out – that was until he finally emptied the fucking thing.

That morning, along with Daz Cooper, we had been booting a ball around on the beach, whilst some other lads were doing the same about twenty- or thirty-yards top side of us and towards the Central Pier. "And that is what I get paid for on a weekend," exclaimed one of them, as he smashed a ball between two jumpers whilst beating the goalkeeper quite easily.

"Have you heard that wanker?" Brian smirked on hearing the kid's egotistical remark, which was obviously said loud enough, to make us assume that he was some semi-professional superstar.

We looked exactly what we were: four rough-arsed lads from Thurnscoe, wearing nothing but a pair of shorts apiece, with Brian the stand-out one as he had his ankle strapped up with some manky bandage.

As for them, they were a few years older and certainly more smartly turned out than we were – with a couple of them wearing England football shirts – and that included Gary Lineker's more talented brother, who was wearing a red one and still showing off his silky skills, catching a ball on the volley and lashing it past the goalkeeper before it rebounded off the sea wall and over into what I suppose was our domain.

"Do you fancy a game?" I asked one of them as I booted their ball back. "Us four and you lot."

We tried kicking off a game using one set of goals against the sea wall, but it was hopeless as Col was always on the goal line, therefore we eventually opted to spread it out a bit and use two sets of nets.

Whilst we had been in dialogue as regards their size, the rules and the fact that the first one to ten wins, we were graced with the presence of Wap, who had dragged what was his new Blackpool girlfriend down to the beach. "You fancy making up a foursome to go out tonight?" he asked me, with reference to me copping for his girlfriend's mate. "She's a nice lass."

The thing about Wap is that although he was one of the shallowest kids you could ever meet – and he was, is that he always appeared extremely sincere. I think it was his face… I think. I had however, seen her before. She was some horrible skank in brown leather trousers who, along with her mate, would shag anything with a pulse. He and Bob Taylor had already doubled-up and engaged in a tag-team session with them on the first night we got there – therefore, the chance of him getting me to cop off with her was absolutely fucking zero.

The football game went exactly as planned and we were two-nil down after as many minutes, with *Roy of the Rovers* kissing the badge on his shirt before blowing kisses to the four or five lasses who were watching. As Brian had already intimated, he was a right posing bastard.

Whereas we started out as four versus four with no goalkeeper – that soon changed, and after watching all his mates pat him on the back, shake his hand, suck his cock or whatever, we changed tactics and opted to play what was always referred to as goalie-when-needed when we had been kids. However, the fact that Col only wanted to score goals and that Daz Cooper wouldn't attempt to tackle never mind dive – especially in the sand, made it my job. That was no problem as I had spent the last three years of senior school between the sticks, but more importantly, when it came to five-a-side – or four-a-side in our case, I could be quite unbeatable as it all boils down to basic reflex as opposed to positional. Also, it gave me a chance to both go through and kick the superstar up in the air a few times, none of which he wanted nor liked.

We were all quite natural footballers, but again, not in the sense where we could have ever taken it any further. I was led to believe that Brian had been released by Sheffield United when he had been a kid, and whilst I knew him, he played at a good level in local amateur football be it in the upper echelons of both the Doncaster & District Senior League and the Mexborough District Sunday League. As for me I was quick but very one-dimensional. On an eleven v eleven scenario you could stick a quick and clever defender on me, and it basically took me out of the game. Daz Cooper was a highly skilful footballer, who due to his size and stature possessed a low centre of gravity, which made it exceedingly difficult for him to be knocked off the ball. As for Col, he must have had some Italian blood in him somewhere along the line as whenever anyone went near him, he generally ended up on the floor.

After their initial onslaught and a string of countless brilliant saves by myself (sic), we consolidated and picked up something of a rhythm in that Brian and Daz wouldn't let them have the ball, so much so, their goalie-when-needed was non-existent and became the fourth outfield player trying to dispossess us, so it was basically a case of sticking Col on their goal line, soaking up the pressure and punting it up to the one-legged Paulo Rossi with the Turkish slippers, who managed to miss around a dozen open goals as we cantered into a 5-2 lead.

"Do you want to change ends?" Brian asked them.

They weren't happy that we had mugged them off and stayed the same and after regrouping they came at us both hammer and tong, bringing the score back to 5-4, before we mugged them off further. Brian and Daz were like a pair of Brazilians', flicking the ball around without it even touching the sand. I even picked up the ball from a volleyed pass by Daz, raced through the lot of them and put the ball in the net. We ended up easily beating them 10-4.

"Do you want to try for the first ones to fifteen?" Col asked them, after obviously getting the scent of blood.

They did and therefore the score became 15-4.

Apart from the badge-kissing superstar, they were fucking shit. However, these hadn't been on their own – they were part of a group of a dozen or so lads that had come up from Rugeley or Cannock – some of whom were reportedly scab miners. It was this that had obviously been gnawing away at Brian.

Wap had been philosophical about it all. "Who's to say that if we were from down there that we wouldn't have gone back to work," he said. "We just don't know, do we?"

He had a valid point – however, it is one that he certainly wouldn't have voiced in Thurnscoe.

I can only imagine what it looked like, four young lads wearing just shorts walking down the middle of the road towards the boarding house, covered in sand whilst all in conversation and bouncing some football.

"What's up with him?" asked one of the girls who had arrived at the boarding house that afternoon, and who had come into the lounge only to witness Brian wrestling with the one-armed-bandit.

I explained that the police had made him come inside as he was disturbing the peace – hence him sulking.

Fast-forward a couple of weeks and I had returned home from her flat in the Willenhall district of the West Midlands to a couple of letters that had dropped through my door. One was from my dad and the other from my nana Durose.

My dad's carefully crafted and neatly penned letter came over as him being very worried while being at the same time quite apologetic. My nans just told me how much her son (my dad) loved me. "Sometimes, you say things you shouldn't," he wrote, whilst at the same time trying to justify his wife's irate actions.

I got it that she was angry. I really did. What I didn't get was how she went about dealing with it. I had been in her life since 1968 – I was just four years old when I first met her. My dad came with baggage and I was exactly that. I thought her quite a lovely woman until I began growing up, and I suppose it was then that I saw certain cracks appear through her paper-thin façade.

"It's bloody Saturday again," he'd often exclaim post-her ranting

"No – it's not just bloody Saturday – it's every-bloody-day," she'd reply.

It was an indirect dig at my presence in their house. That cuckoo in the nest.

"He's going to have to buck up his ideas," I once heard her tell my dad, whilst we were on holiday in St Ives.

"Doesn't Paula like me?" I remember asking him later that evening.

I was just ten years old.

Ten years later, I well and truly had her number. I knew what was going to happen and when it was going to happen. It was just a matter of time. But I always knew.

I recall visiting him in Sheffield's Weston Park Hospital not long after the letter and of us sat on a bench in the park opposite. "I wish I had a kid of yours to bounce around on my knee," he told me.

At that point in my life I needed a child like I needed a hole in the head, but all the same, I knew where he was coming from.

He had already lost a huge amount of weight and the irony about that day was, is that he knew he was going to die. You don't bounce back from something my dad had. The cancer in his stomach, liver and bowels had spread rapidly. It was far too advanced for any chemotherapy to make a difference.

My dad's illness, if you could call it that, must have created a huge amount of stress at home and in later life I remember my brother Shaun recalling the tale of how my dad had been sat on the staircase with his head in his hands, whilst his mum had been screaming and shouting. I also recall my nana telling me that my dad had asked her if he could "come home". When you are really poorly, I suppose you try to cling on to anything that breeds comfort and familiarity. "I told him," she said. "I can't have you here, love."

They couldn't really. My nan and granddad were sixty-two and sixty-five years old respectively, and both very static and far too old to be looking after someone who was struggling and trying to hold on to life. It was all incredibly sad.

One of the outlets for my upset was at 40 Ringway.

My grandma Carman was a no-nonsense woman who knew how I rolled. During the early days of my tenure at my dad's, I often stayed at her house through the week so I could make dayshift. You could say that I provided a connection between the two. Any hatred between them had long-since passed and what was left, just became history. As I always had – I sat opposite her; her in her chair and me in mine, me looking up at the porcelain Dog-Ends ornament that had graced the mantle-piece of her hearth for as long as I could remember and which at the time held all the pens for her crossword puzzles along with the glass cube on the television – of which each of its five visible sides contained photographs of her ten grandchildren.

"How's your dad?" was without fail, the first question she always asked me.

This time however, she knew from conversations with my mum and my auntie Heather, that he was extremely poorly.

My grandma had different levels, which she often moved between. She was the Brian Clough of grandmas – a thoroughly engaging woman who I never ever got bored of listening to. As a child I got either a tut-tut and the shake of my head if I had done bad, or a wink if the opposite had occurred. And she was the only woman that my mum was petrified of – which was made quite obvious when I had been a child. "Helen, that's enough," she'd snap, after my mum had given me a clout. "Pack it in."

She'd then look at me out of the corner of her eye and give a slight shake of the head.

I suppose you could say that was the same with Grandma Ellis, although the latter would have to physically step in to stop the assault, but nevertheless, the dialogue was more of the same. "Helen, pack it in."

My grandma Carman's way of dealing with the subject was by talking about my mum and dad – when they were a couple and when I was a small child. As for me, I loved it.

My dad often spoke about my mum, with a sincerity. As I have said, in a strange kind of way he still loved her and told me as much one Saturday evening during 1975 when we were walking up Barnby Dun's Catling Lane and towards the bus stop. He even possessed negatives from photographs of them, which had long-since been discarded following what was an acrimonious separation and divorce. "These are of me, you and your mam," he used to whisper.

Only two or three of those actual photo's survived the cull.

He used to keep them close to where a lock of my once-blond hair was, along with the letters I had written to him whilst in Houghton Road Infants. He was my hero – a massive presence in my life, but now he was dying.

"Your dad used to drive your mam crazy," smiled my grandma as she recalled a holiday in Ingoldmells, that all our family had been on during the summer of 1966. "Just across from us in the opposite caravan had been some young girls and your dad's outside on the grass rubbing in suntan lotion, whilst your mam's in our caravan banging pots and pans and going crackers as all these girls are eyeing him up."

I was mesmerised by her tales. I always was.

Rather strangely, I can remember certain things from that holiday, such as me sitting outside the caravan on a blanket with my two teenage uncles (our Steve and Rob), who were both laid out and listening to the radio and of my seeing the boating lake in nearby Skegness and on being released from the reins of the pushchair racing into its water. I was told it was my auntie Heather who had fished me out as my mum had been overcome with fits of laughter. All I remember, was going under the water.

"We missed the bus back from that holiday," explained my grandma. "We got the times mixed up."

Both my dad and my mum had said the same. I was led to believe that there had been some confusion with the time's as they had been displayed in the twenty-four-hour clock format and the 14:00 hours that was chalked-down, was taken as 4.00 p.m. I know we managed to get home on some Wallace Arnold bus.

What is strange is that Auntie Heather had just recently married and at the time was carrying a cousin that I never saw. He died as a baby on 30 November that year, aged one day old. As did Jason, who was born the very next year, and who managed a mere four more days of life than his elder brother Michael had, dying on 6 October 1967. I sometimes think that maybe this is the reason why my uncle Jimmy often came over as standoffish and abrupt. Not so much, with me, but to others. Losing your wife at twenty-three years old and two sons that didn't make the week out – and all in the space of three and a half years must have been extremely hard to come back from, if indeed you can come back from it all. He was a guy I loved a lot, but the irony was, that his age coupled with long periods of isolation post-retirement, would always dictate the outcome. However, I have said that already.

As for my grandma, she often stated her dislike of him, which at times had me scratching my head as it was Jimmy who made sure that the lawn in her back garden was in better shape than any Crown bowling green. One of my memories of this was from the summer of 1976 and of me calling around to her house, just as Jimmy had left and finding that she had dutifully utilised his seven-and-a half-year-old son (and her grandson) – our Jonathan, to trim the edge the lawn around the periphery of the blue gravelled garden path – and with nothing more than a pair of small nail scissors.

Outside of what was happening within the family, my life was moving at a huge rate of knots.

An important part of this part of the story emanates from one Friday afternoon and of me sat in Col's Ford Escort outside one of the even-numbered houses on George Street – a street which formed the spine of Thurnscoe's infamous Spike, and which had been built in several sections over different periods of time. Around twenty-five terraced houses at the top of the street had been constructed around the same time as the colliery. These would be demolished sometime during the late-1950s to eventually make way for several late-1960s styled semi-detached homes, which were of a similar construction to those that my dad lived in over in Barnby Dun. The terraced houses at the bottom – followed-on. These included Vincent Terrace, which at one-time I remember standing at a nearby level crossing with my granddad Ellis and watching the colliery locomotive cross Lidget Lane on its way up to the brickworks. During August 1913 tenders had been put out to builders to develop four plots of land that would make up the rest of the street between. It was one of these properties that I had been sat outside whilst looking over at a 1976 bright orange Mark II Ford Capri with its large rectangular Hella H4 headlamps and vinyl roof, whilst Col had been in its adjacent outbuilding which doubled-up as a motor repair garage.

The property belonged to Jimmy Murray – someone that I had played football with during the long hot summer of 1981 with a view to signing on with his pub team The Bomb, and something which culminated in a friendly match versus The Goldthorpe Hotel on the Recreation ground opposite, along with a vicious 20-man brawl.

I had just equalised to make it one-all before setting up Jimmy's brother Mick to smash home the winner and that was it. There were punches flying everywhere – my main recollection being of Mick smacking little Stan Dakin in the face.

As for Jimmy, he was an amiable character with a heart of gold. He would do anything to help you out, and it is credit to the lad how he took his business out of that little garage and set up a what is a very well-run commercial enterprise around the corner – GT Tyres. I also remember him proudly giving me the guided tour when he first extended the place. He was a lovely man, so much so, I was shocked to hear that during 2004, his home had been targeted, with someone throwing an incendiary device through the window. It was something which caused major damage to the interior of his property.

"My car and hundred and twenty quid – what do you reckon?" asked Col, as he pointed over to the Ford Capri.

At the time, Jimmy had just started dabbling with tyres and Col had only gone to get a quote for an £8 (£25.96, circa 2020) slightly worn one. But that was Col for you.

I'm racking my brains here trying to remember, but I think I gave him some money – not so much towards the car, but more to get him out over the following few days, as he absolutely skint himself buying it.

John Gratton's rather apt summation of the vehicle was that it was a "right fucking heap".

It wasn't. That car was the stuff of legend – as you will see.

We always had several different lads hook up with us for the odd night out – but none who you could have ever said were regulars – however, by early-June 1985 both Neil Gollick and Steve Handley had become exactly that.

Neil – who had been affectionately known as Wogger at school, was the younger brother of my near-neighbour Tony and who, like Brian had been in the year below us and a big mate of Col's younger brother Andy Hunter.

I had often seen him on Briton Square, whether it be calling in to see his brother or going next door to Mary Gough's, whose son Dean – a highly-talented tattooist, was of a similar disposition, although much quieter. Neil, like all his brothers possessed a huge frame and was an extremely powerfully built individual. Nevertheless, his deadpan character took some getting used to, as initially, you didn't know if he was being overly serious, standoffish or indeed aggressive.

Unlike us, Neil worked at Houghton Main Colliery, which although it was basically in the next village but one – was in what was the Barnsley Area coalfield. However, on me first meeting him he had been allocated a pit house across from the bus stops at 47 Hanover Street. This was the former home of George and Mary (nee Brown) Porthouse – the former who grew up at 8 Vincent Terrace and the latter who had been Paula's mother's younger sister – and therefore her aunt.

Neil often stated that I had an intense nature – however, the first few times I saw him, whilst knocking about together, he too couldn't have been more indifferent.

I once remember bumping into him in GT Smith's (formerly Laws) supermarket in Goldthorpe and doing his weekly shop. He was extremely organised to the point of it being funny. There was seven of everything – including those flat-tinned Fray Bentos steak pies that were originally processed in Uruguay and that nearly cost as much back then as they do now; and of him diligently assessing which and what tins of vegetables that he was going to have with it and taking what was an age to decide. The next time I saw him he was in the Halfway Hotel and embroiled in a fight with around five or six lads and punching hell out of a lad from Goldthorpe, who was two years older him by the name of Mark Ravenscoft.

The next thing I know is him inviting me around to his for Sunday dinner and whipping up two sachets of cod in parsley sauce and a few days later walking into Yorkshire Bank with a black eye as he and his elder brother Mick had been fighting.

Neil was great fun to be around and extremely genuine and caring, which is a trait that he has never lost. He is just a great lad.

As for Steve, I had signed on at Hickleton Main and had gone through my sixty days' training with him as well as having time working together in the Bag Room on the surface prior to us being deployed underground, therefore it could be said that I knew him quite well.

Steve was around six-feet tall and possessed an uncanny resemblance to the front man out of Spandau Ballet who were a popular band at the time. Just like Neil, Steve had been in a relationship with an older girl that had run its course, and which like many, ended during the twelve-month strike.

Steve had been seeing a dark-haired girl by the name of Janis Agacy who between them had set up home in a row of terraced houses straight opposite St John the Evangelist and St Mary Magdalene Church on Lockwood Road, and just a couple of hundred yards from the exact place on Pit Lane where her cousin, the murderer Alan Conner had raped my sister's sixteen-year-old friend at knifepoint.

Steve fathered a pretty little girl in late-1983 by the name of Jennifer, who during the strike I would often see her mum wheeling around Goldthorpe in a buggy. As for Steve, the last time I recall seeing him, prior to him hooking up with us, had been in the colliery's NUM office on the night of 20 November 1984 – which was around two or three hours before Thurnscoe East had been totally blockaded and violence flared.

My wife's memory of him is spot-on. "He was either the best friend that anyone could ever have, or he just didn't want to know you," she said.

I remember bumping into him whilst we were out one Friday night, not long after I had gone contracting and us dropping him off at their house at 37 Carrfield Lane. His mum, Mary (nee Austin), was a wonderful lady and made us all sandwiches and cups of coffee, whilst we conversed into the small hours. The next time I saw him was several months later in Bolton Club and he looked at me as though I had just taken a shit in his hat. He possessed a very up and down personality. His older brother Tony, however, was a right firebrand of a lad. I remember one instance bumping in to him at Markham Main's shaft side sometime during 1988.

"What are you doing on nights?" I asked him.

"I've just been released on bail," he told me. "I've been in the cop shop all day."

It transpired that he had been arrested that morning for some incident at the weekend, whereby a lad had had either a glass or a bottle rammed in his face.

Tony was a great kid, but certainly someone that I wouldn't want to piss off. As for their Steve, he would indirectly cause me major grief after a series of sinister calls came down the lines and into my phone at 16 Briton Square.

"Your fucking husband thinks he's fucking it, doesn't he?" snarled the voice. "Tell him I'm going to fucking kill him."

I had come home off night shift during mid-1986 to a barrage of questions with my other half doing a bit more than suggesting that I had been having an affair with the guy-at-the-other end-of-the-phone's wife. "You must have really pissed him off," she said.

Obviously – but all the same it did have me scratching my head. I mean, if he had got my number from out of the phone book, he must have had my address – therefore, why tell me he's going to kill me. You know – why not just do it?

The phone calls continued all that week and into the next one, so much so, that after around the twentieth call, I got the police involved.

"Have you been knocking off anyone's wife or girlfriend?" asked the duty sergeant up at Goldthorpe Police Station.

"No," I replied.

I was livid. I wanted the calls tracing as these death threats were becoming quite unnerving, me getting the feeling that my days were to come to an end via some brutal stabbing. Little did I know, however, that was just some fucking halfwit who lived in one of the prefabricated ratholes on Ingsfield Lane.

"Tell me who you are?" I snapped, after the penultimate phone call around 12:30 a.m. "I'll meet you fucking anywhere."

"Ings Lane football field," he said.

"Give me fifteen minutes," I replied.

I remember gathering Col and Neil and us driving down Highgate Lane at speeds of around 70 mph and pulling onto Caernarvon Crescent – a street that I knew well, and me walking down the snicket, through the car park of Ings Lane WMC and into the middle of the football field, whilst the other two lads – one of who was tooled-up, stayed in the shadows. It was, if I am being honest – quite eerie. Everything was in darkness, but I always knew that someone was there watching me.

On the midnight caller failing to show and on me getting back into the house an hour later I received my last phone call ever. "You came mob-handed," it snarled.

"Yeh because I'm going to break your fucking legs," I told him.

He then did the stupidest thing you could imagine. He revealed himself.

"It's Conrad Smith," he candidly stated. With a rather distinct air of menace too, which totally baffled me, as although he paraded as some unpaid assistant doorman at The Goldthorpe Hotel, his was a face that I was more than capable of jumping up and down on.

I had first come across him whilst in Carfield Junior School. He was a strange-looking Herbert who was two school years younger than us and the younger brother of Bernadette – a girl who when I last saw her in December 1981, had worked on the cashier's till in the supermarket within Goldthorpe's Empire Picture House building – that of Supasave. I say strange, as although he must have only been eight years old when I first bumped into him, he had the presence of an undertaker and a rather disproportionate head to his body. He also had a penchant for talking down to you – pontificating, which was something that got me into trouble after I had kicked him up the arse a couple of times. Remember the story earlier in the book, of Nigel Baxter and us doing the school play about bullying. Well it was Conrad that I was adjudged to have bullied. I hadn't really, he had just grassed me up after I had rubbed his face in one of the flower beds.

Childhood reminiscence aside, I was down at his house several times that week. Either there was no-one in – which I fucking very much doubt, or he was upstairs in his bedroom hiding under the duvet as I was the last face he had been expecting at his door. He had been intimidating the wrong person. It was solely a case of mistaken identity. As I said, the kid was a fucking halfwit.

How it all came about is that Col had somehow pissed him off. It could have been any one of a number of things – however, I don't know as I hadn't been there. All I remember was the report from the front page of the *South Yorkshire Times* which mentioned that detectives from Barnsley were searching for an orange-coloured Ford Capri, which four lads jumped out of, leaving one Conrad Smith with a broken leg.

The story I got told was that Conrad had followed the car down Highgate Lane and into Bolton-on-Dearne on his motorcycle, continually overtaking, then purposely slowing down. Basically, annoying the fuck out of the driver and passengers by giving them the bird as he did so. I was led to believe that Col pulled up the car and that Steve Handley got out and launched a half-brick at his head, which culminated in Conrad losing control of his motorcycle and ploughing it into the telephone box at the end of Carrfield Lane.

"Conrad is a keen disco dancer," ended the newspaper report.

The journalist who penned the article must have been pissing himself with laughter.

I recall the police questioning Col about the incident – however, he was far too street-savvy to put his hand up to any assault, never mind one which resulted in some near-death experience and fractured limbs.

As for Steve, it hadn't been his first foray into armed violence as whilst on some night out in Blackpool he went to Col's aid after the latter was being pushed around by some big bloke in a nightclub, and duly left him on the floor in a pool of blood after wrapping a bottle around his face.

As my wife intimated. Steve could be very dark.

Unfortunately, during an incident on Wednesday night in Bolton Club, during the early summer of 1985, neither Neil nor Steve had been with us when we were introduced to Bolton-on-Dearne's local enforcer, Pat Marshall – along with a few of his mates.

I briefly got to know Pat through local football – however, the fact that I was more interested in earning money by working the weekends meant that I never bumped as much as I should have. Nevertheless, there were stories that followed him around – not at least after he had floored some kid with a head-butt in the Mexborough & District Sunday League during the 1984/85 season. It was nothing new in local football. Even I had split someone's face open with a head-butt. Mine, however was during a match against Wath-on-Dearne's Oak Tree Inn in September 1987 after I'd had my hands stamped on – and believe me when I say it, this dirty bastard was the biggest guy on the field.

Pat lived at the top of Caernarvon Crescent and who like the majority of men off Bolton-on-Dearne's scarped pit estate and its Concrete Canyon, generally worked at either one of the collieries. However, the fact that there was a relatively new Lotus Elite parked outside his house at No 2, that he had a pretty common-law wife in Angie Mellor, and that he would punch anyone in the face who looked at him the wrong way, made him quite the stand-out guy.

Angie was the elder sister of Gaynor – an intelligent, witty, and extremely pretty girl.

The tales that followed him around revealed that he was into drugs, something which was highlighted after he had accosted some seventeen-year-old lad off the Concrete Canyon outside the post office on St Andrews Square. The kid – Paddy Milne, I think, had just cashed his DHSS cheque and Pat had beat him senseless prior to taking his money.

He wasn't a big bloke, just aggressively very full-on. I have met people such as him all throughout my life and taking a step back and having five minutes to assess the situation is always the best course of action. You stack the odds in your favour. You take them out where and when they least expect it and of course, how they least expect it. And that is exactly what happened.

That Wednesday night in Bolton Club, was not unlike all the previous Wednesday nights – absolutely packed to the rafters with over-amplified music blaring out of the speakers and girls taking up the dancefloor and trying to manoeuvre around their handbags. What was different however, was the company we were in. Rarely did we come across Thornely Crescent's Three Amigos outside of Thurnscoe. These were Andy Hunter, Andy (Mano) Makings and the local Abortionist's livewire of a grandson – Paul Rice, the latter of who had somehow managed to get Pat's full attention.

Paul was a great kid and fun to be around. He was only slightly built but possessed a volatile and argumentative personality and as such always tended to be involved in some sort of fracas – not that I ever saw it. As I have said – they generally went to different places to us.

I have still no idea of the reasoning behind why what happened, happened, but Pat started on Paul and Andy Hunter stepped in to stop it and copped quite a vicious blow in the face from one of Pat's mates – who was someone that I didn't know. The next thing I saw was that Pat had elbowed Mano in the face and put him on the floor. It all happened within seconds and before Col and I could step in to stop it. Andy – who had done absolutely nothing wrong, was the one who came out the worst as his nose was bleeding heavily. As for Pat, he and his mates were all stood back laughing.

"We need to get him on his way home," I said.

Col said nothing and just took his five minutes.

During the latter months of the strike we had operated behind the picket lines both inflicting violence and creating mayhem. Make no mistake about it. We were more than capable of dealing with some local headcase.

In the here-and-now, my solution is a simple one – however, back then there was a social cohesion between us all that is very hard to explain. It is quite wrong of me to say it, but what happened at Jimmy Murray's is quite a normal action for the times we live in and unfortunately it happens all too often. In 1985 something such as that just never happened. In the here-and-now, Pat's car would have been torched and all his windows put through at the very least, yet they weren't. In fact, it was never even contemplated.

"Yeh, you were naughty, but you weren't a bad lad," my once near-neighbour Sheila Hopkinson told me in later life. "Now the kids are bad. Really bad."

Times have changed and having that heavy industry on your doorstep and everyone knowing each other tended to keep something of a natural order and all you got was the odd blip.

In Col's eyes that blip needed to be rectified and his solution mirrored the one that I had inflicted on Billy Coulson. Within a couple of weeks Pat's common-law wife would be getting picked up in an orange Ford Capri.

If you want to get back at someone, that is exactly how you do it.

Houghton Road Infant School photo's 1970. Andy Moore and Malc Hudson

28.   We All Live in a Yellow Submarine

Lessons were learned in the construction of Thurnscoe's East end and the expansion of Goldthorpe and Bolton-on-Dearne. Not straightaway but learned all the same.

When I was a little lad, I was mesmerised by Denaby. There was just something about it. The busy level crossing with the trains trundling through it, the River Don and the canal, the huge colliery and power station, but most of all it was the steep hill, which at one time comprised rows upon rows of terraced houses. I still remember them being demolished as part of the slum clearance and a series of cardboard boxes being constructed as part of their replacement. Times may change but, in some instances, history will always go on repeating itself and never learn from its mistakes.

Whilst I was doing my initial sixty days training at Markham Main, I often bumped into a lad who had been a year above me at Dearneside Comprehensive. Gary Cartwright was a lad I knew but is fair to say that I didn't know well. He possessed similarities to Tracy Sanderson's elder brother Colin – mainly in that he was just a nice kid. It was through one of his social media outlets that I picked up on a comment he made regarding Goldthorpe. It is the village he grew up in and where he still lives now – tucked away in a cul-de-sac in the shadow of the huge white water tower and close to his family – all of whom have never left those streets in the far end of Goldthorpe which bear the names of the three sisters. He is proud of his roots – a lad that is Goldthorpe through and through. He loves his home, his village, and the people he grew up with – regardless of the "imported scum" who are trying their best to ruin it.

Today, that remark could be construed as being offensive. You can choose to dismiss his comments and tut-tut all you like, but what Gary said is absolutely true. The cheap housing, the subsidised rates, and the quick access onto the UK's two main arterial routes via the Dearne Valley Parkway and the A635 make it quite an attractive place to live for those with financial limitations. And from the local authority's stance, it also makes a nice dumping ground for society's flotsam and jetsam – the so-called filth: the problem families, the homeless, relocated sex offenders and dare I say it – the now-static travellers and economic migrants. This is not just Goldthorpe – it is the eastern Dearne Valley in general.

Just prior to the turn of the twentieth century, the pit being sunk in Thurnscoe attracted thousands of men coming in search of work, which was compounded further by the sinking of the pits in Goldthorpe, Highgate and Barnburgh. Couple that with the lack of housing, poor sanitary conditions and a three or four-shift cycle and there were always going to be problems. When you throw lots of strangers together there always is, regardless of how the political elite try and deflect the subject.

I spend half of the year living out in Cyprus and have done so for the past fifteen or so years. It is no surprise therefore, that I come across quite a few British ex-pats. And there are thousands of them. You listen to them spinning their yarns about X, Y and Z, whilst all the time excreting some form of self-importance by bigging up their lives. They could be anybody – I don't know as I didn't grow up amongst them. It is a similar problem that now faces the people of Goldthorpe, Thurnscoe and Bolton-on-Dearne and something that all three villages faced at the turn of the century. It was also the same with places like Denaby, Mexborough, Wombwell and Wath-on-Dearne much earlier – as their collieries were mining long before the first sod was turned at Hickleton in 1894.

Now here is where the story could become distressful to some people.

Paedophiles were around back then, just as they are now. They are predatory creatures of habit who prey on the weak. They are also highly scheming and move around in the background going quite unnoticed, but nevertheless, they are there amongst us and always plotting their next move. Nowadays a paedophile's movement is linked to the IP server of their computer and its history, along with the pings from their mobile phones –

therefore, they must be highly scheming so as not to get caught. Back then however, it was much simpler to evade capture and was just a case of one person's word (the adult), against the other (the child).

Charlie Ellis, the son of Sampson and Elizabeth (nee Adams), had been born in in the Intake area of Sheffield in 1849 and proudly named after his grandfather. Like many migrant miners, his father had come up from the Sutton-in-Ashfield area of Nottinghamshire to eventually work in the pits, with Charlie doing the same and going underground at the age of twelve.

The second eldest of several children, he grew up at 61 Wombwell Main Row – a few doors down from where another Ellis, this time John, made all the national headlines in the summer of 1959 for strangling his wife to death with a white suspender belt.

It was widely reported that Charlie was very well-known in the town – however, that could solely be down to his father, who not only owned a grocer's shop, butchery and slaughterhouse off Wombwell's High Street (George Street); he was also on the board of Wombwell UDC and a distinguished member of the Darfield and Wombwell Building Society. Sampson had not only achieved quite a lot, he was also an avid teetotaller. One could suppose a great role model for any of his children.

With this son, however – that certainly wasn't the case.

Charlie married an illiterate girl from the terraced sprawl off Bridge Street, in the Towpath area of Swinton, by the name of Anne Elizabeth (nee Beardsley) in 1871 and between them they had two children – Mary who died one day after her birth on 23 March 1872 and Elizabeth, who was born some eighteen months later.

Charlie's presence graced several pubs in and around the town, not at least the nearby Prince of Wales Hotel and the Station Inn. As such, he had regularly been dragged in front of the Barnsley magistrates for numerous drink-related offences. However, his actions on 19 June 1899 – the day of the Miners' Demonstration Day in Barnsley – would be something else.

At fifty years old, he and his wife had resided at 51 Bond's Terrace. It was the same block that an elderly couple who had come over to the area from Lincolnshire by the name of John and Eliza Flatters lived in. It was also the same block that a young married couple in their early-to-mid-twenties by the name of Fred and Martha Lodge (nee Coates) lived and who were about to have their world turned upside down.

Martha was originally from Burton-on-Trent and had married Fred in 1894 and shortly after that they were blessed by the arrival of a little girl by the name of Esther Eliza.

At 4.15 p.m. on what was a warm sunny day, with temperatures topping seventy degrees, the little girl had been happily playing in the yards to the rear of the terraces, before going back into her house to get a toy mail cart.

"I'm just going 'round to the shop to get your dad something for his tea when he comes in from work," she told her daughter. "Play in here while I get back."

A mere thirty minutes later Martha returned, fully expecting to find her daughter still in the house. Slightly puzzled to her whereabouts, she went looking for her only to see her stumbling from the back door of the house where Charlie Ellis resided. She immediately noticed that she possessed what she could only describe as a kind of "lameness in her walk".

Overly concerned, she asked her daughter what the matter was and when she was told became distraught. This was made even worse as her neighbours, John and Eliza Flatters had a nineteen-year-old daughter by the name of Ellen, who had been out to the coal place which was opposite Ellis's house and she had witnessed him with the child on or over his knee in what she could only describe as an indecent manner – straddled. "I told him to put her down and he just looked over at me with a blank expression on his face," she told the little girl's mum. "I did try knocking at your door, but there was no-one in."

As the neighbours assembled a policeman arrived on the scene to try and calm the situation.

"You need to arrest him," screamed Martha, regarding Ellis.

However, they needed proof – medical evidence.

"My husband's still down the pit," she said.

"You need to get your daughter to the doctor's as soon as possible," Sgt. Christopher Taylor told her.

On Fred getting in from work that is exactly what they did. He and his wife rushed their daughter down to the surgery on Clarkes Croft, to the rear of where Wilko's now stands, where she was thoroughly examined by Dr Daniel Bartholomew Foley at 6.20 p.m. The doctor was under no illusion what had happened. The injuries were indeed consistent with the child's statement. At four years and four months old, the little girl had been raped.

The police immediately arrested Charlie Ellis, who pleaded his innocence by stating that he had been in bed all afternoon. He certainly had not.

It is hard perhaps to describe the next bit as it only gets worse.

On first remanding Ellis, the court heard: "The allegations are of a truly shocking nature."

Prior to the case being committed for trial at Sheffield Assizes, John Carrington had prosecuted on behalf of NPCC, whilst Joseph Raley who was employed by Dibb & Clegg, defended Ellis.

You would have thought that the evidence alone would have been cut and dried and consequently seen Ellis swinging from the metaphorical rope, however, that is where you would be wrong.

Maybe the thirty-eight-year-old Newark-born policeman hadn't done as much as he could have – who knows?

There were lots of permeations. It was a time when having a child out of wedlock was seen as nothing short of disgraceful. It was even more so, when the baby was found dead twenty-four hours after it had been born. It was also a time when trivialities such as having a flower in lapel in court would earn you grace and favour by the presiding judge.

All those things were part of the case, as was the fact that the prisoner's father, Sampson – whilst he had been alive, had been extremely well-connected. He had also lived less than 200 yards from the policeman, who resided at 22 Park Street with his Grantham-born wife Merina and their five children.

Medical evidence aside, the star witness for the prosecution was without any doubt, Ellen Flatters. The defence made its play, and she was immediately discredited as being a girl without any morals whatsoever.

She had been in a tempestuous relationship, which was often more off than on – and with a man some fourteen years older than herself who lived on Hope Street in the Low Valley area of town. She had also had a baby, which died shortly after its birth, and in circumstances where there was no reasonable explanation.

Even though she would marry the father some nine years later – James Bromley – the damage had been done. The black clouds hovered in court as the defence led by Henry Turner Waddy KC set about the witness. Not only did Ellen Flatters get dragged through the mire, so did the little girl's mother, Martha: "Did you not thrash your daughter after she had been physically assaulted by a boy on Sunday 18 June – just the day before the alleged incident?"

It was nothing short of a circus. Nowadays, the jury would have took less than ten minutes to convict him, however, in this instance, Ellis walked free.

It was a travesty of justice.

To compound things further, the little girl's mother and father could not rest. They moved from the terrace onto one of the courts off Barnsley's Pontefract Road, before resettling back in Wombwell at 33 Hewson Street. Unfortunately, however, things only got worse. On 18 November 1901, Esther Eliza Lodge died – just seventeen months after the rape.

The child had been poorly for eighteen days prior, eventually dying of cerebral meningitis. Maybe there was more to this as Charlie Ellis dropped dead exactly seventeen months later, supposedly dying of pneumonia.

Not much is known what happened after that although I am almost certain that the couple went their separate ways.

As for Charlie Ellis – he was another who had connections with Thurnscoe. His nephew who had been named after his father, Sampson, had been badly injured as a fifteen-year-old down Wombwell Main, when a pony he was working, fell back on him and broke his thigh. Consequently, he took the route of his father, who had worked as a butcher. Just look at the area to the right of where the marketplace once stood on Wombwell's High Street and its intersection at the foot of George Street – especially, the stone building to the right. The Butcher's Bar.

Sampson went on to marry a girl by the name of Gertrude Parr and moved to Thurnscoe where for years he resided at 38 High Street, eventually becoming manager of the Thurnscoe Lane Sewage Works on the road up into Great Houghton.

As for Ellen Flatters, she had three further illegitimate children to James Bromley – one by the name of Frances Mary who also died, aged twenty months, before finally tying the knot with him in 1908. Not that it lasted. He was dead within ten years.

There is however both a mining and a Thurnscoe connection.

On 25 April 1904, an incident occurred which had James Bromley in front of the magistrates. It was nothing new, he had quite a violent nature as both his future wife and sister-in-law, Sarah would readily admit to – the latter of whom received a couple of black eyes after being subjected to several violent blows. This day however, it had been the turn of his future wife.

Bromley had walked over some fields from Low Valley and past the gas works into the town to meet Ellen Flatters so she could give him some documentation – possibly regarding their newly born daughter, Frances Ellen, who had been named after her dead sister.

At 3.00 p.m. a man employed as a postman had been tending his garden at 1 Smith Street, when he noticed a skirmish. "I saw Bromley strangle the girl and throw her on the floor before kicking her," he told the court. "Then I heard Bromley say 'If it had been dark instead of light she would have got more'."

It would be something that would see Bromley get imprisoned for a month.

The witness in court that day was Albert Pacy Scargill whose great-great-grandfather, Joseph, was also the great-great-great-grandfather of Arthur Scargill.

As for the Thurnscoe connection – then the Bromley's are it.

Ruth Bromley was the girlfriend of Dean Davidson (Conley) when I played football with him during 1990, and her great-grandfather, Thomas, was the younger brother of James.

It would be in the same year that I would re-engage with one of the most dangerous of these creatures of habit.

Terry Gibbons was a lad from Thurnscoe's East end who had been in the same year at school as my younger brother, Joel. The eldest son of his namesake and Dorothy (nee Kitchener). I seem to recall him living in the vicinity of York Street, although I could be wrong. The last I heard, his parents had left Thurnscoe and were living at the top of Kennedy Drive and straight opposite the back door of Tim's old house at 178 Furlong Road.

I knew him mainly through playing football, but all the same I knew him quite well.

In June 1981, when Tim Bright and I were sixteen years old, we used to train with a pub team, The Bomb. We also put together a team of football-mad nine and ten-year olds from Thurnscoe East and promised them that we would fix them up with a few games – one of which was with Heather Garth Primary School – the head teacher being of course, Mr Kneissl.

Terry, along with the likes of my younger brother, his elder half-brother Steve Gibbons (Kitchener), two descendants from Thurnscoe's dark history in Jason Hardman and Paul Allington along with the highly-talented pair of Jason Aspinall and Lee Baker all played in that game, and they absolutely battered their opponents, coming out 7-1 winners – with Steve scoring the best goal of the lot. From well outside the area he hit a curling shot into the top right-hand corner.

They were an awesome bunch of lads.

If you want another bit of history, my cousin Steve Durose played for Heather Garth that day and scored their only goal.

Our Steve played semi-professional football with Frickley Athletic who at the time were managed by former Scottish international and ex-Celtic and Barnsley player Ronnie Glavin who during the 1997/98 season wanted to take him to play for another Northern Premier League side, AFC Emley.

Unfortunately, our Steve had never learned to drive and he couldn't get to Huddersfield to train with them, therefore he had to turn the offer down. A few weeks later, however, they beat Lincoln City in the Second Round of the FA Cup and were drawn to face West Ham United in the next round. Not only would our Steve have been playing at centre-forward that day, but he would also have been marked by Rio Ferdinand. To compound his misery further, the match was shown later that night on the BBC's *Match of the Day*.

A couple of things that I recall about Terry was his timed aggression – nothing major, but aggression all the same. During 1990/91 we had been playing a game in the Dearne & District League on the heavily sloping football pitch behind the scrap metal merchants off Mexborough's Whitelea Road. The game was against the side who were top of that division at the time – the Ring O'Bells from Swinton. Whilst kicking uphill we had come in at half-time 5-1 down. Terry's scrapping on the edge of the area had pulled us a goal back, us eventually going on to draw the match five-all.

The other time was playing in the floodlit five-a-side courts that first replaced Houghton Road School during 1991 and of him hacking at my heels before unintentionally glancing my jaw with his elbow. I had a bruise on my chin for a good couple of weeks after that. Although he had been a tidy schoolboy footballer, he lacked the elegance of his older brother Steve – who was without doubt a fantastic player. However, no-one could say that he wasn't a scrapper.

Then out of the blue I heard that he had been handed a twenty-six year jail sentence.

I was shocked. Twenty-six years?

The murderer of poor Lucy Jones got less time than that and he had beaten his victim senseless before she finally died. He had also lied through his back teeth to the police and point-blank refused to help them with their inquiries.

He got twenty years.

Terry pleaded guilty and as such received a third off his sentence meaning that if he had have gone not guilty and then been found guilty he would have landed a thirty-nine year sentence. It didn't make any sense. So, what the hell did he actually do?

According to the officer in charge of the investigation, a Det. Constable Jo Chambers, he was initially charged with twenty-six offences over a six-year period between 2007 and 2014, including rape and sexual activity with a child.

"He is an extremely dangerous man," she said in a press statement. "He groomed, coerced, threatened and persistently sexually assaulted and raped the two girls, who were both under the age of sixteen and despite pleading guilty, he remained in denial about the vile crimes he committed."

Generally, there is something about a person's sexuality that you can pick up on and it is no accident that females pick up on these things more quickly than males.

My wife said recently: "I remember him – he seemed a really nice lad."

I hold my hands up. There were absolutely no alarm bells whatsoever.

I looked at is police mugshot – and again, nothing. However, if you look at the photograph on his Twitter (social media) handle it generates a completely different perception. His prose – the bald head, the vest top, the sunglasses, the earrings in both ears… His photograph possesses a certain arrogance and has all the hallmarks of a person exhibiting the sexual side of their persona.

Now here is where I have to tread carefully as I have said before, rape cases have a lifetime anonymity for the victim and to reveal the identity is both wrong and more to the point against the law – with the consequence for doing so, one must assume is far worse when the subject surrounds paedophilia. However, in this instance you don't need to be Poirot to put the pieces together.

After Terry left school, he became a welder and on 20 September 1997 married a divorcee who worked as an administrative officer at the DHSS and who at twenty-nine years of age was four years older than himself.

For the time, the couple resided at 12 Crossgate in Mexborough but prior to sentencing, they had lived in a shoe-box sized bungalow at 19 Kingsway. This is a mock-stone-faced property that sticks out like some sore thumb on a street that at one time consisted of numerous prefabricated properties that were built around 1948 and which ran down the periphery of The Avenues and linked Thurnscoe's Houghton Road at the top, with High Street at its bottom.

The property had been bought in January 2006 for just under £90,000.

After Terry's arrest the estate agents William H Brown couldn't sell it. They ended up putting it in an auction at Leeds United's East Stand, where it was eventually sold on 6 April 2018 for £16,000 less than the guide price. The property realised just over half the price paid for it some twelve years earlier.

A lad from Cudworth by the name of Michael Smith purchased it for £49,000.

Terry had lived near-opposite a forty-eight-year-old woman by the name of Shirley Farmer (nee Hall, was Brice) whose whole life was reminiscent of some serial TV drama.

She had a history of alcoholism, an abusive ex-partner, along with a son on the periphery of showbiz, who is in a same-sex marriage and has two adopted disabled kids. It is also well-documented that he, the son, can tap dance on command when the media come calling. A few of Michael's high-profile cha, cha, cha's have been taking legal action against the government to force through his gay marriage; trying to raise a few grand via some Broomstick Ball so he could take his kids to Disneyland; along with trying to get the Cannabis-based medicine Epidoilex on an £8.60 prescription from over the counter at Weldricks. Not for him – for his kids.

Chuck in the paedo across the road, a bash house next door run by Thurnscoe's equivalent to Pablo Escobar, a low-level weed grower up the street by the name of Ricky Stables and it certainly starts to look like BBC tackle.

Shirley had been in the year above us at school and was the twin-sister of Yvonne Hall – the latter of who married a guy three her senior by the name of John Kershaw and who for a time lived at 14 Merrill Road. As for Shirley, she was found collapsed on the bedroom floor and pronounced dead shortly after. It came to light during a hearing on 29 November 2013, that the police had been called to the house via a triple-nine call the night before. She had been on the phone seven minutes, adamant that her ex-partner was trying to force entry into the property.

Det. Sgt. Matthew Penn explained that on responding to the call, his colleagues had to bang on her door and windows for some considerable time before she let them in. They also found no evidence of a crime and struggled to establish exactly why she had called, adding that she appeared both incoherent and intoxicated. In a nutshell, drunk.

That was never the case. She had been suffering from something usually found in alcoholics which is caused by a vitamin deficiency that impairs their judgement.

"Mrs Farmer was suffering from Wernicke-Korsakoff syndrome," explained Consultant Histopathologist, Dr Melanie Levy, post-autopsy. "She was also suffering from acute pneumonia, which affected most of her right lung. The symptoms are very individual and those displayed were of illness, but which would be misinterpreted as being intoxicated."

As had happened with Mark Williamson some eight years earlier – it was the effects from heavy drinking that had caused her death and not the heavy drinking itself.

As for the Bash House next door. That was run by a kid whose parents had lived in Great Houghton all their lives.

Paul Sherrington had been arrested after being found in possession of 2 kg of heroin, over 1 kg of cocaine and 45 and a ½ kg of amphetamines with the police stating that they had a 'street value' of £1.43 million.

By the police stating the *street value* it gives dual purpose. It makes them look heroes, whilst unwittingly handing the dealer the street-cred he craves whilst locked-up in prison. The reality of it was, the police confiscated drugs worth around £88,000.

The son of Ken and Jean (nee Helliwell), Paul was previously married and had moved from 81 Billingley View to the top end of Thurnscoe's property market, buying a house at 19 Howell Gardens in 2002, which was straight off the plot from the developer – Persimmon Homes (East Yorkshire) for £91,950 (£153,454, circa 2020).

His house was on the same street as two taxi drivers; one who used to run us backwards and forwards to Manchester Airport and at one time possessed a Raleigh Vanguard who I rode to Doncaster with as a kid – the other who was none other than James Lloyd, the man who used his part-time job to cruise the streets of Rotherham, looking for female passengers who he could bound and gag, before raping them and stealing their shoes.

I looked at Paul's police mugshot and thought that he looked slightly recognisable. However, if you stare at something too long, you get a kind of familiarity in your subconscious – your psyche, that maybe I knew him, therefore I dismissed it.

These people, however, don't go by their full name – they possess what are termed as *street names*, therefore nothing regarding his actual Christian and surname jumped out at me.

"You know him," I was told. "He's been to your house."

I have never taken drugs – ever, never mind dealt them, therefore how could I possibly know him?

South Yorkshire's drug dealing fraternity at the level Paul was working at is relatively small, therefore they tend to know one another. The business I operate turns over a sizable amount of cash and at one time it was located in the eastern Dearne Valley, therefore it is no coincidence that at some point it brings me into contact with some of the people that Paul would associate with. Drug dealers have a network of people that do X, Y and Z, as have I. Paul's business is an extremely dangerous cash business – mine is not. He needs to protect both himself and his cash. My needs are the exact opposite. I need to ensure that I get mine.

Paul had split from his wife and remarried a Thurnscoe girl who had lived next door to Shirley Farmer at 26 Kingsway – the said property that he had used to bash his product, which became quite clear when the during a search of the premises the police uncovered 20 kg of cutting agent along with other things, such as tools to cut, weigh and package the stuff.

Julie Ann Duggan had lived in the shadow of her elder sister all her life. Although I am sure she loved her, there was always that sibling rivalry. This is made more than clear by some of the comments that she has made through her social media outlet for all to see: "The youngest sister is always the smartest and best-looking."

From personal experience and bar, the odd exception, I reckon Julie's words come across as being dead on the mark.

Her sister, Tracey, had married Kevin Chambers, a kid who had come through the exact same shit as I had, and who had done very well. Between them, their life, bar the odd hiccup, could be seen as nothing short of a success. Kevin was far cleverer than he was ever given credit for. If he'd had the right start, he could have been one of the greatest business development or sales directors in the construction industry. He was that good. There were lads just as adept as he at taking on similar high-powered or middle-management roles within the Class of 1981. The problem that we faced was that we were from a time and place where certain things were expected of us, one of which was, to know thy place.

"If I'd have said that I wanted to go to university to get the degrees needed for the job I do now, our old man would have kicked off big style," Carl Eades once told me. "It was either a case of me going down the pit or being a mechanic, brickie or a plumber. That is as far as he could see. It wasn't his fault it was part of his upbringing."

Kevin's job post-strike bore all the similarities to mine. It was a nothing job that should have been allocated to a seventeen-year-old kid. It was soul destroying, but that would pass. I would say he kept his head down and just got on with it – however, that was never Kev's style.

One of my memories of him was that he suffered from the Monday morning blues on a very regular basis. How he sold that to Markham Main's Personnel Manager, Barry Whaling I have no idea. He just did. His Sunday nights out with the lads made getting up for Monday day shift extremely hard for him. His excuse: reactive salmonella. Kev used that excuse time and time again, so much so, he even had himself believing it.

From my back door on Briton Square I could see his on Hanover Street – with our back gardens nearly touching at the periphery. I remember him coming to work one day, near heartbroken. He and Tracey had bought a Doberman pup they both adored and within a few months it had died. Kev had the task of burying it in his back garden. Never ever think that he was just a laddish, vociferous rogue. He was much more than that – a great kid and someone I got to know extremely well. He wanted out of mining but didn't know how to go about it. The majority of young lads from Thurnscoe had been the same. His would come via voluntary redundancy – a time when the likes of Col, John, Andy Roper, Andy Moore and myself had already left. He took his money and immediately moved into a job with the United Friendly Insurance Company – the exact same company who Graham Pell had worked for when he had been found guilty and jailed for embezzlement. He was a kid that would never stick fast. Put Kev in any environment and he would always succeed.

"J, it's the easiest fucking job in the world," I remember him telling me, one night whilst waiting for his takeaway in the Chop Suey House opposite the Top Spot on Thurnscoe's Station Road. "I'm selling people something that they can't see."

Kev and Tracey made the move from their house across the road from the two bus stops near St Hilda's Church and down into the houses behind The Ship. For a Thurnscoe couple – they had seemingly made it.

I vaguely remember his wife's younger sister as a teenager but that is much as I do. Kevin, however, made a few statements circa 1986 regarding both her pretty looks and how quickly she was growing up. "She's going to cause some kid some right fucking trouble," he said.

As stated, he was far cleverer than he was ever given credit for.

Julie certainly had a resemblance of Tracey, but that was as far as it went. In sharp contrast and solely from looking in from the outside, the younger sister did indeed look like she was in her sister's shadow. She had dropped two kids and by the mid-2000s was living in local authority housing – firstly at 6 Whinside Crescent and latterly on Thurnscoe's Kingsway.

What you see is not always what you get.

What I didn't know was that her first partner had died in late-March 2000, aged thirty-four.

It was her son, Sam that told me that.

According to my ex-girlfriend, his father – a gregarious lad by the name of Steve Morley had carried the dubious nickname of Manface at school. I suppose the reasoning would be self-explanatory.

However, if you want a connection, then there perhaps is one. Just three years later, a lad from 14 Peartree Avenue, by the name of Adrian Mullins had died, aged thirty-eight. Steve's brother and Adrian's sister had, for some time, been in a common-law relationship, which I will get to in a bit.

As for Julie, as much as you love your sister, there is always that rivalry. It is generally always the case and is something that I have seen time and time again. That rivalry would soon by usurped before being smashed into oblivion. Cue: Paul Sherrington.

Drug dealing gives you ready cash and Paul – well, he obviously had it in bundles. The thing is however – is that in his profession, you cannot go throwing it about. Certainly not in Thurnscoe, anyway. Remember my mentioning of the bottom-feeders?

There are people tucked away in the background, that do not like to see progress. Especially, a girl from a council estate with a supposed chip on a shoulder, flashing off her new-found wealth – be it driving around in a new car, regular holidays or something trivial such as sporting a Michael Korrs handbag for each day of the week. As insignificant as these things are, it attracts negative attention.

We had lived on a cul-de-sac and set well and truly amongst them. It was a well-known fact that I had thrown the towel in with mining. My wife had been quite open about it, but that wasn't it. People on the street were inquisitive. They wanted to know where I was going every morning and where I was returning from each evening. We said nothing and just tried to get on with it. My reasoning was simple. I was trying something new and if it failed, then only my wife and I would know of its failure. It got to the point however, when even my eight-year old daughter was being interrogated about my movements with certain neighbours throwing her questions such as "Where's your dad going?" or "What job has he got, now?"

Even though my wife and I kept our mouths shut, there was a time during the early autumn of 1994 when the DHSS became extremely interested in what I was actually doing. It was no secret that I had thrown on the sick and had been ticking over on fortnightly DHSS payments and private health insurance pay-outs whilst waiting for what would eventually be some horrible operation. On my part, bar the fucking operation it had been both pre-planned and very well thought out. Someone, however, had taken it upon themselves to have someone investigate my movements.

I earned zero pounds for six months and by the time the DHSS got involved, I considered quitting. I even had a job lined up with Dragages – a firm who are part of the French conglomerate Bouygues Construction who were driving some tunnels as part of the development of Chek Lap Kok Airport in Hong Kong.

Remember what I said about during the strike, when men were patrolling the streets in Thurnscoe during the early hours to see which lights were being switched on? This wasn't much different.

Sometimes friends may look like they are putting their arms around you, but what you will never see is the metaphorical knife in their hand. It is used solely for stabbing you in the back.

As for Paul, he had sailed under the radar for years and he and his new wife's life looked great on Thurnscoe's Monopoly board. However, with Julie at his side, his future was already mapped out in flashing blue lights and one wrong throw of the dice and he lands a Go to Jail card. And that is exactly what happened. However, in real life there is no rolling doubles to get you out. He got handed a fifteen-year sentence, whittled down to eleven on appeal, along with an asset seizure under the Proceeds of Crime Act 2002.

My thoughts: his arrest was down to jealousy and nothing more.

Although his job was affluent – it was also dangerous. It was a job I would be no fucking good at, that is for sure. I hold my hands up. My nerves would be shot as probably, would everyone else be. I would never go anywhere without a gun and if anything looked at all dodgy, which during a drug deal, it more often than not, does, it would be me with the itchy trigger finger. When Col described me as impetuous, he wasn't wrong. I would make a lousy drug dealer. The world's worst.

One story I was told is that Paul went to do a deal in Liverpool circa 2013 and got robbed at gunpoint. He lost £30,000.

My business has a regular financial outlay regardless of what orders come in. There is a set figure I need to achieve and once that is surpassed, it then becomes profit. The more orders I get, the better I can sleep at night. It is business. As such it is just a case of me factoring our incoming and out goings throughout the year, so it operates on a gross and net profit basis. If a company goes under and hits you, it smarts a bit, but it is hardly likely to put you under. You can never take it personal and as a rule I don't. If someone, however, is just being cute, and trying to scam you out of money what is rightfully yours, then you cannot let that happen. It has happened before, and it will happen again. I am extremely fortunate in the job I do in that once I go after them, they rarely work at the level they once had, as is the tale with a Birmingham-based firm that now have to ply their trade in The Middle East. That £9,000 that they welched on must have cost them half a million in lost contracts.

£30,000? That is a huge lump to swallow. I could not let that go – ever.

Drug dealers tend to get any of the money they are owed through violence. You just beat or torture the life out of them until they pay. In 2007, I was at a funeral in Sheffield and got told the story by a street-level heroin dealer himself, who readily admitted to tying some kid to a chair and putting his bare feet into a washing up bowl before pouring a kettle of boiling hot water them. The reasoning behind his actions? Because he was owed money. Do you want to know how much? £120.

"You have to make a point – you can't let them get away with it," he said.

I had to admire him. At least you know where you stood – or in the other kids' case, didn't.

Ask yourself a question. If someone would do that for that paltry amount – what lengths would they go to if you or I were to offer someone such as that, thousands?

It is an extremely serious business.

Dealers need regular customers and through heroin they get exactly that. The addict or smack head is a person who has been cleverly nurtured to become heavily reliant on the dealer's product. Make no mistake about it, the rush heroin gives you is supposedly unbelievable. It is something that I have been told countless times. Repeated heroin use, however, fucks you up in a big way. It changes the physical structure and physiology of the brain and creates long-term imbalances that are not easily reversed. Repeated use also produces profound degrees of tolerance and physical dependence. The tolerance occurs when more and more of the drug is required to achieve the same effects. With physical dependence, the body adapts to the presence of the drug, and it is then withdrawal symptoms occur.

They say that withdrawal is one hundred times as unpleasurable as the first hit is pleasurable. The pain it creates is unbelievable and this can last weeks. Continual use and it becomes a chronic disorder that goes well beyond physical dependence and is characterised by uncontrollable drug-seeking, no matter the consequences. Remember that last bit. A smack head will do **anything** it takes to score that hit.

During 1995, I was asked by a friend in the industry, called John McKenzie, if I fancied moving my office into an old stone-built school that he had bought in Great Houghton. I had known John since my days, mining up in the Selby coalfield, when he had moved jobs from being a Sales Representative for the high-quality grout manufacturer, Pozament, and had set up his own contracting business that pumped the stuff as ground support – McKenzie Mining.

At fifty-nine years old, I thought him not only a thoroughly charming man, but someone that I respected. He was one of these people who didn't just talk about it – he had gone out there and done it. Therefore, after some lengthy debate with my inner conscience – mainly regarding if I could afford the move into much larger and more expensive premises, I gave him the nod. Unfortunately, two things happened, one of which was John's untimely death from cancer. The other was that the old school property possessed a non-existent security system, and it was eventually targeted by a set of smack heads. They stole several of my computers, which back then were worth a small fortune.

After asking around I knew exactly who had done it and went and confronted their mother who lived on Thurnscoe's Houghton Road – just a few strides down from the bus stop at the Big Lamp.

I was pissed off and duly vented my anger. Nothing physical, but certainly very-fucking-finger-in-the-face. She was petrified or so she claimed and broke down in tears, all apologetic. It wasn't real, however. She had been there before – time and time again. Hers were crocodile tears. She was just another piece of shit in the chain, whose sole aim was covering up for her shitbag sons. Within ten minutes I had the police up in numbers at Briton Square. It was nothing new. Their interest wasn't in the burglary, however – it was in me.

The police eventually left after giving me a severe slap on the wrist – however, I found out that the burglars were more local to my offices than I had envisaged and often frequented a rented house on the top of Great Houghton's School Street. I seem to think that it was No 9.

I will readily admit, I went both well-equipped and intent on doing someone or someone's, serious harm. In my mind, they had affected my livelihood and therefore they deserved what was coming.

I had my brother drive me up there and park away from the property and in the car park of The Old Crown.

As the door was opened, I forced my way into the house and the sight that greeted me was something that I had never seen before. There were five young lads, four of whom were sat on some manky sofa – grey faced, acne-ridden, stinking of sweat and most notably, frightened to death. My initial idea was to hit the first one full-on and to create as much blood and damage as possible and then set about the rest. Screaming and shouting and with my adrenaline pumping through the roof, I grabbed hold of the first one, ready to swing an axe into his face.

"Fucking hell, bro'," our Joel gasped, as he grabbed my shoulder.

I turned around and had a flashback in time. A flashback to the house on Primrose Close. It was me as a ten-year-old kid screaming and shouting. Why? Because the pen I had been using had begun to run out of ink and of my two-year-old brother, who had been standing there, wanting nothing more than to appease me. He had his right arm in the air and was offering me some broken pencil. I remember it, like it was yesterday. He was such a lovely little lad.

"These are just kids," he said. "Look at 'em."

He was right. They hadn't always been like that. At one time they were some mother's son. A smiling face at Christmas. A grandparent's pride and joy. However, that wasn't really the reason I didn't pull the trigger. The ginger-haired smack head that I had been looking for hadn't been there.

Rather strangely this incident, put me in contact with a lad who is no longer here, but who during later life it is quite fair to say, firmly divided opinion. At just turned twenty years old, Sean (Danny) Danforth had lived in one of the flats in the shopping precinct on Windsor Street that belonged to Martin Kantacki. I can only describe Sean in one way and that is how I saw him: a smart, good-looking, but most of all, a very respectful lad. I had been introduced to him by someone off Chapel Lane that I had known since he had been a little lad – Shaun Hiles.

At that time, it was well known that Thurnscoe was still in the last throes of policing itself, and that these two modern day outlaws were part of some uncoordinated three-man vigilante group aimed at eradicating the areas smack head problem.

For his age, Sean was an extremely capable lad and possessed a fast-growing reputation for violence. It was nothing new in Thurnscoe. This, however, was maybe its golden era, and the other person who made up this vicious albeit amiable troika was the twenty-nine-year-old Adam Brinkley. In my eyes, I thought they were all great lads.

I had had a run in with Adam around 1992, even though it had been anything but intentional.

A young lad, Dave Miller (I think), had been in Richard Grundy's bookies on Kingsway and had worked an angle in *pinching a price*. I have never been a gambler so I wasn't really up on the hows and whys, just that my wife, who had been a clerk behind the counter, had taken some flak from the lad, after she had called him on it.

Later that night I had seen him and his mate in the Top Spot, both of whom not only appeared to be disrespectful but seemed quite game in trying to wind me up. I immediately put Miller on the floor with a head butt and the other with a standard blow to the jaw. It was nothing special as they were just a pair of mouthy eighteen-year-olds, who were easily put on their backsides. Unfortunately, there had been a crowd of lads nearby who were making their way over to me. I seem to recall that I hit a few of them before getting crowded out – one of whom had been Adam, and whose nose I had burst. How did I know?

"He's burst my fucking nose," he had shouted.

Pretty self-explanatory, I know.

He certainly hadn't been very happy about it, that's for sure.

Adam had that look of normality in that there was nothing obvious to suggest that he was anything special. That is not me knocking him, that is admiration. He was neither psychotic, aggressive nor mouthy. Neither was he overly tall nor musclebound. As I said, he just looked normal.

I was crowded onto the dancefloor, and thought, *Once I get my back to the wall, I'll be fine*. Unfortunately, there were too many and I was crowded out before being dragged onto the floor and then I had around half a dozen of them around me, mainly clinging on me or laying in the boot – however, the only thing that stood out were two punches I received around the face. Why? Because I had received them from someone that knew how to land a punch. *Maybe a boxer?* I thought.

I had to admit, it was a good night, the sight of my wife on Adam's back trying to punch him in the head was a sight for sore eyes – and believe me when I say it – they were indeed sore. However, it did look funny, with his wife Lynne (nee Ward) trying to pull her off him whilst shouting: "That's his best shirt!"

Julie had just about ripped it off his back. I liked Lynne – she was a lovely lass.

Adam didn't just know how throw a punch – he could take any amount of violence thrust upon him. Nothing seemed to hurt him. He was indeed Thurnscoe's King of the Kerb and had a natural raw talent, which if someone like Brendan Ingle could have got hold of him at a young age, and maybe nurtured it, he could have easily been a British champion. He was just that good.

The week after, everything was great. "I was just trying to save you," he told me.

No, he wasn't. He just wanted the ruck.

I was in good company. He'd gone head-to-head and come out on top with some very serious and highly capable individuals, and had only recently given Pat Marshall a good hiding in The Dearne Hotel before making sure of the points by ramming his head through some window.

The ironic thing about this, is that Adam collected hangers-on. They weren't his friends. They were there for one reason only, and that was to see him fail. There are people out there who are just no good. Wankers. And then it happened. Andy Hunter had been up in Goldthorpe's Rusty Dudley some years later and witnessed him after a drinking session, taking several heavy blows from some land-based Pikey, with a few of his so-called friends and hangers-on all laughing about it afterwards.

The last time I recall seeing Adam was around fifteen years ago walking down Doncaster's Baxtergate towards the marketplace with a face that was almost unrecognisable. Some things in life are certain in that we all get old and we all slow down. It was a sad indictment to who the lad had been. He was really special. My thoughts are, is that he should have got out of Thurnscoe around the same time I had. His life would have been so much different.

Regarding the drug addicts, apart from me wanting the kid responsible for the burglary putting out of action and hospitalised, another potential problem had occurred. I came in from work one day to see the mother of the smack head that I had been screaming and shouting at come out of the empty property at 11 Briton Square – the same house which Norman Robinson and his family had occupied for years before getting into a red Vauxhall Cavalier and driving off. It transpired that one of her other son's was moving into the property.

Briton Square had quite a dark past before I ever lived there. I mean, the house next door at No 10 had been the home of John and Minnie Billam (nee Nortcliffe) – the parents of Raymond – Goldthorpe's very own body in the boot murderer. However, during the last few years of my tenure there had been a different type of people from miners and their families, that came and went with a high degree of frequency. No 10 had seen the death of Annie Whittaker and her house cleared of all her cats – and as with the Robinson's former home at No 11, and Freddie Bevins' former home at No 13, they had been gutted and sold to low-end property speculators.

I had already had the police up at the house a few months earlier for threatening to wrap a wheel brace around some guy's head for parking in front of my drive, whilst he had been looking around the inside of No 11. Needless to say, that he never moved in. Whilst No's 10 and 13 had seen two young couples move in for only a short time – with the lad from No 13 and the girl from No 10 getting quite acquainted with one another, whilst their respective partners had been at work. This led to the relationship at No 13 breaking down and the girlfriend or wife leaving and then me having to jump over the fence and stop Peter Parkinson at No 12, beating the living daylights out of the estranged girlfriend's ex-partner in the rear garden of No. 13. It was interesting, I will give them that. Then, with the relationship at No 10 now on its last legs, I noticed the girl's skirts becoming shorter and shorter as she trammed her kid up and down the street in the buggy to god knows wherever she was going.

"Dad, I've seen that woman who lives in the corner of the Square, kissing with the shopkeeper," my daughter told me.

There you go! It wasn't all the middle-aged lothario had been doing, either.

Whether it was legend or indeed real, the stories that emanated from the acrimonious break-up of that couple were extremely graphic, and whilst the girl's irate husband had been arguing over the telephone with his wife's uber-friendly grocer, the latter had let it be known that his wife was currently on her knees with his dick in her mouth. There are times when I do miss Thurnscoe!

As for the new-soon-to-be occupants at No 11? Cars had been coming backwards and forwards to the property and I was under no illusion that at some point the smack head responsible for the burglary would show his face.

I still remember Shaun Hiles and Sean Danforth stood on Briton Square, the latter in his slippers with a pot of tea in his hand like it was yesterday. He had just got in from work and here he was, peering into the car and through the windows of the house and merrily discussing their immediate eviction.

As I said, at that time, he was a great lad.

"I keep on seeing you driving around," he told my wife on her coming out onto the street. "It's a right car."

She had a white rag top RS 1600i convertible, that stood out like a sore thumb. It was a pile of shite, but to a young kid I suppose it looked the part.

"Do him and you can have it," he got told.

However, that wasn't me who said that – that had been my wife.

"What, really?" he asked.

"Just smash the fuck out of him, get rid of them and it's yours," I nodded.

Rather strangely someone got to the lot of them before I did. The smack heads mother's house on Houghton Road got targeted as well as the smack-house in Great Houghton. Within a fortnight the problem had been removed.

"It's not us," shrugged Sean.

It wasn't.

As for Paul Sherrington, there is a certain law of etiquette within the circles that he works. As strange as this sounds, drug dealers do have certain morals and one of them is to never handle heroin.

"I don't begrudge anyone earning, as everyone as I right to earn," one of Paul's ex-associates recently told me. "However, if they are dealing that stuff, then I want none of it."

I am in a similar mindset.

Under the one of the seats of his VW Golf, the police had found two plastic bags containing two separate kilo blocks of heroin at fifty-seven percent and forty-nine percent purity. Bash that with a cutting agent and that makes 6,000 grams – which at one-fifth of a gram apiece equals 30,000 spikes, which the muppets who are several levels down the layer cake are quite willing to sell to anyone who can cough up a couple of tenners – children included. And as stated, once these are on it, it is near-fucking-impossible to get them off it. Just ask Nigel Baxter's parents. Just ask my uncle Pete. Their children were happy-go-lucky and chippy little Herberts before they got the proposition of heroin – and they both ended up dead.

Never let anyone tell you that paedophiles just deal in sex. They don't. Their main purpose is the exploitation of children and they therefore come in many guises, one of whom is the shitbag right at the bottom of the drug dealing chain – that being the chemical paedophile. These are the pedlars of fucking misery whose main customers are those that have been hooked on their product from being children.

Julie's house at 26 Kingsway had been local authority-owned housing – however, she had bought the property on 28 November 2007 for £35,000 (£51,079, circa 2020) under the government's 'right to buy' scheme. It was a decent investment – however, Paul had made her an offer she couldn't refuse (sic) and one could suppose the thought of her moving directly to the top of Thurnscoe's property chain at Howell Gardens was just too good to turn down. It was a move that would not only put her elder sister well and truly in her shadow, but it would also create a resentment all around. Envy is indeed, one of the magnificent seven deadly sins.

During her husband's trial, Prosecutor, Brian Outhwaite told Sheffield Crown Court that Paul had also been cutting substances at home and preparing them for transfer by packaging them before they were sold on, and that mixing agents for heroin and cocaine were found in a bedroom with a dealing list. Scales with traces of cocaine had also been found in his garage along with more cutting agents and a vacuum plastic bag sealing kit.

I quite like Julie, but only an idiot would assume that she didn't know what was happening.

So, how did her husband come to be at my house?

Prior to him supposedly being robbed at gunpoint he had a business – R&S Construction and Groundworks, and had been doing some building work over at a friend's house – the one who had also been a past-associate of his, and at the time I had been debating having a couple of new drives laid.

As I recall, I mainly spoke with his partner – a very amiable lad who was short and stocky in stature.

Due to the fact of who had put them in touch with me, coupled with the fact that I live in a heavily-gated property in the town centre with CCTV covering every conceivable angle, they had obviously been interested in who I was. My interest in them was short lived, however. They quoted me a price that could have easily funded the sinking of a shaft in the car park of The Ship.

As for Kevin Chambers, there is a story that loosely links him to a vicious sex offender.

During spring 1982, when we were still working on the surface and awaiting our deployment underground, around a dozen of us trainees used to commandeer a set of booths in the pit canteen around 11.00 a.m. There was a lad however, who had been in the same year as me at Dearneside who didn't seem to fit in. In fact, I cannot remember ever seeing him underground. That, however, could have been for a multitude of reasons. He wasn't really a lad that you could ever miss, though.

Gary Smith was part of a big Goldthorpe family, well over six foot tall and possessed one hell of a frame for his age. The most memorable thought I have of him, was of him walking into the pit canteen to order from the counter and Kev ribbing him about aliens. "Woo-woo-woo-woo," he shouted. "Smiffy, there's aliens at one o'clock – woo-woo-woo-woo – can yer see 'em? – Aliens – woo-woo-woo-woo."

Gary had been adamant that he and a friend had seen a UFO over Goldthorpe, which was something that the *South Yorkshire Times* thought it somehow prudent to report on. In fact, it even made the front page. Gary said very little, as outside of his main two friends – Darren Fox and Mick Smith (maybe a relative) in our year – he didn't really associate with anyone, which now brings me on to his elder brother. He was someone two years above us and someone who I thought a bully at school.

Robert Smith cut a coarse and nasty figure, something which must have followed him throughout his adult life, being jailed for eighteen years in September 2018.

Goldthorpe's Hope Avenue is a street that I know well. My mum was born just off it at 5 Welfare View and throughout school I'd had several friends who had lived there. The street itself forms a crescent made up of both a southern and northern arc, with Robert Smith living on the first house of the latter at No 2.

A police investigation was launched in October 2014, after one of his victims told her support worker that Smith had sexually assaulted her on numerous of occasions, adding that he would get extremely angry and start swearing in her face if she did not do what he wanted.

He was immediately arrested, and a further investigation led by Det. Constable Jill Rankin led her to interview a second victim.

Both women were not only from Thurnscoe, but one of them had also been pregnant.

"Absolutely no-one should have to go through this level of abuse, as the mistreatment these women suffered at the hands of Smith was absolutely despicable," added the detective. "This has been a difficult and complicated investigation especially for the victims, who were subjected to violent and horrific attacks over a prolonged period of time."

Smith was found guilty of ten counts of rape against the two women; a further two counts of sexual assault and two counts of assault occasioning actual bodily harm for offences carried out between 2006 and 2014, including throttling one of them around the throat until she became unconscious and threatening to kick the pregnant woman in the stomach, if she didn't do as she was told.

As I said, he was a bully.

Before I leave this subject, there is a story of another local drug dealer.

Dave Bell was a year older than me and lived with his young girlfriend at Saffron Court, which is a newly built property located just off the A633 Valley Way, on the periphery of Wombwell's town centre. It was a house that he had also rather foolishly bought with cash.

I knew him solely through his day job. He was a decent looking, quiet, and unassuming lad, who was a mechanic, that had worked in his father's garage down on Rimington Road – an auto engineers that had a fantastic reputation.

His father, Colin, was a lovely man, who unlike most mechanics, would never ever overcharge or charge for something he hadn't done. I can put my hand on my heart, the man was as honest as the day is long.

A huge motorbike enthusiast, Colin had been born in Jardine Street and firstly went into business in Wombwell with his father Cyril, opening a shop on Park Street in 1960, before running Rimington Autos – a garage which was ranked in the top twenty-five in the UK.

As for his son, Dave, he had been apprehended by the South Yorkshire Police on the Dearne Valley Parkway in July 2006 after the Serious and Organised Crime Agency (SOCA) received a tip off that he was to collect a quantity of drugs.

Remember what I said? The police rely fully on the public to give them intelligence, whether it be someone supposedly making an iffy claim through the DHSS, through to the dealing of narcotics. Generally, it is a neighbour, a so-called friend or indeed a relative. Without a shadow of a doubt, it must be someone who knows the person in question.

On pulling him up they found a kilo of heroin at forty-seven percent purity, wrapped in a bag with Arabic writing on it – which suggested that it had only recently been imported. They weren't wrong. It had, however, been laid on as opposed to being bought. This further added to Dave's woes, as for months afterwards, whilst on remand, his mum and dad had Pakistani drug dealers casing their secluded property on Cork Lane, looking to get some of their £14,000 back plus the £4,500 for the 9,000 ecstasy tablets that were found in the car. He was in a mess. What made things worse, is unlike Paul Sherrington, Dave had the premunition of being robbed, and had therefore travelled backwards and forwards into Sheffield armed with a gun and twenty rounds of ammunition. Unfortunately, that itself, carried a mandatory five-stretch before any of the drugs had been taken into consideration.

At Dave's house, police uncovered 9 kg of a substance commonly mixed with drugs – benzocaine or novocaine, as well as more than 5 kg of crack cocaine and just short of half a kilo of cocaine – all of which added up to around £160,000 and which according to the police a had street value of £497,000 (£748,545, circa 2020).

He was jailed for thirteen years and as with Paul, had an asset seizure under the Proceeds of Crime Act 2002.

Colin Bell was extremely upset and laid part of the blame on his young girlfriend, citing the fact that he had changed since being with her.

"I could understand if he had never had anything," explained his distraught father. "However, me and his mother gave him everything."

The proceeds of crime investigation unit were after confiscating anything they could lay their hands on and had their eye on one of his high-powered motorbikes.

"I told them," said his father. "Me and his mother bought him that."

It was something which was clarified to the investigation unit by Dave's sister – Adrienne (now Sheekey), who just happened to be a detective in the South Yorkshire Police.

Remember what I said earlier: it must be someone who knows the person in question. Normally, it is a neighbour, a so-called friend or indeed a relative who blows the lid on a criminal's activity.

The only thing remotely interesting that happened in Kingsway when I had lived in Thurnscoe tended to surround the bookmakers – which I only got to know through my wife, as she worked there between 1989 and 1996.

The most excitement I'd ever had on there was during the summer of 1979, when we were supposedly camping out and I along with a couple of other lads, found ourselves on the street around 3.00 a.m. with me taking off John Travolta and doing *Greased Lightning* and jumping on the roof of some poor sod's car.

Its owner wasn't best pleased and ended up hanging out of the window and screaming at us. "I know who you are, you little bastards…"

I still can't believe I am remembering all this shit!

Anyway, the bookmakers were part of a small chain owned by an ex-Manvers Main Official (Deputy) by the name of Norman Grundy (now Betfred), whose horrendous motorcycle accident at Denaby Halt, when he was just twenty-six years of age, formed the catalyst for what became a highly successful business, which after his retirement had been handed down to his son, Richard.

Richard was both a lovely and courteous man, who was always on at my wife to move away from Thurnscoe. It was nothing cynical, just that he thought we could do better. It was something that a detective inspector one told me after an incident on Briton Street in 1990, after I had been charged with grievous bodily harm.

I was asked my weekly earnings which related to a form to apply for Legal Aid and the detective nearly fell through the floor when I told him. "What the hell are you living up there for, when you're earning that kind of money?" he shrugged.

Back then, anyone could apply for Legal Aid. Nowadays, the only people who get it tend to be paedophiles, career criminals and migrants.

We had toyed with moving a year earlier and put the wheels in motion. We were going to part exchange our house against a £43,000 (£116,377, circa 2020) detached new-build property on the Meadowgates development opposite Carfield Junior School and recreation ground, with them offering us around £15,000 for ours. It would have been very do-able – however, I saw what I had seen before the twelve-month long Miners' Strike in that nothing is forever, and I got cold feet. On reflection, I felt that I let my wife down on that one and struggled with my conscience for some time after. The reality was, that we would have been happy with one of the cheaper semi-detached houses, but because we were to part exchange – we had been pushed towards one of the highest priced properties on the plot – a detached house with a garage.

My wife's time working in the bookmakers brought her into contact with some pitiful sights. Husband's spending all their wages the same afternoon as they received them and in the case of Steve Morley's brother, Wayne – his then-common-law wife, Lorraine having to wait inside the building whilst his bets went down. There was also the other end of the spectrum too. The old guys dressed in their suit, collar, and ties calling in, not just to place a couple of bets but for the company they found there. There was also the sight of elation and I recall one Saturday afternoon after Stevie Webster's number had come in, and of he and his wife blowing a hole in his winnings whilst doing their weekly shop. "I didn't think you could ever spend ninety-quid in Netto's," he grinned.

There was always a wide variety of colourful people – not at least one of the managers. He was a lad around the same age of myself who I was led to believe lived in West Melton. He was a great conversationalist with the ladies who worked there – Julie Trueman especially. He also had a skin problem in that he possibly suffered from psoriasis and was supposedly in a relationship with a girl that in truth looked anything like a relationship. A mismatch of huge proportions you could say. Although the kid was affable and witty, outside of work, he was something of an enigma. He had supposedly had several mates who he hooked up with to follow Bernard Manning around the northern club circuits, yet had this elderly albeit pretty, well-groomed girlfriend that still lived with her mother – and who, if I am being frank, he very rarely saw. I didn't know him well – no-one did – however, my impression of him was that he could have easily been a closet gay.

Richard Grundy wasn't getting any younger and needed to take a step back and this guy had been a manager at a busy town centre bookmaker and obviously came with good references. One of the things about him however, is that he was also a gambler – and being a gambler, as anyone will tell you, doesn't just involve placing bets on sport.

Richard had had run ins with several customers that had lost heavily. I still remember picking my wife up from work one Saturday evening only to see Richard's burgundy Jaguar XJ6, the subject of a nitro-mos or brake fluid attack and it consequently being stripped down to the bare metal.

It was widely assumed that it was Mick (Woodsy) Woods who had done it.

Mick is someone I know of, rather than know. He is another highly colourful character who lives in the Dunk Houses at the bottom of Highgate Lane and who according to WikiLeaks is a member of the BNP, something which is further emphasised by the fact he flies a Union Jack off a flagpole in his garden. Mick was also there the day Stewart Ball came off his motorbike in Skegness.

"He was always okay with me," explained my wife. "However, he always seemed to have a very serious nature about him."

One would suppose gambling does that to a person.

Around 1980, I still remember him flying past Dearneside one late-afternoon at near-on 70 mph and up towards the shops on Homecroft's intersection with Straight Lane on a Yamaha DT175 Enduro and quickly banking from right-to-left, to fly past its island better than Barry Sheene could have ever done. Shortly after, Mick Moody would try and do the exact same on a brand-new white Yamaha RD400 and failed miserably. We were all looking out of the back of the bus which was parked up and due to take us over to the Sandal area of Wakefield for a FA school's football match and after he came off it watching him boot the hell out of his severely-scraped bike. On another note, we beat Kettlethorpe Comprehensive 6-1. Their goal had been a twenty-yard effort that had gone in off the bar.

As for Mick Woods, he was a bit special – and through our young eyes, an extremely cool kid.

With the new manager in place at the bookmakers – and one much younger than the owner, it would have been the time to show one's mettle and start building something of a reputation with its clientele.

One of the first bits of trouble he had, however, was with Billy Whitehurst.

I was told that Julie Trueman had taken his bet but had refused to pay him out after his horse had come in. There could have been several mitigating factors that had made his bet void – the most obvious being that he had left it to the last minute in a bid to get the best price, and that the slip had passed through the camera just as the race had started. I don't know. Whatever it was, the bet should have given him one hell of a pay-out.

I heard that he went berserk and tried to drag Julie Trueman through the glass partition whilst threatening to rip her head off.

"Now, now, sir," the manager said, whilst quivering in some corner.

Things tend to get exaggerated, but one thing is for sure – both the manager and clerk stayed locked behind that counter whilst he kicked off.

Personally, I think Julie had just being doing what she had been told to do – however, the fact that she had gladly taken the bet at the last minute, was the thing that had caused the disturbance.

Whilst the new manager was appearing to save the owner money in the shop on Kingsway, it could be said that plans were afoot to stage a complicated robbery and one which would see its owner, Richard Gundry, lose a considerable amount of money. For me, it was too well-thought out, in that it was overthought, if that makes any sense, and the story itself moved around far too much for it to have any real validation.

According to the new manager, on the night of the robbery he had been in the pub with some male friends that he claimed not to really know and who had come back to his house. Why invite men whose names you don't know back to your house? He was either gay or the story he was telling was one of fiction.

He claimed that during the early hours his home had been burgled and the keys to both the betting office and the safe were taken. I am not one hundred percent on this, but I seem to feel that the keys were the total sum of the haul and that nothing else was taken from the house. On the burglars getting on Kingsway they were in and out within minutes as they also knew the exact location of the safe – which was buried deep beneath the floor around the kitchenette area to the rear of the building.

"No-one apart from someone who worked there would have ever known where it was," said my wife. "It was even fully covered by a carpet."

The only thing which gave the story any credibility was that the alarm was left to sound. The police thought him guilty, as did the owner – however, they couldn't find any concrete evidence. Maybe the manager had gambled and won – who knows?

His tenure didn't last much long after that. He knew he was being watched.

Two of my grandma's - Helen Carman (nee Gilmer) circa 1952 and Elsie Ellis (was Rayner, nee Cowen) circa 1938. Very forthright and highly protective.

Top. Askern Main Colliery in January 1985. Hundreds of men were transferred to Askern from Hickleton Main both before and after the 1984/85 Miners' Strike (c. PA Photos / Alamy) Bottom Left and Right. The dirty Coalite plant at the mine, both before the strike and after (John Harris).

29. Deviant

During the long-drawn-out summer of 1984, I had spent hours upon hours down at Tim's house at 178 Furlong Road. Throughout 1985, however, I cannot ever remember calling down there.

It was a house I knew well. From Tim moving there from Carrfield Lane, I had seen the place evolve from some ramshackle end-terrace to the stand-out property on the block, with its grey-cemented mock stone facing on the front and the mini extension on the back. Just like Tim's nan and granddad (Beaumont), his dad had had a tickle on the football pools – not enough to go berserk, but a few thousand quid, and he embarked on a modernisation programme that as a kid, I had quite been in awe of. It was a lovely house with some great memories, not at least its cellar which not only housed the coke as part of their home fuel allowance, but masses upon masses of Tim and his dad's fishing tackle – and just like the house we lived in on The Avenues, it had that distinctive damp smell, which never leaves you. Little did we know however, that it was a place which had been the catalyst for one of Bolton-on-Dearne's most bizarre tragedies. Every house holds a secret. An act of violence, a suicide, a rape – even a murder. It could be one of a number of things, and the houses that made up Furlong Road – well they were no different.

After my uncle Paul (Durose) died, Auntie Anne remarried a lovely man by the name of Steve Burrows, who I have since got to know quite well.

Being from Bolton-on-Dearne he had known my auntie and the woman that would become his wife, the majority of his life and made-mention of her grandparents Fred and Emma Watson (nee Ellis), who along with their sons, had made the short move from a council house at 12 Prospect Road to one around the corner on Furlong Road.

No 115 was one of the middle houses of a block of four that was sandwiched between a butcher's – that was owned by the former boyfriend of Doris Turnbull, the young lady who gassed herself and a grocers – that was run by Jim Sharrock and his wife, Connie, and which during my early years, was the Co-op and what looked like an empty drapers shop next door.

"Someone Anne's dad knew had been in the Navy and given them a marmoset – a monkey?" said Steve. "Anne's mam called it Jacko – and as for us lads, we were enthralled by it. We used to trawl the streets catching little dogs to sling in their back yard for it."

When asked why? Steve enthused: "We used to watch the monkey try to shag 'em."

As for Tim's house, the extension his dad had built on the back, became their bathroom, which I always found as cold as the cellar – and which like most houses undergoing a modernisation programme at that time, housed a new off green-coloured bathroom suite. For the record, ours at Lancaster Street was a dark brown.

It was a property that was originally inhabited by Charles Lockwood – a farmer who was part of the family that had sold off parcels of their huge Farm estate during the early- to mid-1920s to help further develop the Washington Road and Hope Avenue areas of Goldthorpe.

During the Second World War the house had been inhabited by a newly married couple – William Kitchener Winder and his wife Edith (nee Hall), whose parents lived a few doors up from them and next to what was once Ken Brown's motorcycle garage. However, a further generation on, and George and Phyllis Blandford (nee Herbert) would set up home at the address – the former who had been born in the Grimsby area and who during the war worked in Sheffield's steel mills. Between them had four boys: David (b. 1942), Brian (b. 1946), Ray (b. 1948) and Don (b. 1956), all of whom left their mark on the area – not least Ray.

Whilst a young lad, my uncle Pete laid claim to seeing a girl whose parents had come into the UK after the Second World War and had come to settle in the eastern Dearne Valley via the St Neots area of Huntingdonshire.

The girl's father had got a job in the pit and the family eventually moved into the house at 123 Merrill Road. Grazyna Matysiak, was a year younger than our Pete and was someone who he described as being extremely pretty.

Ray Blandford cut a different figure entirely, and as with Jozef Kugler – the Lover's Lane Murderer, his appearance was very rock 'n' roll. Whether it was purposely done or not I would not know. He modelled his look on Marlon Brando, in that he was rarely ever seen without his trademark black leather jacket and white T-shirt – something that his younger brother would copy when he got older. His main haunts were the Buxton Arms and Highgate WMC, although he was also known to frequent the Halfway Hotel.

As with Tim and his dad, and living in close proximity to the Brick Ponds, he was a keen angler and whether it had been a tongue in cheek comment or not, it was said that he was the one who had stocked Frank Wells's pond with carp.

Whilst Grazyna had trained to be a shorthand typist, Ray, like many men in Bolton-on-Dearne, worked in heavy industry and was employed by British Rail as a Wagon fitter – although for some unknown reason, he would leave that profession for that of a builder's labourer.

That aside, between them they appeared to have life cracked and had set a date of 29 August 1970 as the day they would be married.

Close your eyes and try to imagine the scene in an early-1970s three-process Technicolor.

That morning, the sun was out with temperatures set to soar well into the seventies. It was the start of a beautiful summers day.

Ray sat on the back step, with mug of tea in his hand reading the *Daily Mirror*. "Just Potty About Each Other – Lord Gardiner marries author Mrs Muriel Box," said the headlines. "It's never too late to fall in love and these newlyweds prove it."

The signs were ominous and that trip to Doncaster Register Office wouldn't be long.

As a succession of red Yorkshire Traction buses passed down Furlong Road – some going to Mexborough and Wath-on-Dearne – some to Thurnscoe, whilst Noel Edmonds could be heard prattling away on the radio. Inside the house his mum was getting ready for what would be her big day. There was a feelgood factor and his elder brother Barry – who was to double as his Best Man, would join him on the step with a brew.

"Wilf Smith's move to Chelsea is off," said Ray, as regards Sheffield Wednesday selling their £100,000 valued defender in some part-exchange deal to balance the books after their relegation into the second division. "John Boyle turned 'Wednesday's offer down."

"I'm not surprised," said Barry, as he looked down Kennedy Drive and at some children playing on the green. "They couldn't even beat Cardiff."

As Radio One played the hits of the time such as Smokey Robinson's *Tears of a Clown*, Deep Purple's *Black Night* and far more appropriately, Three Dog Night's *Mama Told Me Not To Come*, all of which had been hogging the top five places in the charts, his mum summoned both brothers. "You two should both be getting ready," she smiled, before dropping a thought. "It's just a pity your dad couldn't be here to see it."

George Blandford had died three years earlier at forty-seven years of age.

The wedding I am sure, went without a hitch, and as a couple they moved five doors down from his mother, where between them they would have a son by the name of Darryl, who they rather strangely gave the middle name of Rex.

Everything about their relationship appeared structured – however, as Tim's parents set about ripping apart Ray's parents former end-terrace house some seven years later, police along with paramedics arrived on the scene. A dead body had reportedly been found in 168 Furlong Road and in quite suspicious circumstances. There was talk of murder, but that was never the case. Ray was dead, of that there was no doubt. The suspicion surrounded the fact that he had been found in a distressed state and with a polythene bag over his head and some ball in his mouth.

It was a sex act that he had been carrying out on himself that had gone wrong. At just twenty-nine years old he had inadvertently suffocated himself and died of asphyxiation.

At the time, Tim's (step)mum Jill had had us both scratching our heads after she had made reference to him having the golf ball in his mouth.

It was a stupid thing to do and I said as much. *Man About The House* had been on telly that night with George Roper trying his hand at chimney sweeping.

As I have got older, I have become extremely open-minded, but I have to quite frank – I have never fancied either a carrier bag over my head nor a golf ball in my mouth, ever. As for Tim, you'd have to ask him the question, as some of the shit he's been involved in makes Ray Blandford look quite normal.

"I think it was a ping pong ball, love," my auntie Anne recently told me.

Whatever. It makes me want to gip just thinking about it.

I was told that Grazyna suffered a breakdown afterwards, which is quite understandable if true, as it was big news at the time and must have been hugely embarrassing.

It was during 1985 that Tim let me know that he had decided to quit mining. He would be the first one of all my friends to leave the industry – however, the direction that he would take was another thing that had me scratching my head.

"The Army?" I shrugged. "What do you want to go in the Army for?"

My uncle Pete had always maintained that a life in the Army was good – if you are single, that is.

At the time, I had been at a completely different pit with completely different people and doing a job I hated, so much so, I often altered my shift pattern from a 6:00 a.m. start to night shift. Not only did the move – which unlike at Hickleton Main, was seen as being no bother by the Personnel Manager get me off B36s god awful transfer point and back into the rips humping steel or running a haulage system, it also got me on the same shift as both Col and John. Although they had the same mindset as Tim, the Army wouldn't have been a path either of them would have elected to go down.

The strike had changed everything. Even the mice in the pits had gone – in Yorkshire, that is.

I recall one afternoon shift when I had been working down in the intake drift on the Silkstone development, either unloading some colliery arches or just helping the lads stem up the rip by sticking detonators into either Penobel or Polar Ajax explosives, and of our electrician Geoff Lowther shouting down to me over the Tannoy system. "Jamie, I've just shifted your snap – the mice have been at it."

As I often did on afternoon shift, I had called in to Baker Bowes – the bakery on Lidget Lane, and bought a couple of steak pies and had foolishly left them on the bench at the first intake transfer point. This was where the belt loaded onto a noisy armoured flexible conveyor, which in turn dumped spoil on to the East Side Cable Belt. The pies had attracted the mice, the latter of which had had a field day. There were hundreds of the fucking things running around the place – especially on the Concorde Paddy Station just around the corner.

We all expected getting back to work after the strike to find one great massive mouse which had eaten all the others – however, there were none. With no scraps of food to scavenge, they had all eventually starved to death.

As for Geoff Lowther, he was another one of these petrolheads who loved his motorbikes and music and who I saw a few times on a Sunday night over at Bolton Club in between the live act taking a break. He had married a former bus conductress for Larratt Pepper – a blonde-haired girl by the name of Jeanette (Jet) Reynoldson in 1971 – the latter who would become one of my daughters' primary school teachers at Thurnscoe Hill.

"I met her in the New 'Un," he told me. "We were a top end gang, and she was in a bottom end gang. We were all interested in bands and slowly merged together."

Geoff had been off Windsor Street and part of a family that had been no stranger to tragedy – several of them dying as children, with he himself contracting polio.

His wife had been one of those who didn't stick fast, working at both Cora's and SR Gents sewing factories before going back to further education and becoming a teacher – a job she served for twenty-three years.

"Her boss, Headmaster David Williamson, was the most fantastic educationalist ever," Geoff told me. "He understood the working-class children and gained respect that way."

I always liked Geoff. Another selfless lad, who is proud of his socialist roots.

Mr Williamson, who during 1998 had had a cloud hanging over him due to some alleged impropriety that had taken place with a fellow female colleague, had indeed been a very good headmaster and one who had been supported by some outstanding teachers – one of who had been one of my fellow ex-pupil's fathers – Ray Scatchard.

The last time I saw David Williamson was one night during November 1997. He had called in at my office in Great Houghton as I had 100 reams of A4 paper for him.

As for Tim, he explained that dependent on the results from the exams he would have to take, the choices he had were quite rangy.

"So, you'll not be one of those at the front with a gun?" I asked.

"An infantryman? No, fuck that," he replied.

Tim would be the first of my immediate friends to make the break, but it was something a lot of us were contemplating – however, the question was – to do what?

Brian Latham had been pushed around from pillar-to-post having to do this scheme and that scheme with nothing at all to show for it at the end of it. We were living in strange times and on Brian's part it was soul destroying. There were times that he became quite melancholy – not so much when we were out, but certainly at the end of the night. He was a good kid and deserved far better than he got. However, he wasn't alone – there were three million out there with the same problem and with the government tearing away at its pit closure programme faster than anyone could ever have foreseen were staring down the exact same abyss as him. Or so we were led to believe.

A deal could have been done the previous September to slow it down. It was that close.

"No one who doesn't want to leave the industry doesn't have to," explained Margaret Thatcher, during interviews with both the BBC and ITV. "And for those who wish to leave, the NCB will be offering the best terms ever as part of any redundancy package."

What is true is that the NCB never planned to make any compulsory redundancies. They didn't have to. Thatcher's statement may well have been seen as an indictment of *choice* but Scargill knew exactly what she knew and that was by the NCB waving these extraordinary terms in the face of miners, that the NUM would have immediately lost half its members to redundancy.

That being the case, the government's long-term plan of shutting seventy pits could have gone ahead unhindered.

As part of negotiations, you negotiate. It is a process that needs two sides – three if you count the arbitrator.

Scargill could have sanctioned the closure of the twenty uneconomic pits and as part of any deal, worked with the NCB to efficiently streamline the business and get rid of the outdated pay grades and incentives, thereby replacing it with a proper living wage and one that creates a hardworking and flexible workforce. It was a chance for change. A chance to work alongside the company instead continually trying to hamstring it.

History will tell you that that never happened.

Scargill backed the wrong horse when he relied on the deputies and shotfirers Union, NACODS, to bail him out. It was what it was – pure folly.

He told me during the personal meeting that I had with him in 1994. "If they would have come out on strike with us, we would have won it."

History will also tell you that NACODS voted to back us – and with a massive majority, and that Margaret Thatcher became extremely worried. It was also something Ian McGregor readily admitted to afterwards.

If you want outright victory – you must be united. The mining industry was never like that. There will always be someone willing to work when everyone downs tools. Back in the day there was a certain parity – however, even then, people got starved into submission. By the mid-1980s you could forget it. It was just a dog-eat-dog world and we were all part of it.

You can be as uber-socialist as you want, but the reality was – most conversations in the pit revolved around redundancy.

Remember my mention of the mother of the girlfriend that I didn't want and those "Money talks" conversations.

You give some fucker enough of it to fill a carrier bag and it is the ultimate enabler.

Friday's nightshift at Markham Main were very different to those at Hickleton and Askern Main as you went from working an 11.00 p.m. start throughout the week and on to a 6.00 p.m. evening shift – and more often than not I would be asked to work overtime – twelve hours. This would be the only way I could ever get a parity of wages with those on the coal face.

The first time was with Darrell Cooper – and of us tramming timber into B46s face which was being salvaged and removing scrap on the way back out, whilst at the same time illegally riding the bogeys (trams) through sections of tunnel which had collapsed to the point of being virtually unnavigable. It was extremely dangerous if I am being honest.

In my mind working on nightshift was the best. At Markham Main I also saved money by not going out. It was something that Daz and I would end up doing on a regular basis – however, it was certainly never planned like that.

The revolving door at 16 Briton Square saw people come and go – none more than my fifteen-year-old sister. She supposedly came down to clean up for me while I was at work. I say supposedly, as bar the smell of a recycled half-carton of Shake 'N' Vac she slung around the place, which the crappy vacuum that I had at the time, purported to pick up before blowing its dust all over the place, there wasn't much tidying up actually done. The upshot was, that it was just somewhere she could go to have her own space with her mates and listen to the Hi-Fi.

Col's house was always the livelier. I recall a party he once threw around the time and of he and I trying to part their Andy and his younger brother Stephen from fighting. I still have no idea why. The irony was, that Andy had had his leg in a cast and ended up chasing someone around the cul-de-sac on his crutches.

Daz was more than aware that I was struggling to afford the albatross around my neck that was my debt-busting loan and all the household bills on top, and I readily mentioned the possibility of him moving in to mine as his parents' house on the northern-leg of Brunswick Street was vastly overcrowded – especially with him being the second eldest of eight children.

The thought quite appealed to him, but Col thought otherwise.

"Coop's a great kid, J, but you'll be no better off," he said, before adding his second bit of advice. "And your house will never be your own as you'll have his family around all the time, and for what? An extra twenty quid a week."

Col was always the logical one.

"If I were you, I'd ride it out," he said.

To an extent I did. However, there would be times when I had let him stay with his girlfriend – especially when I was elsewhere. And I was elsewhere quite a lot. In fact, half the time there was always somebody else in my bed.

"There's a young girl been around here banging on your door," explained my disgruntled next-door neighbour, one particular evening when I had returned from elsewhere. "Twice."

George Tough had married his wife at St Aiden's Mission Church in the Roker area of Sunderland in 1916 and had been one of the mass exodus of Durham miners that had descended on Hickleton Main straight after the 1926 strike and had not only been allocated a job – but also one of the brand new pit houses at 15 Briton Square. Like many, his wife, Dorothy and family followed him down there – and by family, I am including both his wife's parents, John and Mary Patterson.

Shortly after setting up home in Thurnscoe they had a girl, who by the time I arrived on Briton Square in September 1983, was the only one left in what was an extremely modernised house with its huge bay-window at the front and a newly laid drive up its side – and one which had a W-registered lime-green Volkswagen Beetle parked on it.

The fifty-five-year-old Audrey Beesley (nee Tough) was a heavy-set, horse-faced lady who possessed a rather haughty and high-handed manner along with an accent to match. This maybe came from the fact that she had previously lived in South Africa and had come back over to the UK just before her mum had passed away in 1980.

My relationship with her would be no different to that of my uncle Jimmy (Greaves) in that I thought the world of them until the time I did not. Being on your own for long periods of time, a selfishness tends to set in, and you lose all powers of communication and that being the case, any relationship you have with people begins to flounder. However, back then it couldn't have been any different.

"Young girl?" I shrugged.

"She wasn't that one I saw coming out of your house on Sunday morning," she said.

She wouldn't have been – that was Daz Cooper's girlfriend.

"And it certainly wasn't that one that I saw screaming outside your house on the Friday," she added.

People who live in a cul-de-sac tend to be very nosey and ours was no different. However, this is a story I will certainly get to.

When Audrey had been a nineteen-year-old girl, she had been planning to marry a lad by the name of Jack Rutter from 85 Chapel Lane. He was the son of Marshall and Mona (nee Tyas) – the former of whom back then operated the underground telephone exchange at Hickleton Main.

Jack had served in the Navy as a radio electrician since leaving school and had been on the HMS Amethyst on the Yangtze River on 20 April 1949, when it was attacked by the Chinese People's Liberation Army. This culminated in the boat semi-capsizing and a 101-day siege ensuing, in which twenty-two of its men were killed and eleven wounded before its personnel managed to re-float the vessel and eventually making a final dash for freedom.

Audrey's fiancée had been on the ship throughout the ordeal helping man the wireless cabin and got back to the UK to a hero's welcome. Unfortunately, however, some things are just never meant to be.

Jack got re-posted on to the submarine HMS Affray, which had been one of sixteen of its class, initially designed to fight the Japanese in the Pacific Ocean. The vessel went out on a special-operations training exercise with a reduced crew and never returned. It was found on the very edge of Hurds Deep – a deep underwater valley in the English Channel around 27 km northwest of the island of Alderney. It had unexplainably sunk on 16 April 1951 – just a mere four days under two years since the start of what would be termed in history as the *Yangtze Incident*.

To get to the story of the young girl and indeed Daz's girlfriend, however I feel I must give you some background.

Although I thought the world of Col – and I did, this was around the time when he began doing whatever he felt like doing regardless of the other person, which more often than not, had been me. It is hard to describe the situation without coming over as sniping, but I noticed a change.

When we had moved up to the Second Year of Houghton Road Infant School we had initially been under the tutorage of a fifty-five-year-old lady by the name of Mrs (Doris) Haigh, whose stories were legendary. *The Imps and the Dog* was my ultimate favourite, even though it did give me nightmares up in the cold bedroom of 14 Landsdowne Avenue. For the record this was a rather gory tale of a faithful hound that had been tied up in the kitchen and which had had its limbs lopped off, solely because it kept on barking at these Imps that its owner couldn't see. On eventually seeing the Imps and the damage that they were doing, the owner borrowed some glue from the black-haired school secretary, Mrs Vince, and reattached its limbs and the dog ended up tearing these Imps to pieces. Like I said – gory.

Imps aside, for some strange reason, and just after Christmas 1970, a few of us got moved upstairs to Mrs Brookes' classroom – straight opposite Mrs Vince's office, one of who had been Col.

Back then, we were in the final throws of making the most of the 1946 Free Milk Act and each day a crate of the stuff was carried upstairs into the classroom in what were these little third of a pint (190 ml) bottles. Most of these had been manufactured with the Co-op cloverleaf logo on its side – however, to set these apart there was the odd bottle, which possessed a map of the British Isles on them – and being just six years old, these were seen by us as being the in-thing to have.

As soon as Mrs Brookes gave the okay, there was a scurry of young lads jostling for them and this particular day I had managed to get one back to our table, only to be summoned to the teacher's desk. I can't recall what for, but as soon as I had got back to the table, I realised that I had a standard Co-op logo bottle in front of me. I looked over at Col and his straw had been planted in what had been my bottle – the one with the map on, with almost a quarter of its content slurped. He had swapped bottles and just to make sure I wouldn't take it back he taken a couple of gulps. That was Col in a nutshell. The thing is I mentioned this recently and he remembered it!

During the latter months of the Miners' Strike, Col had shaken off the disappointment of his broken marriage and had early-on post-strike, truly found his feet, so much so, he began to do whatever he pleased. I had already witnessed the fact that he rarely ever took no for an answer, but when it came to him steaming-in and taking the lead on a couple of occasions I had to take a couple of steps back.

"Is your mate just thick-skinned or what?" I was asked by a girl in some nightclub in Blackpool.

She hadn't been interested, but his sheer perseverance wore her down to a nub, and in the end, she must have thought *fuck it*.

That was his not taking *no* for an answer.

In fact, for a time, we nicknamed him *Pepé Le Pew* – you know, after the suave French skunk from the Warner Bros. series of cartoons who is relentless in his search of love and affection, but due to his offensive skunk odour and his aggressive pursuit of romance he never gets the girl. However, it is certainly not from the like of trying. "Every man should have a hobby and mine is making lurv," crooned the skunk.

Yep – that was Col.

As for his steaming in, the first time I had come across it was one Thursday evening in the Church House down in Wath-on-Dearne.

Generally speaking – when there are girls out in twos there is often a half-decent one and one that is not and here was a case in point. One of the girls was Derek Cook's daughter, Lynn – the heiress-apparent to the DC Cook car dealership empire. It was purely a case of who she was that created the interest rather that indeed how she was. She possessed a highly exaggerated laugh, to the point of guffawing, which was as annoying as hell, but the thought of a shiny Datsun parked outside 8 Briton Square easily outweighed that, and his pursuit of her was fucking relentless, so much so, I may as well have not been there. In the end, I let him get on with it and we both came away with nothing.

The second time was on the Sunday a week or two later. We had called in The Goldthorpe Hotel at the back end of the night as there had been some disco on. The pub itself was never anything to write home about and considering it was located in an area, which had been hit by a twelve-month strike and with half the under-twenty-fives out of work, it had become very run down. Whilst we were in there, a DJ played whatever hits were in the chart at the time – maybe Animotion's *Obsession* or Scritti Politti's *The Word Girl* and as always, a load of girls navigated their way around their handbags, whilst monopolising what was the postage stamp dancefloor.

It was I who made the initial contact with these two girls from Bolton-on-Dearne – one off the eastern-arc of Ringway, the other from the top of Canberra Rise. Unlike the scenario in Wath-on-Dearne, there was little to set them apart as they were both quite pretty. However, Col being Col immediately took over proceedings and picked the one he wanted, regardless of what I wanted.

John Gratton once told me a story of them both going to Rhodes one year and explained that they were going to hire motorbikes. Being Mr Safe, Responsible and Totally Fucking Boring, John hired this gutless 50 cc put-put along with the standard piss-pot helmet, whilst just a few minutes later Col rolled into town with his hog and pulled up on this 350 cc trials bike duly wheel-spinning dust in his face as they set off to wherever they were going. "He made me look a right twat," he said.

John had also invested several days of articulate and well-structured patter to entice two girls who were staying in their hotel, to go on some double date.

"I'd been working on them all week," said John. "We're getting ready to go out this particular night and he just fucked off. 'I'm not bothered' he says. I went fucking mental with him."

In the Church House and The Goldthorpe Hotel it had hardly been that, but I must admit, me not being asked, did piss me off. If I had let it go any further, he would have begun treating me like Jacko the fucking monkey – and slinging some dog over the fence just to placate me.

It would be wrong, however, for me to mention names as these were very impressionable young girls and we knew exactly what we were doing. Being on opposite shifts, I saw mine much more than he ever saw his, which when he did, it was a case of all four of us together. The idea was – and this is where the bad bit comes, was to take them to Rebecca's. This was a nightclub near Barnsley railway station on the site where the Gala Bingo now stands. They told their parents that they were stopping at each other's house which is nothing out of the norm and is to my knowledge – what girls often said to their parents when they wanted to be elsewhere. The idea being, that they were to come back to ours at the end of the night.

Outside of a couple of glasses of cider, I had never seen them drink. On this night, however, they certainly did. A lot.

On getting back home, we used the divide and rule philosophy – me and mine in my house – him and his in his. Simplistic but effective. That was until I had some overly anxious half-naked girl with her shoes in her hand banging on my front door and screaming to be let in.

"Where's Col?" I asked. Me being more concerned about being interrupted, rather than anything untoward happening elsewhere.

"I want to come in and stop with you," she told me.

"Again, where's Col?" I asked.

"Can I come and stop with you? I just want to come and stop with you?"

I couldn't get any sense out of her, and Col? Well, he was nowhere to be seen.

The next thing I knew was that we had her on the settee, and I was making her a cup of coffee. Nothing untoward had happened it was just that the girl was all over the place – paranoid one minute, hyper the next.

"I just want to stay with you," she kept on saying.

She eventually calmed down and it was me who ended up putting her to bed.

"What the fuck, Col?" I whispered when he rather sheepishly came to the house around half an hour later.

"I couldn't do anything with her," he shrugged. "She was out of control."

"I had to let her in otherwise we'd have had the police around," I told him. "She's woke half the fucking street up."

I don't think he ever saw her after that.

As for the young girl who Audrey had seen banging on my door – even to this day I still have no idea who that was.

Now, here is a story that links another girl seen coming out of my house and which involves the rape of a child nearly 140 years ago.

Tom Dormand was a twenty-six-year-old from Walbottle in Northumberland who was very well-educated, possessing both a degree in mining engineering and holding a colliery managers certificate. He had followed his elder brother John down to the Dearne Valley along with his twenty-year-old wife, Mary (nee Hardcastle) and one-year-old daughter Lily.

Being ambitious he took up a position as an assistant ventilation engineer at Denaby Main Colliery and in 1881, moved into a house on Thrybergh Terrace with his wife – the latter of who took time out to teach the piano, with one of her first students being her fourteen-year-old neighbour Hannah Cramp. She was the daughter of Jimmy and Mary Ann (nee Kirk), who had themselves had moved up to the area from Leicestershire.

Tom Dormand wasted no time in getting to know his neighbours, not least of all, his wife's young pupil and even offered to teach her arithmetic.

The houses in Denaby Main, were, as I have already said, constructed very close-knit terraces on a steep hillside with paper-thin walls. At around 6.00 p.m. on Monday 17 October 1881, no-one claimed to have heard a thing, which was something that all the street had been talking about when the police eventually arrested Dormand and charged him with rape.

It was certainly nothing new in the village – that is for sure.

After being told, her father – who was a foreman carpenter at the colliery, had made a point of seeing the pit manager for advice and it was he who had said to involve the police. Later on however, when the media got full-wind of the situation and descended on the mine, the manager back-tracked a bit and his company ended-up issuing a statement that falsely stated that Dormand had never been employed in any management capacity – and was only there as an ordinary workman.

"I went into Mr and Mrs Dormand's house, with my slate and book and did some sums," Hannah explained. "After a little while his wife went out and I was sitting on a chair whilst he was seated in another. He took me off the chair, placed me upon his knee and kissed me several times. I resisted him and tried to get to the door – however, he pulled me back and then held me down on the floor."

That is when he raped her.

"I neither cried, shouted, nor screamed, but I suffered a good deal of pain in consequence of his treatment," she added.

There was neither any misunderstanding nor mistake in that he had raped his victim as not only did a Dr William Sykes of Market Street, Mexborough confirm the fact that she had been assaulted, her mother confirmed that Dormand had openly offered her £10 (£1,200, circa 2020) to keep quiet and therefore hopefully sweep the matter under the carpet.

That never happened and he went on trial at York Assizes in November 1881 – however, he was found not guilty.

The girl who was raped was the great grandmother of Susan Wagstaff – the girl who Audrey Beesley had seen come out of my house that Sunday morning and the girl who would go on to marry Darrell Cooper.

30. The Girlfriend

Five months had passed since the end of the strike and financially, I wasn't much better off. I was only a third of my way into paying off my loan and July's payment again took me out of the black and into the red. This time it was £75 (£243.31, circa 2020).

Although I did a lot of stupid things, I wasn't a stupid lad – far from it – however, I just couldn't seem to manage my incomings and outgoings to stay fluid. I knew what the main problem was – I was never in. My other problem was, that any money I earned – I spent. I needed some structure in my life.

I contemplated getting a regular girlfriend, but when you shit on your own doorstep as often as I had, your choices become limited. Nevertheless, I tried my hand at staying in a couple of Saturday nights and that being the case I dragged a succession of female companions in off the street, which worked out about as well as I thought it would.

"I saw that bird that you were knocking off," Col enthused. "She was calling you from a pig to a dog."

That didn't surprise me. I treated every girl that I met, with contempt – and the girl I would come to marry would be no different.

A blond-haired kid a year younger than me from Bolton-on-Dearne by the name of Johnny Lockwood had recently split-up with his girlfriend and to an extent I made sure it was permanent.

I had borrowed Col's car to pick her up from outside Jack Fulton's on Wombwell's High Street to try a night in – however, the choice of having to watch either Val Doonican on the BBC or Russ Abbott on the other, and in monochrome, was enough to contemplate blowing my fucking brains out.

The away leg was pencilled in at her mum and dad's house off Summer Lane on the Monday – however, the thought of coming in off afternoon shift and catching the 226 there and back to drink cups of tea, hold hands on the settee and watch *Panorama*, was hardly a mouth-watering proposition.

"I can't believe the bastard stood me up," she had told Col.

She was an extremely nice girl and certainly didn't deserve me in her life.

I can't remember where I had first met her – however, me walking her to the bus stop after a night out in Bolton Club on the Wednesday night prior sticks in my mind, along with the bollocking I got when I eventually did see her.

I had done the same thing to a girl off Goldthorpe's Pickhills Avenue, who had been in my year at school, around the time we had come back from Blackpool. I don't know whether it was the fact that I just couldn't stay in, or the fact I couldn't be in a relationship. Maybe it was a combination of both – I really could not say. The strange thing is, is that they were actually girls that you could take home to meet your mum. Not so much my mum, but certainly anyone else's. I mean, neither of them spat in the street or had 'love' and 'hate' tattooed on their knuckles. On the contrary – Diane Swift and Jennifer Burden were both very pretty girls.

The bank never let me have an overdraft – that was until the monthly instalment of their loan wanted paying, which meant living off what I had got in until my next wages had been paid. It drove me to the point of insanity and I often wondered how I had put up with the shit I'd had to deal with during the strike.

Col had been out the night that I had elected to stay in and mentioned that he had bumped into Daz Cooper's girlfriend who was of course Sue Wagstaff – the great-granddaughter of Hannah Cramp. "She was with her mate," he told me.

I thought very little of it until he mentioned the fact that she had big eyes.

"Nice legs as well, J," Daz Cooper told me during the week.

I recall nipping up to my mum's and seeing my (step)dad outside the house on the drive with the hood of the car up and water all over the floor. The radiator had gone to an extent that not even two cartons of Holt's Radweld would quell the leak. What was strange is that the radiator had also gone on the motorhome the week before. "I've told her to go slow driving down that pissing road," he snapped. The word "pissing" was without doubt my (step)dad's favourite!

Barnsley MBC had been doing some wanky road surfacing down Highgate Lane using some cheap granular material and my mum had copped for some friendly fire in both radiators.

I rang Col and not only did he source a radiator from Jimmy Murray, he also fitted it and got her back on the road, only for around three weeks later for me to cop some, whilst travelling to Brampton Bierlow on the old Cathill Road that once linked the A635 and the B6273 Pontefract Road at Broomhill.

This road had long since been shut to traffic and replaced by the A6195 Dearne Valley Parkway. Unfortunately, it hadn't been a £10 (£32.45, circa 2020) radiator.

The windscreen blew as though someone had put it through with a twelve-gauge. Salvation was at hand, however, as some parasitical auto-windscreen van had been trawling up and down what was a winding lane on its lookout for roadkill and within minutes copped me parked up just before the old hairpin bend whilst I had been sweeping glass from the seats.

"I've got one in the back," he shouted, before quoting me £40 (£130, circa 2020).

The whole idea of having a girlfriend was to save me fucking money, not cost me.

He fitted it outside the house at 66 Knollbeck Avenue, where just a week earlier I had been invited into its living room by the girl with the big eyes, only to see some bloke sat in a deck chair, reading the *Daily Mirror* with half a pair of glasses on his head.

Her father was hardly the world's greatest conversationalist, that's for sure, as I was the last thing he wanted around his youngest daughter. He didn't say as much, but he certainly implied it.

"You have to look after this lass," my mum told me shortly after. "She's the favourite."

My mother tended to know what I was doing more than I did.

"I can see everything," she used to tell my kids when they were little. "I've got eyes in the back of my head."

Not only did she work alongside a fellow supervisor at the English Rose sewing factory who knew the family extremely well – the elder sister, Jane also worked there, which from my point of view, immediately created complications.

That adage of never shitting on your doorstep.

Lots of girls around my age had gone to work there, and it was no coincidence that they frequented the same places that I did, therefore all this got relayed back and forth, often getting exaggerated out of all proportion. However, the father's reluctance to engage in conversation was a bit more than that. The elder sister had a boyfriend who was from the more affluent area of Wath-on-Dearne, his mother and father living in one of those 1930s-type semi-detached properties within a leafy glade top side of the old Wath Grammar School.

Paul Robinson was a school year older than me – an ex-grammar school lad who come through sixth form, was employed with some local house builder, played for Wath RUFC on a weekend and drove a white Triumph Spitfire. If I am being honest, he was their ideal son-in-law – although a barrister, doctor or some neurosurgeon may have probably trumped that.

As for me, all he saw was just some young miner who lived in some rough shit hole pit village, which had a reputation for being exactly that.

As with mining, you take things in, even at a relatively young age, and you survey all what is around you. Although it was just a trip over the A635 Doncaster-Barnsley road and a mere six miles away, the village of Brampton Bierlow was much different to Thurnscoe. For one, it was inhabited by different types of people and the kind that I had never really come across before – a lot of whom possessed a strong Barnsley dialect. Sentences shortened with apostrophic wording, then stretched out with the exaggerated pronunciation of their vowels and which were often littered with paraphrases from the bible – the *thee's and tha's*. Although theirs was pit village in every sense – I mean, Cortonwood Colliery was supposedly the standard bearer of the strike, it was a totally different world.

The first thing that hit me was a form of flat-cap snobbery – as though they had invented mining.

"If tha not from Ba-a-arnzley and tha dunt work on t'coil face, then tha nor a miner," is how it translated, when one of the friends of the girlfriend's parents quizzed me about who I was and what I did.

That was like a fucking red rag to a bull.

"Cortonwood – it's a scab pit," I said.

"I didn't scab," said the girlfriend's father.

"I'm not saying you did, but there were over one hundred and twenty of you that did."

The elder sister's boyfriend would have never said something as confrontational as that and for all the time I knew him, he never ever spoke out of turn. As for me, I had an opinion and I wasn't shy in voicing it. I certainly wasn't being spoken down to by some pedantic know-your-place twit from Barnsley.

"You don't really embrace yourself with people, do you?" my solicitor Steve Smith once said to me, after the Crown Prosecution Service had been trying to fit me up with a Section 4 for harassing some policeman.

I do – I've just got a nil constitution for dickheads and wankers.

Although the girlfriend's father may have been standoffish, her mother and along with the hoard of great-aunts that visited their house on a regular basis were the exact opposite. I could see where the girlfriend got her outgoing and exuberant personality from and it certainly wasn't him.

Bill and Marlene Mason had lived on the council estate since they had first been married in 1961 – firstly with Marlene's parents, Bill and Edith Wattam (nee Totty) down at 11 Wyn Grove and eighteen months later, in their first home at Knollbeck Avenue. And if you want a coincidence, my sisters ex-father-in-law, Dave Hodgkiss (the father of Shaine Whitehurst), had been born in the very same house, some ten years earlier.

The council estate possessed a rather strange topography and appeared to have been built within a series of dips and valleys, with the houses on its summit both backing onto and overlooking Cortonwood Colliery, which within a couple of years would be flattened and infilled to make way for what would be its state-of-the-art shopping centre.

Julie's house had a long steep path which split the garden on its way down to the back door. The house itself had recently been modernised and comprised a modern kitchenette with an adjoining and well-trafficked dining room along with a wood panelled living room at the other end of a long passage, that I had regularly been dragged into when we were courting.

The first thing that hit me was the warm friendliness of the place, which was generally when her dad was either out or in bed.

When I first met him he had been a Winder at Cortonwood Colliery – however, the way the strike had been managed always dictated that his working life would eventually be away from the village and he, like many, got transferred to Silverwood Colliery, which less than a year earlier had witnessed the most violent scenes of the year-long dispute.

Bill tended to work regular days and like most men, had his dinner on the table when he got in and then went to bed – the idea being to get him up after a couple of hours.

"Leave him in bed," said his daughter, one particular time when we'd had the house to ourselves.

He went crackers when he finally landed in the dining room.

"It's half-past eight," he grumbled, after noticing the time. "It's half-past eight. Why didn't you get me up?"

I think the answer was self-explanatory.

Although he wasn't a nasty man, far from it, what he said in his own house, went. Did I get on with him? About as well as he got on with me, so no.

All his focus was on seeing his eldest daughter marrying the rugger playing grammar school lad from Wath Wood, who drove the white sports car. The furthest my new shiny white lump of metal travelled, was across the kitchen floor.

"Why don't you get it plumbed in, J?" Col asked, on seeing me continually dragging the automatic washing machine across the carpet to hook up to the taps in the bathroom.

"Because I'd rather have two or three nights out than pay out the twenty quid," was my retort.

Col didn't have a washer. He took his clothes down to his mum's or let me wash them. He did have a tumble drier, however.

"It's fucking shit this is, Col," I told him, after waiting two hours for some jeans to be dried one Friday afternoon.

"Yeh, I told you the heater in it was broke," he said.

At times, we lived like a pair of peasants – however, Julie loved the freedom that we all shared as with her living at home, she never had that.

I still remember within the first few weeks of us meeting and the girl with those big eyes sat on the fireplace of the old cream range in my kitchen, with the fire up the chimney back and eating hot dog and tomato sauce sandwiches after dragging me over from Col's after she had spent ten minutes banging on my door without any reply.

"I thought if you weren't in, I'd have ten minutes with Col and get the bus back down home," she said.

That was Julie in a nutshell. She possessed a very outgoing and generous personality and was at times, far too trusting.

She, like many young girls, had left school and worked in the local sewing factories – hers being the same factory that my ex-girlfriend had worked. Rather strangely, she had also worked on the same line.

"I know her," she shrugged. "She told everyone that she was leaving to get married."

"I was on strike, how could I be getting married?"

"Well, that's what she said. I even think we had a collection for her."

This was all news to me.

A week later she was jumping on the 226 with a measuring jug half-full of gravy that her mum had made, to come over and cook my dinner after I had come in from work off Friday's afternoon shift.

"Is he paying thee for the food tha's getting him?" her dad had inquired, knowing that she was on about calling into the butchers on her way over to Thurnscoe.

Neil Gollick hadn't seen her before – however, she certainly must have caught his attention.

"Who's that?" he had inquired, whilst ogling through Col's window and over at the girl in tight short floral short suit who was waving her arse in the air whilst trying to fit the over-elaborate key in the lock.

In the few weeks I had met her I wouldn't have said that I saved any money, but I certainly wasn't spending as much.

"Do you fancy calling and having a lager?" she asked, as I borrowed the orange Capri to take her home.

I pulled up outside the Yorkshire Bank, but I knew as it was the end of the month, that the account would be empty. £70 overdrawn. Again.

"I'll buy us a drink," she said.

It did my head in. I never wanted charity, just a relationship to keep me grounded.

"It's okay," she said. "What's a pint and half of lager cost?"

What I didn't know at the time, is that not only was her elder sister heavily subsidising her boyfriend – her mum and dad were too. They had recently given him the money to buy a suit for his job.

"Why, what exactly does he do?" I inquired.

"He's training to be a quantity surveyor," she replied.

I just shrugged my shoulders.

"He doesn't get paid much – just forty pounds a week," she added.

I paid out more than that on my loan and I said as much, but from that day on I had his number. Whereas I had been the low-rent ponce, scrounging pancakes and gravy in some warm house in Swinton during the dark winter of the strike – he was the upmarket one, swanning around in a brand-new suit and driving a Spitfire.

It sounds as though there was a certain resentment – however, that is so far from the truth.

There was a story I was told, which is another that due to the legal implications surrounding the victims of certain sexual offences – in this case, rape and child rape – that I must tread carefully with. I can, however, be vague.

Julie had been part of gaggle of sixteen-year-olds, including girls by the name of Paula Moyser and Clare Neald, who had been on their way to the Church House in Wath-on-Dearne to enjoy the New Year's Eve celebrations of 1983. Prior to them going out she had made a phone call to another friend who lived in a bungalow on Firth Road, which is a street just up from the Cottage of Content in West Melton. There did, however, become a twist in tale as the stepfather – a man with the name of Geoff – overrode the call and refused point-blank to let her out.

"He was a big bloke – a bully," my wife told me. "Whilst her mam, was not too dissimilar in appearance to your dad's wife Paula, in that she was fat and wore glasses."

The story was that her natural father had died in 1973 at the relatively young age of thirty-six, leaving four pretty daughters aged eight, six, two and one year old. The mother remarried two years later, with the stepfather putting all his efforts into targeting the second oldest girl, who was of course Julie's friend.

"She was extremely clingy and always used to want to stop at our house," she said. "And being fourteen or fifteen, I found it strange."

Later, that New Year's Eve, who should walk into the Church House?

As you would expect, Julie and her friends were pleased to see their friend – however, she wasn't alone. Her mother and stepfather were with her – and Geoff, well, he would step in to break up the friendly banter, and openly referred to Julie as a *slag*.

"He upset me," she said. "I hadn't done anything wrong."

Julie's elder sister had been in the pub with her boyfriend that night, both of whom immediately came to her assistance. "He's told his daughter to keep away from me and that I'm a slag," she said.

Paul, who was quite a big kid, went over to him gave him a tap on the shoulder. "Me and you – outside."

The thing with bullies, is that they rarely like to be fronted – and this was no different. For as big and brash as he was, he didn't fancy the prospect of some young fit lad taking him out into the street and filling him in, and therefore immediately backtracked.

However, he still wasn't done.

"Afterwards he phoned Paula Moyser's mum and told lies about me and her mam believed her and stopped her knocking about with me."

There was much more to that story.

Geoff wanted his second eldest stepdaughter isolated from the pack. As these types of people tend to do, he regarded her as his girlfriend and was raping her on an as-and-when basis – which was something that she told Julie and her friends several years later.

As for Geoff, I am led to believe that the accusations came out – however, the wife and the girl's mother kept it quiet. Maybe she refused to believe it as he is still married to her. Whatever happened, they did leave the area and now live in a bungalow on Flaxpiece Road in Chesterfield.

As for his stepdaughter, she didn't just leave the area, she left the country, got married and currently lives stateside. However, one thing she never did, was have children.

Although she once came to my house in the late-1980s, I never met her. I did get introduced to several other friends, however – one of these was a girl who had been married at sixteen years old.

Andrea Brown was the eldest daughter of Pete and Katherine Wake, a couple who lived over the road at No 59 and the latter of whom, was an ardent member of the village's populous that frequented the Christian Ministries chapel over in West Melton on a Sunday evening.

The reason for Andrea's marriage, is that she had got pregnant and the mother's idea was to further overcrowd the house, by having her, her husband Alan and the new baby temporary live with them, therefore jumping the queue for local authority housing. It was something which obviously worked as within no time at all they were offered a house on the Ellis Crescent part of the council estate.

Her parents were extremely street savvy, especially when it came to manipulating the system.

"What, so none of them work?" I inquired.

"No, never."

Two families – my girlfriend's and theirs, both of whom lived in similar type houses and on the exact same street – one lot worked, the others didn't, and they basically were no worse off than each other. Something didn't sit right with me, even back then, but being a young lad, I wasn't quite as cynical as I am now. I suppose, back then, my thoughts regarding people not working I put down to the state of the country and its large number of unemployed, rather the indolence of the individuals concerned.

Thurnscoe had its parasites and bottom-feeders, but they certainly weren't as brazen-faced about playing the system as this lot from Brampton were. If I am being honest, it was the only thing that I and Julie's dad ever agreed on.

I look back around that time and recall the constant traffic of people coming in and out of their house. The constant stream of auntie's and friends along with the milkman, the pop man, the veg' man, the bread man. They even had an egg man – Goo goo g'joob (sic).

Sometimes the dining room was packed to the rafters and if I had borrowed either Col or my mum's car, I would have my services immediately utilised by the girlfriend's mum – a lady with social graces not unlike my grandma Ellis and who was someone that I adored. "Can you run Auntie Ethel home?" she would ask.

At that time, Marlene had been working on the local authorities Home Help and treated her route as though they were family. "And could you just run me 'round to Mrs so and so's," she'd ask.

Did I mind? Never.

Bill would be sat in his deck chair, cigarette in hand and blowing smoke everywhere as he tried to watch TV or read his newspaper, whilst all these chattering women were continually in and out. How it never drove him crazy, I don't know.

Nevertheless, when I called down, I always got fed and watered. Always.

"My mam wants to know if you're coming down for your tea?" Julie would often ask.

My timekeeping, however, was nothing short of appalling and at times it drove them all to despair – especially her dad.

"We'her is he? Why in't he here?" he'd say.

The old lad could never fathom me out, but I suppose a lot of that came from me living on my own.

This was a time when the likelihood of Daz Cooper moving into my house was distinct possibility, and I recall us going out with him and his girlfriend one evening and them staying at my house whilst I ran Julie home. "So, you just let them stay?" she asked.

I thought nothing of it and the mentioned the prospect of him moving in.

"If he moves in, you know Sue will end up there all the time," she said. "You do know that don't you?"

Julie saw exactly what Col saw, and that was me giving up my house for a nil return.

Coop wasn't mean, far from it, but I was more than aware that he came as a package. I was more concerned about his mates and family, than any girlfriend he would be dragging across the door. Nevertheless, I wasn't averse to him staying over on a weekend – but them using my bed? Well, that was something Julie didn't like, and she said as much one night when we had been in their dining room and yacking into the small hours.

"Are you still up?" her dad exclaimed, as he stuck his head through the door.

Her dad was brilliant for stating the obvious. Maybe it was a Barnsley-thing – I don't know.

He did no more than roust her out of the room, usher her down the passage, gave her a boot up the arse and sent her to bed. The funny thing about that is that she was eighteen at the time!

Marlene had an angry side too, although thankfully, she never directed it at me. Julie's elder sister, however, was a totally different proposition. Sundays back then, consisted of everyone around the table for dinner, watching the *EastEnders* omnibus on TV, whilst washing the pots and then watching both daughters help their mum with the ironing. As for me, I did nothing bar get served cups of tea. It was great.

Whilst Marlene took over ironing duties, a spat ensued where Jane ended up saying something untoward to her mum. The next thing I know is that Marlene's chasing her daughter through the kitchen and down the passage with a red-hot iron in her mitts. Unfortunately, however, her mum forgot to unplug the thing and with the cord not being elastic, it dragged her back and she dropped it on the linoleum, which made her even more livid. What was strange is that after she screamed, shouted and bawled someone out (never me), she had to do something of a tidying-up nature straight after – such as straightening the ornaments on the mantlepiece or a picture frame on the cabinet. It was a habit which regularly had me laughing.

As for Julie, she was becoming more and more territorial about the free use of my house – especially the bed. I recall picking her up one evening in late-September, when as usual, I was around twenty minutes late – however, that didn't matter. She came into the kitchen wearing a new leather jacket, leather skirt, and shoes to match. "I've got yer mate a birthday card," she smiled. "Do you want to write on it, or me?"

Our ultimate destination was to be the scene of the Thurnscoe's most high-profile domestic of 1968 – the Whinwood Hotel and Andy Moore's twenty-first birthday party.

Andy had been whittling on about it for ages – not at least because his father, Tony, had got a new girlfriend – and as these old ones tended to do, they often overshowed their attention in public, which was something that had totally rattled him the week before as he and his then-girlfriend Tracy Moorhouse had been subjected to it.

Although I never lost sight of who Andy was, he and I had reconnected since being transferred to Markham Main. As kids we got brought up in similar circumstances with our mum's hiding from the rent man – him in the houses down Church Street and us in The Avenues, whilst later on in life he would tell me about him and Andy Roper watching Dennis McCabe dutifully constructing his coffins.

They never used to call around for me to watch him make coffins!

As for Julie, she was brilliant. It was as if she had unwittingly decided to up the relationship a couple of notches. We had called in The Red Lion down in Wath-on-Dearne along with The Goldthorpe Hotel and everyone seemed to be around us. It was the best I had felt in ages.

On seeing a rather despondent-looking Andy down in the Whinwood Hotel, she did nothing more than plant him a kiss on the cheek and give him his card, before wishing him Happy Birthday.

"If I were you, mate," he grumbled, "I'd drink your drink and go somewhere else, as this is shit."

I looked around at the meagre turnout of a few friends and relations including his dad and his girlfriend and knew exactly what he meant.

"No, we're staying," Julie told him. "We're yer mates and it's your birthday."

The next thing I know, Julie's up dancing with a handful of people she didn't know, including Andy's girlfriend. She was a girl that just fitted in with everyone. This was the first time I realised that we were a couple.

Within half-an-hour or so, all our friends had come down from the East end and the place was alive. What Andy thought was going to be a poor show, turned out to be the exact opposite. Sometimes things happen like that. I was well-chuffed for him. Nice people deserve nice things and Andy was exactly that.

Julie, however, had her mind set on something and it certainly didn't involve her best friend staying the night at my house. She played her divide and rule card, which was the one that stopped Coop moving in.

"If I can't stay at your house – then she's not staying," she told me.

And it was that simple.

Bill used to get the right hump about the hours his daughter kept.

"I got up at half-past-four and she still weren't in her bed. I'm not happy."

He didn't have to tell me the last part as I was looking back at him.

"It'll not happen again," I told him.

Did it?

Yes, all the time – therefore, it was no surprise when she got caught on.

What did I say about, two steps forward and one step back?

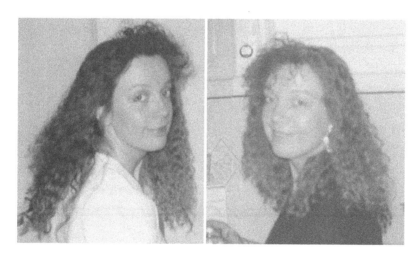

The Girlfriend.

Top. A view looking down Dearne Road, Bolton-on-Dearne with Manvers Main in the background circa 1973 (c. Alamy)
Bottom. A view from Bolton-on-Dearne's Brickyard Ponds looking towards Goldthorpe Colliery's iconic Rapid Loading Bunker circa 1985.

31. The Hand That Rocks The Cradle

I had become far too selfish and certainly too conceited to have a child and I suppose it was both those features that gave the green light for it to become a reality. The reality of the situation was, that I needed a kid like a hole in the head. Nevertheless, the thought quite appealed to me.

It wasn't a rash decision, anything but. Everything was spoken about, including the bad things, such as me possibly walking away from the girlfriend when I eventually got bored and of course, a possible termination. I mean, I had only known her two minutes.

Col was currently fighting a paternity case and had a huge backdated maintenance order hovering over him like a vulture over a corpse, the latter of which was enough to have you contemplate swinging from a rope, therefore those danger signs were always there.

I always remember us sat in my mum's car outside her house and a conversation whereby I had been contemplating buying some cream carpet for the big upstairs bedroom and humming and erring about whether I could afford it or not. "It's only a two-pounds a week," she told me. "I'll pay it for you."

I had only known her a few weeks.

That generous side of her nature, was something that I loved. As was her outgoing personality. She was certainly the type of girl you could settle down with. Unfortunately, for her, I was not.

"What you're doing is wrong," I remember her crying. "It's really wrong."

We had a baby in a pram and all I wanted to do was go out and get away from them both.

That feeling of being trapped was a feeling that I had never contemplated, however that would be several months into the future.

There was a story and one that I didn't know about until recently.

My uncle Rob's wife Joy had had a great-aunt that she had not only never seen but had also never heard of. It is quite true that families back then rarely spoke of tragedies and just recently I was told as much by a lady off Thurnscoe's Windsor Street who candidly explained: "When the grown-ups started talking, we were made to go play outside."

My early childhood was at times, no different.

Joy's great-aunt had been born illegitimate to her great-grandfather's brother, James Severn – a man who rather strangely, dumped the child's mother, Alice Smith, to marry her elder sister, Ethel.

In Alice's own words, she described Ethel as her "beautiful sister", however, their father was not so, and had turned her out, thereby Alice had to throw her mercy on the state – and the child, Ivy Severn Smith, ended up being born in a workhouse in Batley during November 1911.

From what is known, Alice appeared quite intelligent and had moved around for two years after the birth of her daughter, living between addresses in Sheffield and Mexborough. However, the one place it all fell down for her, was with men. As I have said before, the pretty girl always gets drawn to the bad lad.

Jim (John James) Smith (no relation) was exactly that.

Jim Smith was a miner who was two years younger than the twenty-two-year-old Alice. He both used and abused her whilst he dangled the carrot of marriage in her face. The main problem he had was that he was extremely jealous of the child's natural father. James Severn was a big powerful looking guy. He was also well-known, being that he along with his brothers – my auntie Joy's great-grandfather included, were part of the infamous Red Brotherhood. These were a hardcore element of young Mexborough and Denaby miners that came to national attention between 1909 and 1925, and who were renowned for their violence.

It could be assumed that every time he looked at Ivy, James Severn is who he saw.

On the broken promise of him stating that he would marry her after what was a tumultuous nine-week relationship, she ended up moving out her lodgings – a terraced property at 22 Herbert Street, Mexborough which belonged to the slum landlords that were Walter and Isabella Swift. That wasn't before he had tried exploiting her for gain, something which she wanted absolutely nothing to do with.

The straw that broke the camel's back had come on 16 September 1914.

Her relationship with the landlord of the property was more or less exasperated but to add further weight to that, Jim Smith had brought back two men to the house – one who was Thomas Sawyer from Denaby. His idea was for them to have sex with her for money. Alice refused, and all hell broke loose. Not only did he beat her black and blue he also beat her child.

Alice did no more than move out, this time seeking refuge at the home of Hannah Biggs who lived on Mexborough's Kirby Street – the exact same street, where thirty-eight-year-old Brenda Gunn (nee Garfitt) was found murdered after being stabbed to death some sixty-five years later.

Unbeknown to Mrs Biggs, Alice had been at her wit's end. She wanted out but could see no way of doing it. At around 8.30 a.m., she put one hand over her daughter's face and strangled her with the other. She had intended slitting her throat with a kitchen knife but could not bring herself to do it. Her murdered child of two years and nine months laid both cold and very still in the bed for two more hours before the police arrived on the scene.

Alice was extremely forthright about her killing the child and admitted it outright. There was however, one thing she had failed to do and that was to kill herself as is generally the norm when a parent murders their children – as in the case of Carl's *unhappy house* at Pollington.

There was also a story closer to home and which occurred on the wet Wednesday afternoon of 17 November 1976.

Forty-year-old Joseph Scipio Brewster of 29 Croft Road, Brinsworth had parked up his car alongside Howell Wood at the top of Thurnscoe's Clayton Lane and murdered his daughters whilst taking his own life. He had attached a hose to the exhaust of his car and threaded it through the window.

A passer-by saw the fume filled car and on opening its doors to saw the father slumped over the steering wheel and the bodies of three children in the back.

Tracey, Yvette and Andrene Karina – aged nine, seven and six-year-old, had died of carbon monoxide poisoning.

It was claimed that his suicide and their murder had come about after his relationship with his ex-wife Carol (nee Howell) had run its course – whether that was indeed the case, I don't know.

What is true is that she had begun a relationship with Malc Harvey – a diesel fitter at Hickleton Main who had lived just off Derry Grove at 17 Hallgate. He was also the father of one of Thurnscoe Comprehensive's Class of 1981 – Julie Harvey (now Reid).

The couple moved into a flat over one of the shops in Bolton-on-Dearne's St Andrews Square – eventually getting married at Barnsley Register Office on 24 January 1979 where rather interestingly, Barry and Shirley Barnish (nee Wright) were the best man and maid of honour. These were the parents of Ian Barnish – my garrulous adversary in Carfield, and the lad who possessed the exotic footwear.

As for Alice Smith, she continually broke down during her murder trial at Leeds Assizes on 21 November 1914 and on sentencing collapsed in the dock.

She had been sentenced to death by Justice Sir Montague Shearman with a recommendation for mercy. This was eventually commuted to penal servitude for life.

She spent her time in both Walton Gaol (HMP Liverpool) and Aylesbury Prison, where she was initially described as possessing an uncertain temper, being difficult to manage as well as being untruthful, troublesome, and lazy.

Alice was released on licence on 5 February 1919 after serving four years and three months. She would have got out sooner was it not for the fact that she had sent a letter to her other sister Lizzie after four months on the inside, in which she stated that if it took her twenty years, she would get her revenge on Jim Smith.

There was a similar tale a few years later and that was of a girl who had been born in Darfield but who had grown up in the row of terraced houses one up from where I had been born in Mexborough.

Annie Neath was a twenty-eight-year-old domestic servant who had lived at 2 Spencer Street and who on 18 January 1921 gave birth to an illegitimate baby boy and thereafter stabbed it to death with a pair of scissors. He suffered a total of thirteen wounds including one blow that had gone three inches into his brain along with numerous other blows that had penetrated his heart and chest. After she had killed him, she stuck the remains in a dress basket beneath her bed.

Her trial was ground-breaking as it was the first time any women had sat on a jury – however, that didn't alter its outcome and Annie Neath suffered the exact same sentence as Alice Smith.

This happened quite a bit.

In late-February 1914, two women uncovered the body of a child which had been parcelled in a sack and dumped in some disused wash house buildings in a yard off West Street, Conisbrough. The child – a boy, had recently been born weighing 6 lb and 10 oz and had been strangled with a length of calico, which on its discovery, had still been wrapped around its neck.

The story that surrounded the find, concerned a young girl from 34 Church Street, Conisbrough and her elder sister's husband.

From 22 March up until 20 December 1913, it was said that Fred Lyon had been regularly having sex with his fourteen-year-old sister-in-law and had got her pregnant.

Minnie Scott was the daughter of a deceased miner who had worked on the sinking of Cadeby Colliery's shafts and had just turned fifteen-year-old when she was eventually charged with murder.

During her trial at Leeds Assizes on 6 May 1914, Justice Atkin heard that thirty-three-year-old Fred Lyon had had uninterrupted regular access to the girl – and more importantly that access had been obscured as their houses backed on to each other's. On Saturday nights Minnie had been left on her own – with the mother and elder daughter often going out together. That left a window for Fred Lyon to exploit, him often nipping back to the house – his ruse being that he needed to leave the key as Minnie often looked in on his children.

Although the case was vigorously pushed by the NCPCC, Minnie's indictment for murder and her pleading guilty to the concealment of the child made her an unreliable witness.

Lyon was eventually cleared of sex with a minor (rape), whilst Minnie – due to her just being a child, was sentenced to a twelve-month detention order.

I am not sure what happened to Fred and his wife, Ethel Maude, thereafter but what I do know is that Minnie went on to marry twenty-four-year-old Arnall Coope on 6 November 1919 and had four children to him.

Some of the family are still living in the area – Minnie's grandson living at 24 Queen's Avenue, which is a short stroll into Swinton from Mexborough's Roman Terrace.

The nearest my mum had come to something such as that had been after the birth of my sister, which was something that she readily admitted to.

My (step)dad used to get picked up by Hanson's – a private bus operator contracted by the ICI to ferry its workers from the eastern Dearne Valley over to its factory in Huddersfield – much like the millowners in the 1940s and 1950s.

My (step)dad's rendezvous was the bus stop outside The New 'Un – however, on my mum having our Joanne, he had to pack his job in.

"I could have been on the board of directors if I'd stayed," he would often say with a touch of aloofness, thereby adding some civilian myth go with that of his illustrious military career.

"I would have murdered her if he had," my mum had maintained.

Was she the same with me?

Not really. She just told me that I ought to have been drowned at birth.

"Don't worry about it," our Steve (Durose) recently told me. "It's nowt that my mam has never said to me."

I never intimated that my life was idyllic!

Thurnscoe East during the 1940s and 1950s saw a stream of such buses both picking up and dropping off. On 20 March 1951, a tragedy occurred off Windsor Street's junction with its Square. Two young girls ran out into the road from behind a red Yorkshire Traction bus, which had been parked at the bus stop to meet their mums getting of the mill workers bus at the other stop opposite and close to where the old bookmakers shed once stood.

However, as they ran into the road the bus dropping off the mill workers had already set off and with its driver, a Charles William Robinson, being totally unsighted, ended up running over both children and killing them instantly.

Josephine (Josie) McMahon was an eight-year old who lived at 49 Windsor Street whilst her friend, thirteen-year-old Marie Bool, lived across the road at No 52. The driver only managed to stop the vehicle after its front wheels had gone over both children, both of whom sustained absolutely horrific head injuries.

It is hard to imagine the crowds of people and of the distress and heartache of their respective families, with Josephine's younger sister telling me just recently that her distraught father had had to carry her dead sister off the road and into the house.

It must have been nothing short of a truly macabre sight.

"Nobody was allowed to see her," explained Josie's younger sister Lynn (now Sims). "Even on the day of the funeral my mother begged just to be able to hold her hand but was told *no.*"

Neither my grandma Ellis nor my (step)dad never ever mentioned this and it happened right outside their house at 57 Windsor Street, the latter being a year above Josie at Thurnscoe Hill school.

It had been the school holidays and the Tuesday before Easter.

"After the funeral they found her Easter egg half-eaten, rewrapped and purposely turned around to make it look untouched," smiled Lynn. "My mother said afterwards that she wished she had eaten it all!"

There was another *what if.*

"If Josie had gone to the cinema with my mam and dad instead of wanting to go another night with Marie, the accident possibly wouldn't have happened," Lynn further explained.

As I have already said, back then a lot of tragedy got buried in time and nowadays has been forgotten about and it shouldn't do.

A near-neighbour and someone who would have been the cousin of my (step)dad, had been born a mere couple of months after Josie, never even made it to that age, her life being cut short at just sixteen-months old.

Annette Ellis was the daughter of my granddad (Eric) Ellis's elder brother Jimmy and his wife Constance (nee Chapman). Annette came into her short life at 2 Windsor Square cursed with what was described as achondroplasia – a form of short-limbed dwarfism, along with the unwanted baggage of health problems associated with it, and sadly died of bronchial pneumonia on 2 November 1944.

Thurnscoe East has scores of similar tragic stories, especially the further you look back.

The Bridges family from George Street were another family that must have felt cursed.

The rather colourful Arthur Bridges had come up to Thurnscoe from the Depwade area of Norfolk and had married a widow by the name of Ellen Cooper, firstly settling at 3 Hickleton Terrace before becoming the first ever tenants at the newly constructed 3 George Street.

Arthur scrimped and scraped and both ducked and dived to keep his family's head above water – especially during the far-reaching problems associated with the fall-out from the dirt muck strike of 1902 and what would become the mass evictions over at Denaby Main, with poaching certainly being one of his things. In fact, after having his nets and pegs confiscated, he ended up being sentenced to a month in prison after surreptitiously removing several fowls from the home of Checkweighman and future councillor and magistrate Mark Nokes – the police arriving at Arthur's home only to see his wife dishing out a roast chicken dinner.

Arthur's hard work and scheming wasn't always enough to keep his family going and in April 1903 they lost their son John – aged just fifteen-months old.

During the early tenure of the property on George Street, another tragedy would occur. His wife gave birth to twin girls, Alice and Ellen, on 17 October 1911, both of whom died a few days later. This would be shortly followed by Samuel, aged just fourteen years old and nine months – who, according to the *Sheffield Telegraph,* had died underground at Hickleton Main.

It was a time and a place where life appeared cheap and when children dropped like flies.

Arthur was also one of the many who died from injuries sustained from a life working underground.

Never think that the plaque of Hickleton Main's dead covers everyone, however – because it doesn't. Like most things in life it just scratches at the truth.

Arthur went on afternoon shift on 24 October 1922 and ended up being buried alive at around 5.00 p.m. For seventeen hours his colleagues dug and clawed at the coal and muck before they eventually rescued him and hauled him to safety, only for him to die a day or so later at home.

Arthur had several grandchildren, one whom was Stanley Bridges. He and his wife, Janet (nee Till) along with his five great-grandchildren lived on the northern leg of Brunswick Street, which connects Lancaster with Briton Street.

This part of the Thurnscoe's East end had seen masses of families both come and go since its final construction in 1926 and was perhaps seen as the roughest, if not the most run-down of places on the pit estate, with several families down its odd-numbered side living in borderline squalor.

A notable feature was that there always appeared to dozens upon dozens of kids everywhere – which was a nightmare when either the milk man, bread van, Danny's or Misters Softee or Ronskley turned up on the street. If the contents of the milk float or bread van weren't getting pilfered, then it was a case of half a dozen kids hitching a ride down the street on the rear bumpers of the ice cream vans.

Whilst the milkman had been down one of the streets many ginnels seeking payment, half the contents of his float made its way into someone else's property. Still, it wasn't as bad as him having to chase the thing down forty yards down Briton Street after Robert Frost had been out playing the Good Samaritan and had kindly released the handbrake for him.

In March 1973, it was Arthur Bridges great-grandson, David, that became the focal point of attention after he had been seen in the street brandishing some gun – with him firing a pellet into the head of a three-year-old girl, by the name of Sharron Leighton.

I personally struggle to recall the story, however – what I do know is that the little girl was the daughter of Tom and Joan, the latter who was the elder sister of Pauline Cowley (now Duggan).

Tom and Joan Leighton were married in 1968 and moved into 66 Brunswick Street – a house where they had two children, Sharron and Glenn, in 1969 and 1970 respectively. It would be here where they would become the neighbours of Stan and Jean.

The Bridges appeared a happy carefree family with Janet, a lovely lady who seemed to have time for everyone on the street.

I recall on my second stint up in Thurnscoe's East end and of some quarrel between the Bridges and another set of neighbours – the Chapmans. I am unsure as to what exactly occurred – however, I seem to recall that Janet somehow ended up on the floor. As is generally the case with arguments between neighbours, there appeared to be a lot of muted threats being traded, with half the kids on the street inquiring as to the wellbeing of the little lady that everyone loved. Feuding with the Bridges family was nothing new and was something that had certainly occurred in March 1973.

It would be wrong of me to suggest that Janet spoiled her children, but they certainly weren't as restricted as I had been, that's for sure.

For some strange reason, Janet had let her second eldest son go out with a loaded gun.

David would have been around six years old at that time and wouldn't have had the physical strength to retract the spring mechanism of a standard air pistol. Therefore, assuming it was indeed some form of pistol, a 1.77 Gat seems the obvious gun that he became armed with. Although it is still quite heavy, it could easily be retracted by pushing the weapon against any solid object, such as an outhouse wall or indeed a tarmacked pavement.

Most of the lads that I grew up with were all in possession of these types guns as teenagers. Kevin Ince – one of my old mates who went on to be an electrician at Goldthorpe Colliery and who is now an experienced gyroplane pilot had given me my first Gat when I was fourteen.

You could easily shoot each other in the legs and torso with the only result being that the victim took a bit of a sting. Therefore, it would still be highly doubtful if something such as that could penetrate the skin far enough for it to ever create complications.

There is, however, always a danger.

I vividly recall wagging school dinners with the gangly Nigel Coulson and sitting on the abutments of the long since demolished bridge which once carried the Wath Branch Line close to where Doctor Kaye's and Rocky Walls café once stood and of us suddenly being penned in by two lads a few years older firing 2.2 pellets from a high-powered air rifle. They missed their target, but it wasn't for the lack of them trying. A head shot – even at that distance could have easily blinded us or at worst, been fatal.

There was a similar story in Thurnscoe around that time.

Chapel Lane ran parallel with both legs of Brunswick Street – however, unlike Brunswick it only possessed odd-numbered houses which overlooked allotments and playing fields, the latter of which just about always had kids playing football on it.

Tim Bright and I had been part of a bunch of fourteen and fifteen-year-olds kicking a ball about when suddenly the game was disrupted when Mick Hill and Shaun Walker turned up on the field, both of who were armed with an air rifle apiece.

Anthony Cook was possibly the most vociferous of us all and held out his arms and urged one of them to take a pop at him, and from around forty yards Shaun did exactly that and hit his target, which had Anthony going ballistic. "You've fucking shot me, you bastard," he snarled whilst ripping off his shirt to reveal a shoulder that had been both bruised and blooded by the pellet.

From what I've been told, and that is all it is, David didn't just aim and fire at the three-year-old girl – he fired both at close range and at her head, the pellet cutting through Sharron's skull and getting lodged in her brain, meaning that the pellet was maybe discharged from some form of small rifle – a rat gun, perhaps.

"They were playing Cowboys and Indians outside her house on Brunswick Street, when it happened," explained Sharron's auntie Pauline.

The child had to be revived twice in the ambulance whilst on its way over to the head trauma unit at Sheffield's Royal Hallamshire Hospital and was it not for the quick thinking of the paramedics, Sharron would have most certainly died.

She had been in hospital for several months with the lead still lodged in her brain and doing its worst to cause as much damage as possible.

"She was in theatre for hours," Pauline told me. "When she came back to the ward all her beautiful hair had been shaved off and there were tubes coming out of her head. It was heart-breaking to see."

Pauline, the younger sister of Sharron's mum by several years, was livid. Frustrated by the fact that she couldn't help the child and at the upset of her sister, she took her wrath out on Janet Bridges – making her totally culpable for what had occurred.

"After all that, the pellet was still lodged in her brain," she added. "It was too dangerous to remove. It was a very traumatic time. When she eventually came out of the coma she had to learn to eat, talk and walk all over again."

"Sharron's mam never blamed David for it as he was just a child himself," explained Pauline's daughter, Sara. "I recently bumped into him in The Clog (Thurnscoe Social & Ex-Servicemen's Club) and he expressed his guilt about it."

As for Sharron, she suffered irrevocable damage to her brain and still suffers slurred speech, as well as walking with a limp. There is an upside however, in that she proved that she is one of life's fighters.

During her stay in hospital and throughout her rehabilitation, her auntie Pauline said something that maybe spurred her on. "I had always promised her that she could be a bridesmaid at my wedding and wear these silver shoes," she said. "I kept my promise and was so proud of her walking down the aisle."

As for the wedding itself, there were reporters everywhere as it was covered by several outlets of the national media.

Nowadays, Sharron lives over in the Stocksbridge area of northern Sheffield and is married with three children of her own and has a job that entails her working with people that have mental illness.

"I love our Sharron and we have always been protective of her, but she proved everyone wrong," said Sara. "She's a real tough cookie and has never let anything hold her back."

As for me, my problems were just about to start.

"She needs to go to see the doctor," my mum had told me after I let her know that she was to be a grandparent. "She also needs to tell her mam and dad."

It was basic common sense but none of us fancied doing that, therefore it was something that wouldn't happen until the run up to Christmas.

"The doctor will know what to prescribe her," added my mum. "Most probably vitamin and iron tablets."

I did have some reservations surrounding the latter, however.

I remember during Carfield Junior School and of John Weddell in particular. He was possibly the smartest turned-out kid amongst us – with the exception of his yellowish teeth, that is. These, he candidly informed us had been caused due to his mother being administered iron tablets when she had been pregnant with him.

The last time I would ever see John would be around this time.

He and a blond-haired lad a year younger than us – Derek (Jigger) Lidster, had been outside the Church House in Wath-on-Dearne and had been trying to put a Pie and Pea van on its side. They along with a few others had had it precariously rocking from side to side, with the old woman serving, literally screaming her head off at them, whilst trying her best not to get scalded by the tide of hot mushy peas splashing around the van's interior.

John had turned from something of a spoiled brat into a very cynical lad who had truly little respect for anyone – and that included his father.

"I've not spoke to him in ages," he told me whilst I had been down at their new bungalow at 9 Calder Road, solely to pick up an old record player that I had swapped for a pair of brand new matt black coloured cow-horn handlebars.

I looked around his bedroom, which was equipped with all the mod cons that any young kid could have ever wanted – including a new state-of-the-art music centre, and wondered what exactly had gone wrong for him to feel like that about his dad. I mean, in comparison to me, he had everything.

I know John got back speaking to his father on him gearing up to leave school – as his dad, was like the *goose that laid the golden eggs* to lads such as I.

Joey Weddell was a product of Thurnscoe's East end – the second eldest son of Joseph Weddell of 7 Cromwell Street and Harriett Selina Scrimshaw of 11 Queen Street. The pair had been married at St Hilda's Church on 14 September 1929, with Harriett being heavily pregnant, and who after their marriage had moved into a house at 3 Hanover Street.

As with a lot of these families, tragedy would strike and Joey's elder brother by two years, William (Bill), would die of diphtheria in April 1938, aged just eight.

"My dad worked hard from the age of fourteen and virtually brought him and his brother Roy up as his mum [Harriet Scrimshaw] died shortly after losing the eldest son," explained John's elder sister, Bridget (now Ryan).

"My dad and uncle Roy were both beaten badly by their father (her grandfather) but when he had a stroke at fifty-seven years of age, mum and dad had him living with them."

As for their mum, Brenda – she was brought up by her parents Harry and Agnes Hinchcliffe at 20 Queen Street, Thurnscoe, both of whom lived out their lives there until in 1966 and 1979 respectively.

That was a house that proved unlucky for the property's previous occupants, Walter and Emily Finbow (nee Willette). They lost four children there: five-year-old Florence and Ada, aged two years seven months within thirteen days of each other in 1915; seventeen-month-old Harold in 1924; and a seven-week-old baby by the name of Ernest a year later.

"My mum did an amazing thing and went to college to do teacher training, which in those days was massive, especially having two children and my dad working shifts," added Bridget. "They are the salt of the earth."

As for Joey, he would go on to work at both Barnburgh Main and Highgate Colliery before dropping on the job of all jobs – the Training Officer at Manvers Main.

I recall Joey driving me and his son and all over the place – and in two different types of Volkswagen – firstly a Beetle and then a Type 3. One destination was a youth club down Mexborough, if I rightly recall. Then later on in life, he got us along with Gary Salkeld involved in some mini five-a-side tournament to the rear of Wath Grammar School.

I had to admit, Joey was a really upstanding guy – however, not everyone thinks alike, and that envy from beneath always rears its head in some shape or another.

"He's nothing but a shithole," Tim's dad, once sniped with reference to John's father.

We had been in the front room of 178 Furlong Road listening to Booker T's *Soul Limbo*, which was the introduction music to the Test Cricket on TV during the summer of 1981 and his name cropped up. The was possibly down to the fact that his son, John, had been one of the first quota from the Class of 1981 to be set on at the pit.

Pete was one of those people that never said anything bad about anyone without valid reason – so whatever Joey had said or indeed done, must have really wound him up.

It happens. I know there are people out there that I cannot stand and who other people actually like.

As for John, I wouldn't converse with him until towards the back end of the strike. He had been in the Halfway Hotel and explained that he had jacked in his job, bought a van, and had been delivering potatoes.

Fast-forward several years and he had relocated just south of Reading and was working for himself laying commercial block paving.

His sister added that he was now part of Leeds United's Service Crew – one of the most notorious hooligan firms in the history of English football, who when the likes of Tony Waugh and Tim were following them up and down the country, used to meet in the city's *Star and Garter*.

What is strange about that comment is that the lad was never what you would term a *headcase* in any sense of the word; in fact, quite the contrary – he often got bullied. He also switched teams from Leeds United to Sheffield Wednesday all through senior school and for some time thereafter. It is a strange one, that.

I am not sure of my mum's real thoughts of us having a child as I often said, she wasn't the type of person you could ever fully read. She appeared interested, which was a plus and it is fair to say that she pushed extremely hard for us to get married. I don't think that it was so much for the baby, but more because she wanted a wedding. It would be a scenario made for her – with her as the major controlling factor and the centre of attraction.

Am I wrong in saying that? Most definitely. However, it is also the truth.

Just prior to us finding out about the pregnancy, my dad and his family had called to the house.

I recall him knocking on the front door and on me looking down through the upstairs window. He was barely recognisable. He had been wearing a floppy hat to part-cover the god awful mess that the chemo and radiotherapy had made and had lost considerable weight in the few weeks since I'd last seen him – so much so, his fast deterioration and skeletal features began to wear heavy on me and became a huge feature of my upset. The man had been a massive presence in my life and now he was staring at the inevitable. "I wish I had a kid of yours to bounce around on my knee," was the sentence I remember him saying more than anything.

My mum's presence at the house whilst my dad was there was a bit strange.

She along with my (step)dad had called down to Briton Square to get some coal. My mum burned coal just as she spent money and their house always had a fire in 24/7, which was something I certainly recall bollocking her about after my (step)dad had died in April 1995.

She wanted his body along with the coffin in the front room of 51 Lancaster Street – and for around four or five days prior to the funeral. I thought it was morbid as hell and told her as much – however, trying to reason with my mum was always like pissing in the wind.

I recall Dennis McCabe whispering in my ear: "Whatever you do, don't be letting your mam light a fire."

I tried to put that point over – however, two days later I walked into the room only to see some blazing inferno ripping up the chimney back whilst the world's warmest corpse was laid snug in its box.

"Jesus Christ, mam, I told you that you couldn't put a fire in," I said.

"It's just to take the chill out of the room," she replied.

"Yeh, but my dad's going to end up stinking the house out."

As I said, like pissing in the wind.

On my mum calling at the house she immediately saw a pair of white stiletto shoes in the kitchen (remember it was the mid-1980s), meaning that I had a girl in – therefore, the first thing she did was want to bypass me to go in the room and obviously to evaluate her.

"My dad's in there," I told her.

All through my life as a young kid, I had not so much fantasised, but certainly had thoughts about having both my natural parents together as a family – however, for her to see my dad, and at the gateway of death, was a definite non-starter.

Rather strangely, she did the right thing and stayed put whilst my (step)dad filled a few sacks of coal around the back of the house. I have never thought of this before, but that was the nearest that I had been to both parents at the same time since our tenure on Bolton-on-Dearne's Flower Estate.

The thing that always struck me was how quiet my dad's children (Shaun and Louise) were when they were outside of their own domain and whilst at mine, they sat still and rarely spoke.

"They were told not to say owt," my nana Durose told me in later life.

I had lived with them for eight months and never ever noticed anything untoward, in that they were ever made to just sit down and shut up. From a personal point of view, I thought them no different to Joanne and Joel in that they were just lovely kids – the only possible downside being that I had an avid dislike of their mum, which was something that I knew would only get worse.

"When my dad dies, she'll cut me off," I told my girlfriend.

It wasn't just something that I knew. It was also something that my dad knew.

It is hard to gauge how someone is thinking when they are staring into the abyss – but he was anything but stupid.

I remember calling to their house not long after and him giving me an album full of the photographs that he used to get out when I was a kid. It was heart-breaking, as was the fact that as soon as I got through their door he would stick some mid-1960s country and western record on – and one from my past – be it some untitled compilation album of George Jones or The Wilburn Brothers' *Never Alone* – both of which I now have at my house.

As with my grandma Carman, my dad knew how I rolled.

I had a girlfriend who was pregnant and a dad who was dying. It was a time when I began to think a lot.

Hickleton Main NUM officials. Left, Billy Hayes and Right, Kev Hardman - both brilliant men

32. Wings

My idea of being a parent was simple. I just needed to be a better one than mine.

My children were fortunate in that they had everything – even though at certain points in our life we as a couple had nothing.

I looked at the job I was doing underground and could see no future.

Nowadays, they refer to mining as a career, but I must be honest. I certainly never saw it like that – which is strange as in part I am still heavily involved in it.

The progression I was part of at Hickleton Main was nowhere to be seen at Markham as hordes of miners were being shipped in from all over the place – Cadeby Colliery in particular. This brought with it that know-it-all form of pit-snobbery that I had recently seen with those from Cortonwood. Add to that thee fact that it had had a disaster there in 1912, made their self-importance appear all the more important.

Cadeby had been sunk at a similar time as Hickleton Main – however, its neighbouring pit had not. Denaby Main had been around much longer and even though it had in effect, closed – the name still remained.

As part of the NCB's rationalisation of the industry, Denaby had an underground link constructed with Cadeby and by 1956 all coal then came to the surface via the latter. A bit like Goldthorpe and Highgate if-you-like. Further rationalisation followed the exhaustion of Denaby's Barnsley Bed reserves and in 1967 the two collieries became 'Denaby – Cadeby', fully merging on 23 March 1968.

Denaby was synonymous with mining, Cadeby was not. At that point in my life, the only recollection I had of Cadeby Colliery was that the body of some miner's wife had been found in some ditch close to the pit, whilst I had been in the last year of school. She had been murdered.

What I wasn't to know is that one of the lads who transferred over from the pit – a slight looking guy with quite an engaging personality by the name of Dean Roach, had been related to the dead woman.

Anne Marie Harold (nee Roach) went missing from her home on 12 September 1980 and her body was found sixteen days later dumped in some land drain and part-buried under grass and clumps of earth by three members of the nearby Denaby Rifle Club. She had been clubbed over the head and had suffered serious head wounds before being strangled to death with some form of ligature.

The murder bore certain similarities to the death of Doreen Rumble – in that the spot where her body was found was considered something of a Lover's Lane. Doreen had also lived just a couple of hundred yards from where twenty-two-year-old Anne Marie and her husband lived – just off Mexborough's Roman Terrace at 78 Highwoods Road.

Her husband Colin was the son of Alexander Harold – one of the influxes of miners that came down from the north east to work in the pits in the 1950s and 1960s – but strangely not to those in the Dearne Valley, but those in North Nottinghamshire.

It would be here that Colin would marry a girl by the name of Christine Swannack in 1974, with whom he had two children – Simon in 1975 and Daniel in late-1979.

He hardly cut a dashing figure and could only be described as a tall wiry man of gaunt appearance with dark greasy hair and deep-set eyes. However, there is something that stands out. Rather strangely, the second child from his first marriage was born whilst he was not only in a relationship with Anne Marie – but while he had already had a child with her. Sean Harold had been born in February 1979. He may not have been its father, but there were alarm bells everywhere.

Anne Marie had married him at Doncaster Register Office on 28 June 1980 and had managed to stay alive a further seventy-six days.

According to Anne Marie's mother, Theresa Roach – who lived in nearby Conisbrough, her daughter had told her two weeks before her murder: "I've got a feeling that I'm going to die."

At seven months pregnant she was still working as a manageress in some shoe shop in Mexborough, whilst Colin was said to be employed underground and working on the haulage at Manvers Main.

Det. Supt. Peter Owen who led the case, explained that for sixteen days her body lay undiscovered, which he solely put down to the fact that someone had tried their best to hide it. However, the main problem was that there appeared to be absolutely no motive surrounding the murder whatsoever. There had been no sexual interference and the fact that she had money in her purse and all her jewellery intact – such as the gold locket around her neck and both wedding and engagement rings – meant that she hadn't been robbed.

With sex and robbery ruled out, the question facing the police was: Why should anyone want to kill her?

Her twenty-nine-year-old husband had supposedly dropped her off in Mexborough town centre that Friday morning to do some shopping and she never returned.

That day she had been wearing a light blue crew neck T-shirt under a dark blue pinafore dress and a pair of blue wedge-heeled sandals.

"We haven't found anyone who saw her. We have checked the shops, and no one remembers serving her," said the detective. "It is quite baffling."

That really wasn't the case. The finger was firmly pointing at the husband.

"Looking tired and haggard, Colin Harold left the police's murder headquarters at Mexborough's Adwick Road station for the first time since Sunday, when his wife's strangled body was found," stated the South Yorkshire correspondent for the *Daily Mirror*.

As for Colin Harold – he immediately broke protocol. "I would not lift a finger to hurt Anne Marie and I never have. I did not murder my wife."

He even went on to say that he and his family had only been down Cadeby Lane a few days prior to his wife's murder.

"Everybody knew he had murdered her," said Mark Gamble – a lad who had not only been an electrician as part of the batch of transferees from Cadeby Colliery – he and his wife Gail, were also good friends with my girlfriend's elder sister.

My auntie, Irene Bridgen, who at the time lived at 20 Lancaster Street had been coming back from Doncaster to Thurnscoe on the 213 on the day that body had been discovered and on coming through High Melton everyone on the bus noticed the huge police presence around the entrance to Cadeby Lane. "When I found out what happened I remember someone saying the police were interviewing people down Mexborough and in particularly outside the butchers where she was last supposedly seen."

"I felt something awful had happened to her," her mother had told reporters. "She was so devoted to her family."

It took over two years to get to the bottom of it, with South Yorkshire Police even interviewing Peter Sutcliffe (the Yorkshire Ripper) about it – which would give you a slight indication to what state her body was in on it being found.

Colin Harold, however, was finally convicted of the murder of Anne Marie at Leeds Crown Court on 3 December 1982 and was sentenced to life imprisonment. Unfortunately, due to the one hundred-year closure on murder files, we will never find out the real reason why he murdered her until New Year's Day 2084.

At work, I was sick of calling into the Personnel Manager's office to try and get off the lousy job I had been saddled with, only to get knocked back time and time again. "There's nothing at this moment in time," must have been Barry Whaling's favourite saying.

It wasn't just me going in to have a word with him either. Both the Unit Official and the District Overman went in to see him on my behalf – however, his answer to them had been the same to them as it had to me. There were just too many men at the pit doing the same thing, to accommodate promoting someone within.

I wouldn't say it was soul destroying, but it certainly pissed me off. I keep on saying it, but it was a problem that had unknowingly been created by my mum.

"I don't want you going down the pit," she had told me. "Try for something else."

Her decision had robbed me of a mining apprenticeship and the DHSS scab payments through half the strike along with a job on the coal face or in the rips.

Tim had seen this coming and immediately looked to get out.

He would not only be the first of my friends to leave the industry but had also managed to wangle a redundancy payment as the pit he had temporarily been transferred to – Edlington's Yorkshire Main, was about to close. Tim was one of those kids who always seemed to drop on.

"Why can't you be more like Tim?" my mum used to say. "He doesn't mess around at school, play truant or going stealing things out of shops."

Yes, he fucking did – he just never got caught.

I once remember wagging school and stood watching some bloke fishing on the second Brick Pond when one of the Heads of Year tapped me on the shoulder. "Why aren't you in school?" he asked.

Teachers always ask stupid questions. He knew I was watching the guy fishing.

As for Tim, had been less than two yards away from me but part-hidden under the fisherman's big green umbrella.

I got the cane for that along with a letter to my parents which I intercepted as it dropped through the letterbox. Unfortunately, after reading it, I found that the Head of my Year, George Bungard, wished to see them. I can't recall how many times in total my mum was summoned to Dearneside – I just know it was a lot. In fact, Mr Bungard became quite friendly with them, so much so he gave me the bollocking of bollockings prior to him caning me one particular time.

"I hate doing this," he snapped. "I know you're a clever lad from a fine family, but why won't you just behave?"

Paul (Boof) Richardson, Nigel Coulson and I had been clambering all over Mr (Terry) Valentine's car opposite the Fifth Year ROSLA block and had been spitting at each other. They got their hands rattled and kicked out the door. As for me, I got the Spanish Inquisition. I suppose, he knew there was a problem and was just being concerned.

If you want a story of the man and one which has stuck with me all my life, I can give you one.

George was the son of Henry and Ethel Bungard (nee Davies) and was a fully qualified engineer before he became a teacher – his subject being Technical Drawing.

His classroom along with Derek Spink's, the music teacher, was an old wooden annexe which was located both to the rear and far end of the huge, red-bricked building. During November 1977 you could hear a euphonium being oom-pah-pahed and trying to knock out some broken rendition of *God Rest Ye Merry Gentlemen* when he had a knock on the door. One of the girls in the upper years had both a poppy tray and tin in her hands. Mr Bungard did no more than go into the inside of his tweed jacket pocket and pull out is wallet and put a £5 note it in the tin. That is £36.35 in today's money. We were all flabbergasted. He then explained why he had done it and what it was for. My grandma Ellis, who had selflessly worked on behalf of the British Legion since the Second World War, would have been so proud if she would have been there.

He, as with Dennis Owen, the headmaster over at Thurnscoe Comprehensive, were extremely thoughtful people and tried to give a bit back. That is pure class and something that I could never knock.

As for my mum and (step)dad coming to school, it had been for a variety of things which culminated in my expulsion. My parents even had me sit in front of some social worker-type down in the Old Town Hall building on Wombwell's High Street.

The answer was simple: If my home life would have been as good as it had been in 1976, then everything would have followed suit. However, it was not.

Did I tell him that? Nope.

I was more worried about having to go to Borstal, which was something that my (step)dad was always threatening me with, when shit came back to the house – one of the worst, possibly being the Goldthorpe Library heist of 1980.

During my tenure at Dearneside Comprehensive, Goldthorpe Library had been a tall three-storey building that once proudly stood behind what was the Horse & Groom public house and which its car park backed on to Queen Street. Inside the building, the first thing that hit you was that tranquil sound of silence and the smell from the gloss of new books along with its huge open plan design and galleried landing.

It was a great place for the older generation – especially those who had retired, as it stocked all the daily newspapers and high-end magazines such as *Elle, Vogue, Homes and Gardens, What Car?* and that kind of thing. It also had a vast library of vinyl records that you could take out – however, that, if I rightly recall, had a small cost attached to it.

During the Fourth Year (Year 10) of senior school a few of us used to use the place, supposedly as a place to do our homework, as on the second floor there was a table with ample room to study and it also stayed open quite late on a couple of days throughout the week. It also became something of a hang out when we were wagging school dinners – and so long as you were quiet, no one really minded.

My mum certainly didn't – that was until she found out what was happening.

There were three of us calling there quite regularly – myself, Richard Clements-Pearce and his best mate – a dark-haired lad who lived off Bolton-on-Dearne's Concrete Canyon by the name of Danny MacDonald. Danny was just starting out his journey into what could be loosely perceived as an eastern philosophy in that he was a belted master in the Korean martial art of Tae Kwon Do, which one could suppose would serve him well once he was married, and is a story that I am certainly not going into. He could have also been construed as being something as a wolf in sheep's clothing as when you went in a shop with him, he was like some fucking magpie. I saw Danny as one of those kids at school who didn't go without, so it amazed me when I saw him in action. There were other similar kids – the main one being Sean (Bucky) Buck.

Bucky was a short but very smart-looking lad with huge goggle eyes who lived in a big house at the top of Bolton-on-Dearne's Ravensmead Court. In senior school he had, what they now correctly term as *special needs* and was slung in what back then we termed as the *Duggy Class* along with all the other window lickers and illiterates. This was run by the Head of Remedial Education, Mrs (Nellie) Crooks. She was a lady who had lived at 8 Prospect Road up until her death in May 1977. She had also taught at Thurnscoe Hill.

On making his way out of the *Duggy Class* Sean got put in our form. Certainly not in our group as he was still on the *Janet and John* books, but certainly in our form. I will say this with hand on heart, Bucky was the best shoplifter I had ever seen. He was hardly the surgeon of shoplifters – more the butcher, but all the same he was remarkably effective. I recall us all going into Drabble's Newsagents, which once stood at Hall Street's junction with High Street in Goldthorpe, and the main man going straight up to the rows of chocolate displayed on the counter and immediately dragging half its content straight into his sports bag.

Did that just happen? I asked Roger Kitchen, on us getting out of the shop.

He wasn't mean either. What he pilfered, he shared. He was a really good kid.

As for Danny, he was much more professional – more your upmarket gentleman diamond thief than a gun-in-your-face blagger like Bucky.

During the late-1970s, Goldthorpe had two dedicated and well-stocked record shops – Ace Records on Market Street and Duffield's on Doncaster Road – the latter of which, was possibly seen as being the more upmarket.

The first thing I always did when I went in was to check the weekly singles chart and get them to stick a record on. This was something that they always did as any money I did have, generally went on buying a single. If I never had any money, then I'd just take one – as there was some form of carousel to the right side of the counter that stocked ex-Juke Box records and as such, it had a right array of shite that you could sift through before you came across something half-decent.

I remember telling Danny about this particular record that had been written by Paul McCartney and had been the theme song for a film starring Peter Sellars and Ringo Starr which had been on TV one particular Sunday night and seeing it on the carousel. I got spending money off my dad – but absolutely nothing from the parents I lived with, apart from dinner money. This being the case, it rarely went on dinner and was immediately invested at one of a few places: Bernie Blakemore's shop at the end of Furlong Road, King Cod in St Andrew's Square or at Sharp's fish and chip shop at the end of Leadley Street, which generally left me starving for the rest of the week.

"You're like a pissing gannet," my (step)dad used to say at the sight of me tearing away at the tall stack of jam sandwiches whilst watching *Blue Peter*.

Looking back at it – that is all we seemed to eat. Mixed fruit jam, because it was the cheapest. Thin sliced bread, because it was the cheapest. And a 2 kg tub of margarine, because it was the cheapest. How I never had rickets, I'll never know.

As for Danny, he was certainly as good as Bucky, but far more subtle.

"You can't miss it," I told him. "It's got a great big apple on the label."

I didn't even see him take it. He was like lightning. I hadn't even got the bloke behind the counter scratting about for some non-descript single, when he had given me the nod.

The record: *Come and Get It* by Badfinger.

Danny also fancied himself as one of these pedantic undergraduates and unlike Bucky, possessed this studious fascination for high-end literature. As such, he'd had his eye on some big leather-bound books – encyclopaedias, that adorned a few of the shelves. Well, that is what we spent a good fortnight hauling out of Goldthorpe Library and down to his house on Dearne Road. They must have weighed a fucking ton. The hardest part was me having to cover our tracks by filling up the huge void that their subsequent removal had made. I forget how many we took but it was a lot.

He was enormously proud of the study that he had created for himself and I was utterly amazed at the erudite surroundings when I was finally invited into his bedroom. Not that we could have sat down anywhere as there wasn't any room due to all the fucking books.

"How can anyone steal books?" shrugged the Chief Librarian on the headmaster calling up to the library and giving him (or her) the bad news.

Someone had grassed us up.

Mr Dickinson suggested that they did an audit, and not only did they find that half their third-floor reference library was now on the second floor, around forty volumes of books were missing – along with part of their record collection. I mean, I had to get something out of it, didn't I? I remember spending an evening diligently listening to some birds whistling on one particular album that I had lifted. *Woodland Birds*: Field recordings of British birds from February to November.

Why anyone would want to buy something like that I had no idea.

"Mr Dickinson says they have a Wings LP still missing," my mum had told me around a week into my expulsion.

I didn't have it. I certainly had the bird whistling one but not the Wings LP. I think that had been down at Tim's.

My mum went ape shit and while I was out, she and my (step)dad dragged all my bedroom out only to uncover half of Dearneside's stationary budget for 1979.

I had to give my mum her due all she did was load it up into the back of the red Ford Granada and take it through to the Fish and Chip shop at Worsbrough Dale until the heat died down – her fully expecting the police to be brought in.

The Wings LP had been the stumbling block.

"Bring that back and so long as you pay for the damage to the books, the police won't be called," Mr Dickinson had told my mum.

My mum swore blind that I didn't have the Wings LP, although the bird whistling one did have her scratching her head as my record collection was fairly consistent with the era of both The Beatles and The Rolling Stones … *I live in an apartment on the na- na- ninety-ninth floor of my ber -lock… And I sit at home looking out the window imagining the world has stopped… Then in flies a guy, who's all dressed up like a Union Jack… yeah!*

"Where's that one come from?" she asked, regarding the bird whistling LP.

"That's Tim's dad's," I lied.

I could well imagine Pete Bright coming in off night shift from Goldthorpe pit and sticking that pile of shite on his turntable.

"Are you pissing thick or what?" my (step)dad had snapped.

Remember, I am the one that taught him how to do fractions, here!

He had just come back in from a meeting at school and witnessed the huge haul of books in Mr Dickinson's office. And believe me when I say it – those books were nearly touching the ceiling.

"It wouldn't be that pissing bad if tha'd gor 'em to read thi sen – but tha nicked 'em for some chuffer else," added my (step)dad.

Translated from an irate Dick Rayner into the Queen's English, that sort of means: What a foolish thing to do. I could well understand if they were for your personal use and to educate yourself, but alas, they were not.

Danny's parents had to cough up £25 (£127.79, circa 2020) as he had meticulously rung the full collection thereby ripping out all the tickets and had dumped their protective covers. I had nothing to pay, which was a plus, however, Mr Dickinson was still tearing out any hair he had got left, over the missing Wings LP.

In the end he must have thought *fuck it*. And I was sent over to Thurnscoe Comprehensive for an interview with its Headmaster – Mr Dennis Owen. He had washed his hands of me.

The strange thing was, that following my interviews with both the social worker and Mr Owen, my parents had been asked to attend a meeting and both these professionals had allegedly inferred the same: "We can't understand any of this – he seems such a nice, polite, and intelligent lad."

There you go. Never judge a book by its cover (sic).

As for the library – it didn't last long after that and as I have already said, the building was subjected to an arson attack by three young lads from Goldthorpe, one of whom was supposedly the colourful younger brother of Alan Cook – Nigel.

As for Danny MacDonald – although I had certainly heard of some of his misadventures, I hadn't seen him since leaving school. The last I knew, was that he owned some carpet and floor covering business at 71 High Street, Wombwell. Great kid, Danny. I liked him a lot.

As for Tim – him going into The Army would be the start of a journey in life which would at times have me scratching my head. Although I often saw him as having things just drop in his lap, I wouldn't have had his life given for a gold pig. My personal view is that he was the greatest kid you could ever meet – that was until he had a woman in tow. Not so much around this time, but certainly a few years later.

"I don't know why I bother with them [women]," he once told me. "I treat them all like shit, so I can't really like them."

His presence certainly had my then-girlfriend scratching her head.

"He talks down to me," she said. "He is really condescending."

That wasn't just then – that's how it's always been. There was a time however, that whilst he was between girlfriends or wives, that he and my wife got on really well. It never lasted that long, however, as he always succeeded in dragging some wench out of a cupboard, that was just as, or stupider as his other wives prior, and it was a plain case of him reverting to type. He is a remarkably interesting kid, nonetheless.

At this juncture he had hooked up with some girl from Matlock – the hows, wheres and whys however, I forget. She would shortly become the first of his five wives – which I have to say, included one common-law. However, out of that lot, this one was, without a shadow of a doubt, certainly the best.

If you go back to us as young kids, it wouldn't be wrong for me to say that both of us could have been described as being *broken*. Me, through physical abuse and Tim through a mother walking out on him and his sister. If you looked at Colin too, his background had been far from idyllic.

Col had been lucky to get past first base and had struggled for life since the day he was born – the huge scar on his stomach being a testament to the lad's resilience. "My mam didn't think I'd live and always told me to appreciate every day," he said in later life.

However, that's not where Col's story lies.

"As kids we had fuck all," he went on to add. "My dad was either on the sick or in the bookies."

Col had been privy to a recent conversation that I had been having over social media with Andy Moore – nothing too intense, just about when I had lived down in The Avenues and he on Church Street and of our openness about our mums having to hide from the rent man. "If I'd known that back then it might have made me feel a little bit better," Col told me.

There is another story and that is of Colin's natural father, not being Roger – and as such, he is much like myself in that he has two half-brothers and two half-sisters.

"Can you find my real dad for me, J?" he candidly asked me a few years ago. "Gordon Edward Stoney."

I did. He was married and living in Grantham.

Colin was devastated on his return: "He told me that he wasn't my dad and said that he couldn't even have children."

I was frank in my reply: "He's lying to you, mate – he's got a daughter who lives around seven hundred yards from where he lives – I've already checked."

Col went back, only to be told that his daughter was adopted.

The guy was also as frank in his appraisal of Col's mum as I had been over the guy himself – in that he portrayed Iris as some flat-capped femme fatale, which Col quite wrongly set about verbally slighting her.

"Remember what you once told me," I said. "We can't be held responsible for the shit that we have said or done in the past. I mean, look at how we were."

If that didn't placate him, the next bit would.

"At least your mum never beat the living daylights out of you – mine fucking did."

"Dougie Sokell," he told me, in between his growling and grimacing. "She now says my dad is some fucker called Dougie Sokell."

I found two. One in Wakefield and one closer to home that lived in Great Houghton, the latter of whom was exactly where I directed him. There was, however, certainly no *Augie Doggie and Doggie Daddy*-type scenario, and on

Col phoning this gadgy, his backside fell out of his trousers. Apparently, he didn't even know his mum – never mind have a child with her. Col's natural father was in fact, the other Dougie Sokell – the guy from Wakefield.

"Although he had always paid maintenance, he was never allowed to see me," Col said. "He was in the Navy."

As with Tim, Col would remarry and then marry again – however, totally unlike Tim the respective relationships were quite normal and produced a further one and four children. Tim's idea of a relationship was much different. Sex, manipulation, and control. And Tim, well, he was the grandmaster.

I remember his dad's seventieth birthday party quite vividly. Not so much because I nearly ran over one of his nephews on driving into the car park, but more to do with his third wife doing her damnedest to tap me up for a three-in-a-bed.

The Angel in Bolton-on-Dearne and some dimly lit back room where the party was being held had been the venue, and on my wife nipping over to wish Pete a happy birthday, she made her move.

"He's always on about it," she told me.

"He's always on about what?" I shrugged.

"A three-in-a-bed," she said. "Me, you and Tim."

I was no fucking clairvoyant but I could well see how that would pan out. I would be doing her whilst he'd be doing me, and I told my wife as much on driving home.

"What she actually said that?" Julie shrugged.

"I aren't making this shit up," I said.

"I always said he was gay," was her retort.

I wouldn't describe him Tim as being gay. He just likes sex and he isn't too choosy who goes about doing it with and where he sticks it.

"He certainly might not look like him, but he's shagged more women than Kurt Cobain," I recall telling my son, whilst sipping at a Keo outside the rickety old beach bar at Ayia Thekla.

He suddenly became my sixteen-year-old son's uber-hero when I revealed a bit more of who Tim actually was.

"What really – he does that?" he inquired, on me dropping the high-octane titbit of information in his lap.

He and his third wife used to come over to see us quite regularly, and as with the carousel in Duffield's – every time you turned it you got a different record.

Things are great. Things are shit. I love him. I hate him. He is great. He is a wanker.

That was months upon months of appraisal from his wife.

As for me, I admired her honesty. Certainly, not her fucking dress sense, but her honesty.

"As soon as he gets in from work, he calls me a slag and then has me on my knees sucking his cock," she told my wife. "And that's every day. It's getting so I can't even stand fucking looking at it."

And all these women tended to possess some kind of warped loyalty. You know – a bit like the dog that's happy to see its owner when he comes in from work even through it gets a boot up the arse as soon as he comes through the door.

What is strange is that he never hung around with any lads per se, yet he managed to attach himself to all these women. Like I said, he is a remarkably interesting lad.

The three years in the Army would quite suit him – however, married life would not.

"I've made a massive mistake," his first wife told mine. "I should have never married him."

I totally disagreed. I thought their wedding was great, my fondest memory being watching Tim pacing the poop deck and booting the pews, as unbeknown to us, the coach ferrying all his family from Bolton-on-Dearne and Thurnscoe over into the Peak District had broken down. Back then there were no mobile phones, so absolutely no-one knew what was happening. In any case, even if one of them had got to a phone box no one would have been any wiser as St Giles' Church in Matlock didn't possess a phone.

"Fuck it," he said. "We'll get married without them."

The vicar was putting immense pressure on him and had even mentioned postponing the wedding until another date as there was part of the congregation turning up outside the church for the 3.00 p.m. wedding. And as this was happening, his future wife and father-in-law were in limbo and continually circling the area in some horse and cart, so much so, the horse must have been sweating more than the groom.

"I've told them to go around the block again," grinned a dapper-looking Col, who was decked out in his top hat and cloak.

Col had been utilised as some form of Page Boy and only made it down to the church by the skin of his teeth and had Tim kicking off earlier in that he should have had someone more reliable – with Steve Handley's name being candidly mentioned.

The episode at the church was as interesting as his stag-do the week before.

"It's up to you to arrange it," he told me.

"Okay then, how many do you reckon will go."

Tim was under the impression that all his Leeds-supporting football mates from Goldthorpe would be going, therefore a fifty-two-seater bus would be the order of the day.

As for me, I knew only one such mate – Adrian Tait. He was a lad who had been dragged through the mire and indirectly made culpable for the death of an extremely pretty and outgoing fifteen-year-old girl from 8 Monsal Street, Thurnscoe by the name of Mandy Shaw. They had been in a relationship and he had ended it for reasons that I do not know and on 12 May 1981, she took an overdose and killed herself. Tragic.

"Who, Spud?" I asked.

"Not just him – all the Leeds lads."

Did I order a bus? Not a fucking chance.

There were six of us – Me, Col, Bri Latham, Neil Gollick, Tim and his future brother-in-law, Robbie Land – all stood around the pool table in the Cross Daggers off Bolton-on-Dearne's High Street waiting to see who else was going to turn up. And then they did – Steve Handley.

"Is this fucking it?" Tim snapped, obviously noticing the lack of Spud.

"Look, Tim, we're here," said Col. "Let's just drive through to Leeds and leave the cars. We'll get a taxi back."

We did. The taxi pulled up outside the Yorkshire Bank in Goldthorpe at daft o'clock that morning and as we were all potless, we all ended up doing a runner – Tim and Robbie down Market Street and me and Neil over Pit Lane.

Col's last stag-do had had a similar ring to it.

"I'm stressed to fuck, J," Col had told me. "I can't get a bus to take us."

His idea of a stag-do was a daytrip to Blackpool. Me, I was well up for it. The Mad Mouse and the Revolution, along with ten pints of lager, a foul-mouthed comedian and some fish and chips. This was my perfect afternoon.

Unfortunately, he too wanted a fifty-two-seater, mainly for all his boring fire-fighting buddies.

"Come on, Col – can we actually fill it?" I asked, prior to recalling not just Tim's stag-do, but also Ted's.

"Who the fuck is Ted?" he asked.

"John Gratton's mate – some fucking bloke from Trumpton who hired a great trip bus and only three turned up," I told him. "That Ted bloke ended up trying to tap-up John for a third of the cost – about twenty-seven quid, if I remember right."

"I don't know anybody called Ted."

405

"Anyway," I said. "If I get one, can you fill it?"

"Yeh – easy," he said.

Did I hire a bus? No. I got one of the girls in the office to do it.

Did he fill it? No. There was around twenty-four of us – however, with Col, nothing is ever what it seems and as I have often said, he is a kid that always makes life work for him.

"How do you know Col?" I asked one of the lads, whilst stood outside the fish shop lining my stomach before we set off trawling the pubs – me obviously thinking that he was another one of these boring fucking firemen from off his watch.

"I don't know him, mate. I'm with the other stag-do."

There you go, I had unwittingly sorted the bus out for two stag-dos.

That day, however, is something I would not have traded for the world, as Col's brother, Andy, had been there, as had John Gratton.

I can relay a fondness of watching both brothers in dialogue – with Andy still very much suffering from the aftereffects of being run over by the tram. He only had a few quid on him, and I saw their Col hand him £20 and as such, I had done the exact same. The kid was in his element and could not thank us enough. I will say it again. He was such a lovely lad.

The last thing I recall of that day was of John and myself sloping off and doing the Pleasure Beach and later on, having a nap in the exact same spot where just over fourteen years earlier and straight after the Miners' Strike, we had played football against those lads from Staffordshire.

As for Tim's wedding, it was me who stopped him from getting married without his family being there. They turned up just over one hour later and the service became somewhat hurried. The vicar was very reminiscent of *Pinky* and *Perky* and addressed the congregation at 78 rpm, as the other wedding party had been arriving in droves and beginning to clutter up the doorway to the church. Tim had been as anxious as hell and not even a ride back to the hotel on the horse and cart could relieve his stress.

One of his wives I sort of knew – that being his second. I say *sort of*, as her name initially threw me.

"My name is Amah-n-der Lurv-att," she said.

She looked familiar, but apart from that nothing rang any bells with me.

Tim and I had been in business. We had kicked up a mining magazine in 1992, which although it was very sought after, in a gonzo-journalistic kind of way, it had been a commercial failure, which tells you everything that you need to know. I covered the writing and its composition – he the commercial. What should be said, is that being still heavily involved in mining, I knew what we had, and he did not. Tim would tell you straight. I was never in it for the money – more the accolade. Tim's goal had been solely financial – therefore, what he saw was failure. I always felt that he was missing the point.

I still recall a conversation we had in some office off one of the corridors in the old Goldthorpe Town Hall. It was a place where he had been employed as some *suit* on Barnsley MBC's, estates team – allocating repairs to local authority-owned properties. I, on the other hand had thrown in the towel. I had refused to work on Cementation Mining's new cost-cutting week-to-week contract and had focused on setting up the journal that I run now.

"You have the time, as you are unemployed," he condescended, whilst at the same time poo-pooing my idea of rebranding what we had. "At the end of the day, you will never make a living out of a magazine."

I once saw Jeremy Corbyn speak on the subject of the ISIS bride – Shamima Begum and whether or not she would be allowed back into the UK. When put on the spot, the politician's voice dropped in a very matter-of-fact kind of way. Tim often does the same.

Those words, however, wouldn't so much come back to haunt him, but they certainly made sure that I would do everything I could to make it work.

My thoughts were that Tim had been side-tracked. I could say that women were his problem – however, that was not the case. It was *him with women* that was the problem. It is something that takes all his energy and focus and still does, even to this day.

In 1993, however, he had hooked up with some woman from Wakefield who he had candidly described as *insatiable*. All I saw was some tall bird with big feet, a flat chest, and a face that appeared as if it had been plasticised. There was nothing at all that could have possibly intimated her possessing any sex appeal whatsoever.

Mizzz Lur-vatt on the other hand was a complete contrast to what he had and appeared bright, breezy, and full of zest. Well, initially, anyway.

She had been a twenty-four-year-old widow living at 24 Mary Street, Little Houghton. Her husband, Jason Lowe had lost his life on the Wednesday night of 20 July 1994. According to the coroner's inquest, he had lost control of the vehicle that he had been driving and had somehow crashed through the barriers of the A6195 Dearne Valley Parkway between Cat Hill Roundabout and Manvers Way. The car had overturned in water – his death, according to Deputy Coroner, Judith Naylor, being attributed to a combination of drowning and a fracture of the thoracic spine – a broken back, the latter being the reason that he could not get out of his vehicle.

It was hardly straightforward. Amanda had incessantly gone on about some lads in a high-powered sports car turning up at their house and her feeling that he had in fact, been murdered. Amanda did have the tendency to sensationalise or dramatize what you are I could term as *the irrelevant*, but in this instance, her persistence paid off in part, as there were two inquests into his death – the last being on 6 October 1994.

My initial thoughts were that it was indeed a subject worth listening to – that was until you got to know her.

What should also be noted was that some neighbours on the street thought that his death was suicide, which although plain gossip, may have had some bearing on the fact that her husband's parents had very little, or no time at all for their daughter-in-law.

The gossip on the street more than reared its head when she began having quite a number of repairs undertaken at her house. When Tim moved to impress, he didn't fuck around. Falling short of him having two balconies built and a heated swimming pool installed in her loft, she did well out of the relationship. As for Tim, he returned home from work one day to find all his belongings on the front lawn. When I described him as interesting, that is not an understatement.

He and his girlfriend had just got some twenty-five-year mortgage (sic) on a brick-faced Wendy House as part of a new build development on the former site of Yorkshire Main Colliery over in Edlington.

Tim may have been in no man's land, but he fancied his chances with the widow and that is exactly what he did. The only sad thing about the situation was that he and his girlfriend had just had a baby daughter – Kirsten. He therefore did something that I could never have done and walked out on them.

I remember when he and the widow first started out as a couple – my wife invited her out with her friends one night and they ended up in one of the reincarnations of The Docket – Cheers, I think.

"She's really nice," my wife told me. "She made my night."

Amanda, born on 21 October 1969, was the illegitimate child of Linda Bamford and Ralph Levett.

Ralph had still been married to his wife, Linda (nee Beasley) at the time – a woman who he had married in 1965. As a couple they also had a child by the name of Anthony in 1971.

Her parents would eventually marry in 1975, but it was a union that didn't last. Ralph went on to remarry and hooked up with the ex-wife of Hickleton Main Official, Phil Crooks – who was of course the grandson of Charlie – the man who had been jailed in 1911 for the attempted murder of his wife on King Street.

Ralph's grandfather, Walter Ernest Edmund Levett also had a shady past. As with his father he had been a blacksmith by trade, having originally come up to the area from Ipswich. He had married Amy Milns in 1916 and eventually settled at 57 Albert Road in Mexborough.

It would be on 6 October 1941, however, when the fifty-year-old would set tongues wagging, after being on trial at Leeds Assizes. He had been charged with the indecent assault of three young girls at a property on Mexborough's Frederick Street.

It certainly wasn't the worst thing that happened in the area.

On 7 September 1934, Frederick Owen was found hanging from a bedpost in Broadmoor Lunatic Asylum (now Broadmoor Hospital). The sixty-year-old had been found guilty, but insane on a charge of murder at Leeds Assizes. On the evening of 24 April 1923, he had slit the throat of a thirteen-year-old girl by the name of Nora Jeavons at his home at 1 Northgate, Mexborough, with so much force, that he had severed her spinal cord.

The story was, that Owen had been a miner at Barnburgh Main and whilst on the bus travelling through Bolton-on-Dearne, someone had discharged a noxious device – mainly some form of stink bomb, which created a white smoke that filled the vehicle and caused him violent headaches for weeks afterwards.

I had to admit, he looked a scary-looking character. He was certainly someone that I wouldn't want to see standing at the end of my bed, with his thousand-yard stare and brandishing a cut-throat razor in his mitts.

Dr Maxwell Telling spoke on behalf of Owen's defence. He explained that there had been a number of cases of violent temporary insanity – some of which had been exceptional, in that the effects had been delayed. He also knew of one other case that had been brought on by hydrogen sulphate.

Owen claimed that all he remembered that day was coming out of the Red Lion pub on Mexborough's Bank Street around 3.00 p.m. Everything else had been a blur.

It was also said Owen had given a sixpence to a nine-year-old girl by the name of Kathleen Sheriff (now Mills) before raping or attempting to rape her. This was something that had been confirmed by a Dr Lee.

On 18 July 1923, the jury found him guilty of wilful murder but insane, and Justice Frederick Arthur Greer ordered him to be detained at His Majesty's Pleasure. He was initially sent to Armley Gaol before being fast-tracked to Broadmoor.

As for Amanda's other grandparents, John and Margaret Bamford (nee Fell), they had originally lived at Wombwell before making the move to Bolton-on-Dearne – firstly living just off Canberra Rise in a new NCB property, before flitting into local authority housing at 93 Furlong Road around 1958.

Amanda's mum had been born in 1950 and was the twin-sister of David Bamford. The twins would be followed by two further brothers – Percy (b. 1954) and Steven (b. 1961), and it would be here, where a tragic story would unfold.

On New Year's Eve 1954, Amanda's grandparents had been out drinking and dancing – Bolton Club, The Angel, The Collingwood Hotel and to songs such as Billy Haley's *Shake Rattle and Roll* and Perry Como's *Papa Loves Mambo*. On getting home the partying continued and just to get some room and give her one-month-old son some fresh air, the twenty-three-year-old Margaret had pulled the pram outside their door at 6 Princess Close. Unfortunately, she forgot to bring him back in and the very next day he was found dead in his pram. According to the District Coroner, W.H Carlile, the baby – Percy, had died of pneumonia.

After her split with Ralph Levett, Linda would remarry local lothario, Jimmy Grierson – one of Bolton-on-Dearne's most affable of characters. Jimmy, a bricklayer by trade, had been married to Pat Quealey since 1970 and had three children – the youngest being Ian, who, due to his appearance carried the dubious nickname of Anthead. He would receive much notoriety after he along with some other lads were involved in an altercation outside Goldthorpe's Dole Office in the late-1980s whereby a young lad was killed. The case went to Sheffield Crown Court and Ian was found guilty of murder and handed a life sentence. On 30 September 2010, however, he suddenly came to national attention and became the subject of a manhunt after going over the wall from HMP North Sea Camp near Boston.

As for Amanda, my first meeting with her was at her council house in Little Houghton, where after a couple of drinks she introduced us to the family photograph album, which generally speaking, would have been about as palatable as chewing on a fucking light bulb.

Tim being Tim, there was always going to be a twist in the tale.

He had already bragged her off as having done some modelling, which on my part went straight in one ear and out of the other and was about as believable as some of these female profile photos that you see on Facebook. Saying that, most wives have done some form of modelling in a take your knickers off, stick some lipstick on and let me get the camera out kind-of-way. This had been no different.

She opened up an album and there she was parading around in some black mac and stockings. I had to hand it to Tim, he could really unearth some fucking gems.

It was our Tracey (Durose) who eventually had my penny drop.

"She's the same age as you," I had told her.

"I don't know any Amanda Lurr-vatt," said my cousin.

"Her mam married Jimmy Grierson – they live on Station Road – across from Bolton Legion (Bolton On Dearne Ex Servicemens Club)."

"She's not called that, you twit – you're on about Mandy Levitt," she said. "Dark hair, big nose – looks like a witch."

Boom. It was then that I remembered her.

"They used to call me *Witchipoo* at school," she had once told me.

As I have said, kids can be cruel.

Amanda had always acted with an air of pretentiousness – however, this was something that had been further fuelled by Tim. She had been quite tolerable on first meeting her – however, over a period of time, she had become quite noxious – with Tim often purposely ostracising themselves from the crowd.

As an example: I once got a minibus to take us and several couples into Sheffield for a Christmas night's drinking, followed by a curry at the Gulshan Balti House in The Wicker. Although the ride was free and there were two spare seats – he elected to drive behind us in his car.

I never understood that.

As for the fuelling her wants, he had not only thrown money to fund her fixation for owning a floristry business along with cosmetic surgery on her schnozz, he had done everything he could have possibly done to make her think that she was something special, when in fact that was never really the case.

"This is just a stepping-stone," she had said on us walking through the door into their newly purchased property, which had been yet another brick-faced Wendy House – this time in North Athersley.

She had been exuberantly dressed in some white lamming gown and was laid draped across some chair, looking like Fenella Fielding's husky voiced femme fatale from the 1966 film, *Carry on Screaming* – that of *Valeria Watt*, whilst duly welcoming us into her humble abode.

Tim further raised her stock, by candidly showing us around the vast art collection that adorned the walls of their rather contemporary colour-coordinated lounge. Amanda had etched a series of drawings of which he had dutifully framed. "She's very artistic – she can turn her hand to anything," he said.

It does make you wonder if he ever really believed any of the shit he was saying.

Fortunately, she hadn't been there that long and just less than an hour later and spitting feathers, she left the property in haste. Her grandma and Mother of the Year 1954 – Margaret Bamford, had apparently been embroiled in some spat with another woman over in Bolton-on-Dearne and she therefore made the decision to kick up her broom and leave.

Even though it ended abruptly, the marriage lasted much longer than I ever thought it would and to my knowledge Amanda currently lives alone in one of the stone-built terraced houses on Bolton-on-Dearne's Mexborough Road.

I truly think that if Tim hadn't contaminated the relationship from the off with all the control and bullshit, that it would have turned out okay – as the one good thing about her, was her little girl, Lydia Matilda. She was a kid who we all thought the world of.

As for my wedding, the initial dialogue had kicked off – however, seeing as though there was only my mum and (step)dad that knew my girlfriend was pregnant, there wasn't that much arranging to do. "She needs to tell her mam," my mum kept on telling me.

That certainly wasn't happening anytime soon.

The Best Man had been a head-scratcher – however, Tim going into the Army made it quite an easy decision, especially as he informed me about the schedule surrounding his twelve-week training.

One thing I do know is that if Julie would have known how much aggravation a wedding would cause, she would have walked.

Tim Bright outside 16 Briton Square, Thurnscoe circa 1986

Ernie Blakemore and Jim Durose of 129 and 9 The Crescent, Bolton-on-Dearne respectively circa 1960. (c. Pinner Guest)

33. The Dark Princess

Over two years had passed including my twelve months on strike and bar a freshly decorated house with a new room carpet along with a pregnant girlfriend, I was in truth, no further on. I remember always looking around and seeing my friends moving forward with their lives. As for me, all I was doing was living from hand to mouth whilst wishing my life away until 21 April 1986 – which wasn't just my girlfriend or soon-to-be wife's nineteenth birthday, but the date when my loan would be finally paid off.

The girlfriend certainly wasn't as argumentative as the one who had seen me move into the house, that was for sure. That said, I had seen glimpses of the future and that was one of diffidence. The upshot was, that she trusted me about as far as she could throw me.

This was something that reared its head at one of Col's open houses – a kind of off-the-cuff gathering of people, a lot of whom were female.

The night had been interesting not least as I had been driving Col's Ford Capri home from The Goldthorpe Hotel and had literally been chased by some panda car from Dr Boyle's Corner through the pit estate and onto Briton Square.

"He's flashing you," exclaimed Daz Cooper – who had been sat shotgun, whilst his and my girlfriend had been in the back.

The fact that I had already knocked a back few lagers, made stopping on Windsor Street not really in my remit of things to do. However, on getting on to the Square, the police finally stuck on their blue flashing lights, which by the time I had pulled up and got out of the car, we had half the house on the street – one of who, happened to be Neil Gollick.

The violence of the strike was still in everyone's mind, not at least the police's and the last thing they wanted was confrontation.

"You were going at least fifty miles per hour, when you passed us," exclaimed the policeman.

He was right, I was.

"It's a thirty miles per hour zone on Shepherd Lane," he added.

He was right, it was.

All I did, however, was just respond with a nod. Neil and Steve Handley did the rest.

Both lads couldn't have been any different – however, the former appeared as intimidating as the latter was confrontational, given the right (or wrong) circumstances. Neil had a physical presence and didn't need to say a great deal whereas Steve, as with his elder brother, possessed an extremely dark persona and said whatever he fancied saying regardless of who or what they were. "Why don't you get yourselves fucked off," is basically word for word.

It wasn't the first time I would hear him issue that statement to the police. One particular time they turned up at his mum's door on Carrfield Lane in the middle of the night and he ended up giving them both barrels of thunder. At times, the lad just didn't give a fuck.

"I'm just saying," said the policeman, as he and his colleague – a policewoman, suddenly became surrounded, "just try and keep your speed down in future."

Trying not to slur my speech I gave them an "Okay" of sorts and they left.

I look at Briton Square now and try to picture how it was over thirty-five years ago. On my part it is hard to imagine the sight of around fifty-odd people milling around both inside and outside its eighth house with their host inside, resembling the most holy Sultan Tanzimatçı Abdülmecid along with the nineteen wives he had dragged around from The Fairway, sat back on my old orange-striped sofa just sucking it all up.

"Did they say owt about me not having a tax disc?" he shrugged.

"No, I think Neil scared them off," I said.

I had seen Col get pulled up and breathalysed numerous times and smugly walk away. I say smugly, as on three occasions I know he'd had at least four pints of lager.

For some reason, and for as small in stature as he was, he was always under the limit. Always. I could never understand that?

There was an instance where we had been taking Tracy Greaves and John Cardno from the Top Spot over to Goldthorpe one Saturday night when my wife had been at the wheel. Whilst shooting past Dr Boyle's Corner (again), a police car pulled out and whipped on its flashing blue lights eventually pulling us up at the bus stop just before Thurnscoe Bridge Lane's junction with Derry Grove.

My wife was summoned out of the vehicle. She wasn't exactly breathalysed but falling short of sticking her finger on her nose, walking twenty paces toe-to-heel and whilst eyes closed and then reciting the alphabet backwards, she did everything possible to show that she wasn't inebriated.

"I can't believe he never did you," shrugged Cardno, as she climbed back into the car. "He's generally a right horrible bastard."

The fact that she was wearing some red suit, half of which comprised some mini skirt with a twelve-inch hemline may have helped.

Drink driving is not something I have ever been convicted of, which is a good job as throughout my life I have definitely had my moments – not least on 17 December 1990.

I had been working with Cementation Mining on the new Parkgate development at Maltby Colliery when they became some issue which saw us down tools and rather stupidly come out on strike. I say stupidly, as it had been Christmas week.

There had been a heated meeting in the Maltby WMC (The Stute) the very next day, where the NUM showed its complete and utter contempt for private contractors at the mine. I had always kicked up my NUM contributions from the first day I had signed on and even whilst working down in the Vale of Belvoir amidst the rise of the UDM, I had done the same. As I would find with Arthur Scargill, the NUM were a one-dimensional organisation, in that they could never see the bigger picture. The 'M' may have stood for 'Mineworkers', but what it really meant was 'Mineworkers that worked in the direct employ of British Coal'. They didn't give two shits about people such as I, and the NUM man at the meeting said as much. This did nothing to quell the toxic atmosphere, which ten minutes in, had become reminiscent of the meeting in the Coronation WMC after the 1984/85 Miner's Strike had come to an end.

I had picked up a phone call from the Angel with the Dirty Face that was Andy Roper asking me if I was going to attend the meeting. Being that I was part of the crew that were driving one of the half dozen drill and blast headings, it appeared the prudent thing to do and I told him as much. For the record he was on one of the other shifts – although what he actually did at that juncture, I wasn't entirely sure.

Just nine days prior, I had come out of the mine after the Saturday day shift, to a thin blanket of snow and a sky full of the stuff. My remit as always, was to pick my daughter up from my mum's and look after her as my wife worked at the bookmakers at the top of Kingsway. This particular day, however, the majority of staff had been sent home as the horse racing calendar had been decimated with Doncaster, Towcester and Cheltenham all having been abandoned with the only British racecourse operating, being that of Lingfield. That left the day open for some Christmas shopping – however, the weather never let up and come 2.00 p.m., not only could I not get the car off the street, the heavy snow ended up taking one of the windscreen wipers off.

Those nine days later, much of the snow had cleared, but the roads were still treacherous – especially the back roads between Crookhill Park Golf Course and Maltby. As for Andy, he had wanted to know if he could tap a lift.

I knew there had been a problem when I had turned in for work on the Sunday night and seen the skeleton crew that had arrived on site. Timekeeping had been a major issue at Maltby, but I immediately noticed there was something amiss, as I was the only miner in our heading. I could have gone back home – but for what? I was already changed and ready to go underground. I walked onto the job where we had begun constructing a junction with the first of the huge steel frames already been set bar the steel sheets. I finished off the sheeting and packing before setting up a drill and airleg – and with an Official from Bolton-on-Dearne's Caernarvon Crescent – Keith Pears, kindly spotting for me, I fully drilled up the rip with around fifty holes, all of which were then ready to prime with explosives. However, with no manpower to transport the powder kegs I was left scratching my knackers as what to do next, and just to keep busy, I unloaded some trams of steel supports. By the time I had got out of the pit, I knew that a strike had been called.

The person that I recall moaning about it (the strike) in the meeting was Dave Hodgkiss – a guy who lived in some mock stone-fronted property on Wath-on-Dearne's Willow Road. As I said earlier, Dave was the biological father of Shaine Whitehurst and would therefore eventually become my sister's father-in-law. However, at that time I just knew him as some electrician who made Ebenezer Scrooge look like a spendthrift.

Andy and myself stayed in The Stute post-meeting and got drinking with the heading crew that I worked with, two of whom were Bernie McCann and Graham (Shultz) Shaw – possibly two of the most colourful characters you could ever meet and both of whose characters I would use to great effect in later life. It's not often you get to work with two people who had been arrested and charged for taking someone's eye out. I did. The former had done it with a knife and the latter, his fist.

Two lagers quickly became four and then six and then eight – and by that time we were in the Maltby Progressive Club (The Slip) knocking back numbers nine and ten, both absolutely paralytic and talking bollocks.

I can't recall the journey home apart from passing the Welfare sports pitch and running track on Houghton Road.

"You were in a right state last night," exclaimed my wife the very next morning. "How you got home, I don't know."

According to Bernie, I had been well on form. I had run out of money, borrowed twenty quid off him, ordered the taxi, duly walked past it and drove home – therefore, having to navigate the snow-filled backroads through Braithwell.

According to Andy, he handled the steering whilst I did the pedals and gears. How that fucking worked, I had no idea. As I have said, I could only remember passing the running track. It was an act of sheer stupidity but certainly nothing to what I was capable of.

Just a little under twelve months earlier – on the Friday evening of 22 December 1989, nine-year-old Valerie Barrett and her eleven-year-old sister, Donna, of 6 Peartree Avenue, Thurnscoe had just been Christmas carolling. They had collected quite a haul, so much so, the younger sister had been quite full of herself – their ultimate destination being Lorne Road Stores.

On the TV, the Christmas episode of *Only Fools and Horses* had just about been ready to come on, when on Houghton Road, a tragedy unfolded. A red Toyota Corolla being driven at speed towards Great Houghton, hit Valerie as she and her sister had been crossing close to the junction of Horsemoor Road.

A panic ensued whereby the driver got out and commenced screaming at the girls. It wasn't his fault – it was theirs, he claimed.

"Valerie just about had her foot on the kerb when the passenger side of the car hit her," explained Donna. "All I remember was him shouting abuse at us after he'd pulled up the car. He was dressed all in leather and was really, really nasty."

People came rushing out of the nearby houses – one even bringing a quilt, to try and keep Valerie comfortable. There was, however – a major problem. The incident was caught between what was the British ambulance strike – an acrimonious dispute over pay, that took place between 7 September 1989 and 23 February 1990.

The car contained two males and two females, one of whom had been a seventeen-year-old lad off The Spike by the name of Tony Murray. He had been **the** key witness. What would happen following the death of Valerie, however – is that his testimony at the coroner's inquest would never be heard.

"He was never at the inquest," explained Darren Ridsdale. "He wasn't there."

The big question was – why not?

Darren was the son of my near-neighbour, Jimmy and had been talking to the two girls just two minutes prior to Valerie being run over and was on the scene directly.

The inquest was nothing more than a sideshow that made claim to dotting the i's and crossing the t's. The reality was that it was anything but.

Daphne Barrett had lost her child and the police had been worse than useless.

"He's lying! Valerie's mother had shouted at the inquest.

She had need to vent her anger.

"Everybody knew he was lying," said Darren as he shook his head. "The driver didn't speak at the inquest – everything was said through his solicitor. My thoughts are to this day that he had been drunk."

I recently asked Tony Murray three straight questions: i) Who was the driver ii) Where were you going and iii) Where did you come from?

He immediately became confrontational and refused to answer any.

Nowadays, he would have been charged with perverting the course of justice and hauled before a court – however, he wasn't.

Darren told me that Valerie's parents had been distraught and that they ended up walking out of the travesty of justice that was the inquest. Their daughter's death was seen as being accidental and even though it would never bring her back, the family never ever got the closure they deserved.

As I said, I fully blame the police.

Personally, I have been quite lucky in that I have only had a few close calls. I recall some three years later driving home from Ings Lane WMC. I had been parked waiting for the traffic lights to change at Highgate crossroads when a car from Bolton Taxi's drove up behind me and rather than its driver wait for the lights to change – he sped through the slip road on my left side towards Barnsley before making a sharp right to try and beat the lights into Goldthorpe. As it was, he had mistimed the change and ended up hitting me as I legally passed through the junction on my way into Thurnscoe.

I knew I was borderline as I'd dropped a couple of lagers, and after threatening to beat fuck out of the rat-faced bastard, I thought it prudent to leave the scene of the accident, park up my car and had someone take us through to hospital to get my wife checked out for whiplash.

As for the police, the taxi driver told them I was drunk. I wasn't, he was lying. The police, however – only heard one side of the story as I wasn't there. The only thing to counteract his statement, therefore, was the evidence. His car was smashed up, he had stayed, and he was sober.

The police tried catching up with us – both at Barnsley Hospital and much later on in Briton Square. Their remit being that they urgently wanted to breathalyse me. It is just a pity they hadn't worked that hard on the driver of the red Toyota that had killed Valerie Barratt.

It is a strange feeling having the police beating at your door for half-an-hour and putting the flashlights up at your bedroom window and trying and fox their way into getting your attention. The only thing that stopped them illegally gaining entry to the house that night, was our Alsatian – a dog that hated anyone in a uniform.

My wife seems to think that Andy Roper gave the police a statement of our whereabouts post-hospital that night: "His wife was shaken up and they both stayed at mine."

Rather strangely, I had been ready to hit the bat phone after an incident following a night out over at the Burntwood Hotel on Brierley Common a year or so later.

My wife had been the designated driver that night, and whilst following this red three-wheeler all the way home from The Robin Hood nightclub on Southmoor Road and down into Great Houghton, I exacted some pressure on her to get around him.

"He's got to be drunk," shrugged my wife. "He's all over the place."

Rather strangely, that night, Dave Hodgkiss's love child had been in the back seat with my sister, whilst I had been winding up my wife and urging her to show a clean pair of heels to the driver of the plastic pig.

Amidst wild jubilation from me and both back-seat passengers, she began passing him after the Billingley Lane junction into Houghton Road. However, I must have had a rush of blood, and by the time we had eventually passed him the driver of the Reliant Robin had lost control of his vehicle and had ended up on its side in the field.

"What did you do that for, you fucking idiot?" exclaimed my wife.

It was said that I had *allegedly* grabbed the wheel and had thereby *allegedly* cut him up.

I ended up spending the night down at the first office I had in the old Hickleton Main pit baths just in case plod came calling, then around 8.00 a.m. had a mosey down to the foot of King Street, where some garage on the allotments had been temporarily converted into a body shop of sorts.

The said rush of blood not only had the affable Pete Hinchcliffe scratching his head, but cost me £70 (£137, circa 2020) to have the rear wing beat out, filled and resprayed. It had been an expensive night out that is for sure.

Things always catch up with you and sometimes Karma can be a bitch.

On 16 February 1996 I had been invited over to the Piccadilly Hotel and to a dinner put on by the North West branch of the Institute of Civil Engineers as a guest of the directors of some Manchester-based tunnelling firm.

My wife had been whining on about me not spending the night in Manchester. Her reasoning was that we were due to fly to Istanbul on the Sunday morning, and that being the case, we had planned to call in and spend Saturday night at her sister and brother-in-law's in Letchworth prior to flying out from Gatwick.

Rather strangely, it is Jane and Carl who currently live in my old house at 16 Briton Square. It's weird how things turn out!

"Yeh, I'll probably come home," I told her.

Did I? Nope.

I'd got talking with a Scottish mining engineer by the name of Dave Donaldson and ended up knocking back a few too many beers. Therefore, I resigned myself to staying in the room that I'd had pre-booked for me, which then culminated with my wife pissing in my ears about not coming home.

I dragged myself from my slumber and went to retrieve the car from the UMIST car park around 6.30 a.m. only to find it devoid of security guards at its barrier and no-one there to let me out. I beeped the horn numerous times but to no avail. In the end I ripped off the barrier and drove home. It was weeks later when I received an invitation from Manchester's Bootle Street nick for me to come in and have a word with one of their officers about the barrier being ripped off. That, I thought certainly would not be a problem, as I had previously written to UMIST and explained who I was and why I had done it. I had even enclosed a cheque for £30 to cover the cost. Unfortunately for me, the two security guards that had supposedly been on duty that morning must have taken a bollocking for being wherever they had been and had concocted some story to say that they had tried stopping me. What was far worse is that the said that I had tried mowing them over with the car.

It was the fucking lie of all lies and something which saw me in Manchester Magistrates' Court trying to defend a charge of dangerous driving. This would be the first time that I had ever been falsely accused of something, but certainly not the last. I was fined £550 (£1,103, circa 2020), banned for twelve months and forced to take a re-test. I had trusted the system and it had failed me. It was a hard blow to take but looking back at the shit I had gotten away with it was nothing that I didn't deserve.

I shouldn't really say this, but in the here and now and solely through legal disclosure, I would have made sure that the case would never have got to court. However, that is through experience. To gain experience in dealing with shit, you have to have experienced shit.

There is a reason for why I am telling you this, which will soon become apparent.

Now let me introduce you to a different kind of shit – bullshit.

Col's get-together that balmy autumn evening of 1985, had been very much different to the previous ones, one of which had been very male-orientated. That being the case it had seen flashes of confrontation in the form of a sibling rivalry, which I have mentioned already, and where both Andy Hunter and his bare-chested younger brother Steve ended up squaring up to each other. It could have got out of hand, but it didn't. I held Andy back and Col their Steve – whilst in between Geoff Lloyd and Pete Duggan did their level best to exert something of a calming influence. It happens with brothers, which is a subject that I will certainly get on to.

At the more recent get-together, there had been girls everywhere, very few of whom my girlfriend knew, least of all a young blonde-haired girl off the Crossgate access into Lindley Crescent, which was something that had me receive a stiletto down the front of my shins.

In this instance, the girl was someone that had grown up not too far away from my grandparents, but being two years younger than myself, was also someone that I had never really taken any notice of until I had actually taken notice – and even then she had always been in a steady relationship, that even now, has stood the test of time.

Just like her mum, I saw Andrea Mangham as gregarious in nature and extremely pretty. She was, however, perceived by my girlfriend as something quite different – a threat. This had been a glimpse into the future and where I was concerned, she would become extremely territorial – hence the real reason why she never wanted me staying overnight in Manchester.

The ex-girlfriend had had her moments too – in one instance and for some unknown reason kicking off about me saying "Hello" to the girlfriend of Billy Coulson on us alighting the 212 at Doncaster North Bus Station just prior to the Miner's Strike – which was a good fifteen months before she actually dumped him.

What was strange about this are the similarities in their use of me in inflicting hurt on their respective partners. However, what she did to Billy on their relationships end was totally usurped and blown into oblivion by my ex – who was a girl that never did anything by halves. Paula was of course the girl that had told her boyfriend that I had got her pregnant.

My ex-girlfriend didn't just do that to just anyone but to the man she was married to.

How this came about I really have no idea and which in truth, was nearly as bigger shock to me than it must have been for him. On her giving birth to her and her husband's first child, she told him: "She's not yours, she's James's."

For eighteen months, Terry Rich had to live with that lie, and it was only after she had tried to hit him for maintenance and him securing a DNA test that the child was proved to be his.

At that juncture, not only had I been quite oblivious to her statement, but I also had a wife and two-year-old daughter in tow. The nearest I had gotten to anything that my ex had done or said in the two and a half years that I had been married was one day during 1989. My ex had pulled up my wife up the aisles of Kwik Save (now Asda) – the single-storey supermarket where Stone's Garage once stood and mentioned something along the lines of my daughter's resemblance to me.

"You're not going to start inviting her around for coffee," was my glib retort, after being told.

"You must be fucking joking," is exactly what I got back.

I only got to know this just recently. This was after Terry's second wife, Karen Singleton (nee Dawson), engaged me in conversation over social media.

The sole reason that both girls had done this had been one dimensional. They had done it to cause hurt and distress to their respective partners with me as their fucking muppet.

Women can be truly horrible bastards.

Now let me introduce you to the Dark Princess.

Nicola (Nikki) Gough (now Rush) was the youngest of two children to Derek and Mary (nee Hendley) and grew up at Briton Square's fifth house.

As with Andrea, Nikki was extremely pretty. They were also both extremely intelligent – however, whereas Andrea was academically clever, Nicola was street-smart. That, however, is where any similarities ended.

Derek Gough had been a great friend of my father's and part of a group of lads that included Ernie Blakemore, Pinner Guest, and both Pat and Inky Thompson – a set of lads that had hung about together during the late-1950s – early 1960s.

In my mind, Derek had an appearance of the Greek actor and theatre director, Andréas Voutsinas – the man who famously played the flamboyantly gay, Carmen Ghia in Mel Brooks' original 1967 adaption of *The Producers*. Everyone who knew Derek always talked him up. It is something that I have to agree with. He was just an extremely nice man.

As for Mary, she was born and bred in Thurnscoe's East end. She came into the world in 1948 and was the youngest daughter of Tom and Mary (nee Morrisey).

Her father had been one of twelve children, who had lived in cramped conditions at 11 Vincent Terrace – the end house that forms part of the row of terraced houses at the far end of Lidget Lane and which is split by George Street. Unfortunately, however, one of those children Marion, died aged just four days old in October 1936.

A story: On 2 March 1940, two of her uncles – twelve-year-old Gordon Hendley and his six-year old brother, Ronald – ended up in Mexborough Montagu Hospital after they received severe injuries after playing with a hand grenade that they had found.

Gordon had part of his left hand blown off, suffered a broken wrist, and received compound fractures – eleven in total – to his right leg, whilst his younger brother suffered facial injuries – losing several teeth.

As for her mother, Mary Morrisey, she was the daughter of Patrick and Mary Ellen (nee Boylan) – which immediately points to the fact, that both had come over from Ireland – something, which will become more than apparent as you read on.

She was one of nine children who had come up to Thurnscoe from the Mansfield area in 1921 – her father Patrick, like many others, getting employment at Hickleton Main. They would also be the very first family to move into the newly constructed house at 8 Dane Street – a semi-detached property that sat on the periphery of The Bullring.

For the seventeen years I lived across from Mary Gough, she appeared indifferent, expressionless, and deadpan. Miserable, if you like. She was also a lady who kept everything close to her chest. Therefore, unless you were a part of her ridiculously small circle, you got to know little.

Her elder sisters by six and four years respectively were Sheila and Norah – both of whom got brought up at the house opposite – their father dying on 18 May 1970 and their mother, just after I moved onto the Square, in late-1983.

All three girls married within four years of each other. Norah married a miner at Hickleton Main by the name of George Easton in 1963, whilst Sheila married Jim Hinchliffe in 1966. As for Mary, she had married Derek in 1967.

Whereas Sheila and Mary's marriages failed, Norah's did not. She and her husband are still married some fifty-seven years later and living on Bolton-on-Dearne's Broadwater – the very house that they moved into in 1965.

Sheila remarried in 1972 – and from what I have been told, not only was he a miner at Goldthorpe Colliery, but also a part-time fireman. Alvin Roberts was also a divorcee, having previously married a girl by Joyce Law in 1961.

As for the unsociable Mary, she opted for a future of detachment and solitude. To an extent, this was an attribute her son, Dean, shared. Although, not in any way a nasty lad, he was a person that didn't say a deal and tended to keep himself to himself. Nikki on the other hand, showed completely different characteristics in her personality, and at times she was as witty as she was pretty and as inconsiderably forthright as forthright could be.

It was one Saturday morning during mid-1978, that I first recall seeing her. My dad and I had alighted the 276 (107) at the south-eastern bus stop on Thurnscoe's Hanover Street and on him seeing them, immediately began engaging in conversation with their father.

As for me, I thought it quite strange at the time. Both children possessed a kind of non-conformity in their appearance – which rather than being rebellious, could have maybe had something to do with the music that had been around at the time. Dean had a Mohican haircut, whilst Nikki – who had been sat on her father's knee, had dyed hair, and possessed a piercing in her nose.

The thing that I recall about the daughter was that she looked much older than she actually was. I mean a lot older. It was a trait which would follow her all the way through school – hers being not Thurnscoe or Goldthorpe, but the Saint Pius X (Pope Pius) – a Catholic school on the A633 Wath Wood Road.

I didn't know it then, but Derek had just become separated from his wife.

By the time I had moved on to the Square, I began seeing him quite regularly. It was as though he and Mary were still on speaking terms. Whether or not this was so, I really could not say. All the same, he was always polite, and he always acknowledged me with an "Hello".

As regards Nikki, she could appear indifferent, but she always made a point of speaking, which was something that had my ex-girlfriend kicking off at me around the time Nikki's grandmother had died.

It wasn't a case of "Who's that?", more of giving me a kick on the shins and her stomping off home.

"Nikki Gough – get your fucking knickers off," Col used to say, as he copped sight of her through my room window, during the winter of 1984.

"I'm surprised you've not given her one," Carl went on to exclaim.

I gave them the exact same reason that I had given to my ex-girlfriend on the whys and whatnots regarding me never having any relationship with Nikki. The main one being that she had just turned fourteen years old – meaning that she had been a year younger when my ex had kicked off.

"She's never thirteen," my ex-girlfriend had snapped. "She looks older than me."

That snippet of information also had both Col and Carl scratching their heads too.

When I first got to know Neil Gollick straight after the strike, he added weight to the conspiracy. "Weren't you seeing Nicola?" he inquired.

"No, never," I shrugged. "What makes you think that?"

Neil was perhaps the kid closest to the family – mainly through Dean being an aspiring tattooist and Neil being the willing canvas.

"She said you were." he added. "She said that she used to go over to your house and watch television with you."

The me-and-Nicola-thing certainly had me fucking baffled. Age difference aside, that would have been one partnership doomed to fail, with the word's *disaster* chiselled on the stake prior to it being driven into its heart. Before I'd had the time to plan the excavation of the shallow grave, she would have already slit my throat.

Nikki is one of life's conundrums and even now she can have me shaking my head.

I re-engaged with her at some birthday bash for my wife and one of the first things she said to me after the meal had been directed towards her husband, who had been prancing around and pissing everyone off: "Would you do me a favour, James – just go and smack him in the mouth?"

Was I shocked? Nope. Nothing she did, would ever surprise me, but I suppose that's one of those things that makes her – well, 'not boring'.

"Dad, Dad," once exclaimed my eleven-year-old daughter, as she came running into the house. This was just before we left Thurnscoe for good. "Mandy is having a right argument with Nicola."

I had been brushing my teeth at the time and walked on to the drive to see Mandy walking over to Nikki as though she was going to tear her head off.

Parking was, and still is, a contentious issue on Briton Square – however, with Nikki not living there and being the world's most inconsiderate female and parking her shiny new car, so no-one could get either on or off the cul-de-sac, things became more heated than normal.

Shaun Nota and his common-law wife Mandy Heath were originally from the Rotherham area and had recently moved into No 10 – the same house where little Brenda Cole had set herself on fire in 1942 and where the parents of Goldthorpe's body in the boot murderer had once lived. Without sounding disrespectful, Mandy possessed a much larger frame than Nikki and was a fiery character who few people would dare think of messing with. According to her husband that is.

As for me, I wasn't so sure. Nikki was as inconsiderate with her vehicle as she was to any mere mortal who just happened to get in her way, and I wasn't at all surprised when she calmly responded as though she was flicking a bit of fluff from her lapel. "Don't touch what you can't afford."

Shaun's train of thought however, was fully enforced when his wife viciously dinted one of the panels of Nikki's dark blue BMW before moving to wallop her. That was a path that I certainly wouldn't have gone down and was the fucking mistake of all mistakes. Nikki had well and truly grown up amongst us and as such, not a great deal fazed her. Certainly not some fat ginger-haired bitch throwing her weight around, which is exactly what Nikki had told Shaun's wife prior to ramming her up against the peripheral fence of Graham Creighton's house next door and duly beating the living shite out of her. It was brutal, I'll give her that.

I can still picture Shaun escorting his bloodied and beaten wife home, with his arm placed tenderly around her shoulder. "Come on, love," he said.

As for Nikki – she got in her car and sped off. Possibly before the police were called or possibly to have her nails reprofiled, as seven or eight of them must have still been lodged in Mandy's head.

She had one hell of a temper, which if you didn't know, made you wonder where she got it from.

Here goes: On 11 February 1930, the local newspapers carried the story of a forty-six-year-old lady from just off Thurnscoe's Bullring who had been bound over for twelve months after being found guilty of assault and stealing from a store in Doncaster.

It was stated that when the police were called to the shop, the woman was already heavily under the influence of drink and became hysterical, lashing out at anyone and everyone and struck an assistant or two before throwing herself on the floor and fainting. It was all very melodramatic.

The defending solicitor, William Forrest Bracewell – son of the Canon Bracewell of Sheffield, expressed deep remorse on behalf of his client and explained that the she had been in an extremely poor state of health, so poor in fact, that she lived a full healthy life until the ripe old age of seventy-seven, eventually passing away in early-June 1961.

That woman? Mary Ellen Morrisey (nee Boylan), the great-grandmother of Nicola.

I could give you numerous Thurnscoe connections, before I move on with the story – however, for the time being, I reckon two will suffice.

Around the time of Col's get-together, Nikki had been just sharpening her teeth on her life's tumultuous journey and at fifteen years old she had begun a relationship with a lad off the northern leg of Brunswick Street.

Remember the story of the tragedy on the street in 1973? The one about the little girl getting shot in the head and being laid up in hospital in a coma – along with her auntie Pauline's touching promise of her beautiful niece being a bridesmaid at her wedding? It had been Nikki's boyfriend that had unfortunately pulled the trigger.

The other connection is neither as tragic nor as tender and involves the father of one of Nicola's three children. Remember the tale of the drunken half-naked girl in a state of paranoia who had been banging at my front door and waking up all the street? This was the girl who would become the Bryan Mullins's common-law wife and who for a time lived a few doors down from my sister before moving to Wath-on-Dearne.

As for Nicola, she never stuck fast and used all the natural attributes that she was gifted with and ended up marrying a man from the Sprotbrough area of Doncaster by the name of Nigel Rush.

In my mind, it was a union of convenience as opposed to being one of love.

Am I wrong in saying that? Perhaps.

Nigel is a nice enough kid, but in my mind, he and Nikki are not so much a strange union, but about as compatible as chalk and cheese. He is a guy that operates on the fringes of legality, where finance is concerned, and it is here where one could assume that the attraction was. He earns money – and a lot of it.

"The last time I saw her she was driving through Goldthorpe in a Mercedes convertible," my sister recently told me.

And why ever not? The sun had been shining, the hood of the car had been down and those high-fashioned brand-named sunglasses, which were once neatly positioned on her forehead had been firmly dropped in place. Sometimes in life, there is no better feeling than driving away from the rathole from whence you came. However, to emphasise that feeling, one must be seen. Therefore, as the high-performance lump of Affalterbach engineering idly growled, awaiting the sequential shifting of the lights, *our* beautifully attired bête noire, leant forward – her finely-toned posterior barely leaving the well-crafted leather seat, and diligently lifted those £500 rims to glance in the mirror.

One of the golden rules of perfection is the need to check that one's sheer beauty is never solely in the eye of the beholder. Then as the lights moved from red-to-red and amber-to green, those shades were coolly dropped back in place and thereby followed a gentle touch, if not indeed the slightest caress of the accelerator pedal, as the car, slowly navigated its way between the Horse & Groom public house and the police station. Her work here had been done.

"She obviously married well," my sister added.

I made mention of our Joanne seeing her, and the initial response, was of my sister being a "bitch". However, that was never going to be enough. Not for the eloquently spoken Mrs Rush, anyway.

"Is she still living in that pit house?" Nikki inquired.

In life, if you want to put someone in their place, just remind them – not so much where they live, but just how far they have come.

That was absolutely nothing compared with what she said about my brother's wife.

"I can't understand what he's doing with *that*," she once told my wife. "Their Joel's quite a decent-looking lad. I mean, she's just really ugly – I mean really, really ugly."

Nikki was never shy in her assessment of people.

If you want a story of a local transvestite, well I have certainly got one.

On 31 July 1950, a thirty-seven-year-old former woodwork teacher at Dearneside Secondary School – a Londoner by the name of Kenneth Crowe had been beaten to death.

He and his wife Constance (nee Chambers) had been married in 1935 and had two daughters – Pat (b. 1936) and Doreen (b. 1937) – and after their birth lived at 5 Manor Road, Harlington.

After the war, however – he was offered a post as Woodwork Master at the rather upmarket Rotherham Grammar School for Boys by Gilbert E Gunner, and the family eventually relocated to 43 Hounsfield Road, Dalton.

On that fatal Monday night, he had waved them off – they were staying the night in Dinnington before going to Cleethorpes the very next day, Kenneth's intention being to pick them up from outside the Brecks Hotel in Wickersley at 10.20 p.m. the following night.

After dropping off his family he went home.

Meanwhile a twenty-five-year-old by the name of John Patrick Cooney had gone to the Thrybergh WMC (Top Club) on Hollings Lane around 7.20 p.m. – which was located not too far from where some of the rioting took place at Silverwood Colliery in late-September 1984. He had a few pints with a work mate, played snooker and left at closing time – firstly going to his friend's mothers house for some supper and then leaving around 11.00 p.m.

At the end of Arundel Avenue, he bumped into a *lady* wearing a short green coat, a green and white dress, stockings and white stilettos all of which were topped off with brown flowered silk scarf around her neck.

Unbeknown to Cooney, she had been parading up and down Doncaster Road in both directions appearing as though she had been touting for men.

Cooney, a stocky well-built fellow, fancied his chances and got talking to *her* and within minutes the inevitable happened, they were sat kissing on some grassed area before Cooney went in for a *bit more*. To his horror he found that this *lady* was indeed a man – and none other than Kenneth Crowe. Cooney went berserk and beat the living daylights out of him.

According to Chief Supt. J.L. Dunn, Kenneth Crowe's body was discovered on the pavement about 4.00 a.m. by a bus inspector on his way to work.

A doctor pronounced him dead over one-and-a half-hours later, the autopsy showing that not only had Kenneth Crowe suffered serious head injuries – including a broken jaw, but that he had died from asphyxia after being strangled.

The police undertook a rigorous search of his property and uncovered erotic drawings and photographs – some of his wife in bondage and some of him wearing women's clothes.

There was also evidence post-autopsy that Crowe was a sexual pervert, however, the details as to the hows and whys is subject to a 100-year closure.

On hearing of a dead body being found, Cooney – a single man in lodgings, handed himself in the very next day and was charged with manslaughter.

I have seen some of these photographs, and no matter what Cooney's perception of a woman was, you could always tell that the *lady* in question was a man. You had to be blind not to. He was over six-foot-tall, had a pair of great fucking feet and possessed the face of riveter. There was no way at all that you could ever think this could have ever been a woman.

My opinion. I am not totally convinced who the sexual pervert actually was.

The trial at Leeds Assizes was presided over by Justice Sir Donald Leslie Finnemore, who said: "The jury have taken a merciful view of your case, but you have been found guilty of a grave crime, and I am bound to say that it is a case of manslaughter which comes terribly near to a case of murder."

On 22 November 1950, Cooney was found guilty and sentenced to five years.

What would happen, however, is that on 12 March 1962, Cooney would be dragged in front of Rotherham Magistrates' Court on a charge of indecently assaulting a nineteen-year-old girl.

It had been big news at the time as Cooney had been apprehended by Alan Simpson – a mid-distance athlete with Rotherham Harriers & AC who would come fourth in the 1500m at the 1964 Tokyo Olympics In Japan and second in the 1966 British Empire and Commonwealth Games in Kingston, Jamaica.

The girl had been screaming her head off after Cooney had grabbed her from behind, pulled up her dress and began *interfering* with her.

As I said, I am not convinced.

It wasn't the only schoolteacher related murder in the area – that is for sure.

Thirty-three-year-old Bernard Hugh Walden had been a Physics lecturer at Rotherham Technical College who in March 1959, had been offered a senior teaching post as Head of Physics at Dearneside Secondary School. He would, however, never take that job. He was arrested and charged with the double murder of Joyce Moran and her boyfriend, Neil Saxton.

Walden had a major problem in that he had become absolutely infatuated with Joyce, who apart from being a shorthand typist at the college bore a striking resemblance to the actress Rhonda Fleming.

Around 7.30 p.m. on 7 April 1959, he dropped on the twenty-one-year-old chatting through the inquiries hatch to Neil – a former engineering student who was one year her junior.

"The Defiant Ones?" she smiled.

"Yeh – it's on at the Rawmarsh Regal," he told her.

"Yes, and it was the Two Headed Spy last week – not that I saw much of it," she giggled.

"I never heard you complaining," he winked.

"You what – I must have buttoned-up my blouse and pulled my skirt down at least ten times during the first ten minutes. The first I saw of the film was when Gia Scala was playing the piano."

"Why was she in it?" he grinned.

"You know she was you twit."

"Well, she's not in this one – Tony Curtis is though."

Joyce's attention, however had been elsewhere. "Don't look now but Walden's lurking about," she whispered.

"What – Hopalong Cassidy?" he laughed.

Without saying a word, Walden walked over to them before pulling out a .32 ACP Erma KGP-68A (Luger) automatic pistol from his jacket and shot them both dead.

He fired one shot into the back of Neil Saxton – put a further two shots through the inquiries hatch before kicking open the door and letting off several shots as he walked into the room – Bang! Bang! Bang! Bang! Bang! Bang! Joyce was hit six times in rapid succession – four of which were from point blank range with Walden putting the last one in her body whilst literally standing over her.

He turned to see Neil struggling and pointed the gun at him. Click! Click! Click! He had used all his bullets.

Walden swiftly walked out of the building and went on the run for three weeks, of which a nationwide manhunt ensued.

According to Chief Supt. Richard Thompson, Joyce – who had tried hiding behind a desk, had died immediately whereas Neil died in hospital.

The police provided a description of the murderer as being 5'7 in height, having dark curly hair and possessing a limp and who on the day of the double murder had been wearing a blue-grey sports coat and flannels. What was interesting is that he drove a blue Ford Prefect 100E – registration SET 369 – to Leeds railway station, where it was later on, found abandoned.

On locating the vehicle, the police found three revolvers inside, including the murder weapon itself whilst over his lodgings on Spinneyfield – a street in the Whiston area of Rotherham, they uncovered another two.

As the police intensified both their search and inquiries it became apparent that Walden had not only become obsessed with Joyce, but on 29 March – Easter Sunday, he had also asked her to marry him – the offer of which she had declined. Whilst he had lodged on Far Lane in the East Dene area of the town, he had become quite friendly with her family, often running Joyce to work in his car.

A dark secret which was later uncovered, was that Walden had also been convicted of a homosexual offence in 1949.

The police traced his movements – firstly to London, then Torquay, Oxford, Salisbury, Leicester, Sheffield and finally Reading, where a policeman on patrol found him asleep in a bus shelter. He was arrested and charged at Reading Police Station – with Chief Supt. Leonard Allen stating that it was South Yorkshire Police's case and that he would therefore be driven back up north.

During his trial at Sheffield Assizes it was submitted that Walden was suffering from an abnormality of the mind, which diminished his responsibility. It was also said that he was a man who had deliberately cut himself off from his family and childhood friends because he thought he had let them down – embittered that he had only obtained only a third-class degree at university instead of the first-class honours.

"Mr Walden's story was that of a man who nearly made good," explained his barrister, Henry Scott QC. "The son of a working-class family he did well at school and won a scholarship to Oxford University. It was at college, however, that fortune began to dog the young man who was said to have a brilliant future. After two years his mother died from cancer and shortly after, he developed polio and for several vital months, he missed college lectures. He then began to believe that fate was against him. With a third-class degree, he began a teaching career but blamed his failure on the sudden death of his mother and the attack of polio which left him partially crippled. He had been offered a senior teaching post in Barnsley and had that appointment come a few weeks earlier, he may have been able to break his association with Rotherham and in particular the obsession he had with Miss Moran."

Although, whilst on remand at HMP Armley he was diagnosed as suffering from a chronic paranoid disorder, Chief Medical Officer Dr J.L. Walker said that he had been more concerned about his disabled leg than anything else.

During his trial there was also an unsubstantiated claim that he had said: "I am not as other men. I am a cripple and must be armed to put me on fair terms with others… I have an absolute right to kill."

On 1 July 1959, he was sentenced to death – which was something that his defence unsuccessfully appealed against.

A Home Office announcement said: "After giving careful consideration to all the circumstances of the case, the Home Secretary had been unable to find any sufficient ground to justify him in recommending the Queen to intervene with the due course of law."

Bernard Hugh Walden was hanged on 14 August 1959, by Harry Allen – a man who had not only been the Chief Executioner at forty-one executions, but who was from the eastern Dearne Valley, having been born on 5 November 1911 at 50 Braithwell Street, Denaby Main.

As for Nikki's husband, at times Nigel had sailed a bit too close to the wind and on 20 May 2005, he got handed a four-year prison sentence at Leeds Crown Court by Judge Stephen Ashurst QC. He had been found guilty of being one of the movers and shakers in a conspiracy to import 400 kg of cannabis from Morocco.

His arrest followed the seizure of the drugs by Spanish law enforcement officials after a lorry was stopped in Alicante in February 2004.

From what I can gather a confiscation order – a seizure of assets under the Proceeds of Crimes Act 2002 followed, and for a time after Nigel's release he and Nikki were living on-the-fly – firstly in rented accommodation opposite the Seven Lakes Country Park just off the A18 east of Doncaster – where she became the dark hobby of some social media pervert and then in the French Riviera, before she rather abruptly ended it.

"You can all stay, if you want," she told her family against the backdrop of the Tête de Chien. "However, me and the dog are going home."

Certainly not to Thurnscoe, that is for sure, but back to the house off Warning Tongue Lane that they had initially put up for sale.

The detached residence on its block-paved cul-de-sac, which is located between Robin Hood Airport and the affluent Bessacarr area of Doncaster was integral to Nicola's journey and one with traversed a long away from Briton Square and one, which for a time, she took her mother.

For all Nikki's idiosyncrasies, she is a fantastic daughter.

The aloof mannerism and poker-face may have conned those who didn't know her mother, but those who did, had her number. I used to scratch my head at the audacity of Pete and Kathleen Wake who lived opposite my girlfriend's parents in Brampton Bierlow and how brazen-faced they were in conning the authorities into living off the system without having to work. However, there was an honesty in their indolence, in that they never really hid what they did. Mary Gough was different. She acted as though the world owed her a living and set a precedence that her daughter, for some time mirrored.

Personally, I don't think Nikki realised how bright she was until she realised how bright she was. And that was when she had been on her own, both unshackled and without distraction. However, that is Nicola's story to tell and not mine.

My journey in late-1985 would be one of bad timing and heartache and one where I would end up standing directly opposite Nikki's father watching a coffin that contained one of his best friends being lowered into the ground.

My dad had quickly deteriorated to such an extent that it had become hard to look him in the face. His grey and sometimes jaundice exterior had added something of a contrast to the skeletal features which had completely transformed the man that he was, into the cold expressionless corpse that he would inevitably become.

"Mam, I'm going to be a granddad," I remember him telling my nana Durose over the phone. "Our James's girlfriend is having a baby."

I had firstly, albeit tentatively, told his wife the news, whilst she had been making cups of coffee and whose blaring response had the hair on the back of my neck stand on end. As I have said already, I was surprised Paula could manage to walk as far as she could – being that half the time she had her foot in her mouth. It wasn't so much, my girlfriend being pregnant, but the fact that marriage had been mentioned. In my mind, my child needed both a family and a name and I said as much. "And our Louise is going to be a bridesmaid… again?" had been her petulant response. "Maybe it will happen this time, eh?"

Unfortunately, my girlfriend had heard her screech each and every one of her replies – including that one. She did, however, urge me to tell my dad who was ecstatic.

"I'm definitely going to have to get better now," he said.

Although I hid it from everyone, bar my girlfriend, I was absolutely heartbroken all the way through his final three months. It would be the second time that I would come to handle death, but certainly not the last. Like anything in life, you get used to it and things that once created tremendous upset, now can often have me appearing both detached and emotionless, which, when put in certain situations, can be quite unnerving.

"You act as though you don't give a fuck," Tim once told me.

"Have you ever thought that I'm not acting?" was my response.

That apple and that tree, eh?

I recall one Friday afternoon in the playground of Carfield Juniors. We were playing football in the smaller playground – the one which possessed the climbing frame that at one time I had struggled to reach, and between the two sets of superficial goals – the two drainpipes that ran down the outside of the First-Year toilets and one of the layby-shaped openings that used to house one of the three benches.

Nowadays, Owen Scrimshaw is an amateur photographer who works as an Operational Excellence Project Manager at Eurofins Agroscience Services in Derby – however, back then, had been an amiable little lad, with brittle-looking arms and legs, who just loved football.

As for me, I had been happy in the knowledge that the very next day my dad would be picking me up. He had always been an outlet from the misery of home. A place to get away from the shouting and screaming along the futile exercise of trying to appease someone who possessed very little joy – my mum.

She could be the greatest mother in the world. The problem was, that she just couldn't keep it up.

I look at Nikki and there's not so much a similarity, as she's a great mum who is highly protective of her children, but of her mood, which could easily be dictated by any minor irrelevance. She can also act as though she doesn't give damn.

Ever thought that she's not acting? Sound familiar?

The thought of a child, a wedding and my dad dying created an uncertainty in my feelings, which were compounded further after letting my girlfriend's parents know about the imminent arrival. This was made even more problematic by the fact that the girlfriend didn't want to tell her parents and waited until the Christmas tree was up before she did. And even then, it wasn't her who had told them, it had been her sister.

However, by the time that had happened, my dad had been almost ready to die.

The hallucinations that had been created by his intake of morphine had had him seeing spiders racing across the ceiling, and with him being so weak he could hardly turn his head. "I'm glad you've come to see me," he told me. "I need to tell you something."

I gave a shrug, as I let him get his breath before he continued.

"I've not told anyone before, but you need to know," he said. "You have a sister."

"Where?" I asked.

His line of conversation then began wandering. He mentioned seeing a woman he had known and being introduced to a girl. He then told me it had been his daughter.

"What did she look like?" I asked.

"Beautiful," he replied.

Looking back at that statement, it's not really one that is solid enough to hang your hat on as most parents say that about their children. As far-fetched as this may sound, I am sure something of a positive note had at one time been said by the mother of my brother's hideous wife as regards her alleged beauty.

One thing that stands out is the name "Mary". I am ninety-nine percent certain that he made mention of a *Mary*.

I wanted to ask lots more questions, but he wasn't really in a fit state and as I sat at his side the vicar came into the bedroom.

Whilst this had been happening [the run up to his death], I was still young and naïve, but looking back at it there had been a pattern forming.

A couple of weeks earlier my dad had handed me an album crammed full of old photographs from the carrier bags that he had often got out to throughout my childhood for us to reminisce over. These were the times that I had loved.

"That's you down Billy's Lane," he would tell me.

There I was, standing in my sky-blue jersey and a pair of shorts on Tan Pit Lane – a dirt track which runs down the side of the train lines towards Frank Wells's pond just before the stone-built railway bridge off Bolton-on-Dearne's Furlong Road.

"And that's you on your nana's wall at number nine [The Crescent]," he added.

They were all there – however, they had been cropped to fit in the photograph album.

"This Is Your Life," he had said, as he handed it over to me, trying his best to do an impression of Eamonn Andrews.

My initial thoughts were, why spilt up the photographs? Why cut them up? Why even give them me? I mean, I could see them anytime I wanted.

Yes, I could at that time, but soon he would be dead. And he knew deep inside, that everything would change. He wasn't wrong. Everything did change. Quickly.

After his death, his wife couldn't wait to get me out of her life.

"You're a cunt," she screamed as she marched through my gate towards the old battered Mark III Cortina – the very same car that I'd had to reverse out of the car park at Weston Park Hospital – a car which had both my ten-year brother and six-year old sister in it. "You cunt – cunt, bastard, fucking cunt, bastard," she added.

That was word for word. It was obvious that she had still not mastered the use of profanities as adjectives.

What had I done wrong to receive her wrath? Me personally – absolutely nothing. It is what she had always wanted.

I responded by stating that the only person that was a cunt, had been my dad for marrying someone as vile and vulgar as her. A fucking stupid cunt.

You can dwell on things and take it to heart, which is what a lot of people do. Fortunately, I have always surrounded myself by what I term as big people and the day my dad had died had been the time when this would start.

On my dad dying, I recall being up at my mum's house up on Lancaster Street with her appearing quire heartbroken, in as much as she cried.

For me, it was extremely upsetting to see.

My step(dad) sat down next to me and just shook his head. "Me and your dad had our differences – but I wouldn't wish that bloody thing [cancer] on anybody."

"You ought to have seen him when he was younger," added my mum. "He thought he was God's gift strutting around in that white leather jacket. He was like Elvis Presley."

I had heard the story before, but I didn't mind hearing it again.

"Your auntie Heather was on the phone earlier and she told me to tell you that she was sorry," she said. "And your grandma Carman – she asked how you were."

That was it – I broke down.

"Do you want me to go with you?" asked my (step)dad. "To the funeral?"

That said everything about the man he was. He was a truly brilliant bloke.

"Paula will take offence," I told him. "I wouldn't like her to say anything bad to you."

"That'll not bother me," he said.

"Yeh, but it'd bother me," I said.

I obviously hadn't kept in touch with Paula, as there had been too much water gone under the bridge. The odd Christmas card – but that was about it. What was strange, and a pure coincidence, was that my wife rang her one day prior to us going on a meal out with friends. Those friends were Nikki and Nigel. As such, I had told my wife of a photograph that my dad had had – a photo with him, Pat Thomson and Derek Gough on it and standing outside the Tower of London circa 1971. My wife had picked up her phone and asked Paula if she could pick it up so I could get it copied for Nikki.

"She sounded very shaky on the phone," my wife had said. "Very shaky."

Did she give us the photo? Certainly not. She just gave an excuse. "I couldn't find it."

That weekend my wife told Nikki about the photograph and of her talking with Paula during a great night of conversation – but one of the strange things that was said had been at the end of the night and on her giving me a hug.

"I wish I had a sister like you," I told her.

I wasn't lying. I saw her as a great mum, sister and daughter – regardless of her demons.

"I'll definitely be your sister, if you want," she replied.

I never thought anything about it until just recently. Could the sister I never knew be like Nikki? Was she pretty? Did she have a penchant for fine dining, dry New Zealand white wine and expensive shoes? Did possess have a lousy horrible temper, a wicked right hook and detest peas?

It would be interesting to find out.

Unfortunately, the next time I would see my dad he would be boxed up in a coffin in the rear of some funeral parlour in Stainforth.

Mary? Who the hell was Mary?

In the rear garden of 53 Ringway, Bolton-on-Dearne.
Centre - Heather Greaves (nee Carman) and Bridget Weddell (now Ryan)

34.   The Holy Trinity

It is an empty and unsatisfying feeling coming into something right at the end. The area I had grown up in had been dying well before the time that I had started work. Everything that had been good you could associate with mines.

I remember during the early spring of 1981, of being sat in the cabin on the colliery blending plant – which was bossed by Freddie Andrews and looking over and past the Sheffield – York railway lines at the rear gardens of the houses of Lindley Crescent and part-catching a conversation between the grandson of the murdered lady, Mary Ellen Gallagher and some other surface worker.

"I can't see them shutting it," said Don Whitehurst. "They've just paid a fortune to have the shaft lined."

I had only been employed by the NCB a mere six or seven weeks and a subject such as this had raised its head. It wasn't the first time Hickleton Main had been under threat. In June 1968, its workforce of 1,700 were told that the colliery had been haemorrhaging around £14,000 (£256,616, circa 2020) per week and as such, if production didn't get upped then it would close in September.

As I have said, the answer was one of simple economics compounded by a lethargy among its workforce, outdated infrastructure along with a management that was continually hamstrung by the NUM. This was something that had in effect snowballed after nationalisation. If someone didn't want to toil – either on the surface or underground – the truth was, they didn't have to.

I would leave the employ of the NCB (British Coal) and on doing so, I immediately saw the difference between privatisation and nationalisation. Working for Cementation Mining was the ultimate eye-opener and for anyone who wasn't afraid of work, the money and opportunities were nothing short of tremendous. With one 500-yard shaft fully dropped and the mine development commenced I had landed in a completely different world. Two fully circular tunnels, being driven by huge Scottish-manufactured road headers with cranes mounted on either of its sides had just set off from the pit bottom. Outside of the construction of the huge underground junctions where drill and blasting played its part, there was very little manually challenging work as everything was mechanised. The other difference was that every man on site had a huge degree of flexibility in that they would do anything to keep the job going. The reason behind this? They were being paid an absolute fortune.

One of the three things that my uncle Steve (Carman) had said that rang true was: "If you are going to be working underground, you need to try to earn as much as physically possible."

My wages had immediately tripled and within seven months I would be earning a few pounds less than £1,000 (£2,706, circa 2020) per week.

It hadn't quite – but I thought that my time had arrived.

I wasn't the highest paid miner in the UK as there were lads on the construction of the Channel Tunnel earning more, but I was close. That would come some years later after national mining contractor Thyssen had been sold off. The company – a UK subsidiary of Thyssen Schachtbau Gmbh, had its head office at Langthwaite Grange in South Kirkby and a regional office down in Llanelli, South Wales.

Specialist Mining Services (SES) and Quantum Geotechnic bought the major assets whilst I moved in and bought the three companies – mining (GB), tunnelling and geotechnical; the latter of which would be the one that I used.

I had a mate who ran a concrete structures company, and who did a lot of work on the redevelopment of Doncaster Robin Hood Airport (Finningley). His company had run into some trouble and at the time had been owed a substantial amount from a couple of contractors – one being at the Airbus facility over in Broughton, North Wales. It had been something that had his family teetering *on the brink*. I knew the contractor, Manchester-based

Ennis Construction, and went straight to its Managing Director, Roger Seed. "Pay him or you will have a problem," was the gist of my conversation.

I was told that I was unprofessional and was threatened with legal action. It was all par for the course. The last thing he wanted was me on his back and in the end they paid him up.

As for my mate, he saw how I used my contact base but more to the point, also took notice of how under-utilised it was.

"Why don't we put some money together – buy a tunnelling machine and go into business?" he said.

It didn't happen overnight as I saw how he ran his business – mainly from the pub. His perseverance, however, won over and that is the reason that I became the new owner of the Thyssen group of companies. The problem that I had, however, was that I was now running with both the hares and the hounds – the idea being that the company would be better served with me in the background. I had a mining and geotechnical magazine which was reliant on advertising – the money of which, came from the said company's *would be* competitors.

I extended the office, hired in a secretary, and pushed the geotechnical company and within five weeks I had one and a half million pounds worth of work sat on the table. I had created a massive workload for myself – the first being an emergency tunnelling job close to the A1 in Newark.

The problem? None of the guys my mate employed had ever driven a tunnel before. It was therefore a case of me leading a three-man crew armed with nothing more than FL22s and constructing a 25m-long by 1.8m-wide by 1.5m-high electricity tunnel under some huge warehouse. Although, it was a culture shock, as I had not swung a pick in anger in over ten years, from a personal point of view, it was very self-satisfying in that I had reached a goal. May 2004 was a time when I would become the highest paid miner in the UK. I earned £10,000 (£15,947, circa 2020) in one week. That is a miner's true worth. Never think that it is not. A miner deserves every penny he earns from the moment he steps into that cage.

Next up had been a rock anchor / soil nailing job on the A465 Neath to Abergavenny (Heads of the Valley) Trunk Road. Unfortunately, I looked at all the work coming in and me doing it all, and then of my *partner* sat in the pub. It was a bad division of labour.

I had received dozens of telephone calls from lads that I had worked with wanting a job – but for me I needed someone who could both accept and thrive on responsibility. I also needed someone that I could trust – the latter being key.

I had worked at the top-end of contracting within the mines and had got to know some fabulous people, but this was a serious business.

I had found that out a few years earlier after I had lost my driving licence for twelve months. Andy Roper had thrown on the sick from whatever job in mining that he had been doing at the time and showed up at my house to find out what was happening. I wouldn't say he was like a bad penny – because he wasn't. He was just a kid who skimmed the surface to see what he could dig up. A user? Maybe – maybe not. A survivor is a better term. The fact that I needed a driver for the remaining six months of my ban, gave me an idea. It was a mistake. My cash-in-hand offer brought him in contact with my business and was something that I should have never let happen.

We were stood in the middle of some farmland in the Lincolnshire countryside watching some mechanised pipe jack being set up to punch a hole beneath a road as part of a huge gas transmission pipeline project, when he suddenly changed the subject. "I wonder what the girls are doing," he said.

He had been more interested in the girls in the office rather than the job in hand, which was something that would only get worse. Was he lecherous? No, more fucking painful, but the fact that the girls in the office had nicknamed him "Randy Groper" certainly made you think that.

I eventually moved him into the back room with me, which had been the beginning of the end. He couldn't hack it and he broke down. And when I say, broke down – I mean it. "I can't do this anymore," he told me.

I'd had him chasing news and contracts – just plain research, and he became a gibbering wreck of a lad. The thing is, is that he had never worked in a mixed-sex environment before and all he wanted to do was to strut around swinging his dick. All I had done was move to stop it.

The strange thing was, that he would have been much better suited to the contracting arm – but apart from it been a couple of years in the future, he was just someone that I could have never have trusted.

I remember calling down to John Gratton and Julie Trueman's house on Billingley View – the initial phase of the housing development behind The Ship. The pair had become an item around 1997 and had moved in together. Rather strangely, Andy and his second wife Margaret (Morris) had lived next door.

On seeing me, Julie immediately gave me the lay of the land: "Andy lives next door and I know you and he have had words…" she whispered.

"I've never had any words with him," I replied. "He'd certainly fucking know if I had."

It was a plain case of Andy acting out his alter-ego – *the big I am.*

You would often see him standing at the bar in The Ship with a pint of lager in his hand, his head tilted back and looking down his nose at you. In life, bullshit may get you through the door, but it will never keep you in the room. A person will always get found out. Andy's problem was that he should have concentrated on the kid he *is* rather than the one that he thinks he is.

As for the running of the contracting arm – one of Thurnscoe Comprehensive's Class of 1981, would have been quite well-suited.

In early-1992, Cementation Mining needed to push one of its mega contracts in the Selby coalfield. I had been at Whitemoor Mine at the time – the same contract where a set of twins had been working. "Jamie, Dave Parkinson (Project Manager) wants you and both Paul and Brian Russell up at North Selby (Mine) as one of its developments is stalling. You need to see him when you go out of the pit," said the General Foreman, Alan Sherwood.

Paul was nothing short of a stand-up kid and one that would always have your back. He came from good stock – his father, Malc Russell, being a General Foreman with the Amalgamated Construction Company (AMCO). He lived for his job and his enthusiasm knew no bounds. Paul was a kid that just rubbed off on me. I have to admit, if I could have taken someone and showed him how the estimating and quantity surveying worked, he would have picked it up in no time at all. However, the main thing was trust, and this kid had it in spades. He would have been the perfect fit.

As for the job at North Selby Mine – it had been nothing short of a fucking disaster. Our heading had been at the mercy of a mineral transport system that had been continually breaking down. All the conveyors mucked out into a central point which was at another pit – Gascoigne Wood. Although the village of Escrick hadn't been molested by colliery tips or slag heaps – its mine was the last in line and miles away from the exit point for the spoil. It was a case of putting all your eggs in one basket. The engineers at British Coal (NCB) had planned the Selby coalfield in a well-thought-out and prudent manner. Unfortunately, mining isn't like any other profession, and it would be on this job that I saw the worst of the worst when it came to design.

Our tunnelling machine – a Dosco LH1300 had hit its target in the main gate (intake) much quicker than the one driving the tail gate (return), and after building the junction, we turned right to drive the coal face. I was part of a good team, and being over 1,000 yards beneath the surface, we had been working in both extremely hot and wet conditions and had pulled the job back only to see a mess unfold. We were well into driving the coal face, when Cementation's engineers had a brainwave and suggested that the LH1300 in the tail gate set off mining the face as well. The other LH1300, therefore began coming towards us.

It was an act of sheer stupidity. "We are going to get the machines trapped here," I said. "Two Dosco's coming together – we are going to get all the weight coming onto the rings the nearer we get."

It was the ultimate understatement. Weight, just like water, is always drawn to the weakest point. Whilst we were mining, the roof falls became more intense and the floor blow behind the machine was nothing short of phenomenal. I still recall Paul, the fitter and myself dismantling the rear of the Dosco to help get it through the supports that we had set the very same day. The floor had been rising behind us at such a rate, a team of around a dozen men armed with picks and shovels had begun dinting the floor behind us. As I said it was a fucking stupid idea and I was glad when our Steve (Carman) gave me the green light to go down on to his job in Meden Vale (Welbeck Colliery) where they were sinking two bunker shafts.

As for Paul, those twelve weeks working with him and his brother, were as enjoyable as I had ever had. Unfortunately, when I had all this work on the table with the rebranded Thyssen, I had lost touch. He would have made a great Contracts Manager.

The ground anchor job was the eyeopener. I was in discussions with the main contractor, BAM Nuttall for a full week on what machine and the type of anchor and cementitious grout we would be using. In the end I looked at my partner in the pub and just thought *fuck it*. If the job went tits up, I would stand to lose a lot of money. In life, you need people who you can depend on – not a mate who can shift a few pints with you down the pub. It didn't happen overnight but I ended up shelving the company and walked away. It was a very well thought out decision. My mates reinforced concrete structures company went bust not long after.

As for Cementation Mining, the only problem that I had, had been some of the people that I worked with.

Preparatory work – ground freezing in the Vale of Belvoir, began on the mine in 1984, which told you everything that you needed to know: Asfordby New Mine as it was known, was a development that in the main, had been built by scab labour.

I was the only Thurnscoe lad on the development until Andy Roper briefly came and went.

The mentality of the scab is generally one of three traits: that of greed, self-interest and cowardice.

I had been near starving during the dark months of 1984. I had truly gone without and more so than most. At just nineteen years old I had robbed Peter to pay Paul with any pennies that I had – mostly those that had been diverted from paying my rent, to try and maintain my survival. And to listen to some miner bigging himself up and talking about the mega money he had been earning whilst he had been with the NCB, then of him selling his job after cashing in on redundancy and then sneaking in by the back door to go private contracting really pissed me off. As I have already said, I have worked with hundreds of scabs – none of whom, ever admitted to being one. Ralph Thorpe had been no different.

How did I know he was a scab?

He was a Leicestershire miner. Only thirty of them stayed out on strike and it is safe to say that this fucker certainly hadn't been one of them.

He was the scab of greed.

I had been put with him doing some trial and error work whilst trying to push the job, which if I rightly recall had been a senseless decision and as such, one that had been immediately rectified. As the tunnel progressed setting colliery arches, we had been tasked with undermining the floor and circularising the arch.

Personally, I was glad to get shut of the boring fuck pig – however, there is that old well-worn cliché – that of jumping out of the frying pan. I was chucked in a heading with a tunnel crew who were a man light after he had had his leg broken following a roof fall. Little did I realise how depressed working with the wrong people could get someone. I would go from the happiest kid possible, to one who had dark fantasies about shoving a miner into the gathering arms of the road header's apron. I had never truly hated anyone I had worked with. This had been the first, but certainly not the last time, that I would feel like this.

Whilst working in the Yorkshire coalfield, I had never had that problem. In the Leicestershire and Nottinghamshire Area there was always a problem. As I said, there was just a different mentality. In the here and now, I would have thought nothing of confronting the problem with violence, but back then there were hundreds of mitigating factors – the main one being that I would end up losing my job.

At Hickleton Main, there tended to be that pecking order of respect. Being that you lived amongst its workforce it was highly unlikely that you would get spoken to or speak to someone like shit. There was always someone to point you in the right direction. You throw lots of different people together in a different environment and there is always going to be a problem. Straight after the strike the scab problem was immediately seized upon by the management. If any working miner was to be victimised or indeed referred to as a *scab* it would be deemed a sacking offence.

In the Doncaster Area, the management putting that statement into force would be like trying to plait piss, in that it was just a futile exercise. In Nottinghamshire and Leicestershire, however, you were in a minority in that it was *you* who was the scab.

At Shirebrook, and as with the British comedy-drama series *Auf Wiedersehen, Pet*, the scabs, as with the Germans, had been referred to as *Eric's*.

On being transferred to Markham Main in Armthorpe I immediately saw the problems that any miner stupid enough to have broken the strike would come across. In prison, they put what they term as vulnerable prisoners – the paedophiles and such, in their own wing or block. As wrong as I personally think this is, and I do, it does make sense as their longevity would be severely jeopardized if they were to be integrated with the rest. The scabs were mostly treated the same. Generally, the management would move the scab out of harm's way and maybe *pension him off* with a redundancy pay-out or transfer him, as was the case with Maltby Colliery's Gerald Escreet – an electrician who ended up at Asfordby Mine with Cementation.

Escreet had been vilified. Him going back to work on 21 September 1984 had seen around 6,000 pickets trying to block his access to work and some of the worst violence of the strike with Chief Supt. John Nesbitt, stating in *The Guardian* that the picketing had been "very, very heavy and intense." This culminated with Escreet being chased out of the area. In fact, he still lives down there now – some house in the middle of nowhere on Station Road in Waltham-on-the-Wolds.

At Markham Main, however, that certainly wasn't the case. It was an act of nothing short of callousness by the management. It was as if **they** wanted to teach them a lesson. A Banksman isn't a job that puts you out of the way, it is the exact opposite. They come into contact with every miner that descends the mine. I had never witnessed scenes like it. The Banksman didn't just get name-called and jostled, he also got punched and spat it.

Did I engage in it? As with Bob Copping, I did call Escreet a "scab bastard" – however, the only emotion I felt on watching the Banksman get intimidated was one of sadness and the answer is – no, I did not. The man, who had to be in his late fifties, was a gibbering fucking wreck.

I was led to believe that the reason he went back to work was that he had been dogged by his wife.

He was the scab of cowardice.

The NCB enticed men back to work to break the strike then washed their hands of them. It was a case of using people and no different in the way that the police use defence witnesses. One vision that sticks in my mind was seeing Roy Lynk having some sit-in at Silverhill Colliery in October 1992. He had been described by Barrie Clement of *The Independent* as not a man to deal in inconsequential subtleties, but the truth was, he was used by both the government and NCB as nothing more than a muppet – with their sole aim being, to break the strike. Lynk had been instrumental in setting up the breakaway scab union the UDM – however, when the reality of his folly hit home, and pits were closed in his own backyard he decided to act. He felt betrayed.

He was the scab of self-interest.

After the strike, the main talking point at the pit head had been redundancy. The terms on offer for some of the older end had been staggering. It was more money than they had ever seen in their life. Remember me mention the carrier bag?

If a scab had the gall to be bussed through the picket lines at Goldthorpe or Cortonwood for a basic weekly wage of less than £100 he would gladly sell his job for between £20,000 to £30,000 and then try and get a back-door entry into mining through private contracting. This would be something that would come to grate on my fucking soul.

Whereas the car park of Asfordby Mine was full of new and fast cars, the car park at Markham Main had been anything but.

After the strike all my mates had bought vehicles – mostly Ford Capris as with Col, Tim, Daz Cooper and Steve Handley – however, I was still in the process of financial consolidation and it wouldn't be until April 1986 that I would be able to go out and buy the car of my choice.

My dad dying created something of a reality check into how insoluble my finances were.

When you are young, certain things tend to play on your mind. I have only ever mentioned this just recently and to my wife and son – however, the truth was, that I **never** intended going to my dad's funeral and if it hadn't been for my uncle Steve it is highly doubtful that I would have gone. It wasn't a lack of respect – it was something completely different. The simple explanation is one of embarrassment. I didn't have the money for a suit. As with my uncle Paul making sure I saw my dad in the Chapel of Rest in Stainforth before he was laid to rest, our Steve was the one who made sure that I went to the funeral. I owe them both a lot. As I said, I have always made a point of surrounding myself with what I would describe as *big* people. My two uncles were exactly that.

Daz Cooper always tended to be the best dressed amongst us, which was perhaps down to the fact that whilst he had been growing up, there had been a lot of siblings to feed and clothe. "Get a Burton's card, J," he told me. "A couple of quid a week and they'll give you a spending limit of ninety quid."

I saw getting a store card as going against the grain of what I was trying to achieve. Anyway, that wouldn't have been enough for a suit.

I had never had a problem with having a lack of clothes since I had started work. The problem was that I had begun to fill out a bit and some of the clothes that I did have made their way over to Col's as he had been the only one who could fit in them.

"Where's James?" my dad's wife had snapped as the huge black American hearse turned up outside their house. "Where is he?"

"He's here, Paula," my uncle Paul had said, trying to calm things down.

I hated every minute of the funeral. It was bad enough burying my dad but added to that, I felt hugely disrespectful in not having a suit. This would be something that I would never ever let happen again – although there is something that happened, when me having a huge choice of suits created a problem.

My (step)dad's best friend Mick Lowe had passed away. What made it bad was that he had lost his common-law wife around eighteen months earlier. Iris (Bentham) had been from both a time and a place where everything was good. Although totally different in appearance, she reminded me quite a lot of Lily Austin in that she was gregarious in nature and such a lovely lady. Iris sadly passed away after a holiday in July 2006. I am led to believe that the flight had unsettled her deep vein thrombosis, whereby a blood clot formed in her legs and broke off causing some pulmonary embolism.

If you didn't know him, Mick could come over as a big, brash and booming fellow, which was a huge contrast to the person that he really was. My (step)dad thought the world of him and I often recall him and Iris calling over to see us when I was growing up. The first time I ever recall seeing Mick had been in 1969, while I was living on Landsdowne Avenue. I had come racing into the house after being told off by some man for kicking down a bit of broken-down wall behind Scarrot's haberdashery shop. The man had come out of The Clog rather worse for wear and told me that he had called the police and that they were coming to take me away.

"He's having you on," Mick had told me.

I also remember a time when we had lived on the Flower Estate and I had spent half one Sunday morning in the newsagents on St Andrews Square – with Mick and Iris's highly indecisive kids unable to decide how to spend their respective ten pence pieces. This was something which had its proprietor – Trevor Pyott, eventually lose his *rag* and sling them out. "You're messing me about – I'm not serving you," he had snapped.

Mick had been a shadow of himself following Iris's death and I recall the trip from their house at 68 Norfolk Road, Great Houghton to Ardsley Crematorium on 11 January 2009, and of all the old soldiers from the King's Own Yorkshire Light Infantry (KOYLI) smartly turned out in their green berets and striped green and gold ties waiting to greet the procession and to say one last goodbye to their mate. For me, the sight was quite heart-wrenching, as it immediately reminded me of my (step)dad's funeral, with only one word that could ever describe it: respect.

Inside the crematorium, I sat alongside my uncle Pete and Jimmy Bridgen and whilst listening to Mick's memorial service, I looked down and what I noticed, had me aghast.

"I can't believe it," I told our Pete, on us getting outside. "I've got two different fucking suits on."

I had been in a hurry of that there had been no doubt.

As he often had, the ex-Hatfield Main NUM Secretary, Bryan Robson had called around to the house quite unexpected and as such, he had siphoned off some of the time I had allotted myself to drive over to Wath-on-Dearne to pick up my uncle and get over to the crematorium. I had been rushing and after trying on half a dozen suits that were suitable for a funeral, I ended up getting the trousers mixed up and never cottoned on to the fact that they didn't match the jacket.

"Nobody noticed," said our Pete, whilst we drank to Mick's life in the Burlington (Wath) Club on the town's High Street.

The wife certainly did.

"You've got the wrong trousers to the jacket," she said. "How did you do that – I hung all the suits out for you."

At my dad's funeral, that certainly hadn't been the case.

"I'm going to get off," our Steve told me, after he finished his cup of tea. "Are you okay here?"

I was, but not for long.

Paula had always been forthright in her appraisal of the Durose family – especially where pubs, clubs and alcohol was concerned. As that was the case, she made sure that my dad got planted in the ground long before opening time, therefore nullifying any problems that may have arisen straight after the funeral. "I've made sure that your dad's service is in the morning," she said. "I know what the bloody Durose's are like and I'm not having them turning up drunk."

She may have had a point.

After our Steve left, I recall my uncle Les being inconsolable and Paula bawling him out. "This is what I didn't bloody want," she snapped.

He had every right to be upset. He had just seen his eldest brother buried.

"Why don't you just fuck off, Paula," he replied.

People deal with grief in their own way. She should have respected that, and she didn't. Nevertheless, it was interesting to know how the rest of the family felt about her.

I stayed until almost everyone had gone and all that was left had been Paula's brother and his wife.

Russell (Russ) Newton was a lad three years my senior who had grown up in a cramped terrace house at 94 Highgate Lane and who I had met from time to time whilst growing up. He had married a lovely girl by the name of Sue Butterfield just before the strike and had set up home on St Mary's Road, Goldthorpe. Rather strangely, we shared a similar background in that we had both worked at Hickleton Main, although with him working down the Low Main part of the mine I had never really bumped into him. The first time I had, was after what was a particularly violent picket over at Kiveton Park in October 1984 when I had been arguing the toss with Ian Beaney. I have no idea why, as Ian was one of the loveliest kids you could ever meet. Like myself, Russ had been transferred to Markham Main, where, during my early days there, we had worked together on the colliery's Paddy Road – mainly transporting face supports (Chocks).

Russ was totally unlike his elder sister in that he was neither haranguing, cynical nor blaring and I thoroughly enjoyed my time working with him. He was just a very nice kid.

I went to work that night and Paula kindly dropped me off at Markham Main's pit gates. It wouldn't exactly be the last time I would see her – but socially, it certainly was. It had been all part of her grand plan and something that my dad had seen coming. 10.00 p.m. Thursday 19 December 1985 was the exact time and date when she would omit me from both hers and her children's life.

A couple of days later I remember Daz Cooper calling around to the house – not so much for a coffee and a natter, but for him to borrow the trolley-mounted vacuum cleaner that had made its way down from my mum's to mine. He wanted to clean his car.

Generally, Saturday afternoons involved a drive over to Doncaster. Shopping in Top Man and Burton's – browsing around Bradley's or Fox's record shop and a couple of lagers. These were generally sunk in the Nag's Head opposite Woolworth's on St Sepulchre Gate followed by a few up in the King's Head on Bradford Row, where we always made a point of parking up. In fact, even now, that is where I still where I park the car.

Saturday 21 December 1985 was the day I signed up for a Burton card.

"What spending limit have you got on the card?" I asked Daz.

"One hundred and forty-four quid," he told me.

I signed up for £75. Then £90. Then £144.

Although it got me rigged out, it would eventually be something that would spiral out of control until I began earning the money that a miner truly deserves.

I look at Doncaster now, and it is a sad reflection of the lovely, vibrant and busy town that it once was. I can close my eyes and go back in time to sitting on either one of the 14, 37 or 107 Yorkshire Traction buses. Parked at the Sun Inn junction, with the traffic heavily backed up on A638 Great North Road (York Road) and of the driver trying to negotiate his way onto it. Then passing over the bridges that crossed both heavily polluted River Don with its white foam crust and the network of railways before you hit the four-armed roundabout that took you into the town's North Bus Station.

Back then, St Sepulchre Gate was a hive of activity with its red Corporation buses jostling for position with signs above their windscreens advertising exotic destinations such as Balby, Hexthorpe, Hyde Park, The Racecourse, Wheatley Hills and Beckett Road. As a child, I had been fascinated by them all and when my dad had lived on Doncaster's long since demolished South Street we must have travelled on each and every one of them.

I recall the start of the slum clearances in Doncaster's Hyde Park area just as much as I did with the ones in Thurnscoe, Swinton, Denaby and Mexborough – along with the latter's intricate network of terraced houses where West Street, John Street, Cliff Street, Shelley Street and Glass House Lane were flattened in anticipation of the construction of the town's bypass (A6023). The one thing in life that is certain is that everything comes to an end.

The Hyde Park area possesses a dark history – the worst of which had been presided over at Leeds Assizes in January 1948 by Justice Morris – and at a time when he'd had to deal with a similar event in the village he grew up in.

George Henry Whelpton had worked at Edlington's Yorkshire Main and had married Irene Robson in late-1939, whilst during the war he had served out in North Africa

His marriage with Irene did not last and on the war ending and not wanting to go back into mining he got a job as a bus driver with Doncaster Corporation and in the summer of 1947, whilst lodging at 39 Hexthorpe Road, close to Doncaster town centre, he had hooked up with a forty-eight-year-old widow by the name of Alison Gertrude Parkin (nee Cotterill).

It was literally a ten-minute walk over the St James Bridge and down Carr House Road to her home in the Hyde Park area – which in contrast to its terrace sprawl, was a rather salubrious mid-terrace town house at 4 Wainwright Road. It was a home that she had shared with her husband, Roland – a caretaker at Doncaster Museum, who had died in 1938, aged forty-two and her children – two of whom, Joyce and Maurice, still lived with her.

The relationship, according to Whelpton was one that was to result in marriage. That was as soon as his wife, Irene would give him a divorce.

On the evening of 9 October, they had been drinking in the Park Hotel on Carr House Road, whereby they went back to Alison's around 10.00 p.m., where they had supper followed by the promise of a shag. However, what occurred was an argument, which he said had been over money. Basically – she wanted some and he wouldn't give her any. Whether that was indeed true was another thing. What was said is that Alison had caught him coming out of her twenty-three-year-old daughter's bedroom and had accused him of having sex with her. It was possible, as theirs was only an age difference of eight years, him being thirty-one years old. Whelpton's and Allison's on the other hand, was seventeen.

A fight ensued and Whelpton ended up strangling, not only Alison, but both her children – before setting about mutilating both the mother and son.

What made the crime even more horrific is that the body of the boy was found mutilated in the kitchen whilst the two women's bodies were both naked in the room. Maurice's genitals had been cut off and stuffed into his mother's mouth, whilst a cigarette was found in Allison's vagina and another in Joyce's throat.

According to Justice Morris, the three-day trial had been of one of the most revolting stories ever heard in a British Court.

Ralph Cleworth KC defended and tried to push for murder whilst insane due to a head injury that his client had sustained in 1935. However, the jury were having none of it. Whelpton was executed at Armley Gaol on 7 January 1948.

Around the same time, the area had been stunned by a twenty-five-year-old trainee miner, by the name of Edwin Dacey, who had murdered his ten-month old son, Alan.

The baby's body had been found in a sack around 7.00 a.m. on 25 August 1947. It had been dumped under some bushes close to a footbath alongside the River Don between Warmsworth and Hexthorpe. The baby had also had its skull crushed and had been stabbed several times in the abdomen with a carving knife.

Dacey had initially lived with his wife, Iris and her parents – William and Edith Daisy Clifford (nee Jefferies) at 22 Arbitration Street, Doncaster. This was a street that was part of a vast sprawl of terraced houses that at one time was located just off the A630 Balby Road Bridge and which spread over the wider Hyde Park area. That was until his father-in-law turned him out due to his heavy drinking. This had been something echoed by his wife, as in one instance, he had come home worse for wear and tried strangling her.

For two months Dacey had been in lodgings with Irene Muriel Rumbelow at 39 St John's Road, Edlington – however, on that fatal day something must have snapped. His wife Iris had a routine, in much the same as my mum did when I was little. Whereas my mum dropped me off at my grandma Ellis's before she went to work, Iris Dacey dropped her son off at a nursery – her job being in a Doncaster launderette. It was during the drop off when Dacey moved to take the child from her. It would never be seen alive again.

The police arrested him and after several remands his case went to trial, with Justice Morris donning the black cap at sentencing him to be hanged in Armley Gaol on 2 January 1948.

The Medical Officer at the prison, Dr F.H Brisby, suggested Dacey was insane: "It is a clinically reasonable hypothesis to suggest the accused had not realised what he was doing wrong when he attacked the child."

What would happen is that Dacey would be hospitalized with appendicitis giving his defence barrister a chance to successfully appeal the sentence.

Dacey died in early 1982. He had been a patient at Friern Psychiatric Hospital (formerly Colney Hatch Lunatic Asylum) – a psychiatric hospital in the parish of Barnet.

Doncaster may be a sad indictment of how it once was, but it still doesn't have the desperate appearance of its eastern Dearne Valley counterparts.

The advancement of the internet has decimated High Street shopping and nowadays, they are littered with empty shuttered-up premises along with nail bars, takeaways, hairdressers and charity shops – the latter of which aren't really businesses per se and operate on voluntary labour and are often match funded.

Being born in Mexborough I have a fond recollection of the town. Woolworth's, with its wooden floorboards and the plush-looking Burton's with its polished emerald pearl granite faced façade, which back then wouldn't have dreamed of stocking the tawdry assortment of multi-coloured garbage that we had been seen diligently sifting through in December 1985. When I had been a child the shop had been professional tailors – with staff decked out in their collar and ties and who didn't just sell off the peg, but hand-crafted suits for all mice and men.

For any person's father born in the three villages between 1940 and 1950, if you ask them where they got their first suit, they will most probably tell you, "Burton's".

My nana sent my dad and my uncle Graham to get measured up for their first suit. My dad may have come back looking like Dearne Valley's equivalent of Cary Grant, but his younger, much wilder brother – Graham, certainly did not. He walked up the path to their house at 9 The Crescent resembling some Edwardian Dandy, kitted-out in some drape jacketed zoot suit with its high-waist drainpipe trousers cut so short that you could see his socks. "Your granddad went crackers," my dad had told me.

My granddad Sam's constitution when it came to anything to with culture, was at best, zero.

I still remember my younger cousin Paul (Durose) recalling the time when he had been a young lad helping him down at his allotment one Sunday morning and of them walking up Bolton-on-Dearne's Church Street and calling in at the Cross Daggers for a pint. "My granddad gave me some money to put in the jukebox," our Paul explained. "The next thing he hears, is *Madness* singing… 'Naughty boys in nasty schools, headmasters breaking all the rules' [Baggy Trousers]. He went fucking mental."

A true story is that around 1996, just before the Cross Daggers closed its doors for good, our Paul had been offered the chance of running it. My auntie Liz – Elizabeth Pettinger (nee Durose) had been contemplating buying it and sticking him in it as landlord.

"I thought about it for a couple of days and realised that it would be a bad idea," he told me.

Although he would have made a great landlord – and he would, it was the correct decision.

The Cross Daggers was a wonderful building, but remember what my dad's wife had said regarding the Durose family, where pubs, clubs and alcohol were concerned?

Most of my life's bad decisions have come courtesy of a drink and our Paul – although a more sociable and certainly a much mild-mannered person than I could ever be, was in truth, cut from the same cloth. I remember him having some woman-related fall-out with one of his mates in Ings Lane WMC and of him following the kid to the house where he resided on Edinburgh Avenue, looking to get to the root of the problem and thereby confront it face-to-face. Phil Heyes did no more than pull out a shot gun and stick it in his face. "I'll be honest, James – my legs – they just went," he told me.

Having a twelve-gauge stuck in your face would certainly do that to you.

As for me, I thought Phil and his wife, Jayne (nee Goddard) were just very nice people.

Jayne had been in the year above me at school and the first thing that you noticed about her when you saw her, was that she was slightly cross-eyed. This was a flaw that she overcame by exuding a highly sociable persona and certainly when she was out, she also dressed quite provocatively.

Our Paul's wife at the time, had been the exact dull as dishwater opposite, and from what I could gather, fuelled a problem that was never really there. Solely through insecurity, Helen had seen Jayne as a threat and had been pissing in our Paul's ears. Women can be dangerous, and this could have easily gone the wrong way.

She was much older than my cousin and when he had first bumped into her, had both a husband and children. Our Paul didn't discriminate about such trivialities, and much like my uncle Les (Durose), he'd made Bolton-on-Dearne's sloping pit estate, quite a good place to cut his teeth.

His dad – my uncle Paul, had a word with him one particular time after he got wind of his son's escapades in a property near-opposite to the one where he'd had the gun stuck in his face. Our Paul had reportedly been showing an avid interest in a married woman who happened to be the daughter-in-law of Pete and Doreen Hill (nee Cumberbatch) – a couple who lived on the same street as our Paul's family at 50 Caernarvon Crescent. It therefore didn't take long before the word got out – my uncle Paul catching wind of it whilst drinking in The Dearne Hotel.

"Go and see the kid and get it sorted," my uncle Paul immediately told his son.

"I fully expected taking a good hiding," said our Paul. "I'm humming and erring about going down to the house to see him and who should I bump into whilst walking between the lounge and the concert room [in the Dearne Hotel] – fucking, Russ Hill."

My thoughts on what happened next, were hardly in the same category of the gun-wielding husband of Jayne Goddard and was in truth, quite gutless.

"He just put his arms around me a told me not to do it again," shrugged our Paul. "It was a right result."

"Does he still live down there?" I inquired.

"No, does he fuck – he moved to Sprotbrough."

Our Paul had also had to navigate several minefields on the lead up to the woman he eventually married. It wasn't so much the ten-year difference between them nor the fact that she was already married. It was more to do with whom she shared this marital bliss with, that had been the main subject of worry. To my nana Durose that is, and not our Paul.

In 1979, she had tied the knot to the heir apparent to a successful family business up on Hoyland's Stead Road, which was just a 500-yard canter from the home of my nana's. And by canter, I mean it.

"That little bugger's been hedge hopping again," she used to tell me. "I don't like it. I'm worried something bad is going to come of it."

Helen (nee Oliver) had been married to Edwin J. Cook the undertaker, and my nana had been as worried as hell about the consequences of him ending up in the boot of some hearse bound for Ardsley Hill.

"Those kinds of people can do all sorts of things," she added.

She was right. And our Paul had a routine you could set your clock by.

Every Saturday night, you would find them in the exact same seats and sat stage side at Ings Lane WMC. Bert and Irene Rodgers who lived on Broadwater to their right and Jayne and Phil to their left. If it were summer, he would go all Don Johnson and sport his infamous size eleven white slip-on shoes, which we used to refer to as his *Cousin Eddie's* [Christmas Vacation]. Summer aside, he often wore a three-piece pin-striped gangster suit, with only two pieces on show, that being the waistcoat and trousers. And he would always be in his spot for the serious business of the bingo numbers being called. Always.

You could laugh at the notion of anyone getting murdered in that area, but the truth is, that a murderer once lived in the property one door down from my auntie Heather and uncle Jimmy (Greaves) and opposite where the fucking halfwit still lives that had made my life a misery with the eerie unsolicited phone calls to our house in the middle of the night.

Paul Heath was both two school years above me and from Kimberworth and therefore someone that I didn't know. Born on 24 May 1963, he had been someone that you could describe as being nomadic. He had been an apprentice plumber for the local authority when at eighteen years old he would marry a girl from Swinton who was two years his senior on the Friday afternoon of 7 May 1982.

At the time, Nicola Roberts had been a shop assistant in a chemist in Mexborough and lived in one of the relatively new flat roofed properties behind the Ring O'Bells at 36 Park Close when she met the man who would eventually be handed a sentence of life imprisonment. The couple, along with their two daughters, who for obvious reasons I don't wish to name, eventually settled at 90 Ingsfield Lane.

He would, however, come to the attention of the media after events on 19 December 2003.

The man with the dragon tattoo across his back, had hooked up with a petite blonde by the name of Kim Miller, whose life would end in dramatic circumstances after she was found dead in the bathroom of a hotel. The lifeless body of the pretty and near-naked thirty-year-old had been found both strangled and drowned.

The police had received a call from Paul Heath on 11.30 p.m. that fateful Friday claiming to have "just drowned a prostitute".

"I planned to do this for thirty years," he told the arresting officers, whilst sat on the bed in his underwear, calmly smoking a cigarette. "I killed her."

She had been in his hotel room a total of four hours – the agenda, obviously being sex.

"I don't have nothing – this is a cry for help," he said.

He firstly tried to strangle her before finally ending her life by dragging her over to the bath and drowning her.

"It was either her or me," he added. "I am a coward. I couldn't do this to a male."

Failed strangulations during a murder aren't uncommon. Colin Harold's poor wife Anne Marie may well have been killed by a ligature, but she was also found heavily beaten – something which formed a pattern with a couple of other local murders.

Donald Frederick Cheswick was born at 19 Don View – a property which at one time was synonymous with the areas heavy industry and one that proudly stood in the shadow of both Denaby Main and the twin-cooling towers of Mexborough Power Station. These were both bounded by the River Don, the Sheffield and South Yorkshire Canal and the Sheffield – Doncaster railway line. Nowadays, however – the house is just part of some innocuous terrace which you may pass on the way down for a carvery at Mexborough's Pastures Lodge.

Donald Cheswick's fifteen minutes of fame would come the day after the funeral of John F. Kennedy. On the Tuesday night of 26 November 1963, the thirty-two-year-old father of six, brutally murdered his wife.

Rita (nee Dale) who was two years his junior, had recently given birth to a child by the name of Ian at their home at 90 Bank Street. This is property that now no longer stands, but which back then had been built on a steep embankment opposite the fish market and National Westminster Bank.

She was strangled by her husband before he made sure of her death by bludgeoning her.

He appeared in court for the preliminary hearing wearing a green suit, fawn sweater, and open-necked shirt.

Chief Insp. J. Bradshaw told the court that at 7.45 p.m. information had been received at Mexborough Police Station that had them rush to the property and within five minutes they witnessed the dead body of his wife.

"I found that she had many injuries around her neck, face and head," explained Pathologist Dr Gilbert Forbes. "These were for the most part bruises and they extended from skin-deep into the tissues of the neck. An airway was obstructed, and she died from shock haemorrhage and asphyxia due to blunt injuries to the neck."

The reason?

"I wanted to sleep, but she wouldn't let me," he reportedly told the policeman.

There was obviously more to it than that and Donald Cheswick was put on trial at Leeds Assizes on 31 January 1964 only to be found unfit to plead. He was therefore detained indefinitely – going on to eventually be released sometime in the 1970s in dying in 1979, aged forty-eight.

This is something which saw the murderer of Gladys Merrick never go to trial.

The other one of these murders had been much more high profile. This was more to do with the fact that the murderer had been linked to several other murders as well as spending half his time, whilst in Liverpool's high-security Park Lane hospital for the criminally insane, trying to lobby MPs in a bid to get out on license. This alone, resulted in injunctions served against both the *Daily Mail* and *Liverpool Echo* after they published information that could have supposedly jeopardised any chance of his release.

In October 1988, the hospital's director Dr Malcolm McCulloch and other medical staff complained to the Mental Health Review Tribunal who had been discussing the possibility of his release, stating that the press publicity had made it extremely difficult for them to give evidence – the matter of which was reported to the Attorney General.

Peter Pickering was an extremely dangerous and calculative individual – a psychopath. He also possessed a split-personality, and being clever, he could work it in his favour – especially when he had people in the background scurrying around and helping him cover his tracks.

Nevertheless, before the events on 13 July 1972, he had spent nearly half his life behind bars – including nine-and six-year sentences for rape, attempted rape, indecent assault, actual bodily harm as well as malicious wounding with intent to cause grievous bodily harm. What was consistent, was that all his convictions had been against young girls, one case involving a flogging, whereby the doctor said that he had never seen such horrific injuries inflicted on one human being by another.

He may well have looked your tragic Timothy Lumsden-type character – still living at home on 117 Barnsley Road with his overbearing mother, but Pickering was anything but. He was the ultimate sexual predator. "Sex is predominant in my mind – eclipsing all else," he said. "Rape, torture, kill."

Please, remember those last three words.

He knew the local area well, and never strayed that far away from his base and was suspected of numerous unsolved sexual crimes, some of which have only recently come to light. This follows Cold Case information gleaned from the reopening of the murder of fourteen-year-old Elsie Frost in the Lupset area of Wakefield on 9 October 1965 and thirteen-year-old Anne Dunwell in the Hooton Levitt area of Maltby on 6 May 1964.

The horrendous death and mutilation of fourteen-year-old Shirley Ann Boldy has been well-documented, as has the manufactured charge of manslaughter with diminished responsibility that the judge, Sir Bernard Joseph Maxwell MacKenna QC, had to navigate around during his trial at Sheffield Crown Court. There are, however, things that have not.

Wombwell had been the central point – his base from which to operate, with the outlying areas of South and West Yorkshire being his hunting ground. Make no mistake, his mother was in no way innocent in all this, as she knew exactly who he was and what he was doing.

Shirley Ann had gone home for lunch on the penultimate day of school and never returned.

Back then, Wombwell's landscape was much different to what we see now, with new residential developments springing up following the construction of the Dearne Valley Parkway.

Pickering had cased his prey as she made her way back to Wombwell County Secondary School from her home on Hemingfield Road and when the moment arrived had bundled the girl into the back of his van. It is assumed that she made the short journey across Wombwell Park and got accosted around the area of Wentworth View and Elliot Avenue, although without the criminal depositions – which the Department of Prosecutions (again) refused to release, I cannot be certain. What is known is that she was bound and gagged before being driven off to some remote spot far enough away from Wombwell but near enough timewise, to indulge his urge, with the area around the northern periphery of Thurnscoe being his destination.

Howell Wood is ancient woodland that is blessed with soft banks and meandering streams, whilst during spring it boasts the picturesque sight of carpets of violet-blue flowers along with the distant sound of the cuckoo.

During the early days of my parents' separation and our life down on The Avenues, my dad was often in a conundrum of what to do during his weekend visitation / access rights – especially when that day had been a Sunday. I recall times when he would get away from the cold house on Maori Avenue and take me for a walk up Clayton Lane to what he always termed as the *Bluebell Wood*, which back then had been private land and not the scenic country park that it is now.

"When me and your mam were courting, we always used to go on walks," he would tell me. "There used to be a stream in Bella Wood, where we used to take our shoes of and paddle."

His stories always had my attention – however, the most interesting one he had told me had been when we had been on our way to Bridlington where he dropped out the eerie story of the *Ghost Bus*. This had supposedly been seen during the late 1940s – early 1950s and was apparently a bus full of dead people with no driver – a vehicle with no brakes careering down a scarp at speed.

It frightened the life out of me if I am being honest.

The tale had some truth in it and was based on a runaway bus full of holiday makers being ferried to the coast by the Merseyside Touring Company, which after running of control, had crashed on Garrowby Hill on 1 August 1931. The bus had been going at a terrific speed when its brakes failed. It eventually collided with a car coming towards it and overturned in a ditch. What made the story all the more eerie is that when the police arrived there had been no passengers in the car – even though the car's engine was running.

There is an explanation for everything, but I reckon that would definitely ruin the story!

The Bluebell (Howell) Wood was always a great place to listen to his tales and was a place where I often took my children when they were young.

Unfortunately, it too had a dark history – not at least the estranged husband who murdered his three children, whilst taking his own life on some wet miserable Wednesday afternoon in November 1976.

Although this particular day had been sunny with temperatures touching the mid-seventies, the sun certainly hadn't been shining for Shirley Ann, who, when the car reached its destination, had been brutally raped.

What happened next is unclear. It is said that he needed to silence his only witness – however, that could have been done straight after the deed along with the dumping of the body. His next destination, therefore, had been the Church of All Saints located between the villages of Clayton and Hooton Pagnell. A beautiful albeit isolated structure that is surrounded by fields and approached by a gated country road. It is a place I know very well.

During the summer of 1994, whilst on a walk with the wife and kids, a Ford Escort had been parked up the road to the church, with some suspicious activity going on inside, which if truth-be-known, had been quite hard to ignore. I therefore tapped on the window and put an end to the sordid sex show.

That told you everything that you needed to know about Pickering's second destination. He didn't take her there to kill, he took her there for part two of his Holy Trinity. It was here that the psychopath set about torturing her.

The pattern was always the same – however, what the police were unaware of, was how he went about this warped three-phased approach. That was until the murder case for Elsie Frost was reopened in 2015. Their three-year investigation uncovered two lockups – one of which was in the Owlerton area of Sheffield. It was in this building where Pickering had hoarded details of his dark deeds and fantasies. The police found handcuffs, women's underwear, diaries, letters, paintings and exercise books filled with his depraved thoughts – including one which had been eerily etched in ink and had been dated 27 October 1970: "Rape, torture, kill."

"Peter Pickering's problem is that he is a hoarder," said Det. Supt. Nick Wallen from West Yorkshire Police's Homicide and Major Enquiries (cold Case) Team. "Everything he had been writing and drawing over the last forty-to-fifty years whilst in custody, he had kept and then sent to distant relatives, who stored it for him. He had two of these lockups paid for from his mum's estate. They were floor to ceiling with boxes and suitcases. Officers had to read several hundred thousand bits of paper."

There it was in black and white. His relatives had not only been covering his tracks, they had also been withholding material evidence in a murder, as the police were never in any doubt that he had also murdered Elsie Frost. However, I will get to that later.

As part of the inquiry, the detectives looked back through Pickering's conversations with psychiatrists – which resulted in a woman coming forward and Pickering being charged with the rape and false imprisonment of a woman in the Deepcar area of Sheffield on the Sunday morning of 11 June 1972. It was around four weeks before he would drive his grey Mini van up the short access road into the Church of All Saints.

The girl, who was eighteen years old at the time, had been taken to a secluded spot and subjected to a violent rape, followed by her being both handcuffed and tortured.

Sir James Richard William Goss QC presided over the trial at Leeds Crown Court and heard details of how Pickering had burned her breasts, before going on to enact the Holy Ghost element of his three-part metaphor. "I expected him to kill me there and then. I do remember him saying 'I'll have to kill you'," she told the jury. "I was terrified. It was like someone flicked a switch and he went berserk."

Even though the woman described herself as being a 'naïve eighteen-year-old who lived a closeted existence with her strict family', she, unlike Shirly Ann, who was much younger, managed to bullshit him enough, save her life.

"He wanted to know if he had taken my virginity," she added.

That *Me factor* again.

"Notwithstanding that, she had the good sense and wit to try to distract him," Crown Prosecutor Michelle Colbourne QC went on to add. "She assured him that she would not tell anyone and continued to reassure him, and his mood became relaxed."

How long Shirley Ann had to endure her aggressor, whilst down the tracks to the church is anyone's guess but was is known is that she finally met her end in Barnburgh Craggs.

The Craggs run parallel with what is termed as Marr Drag – the fast section of the A635 between Hickleton and Marr Lodge – a place that has seen the road deaths of many people I grew up with. It is therefore accessed from two points, with the western access being opposite the grounds of Hickleton Hall and far eastern access, where it is craggiest and where it therefore takes its name, being that of Hangman Stone Lane.

Three men who had been working in the vicinity had noticed the van reverse into a gap into the Craggs off Hangman Stone Lane. At first, they assumed it was some courting couple as there was movement in the vehicle and as with the road up to All Saints Church, the spot was known to be quite popular.

However, as the men got closer to the vehicle, they saw a disturbing site through its rear window. A teenaged girl lay in the back, naked from the waist down but still wearing white socks and a man wearing yellow marigold gloves who was holding a twelve-inch kitchen knife in his hand. The men heard a scream and saw the girl's legs kicking and shaking. Whilst trying to intervene, the man with the knife managed to start up the vehicle and drive off, almost running them over.

They did, however, manage to record the number plate of the vehicle and went to report what they had witnessed to police.

At 8.35 p.m. on the Thursday after Shirley's death, the van was traced and the man in possession of the vehicle was arrested by police in Wombwell. It was Peter Pickering.

"She mentioned something about her mother, and something snapped inside me," said Pickering. "I tore the clothes off her. I was out of my mind. The least I can do is keep the girl's good name. She fought hard and never asked for any of this. She was a pure girl."

Note the references to virginity and pure. Make no mistake – this man was a total fucking fruit loop.

"The facts of the case are quite the worst and most appalling I have ever had to deal with and I dare say they will come high in that way with your Lordship," Crown Prosecutor, Barry Mortimer QC told Justice Mackenna at

Sheffield Crown Court in December 1972. "They were sub-human acts that could only be described as the acts of a monster."

There was much more to this case, however. He had killed before.

Born premature, Peter Pickering was born in Park Hospital (renamed Trafford General) in the Daveyhulme area of Manchester on 6 October 1937. He grew up at nearby 151 Bradfield Road in Urmston – an innocuous three bedroomed semi-detached house located between junctions 8 and 9 of the M60, that is still there.

His mother – a Wombwell girl by the name of Florence Irene Wilson had married a thirty-three-year-old farmer by the name of Edmund Warrington Pickering at the town's parish church on 14 April 1937. After the Second World War, the family relocated to the Dearne Valley – firstly living at the bottom of Darfield's Snape Hill at 2 Garden Street (now Shayam Stores) between 1948 and 1954 and then at 69 High Street, Wath-on-Dearne – a building that is now the Pizza Palace. This alone, tells you quite a lot. His parents were business-minded people – something which saw Pickering left a substantial legacy after their death.

By 1960, Pickering was supposedly living at the address on Barnsley Road with both his mother and grandmother – Florence Wilson. I say supposedly as the reality was, that he was actually sharing a house on Wombwell's Hough Lane. This was with a man who shared similar interests to himself.

Pickering had been free just five months after being released from a nine-year prison sentence prior to him killing Shirley Ann. These were for sex attacks in Doncaster and Scarborough during 1966.

However, it hadn't been his first sortie into his Holy Trinity. He had been questioned several times regarding other sexually-driven crimes – most notably for the murders of Elsie Frost and Anne Dunwell.

Elsie Frost had been killed in an underpass beneath the railway line that runs between Wakefield Kirkgate railway station and Horbury. She was stabbed five times: twice in the head, twice in the back and once in the hand whilst trying to protect herself. One of the wounds in her back, pierced her heart and caused her to bleed to death.

"Peter Pickering, in my view, is a homicidal maniac and I am absolutely convinced that he killed Elsie Frost," said Nick Wallen.

Pickering had been wanted for sexual assaults on two girls at the time of Elsie's murder and the day after she was murdered the police had put Pickering's home in Wombwell under twenty-four-hour surveillance. Unfortunately, Pickering was one step ahead of the police. He knew they were there and came and went dressed as a woman, eventually escaping custody following a car chase.

As for the murder of Anne Dunwell, the case was reopened in 2002 as the *oldest unsolved murder in South Yorkshire* – something which you could look at one or two ways in that the statement was either right or it was wrong. Gladys Merricks murder in Goldthorpe in 1943 sits as being the oldest unsolved murder, but the truth is – there was a confession to Gladys's murder on 30 January 1951.

On 3 September 1949, a prisoner and escort scenario ensued when Chief Insp. Fenton Schofield and Det. Insp. George Maskill picked their subject up from Manchester and took him to Doncaster Police Station for questioning. After being questioned for six hours, the man was eventually admitted to Sheffield's Middlewood Hospital.

Nearly eighteen months later and that thirty-two-year-old man was in front of Sheffield Magistrates with Insp. Philip Bennison telling the *South Yorkshire Times*: "We believe this man is a psychopath."

Douglas Fair had indeed confessed to the murder of Gladys Merricks and had been held overnight and questioned by Sheffield CID.

Unfortunately, however, Douglas Fair was never mentally fit for trial – and as I have already said, he spent the majority of his life between both Middlewood and Broadmoor Hospital's.

He also suffered from ischaemic heart disease and hypertension in later life and whilst he had been a patient in a mental care home on Coatham Road in Redcar. He died in Middlesbrough General Hospital on 26 December 1997, aged seventy-eight – the cause of death being renal failure.

Mary Elizabeth Fair (now Gunn) – the little girl and daughter of Douglas Fair, who had lived at 43 Chapel Lane, Thurnscoe during wartime and whose mother Ellen had to endure not at least her husband's psychotic personality but threats to kill her – had been at her father's bedside.

Douglas Fair, as with Peter Pickering, had possessed very similar traits.

Remember what clothing Gladys had been wearing on her body being discovered?

DNA exonerated Pickering of her murder of Anne Dunwell – however, what it did reveal was that her killer had possessed a sexually transmitted disease.

"Just before the May Day Bank Holiday of 1964, the girl had gone on a shopping trip with her grandmother, who bought her a new, pale blue coat with a Peter Pan collar," read a report in the *Yorkshire Post* in May 2014. "The thirteen-year-old got to wear it a few days later when she set off from her home on Sandringham Avenue, Whiston, near Rotherham, to visit her aunt and uncle – John and Irene Varah around three and a half miles away in Howard Road, Bramley.

"It was a simple five-minute bus journey down the A614 Bawtry Road and no different to alighting the bus outside Taylor's Shoe Shop in Goldthorpe and getting off at Brough's in Thurnscoe.

"She had been planning to stay for a few days but knowing her grandfather was working the night shift at one of the Sheffield steelworks, the teenager decided to go back and keep her grandmother company."

It was a decision that would cost the little girl her life.

Anne, the daughter of Samuel and Elsie (nee Jones) had moved in with her grandparents following the death of her mother, who had sadly died when she was just five years old.

Witnesses remembered seeing a young girl standing near a bus stop shortly after 9.15 p.m. on 6 May. Remember that last bit – the *bus stop*.

No one quite knows what happened next, except Anne, who spent most weekends with her father at his home in Berkley Street, Attercliffe.

At 7.30 a.m. the following day, a lorry driver by the name of Thomas Wilson who had been travelling to work, made a gruesome discovery whilst driving down Slade Hooton Lane. This is a winding and remote country lane near Hooton Levitt – located just south of Maltby and which was the complete opposite direction that the girl had intended travelling.

"I was driving down the lane when I saw what I thought was a tailor's dummy with its feet in the hedge and back on a manure heap," he told police. "I thought it was a practical joke and drove on. When I got to work, I told my brother-in-law what I had seen and just to make sure we drove back. We went within two yards of the body, which had a stocking round its neck, and noticed that the legs were badly bruised. There were also bruises on the face – and the arms seemed as if they had been placed behind the back."

"Anne suffered a dastardly and perverted sexual assault and appeared to have been dumped from the motor vehicle while still alive," said Head of West Riding CID – Det. Chief Supt. Clifford Lodge, who had been leading the manhunt.

The body was that of a young female and was naked – except for a pair of stockings one of which had been wrapped tightly around the neck. It was some hours later that it was revealed to be the body of Anne Dunwell. The post-mortem was to reveal that she had suffered a savage sexual attack, before ultimately being strangled with her own stocking. No other clothing was found near the body.

Again, it not only bore similarities to Gladys Merricks, but was also a killing absolutely identical to that of Heather Rata – the girl who had been murdered by Ken Rolfe, formerly of East Croft, Bolton-on-Dearne.

A massive police hunt was launched, with a mass widespread search of the surrounding areas being undertaken and enquiries made in the area to establish Anne's final movements. Within a week hundreds of actions had been completed and thousands of statements taken. Anne's last known movements had been traced. It was established that she never caught the 9.29 p.m. bus home as no one could recall a girl matching her description being on the vehicle.

Someone matching her description had been seen near the bus stop at around the crucial time, however.

Had she been abducted off the street as in the case of Shirley Ann Boldy some eight years later or had she got into a car after accepting a lift from her killer?

Anne's family firmly believed that she would never have accepted a lift from a stranger.

Therefore, police worked on the theory that Anne had either been forcibly snatched from the bus stop or had begun to walk towards home and had accepted a lift from her killer – not some random stranger, but someone that she knew.

Five days into the investigation, the search area moved to Ulley Reservoir, some six miles from where Anne's body was found. Ramblers had found some items of clothing, including a pale blue coat with the unmistakable Peter Pan type (Twiggy) collar, at the water's edge – and this was soon identified as belonging to the girl. A specialist team of police frogmen from Nottingham searched the reservoir and were soon to find other items that were identified as having belonged to Anne. This included the wicker basket that she was carrying when she was last seen alive.

It would be many years later, thanks to advancements in forensic science, that the clothing was to provide useful evidence and give an insight into Anne's killer.

Detectives were also left to sift through a multitude of potential suspects, suspect vehicles, and potentially crucial sightings. This was after an appeal had been made to courting couples who had possibly been in the area of the murder scene at the time, and therefore may have seen something of relevance to come forward.

One such couple did. They reported seeing a dark-haired man between twenty-one and twenty-seven years old, and a girl both parked in blue saloon car in a clearing in Slacks Lane – a lane near to the bus stop where Anne was last seen at about 11.00 p.m. The courting couple remembered the sighting vividly because the couple in the saloon car had been struggling – and their car headlights had picked this out as they had passed. This *struggling* couple were never neither identified nor came forward for elimination.

It was always assumed that this had been Anne and her killer.

By the end of May, detectives were no further in their investigation despite having spoken to more than 10,000 people during the enquiry. They did, however, have a suspect that they wished to trace, and an identikit picture was placed in the local press.

This person of interest was also described as being of medium build and between 5'5 and 5'6, with a thin, pockmarked face and nose. He had short dark brown hair worn in a wavy, brushed back style, and was clean-shaven.

The man also drove a dark grey Mini van and was known to offer lifts to young girls – including pupils of Wickersley Secondary Modern – Anne's school. Several names were given to the incident room as the potential killer, and although these were investigated, no arrests were ever made.

Despite the massive investigation the enquiry into Anne's murder was gradually scaled down and then remained a cold case for many years.

There was, however, something that brought Clifford Lodge back into the area soon after, thinking that the killer may have struck again as there were similarities with another murder in Doncaster on 31 August 1964.

The half-naked body of twelve-year-old Lynn Midgley of Albany Road, Balby had been found dumped in a copse off some field near Florence Avenue. The little girl had been both sexually assaulted and strangled. There was no connection, however – Lynn had been killed by a fourteen-year-old by the name of David Albert Bennett. The boy had been diagnosed with having an illness that had caused him brain damage and was sentenced at Sheffield Assizes on 23 October 1964 after he pleaded guilty of manslaughter with diminished responsibility. He was to be detained for life.

With the huge advances in investigative work and forensic science, South Yorkshire Police made the decision to re-open the enquiry in 2002. The original statements and actions were looked at, and an appeal along with the reconstruction of Anne Dunwell's last known movements was shown on *Crimewatch UK*. Even after all this time, new witnesses came forward offering information.

This included a woman who had been fifteen at the time of Anne's murder. She was not only someone who had gone to school with her but who had seen her on the night she died walking along the A614 Bawtry Road in Wickersley and heading towards Whiston at about 9.45 p.m. This seemed to confirm police suspicions that Anne had never boarded the bus that evening and had instead begun to walk towards home. Therefore, she was halfway home when she had met her killer.

Also highlighted, was a different person of interest, that was also never traced, and who rapidly became the prime suspect in Anne's murder. A witness who had been spoken to at the time of the original 1964 investigation had been re-interviewed about her statement and was now able to provide additional information. The witness had described seeing a girl – likely Anne – walking towards a van parked near The Ball Inn on the evening of Anne's murder. In addition, this witness now recalled that the driver of the man was wearing cufflinks. This became significant because it tallied with other descriptions of a person of interest who had been reported in 1964, but one who was never traced.

This man had been seen in the public house just a week before Anne was killed, where a barmaid recalled serving him a brandy. The witness who gave the description recalled talking at length to the man, who had mentioned that he had worked in Rotherham and Doncaster at times.

Remember that bit. He had worked in Rotherham and Doncaster.

What was interesting is that the Ball Inn had held live entertainment on Wednesday evenings and had therefore been full of people who had travelled from all over the area – yet despite so many people being in the pub, this man had stood out. Why? Not only had the man given off the impression that he was well-educated, he was also chain-smoking Craven A cigarettes, which he kept in a silver case, and he wore distinctive jewellery – including those cufflinks.

A detailed physical description was given of the man, that concurred with the others but what stood out was that he had spoken with a soft Scottish accent which police believed was conversant with someone from the Inverness area.

"Perhaps the most important breakthrough in the re-opened enquiry in 2002 was the obtaining of a workable DNA profile from the clothing that had been used to strangle Anne. Forensic scientists were able not only to obtain a DNA sample of the killer from traces of semen found in the knots but were also able to show that the killer suffered from gonorrhoea," explained Nick Wallen.

What threw the investigation is that it appeared highly likely that Anne's killer was from the Yorkshire area, and was expressly familiar with the areas of Bramley and Whiston. Everything about the murder suggested a local knowledge – someone either having lived around the area or worked there.

It is likely that the killer of Anne Dunwell had offended before – if he had, it would have been most likely for sexual offences, or offences of violence.

Some reports say that following the re-investigation, the pool of suspects in Anne's murder had been narrowed down to just two – both of whom were dead. It was said that Peter Pickering was the only one who had still been alive at the time. Everything pointed to him – however, the one thing DNA doesn't do, is lie.

The appeal put out on *Crimewatch UK* produced one new lead and this only came about after police fed the old material through the Holmes forensics computer programme – and police believed that the man they were desperate to trace may have returned to Scotland.

I don't have access to the NPC (National Police Computer) nor any of the evidence such statements or indeed photograph's but rather strangely, I do have a name that fits the profile – a possible suspect, that could exude a bit of levity if the case wasn't so serious.

On 16 August 1960 a case was held in camera at Doncaster Court after defence solicitor Donald Dunn said that the publication of evidence would prejudice the case. The application had been supported by Prosecutor, Richard C. Linney and the court was consequently cleared.

The case involved girls of between fifteen and seventeen years old from Doncaster, Sheffield and Keighley.

Twenty-two-year-old Peter Pickering and a twenty-five-year-old by the name of Richard Dick Weepers (remember the sexually transmitted disease) had both been accused of raping a seventeen-year-old girl and indecently assaulting another female. Pickering was also accused of four other offences: attempting to rape a fifteen-year-old, the assault of a fifteen-year-old girl and another female occasioning them ABH. He was also charged with indecently assaulting another female. Pickering was remanded in custody whilst Weepers had been given bail.

According to the court documentation, both these men lived together on Hough Lane, Wombwell.

What is interesting about Weepers is that not only was he Scottish – he had for a time lived at 1A Castle Street in Inverness.

On 23 March 1953 Pte Richard Weepers – (2229597) of the Royal Scots Fusiliers was jailed after appearing at Aberdeen Sheriff Court. He had pleaded guilty to housebreaking in both Aberdeenshire and Inverness-shire. He and another soldier had been on the run from the Army at the time.

Procurator Fiscal A. MacLeod said that both had been in military detention at Dreghorn Barracks when they cleared out and embarked on a series of offences, both being apprehended in Aberdeen.

Weepers, it was said, had signed on for seven years when he was fifteen years old and had spent time overseas in Germany and India. The impression of being *well-educated and well-travelled*, maybe?

For that offence, he was jailed for three months.

Not long after that he would turn up in the Wanless Street area of the City of Durham in a post office van, which was claimed had been stolen in Edinburgh following him leaving home after some fight with his stepfather.

The Chairman, Alderman Mrs H.H. Rushford told Weepers in court: "It is a dreadful thing to find a nineteen-year-old youth with a record like yours. We think the best thing we can do is to send you to prison."

Weepers would marry a twenty-two-year-old woman in the Consett area of Durham by the name of Brenda Short in 1958 and have a child… but by 1960, he would be living in Wombwell – with Peter Pickering.

Now, where could a man with both Scottish and military roots meet a manipulative free-loading ponce such as Peter Pickering? How did he get to be sharing a home with him in Wombwell?

Weepers had been sentenced to six months. Did he perhaps meet him in Durham or Armley Gaol and their personalities click or was it something else? There had to be some mechanism that took Weepers from a married life in Durham to Hough Lane in Wombwell. What is interesting is that Weepers would also be employed as a bus conductor, who by being based in the town, could have quite easily worked the Barnsley – Rotherham routes as he could those between Thurnscoe and Mexborough or indeed Maltby and Wickersley. He was a man who was not only familiar with just the area, but also its public transport.

As for Anne, she was laid to rest on 13 May 1963 in Tinsley Park Cemetery, Sheffield.

Det. Chief Insp. Dave Stopford of South Yorkshire Police is currently handling the cold case. Weepers died in October 1996, his last address being a one-bedroomed flat in the Duffryn area of Newport. What remains of Anne Dunwell's family deserve closure. Maybe Dave Stopford should try working some familial DNA – and request a swab from Weepers' daughter.

My feelings of the police, however, is that they are heavily restricted by budget and can be both lazy and useless. This is something that becomes very apparent after they dropped into Bolton-on-Dearne as part of another high-profile cold case.

Left to Right. Anne Dunwell, Elsie Frost and Shirley Ann Boldy. All killed in a sexually motivated murder. Anne's murder remains unsolved - however, Douglas Fair formerly of Thunscoe, Kenneth Rolfe formerly of Bolton-on-Dearne and Richard Dick Weepers formerly of Wombwell would have been persons of interest in the investigation of her murder.

Top. St Andrews Square, Bolton-on-Dearne circa 1955. Bottom Left. FW Woolworths on Doncaster Road, Goldthorpe circa. 1961 Bottom Right. Goldthorpe Police Station and Junior and Infant School on the Goldthorpe Lane Ends/High Street Junction circa 1955.

35. Going to Hell

"He said he had murdered him," she said. "He told me he'd rammed a red-hot poker down his throat."

Those were the exact words of Jacqueline Smith (nee Cooper).

Jacqueline and her husband David had been our next-door neighbours when I had been a young boy. They, along with their two young children, had lived at 16 Landsdowne Avenue whilst Guiseppe (Joe) Citarella and his family had been our others at No 12.

Jacqueline also had a son who was killed on 28 January 2012.

She hadn't been referring to the death of her son, however, but of a thirty-three-year-old man by the name of Albert Formstone, who met his end some sixty-one years earlier.

What is strange is that I can draw huge comparisons and indeed connections, with both killings.

Remember the story of the man outside on Lancaster Street, screaming and shouting late one night – and something which had been stirred up by the fact that his wife had been tucked-up inside the house next door and being wooed by Gerry Crossland – if wooed, is indeed the right word. Well, that was the person who had been responsible for the death of Albert Formstone on 31 December 1950.

Bill Cooper had gone into Goldthorpe Police Station with William Round to seek protection from a gang, that had been predominantly led by the Formstones, who had been smashing up their house at 33 Victoria Street and threatening their family.

William Round had hooked up with a widow by the name of Maud Cooper (nee Allen) whose husband William Ephrain had died in 1936, aged thirty-three.

At the time of her husband's death she had lived in one of the stone-built houses at 47 Butcher Street, but after shacking-up with William Round moved into one of the set-back and rather imposing terraced properties that formed Betts Buildings at 101 Lidget Lane. What was strange, is that Maud – who was originally from Derbyshire, encouraged William to leave the area during the Second World War, and for a short time the family relocated to Bolsover – she and William eventually tying the knot in 1943.

Why they came back to the area two years later is unclear, as is the reason the gang, headed by the Formstones decided to single-out Maud's twenty-year-old son.

The story was, that Bill Cooper had been involved in an altercation with Albert Formstone on Boxing Day night, with Formstone dying a few days later.

Although the cause of death was given as meningitis, both Bill Cooper and his fifty-three-year old stepfather were charged with both grievous bodily harm and manslaughter and as such, were remanded pending trial.

Albert Formstone's family originated from Wrexham in North Wales – his grandfather working on the heavily trafficked Shrewsbury – Chester railway line.

It appears that Alfred Formstone's marriage to Barnburgh-born girl Edith Catchpole in 1904 was the catalyst for more of the family to come to work in the mines in the eastern Dearne Valley – their families initially settling in Goldthorpe's north-eastern terraces – that of Co-operative and Victoria Street.

His father and some of his uncles were part of that batch, including Henry's son and namesake, who made the news after being involved in a brawl at a summer dance in Goldthorpe's Welfare Hall on 15 July 1933.

That was certainly nothing new.

On 31 January 1925, Roy Trubshaw made the news after he was sentenced to twelve months in Armley Gaol for grievous bodily harm. Some argument had taken place in The Welfare Hall and he ended up slashing a lad across the face with a cut-throat razor.

As a precursor to the Formstone's, Roy had been something of a headcase and part of a gang from Goldthorpe that frequented the local racetracks. As for the lad he striped – Joseph Baker – he had lived with his parents at 18 Co-operative Street and worked on the haulage down Hickleton Main.

Roy married a couple of times during the 1940s and spent the remainder of his life at 35 St Mary's Road, Goldthorpe, using the three allotments he had nearby, whilst helping run a book. Later in life he would be registered blind and passed away in Bolton-on-Dearne's Dearne Valley Nursing Home in 1995, aged ninety-three.

It could be, that Roy was related to Walter Henry Trubshaw – the man who slayed his family on Mexborough's Adwick Road in 1904 – however, I cannot be certain.

"The Formstone's were a bad lot," explained Walt Claydon – the reluctant hero who left the employ of Barnsley MBC and opened the Home and Garden DIY centre on Barnburgh Lane in 1978.

"Against both her parents' wishes, an old friend of mine, Mary Whitworth, married Ernie Formstone and true to their word, he was a complete bastard with her, and she ended up divorcing him."

Remember the story about Henry and Mary Formstone – the couple who lost the two children at 14 Cooperative Street in 1913? Well they had Ernie a year later, who when he was twenty years old was part of a high-profile case whereby he had been one of two men charged with indecently assaulting an eighteen-year-old girl by the name of Elizabeth Parton, while she had been walking home from Goldthorpe Feast.

In the post-war years however, he had been part of the gang who had been terrorizing William Round and his family. As for Mary – her parents had been the steward and stewardess in the Golden Nugget WMC (Pigeon Club) on Co-operative Street.

The Formstones had had some indifferent history, prior to Albert being killed – most notably, four of his grandfather's brothers.

On 7 September 1853, nine-year-old James Formstone, died after getting caught beneath a train laden with lime on the Chester – Shrewsbury railway line.

"He was either attempting to get upon the wagons or got too close to them," explained the County Coroner, Bevis Haywood Thelwall. "He was knocked down and the carriages went over his body, mangling it in quite a shocking manner."

On 27 June 1866, Henry Formstone was found guilty of being involved in a robbery from the Great Western Railway Company at Chester Railway Station and sentenced to hard labour in the city's Gaol.

On 30 September 1883, thirty-three-year-old William Formstone had had a major quarrel with his wife and had slung her and the kids out, only for her to return to find that he had somehow fractured his skull and set himself on fire – the police explaining that his body had been burning for at least forty-five minutes, when they had finally forced entry into the house.

And on 22 October 1918, sixty-six-year-old James Formstone – the younger brother of the dead brother of the same name – had been sentenced to hard labour after being found guilty of manslaughter.

All good stuff, eh?

As for Albert Formstone, he married the daughter of Enoch and Jane Haynes (nee Fudge) – the latter of whose descendants would go on to marry one of the sons, whose mother had been stabbed to death in what was known as *The Lover's Lane Murder* in 1963.

The Haynes family, just like the Formstones, had lived in Goldthorpe's north-eastern terraces – their homes being opposite one another at 102 and 109 Main Street respectively – moving into 47 Nora Street after their marriage and later on to 113 Doncaster Road – the exact house which Albert Formstone got carried home to, both unconscious and covered in blood, before finally checking out in Mexborough Montagu Hospital.

Doreen Haynes had married a man off Mexborough's Roman Terrace by the name of Robert Lenton, who sadly died two years after their marriage in 1934, aged twenty-eight.

It is unclear when Albert Formstone began seeing Doreen Lenton – however, one thing that is certain, is that she became pregnant and a quick marriage ensued, prior to her dropping the little bundle of joy (sic) that was Joseph (Joe) in late-1946.

Albert Formstone was not only part of Goldthorpe's post-war gang culture, he was also an active member of the Goldthorpe branch of Barnsley FC Supporters Club – and at a time, when the two went hand in hand. After five years of war, people wanted an outlet and Britain's post-war boom saw attendances at football rise. Back then, both Christmas Day and Boxing Day had a full card of matches, when the same two teams met both home and away. In this instance, Albert's team were neck and neck with their local rivals in League Division II and the bragging rights had been well and truly up for grabs.

That Christmas Day, Albert Formstone had been one of the 28,742 attendance at Doncaster Rovers' Belle Vue ground eagerly geeing his football team on and trying their best at coming back from a 3-0 deficit at half time, only for the home side to hold on and come out 3-2 winners.

The very next day, retribution was on the cards and 33,894 turned up to see Barnsley get their revenge. However, that never happened, and Doncaster Rovers came away with a 1-0 victory. Albert's Christmas was ruined – however, panning someone's face in might have helped take the *edge* off.

"Everybody will tell you how nasty the Formstones were," added Walt.

The four-year-old Joe would have been tucked up in bed, when his father had gone mob-handed to William Round's home, allegedly shouting his stepson out for a fight.

Albert Formstone, however, was no match for what he was about to meet.

Bill Cooper had been not only been thirteen years younger – he had also been armed.

He may have slightly embellished the story of the poker to anyone who cared to listen, but there had been a smidgen of truth to his story.

"Get out of the house and fight me, you yellow fucking bastard," Formstone was alleged to have shouted.

What isn't known is the motivation of why Formstone had gone mob-handed to William Round's home to fight his stepson, as there must have been some reasoning behind the events leading up to the altercation. What is known, however, is that Formstone, pissed off with him ignoring his abuse, went around the side of the end terrace and up the backings, intent on dragging him out of his house to give him a good leathering. It was a mistake. Bill Cooper had been ready for him and duly wrapped a poker around his face putting him firmly on the deck. It was then, when Cooper and his stepfather, were alleged to have started putting the boot in.

According to Barnsley Pathologist, Dr David Price, who conducted the post-mortem examination – Albert Formstone had two black eyes along with compound fractures to his nose, both cheeks and upper jaw. He had been badly beaten up.

A total of twenty-seven witnesses had been involved in what would be a highly complex trial at Leeds Assizes – however, no-one who actually witnessed the altercation went to the police.

Several people came out of the woodwork in later years, claiming the beating had been extremely vicious. The Formstone's, however, had intended to take matters into their own hands, so much so, both Bill Cooper and his stepfather had had to hand themselves in to the police and request protection.

It does appear, however, that Albert Formstone got what had been coming to him.

Now, it is here, where the story eventually comes into the here and now.

During 1978, two lads wearing the royal blue jerseys of Dearneside Comprehensive began alighting the 273 at the Stuart Street/ Norman Street bus stop, which was just a few yards away from where three years into the future I would overtake Wayne Tansley on his Suzuki ER50 moped – and in true Quadrophenian style, hem him in before kicking him off it, causing him to crash the bike. That had been a bit of retribution for him running out in the middle of Lancaster Street and throwing a half brick at my head when I had been riding between both arms of Hanover Street a few days earlier. As I said – a great kid, Wayne!

That aside, these two sharp-faced Herberts appeared weedy in frame and possessed a rather pontificating nature about them. One of them was also cross-eyed.

Michael and Martin were two of the three offspring of Joseph Formstone – the four-year-old lad whose father had been both beaten up and killed by Bill Cooper.

"My granddad wants to meet you," came a recent, albeit eerie request via social media.

That wasn't a problem and I told him as much.

"And so do I, smart arse," it added.

It is here where social media falls down. A person may be some whiny little bitch in real life, but on outlets such as Twitter, Instagram and indeed Facebook, they can pretend to be something that they are certainly not. And this was one such case.

I looked at the photo on his moniker – the sharp piercing jaw, the arrogant stance and wanted nothing more than to go over to Goldthorpe and fucking waste him.

Craig Formstone was the son of Michael, grandson of Joseph, the great-grandson of Albert and in my opinion nothing more than a fucking troll.

A bout of messages ensued, which he thought about responding to but thankfully didn't. His grandfather, however, thought it prudent to send me a letter through the amiable managing partner of Walter Brook & Co. solicitors, which made its way directly into my bin.

Why? Because he knew I was going to tell the story. The story of a trouble causer who got his comeuppance.

There is more to the story, however – much more, in that the gang led by the Formstones may have had a valid reason for the threats and violence.

"Bill Cooper was a nasty piece of work," said Jacqueline Smith. "A big fat horrible bastard."

He had been forty-five-years-old when he had married Jacqueline's thirty-three-year-old sister, Rita, in a marriage that lasted less than two years. There was a reason for this, too.

What should be known is that Rita's family – the Coopers – were in no way related to Bill's family. The only thing they shared apart from the barrel-making cognomen, was a house on Highgate's William Street.

"My sister was terrified of him," she added.

Now, it is here where I do have to tread very carefully.

"I used to babysit for her kids – the Chamberlain twats, Richard and Herbert!" was the glib retort given to me by Rita's nephew and Daz Cooper's elder brother, Jimmy.

Rita had had four children to her second (common-law) husband, Walter Chamberlain – two who lived with their father and two who did not.

She also had kids to her first husband – one of whom had been three years above me in Dearneside Comprehensive.

"He frequently used Highgate Club and the Halfway Hotel and there was always a lot of gossip at the time," Inky Thomson told me.

Her time in Dearneside had ended rather abruptly when she was taken into care by the social services, following sexual abuse from her stepfather. What was true is that Bill Cooper was a predatory paedophile – something which saw him handed a huge prison term. According to Jacqueline, he got sentenced to thirty-six years, but only did twelve – the reasons of which I do not know.

According to Inky, he had worked as a dustbin man and lived on Probert Avenue after his release from prison.

"He always maintained that he'd not committed the crime but had taken the wrap for another family member," Inky told me. "Not that anyone believed him, however."

The last I heard, the girl had married and for a time lived off Cusworth Lane in Scawsby, before moving out to Skipton.

As for Jacqueline, she would suffer the ultimate tragedy any parent could suffer.

When I had been in the last year of Houghton Road's infant school, I had been tasked with dropping off a letter at one of houses just around the first arc of Thornley Crescent. In early-1972, it was beginning to look a desperate place with its unkempt gardens, rubbish strewn all over and curtains hanging from windows. I look at the exact same spot where that address once stood, and it looks in a better state. Not much, but better all the same. The white door of the exterior electric box has been ripped off, there are kids' toys in the garden and the white scrawl on the green plastic dustbin tells me that its next-door neighbour is the mother of the thirty-six-year-old lad who was knifed less than fifty yards from where I had lived next door to her on Landsdowne Avenue.

It is hard to visualise a time and a place that was erased when you were a child.

I remember the Wednesday night of 5 November 1969 and of the one and only bonfire we ever had whilst growing up, and all the people there, eating buttered baked potatoes.

I had come in from school and watched both *Jackanory* and the Francesco Stefani-directed spooky load of rubbish that was the *Singing Ringing Tree* on TV, but all I really wanted, was to see the huge pile of wood in the front garden set alight. Even when my granddad Ellis had picked me up and taken me to pick up some Standard Fireworks and had called into Margarite (Ma) Greaves's café in the market place behind her home at 9 Shepherd Lane and bought me a bottle of Coca-Cola that is all I had thought about. I wasn't disappointed.

I think back to Landsdowne Avenue and its residents, not least the haughty rather know-it-all that was little Hannah Citerella who had been in the year above me and who lived next door – or the sweet little bespectacled girl who lived in the odd-numbered terrace opposite.

Michelle Ridyard (now Stevens) was a girl that I had gone all the way through the infants with. She had come into the world at No 5 and had been delivered by Pam Jackson who had lived three doors up from us and in the house that the Gethen family had vacated in 1959.

It is things such as this that help shape a community. Unfortunately, however, time isn't always kind and the Thurnscoe I grew up in would change dramatically.

It has always had its rough edge, not at least the Gethen family themselves – with its colourful head of the household that was Carmi who possessed a string of convictions as long as his arm – not at least for theft. However, it would be his grandson who would come to national attention and in a rather macabre way.

Carmi had married Doris Daykin in 1929 and had seven children – one of whom was Eric, who had been born in 1937.

Eric married twice – to Florence Turton in 1958, and Ann Law in 1993.

The first marriage produced nine children; his second, three – the youngest who was James.

At 3.15 a.m. on Sunday 15 August 2010 police were called to a property at 3 Beever Street, Goldthorpe and found the dead body of a thirty-nine-year-old woman who had literally had her skull caved in.

Ann Gethen had been killed by her then-fifteen-year old son, who, while she had been sitting on the settee, had beat her senseless with a baseball bat.

His complex trial at Sheffield Crown Court, was presided over by Justice Sir Charles Peter Lawford Openshaw QC – the man who would a year later go on to preside over Goldthorpe's *body in the boot* murder.

Through his defence barrister, Adrian Waterman QC, James Edward Gethen pleaded to manslaughter on the grounds of diminished responsibility and on 14 December 2011, after several adjournments due to medical reports, he was given an indeterminate sentence – having to serve a minimum term of five years.

"The attack involved a sustained and savage attack on his mother in the living room of the family home during the course of which the defendant used a baseball bat to strike a number of blows to her head, which killed her almost instantaneously," said Crown Prosecutor, Michael Smith QC.

Mrs Gethen died from massive head injuries and afterwards her son was alleged to have said: "I hit my mum round the head with a baseball bat. I could see her brains and everything. I don't care what I've done. I'm not bothered. I hope she's dead."

Mr Waterman said that the defendant accepted that he hit his mother with the bat and at the time had deliberately intended to hit her.

Mr Smith told the court the teenager had been born prematurely and contracted meningitis at just fifteen weeks old and that two psychiatrists had assessed him and concluded that the meningitis had indeed had a significant effect on his development, leaving him with severe behavioural and learning problems.

Although he went to a mainstream school, he exhibited episodes of disruptive behaviour and unprovoked compulsive violence on an almost daily basis. He was sexually abusive towards girls of his age and once attempted to strangle a fellow pupil with a ligature. He was eventually excluded and moved to a special school – h =owever, it made little difference. He continued to have anger management problems

Consultant Psychologist, Dr Paul Kent said: "This young man has an extremely complex and significant history of psychiatric disorders."

Mr Justice Openshaw said that one of the psychiatrists had described the teenager as "highly dangerous with an uncertain prognosis" and on sentencing him said: "There's a very high risk that he may cause serious harm to someone else. Neither I nor the doctors can say when, if ever, that danger may pass."

Although James Gethen's complex family life was touched upon, it didn't even scratch the surface of why what happened, happened.

Due to the legal restrictions regarding minors – as Gethen had of course been fifteen-years-old at the time, a lot of information was kept out of the public domain.

What was said is that his mother was a woman who had been thirty-four years younger than his father – the latter who had died on Boxing Day 2009, aged seventy-one and that James Gethen had had an extreme reaction to his death and that he had even "tried to enter the grave" and "wished at the time to be buried with his father".

Looking in from the outside, you have a twenty-year-old woman who had married a fifty-six-year-old man who had nine children from his previous marriage – and who after his death was living in a fire-damaged, boarded-up house in Goldthorpe's north eastern terraces.

This was anything but normal.

"When I lived at 51 Brunswick Street, I lived next door to them, and what I do know is that thirteen kids got sexually abused in there, up to 2006," explained Michelle Waldron. "Those that were abused, all lived on the street. The Social Services could have stopped a lot of it and didn't."

And there you had it. A failure of the system.

The house where Michelle Ridyard had lived – like the rest of The Avenues, would be demolished and yet another series of brick-built Wendy Houses would take their place. The void Michelle's house left would be occupied by what would become Marlborough Close – No 27 being the home of the-then thirty-seven-year-old Gary McKeown – the killer of Jacqueline Smith's son, Philip.

I had been left the area twelve years and I knew neither lad. Nor was I aware of how bad the village had become.

I recall going on a site visit to a mini tunnelling job in Lowestoft with some company director who lived over Brierley Common and him dropping me off on Briton Square.

"I can't believe you live on here?" he said.

That was April 1997.

It was nothing new, and as I have already said, something similar had been said to me before on 14 October 1990 and by a Detective Inspector at Wombwell Police Station after he had charged me with malicious wounding with intent to cause grievous bodily harm.

It was a reality check into what both I and the village had become.

I had been in bed late one Saturday night when I was awoken by what I assumed was a few lads outside my home, intent on causing trouble. It wasn't too dissimilar to the story of Albert Formstone, where their vitriol had been firmly aimed at me.

I hadn't been out to cause any trouble and nor had I been drinking. I had just been at home with my family.

At that time in my life I was still relatively young and therefore naive, although it had to be said, that I had already commenced a journey where I had begun not to worry too much about the consequences of violence. Therefore, giving someone or indeed someone's a kick in was par for the course. I worked in an overly aggressive environment where lads were often in and out of prison, some of whom were extremely capable units who could well and truly handle themselves and this alone, rubbed off on me and therefore the reality of the situation was simple. In my mind, I had to go out and confront them – especially as my four-year-old daughter was asleep in the front bedroom, and the last thing I wanted was a brick going through the window.

Nowadays, I am much older and hopefully, wiser, and although the outcome would be very much the same, I am much clearer with how I go about things. I always have an end game in that I know the outcome as soon as the first ball is bowled. Back then, however, that naivete was there for all to see. As I have already mentioned, I had crossed the divide coming from Bolton-on-Dearne into Thurnscoe and as a child had to endure being jumped by gangs of lads wanting nothing more than to lay the boot in. It is like anything else, after a while you get accustomed to it and it becomes the norm. To be confronted, say in a pub, by a group of lads, I will immediately weigh up the odds and if they do not favour me, I will try my best to neutralise the situation. I'll make no bones about it, they will be fucking dealt with, but it will always be on my terms. It is that end game that I mentioned.

In this instance, I had no idea who or what I was going out to, and here is the thing – I don't subscribe to poor odds, and I don't just mean by levelling the playing field – I mean I tip it firmly in my favour. I will never go out to something that I cannot walk back from.

I went out loaded – tooled-up. By the time I had got dressed and gone out into the street they were at the Square's end. There were four of them. The idea is as always to hit the first one with as much force as physically possible and hopefully maximise the damage moving straight on to the next. Gangs go in gangs for a reason – their numbers provide an intimidation that can dilute the possibility of any kick back. Immediately taking two out, cuts those odds in half and that is exactly what happened.

Rather strangely, one of them went for me first and I wrapped a hammer around his head, putting him on the floor and giving him a wound that required thirteen stitches. I then hit another in the lower back and had him hopping around and clutching the area around his kidneys. As for the other two – they were nothing more than a pair of fucking cowards and ran off. With one on the floor and blood pissing out of his head and the other acting like some drama queen I turned my back on them and walked home.

I was totally without feeling – emotionless. It certainly wasn't the worst beating I have ever handed someone, far from it – however, it was the first time I had ever gone out with that end game in mind. As with Albert Formstone – if you go to someone's home intent on causing trouble, you cannot expect to come out of it unscathed.

There is generally always a reasoning behind why something happens, and this was no different.

I had spent the early part of the year helping the football team that ran out of The Fairway get promotion. I liked a lot of the lads, but the problem that I had with it, is that I thought they were continually overlooking a couple of good young footballers one of whom was a quiet lad by the name of Tony Whitham, who at the time had lived on York Street. I had got quite pally with the owner of the pub that was at one time The Docket, and which had since been renamed The Stadium, and he offered up both the pub and its changing rooms.

As for me, I threw a bit of money at buying a football kit and pooling together some good young lads around the same age as Tony – some of whom became great local footballers.

At the time, Littlewood's football pools were the only form of fantasy escapism for the working man, and I had been no different. Our local agent had lived at 81 Briton Street – a frail, dithering, bald-headed man by the name of Johnny Thwaites.

Johnny was a man who it would be fair to say, just loved his family in that he spoiled his children to such an extent – they could do no wrong. That is not a failing, just pure, albeit misguided, love. It would be on my doorstep where he would dangle his youngest son's attributes in my face telling me that he had not only been a brilliant schoolboy boxer who had fought for the All-England title – he was also supposedly an excellent footballer.

Johnny's son and namesake had been a decent looking kid that had a facial appearance of the footballer Mick Harford, with the prominent forehead, sloping eyes and the nose. As soon as I okayed it, I had his lad and a few of his mates down at my house wanting to sign up for the team. These, he told me, had all been part of some all-conquering schoolboy side a few years prior. I knew some of them, but not all, and Johnny's young lad – well he was the outspoken leader of what would become a rather unhealthy clique. I say clique, as the young lad and his mates – although very good, played a game that was basically between themselves in that they wouldn't pass the ball to anyone who wasn't one of them. My solution had been a simple one. After being sick and tired of telling him what I wanted, I made him substitute for an away game on a sloping pitch against Darfield WMC.

"Right lads, let's go," he said, whilst in the dressing room, and he walked off taking six of his mates with him and leaving the team short.

Rather strangely, what he wanted never happened. He was expecting more to follow him and the rag-tag assortment of fill-ins played out of their skin to force a 2-2 draw, with Andy Peat – the son of Valerie – a 100 m sprinter, who competed in the 1968 Olympics in Mexico, scoring both our goals.

The spoiled brat's grand plan hadn't worked.

A week later, four of those five lads had been outside my home. Unfortunately, Johnny's kid – the ringleader, hadn't been one of them.

I look back on the events leading up to that night and firmly put the blame on his father. He spoiled his children to such an extent they felt a God-given right to be granted all of life's wishes. His kid couldn't get his own way, so he walked. He couldn't get a reaction, therefore he caused trouble. It is what is commonly referred to as a foot stamping bitch.

His elder sister had been no different. Debbie Thwaites was one hell of a conundrum.

Just before we left the area, her life ended in rather suspicious circumstances. It was alleged that she fell from a hotel balcony, whilst holidaying abroad with what I am informed was her same-sex partner. Unfortunately, in situations such as this, the only person that knows their intention is the person that is dead, therefore no-one really knows whether it was an accident, foul play or indeed suicide. My wife had been working as a clerk in the Thurnscoe East Post Office, when her distraught father came in through the door with her little boy and handed in her invalidity book. Debbie hadn't worked – she had had what is nowadays termed as mental problems (depression) and had been claiming sick money. Her father I am told was a broken man.

I was also told a story by my ex-girlfriend during 1982, that it was common knowledge that Debbie had also slashed her wrists, following what was the abrupt ending of a relationship with some lad off The Spike.

Whether or not her mental history was relayed at the coroner's inquest is unclear, so who knows?

It was a similar story with a girl who had lived on Thurnscoe's Thornley Crescent prior to its modernisation and rebrand. Cheryl Louise Norris's body was found at the foot of a high-rise tower block on St James Street, Doncaster in the early hours of 11 July 2018. It was claimed that she had fallen from a great height and that two people were arrested as part of the investigation, but later released without charge. Everything was hazy as is often the case when the main witness is dead.

It was a sad ending to what was once a pretty little girl, but the truth was, according to one of her aunts, that everything was stacked against her right from the start.

Her mother was born Audrey Wassell and married Vic Whitaker in 1964 with whom she had several children. For reasons that I am unclear of, they split up and in the early-1980s Audrey met a man by the name of Dave Norris who, according to her sister Lily Dorrit, had been in prison and serving a sentence for manslaughter. They had two children, Davina Lily in 1983 and Cheryl Louise in 1985.

"They had a hard time as kids," explained their aunt. "Audrey didn't give two shits about them nor her other kids."

After Cheryl had been born, Audrey shacked-up and then married Ronald Teale and in 1997 married John Round – the second or third cousin of Bill Cooper.

The thirty-two-year-old Cheryl was known to the police as a both a heroin addict and shoplifter. Her sister, Davina Lily had been no different – however, her path to premature wastage dramatically stalled, when on 12 October 2012 she was sentenced to five years at Burnley Crown Court for malicious wounding with intent to cause grievous bodily harm. Supposedly a part-time carer who had relocated to Frederick Street in Accrington, the twenty-nine-year-old had poured boiling hot water over a sixty-one-year-old man before smashing the kettle around his skull.

The reasoning?

In what was described to have been an unprovoked attack, which left the elderly man with fourteen separate first degree burns, a serious head injury and permanent scarring – it had come about as he had refused to give her money to fund her heroin habit.

"This was a very serious assault on this man and an abuse of his trust," said Judge Beverley Lunt – who in the past had received rather bad press for passing lenient sentences. "You were supposed to care for him but behaved in an extraordinarily violent manner and caused him very serious injuries."

Davina had been defended by Adam Watkins QC, who explained that although she had convictions for theft and harassment, she like Debbie Thwaites, had also suffered from depression and had a long history of self-harm.

Heroin, as I have already stated, always has that tendency, to ruin lives.

"Murder victim Philip Alan Smith was stabbed nine times with a kitchen knife before being slashed across the face by defendant Gary McKeown," said a report in the *South Yorkshire Times*.

It was something echoed by Philip's elder sister Mandy Holmes – the daughter of my ex-next-door neighbour, Jacqueline Smith.

"From what the CID told us, McKeown had left the South Elmsall area after he had slashed someone's face – that is how he and his family came to live in Thurnscoe," she said.

McKeown had not long since moved houses from Malborough Close to 84 Church Street – a house which its front door faces onto Houghton Road and which the side/back door looks out on to the street that it forms part of.

If you read through court transcript, the reasoning behind the whys and wherefores of Philip going to the home of Gary McKeown is hazy at best. The Crown Court were told that the fight was because Gary McKeown – a small-time local drug dealer, was buying his gear from other people and Philip – allegedly another small-time dealer, had supposedly gone around to sort him out. I am told that was never the case. It was a lie.

Mandy's twenty-two-year-old brother, Ben Smith had been seeing a local girl by the name of Lauren Sutton. The problem, however, is that she had also been seeing Gary McKeown's nephew.

"Our Ben found out about this and was texting the nephew. They met up and had a fight which resulted in Gary McKeown's nephew biting our Ben's eye which was a right mess," Mandy explained. "Then a series of text messages were exchanged between the two – however, later on, our Ben realised that he had been texting the wrong person. Gary McKeown's nephew had the exact same name as his uncle."

At the time, Philip Smith had been living in Barnsley with his partner and her two children. They had been childhood sweethearts that had lost touch and then reacquainted.

"It was the first serious relationship our Phil had had, and they were both really happy," smiled his sister.

"Extensive house-to-house and forensic enquiries have been taking place to establish the facts in this case," explained Det. Supt. Andy Thompson, straight after the attack.

"Tensions are running quite high. I understand a gang of youths came down to sort this man out and he has been stabbed near to his home and not far from what used to be known as Ivor's Fish and Chip Shop."

"This case resulted from problems in a close-knit community," added Det. Chief Insp. Tom Whiteley. "There was a confrontation which escalated, leading to a violent incident in which Philip Smith suffered multiple stab wounds."

"Our Phil only came to Thurnscoe once or twice a week, but on this particular day – on 28 January 2012, he saw the state of his brother's eye and was fuming. He certainly wasn't a trouble causer but could handle himself if needed and he and Ben went to Gary McKeown's home on Chapel Street to try and sort the problem."

It was a mistake. An argument ensued and with McKeown armed with a knife, they started a fight which went to ground and then the inevitable happened. McKeown rammed the knife into one side of Philip Smith's body. It was an action that he repeated several times.

"What a lot of people don't know is that my brother was stabbed a total of nine times with that much force that he cut through our Phil's ribs," added Mandy. "And whilst our Phil was laid bleeding on his kitchen floor, Gary McKeown sat on him and slashed his face from underneath his nose to his ear."

In McKeown's mind the slash across the face had possibly been a statement. The reality, however, was that it was an act of nothing more than sheer petulance.

Ben helped drag his elder brother out of the house and on to the street, where he duly collapsed. He was taken to Barnsley Hospital but was pronounced dead on arrival.

According to Mandy, the emergency services had immediately been called – however, it took the ambulance forty minutes to arrive at the scene. "I always said, that if they had got there sooner, he might not have died."

As for McKeown, who was depicted as something of a career criminal by the police, he obviously knew how to play the judicial system. And believe me when I say it, that system can be played.

As with the Formstone death – and to a lesser scale, my experience in 1990 – the main reason that justice was never fully served was that the so-called aggressors went to the defendants' home intent on causing harm or distress.

To walk to their home armed with bats does nothing more than telegraph those intentions. It is certainly something that I would never do. As for the bat, it looks effective, but it has its limitations. I have been hit with something similar – in my case a three-foot long, six-by-four-inch roofbeam. My focus at the time had been elsewhere and to set about hitting some twenty-three-year-old that had been in front of me. I never saw the man come from behind and took a blow to the back of my had that created a pain quite unprecedented. Although it never knocked me unconscious, the following few days were terrible, as you just cannot rest your head. However, where the blow struck tells you everything. It had taken place out in the open and more to the point its target had been unsighted. It was literally speaking – a free shot. A bat is only good given plenty of space and as a surprise tactic. Outside of that it looks intimidating but that is all it is. In a confined space all the man who is holding the knife must do is get close and unfortunately, there is only one winner in that situation.

It is easy to say what I would have done different, as it was a situation that hadn't involved me. I look at the simple facts. The catalyst for the killing had been the fight. The truth is, is that everyone takes a belt at some point in time. There is certainly no shame in it. You just move on.

Earlier on in the story I mentioned a botched murder in which I had been the prime suspect. The reasoning was, that the so-called *victim* had threatened – not so much me, but my wife and youngest child, through a third and fourth party. The go-between had been the owner of the house where little Brenda Cole had set herself on fire in 1942 – that of 10 Briton Square, Thurnscoe.

"He said that he knows that they are on their own and that he will come to the house in the middle of the night and pour petrol through your letterbox," explained Shaun Nota.

I had been bailed away from home at the time. This was due to the fact that I had gone after the man after he had slashed my forehead with a knife. The police were under no illusions that when the right time presented itself, I would maim him.

In some respect, Gary McKeown had a genuine argument of self-defence. Men had not only gone to his house to hurt him – they had also gone armed. The problem McKeown faced, however, was that self-defence doesn't really mean stabbing someone numerous times and then tearing a knife across their face.

In my mind it wasn't manslaughter, but murder. Regardless of Philip Smith's actions and whatever his legal defence state, that intent was always there.

The problem both the South Yorkshire Police and the Crown Prosecution had was that McKeown could have easily walked from a murder charge due to him being in his own home and defending himself from armed men.

The reality was to hopefully cop a plea and after three days of what could have been a highly complex two-week trial, Gary McKeown changed his plea from not guilty to murder, to one of pleading guilty to manslaughter. He got handed a six-year sentence, meaning that he would be out in three. It was an exceptionally good result.

In my opinion, no amount of time is just punishment. Even the eye-for-an-eye has its limitations, and although it can give one some form of closure it is a scenario that still doesn't bring your loved ones back.

Mandy's mention of the polyamorous young girl connects to another story, which for me, sits very close to home.

Remember the mention of the houses just around the first arc of Thornley Crescent and the one where the white door of the exterior electric box had been ripped off along with the white scrawl on the green plastic dustbin – that of Jacqueline Smith's neighbour. Well, the occupier of that property is mother to the girl, that was maybe the catalyst for Philip Smith being killed.

I spent my formative years in school in the same class as Jacqueline (Jackie) Sutton – the middle one of five children to Jack and Sheila (nee Norris).

She was certainly rough and ready, appeared tall in frame and had a rather distinguished voice, as well as having an elder brother that frightened the life out of me or any other kid that got in his way. I quite liked her sweary, underhanded nature and couldn't-give-a-shit attitude. She was a part of that time and place which has long since gone.

Just before I left Thurnscoe for good she briefly made a reappearance in my life, not so much in body, but certainly in soul. My thirteen-year-old daughter had been hanging around with her daughter and had become somewhat entranced by her.

"Jackie Sutton?" I shrugged.

"Yeh, she's right funny," said my daughter. "And she swears right bad."

That didn't surprise me. She wasn't quite as bad as Jimmy Frost, but she was only eight years old the last time I had seen her. She had obviously had time to sharpen up her act.

My daughter was on the start of a very rocky road that was only heading one way and unfortunately, that was to ruin. Have you ever heard the 1995 song written and produced by the alternative rock band Garbage that is titled *Only Happy When It Rains* along with its rather catchy chorus of *Pour your misery down on me*?

Out of all the females I have encountered through my life, there are only three that I have ever considered to be extraordinarily complex – and unfortunately, my daughter is one of them. My son may well be like my father, but my daughter is the Encarnación exacta and epitome of my mum. A dark-eyed sorceress with a pretty face and

461

small frame, who could be very witty one minute and for no apparent reason, highly toxic, confrontational and moody the next. And she can flip-flop her personality to suit her agenda.

From a superficial point of view, Jackie's daughter had nothing and my daughter everything. In the hormone charged, overactive and complex mind of a prepubescent child, however, the superficial didn't count over in the prefabricated coven on the REEMA estate, that had been 53 School Street.

To a teenage girl, Jackie was nothing short of mesmeric. Her laid-back outlook in life and zero house rules absolutely fascinated my daughter – not at least the smoking and the Ouija board.

"I'm stopping at Jackie's house tonight," exclaimed my daughter.

"No, you're not," came my reply.

I had never said a thing about who Jackie was – or indeed still is – however, my wife well and truly had her number,

What is true, is that you can guide your child into adulthood, but the one thing you cannot do is force it – and we certainly made our mistakes, not at least when we left the security blanket which that had been the tight-knit community of Thurnscoe.

There is no right or wrong way of doing things as all children are individuals, therefore, you have to steer your ship in the best way you feel possible. The main storm that was to come crashing against its boughs came in the shape of boys. I had treated the opposite sex disgracefully and that includes the young girl I married. This, if I am being honest, was my Karma coming to get me.

I have had a life that has given me some beautiful memories – but there is one thing that stands out above all and that was just before I had left the employ of British Coal (NCB).

I worked long hours through the week and did as much weekend work as I could get to earn a decent wage. Apart from the empty promise of advancement that had been dangled in front of my face like some carrot, I loved what I did. Traipsing from district to district under Armthorpe's sprawling new model village on the *dead shift*, I would tick off a long sheet of tasks that had been requested by the mechanical engineer. However, on a Friday I always dropped back onto afternoon shift and a 12.00 p.m. start.

The first draw out of the mine, a rushed shower in the pit baths and a drive through Doncaster town centre and down Marr drag – I always knew what I was coming home to. That pretty face at the window frantically waving at me – my three-year old daughter waiting up for her dad. My remit was as always, to drive down to Bolton Fisheries on Furlong Road – with her in a dressing gown and excited, mainly due to the fact that I had only seen her for a few hours through the week and on the Friday night we would let her have what was always termed as a *stopping-up ticket* with her eventually falling asleep after watching *Red Dwarf* and *Cheers* on TV and one of us having to carry her to bed.

In the grand scheme of things, it was nothing, but looking back at it now, it was everything. I considered her the most beautiful child on earth and unlike me, my brother and sister – she would never be denied anything. Remember that quote I made of misguided love? Spoiling a child does have its pitfalls.

At fifteen-and-a-half years old she would walk out of our life, for no reason other than she wanted her freedom. I could relay stories of heartache and the guilt trips we had had, but I would be straying off topic, as it's not really relevant to this story. However, there are some things that are.

My mum had three marriages: My father, Jim Durose, in November 1963; Richard Bryan Rayner in January 1969; and Vic Antcliff in September 1997. Each of these were completely different to one another – although it is quite fair to say that the last one ended in far more acrimonious circumstances than the first.

I still remember being sat at the table inside 29 Derry Grove – a property that still belongs to my sister, Joanne. Vic had had enough. He could not cope with my mum. He wanted her sectioned on a first-class ticket to Sheffield's Middlewood Hospital.

His reasoning was as pithy and shallow as I had ever heard and totally summed up the man.

"Fuck him," I told my sister. "I had to fucking live with it."

My dad had been an aggressive alpha male who could not be controlled. My (step)dad was one of the nicest men you could ever imagine and could. As for Vic, he was neither. Twice married and divorced to the same woman, his whirlwind and rather embarrassing relationship with my mum had initially made me take a few steps back.

Whirlwind in that after my (step)dad had died my mother had a nervous breakdown and became some pathetic withering creature who resolutely recanted the sham that her marriage had been, with a sincerity that was enough to make you chuck up your guts. And as for being fucking needy? Don't even go there.

"It's a fucking pity she didn't think like that when my (step)dad was here," I told my wife.

I was recently given a reminder of the time I had to rush up to 51 Lancaster Street to see my sister with half her hair torn out of her scalp and some fucking lunatic turning the furniture over and screaming like some banshee.

I had to sit on my mum and pin her down.

We managed to get her into an ambulance and over to Doncaster Infirmary. It was then I called her sister – my auntie Heather (Greaves). On her arrival, my mum flipped, thereby racing off across the car park and over on to Thorne Road in just her dressing gown.

My auntie Heather wanted absolutely none of it and turned her back on her sister.

My (step)dad had loved her in a way that I could never understand. If my wife had treated me as bad as he had been treated, she would have been propping up a set of flagstones in the back yard.

You think I am kidding?

That following New Year after my (step)dad had died, I took my family on a seven-day package tour to China and stayed in Beijing, keeping in touch with my mum on a twice-daily basis. However, by the time we hit the tarmac at Heathrow, this falling-to-pieces old lady who had been heavily drinking and chain-smoking herself to death, in between spouting gibberish about the beautiful relationship she'd had with her husband, had managed to have something of an overhaul that would have put both Thornley Crescent and Taylor Street to shame.

"He's just like your (step)dad," she cooed.

She had a boyfriend who was fuck all like my (step)dad and just some bottom-feeding shitbag intent on sucking on the crumbs of what had been my (step)dad's patience and endeavour.

My mum had flicked a switch, and everything had been forgotten.

I genuinely thought I had gone into the wrong house. From being as morose as fuck, she had turned into Doris Day and I fully expected her to break out into song: *Once I had a secret love... that lived within the heart of me...*

The relationship lasted as long as it took for my mum to find someone a bit more affluent – with Vic Antcliff allegedly ticking all the right boxes. However, by then, I had taken several steps back.

My mum's next-door neighbour Kay Brook (nee Elliot) filled us in with all vomit-inducing detail of how the relationship was progressing, with tales of a pair of idiots spraying each other with a hosepipe in the back yard before openly consummating their love for one another, so that half the street could hear.

Forrest Gump's mother was an amateur compared to the diamond-backed rattlesnake that was my mother. She bit, and you died a slow horrible fucking death.

"So, what are you saying?" Vic gibbered at the table. "That you're not willing to have her sectioned?"

Vic had given her exactly what she had always wanted from my (step)dad – mainly some semi-detached bungalow off Highgate Lane that had been Jerry-built by Walter Dunk and Son.

I look back at the final days of their marriage and at the time I threatened to beat the living daylights out of him after my mum had cried wolf and said that he had tried to drown her in the bath.

Had he? No idea.

There was a fine line between what my mum saw and what was real. If the sky was blue, she would disagree and argue it was red. As for Vic, he was just some stupid old twit who my mum had *played*.

As for my daughter, the dark stare of hate and the confrontational personality is all there to see.

"Dad, Dad," she shouted down the phone. "Shaun's come in from the pub and is smashing the house up."

She had been seeing a lovely young lad who lived a couple of doors down from where the murderer, torturer and rapist, Peter Pickering had lived in Wombwell and they had recently moved into a house together, just a few doors up from The Dearnesman pub in West Melton. The lad had been at his wit's end, turned the house upside down and given her a clout.

I was always the one at the end of that *Bat Phone*. Always.

Just the week prior, I had taken my son to see the rock band Feeder over in Dublin and whilst flying out there my wife had been down at my daughters. Shaun – who had been twenty-one years old at the time, was sat on the end of the bed crying. "Julie, I can't cope with her anymore," he told her.

I think they had been living together around eight or nine weeks.

"She's always threatening her boyfriend, with you," my mum had often told me, regarding my daughter.

That, however, had been a different boyfriend. A manipulative piece of shit who I really should have wasted on the spot but didn't through the naivete that was me trying to offer reason. Not with him as he got it in the end – but with my daughter. Dealing with other people's shit is a piece of cake. When it is your immediate family – it is like some cancer that eats away at you.

Violence, or the threat of it, will, ninety-five percent of the time, get you what you want. The threat of it, is the ultimate mechanism of enablement. Ask any armed robber or even some shit bag rapist how he gets what he wants. It is always through the threat of violence. Anyway, I am digressing.

Shaun Tout, a descendant of Raymond Adams family – the man who gunned down Joe McHugh outside his home on Windsor Street in 1968, was just a smashing kid. He had, however, belted my daughter and that needed rectifying. As did the fact that he had been swinging around a baseball bat (that bat again!) and more than implied, that if I arrived on site, that is what I would be getting.

What I was about to witness that evening was something that I would never see again. It was heart breaking. Knowing that I was on my way down, his father had pulled him from the wreckage that he had created within his home and taken him over to their house and that information was relayed direct to me via mobile phone. I therefore went straight to the lads parents' house.

"Where is he?" I asked his father as I got out of my vehicle.

"Tha' not touching him, James," he told me.

"And why's that?"

"Because I'll hit thee," he said.

That young lad sat in the car, whilst I set about giving his father what would have possibly been the biggest, good hiding of his life. It was brutal. There was blood everywhere.

The upshot was that the father had just protecting his son and nothing more.

You invite my daughter into your life and there is only one outcome. Misery.

I look back at the events and can only shake my head. My daughter, just like my mum had with my (step)dad, had been far too headstrong for him. She needed someone who took no shit and she got it. Well, sort of.

"A professional boxer who survived being stabbed in the heart with a screwdriver said yesterday: "I'm lucky to be alive.""

"Light welterweight Gwyn Wale was attacked in the street on 25 August 2011 when friendly banter with another man turned ugly," read a report in the *Yorkshire Post*.

"As the two men fought, twenty-seven-year old Gwyn, knocked out the two front teeth of William Edward Lowe – only for him to reply by sticking a six-inch screwdriver into Mr Wale's chest and back. One wound punctured the sac surrounding the boxer's heart and only the prompt arrival of emergency services and the skill of surgeons at Sheffield's Northern General Hospital saved his life."

Gwyn had married my daughter a year or so after a toxic first relationship, whereby after we had taken them away on a winter city break, he had left her with no money in some freezing cold rat hole of a flat they had rented up in the Blantrye area of south west Scotland.

It had been his brainwave to leave the eastern Dearne Valley and try and escape the clutches of the bailiff's working on behalf of the Northern Rock Building Society after she had had the house in West Melton that she had shared with Shaun Tout, repossessed. My daughter's main problem was that she'd always had life on a plate and fully expected us to sort out her shit, which to an extent we always had.

I quite liked Gwyn. A very capable unit, who, if he would have been nurtured properly, could have had a great career. Unfortunately, part of his problem was that his roots were in the Brampton Bierlow area of Barnsley – the small community that was ripped apart after Cortonwood Colliery threw down the gauntlet for a fight and then reneged after it had got every fucker else involved.

He was the big attraction on the village's lower council sprawl – an estate that was home to work-shy grifters and the flat-capped *thee and tha's* that talked the talk in the Tap Room of the Bull's Head. Although from the same village, my wife's father had always worked and he looked down with scorn at those who did not. As I have said, it was the only real thing that he and I had in common during my first few years of knowing him.

Gwyn was the ultimate ducker and diver – something that he had been accustomed to in the boxing ring. It is a sport where you cannot hide, and it doesn't take long before some two-bit show pony gets found out.

Gwyn informed me that he was the youngest ever professional boxer in the UK. It may well be a point that requires clarification from those in the know, but the fact of the matter was, that his very young age in leaving the amateur circuit was more of personal gain, than of being overly skilled in the said profession. His father was his trainer, which to me – answered a lot of questions.

"He talks a right load of fucking shit," said Tim as regards Gwyn's father.

We had gone up to Motherwell to see him fight on a boxing card which pitted him against some journeyman-cum-punchbag that had been Billy Smith on 29 September 2006.

Tim knew far more about boxing than anyone I knew, and whilst in school he became a very capable fighter – in one instance brawling with the tall gangly lad that was Danny McBride and the well-built Steve Perry – and rather strangely both at the same time. It was an interesting assault that had started outside the ROSLA block and ended up inside, with me trying to part them. Danny had been taken out with two punches and wanted none of it. Steve – a lad from Highgate, not only fancied his chances bust must have thought he was in Pamplona and was ramming Tim up against the wall like some bull. He even had the building shaking.

It was certainly a better fight than Gwyn gave the young lad in Motherwell – the latter who ended up committing suicide following the death of his brother.

When I had first met Gwyn, I had no illusions about who he was and what he was about. He may have been very alpha male and *knock 'em out*, but his main downside was that he tended to look at what other people were getting. He really should have been focusing on himself. The Brampton poster-boy's pet hate at the time was the UK's No 1. He absolutely detested Amir Khan.

"I'd smash him up," he claimed. "He's only where he is because he's a fucking Paki and can sell the tickets."

After fighting Stefy Bull in some regional title fight, which went the distance at the Doncaster Dome, the lad really fancied himself. I will give Gwyn his due, his confidence was sky-high. The kid wasn't scared of anything. He had more than intimated that the result of his fight with Stefy had been rigged and that his opponent deserved nothing. Most people that saw it, say the same.

It was then I saw Amir Khan totally outclass Gwyn's recent opponent in one of the most one-sided fights that I had ever witnessed. He absolutely fucking tore into him. As for Stefy Bull – he wanted none of it. It was nothing short of embarrassing. Dean Carter or Tommy Carey would have put on a better show and they aren't even boxers. They certainly wouldn't have gone down that much is for sure!

It was then I became aware of Gwyn's limitations. Boxers are brilliant against non-boxers. I know, I am one of those the non-boxers that has taken a hit from a few. Stick them in against someone who is good, and it is a totally different story. You only get good by combining natural skill with hard work, dedication and a great trainer. Gwyn certainly had the skill. Unfortunately, he lacked the other three elements. My daughter saw part of the problem as being his father. Carly was wrong on many things, but even a stopped clock tells the correct time twice a day.

He firmly believed that his father was helping him. I really don't thing that was ever the case.

Gwyn hadn't taken long to move into my daughter's house on Barnsley Road – a property which we had kitted out and paid the legal fees for. It was a time when I realised what Gwyn was all about. The mask, the combat gear, and the baseball bat (again) in the cellar. He robbed drug dealers. Mainly cannabis grows. However, his father had been diagnosed with some life-threatening disability that made morphine readily available, therefore Gwyn sold that for him too. Rather strangely that deaths door diagnosis was about fifteen years ago and to my knowledge Mick Wale is still knocking about. Remember what I said about Brampton Bierlow's work-shy populous of grifters?

"I've got faith in him, Mam," my daughter used to say.

That comment was regarding Gwyn and certainly not his father.

We took them to Paris in some four-day break from hell, along with both my in-laws to celebrate our tenth anniversary. That was a fucking mistake.

My son shared what was a twin bedroom with my daughter and Gwyn which overlooked the busy Rue Cler. He also relayed a story of her both punching and name calling him regarding his lowly position in the UK's light welterweight rankings. "Fucking forty-fucking-seventh, you, useless wanker," she had snarled.

My daughter had a brutality in both her speech and her actions.

On getting back into the UK, we received a phone call to say that Gwyn had walked out on her and that he had taken all her wages thereby leaving her with no money. She stressed the fact that she had done with him and that was it.

I felt guilty. Her mother felt guilty. We always did. We were always made to feel guilty.

Life is full of ifs and buts. In part, I had been dragged up, neglected, starved and beat. She'd had none of that, yet you always look at yourself and the mistakes – and we made hundreds of them. I still don't think it would have changed anything, but you still think.

I remember telling her over the phone: "Him taking your wages will be the best money you've ever spent."

I remember speaking with some estate agent about a newly modernised flat in some three or four-storey stone building in Hamilton and transferring £1,000 (£1,506, circa 2020) via BACS into some account through the Royal Bank of Scotland on Doncaster's High Street as a bond along with first month's rent. I also remember receiving a telephone call just over a year later from some old lady who informed us that my daughter had taken an overdose.

To my knowledge that was the first supposed *cry* for help. The last *cry* I know about was her threatening to throw herself off the flyover at Mexborough. I say supposed as there are two types of suicidal people. The ones that do it and those that do not.

Rather strangely, my sister-in-law's brother was on suicide watch. Very much the runt of the litter, in a genetically charged masculine set of siblings, my brother mentioned that he had tried offing himself a few times. Firstly, through gambling and secondly through love (sic). The reality of this, is that if his horses had come in and his girlfriend hadn't dumped him then everything would have been tickety boo. Remember me mention of the *being spoiled*. Certain people will do anything it takes to get what they want. Even slashing their wrists.

Regarding my daughter, our decision was to relocate her to a barn conversion opposite some DHSS-funded new build that Mary Gough rented in Crowle – a market town to the east of Doncaster. It was a move in which I had to give the vendor six months' rent up front. We needed her close by, if only to keep an eye on her. We did care. We really did.

All we were ever seen as was some convenient cash cow that she could tap up, on an as and when basis, and the problem we experienced having her back on our doorstep caused me, personally, some of the most upset ever.

Our son had just turned sixteen years old and was due to start music college. He had a great life with lots of friends and a brand-new Italian moped, that had resembled some 250cc motorbike, with its accompanying racing fairings and derestricted engine that enabled it to top out around 50 mph. Me and his mum were so proud of him having his independence. He used that bike to go and visit is ultra-cool and beautiful sister on a regular basis, so much so, he began staying there. A problem arose after a few weeks as when in our company, he had started to become extremely morose.

We were good friends with a young couple who had relocated from the suburbs of northern Sheffield and often went out for a curry together. My friend's girlfriend, Lauren Hill, was around the same age as my daughter and they struck up some form of relationship, which if truth-be-told, was heavily strained from the start by the fact that my daughter saw herself as just being used a some form of base for Lauren to dump herself and her two kids throughout the day.

Nevertheless, Lauren being there gave us an insight into what we would be dealing with, which was something that resulted in my wife getting feedback that made us feel uneasy.

"I'm going to knife-up my dad," was one such sentence, and this had allegedly come from my son's mouth.

Lessons learned from Jackie Sutton's home and the demonic Ouija board had been played out in the house and my son had become extremely obsessed with the paranormal and speaking with the dead. He was young and impressionable. My daughter is extremely manipulative and was massaging his ego to such an extent, I barely recognised him.

I rarely went to the house in question, which was another huge mistake.

My daughter may have looked like some glamourous model helped on by the mum and dad-funded clothes and shoes, but in her head bar the cynicism, she was still the same – the fifteen-year-old that had left us in the early hours of 4 January 2001. She had not progressed one iota. She had only got worse.

"I wanted to be a model and you stopped me," she snarled. "You've stopped everything I wanted to do."

I still recall being sat in The Everest – an Asian restaurant on Doncaster's Netherhall Road. She and Gwyn had gate-crashed our evening-out with my younger brother, Shaun and his girlfriend, around the time her house was due to be repossessed. The next thing I know the table had been turned over and she was attacking her mother.

This wasn't my daughter. This was my mum.

Gwyn was gobsmacked.

"What's that all about?" he shrugged afterwards.

She blamed her mother for everything. One of the main reasons, being that she was still with me. Her thoughts were that her mum was easy to control. Her dad, however, didn't do control.

She could have had everything – she did have everything, but what she really wanted, was the freedom to do whatever the hell she pleased – however, she neither had the work ethic nor the nous to do it. She was ever reliant on someone else.

All her short tenure in Crowle would do, was let her know how far her younger brother had come. He had everything and she saw it as her duty to destroy it. She had failed and so would he. She would try and lay the blame of the children's two failures at our feet.

There was another thing, however. What I had been totally unaware of was the drugs.

The two poor souls that were the Norris sisters may well have been dragged up and neglected, but my daughter had not. Our unrequited love had given her multiple chances, all of which she would spurn.

"I've been diagnosed with a bipolar disorder," was one of her many excuses.

In my mind, bipolar is basically a medical term for someone who is just a miserable bastard, as is ADDS for some naughty little twat that needs a boot up the arse. These diagnoses are great for milking the other cash cow that is the DHSS, however. You just need to look no further than two twisted, fucking bottom-feeders that are my nieces and the hideous tub of lard that parades as their mother for verification of that.

The first I knew about the drugs was after we had had the estate agent call us to explain that the keys to my daughter's property had been returned.

I couldn't believe it. For six months we had paid her rent, her brother helping her further by both taking food from our house and lending her money.

When we arrived at the house it looked as though it had been burgled and what had us scratching our heads was the fact that my son's moped was still parked up outside. She had not only left but taken her sixteen-year-old brother with her – which is something that he has never forgiven her for. Back then she may have had mesmeric hold over him but in the here and now he looks down on her with pure disdain and hasn't spoken to her in years. It is all incredibly sad.

The frustrating thing was that we were due to fly out to Cyprus that night and I remember being in the airport and being absolutely devastated. I didn't want to go. I needed to find my son. This was made worse by the fact that my dad's son – our Shaun had texted me: "Did you know they were both smoking blow?"

I knew nothing. My response, however, was as black as the last time, he had pissed me off. "You're supposed to be the fucking adult," I told him. "Why have you waited until now to tell me?"

My brother was intellectually off the scale when it came to knowledge garnered from a book but acted like some total fucking retard when it came to anything of importance.

"Yeh, man – sorry, it was a bad call."

For years, I had a quid pro quo sort of side-line. You throw a name at me and I will find them. Always. My daughter however, had no money, nor credit cards, no nothing. Remember what I said. She always had to rely on another person or persons. I knew I wouldn't find her via normal means, therefore from Cyprus, I managed to hack into her email account whilst my wife phoned everyone that she knew. Within a few minutes my wife had feedback that Gwyn had been back on the scene.

The numerous emails told me quite a lot. She had not only been hedging her bets with some other potential relationship, there was also many references to drugs. They were everywhere. She had even openly admitted to smuggling the shit in from Amsterdam – a jaunt that was helped paid for, by her sixteen-year-old brother.

My son had phoned his mum to see if he could call at one of our friends to lend him some money. We had been away at the time and had left him £60 spending money and a fridge full of food. It wasn't until afterwards that we found out that his sister had tapped it off him.

Next phone call. Gwyn Wale's home.

I got his mother on the line and she denied everything and anything, from the relationship down to the drugs. As for me, I got the feeling I was being spoken down to. I certainly couldn't be having that. "Put your fucking husband on the phone," were the last words I ever said to her.

The husband shit himself. He gave his son up straight away but pleaded for me to wait a bit and go down whilst Gwyn was at work. Apparently, he didn't want his son getting in trouble.

That really wasn't the case.

Not that long before, ITN had had a news crew outside our house, which had been quickly followed by BBC North – a shooting and a major arson, which was all supposedly linked to the botched murder that I have mentioned. The truth was, he wanted none of it. "Our Gwyn's besotted with your Carly," were to be his final words until I rammed the metaphorical pencil in his eye.

"'You got an email?" I asked him. "Then, I'll show you exactly how fucking besotted she is with him."

I forwarded every email I could get of my daughters' other *relationship*, and within minutes I had his younger brother, Josh Wale on the phone. "I'll wait until after you go down and then I'll tell our Gwyn," he said. "This is going to devastate him."

Fucking boo-hoo. I didn't give a rats ass. It was the non-ruination of my son's life that I was fighting for not his.

My sister was nothing short of brilliant as she had been when her niece had first left home. Our Joanne suggested me not going. It was a good call and she and my wife went to some property on in Mexborough's Blenheim Crescent, which wasn't that far from the house that I had been born in.

The property itself was some two-up-two down with no carpets whatsoever.

The young lad that had had the world at his feet was like some DHSS skank dressed in a vest top and shorts and sat in the only seat in the house, which was some striped deck chair. My wife described it as nothing short of heart wrenching. My daughter had been cooking their dinner when they arrived on site with pans boiling away on the cooker. That beautiful little girl who use to eagerly wait for her dad coming home on a Friday night, assessed all the options – the main one to be to sling boiling hot water over her mum. Unlike in the sad case of Davina Norris, our Joanne was quick to react and immediately emptied the pans in the sink. My daughter, however, was like some caged animal and attacked her mum – which was another thing my sister nipped in the bud.

The ensuing drama ended up with my daughter not too far away from where Donald Cheswick murdered his wife in 1963. She was threatening to throw herself off the Bank Street flyover and on to the A6023.

This came after Gwyn's father had been the bearer of bad tidings: "She's using you, son."

How they ever made that relationship work after that is either real love or a testament to both their stupidity.

Rather strangely, it was Gwyn's attacker on Brampton Bierlow's Becknoll Road that added to the drugs story.

My wife had received a phone call explaining that Gwyn had been stabbed and that he was in critical condition. The life he led was never going to give him what he wanted.

"He's just a little fucking drug dealer," some fat kid had told me, after I had initially put the wind up him after introducing myself in Sheffield Crown Court.

"I'm the father-in-law of the kid you stabbed up," I had told him.

I had sat across from William Edward Lowe and all I thought was how the fucking hell would a kid such as Gwyn end up being taken down by this piece of shit.

"He likes his nose candy," he added, referring to cocaine. "And his dad's a right little wanker."

All I wanted to know, is if my daughter had made a statement. All I was doing there was looking out for my own. She had been charged as a sixteen-year old for making a false statement and trying to pervert the course of justice whilst trying to get her own way. To be a major witness in a Crown Court trial with that on your resume is a non-starter, and as such, any defence barrister would have torn her apart.

"No, mate, your Carly hasn't made a statement."

The kid may have come over as just some everyday shit bag, but I will give him his due, he never revealed why the argument had taken place. He certainly told me how he stabbed him, however. He made a right mess of the lad.

"Forty-five-year-old Lowe of Edward Street, Great Houghton, near Barnsley was jailed for four years yesterday after he admitted grievous bodily harm," said the report in the *Yorkshire Post*.

"This could quite easily have been a fatal incident," said Judge Simon Lawler QC on sentencing him. "You are lucky your victim went to hospital quickly and there was the skill of the surgeons in managing to repair the injury and stem the blood loss."

Unfortunately, that never happened in the case of poor Philip Smith.

Carly came back into our life and offered us up four grandchildren. It was Gwyn who came through our rear gates holding out the olive branch in the guise of a bunch of cheap petrol station flowers. "Am I okay to come on your property?" he asked, as I opened the door.

"Yeh, come in," I told him.

"I am really sorry for what we have done to you both and I just want to apologise," he said.

My retort was simple. In my mind family always get a pass and if an apology is sincere, I have no problem with receiving one. I gave the lad a hug and everything was forgiven. It would be a time in our life that we had four lovely children around us – the eldest one who thought the world of me.

Unfortunately, and just like my mother, my daughter couldn't keep up the act.

My wife took the kids out to McDonald's and to one of those play areas along with Lauren and her children …as for my daughter – she didn't like it.

"I'm not stopping you from seeing them, but you'll not be taking them over your way again until I can trust you," she had told her mum. "So, if you want to see them again, you'll have to come over here whilst under my supervision."

I tried to rectify it, but all I ended up with, his having the police serve me with some half-assed restraining order. Of why, I have no idea, as I have never once been to Carly and Gwyn's home.

It was all about control. It always has been.

How you deal with these people who like to control, is that you move to take that control off them.

"Go get yourself fucked, Carly," was my wife's response.

The saddest sight in all this was having to return all their [the kids] Christmas presents.

It is all very sad.

Perfection - my daughter, Carly at four years old

36.   The Kiss of Death

For our first year or so at Lancaster Street our telephone system had shared a party-line with a couple of properties on Brunswick Street. What was true is that at certain times, you could end up being privy to someone else's conversation, although I can never recall latching on to anything that I shouldn't have.

I have in my everyday life, however. I remember being sat behind the desk during early-1995, in what was my first office in Hickleton Main's old pit baths around the area where we used to fill our water bottles. I had been on the phone to Dosco – a mining machine manufacturer that was once based near Newark. I had put my phone down at the end of our conversation only to pick it up a few minutes later to find that the guy I had been talking to, was still on the phone. He had been in a conversation with someone else and trying to do some dirty back door deal.

For years, I recorded every phone call that came into my office.

"I never said that!" they would shriek.

"Yeh you did, pal. I don't make these stories up and I never write down anything without a source. I record everything and believe me when I say this: You did say it."

I have an inquisitive nature and my thirst for information is something else.

There were two girls on each of these Brunswick Street party lines.

Susan (Sue) Helm (nee Hopes) was part of Thurnscoe Comprehensive's Class of 1981. Although, I knew who she was, we had never been close, which is quite a shame as she converses at a completely different level. She also rarely says anything that is not worth repeating and possesses a blinding memory.

It was Sue who mentioned the party line and the fact that when I had been fourteen years old I had been in a relationship with its other third-party, Joanne Russell (now Greaves) – a girl who I have previously mentioned, and who rather coincidentally, had also been one of the office cleaners down at the newly reconstructed pit baths during the time of my phone call to Dosco.

Reading between the lines, and without me saying a deal, Sue also touched on the internal wrangling within her family that is much the same with mine. As I said, her intuition is nothing short of amazing.

Mine revolved around some *problem* that I never ever thought was there, and which was sparked from what I assume is a bitterness brought on by envy. One of the many downside's of where we once lived is that there can be a kind of innate inverted snobbery, where people look down their nose at certain people with conceit. You only have to look at the barbed comments on social media that has been aimed at the owners of the high-end properties on Thurnscoe's High Street such as Brian Moffatt, Mark Jarvis and Shaun Moreby – all kids that I grew up with. They got there through hard work and determination and nothing else. The snide and poisonous comments are made by the bottom-feeding trolls, their main aim being to try and drag them down to their level. It is all part of a low rent working class culture that has very little place in today's society, as everything is available – that is, if you are prepared to work for it.

I recall the journey from our home on The Avenues and to my grandma Ellis's on Lindley Crescent at 6.00 a.m. throughout early 1970. My mum had got a job and my grandma took me to school and looked after my sister. I dreamed of living on High Street, in some huge house with its beautiful gardens and big windows that look out on to the rookery that partially hides the imposing structure that was once Thurnscoe Hall. As I said, in 1996 I had been considering buying one.

I moved away well over twenty-years ago into a similar property living a life between two countries, one of which is the gateway to the Middle East. It is a life that apparently gnaws at my brother's wife and her two deluded offspring, as I cannot imagine the hatred being anything else.

My brother lives in some rented accommodation on Thornwood Close – a development that is situated just off Low Grange Road and close to where the Whinwood Hotel once stood.

The reason I have rarely been down his that his wife has always seen me as a threat.

From a personal point of view, I find her poisonous, conceited, ignorant and lazy. She is also extremely controlling – which is a fact that has seen her throw out both her children and driven my brother into some deep depression where he has ballooned-out to the size of a Zeppelin and talks to very few people.

Do I feel sorry for him? No. Although she is the driving force behind his misery, he is the sole architect of who he has become.

I still recall us sat around the table one teatime around late-1978. There had been no food in the house, bar the resident half-empty tub of margarine in the fridge and the odd tin in the cupboard. My mum's brainwave had been to open a packet of dehydrated chicken soup and make it go around all three kids, which she did by adding more water and thickening it up with the use of flour. As you could imagine, it was hardly haute cuisine, which saw our Joel having to chew at his soup. It did of course, look quite funny and after a while his actions had both me and his elder sister in stitches. I had to admit, she had fed us some right shite before, but this had to be *up there*. For some reason, she assumed that the jocularity had been at her expense and punched me full in the face. It was a right crack which had blood everywhere. After trying to evade getting walloped a second time, I had raced upstairs and locked my bedroom door, which I assumed its little latch would give me some form of sanctuary. It didn't. She kicked it open, took my guitar off the wall and smashed it around my head and back before wrecking the record player and just about everything else in the room. And these were things that she and my (step)dad had struggled to pay for. My bedroom looked like a live set from *The Who*, but she still wasn't done. I could hear the noise coming from downstairs and both younger kids taking a clip, before having to wade through their slop in silence.

Our Joel was a lovely little lad of that there is no doubt and I can draw the odd comparison with my son who once thought the world of his uncle. Why he doesn't now, is my son's story to tell and not mine.

Joel had turned his future wife away from our door for months, but in the end her sheer perseverance won through. You have to understand that his home life at the time was nothing short of horrendous when she finally forced her way into his life.

Both my mum and his dad – my (step)dad – despised her. "I can't stand looking at her face," he used to say, before mimicking her pathetic droll voice.

I had to admit, he could take her off great.

Due to her masculine frame, zero waist and large head, my mum often referred to her as the *Hunny Monster*, which was a character from a TV advert for *Sugar Puffs* that had been around at the time.

My family are no different to Sue's, that is for sure.

What she did tell me, however, is that during her time as a sewing machinist at Mexborough's SR Gents she had worked with a twenty-one-year-old girl off Goldthorpe's Kennedy Drive who had been raped after walking home from the Kiss of Life in December 1983. She had been attacked close the underbridge that takes Furlong Road beneath the Sheffield – York railway line and dragged down Tan Pit Lane (Billy's Lane) and on to ground where Furlong Court now stands.

As for the Kiss of Life – it stood opposite Manvers Main Coking Plant and was an establishment that I never went into in its former state. I say former – as for years, especially after the demolition of the plant, it has been The Staithes pub and restaurant. Back then, however, it had been a tacky late-night bar with dancing, and not what you could ever describe as a nightclub. I remember Neil Gollick coming around to my house in November 1985, prior to us going out: "I went last night – it's fucking shit – it ought to be called the Kiss of Death."

You had to love Neil.

I am reliably informed that around chucking out time, a bus had been provided free of charge, which picked up outside and dropped off in and around Wath-on-Dearne. For people who had farer to travel – taxis were always available. One such taxi driver, however, hadn't been interested in picking up fares. This one had used his part-time job as a façade – a cover to cruise the streets of the eastern Dearne Valley in his hunt for women.

"James Lloyd, a fifty-year-old father of two, hung his head in the dock at Sheffield Crown Court as he was told that he would spend at least fifteen years in jail for crimes that had terrorised South Yorkshire," read a report in *The Times* on 5 September 2006.

He was the father of a seventeen-year-old son and twelve-year-old daughter and had lived on 1 Ullswater Close, Bolton-on-Dearne, prior to moving into a four-bedroom detached house at Howell Gardens in Thurnscoe.

Rather strangely, a lot of locals do not know who he is or indeed who he was. James Lloyd was never really known as that name more by his other – that of Desmond, a lad who had grown up in the rather innocuous surroundings of 207 Furlong Road. He has Thurnscoe connections too. On 23 December 1978 he married Jackie Cole – the daughter of Jonathan and Lilian Cole and for a time resided at 2 Hanover Square.

"One of the rapist's youngest victims, waited twenty years to see Lloyd brought to justice. She waived her right to anonymity to tell how Lloyd raped her before stealing her high-heeled shoes as a bizarre trophy. She was one of four women aged between eighteen and fifty-three that he admitted raping in the Rotherham and Barnsley area between 1983 and 1986. He also admitted four attempted rapes."

He admitted raping a woman at Goldthorpe in December 1983; a twenty-one-year-old woman near Silverwood Colliery in October 1984; an eighteen-year-old at Hoyland in December 1984; and another eighteen-year-old in Swinton, the latter of who was the one who waived anonymity.

He also admitted two attempted rapes in February 1983 and June 2004 and attempting to rape another woman in June 2004.

Prior to being both charged and sentenced, Lloyd had tried committing suicide twice, once by hanging himself and the second whilst on remand, whereby he ended up spending a week in intensive care, before being shipped out to HMP Hull.

Judge Alan Goldsack QC is someone that I am certainly familiar with. He had been a young crown prosecutor during one of my trials in Sheffield Crown Court, whereby I had a charge of grievous bodily harm overturned and walked away with nothing more than a slap on the wrists. For the record, George England QC had been my defence barrister that day.

Goldsack – who is nowadays termed by Sheffield's criminal fraternity as the *Hanging Judge*, handed Lloyd an indeterminate sentence and ordered that he should spend at least fourteen-and-a-half years in prison before being assessed for release.

Never think that is justice, because it is not.

I think all the self-appraised back patting that was led by Det. Insp. Angie Wright's investigation was not only very premature but was extremely half-assed and was something which Lloyd's legal team seized upon. The reality was that the rapist went on to spend seven years and 263 days in prison, after the Court of Appeal in London reduced his minimum term. They decided in their wisdom, that the original sentence was too severe in the light of his guilty plea.

The police state that all the attacks took place during the first three years of his relationship with his current wife whom he married on 3 August 1985, and when he was working part-time as a taxi-driver at nights.

I am certainly not convinced.

Justine Louise Kelly (now Armstrong, was Cornes) lived at Gorse Close in Brampton Bierlow at the time of his trial and bravely spoke out. She had been just eighteen years old when he had grabbed her from behind and held a knife to her throat. The Towpath, The Ship, The Station. She had been just another young girl enjoying a night out in Swinton during a balmy August evening of 1986, when she had been dragged onto some waste ground.

"I was desperate to get away and fought like a tiger," she told the court. "I was covered in cuts and strangulation marks as he attacked me. There was no one else around."

What was unknown at the time is that Justine fitted perfectly within Lloyd's template of lust. She was only 5'5, possessed a slim frame and more importantly – she wore three-inch black patent heels.

"Although he was only a few inches taller he was very strong," she said.

The other part of his Motive Operandi (MO) had several other layers outside of the obvious.

i) He preyed on women walking home alone after a night out.

ii) He generally dragged them into bushes and grassy areas.

iii) He threatened them with violence – at knifepoint or with strangulation.

iv) He tied them up and sexually assaulted them.

v) He stole their belongings, most notably, shoes, stockings, tights.

"He tied my hands behind my back with some stockings, put something woolly in my mouth and put a rope around my neck," added Justine. "He also made me put my head between my knees and then roped it around my neck and knees. Struggling all the while, I managed to get my left hand free and pulled the rope from my neck and we both fell down."

It had been one hell of a struggle.

"He then sat on top of me and held my hands across my chest, put my coat over my face so that I couldn't see him and then pulled my knickers down. Chillingly he then told me, 'I'm going to have sexual intercourse with you'. He used those exact words. And with that he raped me."

He then rifled through her handbag, stole some of its contents along with her shoes. This hadn't just been rape – it had also been armed robbery, something the police should have pushed like hell for the Crown Prosecution to pursue. The fact that they did not says everything about their laxity.

"This is the best result so far from familial searching and it will have a massive effect across the country because this proves it brings results and other forces will want to use it," said Det. Insp. Angie Wright.

"It is a fantastic result for forensic science because it is a new technique they are developing and without results like this it does not get credibility. They are really pushing for rape victims to get justice and this is the way forward."

Don't fucking kid yourself.

This case was all about the hurrah of new scientific methods of policing and self-appraised back patting. It had little to do with the victims. If that were the case, Lloyd would never have got out. Sheffield's so-called hanging judge did his duty by hamstringing the do-gooders by handing him an indeterminate sentence, meaning that there was no leverage for early release in that he would serve his sentence. The fact that the police and Crown Prosecution Service (CPS) were fine with him coughing up to four rapes and two botched ones said it all. They left him wiggle room and lots of it.

After William Edward Lowe was sentenced to four years after stabbing Gwyn Wale through the heart and suffering and two life-threatening wounds, Gwyn's father told the local media that **they** were happy with the result.

If it was not for the speed and skill of both the paramedics and surgeons that lad would have died. I saw both the mess that the *trying to save him* caused. The scars down his chest are a constant reminder of that.

So, why were **they** happy?

Especially given that Lowe went down the same route as James Lloyd and had his legal team appeal his sentence. He had his term cut to three years and sixty days and was therefore out in just over a year.

This isn't fucking justice.

"By the time James Lloyd met his current wife, Patricia (nee Willis) in 1984, his offending had already stopped," said Paul Whitehouse of *The Yorkshire Post*.

For as much as his wife pushed his buttons – and believe me when I say it, she really, really did – I personally don't think that was ever the case.

"When detectives searched Lloyd's possessions, they found a series of videos of him and his wife, having sex," reported Helen Carter of *The Guardian*. "She was often tied up and appeared to be unconscious. Lloyd was seen to stop what he was doing and replace his wife's stilettos if one of them fell off. But in a statement read to the court, she said she consented to all the acts in the videos and denied that her husband had drugged her."

"It may be your sexual fantasy to have simply been contained within the relationship. Were it to end, however, you may well have been tempted to carry them out with other women, giving them no choice whether to consent or not," added Judge Goldsack. "These assaults are every woman's nightmare. They are terrifying offences – set upon by a stranger while walking home, with no help available and not knowing whether the assault will end with sexual degradation or go further."

He may have been referring to sex predator and murderer, Peter Pickering in his last sentence.

"Those unlucky enough to become his victims suffered increasingly violent ordeals, which progressed from threats of violence to the use of a knife," added the *Yorkshire Post's*, Paul Whitehouse. "He carefully planned each of his attacks and was confident enough to spend a relatively long time with each of his victims, binding their hands in a similar way and stealing their property."

When police searched his home in Thurnscoe, and his office at Dearne Valley Printers on Doncaster Road in Wath-on-Dearne, they found 126 pairs of stiletto-heel shoes along with a document entitled *The Perfect Victim*, detailing rapes identical to those committed by Lloyd. There were indeed similarities with Pickering – not just his attacks, but parallels of his eerily penned document of rape, torture and kill.

"He certainly had a horrendous fetish for high heels," explained Angela Wright. "It was just so many really, really high heels, and they had obviously been worn and belonged to someone at one point. It was quite clear to me that there were more victims than had come forward."

You don't say?

There is another point in something that she said, however: "There was also stockings and tights Lloyd had used to tie up his victims."

And there you had it.

They had 126 pairs of shoes – all different sizes, along with hosiery used as a ligature.

How much fucking evidence did they need?

The arithmetic just does not stack up to go to trial with just four rapes and two attempted ones. The police admitted as much and said that the true number of his victims could be as many as 120. So why just four? Why not DNA test all the shoes and the hosiery that they had confiscated and build up a true number? For me it was extremely shoddy policework.

There was absolutely no evidence to suggest that he ever stopped attacking women after his marriage. None whatsoever. There is a reason why a serial rapist is called a serial rapist. They need to feel that power over their victims. They don't just turn that power off like some tap and say: "Hey, that's it, I'm done – I aren't doing this no more." They can't. The power is the aphrodisiac in as much as the sex. They can't give it up in as much as a smack addict can give up their smack.

If you want the best evidence ever that Lloyd never stopped, just sit back and look at the haul of shoes taken from his office. There is little to suggest that any of those shoes were styled in the early 1980s. And you don't have to be fucking Hercule Poirot to notice this. Just ask any of the girls who I grew up with.

James Lloyd had been doing this all his life.

You want an identical case: "Police are still hunting for a man who is alleged to have attacked and twice raped a twenty-two-year old woman at Worsbrough Dale," read a report in the *South Yorkshire Times*.

At 11.30 p.m. on 6 August 1977, the lady had been walking down Knowle Road and not too far away from where my mum had had the fish and chip shop, when she noticed that she was being followed. The man approached her, hit her in the face and forced her on to waste ground alongside some garages.

The woman, who was making her way home from the Queen Victoria Hotel in Barnsley, was held by the man for an hour and threatened to strangle her if she resisted.

"The more crimes he committed the more violent he got," Det. Insp. Angela Wright had said at the press conference after Lloyds sentencing.

The police circulated a description of a smartly turned out man in his early twenties around 5'7 or 5'8.

At that time James Lloyd had been twenty-one years old. Also, note the length of time he spent with his victim along with his height. Everything points to Lloyd.

As for his family – it was said that they faced financial ruin.

Not really.

His wife – the daughter of Ken and Jane Willis (nee Cahill) formerly of 50 Barnburgh Lane (25 Poplar Avenue), Goldthorpe, of whose anonymity was waived at the trial – due to the fact that she refused to testify against her husband, did leave Thurnscoe. She isn't in some rat hole bedsit or flat, however. She now lives in one of the three-storey houses on the site of Bolton-Dearne's old woodyard – a property which she paid £124,950 for on 12 January 2011.

So, did she or his previous wife either know or suspect? Unfortunately, only they know the answer to that.

There is a similar case, although minor in comparison.

On 15 April 1966 at Rotherham West Riding Magistrates Court, twenty-nine-year-old Arthur Alan Johnson of Boswell Road, Wath-on-Dearne was found guilty of the indecent assault of a seventeen-year-old receptionist and a twenty-five-year-old sewing machinist along with five cases of indecent exposure.

"It happens when I am out in the car," he told the police. "I pass a girl and I just seem to get an impulse. I park up my car and then get out and do it."

According to the police, this had just been the tip of the iceberg. It had been a time when the Wath-on-Dearne, Swinton and Mexborough areas had been on high alert following a string of similar offences.

"Several of these were against women and girls standing in bus stops," said Chief Insp. R. Greaves. "In Johnson's case he had come up behind them as they walked up the street."

Extensive police enquiries were made and descriptions appeared to point to the same man being responsible.

"Surveillance was undertaken in and around the Manvers Main Coking Plant and the seventeen-year-old girl that had been assaulted eventually identified Johnson as the man who had assaulted her," added the chief inspector.

On his arrest he told the police: "I may as well admit it – it was me. I have done quite a few others too, although I don't know how many."

"There is obviously something mentally wrong with Mr Johnson and since these events he has seen several doctors and two psychiatrists," said his defence solicitor Mr R. Elmhurst. "His wife was completely horrified when she heard about it all and I am assured by her that their married life is happy in every way."

Johnson, somehow escaped prison and was fined £125 (£2,440, circa 2020).

As for his marriage – I am led to believe that it survived and the last I knew they were living opposite Mexborough's New Pastures Primary School and just around the corner from the house where Harold Marsden had cut off his daughter's head.

In the autumn of 1979, there had been a spate of thefts in Dearneside Comprehensive, one of which was nothing to do with me and one which I had been the victim.

Our mid-Monday morning's lesson had been *Games* and long before the final construction of the new gymnasium and Sports Hall in 1980, children had changed into their football gear in the upper cloakroom that was located close to where Mr (Ken) Dean and Mr (Paul) Charleworth's respective metal and woodwork classrooms were.

"Any valuables, hand them in," shouted, Mr (Jack) Taylor as he watched kids dropping various bits of shite into the clear polythene bag he was holding. "And I'm not saving any fags – Paul Richardson."

Whilst out on the field the cloakroom had been ransacked and we came in around 12.10 pm to find clothes scattered around and pockets emptied. I'd had five pink dinner tickets worth £1.25 (£7.25, circa 2020) along with my bus fare home lifted. What was even worse is that I hadn't written my name and form number on the back of any of them.

"Why didn't you hand in your stuff for me to save?" asked Mr Taylor. "I did ask you."

I had to admit, the bloke was brilliant. Within ten minutes the Deputy Headmaster, Mr (Howard) Baxter had been summoned and was asking staff which shitbags had been allowed out of class to go to the toilets. Within two hours I had had my dinner tickets returned. Unfortunately, there were only four of them as one had been weighed in for a meal on the second sitting comprising spam fritter and chips followed jelly and ice cream. Mr Baxter was always thorough, so much so, he had found out who had been behind me in the queue whilst purchasing them just to tally the numbers with the one the prime suspect had chucked in. On dragging him out of class he had the tallying tickets which were returned to me, and what followed was a bollocking – and not just to the thief. "Next time, write on the back of them and don't leave them in your pocket," he said.

The cloakroom bandit was the youngest son of Edward and Margaret Tarmey (nee Yardley) who at one time had lived on the Concrete Canyon at 96 Broadwater – Chris.

My recollection of him was as a little vociferous kid who I seem to recall lived not too far away from where Ken Rolfe had lived on the Ringway estate. Well, that was the house Kenny Barrett and myself had tried gaining access to when I had found out who had done it. My idea, post kicking him in the head was to take all his belongings. The upshot was, however, is that the kid had fuck all. There was nothing in the house worth taking bar half a loaf of bread – and even that was stale. And I thought my life was bad!

He offered to pay me back. "I'll nick something for you," he told me.

Kenny can maybe recall the story a bit better – especially as I got trapped in one of their small downstairs windows. Kenny had been alright as he made a Japanese POW look obese.

"What's up?" he asked, whilst watching me dangling.

"I'm fucking stuck," I told him.

It had been a similar tale when Alan Cook and myself tried gaining access to St Hilda's Church Hall a year earlier, whereby I scraped my ribs on the catch on one of its windows – the scars of which are still there today.

The last time I saw Kenny was during a Christmas Party at the Spit & Whisper in 1999 and one of the things he asked was: "Can you remember getting trapped and hanging from Tarmey's window?"

Chris had an elder brother who during late-November 1977 had been on trial for a crime which nowadays would probably see him doing ten years inside.

Graham Tarmey had been twenty years old when he and two youths accosted a pregnant young woman on Mexborough's Sticking Hill, dragged her into a field and attempted to rape her.

The details are sketchy in that I am not sure whether she had been travelling towards Bolton-on-Dearne or Adwick Road Allotments.

"Graham and me pulled her into that field," one of the youths had told the police. "I held her arms whilst Graham got on top of her. When he started undressing her, I left them to it."

A jury at Doncaster Crown Court were unanimous in finding him guilty and he was sentenced to six months in prison.

I have mentioned those allotments before as they have been the scene for suicides, rapes and more recently one of the most horrific murders in the area.

"It was the most brutal act of slaughter I have ever seen," said South Yorkshire Police's Det. Insp. Bob Meek. "It is all the more chilling when you realise that he must have spent half an hour inflicting those terrible wounds."

Although he was only two years younger than myself, I never knew Anthony Arkwright.

He is the middle-born son of Richard and Vida (nee Puidokas), the latter who abandoned her children and remarried a man over in Bradford by the name of Richard Waine in 1974.

Arkwight was dogged with rumours that he had been the product of an incestuous relationship between his mother and grandfather and from a relatively young age had been in local authority care, part of which involved living in a children's home – his entire childhood being very distorted and disturbed.

His Lithuanian-born grandfather, Stasys had married Ursule Vekerotaite in 1949 – but divorced sometime after, with Arkwright's grandmother remarrying a man by the name of Richard Hill in 1965.

Possessing an appearance not too dissimilar to Billy Idol – the front man of punk band Generation X, he had already served a thirty-month youth custody sentence for burglary, theft, and arson along with a six-month stint in prison. By the time he was twenty-one years old, however, this dysfunctional young man appeared to have got his life back on track and was working in the scrapyard (now JBM Recycling) off Swinton's White Lea Road, whilst living in a council flat on Wath-on-Dearne's Denman Road.

On Friday 26 August 1988, however, his life would change forever.

He had suddenly been sacked from his job – the two-fold reason being poor attendance and a bad attitude and thereby went on a drinking spree in Mexborough.

The signs were ominous. It was a night, when the 1981 version of *The Postman Always Rings Twice* would be shown on TV – Jack Nicholson being the drifter and Jessica Lange, the sexually charged femme fatale intent on ridding herself of her aged husband, by having him murdered.

At around 4.30 p.m. Arkwright walked up to his sixty-eight-year-old grandfather's allotment off Adwick Road and on finding him there callously stabbed him in the neck with a blow that instantly paralysed him. He had severed his spinal cord. Still conscious he then dragged his grandfather into the shed before finishing him off with an axe and 14 lb sledge hammer, the latter of which he used to completely crush his skull.

It is widely assumed that he then walked 700 yards to his grandfather's home at 12 Ruskin Avenue with a view to taking all his money, Arkwright firmly believing that his grandfather had been in part, responsible for his lousy upbringing. It would be there that he not only stole £3,000 (£8,517, circa 2020), but murdered his grandfather's seventy-three-year old housekeeper, Elsa Kronadiate, battering her around the skull with the self-same axe he had used to attack his grandfather.

Both bodies lay undiscovered for six days.

Arkwright had also had problems with his neighbours – Raymond Ford and wheelchair-bound Marcus Wright.

At 3.00 a.m. on 28 August, fully naked apart from a devil's mask, he gained access into forty-five-year-old Raymond Ford's home through a window that a few days earlier he had slung a dustbin through. The retired schoolteacher lived in relative squalor and was not only an extremely heavy drinker but suffered with depression. It had been Ford who had mentioned to police that he believed that Arkwright had been responsible for the burglary of his home – where both an antique clock and a microwave oven had been stolen. Arkwright not only stabbed him over 250 times but disembowelled him, draping his intestines all around the room, before calmly leaving the building to go home and shower.

What was interesting is that at 8.00 a.m. the police arrived at Arkwright's flat, totally unaware of the three murders and arrested him on suspicion of burglary. After interviewing him a total of three hours he was released on bail.

Early next morning, Marcus Law would undergo a similar same fate. The twenty-five-year-old, who was born in Germany as his father had been stationed overseas in the Armed Forces, lived in a specially adapted bungalow for wheelchair access as he had become paralysed following a motorcycle accident some years earlier. On entering his home Arkwright attacked him and stabbed him a total of seventy times, slicing open his stomach and ramming one of his crutches through it.

What was strange is that it was Arkwright that tipped off the police by telling Law's mother: "Sorry about poor old Marcus – he's killed himself."

Arkwright was arrested on suspicion of murder but with little evidence other than that of a rambling man, he toyed with the police for hours whilst playing with a pack of cards. It was then he showed his hand – not at least the *Four of Hearts* and intimated that there wasn't just one corpse, but four.

He told the detectives: "I can read the future from these cards. This is the master card – it means that you have four bodies and a madman on the loose. I can see Marcus Law, but the others are indescribable. They are just too horrible to describe."

Knowing that Arkwright was due in court on a charge of burglary the following week they decided to speak with Raymond Ford. It was PC David Winter who found his mutilated body after accessing the property via the same broken window.

That was the start of a huge murder inquiry, which saw Arkwright angling for publicity – something that the police did well to contain. His case went to trial at Sheffield Crown Court in July 1989 and he was sentenced to life imprisonment by Judge Sir Leslie Kenneth Boreham QC – the man who oversaw the trial of Peter Sutcliffe. Arkwright's sentence was later increased to that of a whole life tariff, meaning that he will thankfully never get out of prison.

Those allotments in Mexborough have a history that stretches back to a time long before Anthony Arkwright.

Prior to Christmas 1927, they had seen a bit of a police presence there as there had been complaints regarding thefts of property. What the police were about to find however, was something completely different – that of Peeping Tom's. Namely two Mexborough miners by the names of Stephen Scroop and William Riley who had been spying on courting couples.

This was nothing new as three years prior on 6 December 1924, a couple that were engaged to be married by the name of Jimmie Doyle and Doris May Wilford, had been subjected to much of the same. They had been on Doncaster Cricket Field (near the Racecourse) around 10.30 p.m., when they noticed two people crouched down behind a wall. One of these had even been wearing kneepads that had been custom made especially for the occasion. On having a closer look, Jimmie ended up getting involved in an altercation, whereby a thirty-eight-year-old man from the Mill Lane area of South Kirkby ended up getting stabbed through the heart.

The trial, which had nationwide coverage, exposed the fact that there were hundreds of these so-called Peeping Tom's operating in the Doncaster area alone and the death of Albert Needham was not seen as murder, but manslaughter – even though Jimmie Doyle had gone out armed with a knife.

The other voyeur had been a thirty-two-year-old Assistant Cemeteries Superintendent who worked for the Doncaster Corporation by the name of William Thrustle.

With Sir Edward Marshall Hall QC defending, Doyle was rather bizarrely given a not guilty verdict amidst cheers from the gallery.

The area around Doncaster racecourse has been witness to many other sexually motivated deaths one of which was a Thurnscoe woman, whose body was found in long grass just twenty-five yards from the A638 Great North Road.

On 26 November 1957, sixty-one-year-old Harry Smith had been sentenced at Sheffield Assizes after being found guilty of killing forty-two-year-old Dorothy (Dot) Hendley.

There are different pods of the Hendley family in and around Thurnscoe and Goldthorpe – all of whom are related in some way or another. It is, however, Dorothy's family that slightly complicates the story that I am going to relate.

On 4 February 1888, James Smith married Charlotte Walton – the latter of whom was not only just sixteen years old, but was also pregnant with their daughter, Rose.

The family relocated from the Tideswell area of Derbyshire and came to Thurnscoe – setting up home at 2 Clarence Terrace. Unfortunately, James died in 1909, aged forty-five, leaving a widow and several children, one of whom was Dorothy.

Charlotte didn't stick fast and on 21 February 1911 she remarried a thirty-eight-year-old miner by the name Joseph Rooth and moved up the road and into 23 Hickleton Terrace, where in June 1914 – they sadly had a six-month old daughter die, by the name of Ruby Rooth.

Dorothy, however, would end up marrying a young man from off The Spike in 1934. Thomas (Tom) Hendley was the son of Charles and Emily (nee Lloyd) – a couple that had been married in St Andrews Church, Bolton-on-Dearne on 19 August 1912 – with Emily having lived with her parents in Goldthorpe's north-eastern terraces at 30 Co-operative Street.

Tom and Dorothy set up home at 5 York Terrace before moving to 36 Tudor Street – that was until the outbreak of the Second World War. What I am unsure of, however, is what happened during the war. I know that for a time they relocated to Scunthorpe's Fox Street, which suggests that maybe he left mining and worked in one of the town's steelworks or armament factories. What I do know, is that Dorothy Hendley eventually left him – and moved around several addresses in Doncaster town centre before her dead body was uncovered on the Wednesday evening of 24 July 1957. She had been strangled to death.

Her assailant was a sixty-one-year-old labourer by the name of Harry Smith.

Home Office Pathologist, Dr David Price made an on-the-spot examination whilst the Head of Doncaster CID, Det. Insp. Arthur Howard headed up the murder investigation.

It was Sgt. George Herbert, however, who had been the first to be alerted to the crime as at around 8.30 p.m. Smith came into the Doncaster Police Headquarters with his face covered in scratches.

"I've had an argument with Dot Hendley and I am afraid I have done her some harm," he explained. "I have left her down at the Racecourse. I am sure I've done her in. There is no doubt about it. I have covered her up. She won't move far."

The policeman described Smith as being, "Cool, calm and collected," whilst in the court room during his trial it was described as a "most sordid case".

What would transpire is that Dorothy Hendley was a prostitute, who had said something *objectionable* to him. You can read into that however you will. I have had loads of women say objectionable things to me, not at least by the descendants of Dorothy Hendley. I didn't strangle them, however.

The truth is in the criminal depositions – however, as soon as I started rooting around the Department of Prosecution's files in the National Archives, those files got nailed-down with a 100-year closure.

As for Smith, he was found guilty of manslaughter and sentenced to seven years, which was later reduced to eighteen months on appeal.

Whilst I had been working down in the Vale of Belvoir, one of the men on the opposite shift in our heading had been a lad from the Woodlands area of Doncaster. He was a tall, gangly and vociferous kid, around one school year older than me, whose most striking feature was that he possessed a nose which could easily put mine to shame.

On starting work on the development, I had got to know Alan Plant quite well, with the thing I most recall about him is driving home from work on the A6097, A46 and A614 at speeds more than 100 mph. It was something that towards the end of the job saw him involved in a near fatal road crash with two Conisbrough lads as his passengers. It is, however, his brother, where this story is going.

Gary Plant was a man that I didn't know but someone that held something of a legendary nudge-nudge kind of status in Doncaster's mining fraternity. He had married Jacqueline (Jackie) Froggatt in 1980 and between them had two children: Sherri Ann in 1981 and Susan Anne in 1984. However, shortly after the birth of their second child, Jackie would end up dead. I was told that he had strangled his wife. As I have said, domestic incidents happen every day, although not all end with a murder investigation.

From what I am told, he was charged with manslaughter and served minimal time in prison – with one of the things that was said, being that there was both mitigating circumstances coupled with the fact that he never tried to hide it.

The most interesting domestic in that area occurred some twenty-two years earlier.

At 6.00 p.m. on Friday 5 April 1962, the body of Mavis Chappell (nee Hughes) had been found in the bedroom of their home in Charles Street, Skellow.

Her husband was immediately put in the frame and an all-points bulletin was sent out for someone fitting his description – a man between 5'4 and 5'6 and slightly built, wearing a grey-green overcoat, dark suit, white shirt and black shoes, with short brown hair and sideboards.

Her death certainly wasn't as cleanly executed as either Dot or Jackie's, that is for sure. The twenty-one-year-old had been bludgeoned to death with a pickaxe whilst she had been laid in bed.

On 5 June at Sheffield Assizes and in a trial presided over by Justice Roskill QC, Chappell pleaded guilty to murder and was sentenced to life imprisonment.

His defence barrister, Rudolph Lyons QC had told the court that his wife had been pregnant and that he had been that worried about money – so much so, that he had contemplated suicide.

"I did not kill her on purpose – she dared me," Chappell had told Chief Insp. S.C Mogg on his arrest.

He had been employed as a Wire Drawer but was on the brink of bankruptcy as he hadn't been working.

The couple had been married in 1959 and had two children – Stephen and Keith, aged two and one-years-old, respectively.

Now, here is the story of someone who did anything but come clean with the police – that of Goldthorpe's *Body in the Boot Murderer* and a man who will perhaps die in prison.

Raymond (Ray) Vernon Billam was born on 19 September 1948 in a mid-terraced property at 76 Highgate Lane (formerly Bolton Road) to John Anthony and Minnie (nee Nortcliff) – a couple who had married in 1935 and who along with their three eldest children had relocated from 10 Briton Square during the war.

Ray had been married a total of four times: to Susan Haywood in 1969; Janet Potts in 1978; Lesley Townend in 1985; and Joy Stockhill in 1997 – the latter of whose dead body was found in the boot of her purple Ford Fiesta Fusion on Saturday 1 October 2011.

It had hardly been well hidden, that is for sure. The car had been attracting attention as it stood out like some sore thumb, being parked up in a layby on a section of the A635, close to the Doncaster-Barnsley road's first junction into Goldthorpe.

"Raymond Billam is a deceptive, manipulative and very dangerous man, whose wife had endured his abuse for years and which has ultimately resulted in her death," said Det. Chief Insp. Sean Middleton, who led the investigation.

It transpired that Ray's forty-six-year-old wife had left him and hooked up with someone from Goldthorpe's Garden Street by the name of Michael Woodland. She had also got engaged to him a day before her murder.

Ray's brainwave, if you could call it that, was to kill her, shift the body and dump it close to her boyfriend's house thereby ultimately trying to put him in the frame for her murder. It had been an act of pure folly.

His trial at Sheffield Crown Court in March 2012 was presided over by Justice Openshaw QC – a man who had been closer to murder than most. His father, also a Judge, had been murdered by someone that he had sentenced in 1968. At around 8.30 a.m. on 12 May 1981, a loner by the name of John Smith, had laid in wait for him tucked up in the rafters of his garage at his home on Garstang Road, Broughton and had stabbed him a dozen times with a hunting knife.

Ray's story was that his ex-wife had visited him at his home at 12 Guildford Road –a street located just to the west of Sandall Park in the Wheatley Hills area of Doncaster. This, he said, was to discuss their divorce. However, that definitely wasn't happening as Ray still hoped for a reconciliation and therefore would not agree.

As they argued, Ray – a former miner at both Barnburgh and Manvers Main collieries – told her that he would stretch out proceedings as long as he could and added motive to his story by saying that his wife began taunting him – mainly about Micky being better in bed than he was – and that he *saw red* before losing control.

"I called her a slag and she came at me like a crazy woman, scratching, kicking and nipping," he told the jury, whilst trying to gain favour, by turning up to court on a pair of crutches. "I told her to shut her filthy mouth!"

He claimed that when he pushed her away, she *went flying* and fell between a chair and coffee table.

"I stood up and fell over her legs and on top of her knocking a transformer off the coffee table and ended up with its flex in my hands."

It was then that he put it across Joy's throat.

"I told her to shut her mouth once and for all," he added. "It was the way she was laughing and saying *Micky this and Micky that.* Thinking about his name made me sick. I lost control. I had no idea what I had done as it all happened so fast."

That bit of the story could have been quite believable, and if he would have hit a triple-nine and held his hands up, he would now be a free man. Unfortunately, for Ray, that is exactly what he didn't do.

One of the golden rules is to never over complicate things. It is like a lie – in that as soon as a person starts getting deeper into their explanation, it gives you more to pull that person up on. That is why when you are hauled into a police station on any charge you must tell them as little as possible. As Sheffield barrister Chris Tong once told me: "Saying 'I don't know' is quite possibly the best response you could ever give."

It is neither a yes nor a no. It is vague.

Ray was defended by Paul Watson QC with the Crown Prosecutor being Rodney Jameson QC.

The court heard that he had carried his wife's body to the boot of her car, which had been parked behind his house, and drove it to Goldthorpe.

"I wanted to put some space between me and Joy," he said. "I didn't know whether I was going north, south, east or west. I had no idea why I stopped where I did."

Yes, he did. He wanted the boyfriend to cop for her murder, and in part that is exactly what happened. However, when the police realised this, it put him on the back foot, Ray telling his barrister that he was "utterly disgusted and ashamed" of what he had done.

He was asked by the Crown Prosecutor when such "admirable feelings" first arose.

Ray replied: "When I was sat in prison. I had time to reflect on life with Joy. I thought, yes I've got to hold my hands up and say yeah, I did kill her."

In a case of violence, self-defence is the greatest alibi going and that is what he tried. "If she hadn't been kicking and scratching it would never have got to that stage. All of a sudden she was like a woman possessed."

Remember, the Lover's Lane murder. The murderers' story was exactly the same.

Mr Jameson questioned why Ray had not considered an ambulance for the woman he had called the 'love of his life'. "Might she still have been alive while she was lying on the floor?" he asked.

"I don't know," was Ray's reply.

The court heard that Joy had got engaged to her new boyfriend on Ingoldmells beach the previous day and that Ray committed the murder when he realised that he couldn't win his wife back. Evidence was also heard that Ray had started to make frequent phone calls to Joy which became quite hostile, telling her that if he couldn't have her, then no-one else could.

"As a macabre gesture, you removed your ex-wife's new engagement ring, placed it on your mantelpiece, and even recruited a sixteen-year-old to help you remove the body," said Mr Jameson. "Then, as a calculating attempt to frame her boyfriend you parked up her car on Doncaster Road, Goldthorpe, which was just a few hundred yards from his home."

It nearly worked. Because Ray had hidden the body, the innocent Mr Woodland had been the first person arrested on suspicion of Joy's murder and as a result spent twenty-four hours in custody before police realised that the ex-husband had been conning them.

Ray – who admitted manslaughter – was convicted of murder. The jury had been unanimous in its decision.

"Nothing could justify taking up that cable and holding it forcibly against her neck, as she clawed desperately at his forearms to free herself," said Justice Openshaw.

"I am satisfied that you killed her in a fit of sexual jealousy, founded essentially on the fact that she had left you for another man."

The judge jailed him for life with a minimum term of eighteen years, meaning that he may die in prison.

A statement from his ex-wife's family read: "Throughout his trial, he has sought to discredit our mum's name and convince the jury his actions were justified. His attempts to convince the jury that she was the love of his life and that he would never hurt her were a sham. Only when she decided to leave him and make a new life did he show his true colours. Then, when it was clear she would no longer be around to pay for his lifestyle, he murdered her. Our mum loved her grandchildren so very much; she was so full of life and happy when around them. They will never see her again due to his spitefulness and jealousy. Thankfully, the jury saw through his lies and distortion of the truth."

Four marriages with one wife murdered, maybe married life just wasn't for him.

The Billam's however, were a colourful family.

If you want more violence: On 11 December 1959, Ray's younger brothers, nineteen-year-old George of South Drive and seventeen-year-old Jimmy, off Heath Grove had been dragged before Doncaster West Riding Magistrates, after being arrested following a knife fight which resulted in the youngest being stabbed in the neck after some altercation over a fire that the eldest had started in some air raid shelter.

According to Chief Insp. S. Mogg – the case was made worse as George had threatened a fifteen-year-old by the name of Edward Ramsdale, saying that if he gave evidence he would also be stabbed-up.

If you want a bit of entrepreneurism: On 18 March 1966, Jimmy had been dragged before Rotherham West Riding Magistrates – after being caught with 14 miles of overhead telephone wire valued at £560 and nine shillings (£10,940, circa 2020).

How he got caught was interesting. Apart from the fact that all the communication wire on the railway lines between Denaby Main and both Adwick and Wath-on-Dearne had been removed – half of which was in his back garden at York Street, Thurnscoe, two detectives had been making a routine visit to the premises of a metal recycling firm in Leeds – and who should they see but one Mr Billam hawking his wares. And not only did he have a van crammed full of the stuff – even the van it was in had been stolen.

If you want fraud: Ray's son – Raymond (Jnr) of 99 Primrose Close, Bolton-on-Dearne, made the national media as some box-to-box midfielder playing for Ings Lane FC. He had been under investigation by the Department for Work and Pensions as he was supposedly disabled. According to reports he required the aid of crutches to walk and had scammed the DHSS out of £15,066.

In April 2015, he was found guilty of fraud and the District Judge at Barnsley Magistrates Court – John Foster, handed him a twenty-six-week sentence, suspended for two years, along with a community order for 200 hours unpaid work.

As I have said, most of the houses in Thurnscoe's east end have some unwanted history. If you want an example there is no better one than 40 Windsor Street – and the regular sighting of little girl at the landing window. Many have claimed to see it – however, one minute it is there, the next it has gone.

Enter, the Dark Queen.

The Hendleys had been the family on her mother's side, but what of the other?

Nikki Gough's great grandparents on her father's side originally came from the Wigan area of Lancashire. They settled in Thurnscoe after the lockout of 1926 and moved into the said property on Windsor Street.

Their eighteen-year-old daughter, Mary Elizabeth Gough, married a miner by the name of Phillip Nicholson Nuttall in 1934 and all the family lived together at the same property with their three children Mary (b. 1935), Margaret (b. 1937) and Peter (b. 1939).

On the Sunday evening of 3 September 1939, the children had all been put to bed and one hour later – tragedy struck. The two-and-half-year-old Margaret had been found dead. She had climbed onto the landing windowsill and fallen out of the window from a height of 11 feet and on to the concrete path.

The paranormal is often taken with a pinch of salt, but most people will have experienced it at some point in their lives.

Whilst living at 14 Landsdowne Avenue, I awoke in panic and even now, I feel that it was real. I saw two creatures in the bedroom – children with heads that looked like a sheep, one of which had been chewing on a handkerchief – which was one of two that had been given to me by my great-auntie Elsie (nee Carman) for my fifth birthday.

The couple that had lived there before us had been Jimmy and Gladys Ferguson (nee Adams) – a couple that were married in 1927 and had five children: Gerald (b. 1931), Jean (b. 1934), Margaret (b. 1936), Sadie (b. 1938) and Patrick (b. 1944). They had vacated the property shortly before we set up home there, moving into a property with a bathroom at 107 Low Grange Road.

On 20 October 1958, a child had been born in the house. Unfortunately, it had been born dead.

At fifty-five years old, it could have hardly been Gladys's child, therefore I am assuming it was their son Gerald's – who just a few months earlier had been in front of Doncaster West Riding Magistrates Court and fined £15 (£365, circa 2020) for obtaining money by false pretences.

As for that handkerchief, I never saw it again!

"I lived in 147 Deightonby Street as a child from about 1977 to 1981 and loads of strange things happened there, especially in the little bedroom," explained Andrea Element – the eldest of three children to Charlie and Karen (nee Robinson).

"While we lived there, my mam often suffered with really bad with panic attacks and often felt like she was choking. She used to have to sit at window through night for air, as she felt like she couldn't breathe."

This hadn't been helped by the peculiar sighting of an old man at her bedroom door. Nor was it helped by the eerie sightings from the back garden of a child in the window of the back bedroom, covered in what I am assuming was some white shroud as it looked out of the window at the children playing.

Andrea, her brothers and cousins often referred to this as the "White Bird".

"My mam said the little back bedroom was very eerie. When we moved into it looked like it had never ever been decorated and the dog that my nanan had, even refused to even to enter the room."

What was true is that there had been a dead child connected this property, but what intrigued me more, was something else that Andrea told me. "Our next-door neighbour – who used to come and help my mam mentioned that it may have had something to do with something that happened in the house in 1942."

The last bit of information was extremely interesting.

The proprietor of the property had been an official at Hickleton Main by the name of Horace Beardshall – a man who had married Lily Bullock in 1906. After the couple moved to Thurnscoe, Lily had given birth to twins, one of who had been born dead.

Deightonby Street was no different to any other street in that it has washed its hands in the misery of dead children. One of the most notable had been from yet another family who came over to Thurnscoe from Lancashire after the lockout of 1926.

On 26 September 1931, Seven-year-old Joyce Colley had been playing in the rear yard of No 76 and had been stood on a dustbin. She lost her footing and fell awkwardly –causing her to hit her head on the concrete. It was also a blow that fractured her skull. She eventually died in Mexborough Montagu Hospital.

Something similar happened on York street just over eleven years later.

At 6.10 p.m. on 16 November 1942, seven-year-old Sheila Wordsworth of 26 York Street had also died in Mexborough Montagu. She had fractured her skull less than two hours earlier after swinging on a double gate between No's 16 and 18.

As for the Beardshalls – Lily died in Dearnlea old people's home on 16 April 1976, aged ninety. As for Horace, he died aged fifty-nine… both in the said property and in 1942.

In my eyes, the Christmas of 1970 was one of wonderment and one that I rarely forget.

I would often wind up my two kids on driving past the entry to both Crossgate and Lindley Crescent by saying: "Did I ever tell you the story…"

"Yeh Dad, you did," they would sigh.

I recall the Christmas Eve of that year stood within its concrete bus shelter along with my mum, (step)dad and little sister waiting to catch the 23 into Goldthorpe, when it suddenly began snowing. It would be the first White Christmas of my life. It was a memory that has never left me.

A few days earlier it had been our final days of that decade in Houghton Road Infants – and the miracle of Christmas had been there too. All the children had been sat in awe at the foot of Mrs (Doris) Haigh's desk waiting for Father Christmas to come into the class. It may seem nothing, but as kid's it was everything and what most of us asked after the fake Santa had handed out the presents, was of who had been the man behind the beard. The head teacher of the junior school seemed the most obvious – but the upshot was, that none of us really knew.

That would be the day that a lot of friends had been split up.

"Which children would like to change class and go to the upstairs classroom with Mrs Brookes?" asked Mrs Haigh.

There were a few kids who put up their hand. Colin Hunter and myself were one of those, although I did try to renege on that a few seconds after. It was not to be, however, by 4 January 1971, my new classroom would be opposite the head mistress's office and Mrs Vince's –dark-haired school secretary.

Mrs Brookes was one of those teachers that gave loads of encouragement and had us doing all kinds of wonderful things from making models, to acting, to singing. She had something quite unique about her and one of my fondest memories would be that summer and the school trip to Cleethorpes. How she coped with all those children, I do not know – but she did. I recall us all getting stripped on the sand not too faraway from the zoo and racing down to the shoreline and paddling through the sludge and freezing cold water in the Humber Estuary.

In the classroom, one of the songs she taught us was Oscar Brand's New World Song. You may know the one:

When I first came to this land, I was not a wealthy man? And I called my wife, Run For Your Life – and I called my cow, No Milk Now – and I called my shack, Break My Back – but the land was sweet and good, and I did what I could.

One of those little faces had been a girl by the name of Pamela Duke.

I haven't seen Pam since I left Houghton Road school, but we often speak over social media and one thing she mentioned had been an horrific incident that occurred on 4 November 1982.

The dark Thursday evening in question was etched in a lot of people's minds – even now, as it was the catalyst for a series of tragic incidents that left residents of the Whinwood Estate scratching their heads?

I do not so much remember the day – but I certainly the day after as I had been in to see the Training Officer, Ron Lester about going on three-shifts as it had been the week before my eighteenth birthday. My wish may have been granted and I got to spend the next week on afternoon shift – my first ever job as an adult being to man the busy East Gearhead, but the main conversation with Ron had been about the fifty-one-year-old father of one of the lads manning one of the transfer points up on the P80's drift.

A great night of TV that kicked off with *Top of the Pops* – Tears for Fears singing *Mad World* – Eddy Grant at No 1 with the fact that he *didn't want to dance* – followed by *Only Fools and Horses* – the episode where Boycie challenges Del Boy to a winner-takes-all poker game, had been abruptly interrupted. Unbeknown to me at the time there had been an incident around four hundred yards from where I had been sat.

Pam's common-law-husband, Rob Nicholson lived at 15 Deightonby Street – a house that at one time had trains trundling through a cutting at the rear of its back garden and transporting coal from Wath Main over to Hull Docks. In 1982, however, all there had been was a grassed area over an infilled cutting – which suddenly had a massive police presence on it along with a substantial area being cordoned off. And Rob – he had a front seat view. The police had been dealing with a suicide on the Sheffield – York railway line.

"It was Mischievous Night," explained Bob Butler – one of the young lads that had been playing on the bankings that evening. "When the police put all the spotlights up, we obviously became intrigued and started to walk up towards the girder bridge to find out what was happening. The police stopped us and told us to go back home. I remember it like it was yesterday. It was all very sad."

Les Bainbridge of 47 Burnside had donned his best suit, gone up to the railway lines and thrown himself in front of a train.

I am told that there was a reason – as there generally is in cases such as this – however, as it was never made public, it would be quite wrong of me to say. There was, however, a suicide – that although completely different, had perhaps possessed a similar catalyst, and which was something I touched on earlier.

On 20 October 1978, the family at 31 Lancaster Street had to deal with a macabre event that would set all the tongues wagging. George Nicholson had been forty-seven years old when police attended his allotment to find him dead. The father of six children, one of who I regularly saw playing on the park behind the Hanover Street bus stops with her friends, had poured petrol over himself and set himself on fire.

As for the incident on the railway lines, I would get to know the man's son quite well.

Trevor Bainbridge was an affable lad who frequented all the bottom-end pubs along with Grundy's bookmakers – therefore if I didn't see him in one of those, I certainly heard about him the other as it was no secret that he had quite a soft spot for my wife. Standing at around 6'0, with his unkempt blond hair and gregarious personality I saw him as quite harmless and just a really nice lad. It was something echoed by everyone that knew him, therefore on the days following Monday 13 November 1995, it remained a mystery as to why this thirty-two-year-old lad who everyone liked had taken his own life.

Daz Cooper had been with him that weekend and the only thing that could have thrown light on as to *why* – was the loss of his mum a few months prior. It was something that had hit him bad.

"You just don't know what's going on in people's heads," Daz told me.

Very true.

There is another dark story that happened recently.

At 12.48 p.m. on 14 August 2019, a forty-six-year-old man threw himself in front of a train at Goldthorpe (Highgate) Railway Station.

A spokesperson for British Transport Police said: "We were called following a report of a casualty on the tracks. Paramedics also attended but sadly the person was pronounced dead at the scene. The incident is not being treated as suspicious. We are currently working to identify the person and inform their next of kin."

What the police did not – and would not say is that the dead man had been a serving officer with South Yorkshire Police's Doncaster West Neighbourhood Policing Team.

"This is the last we are going to say on the matter," the statement said.

The police are always very selective about what they both do and say.

Michael Wilburn and Linda Guest had married in 1965 and lived on Thurnscoe's High Street soon after having a daughter by the name of Kay, who in September 1969, should have started school in Houghton Road Infants. Unfortunately, that never happened. She died at just four months old.

They would, however, be blessed with the birth of a son in 1973. Lewis Brigham Wilburn was the person that had thrown himself in front of the train at Highgate, and who more importantly, the police were trying their damnedest to keep out of the news.

Lewis had made his final post on social media the night before. He posted a song titled *Who Is It* by Michael Jackson – the singer who during the summer of 1993 had been publicly accused of sexually abusing the thirteen-year-old son of screenwriter, Evan Chandler, and then signed off: "And you all thought I was shallow. Anyway, that's all."

And the reason why she left me – did she find someone else?

Is it a friend of mine (Who is it?) Is it my brother? (Who is it?) Somebody hurt my soul (Who is it?)

I can't take this stuff no more.

I am the damned – I am the dead – I am the agony…

On 11 October 2016, Lewis's seventy-three-year-old father of 4 Princess Road, Goldthorpe, had been handed a fourteen-year sentence, which was reduced to ten on appeal after being convicted at Sheffield Crown Court of attempted rape and indecent assault against three young girls.

That, however, certainly hadn't been the reason.

My two-year-old son, Jamie in the rear garden of 16 Briton Square - whilst his mum natters to near neighbour Gail Gollick at the gates

37. Dubstar

Two legs of Deightonby Street. That was my first ever job. 21 January 1979. Delivering newspapers in two batches. The money was rubbish and the weather absolutely freezing. The previous paper lad – well, it wasn't a lad as such, but a girl that was very-much laddish, had chucked in her job and as I'd had my name down for a couple of weeks, I received a telephone call asking if I fancied it. It sounded great until I had to do it.

The base-venue, a little cluttered shop at 22 Roman Street; my boss, Mrs (Doris) Morrell.

Doris was an old white-haired lady who was both slow and methodical and who always had her hair styled in the Beehive. I had known her since I was seven years old.

"Twenty Number Six tipped, please," had been my general request.

That was until my mum found the Howley's beer-off on Lidget Lane's junction with Queen Street sold them considerably cheaper at 19 ½ pence.

Born on 12 December 1900, this little old lady had probably seen it all: the construction of The Avenues, the two sprawling council estates and of course both pit estates – most notably, Thurnscoe East. As with the landlord of public houses, newsagents were central to the area that they served.

The shop itself was extremely compact and highly disorganised in such away, only the little old lady knew where anything was. If I close my eyes, I can see it now. As you entered through the door straight in front of you there was an array of cards and magazines and immediately to your left a counter full of newspapers, with chocolates, slightly to the right and out of reach to any would be short-arsed thief. To the left there was a glass cabinet, full of all sorts of oddments and at the back, the till and cigarettes. What was strange is that she had magazines and toys hanging from the ceiling on bulldog clips.

Compared to Pyott's newsagents in Bolton-on-Dearne's St Andrews Square, it was a chaotic ensemble of clutter. Even the newsagent at 139 Furlong Road owned by Harry and Mary Burley (nee Goss), had more structure to its layout – and kids were in and out of there all day long. My auntie Heather once caught one of their paper lads both behind the counter and rifling cigarettes one morning she'd gone in.

I had known Jeff Nash from my first few days at Carfield school. He lived on Bolton-on-Dearne's shortest Street – that of Bridge Street and just around the corner from the shop. He was a tall, gangly and buck-toothed lad two years my senior.

Although Mary Burley had been a policewoman – something she often used to threaten us with, Harry had been as deaf as a post, and couldn't hear you coming in and out of the shop. This was something that our Tony and I used to great effect during the summer of 1976. We would wait until the shop was empty and he had gone into the back – then move inside quickly and empty the shelves. I seem to recall coming out with one particular haul that included seven packets of *Pacers*. These were sweets that were shaped exactly like Opal Fruits (now Sunburst) but were both spearmint and peppermint flavoured. They were quite crap if I am being honest.

Doris was just as deaf and much slower but having her premises in the heart of Thurnscoe's East end, she was much the wilier proprietor.

What immediately struck me was that she clacked her mouth all of the time – and every minute or so, she would take a deep noisy intake of breath, which while you were dropping to sleep waiting for her to scrawl the numbers on the newspapers, had a tendency to make you jump.

My slave wages were immediately supplemented – but not so much by a chocolate bar but maybe a Dandy or a Beano and most certainly three of four newspapers from the round.

Trudging through the snow from 6.15 a.m. was the ultimate ball ache. There were 140 letterboxes on the street and the papers, to those who paid for their delivery, weighed a fucking ton. This was even more so on a Friday, when half the round had the *South Yorkshire Times* delivered.

The lower part of Deightonby Street had some interesting letterboxes – especially the block of four between No's 32 and 38. One always had the smell of bacon being fried whilst another had a nasty little dog that obviously suffered from small man syndrome and would inadvertently rip the newspaper to pieces. I thought it great. As soon I felt him grab on to the paper, I used to drag the paper back through the letterbox and smash him against the door. The dog fell for it every time. God knows what the state of the *Daily Mirror* looked like, when the owner came to read it.

A house close-by on the same side of the street suffered a lightning strike a few months later. The lightning struck the chimney and blew out some of the windows. However, by that time, the landscape had changed, and I had chucked the lousy job. Doris hadn't been too well and the position behind the counter had been filled by her nephew, Colin.

Well, you could say, nephew, but he had also been her stepson.

The Morrells were a family that came over from the Birdwell area of Barnsley and in line with their shop keeping aspirations, initially settled at 14 High Street, Goldthorpe. This was a shop that during the 1970s stood opposite the school and which was flanked by Jack Ellis's photography studio and Edmondson's DIY store.

Both the father Edward and his son, Colin worked at Hickleton Main – the latter as a rope man. Colin, however, was one of the 1,000 miners who left the pit to fight in the horror that was the First World War, enrolling into the 1st Yorkshire (West Riding) Royal Engineers on 20 June 1915. He not only progressed to the rank of Sergeant but was awarded the Distinguished Conduct Medal (DCM) in February 1916.

On 25 July 1922, the twenty-seven-year-old war hero married a widow by the name of Florence Smith (nee Fawcett) and a year later she gave birth to a son by the name of Colin – the exact same person, who ended up taking over from Doris.

Unfortunately, Florence died in childbirth in early December 1934 and to compound her husband's misery further, the child she should have been having, was born dead. It wasn't the first child of theirs to die. Colin had had a younger sister by the name of Molly who died in April 1927, aged just seven weeks. This had been whilst they had had the newsagents at 34 Lidget Lane – the extremely busy shop which Irene Ratcliffe (nee Cattell) had owned when I had first started at Hickleton Main.

Rather strangely, they moved from the front street premises and further into the pit estate after the death of their first child and moved between two properties – that being the shop on Roman Street and the family home at 2 Saxon Street. This is the house where Florence would die. It was nothing new. As I have mentioned already – the street has a god-awful history for chid deaths. Remember the story of little Alen Atkinson at No 9 being boiled alive in February 1922. That was just the tip of the iceberg. Just a couple of months later a six-month-old child by the name of John Cottam died, whilst straight opposite at No 8, a little lad by the name of Lawrence Fletcher lost his life, aged sixteen months.

The child mortality rate in Thurnscoe was dire – Colin himself killing a child. He ran over eleven-year-old, Jack Godley of 73 George Street on 23 February 1933. It was said that the little lad ran across Lidgett Lane, close to where the Pit Shop now stands, and that Colin hit him head on. Although he was exonerated by the District Coroner, you have a feeling of what comes around goes around and Colin was left on his own with two children to bring up.

However, here comes the twist in the tale.

Colin's wife, Florence had a younger sister by the name of Doris – the exact same white-haired old lady who effectively policed her counter with an authority that Harry Burley could have only dreamed of. Doris, however, hadn't always been the doddering old lady that clacked, puffed and wheezed whilst chalking up the newspapers. Far from it. She was from a respectable family of that there was no doubt, with her father, David serving on

Thurnscoe UDC as Vice Chairman of the Education committee as well as being a prominent leader of the Wesleyan Chapel until his death in December 1913. However, as with girls from my generation, such as Angie Mellor, Wendy Fereday, Nikki Gough and so on – no matter how pretty or intelligent they are, they are always attracted to the bad lad. And Doris had been no different. She had been in a relationship with a man from Sheffield who was a serious – or seriously bad gambler and she ducked and dived to aid his addiction. However, the walls would come tumbling down on her affair, when she was arrested, charged and eventually sentenced on Friday 22 April 1932 for a series of offences – not at least forgery, fraud… and rather interestingly, blackmail.

On 10 March 1926, her mother Annie, had remarried a man by the name of William Tinker and moved into a property at 31 Laurel Terrace, Skellow. The marriage at All Saints Church in the quaint little village of Owston just off the A19 topside of Doncaster was very strange. Not only was her new husband eight years younger than her – but was both illiterate and blind. It would be something that over a fourteen-month period, Doris would fully exploit.

William Tinker was originally from Allerton Bywater and for a time, during the early years of their respective marriages, had been the near neighbour of the Fawcett's – Tinker becoming a shopkeeper after being injured in the pit.

The West Riding police had been alerted after Tinker nearly fell through the floor after finding out that the contents of his Post Office Savings account only had £2, four shillings and eight pennies (£135.50, circa 2020) left in the account.

On thirty different occasions Doris had made withdrawals from the account by forging her stepfather's signature, duly robbing him of £323 (£19,892, circa 2020).

Doris's day job at the time was as a typist, although it was also stated that she had been an uncertified teacher and had been considering moving into the poultry business – something that her grandfather John Carr had been involved in. However, the stolen money certainly hadn't been used for that. Doris had set up accounts with some farm supplier down in Bedford and using her stepfather's details she had managed to fleece them out of £41 and 12 shillings (£2,562, circa 2020).

The case at Leeds Assizes on 22 April 1932 had been presided over by Justice Sir John Anthony Hawke QC. He was the high-profile judge who overturned the verdict on appeal of William Herbert Wallace – a man convicted of the murder of his wife Julia at their home at 29 Wolverton Street in the Anfield district of Liverpool in 1931.

"I have grave doubts about not sentencing you to penal servitude," the judge told her.

The background to Doris's case was interesting in that the Crown Prosecutor, Charles Paley-Scott QC, referred to her bad character, stating that she had previously been charged with blackmail and trying to demand money by menaces, after threatening to expose a Sheffield-based businessman. What of, isn't exactly clear, but the case was adjourned sine-die on the pretext that she wouldn't molest him further.

The fact of how respectable her family were, weighed in her favour and she was handed a slap on the wrists by way of an eighteen-month suspended sentence.

It is unclear what happened to Doris's mother and her stepfather straight after that, as Annie passed away in one of the bungalows on what is now Thurnscoe's Kingsway Grove in November 1933 and by the outbreak of war, William Tinker was living back in Allerton Bywater.

You kind of got a feeling that there was much more to Doris.

In fact, on 30 May 1935, she had been one of the witnesses in a strange case that involved the death of a sixty-one-year-old lady by the name of Elizabeth Hayselden who was found dead in the cellar of 84 Furlong Road, Bolton-on-Dearne. She had apparently died from asphyxia – her body being found face-down in the coal.

It is also unclear, when exactly, she shacked up with Colin Morrell – however, what is certain is that she was living over the shop on 22 Roman Street at least ten years before she actually married him in 1948. This was the year when the younger Colin, who was by then a timber dealer, had been both remanded and jailed for the theft of a bread van and its contents that had been valued at £391 (£15,420, circa 2020).

The one thing that you cannot say is that the Morrell family weren't colourful.

Colin had a younger sister who would go on to marry the son and namesake of the man who would go on to be an undermanager at Hickleton Main. This was the same man who would receive the Edward Medal from the King himself – following the successful rescue of Arthur Bridges in 1923. Lily Morrell married James Parkin in 1922, both of whom would go on to run a newsagent in Leeds.

As for Doris, she died on Christmas Eve, 1984.

What was far sadder, however, was that Harry and Mary Burley had a sixteen-year-old son who had died earlier that year on 7 April.

Robert, a bespectacled fellow, had been very academically gifted. He was a lad that was regarded as something of a *geek*, both playing the trumpet in a brass band and having half the school standing around him in the playground, whilst he completed the Rubik Cube in less than two minutes. How do I know that? I was one of those watching on in admiration. I am informed by his best friend, Rich Hall, that the cause of death was meningitis. I was also told that it was something that his father struggled to deal with afterwards and shortly after his death they ended up selling the shop.

The new owners were Douglas and Margaret Gibbard (nee Cox) – the parents of Jayne and Julie – the latter of whom was one of the pretty little things from the year below me at school. They moved from 23 Carfield Lane and set up shop, converting half of it into a florists.

"My dad took a huge risk," Julie had told me. "He had just been finished from Goldthorpe Pit and put most of his redundancy money into buying it."

It was all very sad. However, there is always something that trumps it and which is something that I will get on to.

Around the time of my flirtation with actually working for a living and trudging through the snow at daft o'clock in the morning, I was part of that group of young lads (that have already been mentioned) which wreaked havoc both inside and outside school – one of these being a ginger-haired lad by the name of Stuart Kerry.

Stuart and his family lived in a semi-detached house within one of the several cul-de-sacs that made-up Bolton-on-Dearne's Ringway estate – that of 9 East Croft. It was there during dinnertime, where in between taking anything that wasn't nailed down, that we went to get out of the cold.

His parents were Roy and Pat (nee Hawley), the latter of who was a lovely lady, and who like a lot of people during that time in my life, I never genuinely appreciated.

"What's a matter with you – are yer sat on a bleeding feather or what?" I once recall her saying.

Pat tended to leave her false teeth out and as such, when she spoke, her gurning created a mildly amusing incoherence that once Roger (Kitch) Kitchen started sniggering, had us all in stitches.

It would be fair to say that Kitch had been the dominant and central figure of the dinnertime crowd that I hung about with. He was flanked by me, Stuart, Sean Buck and more often than not, a few lads from the school year below. These were Richard (Puggy) Pugh, Kenny Barrett (or Benny Carrot) and Allen (Bungy) Guest – the latter of who lived in a house that literally backed onto The Dearne Hotel. Bungy was interesting in that he was the younger brother to a rather strange looking pair of twin sisters – Diane and Jane. These were a year older than us and who due to their appearance – which could be construed as Albinism, coupled with their National Health prescribed eyewear, were both heartlessly referred to as Pink Eyes.

Rather strangely, my last thoughts of them were watching them climbing on to the top of their next-door neighbours' outhouse.

And there you had it. Again, kids can be cruel, and, in this instance, there was no one more so than I. I look back and outside of my family I have very few regrets. One of the few that I do have, however, are tied in with situations such as the one I am now going to relate.

There are certain types of bully – the one that inflicts physical pain and the other that exacts it mentally. Throughout my childhood I had been both. I put this solely down to my violent upbringing.

When a parent tries to get children to behave better by hitting them, that parent is telling them that hitting people who are smaller and weaker than you, is an acceptable way of getting what you want from them. That is not me saying that but a renowned psychologist by the name of Dr Denise Cummins. She also goes on to say that the more physical punishment a child receives, the more defiant they become toward parents and authority. She is right on both counts.

Fortunately, two things stopped it from getting out of control. The first being that I was never that big a kid to throw my weight around and the other was the lack of confidence that these beatings at home brought. The downside to the latter, however, is that a lack of confidence is all the ingredients needed for a self-doubting and deceitful personality. Not all the time, but it was definitely there if I needed it.

Around this time, news had been circling the jungle telegraph regarding one of Dearneside's Class of 1973 being caught in an uncompromising position with another man in Doncaster's North Bus Station toilets. I would say they were cottaging, but that sounds quite quaint and countryfied, which is something the North Bus Station bogs certainly were not. They weren't a place where you felt comfortable, that's for sure. Even if you could shake off the stink, there was always someone in there who could make you feel ill at ease, with the same amenities over in the town's South Bus Station – being just as dire.

What is strange is that outside of the toilets, the bus station was a place which generated many fond memories. After a busy day's shopping on a Saturday, I recall both waiting for and watching both the 212 and 213 carefully navigating its way underneath the tight and sloping brick-arched entrance into the station and of the bus drivers café and the taxi rank, which were located within two other concealed arches along with the steps up on to the North Bridge and the Trades and Labour WMC.

Kitch dented any nice thoughts of this, by dark tales surrounding a guy who frequented the self-same lavatories and who had the unwanted moniker of the *Mad Wanker*.

As I have already said, perverts roamed the plains back then, just as they do now and every time you opened a local newspaper they were there.

It is hard to imagine a nineteen-year-old miner in Thurnscoe's Flower Park being arrested three times in one week for indecent behaviour – which is a more apt word for wanking in public, but it happened. On 17 January 1924, the authorities decided they had had enough and banged him away three months.

Fast-forward exactly twenty-six years and fifty-year-old John Charles (Jack) Kay of 264 Furlong Road – one of the terraced houses that formed part of Packey's Puzzle, was arrested for the same thing.

I recall a similar thing happening when I had been in the First Year (Year 7) of Dearneside when a couple of girls began to put it around that some man had allegedly been flashing his jewels at them whilst on their way to school.

More often than not, Richard Clements-Pearce and I had often disembarked the 213 outside Stan Brettoner's Cycle shop and called in at Drabble's Newsagents before cutting through the snicket that linked Hall Street and the steep and rather snaking Orchard Street. This street essentially took out the four-way hairpin junction at the bottom of Straight Lane and that being the case, it was the main thoroughfare for kids travelling between the school and Goldthorpe's north-eastern terraced sprawl.

Can you recall the story of the little girl that went missing from Ringway in 1949?

Well, it was her fifty-seven-year-old father, Herbert Boreham, that became the focus of the police during the late-spring of 1977. This was after four schoolgirls reported him to one of the teachers – with the Deputy Headmistress Mrs (Florence) Headley making sure that matter was immediately dealt with.

Four years prior to the events on the Friday morning of 13 May 1977, it had been stated that Herbert had been living on his own – his wife, Christine having left him in 1973. The four schoolgirls had seen him exposing himself through the bedroom window of 9 Orchard Street dressed only in a T-shirt. He initially disputed the claims but seeing that half Goldthorpe had seen him do it, he eventually coughed to the offence and admitted that he had been doing it a while.

"I can remember that happening," Angie Mellor recently told me.

Herbert, who along with his wife were known to be part of the regular congregation at Furlong Road's Methodist Chapel, passed away in April 2005, aged eighty-five and was cremated at Ardsley Crematorium.

As for James Teasdale – the terror of the Flower Park, he would marry a woman by the name of Violet Hughes in 1935 and between them moved into the bungalow next door to where Doris Morrell's mother had lived on Thurnscoe's Kingsway Grove. And Jack Kay? To my knowledge he never married and lived with his mum up until her death in 1955, passing away himself in late-January 1971.

When I had been a kid, there had been a huge stigma attached to anything gay, and for someone who was just a few years older than us and who had been at the same school made it ten times worse.

It would be wrong of me to *out* the kid, even though he has lived with his male partner for years and even now still lives in the area – a house a few doors down from where the butchers once stood, off the A635 crossroads at Highgate.

The fact that it was Paul (Boof) Richardson that alerted us to the story, quite wrongly made him the obvious candidate to be the not-so-secret gay that we would saddle with the same Christian name as that of the ex-pupil who had been caught in the bus station toilets.

At first, calling him "Roy" or "Roy-Boy" was plain banter. However, over the following weeks it became much murkier and you could tell the lad was getting quite upset.

Boof, the youngest child of three to Collis and Janet Richardson (nee Wordsworth), possessed a scrag-styled long-blond hair and had a highly humorous nature about him. This had probably been picked up from his older brother, Mick and the entourage of sophisticated nicotine loving petrolheads that he knocked around with, one of whom was one of the strangest looking Herbert's you could ever wish to meet – that being Ian Gilbert, who carried the rather dubious nickname of Dr Phibes.

Boof smoked like a chimney and was Status Quo-mad. He was also a kid that you could tell a mile off as he always tended to wear some fluorescent yellow cagoule, which had a large oblong breast pocket where he generally kept his fags and matches. As his mother's maiden name could suggest, he was also very articulately spoken and often used to rip certain words apart and purposely mispronounce them. His favourites were: nutter, which became *tunner*; knob, which became *bon*; along with his pièce de résistance and the one which became the butt of all the piss-take – that of being a bummer (gay). He referred to bummer as *buma*.

On getting to Dearneside, all the pupils from the surrounding junior schools got mixed and I ended up in Form 1W with Boof and another lad from Bolton Juniors by the name of Carl Ottewell, the latter whose life would be cut short at just forty years old.

Carl had been a construction supervisor with consulting engineer Atkins and had been one of fifty-eight people that had drowned when an unlicensed twin-decked wooden Dhow – the Al Dana, capsized in the Persian Gulf off the coast of Bahrain on 30 March 2006. He had been one of fifteen Britons on board to celebrate the topping out of the Bahrain World Trade Centre towers. His wife was Jeanette (nee Shaw), a pretty little girl who had lived a few doors up from me on the Flower Estate and rather coincidentally had also been in the exact same form as us. She is also someone I will get on to in a bit.

As for Boof, he had lived on Bolton-on-Dearne's Concrete Canyon at 6 South Drive. Although I often remember hanging around down there and playing in what I assumed was the old dismantled screening plant of Wath Main, as well as on the River Dearne's floodplains, I can only remember calling at his house, or their *cave* as he always termed it, just the once. It was Sean Buck who had escalated the piss take, when he candidly mentioned a particular time that he had called for him and on Boof opening the door to greet him, he had immediately noticed some old falling-to-bits cooker in the kitchen, which was both caked up with grease and that had a frying pan on one of the rings with a smiley face drawn into the fat.

It was something that was immediately seized upon.

Not only did we make out that he was he a closet *buma*, but one that lived in Dickensian surroundings. We contrived a load of exaggerated bullshit to compound his families alleged poverty by letting everyone know that his house didn't even have electric and that the washing machine, fridge, record player and hoover all ran on coal, and that it was Boof's job to keep them stoked up. I made things ten-times worse one weekend when I came to school armed with some eight-page satirical albeit heartless magazine that I had penned, and which had been aimed at poor, perverted *buma's*. It may have been an effort worthy of an A-Level grade, but the upset it caused the lad was immense. This never let up for months, with Stuart Kerry suddenly becoming tarred with the same brush, when not only was it revealed that his dad was also called Roy – his mum had mesmerised us by asking him to get her a match, so she could light their fridge. We couldn't believe it. Their fucking fridge actually ran on gas.

The reality of the situation, however – is that at the time, these two lads had a much better homelife than I. As for me, I had just been just deflecting my lousy existence by pulling down theirs. It was something that as I got older, I would come to despise.

I last saw Paul in The Goldthorpe Hotel sometime after the Miners' Strike. As with most lads from our year he had opted for a life underground and had signed on at the pit most of my family had worked at – that being Barnburgh Main. He looked well and went on to say that he had just passed his driving test and bought a car. I was pleased for the lad and told him as much.

I hadn't always been a twat with him. I recall coming back into the UK from some annual holiday in Spain and giving him a pack of Rothman's Regals. These were a batch of pretentious ultra-long cigarettes that our Tony, Jonathan and I had stolen from one of the rooms in the hotel. What I should have done, however, is apologised to him. He never deserved any of the piss-take aimed at him as he was such a brilliant lad. Like I said, I don't have many – but that is one of my life's few regrets.

Stuart had nowhere near the amount flack Boof had had aimed at him, but what he and his family would have to endure would be quite something else.

He was the second youngest of five children, with his two-elder sister's – Sharon and Susan, being one and two years older than us respectively and the two I knew the best. He also had a cool elder brother by the name of Mick along with his youngest sister, Mandy. It would be on 17 December 2001 that the Kerry's lives would be turned upside down – Stu's youngest sister, in particular.

In 1995, Mandy had married a man eight years her senior by the name of Andrew Goddard, and between them they had three children, the family eventually residing at 49 John Street, Thurnscoe.

At one time, the street formed one of the three accesses up to the once long sweeping and arced crescent that proudly stood high above the rest of the village.

Like anything, the years had taken their toll and what had once been a modern and innovative council estate had become outdated, fallen into disrepair and was in urgent need of modernisation. Although the estate looked surprising fresh post-facelift, with its main thoroughfares blocked off and the creation of cul-de-sacs, the estate sadly lost its identity as both Thornley Crescent and Taylor Street, were unceremoniously wiped off the map. Following the decimation of the Doncaster Area coalfield, not at least the infilling and capping off of Hickleton Main, change was inevitable – however, for a time, part of the community managed to survive.

Mandy was no stranger to living in a close-knit community, some of whom had done their level best at making the very best of what they had, and though herself partially disabled, she had tried to recreate exactly that. However, like most of us, she wanted to create something that bit better for her children. This goes some way to explaining why our children are often referred to as the *spoilt generation*.

Each Christmas, the residents of John Street got their heads together, pulled out all the stops and in a US-themed bout of festivity, went all *Deck the Halls*, and completely lit up the cul-de-sac with extravagant Yuletide illuminations – so much so, the street became well-known within the local area and was eventually labelled *Christmas Street*.

That fateful Monday evening, nothing appeared out of the ordinary. The only things that ran across the grain had possibly been on TV. On the set of the BBC's *EastEnders*, Sharon Mitchell had seemed a bit pissed off with her moody husband, Phil, whilst on the other side, the original *Top Gear* had aired for the very last time with Tiff Needell racing a Mini Cooper.

However, around 10.20 p.m. and whilst watching TV, Mandy and Andrew's lives would change forever. A loud bang had suddenly plunged the house into darkness. The power had tripped. The reasoning behind the power failure soon became apparent. A fire quickly took hold and spread throughout the dining room engulfing the downstairs of the compact semi-detached house with a dense smoke within in a matter of seconds. This was made a hundred times worse by the toxicity of burning plastic.

The flammable nature of the decorations, the rapidity and ferociousness of the flames, the billowing of black smoke and the panic and confusion it had created, had all the ingredients of a tragedy waiting to happen.

Neighbours heard screaming coming from the property has the intense heat began popping the windows.

Anyone who has experienced a fire will probably tell you that the panic creates an indecisiveness in that you are always in two minds – one of which is that you always feel that you can contain it. In this instance, that was never the case.

It was never publicly mentioned, but the panic and indecision lost valuable tens of seconds and by the time Andrew knew that the fire was out of control he had been unable to gain immediate access to the staircase.

It was said that he climbed out of the window and went back into the house through the front door, before running up the stairs in his bid to rescue his children. Unfortunately for their father, they too had been in a state of panic and had become disorientated one hiding under the duvet and the other seeking sanctuary in the bathroom.

Andrew managed to both find and grab his five-year-old daughter, Jade, by the sleeve of her pyjama top and dragged her to the window, but in the smoke and confusion she slipped from his grasp. He had lost her.

It is hard to gauge both the *could haves* and the *would haves*, when you are not the one placed in the position that Andrew had been placed in. The thick smoke omitted not only a deadly carbon monoxide, but dangerous chemicals such as hydrochloric acid, sulphur dioxide and furans along with poisonous cancer-causing dioxins that supress the immune system.

"Everyone was out trying to help. Some were round the front and some were round the back," explained near-neighbour Gary Rhodes. "We went in and it was pitch black. I couldn't see a thing – it was just heat and smoke. I tried to breathe but I couldn't. I had to come back out. We managed to find a couple of ladders, but we could see how thick and intense the smoke was. Some of the lads started throwing bricks at the windows to try and get some air in so they could breathe and to let smoke out."

All that does, however, is provide oxygen for the flames.

Mandy had been pulled to safety through a ground floor window and her four-year-old son, Nathan, had been dragged out the house by his feet after falling down the blazing staircase – however, the tragedy was that both his elder siblings had become trapped.

"I went up a ladder and the window popped," added Gary. "Andrew was at the window and he couldn't breathe. I grabbed him, pulled him out and I jumped, holding on to him. We both dropped twenty-feet and landed on the bonnet of his car."

It had been a plain case of Gary forcibly saving the life of a man who was trying to sacrifice his own, in a desperate effort to save his child. It was a truly heart-breaking situation.

"We went back in for the other two, but by that time the fire was so intense we couldn't get in. We kept trying and trying. We could hear the kids screaming. It was terrible. We really did our best, but our best was never going to be good enough."

Although the younger brother survived and was initially put in an induced coma on a life support machine in Leeds General Infirmary's burns and fire unit, both his elder siblings did not. Jade and her six-year-old brother, Alex, sadly died.

Post-mortems suggested that although both children died from smoke inhalation, they had received such extensive burn injuries that it would have been unlikely if they had survived.

Residents described the terrible scene in which Mandy's husband had been clearly devastated and was blaming himself for not getting the children out of the house.

Initial police investigations centred on a possible fault in the Christmas decorations.

There was a twist in the tale, however, and during an inquest held by District Coroner, Chris Dorries, some six months after the tragedy, an electrical engineer explained that there was absolutely no evidence to suggest that the electrical system at the house was overloaded or dangerous.

"After we heard the massive bang and the lights went out, we saw smoke coming from the dining room," Andrew recently explained. "I shouted 'fire' and ran to the kids. The smoke alarm was ringing, there was smoke was everywhere and it was inky dark. Our Jade was standing at the top of the stairs. I grabbed her hand and turned towards the boys' room.

"We could barely breathe. I opened the bedroom window and got out on the windowsill shouting for help. I was still holding my daughter's hand, but her hand left my grip. Mandy was screaming 'I want my babies!' while neighbours held her back from the burning house. I was having difficulty breathing and the back of my throat was burning. Everything was going very fast but moving in slow motion at the same time. It felt like I was trapped underwater. There was a man shouting in my face, but I couldn't hear him. The next thing I know is that I was pulled out of the window and landed on the car below. I tried to stand up, but I collapsed.

"Our daughter's body was later found in the bathroom. She must have been disorientated by the smoke and turned right when she left the boys room instead of heading for the stairs. Our oldest lad stayed curled up in bed tucked under his duvet. Only Nathan turned down the stairs."

Andrew was taken to Barnsley hospital where he was later told that both Jade and Alex had died.

"I kept thinking I should have held Jade tighter," added Andrew. "It's a father's responsibility to protect his children and I wish I could have protected them that night. I watched every news broadcast in the hospital that week, seeing what happened to the kids. The fire was all over the news at the time. I can't explain why I needed to watch it, but I did. I had to watch all these people talking about my kids."

"I still had visions of losing our Nathan until he came out of the coma," explained his mum.

"I used to sit by his bed holding his hand and praying that he would be OK. I kept saying 'Mummy loves you'. We all stood around his bed waiting for him to wake up. He had blisters and scars on his hands where he had been burned – however, the trauma and stress caused his mind to blank out. He can't remember anything before the fire. He knew he had a brother and a sister, but he couldn't remember them. I think it protected him."

As for Alex and Jade – they are buried together in the cemetery at Bolton-on-Dearne.

"Alex was in a camouflage coffin because he loved Action Man and Jade was in a Barbie pink coffin," their mum explained. "Everyone cried as their coffins were lowered into the ground."

As for the cause of the fire, it was said that it was probably an electrical fault somewhere in the wiring. But that said, there wasn't enough of the house left to conclusively say how the fire started.

"Originally, we thought it was the lights on a Christmas tree – however, they ran tests which showed that nothing had overloaded. They didn't think it was the Christmas lights that sparked it but some internal wiring," concluded Andrew.

Unfortunately, this was a case of Thurnscoe's god-awful history repeating itself and possessed similarities to something which happened thirty-one years earlier on the weekend of the Sheffield derby. A match at Bramall Lane where in front of just under 40,000, United had come out 3-2 winners.

Although its backings are still evident, Orchard Street was a street that is no longer there and formed part of Thurnscoe's slum clearances – the said street, finally being flattened in the early-1970s. Its thirty-three properties ran both parallel with and behind Houghton Road, from the north of Butcher Street into the northern end of Church Street taking in another long-demolished street – that of Albert, as it did so.

I don't possess any memories of it, although I have been informed that when I had been a toddler, I had frequently run around the downstairs rooms in that of No 23, which had been the first marital home of Pat and Rose Thomson (nee Depledge) – the couple that had been the main witnesses at my mum and dad's wedding on 13 November 1963.

As short as the street was, up until the day it was demolished it had witnessed the death of around fifty children, two of which had been found dead on arrival at Mexborough Montagu Hospital after being pulled out of a burning a house. It had been just three doors down from where the Thomson's had lived.

It could be said that Marjorie (Madge) Cooke was a great example of the changing times and the counterculture that was creating social change throughout much of the country. Unmarried and living with a partner, she was perhaps, sticking two fingers up at the system. That, however, was certainly not the case. The reality of the situation was that her then-common-law husband John Hudson had still been legally married.

What is certainly known is that he had lived at the address with his first wife Mabel (nee Whittaker) until 1962 and that a year later Madge got caught on with her first child. What is also known is that Mabel left her husband taking their three children with her, clearing the way for Madge to move into the house. Whether or not John and Madge had been having an affair whilst he had still been with Mabel appears highly likely – although it is not something that has been confirmed.

John Hudson, who was also the father of their four small children, had been at work on the fateful Sunday evening of 4 October 1970, when a fire had somehow started in one of the two downstairs rooms. As with the Goddard's compact home on John Street, the fire spread rapidly and showed no mercy.

There had been two conflicting versions of the tragedy, the one after it happened and the other at the coroner's inquest – both possessing different events but having the same outcome, that being two dead children.

What was heard at the Goldthorpe inquest was that Madge had had been in the front bedroom when she had been awoken by the smell of smoke.

"I could see massive flames coming from the kitchen," she told the Doncaster District Coroner, Kenneth Potter. "I had gone to bed with my eighteen-month-old son, John, and must have fallen asleep."

She had also awoken to find her two-and-a-half-year-old daughter, Maxine, in the bedroom with her and her son playing on the stairs, with the two older children – four-year-old Neil and six-year-old Diane, in the back bedroom.

"I took the youngest two to the front bedroom window to get them some fresh air and call for help."

Her cries were heard by twenty-four-year-old Sandra Mead – the daughter of Denaby miner Sam and his wife Edna (nee Webster) over the road at No 2 – who raced to her aid. Sandra defied all odds and climbed onto the window ledge before scaling up a cable that was attached to the outside of the property to receive both youngest children.

498

"I heard Madge screaming and ran outside. I could see her through the bedroom window," Sandra had explained. "She was shouting – 'My house is on fire – my washing machine has set the house on fire'."

Rather strangely, there was no mention of this at the inquest.

"I rushed across the road to try and get in through the front window, but the fire was too bad. I climbed on to the window ledge and up some cabling affixed to the house, so that Madge could pass the children to me," Sandra had told the inquest. "When they were safe, I ran into the backings to try and get into the house that way – but again it was no good."

The ferocity of the heat and flames beat Madge back from saving her other two children in the back bedroom.

The neighbours out on the street witnessed the haunting sight of the helpless mother hysterically screaming through the window and for someone to help her children, and with the flames quite visible behind her, there was nothing left for her to do but leap out onto the pavement. Although she survived the fall, she was not only left with the mental scars of losing two of her children, she landed badly – firstly hitting the downstairs window ledge before flipping head-first on to the pavement, the injuries of which, would leave her severely disabled.

Firemen from Goldthorpe arrived on the scene and wearing breathing apparatus they finally succeeded in reaching the two older children. They attempted mouth to mouth resuscitation, but it was no good. They were taken to Mexborough Montagu Hospital where they were found to be dead on arrival. They had both been overcome by smoke and died of carbon monoxide poisoning.

So, how did it happen?

Our house at Landsdowne Avenue, which was just a trip through the ginnel past the *Tin Chapel* was remarkably similar in build. It had two coal burning fireplaces – one in the kitchen and the other in the room, and much like ours had been, their house was also extremely compact, but more so, being a two-up-two-down.

The squalor could be construed as being the same, with Pat and Rose Thomson's daughter Julie saying that she remembers watching several families vacate the houses through their front bedroom window in what was termed as a moonlight flit scenario. People generally came and went as these properties were often seen as a stopgap.

Throughout the Sunday, the late-October weather had been very predictable with temperatures rarely topping fifty degrees and with rain expected later. The fact that Madge had been doing her washing more than likely meant that a fire had been in both to heat the back boiler and dry the clothes – the boiler being more likely to have been in the kitchen fireplace than the room.

Madge had gone upstairs just after Bob Monkhouse's *The Golden Shot* had been on TV with his special guest star Des O'Connor – and by the time *Please Sir!* had started in an episode titled *Knick, Knack, Taffy Whack!* the house had been full of smoke.

It was found at the inquest that **three gas rings on the cooker had been left on** and that there had been three piles of clothes ready for washing on the floor. Back then, safety in the home wasn't preached like it is now and although the gas leaking through the rings on the cooker, according to John Edgeley – a man who had been a service engineer with the East Midlands Gas Board – strangely stated that this *wasn't* an issue, the house was decimated by fire.

Nevertheless, no fault was apportioned, and the jury returned verdicts of accidental death.

I am reliably informed that in the here and now, there would have been a much more thorough investigation and that the house would have been immediately cordoned off as a crime scene. An open fire, three gas rings on, four young kids in the house unsupervised, and their mother upstairs asleep unfortunately wreaks of negligence.

"Neither of you is fit to have a child," snapped the Chairman at Doncaster West Riding Court, Mr O.S. Howden, on 12 June 1956.

Those words were said to both forty-five-year-old John Henry Cooke and his thirty-four-year-old wife, Evelyn – an estranged couple that had been summoned to court for the severe neglect of their three children by Inspector George Fisher of the NSPCC.

One of these children had been fourteen-year-old Madge Cooke – the girl who would become the wife of John Hudson.

On the outcome of the trial the mother, Evelyn – who had been living with a man in the Wood View area of Edlington – was sent to prison and her three children put into the care of the West Riding Children's home.

It was nothing new, as the couple had already had their other five other children put into care.

It transpired that when the case had first been reported in January that year, a female officer from the NPCC, Mrs P. Pickering, had arrived at their home at 31 Thornley Crescent, and found there was no gas on and that the three children had to stay in a dark room with what was described in court as an "unprotected fire".

Is that ringing any bells?

It was also said that the mother left the children for long periods – sometimes up to two weeks at a time thereby leaving Madge to look after her two young sisters.

"Marjorie (Madge) has practically had the upbringing of the baby. She has fed, nursed and bathed these two children almost entirely except when she was at school," said Mrs Pickering. "And her school attendance record is shocking."

She added that on that bitter day in January, she had found the children dressed in nothing more than rags: "Marjorie was wearing only a filthy vest full of holes, a cotton skirt, a shrunken woollen jumper, a ragged coat and boots with neither any socks nor stockings."

Her mother, who pleaded guilty to neglect, explained that she had got into bad company and expressed regret but said that there was no way that she would be going back to her husband.

What also came out in court is that the father had been sentenced to six months in prison for the neglect of his children some seven years earlier, in 1949.

What is sad, is that neither of the surviving children – Maxine and John, had much, if indeed any knowledge of this. What is strange is that it took me ten minutes to find out. What makes it all the sadder, is that they have had fifty.

Diane Hudson had been in the year above me at Houghton Road Infant School and as hard as I try, I cannot recall her – nor can I recall being told about the tragedy in school, which is strange as around the exact time, one of our teachers sons – David Follows, fell out of a tree and broke his leg and I remember that. I do, however, remember Diane's cousin Shaun, who had been in the same year as her.

Shaun had been a stocky little Herbert who possessed a broad accent and quite a bullying nature, something which saw the fearless and much smaller Dean Carter, wrestle him to the ground in Houghton Road Infant School's playground and punch the living daylights out of him. Never think that violence is just part of the here and now. Our generation got brought up on it.

I recall The Mod chants in the school playground with groups of kids walking around arm in arm and shouting: "We won the war in 1964". There was also the more menacing chant of: "Anybody in my way gets a kick".

It wasn't just Thurnscoe either. On the Friday afternoon 4 May 1973, Carfield Primary School's larger playground became a battleground of fighting and stone throwing, which had the male teachers – including the Headmaster, Mr Cooke, and both Mr Kneissl and Mr Swales having to intervene.

Leeds United had been due to play Sunderland in the FA Cup Final the very next day and half the boys in school supported them. The other half must have taken exception to the fact and not only wanted Sunderland to beat them but also fight them. Even though it was just *kid's shit*, it became quite brutal as a few kids that were hit by missiles.

As for the Hudson's, the family lost everything in the fire with neighbours putting them up until Dearne UDC could accommodate them in a property on Thornley Crescent. Madge and John eventually moved into 22 Garden Street – which had been the former home of Ernest and Elizabeth Roper (nee Hague), and eventually tied the knot in 1975.

Madge died in 2008 and John in 2010, and if you want a beautiful ending, there is perhaps one. They were reunited and laid to rest with their two children in Thurnscoe Cemetery.

If you want a series of coincidences, I can certainly give you a few of those.

There were huge similarities with the Goddard family's tragedy: two children – a boy and girl of a similar age; the fact that the male partner had both been married before and was much older; a disabled wife, along with a jump from the window. There was also the fact that from their home at 22 Garden Street you could see the Goddard family's home at 49 John Street, which rather eerily looks out onto a newly named street – that of Orchard Way. However, the connection which had me scratching my head was nothing to do with the Goddard family and everything to do with the Hudsons.

John and his first wife had had a child that had died at just two days old – and rather strangely at 37 Chapel Street, Thurnscoe. This had been the same house which had witnessed the deaths of three children with the same surname of Hudson – this one being the family of Malcolm. This family were one that had been cursed with misfortune. Geoffrey and Dennis had been twins who died in the house at just two days old on 26 November 1931, whilst their elder brother Frank had died aged twenty-seven months old on 29 September 1932.

The following year, a new baby would come into the world – and as with my grandfather, he would be named after one of his older dead brothers. Dennis would become the father of Malcolm, but not before witnessing the premature death of two of his younger brothers, Eric and James at eighteen-months and nine-months old in 1944 and 1946, respectively. By this time, however, the family had been living in the fifth row of terraces at 14 Marlborough Avenue – the street where I would first come across a kid some five years older than myself, who had been the next-door neighbour to the other Hudson family on Orchard Street.

A bulky looking kid with a rather posh and pontificating persona, he was not unlike Andy Roper in that he never moved far the place he grew up – and even now, lives just a stone's throw away at 39 Church Street. He had a certain mannerism to Pat and Inky Thomson's younger brother, Karl, in that to a young kid, he appeared highly knowledgeable.

Leonard G.C. Chandler Esq. used to hang about around The Avenues and Houghton Road's compact shopping centre and always seemed to have a bag of sweets with him, which he was never shy in passing around.

"He's a bit queer, him," my mum used to say. "And he's too old for you to be playing out with."

Back then, I thought he was a great kid. He appeared extremely intelligent and was very generous with it. He also reckoned that he could get the old broken-down car started that was outside Reg Mower's old house at 18 Landsdowne Avenue and that he could even drive us to the seaside.

Andy Moore's recollection of him isn't that far out either. After the demolition of Orchard Street, he became Andy's next-door-but-one neighbour. "He used to play cricket with us when the pitch used to be at the back of the running track on Houghton Road," he told me.

"He could smash the ball miles – and he bowled a bit too," added Gary Bright. "We once played at a match for Hickleton Main at the far side of the running track and the side who we were playing, possibly had the best bowler in the league. Lenny cracked two straight sixes straight over his head, before walking over to the bowler and duly apologising to him."

Unfortunately, however, these were just our fond memories of him and memories which would be tainted by allegations that followed him around all his life. From being caught red-handed doing his Peeping Tom act, through to being caught undertaking some indecent act in the toilets of Houghton Road School.

"He is a strange person and not to be trusted," explained Phil Hardman's elder brother, Barry. "I once witnessed him walking up Butcher Street and slow down his walk when passing houses – just so he could look inside."

It was something echoed by Kevin Deakin, who had been a shaft man at Barnburgh Main and who at the time lived at 13 Peartree Avenue.

"When I was first married and lived in the old houses on Church Street, I remember one night being sat watching the telly with our lass (Elizabeth, nee Rice) in the front room, when we heard the flap on the letter box drop," added Barry Hardman. "I raced out of the back door and there he was. The first thing he said was, 'Wot's up are Baz?'"

"The lads in the cricket team were right fuckers with him," added Gary Bright. "We once stuck him in a locker after playing a Cantley Park. This, however, was long before all the allegations came out."

There were numerous stories that followed him around – however, the last time I saw him to speak to, was a few months after the Miners' Strike. He had been in the lounge of The Fairway and rather strangely decked out in some crumpled fawn suit which had been complimented with a white shirt that was in dire need of a wash, along with a tie that rather clumsily hung down over his midriff – whilst his corpulent frame had been propped up on some cheap black rubber soled brogues. Although it wasn't particularly hot evening, he was perspiring to the point that both his hair and face were wet through.

"You're looking pukka, Len," I said, acknowledging his effort.

"I've just been for an interview [for a job]," he told me. "I'll be heading up their sales team. I've been promised four hundred pounds a week."

At the time it seemed about as likely as him auditioning for the lead trombonist with *Sigue Sigue Sputnik*, but nevertheless, I placated him.

My wife used to see him regularly when she had worked in the bookmakers on Kingsway. And again, the thing she mainly recalls is him offering the staff boiled sweets from a bag.

"You're never eating that, are you?" gasped Julie Trueman.

"Yeh, why?" shrugged my wife.

"You don't know where he's fucking had it," she said.

Rather strangely, my dad's second wife, Paula, is related to him through her auntie Shirley's (nee Brown) marriage to Clarence Chandler in 1961.

I just thank the lord that I'm not part of that fucking gene pool.

Sometimes we can be totally unaware who we live next to, as in the case of Jeanette Ottewell (nee Shaw).

The last time I ever saw Jeanette and her husband as a couple had been in the Dog End of Ings Lane WMC in 1995. I recall her as a pretty dark-haired little lass with mottled skin and a distinguished voice who had lived at 30 Campion Close. Jeanette's closest friend had been an olive-skinned girl by the name of Shani Scatchard (now Lashmar), who I recall often suffered from tremendous bouts of migraine and lived at No 39. Shani was of course the daughter of Martin Scatchard – one of the junior schoolteachers at The Hill School.

It wasn't just the fact that the numbering of the houses on The Flower Estate went 1, 2, 3, as opposed to being odd and even numbered – they even followed suit, even though the name of the Close (street) changed in that there was only one of that number on the entire estate. What was also strange is that some of the addresses were in fact partly on a totally different street. Jeanette's home was in fact on Fairfield, whilst Shani's was just around the corner in a tight cul-de-sac the opposite side of which was Heather Walk. Nevertheless, sandwiched in between Shani and Jeanette's homes lived a woman whose extremely dark past had been well-hidden by the fact that she had left the area she came from and had remarried and therefore lived quite inconspicuously at 34 Campion Close. I say inconspicuously, as when asked, neither Jeanette nor Shani's parents knew who she was.

The woman had previously lived at 68 Washington Road, Goldthorpe being employed as a sewing machinist at SR Gents in Mexborough, a fact which was corroborated by the cousin of my cousin, who used to give her a lift to and from work. "She drank a lot," said Tracy Greaves. "She also had a very strained relationship with her children."

The last bit was certainly true as the eldest child had been taken into care at an early age.

Paul White had married his thirty-one-year-old wife, Teresa Ann (nee Chadwick, now Gretorex) in 1988 – however, it was another one of these marriages where the woman had been much older than the man. Ten years older in this case.

Whilst we had been gearing up for the school Christmas holidays of 1977 – all being gathered in Dearneside's Lower Hall to watch Gene Wilder and Richard Prior in the *Silver Streak*, a huge child exploitation trial had been going on at Doncaster Crown Court. This had involved a nineteen-year-old by the name of Paul Stanton and his twenty-year-old wife, Teresa – each of whom apportioned the blame on each other.

The couple had lived on the exact same street that I had been born – that of Barker Street, which was the street where the offences took place.

The complex trial had all the hallmarks of the trial of Ian Brady and Myra Hindley, but without the murders, and was littered with a series of perverse acts, brutality, threats and lies. During the trial, it was suggested that Teresa had in fact been the dominant partner, which was something that she refuted.

Her husband was described as twice the size of his wife and possessed a violent background, recently serving six months in prison for a vicious assault on her, which would become the major contributing fact to him copping for three-years inside.

The Stanton's themselves had been a well-known family in the area, sometimes for all the wrong reasons.

Paul's great-grandfather, John Henry Stanton had lived at 4 Furlong Road, Bolton-on-Dearne with his wife Sarah (nee Whitehouse) along with his grandfather – also called John, who had been the eldest of nine children.

John Henry had been killed in a fight outside the Albion Inn on Mexborough's High Street on 28 October 1911, taking a blow to the face of which the impact caused him to fall back, hit the floor and fracture his skull. The aggressor was a twenty-two-year-old pit Corporal and former amateur boxer by the name of Jimmy Cairns, a lad who ended up doing nine-months hard labour after being found guilty of manslaughter.

Paul's grandfather, just like himself, had had a younger brother who died aged six years old. This had been in 1913. Paul's younger brother's death, however, became part of a murder trial at Sheffield Crown Court, after it was found that an eleven-year-old boy had purposely drowned him in the Mexborough-Swinton Canal. It was a case which the Crown Prosecutor Donald Herrod QC described as both "tragic and heartrending".

During April 1972, David Stanton had been playing with the elder child, who not only threw him in the canal but readily admitted to drowning him.

"I carried David to the canal and dropped him in," said the boy. "He went into the middle of the canal and tried to swim back but when he came back, I got hold of his hair and bumped his head on the side twice. I then got two stones. I chucked an orange one, but it missed. I then threw a white one which hit him in the middle of the head. Then he drowned."

When asked why he had done it the boy just replied: "I don't know."

As part of the defence led by Gilbert Gray QC – psychiatrist Dr William Allen Weston explained that the elder boy had suffered organic brain damage which would substantially impair his responsibility.

As for the trial of Paul Stanton, the lies wreaked out the place, with one of the witnesses for the Crown, Police Sgt. Trevor Higgins declining to give an opinion when asked if he thought Teresa had been afraid of her husband.

Barker Street was part of the terraced slums, much of which have now been cleared – however, this street, which was built in two phases around the turn of the century, still stands. I am told that my dad had bought our house at No 15 in 1964, with £500 (£10,566, circa 2020) being the figure that was quoted. I have virtually no recollections of living there, only the stories that were told to me by my parents. I vaguely remember my mum holding some stainless-steel pans which had turquoise blue lids and being shown some rabbits, that were the pets of the girl next door. Outside of that, nothing.

As for the street itself, it is formed by two banks of terraced houses with no thoroughfare – just a huge fence at its end. It is a street, much like those on Thurnscoe's Avenues in that practically everyone knew everyone. However, by 1977, a very different *type of people* began occupying these properties.

The collier from Barnburgh Main or the fitter from Manvers Main coal preparation plant generally had more aspirations than living in some claustrophobic two-up-two-down with a toilet in the yard and a scrap yard at the street's end. Therefore, it is not wrong for me to assume that Mexborough UDC began filling these fast emptying properties with the unemployed or unemployable – one of these being Paul Stanton and his wife, Teresa.

It is also not inappropriate to assume that to gain a young girl's trust, a female would always be the better option. Remember the "Charley Says" adverts: A man asks you to go see some puppies – especially a burly, well-developed man such as Paul Stanton – and alarm bells immediately start ringing. A petite woman asks the question and it is perhaps a completely different story. The upshot was that an eleven-year-old girl somehow got through the front door of the Stanton's two-up-two-down.

In court, Teresa had readily admitted to using threats to incite the child to commit an act of gross indecency (fellatio) on her husband but claimed that she had acted on her husband's instructions and out of fear of the consequences if she did not. There was also intercourse involved, with Teresa playing more than the part of an innocent onlooker.

She did, however, describe past occasions when her husband had beaten her, threatened her with a shotgun and allegedly forced her to take part in unnatural sexual practices and said she had feared more of the same if she refused to carry out his wishes.

The husband, who was the son of Mexborough bookmaker, Gordon Stanton, openly claimed in court that it was Teresa that had introduced him to acts of perversion and that prior to him meeting her, he had only ever had one previous girlfriend. As for his wife, she had not only previously lived with Paul Stanton's elder brother but according to his defence counsel Malcolm Swift QC, had during their eighteen-month marriage "consorted with several other men and committed the grossest infidelity". It was also claimed that Teresa had often deprived her husband of sex and that it was she, not he, who was in fact the dominant partner.

Teresa's dominance was firmly substantiated by the child, who said that she had twisted her arm and threatened to throw her out of the window if she did not take her clothes off and do as she was told.

The child said in court: "I told her that I would tell my mam but she said, 'you won't be in a fit state to tell your mam when I've done with you'."

The defence counsel added to this by stating that the husband had always maintained that it was Teresa who had been the evil partner in the marriage and that he had just complied with her desires.

Teresa's statement, which was read out in court stated the exact opposite: "Whenever the two of us are in the house together, the doors are locked because Paul knows, that if I have the opportunity, I will leave him. He normally walks around completely naked and asks me to perform unnatural practices and if I refuse, I know I shall get a good hiding. The only time I refused, I got such a hiding, whereby he split open my head and put me in bed for two days."

The Crown Prosecutor, Arthur Hutchinson QC, had a complex case to deal with as Teresa was the main witness to help put the husband away, yet he obviously knew that she was lying and described the overall case as "disgusting, sordid and offensive".

"These two people are birds of a feather who both get satisfaction from hurting each other and misbehaving with children," he said.

It had been argued that Teresa hated her husband – however, that wasn't true.

"He is sick, and I can't stand it anymore," she said in her statement to the police.

It was, however, later found that she had been writing him love letters, whilst he had been on remand.

"This case is almost unique in the reliance placed by the prosecution on what Teresa Ann Stanton had told the police," added the prosecutor. "But regardless of the jury's verdict in this trial, these offences had been planned by Teresa, incited by her, and carried out by her. My submission is that during the course of this eventful marriage and during the course of this regrettable evening, she was indeed the dominant partner."

At the end of the trial and after five hours' deliberation Teresa had been found not guilty on both charges of inciting a child to commit an act of gross indecency. How that came about, I haven't a fucking clue as she had freely admitted in court of using threats to force the child to do them.

The British justice system is far from perfect.

Alex, Jade and Nathan Goddard (c. Alamy)

38. Peep Show (Unedited)

On the Sunday morning of 11 October 2020, I had taken a detour through Goldthorpe on my way to see my mother- and father-in-law over in Brampton Bierlow.

It would be wrong of me to say that it is unrecognisable, as in the main, and structure-wise, the village is more or less how it looked over 120 years ago. The exception being that Goldthorpe Junior and Infant School has been demolished and re-sited further up Doncaster Road and most of what was once known as Goldthorpe Lane Ends has been flattened including Main Street. There will be more to come – it is inevitable.

The Goldthorpe Hotel and The Horse & Groom are boarded up but still standing – however, their clock is ticking. Within twenty years, Goldthorpe's north-eastern terraces will all have Compulsory Purchase Orders (CPO's) served, prior to them coming down.

The Thursday evening of 18 December 1980 had been a time when I had sat in the Dog End of The Horse & Groom after buying my first ever drink. Blondie's *The Tide is High* had been playing in the background and there I was – sat amongst several lads my age – including Tim Bright, just turned sixteen-years-old and sipping at a lager.

We had been on our way to the school's Fifth-Year Christmas Party – a dance and live music at the Goldthorpe Parish Hall. A four- or five-piece band knocking out covers of old Motown, northern soul, and sixties numbers.

Around that time, I had been in a short relationship with a girl off Bolton-on-Dearne's Chapel Street who rather interestingly lived next door to the house where 81-year old Elizabeth Carrington (nee Dunbar) hanged herself in January 1956. In fact, Elizabeth's father-in-law along with her brother- and sister-in-law – her sister-in-law's father and their son, Douglas had died in the house where the-then girlfriend had lived at No 17 – the nephew passing away on Tuesday 9 March 1976.

Her parents, Joe and Susan Wright (nee Lawrence) were lovely people, something which had been fully reinforced by the fact that they had adopted a little lad after he had been in their foster care, with her father at the time, working with my uncle Paul at Barnburgh Main.

I often recall the journey home from their house and alighting the last bus into Thurnscoe from the sheltered bus stop outside The Collingwood on a Friday and Saturday night, being that the 226 was often late. As the bus turned left at Goldthorpe's traffic lights, the first thing that hit you was the sight of the huge crowds of people milling around at the two bus stops – some eating out of polystyrene trays or carrying parcels or carrier bags of food that they had bought from either Sharps fish and chip shop or the Chinese. Nowadays, it is hard to envisage a bus crammed full of people and its driver asking the standing customers to move to the back of the bus as it pulled up further down Barnsley Road to pick up fares outside Highgate Club and The Halfway Hotel. Back then, everything seemed alive.

Not long before I had left Thurnscoe, I often remember seeing the buses on a weekend night negotiating their way up both Windsor and Briton Street – both empty and devoid of passengers. That was before the bus company – Yorkshire Traction, withdrew its services from going into Thurnscoe East completely, as it had been subjected to regular attacks from youths throwing bricks and stones.

By then, however, even the bus company's number one passenger, Robert Frost, had stopped using the service.

"If tha dunt pack it in, now, I'll throw you off," said the driver.

In one particular instance, the twelve-year old Rob had got on the 273 outside Windsor Stores and had been sat in the front seat near the door and mimicking its driver. Not content with imitating the steering, his foot movements and all the semi-automatic gear changes he had also been doing the accompanying vroom-vroom noise of the engine, which had had the majority of the passengers in stitches.

Special needs or not, he was an extremely humorous lad, not that the driver appreciated him, however. He slung him off just outside Highgate Club.

Tommy Mitchell, was the son of his namesake – a bespectacled former professional cricketer who had played for a brilliant Derbyshire county side and five times for England during the 1930s and who had lived at 36 Hanover Street, on getting a job at Hickleton Main after the Second World War.

Tommy (Jnr) had married Janet (Jan) Fells in 1957 and lived at 7 Roman Street – a property where they still live to this day and which coincidentally had been the house that directly connected to that of the Frost's. Being good friends of Barry and Carol (Oldfield) and of course my parents, I knew them quite well and even now we still exchange Christmas cards every December.

Tommy had been employed as a Winder on Hickleton Main's No's 1 and 2 shaft and whilst I had been waiting to be fully deployed underground during the spring of 1982, he invited me and Daz Eades into his operators cabin and took time out show us exactly what his job entailed.

"And that's all you do?" asked Daz.

"Easy isn't it?" he winked.

It may have just looked like a case of pressing a couple of buttons and releasing a few levers, but it wasn't. It was hardly as complex as driving a road header or indeed drilling and blasting a rip, but bollocks up that symmetry, and it is not just production, but people's lives that are at stake. As shaft sinking is to the construction of a tunnel – being a Winder is basically the vertical process of operating a rope-hauled Paddy.

Tommy was gregarious in nature and possessed the two-fold distinction of having an uncanny resemblance to Yul Brynner and owning an immaculately clean red Reliant Rialto three-wheeler, the latter of which was obviously seen as some joke by some disrespectful youths and had been turned on its head just before I had left the area.

Like Mick Wharton – another of his good friends, he talked to you rather than at you and exuded a kind of respect that makes you proud to have known him. A great bloke if I am being honest – and I don't say that lightly.

We had all gone for a week away in Skegness during May 1980. Dexy's Midnight Runners had just reached the top of the charts with their iconic *Geno* and Steve Wharton and I had spent the bulk of the holiday trawling the town's shopping centre, market and amusement arcades to get out of the rain.

Tommy and Janet had rented a flat quite near to us, and seeing as though the English-weather was predictable in it gloom, they saw us sheltering within the doorway of our flat and invited us in. It was there at Steve's request that Tommy relayed us tale after tale – not at least regarding the youngest member of the Frost family, and being an extremely witty guy, he had us in stitches.

I can't recall the owner of the vehicle or indeed where it was as forty years is a long time. However, the story that I do recall is of its owner starting his car and going back inside the house. Whether he was waiting for the windscreen to demist or that he had forgotten something, I cannot say. What I do know is that when the owner had eventually set off driving and had gone some considerable distance a body suddenly arose from the rear of the car and excitedly presented itself between both front seats. "Where are we going, Jack?" Rob boomed.

The driver had a near-coronary, lost control of his vehicle and ended up mounting the kerb and narrowly missing a lamppost.

I could just imagine Rob doing it.

"What's up wi' thee?" he would have innocently shrugged after being dragged out of the car and booted up the arse.

Whereas Rob was harmless and at times, side-splittingly funny, there were lads out there with special needs – mental health issues, that were the complete opposite.

Thurnscoe's Lidget Lane has had an array of businesses and shops throughout the years one of which was a bookmaker that was at one time owned by Seymour & Story – which during the time that I had first lived in Thurnscoe had been a grocers and had had its upstairs accommodation occupied by Stanley and Emily McGlasson (nee Hendley). These were a couple, who along with their son, twenty-year-old, (John) Michael, all died in December 1969.

According to Dr (Kenneth) Kaye, Stanley had collapsed on 9 December due to a brain haemorrhage which had been caused by Vertebrobasilar insufficiency and Arteriosclerosis.

On 14 December, Michael – an assistant in the shop, was found dead in his bedroom. A gas pipe had been disconnected from the fire and following two inquests – 31 December and 20 January 1970, his death was acknowledged as suicide. He had died of cardiorespiratory failure due to carbon monoxide poisoning.

Emily McGlasson – was the elder sister of the two little lad's that had been severely injured by a hand grenade going off in the rear yard of 11 Vincent Terrace and therefore the great aunt of the Dark Queen. Emily had been married before and for a time had lived at 7 Windsor Square along with her first husband Jack Hooley and their four children – one whom who had been named after the father.

Her husband, originally from Great Houghton, had worked at Hickleton Main prior to the war breaking out and had joined up with the 2/5th Battalion of the Leicestershire Regiment, becoming a corporal and fighting in the Tunisian Campaign, including the Battle of Kasserine Pass, and later-on being part of the Allied invasion of Italy. Unfortunately, and just like my (step)dad's father, he had been fatally wounded. He died on 28 October 1943 near the Trigno river in the run up to the Battle of Monte Cassino.

If you want another Thurnscoe connection, then I have two.

During the North African campaign, my ex-next-door neighbours' brother from 15 Briton Square – Ernest Tough, had been a 20-year-old seaman when he was captured by the Nazis and interred at Le Kef in Tunisia in September 1942. Sadly, the same week his parents had received the telegram from the War Office, there had been a sadness amongst the East end's populous of Mackem's – the families such as the Tough's that had come down to Thurnscoe from Durham after the 1926 strike. Thirty-year-old Bernard Davison of 38 Lancaster Street had been killed in an accident at Hickleton Main after being crushed in the Middle East district of the Barnsley Seam.

As for Jack Hooley (Jnr), he had some mental illness and would eventually be committed to Sheffield's Middlewood Hospital, where he would die on 25 November 1976, aged forty.

He followed in his father's footsteps and went into The Army but on being discharged both his demeanour and mannerisms had severely changed.

"Tha went into the Army a man and tha came out a woman," his stepfather – Stan McGlasson, had allegedly told him.

On leaving The Army he returned to live with his mother and Stan at 11 Hall Broome Gardens, Bolton-on-Dearne – a prefabricated property that sits on the corner of the access into Crofton Drive. It would be here where the police arrested him following allegations of a sexual assault and whereby after the trial, he would be committed to Middlewood for a medical assessment.

According to his parents, he had gone well and truly off the rails and had begun speaking in an highly exaggerated manner and dressing outlandishly, which for the time was nothing really out of the ordinary, as it was the era of the Teddy Boy. It was said, however – that they were absolutely terrified of what the lad would do next.

After the stint in the mental hospital he had twelve-months on probation.

In his defence, it was said that he had received a head injury whilst working in the pit – although I am not sure which one, as he had been employed at both Goldthorpe and Barnburgh Main collieries.

He received treatment at Middlewood but on getting out it happened again. Firstly, getting remanded for theft and criminal damage and then the big one. On Friday 6 September 1957, the twenty-one-year-old was sent to prison for six months for the indecent assault of his fifteen-year-old cousin – something that had happened on at least two occasions – one being at his parents' house on Hall Broome Gardens.

Around this time, there had been a lot of this about, not least on 23 June 1954, when twenty-one-year-old Paul Kerley of 27 Beever Street, Goldthorpe was sentenced at Doncaster West Riding Court and fined £20 (£563, circa

2020) for the indecent assault on a young girl. Kerley's niece was the aunt of the two ex-Thurnscoe girls that had been introduced to hard drugs in the 1990s – Cheryl and Davina Norris – the former who had allegedly been thrown from a Doncaster tower block and the latter who served five years for grievous bodily harm.

Thurnscoe has had a few of them – not at least fifty-three-year-old Daniel Jones of 30 Taylor Street, twenty-three-year-old James Kitchener of 38 Cromwell Street, thirty-eight-year-old Oswald Parker of 3 Wensley Street and sixty-eight-year old Tom Archer – who at one time had been lodging with Edwin and Beatrice Barrow (nee Arrowsmith) at 29 George Street up on The Spike.

On 20 January 1931, Jones had been found guilty of indecent assault and fined £2 (£131, circa 2020), whilst on 24 September 1940, Kitchener, who had just recently been married to Rose Havenhand and had a young child, was found guilty of indecent assault at Doncaster West Riding Court and sent to prison for a month. He had only recently been in court and found guilty of stealing money from a near-neighbour. To my knowledge, Kitchener – who moved to 62 Brunswick Street with his family, sired at least twelve children and was the grandfather of Terry Gibbons.

Pauline Duggan – the aunt of Sharron Leighton, the little girl who got shot in the head on Brunswick Street, said: "You couldn't walk past the Kitchener's house without getting a burst nose off one of their kids."

As for Parker – on 30 August 1941, he was sent down for six months after being found guilty of three charges of indecent conduct towards young girls. Formerly of Birdwell, he had married Hilda Bradbury on 14 May 1932 and had a son by the name of Roy a year later. Oswald would live at 44 Merrill Road up until his death in September 1963.

On 16 January 1934, Tom Archer got sentenced to nine-months after being found guilty of indecently assaulting a twelve-year-old girl at a house where he had lodged in Thurnscoe.

The most interesting one was perhaps one that happened in an overcrowded house at 27 Tudor Street, which forty-one-year-old Godfrey and Emma Cropper (nee Tagg) had supposedly been the tenants. I say, supposedly as George was doing six months after he and George (Jones) Cunningham – the latter of who was the uncle of Colin Tutin and John Cunningham, being found guilty after they had been caught stealing coal from the offices of Thurnscoe UDC.

As for Emma – on 29 September 1934, she had been due to go on trial for obtaining goods by false pretences, when she had been jailed for a month for aiding and abetting a paedophile. Basically it was perverting the course of justice, by lying in court to protect another one of her lodgers – that being fifty-year-old Joe Bennett – who was serving six months hard labour after being found guilty of indecently assaulting a fourteen-year-old-girl.

The other people living in the house at the time were John Robert Davies and Mary Ellen Gallagher along with their two children and his brother- and sister-in-law, James and Violet Ball (nee Gower) and their three children – Jimmy, Albert and Raymond.

It was Davies who had murdered his wife on Church Street in 1954.

As for the Cropper's, their life had been nothing short of a soap opera – that was up until 12.45 a.m. on 5 August 1956, when George was found near beaten to death in Doncaster's Frenchgate, dying later that day in Doncaster Royal Infirmary.

A man by the name of Arthur Charles Kettlewood who lived in the Beckett Road area of the town was charged with his manslaughter, with Chief Supt. A. Bruton stating that whilst outside the White Swan public house the sixty-three-year-old Godfrey had apparently grabbed hold of him and thrown the first punch, with Kettlewood merely acting in self-defence. Well, that was what the jury obviously thought at Sheffield Assizes on 20 November, when the twenty-eight-year-old Carlton Road plumber was found not guilty and duly discharged.

Godfrey had been active during the lock-out of 1926 and had been summoned to court under the Emergency Powers Act after being one of a few that were accused of bricking a bus taking safety workers from Hickleton Main to Bullcroft Colliery on 17 October. Three days later, he had been amongst it again as the scab problem raised its head in Goldthorpe and a hostile crowd of 2,000 massed at the bottom of Straight Lane waiting for the bus coming up the hill past the Buxton Arms on its way to Barnburgh Main. There were initially just thirty policemen on duty – including two that were mounted, and it wasn't until reinforcements came from Mexborough that order was eventually restored. There had been fighting and stone throwing – with the most serious attacks being on both Straight Lane and Barnburgh Lane.

Emma had died in some sixteen years before her husband when they had lived at 22 Wentworth Road near-opposite Jump WMC in Blacker Hill, aged forty-seven.

As for Goldthorpe and Bolton-on-Dearne, there has been a few convicted deviants.

In July 1930, seventy-year-old David Roystone of 17 Beever Street – a dataller at Goldthorpe Colliery, was found guilty of two charges of indecent assault against several girls and sent to prison for three months and on 1 December 1947, a forty-six-year-old had been on trial for indecently assaulting two girls at Mexborough Technical College where he had been employed as a P.E teacher.

William Christopher Wright had lodged with Samuel and Eva Crowe at 101 The Crescent, Bolton-upon-Dearne and was found guilty – not of indecent assault, but common assault and Justice Hallett who presided over the case, fined him £20 (£844, circa 2020).

Where teachers are concerned, he wouldn't be the first and he wouldn't be the last.

On 9 May 1919, thirty-eight-year-old Henry Bradley – an assistant schoolmaster at Wath National Schools and whose mother was the Innkeeper at the White Bear public house, had been in front of the bench at Rotherham West Riding Court.

He had initially been due to go in front of the school governors after allegations had been made about him, but absconded, with a warrant going out for his arrest straight after.

On his arrest he was remanded on four charges of assaulting children in the school, including the indecent assault of a twelve-year-old girl on two separate occasions – 10 and 17 March.

There is one that stands out and which the authorities should have seen but did not.

On Monday 28 January 1957, a warrant went out for the arrest of seventeen-year-old Raymond Clarke of 102 Buckleigh Road, Wath-on-Dearne after he had failed to answer charges to both shop and house breaking – around ten in all, along with the rape and attempted rape of a thirteen-year-old girl.

He had been arrested on 8 January but absconded bail – leaving his sister, twenty-two-year-old Joyce Straw of 26 Firth Road, Wath-on-Dearne, to forfeit the £10 (£252, circa 2020) surety that she had put up.

After being sentenced, he along with four other youths eventually escaped from HMP Lowdham Grange (Borstal) in Nottinghamshire on 13 October 1957.

Raymond – a former haulage hand at Wath Main, was caught a few days later and ended up serving his sentence, and on 13 June 1959 married a spinner at the Worsted Mill over in Bradford by the name of Barbara Higgins who was the sixteen-year old daughter of Douglas and Mary (nee Jay) of 34 Coronation Road, Hoyland.

It was a mistake. Clarke was bad news. On 26 November 1963, his young wife was found dead at their home at 46 Packman Road, West Melton.

"The body of Mrs Clark was discovered a 7.00 p.m. last night by police officers as a result of information received that the woman was thought to be dead," explained Head of Rotherham West Riding Police, Chief Supt. Charles Woodham. "We shall be working on this for some time."

It was stated that her twenty-four-year-old husband had recently appeared in court on a charge of trying to obtain drugs by means of a forged prescription and had been both arrested and remanded."

Clarke was eventually charged with the murder of his wife.

Some more stomach churners for you:

i) On 7 August 1929 William Park from Conisbrough was sentenced to four months imprisonment with hard labour after being found guilty of indecently assaulting a seven-year-old girl.

ii) On 1 April 1939, twenty-eight-year-old Albert Parton of Leslie Avenue, Conisbrough had been remanded at Doncaster West Riding Court after being charged with the indecent assault of a four-year-old-girl at North Cliff Craggs on 6 March. According to Ald. George Probert, it was one of the worst cases that he had ever heard.

Parton was eventually found guilty and committed to Oulton Hall Mental Hospital near Leeds.

Oulton Hall was also the destination of seventeen-year-old Frank Goddard of 23 West Street, Darfield – a youth with mental issues (special needs), when on 28 March 1938, he was found guilty of indecently assaulting a three-year-old girl.

iii) On 2 April 1941, John Hartley of 6 The Bungalows, Rotherham Road, Great Houghton, had to be carried out of Barnsley West Riding Court after collapsing following the judge's decision to spare him from a prison sentence. The seventy-eight-year-old pleaded guilty to the indecent assault of a young girl and was fined £5 (£282, circa 2020) plus costs.

iv) On 19 February 1957, William Edward Greenall of 11 Pope Avenue, Conisbrough was sent down after being charged with indecently assaulting three girls that had been employed in a Denaby factory. The thirty-five-year old had previous and had been convicted of a similar offence two years earlier.

v) On 1 March 1957, fifty-two-year-old bricklayer, John Monk had been sent for trial at Sheffield Assizes following the indecent assault of a nine- and ten-year-old-girl in his caravan at Drabble's Field, Conisbrough – whilst twenty days later, forty-eight-year-old George Wilson of Loversall Street, Denaby would follow the same route after being charged with the rape of a fifteen-year-old girl.

vi) On 9 July 1957, John Derek Hobson – a twenty-six-year-old bricklayer from 7 Charles Street, Swinton, was sentenced to three years at Leeds Assizes.

Hobson had been found guilty of indecently assaulting young girls at Mexborough and Whiston respectively and occasioning them bodily harm along with the wounding of a twenty-three-year-old off duty soldier – who he had stabbed in the head after he had intervened to stop the second assault.

At 10.40 p.m. on Tuesday 19 March, eighteen-year-old Jennifer Turner had been walking along a footpath that linked the snicket between 139 and 141 Maple Road and Barber's Path just west of Mexborough Montagu Hospital, when she was pushed to the ground and indecently assaulted.

"He had an article that looked like a dagger which he pushed against my neck," she told the court. "He told me to undo my coat and then lifted up my skirt."

At 9.55 p.m. on Sunday 16 June, sixteen-year-old Diane Thomas had been wearing a square-necked summer dress and had been walking her dog across Whiston Meadows towards Long Lane when she, just like Jennifer, had been grabbed from behind.

Hobson threatened her with the same dagger-like-knife and threw her on to the floor, held her down and supposedly said: "If you don't keep quiet, I will kill you."

He then tore her dress down to the waist and ripped off her underclothes. As she resisted, he forced the dagger against her eye and struck her several times.

Hobson, who had married Freda Mary Colton in 1952 and had two daughters – Barbara and Teresa at the time, stated that he "never intended to ravish the girls".

Crown Prosecutor, J.E Wilson intimated that Hobson had suddenly stopped, straightened up and ran away.

He was caught after the off-duty soldier – a man by the name of Roy Nettleship, chased him and dragged him off his motorbike duly receiving a knife in his head for his troubles.

vii) Never think that the influx of migrants and the problems regarding, grooming, rape and indeed paedophilia, has only been present in the here and now as it has not. There were similar problems, not at least in the late-1950s when South Yorkshire (then West Riding) – in particular, Barnsley and Mexborough, opened its doors to foreign nationals who had supposedly escaped the Hungarian Uprising – not at least the Lovers Lane murderer, Josef Kugler.

At 8.45 p.m. on Thursday 18 July 1957, a seventeen-year-old by the name of Janos Halanyos had been one of three of these refugees who had sexually assaulted a fourteen-year-old girl outside Young's jewellers on Mexborough's High Street.

Halanyos – who was described as a factory hand who lived on Doncaster's Christchurch Road, was very matter-of-fact in his manner and said on being arrested: "I came from Doncaster to meet my friends on High Street, Mexborough. We took a walk together and I met a young girl who I have seen on several occasions before. I did it because she was a pretty girl with nice breasts, and I wanted to touch them."

After his initial arrest Chief Insp. Vaughan of Mexborough Police Station stated that Halanyos was not only a flight risk but had an extremely violent temper and on several occasions had been warned about striking female workers when he had been staying at the Miners' Hostel on Mexborough's Adwick Road along with around 230 other Hungarian nationals. That was prior to him being evicted on 30 June.

At its peak, the hostel accommodated 365.

viii) On 26 May, another Hungarian from the hostel – this time twenty-eight-year old Janos Kovac was sentenced at Leeds Assizes for what was described as a serious assault of a fifteen-year-old girl in Mexborough. He had walked her home and on being invited inside it was alleged that he had raped her.

On 3 May, yet another Hungarian from the hostel – this time eighteen-year-old Laslio Gaspar, had been sentenced for indecently assaulting a woman in the town centre.

It was a time when there had been a lot of animosity towards the Hungarian's as they were often seen to be repaying the generosity and kindness that the locals had initially shown them with ingratitude. This was something which had been expressed in Thurnscoe, when the NUM at Hickleton Main in a round-a-bout way knocked-back the idea of employing any Hungarian nationals, when Branch secretary Sid Auty said: "We cannot accommodate them. We have just asked thirty of the older men to retire early to make room for 140 men from Thorne Colliery."

It was nothing like the woke-driven, left-wing rhetoric of today. Back then, it was a case of socialism beginning at home.

It had been a similar situation at Barnburgh Main when their Branch Secretary, Herbert Swift candidly stated: "It has been discussed at three meetings, but the men have finally decided to reject the Hungarian's. We have never had foreign labour at the pit."

The Branch Secretary at Wath Main, Vince Hutchinson intimated much the same and said: "Our problem is looking after our own men – not Hungarian's."

Later-on that month, another four young men – all mining trainees from the hostel, broke into Mexborough Athletic's clubhouse at Hampden Road and stole beer from the cellar, whilst at the hostel itself there were continual problems – with the police often called in after fighting and theft amongst themselves.

On the Sunday night of 2 June, things got out of hand when upwards of a hundred Hungarian's and youths from Mexborough and Denaby were involved in a mass brawl outside Mexborough Post Office, which escalated into a major confrontation with weapons being brandished on Bank Street's junction with Adwick Road. On the Friday night there had been a similar problem when a twenty-eight-year-old Hungarian by the name of Josef Ragoncsa had been knifed.

Only a week before, it had kicked off outside the Montagu Arms Hotel whereby a couple of police officers were violently attacked with the Chairman at Doncaster West Riding Court A.E Emberton candidly stating afterwards: "We have enough of their kind in this country without importing them."

It wasn't the first time, and it would not be the last – and even back then, the media were trying its level best not to escalate the problem.

As for Halanyos – although he was recommended for deportation, that never happened, and after serving time in prison he fled to London – and for a time resided in digs on Moscow Road in the Bayswater area of the city.

"The way he set about me he must have gone berserk," explained Station Foreman, Albert Young, when he described how he had been assaulted on a platform at Oxford Circus London Underground Station. "I have never seen anything like it. When I confronted him, he spat in my face and practically jumped on me and then commenced kicking me in the stomach."

On 9 June 1957, forty-two-year-old Marton Kucheida was found in a wood near Conisbrough after he had been missing from the hostel for ten days. He had slashed his wrists and arms in a failed suicide attempt and was remanded to Armley Gaol pending a psychiatric report.

On 15 October 1957, seventeen-year-old Gabor Csabo was one of three Hungarian trainee miners at the hostel who was found guilty of grievous bodily harm and the assault of two Mexborough youths. The others were twenty-five-year-old Janos Dornay and nineteen-year-old Lajos Bokor.

A week later revenge was in the air and Dornay was subjected to a vicious assault on Manvers Road from one of the Mexborough youths that he had been accused of assaulting, which nearly resulted in a riot as half the street ended up getting involved.

On the Friday night of 31 January 1958, in Lees Buildings (lodging house) on Main Street, Mexborough, the proprietor John McCarthy was knifed after asking five Hungarian's who were sharing the downstairs dormitory to keep it down as they had been jumping up and down and shouting and screaming.

The assailant, thirty-three-year-old Attila Surayni, who had previously been recommended for deportation after picking up two convictions, was found guilty of grievous bodily harm and handed a three-month jail sentence.

Another Hungarian, this time Sandar Toth, was sent to prison for six months for assaulting twenty-two-year-old Joan Bennett of Shelley Street, Mexborough after she had broken-off her relationship with him.

On Sunday 29 June 1958, Joan had been returning from church along Swinton Road when he punched her in the face after she had spurned his advances.

ix) On 9 April 1958, sixty-eight-year-old Robert Henry Gledhill of 81 Oak Road, Wath-on-Dearne had been remanded after being charged with indecently assaulting a ten-year-old girl. It certainly hadn't been the first time either.

On 6 September 1941, he had been sent to prison for six months after being found guilty of the indecent assault of two girls – one six-years old and the other four.

His wife Esther (nee Heaton) had left him ten years prior.

x) On Wednesday 18 June 1958, fifty-three-year-old Norman Bradburn of 23 Winifred Road, Wath-on-Dearne was sentenced to eighteen-months imprisonment for sexually assaulting a twenty-nine-year-old married woman at Mexborough.

xi) Twenty-three-year-old Keith Terence Rigby of 73 Tickhill Street, Denaby was yet another deviant and was jailed for the indecent assault of a nine-year-old boy – the offences occurring between 27 March and 19 April 1959.

xii) On 11 June 1959, four lads for Conisbrough had been charged with the unlawful sexual intercourse of a fifteen-year-old girl – in a sort of gang bang scenario. These were twenty-two-year-old John Winfield of

Halifax Avenue, twenty-year-old William Straw of Fullerton Avenue, and seventeen-year-old Alan Wesley of Chambers Avenue. The charges were dropped against a seventeen-year-old by the name of Brian Cartwright of Halifax Avenue – and reading between the lines, possibly through lack of disclosure.

It had been claimed that the girl had been a willing party and after the trial she had been sent to an approved school as part of a child protection order.

Something similar had occurred at Bolton-on-Dearne on the Sunday evening of 20 November 1938, when three lads raped a fourteen-year-old girl in a caravan at Bolton Feast.

"It is about the worst case of indecent assault that the bench could have brought before them," explained Det. Supt. T. Gordon after two eighteen-year-old's – Charlie Robinson and George Wilkinson, along with a seventeen year old by the name of Albert Walker had been sentenced to three months in jail.

"It appeared that one of these youths – I don't care which, gave the girl a free ticket for an aerial flight. What agreement there was I do not know, but the following day the girl went to the caravan which was occupied by the three youths – all of whom sexually assaulted her. They then made statements against each other."

From what was said, it appeared that the girl's mother had gone to the fairground and had been hammering on the door of the caravan – with all three lads exclaiming that her daughter had not been in. It wasn't until a crowd had gathered and she had threatened to call the police that the child came out.

xiii) Two twenty-year old's – Leslie Ware of 28 Oak Road, Mexborough and Tom Squires of 3 The Croft, Swinton had been arrested and charged with stealing two portable radio sets from Harry Croft's radio and television shop on 13 March 1959, along with a motorcycle and the damage to a plate-glass window of the Redifusion Services shop in Rotherham – however, the story didn't end there.

Now for the warped bit. On 20 April 1959, they had both been arrested and remanded in custody after being accused of indecent offences with each other along with the indecent assault of a six-year-old girl. Ware's older brother William had also been remanded for an indecent offence – his being with his brother Leslie.

If you want a connection – it would be that Tom Squires had been the next-door neighbour of George Bungard – the Head of our Second- and Third Year's and of course the lovely patriotic poppy-wearing fellow that had been our teacher for Technical Drawing at Dearneside Comprehensive.

Leslie Ware married Joyce Purvis in 1961, whilst his elder brother married Jean Oldham in 1968. As for Tom Squires, I could not say. He dropped off the radar.

xiv) On 6 June 1958, fifty-three-year-old Sidney Jones of Cadeby Avenue, Conisbrough was jailed after being found guilty of indecently assaulting a twenty-one-year-old housewife in a cinema at Mexborough. Originally from Durham, he had seven previous convictions for indecent assault. These included: one against his fourteen-year-old cousin in November 1927; for groping several ladies in Doncaster marketplace during the Saturday afternoon of 22 July 1939; and on 13 January 1942, he was sentenced to six months after being found guilty on three charges of indecently assaulting women.

xv) And if you want another set of dirty bastards – on New Years' Eve 1958, fifty-year-old male nurse, Jack Oliver of Sykes Street, Platts Common, Hoyland and a sixty-year-old bricklayer by the name of Frank Charles Cartwright from Unwin Street, Darnall were fined £20 (£472, circa 2020) apiece after being caught giving each other blow jobs in some Sheffield cinema. Please, don't ask me which picture house it was or what film was playing as I don't know!

I certainly don't have any recollections of anything untoward happening in any of our local picture house's – however, saying that – they were reaching the end of their lives by the end of the late-1960's. My only recollection of Goldthorpe's Empire ever being a cinema was during 1971, after I had been allowed to go and see a re-run of Walt Disney's 1950 feature film, *Treasure Island* with Robert Newton doing his iconic portrayal of the pirate, Long

John Silver. By then, however, the place was run down, the seats fusty and the film played to only a small audience of kids – me being part of a group that was led by my elder cousin, Tony, who along with a couple of his mates from Goldthorpe Junior School were threatened with ejection by the manager after their game of hide and seek had been cut short.

Back in the day, however – there were people out there that the press had labelled *Cinema Pests*.

"Complaints are being made of the return of the Cinema Pest who takes advantage of the darkness in picture-houses to annoy women," said a report in the *Sheffield Independent* on 27 September 1928.

If you want a local example: On 3 March 1928, Wombwell's Empire picture palace had set the scene for forty-two-year-old miner – Ernest Bakewell of 134 Hough Lane, to harass three young ladies, whilst watching *The White Black Sheep* – a drama of the desert by all accounts… directed by Sidney Olcott and starring Richard Barthelmess and Patsy Ruth Miller.

Twenty-three-year-old Ada Keen of Hope Street, Low Valley received the most attention and as soon as the lights were lowered, she began to have a wandering hand initially rub up the inside of her leg. Trying her best to ignore the advances, it went a little further whereby she ended up ramming a hat pin into the back of his head before finally slapping his face and calling the manager.

He was duly arrested and Supt. Wilfred Blacker told the court prior to the case going to Leeds Assizes for trial that it had been a "most dastardly" assault and added: "The incidents continued at intervals all throughout the performance."

Bakewell, who was bound over in the sum of £10 (£633, circa 2020) for twelve months, passed away on 4 February 1969, aged eighty-three.

There was one incident, that although it should not have – it did raise a smile – more with the brazen-faced denials and the contemptuous and supercilious repose of the man than anything else.

Thirty-year-old Douglas Marcel Booth-Frazier, was an accomplished concert pianist and an Associate of both the London College of Music and the Royal College of Music and had been the Master of Music at Barnsley's Holgate Grammar School up until 14 March 1930, when he was suspended by Headmaster Arthur John Schooling, following allegations of gross indecency.

"I absolutely refute it," he had said on being charged. "It is outrageous. They are preposterous, abominable, and despicable charges. It is a conspiracy."

Make no mistake about it, this man was a highly-talented individual – a flawed genius, his obsession for homosexuality in a world where it was still illegal, being his one great downfall.

His talent was phenomenal of that there wasn't any doubt, but he did possess a tendency for exaggeration.

On 2 May 1946, he was at Bedford Court doing a piano recital to a packed assembly hall under the name of Dr Marcel Frazier Ph.D., B.A., L.R.A.M., A.R.C.M.

He had, however, been born at 3 Beardall Street in Hucknall under the name of Douglas – to John and Emily Booth (nee Smith), his father being an Inspector in the police. However, by the time of his death in 1959, he had been Marcel Frazier. Rather strangely, he had also been fourteen years younger, which was something that various news outlets picked upon throughout the years – him continually lying about his age.

Not unlike Władziu Valentino Liberace, who would come into the world, just a couple of months after he had returned from the First World War, Douglas had been something of a child prodigy, playing complex recitals to packed audiences well before his sixteenth birthday.

At just seventeen years old, he had signed on with the 87th Battalion at Mansfield on 17 October 1917.

A Det. Insp. Tom Hodgson of Barnsley Borough Police, said that Douglas had been educated at Mansfield Grammar School and that he had served as a Private in the Royal Army Medical Corps after which he held various teaching appointments, leaving his home at 38 Harrington Street in Mansfield and becoming Resident Lecturer in

Music and French at Rishworth College for boys in September 1925. This is a huge imposing building which still overlooks the River Ryburn near Ripponden.

He had previously been the organist at St Barnabas Church in Pleasley Hill and at St Mark's Church on Nottingham Road, Mansfield, and just the year before had scored one hundred marks out of one hundred whilst playing for his diploma at the London Victoria College of Music. He had, however, become somewhat disillusioned with the town and its people.

On 26 April 1925, he responded to an article in the *Mansfield Reporter* that concerned a thirteen-year-old violinist who was the son of John and Gertrude Becher (nee Gale) of which the paper reported the details of the recital as nothing more than its attendance being sparse.

"As long as Mansfield is full of whist drives and dances its musical education will be nil," he said. "Here you had a wonderful young boy doing a tremendous recital and all you can pick up on is the lack of people in attendance. It certainly wasn't the terrible cheap-jack stuff which the modern cheap composers are churning out every day and which are being sung in the theatres and music halls. That is not music and it is high time it was abolished, and it substituted with the real music of the world."

It would be in June 1929, when he would become the first Master of Music at the newly constructed Wombwell Middle School – initially lodging at 1 Victoria Road.

If you want a bit more history, the school's first ever geography teacher had been John Corley – the younger brother of Thomas who would become a teacher at Dearneside, both of whom had been brought up in the end-terraced property at 112 Furlong Road, Bolton-on-Dearne.

Teachers tend to move around a bit and as Douglas's reasoning behind his movement will soon become apparent, John Corley's – although solely professional, would have tragic circumstances.

Being part of Goldthorpe's Roman Catholic Community (Sacred Heart), the Corley's were a well-known family and even after he married Dorothy Livermore and took up teaching posts in the south of England, John's career had still been locally reported. As was the tragic death of their twenty-three-month-old daughter, Daphne on 9 May 1936. The family had been involved in a head-on collision on the A414 Ongar – Chelmsford Road, whilst on their way to London.

Witnesses from nearby houses saw the former student of Mexborough Secondary School, get out of the car staggering – his face all covered in blood and holding the dead child in his arms. She had died of a fractured skull and was pronounced dead on arrival, whilst his wife had laid in a coma for seventeen hours.

Douglas left Wombwell after just a few months when he was appointed Music Master at Holgate Grammar School.

I had been there a few times. It was a huge imposing red bricked building which sadly isn't there anymore, it being demolished in 2012. My first time there was as fifth man – a reserve for Carfield's Chess Team in early 1976 – ten and eleven-year-old juniors playing against fifteen and sixteen-year-old seniors. As I recall, Mr Capaldi bundled us into his Volkswagen and on getting there we were taken into what seemed at the time like a huge library. As for the game, we beat them easily, our only defeated player being Richard Purcell. I ended up playing the same kid straight after and thrashed him in less than twenty moves, my main recollection being that he offered me a few sweets from his packet of wine gums, whilst I had been taking his pieces. He was a really nice kid if I am being honest!

Later, and whilst in Dearneside, I remember going over there with the school football team and getting walloped 3-0. I think that was the game Alan Bainbridge filled in at left-back, and then a couple of weeks later beating them at our place 6-3.

Although Douglas left under something of a cloud at Wombwell, it would not come to light until the police got involved. Under the name of Douglas Marcel Booth-Frazier, he was charged with several offences against schoolboys between 3 November 1929 and 13 March 1930, seven of which occurred in picture houses around Barnsley and another five whilst in the classroom – three of which he was additionally charged with gross indecency.

"When the prisoner was searched, we found face powder on him – and at his home we found tinted face cream, a box of powder and a powder puff," said Supt. Blacker – pointing to the fact that he was indeed a homosexual.

Douglas had rooms in a stone-built end-terrace at 116 Park Road, in a once-affluent area of the town, close to Locke Park – the women's make-up he had told the police had belonged to his landlady, who had recently died.

In a two-day trial at Leeds Assizes on 13 May which was presided over by Justice Sir Henry Alfred McCardie, the jury had to hear evidence from eleven boys – including a twelve-year-old's testimony regarding the events of 13 March, which was described in court as a *grave offence* falling just short of sodomy.

He was found guilty on sixteen charges.

Justice McCardie said: "I do not inflict a light sentence of imprisonment upon you, because you have corrupted not one, but eleven boys, and inflicted upon them grave moral corruption, and every one of these little fellows who stood in the witness box goes through life with the stain of your pollution upon him."

Douglas was sentenced to twenty months hard labour.

As for the controversial judge – he ended up committing suicide on 26 April 1933, shooting himself in the head with a twelve-gauge. It was said that he had racked up huge gambling debts and was being blackmailed, but how true that is I do not know.

Douglas's life thereon afterwards was ruined. His tragic existence comprised several convictions for importuning in public lavatories – mainly in Coventry and Southsea, along with several attempted suicides – including two where he had overdosed, one of which involved him receiving treatment in Warwick Hospital for Aspirin poisoning. He had taken 150 tablets.

"You reach extremes where you cannot go on any longer," he had told the court.

There was much worse than Douglas – that is for sure. On 17 May 1939, music teacher and former choirmaster, William Henry Dawson Lyne was sentenced to six months in prison.

The unmarried forty-five-year-old of 123 Worksop Road, Swallownest had been charged with indecently assaulting three girls aged, eight, ten and eleven on 8 May 1939.

As for the so-called Cinema Pest's, one my dad's second cousin's, Maurice Durose had been committed to trial at Nottingham Quarter Sessions on 21 May 1948, when as a seventeen-year-old living at 36 Greenwood Drive, Kirkby-in-Ashfield, he was alleged to have indecently assaulted two sisters aged sixteen and seventeen along with their sixteen-year-old friend in the Regent Cinema in East Kirkby on 31 March. It was something that saw him sentenced to three years in Borstal. Not that, that ever stopped him. On 31 August that year, he was apprehended by police after going over the wall and breaking into F.W Woolworths on Lumley Road, Skegness.

Apart from him being 5'6 in height and the fact that he was released from his third term inside on 10 January 1952, I don't know a great deal about him apart from the fact that on getting out of jail he signed up with the Royal Armoured Corps and served in Hannover, Germany… and that he died of kidney failure in Queen Alexandra Military Hospital on 9 June 1958, aged twenty-seven.

As I have already mentioned – several members of the Durose family came north from the Kirkby-in-Ashfield area to work in the mines – my great grandfather first settling at 32 Cliff View, Denaby before moving to 13 Wellington Street, Goldthorpe.

Like my great grandfather, William (Bill) Durose had been born in Kirkby-in-Ashfield, but as he was ten years his junior, he had come up to South Yorkshire with his father, Charlie and common-law wife, Lizzie (nee Birtles). And whereas my grandparents initially headed for the eastern Dearne Valley, he and his father got jobs at Silverwood Colliery, and moved into one of the newly constructed properties at 31 Cross Street – part of several rows of terraced houses located just off Whinney Hill (now the A630 Doncaster Road) between Dalton and Thrybergh.

Bill's father was 6'2 and described as being both powerfully-built and extremely violent, and much like the Durose's within my immediate family, he was a hard drinker. It was a dark combination of all three that had seen him serve time in prison – namely for beating up a policeman outside the Forest Tavern on Skegby Road, Kirkby-in-Ashfield on 9 November 1886.

"The scene of the tragic affair revealed a deplorable state of things, the interior of the dwelling presenting a squalid and despicable appearance," read a report in *The South Yorkshire Times* on 7 December 1907. "The kitchen was sparsely furnished and devoid of all home comforts. There were only three or four ordinary dirty-looking chairs and a rickety uncovered table in the kitchen, the walls of which were covered with a dirty-looking paper. The indications generally pointed to the fact that all the joy and happiness of the home had been ruined by the depredations of drink."

Basically, their house was a shit tip.

At 11.00 p.m. on 29 November, twenty-one-year old Bill Durose had been involved in an altercation with his fifty-three-year-old father, the latter of whom had sustained several blows to the head – one of which had connected just behind his lower ear and had caused bleeding to the brain. The son had killed his father – the root cause being booze.

"The family were of a very quarrelsome disposition," a neighbour explained. "They went to Rotherham on Friday and didn't get in until 10.00 p.m."

"Charlie was a very powerful man and was a threat to anybody, whether they wanted it or not," explained his stepdaughter, Susannah (Davies). "It was more often a blow of the fist rather than a word."

Charlie had been living with Susannah's mother, Lizzie for twenty-seven years and had moved around a considerable amount, before settling in Thrybergh – having five children between them – Charlie (Jnr), Bill, Elizabeth, Lydia and Sam.

The story was, that Bill and both his parents had been extremely drunk – especially, his mother who by all accounts, possessed a black eye from an earlier quarrel with her husband and was not only unable to recall any account of the night but had also been too intoxicated to even speak. The son had laid down on the hearth rug in front of the fire, and apparently his father had taken exception to this and got up out of his chair, called him a *cunt* and told him to get up before kicking him in the back and grabbing himself another drink.

"Go sit back down," said Bill. "I don't want any bother."

His father was stumbling all over the place, therefore his son went to put him in the chair – however, on him sitting back down he fell off, breaking it in the process. A scuffle therefore ensued with the father hitting the son. Unfortunately, for the father, Bill managed to hit him several times, with the fatal blow catching him on the side of the head.

"Oh, Bill what have you done?" exclaimed his sister as their father lay motionless.

"The old fucker hit me in the mouth, so I hit him back," he said.

Bill's shirt was ripped at the collar and there were scratches around his neck and blood dripping from a split lip.

Elizabeth became hysterical after failing to wake him and within minutes she had half the street out in the yard prior to two policemen turning up on the scene, whereby Bill Durose was eventually charged with killing his father.

The inquest took place at the Grapes Hotel in Dalton and after a post-mortem examination performed by Dr John Ewing Adams it was suggested that as there had been no fracture of the skull, Charlie Durose had died of shock.

The trial at Leeds Assizes on 25 March 1908, was presided over by Justice Sutton and Bill Durose was found not guilty of manslaughter and duly discharged.

I mentioned the Hungarians during the 1950s. There was, however, a more interesting story around a similar time – that involved a Pole.

Imagine a thirty-nine-year-old woman, possessing huge similarities to Kim Hartman's characterisation of Private Helga Geerhart – Herr Flick's sado-masochistic love interest in the BBC Sitcom *Allo Allo*. The peroxide plaited and tied back blonde hair, the sexually pragmatic German accent, the conservative dress sense, and matter-of-fact front that conceals an erotic underlayer of seduction along with a frivolous and licentious nature. Throw in a disabled non-functioning husband and you have all the ingredients for a disaster.

A doppelgänger, Charlotte Ball (nee Boldt) may well have been, but there was more. She was bewitching, tantalising and indeed sexual dynamite, her husband getting off on a relationship that saw another man (men) invited into the fold. A Bitter Moon-type secret that only the three of them would ever know about – the wife, the lover, and the cuckold. However, it did not work out like that. It rarely does.

"All three were always very quiet and kept to themselves," said their landlord, John Robert Varty, during a murder trial at Leeds Assizes on 27 November 1953.

That certainly hadn't been the case.

The husband, Herbert Ball – although disabled and only able to walk with the assistance of crutches, was employed at the Remploy furniture factory on Pogmoor Road in the Dodworth area of Barnsley.

Post-war Barnsley was much like the rest of the country, where TV, radio and indeed music was changing the way people thought and which saw styles change and certain inhibitions dropped.

At thirty-three, Charlotte – who was of German nationality, had met her future husband whilst he had been on military service, eventually marrying him in the Lower Saxony town of Celle in 1947.

A life in England beckoned.

Some three years older than Charlotte, Wilhelm Lubina had been born in Poland and was drafted into the German army on his country being invaded, and whilst serving in France, he was said to have deserted.

On getting to England he sought employment as a miner and worked at Elsecar Main Colliery. He was said to have met the Ball's in a public house in Dodworth in 1948 and they became friends – not at least with Charlotte, as they could both converse in German.

Herbert and Charlotte lived in a one-bedroomed flat at Dodworth Hall (Grange) – however, according to the owner, the other tenants in the building had been taking exception to the couple being there – which is something that I will get on to shortly.

The Ball's eventually moved out and into a large three-storey house at 15 Springfield Street, which was a property owned by Mr Varty that was located just off Dodworth Road, whereby they rented the upstairs two-bedroomed flat.

On 2 May 1953, Lubina would be taken in by Ball and his wife. Whether this was as a sub-tenant-cum-lodger or as his wife's full-time lover I could not say. What is known, is that there was a sexual relationship, which was something that had been confirmed at Barnsley West Riding Court during the pre-trial on 23 July 1953, when Prosecutor, R.L.D Thomas established that Lubina and Mrs Ball had indeed been having some form of affair.

Herbert Ball, however – would not be drawn on the subject, and the nearest he ever got to discussing it, was when he told the court, that around twelve-months prior, he was supposed to have been meeting his wife in a public house in Barnsley and that she did not show. He had later found out that she had been with Lubina in another.

There was far more to the story, which maybe goes back to their period of tenancy at Dodworth Hall.

Dick Whittington maybe the loveable fable of a young man who sought to find his fortune in London and a tale which was penned by Oscar Weigle – however, Barnsley had its very own version of a man with the same name who would most certainly find that the streets he travelled, would be paved with gold.

As the Dick in the story found himself a cat, the one in Barnsley also found a four-limbed friend – not so much a cow – but a cash cow.

Born on 19 November 1923, Richard (Dick) Whittington was a chancer and opportunist and described by his elderly wife as a "good-looking young rotter".

He had initially lived off the A628 in the Lundwood area of Barnsley, in a local authority-owned property at 112 Priory Road and worked on the haulage at one of the nearby collieries. That, however – was only temporary.

Herbert Harry Asquith had not only been a magistrate but also one of the major shareholders and directors of Barnsley-based glass manufacturers Messrs Redfearn Bros. and had married the twenty-five-year-old daughter of a music teacher (Professor of Music) on 9 September 1908.

His wife, Ethel Thornsby, had lived at 35 Summer Lane, Wombwell and whose grandfather was the very well-respected Thomas Muscroft Thornsby. He owned a hugely successful printing business, was Vice President of the South Yorkshire Club Union and also been a football linesman and referee in the First and Second Division respectively.

From what I have picked up, Mr and Mrs Asquith moved into Dodworth Hall during the 1920s – a property which was originally the home of the Rev Thomas Thornley-Taylor. Note the Thurnscoe connection? According to the records, the couple never had children and her husband duly passed away on 12 February 1941, aged fifty-six.

It took the wealthy widow less than six-and-a-half years to find love again. Unfortunately, it came in the guise of her chauffer and handy man – that being the twenty-five-year-old Richard Whittington, whom she ended up marrying on 14 May 1948. Just for the record she was forty-one years older than him.

The marriage was nothing short of a farce and by 4 August 1950 it was over – but not before the "good looking young rotter" had dragged her through the mire, whilst at the same time creaming as much out of her as he could.

"It seems clear that at the time of the marriage he treated her with extreme cruelty in the most depraved way," said Commissioner R.C Essenhigh at the Sheffield Divorce Court. "On one occasion he had induced her to make out a cheque for £3,000 (£110,000, circa 2020) and on another, accompanied by his brother he went to Dodworth Hall, dragged his wife out of bed and forced her to sign over a taxicab business of which she was the owner."

Her reasoning behind her filing for a divorce cited both adultery and cruelty, but that wasn't the half of it.

Whittington had numerous convictions and had spent time in prison – mainly for assault and driving offences, but if you scratch the surface, you will always find something more.

Around 10.30 p.m. on Sunday 22 April 1951, he had a twenty-three-year-old girl from Worsbrough View, Tankersley – the same street as Winifred Shingler, pinned down in the rear of his car and screaming for help.

He had offered to take Ruth Buckley and two of her friends home from Shaw Inn (Shaw Lane Sports Club) and after dropping them off at the bus stop commenced the journey down the A61 Sheffield Road, whereby after negotiating a few junctions and passing The Cock Inn, he had pulled up in a siding down Pilley Lane. A kiss and a cuddle were on the agenda and as that was the case, they both ended up in the back seat of the car. His intentions, however – were one dimensional in that he intended to have sex with her, whether she wanted it or not.

After much touching, groping, and slapping he told her straight: "I chose you out of all of them and I always get what I want."

She managed to get out the car, but he dragged her back inside.

A man out walking had intervened, but Whittington had told him that if he "didn't fuck off" he would "run him over", and as that was the case the man alerted the police, who when they arrived saw a distressed Ruth in the back seat, not only sporting a black eye but with her clothes torn off.

Whittington was arrested and charged with assault and attempted rape.

On 11 July 1951 at Leeds Assizes, and in a trial presided over by Justice Jones, Richard Whittington-Asquith (as he had adopted his elderly wife's surname) was found not guilty of attempted rape and indecent assault but guilty of the assault. He was sentenced to nine months.

On getting out of prison, he was in bother again, as during the summer of 1952, the car he had been driving had hit a motorcycle on Staincross crossroads (B6428/B6131 Towngate / Blacker Road) in Mapplewell, the collision of which, killed a twenty-four-year-old nurse from Wentbridge by the name of Joyce Fletcher. She had been riding pillion.

Fortunately for him, the driver of the motorcycle – twenty-three-year-old Donald Elliot, who just happened to be an off-duty policeman from Chapeltown, had been driving without insurance and it was therefore he, who had been made culpable for the accident, even though he got off with a charge of driving without due care and attention.

Trivialities aside, around this time Whittington still had some involvement over at Dodworth Hall, not at least with him being the Estates Manager (Thornley Taylor Estates) and picking up rent money from the tenants and organising the repairs to their properties, one of which was occupied by none other than Herbert and Charlotte Ball. That was up until 8 December 1952.

By then tensions had become untenable, with Whittington apparently getting frustrated by the fact that they had still been there after he had served them with a notice to quit.

"I have been getting complaints about them from the other tenants – I gave them notice and she just burned it," he said.

Why? Was always going to be the next question.

On the said Sunday night, he had been banging on the door of their flat and supposedly shouted: "If you don't clear out my fist will be coming through this door."

As Charlotte opened the door, he gave her a winder under the chin which put her on her backside before going over to the husband and dragging him out of bed. He then commenced throwing their belongings out into the passage.

On 5 January 1953, it was ascertained at Barnsley West Riding Court, that Charlotte had run to the police station in just her night-dress as he had been assaulting her husband and that when the police arrived on the scene, Whittington was arrested and charged.

There had to be more to this story, especially as Whittington would be found guilty of assault and given nothing more than a slap on the wrists: a fine of £5 (£145, circa 2020).

He had major form and had just recently been released from Armley Gaol after serving a nine-month sentence. And now he had been found guilty of not only assaulting a woman but her crippled husband too – along with illegally entering their home to actually do it. As I have said – I am not convinced. There had to be much more to the story.

Mrs Whittington-Asquith (nee Thornsby) was in financial trouble and within six months she would be filing for bankruptcy. As for Whittington himself, he spent money like a drunken sailor and had bled her dry. My thoughts are – and that is what they are, is that he had begun to ask for all the rents on the estate to be paid in cash – which was something that had seen Charlotte – on the behest of her husband, go to Wilhelm Lubina and ask him for money.

I personally think that prior to this, there had been some payment in kind, in that Whittington had been having regular sex with Charlotte Ball either as payment or part-payment of the rent and now, he just wanted the money. Why else would a tenant petulantly burn an eviction notice? She had to have had something on him.

Back to the main story: On 25 June 1953 – a time when the trial of the fifty-five-year-old necrophile, John Christie was on all the front pages, after being found guilty at The Old Bailey of the murder of his wife, Ethel (nee Simpson) along with seven other people, Wilhelm Lubina would end up murdering Charlotte Ball.

Thirty-year-old Bertha Varty (nee Birkell) – the wife of the landlord, had seen him coming in from work around 3.00 p.m. and maybe an hour prior to that, Charlotte, dressed in a dark red summer dress, stockings and heels, come into the house with some shopping and fumble for the key prior to her opening the door. That Thursday afternoon, the sun had been out with temperatures hitting nearly eighty-five degrees and although Bertha and

Charlotte were as different as chalk and cheese in that they had absolutely nothing in common, the weather could always form part of some polite conversation.

"Yes – the weather is good – I like the sun," Charlotte could have said, in her mysterious Prussian accent.

Whatever the conversation, the soon-to-be-pregnant Bertha, couldn't have helped but be intrigued by the ménage à trois upstairs, not at least in the atomic blonde with the crippled husband who had a tendency to turn heads wherever she went.

The facts were, however – that on getting in from work and picking up the paper, Charlotte, set about making Lubina a sandwich.

Had John Christie – a man who had temporarily lived above the shop at 61 Hinde House Lane, Sheffield – which was owned by his brother-in-law, Arthur Cecil Bartle – a man who was the cousin of the father of Joseph Bartle of 41 Thornley Crescent, Thurnscoe, been a topic of conversation? Or was it her husband or indeed another man they had been talking about? Whatever it had been – the conversation had created a problem, as exactly two hours and twenty minutes later she was dead. He had stabbed her six times, including two blows through the lungs and a fatal one which penetrated her heart. What made this even more pathetic than it already was, hadn't just been the failed suicide of the murderer himself – as he was found with seven stab wounds in his right temple and three in his chest – but the fact that the husband, Herbert Ball, had seen it all happening from the foot of the stairs, and due to his disability, had been unable to negotiate the staircase to stop it happening.

If you have ever been involved in a trial – especially at Crown Court, lots of information goes missing and is purposely left out – mainly on a quid pro quo basis, but mostly it always favours the defendant. This trial, which had been presided over by Justice Sir Wintringham Norton Stable, was no different.

In the main, the subject of the ménage à trois was diligently sidestepped by both the defence and the prosecution – H.B.H. Hylton-Foster QC and S. Temple Mills QC respectively, although it did manage to raise its head a couple of times.

Herbert Ball mumbled to the court that he had found a letter to his wife from a "Bill" who wished to see her again after she had been "with him" in Leeds. He said that he had discussed the matter with Charlotte and that she had written to this "Bill" and told him that she never wanted to see him again.

The identity of "Bill" was never mentioned, although you don't have to be Poirot to make the connection: Bill is of course short for William... and indeed Wilhelm.

On searching Wilhelm Lubina's room, the police – who were headed by Det. Insp. John James Marshall, found that he had five photographs of Charlotte in a box by his bed along with a love letter. Remember me mentioning the fact that most women have done some form of modelling from time to time? These photographs, risqué in nature – had been no different.

It was also confirmed that Lubina loved Charlotte and that he had been extremely jealous of her association with other men – and there had been many.

"A man can have a friend. A woman can have a husband and a friend – but not many friends," Lubina had told the court.

So, had Richard Whittington been one of these *friends*? Herbert Ball had denied that on occasions he had sent his wife to Lubina for money, not at least to make the shortfall on the rent for the flat at Dodworth Hall. The dots (facts) were there but when asked in court, the husband refused to be drawn on their links.

Lubina had allegedly told Charlotte that he was leaving, and a quarrel developed whereby she supposedly lashed out at him several times. He had also told the court that during this onslaught, he grabbed something from the table and hit her – however, he hadn't been sure how many times. "I never wanted to kill her. I just lost control," he had said.

Mr Varty said he saw Mrs Ball stagger from the living room screaming, whilst Lubina had been striking her, with Charlotte eventually collapsing in a pool of blood on the landing.

He then saw Lubina stand in front of the mirror and make a half-assed attempt to take his own life.

Pathologist, Dr David Ernest Price said that Charlotte had died from shock and haemorrhage following the stab wounds to the chest.

The verdict was a formality and on Justice Stable donning the black cap, Lubina remained unmoved as the death sentence was passed.

He was duly executed at Armley Gaol on Wednesday 27 January 1954 by Denaby-hangman Harry Allen and his assistant, Steve Wade – the latter of whom had lived at 90 Thorne Road, Edenthorpe, prior to his death from stomach cancer on 22 December 1956.

As for Richard Whittington. He died in February 1964 in a property at 338 Meanwood Road in the Headingley area of Leeds, aged forty.

I could give you a similar case.

Thirty-four-year-old Gordon Dunhill Davy had been brought up in the stone cottage next door to the Market Hotel on Elsecar's Wentworth Road.

At 4.50 a.m. on Sunday 22 January 1961, he stabbed Kathleen Conway to death. The thirty-year-old blonde had lived in a property on Murdock Road in the Southey Green area of Sheffield for the past twelve months and had been separated from her husband, Joseph for the past six, whereby she had got involved with Davy.

"A small boy ran a quarter of a mile through the rain in his pyjamas and dressing gown early yesterday to fetch help for his dying mother," read a report in the *Daily Mirror* the following day. "Curly-haired Charles Conway – eleven, dashed along the streets in his stockinged feet until he bumped into a policeman."

Within seconds five police cars shot over to a property – however, they were too late.

The boy's mother had died from multiple stab wounds – and Davy was charged with her murder.

According to Chief Supt. G.A Carnill – Head of Sheffield CID, Davy – a divorcee who married Olive Russell in 1948, had been told that the relationship was over.

"Kathleen came in on Saturday night and said that I had to go. We talked and disagreed and then went to bed," said Davy. "I suddenly woke up at 4.30 a.m. I don't know whether I was asleep or mad, or what I was. I fetched the knife and stabbed her."

"My wife and I had been separated but we had been planning a reconciliation," said her distraught thirty-four-year-old husband, Joseph Frederick Conway. "We had been out on Saturday night with her sister, Mavis Atkinson. They dropped me off at my mother's and that was the last time I saw my wife alive."

Davy was sentenced to life on 27 February that year.

He died on 28 November 1986 – his last address being 14 Mackie Hill Close, Crigglestone, Wakefield.

This unedited chapter was written after the book was completed.

Top. The Dearne Hotel on St Andrews Square / Carr Head Lane, Bolton-on-Dearne - built in the summer of 1956 along with the Co-op supermarket. Bottom. Brothers David and Paul Martin standing outside their home at York Terrace, Thurnscoe with the Thurnscoe Memorial Club (The Bomb) and the Coronation WMC (The Corra) in the background. The Bomb opened its doors in September 1956 - The Corra in 1958.

39. Lucky Man

"I would give everything I own just to see them one last time," said Julie Gibbard (now Thompson).

It is a similar sentiment that echoes with a lot of people regarding their parents once they have gone, and one that to some extent rings true.

What would you do if you could go back in time? For me, there are hundreds of things that I could do.

I rarely spoke to my mum after she and Vic Antcliffe had parted company. It was an acrimonious split, which my daughter no doubt helped fuel. After that, my mum sold up and drove down to Spain's Costa Del Sol. It was a move that my (step)dad had only ever dreamed of.

I remember him and I being stood in some dirty run-down bar in L'Escala – a little known fishing village on the Catalonian coast during summer 1987 and knocking back more than a few a few San Miguel's. As he often did, he told me that this was the kind of life he wanted. Unfortunately, when my mum took the plunge, he had been gone several years. She had not only waited until he had died but had had time to recycle another husband. However, by then I had lost interest in her.

"You need to have a word with your mum," I was told.

After my daughter had left home, the trouble she caused had been immense. For a short while she had stopped with my mum on the Dunk Estate at 38 Roche Drive, during which time my mum had called the police as her husband had supposedly tried drowning her in the bath.

Had he? I really have no idea.

In later years, my mum drank heavily and that alone distorts reality.

We had tried to calm it, but a drinker only has one friend and that I am afraid is the bottle of which it comes out of. I drink as much as the next man – however, what I don't have is an addictive personality. Like anything else, I can detach myself from it in that I can do without. "I can take it or leave it", I suppose is the phrase. My mum, however, could not. It was the same with smoking. She was like a baby with a dummy and went through those French cigarettes one after the other with their customary blue packets of *Gitanes* or *Gauloises* often being scattered about the place.

Whilst my sixteen-year-old daughter had stayed there, my mum had started handing out the customary backhander, which was something that my wife had been there to witness this particular day. "She'd done nothing wrong," I had been told.

The law of averages where my daughter is concerned could quite easily state if that one wasn't deserved, then there would be three or four others which had been missed and that were. Still, she had put my wife and I through the mill and never once taken a good hiding – then again, I am not my mum.

There is the adage of the messenger boy getting shot and that is exactly what happened. As soon as I mentioned to my mum about her hitting my daughter and that it had to stop – fucking boom.

I had grown up with the screaming and shouting, and my mum, fuelled on cheap wine, along with her piercing dark brown eyes and brandishing a paring knife could have appeared quite unnerving, however, to me it was nothing.

"If you wanna do it, then fucking do it," I told her.

The fear and control she once had over me had long since gone.

The screaming and shouting were all par for the course and after a while you just grow oblivious to it. Even her Alsatian never flinched at its volume.

However, as my daughter had been collecting her things, my mum hit the triple-nine then started smashing the house up. It was nothing more than a tantrum. Something that she could deflect blame on. If she couldn't sort me one way, she would do it another. I had done nothing, but when the police arrived, they arrested me. Thankfully, I had made a phone call to my sister and she was there to remove the kids. I say kids, as my nine-year-old son had been with me, having just picked him up from his other set of grandparents.

I was told that my sister flipped her lid with my mum. "What are you going to do – beat them, like you did us?" she had supposedly said.

It was my kids that told me that.

In a family crisis, my sister was good – however there was the last one, where she was not so.

I spent several hours locked up in Barnsley police cells – the duty solicitor that night being none other than the infamous Walter Brooke. "It sounds like your mother really needs some help," he told me.

She did, but she would never accept it. It is just how she was.

On being released, I told the arresting policeman, a PC Robinson, exactly what I told him on him cuffing me: "You're making a mistake – I haven't done a thing wrong – I am just picking up my daughter."

Another fucking halfwit.

I said to my wife on her picking me up: "I don't really think that things can get any worse."

I was certainly wrong on that score. For me it was just another low point where my mum was concerned. It would be a time when I would never speak to her for several years. I have often said it. When she was good, she was really good. Unfortunately, the opposite applied all too often. All a kid ever wants is their parents to love them. Well, that is all I ever wanted.

For years there was no interaction, no phone calls, no letters, no nothing.

What is strange is that whenever things were okay with me and my mum, the opposite applied to my brother. As soon as there was a problem with us, he was there. Read into that how you will. He hadn't been around when his dad was badly – and had kept away for months. What is ironic, however, is that in the months up to my (step)dad dying, my mum had been nothing short of perfect. It is a shame his dying had to bring the best out in her.

A lot of the arguments in later life was with how my mum treated the grandkids. Not mine – as outside of her, they were kids that had everything. My brothers. She despised our Joel's kids and absolutely hated the sight of his eldest, Nicole. Hayley had been younger, so there hadn't been that kind of animosity, but nevertheless, she certainly wasn't keen. Our Joanne's son, however, had been the favourite.

It is a thing that Steve Bradley once mentioned about his mother – Mary. "The thing that fucked me off about my mam is that she didn't treat the grandkids the same," he told me.

I have never really asked anyone who I grew up with about how their parents treated their kids. It would be quite interesting to hear, however.

My son always said that our Joanne's lad, Josh (Whitehurst), idolised me as a kid – in much the same way as my daughter's eldest had. He was an extremely humorous little Herbert in that half the time didn't know what he was doing. There were times when I took him everywhere with me – be it over to the printers in Derbyshire, down to London, up to Scotland and even over to Cyprus. Like his grandma – my mum, he had an addictive personality, in that once he had his mind set on something, that was it. And as for clumsy, don't even go there. He was such a lovely little lad.

"I can't believe your dad took him there," my sister had said to my daughter.

I had taken him and my son to the London Dungeon. I had to admit it was interesting bordering on the very ghoulish, the latter of which gave my little nephew nightmares.

"What's *The Shining*, Uncle James?" he asked in his gruff voice, as we drove up to Scotland to pick up my daughter a couple of days before Christmas Day 2007.

"It's a dead scary film that I always watch before Christmas," I told him.

Did he watch it? No, I couldn't find it, so we watched some other scary film which ended up with him sleeping with the light on all night.

Still, it wasn't as bad as the Boxing Day night when my brother and his wife had stopped in 2001. That resembled something out of a horror movie with their two daughters standing on the landing in the middle of the night and both howling and wailing like a pair of fucking inmates from Middlewood.

"What's the matter?" I asked them.

They didn't talk as such – and just howled and wailed. It was all very disturbing.

"Look, go and wake your mum and dad up," I told them.

"We are sc-a-a-red," said the eldest. "We da-a-a-r-n't."

"Scared of what? I'm here."

There was no consoling them. They were at it all night. Weird as fuck if you ask me.

As for my mum's Iberian lifestyle, it was hardly Simon Cowell and consisted of a wooden chalet on some gated campsite that was little more than a glorified shed.

My brother and his family tried holidaying there – however, the fact that my mum and his wife hated each other's guts made the latter's week-long stay last around six days shorter than it should have – my brother having to part them from fighting on Day One.

My mum may have had a point. His wife's daily routine was a bit like your archetypal miner on dayshift, in that she liked a couple of hours' kip on an afternoon. What was strange is that when I knew her, she hadn't worked for years and spent the majority of her children's life drawing sick pay – in a situation not too dissimilar to that of Debbie Thwaites. However, not only did she have to have a sleep in the afternoon – so did her kids. It was obviously something that had driven my mum to despair. Overall, them being there was just an accident waiting to happen.

We had a phone call. My brother's wife was at the airport in her pyjamas wanting a flight back into the UK. The problem was, however, is that she didn't have any money.

I don't know how she got back as I certainly never lent her anything.

The time between me leaving my mums in the police car to seeing her in Spain I reckon was around six years, although I had texted her a few times, and that was amiable enough.

I recall going to Billy Swift's funeral at St Hilda's church. He was the father-in-law of Carl Eades. He had been a humorous little fellow with the club foot that I had often seen as a young lad in Hickleton Main's screening plant and who in later life I regarded as just a lovely man.

Also there, had been Janet Michell – the daughter-in-law of the famous cricketer, Tommy.

"I will tell you something, James – I get on with your mam a lot better, now that I'm just writing to her," she told me.

My auntie Carol (Oldfield) had also been there at the time, which is something else I remember, as that the first thing she did on seeing me was to give me a hug.

As I have said, Carol was one of those angels, who made my growing up, so much nicer.

My son used to phone his grandma on and off, which was quite nice and in the end our Joanne took him over there on a flight out of Leeds Bradford Airport.

"How did it go?" I asked him on his return.

"My grandma was really nice."

I didn't doubt that – my mum could be like that.

"She's stopped drinking," he told me.

"What, she's stopped drinking, or you didn't see her drinking?" I said.

"No, she's stopped – she's really poorly."

That was the gamechanger.

My mum had smoked since she was ten years old. "Me and Margaret Dawson used to go over the Seven Fields with our packet of cigs," she used to tell me.

She had advanced lung cancer and with that there is only one winner and it is certainly not the person who has it.

I flew over to my mums with the idea of driving her back home, however, when I got there, her appearance had resembled my dad. She was never a big woman – far from it – however, what I would see was someone that had completely wasted away. It was so sad. To compound the fact further, my sister had purposely kept things from me.

I had been picked up from the airport by someone by the name of Alan who my mum regarded as her boyfriend. He was a stocky bloke with a chip on his shoulder who as soon as he met me went on the defensive. "You weren't what I was expecting," he said.

I had a similar thing aimed at me more recently after I bumped into my son's immediate boss at the cashier tills in Scunthorpe's Tesco. "Your dad looked nothing like I thought, he would," he told him.

Ever feel that you are getting an inferiority complex?

Maybe I should shave my head, have tattoos around my neck and start twitching a bit.

Alan's conversation covered most things – but basically it all boiled down to the fact that while he had been growing up in Huddersfield, he had been a bit of a rum customer – and whilst in his prime, few people dared fuck with him.

It was a similar scenario on my second meeting with the husband of Thurnscoe's Dark Queen, in that he more or less handed me his resume which stated how much of a bad ass he was: "When I was sixteen… I went down to London… got a degree and (wait for it)… learned Jujitsu."

Believe me when I say it – this guy was certainly no fucking *Grasshopper* out of *Kung Fu*.

Nikki had obviously told him that I had leathered a few people whilst I had lived in Thurnscoe and maybe, he felt a bit intimidated. Who knows?

This guy was not too dissimilar, but I didn't really cotton on to it until the day I drove home.

The chalet was compact, and I mean compact, made even more so by the three dogs – one of which was an idiot Dalmatian that I had to retrieve on the drive home. Our dogs have always done as they are told – this fucking thing didn't. I suppose there is a first time for everything and chasing it up the hard shoulder and over on to the fast lane of the motorway, was an experience I would not like to repeat. Believe me when I say it, the kick up the arse it received when I caught the fucking thing made sure it never did it again.

I think Karen Simpson – Andrea Mangham's sister-in-law, ended up with it, although I could be wrong.

That aside, when I saw the state of my mum, I knew she couldn't travel. "Mum, you need to go back to hospital," I had told her.

Here she was, thinking that I would take her back to England and everything would be alright – and there I was telling her "no". It was horrible. If I could have made things right, I would have.

I had arrived late at night and early next morning I took the dogs out for a walk – one of which was her Alsatian. I thought long and hard about what was best, and when I relayed my thoughts, that is exactly what happened. "I'll drive home and re-house the dogs and then I will come back for you," I said.

"So, I'm not going home?" asked my mum.

I looked at the two huge oxygen tanks, the dogs, my sister, and the idiot boyfriend who wanted to tag along for the free ride into the UK. "The journey will be too much for you, Mum," is what I said. "You need to go back to the hospital. I will sort everything out and come back."

It is exactly what I did do, but that morning after I had walked the dogs, she asked me to sit at the side of her and on summoning me, duly patted the bed. "I love you," she said.

I have racked my brains and cannot recollect any time that she had ever said that before. Maybe she had and maybe I had forgotten – I don't know.

My son phones his mum every day – and on ringing off, 'Love you, Mam' – 'Love you, son' is always the last thing that is said.

We ended up with the Alsatian, which had similar traits to my mum – in that for the first few weeks it did whatever the hell it wanted to do, including taking chunks out of my wife and attacking the postman. It did, however, turn out to be an incredibly good dog. It is like anything in life – you treat them right and more often than not you will get it back.

On flying back into Spain – as her boyfriend wanted to see his family, so he took the car – I came back with my two uncles who were of course my mum's younger brothers, Rob and Steve. The reality was, that we had come to see her die. On my mum waking up in hospital and seeing her brothers and trying to reach out… well, I can detach myself from most things, but that for me was really upsetting. She died a day later. Unlike my (step)dad, there were no last words – just death. I felt for a pulse in her neck and she had gone.

The first five phone calls I received post her dying, were: i) my nana Durose ii) my auntie Liz (Durose) iii) my auntie Carol (Oldfield) iv) my friend, Tim (Bright) and v) my former accountant, Giles Brearley. And all in that order.

Her funeral was interesting as there was quite a turn-out of expats. As I have said, expats are generally some of the biggest sets of wankers you could ever come across, as their lives are nothing like they make them out to be. I speak from experience here. We have a few in our village over in Cyprus, one of whom claims to eat only haut cuisine food and drink fine wines. By all accounts he is supposedly a millionaire stamp collector. The fact that he drives around in a purple heap of shit that I wouldn't give £200 for and lives in some jerry-built concrete bungalow, had me scratching my head, so much so, I did a recce on his former life in England. It turned out that he was absolutely nothing like who he said he was and had lived in some rat hole ex-council house in Birmingham. There is nothing wrong with that, so why lie?

My sixteen-year-old son was the only one who wanted to see his grandma before the cremation, and which was something that made me proud.

Her funeral went like clockwork and it was a case of back to the bar on the campsite, for a buffet and a drink. I had only shifted around four bottles of San Miguel when I suddenly had company at my side. "Your mam told me that you are a nasty bastard, now, let's me and you go outside," he said.

I couldn't believe it. I was being offered out. And not only at my mum's funeral, but by her boyfriend.

I shouted over to my sister. "Do me a favour and have a word with him," I said.

She must have said something to him as he left. However, the more I thought of it, the more it rankled me. I couldn't let it go.

"So, what did you say to him," I asked my sister.

"Nothing – what did you want me to say?"

"Whose car is it?" I asked, as regards the ownership of the Volkswagen MPV that he'd just had valeted after driving it back from the UK.

"It's my mam's," she said.

In life, the way you go about hurting someone is to begin taking things from them. It is something that I have done numerous times. This was a guy who thought his number had come up. He didn't give a shit about my mum. Whilst she had been in hospital he had not been once. He had spent the last week and a bit driving her car around and propping up some bar in West Yorkshire – possibly spinning yarns about his affluent Iberian lifestyle.

I knocked on the door of his glorified shed and he opened it.

"I want the keys to my mum's car," I said.

He was taken aback but all the same he gave them to me. Unfortunately, I couldn't just leave it there and gave him one hell of a head shot which put him on the floor. "You ever speak to me like that again, you fucking piece of shit and I'll come back and finish the job," was exactly what I said.

I don't know what it was, but still, I couldn't leave it. I was in my mum's chalet packing my stuff and just getting irater by the minute. Generally, I can focus and redirect my anger in a meaningful manner. Not this time. I really had to go back and finish him.

I am not sure whether my sister tipped him off or not – the truth is, is that I do not know. However, credit where credit is due – he fully expected my return and on me kicking in his door he was ready in wait with a 2 lb hammer of which he swung at my forehead, the mark of which I still have to this day. On seeing blood, I dragged the tool out of his hand, slung it through his TV set and set about fucking him up properly. It was a mess. He was a mess.

The next thing I know I had my uncle Steve behind me and holding both my arms: "Jamie, lad, what have you done? You can't hurt him anymore – Alan's dead."

That was word for word.

"Chuck his body in the car and I'll dump it," I said.

Our Steve had seen a lot of things, but nothing like this. I had handed out much worse in the past and would do so in the future. This, however, was a side of me that he had never seen before. It had always been there but tucked deep away and waiting until I was well into my mid-thirties before I finally let it out.

"Your mam told me that you are a nasty bastard, now, let's me and you go outside."

My mum was dead, yet her presence had still been there. Why would someone say something such as that to the eldest son at his mother's funeral? Even now, it still has me baffled. It was something that I mentioned to my auntie Anne (Durose) on me getting back home.

"No matter what's gone on – he should have never said owt at your mam's funeral," she told me.

There he was, some big fat bastard laid in a pool of his own blood. I gave him a kick in the ribs, and he made a grunt. He hadn't been dead, just unconscious.

Our Steve and Rob did well and managed to convince him to keep schtum and not report it to the Spanish police. As for my mum's MPV – on driving it back to the UK I gave it my brother and walked away from it all.

I would give everything I own just to see them one last time.

Unfortunately, for me Julie – one lifetime is enough.

I would, however, like to stroll the tarmacked streets of The Avenues during the late 1960s and call into my grandparents at 63 Lindley Crescent if only to be a fly on the wall. These were two wonderful people that made part of my life so pleasurable. I would also love to take a walk up into the village's East end and go through the main doors of The Fairway one last time and stand at its bar have a pint with my (step)dad – if not to just to listen to his tall stories.

Even now, when The Tornadoes' *Telstar* gets played on the radio – the first thing I think of is my (step)dad. "1963 – I was in Aden when I first heard that," he would wink.

It is something that always makes me smile.

And how I would love another Thursday night sat in the room at 40 Ringway and listening to my grandma relaying me the past.

I reckon I am just getting sentimental now.

AUTHOR'S NOTES

For years I had promised myself that I would write a book that covered my local area during the time of the 1984/85 Miners' Strike – however, apart from some incoherent scribbling around 2003, it was something that never went anywhere.

In 2017, one of my best friends, Colin Hunter called me on it whilst I was between projects. It was then that I said that I would take it forward.

As well as possessing a start, an end and a middle bit, a story has to have a point. And as it is a factual story – it also has to read true.

I thought about the structure and content of the book for quite some time – its lack of point and the truth being something of a stumbling block.

In my experience it is not until you start writing at length that you find the direction in which it is going. The problem you then have is that you find that its style has changed and that a lot of what you have written needs binning. It is exactly what happened here.

When I write a book I never start from the beginning.

A small part of my original start to this book had been discarded and later on reinstated and is buried somewhere within the second chapter. The other part – the rape of a thirteen-year-old girl by a shopkeeper with one leg, I left out. What is strange about its omission is that it is quite an interesting story in that the girl's father died in the Oaks Pit Disaster and the mother remarried one of the Weldrick family – who now own a chain of chemists in the north of England.

There has been a lot of similar omissions – some which I reinserted in an additional chapter I wrote whilst waiting for the original thirty-eight files to come back from the publisher. The fragmentary styled Chapter 38 – Peep Show is my equivalent of The Beatles' *White Album* – a huge array of heavily researched and horrible historical information – a small part of which in my humble opinion is extremely interesting. I purposely left it unproofed, unedited and thereby totally unmolested.

The first chapter I wrote was Chapter 2: All God's Children, the last – Chapter 12: I'm Mandy, Fly Me.

9 781800 314

children of the sun

to the child who has lived
by the sea and the sand
and woken each day in a sun gilded land

to grown-ups who wish
that they ever could be
a child without care by the sand and the sea

to Ishaan and Iraaj
and Aaron and Ray
who played by the shore on each bright childhood day

Children of the Sun –
growing up in the gulf

Text and Production

Piyu Majumdar

Photography

Paul Thuysbaert
www.ptphotography.com

Photography Assistant

Kalu Thapa (Bahadur)

Design

Nicolle Kennedy & Paul Thuysbaert
nicollekennedy@mac.com

Published in 2009 by JERBOA BOOKS
PO Box 333838 Dubai UAE

www.jerboabooks.com
ISBN 978 9948 435 044

Approved by the National Information Council UAE:
No 3326 23 July 2008

With the support of
Emirates Printing Press, Dubai

A part of the royalty earned will be
donated to the Kids For Wish Kids.

The Kids For Wish Kids club of ASD raises
funds for the Make A Wish Foundation to help
children in the UAE who are living with life
threatening illnesses.

Contents

Gulf Child

The sun warms our backs as we play by the sea
Ali and Adam and Arjun and me
The tumbling blue waves and the lazy white foam
Swirl round our feet in this land we call home

On weekends sometimes to the wadis we go
With Jamila, Jenna and Juhi and Joe
By dark purple rocks the long bullrushes grow
And dragonflies flitter where cool waters flow

Skyscrapers, minarets, souks and the parks
Glittering lights on the creek in the dark
The high rocky jebels, the calm turquoise sea
The pink and gold desert are all home to me

I know, when I grow from this land I'll depart
But I'll hold all these memories wrapped warm round my heart
With values I've learnt from this hot desert land
To be brave and resourceful, give others a hand
I'll stand tall and sturdy
I'll stand bold and tough
And proudly proclaim, 'I grew up in the Gulf!'

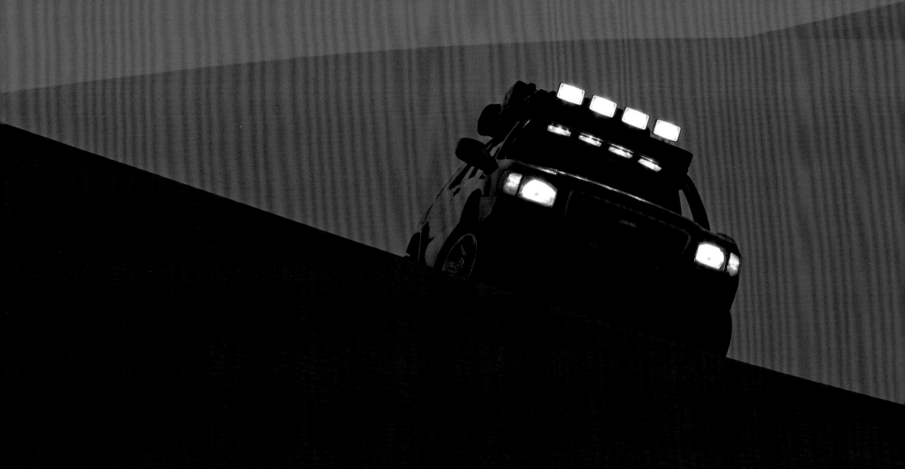

A Day on
the Dunes

There's nothing ahead but the sand and the sky
Up the sand dunes in our four-wheel we fly

We swoosh up the hill all the way to the top
On wobbly wheels for a moment we stop

Perched on a peak I see dunes oh-so-high
And there's nothing below but the sand and the sky

Our car hurtles down, the sand sprays all around
My stomach goes plunging right down to the ground!

There's sand everywhere from the rocketing ride
It covers the windscreen, we can't see outside

Now there's nothing ahead but just sand and more sand
As we coast to a halt on a bit of firm land

We gather our breath, choose the next dune and then –
It's up to the top all over again!

The Camel Ride

At first sight your camel will sit very still

His back looks quite comfy – a little round hill

You climb on his back. Your feet touch the ground.

When suddenly, with a great galumping sound

His back goes up while his front's still down!

Galump, galump, galump, galump

Bumpety, bumpety, bumpety, bump!

You're startled. You're frightened.

You clutch your reins tight

You're slipping. You're sliding. This can't be right!

His front comes up with a bumpety bump

You find yourself clinging quite tight to his hump.

Galump, galump, galump, galump

Bumpety, bumpety, bumpety, bump!

The camel starts walking, your bones creak and groan
You're bounced and you're jounced like a bag full of stones.
Yallah! Yallah! He's starting to run!
The sand dunes whiz by in the hot desert sun.

Galump, galump, galump, galump
Bumpety, bumpety, bumpety, bump!

The camel's head bobs with each step that he takes
A horrible thought makes you quiver and quake
Here you are – so high off the ground
How will you get down? How will you get down?
Will his front come down while his back's in the air?
Will you fall in a heap in dismay and despair?
You worry and fret as you ride through the town
How will you get down? How will you get down?

Galump, galump, galump, galump
Bumpety, bumpety, bumpety, bump!

Busy Busy Me

I am a busy Gulf child

Just as busy as a bee

My every waking hour is filled

With some activity!

Golf on Tuesdays, netball practice
Tennis game at three
The piano teacher comes around
With regularity
Ballet, tap and modern jazz
For flexibility
For extra French and Arabic
Mum pays a hefty fee!
I swim, I skate
I climb, I ride
And sometimes even ski
And in between I play cool games
On my new PSP
My social calendar is full
From party to party
If you need me, please feel free
To call my secretary!

22

Ramadan

The sun sinks down low
And the long day is done
With dates and fresh fruit
Our *Iftar* has begun
All day we have fasted
With joy in our hearts
For pure thoughts and deeds
Set this fair month apart
We feel for the hungry, the helpless and weak
And master our hunger, our thoughts and our speech
When the sun sinks down low
And the day's at an end
We break bread together
With family and friends

Giant Rocks

The rocky jebels soar up high
A purple fist against the sky
Like monoliths they bar the way
In dusty tones of brown and grey

Silent at the desert edge
Their stony heights are tightly wedged
They hint of patience and of strength
They stand for years of endurance
Assaulted by the sun and sand
They still inspire and command.

Storm

Hot and dusty the *shamaal* blows

There's sand in my hair, there's sand in my toes

When the *shamaal* comes, just stay indoors

Bar the windows and shut the doors!

Sandy streets and gritty trees

Sand from the desert swirls in the breeze

A dull, dun sky hides a cowering sun

He'll stay home too till the *shamaal's* done!

The Oasis

Surrounded by sand dunes
And the heat haze of high noon
A treasure lies hidden
From all but a few

The thirsty find aid
The traveller finds shade
As an age-old resting place
Comes into view

Cool water, still water
Precious as pearls
Trickling up from a deep spring below
Sturdy date palms
Wave their feathery arms
A cool breeze picks up as the sun sinks down low

Come rest and recover
This green world discover
Let the desert wind soothe you
To a soft, dreamless sleep

At the oasis kind
Leave your worries behind
As you drink of the waters
So still and so deep

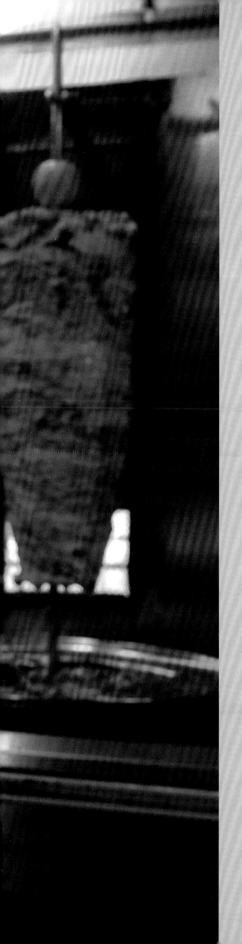

Ode to the Shawarma

Oh, King of Sandwiches

Snacker's delight

Chockful of flavours

With each robust bite

Wrapped in a pale cloak of soft, chewy bread

Tomato, lettuce and tahini spread

Juicy, grilled morsels of meat from a cone

Sliced bit by bit with no hint of bone

A succulent pickle for a sense of tart

And sometimes French fries are tucked into its heart

Oh, harmonious blend of carbs and proteins

Oh tasty concoction of hasty cuisine!

With a surgeon's precision wrapped secure and tight

So nothing spills out with each gargantuan bite!

There are those who will eat at five-starred fancy places

Where Michelin chefs swirl their sauce in their faces

In Paris and London, New York and Dubai

They dine on the finest that money can buy

But the hearty *shawarma* is food for the soul

Satisfaction disguised as a mere sandwich roll

You can eat it by day

You can eat it by night

At picnics, at parties or by candle light!

Some like it hot

While some like it cold

And some eat it from the fridge two days old!

Oh, stately *shawarma* let us sing your praise

In joyful chorus our voices we raise

For no matter where on this planet we roam

This down to earth sandwich reminds us of home!

Up and Away

Each day new towers
Crop up in Dubai
They stretch out their arms
And they reach for the sky

I look up and watch
As the swarms of small men
Shape each new building
Again and again

And there's noise and there's ruckus
There's heat and there's dust
But the towers keep growing
So work there they must

Like ants on an anthill
Impossibly high
They work day and night
Till the towers reach the sky

Dad says
that our national bird is the 'crane'
He laughs when he says it
He doesn't explain

And I watch and I wonder
If sometime real soon
They'll build us a tower
Straight up to the moon

For nothing's impossible
Here in Dubai
Where each day new towers
Reach up to the sky

Eid Mubarak

Eid Mubarak, Eid Mubarak
We wish you all a happy Eid
A time of joy and celebration
Welcome, welcome *Eid sayyid!*

Holy *Ramadan* is over
The month of sacrifice is done
By the sickle moon's pale light
The festivities have begun
My sisters glow in their fine clothes
Their steps so light, their faces bright
Mother's busy in the kitchen
Cooking dishes that delight!

'Ahmed, where do you think you're going?
There is so much to be done!'
'Uncle Khalid gave me eidhia –
I am off to have some fun!'

A time for friends and family
To meet and greet, acknowledge love
A happy time, a feasting time
While the silver moon gleams up above.

Eid Mubarak, Eid Mubarak
A happy *Eid* to everyone
A time of joy and celebration
Joyous *Shawal* has begun!

Across vast barren desert lands
These gentle beasts first led the way
Long, long before this age of man
O'er dunes and sands they once held sway

Down ancient routes, through bone dry tracks
Backs laden down with salt and gold
In caravans a thousand strong
They braved the climes in days of old

For days on end, the land ablaze
Through changing dunes of shifting sand
In blinding storms, chilled winter nights,
Tenaciously cross untamed lands

Accolade

Nature formed that comic shape
Resilient to sand and heat
With humps that store and then restore
And toughened hide and padded feet

Bedu's lifeline, *Bedu's* pride
On him their very lives depend
Today content to ride and race
The camel's rule is at an end

For nature and her wondrous hands
Can hold back neither time nor tide
And ancient ways and long gone days
Relentlessly are swept aside

That noble head, those patient eyes
Unfaltering stride, untiring will

But bonds that once bound beast and man
Untouched by time, holds firm, holds still

What a Racket!

My next door neighbour has a rooster in his yard
He struts and pecks and chases other birds
All day long his voice can be heard
Cock-a-doodle, cock-a-doodle
Cock-a-doodle doo!

My next door neighbour has a pair of cats that fight
Snarling, spitting, hissing till daylight
All night long you can hear them on the roof
Yowl! Yowl! Howl! Howl!
Cock-a-doodle-doo!

My neighbour's dog is a little fluffy tyke

He races and chases poor paper boys on bikes

All day long, his shrill bark goes on and on

Woof! Woof! Yip! Yip!

Yowl! Yowl! Howl! Howl!

Cock-a-doodle! Cock-a-doodle!

Cock-a-doodle-doo!

My next door neighbour has a goat with pointy horns

He chomps through flowers, plants and shrubs

And bushes with sharp thorns

He'll eat your mat, he'll eat your hat

And bleat all day while he does that

Maa! Maa! Baa! Baa!

Yip! Yip! Yelp! Yelp!

Yowl! Yowl! Howl! Howl!

Cock-a-doodle doo!

Mum came home from the hospital today

She brought with her our baby

And she says it's going to stay.

Now we don't hear our neighbours any more

For nothing is as loud as our baby's awful roar –

Bawl! Bawl! Waa! Waa!

Yowl! Yowl! Howl! Howl!

Woof! Woof! Yip! Yip!

Maa! Maa! Baa! Baa!

Cock-a-doodle! Cock-a-doodle! Cock-a-doodle-doo!

Coming
of Age

64

As the world turns
Days slide swiftly away
Life beckons boldly
With dazzling display
I wait on the threshold
With hope, joy and fear
And leave childhood behind me
With each passing year

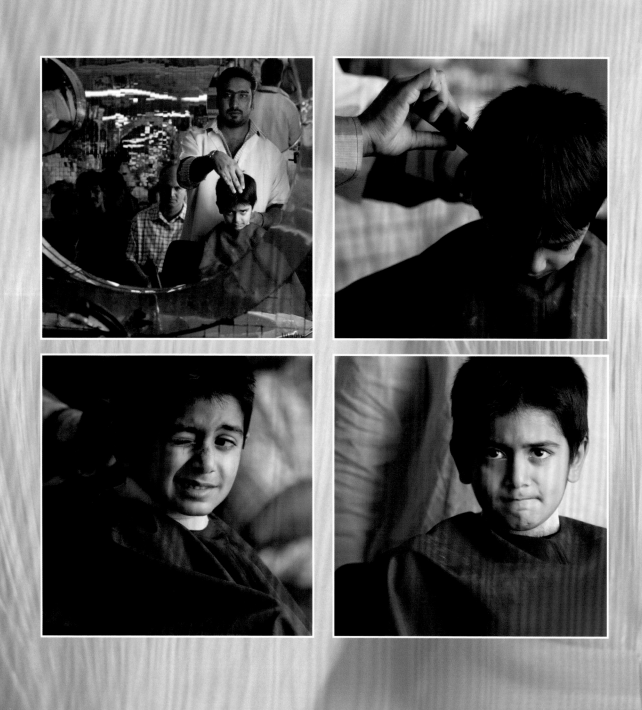

The Haircut

Snip, snip of the scissors so close to my ear
I scrunch up my face and sit stiffly in fear

Bits of hair float like damp feathers below
When with my Dad to the barber we go

Dad tells the man, 'Not too much off the top'.
I grimace and wince through a regular crop

There's hair in my mouth and there's hair in my face
The sheet binds my arms very tightly in place

At last we are done. Off the high seat I leap.
But dad's head massage has sent him straight to sleep!

Leapin'
Lizards

From my room a chirping echo
Went inside to take a dekko
Spotted on the wall – a gecko
Scaly skin and bulging eyes

A gecko'd make a perfect pet
It doesn't eat that much, I bet
You needn't take it to the vet
All it needs are bugs and flies

I ran outside to find a box
And lined it with old tennis socks
Some grass and stones and one big rock
A perfect home, a cosy nook

For a pet I'm longing, dreaming
Now this gecko has me beaming
If only Mother would stop screaming
Climb off that chair and take a look!

Wildebeast

On desert sands where camels roamed

Our mighty herd

Now rules the day

We tear the soil and gouge the land

And for the future

Forge the way

With metal jaws and ribs of steel
We buck and strain
And rev and roar
We paw the ground and slash the trees
We claw deep troughs
On sandy floors
When twilight falls we crouch and wait
Impatient
For the break of dawn
With iron will to tame the dunes
Relentlessly
Our hunt goes on

Horsing Around

Last night Mum and I went to see the Big Race

We dressed up real fancy

Our hats were in place

Mum wore high heels and I wore some too!

(I think she said hers were from some Jimmy Choo)

The races were fun, everyone looked so grand

There were flowers and tents

And a band in a stand

And eating and drinking and laughing and talking

And watching and wandering and walking and gawking

We had a great time, having fun without care –

By the way, did I mention, some horses were there?

Laundry
Lullaby

The ironing man
The ironing man
Brings order to chaos
As only he can!

He takes piles of wrinkled-up, crinkled-up clothes
And irons them flat in neat stacks and straight rows
His huge, heavy iron
Attached to a cord
He wields swift and deft
Like a knight with a sword
He defeats all the furrows
And levels the bends
He cheerfully folds all the clothes end to end
Cuffs, collars, buttons he carefully scans
For nothing's too tough for the ironing man!

Equus

The Arab steed, the Arab steed
Is handsome, brave and pedigreed
Born of an ancient, noble line
He's elegance and grace defined
And sometimes he'll consent to hack
With little children on his back!

The Gold Souk

Shop fronts that glitter and glisten with gold
Bracelets and bangles
Earrings and chains
Delicate traceries, patterns so bold
Gleam with warm welcome in Deira's dark lanes

With rings on her fingers and bells on her toes
A shimmer and shine through the gold *souk* she goes

Twinkling tiaras and rings set with gems
Necklaces crafted from sunbeams and stars
Intricate filigreed belts made by hand
For fairytale princesses in lands afar

With rings on her fingers and bells on her toes
A-shimmer and shine through the gold *souk* she goes.

All Aboard,
All Abroad

Each year when the heat haze
Grips hard this hot land
We head for the airport
A bag in each hand

Day flight or night flight
Whichever you take
The airport is bustling
And always awake!

When school's out for summer
We take to the skies
See family and friends
And to new lands we fly

Midnight or mid-day
No difference it makes
The airport is buzzing
And always awake!

Our dads stay behind
And they work in the sun
We go with our mums
For two whole months of fun

It starts at the airport
Where our flights we take
It's big, bright and shining
And always awake!

A Day in the Park

Islands of green in the land of the sun

To run and to play and have long days of fun

You can swim, you can jog, on your bike you can ride

You can skip, catch and throw

You can swing, climb and slide

Pack up a picnic and take it with you

That's what I like to do

That's what I like to do

Sit on the grass with a sandwich or two

A bag full of crisps and an ant on my shoe

Beach parks and city parks

You'll love them too!

92

Afternoon Tea

They converse politely
They sip their tea lightly
Their ankles crossed tightly
Napkins on their knees
They raise their cups gently
They blot their lips faintly
Look at our mummies at Afternoon Tea!

Cucumber sandwiches diced so precise

Scones, cream and jam go together qui

Iced petit-fours perch on bone china bl

Earl Grey? Darjeeling? What shall it be?

Outside the sun shines

The waves murmur sweetly

With shiny flatware they cut up their f

They call for the bills raising fingers dis

Our mummies are busy at Afternoon T

Ayallah

Come my brothers, band together
Raise your swords and play the drums
Sing of days of ancient glory
Sing of battles fought and won

Arm in arm, come dance my brothers
Step together, sword in hand
Our hearts are strong, our heads held high
We are protectors of our land

Dance in step and raise your swords
Sing of stirring acts so brave
Valiant heroes, warriors mighty
Now lie peaceful in their graves

Raise your swords and step together
Singing, dancing, arm in arm
Pledge yourselves to deeds of honour
Keep our country safe from harm.

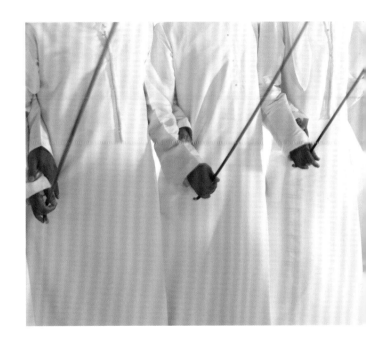

Song of Spice

The spice *souk* sits by the side of the creek
There's hustle and bustle all days of the week
It's easy to find – just follow your nose
Chase that spicy scent wherever it goes…
Through the winding streets, past crowded shops
At the fragrant *souk* you'll finally stop.

Ahlan! Ahlan! the shopkeepers say
Heaped sacks of spices they proudly display

Cardomom and cloves from a faraway place
Sticks of cinnamon, peppercorn and mace
Mounds of dried chillies, shiny and red
Sesame seeds to scatter on bread

Kahwa? Chai? The shopkeepers say
Cups of tea they bring on a tray

Mustard and fenugreek and onion seeds
Coriander piled like rough brown beads
Turmeric gold and cumin from the east
Sumac and saffron fit for a feast.

Shukran! Shukran! the shopkeepers say
As you carry your packages of spices away!

Long
Long Ago

I lived among the desert sands

Our tribe was proud and brave

Our ancient ways would nourish us from cradle to the grave

The sand was hot, the sun was hot.

Our days were hard and long

We travelled with our animals, our bonds were true and strong.

Yes, life was rough. Yes, life was tough

But we loved it so —

It was the only life we knew

Long, long ago…

I took my boat to sea each day
The waves were fierce and high
The sea was cold
The blazing sun shone from a ruthless sky.
Some days we caught a lot of fish
And some days we caught none
We toiled all day from dawn to dusk
Until our work was done.

Yes, life was rough. Yes, life was tough
But we loved it so –
It was the only life we knew
Long, long ago…

I dived into the ink-blue sea
A precious pearl to find
A hempen rope, a wooden clip
I left the world behind
Time and time I dived down deep
The ocean's prize to seek
For every treasured pearl I found
Could feed us for a week

Yes, life was rough. Yes, life was tough
But we loved it so –
It was the only life we knew
So very long ago…

Sand Song

Those sculptured dunes of rose and gold
What age old secrets do they hold?
What fireside *Bedu* tales are told
Of camel treks and caravans?

Under brightening morning skies
In light and shade the sand dunes lie
And shift their shapes with restless sighs
As desert winds their warm brows fan

Valley, ridge, and mound and hill
The molten sun does slowly fill
Lulled by the heat the dunes lie still
Unmoved by toil of beast or man

Once I remember we even had hail

And without fail

We all talked about it for the next ten years

And if there's morning fog

We all run amock

Bumping into each other, hazard lights blinking

Overcome by fear

Sunny Days

Do you know
on average we have 300 days of sunshine in Dubai?
Day after day after day
The sun blazes down from a bland and cloudless sky
Except for an odd day of rain
It's always sunny
It's not funny —
Just look at the weather forecast for a week
'Plenty of sun'
'Very sunny'
'Sunny and warm'
'Sunshine all day'
Go on, take a peek —
You forget there can be any other kind of weather altogether
A storm is an occasion
For a celebration

The constant sun is so dependable,
We can plan our days in careless ease
Living as we please
BUT
When you add humidity to the mix
It leaves us all in a fix
It's like living life in a sauna
When perspiration trickles down every
groove and channel
Even the most hardened resident
would think themselves a goner!

The Camel's Lament

The sun is hot

We mustn't grumble

Trek through dunes

Without a stumble

Walk all day

We mustn't grumble

Hardy desert beings are we!

Not much food
We mustn't grumble
Thorny scrubs
Our tummies rumble
Water's scarce
We mustn't grumble
Patient plod-alongs are we!

Sandstorm stings
We mustn't grumble
Huddle close
Demure and humble
Eyes shut tight
We mustn't grumble
Uncomplaining creatures we!

123

Winters freeze
We mustn't grumble
Under blankets
Flail and fumble
Cold or hot
We mustn't grumble
Beasts of burden tough are we

Stiff upper lips
We mustn't grumble
Talk of weather
In low rumbles
Could be worse
We mustn't grumble
Veterans of the wild are we!

Satwa
Sights

There's a bearded man in a little shop
He'll fix your shoes and glue the soles
If you need an extra front door key
You can get it cut at the shop next door
A watch strap or a battery?
Ahmed, near-by, is the man to see
You'll find them all sat side by side
In a crooked street in Satwa

Plastic buckets, cheap handbags

Vegetables and frozen fish

Cotton, rayon, silk and lace

In every colour you could wish

Photocopy? Post a letter?

Need a pill to make you better?

T.V. bust? Do you need new tyres?

Hammer, nails or rolls of wire?

You'll find someone who'll sort you out in that

crooked street in Satwa

They say you can get anything
From an elephant to a shiny pin
(And I have bought some funny things!)
In that crooked street in Satwa!

Aqua Marine

They glide swift and sleek
Like a hawk in full flight
The sails catch the breeze
And the sea glitters bright
I sit on the beach
And watch white yachts sail by
In the blue of the sea
In the blue of the sky

Day's End

The setting sun still hugs the land
Its last rays warm the rocks and sand
All day we've played in sand-smeared glee
Outrun the waves, outpaced the sea

And now our play, at last, is done

We sink to rest just like the sun

Refrain

And so its goodbye from the sand and the sea

From Ali and Adam and Arjun and me

We watch our land change and we watch our land grow

As we play by the foam on this golden seashore

For childhood is fleeting

A blink of the eye

These long sunny days too soon will pass by

But Jamila, Jenna and Juhi all know

That our hearts will remain in this land we love so

Notes for the needy

Eid Al Fitr – This Islamic festival commemorates the end of the period of fasting during the month of Ramadan. There are feasts and celebrations and homes, buildings and streets are beautifully decorated. The festivals begin with the sighting of the new moon marking the month of Shawaal – the 10th in the Islamic calendar.

Ramadan – A religious observance for Muslims that takes place during the month of Ramadan, the 9th month in the Islamic calendar. During this month Muslims fast from dawn to dusk and also refrain from all activities that are not compatible with Islamic values.

Shawarma – A popular and readily available Middle Eastern sandwich made of chicken or lamb. The classic shawarma consists of pita bread, hummus, tomato, cucumber, tahini wrapped around the shaved meat.

The Ayallah – A traditional dance from the U.A.E. The dance depicts victory in battle and is performed by groups of men holding sticks or swords, singing and reciting stirring poetry. The dance may be accompanied by drums, tambourines, bagpipes and flutes.

Souk – Open air markets in Arab cities sometimes specialising in particular products such as vegetables, fish, fabrics, spices or gold.

Al Satwa – An area within the city of Dubai populated by inhabitants from all over the world. There are many small shops and narrow streets where all kinds of things are sold. There are several such areas in the major cities of the Gulf. In Dubai, Satwa is gradually being demolished to make way for newer developments.

Photographer's Note: The photographs in the book were taken with the world's first integrated medium-format digital camera, the Hasselblad HD1 and HD3II with 22 and 39 megapixel sensors.

Abra – a traditional boat made of wood, used to transport people across Dubai Creek in Dubai, United Arab Emirates

Aish – what?

Ahlan – welcome

Aiwa – Yes

Al Arabiah – Arabic

Bedu – (plural Bedouin) nomadic Arabian tribes who live in the desert and herd goats, sheep and other animals

Chai – tea

Dhow – traditional Arabic sailing vessel plying the coasts of the Arabic peninsula, India and East Africa

Eidhia – money given as gifts to children during Eid celebrations

Fayn – Where?

Hamour – (Grouper) popular fish in gulf cuisine found in the region

Henna – A flowering plant used to produce an orange dye that is used for decorating the body

Iftar – The evening meal that is eaten after breaking the fast during the month of Ramadan

Ismalhee – Excuse me

Ithnen – the number two in Arabic

Jebel – mountain

Kahwa – coffee

Keef halak – how are you?

La – no

Lay Ish – why?

Maalish – never mind

Marhaba – hello

Meen – who?

Meta – when?

Min fadlak – please

Mubarak – greetings

Saba hal Khair – good morning

Sayara – vehicle

Shumaal – dust storm

Sayyid – happiness

Sheri – fish found in Gulf region

Shukran – thank you

Shuway-shuway – a little

Sumac – a deep red, tart spice used in Arabic cooking

Tayara – aeroplane

Tayeeb – o.k.

Talatha – the number three

Wahid – the number one

Wadi – dried river bed

Yallah – let's go!

Acknowledgements

Aktoplak family

Matar Humid Bin Abid

Faisal Al Bahar

Tarik Al Khamis

Sara and Al Mousawe family

Al Shaali family

Khalid and Amin Ali

Lesley Clegg

Jimmy and the Craig family

Ahne Crawford-Ridley and Phil Ridley

Karon Collins

Rachel and Belinda Farah

Michael Hanania

Alison Henry

Dee and David Hewitt

Maria Regina and Elissa Kadamani

Dara Kazerouni

Yasmina and the Koerfgen family

Geeta Krishnamoorthy

Julia and the Lampke family

Layla, Frank and the Laubach family

Henri Lemaire

Lootah family and cousins

Juliette and Marier family

Colby Marion

Celeste, Zack, Julian and the Maawad family

Christopher Maroun

Tia McSherry

Sarah Mugharbil

Ursula Musch and her camels

Karim Mushtaq

Nabil Arabi El Eter

Adam, Hannah, Ahmed and the Nazari family

Naqvi famliy

Matheus Oliviera

Aayush Prakash

William Pranno

Shreyan Ramsinghani

Halina Rignall

Sayeed and Al Mazoud band

Elena, Olivia and Amy Sherman

Gertrudes Silvan

Blaise and Snelling family

Khalil and Somani family

Griffin, Cooper and Stermer family

Sarah and Tabra family

Julian Thompson

Aaron and Ray Thuysbaert

Laura and Warner family

Brittany, Dylan and Vanessa Welch

The Wiltshire family and baby Gabriella

Also many thanks to

The camels of Ursula and Matar

The chickens, goats and cows behind Al Wasl Road

The horses of Dubai Equestrian Club

The lizard at No.19 Meadows 7

And let's not forget

American School of Dubai

Dubai International Airport

The Ritz Carlton Dubai

Dubai Equestrian Club

Dubai Racing Club, Nad Al Sheba

Prolab – Jayne Reader

No children or animals or insects were harmed in the making of our book – the only casualty was Paul's assistant Bahadur who was butted by a goat during the shooting of "What a Racket" but took it like a man!!

Special thanks to

our spouses and children for their patience and encouragement

and;

Nicolle Kennedy for her support and enthusiasm.

Isobel Abulhoul and Jane Hodges for their vision and faith!

VK Tensingh.

Barbara Devine, Pat Al Fakhri and the Water Colour Class of 2004-2005.

Mike Skipper who taught me about photography and giving selflessly. PT

Made in Dubai

We had been searching for chickens for weeks. It seemed that everyone we knew in the Emirates had once lived next door to a house with chickens. Yet no one could actually lead us to a place where we could find some!
We rummaged in the back streets of Satwa and got nothing but black looks. We poked around the small alleys behind Jumeirah Mosque and found several pigeons.
Helpful friends gave us leads – Go to Al Barsha. Search in Mirdiff. Have you thought of Deira?
Alas our meanderings brought us neither fowl nor anything fair! But serendipity played a hand. Purely by luck we drove past a house in the centre of Jumeirah and spied goats tethered outside. Be still our beating hearts!! Surely where there were goats, there would be chickens?!
We tentatively approached the gate. In a sweep of bright feathers a rooster flew onto the wall and glared down at us in yellow-eyed spite. We could hear a great cacophony of clucks from the yard. Somewhere a cow mooed. We had found exactly what we needed to illustrate "What a Racket"!

Exhilarating. Maddening. Inspiring. The production of Children of the Sun has been an adventure to remember. A labour of love that was two years in the making, the book grew and morphed from the original 14 poems to more than double. Soon we were faced with the daunting challenge of arranging almost 30 photo shoots between us to create a book that melded poetry with photographs to encapsulate a childhood in the Gulf.

We scoured the Emirates in search of unique and authentic pictures. Liwa's majestic dunes, Jebel Dhanna's wide beaches, Hatta's iconic pools, the oases of Al Ain, the stunning mountains of the East Coast all found a place with a poem to match. We tirelessly tracked camels, goats, camels, chickens, camels, Oryx, camels, fish, camels, lizards, camels, crickets in an attempt to cover all creatures great and small – did I mention camels?

The enormous number of photographs required a plethora of models and over 60 children and adults feature in the book. We depended entirely on the kindness of friends, acquaintances and even random strangers who all volunteered to model for us for no other remuneration than the pleasure of taking part in an exciting project. In Ras Al Khaimah a gracious Emirati family warmly welcomed us to their Eid celebrations, posed for photographs and then sent us home with enormous lunch boxes of food! A dozen parents from the American School Dubai brought their children to the beach on a sultry May afternoon and waited patiently untill the perfect shot was taken.
The shopkeepers of Satwa came forward gladly and even gave us free snacks and tea!

The people of the Emirates embraced our project wholeheartedly. In the making of the book we found help when we most needed it, friendship when we least expected it and tons of advice whether we wanted it or not! Our thrilling journey has served all the more to show the many colours that make up the close-knit fabric of our lives here and we can proudly proclaim, like the Gulf Child, our book "grew up in the Gulf".

Piyu Majumdar and Paul Thuysbaert have lived in the Gulf with their families for almost two decades.

A copywriter by profession, Piyu Majumdar works as a teaching assistant at the American School of Dubai and has made children her focus for many years. Her two children grew up in Oman and the Emirates and still call the Gulf their home.

Paul Thuysbaert is a renowned professional photographer whose assignments have taken him all over the Gulf and the world. His own children continue to delight and inspire him day after day.

Both Piyu and Paul believe that their children have enjoyed a vibrant and exciting childhood in the Gulf and their book is a tribute to this unique region, its people and its all-embracing culture.

Let There be Light!

Our intrepid lightsman
Bahadur the Bold
Has patience and humour
And a heart made of gold.
Up dunes and down wadis
Through souks and parks
He trekked with the lights
Bringing brightness to dark
Kid, camels and chickens
Palm trees, frozen fish
He'd light with great ease
Any object you wish
His steps never flagged
From the start to the end –
Couldn't have done it
Without you my friend!

Close your eyes and count to ten
While new pages soon we pen
And bring them to you once again!